Colin MacFarquhar, George Gleig

Encyclopµdia britannica : or, A dictionary of arts, sciences, and miscellaneous literature : constructed on a plan, by which the different sciences and arts are digested into the form of distinct treatises or systems .

Colin MacFarquhar, George Gleig

Encyclopµdia britannica : or, A dictionary of arts, sciences, and miscellaneous literature : constructed on a plan, by which the different sciences and arts are digested into the form of distinct treatises or systems .

ISBN/EAN: 9783741168109

Manufactured in Europe, USA, Canada, Australia, Japa

Cover: Foto ©Andreas Hilbeck / pixelio.de

Manufactured and distributed by brebook publishing software
(www.brebook.com)

Colin MacFarquhar, George Gleig

Encyclopμdia britannica : or, A dictionary of arts, sciences, and miscellaneous literature : constructed on a plan, by which the different sciences and arts are digested into the form of distinct treatises or systems .

Legacy
from
W. Cunningham Esq. of Galway
to
The Rev. G. Cunningham

ENCYCLOPÆDIA BRITANNICA;

OR, A

DICTIONARY

OF

ARTS, SCIENCES,

AND

MISCELLANEOUS LITERATURE;

Conſtructed on a PLAN,

BY WHICH

THE DIFFERENT SCIENCES AND ARTS

Are digeſted into the FORM of Diſtinct

TREATISES OR SYSTEMS,

COMPREHENDING

The HISTORY, THEORY, and PRACTICE, of each,
according to the Lateſt Diſcoveries and Improvements;

AND FULL EXPLANATIONS GIVEN OF THE

VARIOUS DETACHED PARTS OF KNOWLEDGE,

WHETHER RELATING TO

NATURAL and ARTIFICIAL Objects, or to Matters ECCLESIASTICAL,
CIVIL, MILITARY, COMMERCIAL, &c.

Including ELUCIDATIONS of the moſt important Topics relative to RELIGION, MORALS,
MANNERS, and the OECONOMY of LIFE:

TOGETHER WITH

A DESCRIPTION of all the Countries, Cities, principal Mountains, Seas, Rivers, &c.
throughout the WORLD;

A General HISTORY, *Ancient* and *Modern*, of the different Empires, Kingdoms, and States;

AND

An Account of the LIVES of the moſt Eminent Perſons in every Nation,
from the earlieſt ages down to the preſent times.

Compiled from the writings of the beſt Authors, in ſeveral languages; the moſt approved Dictionaries, as well of general ſcience as of its particular branches; the Tranſactions, Journals, and Memoirs, of learned Societies, both at home and abroad; the MS. Lectures of Eminent Profeſſors on different ſciences; and a variety of Original Materials, furniſhed by an Extenſive Correſpondence.

THE THIRD EDITION, IN EIGHTEEN VOLUMES, GREATLY IMPROVED.

ILLUSTRATED WITH FIVE HUNDRED AND FORTY-TWO COPPERPLATES.

VOL. IV.

INDOCTI DISCANT, ET AMENT MEMINISSE PERITI.

Encyclopædia Britannica.

C

C, THE third letter, and second consonant, of the alphabet, is pronounced like *k* before the vowels *a*, *o*, and *u*; and like *s* before *e*, *i*, and *y*. C is formed, according to Scaliger, from the κ of the Greeks, by retrenching the stem or upright line; though others derive it from the כ of the Hebrews, which has in effect the same form; allowing only for this, that the Hebrews, reading backwards, and the Latins, &c. forwards, each have turned the letter their own way. However, the C not being the same as to sound with the Hebrew *caph*, and it being certain the Romans did not borrow their letters immediately from the Hebrews or other orientals, but from the Greeks, the derivation from the Greek κ is the more probable. Add, that F. Montfaucon, in his Palæographia, gives us some forms of the Greek κ, which come very near that of our C; thus, for instance, ς; and Suidas calls the C the Roman kappa. The second sound of C resembles that of the Greek σ; and many instances occur of ancient inscriptions, in which σ has the same form with our C. All grammarians agree, that the Romans pronounced their Q like our C, and their C like our K. F. Mabillon adds, that Charles the Great was the first who wrote his name with a C; whereas all his predecessors of the same name wrote it with a K; and the same difference is observed in their coins.

As an abbreviature, C stands for Caius, Carolus, Cæsar, *condemno*, &c. and CC for *consulibus*.

As a numeral, C signifies 100, CC 200, &c.

C, in music, placed after the cliff, intimates that the music is in common time, which is either quick or slow, as it is joined with allegro or adagio; if alone, it is usually adagio. If the C be crossed or turned, the first requires the air to be played quick, and the last very quick.

CAABA, or Caabah, properly signifies a square stone building; but is particularly applied by the Mahometans to the temple of Mecca, built, as they pretend, by Abraham and Ismael his son.

Before the time of Mahomet, this temple was a place of worship for the idolatrous Arabs, and is said to have contained no less than 360 different images, equalling in number the days of the Arabian year. They were all destroyed by Mahomet, who sanctified the Caaba, and appointed it to be the chief place of worship for all true believers. The temple is in length from north to south about 24 cubits; its breadth from east to west is 23; and its height 27. The door, which is on the east side, stands about four cubits from the ground; the floor being level with the bottom of the door. In the corner next this door is the *black stone*, so much celebrated among the Mahometans. On the north side of the caaba, within a semicircular inclosure 50 cubits long, lies the *white stone*, said to be the sepulchre of Ishmael, which receives the rain-water from the caaba by a spout formerly of wood, but now of gold. The black stone, according to the Mahometans, was brought down from heaven by Gabriel at the creation of the world; and originally of a white colour; but contracted the blackness that now appears on it, from the guilt of those sins committed by the sons of men. It is set in silver, and fixed in the south-east corner of the caaba, looking towards Basra, about seven spans from the ground. This stone, upon which there is the figure of a human head, is held in the highest estimation among the Arabs; all the pilgrims kissing it with great devotion, and some even calling it the *right hand of God*. Its blackness, which is only superficial, is probably owing to the kisses and touches of so many people. After the Karmatians had taken Mecca, they carried away this precious stone, and could by no means be prevailed upon to restore it; but finding at last that they were unable to prevent the concourse of pilgrims to Mecca, they sent it back of their own accord, after having kept it 22 years.

The double roof of the caaba is supported within by three octagonal pillars of aloes-wood; between which, on a bar of iron, hang some silver lamps. The outside is covered with rich black damask, adorned with an embroidered band of gold, which is changed every year, and was formerly sent by the khalifs, afterwards by the sultans of Egypt, and is now provided by the Turkish emperors. The caaba, at some distance, is almost surrounded by a circular inclosure of pillars, joined towards the bottom by a low ballustrade, and towards the top by bars of silver. Just without this inner inclosure, on the south, north, and west sides of the caaba, are three buildings, which are the oratories or places where three of the orthodox sects assemble to perform their devotions. Towards the south-east stands an edifice which covers the well Zemzem, the treasury, and the cupola of Al Abbas. Formerly there was another cupola, that went under the name of the *hemicycle*, or *cupola of Judea*: but whether or not any remains of that are now to be seen is unknown; nor is it easy to obtain information in this respect, all Christians being denied access to this holy place. At a small distance from the caaba, on the east side, is the *station* or *place* of Abraham; where is another stone much respected by the Mahometans; and where they pretend to to shew the footsteps of the patriarch, telling us he stood on it when he built the caaba. Here the fourth sect of Arabs, viz. that of Al Shafei, assemble for religious purposes.

The square colonnade, or great piazza, that at a considerable distance incloses these buildings, consists, according to Al Jannabi, of 448 pillars, and has no less than 38 gates. Mr Sale compares this piazza to that of the royal exchange at London, but allows it to be much larger. It is covered with small domes or cupolas, from the four corners of which rise as many minarets or steeples, with double galleries, and adorned with gilded spires and crescents after the Turkish manner, as are also the cupolas which cover the piazza and other buildings. Between the columns of both inclosures hang a great number of lamps, which are constantly lighted at night. The first foundations of this second inclosure were laid by Omar the second khalif, who built no more than a low wall, to prevent the court of the caaba from being incroached upon by private buildings; but by the liberality of succeeding princes, the whole has been raised to that state of magnificence in which it appears at present.

This temple enjoys the privilege of an asylum for all sorts of criminals; but it is most remarkable for the pilgrimages made to it by the devout mussulmans, who pay so great a veneration to it, that they believe a single sight of its sacred walls, without any particular act of devotion, is as meritorious, in the sight of God, as the most careful discharge of one's duty, for the space of a whole year, in any other temple.

CAAMINI, in botany, a name given by the Spaniards and others to the finest sort of Paraguayan tea. It is the leaf of a shrub which grows on the mountains of Maracaya, and is used in Chili and Peru as the tea is with us. The mountains where this shrub grows naturally are far from the inhabited parts of Paraguay; but the people of the place know so well the value and use of it, that they constantly furnish themselves with great quantities of it from the spot. They used to go out on these expeditions many thousands together; leaving their country in the mean time exposed to the insults of their enemies, and many of themselves perishing by fatigue. To avoid these inconveniences, they have of late planted these trees about their habitations; but the leaves of these cultivated ones have not the fine flavour of those that grow wild. The king of Spain has permitted the Indians of Paraguay to bring to the town of Saintfoy 12,000 arobes of the leaves of this tree every year, but they are not able to procure so much of the wild leaves annually: about half the quantity is the utmost they bring of this: the other half is made up of the leaves of the trees in their own plantations; and this sells at a lower price, and is called *palos*. The arobe is about 25 pound weight; the general price is four piasters; and the money is always divided equally among the people of the colony.

CAANA, or Kaana, a town in Upper Egypt, seated on the eastern banks of the river Nile, from whence they carry corn and pulse for the supply of Mecca in Arabia. E. Long. 32. 23. N. Lat. 24. 30. Here are several monuments of antiquity yet remaining, adorned with hieroglyphics.

CAB, an Hebrew dry measure, being the sixth part of a seah or satum, and the 18th part of an ephah. A cab contained 2½ pints of our corn-measure: a quarter cab was the measure of dove's dung, or more properly a sort of chick-pease called by this name, which was sold at Samaria, during the siege of that city, for five shekels.

CABAL, an apt name currently given to the infamous ministry of Charles II. composed of five persons, Clifford, Ashley, Buckingham, Arlington, and Lauderdale; the first letters of whose names, in this order, furnished the appellation by which they were distinguished.

CABALIST, in French commerce, a factor or person who is concerned in managing the trade of another.

CABALLARIA, in middle-age writers, lands held by the tenure of furnishing a horseman, with suitable equipage, in time of war, or when the lord had occasion for him.

CABALLEROS, or Cavalleros, are Spanish wools, of which there is a pretty considerable trade at Bayonne in France.

CABALLINE, denotes something belonging to horses: thus caballine aloes is so called, from its being chiefly used for purging horses; and common brimstone is called *sulphur caballinum* for a like reason.

CABALLINUM (anc. geog.), a town of the Ædui in Gallia Celtica; now *Chalon sur Saone*, which see.

CABALLINUS (anc. geog.), a very clear fountain of mount Helicon in Bœotia; called *Hippocrene* by the Greeks, because opened by Pegasus on striking the rock with his hoof, and hence called *Pegasius*.

CABALLIO, or Cabellio (anc. geog.), a town of the Cavares in Gallia Narbonensis, situated on the Druentia. One of the Latin colonies, in the Notitiæ called *Civitas Cabellicorum*. Now *Cavaillon* in Provence.

CABBAGE, in botany. See Brassica; and Agriculture, n° 40, and 169. In the Georgical essays, we find this plant greatly recommended as an excellent food for cattle, producing much dung, and being an excellent substitute for hay. The author prefers the Scotch kind, as being most durable, and preferable on all other accounts. He also recommends autumn-sowed plants in preference to those sowed in the spring; the former producing a much more weighty crop than the latter. The expence of raising an acre of good cabbages he values at 14*l.* 15*s.* and its produce at 24*l.*

Cabbage-Tree, or *True Cabbage-Palm*. See Areca.

Cabbage-bark Tree. See Geoffræa.

CABBALA, according to the Hebrew style, has a very distinct signification from that wherein we understand it in our language. The Hebrew cabbala signifies tradition; and the Rabbins, who are called *cabbalists*, study principally the combination of particular words, letters, and numbers, and by this means pretend to discover what is to come, and to see clearly into the sense of many difficult passages of scripture. There are no sure principles of this knowledge, but it depends upon some particular traditions of the ancients; for which reason it is termed *cabbala*.

The cabbalists have abundance of names which they call *sacred*; these they make use of in invoking of spirits, and imagine they receive great light from them. They

They tell us, that the secrets of the cabbala were discovered to Moses on mount Sinai; and that these have been delivered to them down from father to son, without interruption, and without any use of letters; for to write them down, is what they are by no means permitted to do. This is likewise termed the *oral law*, because it passed from father to son, in order to distinguish it from the written laws.

There is another cabbala, called *artificial*, which consists in searching for abstruse and mysterious significations of a word in Scripture, from whence they borrow certain explanations, by combining the letters which compose it: this cabbala is divided into three kinds, the gematria, the notaricon, and the temura or themurah. The first whereof consists in taking the letters of a Hebrew word for ciphers or arithmetical numbers, and explaining every word by the arithmetical value of the letters whereof it is composed. The second sort of cabbala, called *notaricon*, consists in taking every particular letter of a word for an entire diction; and the third, called *themura*, i. e. change, consists in making different transpositions or changes of letters, placing one for the other, or one before the other.

Among the Christians, likewise, a certain sort of magic is, by mistake, called *cabbala*; which consists in using improperly certain passages of Scripture for magic operations, or in forming magic characters or figures with stars and talismans.

Some visionaries among the Jews believe, that Jesus Christ wrought his miracles by virtue of the mysteries of the cabbala.

CABBALISTS, the Jewish doctors who profess the study of the cabbala.

In the opinion of these men, there is not a word, letter, or accent in the law, without some mystery in it. The Jews are divided into two general sects; the karaites, who refuse to receive either tradition or the talmud, or any thing but the pure text of scripture; and the rabbinists, or talmudists, who, besides this, receive the traditions of the ancients, and follow the talmud.

The latter are again divided into two other sects; pure rabbinists, who explain the scripture in its natural sense, by grammar, history, and tradition; and cabbalists, who, to discover hidden mystical senses, which they suppose God to have couched therein, make use of the cabbala, and the mystical methods above mentioned.

CABECA, or Cabesse, a name given to the finest silks in the East Indies, as those from 15 to 20 *per cent.* inferior to them are called *barras*. The Indian workmen endeavour to pass them off one with the other; for which reason, the more experienced European merchants take care to open the bales, and to examine all the skains one after another. The Dutch distinguish two sorts of cabecas; namely, the moor cabeca, and the common cabeca. The former is sold at Amsterdam for about 21½ schellinghen Flemish, and the other for about 18½.

Cabeca de Vide, a small sea-port town of Alentejo in Portugal, with good walls, and a strong castle. W. Long. 6. 43. N. Lat. 39. 0.

CABENDA, a sea port of Congo in Africa, situated in E. Long. 12. 2. S. Lat. 4. 5.

CABES, or Gabes, a town of Africa, in the kingdom of Tunis, seated on a river near the gulf of the same name. E. Long. 10. 55. N. Lat. 33. 40.

CABEZZO, a province of the kingdom of Angola, in Africa; having Oacco on the north, Lubolo on the south, the Connza on the north-east, and the Reinha on the south-west. It is populous, and well stored with cattle, &c. and hath a mine of iron on a mountain from thence called the *iron mountain*, which yields great quantities of that metal; and this the Portuguese have taught the natives to manufacture. This province is watered by a river called *Rio Longo*, and other small rivulets, lakes, &c. The trees here are vastly large; and they have one sort not unlike our apple-trees, the bark of which being slashed with a knife, yields an odoriferous resin of the colour and consistency of wax, and very medicinal in its nature, only a little too hot for Europeans, unless qualified by some cooling drug.

CABIDOS, or Cavidos, a long measure used at Goa, and other places of the East Indies belonging to the Portuguese, to measure stuffs, linens, &c. and equal to 4/5ths of the Paris ell.

CABIN, a room or apartment in a ship where any of the officers usually reside. There are many of these in a large ship; the principal of which is designed for the captain or commander. In ships of the line this chamber is furnished with an open gallery in the ship's stern, as also a little gallery on each quarter. The apartments where the inferior officers or common sailors sleep and mess are usually called Births; which see.

The bed-places built up for the sailors at the ship's side in merchantmen are also called *cabins*.

CABINDA, the chief port of the kingdom of Angoy in Loango in Africa. It is situated at the mouth of a river of the same name about five leagues north of Cape Palmerino, on the north side of the mouth of the river Zaire. The bay is very commodious for trade, wooding, and watering.

CABINET, the most retired place in the finest part of a building, set apart for writing, studying, or preserving any thing that is precious.

A complete apartment consists of a hall, anti-chamber, chamber, and cabinet, with a gallery on one side. Hence we say, a cabinet of paintings, curiosities, &c.

Cabinet, also denotes a piece of joiner's workmanship, being a kind of press or chest, with several doors and drawers.

There are common cabinets of oak or of chesnut, varnished cabinets of China and Japan, cabinets of inlaid work, and some of ebony, or the like scarce and precious woods. Formerly the Dutch and German cabinets were much esteemed in France; but are now quite out of date, as well as the cabinets of ebony which came from Venice.

Cabinet is also used in speaking of the more select and secret councils of a prince or administration. Thus we say, the secrets, the intrigues of the cabinet. To avoid the inconveniences of a numerous council, the policy of Italy and practice of France first introduced cabinet councils. King Charles I. is charged with first establishing this usage in England. Besides his privy council, that prince erected a kind of cabinet council, or junto, under the denomination of a council of state; composed of archbishop Laud, the earl of

Strafford, and lord Collington, with the secretaries of state. Yet some pretend to find the substance of a cabinet council of much greater antiquity, and even allowed by parliament, who anciently settled a quorum of persons most confided in, without whose presence no arduous matter was to be determined; giving them power to act without consulting the rest of the council. As long since as the 28th of Henry III. a charter passed in affirmance of the ancient rights of the kingdom; which provided, that four great men, chosen by common consent, who were to be conservators of the kingdom, among other things, should see to the disposing of monies given by parliament, and appropriated to particular uses; and parliaments were to be summoned as they should advise. But even of these four, any two made a quorum; and generally the chief justice of England, and chancellor, were of the number of the conservators. Matth. Par. 28. Hen. III. In the first of Henry VI. the parliament provides, that the quorum for the privy council be six, or four at least; and that in all weighty considerations, the dukes of Bedford and Gloucester, the king's uncles, should be present; which seems to be erecting a cabinet by law.

CABIRI, a term in the theology of the ancient Pagans, signifying great and powerful gods; being a name given to the gods of Samothracia. They were also worshipped in other parts of Greece, as Lemnos and Thebes, where the cabiria were celebrated in honour of them; these gods are said to be, in number, four, viz. Axieros, Axiocersa, Axiocersus, and Casmilus.

CABIRIA, festivals in honour of the Cabiri, celebrated in Thebes and Lemnos, but especially in Samothracia, an island consecrated to the Cabiri. All who were initiated into the mysteries of these gods, were thought to be secured thereby from storms at sea, and all other dangers. The ceremony of initiation was performed by placing the candidate, crowned with olive branches, and girded about the loins with a purple ribband, on a kind of throne, about which the priests, and persons before initiated, danced.

CABLE, a thick, large, strong rope, commonly of hemp, which serves to keep a ship at anchor.

There is no merchant-ship, however weak, but has at least three cables; namely, the chief cable, or cable of the sheet-anchor, a common cable, and a smaller one.

Cable is also said of ropes, which serve to raise heavy loads, by the help of cranes, pullies, and other engines. The name of *cable* is usually given to such as have, at least, three inches in circumference; those that are less are only called *ropes*, of different names according to their use.

Every cable, of whatsoever thickness it be, is composed of three strands; every strand of three ropes; and every rope of three twists: the twist is made of more or less threads, according as the cable is to be thicker or thinner.

In the manufacture of cables, after the ropes are made, they use sticks, which they pass first between the ropes of which they make the strands, and afterwards between the strands of which they make the cable, to the end that they may all twist the better, and be more regularly wound together; and also, to prevent them from entwining or entangling, they hang, at the end of each strand and of each rope, a weight of lead or of stone.

The number of threads each cable is composed of is always proportioned to its length and thickness; and it is by this number of threads that its weight and value are ascertained: thus, a cable of three inches circumference, or one inch diameter, ought to consist of 48 ordinary threads, and to weigh 192 pounds; and on this foundation is calculated the following table, very useful for all people engaged in marine commerce, who fit out merchantmen for their own account, or freight them for the account of others.

A table of the number of threads and weight of cables of different circumferences.

Circumf.	Threads.	Weight.
3 inches	48	192 pounds.
4	77	308
5	121	484
6	174	696
7	238	952
8	311	1244
9	393	1572
10	485	1940
11	598	2392
12	699	2796
13	821	3284
14	952	3808
15	1093	4372
16	1244	4976
17	1404	5616
18	1574	6296
19	1754	7016
20	1943	7772

Sheet-Anchor Cable, is the greatest cable belonging to a ship.

Stream Cable, a hawser or rope, something smaller than the bowers, and used to moor the ship in a river, or haven, sheltered from the wind and sea, &c.

Serve or Plait the Cable, is to bind it about with ropes, clouts, &c. to keep it from galling in the hawse.

To splice a Cable, is to make two pieces fast together, by working the several threads of the rope the one into the other.

Pay more Cable, is to let more out of the ship. *Pay cheap the Cable*, is to to hand it out apace. *Veer more Cable*, is to let more out, &c.

Cable's *Length*, a measure of 120 fathoms, or of the usual length of the cable.

CABLED, in heraldry, a term applied to a cross formed of the two ends of a ship's cable; sometimes also to a cross covered over with rounds of rope; more properly called a *cross corded*.

Cabled *Flute*, in architecture, such flutes as are filled up with pieces in the form of a cable.

CABO de Istria, the capital town of the province of Istria, in the territory of Venice; and the see of a bishop. It is seated on a small island in the gulf of Venice, and is joined to the main land by draw-bridges. E. Long. 14. 18. N. Lat. 45. 49.

CABOCHED, in heraldry, is when the heads of beasts are borne without any part of the neck, full-faced.

CABOLETTO, in commerce, a coin of the republic of Genoa, worth about 3d. of our money.

CABOT (Sebastian), the first discoverer of the continent of America, was the son of John Cabot a Venetian. He was born at Bristol in 1477; and was taught by his father arithmetic, geometry, and cosmography.

graphy. Before he was 20 years of age he made several voyages. The first of any consequence seems to have been made with his father, who had a commission from Henry VII. for the discovery of a north-west passage to India. They sailed in the spring of 1497; and proceeding to the north-west they discovered land, which for that reason they called *Primovista*, or *Newfoundland*. Another smaller island they called *St John*, from its being discovered on the feast of St John Baptist; after which, they sailed along the coast of America as far as Cape Florida, and then returned to England with a good cargo, and three Indians aboard. Stowe and Speed ascribe these discoveries wholly to Sebastian, without mentioning his father. It is probable that Sebastian, after his father's death, made several voyages to these parts, as a map of his discoveries, drawn by himself, was hung up in the privy garden at Whitehall. However, history gives but little account of his life for near 20 years; when he went to Spain, where he was made pilot-major, and intrusted with reviewing all projects for discoveries, which were then very numerous. His great capacity and approved integrity induced many eminent merchants to treat with him about a voyage by the new found straits of Magellan to the Moluccas. He therefore sailed in 1525, first to the Canaries; then to the Cape Verd islands; thence to St Augustine and the island of Patos; when some of his people beginning to be mutinous, and refusing to pass through the straits, he laid aside the design of sailing to the Moluccas; left some of the principal mutineers upon a desart island; and, sailing up the rivers of Plate and Paraguay, discovered, and built forts in, a large tract of fine country, that produced gold, silver, and other rich commodities. He thence dispatched messengers to Spain for a supply of provisions, ammunition, goods for trade, and a recruit of men: but his request not being readily complied with, after staying five years in America, he returned home; where he met with a cold reception, the merchants being displeased at his not having pursued his voyage to the Moluccas, while his treatment of the mutineers had given umbrage at court. Hence he returned to England; and being introduced to the Duke of Somerset, then lord protector, a new office was erected for him: he was made governor of the mystery and company of the merchant-adventurers for the discovery of regions, dominions, islands, and places unknown; a pension was granted him, by letters-patent, of 166l. 13s. 4d. per annum; and he was consulted in all affairs relative to trade. In 1522, by his interest, the court fitted out some ships for the discovery of the northern parts of the world. This produced the first voyage the English made to Russia, and the beginning of that commerce which has ever since been carried on between the two nations. The Russia company was now founded by a charter granted by Philip and Mary; and of this company Sebastian was appointed governor for life. He is said to be the first who took notice of the variation of the needle, and who published a map of the world. The exact time of his death is not known, but he lived to be above 70 years of age.

CABRA, a town of the kingdom of Tombut in Africa. It is a large town, but without walls; and is seated on the river Niger, about 12 miles from Tombut. The houses are built in the shape of bells; and the walls are made with stakes or hurdles, plastered with clay, and covered with reeds after the manner of thatch. This place is very much frequented by negroes who come here by water to trade. The town is very unhealthy, which is probably owing to its low situation. The colour of the inhabitants is black, and their religion a sort of Mahometanism. They have plenty of corn, cattle, milk, and butter; but *salt* is very scarce. The judge who decides controversies is appointed by the king of Tombut. E. Long. 0. 50. N. Lat. 14. 21.

CABUL, or GABOUL, a city of Asia, and capital of the province of Cabulistan. It lies in E. Long. 68. 15. N. Lat. 33. 30. on the frontiers of Great Bukharia, on the south side of the mountains which divide the territories of the Mogul from that part of Great Tartary. It is one of the finest places in that part of the world; large, rich, and very populous. As it is considered as the key of the great Mogul's dominions on that side, great care is taken to keep its fortifications in repair, and a numerous garrison is maintained for its security. It lies on the road between Samarcand and Lahor; and is much frequented by the Tartars, Persians, and Indians. The Usbec Tartars drive there a great trade in slaves and horses, of which it is said that no fewer are sold than 60,000 annually. The Persians bring black cattle and sheep, which renders provisions very cheap. They have also wine, and plenty of all sorts of eatables. The city stands on a little river which falls into the Indus, and thereby affords a short and speedy passage for all the rich commodities in the country behind it, which, when brought to Cabul, are there exchanged for slaves and horses, and then conveyed by merchants of different countries to all parts of the world. The inhabitants are most of them Indian pagans, though the officers of the Mogul and most of the garrison are Mahometans.

CABULISTAN, a province of Asia, formerly belonging to the Great Mogul; but ceded in 1739 to Kouli Khan, who at that time governed Persia. It is bounded on the north by Bukharia, on the east by Cashmire, on the west by Zabulistan and Candahar, and on the south by Multan. It is 350 miles in length, 150 in breadth, and its chief town is Cabul. This country in general is not very fruitful; but in the vales they have good pasture-lands. The roads are much infested with banditti; which obliges the natives to have guards for the security of travellers. The religion of the Cabulistans is pagan; and their extraordinary time of devotion is the full moon in February, and continues for two days. At this time they are clothed in red, make their offerings, dance to the sound of the trumpet, and make visits to their friends in masquerade dresses. They say, their god Crusman killed a giant who was his enemy, and that he appeared like a little child; in memory of which, they cause a child to shoot at the figure of a giant. Those of the same tribe make bonfires, and feast together in a jovial manner. The moral part of their religion consists in charity; for which reason, they dig wells and build houses for the accommodation of travellers. They have plenty of provisions, mines of iron, myrobolans, aromatic woods, and drugs of many kinds. They carry on a great trade with the neighbouring countries; by which means they are very rich, and are supplied with plenty of all things.

CABURNS,

Caburns, Cacalia.

CABURNS, on ſhip-board, are ſmall lines made of ſpun yarn, to bind cables, ſeize tackles, or the like.

CACALIA, in botany; a genus of the polygamia æqualis order, belonging to the ſyngeneſia claſs of plants. The receptacle is naked; the pappus hairy; the calyx cylindrical, oblong, and caliculated, or having a ſmall calyx of very ſhort ſcales only at the baſe.

Species. 1. The ſuaveolens, with a herbaceous ſtalk, is a native of North America. It hath a perennial creeping root which ſends out many ſtalks, garniſhed with triangular ſpear-ſhaped leaves ſharply ſawed on their edges, of a pale green on their under ſide, but a deep ſhining green above, placed alternately. The ſtalks riſe to the height of ſeven or eight feet, and are terminated by umbels of white flowers, which are ſucceeded by oblong ſeeds covered with down. It flowers in Auguſt, and the ſeeds ripen in October. The ſtalks decay in autumn, and new one riſes in the ſpring. This plant multiplies greatly by its ſpreading roots, as alſo by the ſeeds, which are ſpread to a great diſtance by the wind, the down which adheres to them being greatly aſſiſting to their conveyance. The roots which have been caſt out of Chelſea garden, being carried by the tide to a great diſtance, have fixed themſelves to the banks of the river, and increaſed ſo much, that in a few years this ſpecies may probably appear as a native of England. 2. The ficoides is a native of the Cape of Good Hope. It riſes with ſtrong round ſtalks to the height of ſeven or eight feet, woody at bottom, but ſoft and ſucculent upward, ſending out many irregular branches, garniſhed more than half their length with thick, taper, ſucculent leaves, a little compreſſed on two ſides, ending in points, covered with a whitiſh glaucous farina, which comes off when handled. Theſe, when broken, emit a ſtrong odour of turpentine, and are full of a viſcous juice; at the extremity of the branches the flowers are produced in ſmall umbels; they are white, tubulous, and cut into five parts at the top. The leaves of this plant are pickled by the French, who eſteem them much; and in doing this they have a method of preſerving the white farina upon them, which adds greatly to the beauty of the pickle when brought to table. 3. The kleinia, with a compound ſhrubby ſtalk, grows naturally in the Canary iſlands, but has long been cultivated in the Engliſh gardens. It riſes with a thick fleſhy ſtem divided at certain diſtances, as it were, into ſo many joints. Each of theſe diviſions ſwell much larger in the middle than they do at each end; and the ſtalks divide into many irregular branches of the ſame form, which, toward their extremities, are garniſhed with long, narrow, ſpear-ſhaped leaves of a glaucous colour, ſtanding all round the ſtalks without order. As they fall off, they leave a ſcar at the place, which always remains on the branches. The flowers are produced in large cluſters at the extremity of the branches, which are tubulous, and of a faint carnation colour. They appear in Auguſt and September, but continue great part of October, and are not ſucceeded by ſeeds in this country. There have been ſtones and foſſils dug up at a very great depth in ſome parts of England having very perfect impreſſions of this plant upon them; from whence Dr Woodward has ſuppoſed the plants were lodged there at the univerſal deluge; and finding the impreſſions of many other plants and animals which are natives of thoſe iſlands, he concludes that the water flowed hither from the ſouth-weſt. This plant has been called the *cabbage-tree*, from the reſemblance which the ſtalk of it has to the cabbage: others have intitled it *carnation-tree*, from the ſhape of the leaves and the colour of the flowers. Beſides theſe, there are ſeven other ſpecies, viz. the alpina, with kidney-ſhaped leaves; the glabra, with ſmooth leaves; the atriplicifolia, with heart-ſhaped ſinuated leaves; the papillaris, with a ſhrubby ſtalk guarded on every ſide with broken rough foot-ſtalks; the ante-euphorbium, with oblong oval leaves; the ſonchifolia, with lyre-ſhaped indented leaves; and the hitra, with leaves divided into five acute parts.

Cacalia ‖ Cachao.

Culture. The three ſpecies deſcribed above are very eaſily propagated. The firſt will propagate itſelf, as already mentioned, either by roots or ſeeds. The ſecond is eaſily propagated by cuttings during the ſummer months: Theſe ſhould be cut from the plants and laid to dry a fortnight, that the wound may be healed over before they are planted. Moſt people plunge the pots in which theſe are planted into an hot-bed, to promote their putting out roots; but if planted in June or July, they will root as well in the open air. Even branches broken off by accident have frequently put out roots when fallen on the ground, without any care. Theſe branches may be kept ſix months out of the ground, and will take root if planted. This ſhould have a light ſandy earth, and in winter be placed in an airy glaſs-caſe, where they may enjoy the ſun and air in mild weather, but muſt be protected from froſt. During the winter ſeaſon the plants muſt have but little water; and in ſummer, when they are placed in the open air, it ſhould not be given to them too often, nor in great quantity. The third is alſo propagated by cuttings, and the plants require the ſame culture; but muſt have a dry warm glaſs-caſe in winter, and very little water, being ſubject to rot with wet. In ſummer they muſt be placed in the open air in a warm ſheltered ſituation, and in very dry weather refreſhed moderately with water. With this management the plants will flower annually, and grow to the height of eight or ten feet.

CACAO. See Theobroma.

CACCOONS. See Fevillea.

CACERES, a town of Spain, in the province of Eſtremadura, is ſeated on the river Saler, and noted for the exceeding fine wool which the ſheep bear in the neighbourhood. Between this town and Brozas, there is a wood, where the allies defeated the rear-guard of the duke of Berwick, on the 7th of April 1706. E. Long. 6. 47. N. Lat. 39. 15.

CACHALOT, in ichthyology. See Physeter.

CACHAN, or Cashan, a conſiderable town of Perſia in Irac Agemi, where they carry on an extenſive trade in ſilks, ſilver, and gold brocades, and fine earthen ware. It is ſituated in a vaſt plain, 55 miles from Iſpahan. E. Long. 50. 5. N. Lat. 34. 10.

CACHAO, a province of the kingdom of Tonquin in Aſia, ſituated in the heart of the kingdom, and ſurrounded by the other ſeven. Its ſoil is fertile, and in ſome places mountainous, abounding with variety of trees, and particularly that of varniſh. Moſt of theſe provinces carry on ſome branch of the ſilk manufactory, but this moſt of all. It takes its name from the capital, which is alſo the metropolis of the whole kingdom, though in other reſpects hardly comparable to a Chineſe one of the third rank.

Cachao, a city of the province of that name, in the kingdom of Tonquin in Aſia, ſituated in E. Long.

105.

Cachao.

105. 31. N. Lat. 22. 10. at about 80 leagues distance from the sea. It is prodigiously crowded with people, insomuch that the streets are hardly passable, especially on market days. These vast crowds, however, come mostly from the neighbouring villages; upon which account these villages have been allowed their halls in particular parts of the city, where they bring and dispose of their wares. The town itself, though the metropolis of the whole Tonquinese kingdom, hath neither walls nor fortifications. The principal streets are wide and airy, but the rest of them narrow and ill-paved; and except the palace royal and arsenal, the town hath little else worth notice. The houses are low and mean, mostly built of wood and clay, and not above one story high. The magazines and warehouses belonging to foreigners are the only edifices built of brick; and which, though plain, yet, by reason of their height and more elegant structure, make a considerable show among those rows of wooden huts. From the combustibility of its edifices, this city suffers frequent and dreadful conflagrations. These spread with such surprising velocity, that some thousands of houses are often laid in ashes before the fire can be extinguished. To prevent these sad consequences, every house hath, either in its yard or even in its centre, some low building of brick, in form of an oven, into which the inhabitants on the first alarm convey their most valuable goods. Besides this precaution, which every family takes to secure their goods, the government obliges them to keep a cistern, or some other capacious vessel, always full of water on the top of their house, to be ready on all occasions of this nature; as likewise a long pole and bucket, to throw water from the kennel upon the houses. If these two expedients fail of suppressing the flames, they immediately cut the straps which fasten the thatch to the walls, and let it fall in and waste itself on the ground. The king's palace stands in the centre of the city; and is surrounded with a stout wall, within whose cincture are seen a great number of apartments two stories high, whose fronts and portals have something of the grand taste. Those of the king and his wives are embellished with variety of carvings and gildings after the Indian manner, and all finely varnished. In the outer court are a vast number of sumptuous stables for the king's horses and elephants. The appearance of the inner courts can only be conjectured; for the avenues are not only shut to all strangers, but even to the king's subjects, except those of the privy council, and the chief ministers of state: yet we are told, that there are stair-cases by which people may mount up to the top of the walls, which are about 18 or 20 feet high; from whence they may have a distant view of the royal apartments, and of the fine parterres and fish-ponds that are between the cincture and them. The front wall hath a large gate well ornamented, which is never opened but when the king goes in and out; but at some distance from it on each side there are two posterns, at which the courtiers and servants may go in and out. This cincture, which is of a vast circumference, is faced with brick within and without, and the whole structure is terminated by wide spacious gardens; which, though stored with great variety of proper ornaments, are destitute of the grandeur and elegance observed in the palaces of European princes. Besides this palace, the ruins of one still more magnificent are to be observed, and are called *Litterris*. The circumference is said to have been betwixt six and seven miles: some arches, porticoes, and other ornaments, are still remaining; from which, and some of its courts paved with marble, it may be concluded to have been as magnificent a structure as any of the eastern parts can show. The arsenal is likewise a large and noble building, well stored with ammunition and artillery. The English factory is situated on the north side of the city, fronting the river *Singuhoy*. It is a handsome low-built house, with a spacious dining-room in the centre; and on each side are the apartments of the merchants, factors, and servants. At each end of the building are smaller houses for other uses, as store-houses, kitchen, &c. which form two wings with the square in the middle, and parallel with the river, near the bank of which stands a long flag-staff, on which they commonly display the English colours on Sundays and all remarkable days. Adjoining to it, on the south side, is the Danish factory, which is neither so large nor so handsome. On the same side of the river runs a long dike, whose timber and stones are so firmly fastened together, that no part of it can be stirred without moving the whole. This work was raised on those banks to prevent the river, during the time of their vast rains, from overflowing the city; and it has hitherto answered its end; for though the town stands high enough to be in no danger from land-floods, it might yet have been otherwise frequently damaged, if not totally laid under water, by the overflowing of that river. Some curious observations have been communicated to the royal society concerning differences between the tides of those seas and those of Europe, viz. that on the Tonquinese coast ebbs and flows but once in 24 hours; that is, that the tide is rising during the space of 12 hours, and can be easily perceived during two of the moon's quarters, but can hardly be observed during the other two. In the spring tides, which last 14 days, the waters begin to rise at the rising of the moon; whereas in the low tides, which continue the same number of days, the tide begins not till that planet is got below the horizon. Whilst it is passing through the six northern signs, the tides are observed to vary greatly, to rise sometimes very high, and sometimes to be very low; but when it is once got into the southern part of the zodiac, they are then found to be more even and regular.

Cachao || Cachrys.

CACHECTIC, something partaking of the nature of, or belonging to, a cachexy.

CACHEO, a town of Negroland in Africa, seated on the river St Domingo. It is subject to the Portuguese, who have three forts there, and carry on a great trade in wax and slaves. W. Long. 14. 55. N. Lat. 12. 0.

CACHEXY, in medicine, a vicious state of the humours and whole habit. See (the Index subjoined to) MEDICINE.

CACHRYS, in botany: A genus of the digynia order belonging to the pentandria class of plants; and in the natural method ranking under the 45th order, *Umbellatae*. The fruit is subovate, angled, and cork or spongy rinded.

There are five species, viz. the trifida, with bipinnated leaves; the sicula, with double winged leaves; the libanotis, with smooth furrowed seeds; the linearia, with plain channelled fruit; and the hungarica, with a plain, fungous, channelled seed. All these are per-

cenial.

cassial plants, rising pretty high, and bearing large umbels of yellow flowers, and may be propagated by seeds which ought to be sown soon after they are ripe; for if they are kept out of the ground till the next spring, they often miscarry. They must also be sown in a shady border where they are to remain: for the plants, having long tap-roots, will not bear transplanting so well as many others. The Hungarians in the neighbourhood of Erlaw, and those who border on Transylvania, Servia, &c. eat the root of the fifth species in a scarcity of corn for want of other bread.

CACHUNDE, the name of a medicine, highly celebrated among the Chinese and Indians, and made of several aromatic ingredients, the perfumes, medicinal earth, and precious stones: they make the whole into a stiff paste, and form out of it several figures according to their fancy, which are dried for use: these are principally used in the East Indies, but are sometimes brought over to Portugal. In China, the principal persons usually carry a small piece in their mouths, which is a continued cordial, and gives their breath a very sweet smell. It is a highly valuable medicine also, in all nervous complaints; and is esteemed a prolonger to life, and a provocative to venery, the two great intentions of most of the medicines in use in the East.

CACOCHYLIA, or CACOCHYMIA, a vicious state of the vital humours, especially of the mass of blood; arising either from a disorder of the secretions or excretions, or from external contagion. The word is Greek, compounded of κακος *ill*, and χυμος *juice*.

CACOPHONIA, in grammar and rhetoric, the meeting of two letters, or syllables, which yield an uncouth and disagreeable sound. The word is compounded of κακος *evil*, and φωνη *voice*.

CACOPHONIA, in Medicine, denotes a vice or depravation of the voice or speech; of which there are two species, *aphonia* and *dysphonia*.

CACTUS, in botany: A genus of the monogynia order, belonging to the icosandria class of plants; and in the natural method ranking under the 13th order, *Succulentæ*. The calyx is monophyllous; superior, or above the receptacle of the fruit imbricated; the corolla polypetalous; the fruit an unilocular, polyspermous berry. To this genus Linnæus has added the cereus and opuntia. There are 24 species, all natives of the West Indies and Mexico.

The cacti are plants of a singular structure, but especially the larger kinds of them; which appear like a large, fleshy, green melon, with deep ribs, set all over with strong sharp thorns; and, when the plants are cut through the middle, their inside is a soft, pale-green, fleshy substance, very full of moisture. The fruit of all the species is frequently eaten by the inhabitants of the West Indies. "The fruits are about three quarters of an inch in length, of a taper form, drawing to a point at the bottom toward the plant, but blunt at the top where the empalement of the flower was situated." The taste is agreeably acid, which in a hot country must render the fruit more grateful.

The cochineal animals are supported on a species called *cactus cochinillifer*.—The flower of the cactus grandiflora (one of the creeping cereuses) is said to be as grand and beautiful as any in the vegetable system: It begins to open in the evening about seven o'clock, is in perfection about eleven, and fades about four in the morning; so that the same flower only continues in perfection about six hours. The calyx when expanded is about a foot in diameter, of a splendid yellow within, and a dark brown without; the petals are many, and of a pure white; and the great number of recurved stamina, surrounding the style in the centre of the flower, make a grand appearance, to which may be added the fine scent, which perfumes the air to a considerable distance. It flowers in July.

CACUS, in fabulous history, an Italian shepherd upon mount Aventine. As Hercules was driving home the herd of king Geryon whom he had slain, Cacus robbed him of some of his oxen, which he drew backward into his den lest they should be discovered. Hercules at last finding them out by their lowing, or the robbery being discovered to him, killed Cacus with his club. He was Vulcan's son, of prodigious bulk, and half man half satyr.

CADAN, a town of Bohemia, in the circle of Zats, seated on the northern bank of the river Egra, in E. Long. 13. 34. N. Lat. 50. 20.

CADARI, or KADARI, a sect of Mahometans, who assert free-will; attribute the actions of men to men alone, not to any secret power determining the will; and deny all absolute decrees, and predestination. The author of this sect was Mabed ben Kaled Al Gihoni, who suffered martyrdom for it. The word comes from the Arabic, קדר, *cadara*, *power*. Ben Aun calls the Cadarians the Magi, or Manichees of the Mussulmen.

CADE, a cag, cask, or barrel. A cade of herrings is a vessel containing the quantity of 500 red herrings, or 1000 sprats.

Cade-Lamb, a young lamb weaned, and brought up by hand, in a house; called in the North, *pet-lamb*.

Cade-Oil, in the *Materia Medica*, a name given to an oil much in use in some parts of France and Germany. The physicians call it *oleum cadæ*, or *oleum de cada*. This is supposed by some to be the pisselæum of the ancients, but improperly; it is made of the fruit of the oxycedrus, which is called by the people of these places *cada*.

Cade-Worm in zoology, the maggot or worm of a fly called *phryganea*. It is used as a bait in angling. See PHRYGANEA.

CADEA, or THE LEAGUE OF THE HOUSE OF GOD, is one of those that compose the republic of the Grisons, and the most powerful and extensive of them all. It contains the bishopric of Coire, the great valley of Engadine, and that of Bregail or Pregal. Of the 11 great, or 21 small communities, there are but two that speak the German language; that of the rest is called the *Rhetic*, and is a dialect of the Italian. The Protestant religion is most prevalent in this league, which has been allied to the Swiss cantons ever since the year 1498. Coire is the capital town.

CADENAC, a town of France in Quercy, on the confines of Rouergue, seated on the river Lot, in E. Long. 2. 12. N. Lat. 44. 36.

CADENCE, or REPOSE, in music, (from the Latin *cadere* to *fall or descend*); the termination of an harmonical phrase on a repose, or on a perfect chord. See MUSIC, art. 73—76, and 131—137.

CADENCE, in reading, is a falling of the voice below the key-note at the close of every period. In reading, whether prose or verse, a certain tone is assumed which is called the *key-note*; and in this tone the bulk of the words

words are founded; but this note is generally lowered towards the close of every sentence.

Cadence, in the manege, an equal measure or proportion, observed by a horse in all his motions; so that his times have an equal regard to one another, the one does not embrace or take in more ground than the other, and the horse observes his ground regularly.

CADENE, one of the sorts of carpets which the Europeans import from the Levant. They are the worst sort of all, and are sold by the piece from one to two piastres per carpet.

CADENET, a town of France in Provence, and in the Viguirie of Apt. E. Long. 5. 30. N. Lat. 43. 40.

CADES, or Kadesh, (anc. geog.) a town in the Wilderness of Zin, in Arabia Petræa; the first encampment of the Israelites, after their departure from Eziongeber; and from which the Wilderness of Zin was called Cades; the burial-place of Miriam, with the rock and water of Meribah in it. Another *Cades*, a town of the tribe of Judah, Joshua xv. 23. *Cadesbarnea*, called also *Cades*.

CADESBARNEA, (anc. geog.) a town of the Wilderness of Paran, on the confines of Canaan, from which the spies were sent out; sometimes simply called *Cades*, but distinct from the Cades in the Wilderness of Zin.

CADET, the younger son of a family, is a term naturalized in our language from the French. At Paris, among the citizens, the cadets have an equal patrimony with the rest. At Caux, in Normandy, the custom, as with us, is to leave all to the eldest, except a small portion to the cadets. In Spain, it is usual for one of the cadets in great families to take the mother's name.

Cadet is also a military term denoting a young gentleman who chooses to carry arms in a marching regiment as a private man. His views are, to acquire some knowledge in the art of war, and to obtain a commission in the army. Cadet differs from volunteer, as the former takes pay, whereas the latter serves without pay.

CADI, or Cadhi, a judge of the civil affairs in the Turkish empire. It is generally taken for the judge of a town; judges of provinces being distinguished by the appellation of *mollas*.

We find numerous complaints of the avarice, iniquity, and extortion, of the Turkish cadis; all justice is here venal; the people bribe the cadis, the cadis bribe the moulas, the moulas the cadileschers, and the cadileschers the mufti. Each cadi has his serjeants, who are to summon persons to appear and answer complaints. If the party summoned fails to appear at the hour appointed, sentence is passed in favour of his adversary. It is usually vain to appeal from the sentences of the cadi, since the affair is never heard anew, but judgment is passed on the case as stated by the cadi. But the cadis are often cashiered and punished for crying injustice with the bastinado and mulcts; the law, however, does not allow them to be put to death. Constantinople has had cadis ever since the year 1390, when Bajazet I. obliged John Paleologus, emperor of the Greeks, to receive cadis into the city to judge all controversies happening between the Greeks and the Turks settled there. In some countries of Africa, the cadis

are also judges of religious matters. Among the Moors, cadi is the denomination of their higher order of priests or doctors, answering to the rabbins among the Jews.

CADIACI, the Turkish name of Chalcedon. See Chalcedon.

CADILESCHER, a capital officer of justice among the Turks, answering to a chief justice among us.

It is said, that this authority was originally confined to the soldiery; but that, at present, it extends itself to the determination of all kinds of law-suits; yet is nevertheless subject to appeals.

There are but three cadileschers in all the grand signior's territories: the first is that of Europe; the second, of Natolia; and the third resides at Grand Cairo. This last is the most considerable: they have their seats in the divan next to the grand visir.

CADILLAC, a town of France in Guienne, and in Bazadois, near the river Garonne, with a handsome castle, situated in W. Long. 0. 15. N. Lat. 44. 37.

CADIZ, a city and port-town of Andalusia in Spain, situated on the island of Leon, opposite to Port St Mary on the continent, about 60 miles south-west of Seville, and 40 north-west of Gibraltar. W. Long. 6. 40. N. Lat. 36. 30.

It occupies the whole surface of the western extremity of the island, which is composed of two large circular parts, joined together by a very narrow bank of sand, forming altogether the figure of a chain-shot. At the south-east end, the ancient bridge of Suaço, thrown over a deep channel or river, affords a communication between the island and the continent; a strong line of works defends the city from all approaches along the isthmus; and, to render them still more difficult, all the gardens and little villas on the beach were in 1762 cleared away, and a dreary sandy glacis left in their room, so that now there is scarce a tree on the whole island.

Except the *Calle Ancha*, all the streets are narrow, ill-paved, and insufferably stinking. They are all drawn in straight lines, and most of them intersect each other at right angles. The swarms of rats that in the nights run about the streets are innumerable; whole droves of them pass and repass continually, and their their midnight revels are extremely troublesome to such as walk late. The houses are lofty, with each a vestibule, which being left open till night, serve passengers to retire to; this custom, which prevails throughout Spain, renders these places exceedingly offensive. In the middle of the house is a court like a deep well, under which is generally a cistern, the breeding-place of gnats and musquitoes; the ground-floors are warehouses, the first stories compting-house or kitchen, and the principal apartment up two pair of stairs. The roofs are flat, covered with an impenetrable cement, and few are without a *mirador* or turret for the purpose of commanding a view of the sea. Round the parapet-wall at top are placed rows of square pillars, meant either for ornament according to some traditional mode of decoration, or to fix awnings to, that such as sit there for the benefit of the sea-breeze may be sheltered from the rays of the sun; but the most common use made of them, is to fasten ropes for drying linen upon. High above all these pinnacles, which give Cadiz a most singular appearance, stands

Cadiz.

the tower of signals. Here flags are hung out on the first sight of a sail, marking the size of the ship, the nation it belongs to, and, if a Spanish Indiaman, the port of the Indies it comes from. The ships are acquainted with the proper signals to be made, and these are repeated by the watchmen of the tower; as painted lists are in every house, persons concerned in commerce soon learn the marks.

The city is divided into twenty-four quarters, under the inspection of as many commissioners of police; and its population is reckoned at one hundred and forty thousand inhabitants, of which twelve thousand are French, and at least as many more Italians. The square of Saint Antonio is large, and tolerably handsome, and there are a few smaller openings of no great note. The public walk, or Alameda, is pleasant in the evening: it is fenced off the coach-road by a marble rail. The sea-air prevents the trees from thriving, and destroys all hopes of future shade.

From the Alameda, continuing your walk westwards, you come to the Campofanto, a large esplanade, the only airing-place for coaches; it turns round most part of the west and south sides of the island, but the buildings are straggling and ugly; the only edifice of any show is the new orphan-house; opposite to it is the fortress of St Sebastian, built on a neck of land running out into the sea. The round tower at the extremity is supposed to have saved the city, in the great earthquake of 1755, from being swept away by the fury of the waves. The building proved sufficiently solid to withstand the shock, and break the immense volume of water that threatened destruction to the whole island. In the narrow part of the isthmus the surge beat over with amazing impetuosity, and bore down all before it; among the rest, the grandson of the famous tragic-poet Racine, who strove in vain to escape, by urging his horse to the utmost of his speed. On St Sebastian's feast, a kind of wake or fair is held in the fort; an astonishing number of people then passing and repassing, on a string of wooden bridges laid from rock to rock, makes a very lively moving picture.

From hence to the wooden circus where they exhibit the bull-feasts, you keep turning to the left close above the sea, which on all this side dashes over large ledges of rock; the shore seems here absolutely inaccessible. On this shore stands the cathedral, a work of great expence, but carried on with so little vigour, that it is difficult to guess at the term of years it will require to bring it to perfection. The vaults are executed with great solidity. The arches, that spring from the clustered pilasters to support the roof of the church, are very bold; the minute sculpture bestowed upon them seems superfluous, as all the effect will be lost from their great height, and from the shade that will be thrown upon them by the filling up of the interstices. From the sea, the present top of the church resembles the carcase of some large monster cast upon its side, rearing its gigantic blanched ribs high above the buildings of the city. The outward casings are to be of white marble, the bars of the windows of bronze.

Next, crossing before the land-gate and barracks, a superb edifice for strength, convenience, and cleanliness, you come down to the ramparts that defend the city on the side of the bay. If the prospect to the ocean is solemn, that towards the main land is animated in the highest degree; the men of war ride in the eastern bosom of the bay; lower down the merchantmen are spread far and near; and close to the town an incredible number of barks, of various shapes and sizes, cover the surface of the water, some moored and some in motion, carrying goods to and fro. The opposite shore of Spain is studded with white houses, and enlivened by the towns of St Mary's, Port-real, and others, behind which, eastward, on a ridge of hills, stands Medina Sidonia, and further back rise the mountains of Granada. Westward, Rota closes the horizon, near which was anciently the island and city of Tartessus, now covered by the sea, but at low-water some part of the ruins are still to be discerned. In a large bastion, jutting out into the bay, they have built the custom-house, the first story of which is level with the walk upon the walls. When it was resolved to erect a building so necessary to this great emporium of trade, the marquis di Squillace gave orders that no expence should be spared, and the most intelligent architects employed, in order to erect a monument, which by its taste and magnificence might excite the admiration of posterity: the result of these precautions proved a piece of vile architecture, composed of the worst of materials.

Cadiz, Cadmus.

The stir here is prodigious during the last months of the stay of the flota. The packers possess the art of pressing goods in great perfection; but, as they pay the freight according to the cubic palms of each bale, they are apt to squeeze down the cloths and linens so very close and hard, as sometimes to render them unfit for use. The exportation of French luxuries in dress is enormous; Lyons furnishes most of them; England sends out bale goods; Brittany and the north, linens. Every commercial nation has a consul resident at Cadiz; those of England and France are the only ones not allowed to have any concern in trade.

In 1596, Cadiz was taken, pillaged, and burnt by the English; but in 1702 it was attempted in conjunction with the Dutch, without success.

CADIZADELITES, a sect of Mahometans very like the ancient stoics. They shun feasts and diversions, and affect an extraordinary gravity in all their actions; they are continually talking of God, and some of them make a jumble of Christianity and Mahometanism; they drink wine, even in the *fast* of the ramazan; they love and protect the Christians; they believe that Mahomet is the Holy Ghost, practise circumcision, and justify it by the example of Jesus Christ.

CADMEAN LETTERS, the ancient Greek or Ionic characters, such as they were first brought by Cadmus from Phœnicia; whence Herodotus also calls them *Phœnician letters*.—According to some writers, Cadmus was not the inventor, nor even importer of the Greek letters, but only the modeller and reformer thereof; and it was hence they acquired the appellation *Cadmean* or *Phœnician letters*; whereas before that time they had been called *Pelasgian letters*.

CADMIA. See CALAMINE.

CADMUS, in fabulous history, king of Thebes, the son of Agenor king of Phœnicia, and the brother of Phœnix, Cilix, and Europa. He carried into Greece the 16 simple letters of the Greek alphabet; and there built Thebes, in Bœotia. The poets say, that

that he left his native country in search of his sister Europa, whom Jupiter had carried away in the form of a bull; and that, inquiring of the Delphic oracle for a settlement, he was answered, that he should follow the direction of a cow, and build a city where she lay down. Having arrived among the Phocenses, he was met by a cow, who conducted him through Bœotia to the place where Thebes was afterwards built: but as he was about to sacrifice his guide to Pallas, he sent two of his company to the fountain Dirce for water; when they being devoured by a serpent or dragon, he slew the monster, and afterwards, by the advice of Pallas, sowed his teeth, when there sprung up a number of armed soldiers, who prepared to revenge the death of the serpent; but on his casting a stone among these upstart warriors, they turned their weapons against each other with such animosity, that only five survived the combat, and these assisted Cadmus in founding his new city. Afterwards, to recompence his labours, the gods gave him Harmonia, or Hermione, the daughter of Mars and Venus; and honoured his nuptials with presents and peculiar marks of favour. But at length resigning Thebes to Pentheus, Cadmus and Hermione went to govern the Encheleenses: when grown old, they were transformed into serpents; or, as others say, sent to the Elysian fields, in a chariot drawn by serpents. See THEBES.

CADMUS of Miletum, a celebrated Greek historian, was, according to Pliny, the first of the Greeks who wrote history in prose. He flourished about 550 before Christ.

CADORE, or PIEVE DI CADORE, a town of Italy, in the territory of Venice, and capital of a district called *Cadorino*; famous for the birth of Titian the painter. E. Long. 13. 45. N. Lat. 46. 25.

CADORINO, a province of Italy, in the territory of Venice; bounded on the east by Friuli Proper, on the south and west by the Bellunese, and by the bishopric of Brixen on the north. It is a very mountainous country, but pretty populous. The only town is Pieve de Cadore.

CADRITES, a sort of Mahometan friars, who once a-week spend a great part of the night in turning round, holding each others hand, and repeating incessantly the word *hai*, which signifies *living*, and is one of the attributes of God; during which one of them plays on a flute. They never cut their hair, nor cover their heads; and always go barefooted: they have liberty to quit their convent when they please, and to marry.

CADSAND, an island on the coast of Dutch Flanders, situated at the mouth of the Scheld, whereby the Dutch command the navigation of that river.

CADUCEUS, in antiquity, Mercury's rod or sceptre, being a wand entwisted by two serpents borne by that deity as the ensign of his quality and office, given him, according to the fable, by Apollo, for his seven-stringed harp. Wonderful properties are ascribed to this rod by the poets; as laying men asleep, raising the dead, &c.

It was also used by the ancients as a symbol of peace and concord: the Romans sent the Carthaginians a javelin and a caduceus, offering them their choice either of war or peace. Among that people, those who denounced war were called *feciales*; and those who went to demand peace, *caduceatores*, because they bore a caduceus in their hand.

The caduceus found on medals is a common symbol, signifying good conduct, peace, and prosperity. The rod expresses power, the two serpents prudence, and the two wings diligence.

CADUCI, (from *cado* to "fall"); the name of a class in Linnæus's *calycina*, consisting of plants whose calyx is a simple perianthium, supporting a single flower or fructification, and falling off either before or with the petals. It stands opposed to the *classes persistentes* in the same method, and is exemplified in mustard and ranunculus.

CADURCI, CADURCUM, *Cadurcus*, and *Cadurx*, (anc. geog.), a town of the Cadurci, a people of Aquitania; situated between the rivers Oldus, running from the north, and the Tarnis from the south, and falling into the Garumna: now *Cahors*, capital of the territory of the Quercí, in Guienne. A part of the Cadurci, to the south near the Tarnis, were called *Eleutheri*.

CADUS, in antiquity, a wine-vessel of a certain capacity, containing 80 amphoræ or firkins; each of which, according to the best accounts, held nine gallons.

CADUSII (anc. geog.), a people of Media Atropatene, situated to the west in the mountains, and reaching to the Caspian sea; between whom and the Medes, perpetual war and enmity continued down to the time of Cyrus.

CÆCILIA, in zoology, a genus of serpents belonging to the amphibia class. The cæcilia has no scales; it is smooth, and moves by means of lateral rugæ or prickles. The upper lip is prominent, and furnished with two tentacula. It has no tail. There are but two species of this serpent, viz. 1. The tentaculata, has 135 rugæ. It is about a foot long, and an inch in circumference, preserving an uniform cylindrical shape from the one end to the other. The teeth are very small. It has such a resemblance to an eel, that it may easily be mistaken for one; but as it has neither fins nor gills, it cannot be classed with the fishes. It is a native of America, and its bite is not poisonous. 2. The glutinosa, has 340 rugæ or prickles above, and 10 below, the anus. It is of a brownish colour, with a white line on the side, and is a native of the Indies.

CÆCUM, or COECUM, the blind gut. See ANATOMY, N° 93.

CÆLIUM (anc. geog.), an inland town of Peucetia, a division of Apulia; a place four or five miles above Barium or Bari, and which still retains that name.

CÆLIUS MONS, (Itinerary), a town of Vindelicia, on the right or west side of the Ilargus. Now *Kelmunz*, a small town of Suabia, on the Iller.

CÆLIUS MONS at Rome. See COELIUS.

CÆLIUS (Aurelianus), an ancient physician, and the only one of the sect of the methodists of whom we have any remains. He was of Sicca, a town of Numidia; but in what age he lived, cannot be determined: it is probable, however, that he lived before Galen; since, though he carefully mentions all the physicians before him, he takes no notice of Galen. He had read over very diligently the ancient physicians of all sects; and we are indebted to him for the knowledge of many dogmas which are not to be found but in his books *de acribus et tardis passionibus*. He wrote, as he himself tells us, several other works; but they are all perished.

CAEN, an handsome and considerable town of France, capital of Lower Normandy, with a celebrated university, and an academy of literature. It contains 60 streets, and 12 parishes. It has a castle with four towers, which were built by the English. The town-house is a large building with four great towers. The royal square is the handsomest in all Normandy, and has fine houses on three sides of it; and in the middle is the statue of Louis XIV. in a Roman habit, standing on a marble pedestal, and surrounded with an iron balustrade. It is seated in a pleasant country on the river Orne, about eight miles from the sea. William the conqueror was buried here, in the abbey of St Stephen, which he founded. W. Long. 0. 17. N. Lat. 49. 11.

CÆRE, (anc. geog.), a town of Etruria, the royal residence of Mezentius. Its ancient name was *Arzylle*. In Strabo's time not the least vestige of it remained, except the baths called *caretana*. From this town the Roman censor's tables were called *cerites tabulæ*. In these were entered the names of such as for some misdemeanor forfeited their right of suffrage, or were degraded from a higher to a less honourable tribe. For the people of Cære hospitably receiving those Romans who, after the taking of Rome by the Gauls, fled with their gods and the sacred fire of Vesta, were, on the Romans recovering themselves from this disaster, honoured with the privilege of the city, but without a right of voting.

CÆRITES TABULÆ. See the preceding article.

CAERFILLY, a town of Glamorganshire in South Wales, seated between the rivers Taff and Rumney, in a moorish ground, among the hills. It is thought the walls, now in ruins, were built by the Romans; there being often Roman coins dug up there. W. Long. 3. 12. N. Lat. 51. 25.

CAERLEON, a town of Monmouthshire in England, and a place of great antiquity. It was a Roman town, as is evident from the many Roman antiquities found here. It is commodiously situated on the river Usk, over which there is a large wooden bridge. The houses are generally built of stone, and there are the ruins of a castle still to be seen. W Long. 3. 0. N. Lat. 51. 40.

CAERMARTHEN-SHIRE, a county of Wales, bounded on the north by Severn sea or St George's Channel, Cardiganshire on the south, the shires of Brecknock and Glamorgan on the east, and Pembrokeshire on the west. Its greatest length is between 30 and 40 miles, and its breadth upwards of 20. The air is wholesome, and the soil less rocky and mountainous than most other parts of Wales, and consequently is proportionally more fertile both in corn and pasture. It has also plenty of wood, and is well supplied with coal and limestone. The most considerable rivers are the Towy, the Cothy, and the Tave; of which, the first abounds with excellent salmon. The principal towns are Caermarthen the capital, Kidwely, Lanimdovery, &c. This county abounds with ancient forts, camps, and tumuli or barrows. Near to Caermarthen, towards the east, may be seen the ruins of Kastell Kerrey, which was situated on a steep and inaccessible rock; and also several vast caverns, supposed to have been copper-mines of the Romans. Near this spot is a fountain which ebbs and flows twice in 24 hours like the sea.

CAERMARTHEN, a town of Wales, and capital of the county of that name. It is situated on the river Towy, over which it has a fine stone-bridge. It is of great antiquity, being the Maridunum of Ptolemy. It is a populous, thriving, and polite place, many of the neighbouring gentry residing there in the winter. It is a corporation and county of itself, with power to make by-laws. Here were held the courts of chancery and exchequer for South Wales, till the whole was united to England in the reign of Henry VIII. Here was born the famous conjurer Merlin; and near the town is a wood called *Merlin's grove*, where he is said to have often retired for contemplation. Many of his pretended prophecies are still preserved in the country. The town gives the title of *marquis* to his grace the duke of Leeds. It sends one member to parliament, and the county another.

CAERNARVON-SHIRE, a county of Wales, bounded on the north and west by the sea, on the south by Merionethshire, and on the east is divided from Denbighshire by the river Conway. It is about 40 miles in length, and 20 in breadth; and sends one member to parliament for the shire, and another for the borough of Caernarvon. The air is very piercing; owing partly to the snow, that lies seven or eight months of the year upon some of the mountains, which are so high that they are called the *British Alps*; and partly to the great number of lakes, which are said not to be fewer than 50 or 60. The soil in the valleys on the side next Ireland is pretty fertile, especially in barley; great numbers of black cattle, sheep, and goats, are fed on the mountains; and the sea, lakes, and rivers, abound with variety of fish. The highest mountains in the county are those called *Snowdon hills*, and *Pen-maen-mawr*, which last hangs over the sea. There is a road cut out of the rock on the side next the sea, guarded by a wall running along the edge of it on that side; but the traveller is sometimes in danger of being crushed by the fall of pieces of the rock from the precipices above. The river Conway, though its course from the lake out of which it issues to its mouth is only 12 miles, yet is so deep, in consequence of the many brooks it receives, that it is navigable by ships of good burden for eight miles. Pearls are found in a large black muscle taken in this river. The principal towns are Bangor, Caernarvon the capital, and Conway. In this county is an ancient road said to have been made by Helena the mother of Constantine the Great; and Matthew of Westminster asserts, that the body of Constantius the father of the same Constantine was found at Caernarvon in the year 1283, and interred in the parish-church there by order of Edward I.

CAERNARVON, a town of Wales, and capital of the county of that name. It was built by Edward I. near the site of the ancient Segontium, after his conquest of the country in 1282, the situation being well adapted to overawe his new subjects. It had natural requisites for strength; being bounded on one side by the arm of the sea called the *Menai*; by the estuary of the

Seiont

stiont on another, exactly where it receives the tide from the former; on a third side, and a part of the fourth, by a creek of the Menai; and the remainder has the appearance of having the insulation completed by art. Edward undertook this great work immediately after his conquest of the country in 1282, and completed the fortifications and castle before 1284; for his queen, on April 25th in that year, brought forth within its walls Edward, first prince of Wales of the English line. It was built within the space of one year, by the labour of the peasants, and at the cost of the chieftains of the country, on whom the conqueror imposed the hateful task. The external state of the walls and castle, Mr Pennant informs us, are at present exactly as they were in the time of Edward. The walls are defended by numbers of round towers, and have two principal gates: the east, facing the mountains; the west, upon the Menai. The entrance into the castle is very august, beneath a great tower, on the front of which appears the statue of the founder, with a dagger in his hand, as if menacing his new-acquired unwilling subjects. The gate had four portcullises, and every requisite of strength. The towers are very beautiful. The Eagle tower is remarkably fine, and has the addition of three slender angular turrets issuing from the top. Edward II. was born in a little dark room in this tower, not twelve feet long nor eight in breadth; so little did, in those days, a royal consort consult either pomp or conveniency. The gate through which the affectionate Eleanor entered, to give the Welsh a prince of their own, who could not speak a word of English, is at the farthest end, at a vast height above the outside ground; so could only be approached by a draw-bridge. The quay is a most beautiful walk along the side of the Menai, and commands a most agreeable view.

Caernarvon is destitute of manufactures, but has a brisk trade with London, Bristol, Liverpool, and Ireland, for the several necessaries of life. It is the residence of numbers of genteel families, and contains several very good houses. Edward I. bestowed on this town its first royal charter, and made it a free borough. Among other privileges, none of the burgesses could be convicted of any crime committed between the rivers Conway and Dyse, unless by a jury of their own townsmen. It is governed by a mayor, who, by patent, is created governor of the castle. It has one alderman, two bailiffs, a town-clerk, and two serjeants at mace. The representative of the place is elected by its burgesses, and those of Conway, Pwllheli, Nefyn, and Crickaeth. The right of voting is in every one, resident or non-resident, admitted to their freedom. The town gives title of *earl* and *marquis* to the duke of Chandos, and has a good tide-harbour.

CAERWIS, a market-town of Flintshire in North Wales, situated in W. Long. 3. 25. N. Lat. 53. 20.

CÆSALPINIA BRASILETTO, or *Brasil-wood*; a genus of the monogynia order, belonging to the decandria class of plants; and in the natural method ranking under the 33d order, *Lomentaceæ*. The calyx is quinquefid, with the lowest segment larger in proportion. There are five petals, with the lowest more beautiful than the rest. It is a leguminous plant. Of this there are three species, the most remarkable of which is the brasiliensis, commonly called *Brasiletto*. It grows naturally in the warmest parts of America, from whence the wood is imported for the dyers, who use it much. The demand has been so great, that none of the large trees are left in any of the British plantations; so that Mr Catesby owns himself ignorant of the dimensions to which they grow. The largest remaining are not above two inches in thickness, and eight or nine feet in height. The branches are slender and full of small prickles; the leaves are pinnated; the lobes growing opposite to one another, broad at their ends, with one notch. The flowers are white, papilionaceous, with many stamina and yellow apices, growing in a pyramidal spike, at the end of a long slender stalk; the pods inclose several small round seeds. The colour produced from this wood is greatly improved by solution of tin in aqua regia*. The second sort is a native of the same countries with the first, but is of a larger size. It sends out many weak irregular branches, armed with short, strong, upright thorns. The leaves branch out in the same manner as the first; but the lobes, or small leaves, are oval and entire. The flowers are produced in long spikes like those of the former, but are variegated with red. These plants may be propagated from seeds, which should be sown in small pots filled with light rich earth early in the spring, and plunged in a bed of tanner's bark. Being tender, they require to be always kept in the stove, and to be treated in the same manner as other exotics of that kind.

Plate CXV.

* See *Colour-making* and *Dyeing*.

CÆSALPINUS of Arezzo, professor at Pisa, and afterwards physician to pope Clement VIII. one of the capital writers in botany. See BOTANY, p. 419, 420.

CÆSAR (Julius), the illustrious Roman general and historian, was of the family of the Julii, who pretended they were descended from Venus by Æneas. The descendants of Ascanius son of Æneas and Creusa, and surnamed *Julus*, lived at Alba till that city was ruined by Tullus Hostilius king of Rome, who carried them to Rome, where they flourished. We do not find that they produced more than two branches. The first bore the name of *Tullus*, the other that of *Cæsar*. The most ancient of the Cæsars were those who were in public employments in the 11th year of the first Punic war. After that time we find there was always some of that family who enjoyed public offices in the commonwealth, till the time of Caius Julius Cæsar, the subject of this article. He was born at Rome the 12th of the month Quintilis, year of the city 653, and lost his father an. 669. By his valour and eloquence he soon acquired the highest reputation in the field and in the senate. Beloved and respected by his fellow-citizens, he enjoyed successively every magisterial and military honour the republic could bestow consistent with its own free constitution. But at length having subdued Pompey the great rival of his growing power, his boundless ambition effaced the glory of his former actions: for, pursuing his favourite maxim, "that he had rather be the first man in a village than the second in Rome," he procured himself to be chosen perpetual dictator; and, not content with this unconstitutional power, his faction had resolved to raise him to the imperial dignity; when the friends of the civil liberties of the republic rashly assassinated him in the senate-house, where they should only have seized him and brought him to a legal trial for usurpation. By this

impolitic

Cæfar.

impolitic meafure they defeated their own purpofe, involving the city in confternation and terror, which produced general anarchy, and paved the way to the revolution they wanted to prevent; the monarchial government being abfolutely founded on the murder of Julius Cæfar. He fell in the 56th year of his age, 43 years before the Chriftian æra. His commentaries contain a hiftory of his principal voyages, battles, and victories. The London edition in 1712, in folio, is preferred.

The detail of Cæfar's tranfactions (fo far as is confiftent with the limits of this work) being given under the article Rome, we fhall here only add a portrait of him as drawn by a philofopher *.

* From the Monarque Philofophe of M. [illegible].

" If, after the lapfe of 18 centuries, the truth may be publifhed without offence, a philofopher might, in the following terms, cenfure Cæfar without calumniating him, and applaud him without exciting his blufhes.

" Cæfar had one predominant paffion: it was the love of glory; and he paffed 40 years of his life in feeking opportunities to fofter and encourage it. His foul, entirely abforbed in ambition, did not open itfelf to other impulfes. He cultivated letters; but he did not love them with enthufiafm, becaufe he had not leifure to become the firft orator of Rome. He corrupted the one half of the Roman ladies, but his heart had no concern in the fiery ardours of his fenfes. In the arms of Cleopatra, he thought of Pompey; and this fingular man, who difdained to have a partner in the empire of the world, would have blufhed to have been for one inftant the flave of a woman.

" We muft not imagine, that Cæfar was born a warrior, as Sophocles and Milton were born poets. For, if nature had made him a citizen of Sybaris, he would have been the moft voluptuous of men. If in our days he had been born in Penfylvania, he would have been the moft inoffenfive of quakers, and would not have difturbed the tranquillity of the new world.

" The moderation with which he conducted himfelf after his victories, has been highly extolled; but in this he fhowed his penetration, not the goodnefs of his heart. Is it not obvious, that the difplay of certain virtues is neceffary to put in motion the political machine? It was requifite that he fhould have the appearance of clemency, if he inclined that Rome fhould forgive him his victories. But what greatnefs of mind is there in a generofity which follows on the ufurpation of fupreme power?

" Nature, while it marked Cæfar with a fublime character, gave him alfo that fpirit of perfeverance which renders it ufeful. He had no fooner begun to reflect, than he admired Sylla; hated him, and yet wifhed to imitate him. At the age of 15, he formed the project of being dictator. It was thus that the prefident Montefquieu conceived, in his early youth, the idea of the fpirit of laws.

" Phyfical qualities, as well as moral caufes, contributed to give ftrength to his character. Nature, which had made him for command, had given him an air of dignity. He had acquired that foft and infinuating eloquence, which is perfectly fuited to feduce vulgar minds, and has a powerful influence on the moft cultivated. His love of pleafure was a merit with the fair fex; and women, who even in a republic can draw to them the fuffrages and attention of men, have the higheft importance in degenerate times. The ladies of his age were charmed with the profpect of having a dictator whom they might fubdue by their attractions.

" In vain did the genius of Cato watch for fome time to fuftain the liberty of his country. It was unequal to contend with that of Cæfar. Of what avail were the eloquence, the philofophy, and the virtue of this republican, when oppofed by a man who had the addrefs to debauch the wife of every citizen whofe intereft he meant to engage; who, poffeffing an enthufiafm for glory, wept, becaufe, at the age of 30, he had not conquered the world like Alexander; and who, with the haughty temper of a defpot, was more defirous to be the firft man in a village than the fecond in Rome.

" Cæfar had the good fortune to exift in times of trouble and civil commotions, when the minds of men are put into a ferment; when opportunities of great actions are frequent; when talents are every thing, and thofe who can only boaft of their virtues are nothing. If he had lived an hundred years fooner, he would have been no more than an obfcure villain; and, inftead of giving laws to the world, would not have been able to produce any confufion in it.

" I will here be bold enough to advance an idea, which may appear paradoxical to thofe who weakly judge of men from what they achieve, and not from the principle which leads them to act. Nature formed in the fame mould Cæfar, Mahomet, Cromwell, and Kouli Khan. They all of them united to genius that profound policy which renders it fo powerful. They all of them had an evident fuperiority over thofe with whom they were furrounded; they were confcious of this fuperiority, and they made others confcious of it. They were all of them born fubjects, and became fortunate ufurpers. Had Cæfar been placed in Perfia, he would have made the conqueft of India; in Arabia, he would have been the founder of a new religion; in London, he would have ftabbed his fovereign, or have procured his affaffination under the fanction of the laws. He reigned with glory over men whom he had reduced to be flaves; and, under one afpect, he is to be confidered as a hero; under another, as a monfter. But it would be unfortunate, indeed, for fociety, if the poffeffion of fuperior talents gave individuals a right to trouble its repofe. Ufurpers accordingly have flatterers, but no friends; ftrangers refpect them; their fubjects complain and fubmit; it is in their own families that humanity finds her avengers. Cæfar was affaffinated by his fon, Mahomet was poifoned by his wife, Kouli Khan was maffacred by his nephew, and Cromwell only died in his bed becaufe his fon Richard was a philofopher.

" Cæfar, the tyrant of his country; Cæfar, who deftroyed the agents of his crimes, if they failed in addrefs; Cæfar, in fine, the hufband of every wife, and the wife of every hufband; has been accounted a great man by the mob of writers. But it is only the philofopher who knows how to mark the barrier between celebrity and greatnefs. The talents of this fingular man, and the good fortune which conftantly attended him till the moment of his affaffination, have concealed the enormity of his actions."

Cæsar, in Roman antiquity, a title borne by all the

the emperors, from Julius Cæſar to the deſtruction of the empire. It was alſo uſed as a title of diſtinction for the intended or preſumptive heir of the empire, as *king of the Romans* is now uſed for that of the German empire.

This title took its riſe from the ſurname of the firſt emperor, C. Julius Cæſar, which, by a decree of the ſenate, all the ſucceeding emperors were to bear. Under his ſucceſſor, the appellation of *Auguſtus* being appropriated to the emperors, in compliment to that prince, the title *Cæſar* was given to the ſecond perſon in the empire, though ſtill it continued to be given to the firſt; and hence the difference betwixt Cæſar uſed ſimply, and Cæſar with the addition of Imperator Auguſtus.

The dignity of Cæſar remained to the ſecond of the empire, till Alexius Comnenus having elected Nicephorus Meliſſenus Cæſar, by contract; and it being neceſſary to confer ſome higher dignity on his own brother Iſaacius, he created him Sebaſtocrator, with the precedency over Meliſſenus; ordering, that in all acclamations, &c. Iſaacius Sebaſtocrator ſhould be named the ſecond, and Meliſſenus Cæſar the third.

Cæsar (Sir Julius), a learned civilian, was deſcended by the female line from the duke de Ceſarini in Italy; and was born near Tottenham in Middleſex, in the year 1557. He was educated at Oxford, and afterwards ſtudied in the univerſity of Paris, where, in the year 1581, he was created doctor of the civil law, and two years after was admitted to the ſame degree at Oxford, and alſo became doctor of the canon law. He was advanced to many honourable employments, and for the laſt 20 years of his life was maſter of the rolls. He was remarkable for his extenſive bounty and charity to all perſons of worth, ſo that he ſeemed to be the almoner-general of the nation. He died 1639, in the 79th year of his age. It is very remarkable that the manuſcripts of this lawyer were offered (by the executors of ſome of his deſcendants) to a cheeſemonger for waſte-paper; but being timely inſpected by Mr Samuel Paterſon, this gentleman diſcovered their worth, and had the ſatisfaction to find his judgment confirmed by the profeſſion, to whom they were ſold in lots for upwards of 500 *l.* in the year 1757.

Cæsar Auguſta or *Cæſarea Auguſta*, (anc geog.), a Roman colony ſituated on the river Iberus in the hither Spain, before called *Salduba*, in the territories of the Edetani. Now commonly thought to be Saragoſa.

CÆSAREA, the name of ſeveral ancient cities, particularly one on the coaſt of Phœnice. It was very conveniently ſituated for trade; but had a very dangerous harbour, ſo that no ſhips could be ſafe in it when the wind was at ſouth-weſt. Herod the Great king of Judea remedied this inconveniency at an immenſe expence and labour, making it one of the moſt convenient havens on that coaſt. He alſo beautified it with many buildings, and beſtowed 12 years in the finiſhing and adorning it.

CÆSARIAN operation. See Midwifery.

CÆSARIANS, *Cæſarienſes*, in Roman antiquity, were officers of miniſters of the Roman emperors. They kept the accounts of the revenues of the emperors; and took poſſeſſion, in their name, of ſuch things as devolved or were confiſcated to them.

CÆSARODUNUM (anc. geog.), a town of the Turones in Celtic Gaul; now *Tours*, the capital of Touraine. See Tours.

CÆSAROMAGUS (anc. geog.), a town of the Trinobantes in Britain; by ſome ſuppoſed to be *Chelmsford*, by others *Brentford*, and by others *Burſtet*.

CÆSENA (anc. geog.), a town of Gallia Ciſpadana, ſituated on the rivers Iſapis and Rubicon; now Cesena, which ſee.

CÆSIA sylva (anc. geog.), a wood in Germany, part of the great Sylva Hercynia, ſituated partly in the duchy of Cleves, and partly in Weſtphalia between Weſel and Kresfeld.

CÆSONES, a denomination given to thoſe cut out of their mother's wombs. Pliny ranks this as an auſpicious kind of birth; the elder Scipio Africanus, and the firſt family of Cæſars, were brought into the world in this way.

CÆSTUS, in antiquity, a large gauntlet made of raw hide, which the wreſtlers made uſe of when they fought at the public games.—This was a kind of leathern ſtrap, ſtrengthened with lead or plates of iron, which encompaſſed the hand, the wriſt, and a part of the arm, as well to defend theſe parts as to enforce their blows.

Cæstus, or *Ceſtus*, was alſo a kind of girdle, made of wool, which the huſband untied for his ſpouſe the firſt day of marriage, before they went to bed.

This relates to Venus's girdle, which Juno borrowed of her to entice Jupiter to love her. See Cestus.

CÆSURA, in the ancient poetry, is when, in the ſcanning of a verſe, a word is divided ſo, as one part ſeems cut off, and goes to a different foot from the reſt; as,

Menti|ri noli, nun|quam mendacia | proſunt.

where the ſyllables *ri*, *li*, *quam*, and *men*, are cæſuras.

Cæsure, in the modern poetry, denotes a reſt or pauſe towards the middle of an Alexandrian verſe, by which the voice and pronunciation are aided, and the verſe, as it were, divided into two hemiſtichs. See Pause.

CÆTERIS paribus, a Latin term in frequent uſe among mathematical and phyſical writers. The words literally ſignify, *the reſt* (or *other things*) *being alike or equal*. Thus we ſay the heavier the bullet, *cæteris paribus*, the greater the range; *i. e.* by how much the bullet is heavier, if the length and diameter of the piece and ſtrength of the powder be the ſame, by ſo much will the utmoſt range or diſtance of a piece of ordnance be the greater. Thus alſo, in a phyſical way, we ſay, the velocity and quantity circulating in a given time through any ſection of an artery, will, *cæteris paribus*, be according to its diameter, and nearneſs to or diſtance from the heart.

CÆTOBRIX (anc. geog.), a town of Luſitania, near the mouth of the Tagus on the eaſt ſide; now extinct. It had its name from its fiſhery; and there are ſtill extant fiſh-ponds on the ſhore, done with plaſter of Paris, which illuſtrate the name of the ruined city.

CAFFA, in commerce, painted cotton-cloths manufactured in the Eaſt Indies, and ſold at Bengal.

Caffa, or *Kaffa*, a city and port-town of Crim-Tartary, ſituated on the ſouth-eaſt part of that peninſula. E. Long. 37. 0. N. Lat. 44. 55.

It

It is the most considerable town in the country, and gives name to the straits of Caffa, which runs from the Euxine or Black Sea, to the Palus Meotis, or sea of Asoph.

CAFFILA, a company of merchants or travellers, who join together in order to go with more security through the dominions of the Grand Mogul, and through other countries on the continent of the East Indies.

The Caffila differs from a caravan, at least in Persia: for the caffila belongs properly to some sovereign, or to some powerful company in Europe, whereas a caravan is a company of particular merchants, each trading upon his own account. The English and Dutch have each of them their caffila at Gambrow. There are also such caffilas, which cross some parts of the deserts of Africa, particularly that called the *sea of sand*, which lies between the kingdom of Morocco and those of Tombut and Gago. This is a journey of 400 leagues; and takes up two months in going, and as many in coming back; the caffila travelling only by night, on account of the excessive heat of that country. The chief merchandise they bring back consists in gold dust, which they call *attibar*, and the Europeans *tibir*.

Caffila on the coast of Guzerat or Cambaya, signifies a small fleet of merchant-ships.

CAFFRARIA, the country of the Caffres or Hottentots, in the most southerly parts of Africa lying in the form of a crescent about the inland country of Monomopata, between 35° south latitude and the tropic of Capricorn: and bounded on the east, south, and west, by the Indian and Atlantic oceans. See Hottentots.

Most of the sea-coasts of this country are subject to the Dutch, who have built a fort near the most southern promontory, called the *Cape of Good-Hope*.

CAG, or Kag, a barrel or vessel, that contains from four to five gallons.

CAGANUS, or Cacanus, an appellation anciently given by the Huns to their kings. The word appears also to have been formerly applied to the princes of Muscovy, now called *czar*. From the same also, probably, the Tartar title *cham* or *can*, had its origin.

CAGE, an inclosure made of wire, wicker, or the like, interwoven lattice-wise, for the confinement of birds or wild beasts. The word is French, *cage*, formed from the Italian *gaggia*, of the Latin *cavea*, which signifies the same: *a caveis theatralibus in quibus includebantur feræ*.

Beasts were usually brought to Rome shut up in oaken or beechen cages, artfully formed, and covered or shaded with boughs, that the creatures, deceived with the appearance of a wood, might fancy themselves in their forest. The fiercer sort were pent in iron cages, lest wooden prisons should be broke through. In some prisons there are iron cages for the closer confinement of criminals. The French laws distinguish two sorts of bird-cages, viz. high or singing cages, and low or dumb-cages; those who expose birds to sale are obliged to put the hens in the latter, and the cocks in the former, that persons may not be imposed on by buying a hen for a cock.

Cages (*caveæ*), denote also places in the ancient amphitheatres, wherein wild beasts were kept, ready to be let out for sport. The *caveæ* were a sort of iron cages different from dens, which were under ground and dark; whereas the *caveæ* being airy and light, the beasts rushed out of them with more alacrity and fierceness than if they had been pent under ground.

Cage, in carpentry, signifies an outer-work of timber, enclosing another within it. In this sense we say, *the cage of a wind-mill*. The cage of a stair-case denotes the wooden sides or walls which inclose it.

CAGEAN, or Cagayan, a province of the island of Lyticon, or Manila, in the East Indies. It is the largest in the island, being 80 leagues in length, and 40 in breadth. The principal city is called *New Segovia*, and 15 leagues eastward from this city lies cape Bajador. Doubling that cape, and coasting along 20 leagues from north to south, the province of Cagean ends, and that of Illocos begins. The peaceable Cageans who pay tribute are about 9000; but there are a great many not subdued. The whole province is fruitful: the men apply themselves to agriculture, and are of a martial disposition; and the women apply to several works in cotton. The mountains afford food for a vast number of bees; in consequence of which wax is so plenty, that all the poor burn it instead of oil. They make their candles after the following manner: they leave a small hole at each end of a hollow stick for the wick to run through; and then, stopping the bottom, fill it with wax at the top: when cold, they break the mould, and take out the candle. On the mountains there is abundance of brasil, ebony, and other valuable woods. In the woods are store of wild beasts, as boars; but not so good as those of Europe. There are also abundance of deer, which they kill for their skins and horns to sell to the Chinese.

CAGLI, an ancient episcopal town of Italy, in the duchy of Urbino, situated at the foot of the Appennine mountains. E. Long. 14. 12. N. Lat. 43. 30.

CAGLIARI (Paolo), called *Paulo Veronese*, an excellent painter, was born at Verona in the year 1532. Gabriel Cagliari his father was a sculptor, and Antonio Badile his uncle was his master in painting. He was not only esteemed the best of all the Lombard painters, but for his extensive talents in the art was peculiarly styled *Il pittor felice*, "the happy painter;" and there is scarcely a church in Venice where some of his performances are not to be seen. De Piles says, that "his picture of the marriage at Cana, in the church of St George, is to be distinguished from his other works, as being not only the triumph of Paul Veronese, but almost the triumph of painting itself." When the senate sent Grimani, procurator of St Mark, to be their ambassador at Rome, Paul attended him, but did not stay long, having left some pieces at Venice unfinished. Philip II. king of Spain, sent for him to paint the Escurial, and made him great offers; but Paul excused himself from leaving his own country, where his reputation was so well established, that most of the princes of Europe ordered their several ambassadors to procure something of his hand at any rate. He was indeed highly esteemed by all the principal men in his time; and so much admired by the great masters, as well his contemporaries as those who succeeded him, that Titian himself used to say, he was the ornament of his profession. And Guido Reni being asked which of the masters his predecessors he would choose to be, were it in his power, after Raphael and Corregio,

gio, named Paul Veronese; whom he always called his Paolino. He died of a fever at Venice in 1588, and had a tomb and a statue of brass erected to his memory in the church of St Sebastian. He left great wealth to his two sons Gabriel and Charles, who lived happily together, and joined in finishing several of their father's imperfect pieces with good success.

CAGLIARI, an ancient, large, and rich town, capital of the island of Sardinia in the Mediterranean. It is seated on the declivity of an hill, is an university, an archbishopric, and the residence of the viceroy. It has an excellent harbour, and a good trade; but is a place of no great strength. It was taken, with the whole island, by the English in 1708, who transferred it to the emperor Charles VI.; but it was retaken by the Spaniards in 1717, and about two years afterwards ceded to the duke of Savoy in lieu of Sicily, and hence he has the title of *king of Sardinia*. E. Long. 9. 14. N. Lat. 39. 12.

CAGUI, in zoology, a synonyme of two species of monkeys, viz. the jacchus and oedipus. See SIMIA.

CAHORS, a considerable town of France, in Querci in Guienne, with a bishop's see and an university. It is seated on a peninsula made by the river Lot, and built partly on a craggy rock. The principal street is very narrow; and terminates in the market-place, in which is the town-house. The cathedral is a Gothic structure, and has a large square steeple. The fortifications are regular, and the town is surrounded with thick walls. E. Long. 1. 6. N. Lat. 44. 26.

CAHYS, a dry measure for corn, used in some parts of Spain, particularly at Seville and at Cadiz. It is near a bushel of our measure.

CAJANABURG, the capital of the province of Cajania or East Bothnia in Sweden, situated on the north-east part of the lake Cajania, in E. Long. 27. 0. N. Lat. 64. 50.

CAIPHAS, high-priest of the Jews after Simon, condemned Christ to death; and was put out of his place by the emperor Vitellius, for which disgrace he made away with himself.

CAJAZZO, a town of the province of Lavoro in the kingdom of Naples, situated in E. Long. 15. 0. N. Lat. 41. 15.

CAICOS, the name of some American islands to the north of St Domingo, lying from W. Long. 112. 10. to 113. 16. N. Lat 21. 40.

CAJEPUT, an oil brought from the East Indies resembling that of Cardamoms.

CAIETA, (anc. geog.), a port and town of Latium, so called from *Æneas's* nurse; now *Gaeta*, which see.

CAJETAN (Cardinal), was born at Cajeta in the kingdom of Naples in the year 1469. His proper name was *Thomas de Vio*; but he adopted that of *Cajetan* from the place of his nativity. He defended the authority of the Pope, which suffered greatly at the council of Nice, in a work entitled *Of the power of the Pope*; and for this work he obtained the bishopric of Cajeta. He was afterwards raised to the archiepiscopal see of Palermo, and in 1517 was made a cardinal by Pope Leo X. The year after, he was sent as legate into Germany, to quiet the commotions raised against indulgences by Martin Luther; but Luther, under protection of Frederic elector of Saxony, set him at defiance; for though he obeyed the cardinal's summons in repairing to Augsburg, yet he rendered all his proceedings ineffectual. Cajetan was employed in several other negociations and transactions, being as ready at business as at letters. He died in 1534. He wrote Commentaries upon Aristotle's philosophy, and upon Thomas Aquinas's theology; and made a literal translation of the Old and New Testaments.

CAIFONG, a large, populous, and rich town of Asia, in China, seated in the middle of a large and well cultivated plain. It stands in a bottom; and when besieged by the rebels in 1642, they ordered the dykes of the river Hoangho to be cut, which drowned the city, and destroyed 300,000 of its inhabitants. E. Long. 113. 27. N. Lat. 35. 0.

CAILLE (Nicholas Louis de la), an eminent mathematician and astronomer, was born at a small town in the diocese of Rheims in 1713. His father had served in the army, which he quitted, and in his retirement studied mathematics; and amused himself with mechanic exercises, wherein he proved the happy author of several inventions of considerable use to the public. Nicholas, almost in his infancy, took a fancy to mechanics, which proved of signal service to him in his maturer years. He was sent young to school at Mantes-sur-Seine, where he discovered early tokens of genius. In 1729, he went to Paris; where he studied the classics, philosophy, and mathematics. Afterwards he went to study divinity at the college de Navarre, proposing to embrace an ecclesiastical life. At the end of three years he was ordained a deacon, and officiated as such in the church of the college de Mazarin several years; but he never entered into priests orders, apprehending that his astronomical studies, to which he became most assiduously devoted, might too much interfere with his religious duties. In 1739, he was conjoined with M. de Thury, son to M. Cassini, in verifying the meridian of the royal observatory through the whole extent of the kingdom of France. In the month of November the same year, whilst he was engaged day and night in the operations which this grand undertaking required, and at a great distance from Paris, he was, without any solicitation, elected into the vacant mathematical chair which the celebrated M. Varignon had so worthily filled. Here he began to teach about the end of 1740; and an observatory was ordered to be erected for his use in the college, and furnished with a suitable apparatus of the best instruments. In May 1741, M. de la Caille was admitted into the royal academy of sciences as an adjoint member for astronomy. Besides the many excellent papers of his dispersed up and down in their memoirs, he published Elements of geometry, mechanics, optics, and astronomy. Moreover, he carefully computed all the eclipses of the sun and moon that had happened since the Christian era, which were printed in a book published by two Benedictines, entitled *l'Art de verifier les dates*, &c. Paris, 1750, in 4to. Besides these, he compiled a volume of astronomical ephemerides for the years 1745 to 1755; another for the years 1755 to 1765; a third for the years 1765 to 1775; an excellent work entitled *Astronomiae fundamenta novissimis solis et stellarum observationibus stabilita*; and the most correct solar tables that ever appeared. Having gone through a seven years series of astronomical observations in his own observatory, he formed a project of going to observe the southern stars at the

Caille.

Cape of Good Hope. This was highly approved by the academy, and by the prime minister Comte de Argenson, and very readily agreed to by the states of Holland. Upon this, he drew up a plan of the method he proposed to pursue in his southern observations; setting forth, that, besides settling the places of the fixed stars, he proposed to determine the parallax of the moon, Mars, and Venus. But whereas this required correspondent observations to be made in the northern parts of the world, he sent to those of his correspondents who were expert in practical astronomy previous notice, in print, what observations he designed to make at such and such times for the said purpose. At length, on the 21st of November 1750, he sailed for the Cape, and arrived there on the 19th of April 1751. He forthwith got his instruments on shore; and, with the assistance of some Dutch artificers, set about building an astronomical observatory, in which his apparatus of instruments was properly disposed of as soon as it was in a fit condition to receive them.

The sky at the Cape is generally pure and serene, unless when a south-east wind blows. But this is often the case; and when it is, it is attended with some strange and terrible effects. The stars look bigger, and seem to caper; the moon has an undulating tremor; and the planets have a sort of beard like comets. Two hundred and twenty-eight nights did our astronomer survey the face of the southern heavens; during which space, which is almost incredible, he observed more than 10,000 stars; and whereas the ancients filled the heavens with monsters and old-wives tales, the abbe de la Caille chose rather to adorn them with the instruments and machines which modern philosophy has made use of for the conquest of nature*. With no less success did he attend to the parallax of the moon, Mars, Venus, and the sun. Having thus executed the purpose of his voyage, and no present opportunity offering for his return, he thought of employing the vacant time in another arduous attempt; no less than that of taking the measure of the earth, as he had already done that of the heavens. This indeed had, through the munificence of the French king, been done before by different sets of learned men both in Europe and America; some determining the quantity of a degree under the equator, and others under the arctic circle: but it had not as yet been decided whether in the southern parallels of latitude the same dimensions obtained as in the northern. His labours were rewarded with the satisfaction he wished for; having determined a distance of 410,814 feet from a place called *Klip-Fontyn* to the Cape, by means of a base of 38,802 feet, three times actually measured: whence he discovered a new secret of nature, namely, that the radii of the parallels in south latitude are not the same as those of the corresponding parallels in north latitude. About the 33d degree of south latitude he found a degree on the meridian to contain 342,222 Paris feet. He returned to Paris the 27th of September 1754; having in his almost four years absence expended no more than 9144 livres on himself and his companion; and at his coming into port, he refused a bribe of 100,000 livres, offered by one who thirsted less after glory than gain, to be sharer in his immunity from custom-house searches.

* See the *Planisphere in the Cœlum australe stelliferum.*

After receiving the congratulatory visits of his more intimate friends and the astronomers, he first of all thought fit to draw up a reply to some strictures which professor Euler had published relative to the meridian, and then he settled the results of the comparison of his own with the observations of other astronomers for the parallaxes. That of the sun he fixed at 9½″; of the moon, at 56′ 56″; of Mars in his opposition, 36″; of Venus, 38″. He also settled the laws whereby astronomical refractions are varied by the different density or rarity of the air, by heat or cold, and dryness or moisture. And, lastly, he showed an easy, and by common navigators practicable, method of finding the longitude at sea by means of the moon, which he illustrated by examples selected from his own observations during his voyages. His fame being now established upon so firm a basis, the most celebrated academies of Europe claimed him as their own: and he was unanimously elected a member of the royal society at London; of the institute of Bologna; of the imperial academy at Petersburg; and of the royal academies of Berlin, Stockholm, and Gottingen. In the year 1760, Mr de la Caille was attacked with a severe fit of the gout; which, however, did not interrupt the course of his studies; for he then planned out a new and immense work, no less than a history of astronomy through all ages, with a comparison of the ancient and modern observations, and the construction and use of the instruments employed in making them. In order to pursue the task he had imposed upon himself in a suitable retirement, he obtained a grant of apartments in the royal palace of Vincennes; and whilst his astronomical apparatus was erecting there, he began printing his Catalogue of the southern stars, and the third volume of his Ephemerides. The state of his health was, towards the end of the year 1763, greatly reduced. His blood grew inflamed; he had pains of the head, obstructions of the kidneys, loss of appetite, with an oppletion of the whole habit. His mind remained unaffected, and he resolutely persisted in his studies as usual. In the month of March, medicines were administered to him, which rather aggravated than alleviated his symptoms; and he was now sensible, that the same distemper which in Africa, ten years before, yielded to a few simple remedies, did in his native country bid defiance to the best physicians. This induced him to settle his affairs: his manuscripts he committed to the care and discretion of his esteemed friend M. Maraldi. It was at last determined that a vein should be opened; but this brought on an obstinate lethargy, of which he died, aged 49.

Caille ‖ Caiman islands.

CAIMACAN, or CAIMACAM, in the Turkish affairs, a dignity in the Ottoman empire, answering to lieutenant, or rather deputy, amongst us.

There are usually two Caimacams; one residing at Constantinople, as governor thereof; the other attending the grand vizir in quality of his lieutenant, secretary of state, and first minister of his council, and gives audience to ambassadors. Sometimes there is a third caimacan, who attends the sultan; whom he acquaints with any public disturbances, and receives his orders concerning them.

CAIMAN ISLANDS, certain American islands lying south of Cuba, and north-west of Jamaica, between 81° and 86° of west longitude, and in 21° of north latitude. They are most remarkable on account of the

Caia ‖ Cairns.

fishery of tortoise, which the people of Jamaica catch here, and carry home alive, keeping them in pens for food, and killing them as they want them.

CAIN, eldest son of Adam and Eve, killed his brother Abel; for which he was condemned by God to banishment and a vagabond state of life. Cain retired to the land of Nod, on the east of Eden; and built a city, to which he gave the name of his son Enoch.

CAINITES, a sect of heretics in the 2d century, so called on account of their great respect for Cain. They pretended that the virtue which produced Abel was of an order inferior to that which had produced Cain, and that this was the reason why Cain had the victory over Abel and killed him; for they admitted a great number of genii, which they called *virtues*, of different ranks and orders. They made profession of honouring those who carry in Scripture the most visible marks of reprobation; as the inhabitants of Sodom, Esau, Korah, Dathan, and Abiram. They had, in particular, a very great veneration for the traitor Judas, under pretence that the death of Jesus Christ had saved mankind. They had a forged gospel of Judas, to which they paid great respect.

CAIRNS, or Carnes, the vulgar name of those heaps of stones which are to be seen in many places of Britain, particularly Scotland and Wales.—They are composed of stones of all dimensions thrown together in a conical form, a flat stone crowning the apex; (see Plate CXXVII.).

Various causes have been assigned by the learned for these heaps of stones. They have supposed them to have been, in times of inauguration, the places where the chieftain-elect stood to show himself to best advantage to the people; or the place from whence judgment was pronounced; or to have been erected on the road-side in honour of Mercury; or to have been formed in memory of some solemn compact, particularly where accompanied by standing pillars of stones; or for the celebration of certain religious ceremonies. Such might have been the reasons, in some instances, where the evidences of stone-chests and urns are wanting: but these are so generally found, that they seem to determine the most usual purpose of the piles in question to have been for sepulchral monuments. Even this destination might render them suitable to other purposes; particularly religious, to which by their nature they might be supposed to give additional solemnity.—According to Toland, fires were kindled on the tops or flat stones, at certain times of the year, particularly on the eves of the 1st of May and the 1st of November, for the purpose of sacrificing; at which time all the people having extinguished their domestic hearths rekindled them from the sacred fires of the cairns. In general, therefore, these accumulations appear to have been designed for the sepulchral protection of heroes and great men. The stone-chests, the repository of the urns and ashes, are lodged in the earth beneath: sometimes only one, sometimes more, are found thus deposited; and Mr Pennant mentions an instance of 17 being discovered under the same pile.

Cairns are of different sizes, some of them very large. Mr Pennant describes one in the island of Arran, 114 feet over and of a vast height. They may justly be supposed to have been proportioned in size to the rank of the person, or to his popularity: the people of a whole district assembled to show their respect to the deceased; and, by an active honouring of his memory, soon accumulated heaps equal to those that astonish us at this time. But these honours were not merely those of the day; as long as the memory of the deceased endured, not a passenger went by without adding a stone to the heap: they supposed it would be an honour to the dead, and acceptable to his manes.

Quanquam festinas, non est mora longa; licebit,
Injecto ter pulvere, curras.

To this moment there is a proverbial expression among the highlanders allusive to the old practice: a suppliant will tell his patron, *Curri mi clach er do chairn*, "I will add a stone to your cairn;" meaning, When you are no more, I will do all possible honour to your memory.

Cairns are to be found in all parts of our islands, in Cornwal, Wales, and all parts of North Britain; they were in use among the northern nations; Dahlberg, in his 323d plate, has given the figure of one. In Wales they are called *carnedden*; but the proverb taken from them there, is not of the complimental kind: *Karn ar dy ben*, or, "A cairn on your head," is a token of imprecation.

Cairo.

CAIRO, or Grand Cairo, the capital of Egypt, situated in a plain at the foot of a mountain, in E. Long. 32. 0. N. Lat. 30. 0. It was founded by Jawhar, a Magrebian general, in the year of the Hegira 358. He had laid the foundations of it under the horoscope of Mars; and for that reason gave his new city the name of *Al Kahirah*, or the *Victorious*, an epithet applied by the Arab astronomers to that planet. In 362 it became the residence of the kalifs of Egypt, and of consequence the capital of that country, and has ever since continued to be so. It is divided into the New and Old cities. Old Cairo is on the eastern side of the river Nile, and is now almost uninhabited. The New, which is properly Cairo, is seated in a sandy plain about two miles and a half from the old city. It stands on the western side of the Nile, from which it is not three quarters of a mile distant. It is extended along the mountain on which the castle is built, for the sake of which it was removed hither, in order, as some pretend, to be under its protection. However, the change is much for the worse, as well with regard to air as water, and the pleasantness of the prospect. Bulack may be called the port of Cairo; for it stands on the bank of the Nile, about a mile and a half from it, and all the corn and other commodities are landed there before they are brought to the city. Some travellers have made Cairo of a most enormous magnitude, by taking in the old city Bulack, and the new; the real circumference of it, however, is not above ten miles, but it is extremely populous. The first thing that strikes a traveller is the narrowness of the streets, and the appearance of the houses. These are so daubed with mud on the outside, that you would think they were built with nothing else. Besides, as the streets are unpaved, and always full of people, the walking in them is very inconvenient, especially to strangers. To remedy this, there are a great number of asses, which always stand ready to be hired for a trifle, that is, a penny a mile. The owners drive

Cairo them along, and give notice to the crowd to make way. And here it may be observed, that the Christians in this, as well as other parts of the Turkish dominions, are not permitted to ride upon horses. The number of the inhabitants can only be guessed at; but we may conclude it to be very great, because in some years the plague will carry off 100,000, without their being much missed. The houses are from one to two or three stories high, and flat at the top; where they take the air, and often sleep all night. The better sort of these have a court on the inside like a college. The common run of houses have very little room, and even among great people it is usual for 20 or 30 to lie in the small hall. Some houses will hold 300 persons of both sexes, among whom are 20 or 30 slaves, and those of ordinary rank have generally three or four.

There is a canal called *Halis*, which runs along the city from one end to the other, with houses on each side, which make a large straight street. Besides this, there are several lakes, which are called *birks* in the language of the country. The principal of these, which is near the castle, is 500 paces in diameter. The most elegant houses in the city are built on its banks; but what is extraordinary, eight months in the year it contains water, and the other four it appears with a charming verdure. When there is water sufficient, it is always full of gilded boats, barges, and barks, in which people of condition take their pleasure towards night, at which time there are curious fire-works, and variety of music.

New Cairo is surrounded with walls built with stone, on which are handsome battlements, and at the distance of every hundred paces there are very fine towers, which have room for a great number of people. The walls were never very high, and are in many places gone to ruin. The basha lives in the castle, which was built by Saladine seven hundred years ago. It stands in the middle of the famous mountain Moketan, which terminates in this place, after it had accompanied the Nile from Ethiopia hither. This castle is the only place of defence in Egypt; and yet the Turks take no notice of its falling, insomuch that in process of time it will become a heap of rubbish. The principal part in it is a magnificent hall, environed with 12 columns of granite, of a prodigious height and thickness, which sustain an open dome, under which Saladine distributed justice to his subjects. Round this dome there is an inscription in relievo, which determines the date and by whom it was built. From this place the whole city of Cairo may be seen, and above 30 miles along the Nile, with the fruitful plains that lie near it, as well as the mosques, pyramids, villages, and gardens, with which these fields are covered. These granite pillars were the work of antiquity, for they were got out of the ruins of Alexandria. There are likewise in the mosques and in the principal houses no less than 40,000 more, besides great magazines, where all kinds are to be had at very low rates. A janissary happened to find five in his garden, as large as those in the castle; but could not find any machine of strength sufficient to move them, and therefore had them sawed in pieces to make mill-stones. It is believed that there have been 30 or 40,000 of these pillars brought from Alexandria, where there are yet many more to be had.

The gates of Cairo are three, which are very fine and magnificent. Cairo.

There are about 300 public mosques in this city, some of which have six minarets. The mosque of Azhar hath several buildings adjoining, which were once a famous university, and 14,000 scholars and students were maintained on the foundation; but has now not above 1400, and those are only taught to read and write. All the mosques are built upon the same plan, and differ only in magnitude. The entrance is thro' the principal gate into a large square, open on the top, but well paved. Round this are covered galleries, supported by pillars; under which they say their prayers, in the shade. On one side of the square there are particular places with basons of water, for the conveniency of performing the ablutions injoined by the Koran. The most remarkable part of the mosque, besides the minaret, is the dome. This is often bold, well proportioned, and of an astonishing magnitude. The inside stones are carved like lace, flowers, and melons. They are built so firm, and with such art, that they will last 600 or 700 years. About the outward circumference there are large Arabic inscriptions, in relievo, which may be read by those who stand below, though they are sometimes of a wonderful height.

The khanes or caravanseras are numerous and large, with a court in the middle, like their houses. Some are several stories high, and are always full of people and merchandise. The Nubians, the Abyssinians, and other African nations, which come to Cairo, have one to themselves, where they always meet with lodging. Here they are secure from insults, and their effects are all safe. Besides these, there is a bazar, or market, where all sorts of goods are to be sold. This is in a long broad street; and yet the crowd is so great, you can hardly pass along. At the end of this street is another short one, but pretty broad, with shops full of the best sort of goods, and precious merchandise. At the end of this short street there is a great khane, where all sorts of white slaves are to be sold. Farther than this is another khane, where a great number of blacks, of both sexes, are exposed to sale. Not far from the best market-place is an hospital, and a mosque for mad people. They also receive and maintain sick people into this hospital, but they are poorly looked after.

Old Cairo has scarce any thing remarkable but the granaries of Joseph; which are nothing but a high wall, lately built, which includes a square spot of ground, where they deposite wheat, barley, and other grain, which is a tribute to the basha, paid by the owners of land. This has no other covering but the heavens, and therefore the birds are always sure to have their share. There is likewise a tolerable handsome church, which is made use of by the Copts, who are Christians and the original inhabitants of Egypt. Joseph's well is in the castle, and was made by king Mohammed about 700 years ago. It is called *Joseph's well*, because they attribute every thing extraordinary to that remarkable person. It is cut in a rock, and is 280 feet in depth. The water is drawn up to the top by means of oxen, placed on platforms, at proper distances, which turn about the machines that raise it. The descent is so sloping, that, though there are no steps, the oxen can descend and ascend with ease.

The

The river Nile, to which not only Cairo, but all Egypt is so much indebted, is now known to have its rise in Abyssinia. The increase of the Nile generally begins in May, and in June they commonly proclaim about the city how much it is risen. Over against old Cairo the basha has a house, wherein the water enters to a column, which has lines at the distance of every inch, and marks at every two feet as far as 30. When the water rises to 22 feet, it is thought to be of a sufficient height; when it rises much higher, it does a great deal of mischief. There is much pomp and ceremony used in letting the water into the canal, or hali, above-mentioned. The basha gives the first stroke towards the removal of the dike or dam. When the water has filled the canal and lakes in the city, and the numerous cisterns that are in the mosques and private houses, it is let into a vast plain, to the north-east; the extent of which is 50 miles. When the country is covered with water, it is no unpleasant sight to view the towns appearing like little islands, and the people passing and repassing in boats.

The inhabitants of Cairo are a mixture of Moors, Turks, Jews, Greeks, and Cophts, or Coptis. The only difference between the habit of the Moors and Coptis is their turbans; those of the Moors being white, and of the Coptis white striped with blue. The common people generally wear a long black loose frock, sewed together all down before. The Jews wear a frock of the same fashion, made of cloth; and their caps are like a high crowned hat, without brims, covered with the same cloth, but not so taper. The Jewish women are not very unlike the men, but more light and long. The Greeks are habited like the Turks, only their turbans differ.

Provisions of all kinds are exceeding plenty; for 20 eggs may be bought for a parrah or penny, and bread is six times as cheap as with us. They have almost all sorts of flesh and fish; and in particular have tame buffaloes, which are very useful. They bring goats into the streets in great numbers, to sell their milk. Their gardens are well stocked with fruit-trees of various kinds, as well as roots, herbs, melons, and cucumbers. The most common flesh meat is mutton. The goats are very beautiful, and have ears two feet in length; but their flesh is in no great esteem.

CAIROAN, or CAIRWAN, a city of Africa, in the kingdom of Tunis, seated in a sandy barren soil, about five miles from the gulph of Capres. It has neither spring, well, nor river; for which reason they are obliged to preserve rain-water in tanks and cisterns. It was built by the Aghlabites; and is the ancient Cyrene*, but hath now lost its splendour. There is still, however, a very superb mosque, and the tombs of the kings of Tunis are yet to be seen. E. Long. 9. 12. N. Lat. 35. 40.

* See Barbary.

CAISSON, in the military art, a wooden chest, into which several bombs are put, and sometimes filled only with gunpowder: this is buried under some work whereof the enemy intend to possess themselves, and, when they are masters of it, is fired, in order to blow them up.

CAISSON is also used for a wooden frame or chest used in laying the foundations of the piers of a bridge.

CAITHNESS, otherwise called the *shire of Wick*, is the most northern county of all Scotland; bounded on the east by the ocean, and by Strathnavern and Sutherland on the south and south-west; from these it is divided by the mountains Orde, and a continued ridge of hills as far as Knockfin, then by the whole course of the river Hallowdale. On the north it is washed by the Penthland or Putland frith, which flows between this county and the Orkneys. It extends 35 miles from north to south, and about 20 from east to west. The coast is rocky, and remarkable for a number of bays and promontories. Of these, the principal are Sandside-head to the west, pointing to the opening of Pentland frith; Orcas, now Hulborn-head, and Dunnet-head, both pointing northward to the frith. Dunnet-head, is a peninsula about a mile broad, and seven in compass; affording several lakes, good pasture, excellent mill-stones, and a lead-mine. Scribsiter bay, on the north-west, is a good harbour, where ships may ride securely. Rice-bay, on the east side, extends three miles in breadth; but is of dangerous access, on account of some sunk rocks at the entrance. At the bottom of this bay appear the ruins of two strong castles, the seat of the Earl of Caithness, called *Castle Sinclair*, and Gernego, joined to each other by a draw-bridge. Duncan's bay, otherwise called *Dungsby-head*, is the north-east point of Caithness, and the extremest promontory in Britain. At this place, the breadth of the frith does not exceed 12 miles, and in the neighbourhood is the ordinary ferry to the Orkneys. Here is likewise Clytheness pointing east, and Noshead pointing north-east. The sea in this place is very impetuous, being in continual agitation from violent counter-tides, currents, and vortices. The only island belonging to this county is that of Stroma, in the Pentland frith, at the distance of two miles from the main land, extending about a mile in length, and producing good corn. The navigation is here rendered very difficult by conflicting tides and currents, which at both ends of the island produce a great agitation in the sea. At the south end, the waves dance so impetuously, that the sailors term them the *merry men of May*, alluding to the house of one Mr May, on the opposite shore of Caithness, which served them as a land-mark, in the dangerous passage between the island and the continent. The property of this island was once disputed between the earls of Orkney and Caithness; but adjudged to the latter, in consequence of an experiment, by which it appeared, that venomous creatures will live in Stroma, whereas they die immediately if transported to the Orkneys. The county of Caithness, though chiefly mountainous, flattens towards the sea-coast, where the ground is arable, and produces good harvests of oats and barley, sufficient for the natives, and yielding a surplus for exportation. Caithness is well watered with small rivers, brooks, lakes, and fountains, and affords a few woods of birch, but is in general bare of trees; and even those the inhabitants plant are stunted in their growth. Lead is found at Dunnet, copper at Old Urk, and iron ore at several places; but these advantages are not improved. The air of Caithness is temperate, tho' in the latitude of 58, where the longest day in summer is computed at 18 hours; and when the sun sets, he makes so small an arch of a circle below the horizon, that the people enjoy a twilight until he rises again. The fuel used by the inhabitants of Caithness consists of peat and turf, which the ground yields in great plenty. The

Caithness. forests of Morvine and Berridale afford abundance of red-deer and roe-bucks: the country is well stored with hares, rabbits, growse, heathcocks, plover, and all sorts of game, comprehending a bird called *snow-fleet*, about the size of a sparrow, exceedingly fat and delicious, that comes hither in large flights about the middle of February, and takes its departure in April. The hills are covered with sheep and black cattle; so numerous, that a fat cow has been sold at market for 4s. Sterling. The rocks along the coasts are frequented by eagles, hawks, and all manner of sea-fowl, whose eggs and young are taken in vast quantities by the natives. The rivers and lakes abound with trout, salmon, and eels; and the sea affords a very advantageous fishery. Divers obelisks and ancient monuments appear in this district, and several Romish chapels are still standing. Caithness is well peopled with a race of hardy inhabitants, who employ themselves chiefly in fishing, and breeding sheep and black cattle: they are even remarkably industrious; for between Wick and Dunbeath, one continued track of rugged rocks, extending 12 miles, they have forced several little harbours for their fishing boats, and cut artificial steps from the beach to the top of the rocks, where they have erected houses, in which they cure and dry the fish for market.

According to Mr Pennant, this county is supposed to send out in some years about 20,000 head of black cattle, but in bad seasons the farmer kills and salts great numbers for sale. Great numbers of swine are also reared here. These are short, high-backed, long bristled, sharp, slender, and long-nosed; have long erect ears, and most savage looks. Here are neither barns nor granaries: the corn is threshed out, and preserved in the chaff in bykes; which are stacks, in the shape of bee-hives, thatched quite round, where it will keep good for two years. Vast numbers of salmon are taken at Castle-hill, Dunnet, Wick, and Thurso. A miraculous draught at this last place is still talked of, not less than 2500 being taken at one tide within the memory of man; and Mr Smollet informs us, that, in the neighbourhood, above 300 good salmon have been taken at one draught of the net. In the month of November, great numbers of seals are taken in the caverns that open into the sea, and run some hundreds of yards under ground. The entrance of these caverns is narrow, but the inside lofty and spacious. The seal-hunters enter these in small boats with torches, which they light as soon as they land, and then with loud shouts alarm the animals, which they kill with clubs as they attempt to pass. This is a hazardous employment; for should the wind blow hard from sea, these adventurers are inevitably lost. Sometimes a large species of seals, 12 feet long, have been killed on this coast; and it is said the same kind are found on the rock Hiskir, one of the western islands. During the spring, great quantities of lump-fish resort to this coast, and are the prey of the seals, as appears from the number of skins of these fishes which at that season float ashore. At certain times also the seals seem to be visited by a great mortality; for, at those times, multitudes of them are seen dead in the water. Much limestone is found in this country, which when burnt is made into a compost with turf and sea-plants. The common people are kept in great servitude, and most of their time is given to the lairds, an invincible impediment to the prosperity of the country. The women are also condemned to a shameful drudgery; it not being uncommon to see them trudging in droves of 60 or 70 to the fields with baskets of dung on their backs, which are filled at pleasure from the dunghills by their lords and masters with their pitchforks. Caius.

The last private war in Scotland was occasioned by a dispute relating to this county. An earl of Breadalbane married an heiress of Caithness: the inhabitants would not admit her title, but set up another person in opposition. The earl, according to the custom of those times, designed to assert his right by force of arms: he raised an army of 1500 men; but thinking the number too great, he dismissed first one 500, and then another. With the remainder he marched to the borders of Caithness. Here he thought proper to add stratagem to force. He knew that the enemy's army waited for him on the other side of the promontory of Ord. He knew also, that whisky was then the nectar of Caithness; and therefore ordered a ship laden with that precious liquor to pass round, and wilfully strand itself on the shore. The directions were punctually obeyed; and the crew in a seeming fright escaped in the boats to the invading army. The Caithness men made a prize of the ship; but making too free with the freight, became an easy prey to the earl, who attacked them during their intoxication, and gained the county, which he disposed of very soon after his conquest.

CAIUS, Kaye, or *Kay*, (Dr John), the founder of Caius college in Cambridge, was born at Norwich in 1510. He was admitted very young a student in Gonville-hall in the above mentioned university; and at the age of 21 translated from Greek into Latin some pieces of divinity, and into English Erasmus's paraphrase on Jude, &c. From these his juvenile labours, it seems probable that he first intended to prosecute the study of divinity. Be that as it may, he travelled to Italy, and at Padua studied physic under the celebrated Montanus. In that university he continued some time, where we are told he read Greek lectures with great applause. In 1543, he travelled through part of Italy, Germany, and France; and returning to England commenced doctor of physic at Cambridge. He practised first at Shrewsbury, and afterwards at Norwich; but removing to London, in 1547 he was admitted fellow of the college of physicians, to which he was several years president. In 1557, being then physician to queen Mary, and in great favour, he obtained a licence to advance Gonville-hall, where he had been educated, into a college; which he endowed with several considerable estates, adding an entire new square at the expence of 1834l. Of this college he accepted the mastership, which he kept till within a short time of his death. He was physician to Edward VI. queen Mary, and Queen Elizabeth. Towards the latter end of his life he retired to his own college at Cambridge; where, having resigned the mastership to Dr Legge of Norwich, he spent the remainder of his life as a fellow-commoner. He died in July 1573, aged 63; and was buried in the chapel of his own college. Dr Caius was a learned, active, benevolent man. In 1557, he erected a monument in St Paul's to the memory of the famous Linacre. In 1563, he obtained a grant for the college of physicians to take the bodies of two male-

factors

factors annually for dissection; and he was the inventor of the *insignia* which distinguish the president from the rest of the fellows. He wrote, 1. Annals of the college from 1555 to 1572. 2. Translation of several of Galen's works. Printed at different times abroad. 3. *Hippocrates de Medicamentis*, first discovered and published by our author; also *De ratione victus*, Lov. 1556, 8vo. 4. *De medendi Methodo*. Basil, 1544. Lond. 1556, 8vo. 5. Account of the sweating sickness in England. Lond. 1556. 1721. It is entitled *De ephemera Britannica*. 6. History of the university of Cambridge. Lond. 1568, 8vo. 1574, 4to. in Latin. 7. *De thermis Britannicis*. Doubtful whether ever printed. 8. Of some rare plants and animals. Lond. 1570. 9. *De canibus Britannicis*, 1570, 1729. 10. *De pronunciatione Græcæ et Latinæ Linguæ*. Lond. 1574. 11. *De libris propriis*. Lond. 1570. Besides many other works which never were printed.

CAKE, a finer sort of bread, denominated from its flat round figure.

We meet with different compositions under the name of *cakes*; as *seed-cakes*, made of flour, butter, cream, sugar, coriander and caraway seeds, mace, and other spices and perfumes baked in the oven; *plum-cake*, made much after the same manner, only with fewer seeds, and the addition of currants; *pan-cakes*, made of a mixture of flour, eggs, &c. fried; *cheese-cakes*, made of cream, eggs, and flour, with or without cheese-curd, butter, almonds, &c. *oat-cakes*, made of fine oaten flour, mixed with yest and sometimes without, rolled thin, and laid on an iron or stone to bake over a slow fire; *sugar-cakes*, made of fine sugar beaten and searced with the finest flour, adding butter, rosewater, and spices; *rose-cakes*, *placenta rosacea*, are leaves of roses dried and pressed into a mass, sold in the shops for epithems.

The Hebrews had several sorts of cakes, which they offered in the temple. They were made of the meal either of wheat or barley; they were kneaded sometimes with oil and sometimes with honey. Sometimes they only rubbed them over with oil when they were baked, or fried them with oil in a frying pan upon the fire. In the ceremony of Aaron's consecration, they sacrificed a calf and two rams, and offered unleavened bread, and cakes unleavened, tempered with oil, and wafers unleavened anointed with oil; the whole made of fine wheaten flour. Ex. xxix. 1, 2.

CAKET, a town of Asia, in Persia, in the province of Gurgistan near Mount Caucasus. Its trade consists chiefly in silks. E. Long. 46. 15. N. Lat. 43. 30.

CALABASH, in commerce, a light kind of vessel formed of the shell of a gourd, emptied and dried, serving to put divers kinds of goods in, as pitch, rosin, and the like. The word is Spanish, *Calabaça*, which signifies the same. The Indians also, both of the North and South Sea, put the pearls they have fished in calabashes, and the negroes on the coast of Africa do the same by their gold-dust. The smaller calabashes are also frequently used by these people as a *measure*, by which they sell these precious commodities to the Europeans. The same vessels likewise serve for putting in liquors; and do the office of cups, as well as bottles, for soldiers, pilgrims, &c.

Calabash-Tree, in botany. See Crescentia.

African Calabash-Tree. See Adansonia.

CALABRIA, a country of Italy, in the kingdom of Naples, divided into Calabria Ultra, and Calabria Citra, commonly called *Ulterior* and *Citerior*, or Farther and Hither Calabria. Calabria Citerior is one of the 12 provinces of the kingdom of Naples; and bounded on the south by Calabria Ultra, on the north by Basilicata, and on the west and east by the sea: Cosenza is the capital. Calabria Ultra is washed by the Mediterranean sea on the east, south, and west, and bounded by Calabria Citra on the north. Reggio is the capital town.

This country has been almost entirely desolated by the earthquakes of 1783. The reiterated shocks extended from Cape Spartivento to Amantea above the gulf of St Eufemia, and also affected that part of Sicily which lies opposite to the southern extremity of Italy. Those of the 5th and 7th of February, and of the 28th of March, were the most violent, and completed the destruction of every building throughout the abovementioned space. Not one stone was left upon another south of the narrow isthmus of Squillace; and what is more disastrous, a very large proportion of the inhabitants was killed by the falling of their houses, near 40,000 lives being lost. Some persons were dug out alive after remaining a surprising length of time buried among the rubbish. Messina became a mass of ruins; its beautiful palazzata was thrown in upon the town, and its quay cracked into ditches full of water. Reggio almost destroyed; Tropea greatly damaged; every other place in the province levelled to the ground.

Before and during the concussion the clouds gathered, and then hung immoveable and heavy over the earth. At Palmi the atmosphere wore so fiery an aspect, that many people thought part of the town was burning. It was afterwards remembered that an unusual heat had affected the skin of several persons just before the shock; the rivers assumed a muddy ash-coloured tinge, and a sulphureous smell was almost general. A frigate passing between Calabria and Lipari felt so severe a shock, that the steersman was thrown from the helm, and the cannons were raised up on their carriages, while all around the sea exhaled a strong smell of brimstone.

Stupendous alterations were occasioned in the face of the country; rivers choaked up by the falling in of the hills, were converted into lakes, which if not speedily drained by some future convulsion, or opened by human labour, will fill the air with pestilential vapours, and destroy the remnants of population. Whole acres of ground, with houses and trees upon them, were broken off from the plains, and washed many furlongs down the deep hollows which the course of the rivers had worn; there, to the astonishment and terror of beholders, they found a new foundation to fix upon, either in an upright or an inclining position. In short, every species of phenomenon, incident to these destructive commotions of the earth, was to be seen in its utmost extent and variety in this ruinated country. Their Sicilian majesties, with the utmost expedition, dispatched vessels loaded with every thing that could be thought of on the occasion for the relief and accommodation of the distressed Calabrians; a general officer went from Naples with engineers and troops to direct the operations of the persons employed in clearing away and rebuilding the houses, and to defend the

property

property of the sufferers. The king ordered this officer to take all the money the royal treasures could supply or borrow; for, rather than it should be wanting on this pressing call, he was determined to part with his plate, nay, the very furniture of his palace. A messenger sent off from a town near Reggio on the 6th of February, travelled four days without shelter, and without being able to procure a morsel of bread; he supported nature with a piece of cheese which he had brought in his pocket, and the vegetables he was lucky enough to find near the road. To add to all their other sufferings, the Calabrians found themselves and the miserable wreck of their fortunes exposed to the depredations of robbers and pirates. Villains landed from boats and plundered several places, and thieves went even from Naples in search of booty: In order to strike a greater terror, they dressed themselves like Algerines; but were discovered and driven off. To this accumulated distress succeeded a most inclement season, which obstructed every effort made to alleviate it; and almost daily earthquakes kept the inhabitants in continual dread, not of being destroyed by the fall of houses, for none were left, but of being swallowed up by the splitting of the earth, or buried in the waves by some sudden inundation.

For further particulars concerning this dreadful catastrophe, and the phenomena attending it, see EARTHQUAKE.

CALADE, in the manege, the descent or sloping declivity of a rising manege ground, being a small eminence, upon which we ride down a horse several times, putting him to a short gallop, with his fore-hams in the air, to learn him to ply or bend his haunches, and form his stop upon the aids of the calves of the legs, the stay of the bridle, and the caveson seasonably given.

CALAGORINA, or CALAGURIS, distinguished by the surname *Nasica* (anc. geog.), a city of the Vascones in the Hither Spain; now *Calahorra*.

CALAHORRA, an episcopal town of Spain, in Old Castile, seated in a fertile soil, on the side of a hill which extends to the banks of the river Ebro. W. Long. 2. 7. N. Lat. 42. 12.

CALAIS, a strong town of France, in Lower Picardy, with a citadel and a fortified harbour. It is built in the form of a triangle, one side of which is towards the sea. The citadel is as large as the town, and has but one entrance. It is a trading place, with handsome streets, and several churches and monasteries; the number of inhabitants is reckoned to be 4000.

Calais was taken by Edward III. in 1347. Hither he marched his victorious army from Crecy, and invested the town on the 8th of September. But finding that it could not be taken by force without the destruction of great multitudes of his men, he turned the siege into a blockade; and having made strong entrenchments to secure his army from the enemy, huts to protect them from the inclemency of the weather, and stationed a fleet before the harbour to prevent the introduction of provisions, he resolved to wait with patience till the place fell into his hands by famine. The besieged, discovering his intention, turned seventeen hundred women, children, and old people, out of the town, to save their provisions; and Edward had the goodness, after entertaining them with a dinner, and giving them twopence a-piece, to suffer them to pass. The garrison and inhabitants of Calais having at length consumed all their provisions, and even eaten all the horses, dogs, cats, and vermin, in the place, the governor John de Vienne appeared upon the walls, and offered to capitulate. Edward, greatly incensed at their obstinate resistance, which had detained him eleven months under their walls, at an immense expence both of men and money, sent Sir Walter Manny, an illustrious knight, to acquaint the governor, that he would grant them no terms; but that they must surrender at discretion. At length, however, at the spirited remonstrances of the governor, and the persuasions of Sir Walter Manny, Edward consented to grant their lives to all the garrison and inhabitants, except six of the principal burgesses, who should deliver to him the keys of the city, with ropes about their necks. When these terms were made known to the people of Calais, they were plunged into the deepest distress; and after all the miseries they had suffered, they could not think without horror of giving up six of their fellow-citizens to certain death. In this extremity, when the whole people were drowned in tears, and uncertain what to do, Eustace de Pierre, one of the richest merchants in the place, stepped forth, and voluntarily offered himself to be one of these six devoted victims. His noble example was soon imitated by other five of the most wealthy citizens. These true patriots, barefooted and bareheaded, with ropes about their necks, were attended to the gates by the whole inhabitants, with tears, blessings, and prayers, for their safety. When they were brought into Edward's presence, they laid the keys of the city at his feet, and falling on their knees implored his mercy in such moving strains, that all the noble spectators melted into tears. The king's resentment was so strong for the many toils and losses he had suffered in this tedious siege, that he was in some danger of forgetting his usual humanity; when the queen, falling upon her knees before him, earnestly begged and obtained their lives. This great and good princess conducted these virtuous citizens, whose lives she had saved, to her own apartment, entertained them honourably, and dismissed them with presents. Edward took possession of Calais August 4th; and in order to secure a conquest of so great importance, and which had cost him so dear, he found it necessary to turn out all the ancient inhabitants, who had discovered so strong an attachment to their native prince, and to people it with English.

Calais remained in subjection to England till the reign of queen Mary, when it was retaken by the duke of Guise. This general began the enterprise by ordering the privateers of Normandy and Bretagne to cruise in the channel, more especially in the very straits of Calais: he then detached the duke of Nevers, with a considerable army, towards the country of Luxemburgh; a motion which drew the attention of the Spaniards that way: when all things were ready, he procured an application from the people of Boulogne, for a body of troops to secure them against the incursions of the Spaniards; he sent a strong detachment at their request, which was followed by another, under colour of supporting them, then repaired thither in person, secure that his officers would follow his instructions; and thus, on the first day of the new year, 1557, Calais was invested. He immediately at-

Calais

tacked fort St Agatha, which the garrison quitted, and retired into the fort of Nicolai, which, together with the Risbank, the besiegers attacked at the same time, granted good terms to the officer who commanded in the former, but obliged the garrison of the latter to surrender prisoners of war. By these means he opened a communication with the sea; and having received from on board the ships an immense quantity of hurdles, his infantry, by the help of them, passed the morasses that lie round the town. He then made a false attack at the water-gate, which drew the attention of the garrison, who fatigued themselves exceedingly in making entrenchments behind the breach; but when they had finished their work, he began to fire upon the castle, where the walls were very old, and had been neglected on account of the breadth of the ditch, which was also very deep when the tide was in; but a great breach being made, the duke caused it to be attacked in the night, and during the ebb the soldiers passing almost up to the shoulders. The place was easily carried, though the governor made three vigorous attacks before the break of day, in order to dislodge them; but the French, though they lost a considerable number of men, kept their posts. The governor then saw that it was impracticable to defend the place any longer, and therefore made the best terms for himself that he could obtain, which, however, were not very good: and thus in eight days the duke of Guise recovered a fortress which cost the victorious Edward III. a whole year's siege, and which had been now 210 years in the possession of the English, without so much as a single attempt to retake it. There are very different accounts given of this matter: Some English historians say, that king Philip penetrated the design of the French upon this fortress, gave notice of it in England, and offered to take the defence of it upon himself; but that this, out of jealousy, was refused, it being believed to be only an artifice to get a place of such consequence into his own hands. The truth of the matter seems to be this: The strength of Calais consisted in its situation and outworks, which required a very numerous garrison; but this being attended with a very large expence, the best part of the troops had been sent to join Philip's army, so that the governor had not above 500 men, and there were not more than 250 of the townsmen able to bear arms. As to ammunition, artillery, and provisions, the French found there abundance, but with so slender a garrison, that it was impossible to make a better defence; and therefore, when the lord Wentworth, who was governor, and whom the French call lord Dumfort, was tried by his peers for the loss of this place, he was acquitted. The duke obliged all the English inhabitants to quit Calais; and bestowed the government of it upon des Termes, who was soon after made a marshal of France.

The fortifications of Calais are good; but its greatest strength is its situation among the marshes, which may be overflowed at the approach of an enemy. The harbour is not so good as formerly, nor will it admit vessels of any great burden. In times of peace, there are packet-boats going backward and forward twice a week from Dover to Calais, which is 21 miles distant. E. Long. 2. 6. N. Lat. 50. 58.

Calais and Zetes, in fabulous history, sons of Boreas and Orythia, to whom the poets attributed wings: they went on the voyage of Colchis with the Argonauts, delivered Phineus from the harpies, and were slain by Hercules.

Calais to Calamine.

CALAMANCO, a sort of woollen stuff manufactured in England and Brabant. It has a fine gloss; and is checkered in the warp, whence the checks appear only on the right side. Some calamancoes are quite plain, others have broad stripes adorned with flowers, some with plain broad stripes, some with narrow stripes, and others watered.

CALAMARIÆ, in botany, an order of plants in the *Fragmenta methodi naturalis* of Linnæus; in which he has the following genera, viz. bobartia, scirpus, cyperus, eriophorum, carex, schœnus, flagellaria, juncus. See Botany.

CALAMATA, a considerable town of Turky in Europe, in the Morea, and province of Belvedera. It was taken by the Venetians in 1685; but the Turks retook it afterwards with all the Morea. It stands on the river Spinarza, eight miles from the sea. E. Long. 22. 15. N. Lat. 37. 8.

CALAMINE, Calamy, *Lapis Calaminaris*, or *Cadmia Fossilis*, a sort of stone or mineral, containing zinc, iron, and sometimes other substances. It is considerably heavy, and the more so the better; moderately hard and brittle, or of a consistence betwixt stone and earth: the colour is sometimes whitish or grey; sometimes yellowish, or of a deep yellow; sometimes red; sometimes brown or blackish. It is plentiful in several places of Europe, as Hungary, Transylvania, Poland, Spain, Sweden, Bohemia, Saxony, Goslar, France, and England, particularly in Derbyshire, Gloucestershire, Nottinghamshire, and Somersetshire, as also in Wales. The calamine of England, however, is by the best judges allowed to be superior in quality to that of most other countries. It seldom lies very deep, being chiefly found in clayey grounds near the surface. In some places it is mixed with lead-ores. It is the only true ore of zinc, and is used as an ingredient in making of brass.—Newmann relates various experiments with this mineral, the only result of which was to show that it contained iron as well as zinc. The most remarkable are the following. A saturated solution of calamine in the marine acid, concentrated by evaporating part of the liquor, exhibits in the cold an appearance of fine crystals, which on the application of warmth dissolve and disappear. A little of this concentrated solution tinges a large quantity of water of a bright yellow colour; and at the same time deposits by degrees a fine, spongy, brownish precipitate. Glue dissolved in this solution, and afterwards inspissated, forms an extremely slippery tenacious mass, which does not become dry, and, were it not too expensive, might be of use for entangling flies, caterpillars, &c. Sulphur boiled in the solution seems to acquire some degree of transparency.—This mineral is an article in the materia medica; but, before it comes to the shops, is usually roasted or calcined, in order to separate some arsenical or sulphureous matter which in its crude state it is supposed to contain, and to render it more easily reducible into a fine powder. In this state it is employed in collyria against defluxions of thin acrid humours upon the eyes, for drying up moist running ulcers, and healing excoriations. It is the basis of an official epulotic Cerate.

Though the lapis calaminaris is the only native ore of zinc, there is another substance from which that semi-metal is also obtained. This is called *cadmia fornacum*, or *cadmia of the furnaces*, to distinguish it from the other. This is a matter sublimed when ores containing zinc, like those of Rammelsberg, are smelted. This cadmia consists of the flowers of the semi-metal sublimed during the fusion, and adhering to the inner surfaces of the walls of furnaces, where they suffer a semi-fusion, and therefore acquire some solidity. So great a quantity of these are collected, that they form very thick incrustations, which must be frequently taken off. The name of *cadmia of the furnaces* has also been given to all the soots and metallic sublimates formed by smelting in the great, although there is certainly a difference in these matters.

CALAMINT, in botany. See MELISSA, and MENTHA.

CALAMUS, in botany; A genus of the monogynia order, belonging to the hexandria class of plants; and in the natural method ranking under the 5th order, *Tripetaloideæ*. The calyx is hexaphyllous, there is no corolla, the fruit is a dry monospermous berry, imbricated backwards. There is but one species, the rotang. The stem is without branches, has a crown at top, and is every where beset with straight spines. This is the true Indian cane, which is not visible on the outside; but the bark being taken off discovers the smooth stick, which has no marks of spine on the bark, and is exactly like those which the Dutch sell to us; keeping this matter very secret, lest travellers going by should take as many canes out of the woods as they please. Sumatra is said to be the place where most of these sticks grow. Such are to be chosen as are of proper growth between two joints, suitable to the fashionable length of canes as they are then worn: but such are scarce.—The calamus rotang is one of several plants from which the drug called Dragon's-blood is obtained.

CALAMUS, in the ancient poets, denotes a simple kind of pipe or fistula, the musical instrument of the shepherds and herdsmen; usually made either of an entire stalk or a reed.

CALAMUS *Aromaticus*, or *Sweet-scented Flag*, in the materia medica, a species of flag called *acorus* by Linnæus. See ACORUS.

CALAMUS *Scriptorius*, in antiquity, a reed or rush to write with. The ancients made use of styles to write on tables covered with wax; and of reed, or rush, to write on parchment, or Egyptian paper.

CALAMY (Edmund), an eminent Presbyterian divine, born at London in the year 1600, and educated at Pembroke-hall, Cambridge, where his attachment to the Arminian party excluded him from a fellowship. Dr Felton bishop of Ely, however, made him his chaplain; and, in 1639, he was chosen minister of St Mary Aldermary, in the city of London. Upon the opening of the long parliament, he distinguished himself in defence of the Presbyterian cause; and had a principal hand in writing the famous *Smectymnuus*, which, himself says, gave the first deadly blow to episcopacy. The authors of this tract were five, the initials of whose names formed the name under which it was published; viz. Stephen Marshal, Edmund Calamy, Thomas Young, Matthew Newcomen, and William Spurstow. He was after that an active member in the assembly of divines, was a strenuous opposer of sectaries, and used his utmost endeavours to prevent those violences committed after the king was brought from the isle of Wight. In Cromwell's time he lived privately, but was assiduous in promoting the king's return; for which he was afterwards offered a bishopric, but refused it. He was ejected for nonconformity in 1662; and died of grief at the sight of the great fire of London.

CALAMY (Edmund), grandson to the preceding (by his eldest son Mr Edmund Calamy, who was ejected out of the living of Moreton in Essex on St Bartholomew's day 1662), was born in London, April 5th 1671. After having learned the languages, and gone through a course of natural philosophy and logic at a private academy in England, he studied philosophy and civil law at the university of Utrecht, and attended the lectures of the learned Grævius. Whilst he resided here, an offer of a professor's chair in the university of Edinburgh was made him by Mr Carstairs, principal of that university, sent over on purpose to find a person properly qualified for such an office. This he declined; and returned to England in 1691, bringing with him letters from Grævius to Dr Pocock canon of Christ-church and regius professor of Hebrew, and to Dr Bernard Savilian professor of astronomy, who obtained leave for him to prosecute his studies in the Bodleian library. Having resolved to make divinity his principal study, he entered into an examination of the controversy between the conformists and nonconformists; which determined him to join the latter: and coming to London in 1692, he was unanimously chosen assistant to Mr Matthew Sylvester at Blackfriars; and in 1694, he was ordained at Mr Annesly's meeting-house in Little St-Helens, and soon after was invited to become assistant to Mr Daniel Williams in Hand-Alley. In 1702, he was chosen to be one of the lecturers in Salter's-hall; and, in 1703, succeeded Mr Vincent Alsop as pastor of a great congregation in Westminster. He drew up the table of contents to Mr Baxter's history of his life and times, which was sent to the press in 1696; made some remarks on the work itself, and added to it an index; and, reflecting on the usefulness of the book, he saw the expediency of continuing it, for Mr Baxter's history came no lower than the year 1684. Accordingly he composed an abridgement of it, with an account of many other ministers who were ejected after the restoration of Charles II.; their apology, containing the grounds of their nonconformity and practice as to stated and occasional communion with the church of England; and a continuation of their history till the year 1691. This work was published in 1702. He afterwards published a moderate defence of nonconformity, in three tracts, in answer to some tracts of Dr Hoadley. In 1709, Mr Calamy made a tour to Scotland, and had the degree of doctor of divinity conferred on him by the universities of Edinburgh, Aberdeen, and Glasgow. In 1713, he published a second edition of his Abridgement of Mr Baxter's history of his life and times; in which, among other additions, there is a continuation of the history through king William's reign, and queen Anne's, down to the passing of the occasional bill; and in the close is subjoined the reformed liturgy, which was drawn

drawn up and presented to the bishops in 1661, "that the world may judge (he says in his preface) how fairly the ejected ministers have been often represented as irreconcilable enemies to all liturgies." In 1718, he wrote a vindication of his grandfather, and several other persons, against certain reflections cast upon them by Mr Archdeacon Echard in his History of England; and in 1728 appeared his Continuation of the account of the ministers, lecturers, masters, and fellows of colleges, and schoolmasters, who were ejected, after the restoration in 1660, by or before the act of uniformity. He died June 3d 1732, greatly regretted not only by the dissenters, but also by the moderate members of the established church, both clergy and laity, with many of whom he lived in great intimacy. Besides the pieces already mentioned, he published a great many sermons on several subjects and occasions. He was twice married, and had 13 children.

CALANDRE, a name given by the French writers to an insect that does vast mischief in granaries. It is properly of the scarab or beetle class; it has two antennæ or horns formed of a great number of round joints, and covered with a soft and short down; from the anterior part of the head there is thrust out a trunk, which is so formed at the end, that the creature easily makes way with it through the coat or skin that covers the grain, and gets at the meal or farina on which it feeds; the inside of the grains is also the place where the female deposits her eggs, that the young progeny may be born with provision about them. When the female has pierced a grain of corn for this purpose, she deposits in it one egg, or at the utmost two, but she most frequently lays them single: these eggs hatch into small worms, which are usually found with their bodies rolled up in a spiral form, and after eating till they arrive at their full growth, they are changed into chrysales, and from these in about a fortnight comes out the perfect calandre. The female lays a considerable number of eggs; and the increase of these creatures would be very great: but nature has so ordered it, that while in the egg state, and even while in that of the worm, they are subject to be eaten by mites; these little vermin are always very plentiful in granaries, and they destroy the far greater number of these larger animals.

CALAS (John), the name of a most unfortunate Protestant merchant at Thoulouse, inhumanly butchered under forms of law cruelly prostituted to shelter the sanguinary dictates of ignorant Popish zeal. He had lived 40 years at Thoulouse. His wife was an English woman of French extraction: and they had five sons; one of whom, Lewis, had turned Catholic through the persuasions of a Catholic maid who had lived 30 years in the family. In October 1761, the family consisted of Calas, his wife, Mark Anthony their son, Peter their second son, and this maid. Anthony was educated for the bar; but being of a melancholy turn of mind, was continually dwelling on passages from authors on the subject of suicide, and one night in that month hanged himself on a bar laid across two folding doors in their shop. The crowd collected by the confusion of the family on so shocking a discovery, took it into their heads that he had been strangled by the family to prevent his changing his religion, and that this was a common practice among protestants. The officers of justice adopted the popular tale, and were supplied by the mob with what they accepted as evidences of the fact. The fraternity of white penitents got the body, buried it with great ceremony, and performed a solemn service for him as a martyr; the Franciscans did the same: and after these formalities no one doubted the guilt of the devoted heretical family. They were all condemned to the torture, to bring them to confession: they appealed to the parliament; who, as weak and as wicked as the subordinate magistrates, sentenced the father to the torture ordinary and extraordinary, to be broken alive upon the wheel, and then to be burned to ashes. A diabolical decree! which, to the shame of humanity, was actually carried into execution. Peter Calas, the other son, was banished for life; and the rest were acquitted. The distracted widow found some friends, and among the rest M. Voltaire, who laid her case before the council of state at Versailles, and the parliament of Thoulouse were ordered to transmit the proceedings. These the king and council unanimously agreed to annul; the capitoul, or chief magistrate of Thoulouse, was degraded and fined; old Calas was declared to have been innocent; and every imputation of guilt was removed from the family, who also received from the king and clergy considerable gratuities.

CALASH, or Caleche, a small light kind of chariot or chair, with very low wheels, used chiefly for taking the air in parks and gardens. The calash is for the most part richly decorated, and open on all sides for the conveniency of the air and prospect, or at most inclosed with light mantlets of wax-cloth to be opened and shut at pleasure. In the Philosophical Transactions we have a description of a new sort of calash going on two wheels, not hung on traces, yet easier than the common coaches, over which it has this further advantage, that whereas a common coach will overturn if one wheel go on a surface a foot and an half higher than the other, this will admit of a difference of 3½ feet without danger of overturning. Add, that it would turn over and over; that is, after the spokes being so turned as that they are parallel to the horizon, and one wheel flat over the head of him that rides in it, and the other flat under him, it will turn once more, by which the wheels are placed *in statu quo*, without any disorder to the horse or rider.

CALASIO (Marius), a Franciscan, and professor of the Hebrew language at Rome, of whom there is very little to be said, but that he published there, in the year 1621, a Concordance of the Bible, which consisted of four great volumes in folio. This work has been highly approved and commended both by Protestants and Papists, and is indeed a most admirable work. For besides the Hebrew words in the Bible, which are in the body of the book, with the Latin version over against them; there are, in the margin, the differences between the septuagint version and the vulgate; so that at one view may be seen wherein the three Bibles agree, and wherein they differ. Moreover, at the beginning of every article there is a kind of dictionary, which gives the signification of each Hebrew word; affords an opportunity of comparing it with other oriental languages, viz. with the Syriac, Arabic, and Chaldee; and is extremely useful for determining more exactly the true meaning of the Hebrew words.

CALASIRIS, in antiquity, a linen tunic fringed at the bottom, and wore by the Egyptians under a white woollen garment: but this last they were obliged to pull off when they entered the temples, being only allowed to appear there in linen garments.

CALATAJUD, a large and handsome town of Spain, in the kingdom of Arragon; seated at the confluence of the rivers Xalon and Xiloca, at the end of a very fertile valley, with a good castle on a rock. W. Long. 2. 9. N. Lat. 41. 22.

CALATHUS, in antiquity, a kind of hand-basket made of light wood or rushes; used by the women sometimes to gather flowers, but chiefly, after the example of Minerva, to put their work in. The figure of the calathus, as represented on ancient monuments, is narrow at the bottom, and widening upwards like that of a top. Pliny compares it to that of a lily. The Calathus or work-basket of Minerva is no less celebrated among the poets than her distaff.

Calathus was also the name of a cup for wine, used in sacrifices.

CALATOR, in antiquity, a cryer, or officer appointed to publish something aloud, or call the people together. The word is formed from καλω, voco, *I call*. Such ministers the pontifices had, whom they used to send before them when they went to sacrifice on *feriæ* or holidays, to advertise the people to leave off work. The magistrates also used *calatores*, to call the people to the comitia, both *curiata* and *centuriata*. The officers in the army also had *calatores*; as had likewise many private families, to invite their guests to entertainments.

CALATRAVA, a city of New Castile, in Spain, situated on the river Guadiana, 45 miles south of Toledo. W. Long. 4. 00. N. Lat. 39. 0.

Knights of Calatrava, a military order in Spain, instituted under Sancho III. king of Castile, upon the following occasion. When that prince took the strong fort of Calatrava from the moors of Andalusia, he gave it to the templars, who, wanting courage to defend it, returned it him again. Then Don Reymond, of the order of the Cistercians, accompanied with several persons of quality, made an offer to defend the place, which the king thereupon delivered up to them, and instituted that order. It increased so much under the reign of Alphonsus, that the knights desired they might have a grand master, which was granted. Ferdinand and Isabella afterwards, with the consent of pope Innocent VIII. re-united the grand-mastership of Calatrava to the Spanish crown; so that the kings of Spain are now become perpetual administrators thereof.

The knights of Calatrava bear a cross gules, flower-delised with green, &c. Their rule and habit was originally that of the Cistercians.

CALAURIA (anc. geog.), an island of Greece in the Saronic bay, overagainst the port of Troezen, at the distance of 40 stadia. Hither Demosthenes went twice into banishment; and here he died. Neptune was said to have accepted this island from Apollo in exchange for Delos. The city stood on a high ridge nearly in the middle of the island, commanding an extensive view of the gulf and its coasts. There was his holy temple. The priestess was a virgin, who was dismissed when marriageable. Seven of the cities near the island held a congress at it, and sacrificed jointly to the deity. Athens, Ægina, and Epidaurus were of this number, with Nauplia, for which place Argos contributed. The Macedonians, when they had reduced Greece, were afraid to violate the sanctuary, by forcing from it the fugitives, his suppliants. Antipater commanded his general to bring away the orators, who had offended him, alive; but Demosthenes could not be prevailed on to surrender. His monument remained in the second century, within the inclosure of the temple. The city of Calauria has been long abandoned. Traces of buildings, and of ancient walls, appear nearly level with the ground; and some stones, in their places, each with a front and back, forming a little circle, once perhaps a bath. The temple, which was of the Doric order, and not large, as may be inferred from the fragments, is reduced to an inconsiderable heap of ruins. The island is now called *Poro*. It stretches along before the coast of the Morea in a lower ridge, and is separated from it by a canal only four stadia or half a mile wide. This, which is called Poro or the Ferry, in still weather may be passed on foot, as the water is not deep. It has given its name to the island; and also to the town, which consists of about 200 houses, mean and low, with flat roofs; rising on the slope of a bare disagreeable rock.

CALCADA, or *St Dimingo Calcada*, a town of Spain, situated in W. Long. 3. 5. N. Lat. 42. 36.

CALCAR, a very strong town of Germany, in the circle of Westphalia, and duchy of Cleves. It belongs to the king of Prussia, and is seated near the Rhine, in E. Long. 5. 42. N. Lat. 51. 45.

Calcar, in glass-making, the name of a small oven, or reverberatory furnace, in which the first calcination of sand and salt of potashes is made for the turning them into what is called *frit*. This furnace is made in the fashion of an oven, ten feet long, seven broad in the widest part, and two feet deep. On one side of it is a trench six inches square, the upper part of which is level with the calcar, and separated only from it at the mouth by bricks nine inches wide. Into this trench they put sea-coal, the flame of which is carried into every part of the furnace, and is reverberated from the roof upon the frit, over the surface of which the smoke flies very black, and goes out at the mouth of the calcar; the coals burn on iron-grates, and the ashes fall through.

Calcar (John de), a celebrated painter, was the disciple of Titian, and perfected himself by studying Raphael. Among other pieces he drew a nativity, representing the angels around the infant Christ; and so ordered the disposition of his picture, that the light all proceeds from the child. He died at Naples, in 1546, in the flower of his age. It was he who designed the anatomical figures of Vesal, and the portraits of the painters of Vesari.

CALCAREOUS, something that partakes of the nature and qualities of calx, or lime. We say, a *calcareous* earth, *calcareous* stone. See *Chemistry-Index*.

CALCEARIUM, in antiquity, a donative or largess bestowed on Roman soldiers for buying shoes. In monasteries, *calcearium* denoted the daily service of cleaning the shoes of the religious.

CALCEOLARIA, in botany; a genus of the monogynia order, belonging to the diandria class of plants. The corolla is ringent and inflated; the capsule has two cells, and two valves; the calyx four parted and equal.

CALCHAS, in fabulous history, a famous diviner, followed the Greek army to Troy. He foretold that the siege would last ten years; and that the fleet, which was detained in the port of Aulis by contrary winds, would not sail till Agamemnon's daughter had been sacrificed to Diana. After the taking of Troy, he retired to Colophon; where, it is said, he died of grief, because he could not divine what another of his profession, called *Mopsus*, had discovered.

CALCINATION, in chemistry, the reducing of substances to a calx by fire. See *Chemistry-Index*.

CALCINATO, a town of Italy, in the duchy of Mantua, remarkable for a victory gained over the Imperialists by the French in 1706. E. Long. 9. 55. N. Lat. 45. 25.

CALCULARY *of a Pear*, a congeries of little strong knots dispersed through the whole parenchyma of the fruit. The calculary is most observed in rough-tasted or choak-pears. The knots lie more continuous and compact together towards the pear where they surround the ACETARY. About the stalk they stand more distant; but towards the cork, or stool of the flower, they still grow closer, and there at last gather into the firmness of a plumb-stone. The calculary is no vital or essential part of the fruit; the several knots whereof it consists being only so many concretions or precipitations out of the sap, as we see in urines, wines, and other liquors.

CALCULATION, the act of computing several sums, by adding, subtracting, multiplying, or dividing. See ARITHMETIC.

CALCULATION is more particularly used to signify the computations in astronomy and geometry, for making tables of logarithms, ephemerides, finding the time of eclipses, &c. See ASTRONOMY, GEOMETRY, and LOGARITHMS.

CALCULUS, primarily denotes a little stone or pebble, anciently used in making computations, taking of suffrages, playing at tables, and the like. In after-times, pieces of ivory, and counters struck of silver, gold, and other matters, were used in lieu thereof, but still retaining the ancient names. Computists were by the lawyers called *calculones*, when they were either slaves or newly freed men; those of a better condition were named *calculatores* or *numerarii*: ordinarily there was one of these in each family of distinction. The Roman judges anciently gave their opinions by calculi, which were white for absolution, and black for condemnation. Hence *calculus albus*, in ancient writers, denotes a favourable vote, either in a person to be absolved and acquitted of a charge, or elected to some dignity or post; as *calculus niger* did the contrary. This usage is said to have been borrowed from the Thracians, who marked their happy or prosperous days by white, and their unhappy by black, pebbles, put each night into an urn.

Besides the diversity of colours, there were some calculi also which had figures or characters engraven on them, as those which were in use in taking the suffrages both in the senate and at assemblies of the people. These calculi were made of thin wood, polished and covered over with wax. Their form is still seen in some medals of the Cassian family; and the manner of casting them into the urns, in the medals of the Licinian family. The letters marked upon these calculi were U. R. for *uti rogas*, and A. for *antiquo*; the first of which expressed an approbation of the law, the latter a rejection of it. Afterwards the judges who sat in capital causes used calculi marked with the letter A. for *absolvo*; C. for *condemno*; and N. L. for *non liquet*, signifying that a more full information was required.

Calculus is also used in ancient grammatic writers for a kind of weight equal to two grains of cicer. Some make it equivalent to the siliqua, which is equal to three grains of barley. Two calculi made the ceratium.

Calculus Differentialis is a method of differencing quantities, or of finding an infinitely small quantity, which, being taken infinite times, shall be equal to a given quantity: or, it is the arithmetic of the infinitely small differences of variable quantities.

The foundation of this calculus is an infinitely small quantity, or an infinitesimal, which is a portion of a quantity incomparable to that quantity, or that is less than any assignable one, and therefore accounted as nothing; the error accruing by omitting it being less than any assignable one. Hence two quantities, only differing by an infinitesimal, are reputed equal. Thus, in Astronomy, the diameter of the earth is an infinitesimal, in respect of the distance of the fixed stars; and the same holds in abstract quantities. The term, infinitesimal, therefore, is merely respective, and involves a relation to another quantity; and does not denote any real ens, or being. Now infinitesimals are called *differentials*, or *differential quantities*, when they are considered as the differences of two quantities. Sir Isaac Newton calls them *moments*; considering them as the momentary increments of quantities, e. g. of a line generated by the flux of a point, or of a surface by the flux of a line. The differential calculus, therefore, and the doctrine of fluxions, are the same thing under different names; the former given by M. Leibnitz, and the latter by Sir Isaac Newton: each of whom lay claim to the discovery. There is, indeed, a difference in the manner of expressing the quantities resulting from the different views wherein the two authors consider the infinitesimals; the one as moments, the other as differences: Leibnitz, and most foreigners, express the differentials of quantities by the same letters as variable ones, only prefixing the letter *d*: thus the differential of x is called dx; and that of y, dy: now dx is a positive quantity, if x continually increase; negative, if it decrease. The English, with Sir Isaac Newton, instead of dx write $\dot{x}$ (with a dot over it;) for dy, $\dot{y}$, &c. which foreigners object against, on account of that confusion of points, which they imagine arises when differentials are again differenced; besides, that the printers are more apt to overlook a point than a letter. Stable quantities being always expressed by the first letters of the alphabet $da=0$, $db=0$, $dc=0$; wherefore $d(x+y-a)=dx+dy$, and $d(x-y+a)$ $dx-dy$. So that the differencing of quantities is easily performed, by the addition or subtraction of their compounds.

To difference quantities that multiply each other; the rule is, first, multiply the differential of one factor into the other factor, the sum of the two factors is the differential sought: thus, the quantities being xy, the dif-

differential will be $x\,dy+y\,dx$, i. e. $d(xy)=x\,dy+y\,dx$. Secondly, if there be three quantities mutually multiplying each other, the factum of the two must then be multiplied into the differential of the third: thus suppose vxy, let $vx=t$, then $vxy=ty$; consequently $d(vxy)=t\,dy+y\,dt$: but $dt=v\,dx+x\,dv$. These values, therefore, being substituted in the antecedent differential, $t\,dy+y\,dt$, the result is, $d(vxy)=vx\,dy+vy\,dx+xy\,dv$. Hence it is easy to apprehend how to proceed, where the quantities are more than three. If one variable quantity increase, while the other y decreases, it is evident $y\,dx-x\,dy$ will be the differential of xy.

To difference quantities that mutually divide each other; the rule is, first, multiply the differential of the divisor into the dividend; and, on the contrary, the differential of the dividend into the divisor; subtract the last product from the first, and divide the remainder by the square of the divisor; the quotient is the differential of the quantities mutually dividing each other. See Fluxions.

Calculus Exponentialis, is a method of differencing exponential quantities, or of finding and summing up the differentials or moments of exponential quantities; or at least bringing them to geometrical constructions.

By exponential quantity, is here understood a power, whose exponent is variable; v. g. x^x, a^x, x^y, where the exponent x does not denote the same in all the points of a curve, but in some stands for 2, in others for 3, in others for 5, &c.

To difference an exponential quantity; there is nothing required but to reduce the exponential quantities to logarithmic ones; which done, the differencing is managed as in logarithmic quantities.—Thus, suppose the differential of the exponential quantity x^y required, let

$$x^y=z$$

Then will $y\,lx=lz$

$$lx\,dy+\frac{y\,dx}{x}=\frac{dz}{z}$$

$$z\,lx\,dy+\frac{zy\,dx}{x}=dz$$

That is, $x^y\,lx\,dy+yx^{y-1}\,dx=dz$.

Calculus Integralis, or Summatorius, is a method of integrating, or summing up moments, or differential quantities; i. e. from a differential quantity given, to find the quantity from whose differencing the given differential results.

The integral calculus, therefore, is the inverse of the differential one: whence the English, who usually call the differential method *fluxions*, give this *calculus*, which ascends from the fluxions, to the flowing or variable quantities: or, as foreigners express it, from the differences to the sums, by the name of the *inverse method of fluxions*.

Hence, the integration is known to be justly performed, if the quantity found, according to the rules of the differential calculus, being differenced, produce that proposed to be summed.

Suppose $\int$ the sign of the sum, or integral quantity, then $\int y\,dx$ will denote the sum, or integral of the differential $y\,dx$.

To integrate, or sum up a differential quantity: It is demonstrated, first, that $\int dx=x$; secondly, $\int(dx+dy)=x+y$; thirdly, $\int(x\,dy+y\,dx)=xy$; fourthly, $\int(m\,x^{m-1}\,dx)=x^m$; fifthly, $\int(n:m)\,x^{\frac{n-m}{m}}dx=x^{\frac{n}{m}}$; sixthly, $\int(y\,dx-x\,dy):y^2=x:y$. Of these, the fourth and fifth cases are the most frequent, wherein the differential quantity is integrated, by adding a variable unity to the exponent, and dividing the sum by the new exponent multiplied into the differential of the root; v. g. the fourth case, by $m-(1+1)\,dx$, i. e. by $m\,dx$.

If the differential quantity to be integrated doth not come under any of these formulas, it must either be reduced to an integral finite, or an infinite series, each of whose terms may be summed.

It may be here observed, that, as in the analysis of finites, any quantity may be raised to any degree of power; but *vice versa*, the root cannot be extracted out of any number required: so in the analysis of infinites, any variable or flowing quantity may be differenced; but *vice versa*, any differential cannot be integrated. And as, in the analysis of finites, we are not yet arrived at a method of extracting the roots of all equations, so neither has the integral calculus arrived at its perfection: and as in the former we are obliged to have recourse to approximation, so in the latter we have recourse to infinite series, where we cannot attain to a perfect integration.

Calculus Literalis, or *Literal Calculus*, is the same with specious arithmetic, or algebra, so called from its using the letters of the alphabet; in contradistinction to numeral arithmetic, which uses figures. In the literal calculus given quantities are expressed by the first letters, *a b c d*; and quantities sought by the last *z y x*, &c. Equal quantities are denoted by the same letters.

Calculus Minervæ, among the ancient lawyers, denoted the decision of a cause, wherein the judges were equally divided. The expression is taken from the history of Orestes, represented by Æschylus and Euripides; at whose trial, before the Areopagites, for the murder of his mother, the votes being equally divided for and against him, Minerva interposed, and gave the casting vote or calculus in his behalf.

M. Cramer, professor at Marpurg, has a discourse express, *De Calculo Minervæ*; wherein he maintains, that all the effect an entire equality of voices can have, is to leave the cause *in statu quo*.

Calculi Tiburtini, a sort of figured stone, formed in great plenty about the cataracts of the Anio, and other rivers in Italy; of a white colour, and in shape oblong, round, or echinated. They are a species of the *stiria lapidea*, and generated like them; and so like sugar-plums in the whole, that it is a common jest at Rome to deceive the unexperienced by serving them up at deserts.

Calculus, in Medicine, the disease of the stone in the bladder, or kidneys. The term is Latin, and signifies a *little pebble*. The calculus in the bladder is called *lithiasis*; and in the kidneys, *nephritis*. See Medicine and Surgery.

Human calculi are commonly formed of different

strata

crusts or incrustations; sometimes smooth and heavy like mineral stones; but oftener rough, spongy, light, and full of inequalities or protuberances: chemically analysed, or distilled in an open fire, they nearly yield the same principles as urine itself, or at least an empyreumatic volatile urinous matter, together with a great deal of air. They never have, nor can have, naturally, any foreign matter for a basis; but they may by accident; an instance of which is related by Dr Percival*. A bougie had unfortunately slipped into the bladder, and upon it a stone of a considerable size was formed in less than a year. This stone had so much the appearance of chalk, that the doctor was induced to try whether it could be converted into quicklime. His experiment succeeded, both with that and some other calculi; from which he conjectures, that hard waters which contain calcareous earth may contribute towards the formation of these calculi.

* Essays, Vol. III. p. 163.

CALCUTTA, the capital of the province of Bengal, and of all the British possessions in the East Indies, is situated on the river Hugguely, a branch of the Ganges, about 100 miles from the sea, in N. Lat. 23. and 88. 28. E. Long. from Greenwich. It is but a modern city, built on the site of a village called *Govindpour*. The English first obtained the Mogul's permission to settle in this place in the year 1690; and Mr Job Channock, the company's agent, made choice of the spot on which the city stands, on account of a large shady grove which grew there; though in other respects it was the worst he could have pitched upon; for three miles to the north east, there is a salt-water lake, which overflows in September, and when the flood retires in December, leaves behind such a quantity of fish and other putrescent matter, as renders the air very unhealthy. The custom of the Gentoos throwing the dead bodies of their poor people into the river is also very disgustful, and undoubtedly contributes to render the place unhealthy, as well as the cause already mentioned.

Calcutta is now become a large and populous city, being supposed at present to contain 500,000 inhabitants. It is elegantly built, at least the part inhabited by the English; but the rest, and that the greatest part, is built after the fashion of the cities of India in general. The plan of all these is nearly the same; their streets are exceedingly confined, narrow, and crooked, with a vast number of ponds, reservoirs, and gardens interspersed. A few of the streets are paved with brick. The houses are built, some with brick, others with mud, and a still greater number with bamboos and mats; all which different kinds of fabrics standing intermixed with one another, form a very uncouth appearance. The brick houses are seldom above two stories high, but those of mud and bamboos are only one, and are covered with thatch. The roofs of the brick houses are flat and terraced. These, however, are much fewer in number than the other two kinds; so that fires, which often happen, do not sometimes meet with a brick house to obstruct their progress in a whole street. Within these 20 or 25 years Calcutta has been greatly improved both in appearance and in the salubrity of its air: the streets have been properly drained, and the ponds filled; thereby removing a vast surface of stagnant water, the exhalations of which were particularly hurtful. The citadel is named Fort William, and is superior as a fortress to any in India; but is now on too extensive a scale to answer the purpose for which it was intended, viz. the holding a post in case of extremity. It was begun on this extended plan by lord Clive immediately after the battle of Plassey. The expence attending it was supposed to amount to two millions Sterling.

Calcutta is the emporium of Bengal, and the residence of the governor-general of India. Its flourishing state may in a great measure be supposed owing to the unlimited toleration of all religions allowed here; the Pagans being suffered to carry their idols in procession, the Mahommedans not being discountenanced, and the Roman Catholics being allowed a church.— At about 2 miles distance from the town is a plain where the natives annually undergo a very strange kind of penance on the 9th of April; some for the sins they have committed, others for those they may commit, and others in consequence of a vow made by their parents. This ceremony is performed in the following manner. Thirty bamboos, each about the height of 20 feet, are erected in the plain above mentioned. On the top of these they contrive to fix a swivel, and another bamboo of thirty feet or more crosses it, at both ends of which hangs a rope. The people pull down one end of this rope, and the devotee placing himself under it, the Brahmin pinches up a large piece of skin under both the shoulderblades, sometimes in the breasts, and thrusts a strong iron hook through each. These hooks have lines of Indian grass hanging to them, which the priest makes fast to the rope at the end of the cross bamboo, and at the same time puts a sash round the body of the devotee, laying it loosely in the hollow of the hooks, lest by the skin's giving way, he should fall to the ground. When this is done, the people haul down the other end of the bamboo; by which means the devotee is immediately lifted up 30 feet or more from the ground, and they run round as fast as their legs can carry them. Thus the devotee is thrown out the whole length of the rope, where, as he swings, he plays a thousand antic tricks; being painted and dressed in a very particular manner, on purpose to make him look more ridiculous. Some of them continue swinging half an hour, others less. The devotees undergo a preparation of four days for this ceremony. On the first and third they abstain from all kinds of food; but eat fruit on the other two. During this time of preparation they walk about the streets in their fantastical dresses, dancing to the sound of drums and horns; and some, to express the greater ardour of devotion, run a rod of iron quite through their tongues, and sometimes through their cheeks also.

Before the war of 1755, Calcutta was commonly garrisoned by 300 Europeans, who were frequently employed in conveying the company's vessels from Patna, loaded with salt-petre, piece-goods, opium, and raw silk. The trade of Bengal alone supplied rich cargoes for 50 or 60 ships annually, besides what was carried on in small vessels to the adjacent countries. It was this flourishing state of Calcutta that probably was one motive for the Nabob Surajah Dowla to attack it in the year 1756. Having had the fort of Cossimbuzar delivered up to him, he marched against Calcutta with all his forces, amounting to 70,000 horse and foot,

with

Calcutta. with 400 elephants, and inveſted the place on the 15th of June. Previous to any hoſtilities, however, he wrote a letter to Mr Drake the governor, offering to withdraw his troops, on condition that he would pay him his duty on the trade for 15 years paſt, defray the expence of his army, and deliver up the black merchants who were in the fort. This being refuſed, he attacked one of the redoubts at the entrance of the town; but was repulſed with great ſlaughter. On the 16th he attacked another advanced poſt, but was likewiſe repulſed with great loſs. Notwithſtanding this diſappointment, however, the attempt was renewed on the 18th, when the troops abandoned theſe poſts, and retreated into the fort; on which the Nabob's troops entered the town, and plundered it for 24 hours. An order was then given for attacking the fort; for which purpoſe a ſmall breaſt-work was thrown up, and two twelve pounders mounted upon it; but without firing oftener than two or three times an hour. The governor then called a council of war, when the captain of the train informed them, that there was not ammunition in the fort to ſerve three days; in conſequence of which the principal ladies were ſent on board the ſhips lying before the fort. They were followed by the governor, who declared himſelf a quaker, and left the place to be defended by Mr Holwell the ſecond in council. Beſides the governor, four of the council, eight gentlemen in the company's ſervice, four officers, and 100 ſoldiers, with 52 free merchants, captains of ſhips, and other gentlemen, eſcaped on board the ſhips, where were alſo 59 ladies, with 33 of their children. The whole number left in the fort were about 250, effective men, with Mr Holwell, four captains, five lieutenants, ſix enſigns, and five ſerjeants; as alſo 14 ſea-captains, and 29 gentlemen of the factory. Mr Holwell then having held a council of war, divided three cheſts of treaſure among the diſcontented ſoldiers; making them large promiſes alſo, if they behaved with courage and fidelity; after which he boldly ſtood on the defence of the place, notwithſtanding the immenſe force which oppoſed him. The attack was very vigorous; the enemy having got poſſeſſion of the houſes, galled the Engliſh from thence, and drove them from the baſtions; but they themſelves were ſeveral times diſlodged by the fire from the fort, which killed upwards of 12,000 men, with the loſs of only five Engliſh ſoldiers the firſt day. The attack, however, was continued till the afternoon of the 20th; when many of the garriſon being killed and wounded, and their ammunition almoſt exhauſted, a flag of truce was hung out. Mr Holwell intended to have availed himſelf of this opportunity to make his eſcape on board the ſhips, but they had fallen ſeveral miles down from the fort, without leaving even a ſingle boat to facilitate the eſcape of thoſe who remained. In the mean time, however, the back-gate was betrayed by the Dutch guard, and the enemy, entering the fort, killed all they firſt met, and took the reſt priſoners.

The fort was taken before ſix in the evening; and, in an hour after, Mr Holwell had three audiences of the Nabob, the laſt being in the durbar or council. In all of theſe the governor had the moſt poſitive aſſurances that no harm ſhould happen to any of the priſoners; but he was ſurpriſed and enraged at finding only 50,000 l. in the fort, inſtead of the immenſe treaſures he expected; and to this, as well as perhaps to the reſentment of the jemmidaars or officers, of whom many were killed in the ſiege, we may impute the cataſtrophe that followed. Calcutta.

As ſoon as it was dark, the Engliſh priſoners, to the number of 146, were directed by the jemmidaars who guarded them, to collect themſelves into one body, and ſit down quietly under the arched veranda, or piazza, to the weſtward of the black-hole priſon. Beſides the guard over them, another was placed at the ſouth-end of this veranda, to prevent the eſcape of any of them. About 500 gunmen, with lighted matches, were drawn up on the parade; and ſoon after the factory was in flames to the right and left of the priſoners, who had various conjectures on this appearance. The fire advanced with rapidity on both ſides; and it was the prevailing opinion of the Engliſh, that they were to be ſuffocated between the two fires. On this they ſoon came to a reſolution of ruſhing on the guard, ſeizing their ſcymitars, and attacking the troops upon the parade, rather than be thus tamely roaſted to death; but Mr Holwell advanced, and found the Moors were only ſearching for a place to confine them in. At that time Mr Holwell might have made his eſcape, by the aſſiſtance of Mr Leech, the company's ſmith, who had eſcaped when the Moors entered the fort, and returned juſt as it was dark, to tell Mr Holwell he had provided a boat, and would inſure his eſcape, if he would follow him through a paſſage few were acquainted with, and by which he then entered. This might eaſily have been accompliſhed, as the guard took little notice of it; but Mr Holwell told Mr Leech, he was reſolved to ſhare the fate of the gentlemen and the garriſon; to which Mr Leech gallantly replied, that "then he was reſolved to ſhare Mr Holwell's fate, and would not leave him."

The guard on the parade advanced, and ordered them all to riſe and go into the barracks. Then, with their muſkets preſented, they ordered them to go into the black-hole priſon; while others, with clubs and ſcymitars, preſſed upon them ſo ſtrong, that there was no reſiſting it; but, like one agitated wave impelling another, they were obliged to give way and enter; the reſt following like a torrent. Few among them, the ſoldiers excepted, had the leaſt idea of the dimenſions or nature of a place they had never ſeen; for if they had, they ſhould at all events have ruſhed upon the guard, and been cut to pieces by their own choice as the leſſer evil.

It was about eight o'clock when theſe 146 unhappy perſons, exhauſted by continual action and fatigue, were thus crammed together into a dungeon about eighteen feet ſquare, in a cloſe ſultry night in Bengal; ſhut up to the eaſt and ſouth, the only quarters from whence air could reach them, by dead walls, and by a wall and door to the north; open only to the weſt by two windows, ſtrongly barred with iron, from which they could receive ſcarce any circulation of freſh air.

They had been but few minutes confined before every one fell into a perſpiration ſo profuſe, that no idea can be formed of it. This brought on a raging thirſt, which increaſed in proportion as the body was drained of its moiſture. Various expedients were thought

thought of to give more room and air. Every man was stripped, and every hat put in motion: they several times sat down on their hams; but at each time several of the poor creatures fell, and were instantly suffocated or trod to death.

Before nine o'clock every man's thirst grew intolerable, and respiration difficult. Efforts were again made to force the door; but still in vain. Many insults were used to the guards, to provoke them to fire in upon the prisoners, who grew outrageous, and many delirious. "Water, water," became the general cry. Some water was brought; but these supplies, like sprinkling water on fire, only served to raise and feed the flames. The confusion became general, and horrid from the cries and ravings for water; and some were trampled to death. This scene of misery proved entertainment to the brutal wretches without, who supplied them with water, that they might have the satisfaction of seeing them fight for it, as they phrased it; and held up lights to the bars, that they might lose no part of the inhuman diversion.

Before eleven o'clock, most of the gentlemen were dead, and one third of the whole. Thirst grew intolerable: but Mr Holwell kept his mouth moist by sucking the perspiration out of his shirt-sleeves, and catching the drops as they fell, like heavy rain, from his head and face. By half an hour after eleven, most of the living were in an outrageous delirium. They found that water heightened their uneasinesses; and "Air, air," was the general cry. Every insult that could be devised against the guard, all the opprobrious names that the viceroy and his officers could be loaded with, were repeated, to provoke the guard to fire upon them. Every man had eager hopes of meeting the first shot. Then a general prayer to heaven, to hasten the approach of the flames to the right and left of them, and put a period to their misery. Some expired on others; while a steam arose as well from the living as the dead, which was very offensive.

About two in the morning, they crowded so much to the windows, that many died standing, unable to fall by the throng and equal pressure round. When the day broke, the stench arising from the dead bodies was unsufferable. At that juncture, the Soubah, who had received an account of the havoc death had made among them, sent one of his officers to enquire if the chief survived. Mr Holwell was shown to him; and near six an order came for their release.

Thus they had remained in this infernal prison from eight at night until six in the morning, when the poor remains of 146 souls, being only 23, came out alive; but most of them in a high putrid fever. The dead bodies were dragged out of the hole by the soldiers, and thrown promiscuously into the ditch of an unfinished ravelin, which was afterwards filled with earth.

The injuries which Calcutta suffered at this time, however, were soon repaired. The place was retaken by Admiral Watson and Colonel Clive, early in 1757: Surajah Dowla was defeated, deposed, and put to death; and Meer Jaffier, who succeeded him in the Nabobship, engaged to pay an immense sum for the indemnification of the inhabitants. Since that time the immense acquisition of territory by the British in this part of the world, with the constant state of security enjoyed by this city, have given an opportunity of embellishing and improving it greatly beyond what it was before.—Among these improvements we may reckon that of Sir William Jones; who, on the 15th of January 1784, instituted a society for inquiring into the history civil and natural, the antiquities, arts, sciences, and literature of Asia; and thus the literature of Europe, and along with it, it is to be hoped, the arts of humanity, beneficence, and peace, have at length obtained a footing in the rich empire of Indostan, so long a prey to the rapine and violence of tyrants and usurpers.

CALDARIUM, in the ancient baths, denoted a brazen vessel or cistern, placed in the hypocaustum, full of hot water, to be drawn thence into the *piscina* or bath, to give it the necessary degree of heat. In this sense, the *caldarium* stood contradistinguished from the *tepidarium* and *frigidarium*.

Caldarium also denoted the stove, or sudatory, being a close vaulted room, wherein by hot dry fumes, without water, people were brought to a profuse sweat. In which sense, *caldarium* was the same with what was otherwise denominated *vaporarium*, *sudatorium*, and *laconicum*; in the Greek baths, *hypocaustum*, [illegible].

CALDERINUS (Domitius), a learned critic, born at Caldería near Verona. He read lectures upon polite literature at Rome with great reputation; and was the first who ventured to write upon the most difficult of the ancient poets. He died very young in 1477.

CALDERON, De la Barca, (Don Pedro), a Spanish officer, who, after having signalized himself in the military profession, quitted it for the ecclesiastical, and then commenced dramatic writer. His dramatic works make 9 vols in 4to, and some Spanish authors have compared him to Shakespeare. He flourished about the year 1640.

CALDERWOOD (David), a famous divine of the church of Scotland, and a distinguished writer in behalf of the Presbyterians, was descended of a good family in that kingdom; and being early designed for the ministry, he applied with great diligence to the study of the Scriptures in their original tongues, the works of the fathers, the councils, and the best writers on church-history. He was settled about the year 1604 at Crelling near Jedburgh. King James I. of Great Britain, being desirous of bringing the church of Scotland nearer to a conformity with that of England, laboured earnestly to restore the episcopal authority, and enlarge the powers of the bishops who were then in Scotland. This design was very warmly opposed by many of the ministers, and particularly by Mr David Calderwood; who, when Mr James Law, bishop of Orkney, came to visit the presbyteries of Merse and Teviotdale, declined his jurisdiction by a paper under his hand dated May 5th 1608. But the king having its success much at heart, sent the earl of Dunbar, then high-treasurer of Scotland, with Dr Abbot afterwards archbishop of Canterbury, and two other divines, into that kingdom, with instructions to employ every method to persuade both the clergy and laity of his majesty's sincere desire to promote the good of the church, and of his zeal for the Protestant religion. Mr Calderwood did not assist at the general assembly held at Glasgow June 8th 1610, in which lord Dunbar lor preſided as commiſſioner; and it appears from his writings, that he looked upon every thing tranſacted in it as null and void. In May following, king James went to Scotland; and on the 17th of Jone held a parliament at Edinburgh: at that time the clergy met in one of the churches, to hear and adviſe with the biſhops; which kind of aſſembly, it ſeems, was contrived in order to reſemble the Engliſh convocation. Mr Calderwood was preſent at it, but declared publicly that he did not take any ſuch meetings to reſemble a convocation; and being oppoſed by Dr Whitford and Dr Hamilton, who were friends to the biſhops, he took his leave of them in theſe words: "It is abſurd to ſee men ſitting in ſilks and ſattins, and to cry poverty in the kirk, when purity is departing." The parliament proceeded in the mean while in the diſpatch of buſineſs; and Mr Calderwood, with ſeveral other miniſters, being informed that a bill was depending to empower the king, with the advice of the archbiſhops, biſhops, and ſuch a number of the miniſtry as his Majeſty ſhould think proper, to conſider and conclude as to matters decent for the external policy of the church, not repugnant to the word of God; and that ſuch concluſions ſhould have the ſtrength and power of eccleſiaſtical laws: againſt this they proteſted, for four reaſons. 1. Becauſe their church was ſo perfect, that, inſtead of needing reformation, it might be a pattern to others. 2. General aſſemblies, as now eſtabliſhed by law, and which ought always to continue, might by this means be overthrown. 3. Becauſe it might be a means of creating ſchiſm, and diſturb the tranquillity of the church. 4. Becauſe they had received aſſurances, that no attempts ſhould be made to bring them to a conformity with the church of England. They deſired therefore, that, for theſe and other reaſons, all thoughts of paſſing ſuch a law might be laid aſide: but in caſe this be not done, they proteſt for themſelves and their brethren who ſhall adhere to them, that they can yield no obedience to this law when it ſhall be enacted, becauſe it is deſtructive of the liberty of the church; and therefore ſhall ſubmit to ſuch penalties, and think themſelves obliged to undergo ſuch puniſhments, as may be inflicted on them for diſobeying that law. This proteſt was ſigned by Mr Archibald Simſon on behalf of the members who ſubſcribed another ſeparate roll, which he kept for his juſtification. This proteſt was preſented to the clerk regiſter, who refuſed to read it before the ſtates in parliament. However, though not read, it had its effect; for although the bill had the conſent of parliament, yet the king thought fit to cauſe it to be laid aſide, and not long after called a general aſſembly at St Andrew's. Soon after the parliament was diſſolved, and Mr Calderwood was ſummoned to appear before the high-commiſſion court at St Andrew's, on the 8th of July following, to anſwer for his mutinous and ſeditious behaviour. July 10th, the king came to that city in perſon; when Mr Calderwood, being called upon, and refuſing to comply with what the king in perſon required of him, was committed to priſon. Afterwards the privy council, according to the power exerciſed by them at that time, directed him to baniſh himſelf out of the king's dominions before Michaelmas next; and not to return without licence. Having applied to the king for a prorogation of his ſentence without ſucceſs, becauſe he would neither acknowledge his offence, nor promiſe conformity for the future, he retired to Holland, where, in 1623, he publiſhed his celebrated piece entitled *Altare Damaſcenum*. Mr Calderwood having in the year 1624 been afflicted with a long fit of ſickneſs, and nothing having been heard of him for ſome time, one Mr Patrick Scot, as Calderwood himſelf informs us, took it for granted that he was dead; and thereupon wrote a recantation in his name, as if, before his deceaſe, he had changed his ſentiments. This impoſture being detected, Scot went over to Holland, and ſtaid three weeks at Amſterdam, where he made a diligent ſearch for the author of Altare Damaſcenum, with a deſign to have diſpatched him. But Calderwood had privately retired into his own country, where he lived ſeveral years. Scot gave out that the king had furniſhed him with the matter for the pretended recantation, and that he only put it in order. During his retirement, Mr Calderwood collected all the memorials relating to the eccleſiaſtical affairs of Scotland, from the beginning of the reformation there down to the death of king James; which collection is ſtill preſerved in the univerſity library of Glaſgow; that which was publiſhed under the title of "The true hiſtory of Scotland," is only an extract from it. In the advertiſement prefixed to the laſt edition of his Altare Damaſcenum mention is made of his being miniſter of Pencaitland near Edinburgh in 1638; but we find nothing ſaid there, or any where elſe, of his death.

CALDRON, a large kitchen utenſil, commonly made of copper; having a moveable iron handle, whereby to hang it on the chimney-hook. The word is formed from the French *chaudron*, or rather the Latin *caldarium*.

Boiling in CALDRONS, *(caldariis decoquere)*, is a capital puniſhment ſpoken of in the middle-age writers, decreed to divers ſorts of criminals, but chiefly to debaſers of the coin. One of the torments inflicted on the ancient Chriſtian martyrs, was boiling in caldrons of water, oil, &c.

CALDWALL (Richard), a learned Engliſh phyſician, born in Staffordſhire about the year 1513. He ſtudied phyſic in Brazen-Noſe college Oxford; and was examined, admitted into, and made cenſor of, the college of phyſicians at London, all in one day. Six weeks after he was choſen one of the elects; and in the year 1570, was made preſident of that college. Mr Wood tells us, that he wrote ſeveral pieces in his profeſſion; but he does not tell us what they were, only that he tranſlated a book on the art of ſurgery, written by one Horatio More, a Florentine phyſician. We learn from Cambden, that Caldwall founded a chirurgical lecture in the college of phyſicians, and endowed it with a handſome ſalary. He died in 1585.

CALEA, in botany: A genus of the polygamia æqualis order, belonging to the ſyngeneſia claſs of plants; and in the natural method ranking under the 49th order, *Compoſitæ*. The receptacle is paleaceous, the pappus hairy, and the calyx imbricated.

CALEB, one of the deputies ſent by the Iſraelites to take a view of the land of Canaan. He made a good report of the country, and by this means revived the ſpirits of the dejected people; on which account, he and Joſhua were the only perſons who, after their leaving Egypt, ſettled in the land of Canaan. Caleb

had,

had, for his share, the mountains and the city of Hebron, from which he drove three kings. Othoniel his nephew having taken the city of Debir, Caleb gave him his daughter Achsah in marriage; and died, aged 114.

CALEDONIA, the ancient name of Scotland. From the testimonies of Tacitus, Dio, and Solinus, we find, that the ancient Caledonia comprehended all that country lying to the north of the rivers Forth and Clyde. In proportion as the Silures or Cimbri advanced towards the north, the Caledonians, being circumscribed within narrower limits, were forced to transmigrate into the islands which crowd the western coasts of Scotland. It is in this period, probably, we ought to place the first great migration of the British Gael into Ireland; that kingdom being much nearer to the promontory of Galloway and Cantire, than many of the Scottish isles are to the continent of North Britain.

To the country which the Caledonians possessed, they gave the name of *Gael-doch*; which is the only appellation the Scots, who speak the Gaelic language, know for their own division of Britain. *Gael-doch* is a compound, made up of *Gaël* or *Gaïl*, the first colony of the ancient Gauls who transmigrated into Britain, and *doch*, a district or division of a country. The Romans, by transposing the letter *l* in *Gael*, and by softening into a Latin termination the *ch* of *doch*, formed the well known name of Caledonia.

When the tribes of North Britain were attacked by the Romans, they entered into associations, that, by uniting their strength, they might be more able to repel the common enemy. The particular name of that tribe, which either its superior power or military reputation placed at the head of the association, was the general name given by the Romans to all the confederates. Hence it is that the *Meatæ*, who with other tribes inhabited the districts of Scotland lying southward of the frith, and the *Caledonians*, who inhabited the west and north-west parts, have engrossed all the glory which belonged in common, though in an inferior degree, to all the other nations settled of old in North Britain. It was for the same reason that the name of *Meatæ* was entirely forgotten by foreign writers after the third century, and that of the *Caledonians* themselves but seldom mentioned after the fourth.

Britons, Caledonians, Meatæ, Barbarians, are the names constantly given to the old inhabitants of North Britain, by Tacitus, Herodian, Dio, Spartian, Vopiscus, and other ancient writers. The successors of these Britons, Caledonians, Meatæ, and Barbarians, are called Picts, Scots, and Attacots, by some Roman writers of the fourth century.

The origin of the appellation *Scoti* and *Picti*, introduced by latter Roman authors, has occasioned much controversy among the antiquarians of these days. The dispute seems now to be fully decided by some learned critics of the present century, whose knowledge of the Gaelic language assisted their investigation. See SCOTLAND, PICTS, and HIGHLANDERS.

CALEDONIA, the name of a settlement made by the Scots on the west side of the gulph of Darien, in 1698; out of which they were starved at the request of the East-India company: for the English government prohibited the other colonies sending them any provisions; so they were obliged to leave it in 1700.

New CALEDONIA, an island in the south-sea, lately discovered by captain Cook, and, next to New Holland and New Zealand, is the largest island that hath yet been discovered in that sea. It extends from 19. 37. to 22. 30. S. Lat. and from 163. 37. to 167. 14. E. Long. Its length from north-west to south-east is about 80 leagues; but its greatest breadth does not exceed ten leagues. This island is diversified by hills and valleys of various size and extent. From the hills issue abundance of rivulets, which contribute to fertilize the plains. Along its north-east shore the land is flat; and being well watered, and cultivated by the inhabitants after their manner, appeared to great advantage to captain Cook's people. Was it not, indeed, for those fertile spots on the plains, the whole country might be called *a dreary waste*: the mountains and higher parts of the land are in general incapable of cultivation. They consist chiefly of rocks, many of which are full of mundic; the little soil that is upon them is scorched and burnt up by the sun; it is, however, covered with coarse grass and other plants, and here and there covered with trees and shrubs. The country in general bears a great resemblance to those parts of New South Wales which lie under the same parallel of latitude. Several of its natural productions are the same, and the woods are without underwood as well as in that country. The whole coast seems to be surrounded by reefs and shoals, which render all access to it extremely dangerous; but at the same time guard the coasts against the attacks of the wind and sea; rendering it easily navigable along the coast by canoes, and causing it abound with fish. Every part of the coast seems to be inhabited; the plantations in the plains are laid out with great judgment, and cultivated with much labour. They begin their cultivation by setting fire to the grass, &c. with which the ground is covered, but have no notion of preserving its vigour by manure; they, however, recruit it by letting it lie for some years untouched. On the beach was found a large irregular mass of rock, not less than a cube of ten feet, consisting of a close-grained stone speckled full of garnets somewhat bigger than pins heads, from whence it seems probable that some valuable minerals may be found on this island. It differs from all the other islands yet discovered in the South Sea, by being entirely destitute of volcanic productions. Several plants of a new species were found here; and a few young breadfruit trees, not then sufficiently grown to bear fruit, seemed to have come up without culture: plantains and sugar-canes are here in small quantity, and the cocoa-nut trees are small and thinly planted. A new species of passion-flower was likewise met with, which was never known to grow wild any where but in America. Several *Caputi* (MELALEUCA) trees were also found in flower. Musquetoes here are very numerous. A great variety of birds were seen of different classes, which were for the most part entirely new; particularly a beautiful species of parrot before unknown to zoologists. A new species of fish, of the genus called by Linnæus *tetraodon*, was caught here; and its liver, which was very large, prefented at supper. Several species of this genus being reckoned poisonous, and the present species being re-

Caledonia. markably ugly, Meſſ. Forſters hinted their ſuſpicions of its quality; but the temptation of a freſh meal, and the aſſurances of captain Cook that he had formerly eaten this identical ſort of fiſh without harm, got the better of their ſcruples, and they eat of it. Its oilineſs, however, though it had no other bad taſte than what proceeded from this, prevented them from taking more than a morſel or two. In a few hours after they had retired to reſt, they were awakened by very alarming ſymptoms, being all ſeized with an extreme giddineſs; their hands and feet were numbed, ſo that they were ſcarcely able to crawl; and a violent langour and oppreſſion ſeized them. Emetics were adminiſtered with ſome ſucceſs, but ſudorifics gave the greateſt relief. Some dogs who had eaten the remainder of the liver were likewiſe taken ill; and a pig which had eaten the entrails died ſoon after, having ſwelled to an unuſual ſize. The effects of this poiſon on the gentlemen did not go entirely off in leſs than ſix weeks.—Abundance of turtle was ſeen here. The natives had not the leaſt notion of goats, hogs, dogs, or cats, and had not even a name for any of them.

The inhabitants are very ſtout, tall, and in general well proportioned; their features mild; their beards and hair black, and ſtrongly friezled, ſo as to be ſomewhat woolly in ſome individuals; their colour is ſwarthy, or a dark cheſnut brown. A few were ſeen who meaſured ſix feet four inches. They are remarkably courteous, not at all addicted to pilfering and ſtealing; in which character of honeſty they are ſingular, all the other nations in the South Sea being remarkably thieviſh. Some wear their hair long, and tie it up to the crown of their heads; others ſuffer only a large lock to grow on each ſide, which they tie up in clubs; many others, as well as all the women, wear it cropt ſhort. They make uſe of a kind of comb made of ſticks of hard wood, from ſeven to nine or ten inches long, and about the thickneſs of knitting needles; a number of theſe, ſeldom exceeding 20, but generally fewer, are faſtened together at one end, parallel to and near one tenth of an inch from each other; the ends, which are a little pointed, will ſpread out or open like the ſticks of a fan. Theſe combs they always wear in their hair on one ſide of their head. Some had a kind of concave cylindrical ſtiff black cap, which appeared to be a great ornament among them, and was ſuppoſed to be worn only by the chiefs and warriors. A large ſheet of ſtrong paper, whenever they got one in exchange, was commonly applied to this purpoſe. The men go naked; only tying a ſtring round their middle, and another round their neck. A little piece of a brown cloth made of the bark of a fig-tree, ſometimes tucked up to the belt, and ſometimes pendulous, ſcarcely deſerves the name of a covering; nor indeed does it ſeem at all intended for that purpoſe. This piece of cloth is ſometimes of ſuch a length, that the extremity is faſtened to the ſtring round the neck; to this ſtring they likewiſe hang ſmall round beads of a pale green nephritic ſtone. Coarſe garments were ſeen among them made of a ſort of matting; but they ſeemed never to wear them, except when in their canoes and unemployed. The women ſeemed to be in a ſervile ſtate: they were the only perſons of the family who had any employment, and ſeveral of them brought bundles of ſticks and fuel on their back: thoſe who had children carried them on their backs in a kind of Caledonia. ſatchel. The women alſo were ſeen to dig up the earth in order to plant it. They are in general of a dark cheſnut, and ſometimes mahogany brown; their ſtature middle-ſized, ſome being rather tall, and their whole form rather ſtout, and ſomewhat clumſy. Their dreſs is the moſt disfiguring that can be imagined, and gives them a thick ſquat ſhape; it is a ſhort petticoat or fringe, conſiſting of filaments or little cords, about eight inches long, which are faſtened to a very long ſtring, which they have tied ſeveral times round their waiſt. The filaments, or little ropes, therefore, lie above each other in ſeveral layers, forming a kind of thick thatch all round the body, but which does not near cover the thigh: theſe filaments were ſometimes dyed black; but frequently thoſe on the outſide only were of that colour, the reſt being of a dirty grey. There was not a ſingle inſtance, during the ſhip's ſtay in this iſland, of the women permitting any indecent familiarity with an European: they took pleaſure in practiſing the arts of a jilting coquette, but never became abſolute wantons. The general ornaments of both ſexes are ear-rings of tortoiſe ſhell; necklaces, or amulets, made both of ſhells and ſtones; and bracelets made of large ſhells, which they wear above the elbows.

The houſes, or huts, in New Caledonia, are circular, ſomething like a bee-hive, and full as cloſe and warm; the entrance is by a ſmall door, or long ſquare hole, juſt big enough to admit a man bent double: the ſide-walls are about four feet and a half high; but the roof is lofty, and peaked to a point at the top, above which is a poſt or ſtick of wood, which is generally ornamented either with carving or ſhells, or both. The framing is of ſmall ſpars, reeds, &c. and both ſides and roof are thick, and cloſe covered with thatch made of coarſe long graſs. In the inſide of the houſe are ſet up poſts, to which croſs ſpars are faſtened, and platforms made, for the conveniency of laying any thing on. Some houſes have two floors, one above another; the floor is laid with dried graſs, and here and there mats are ſpread for the principal people to ſit or ſleep on. In theſe houſes there was no paſſage for the ſmoke but through the door; they were intolerably ſmoky, and ſo hot as to be inſupportable to thoſe unaccuſtomed to them: probably the ſmoke is intended to drive out the muſquetos which ſwarm here. They commonly erect two or three of theſe huts near each other under a cluſter of lofty fig-trees, whoſe leaves are impervious to the rays of the ſun.

The canoes uſed here are very heavy clumſy veſſels; they are made of two trees hollowed out, having a raiſed gunnel about two inches high, and cloſed at each end with a bulk head of the ſame height; ſo that the whole is like a long ſquare trough about three feet ſhorter than the body of the canoe. Two canoes thus fitted are faſtened to each other about three feet aſunder, by means of croſs-ſpars, which project about a foot over each ſide. Over theſe is laid a deck or heavy platform made of plank and ſmall round ſpars, on which they have a fire-hearth, and generally a fire burning; they are navigated by one or two lateen ſails, extended to a ſmall lateen yard, the end of which is fixed in a notch or hole in the deck.

Notwithſtanding the inoffenſive diſpoſition of the inhabitants of New Caledonia, they are well provided with

with offensive weapons; as clubs, spears, darts, and slings for throwing stones. Their clubs are about two feet and an half long, and variously formed; some like a scythe, others like a pick-ax; some have a head like a hawk, and others have round heads; but all are neatly made; many of their darts and spears are no less neat, and ornamented with carvings. The slings are as simple as possible; but they take some pains to form the stones that they use into a proper shape, which is something like an egg, supposing both ends to be like the small one. They drive the dart by the assistance of short cords knobbed at one end and looped at the other, called by the seamen *beckets*. These contain a quantity of red wool taken from the vampyre, or great Indian bat. Bows and arrows are wholly unknown among them.

Their language bears no affinity to that spoken in the other South-sea islands, the word *arrikee* and one or two more excepted. This is the more extraordinary, as different dialects of one language were spoken not only in the easterly islands, but at New Zealand.

A musical instrument, a kind of whistle, was procured here. It was a little polished piece of brown wood about two inches long, shaped like a kind of bell, tho' apparently solid, with a rope fixed at the small end; two holes were made in it near the base, and another near the insertion of the rope, all which communicated with each other; and by blowing in the uppermost, a shrill sound like whistling was produced: no other instrument was seen among them that had the least relation to music.

Many of the New Caledonians were seen with prodigiously thick legs and arms, which seemed to be affected with a kind of leprosy; the swelling was found to be extremely hard, but the skin was not alike harsh and scaly in all those who were afflicted with the disorder. The preternatural expansion of the arm or leg did not appear to be a great inconvenience to those who suffered it; and they seemed to intimate that they very rarely felt any pain in it; but in some the disorder began to form blotches, which are marks of a great degree of virulence.

Here they bury their dead in the ground. The grave of a chief who had been slain in battle here resembled a large mole-hill, and was decorated with spears, darts, paddles, &c. all stuck upright in the ground round about it. Lieutenant Pickersgill was showed a chief whom they named *Tea-booma*, and styled their *arrekee* or *king*; but nothing further is known of their government, and nothing at all of their religion.

CALEFACTION, the production of heat in a body from the action of fire, or that impulse impressed by a hot body on others around it. This word is used in pharmacy, by way of distinction from *coction*, which implies boiling; whereas calefaction is only heating a thing.

CALENBERG, a castle of Germany, in the duchy of Brunswic and principality of Calenberg. It is seated on the river Leine, and is 15 miles south of Hanover. It is subject to the duke of Brunswic Lunenberg, elector of Hanover, and king of Great Britain. E. Long. 9. 45. N. Lat. 52. 20.

CALENBERG, a principality of Lower Saxony, and one of the three parts of the duchy of Brunswic, is bounded on the north by the duchy of Verden, on the east by the principality of Zell, on the south by the principalities of Grubenhagen and Wolfenbuttle, and on the west by Westphalia. It belongs to the elector of Hanover.

CALENDAR, in astronomy and chronology. See KALENDAR.

CALENDAR of prisoners, in law, a list of all the prisoners names in the custody of each respective sheriff*.

CALENDARIUM FLORÆ, in botany, a calendar containing an exact register of the respective times in which the plants of any given province or climate germinate, expand, and shed their leaves and flowers, or ripen and disperse their seeds. For particulars on this curious subject, see the articles DEFOLIATIO, EFFLORESCENTIA, FRONDESCENTIA, FRUCTESCENTIA, and GERMINATIO.

CALENDER, a machine used in manufactories to press certain woollen and silken stuffs and linens, to make them smooth, even, and glossy, or to give them waves, or water them, as may be seen in Mohairs and tabbies. This instrument is composed of two thick cylinders or rollers, of very hard and well polished wood, round which the stuffs to be calendered are wound: these rollers are placed cross-wise between two very thick boards, the lower serving as a fixed base, and the upper moveable by means of a thick screw with a rope fastened to a spindle which makes its axis; the uppermost board is loaded with large stones weighing 20,000 lb. or more. At Paris they have an extraordinary machine of this kind, called the *royal calender*, made by order of M. Colbert. The lower table or plank is made of a block of smooth marble, and the upper is lined with a plate of polished copper.—The alternate motion of the upper board sometimes one way and sometimes another, together with the prodigious weight laid upon it, gives the stuffs their gloss and smoothness; or gives them the waves, by making the cylinders on which they are put roll with great force over the undermost board. When they would put a roller from under the calender, they only incline the undermost board of the machine. The dressing alone, with the many turns they make the stuffs and linens undergo in the calender, gives the waves, or waters them, as the workmen call it. It is a mistake to think, as some have asserted, and Mr Chambers among others, that they use rollers with a shallow indenture or engraving cut into them.

CALENDER or MONTEITH, a district in the south-west corner of Perthshire in Scotland, from which a branch of the ancient family of Livingston had the title of Earl. The chief seat of the family near Falkirk is also called *Calender*. Both estate and title were forfeited for being engaged in the rebellion 1715.

CALENDERS, a sort of Mahometan friars, so called from Santon Calenderi their founder. This Santon went bare-headed, without a shirt, and with the skin of a wild beast thrown over his shoulders. He wore a kind of apron before, the fringes of which were adorned with counterfeit precious stones. His disciples are rather a sect of Epicureans than a society of religious. They honour a tavern as much as they do a mosque; and think they pay as acceptable worship to God by the

* See the article [illegible].

the free use of his creatures, as others do by the greatest austerities and acts of devotion. They are called, in Persia and Arabia, *Abdals*, or *Abdallat*, i. e. persons consecrated to the honour and service of God. Their garment is a single coat, made up of a variety of pieces, and quilted like a rug. They preach in the market-places, and live upon what their auditors bestow on them. They are generally very vicious persons; for which reason they are not admitted into any houses.

CALENDS, in Roman antiquity. See Kalends.

CALENDULA, the marigold: A genus of the polygamia necessaria order, belonging to the syngenesia class of plants; and in the natural method ranking under the 49th order, *Compositæ*. The receptacle is naked, there is no pappus, the calyx is polyphyllous and equal, the seeds of the disk membranaceous. Of this there are eight species, none of them natives of Europe. The common kind is so well known as to need no definition; and none of the others merit any, except the fruticosa, which hath lately been introduced from the Cape of Good Hope. It hath a slender shrubby perennial stalk, which rises to the height of seven or eight feet, but requires support: this sends out a great number of weak branches from the bottom to the top, which hang downward unless they are supported: they are garnished with oval leaves, having short flat footstalks; these are of a shining green colour on their upper side, but paler underneath: the flowers come out at the end of the branches, on short naked footstalks. This is easily propagated by cuttings which may be planted at any time in summer in a shady border, or otherwise shaded with mats in the heat of the day: in five or six weeks these will have taken root, when they should be separately taken up, each put in a separate pot, and placed in the shade till they have taken fresh root; then they may be placed, with other hardy exotic plants, in a sheltered situation, where they may remain till the frost begins, when they must be removed into the green-house, placing them near the windows, that they may enjoy the free air; for this plant only requires protection from frost. The seeds of the common sort may be sown in March or April, where the plants are to remain; and will require no other culture but to keep them clear of weeds, and to thin the plants where they are too thick. The flowers of the common marigold are supposed to be aperient and attenuating, as also cardiac, alexipharmac, and sudorific; they are principally celebrated in uterine obstructions, the jaundice, and for throwing out the small-pox. Their sensible qualities, however, give little foundation for these virtues: they have scarce any taste, and have no considerable smell. The leaves of the plant discover a viscid sweetishness, accompanied with a more durable saponaceous pungency and warmth; these seem capable of answering some useful purposes as a stimulating, aperient, and antiscorbutic medicine.

CALENTIUS (Elisius), a Neapolitan poet and prose author. He was preceptor to Frederic the son of Ferdinand king of Naples, and the earliest writer on the illegality of putting criminals to death, except for murder. He died in 1503.

CALENTURE, a feverish disorder incident to sailors in hot countries; the principal symptom of which is their imagining the sea to be green fields: hence, attempting to walk abroad in these imaginary places of delight, they are frequently lost. Vomiting, bleeding, a spare diet, and the neutral salts, are recommended in this disorder; a single vomit commonly removing the delirium, and the cooling medicines completing the cure.

CALEPIN (Ambrosius), an Augustin monk of Calepio, whence he took his name, in the 16th century. He is author of a dictionary of eight languages, since augmented by Passerat and others.

CALES (anc. geog.), a municipal city of some note in Campania, at no great distance from Casilinum. The epithet *Calenus* is by Horace and Juvenal applied to a generous wine which the territory produced.

CALETES (anc. geog.), a people of Gallia Celtica, on the confines of Belgica, situated between the sea and the Sequana. Now called *le Pais de Caux*, in Normandy.

CALETURE, a fort on the island of Ceylon, at the mouth of a river of the same name. The Dutch became masters of it in 1655; but were afterwards obliged to leave it. E. Long. 80. 51. N. Lat. 6. 38.

CALF, in zoology, the young of the ox kind.

There are two ways of breeding calves that are intended to be reared. The one is to let the calf run about with its dam all the year round; which is the method in the cheap breeding countries, and is generally allowed to make the best cattle. The other is to take them from the dam after they have sucked about a fortnight: they are then to be taught to drink flat milk, which is to be made but just warm for them, it being very dangerous to give it them too hot. The best time of weaning calves is from January to May: they should have milk for 12 weeks after; and a fortnight before that is left off, water should be mixed with the milk in larger and larger quantities. When the calf has been fed on milk for about a month, little whisps of hay should be placed all about him in cleft sticks to induce him to eat. In the beginning of April they should be turned out to grass; only for a few days they should be taken in for the night, and have milk and water given them: the same may also be given them in a pail sometimes in the field, till they are so able to feed themselves that they do not regard it. The grass they are turned into must not be too rank, but short and sweet, that they may like it, and yet get it with some labour. Calves should always be weaned at grass; for if it be done with hay and water, they often grow big-belly'd on it, and are apt to rot. When those among the males are selected which are to be kept as bulls, the rest should be gelt for oxen: the sooner the better. Between 10 and 20 days is a proper age. About London almost all the calves are fatted for the butcher. The reason of this is, that there is a good market for them; and the lands there are not so profitable to breed upon as in cheaper countries. The way to make calves fat and fine is, the keeping them very clean; giving them fresh litter every day; and the hanging a large chalk-stone in some corner where they can easily get at it to lick it, but where it is out of the way of being fouled by their dung and urine. The coops are to be placed so as not to have too much sun upon them, and so high above the ground that the urine may run off. They also bleed them once when they are a month old, and a second time before they kill them; which is a great addition to the beauty and whiteness of their flesh: the bleeding is by some repeated much oftener, but this is sufficient. Calves are very apt to be loose in their bowels; which wastes and very much injures them. The remedy is to give them chalk scraped among milk, pouring it down with a horn. If this does not succeed, they give them bole armenic in large doses, and use the cold bath every morning. If a cow will not let a strange calf suck her, the common method is to rub both her nose and the calf's with a little brandy; this generally reconciles them after a few smellings.

Golden Calf, an idol set up and worshipped by the Israelites at the foot of Mount Sinai in their passage through the wilderness to the land of Canaan. Our version makes Aaron fashion this calf with a graving tool after he had cast it in a mould: the Geneva translation makes him engrave it first, and cast it afterwards. Others, with more probability, render the whole verse thus: "And Aaron received them (the golden ear-rings), and tied them up in a bag, and got them cast into a molten calf:" which version is authorised by the different senses of the word *tsur*, which signifies to tie up or bind, as well as to shape or form; and of the word *cheret*, which is used both for a graving tool and a bag. Some of the ancient fathers have been of opinion that this idol had only the face of a calf, and the shape of a man from the neck downwards, in imitation of the Egyptian Isis. Others have thought it was only the head of an ox without a body. But the most general opinion is, that it was an entire calf in imitation of the Apis worshipped by the Egyptians; among whom, no doubt, the Israelites had acquired their propensity to idolatry. This calf Moses is said to have *burnt with fire*, reduced to powder, and strewed upon the water which the people were to drink. How this could be accomplished hath been a question. Most people have thought, that as gold is indestructible, it could only be burnt by the miraculous power of God; but M. Stahl conjectures that Moses dissolved it by means of liver of sulphur *. The Rabbins tell us that the people were made to drink of this water in order to distinguish the idolaters from the rest; for that as soon as they had drunk of it, the beards of the former turned red. The cabbalists add, that the calf weighed 125 quintals; which they gather from the Hebrew word *massekah*, whose numerical letters make 125.

* See Chemistry Index.

Calf-Skins, in the leather manufacture, are prepared and dressed by the tanners, skinners, and curriers, who sell them for the use of the shoe-makers, saddlers, book-binders, and other artificers, who employ them in their several manufactures.

Calf-Skin dressed in sumach, denotes the skin of this animal curried black on the hair side, and dyed of an orange colour on the flesh side, by means of sumach, chiefly used in the making of belts.

The English calf-skin is much valued abroad, and the commerce thereof very considerable in France and other countries; where divers attempts have been made to imitate it, but hitherto in vain. What is like to baffle all endeavours for imitating the English calf in France is, the smallness and weakness of the calves about Paris; which at fifteen days old are not so big as the English ones when they come into the world.

Sea-Calf. See Phoca.

CALI, a town of Popayan in South America, seated in a valley of the same name on the river Cauca. The governour of the province usually resides there. W. Long. 78. 5. N. Lat. 3. 15.

CALIBER, or Calibre, properly denotes the diameter of any body; thus we say, two columns of the same caliber, the caliber of the bore of a gun, the caliber of a bullet, &c.

Caliber-Compasses, a sort of compasses made with arched legs to take the diameter of round or swelling bodies. See Compasses.

Caliber-compasses, are chiefly used by gunners, for taking the diameters of the several parts of a piece of ordnance, or of bombs, bullets, &c. Their legs are therefore circular; and move on an arch of brass, whereon is marked the inches and half inches, to shew how far the points of the compasses are opened asunder.

Some are also made for taking the diameter of the bore of a gun or mortar.

The gaugers also sometimes use calibers, to embrace the two heads of any cask, in order to find its length.

The calliber used by carpenters and joiners, is a piece of board notched triangular-wise in the middle for the taking of measure.

Caliber-Rule, or *Gunner's Callipers*, is an instrument wherein a right line is so divided as that the first part being equal to the diameter of an iron or leaden ball of one pound weight, the other parts are to the first as the diameters of balls of two, three, four, &c. pounds are to the diameter of a ball of one pound. The caliber is used by engineers, from the weight of the ball given, to determine its diameter or caliber, or *vice versa*.

The gunner's callipers consist of two thin plates of brass joined by a rivet, so as to move quite round each other: its length from the centre of the joint is between six inches and a foot, and its breadth from one to two inches; that of the most convenient size is about nine inches long. Many scales, tables, and proportions, &c. may be introduced on this instrument; but none are essential to it, except those for taking the caliber of shot and cannon, and for measuring the magnitude of salient and entering angles. The most complete callipers is exhibited Plate CXII. the furniture and use of which we shall now briefly describe. Let the four faces of this instrument be distinguished by the letters A, B, C, D: A and D consist of a circular head and leg; B and C consist only of a leg.

On the circular head adjoining to the leg of the face A are divisions denominated *shot diameters*; which show the distance in inches and tenths of an inch of the points of the callipers when they are opened; so that if a ball not exceeding ten inches be introduced between them, the bevil edge E marks its diameter among these divisions.

On the circular bevil part E of the face B is a scale of divisions distinguished by *lb. weight of iron shot*. When the diameter of any shot is taken between the points of the callipers, the inner edge of the leg A shows its weight in avoirdupoise pounds, provided it be lb. ¼, 1, 1½, 2, 3, 4, 5½, 6, 8, 9, 12, 16, 18, 24, 26, 32, 36, or 42; the figures nearest the bevil edge answering to the short lines in the scale, and those behind them to the longer strokes. This scale is constructed

ſtructed on the following geometrical theorem, viz. that the weights of ſpheres are as the cubes of their diameters.

On the lower part of the circular head of the face A is a ſcale of diviſions marked *bores of guns*; for the uſe of which, the legs of the callipers are ſlipped acroſs each other, till the ſteel points touch the concave ſurface of the gun in its greateſt breadth; then the bevil edge F of the face B will cut a diviſion in the ſcale ſhowing the diameter of the bore in inches and tenths.

Within the ſcales of *ſhot* and *bore* diameters on the circular part of A, are diviſions marked *powders*: the inner figures $\frac{1}{2}$, 1$\frac{1}{2}$, 3, 5$\frac{1}{2}$, 8, 12, 18, 26, 36, correſpond to the longeſt lines; and the figures 1, 2, 4, 6, 9, 16, 24, 32, 42, to the ſhort ſtrokes. When the bore of a gun is taken between the points of the callipers, the bevil edge F will either cut or be near one of theſe diviſions, and ſhow the weight of iron-ſhot proper for that gun.

On the upper half of the circular head of the face A are three concentric ſcales of degrees; the outer ſcale conſiſting of 180 degrees numbered from right to left, 10, 20, &c. the middle numbered the contrary way, and the outer ſcale beginning at the middle with 0, and numbered on each ſide to 90 degrees. Theſe ſcales ſerve to take the quantity of an angle, either entering or ſaliant. For an entering or internal angle, apply the legs of the callipers ſo that its outward edges coincide with the legs of the given angle, the degree cut by the bevil edge F in the outer ſcale ſhows the meaſure of the angle ſought: for a ſaliant or external angle, ſlip the legs of the callipers acroſs each other, ſo that their outward edges may coincide with the legs forming the angle, and the degree marked on the middle ſcale by the bevil edge E will ſhow the meaſure of the angle required. The inner ſcale will ſerve to determine the elevation of cannon and mortars, or of any oblique plane. Let one end of a thread be fixed into the notch on the plate B, and any weight tied to the other end: apply the ſtraight ſide of the plate A to the ſide of the body whoſe inclination is ſought; hold it in this poſition, and move the plate B, till the thread falls upon the line near the centre marked *Perp.* Then will the bevil edge F cut the degrees on the inner ſcale, ſhowing the inclination of that body to the horizon.

On the face C near the point of the callipers is a little table ſhowing the proportion of troy and avoirdupoiſe weights, by which one kind of weight may be eaſily reduced into another.

Near the extreme of the face D of the callipers are two tables ſhowing the proportion between the pounds weight of London and Paris, and alſo between the lengths of the foot meaſure of England and France.

Near the extreme on the face A is a table containing four rules of the circle and ſphere; and geometrical figures with numbers annexed to them: the firſt is a circle including the proportion in round numbers of the diameter to its circumference: the ſecond is a circle inſcribed in a ſquare, and a ſquare within that circle, and another circle in the inner ſquare: the numbers 28, 22, above this figure exhibit the proportion of the outward ſquare to the area of the inſcribed circle; and the numbers 14, 11, below it ſhow the proportion between the area of the inſcribed ſquare and the area of its inſcribed circle. The third is a cube inſcribed in a ſphere: and the number 89$\frac{3}{5}$ ſhows that a cube of iron, inſcribed in a ſphere of 12 inches in diameter, weighs 89$\frac{3}{5}$. The fourth is a ſphere in a cube, and the number 243 expreſſes the weight in pounds of a ſphere inſcribed in a cube whoſe ſide is 12 inches: the fifth repreſents a cylinder and cone of one foot diameter and height: the number in the cylinder ſhows, that an iron cylinder of that diameter and height weighs 364.5 lb. and the number 121.5 in the cone expreſſes the weight of a cone, the diameter of whoſe baſe is 12 inches, and of the ſame height: the ſixth figure ſhows that an iron cube, whoſe ſide is 12 inches, weighs 464 lb. and that a ſquare pyramid of iron, whoſe baſe is a ſquare foot and height 12 inches, weighs 154$\frac{2}{3}$ lb. The numbers which have been hitherto fixed to the four laſt figures were not ſtrictly true; and therefore they have been corrected in the figure here referred to; and by theſe the figures on any inſtrument of this kind ſhould be corrected likewiſe.

On the leg B of the callipers, is a table ſhowing the weights of a cubic inch or foot of various bodies in pounds avoirdupoiſe.

On the face D of the circular head of the callipers is a table contained between five concentric ſegments of rings: the inner one marked *Guns* ſhows the nature of the gun or the weight of ball it carries; the two next rings contain the quantity of powder uſed for proof and ſervice to braſs guns, and the two outermoſt rings ſhow the quantity for proof and ſervice in iron cannon.

On the face A is a table exhibiting the method of computing the *number of ſhot or ſhells* in a triangular, ſquare, or rectangular pile. Near this is placed a table containing the principal rules relative to the *fall of bodies*, expreſſed in an algebraic manner: nearer the centre we have another table of rules for raiſing water, calculated on the ſuppoſition, that one horſe is equal in this kind of labour to five men, and that one man will raiſe a hogſhead of water to eight feet of height in one minute, and work at that rate for ſome hours. N. B. Hogſheads are reckoned at ſixty gallons.

Some of the leading principles in gunnery, relating to *ſhooting* in cannon and mortars, are expreſſed on the face B of the callipers. Beſides the articles already enumerated, the ſcales uſually marked on the ſector are laid down on this inſtrument: thus, the line of inches is placed on the edge of the callipers, or on the ſtraight borders of the faces C, D: the logarithmic ſcales of numbers, ſines, verſed ſines, and tangents, are placed along theſe faces near the ſtraight edges: the line of lines is placed on the ſame faces in an angular poſition, and marked *Lin.* The lines of plains or ſuperficies are alſo exhibited on the faces C and D, tending towards the centre, and marked *Plan.* Finally, the lines of ſolids are laid on the ſame faces tending towards the centre, and diſtinguiſhed by *Sol.*

CALICOULAN, or QUILLON, a town of Aſia, in the Eaſt Indies, on the coaſt of Malabar, and in the peninſula on this ſide the Ganges, where the Dutch have a factory. E. Long. 75. 21. N. Lat. 9. 5.

CALICUT, a kingdom of India, on this ſide the Ganges, upon the coaſt of Malabar. It is about 63 miles long, and as much broad. It has many woods, rivers, and marſhes, and is very populous; but does not produce much corn, abundance of rice being im-

Plate CXII.

CALIBER Rule.

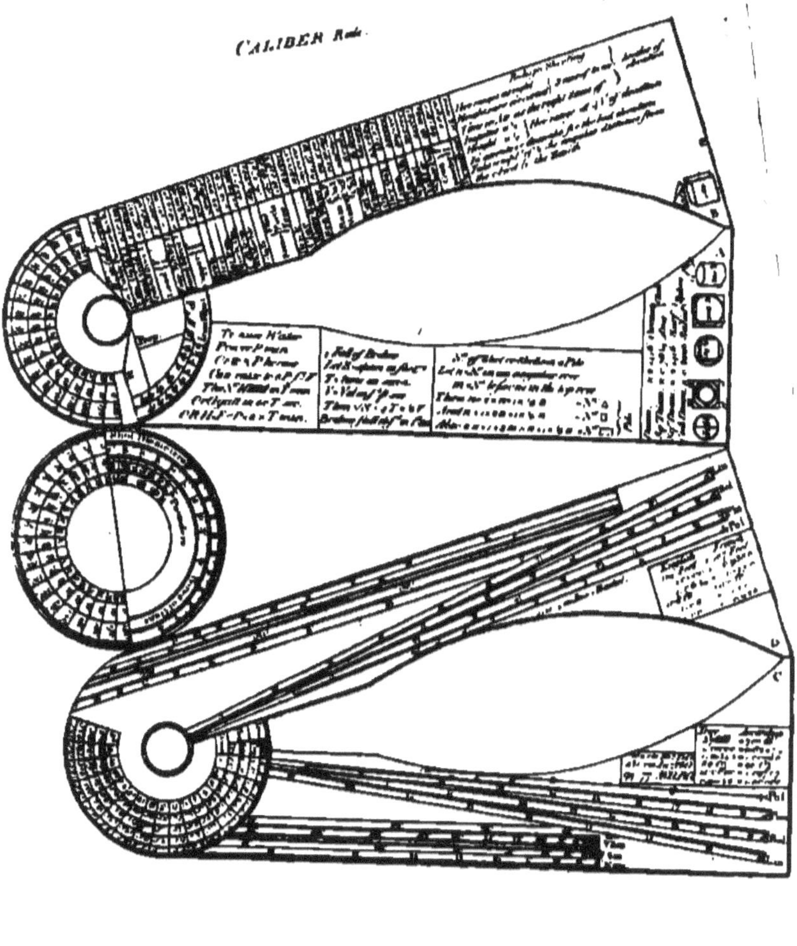

ported from Canara. The land along the sea-coast is low and sandy, and produces a number of cocoa-trees. The higher grounds produce pepper and cardamoms of a very good quality. They have likewise timber for building, white and yellow sanders, cassia lignea, cassia fistula, nux vomica, and cocculus indicus. The woods abound with parrots and monkeys, as well as different kinds of game. They have also plenty of fish, several sorts of medicinal drugs, and their mountains produce iron. The *samorin*, or king, of Calicut, was once master of all the coast of Malabar; but at his death, he left it by will among four of his nephews. He who governs Calicut has a palace of stone, and there is some appearance of grandeur about his court. He carries on a considerable trade, which makes the people of Calicut richer than their neighbours. In former times they had several strange customs, some of which are still kept up; particularly the samorin's wife must be first enjoyed by the high priest, who may have her three nights if he pleases. The nobles permit the other priests to take the same liberty, but the lower people cannot have that honour. A woman may marry a number of husbands; each of whom has her ten days or more by turns, as they agree among themselves; and provides her all things necessary during that time. When she proves with child, she names the father; who, after the child is weaned, takes care of his education. These people have no pens, ink, or paper; but write with a bodkin on flags that grow by the sides of the rivers. By this means the letters are in some sense engraved; and so tough are the flags, that they will last for a great number of years. This was the first land discovered by the Portuguese in 1498.

Calicut, a town of Asia, in the kingdom of that name on the coast of Malabar. It contains a great number of mean low houses, each of which has a garden. The English had a factory here, but it is removed to Tillicherry. E. Long. 76. 4. N. Lat. 11. 21.

CALIDÆ plantæ (from *calor* heat); plants that are natives of warm climates. Such are those of the East Indies, South America, Egypt, and the Canary Islands. These plants, says Linneus, will bear a degree of heat which is as 40 on a scale in which the freezing point is 0, and 100 the heat of boiling water. In the 10th degree of cold they cease to grow, lose their leaves, become barren, are suffocated, and perish.

CALIDUCT, in antiquity, a kind of pipes or canal disposed along the walls of houses or apartments, used by the ancients for conveying heat to several remote parts of the house from one common furnace.

CALIFORNIA, the most northerly of all the Spanish dominions on the continent of America, is sometimes distinguished by the name of *New Albion*, and the *Isles Carolinas*: but the most ancient appellation is *California*; a word probably owing to some accident, or to some words spoken by the Indians and misunderstood by the Spaniards. For a long time California was thought to be an island; but Father Caino, a German Jesuit, discovered it to be a peninsula joining to the coast of New Mexico and the southern parts of America. This peninsula extends from Cape St Sebastian, lying in north latitude 43. 30. to Cape St Lucas which lies in north latitude 22. 32. It is divided from New Mexico by the gulph, or as some call it the *lake*, of California, or *Vermilion Sea*, on the east; on the north, by that part of the continent of North America which is least known; and on the west and south, by the Pacific Ocean or great South Sea. The coasts, especially towards the Vermilion Sea, are covered with inhabited islands, on some of which the Jesuits have established settlements, such as St Clement, Pazaros, St Anne, Cedars (so called from the great number of these trees it produces), St Joseph, and a multitude of others. But the islands best known are three lying off Cape St Lucas, towards the Mexican coast. These are called *Los Tres Marias*, "the three Maries." They are but small, have good wood and water, salt pits, and abundance of game; therefore the English and French pirates have sometimes wintered there, when bound on cruises in the South Seas.

As California lies altogether within the temperate zone, the natives are neither chilled with cold nor scorched with heat; and indeed the improvements in agriculture made by the Jesuits afford strong proofs of the excellency of the climate. In some places the air is extremely hot and dry; and the earth wild, rugged, and barren. In a country stretching about 800 miles in length, there must be considerable variations of soil and climate; and indeed we find, from good authority, that California produces some of the most beautiful lawns, as well as many of the most inhospitable desarts, in the universe. Upon the whole, although California is rather rough and craggy, we are assured by the Jesuit Vinegas, and other good writers, that with due culture it furnishes every necessary and conveniency of life; and that, even where the atmosphere is hottest, vapours rising from the sea, and dispersed by pleasant breezes, render it of a moderate temperature.

The peninsula of California is now stocked with all sorts of domestic animals known in Spain and Mexico. Horses, mules, asses, oxen, sheep, hogs, goats, and all other quadrupeds imported, thrive and increase in this country. Among the native animals is a species of deer of the size of a young heifer, and greatly resembling it in shape; the head is like that of a deer, and the horns thick and crooked like those of a ram. The hoof of the animal is large, round, and cloven, the skin spotted, but the hair thinner and the tail sharper than those of a deer. Its flesh is greatly esteemed. There is another animal peculiar to this country, larger and more bulky than a sheep, but greatly resembling it in figure, and, like it, covered with a fine black or white wool. The flesh of this animal is nourishing and delicious; and, happily for the natives, it is so abundant, that nothing more is required than the trouble of hunting, as these animals wander about in droves in the forests and on the mountains. Father Torquemado describes a creature which he calls a *species of large deer*, something like a buffalo, of the size of a steer, and nearly of the figure of a stag. Its hair is a quarter of a yard in length, its neck long and awkward, and on its forehead are horns branched like those of a stag. The tail is a yard in length and half a yard in breadth; and the hoofs cloven like those of an ox. With regard to birds, we have but an imperfect account; only, in general, Father Venegas tells us that the coast is plentifully stored with peacocks, bustards, geese, cranes, and most of the birds common in other parts of the world. The quantity of fish which resort to these coasts are incredible. Salmon, turbot, barbel, skate, mackerel, &c. are caught here with very little trouble; together with pearl oysters, common oysters, lobsters, and a variety of exquisite shell-fish. Plenty of turtle are also caught on the coasts. On the South Sea coasts are some shell-fish peculiar to it, and perhaps the most beautiful in the world; their lustre surpassing that of the finest pearl, and darting their rays through a transparent varnish of an elegant vivid blue, like the lapis lazuli. The fame of California for pearls soon drew forth great numbers of adventurers, who searched every part of the gulph, and are still employed in that work, notwithstanding fashion has greatly diminished the value of this elegant natural production. Father Torquimado observes that the sea of California affords very rich pearl fisheries; and that the *bassas*, or beds of oysters, may be seen in three or four fathom water, almost as plain as if they were on the surface.

The extremity of the peninsula towards Cape St Lucar is more level, temperate, and fertile, than the other parts, and consequently more woody. In the more distant parts, even to the farthest missions on the east coast, no large timber hath yet been discovered. A species of manna is found in this country, which, according to the accounts of the Jesuits, has all the sweetness of refined sugar without its whiteness. The natives firmly believe that this juice drops from heaven.

The Californians are well made, and very strong. They are extremely pusillanimous, inconstant, stupid, and even insensible, and seem extremely deserving of the character given to the Indians in general, under the article America. Before the Europeans penetrated into California, the natives had no form of religion. The missionaries indeed tell us many tales concerning them, but they so evidently bear the marks of forgery as not to be worth repeating. Each nation was then an assemblage of several cottages more or less numerous, that were all mutually confederated by alliances, but without any chief. They were strangers even to filial obedience. No kind of dress was used by the men; but the women made use of some coverings, and were even fond of ornamenting themselves with pearls and such other trinkets as the country afforded. What mostly displayed their ingenuity was the construction of their fishing nets, which are said by the Jesuits to have even exceeded in goodness those made in Europe. They were made by the women, of a coarse kind of flax procured from some plants which grow there. Their houses were built of branches and leaves of trees; nay, many of them were only inclosures of earth and stone, raised half a yard high, without any covering; and even these were so small, that they could not stretch themselves at length in them. In winter, they dwelt under ground in caves either natural or artificial.

In 1526, Ferdinand Cortez having reduced and settled Mexico, attempted the conquest of California; but was obliged to return, without even taking a survey of the country, a report of his death having disposed the Mexicans to a general insurrection. Some other attempts were made by the officers of Cortez, but these were also unsuccessful; and this valuable coast was long neglected by the Spaniards, who, to this day, have but one settlement upon it. In 1595, a galleon was sent to make discoveries on the Californian shore; but the vessel was unfortunately lost. Seven years after, the count de Monteroy, then viceroy of New Spain, sent Sebastian Biscayno on the same design with two ships and a tender; but he made no discovery of importance. In 1684, the marquis de Laguna, also viceroy of new Spain, dispatched two ships with a tender to make discoveries on the lake of California. He returned with an indifferent account, but was among the first that asserted that California was not an island; which was afterwards confirmed by Father Caino, as already related. In 1697, the Spaniards being discouraged by their losses and disappointments, the Jesuits solicited and obtained permission to undertake the conquest of California. They arrived among the savages with curiosities that might amuse them, corn for their food, and clothes for which they could not but perceive the necessity. The hatred these people bore the Spanish name could not support itself against these demonstrations of benevolence. They testified their acknowledgments as much as their want of sensibility and their inconstancy would permit them. These faults were partly overcome by the religious institutors, who pursued their project with a degree of warmth and resolution peculiar to the society. They made themselves carpenters, masons, weavers, and husbandmen; and by these means succeeded in imparting knowledge, and in some measure a taste for the useful arts, to this savage people, who have been all successively formed into one body. In 1745, they composed 43 villages, separated from each other by the barrenness of the soil and the want of water. The inhabitants of these small villages subsist principally on corn and pulse, which they cultivate; and on the fruits and domestic animals of Europe, the breeding of which last is an object of continual attention. The Indians have each their field, and the property of what they reap; but such is their want of foresight, that they would squander in a day what they had gathered, if the missionary did not take upon himself to distribute it to them as they stand in need of it. They manufacture some coarse stuffs; and the necessaries they are in want of are purchased with pearls, and with wine nearly resembling that of Madeira, which they sell to the Mexicans and to the galleons, and which experience hath shown the necessity of prohibiting in California. A few laws, which are very simple, are sufficient to regulate this rising state. In order to enforce them, the missionary chooses the most intelligent person of the village; who is empowered to whip and imprison; the only punishments of which they have any knowledge. In all California there are only two garrisons, each consisting of 30 men and a soldier with every missionary. These troops were chosen by the legislators, though they are paid by the government. Were the court of Madrid to push their interest with half the zeal of the Jesuits, California might become one of the most valuable of their acquisitions, on account of the pearls and other valuable articles of commerce which the country contains. At present the little Spanish town near Cape St Lucar is made use of for no other purpose than as a place of refreshment for the Manila ships, and the head residence of the missionaries.

CALIGA, in Roman Antiquity, was the proper sol-

soldier's shoe, made in the sandal fashion, without upper leather to cover the superior part of the foot, tho' otherwise reaching to the middle of the leg, and fastened with thongs. The sole of the caliga was of wood, like the sabot of the French peasants, and its' bottom stuck full of nails; which clavi are supposed to have been very long in the shoes of the scouts and sentinels; whence these were called by way of distinction, *caligæ speculatoriæ*; as if by mounting the wearer to a higher pitch, they gave a greater advantage to the sight: though others will have the *caligæ speculatoriæ* to have been made soft and woolly, to prevent their making a noise. From these *caligæ* it was that the emperor Caligula took his name, as having been born in the army, and afterwards bred up in the habit of a common soldier.

According to Du Cange, a sort of *caligæ* was also worn by monks and bishops, when they celebrated mass pontifically.

CALIGATI, an appellation given by some ancient writers to the common soldiers in the Roman armies, by reason of the caliga which they wore. The caliga was the badge or symbol of a soldier; whence to take away the caliga and belt, imported a dismissing or cashiering.

CALIGO, or CALIGATIO, in Medicine, an opacity, or cloudiness of the anterior surface of the crystalline, causing a dimness or suffusion of sight.

CALIGULA, the Roman emperor and tyrant, A. D. 37, began his reign with every promising appearance of becoming the real father of his people; but at the end of eight months he was seized with a fever, which, it is thought, left a frenzy on his mind: for his disposition totally changed, and he committed the most atrocious acts of impiety, cruelty, and folly; such as proclaiming his horse consul, feeding it at his table, introducing it to the temple in the vestments of the priests of Jupiter, &c. and causing sacrifices to be offered to himself, his wife, and the horse. After having murdered many of his subjects with his own hand, and caused others to be put to death without any just cause, he was assassinated by a tribune of the people as he came out of the amphitheatre, A. D. 41, in the 29th year of his age, and 4th of his reign.

CALIN, a compound metal, whereof the Chinese make tea-canisters, and the like. The ingredients seem to be lead and tin.

CALIPH, or KHALIF, the supreme ecclesiastical dignity among the Saracens; or, as it is otherwise defined, a sovereign dignity among the Mahometans, vested with absolute authority in all matters relating both to religion and policy. In the Arabic it signifies *successor* or *vicar*; the caliphs bearing the same relation to Mahomet that the popes pretend they do to Jesus Christ or St Peter. It is at this day one of the Grand Signior's titles, as successor of Mahomet; and of the Sophi of Persia, as successor of Ali. One of the chief functions of the caliph, in quality of imam or chief priest of Mussulmanism, was to begin the public prayers every Friday in the chief mosque, and to deliver the *khotbah* or sermon. In after-times, they had assistants for this latter office; but the former the caliphs always performed in person. The caliph was also obliged to lead the pilgrims to Mecca in person, and to march at the head of the armies of his empire. He granted investiture to princes; and sent swords, standards, gowns, and the like, as presents to princes of the Mahometan religion; who, though they had thrown off the yoke of the caliphate, nevertheless held of it as vassals. The caliphs usually went to the mosque mounted on mules; and the sultans seigniories, though masters of Bagdad, held their stirrups, and led their mule by the bridle some distance on foot, till such time as the caliphs gave them the sign to mount on horseback. At one of the windows of the caliph's palace, there always hung a piece of black velvet 20 cubits long, which reached to the ground, and was called the *caliph's sleeve*; which the grandees of his court never failed to kiss every day, with great respect. After the destruction of the caliphate by Hulaku, the Mahometan princes appointed a particular officer, in their respective dominions, who sustains the sacred authority of caliph. In Turky, he goes under the denomination of *mufti*, and in Persia under that of *sadne*.

CALIPHATE, the office or dignity of caliph: See the preceding article. The succession of caliphs continued from the death of Mahomet till the 655th year of the Hegira, when the city of Bagdad was taken by the Tartars. After this, however, there were persons who claimed the caliphate, as pretending to be of the family of the Abassides, and to whom the sultans of Egypt rendered great honours at Cairo, as the true successors of Mahomet: but this honour was merely titular, and the rights allowed them only in matters relating to religion; and though they bore the sovereign title of *caliphs*, they were nevertheless subjects and dependents of the sultans. In the year of the Hegira 361, a kind of caliphate was erected by the Fatemites in Africa, and lasted till it was suppressed by Saladdin. Historians also speak of a third caliphate in Geaure or Arabia Felix, erected by some princes of the family of the Jobites. The emperors of Morocco assume the title of *grand cherifs*; and pretend to be the true caliphs, or successors of Mahomet, though under another name.

CALIPPIC PERIOD, in chronology, a series of seventy-six years, perpetually recurring; which clapsed the middle of the new and full moons, as its inventor Calippus, an Athenian, imagined, return to the same day of the solar year. Meton, an hundred years before, had invented the period, or cycle, of nineteen years; assuming the quantity of the solar year 365 *d.* 6 *h.* 18' 56'' 50''' 21'''' 34'''''; and the lunar month, 29 *d.* 12 *h.* 45' 47'' 26''' 48'''' 30''''': but Calippus, considering that the Metonic quantity of the solar year was not exact, multiplied Meton's period by 4, and thence arose a period of 76 years, called the *Calippic*. The Calippic period, therefore, contains 27759 days: and since the lunar cycle contains 235 lunations, and the *Calippic period* is quadruple of this, it contains 940 lunations. This period began in the third year of the 112th Olympiad, or the 4384th of the Julian period. It is demonstrated, however, that the Calippic period itself is not accurate; that it does not bring the new and full moons precisely to their places: 8 *h.* 5' 52'' 60''', being the excess of 940 lunations above 76 solar years; but brings them too late, by a whole day in 225 years.

CALISTA, in fabulous history, the daughter of Lycaon king of Arcadia, and one of the nymphs of

Diana. Being beloved by Jupiter, that god assumed the form of the goddess of chastity, by which means he debauched her: but her disgrace being revealed, as she was bathing with her patroness, the incensed deity turned her and the son with which she was pregnant into bears; when Jupiter, in compassion to her sufferings, took them up into the heavens, and made them the constellations Ursa Major and Ursa Minor

CALIX. See CALYX.

CALIXTINS, a name given to those, among the Lutherans, who follow the sentiments of George Calixtus, a celebrated divine, and professor at Helmstadt, in the dutchy of Brunswick, who died in 1656; he opposed the opinion of St Augustin, on predestination, grace, and free-will, and endeavoured to form an union among the various members of the Romish, Lutheran, and reformed churches; or, rather, to join them in the bonds of mutual forbearance and charity.

CALIXTINS also denote a sect in Bohemia, derived from the Hussites, about the middle of the 15th century, who asserted the use of the cup, as essential to the eucharist. And hence their name; which is formed from the Latin *calix*, a cup.

The Calixtins are not ranked by Romanists in the list of heretics, since in the main they still adhered to the doctrine of Rome. The reformation they aimed at terminated in the four following articles. 1. In restoring the cup to the laity. 2. In subjecting the criminal clerks to the punishment of the civil magistrate. 3. In stripping the clergy of their lands, lordships, and all temporal jurisdiction. 4. In granting liberty to all capable priests to preach the word of God.

CALKA, a kingdom of Tartary, in Asia, to the east of Siberia.

CALKING. See CAULKING.

CALKINS, the prominent parts at the extremities of a horse-shoe, bent downwards, and forged to a sort of point.

Calkins are apt to make horses trip; they also occasion bleymes, and ruin the back sinews. If fashioned in form of a hare's ear, and the horn of a horse's heel be pared a little low, they do little damage; whereas, the great square calkins quite spoil the foot.

Calkins are either single or double, that is, at one end of the shoe, or at both: these last are deemed less hurtful, as the horses can tread more even.

CALL, among hunters, a lesson blown upon the horn, to comfort the hounds.

CALL, an English name for the mineral called Tungsten or Wolfram by the Germans.

CALL, among sailors, a sort of whistle or pipe, of silver or brass, used by the boatswain and his mates to summon the sailors to their duty, and direct them in the different employments of the ship. As the call can be sounded to various strains, each of them is appropriated to some particular exercise; such as hoisting, heaving, lowering, veering away, belaying, letting go a tackle, &c. The act of winding this instrument is called piping, which is as attentively observed by sailors as the beat of the drum to march, retreat, rally, charge, &c. is obeyed by soldiers.

CALL, among fowlers, the noise or cry of a bird, especially to its young, or to its mate in coupling-time. One method of catching partridges is by the natural call of a hen trained for the purpose, which drawing the cocks to her, they are entangled in a net. Different birds require different sorts of calls; but they are most of them composed of a pipe or reed, with a little leathern bag or purse, somewhat in form of a bellows; which, by the motion given thereto, yields a noise like that of the species of bird to be taken. The call for partridges is formed like a bone bored through, and fitted with a pipe or swan's quill, &c. to be blown with the mouth, to make the noise of the cock partridge, which is very different from the call of the hen. Calls for quails, &c. are made of a leathern purse in shape like a pear, stuffed with horse-hair, and fitted at the end with the bone of a cat's, hare's, or coney's leg, formed like a flagelet. They are play'd, by squeezing the purse in the palm of the hand, at the same time striking on the flagelet part with the thumb, to counterfeit the call of the hen-quail.

Call of the House. See CALLING.

CALLA, WAKE-ROBIN, or *Ethiopian Arum*: A genus of the polyandria order, belonging to the gynandria class of plants; and in the natural method ranking under the 2d order, *Piperitæ*. The spatha is plain; the spadix covered with florets; there is no calyx; no petals; and the berries are monospermous. Of this there is but one species. It hath thick, fleshy, tuberous roots, which are covered with a thin brown skin, and strike down many strong fleshy fibres into the ground. The leaves have footstalks more than a foot long, which are green and succulent. The leaves are shaped like the point of an arrow; they are eight or nine inches in length, ending in a sharp point, which turns backward; between the leaves arise the footstalk of the flower, which is thick, smooth, of the same colour as the leaves, rises above them, and is terminated by a single flower, shaped like those of the arum, the hood or spatha being twisted at bottom, but spreads open at the top, and is of a pure white colour. When the flowers fade, they are succeeded by roundish fleshy berries, compressed on two sides, each containing two or three seeds. This plant grows naturally at the Cape of Good Hope. It propagates very fast by offsets, which should be taken off in the latter end of August, at which time the old leaves decay; for at this time the roots are in their most inactive state. They are so hardy as to live without any cover in mild winters, if planted in a warm border and dry soil; but, with a little shelter in hard frost, they may be preserved in full growth very well.

Calla-Sasory, a town of Asia, in the island of Bouton in the East Indies. It is seated about a mile from the sea, on the top of a small hill surrounded with cocoa nut-trees. See BOUTON.

CALLAO, a strong town of South America, in Peru. It is the port of Lima, from which it is distant about five miles. The town is built on a low flat point of land on the sea-shore. It is fortified; but the fortifications were much damaged by the last great earthquake, and have not since been repaired. The town is not above nine or ten feet above the level of high-water mark; but the tide does not commonly rise or fall above five feet. The streets are drawn in a line; but are full of dust, which is very troublesome. In a square near the sea-side are the governor's house, the viceroy's palace, the parish-church, and a battery of three pieces of cannon. On the north side are the warehouses for the merchandise brought from Chili, Mexico, and other parts of Peru. The other churches are built with reeds, and covered with timber or clay, but they look tolerably neat. There are five monasteries and an hospital, though the number of families does not exceed 400. The trade of Callao is considerable. From Chili they bring cordage, leather, tallow, dried fish, and corn; from Chiloe, cedar-planks, woollen manufactures, and carpets; from Peru, sugars, wines, brandy, masts, cordage, timber for shipping, cacao, tobacco, and molasses; from Mexico, pitch, tar, woods for dyeing, sulphur, balsam of Peru both white and brown, as well as commodities from China. At the port of Callao the watering is easy, but the wood is a mile or two distant. Earthquakes are very frequent in these parts, which have done vast mischief to Lima and Callao. W. Long. 76. 15. S. Lat. 12. 29.

CALLE (anc. geog.), a town of Hither Spain, situated on an eminence which hangs over the river Durius; whose port was at the mouth of the river. Now *Porto*, *Oporto*, or *Port a Port*.

CALLEN, a town of Ireland, in the county of Kilkenny and province of Leinster, about ten miles south-west of Kilkenny. W. Long. 7. 22. N. Lat. 52. 25.

CALLICARPA. See JOHNSONIA.

CALLICO, in commerce, a sort of cloth resembling linens made of cotton. The name is taken from that of Callicut, a city on the cost of Malabar, being the first place at which the Portuguese landed when they discovered the India trade. The Spaniards still call it *calico*.

Callicoes are of different kinds, plain, printed, painted, stained, dyed, chints, muslins, and the like, all included under the general denomination of *callicoes*. Some of them are painted with various flowers of different colours: others are not stained, but have a stripe of gold and silver quite through the piece, and at each end is fixed a tissue of gold, silver, and silk, intermixed with flowers. The printing of callicoes was first set on foot in London about the year 1676.

CALLICRATES, an ancient sculptor, who engraved some of Homer's verses on a grain of millet, made an ivory chariot that might be concealed under the wing of a fly, and an ant of ivory in which all the members were distinct: but Ælian justly blames him for exerting his genius and talents in things so useless, and at the same time so difficult. He flourished about the year 472 before Christ.

CALLIGONUM, in botany: A genus of the digynia order belonging to the polyandria class of plants; and in the natural method ranking under the 12th order, *Holoraceæ*. The calyx is pentaphyllous, without petals or styles; the fruit hispid and monospermous. There is but one species, which is found on Mount Ararat.

CALLIGRAPHUS anciently denoted a copyist, or scrivener, who transcribed fair, and at length, what the notaries had taken down in notes or minutes. The word is compounded of καλλος, *beauty*, and γραφω, *I write*. The minutes of acts, &c. were always taken in a kind of cypher, or short-hand; such as the notes of Tyro in Gruter: by which means the notaries, as the Latins called them, or the ταχυγραφοι and σημειογραφοι, as the Greeks called them, were enabled to keep pace with a speaker or person who dictated. These notes, being understood by few, were copied over fair, and at length, by persons who had a good hand, for sale, &c. These persons were called *calligraphi*; a name frequently met with in the ancient writers.

CALLIGRAPHY, the art of fair writing. Callicrates is said to have written an elegant distich on a sesamum seed. Junius speaks of a person, as very extraordinary, who wrote the apostles creed, and beginning of St John's Gospel, in the compass of a farthing. What would he have said of our famous Peter Bale, who in 1575 wrote the Lord's prayer, creed, ten commandments, and two short prayers in Latin, with his own name, motto, day of the month, year of the Lord, and reign of the queen, in the compass of a single penny, inchased in a ring and border of gold, and covered with a crystal, all so accurately wrought as to be very legible?

CALLIMACHUS, a celebrated architect, painter, and sculptor, born at Corinth, having seen by accident a vessel about which the plant called *acanthus* had raised its leaves, conceived the idea of forming the Corinthian capital. (See ACANTHUS, and Plate XXXIV. fig. 4.) The ancients assure us, that he worked in marble with wonderful delicacy. He flourished about 540 B. C.

CALLIMACHUS, a celebrated Greek poet, native of Cyrene in Libya, flourished under Ptolemy Philadelphus and Ptolemy Evergetes kings of Egypt, about 280 years before Christ. He passed, according to Quintilian, for the prince of the Greek elegiac poets. His style is elegant, delicate, and nervous. He wrote a great number of small poems, of which we have only some hymns and epigrams remaining. Catullus has closely imitated him, and translated into Latin verse his small poem on the locks of Berenice. Callimachus was also a good grammarian and a learned critic. There is an edition of his remains, by Mad. le Fevre, quarto; and another in two volumes octavo, with notes by Spanheim, Grævius, Bently, &c.

CALLING *the* HOUSE, in the British parliament, is the calling over the members names, every one answering to his own, and going out of the house, in the order in which he is called: this they do in order to discover whether there be any persons there not returned by the clerk of the crown, or if any member be absent without leave of the house.

CALLINICUS of Heliopolis, inventor of a composition to burn in the water, called the *Greek*, and since *Wild, Fire*. See *Grecian* FIRE.

CALLINUS of Ephesus, a very ancient Greek poet, inventor of elegiac verse; some specimens of which are to be found in the collection of Stobeus. He flourished about 776 years before Christ.

CALLIONYMUS, the DRAGONET, in ichthyology, a genus of fishes belonging to the order of jugulares. The upper lip is doubled up; the eyes are very near each other; the membrane of the gills has six radii; the operculum is shut; the body is naked; and the belly-fins are at a great distance from each other. There are three species of callionymus, viz. 1. The lyra, with the first bone of the back-fin as long as the body of the animal, and a cirrhus at the anus. It is found as far north as Norway and Spitsbergen, and as far

far ſouth as the Mediterranean ſea, and is not unfrequent on the Scarborough coaſts, where it is taken by the hook in 30 or 40 fathoms water. It is often found in the ſtomach of the cod-fiſh. 2. The dracunculus, with the firſt bone of the back-fin ſhorter than its body, which is of a ſpotted yellow colour. It frequents the ſhores of Genoa and Rome. 3. The indicus has a ſmooth head, with longitudinal wrinkles; the lower jaw is a little longer than the upper one; the tongue is obtuſe and emarginated; the apertures of the gills are large: it is of a livid colour, and the anus is in the middle of the body. It is a native of Aſia.

CALLIOPE, in the Pagan mythology, the muſe who preſides over eloquence and heroic poetry. She was thus called from the ſweetneſs of her voice, and was reckoned the firſt of the nine ſiſters. Her diſtinguiſhing office was to record the worthy actions of the living; and accordingly ſhe is repreſented with tablets in her hand.

CALLIPÆDIA, the art of getting or breeding fine and beautiful children. We find divers rules and practices relating to this art, in ancient and modern writers. Among the magi, a ſort of medicine called *eruyſia* was adminiſtered to pregnant women, as a means of producing a beautiful iſſue. Of this kind were the kernels of pine-nuts ground with honey, myrrh, ſaffron, palm-wine, and milk. The Jews are ſaid to have been ſo ſolicitous about the beauty of their children, that care was taken to have ſome very beautiful child placed at the door of the public baths, that the women at going out being ſtruck with his appearance, and retaining the idea, might all have children as fine as he. The Chineſe take ſtill greater care of their breeding women, to prevent uncouth objects of any kind from ſtriking their imagination. Muſicians are employed at night to entertain them with agreeable ſongs and odes, in which are ſet forth all the duties and comforts of a conjugal and domeſtic life; that the infant may receive good impreſſions even before it is born, and not only come forth agreeably formed in body, but well diſpoſed in mind. Callipædia, nevertheleſs, ſeems to have been firſt erected into a juſt art by Claude Quillet de Chinon, a French abbot, who, under the fictitious name of *Calvidius Letus*, has publiſhed a fine Latin poem in four books, under the title of *Callipædia, ſeu de pulchra prolis habendæ ratione*; wherein are contained all the precepts of that new art. There is a tranſlation of it into Engliſh verſe by Mr Rowe.

CALLIPOLIS, (anc. geog.) the name of ſeveral cities of antiquity, particularly one upon the Helleſpont, near the Propontis, and oppoſite to Lampſacus in Aſia. Now GALLIPOLI.

CALLIPPIC PERIOD. See CALIPPIC.

CALLIRRHOE, (anc. geog.), ſurnamed *Enneacrunos*, from its nine ſprings or channels; a fountain not far from Athens, greatly adorned by Piſiſtratus, where there were ſeveral wells, but this only the running ſpring. Callirrhoe was alſo the name of a very fine ſpring of hot water beyond Jordan near the Dead ſea, into which it empties itſelf.

CALISIA, in botany: A genus of the monogynia order, belonging to the triandria claſs of plants; and in the natural method ranking under the 6th order, *Enſatæ*. The calyx is triphyllous; the petals are three; the antheræ are double; and the capſule is bilocular. There is but one ſpecies, a native of America.

CALLISTEA, in Grecian antiquity, a Leſbian feſtival, wherein the women preſented themſelves in Juno's temple, and the prize was aſſigned to the faireſt. There was another of theſe contentions at the feſtival of Ceres Eleuſinia among the Parrhaſians, and another among the Eleans, where the moſt beautiful man was preſented with a complete ſuit of armour, which he conſecrated to Minerva, to whoſe temple he walked in proceſſion, being accompanied by his friends, who adorned him with ribbons, and crowned him with a garland of myrtle.

CALLISTHENES the philoſopher, diſciple and relation of Ariſtotle, by whoſe deſire he accompanied Alexander the Great in his expeditions; but proving too ſevere a cenſurer of that hero's conduct, he was put by him to the torture (on a ſuſpicion of a treaſonable conſpiracy), and died under it, 328 years before Chriſt.

CALLISTRATUS, an excellent Athenian orator, was baniſhed for having obtained too great an authority in the government. Demoſthenes was ſo ſtruck with the force of his eloquence, and the glory it procured him, that he abandoned Plato, and reſolved from thenceforward to apply himſelf to oratory.

CALLITRICHE, or STAR GRASS, in botany: A genus of the digynia order, belonging to the monandria claſs of plants; and in the natural method ranking under the 11th order, *Holeraceæ*. There is no calyx, but two petals, and the capſule is bilocular and tetraſpermous.

CALLOO, a fortreſs in the Netherlands, in the territory of Waes, on the river Scheld, ſubject to the houſe of Auſtria. The Dutch were defeated here by the Spaniards in 1638. E. Long. 4. 10. N. Lat. 51. 15.

CALLOSUM CORPUS, in anatomy, a whitiſh hard ſubſtance, joining the two hemiſpheres of the brain, and appearing in view when the two hemiſpheres are drawn back. See ANATOMY, N° 132.

CALLOT (James), a celebrated engraver born at Nancy in 1593. In his youth he travelled to Rome to learn deſigning and engraving; and from thence went to Florence, where the grand duke took him into his ſervice. After the death of that prince, Callot returned to his native country; where he was very favourably received by Henry duke of Lorrain, who ſettled a conſiderable penſion upon him. His reputation being ſoon after ſpread all over Europe, the infanta of the Netherlands drew him to Bruſſels, where he engraved the ſiege of Breda. Louis XIII. made him deſign the ſiege of Rochelle, and that of the iſle of Rhe. The French king, having taken Nancy in 1631, made Callot the propoſal of repreſenting that new conqueſt, as he had already done the taking of Rochelle: but Callot begged to be excuſed; and ſome courtiers reſolving to oblige him to do it, he anſwered, that he would ſooner cut off his thumb than do any thing againſt the honour of his prince and country. This excuſe the king accepted; and ſaid, that the duke of Lorrain was happy in having ſuch faithful and affectionate ſubjects. Callot followed his buſineſs ſo cloſely, that, though he died at 43 years of age, he is ſaid to have left of his own execution about 1500 pieces. The following are a few of the principal. 1. The *murder of the innocents*, a small oval plate, engraved at Florence. Callot engraved the same subject at Nancy, with some difference in the figures on the back-ground. The former is the most rare: a fine impression of it is very difficult to be found. 2. The *marriage of Cana in Galilee*, from Paulo Veronese, a middling-sized plate lengthwise. 3. The *passion of Christ*, on twelve very small upright plates: first impressions very scarce. 4. *St John in the island of Patmos*, a small plate, nearly square. 5. The *temptation of St Anthony*, a middling-sized plate, lengthwise. He also engraved the same subject larger; which, though not the best, is notwithstanding the scarcest print. There is a considerable difference in the treatment of the subject in the two prints. 6. The *punishments*, wherein is seen the execution of several criminals. The marks of the best impressions of this plate are, a small square tower which appears above the houses, towards the left, and a very small image of the Virgin placed in an angle of the wall, near the middle of the print. 7. The *miseries of war*, eighteen small plates, lengthwise. There is another set on the same subject, consisting of seven plates less than the former. 8. The *great fair of Florence*, so called because it was engraved at Florence. As several parts of this plate were not equally bitten by the aquafortis, it is difficult to meet with a fine impression. Callot, on his return to Nancy, re-engraved this plate without any alteration. The copy, however, is by no means equal to the original. The first is distinguished from the second by the words *in Firenza*, which appear below at the right hand corner of the plate. The second has these words in the same place, *Fe Florentia, & excudit Nanceii*. There is also a large copy of this print, reversed, published by Savery; but the difference is easily distinguished between it and the true print. 9. The *little fair*, otherwise called the *players at bowls*; where also some peasants are represented dancing. This is one of the scarcest of Callot's prints; and it is very difficult to meet with a fine impression of it, for the distances and other parts of the plate failed in the biting it with the aquafortis. 10. The *tilting, or the new street at Nancy*, a middling-sized plate, lengthwise. 11. The *Garden of Nancy*, where young men are playing with a balloon, the same. 12. *View of the Pont Neuf*, a small plate, lengthwise. 13. *View of the Louvre*, the same. 14. *Four landscapes*, small plates, lengthwise.

CALLUS, or CALLOSITY, in a general sense, any cutaneous, corneous, or osseous hardness, whether natural or preternatural; but most frequently it means the callus generated about the edges of a fracture, provided by nature to preserve the fractured bones, or divided parts, in the situation in which they are replaced by the surgeon. A callus, in this last sense, is a sort of jelly, or liquid viscous matter, that sweats out from the small arteries and bony fibres of the divided parts, and fills up the chinks or cavities between them. It first appears of a cartilaginous substance; but at length becomes quite bony, and joins the fractured part so firmly together, that the limb will often make greater resistance to any external violence with this part than with those which were never broken.

CALLUS is also a hard, dense, insensible knob, rising on the hands, feet, &c. by much friction and pressure against hard bodies.

CALM, the state of rest which appears in the air and sea when there is no wind stirring. A calm is more dreaded by a sea-faring man than a storm if he has a strong ship and sea-room enough; for under the line excessive heat sometimes produces such dead calms, that ships are obliged to stay two or three months without being able to stir one way or other. Two opposite winds will sometimes make a calm. This is frequently observed in the gulph of Mexico, at no great distance from the shore, where some gust or land-wind will so poise the general easterly wind, as to produce a perfect calm.

Calms are never so great on the ocean as on the Mediterranean, by reason the flux and reflux of the former keep the water in a continual agitation, even where there is no wind; whereas there being no tides in the latter, the calm is sometimes so dead, that the face of the water is as clear as a looking-glass; but such calms are almost constant presages of an approaching storm. On the coasts about Smyrna, a long calm is reputed a prognostic of an earthquake.

It is not uncommon for the vessels to be calmed, or becalmed, as the sailors express it, in the road of the constant Levantine winds, in places where they ride near the land. Thus between the two capes of Cartouche toward the main, and cape Antonio in Cuba, the sea is narrow, and there is often a calm produced by some gust of a land-wind, that poises the Levantine wind, and renders the whole perfectly still for two or three days. In this case, the current that runs here is of use to the vessels, if it sets right; when it sets easterly, a ship will have a passage in three or four days to the Havannah; but if otherwise, it is often a fortnight or three weeks sail, the ship being embayed in the gulf of Mexico.

When the weather is perfectly calm, no wind at all stirring, the sailors try which way the current sets, by means of a boat which they send out, and which will ride at anchor though there is no bottom to be found, as regularly and well as if fastened by the strongest anchor to the bottom. The method is this: they row the boat to a little distance from the ship, and then throw over their plummet, which is about forty pounds weight; they let this sink to about two hundred fathoms; and then, though it never reaches the bottom, the boat will turn head against the current, and ride as firmly as can be.

Calm Latitudes, in sea language, are situated in the Atlantic ocean, between the tropic of Cancer and the latitude of 29° N. or they denote the space that lies between the trade and variable winds, because it is frequently subject to calms of long duration.

CALMAR, a strong sea-port of Sweden, in the province of Smaland, divided into two towns, the old and the new; but of the former there remains only the church and a few houses. The new town is built a little way from the other, and has large handsome houses. E. Long. 16. 15. N. Lat. 56. 48.

CALMET (Augustine), one of the most learned and laborious writers of the 18th century, was born at Mesnil le Horgne, a village in the diocese of Toul in France, in the year 1672, and took the habit of the Bene-

Benedictines in 1688. Among the many works he published are, 1. A literal exposition, in French, of all the books in the Old Testament, in nine volumes folio. 2. An historical, critical, chronological, geographical, and literal, dictionary of the Bible, in four vols folio, enriched with a great number of figures of Jewish antiquities. 3. A civil and ecclesiastical history of Lorrain, three vols folio. 4. A history of the Old and New Testament, and of the Jews, in two volumes folio, and seven vols duodecimo. 5. An universal sacred and profane history, in several volumes quarto. He died in 1757.

CALMUCKS. See Kalmucks.

CALNE, a town of Wiltshire in England, seated on a river of the same name. It has a handsome church, and sends two members to parliament. W. Long. 1. 59. N. Lat. 51. 30.

CALNEH, (anc. geog.) a city in the land of Shinar, built by Nimrod, and the last city mentioned (Gen. x. 10.) as belonging to his kingdom. It is believed to be the same with Calno mentioned in Isaiah (x. 9.), and with Canneh in Ezekiel (xxvii. 23.) with still greater variation. It is observed, that it must have been situated in Mesopotamia, since these prophets join it with Haran, Eden, Assyria, and Chilmad, which carried on a trade with Tyre. It is said by the Chaldee interpreters, as also by Eusebius and Jerom, to be the same with Ctesiphon, standing upon the Tigris, about three miles distant from Seleucia, and that for some time it was the capital city of the Parthians.

CALOGERI, in church-history, monks of the Greek church, divided into three degrees: the novices, called *archari*; the ordinary professed, called *microschemi*; and the more perfect, called *megaloschemi*: they are likewise divided into cœnobites, anchorets, and recluses. The cœnobites are employed in reciting their offices from midnight to sun-set; they are obliged to make three genuflexions at the door of the choir, and, returning, to bow to the right and to the left, to their brethren. The anchorites retire from the conversation of the world, and live in hermitages in the neighbourhood of the monasteries; they cultivate a little spot of ground, and never go out but on Sundays and holidays to perform their devotions at the next monastery. As for the recluses, they shut themselves up in grottos and caverns on the tops of mountains, which they never go out of, abandoning themselves entirely to Providence: they live on the alms sent them by the neighbouring monasteries.

CALOMEL, or dulcified sublimate of mercury. See Pharmacy, *Index*.

CALOPHYLLUM, in botany: A genus of the monogynia order belonging to the polyandria class of plants: and in the natural method classed under those called *dubiæ* by Linnæus. The corolla is tetrapetalous; the calyx tetraphyllous and coloured; the fruit a globose plum. There are two species, both natives of India.

CALOTTE, a cap or coif of hair, sattin, or other stuff: an ecclesiastical ornament in most Popish countries. See Cap.

Calotte, in architecture, a round cavity or depressure, in form of a cap or cup, lathed and plastered, used to diminish the rise or elevation of a moderate chapel, cabinet, alcove, &c. which, without such an expedient, would be too high for other pieces of the apartment.

CALPE, a mountain of Andalusia in Spain; at the foot of which, towards the sea, stands the town of Gibraltar. It is half a league in height towards the land, and so steep that there is no approaching it on that side.

CALPURNIUS (Titus), a Latin Sicilian poet, lived under the emperor Carus and his son. We have seven of his eclogues remaining.

CALQUING, or Calking, a term used in painting, &c. where the back-side of any thing is covered over with a black or red colour, and the strokes or lines traced through on a waxed plate, wall, or other matter, by passing lightly over each stroke of the design with a point, which leaves an impression of the colour on the plate or wall.

CALTHA, in botany: A genus of the monogynia order belonging to the polyandria class of plants; and in the natural method ranking under the 26th order, *Multisiliquæ*. There is no calyx; there are five petals; no nectaria; the capsules are many, and polyspermous. There is only one species known, which grows naturally in moist boggy lands in many parts of England and Scotland. There is a variety, with very double flowers, which for its beauty is preserved in gardens. It is propagated by parting the roots in autumn. It should be planted in a moist soil and shady situation; and as there are often such places in gardens where few other plants will thrive, so these may be allowed room, and during their season of flowering will afford an agreeable variety. The flowers gathered before they expand, and preserved in salted vinegar, are a good substitute for capers. The juice of the petals, boiled with a little alum, stains paper yellow. The remarkable yellowness of the butter in spring is supposed to be caused by this plant: but cows will not eat it, unless compelled by extreme hunger; and then, Boerhaave says, it occasions such an inflammation, that they generally die. Upon May-day, the country people strew the flowers upon the pavement before their doors. Goats and sheep eat this plant; horses, cows, and swine, refuse it.

CALTROP, in botany. See Tribulus.

Caltrop, in military affairs, an instrument with four iron points, disposed in a triangular form, so that three of them are always on the ground, and the fourth in the air. They are scattered over the ground where the enemy's cavalry is to pass, in order to embarrass them.

CALVARIA, in anatomy, the hairy scalp or upper part of the head, which, either by disease or old age, grows bald first.

CALVART (Denis), a celebrated painter, was born at Antwerp in 1585; and had for his masters Prospero Fontana and Lorenzo Sabbatini. He opened a school at Bologna, which became celebrated; and from which proceeded Guido, Albani, and other great masters. Calvart was well skilled in architecture, perspective, and anatomy, which he considered as necessary to a painter, and taught them to his pupils. His principal works are at Bologna, Rome, and Reggio. He died at Bologna in 1619.

CALVARY, a term used in Catholic countries for a

a kind of chapel of devotion raised on a hillock near a city, in memory of the place where Jesus Christ was crucified near the city of Jerusalem. The word comes from the Latin *calvarium*; and that from *calvus*, bald; in regard the top of that hillock was bare and destitute of verdure: which is also signified by the Hebrew word *golgotha*. Such is the Calvary of St Valerian near Paris; which is accompanied with several little chapels, in each of which is represented in sculpture one of the mysteries of the passion.

Calvary, in heraldry, a cross so called, because it resembles the cross on which our Saviour suffered. It is always set upon steps.

CALVERT (George), afterwards lord Baltimore, was born at Kipling in Yorkshire about the year 1582, and educated at Oxford, where he took the degree of bachelor of arts, and afterwards travelled. At his return, he was made secretary to Sir Robert Cecil: he was afterwards knighted, and in 1618 appointed one of the principal secretaries of state. But after he had enjoyed that post about five years, he willingly resigned it; freely owning to his majesty that he was become a Roman-catholic, so that he must either be wanting to his trust, or violate his conscience in discharging his office. This ingenuous confession so affected king James, that he continued him privy-counsellor all his reign, and the same year created him baron of Baltimore in the kingdom of Ireland. He had before obtained a patent for him and his heirs, for the province of Avelon in Newfoundland: but that being exposed to the insults of the French, he abandoned it, and afterwards obtained the grant of a country on the north part of Virginia from Charles I. who called it *Maryland*, in honour of his queen: but he died in April 1632 (aged 50), before the patent was made out. It was, however, filled up to his son Cecil Calvert lord Baltimore; and bears date June 20th 1632. It is held from the crown as part of the manor of Windsor, on one very singular condition, viz. to present two Indian arrows yearly, on Easter Tuesday, at the castle, where they are kept and shown to visitors.—His lordship wrote, 1. A Latin poem on the death of Sir Henry Upton. 2. Speeches in parliament. 3. Various letters of state. 4. The answer of Tom Tell-truth. 5. The practice of princes. And, 6. The lamentation of the kirk.

CALVI, a town of the province of Lavoro, in the kingdom of Naples, situated near the sea, about fifteen miles north of the city of Naples. E. Long. 14. 45. N. Lat. 41. 15.

Calvi is also the name of a sea-port in the island of Corsica, situated on a bay, on the west side of the island, about 40 miles south-west of Bastia. E. Long. 9. 5. N. Lat. 42. 16.

CALVIN (John), the celebrated reformer of the Christian church from Romish superstitions and doctrinal errors, and founder of the sect since called *Calvinists*, was born in 1509. He was the son of a cooper of Noyon in Picardy; and his real name was *Chauvin*, which he chose to latinize into *Calvinus*, styling himself in the title-page to his first work (a Commentary on *Seneca de clementia*), "Lucius Calvinus, Civis Romanus;" an early proof of his pride, at about 24 years of age. In 1529, he was rector of Pont l'Eveque; and in 1534 he threw up this benefice, separating himself entirely from the Romish church. The persecution against the Protestants in France (with whom he was now associated) obliged him to retire to Basle in Switzerland: here he published his famous Institutes of the Christian religion in 1535. The following year, he was chosen professor of divinity, and one of the ministers of the church, at Geneva. The next year, viz. 1537, he made all the people solemnly swear to a body of doctrines; but finding that religion had not yet had any great influence on the morals of the people, he, assisted by other ministers, declared, that since all their admonitions and warnings had proved unsuccessful, they could not celebrate the holy sacrament as long as these disorders reigned; he also declared, that he could not submit to some regulations made by the synod of Berne. Upon which the Syndics having summoned the people, it was ordered that Calvin and two other ministers should leave the city within two days. Upon this Calvin retired to Strasburg, where he established a French church, of which he was the first minister, and was also chosen professor of divinity there. Two years after he was chosen to assist at the diet appointed by the emperor to meet at Worms and at Ratisbon in order to appease the troubles occasioned by the difference of religion. He went with Bucer, and entered into a conference with Melancton. The people of Geneva now entreated him to return; to which he consented, and arrived at Geneva, September 13th 1541. He began with establishing a form of ecclesiastical discipline, and a consistorial jurisdiction, with the power of inflicting all kinds of canonical punishments. This was greatly disliked by many persons, who imagined that the papal tyranny would soon be revived. Calvin, however, asserted on all occasions the rights of his consistory with inflexible strictness; and he caused Michael Servetus to be burnt at the stake for writing against the doctrine of the Trinity. But though the rigour of his proceedings sometimes occasioned great tumults in the city, yet nothing could shake his steadiness and inflexibility. Amongst all the disturbances of the commonwealth, he took care of the foreign churches in England, France, Germany, and in Poland; and did more by his pen than his presence, sending his advice and instructions by letter, and writing a great number of books. This great reformer died on the 27th of May 1564, aged 55. His works were printed together at Amsterdam in 1671, in nine volumes folio: the principal of which are his Institutions, in Latin, the best edition of which is that of Robert Stephens in 1553, in folio; and his Commentaries on the Holy Scriptures.—Calvin is universally allowed to have had great talents, an excellent genius, and profound learning. His style is grave and polite. Independent of his spiritual pride, his morals were exemplary; for he was pious, sober, chaste, laborious, and disinterested. But his memory can never be purified from the stain of burning Servetus: it ill became a reformer to adopt the most odious practice of the corrupt church of Rome.

CALVINISM, the doctrine and sentiments of Calvin and his followers. Calvinism subsists in its greatest purity in the city of Geneva; and from thence it was first propagated into Germany, France, the United Provinces, and England. In France it was abolished by the revocation of the edict of Nants in 1685.

It has been the prevailing religion in the United Provinces ever since the year 1571. The theological system of Calvin was adopted, and made the public rule of faith in England, under the reign of Edward VI. and the church of Scotland was modelled by John Knox, the disciple of Calvin, agreeably to the doctrine, rites, and form of ecclesiastical government, established at Geneva. In England it has declined since the time of queen Elizabeth; though it still subsists, some say a little allayed, in the articles of the established church; and in its rigour in Scotland.

The distinguishing theological tenets of Calvinism, as the term is now generally applied, respect the doctrines of PREDESTINATION, or particular ELECTION and REPROBATION, original SIN, particular REDEMPTION, effectual, or, as some have called it, irresistible GRACE in regeneration, JUSTIFICATION by faith, PERSEVERANCE, and the TRINITY. See each of these articles.

Besides the doctrinal part of Calvin's system, which, so far as it differs from that of other reformers of the same period, principally regarded the absolute decree of God, whereby the future and eternal condition of the human race was determined out of mere sovereign pleasure and free-will; it extended likewise to the discipline and government of the Christian church, the nature of the Eucharist, and the qualification of those who were intitled to the participation of it. Calvin considered every church as a separate and independent body, invested with the power of legislation for itself. He proposed that it should be governed by presbyteries and synods, composed of clergy and laity, without bishops, or any clerical subordination; and maintained, that the province of the civil magistrate extended only to its protection and outward accommodation. In order to facilitate an union with the Lutheran church, he acknowledged a real, though spiritual, presence of Christ, in the Eucharist, that true Christians were united to the man Christ in this ordinance, and that divine grace was conferred upon them, and sealed to them, in the celebration of it; and he confined the privilege of communion to pious and regenerate believers. In France the Calvinists are distinguished by the name of *Huguenots*; and, among the common people, by that of *Parpaillots*. In Germany they are confounded with the Lutherans, under the general title *Protestants*; only sometimes distinguished by the name *Reformed*.

CALVINISTS, in church-history, those who follow the opinions of CALVIN. See the two preceding articles.

*Crypto-*CALVINISTS, a name given to the favourers of Calvinism in Saxony, on account of their secret attachment to the Genevan doctrine and discipline. Many of them suffered by the decrees of the convocation of Torgaw, held in 1576. The Calvinists in their progress have divided into various branches, or lesser sects.

CALVISIUS (Seth), a celebrated German chronologer in the beginning of the 17th century. He wrote *Elenchus calendarii Gregoriani, et duplex calendarii melioris forma*, and other learned works, together with some excellent treatises on music. He died in 1617, aged 61.

CALVITIES, or CALVITIUM, in medicine, baldness, or a want of hair, particularly on the sinciput, occasioned by the moisture of the head, which should feed it, being dried up, by some disease, old age, or the immoderate use of powder, &c. See ALOPECIA.

CALUMET, a symbolical instrument of great importance among the American Indians.—It is nothing more than a pipe, whose bowl is generally made of a soft red marble; the tube of a very long reed, ornamented with the wings and feathers of birds. No affair of consequence is transacted without the calumet. It ever appears in meetings of commerce or exchanges; in congresses for determining of peace or war; and even in the very fury of a battle. The acceptance of the calumet is a mark of concurrence with the terms proposed; as the refusal is a certain mark of rejection. Even in the rage of a conflict this pipe is sometimes offered; and if accepted, the weapons of destruction instantly drop from their hands, and a truce ensues. It seems the sacrament of the savages; for no compact is ever violated which is confirmed by a whiff from this holy reed. When they treat of war, the pipe and all its ornaments are usually red, or sometimes red only on one side. The size and decorations of the calumet are for the most part proportioned to the quality of the persons to whom they are presented, and to the importance of the occasion. The calumet of peace is different from that of war. They make use of the former to seal their alliances and treaties, to travel with safety, and to receive strangers; but of the latter to proclaim war. It consists of a red stone, like marble, formed into a cavity resembling the head of a tobacco pipe, and fixed to a hollow reed. They adorn it with feathers of various colours; and name it the calumet of the sun, to which luminary they present it, in expectation of thereby obtaining a change of weather as often as they desire. From the winged ornaments of the calumet, and its conciliating uses, writers compare it to the caduceus of Mercury, which was carried by the caduceatores, or messengers of peace, with terms to the hostile states. It is singular, that the most remote nations, and the most opposite in their other customs and manners, should in some things have, as it were, a certain consent of thought. The Greeks and the Americans had the same idea, in the invention of the caduceus of the one, and the calumet of the other.

Dance of the CALUMET, is a solemn rite among the Indians on various occasions. They dare not wash themselves in rivers in the beginning of summer, nor taste of the new fruits, without performing it; and the same ceremony always confirms a peace or precedes a war. It is performed in the winter-time in their cabins, and in summer in the open fields. For this purpose they choose a spot among trees to shade them from the heat of the sun, and lay in the middle a large mat, as a carpet, setting upon it the manitor, or god, of the chief of the company. On the right hand of this image they place the calumet, as their great deity, erecting around it a kind of trophy with their arms. Things being thus disposed, and the hour of dancing come, those who are to sing take the most honourable seats under the shade of the trees. The company is then ranged round, every one, before he sits down, saluting the manitor, which is done by blowing

upon

upon it the smoke of their tobacco. Each person next receives the calumet in rotation, and holding it with both hands, dances to the cadence of the vocal music, which is accompanied with the beating of a sort of drum. During this exercise, he gives a signal to one of their warriors, who takes a bow, arrow, and axe, from the trophies already mentioned, and fights him; the former defending himself with the calumet only, and both of them dancing all the while. This mock engagement being over, he who holds the calumet makes a speech, in which he gives an account of the battles he has fought, and the prisoners he has taken, and then receives a cloak, or some other present, from the chief of the ball. He then resigns the calumet to another, who having acted a similar part, delivers it to a third, who afterwards gives it to his neighbour, till at last the instrument returns to the person that began the ceremony, who presents it to the nation invited to the feast, as a mark of their friendship, and a confirmation of their alliance, when this is the occasion of the entertainment.

CALUBINY, the crime of accusing another falsely, and knowingly so, of some heinous offence.

Oath of CALUMNY, *Juramentum* (or rather *Jusjurandum*) *Calumniæ*, among civilians and canonists, was an oath which both parties in a cause were obliged to take; the plaintiff that he did not bring his charge, and the defendant that he did not deny it, with a design to abuse each other, but because they believed their cause was just and good; that they would not deny the truth, nor create unnecessary delays, nor offer the judge or evidence any gifts or bribes. If the plaintiff refused this oath, the complaint or libel was dismissed; if the defendant, it was taken *pro confesso*. This custom was taken from the ancient athletæ; who, before they engaged, were to swear that they had no malice, nor would use any unfair means for overcoming each other. The *juramentum calumniæ* is much disused, as a great occasion of perjury. Anciently the advocates and proctors also took this oath; but of late it is dispensed with, and thought sufficient that they take it once for all at their first admission to practice. See also LAW, Part III. n° clxxxiv. 7.

CALVUS (Cornelius Licinius), a celebrated Roman orator, was the friend of Catullus; and flourished 64 B. C. Catullus, Ovid, and Horace, speak of him.

CALX properly signifies *lime*, but is also used by chemists and physicians for a fine powder remaining after the calcination or corrosion of metals and other mineral substances. All metallic calces, at least all those made by fire, are found to weigh more than the metal from which they were originally produced. See the article FIRE.

CALX *Nativa*, in natural history, a kind of marly earth, of a dead whitish colour, which, if thrown into water, makes a considerable bubbling and hissing noise, and has, without previous burning, the quality of making a cement like lime or plaster of Paris.

CALX *Viva*, or *Quick-lime*, that whereon no water has been cast, in contradistinction to lime which has been slaked by pouring water on it.

CALYBITES, the inhabitant of a cottage, an appellation given to divers saints on account of their long residence in some hut, by way of mortification. The word is formed from [illegible], *tego*, *I cover*; whence [illegible], *a little cot*.—The Romish church commemorates St John the calybite on the 15th of December.

CALYCANTHEMÆ, in botany, an order of plants in the *Fragmenta methodi naturalis* of Linnæus, in which are the following genera, viz. epilobium, œnothera, jussiæa, ludwigia, oldenlandia, isnarda, &c. See BOTANY, sect. vi. 17.

CALYCANTHUS, in botany: A genus of the polygynia order, belonging to the icosandria class of plants; and in the natural method classed with those of which the order is doubtful. The calyx is monophyllous, urceolate, or blown up; squarrose, or frizzled with small coloured leaves, the corolla consisting of the leaves on the calyx; the styles are numerous, each with a glandular stigma; the seeds are many, each with a train, within a succulent calyx. There are two species; namely, 1. The præcox, which is not quite inured to this climate; and, 2. The floridus, a flowering calycanthus, or Carolina allspice tree, a native of Carolina. It seldom grows, at least with us, to more than five feet high. It divides into many branches irregularly near the ground. They are of a brown colour, and being bruised emit a most agreeable odour. The leaves that garnish this delightful aromatic are of an oval figure, pointed: They are near four inches long, and are at least two and a half broad, and are placed opposite by pairs on the branches. At the end of these stand the flowers, of a kind of chocolate-purple colour, and which are possessed of the opposite qualities of the bark on the branches. They stand single on their short footstalks, come out in May and June, and are succeeded by ripe seeds in England. The propagation of this shrub is not very difficult; though more than common care must be taken, after small plants are obtained, to preserve them till they are of a size to be ventured abroad. The last year's shoots, if laid in the ground, the bark especially being a little bruised, will strike root within the compass of twelve months, particularly if the layers are shaded, and now and then watered in the summer's drought. In the spring they should be taken off, and planted in pots; and if these are afforded a small degree of heat in a bed, they will strike so much the sooner and stronger. After they have been in this bed a month or six weeks, they should be taken out. In the heat of the summer they should be placed in the shade; and if the pots are plunged into the natural ground, it will be so much the better. At the approach of the succeeding winter's bad weather, the pots should be removed into the green-house, or some shelter, and in the spring may resume their old stations: and this should be repeated till they are of a proper size and strength to be planted out to stand. If the pots in which they were first planted were small, they may be shifted into larger a spring or two after; and, when they have got to be pretty strong plants, they may be turned out, mould and all, into the places where they are to remain. By this care of potting them, and housing them during the severe weather in winter, the young crop will be preserved; otherwise, if they were planted immediately abroad, the first hard frost the ensuing winter would destroy them all: Tanner's bark about their roots will be the most proper

security;

security; as they are at best, when full grown, but tender plants, and must have the warmest situation and the driest soil.

CALYCIFLORÆ, in botany, the 16th order in Linnæus's *Fragmenta methodi naturalis*, consisting of plants which, as the title imports, have the stamina (the flower) inserted into the calyx. This order contains the following genera, viz. eleagnus, hippophæ, osyris, and trophis. See BOTANY, sect. vi. 16.

CALYCISTÆ (from *calyx* the flower-cup), systematic botanists, so termed by Linnæus, who have arranged all vegetables from the different species, structure, and other circumstances, of the calyx or flower-cup. The only systems of this kind are the *Character plantarum novus*, a posthumous work of Magnolius, professor of botany at Montpelier, published in 1720; and Linnæus's *Methodus calycina*, published in his *Classes plantarum*, at Leyden, in 1738. See BOTANY, p. 435.

CALYDON, (anc. geog.), a town of Ætolia, situated seven miles and a half from the sea, and divided by the river Evenus: the country was anciently called *Æolis*, from the Æolians its inhabitants. This country was famous for the story of Meleager and the Calydonian boar.

CALYPSO, in fabulous history, a goddess, who was the daughter of Oceanus and Tethys, or, as others say, of Atlas. She was queen of the island of Ogygia, which from her was called the island of *Calypso*. According to Homer, Ulysses suffered shipwreck on her coast, and staid with her several years.

CALYPTRA, among botanists, a thin membranaceous involucrum, usually of a conic figure, which covers the parts of fructification. The capsules of most of the mosses have calyptræ.

CALYX, among botanists, a general term expressing the cup of a flower, or that part of a plant which surrounds and supports the other parts of the flower.

The cups of flowers are very various in their structure, and on that account distinguished by several names, as *perianthium*, *involucrum*, *spatha*, *gluma*, &c. See BOTANY, p. 439.

CALZADA, a town of Old Castile in Spain, seated on the river Leglera. W. Long. 2. 47. N. Lat. 42. 18.

CAMÆA, in natural history, a genus of the semipellucid gems approaching to the onyx structure, being composed of zones, and formed on a crystalline basis; but having their zones very broad and thick, and laid alternately one on another, with no common matter between; usually less transparent, and more debased with earth, than the onyxes.

1. One species of the camæa is the dull-looking onyx, with broad black and white zones; and is the camæa of the moderns, and the Arabian onyx. This species is found in Egypt, Arabia, Persia, and the East Indies. 2. Another species of the camæa is the dull broad zoned, green and white camæa, or the jaspi-cameo of the Italians; it is found in the East Indies, and in some parts of America. 3. The third is the hard camæa, with broad white and chesnut coloured veins. 4. The hard camæa, with bluish, white, and flesh-coloured broad veins, being the sardonyx of Pliny's time, only brought from the East Indies.

CAMAIEU, or CAMAYEU, a word used to express a peculiar sort of onyx; also by some to express a stone, wherein are found various figures, and representations of landscapes, &c. formed by a kind of *lusus naturæ*; so as to exhibit pictures without painting. The word comes from *camehuia*, a name the Orientals give to the onyx, when they find in preparing it, another colour; as who should say, *a second stone*. It is of these *camaieux* Pliny is to be understood when he speaks of the manifold picture of gems, and the party-coloured spots of precious stones: *Gemmarum pictura tam multiplex, lapidumque tam discolores maculæ*.

CAMAIEU is also applied by others to those precious stones, as onyxes, cornelians, and agates, whereon the lapidaries employ their art to aid nature, and perfect those representations. See CAMÆA.

CAMAIEU is also frequently applied to any kind of gem, whereon figures may be engraven either indentedly or in relievo. In this sense the lapidaries of Paris are called in their statutes, *cutters of camayeux*.

A society of learned men at Florence undertook to procure all the *cameos* or *camayeux*, and intaglios in the great duke's gallery to be engraven; and began to draw the heads of divers emperors in *cameos*.

CAMAIEU is also used for a painting, wherein there is only one colour; and where the lights and shadows are of gold, wrought on a golden or azure ground. When the ground is yellow, the French call it *cirage*; when grey, *grisaille*. This kind of work is chiefly used to represent basso relievos; the Greeks call pieces of this sort *μονοχρωματα*.

CAMALDULIANS, CAMALDUNIANS, or CAMALDOLITES, an order of religious, founded by Romuald, an Italian fanatic, in 1023, in the horrible desert of Camaldoli, otherwise called Campo-Malduli, situate in the state of Florence, on the Appennines. Their rule is that of St Benedict; and their houses, by the statutes, are never to be less than five leagues from cities. The *Camaldulians* have not borne that title from the beginning of their order; till the close of the eleventh century they were called *Romualdins*, from the name of their founder. Till that time, *Camaldulians* was a particular name for those of the desert Camaldoli; and D. Grandi observes, was not given to the whole order, in regard it was in this monastery that the order commenced, but because the regulation was best maintained here.

Guido Grandi, mathematician of the great duke of Tuscany, and a monk of this order, has published *Camaldulian* Dissertations, on the origin and establishment of it.

The *Camaldulians* were distinguished into two classes, of which the one were CŒNOBITES, and the other EREMITES.

CAMALODUNUM (anc. geog.), a town of the Trinobantes, the first Roman colony in Britain, of veterans, under the emperor. From the Itineraries it appears to have stood where now Malden stands. It continued to be an open place under the Romans; a place of pleasure rather than strength; yet not unadorned with splendid works, as a theatre and a temple of Claudius: which the Britons considered as badges of slavery, and which gave rise to several seditions and commotions. It stands on a bay of the sea, at the mouth of the Chelmer, in the county of Essex; the modern name is contracted from the ancient.

CAMARANA, an island of Arabia, in the Red Sea, whose inhabitants are little and black. It is the best

best of all the islands in this sea, and here they fish for coral and pearls. N. Lat. 15. 0.

CAMASSEI, or CAMACE, (Andrea), painter of history and landscape, was born at Bevagna, and at first learned the principles of design and colouring from Domenichino; but afterwards he studied in the school of Andrea Sacchi, and proved a very great painter. He was employed in St Peter's at Rome, as also at John Lateran; and his works are extremely admired, for the sweetness of his colouring, the elegance of his thoughts and design, and likewise for the delicacy of his pencil. Sandrart laments that the world was deprived of so promising a genius, in the very bloom of life, when his reputation was daily advancing. He died in 1657. At St John Lateran are to be seen, the Battle of Constantine and Maxentius; and the Triumph of Constantine; which are noble and grand compositions; and they afford sufficient proofs of the happiness of his invention and the correctness of his execution. Also at Wilton, the seat of the earl of Pembroke, there is a picture of Venus with the Graces, said to be by the hand of Camassei.

CAMARCUM, (anc. geog.), the capital of the Nervii, a people of Gallia Belgica, (Antonine, Peutinger); before whose time no mention was made of it. Now Cambray, capital of the Cambresis, in French Flanders. E. Long. 3. 15. Lat. 50. 15.

CAMARINA, (anc. geog.), a city of Sicily, built by the Syracusans on an eminence near the sea, in the south of Sicily, to the west of the promontory Pachynum, between two rivers, the Hipparis and Oanus. Of so famous a city nothing now remains but its name and ancient walls, a mile and a half in compass, with the slight remains of houses: now called *Camarana*.

Camarina Palus, a marsh or lake, near the city Camarina, and from which it took its name. In a time of drought, the stench of the lake produced a pestilence; upon which the inhabitants consulted the oracle, whether they should not quite drain it. The oracle dissuaded them: they notwithstanding drained it, and opened a way for their enemies to come and plunder their city: hence the proverb, *Ne moveas Camarinam*, that is, not to remove one evil to bring on a greater. Now *Lago di Camarana*, situate in a beautiful plain, under the very walls of Camarina, and of a triangular form.

CAMAYEU. See CAMAIEU.

CAMBAIA, or CAMBAY, a town of Asia, in India, and in the peninsula on this side the Ganges; capital of a province of the same name; but more commonly called *Guzarat*. It is seated at the bottom of a gulph of the same name, on a small river; is a large place with high walls, and has a pretty good trade. The product and manufactures are inferior to few towns in India; for it abounds in corn, cattle, and silk; and cornelian and agate stones are found in its rivers. The inhabitants are noted for embroidery; and some of their quilts have been valued at 40l. It is subject to the Great Mogul. E. Long. 72. 15. N. Lat. 22. 50.

CAMBAYES, in commerce, cotton cloths made at Bengal, Madras, and some other places on the coast of Coromandel. They are proper for the trade of Marseilles, whither the English at Madras send great numbers of them. Many are also imported into Holland.

CAMBER, according to our monkish historians, one of the three sons of Brute, who, upon his father's death, had that part of Britain assigned him for his share, called from him *Cambria* now *Wales*.

Camber-Beam, among builders, a piece of timber in an edifice cut archwise, or with an obtuse angle in the middle, commonly used in platforms, as church-leads, and on other occasions where long and strong beams are required.

CAMBERED-DECK, among ship-builders. The deck or flooring of a ship is said to be cambered, or to lie cambering, when it is higher in the middle of the ship's length, and droops toward the stem and stern, or the two ends. Also when it lies irregular; a circumstance which renders the ship very unfit for war.

CAMBERT, a French musician in the 17th century, was at first admired for the manner in which he touched the organ, and became superintendant of the music to Anne of Austria the queen-mother. The abbe Perrin associated him in the privilege he obtained of his majesty, of setting up an opera in 1669. Cambert set to music two pastorals, one entitled *Pomona*, the other *Ariadne*, which were the first operas given in France. He also wrote a piece entitled *The pains and pleasures of love*. These pieces pleased the public; yet, in 1672, Lully obtaining the privilege of the opera, Cambert was obliged to come to England, where he became superintendant of the music to king Charles II. and died there in 1677.

CAMBIO, an Italian word which signifies *exchange*; commonly used at Provence, and in some other countries, particularly Holland.

CAMBIST, a name given in France to those who trade in notes and bills of exchange. The word cambist, though a term of antiquity, is even now a technical word, of some use among merchants, traders, and bankers. Some derive it from the Latin *cambium*, or rather *cambio*.

CAMBLET, or CHAMBLET, a stuff sometimes of wool, sometimes silk, and sometimes hair, especially that of goats, with wool or silk: in some, the warp is silk and wool twisted together, and the woof hair.

The true or oriental camblet is made of the pure hair of a sort of goat, frequent about Angora, and which makes the riches of that city, all the inhabitants whereof are employed in the manufacture and commerce of camblets. It is certain we find mentioned in middle-age writers stuffs made of camel's hair, under the denominations of *camelotum* and *camelinum*, whence probably the origin of the term; but these are represented as strangely coarse, rough, and prickly, and seem to have been chiefly used among the monks by way of mortification, as the hair-shirt of later times.

We have no camblets made in Europe of the goats hair alone; even at Brussels, they find it necessary to add a mixture of woollen thread.

England, France, Holland, and Flanders, are the chief places of this manufacture. Brussels exceeds them all in the beauty and quality of its camblets: those of England are reputed the second.

Figured CAMBLETS, are those of one colour whereon are stamped various figures, flowers, foliage, &c. by means of hot irons, which are a kind of moulds, passed together with the stuff, under a press. These are chiefly brought from Amiens and Flanders; the commerce of these was anciently much more considerable than at present.

Watered-Camblets, those which, after weaving, receive a certain preparation with water; and are afterwards passed under a hot-press, which gives them a smoothness and lustre.

Waved-Camblets, are those whereon waves are impressed, as on tabbies; by means of a calender, under which they are passed and repassed several times.

The manufacturers, &c. of camblets are to take care they do not acquire any false and needless plaits; it being almost impossible to get them out again. This is notorious, even to a proverb: we say, a person is like camblet, he has taken his plait.

CAMBODIA, a kingdom of Asia, in the East Indies, bounded on the north by the kingdom of Laos, on the east by Cochin-China and Chiapa, and on the south and west by the gulph and kingdom of Siam; divided by a large river called *Mecon*. The capital town is of the same name, seated on the western shore of the said river, about 150 miles north of its mouth. This country is annually overflowed in the rainy season, between June and October; and its productions and fruits are much the same with those usually found between the tropics. E. Long. 104. 15. N. Lat. 13. 40.

CAMBODUNUM, (Itinerary); a town of the Brigantes, in Britain; now in ruins, near Almonbury, in York-shire. Wesseling, (Talbot.) Also a town of Vindelicia, on the Cambus: now Kempten, in Suabia.

CAMBOGIA, in botany: A genus of the monogynia order, belonging to the polyandria class of plants; and in the natural method ranking under the 38th order, *Tricoccae*. The corolla is tetrapetalous; the calyx tetraphyllous; and the fruit is a pome with eight cells, and solitary seeds. There is but one species, the gotta, a native of India, which yields the gum-resin known by the name of *gamboge* in the shops. See Gamboge.

CAMBRASINES, in commerce, fine linen made in Egypt, of which there is a considerable trade at Cairo, Alexandria, and Rosetta, or Rasehit. They are called *cambrasines* from their resemblance to cambrics.

CAMBRAY, an archiepiscopal city, the capital of the Cambresis, in the Low Countries, seated on the Scheld. It is defended by good fortifications, and has a fort on the side of the river; and as the land is low on that side, they can lay the adjacent parts under water by means of sluices. Its ditches are large and deep, and those of the citadel are cut into a rock. Clodion became master of Cambray in 445. The Danes burnt it afterwards; since which time it became a free imperial city. It has been the subject of contest between the emperors, the kings of France, and the earls of Flanders. Francis I. let it remain neutral during the war with Charles V. but this last took possession of it in 1543. After this it was given to John of Montluc by Henry III. of France, whom he created prince of Cambray; but the Spaniards took it from Montluc in 1593, which broke his heart. It continued under the dominion of the House of Austria till 1677, when the king of France became master of it, in whose hands it has continued ever since.

The buildings of Cambray are tolerably handsome, and the streets fine and spacious. The place or square for arms is of an extraordinary largeness, and capable of receiving the whole garrison in order of battle. The cathedral dedicated to the Virgin Mary is one of the finest in Europe. The body of the church is very large, and there are rich chapels, the pillars of which are adorned with marble tombs that are of exquisite workmanship, and add greatly to the beauty of the place. There are two galleries, one of which is of copper, finely wrought. The door of the choir is of the same metal, and well carved. The steeple of this church is very high, and built in the form of a pyramid; and from its top you have a view of the city, which is one of the finest and most agreeable in the Low Countries. There are nine parishes, four abbeys, and several convents for both sexes. The citadel is very advantageously situated on high ground, and commands the whole city. Cambray is one of the most opulent and commercial cities in the Low Countries; and makes every year a great number of pieces of cambric, with which the inhabitants drive a great trade. E. Long. 3. 20. N. Lat. 50. 11.

Cambray (M. de Fenelon, archbishop of). See Fenelon.

CAMBRESIS, a province of France, in the Netherlands, about 25 miles in length. It is bounded on the north and east by Hainault, on the south by Picardy, and on the west by Artois. It is a very fertile and populous country; and the inhabitants are industrious, active, and ingenious. The trade consists principally in corn, sheep, very fine wool, and fine linen cloth. Cambray is the capital town.

CAMBRIA, a name for the principality of Wales.

CAMBRIC, in commerce, a species of linen made of flax, very fine and white; the name of which was originally derived from the city of Cambray, where they were first manufactured. They are now made at other places in France.

The manufacture of cambrics hath long since proved of extraordinary advantage to France. For many years it appeared that England did not in this article contribute less than 200,000 *l.* per annum to the interest of France. This proved motive sufficient to induce the parliament of Great Britain to enact many salutary laws to prevent this great loss of our wealth. See 18 Geo. II. c. 36. and 21 Geo. II. c. 26. See also stat. 31 Geo. II. c. 32. and 4 Geo. III. c. 37. which regulates the cambric manufactory, not long since introduced into Winchelsea in Sussex; but very soon abolished. The cambrics now allowed in this country are manufactured in Scotland and Ireland. Any persons convicted of wearing, selling (except for exportation), or making up for hire any cambric or French lawns, are liable to a penalty of 5 *l.* by the two first statutes cited above.

CAMBRIDGE, a town of England, and capital of the county of that name. It takes the name of Cambridge from the bridge over the Cam, which divides the town into two parts. Either it or a place in the neighbourhood was styled *Camboritum* in the time of the Romans. It suffered much during the wars with the Danes. Here was a castle built by William the Conqueror, of which the gatehouse yet remains, and is now the county goal. By Doomsday-book it appears, that it then had ten wards, containing 387 houses. In William Rufus's reign it was quite destroyed by Roger de Montgomery; but Henry I. bestowed flowed many privileges upon it to encourage its resturation, particularly an exemption from the power of the sheriff, on condition of its paying yearly into the exchequer 100 merks (equivalent to 1000 pounds now), and from tolls, lastage, pontage, passage, and stallage, in all fairs of his dominions. It was afterwards often plundered in the barons wars by the outlaws from the isle of Ely, till Henry III. secured it by a deep ditch. In 1381, Richard II. held a parliament here. In the rebellion of Wat Tyler and Jack Straw against that prince, the university records were taken and burnt in the market-place.

The modern town is about one mile long from S. to N. and about half a mile broad in the middle, diminishing at the extremities. It has 14 parish-churches, of which two are without any towers. It contains above 1500 houses; but the private buildings are neither elegant or large, owing chiefly to their being held on college or corporation leases. It is governed by a mayor, high-steward, recorder, 13 aldermen, and 24 common council-men, a town-clerk, &c. Its chief trade is water carriage from hence to Downham, Lynn, Ely, &c. The Jews being encouraged to settle in England by William I. and II. were very populous here for several generations, and inhabited that street now called the *Jewry*. They had a synagogue, since converted to a parish church, called from the shape of its tower *Round Church*; though others are of opinion, that it was built by the Knights Templars, it bearing a resemblance to the temple church in London. The market-place is situated in the middle of the town, and consists of two spacious oblong squares united together; at the top of the angle stands the shire-hall, lately erected at the expence of the county. At the back of the shire-hall is the town-hall and gaol. In the market place, fronting the shire-hall, is a remarkable handsome stone conduit, to which water is conveyed by an aqueduct, which was the benefaction of the celebrated Hobson, a carrier in the reign of James I. who was a native of this town. A fine road for the benefit of the inhabitants and students was made a few years since for 4 miles, from this town to Gogmagog-hills, pursuant to the will of Mr Worts. The late Dr Addenbroke also left it 4000 l. towards building and furnishing an hospital for the cure of poor diseased people gratis; of which charity the master of Catharine-hall is a trustee; which hospital has been erected at the south-east end of the town. At a little distance from Benet-college is the botanic garden of 5 acres, and a large house for the use of the governors and the residence of the curator, given to the university by the late Dr Walker, who settled an estate on it towards its support; to which the late Mr Edward Betham added a very considerable benefaction. The town has fairs on June 24. and Aug. 24.

The glory of Cambridge is its university; but when it had its beginning is uncertain. At first there was no public provision for the accommodation or maintenance of the scholars; but afterwards inns began to be erected by pious persons for their reception, and in the time of Edward I. colleges began to be built and endowed. This university, not inferior to any in Christendom, consists of 12 colleges and 4 halls, which have the same privileges as the colleges. The whole body, which is commonly about 1500, enjoys very great privileges granted by several of our sovereigns; but it was James I. who impowered it to send two members to parliament, as the town had done from the first. The university is governed, 1. By a chancellor, who is always some nobleman, and may be changed every three years, or continued longer by the tacit consent of the university. 2. By a high-steward, chosen by the senate, and holding his place by patent from the university. 3. By a vice-chancellor, who is the head of some college or hall, and chosen yearly by the body of the university, the heads of the colleges naming two. 4. By two proctors chosen every year, according to the cycle of colleges and halls; as are two taxors, who with the proctors regulate the weights and measures, as clerks of markets. The proctors also inspect the behaviour of the scholars, who must not be out of their colleges after nine at night. Here are also 2 moderators, 2 scrutators, a commissary, public orator, 2 librarians, a register, a school-keeper, 3 esquire beadles and a yeoman beadle, 18 professors, and the caput, consisting of the vice-chancellor, a doctor of divinity, a doctor of laws, a doctor of physic, a regent, and a non regent master of arts. Henry VI. granted it the power to print all books of any kind within itself, a privilege which Oxford had not. The senate-house of the university is an elegant building of the Corinthian order, cost near 16,000 l building; in which, on the north side is a fine statue of George I. erected in 1739 at the expence of the late Lord Townsend; opposite to this on the south side is another of George II. erected in 1763 at the expence of the late Duke of Newcastle: at the east end, on each side of the entrance, are two others; one, the late duke of Somerset, after the Vandyke taste; the other, an Italian emblematical figure of Gloria. This is allowed to be the most superb room in England, being 101 feet long, 42 broad, and 32 high; and it has a gallery which can contain 1000 persons. This building forms the north side of a quadrangle, as the schools and public library do the west, the schools being the ground floor, and the library over them surrounding a small court. North of the philosophy school is the repository of Dr Woodward's fossils, ores, shells, &c. The doctor, together with that collection and a part of his library, left a sum of money to this university for erecting a professorship for natural philosophy, with a provision of 150 l. a-year for ever. At the south-east corner of this building is an elegant geometrical stone staircase which leads to the old library, and consists of 18 classes; at the end of which is an elegant square room, in which are deposited the MSS. and a valuable cabinet of oriental books and curiosities, &c. This room opens to two other rooms, containing 26 large classes consisting of 30,000 volumes presented the university by George I. being the entire collection of Dr Moor bishop of Ely, and purchased of the doctor's executors by his majesty for 6000 guineas; before which his majesty gave the university 2000 l. to defray the expence of fitting up the apartments and erecting classes for their reception; they consist of the first editions of the Greek and Latin classics and historians, and the greatest part of the works of the first printers; large collections of prints of the greatest masters; and a valuable MS. of the Gospels and Acts of the Apostles on vellum, in Greek and Latin capitals, given the university by Theodore

Beza,

Cambridge

Beza, and supposed to be as old as any MS. extant. The other part of the library has been rebuilt in an elegant manner, and forms the west side of the intended quadrangle. The books which are contained in the last room are part of the old library augmented with a considerable number of the best modern books, several of which are presents from foreign sovereigns and eminent men. The south side of this quadrangle is designed for a building to contain the printing-office, &c. of the university, for which preparations began lately to be made by pulling down the old buildings on the spot. St Mary's church forms the east side of this quadrangle: here the university have their public sermons; and the pulpit, which stands in the centre of the church and faces the chancel, has no sounding-board. In a grand gallery over part of the chancel is a seat for the chancellor, vice-chancellor, &c. George I. when he gave the books, also established a professor of modern history and modern languages in this university, with a salary of 400l. for himself and two persons under him qualified to instruct in that branch 20 scholars, to be nominated by the king, each of which is obliged to learn two at least of the languages. A fellowship is founded at Magdalen college, appropriated to the gentlemen of Norfolk, and called *the travelling Norfolk fellowship*. All the libraries in Cambridge, except that of the king's-college, are lending libraries; and those at Oxford are studying libraries. The different colleges are as follows.

1. St Peter's, the most ancient, and the first on entering the town from London, consisting of two courts, separated by a cloister and gallery. The largest is 144 feet long, 84 broad. The buildings in this court have been lately repaired in an elegant manner. The lesser court is divided by the chapel, which is a fine old building 54 feet long, 27 broad, and 27 high. This college was founded 1257. There are three colleges in Oxford which dispute the antiquity with this. Cambridge and Oxford were universities long before they were possessed of any colleges in their own right, the students then lodging and boarding with the townsmen, and they then hired hotels for their exercises and disputations. A hotel or hall, now denominated *Pythagoras's school*, situated on the west side of the river, is one of the ancient hotels that remains undemolished, and in which Erasmus read his first Greek lectures in England. 2. Clare-hall, on the bank of the river, over which it has an elegant stone-bridge, was founded 1326, consisting of one grand court 150 feet long and 111 broad. The front of this building that faces the fields has the appearance of a palace. To this college a new chapel has been added. 3. Pembroke hall is near St Peter's college, and was founded in 1343, consists of two courts. It has an elegant chapel built by Sir Christ. Wren. 4 Corpus Christi or Benet college, founded in 1350, has but a mean appearance, but is possessed of a remarkably large collection of valuable and curious ancient manuscripts. 5. Trinity-hall, on the north of Clare-hall, near the river, was founded in 1351: it is a small but remarkably neat building. 6. Gonvil and Caius college is near the middle of the town, north of the senate-house, and has three courts. It was founded 1348, and augmented 1557. 7. King's-college, the most noble foundation in Europe, was first endowed by Henry VI. The old court resembles a decayed castle more than a college. The new building is very magnificent, near 300 feet long. The chapel is one of the finest pieces of Gothic architecture now remaining in the world. It is 304 feet long, 73 broad on the outside and 40 within, and 91 high; and yet not a single pillar to sustain its ponderous roofs, of which it has two: the first is of stone, most curiously carved; the other of wood, covered with lead, between which is a vacancy of 10 feet. There is such a profusion of carvings both within and without as is no where to be equalled. Henry VII. enlarged it 188 feet in length, and Henry VIII. gave the elegant stalls and organ gallery, with its inimitable carvings, where are the coats of arms of that king and those of Anne Boleyn quartered. He gave also the elegant painted glass windows, which are in fine preservation, and were permitted by Cromwell to be preserved when almost every other in England was destroyed, as he had a particular regard for this university where he had his education, and for the town which he had represented in parliament. A new altar has been lately erected, which corresponds with the architecture of the building, embellished with an antique painting of Christ taking down from the cross, purchased in Italy, and presented the college by the earl of Carlisle. In this chapel are put up the Spanish colours taken at the reduction of Manilla by Colonel Draper, a member of this college. This college has an ancient stone-bridge over the Cam. 8. Queen's-college, near the river, south of King's, was founded 1448, and consists of two courts, with a fine grove and gardens on both sides of the river, connected with each other and the college by two wooden bridges, one of which is of a curious structure. 9. Catharine-hall is east of Queen's, and its principal front on the west, the most extensive and regular in the university. It contains only one court 180 feet long and 110 broad, and was founded in 1475. 10 Jesus college is at the east end of the town, surrounded by groves and gardens. The principal front faces the south 180 feet long, regularly built and sashed; it was originally a benedictine convent, and converted to the present use 1576. 11. Christ's college is opposite to St Andrew's church, on the east side of the town; and was founded by Henry VII.'s mother in 1505. It has lately had a thorough repair, and is now a neat and beautiful structure. 12. St John's college was founded by the same lady in 1509, on the site of a dissolved priory. It consists of three courts, and has a large library filled with scarce and valuable books. To this college belongs a fine stone-bridge over the river, which leads to their grand walks. 13. Magdalen college, the only one that stands on the north side of the river, near the great bridge, consists of two courts, and was founded in 1519. 14. Trinity college is east of the river, having St John's college on the north and Caius's college and Trinity-hall on the south. It contains two large quadrangles, the first of which is 344 feet long and 280 broad. It has two noble entrances; and on the north side of it is the chapel 204 feet long, 34 broad, and 44 high. It has every grand ornament, and the much admired statue of Sir Isaac Newton, who was a student in this college. The hall is above 100 feet long, 40 broad, and 50 high. The inner court is esteemed the finest in the university, and surpasses

passes

Cambridge.

paſſes any in Oxford. It is very ſpacious, and has an elegant cloiſter of ſtone pillars, ſupporting grand apartments; on the weſt is the library, the moſt elegant ſtructure of the kind in the kingdom, 190 feet long, 40 broad, and 38 high within. Its entrance is by a ſtair-caſe, the ſteps black marble, and the walls incruſted with ancient Roman monuments. The entrance into the library is by folding doors at the north end. Its inſide appearance is inexpreſſibly grand, having at the ſouth end (lately erected) a beautiful painted glaſs window of his preſent majeſty in his robes; and the claſſes are large, beautiful, and noble, well ſtocked with books, manuſcripts, &c. Its outſide has every ſuitable embelliſhment, and was erected by Sir Chriſtopher Wren at the expence of near 20,000 l. Under this building is a ſpacious piazza of equal dimenſions; out of which opens three gates to a lawn that leads to the river, over which is a new elegant cycloidal bridge of three arches, leading to extenſive walks. In the middle is a remarkable viſta. This college was founded on the ſite of two other colleges and a hall in 1546 by Henry VIII. 15. Emanuel college is at the ſouth-eaſt end of the town; conſiſts of two courts, the principal of which is very neat; and was built on the ſite of a Dominican convent. It has been lately in a great part rebuilt and elegantly embelliſhed. 16. Sidney-Suſſex college is in Bridge-ſtreet. Its hall is elegant, but chapel remarkable only for ſtanding north and ſouth, as others do eaſt and weſt.

CAMBRIDGESHIRE, an inland county of England, bounded on the eaſt by Norfolk and Suffolk, on the ſouth by Eſſex and Hertfordſhire, on the weſt by Bedfordſhire and Huntingdonſhire, and on the north by Lincolnſhire. Prior to the arrival of the *Romans* it was included in the antient diviſion of the Iceni; and after their conqueſt in the third province of Flavia Cæſarienſis, which reached from the Thames to the Humber. During the Heptarchy it belonged to the kingdom of Eaſt Angles, the ſixth kindom, which began in 575, and ended in 792, having had 14 kings; and it is now included in the Norfolk circuit, the dioceſe of Ely, and province of Canterbury, except a ſmall part which is in the dioceſe of Norwich. It is about 40 miles in length from north to ſouth, and 25 in breadth from eaſt to weſt, and is 130 miles in circumference, containing near 570,000 acres. It has about 17,400 houſes, 140,000 inhabitants, is divided into 17 hundreds, in which are one city, Ely; 8 market towns, viz. Cambridge which is the ſhire town and a celebrated univerſity, Caxton, Linton, Merch, Newmarket, Soham, Wiſbeach, Thorney, and part of Royſton; 280 villages, 64 pariſhes, ſends 2 members to parliaments (excluſive of 2 for the town and 2 for the univerſity), pays one part of the land tax, and provides 480 men in the militia. Its only rivers are the Cam, the Nene, and the Ouſe. A conſiderable tract of land in this county is diſtinguiſhed by the name of the Iſle of Ely. It conſiſts of fenny ground, divided by innumerable channels and drains; and is part of a very ſpacious level, containing 300,000 acres of land, extending into Norfolk, Suffolk, Huntingdonſhire, and Lincolnſhire. The Iſle of Ely is the north diviſion of the county, and extends ſouth almoſt as far as Cambridge. The whole level of which this is part, is bounded on one ſide by the ſea, and on the others by uplands; which, taken together, forms a rude kind of ſemicircle reſembling a horſe-ſhoe. The air is very different in different parts of the county. In the fens it is moiſt and foggy, and therefore not ſo wholeſome; but in the ſouth and eaſt parts it is very good, theſe being much drier than the other: but both, by late improvements, have been rendered very fruitful, the former by draining, and the latter by cinquefoil: ſo that it produces plenty of corn, eſpecially barley, ſaffron, and hemp, and affords the richeſt paſtures. The rivers abound with fiſh, and the fens with wild fowl. The principal manufactures of the country are malt, paper, and baſkets. As the above tract appears to have been dry land formerly, the great change it has undergone muſt have been owing either to a violent breach and inundation of the ſea or to earthquakes. As the towns in and about the fens were great ſufferers by the ſtagnation of the waters in ſummer, and want of proviſions in winter, many attempts were made to drain them, but without ſucceſs, until the time of Charles I. in which, and that of his ſon, the work was happily completed, and an act of parliament paſſed, by which a corporation was eſtabliſhed for its preſervation and government. By the ſame act, 83,000 acres were veſted in the corporation and 10,000 in the king. In theſe fens are a great many DECOYS, in which incredible numbers of ducks, and other wild fowl, are caught during the ſeaſon.

Cambridge, Camden.

New Cambridge, a town of New England about three miles from Boſton, remarkable for an univerſity conſiſting of three colleges. W. Long. 70. 4. N. Lat. 42. 0.

Cambridge Manuſcript, a copy of the Goſpels and Acts of the Apoſtles in Greek and Latin. Beza found it in the monaſtery of Irenæus at Lyons in the year 1562, and gave it to the univerſity of Cambridge in 1582. It is a quarto ſize, and written on vellum; 66 leaves of it are much torn and mutilated, ten of which are ſupplied by a later tranſcriber. Beza conjectures, that this manuſcript might have exiſted ſo early as the time of Irenæus: Wetſtein apprehends, that it either returned or was firſt brought from Egypt into France; that it is the ſame copy which Druthmar, an ancient expoſitor who lived about the year 840, had ſeen, and which, he obſerves, was aſcribed to St Hilary; and that R. Stephens had given a particular account of it in his edition of the New Teſtament in 1550. It is uſually called *Stevens's ſecond manuſcript*. Mill agrees with F. Simon in opinion, that it was written in the weſtern part of the world by a Latin ſcribe, and that it is to a great degree interpolated and corrupted: he obſerves, that it agrees ſo much with the Latin Vulgate, as to afford reaſon for concluding, that it was corrected or formed upon a corrupt and faulty copy of that tranſlation. From this and the Clermont copy of St Paul's Epiſtles, Beza publiſhed his larger Annotations in 1582.

CAMBYSES. See (*Hiſtory of*) PERSIA.

CAMDEN (William), the great antiquarian, was born in London in the year 1551. His father was a native of Litchfield in Staffordſhire, who ſettling in London, became a member of the company of painter-ſtainers, and lived in the Old Bailey. His mother was of the ancient family of Curwen, of Workington in Cumberland. He was educated firſt at Chriſt's hoſpital, and afterwards at St Paul's ſchool; from thence he was ſent, in 1566, to Oxford, and entered ſervitor of Magdalen college; but being diſappointed of a demy's

Camden.

ny's place, he removed to Broad-gate hall, and somewhat more than two years after, to Christ-church, where he was supported by his kind friend and patron Dr Thornton. About this time he was a candidate for a fellowship of All-Souls college, but lost it by the intrigues of the Popish party. In 1570, he supplicated the regents of the university to be admitted bachelor of arts; but in this also he miscarried. The following year Mr Camden came to London, where he prosecuted his favourite study of antiquity, under the patronage of Dr Goodman, dean of Westminster, by whose interest he was made second master of Westminster school in 1575. From the time of his leaving the university to this period, he took several journeys to different parts of England, with a view to make observations and collect materials for his *Britannia*, in which he was now deeply engaged. In 1581 he became intimately acquainted with the learned president Brisson, who was then in England; and in 1586 he published the first edition of his Britannia; a work which, though much enlarged and improved in future editions, was even then esteemed an honour to its author, and the glory of his country. In 1593 he succeeded to the head mastership of Westminster school on the resignation of Dr Grant. In this office he continued till 1597, when he was promoted to be Clarencieux king at arms. In the year 1600 Mr Camden made a tour to the north, as far as Carlisle, accompanied by his friend Mr (afterwards Sir Robert) Cotton. In 1606 he began his correspondence with the celebrated president de Thou, which continued to the death of that faithful historian. In the following year he published his last edition of the Britannia, which is that from which the several English translations have been made; and in 1608, he began to digest his materials for a history of the reign of queen Elizabeth. In 1609, after recovering from a dangerous illness, he retired to Chiselhurst in Kent, where he continued to spend the summer months during the remainder of his life. The first part of his annals of the queen did not appear till the year 1615, and he determined that the second volume should not appear till after his death (A). The work was entirely finished in 1617; and from that time he was principally employed in collecting more materials for the further improvement of his Britannia. In 1622, being now upwards of 70, and finding his health decline apace, he determined to lose no time in executing his design of founding an history-lecture in the university of Oxford. His deed of gift was accordingly transmitted by his friend Mr Heather to Mr Gregory Wheare, who was, by himself, appointed his first professor. He died at Chiselhurst in 1623, in the 73d year of his age; and was buried with great solemnity in Westminster-abbey in the south aisle, where a monument of white marble was erected to his memory. Camden was a man of singular modesty and integrity; profoundly learned in the history and antiquities of this kingdom, and a judicious and indefatigable historian. He was reverenced and esteemed by the literati of all nations, and will be ever remembered as an honour to the age and country wherein he lived. Besides the works already mentioned, he was author of an excellent Greek grammar, and of several tracts in Hearne's collection. But his great and most useful work, the *Britannia*, is that upon which his fame is chiefly built. The edition above mentioned, to which he put his last hand, was correctly printed in folio, much augmented, amended where it was necessary, and adorned with maps. It was first translated into English, and published in folio at London, in 1611, by the laborious Dr Philemon Holland, a physician of Coventry, who is thought to have consulted our author himself; and therefore great respect has been paid to the additions and explanations that occur therein, on a supposition that they may belong to Camden. But in a later edition of the same translation, published in 1636, the Doctor has taken liberties which cannot either be defended or excused. A new translation, made with the utmost fidelity from the last edition of our author's work, was published in 1695, by Edmund Gibson of Queen's College in Oxford, afterwards bishop of Lincoln; in which, besides the addition of notes, and of all that deserved to be taken notice of in Dr Holland's first edition, which, though thrown out of the text, is preserved at the bottom of the page, there are many other augmentations and improvements, all properly distinguished from the genuine work of the author, as they ought to be; and the same judicious method obtained in the next edition of the same performance, which was justly considered as the very best book of its kind that had been hitherto published. But the public has recently been put in possession of a new translation, and still more improved edition, by that learned and industrious topographer Mr Gough, under whose hands it has been enlarged to near double the size of the last of the preceding editions.

Camden, Camel.

CAMEL, in zoology. See CAMELUS.

CAMEL, in merchandise, a kind of machine used in Holland for raising or lifting ships, in order to bring them over the Pampus, which is at the mouth of the river Y, where the shallowness of the water hinders large ships from passing. It is also used in other places, particularly at the dock of Petersburg, the vessels built here being in their passage to Cronstadt lifted over the bar by means of camels. These machines were originally invented by the celebrated De Wit, for the purpose above mentioned; and were introduced into Russia by Peter the Great, who obtained the model of them when he worked in Holland as a common shipwright. A camel is composed of two separate parts; whose outsides are perpendicular, and whose insides are concave, shaped so as to embrace the hull of a ship on both sides. Each part has a small cabin with sixteen pumps and ten plugs, and contains twenty men. They are braced to a ship underneath by means of cables, and entirely enclose its sides and bottom; being then towed to the bar,

(A) The reign of queen Elizabeth was so recent when the first volume of the Annals was published, that many of the persons concerned, or their dependents, were still living. It is no wonder, therefore, that the honest historian should offend those whose actions would not bear inquiry. Some of his enemies were clamorous and troublesome; which determined him not to publish the second volume during his life; but that posterity might be in no danger of disappointment, he deposited one copy in the Cotton Library, and transmitted another to his friend Dupuy at Paris. It was first printed at Leyden in 1625.

African Camel, or Dromedary.

Bactrian Camel.

[illegible]

bar, the plugs are opened, and the water admitted until the camel sinks with the ship and runs a-ground. Then, the water being pumped out, the camel rises, lifts up the vessel, and the whole is towed over the bar. This machine can raise the ship eleven feet, or, in other words, make it draw eleven feet less water.

CAMELFORD, a borough town of Cornwall in England, consisting of about 100 houses, badly built; but the streets are broad and well paved. W. Long. 5. 4. N. Lat. 50. 40. It sends two members to parliament; and gives title of baron to Thomas Pitt, elder, brother of the great earl of Chatham.

CAMELLIA, in botany: A genus of the polyandria order, belonging to the monodelphia class of plants; and in the natural method ranking under the 37th order, *Columniferæ*. The calyx is imbricated and polyphyllous, with the interior leaves larger than the exterior ones. Of this genus there is but one species, a native both of China and Japan. Thunberg, in his *Flora Japonica*, describes it as growing every where in the groves and gardens of Japan, where it becomes a prodigiously large and tall tree, highly esteemed by the natives for the elegance of its large and very variable blossoms, and its evergreen leaves; it is there found with single and double flowers, which also are white, red, and purple, and produced from April to October. Representations of this flower are frequently met with in Chinese paintings. With us, the *Camellia* is generally treated as a stove plant, and propagated by layers; it is sometimes placed in the greenhouse; but it appears to us to be one of the properest plants imaginable for the conservatory. At some future time it may, perhaps, not be uncommon to treat it as a *Laurustinus* or *Magnolia*: the high price at which it has hitherto been sold, may have prevented its being hazarded in this way. The blossoms are of a firm texture, but apt to fall off long before they have lost their brilliancy; it therefore is a practice with some to stick such deciduous blossoms on some fresh bud, where they continue to look well for a considerable time. Petiver considered this plant as a species of tea-tree; and future observations will probably confirm his conjecture.

CAMELODUM. See CAMALODUNUM.

CAMELOPARDALIS, in zoology, the trivial name of a species of CERVUS.

CAMELUS, or CAMEL, in zoology, a genus of quadrupeds belonging to the order of pecora. The characters of the camel are these: It has no horns; it has six fore-teeth in the under jaw; the laniarii are wide set, three in the upper, and two in the lower jaw; and there is a fissure in the upper lip, resembling a cleft in the lip of a hare. The species are:

1. The dromedarius, or Arabian camel, with one bunch or protuberance on the back. It has four callous protuberances on the fore-legs, and two on the hind ones. This species is common in Africa, and the warmer parts of Asia; not that it is spread over either of the continents. It is a common beast of burden in Egypt, and along the countries which border on the Mediterranean Sea; in the kingdom of Morocco, Sara or the Desert, and in Ethiopia: but no where south of those kingdoms. In Asia, it is equally common in Turky and Arabia; but is scarcely seen farther north than Persia, being too tender to bear a more severe climate. India is destitute of this animal.

2. The Bactrianus, or Bactrian camel, has two bunches on the back, but is in all other respects like the preceding; of which it seems to be a mere variety, rather than a different species; and is equally adapted for riding or carrying loads. It is still found wild in the deserts of the temperate parts of Asia, particularly in those between China and India. These are larger and more generous than the domesticated race. The Bactrian camel, which is very common in Asia, is extremely hardy, and in great use among the Tartars and Mongols, as a beast of burden, from the Caspian Sea to the empire of China. It bears even so severe a climate as that of Siberia, being found about the lake Baikal, where the Burats and Mongols keep great numbers. They are far less than those which inhabit Western Tartary. Here they live during winter on willows and other trees, and are by this diet reduced very lean. They lose their hair in April, and go naked all May, amidst the frosts of that severe climate. To thrive, they must have dry ground and salt marshes. There are several varieties among the camels. The Turkman is the largest and strongest. The Arabian is hardy. What is called the Dromedary, Maihary, and Raguahl, is very swift. The common sort travel about 30 miles a day. The last, which has a less bunch, and more delicate shape, and also is much inferior in size, never carries burdens; but is used to ride on. In Arabia, they are trained for running-matches: and in many places for carrying couriers, who can go above 100 miles a day on them; and that for nine days together, over burning deserts, unhabitable by any living creature. The African camels are the most hardy, having more distant and more dreadful deserts to pass over than any of the others, from Numidia to the kingdom of Ethiopia. In Western Tartary there is a white variety, very scarce, and sacred to the idols and priests. The Chinese have a swift variety, which they call by the expressive name of Fong Kyo Fo, or camels with feet of the wind. Fat of camels, or, as those people call it, oil of bunches, being drawn from them, is esteemed in many disorders, such as ulcers, numbness, and consumptions. This species of camel is rare in Arabia, being an exotic, and only kept by the great men.

Camels have constituted the riches of Arabia from the time of Job to the present day. The patriarch reckoned 6000 camels among his pastoral treasures, and the modern Arabs estimate their wealth by the numbers of these useful animals. Without them great part of Africa would be wretched; by them the whole commerce is carried through arid and burning tracts, impassable but by beasts which Providence formed expressly for the scorched deserts. Their soles are adapted to the sands they are to pass over, their toughness and spungy softness preventing them from cracking. Their great powers of sustaining abstinence from drinking, enable them to pass over unwatered tracts for many days, without requiring the least liquid; and their patience under hunger is such, that they will travel many days fed only with a few dates, or some small balls of bean or barley-meal, or on the miserable thorny plants they meet with in the deserts.

The Arabians regard the camel as a present from heaven, a sacred animal, without whose assistance they could neither subsist, carry on trade, nor travel. Camel's mel's milk is their common food. They also eat its flesh, that of the young camel being reckoned highly savoury. Of the hair of those animals, which is fine and soft, and which is completely renewed every year, the Arabians make stuffs for clothes, and other furniture. With their camels, they not only want nothing, but have nothing to fear. In one day, they can perform a journey of fifty leagues into the desert, which cuts off every approach from their enemies. All the armies of the world would perish in pursuit of a troop of Arabs. Hence they never submit, unless from choice, to any power. With a view to his predatory expeditions, the Arab instructs, rears, and exercises his camels. A few days after their birth, he folds their limbs under their belly, forces them to remain on the ground, and, in this situation, loads them with a pretty heavy weight, which is never removed but for the purpose of replacing a greater. Instead of allowing them to feed at pleasure, and to drink when they are dry, he begins with regulating their meals, and makes them gradually travel long journeys, diminishing, at the same time, the quantity of their aliment. When they acquire some strength, they are trained to the course. He excites their emulation by the example of horses, and, in time, renders them more robust. In fine, after he is certain of the strength, fleetness, and sobriety of his camels, he loads them both with his own and their food, sets off with them, arrives unperceived at the confines of the desert, robs the first passengers he meets, pillages the solitary houses, loads his camels with the booty, and, if pursued, he is obliged to accelerate his retreat. It is on these occasions that he unfolds his own talents and those of the camels. He mounts one of the fleetest, conducts the troop, and makes them travel night and day, without, almost, either stopping, eating, or drinking; and, in this manner, he easily performs a journey of three hundred leagues in eight days. During this period of motion and fatigue, his camels are perpetually loaded, and he allows them each day, one hour only of repose, and a ball of paste. They often run in this manner nine or ten days, without finding water; and when, by chance, there is a pool at some distance, they scent the water half a league off. Thirst makes them double their pace, and they drink as much at once as serves them for the time that is past, and as much to come; for their journeys often last several weeks, and their abstinence continues an equal time.

Of all carriages, that by camels is the cheapest and most expeditious. The merchants and other passengers unite in a caravan, to prevent the insults and robberies of the Arabs. These caravans are often very numerous, and are always composed of more camels than men. Each camel is loaded in proportion to his strength; and, when overloaded, he refuses to march, and continues lying till his burden is lightened. The large camels generally carry a thousand, or even twelve hundred pounds weight, and the smallest from six to seven hundred. In these commercial travels, their march is not hastened: As the route is often seven or eight hundred leagues, their motions and journeys are regulated. They walk only, and perform about from ten to twelve leagues each day. Every night they are unloaded, and allowed to pasture at freedom. When in a rich country, or fertile meadow, they eat, in less than an hour, as much as serves them to ruminate the whole night, and to nourish them during twenty-four hours. But they seldom meet with such pastures; neither is this delicate food necessary for them. They even seem to prefer wormwood, thistles, nettles, broom, cassia, and other prickly vegetables, to the softest herbage. As long as they find plants to browse, they easily dispense with drink. This facility of abstaining long from drink proceeds not, however, from habit alone, but is rather an effect of their structure. Independent of the four stomachs, which are common to ruminating animals, the camels have a fifth bag, which serves them as a reservoir for water. This fifth stomach is peculiar to the camel. It is so large as to contain a vast quantity of water, where it remains without corrupting, or mixing with the other aliments. When the animal is pressed with thirst, and has occasion for water to macerate his dry food in ruminating, he makes part of this water mount into his paunch, or even as high as the œsophagus, by a simple contraction of certain muscles. It is by this singular construction that the camel is enabled to pass several days without drinking, and to take at a time a prodigious quantity of water, which remains in the reservoir pure and limpid, because neither the liquors of the body, nor the juices of digestion, can mix with it. Travellers, when much oppressed with drought, are sometimes obliged to kill their camels in order to have a supply of drink from these reservoirs. These inoffensive creatures must suffer much; for they utter the most lamentable cries, especially when overloaded. But, though perpetually oppressed, their fortitude is equal to their docility. At the first signal, they bend their knees and lie down to be loaded, which saves their conductor the trouble of raising the goods to a great height. As soon as they are loaded, they rise spontaneously, and without any assistance. One of them is mounted by their conductor, who goes before, and regulates the march of all the followers. They require neither whip nor spur. But, when they begin to be tired, their courage is supported, or rather their fatigue is charmed, by singing, or by the sound of some instrument. Their conductors relieve each other in singing; and, when they want to prolong the journey, they give the animals but one hour's rest; after which, resuming their song, they proceed on their march for several hours more, and the singing is continued till they arrive at another resting place, when the camels again lie down; and their loads, by unloosing the ropes, are allowed to glide off on each side of the animals. Thus they sleep on their bellies in the middle of their baggage, which, next morning is fixed on their backs with equal quickness and facility as it had been detached the evening before.

Fatigue, hunger, thirst, and meagreness, are not the only inconveniencies to which these animals are subjected: To all these evils they are prepared by castration. One male is only left for eight or ten females; and the labouring camels are generally geldings. They are unquestionably weaker than unmutilated males; but they are more tractable, and at all seasons ready for service. While the former are not only unmanageable, but almost furious, during the rutting season, which lasts forty days, and returns annually in the spring. It is then said, that they foam

con-

Camelus.

continually, and than one or two red vesicles, as large as a hog's bladder, issue from their mouths. In this season they eat little, attack and bite animals, and even their own masters, to whom at all other times they are very submissive. Their mode of copulating differs from that of all other quadrupeds; for the female, instead of standing, lies down on her knees, and receives the male in the same position that she reposes, or is loaded. This posture, to which the animals are early accustomed, becomes natural, since they assume it spontaneously in coition. The time of gestation is near twelve months, and, like all large quadrupeds, the females bring forth only one at a birth. Her milk is copious and thick; and, when mixed with a large quantity of water, affords an excellent nourishment to men. The females are not obliged to labour, but are allowed to pasture and produce at full liberty. The advantage derived from their produce and their milk is perhaps superior to what could be drawn from their working. In some places, however, most of the females are castrated, in order to fit them for labour; and it is alleged, that this operation, instead of diminishing, augments their strength, vigour, and plumpness. In general, the fatter camels are, they are the more capable of enduring great fatigue. Their bunches seem to proceed from a redundance of nourishment: for, during long journeys, in which their conductor is obliged to husband their food, and where they often suffer much hunger and thirst, these bunches gradually diminish, and become so flat, that the place where they were is only perceptible by the length of the hair, which is always longer on these parts than on the rest of the back. The meagreness of the body augments in proportion as the bunches decrease. The Moors, who transport all articles of merchandise from Barbary and Numidia, as far as Æthiopia, set out with their camels well laden, which are very fat and vigorous; and bring back the same animals so meagre, that they commonly sell at a low price to the Arabs of the Desert, to be again fattened.

We are told by the ancients, that camels are in a condition for propagating at the age of three years. This assertion is suspicious; for, in three years, they have not acquired one half of their growth. The penis of the male, like that of the bull, is very long, and very slender. During erection, it stretches forward, like that of all other quadrupeds; but, in its ordinary state, the sheath is drawn backward, and the urine is discharged from between the hind legs; so that both males and females urine in the same manner. The young camel sucks his mother twelve months; but, when meant to be trained, in order to render him strong and robust in the chace, he is allowed to suck and pasture at freedom during the first years, and is not loaded, or made to perform any labour, till he is four years old. He generally lives forty and sometimes fifty years, which duration of life is proportioned to the time of his growth. There is no foundation for what has been advanced by some authors, that he lives one hundred years.

By considering, under one point of view, all the qualities of this animal, and all the advantages derived from him, it must be acknowledged that he is the most useful creature subjected to the service of man. Gold and silk constitute not the true riches of the East. The camel is the genuine treasure of Asia. He is more valuable than the elephant; for he may be said to perform an equal quantity of labour at a twentieth part of the expence. Besides, the whole species are under subjection to man, who propagates and multiplies them at pleasure. But he has no such dominion over the elephants, whom he cannot multiply, and the individuals of whom he conquers with great labour and difficulty. The camel is not only more valuable than the elephant, but is perhaps equal in utility to the horse, the ass, and the ox, when their powers are united. He carries as much as two mules; though he eats as little, and feeds upon herbs equally coarse as the ass. The female furnishes milk longer than the cow. The flesh of a young camel is as good and wholesome as veal: The Africans and Arabs fill their pots and tubs with it, which is fried with grease, and preserved in this manner during the whole year for their ordinary repasts; The hair is finer and more in request than the best wool. Even their excrements are useful: for sal ammoniac is made of their urine; and their dung, dried in the sun and pulverised, serves for litter to themselves, as well as to horses, with which people frequently travel in countries where no hay or straw can be had. In fine, their dung makes excellent fuel, which burns freely, and gives as clear and nearly as hot a flame as dry wood, which is of great use in the deserts, where not a tree is to be found, and where, for want of combustible materials, fire is as scarce as water.

Camelus.

3. The Glama, Llama, or South-American camel-sheep, has an almost even back, small head, fine black eyes, and very long neck, bending much, and very protuberant near the junction with the body: in a tame state, with smooth short hair; in a wild state, with long coarse hair, white, grey, and russet, disposed in spots; with a black line from the head along the top of the back to the tail, and belly white. The spotted may possibly be the tame, the last the wild, llamas. The tail is short; the height from four to four feet and a half; the length from the neck to the tail, six feet. The carcase divested of skin and offals, according to the editor of Mr Byron's voyage, weighed 200lb. In general, the shape exactly resembles a camel, only it wants the dorsal bunch. It is the camel of Peru and Chili; and, before the arrival of the Spaniards, was the only beast of burden known to the Indians. It is very mild, gentle, and tractable. Before the introduction of mules, they were used by the Indians to plough the land: at present they serve to carry burdens of about 100lb. They go with great gravity; and, like their Spanish masters, nothing can prevail upon them to change their pace. They lie down to the burden; and when wearied, no blows can provoke them to go on. Feuillee says, they are so capricious, that if struck, they instantly squat down, and nothing but caresses can make them arise. When angry, they have no other method of revenging their injuries than by spitting; and they can ejaculate their saliva to the distance of ten paces: if it falls on the skin, it raises an itching and a reddish spot. Their flesh is eaten, and is said to be as good as mutton. The wool has a strong disagreeable scent. They are very sure-footed; therefore used to carry the Peruvian ores over the ruggedest hills and narrowest paths of the Andes. They

inhabit that vast chain of mountains their whole length to the straits of Magellan; but except where these hills approach the sea, as in Patagonia, never appear on the coasts. Like the camel, they have powers of abstaining long from drink, sometimes for four or five days; like that animal, their food is coarse and trifling. —In a wild state, they keep in great herds in the highest and steepest parts of the hills; and while they are feeding, one keeps centry on the pinnacle of some rock; if it perceives the approach of any one, it neighs; the herd takes the alarm, and goes off with incredible speed. They outrun all dogs, so there is no other way of killing them but with the gun. They are killed for the sake of their flesh and hair; for the Indians weave the last into cloth. From the form of the parts of generation in both sexes, no animal copulates with such difficulty. It is often the labour of a day, *antequam actum ipsum venereum incipiant, et absolvant.*

4. The Pacos, or sheep of Chili, has no bunch on the back. It is covered with a fine valuable wool, which is of a rose red colour on the back of the animal, and white on the belly. They are of the same nature with the preceding; inhabit the same places, but are more capable of supporting the rigour of frost and snow: they live in vast herds; are very timid, and excessively swift. The Indians take the pacos in a strange manner: they tie cords with bits of cloth or wool hanging to them, above three or four feet from the ground, cross the narrow passes of the mountains, then drive those animals towards them, which are so terrified by the flutter of the rags, as not to dare to pass, but, huddling together, give the hunters an opportunity to kill with their slings as many as they please. The tame ones will carry from 50 to 75 lb.; but are kept principally for the sake of the wool and the flesh, which is exceedingly well tasted.

CAMERA Æolia, a contrivance for blowing the fire, for the fusion of ores, without bellows; by means of water falling through a funnel into a close vessel, which sends from it so much air or vapour as continually blows the fire: if there be the space of another vessel for it to expatiate in by the way, it there lets fall its humidity, which otherwise might hinder the work. This contrivance was named *camera Æolia* by Kircher.

Camera Lucida, a contrivance of Dr Hook for making the image of any thing appear on a wall in a light room, either by day or night. Opposite to the place or wall where the appearance is to be, make a hole of at least a foot in diameter, or if there be a high window with a casement of this dimension in it, this will do much better without such hole or casement opened. At a convenient distance, to prevent its being perceived by the company in the room, place the object or picture intended to be represented, but in an inverted situation. If the picture be transparent, reflect the sun's rays by means of a looking-glass, so as that they may pass through it towards the place of representation; and to prevent any rays from passing aside it, let the picture be encompassed with some board or cloth. If the object be a statue, or a living creature, it must be much enlightened by casting the sun's rays on it, either by reflection, refraction, or both. Between this object and the place of representation put a broad convex glass, ground to such a convexity as that it may represent the object distinctly in such place. The nearer this is situated to the object, the more will the image be magnified on the wall, and the further the less; such diversity depending on the difference of the spheres of the glasses. If the object cannot be conveniently inverted, there must be two large glasses of proper spheres, situated at suitable distances, easily found by trial, to make the representations erect. This whole apparatus of object, glasses, &c. with the persons employed in the management of them, are to be placed without the window or hole, so that they may not be perceived by the spectators in the room, and the operation itself will be easily performed. Phil. Trans. N° 38. p. 741. seq.

Camera Obscura, or Dark Chamber, in *Optics*, a machine, or apparatus, representing an artificial eye; whereon the images of external objects, received thro' a double convex glass, are exhibited distinctly, and in their native colours, on a white matter placed within the machine, in the focus of the glass.

The first invention of this instrument is ascribed to Baptista Porta. See his *Magia Naturalis*, lib. xvii. cap. 6. first published at Franckfort about the year 1589 or 1591; the first four books of this work were published at Antwerp in 1560.

The *camera obscura* affords very diverting spectacles; both by exhibiting images perfectly like their objects, and each clothed in their native colours; and by expressing, at the same time, all their motions; which latter no other art can imitate. By means of this instrument, a person unacquainted with designing will be able to delineate objects with the greatest accuracy and justness, and another well versed in painting will find many things herein to perfect his art. See the construction under Dioptrics.

CAMERARIA, in botany: A genus of the monogynia order, belonging to the pentandria class of plants; and in the natural method ranking under the 30th order, *Contortæ*. There are two horizontal follicles at the base of the seed-case. The seeds are inserted into a proper membrane. Of this there are two species; the latifolia, and the angustifolia. The first is a native of the island of Cuba, and rises with a shrubby stalk to the height of 10 or 12 feet, dividing into several branches, garnished with roundish pointed leaves placed opposite. The flowers are produced at the end of the branches in loose clusters, which have long tubes enlarging gradually upward, and at the top are cut into five segments, broad at their base, but ending in sharp points; the flower is of a yellowish white colour. The second sort has an irregular shrubby stalk, which rises about eight feet high, sending out many branches which are garnished with very narrow thin leaves placed opposite at each joint. The flowers are produced scatteringly at the end of the branches, which are shaped like those of the former sort, but smaller. It is a native of Jamaica. Both these plants abound with an acrid milky juice like the spurge. They are propagated by seeds, which must be procured from the places of their growth. They may also be propagated by cuttings planted in a hot-bed during the summer-months: they must have a bark-stove, for they are very tender plants; but in warm weather they must have plenty of air.

CAMERARIUS (Joachim), one of the most learned

ed writers of his time, was born in 1500, at Bamberg, a city of Franconia; and obtained great reputation by his writings. He translated into Latin Herodotus, Demosthenes, Xenophon, Euclid, Homer, Theocritus, Sophocles, Lucian, Theodoret, Nicephorus, &c. He published a catalogue of the bishops of the principal sees; Greek epistles; Accounts of his journeys, in Latin verse; a Commentary on Plautus; the Lives of Helius Eobanus Hessus, and Philip Melancthon, &c. He died in 1574.

Camerarius (Joachim), son of the former, and a learned physician, was born at Nuremberg in 1534. After having finished his studies in Germany, he went into Italy, where he obtained the esteem of the learned. At his return he was courted by several princes to live with them; but he was too much devoted to books, and the study of chemistry and botany, to comply. He wrote an hortus medicus, and several other works. He died in 1598.

CAMERATED, among builders, the same with vaulted or arched.

CAMERET-bay, in the province of Brittany in France, forms the harbour of Brest. See Brest.

CAMERINO, a town of the ecclesiastical state in Italy, situated in E. Long. 13. 7. N. Lat. 45. 5.

CAMERLINGO, according to Ducange, signified formerly the pope's or emperor's treasurer: at present, camerlingo is no where used but at Rome, where it denotes the cardinal who governs the ecclesiastical state and administers justice. It is the most eminent office at the court of Rome, because he is at the head of the treasury. During a vacation of the papal chair, the cardinal camerlingo publishes edicts, coins money, and exerts every other prerogative of a sovereign prince; he has under him a treasurer-general, auditor-general, and 12 prelates called *clerks of the chamber*.

CAMERON (John), one of the most famous divines among the Protestants of France in the 17th century, was born at Glasgow in Scotland, where he taught the Greek tongue; and having read lectures upon that language for about a year, travelled, and became professor at several universities, and minister at Bourdeaux. He published, 1. Theological lectures; 2. *Icon Johannis Cameronis*; and some miscellaneous pieces. He died in 1625, aged 60.

CAMERONIANS, a sect or party in Scotland, who separated from the Presbyterians in 1666, and continued to hold their religious assemblies in the fields.

The Cameronians took their denomination from Richard Cameron, a famous field-preacher, who, refusing to accept the indulgence to tender consciences, granted by king Charles II. as such an acceptance seemed an acknowledgment of the king's supremacy, and that he had before a right to silence them, made a defection from his brethren, and even headed a rebellion, in which he was killed. His followers were never entirely reduced till the Revolution, when they voluntarily submitted to king William.

The Cameronians adhered rigidly to the form of government established in 1648.

Cameronians, or *Cameronites*, is also the denomination of a party of Calvinists in France, who asserted that the will of man is only determined by the practical judgement of the mind; that the cause of mens doing good or evil proceeds from the knowledge which God infuses into them; and that God does not move the will physically, but only morally, in virtue of its dependence on the judgement of the mind. They had this name from John Cameron, a famous professor, first at Glasgow, where he was born, in 1580, and afterwards at Bourdeaux, Sedan, and Saumur; at which last place he broached his new doctrine of grace and free-will, which was followed by Amyraut, Cappel, Bochart, Daillé, and others of the more learned among the reformed ministers, who judged Calvin's doctrines on these points too harsh. The Cameronians are a sort of mitigated Calvinists, and approach to the opinion of the Arminians. They are also called *Universalists*, as holding the universality of Christ's death; and sometimes *Amyraldists*. The rigid adherents to the synod of Dort accused them of Pelagianism, and even of Manicheism. The controversy between the parties was carried on with a zeal and subtilty scarce conceivable; yet all the question between them was only, Whether the will of man is determined by the immediate action of God upon it, or by the intervention of a knowledge which God impresses into the mind? The synod of Dort had defined that God not only illuminates the understanding, but gives motion to the will by making an internal change therein. Cameron only admitted the illumination, whereby the mind is morally moved, and explained the sentiment of the synod of Dort so as to make the two opinions consistent.

CAMES, a name given to the small slender rods of cast-lead, of which the glaziers make their turned lead.

Their lead being cast into slender rods of twelve or fourteen inches long each, is called the *came*; sometimes also they call each of these rods a *came*, which being afterwards drawn through their vice, makes their turned lead.

CAMILLUS (Marcus Furius) was the first who rendered the family of *Furius* illustrious. He triumphed four times, was five times dictator, and was honoured with the title of the *second founder of Rome*. In a word, he acquired all the glory a man can gain in his own country. Lucius Apuleius, one of the tribunes, prosecuted him to make him give an account of the spoils taken at Veii. Camillus anticipated judgment, and banished himself voluntarily. During his banishment, instead of rejoicing at the devastation of Rome by the Gauls, he exerted all his wisdom and bravery to drive away the enemy; and yet kept with the utmost strictness the sacred law of Rome, in refusing to accept the command which several private persons offered him. The Romans, who were besieged in the capitol, created him dictator in the year 363; in which office he acted with so much bravery and conduct, that he entirely drove the army of the Gauls out of the territories of the commonwealth. He died in the 81st year of his age, 365 years before the Christian æra.

CAMILLI and Camillæ, in antiquity, boys and girls of ingenuous birth, who ministered in the sacrifices of the gods; and especially those who attended the *flamen dialis*, or priest of Jupiter. The word seems borrowed from the language of the ancient Hetrurians, where

where it signified minister, and was changed from *casmillus*. The Tuscans also gave the appellation *Camillus* to Mercury, in quality of minister of the gods.

CAMINHA, a maritime town of Portugal, in the province of Entre-Duero-e-Minho, with the title of a duchy. It is situated at the mouth of the river Minho, in W. Long. 9. 15. N. Lat. 41. 44.

CAMIS, or Kamis, in the *Japanese Theology*, denote deified souls of ancient heroes, who are supposed still to interest themselves in the welfare of the people over whom they anciently commanded.

The camis answer to the heroes in the ancient Greek and Roman theology, and are venerated like the saints in the modern Romish church.

Besides the heroes or camis beatified by the consent of antiquity, the *mikaddos*, or pontiffs, have deified many others, and continue still to grant the apotheosis to new worthies; so that they swarm with *camis*: the principal one is *Tensio Dai Sin*, the common father of Japan, to whom are paid devotions and pilgrimages extraordinary.

CAMISADE, in the art of war, an attack by surprise in the night, or at the break of day, when the enemy is supposed to be a-bed. The word is said to have taken its rise from an attack of this kind; wherein, as a badge or signal to know one another by, they bore a shift, in French called *chemise*, or *camise*, over their arms.

CAMISARDS, a name given by the French to the Calvinists of the Cevennes, who formed a league, and took up arms in their own defence, in 1688.

CAMLETINE, a slight stuff, made of hair and coarse silk, in the manner of camblet. It is now out of fashion.

CAMMA, and Gobby, two provinces of the kingdom of Loango in Africa. The inhabitants are continually at war with each other. The weapons they formerly used in their wars were the short pike, bows and arrows, sword and dagger; but since the Europeans have become acquainted with that coast, they have supplied them with fire-arms. The chief town of Gobby lies about a day's journey from the sea. Their rivers abound with a variety of fish; but are infested with sea-horses, which do great mischief both by land and water. The principal commerce with the natives is in logwood, elephants teeth, and tails, the hair of which is highly valued, and used for several curious purposes.

CAMMIN, a maritime town of Germany, in Brandenburg Pomerania, situated in E. Long. 15°. N. Lat. 54°.

CAMOENS (Louis de), a famous Portuguese poet, the honour of whose birth is claimed by different cities. But according to N. Antonio, and Manuel Correa, his intimate friend, this event happened at Lisbon in 1517. His family was of considerable note, and originally Spanish. In 1370, Vasco Perez de Caamans, disgusted at the court of Castile, fled to that of Lisbon, where king Ferdinand immediately admitted him into his council, and gave him the lordships of Sardoal, Punnete, Marano, Amendo, and other considerable lands; a certain proof of the eminence of his rank and abilities. In the war for the succession, which broke out on the death of Ferdinand, Caamans sided with the king of Castile, and was killed in the battle of Aljabarota. But though John I. the victor, seized a great part of his estate, his widow, the daughter of Gonsalo Tereyro, grand master of the order of Christ, and general of the Portuguese army, was not reduced beneath her rank. She had three sons who took the name of *Camoens*. The family of the eldest intermarried with the first nobility of Portugal; and even, according to Castera, with the blood royal. But the family of the second brother, whose fortune was slender, had the superior honour to produce the author of the Lusiad.

Early in his life the misfortunes of the poet began. In his infancy, Simon Vaz de Camoens, his father, commander of a vessel, was shipwrecked at Goa, where, with his life, the greatest part of his fortune was lost. His mother, however, Anne de Macedo of Santarene, provided for the education of her son Louis at the university of Coimbra. What he acquired there, his works discover; an intimacy with the classics, equal to that of a Scaliger, but directed by the taste of a Milton or a Pope.

When he left the university, he appeared at court. He was handsome; had speaking eyes, it is said; and the finest complexion. Certain it is, however, he was a polished scholar, which, added to the natural ardour and gay vivacity of his disposition, rendered him an accomplished gentleman. Courts are the scenes of intrigue; and intrigue was fashionable at Lisbon. But the particulars of the amours of Camoens rest unknown. This only appears: he had aspired above his rank, for he was banished from the court; and in several of his sonnets he ascribes this misfortune to love.

He now retired to his mother's friends at Santarene. Here he renewed his studies, and began his poem on the discovery of India. John III. at this time prepared an armament against Africa. Camoens, tired of his inactive obscure life, went to Ceuta in this expedition, and greatly distinguished his valour in several rencounters. In a naval engagement with the Moors in the straits of Gibraltar, in the conflict of boarding, he was among the foremost, and lost his right eye. Yet neither hurry of actual service nor the dissipation of the camp could stifle his genius. He continued his *Lusiadas*, and several of his most beautiful sonnets were written in Africa, while, as he expressed it,

One hand the pen, and one the sword, employ'd.

The fame of his valour had now reached the court, and he obtained permission to return to Lisbon. But, while he solicited an establishment which he had merited in the ranks of battle, the malignity of evil tongues, as he calls it in one of his letters, was injuriously poured upon him. Though the bloom of his early youth was effaced by several years residence under the scorching heavens of Africa, and though altered by the loss of an eye, his presence gave uneasiness to the gentlemen of some families of the first rank where he had formerly visited. Jealousy is the characteristic of the Spanish and Portuguese; its resentment knows no bounds, and Camoens now found it prudent to banish himself from his native country. Accordingly, in 1553, he sailed for India, with a resolution never to return. As the ship left the Tagus, he exclaimed, in the words of the sepulchral monument of Scipio Africanus, *Ingrata patria, non possidebis ossa mea!* "Ungrateful

Camoens.

ful country, thou shalt not possess my bones!" But he knew not what evils in the East would awake the remembrance of his native fields.

When Camoens arrived in India, an expedition was ready to sail to revenge the king of Cochin on the king of Pimenta. Without any rest on shore after his long voyage, he joined this armament, and in the conquest of the Alagada islands displayed his usual bravery.

In the year following, he attended Manuel de Vasconcello in an expedition to the Red Sea. Here, says Faria, as Camoens had no use for his sword, he employed his pen. Nor was his activity confined in the fleet or camp. He visited Mount Felex and the adjacent inhospitable regions of Africa, which he so strongly pictures in the Lusiad, and in one of his little pieces where he laments the absence of his mistress.

When he returned to Goa, he enjoyed a tranquillity which enabled him to bestow his attention on his Epic Poem. But this serenity was interrupted, perhaps by his own imprudence. He wrote some satires which gave offence; and, by order of the viceroy Francisco Barreto, he was banished to China.

The accomplishments and manners of Camoens soon found him friends, though under the disgrace of banishment. He was appointed commissary of the defunct in the island of Macao, a Portuguese settlement in the bay of Canton. Here he continued his Lusiad; and here also, after five years residence, he acquired a fortune, though small, yet equal to his wishes. Don Constantine de Braganza was now viceroy of India; and Camoens, desirous to return to Goa, resigned his charge. In a ship, freighted by himself, he set sail; but was shipwrecked in the gulph near the mouth of the river Mekon on the coast of China. All he had acquired was lost in the waves: his poems, which he held in one hand, while he swimmed with the other, were all he found himself possessed of when he stood friendless on the unknown shore. But the natives gave him a most humane reception: this he has immortalised in the prophetic song in the tenth Lusiad; and in the seventh, he tells us, that here he lost the wealth which satisfied his wishes.

> *Agora da esperança ja adquirida, &c.*
> Now blest with all the wealth fond hope could crave,
> Soon I beheld that wealth beneath the wave
> For ever lost;——
> My life, like Judah's heaven-doom'd king of yore,
> By miracle prolong'd——

On the banks of the Mekon, he wrote his beautiful paraphrase of the psalm, where the Jews, in the most strain of poetry, are represented as hanging their harps on the willows by the rivers of Babylon, and weeping their exile from their native country. Here Camoens continued some time, till an opportunity offered to carry him to Goa. When he arrived at that city, Don Constantine de Braganza, the viceroy, whose characteristic was politeness, admitted him into intimate friendship, and Camoens was happy till count Redondo assumed the government. Those who had formerly procured the banishment of the satirist, were silent while Constantine was in power; but now they exerted all their arts against him. Redondo, when he entered on office, pretended to be the friend of Camoens; yet, with all that unfeeling indifference with which he made his most horrible witticism on the Zamorim, he suffered the innocent man to be thrown into the common prison. After all the delay of bringing witnesses, Camoens, in a public trial, fully refuted every accusation of his conduct while commissary at Macao, and his enemies were loaded with ignominy and reproach. But Camoens had some creditors; and these detained him in prison a considerable time, till the gentlemen of Goa began to be ashamed that a man of his singular merit should experience such treatment among them. He was set at liberty; and again he assumed the profession of arms, and received the allowance of a gentleman volunteer, a character at this time common in Portuguese India. Soon after, Pedro Barreto, appointed governor of the fort at Sofala, by high promises, allured the poet to attend him thither. The governor of a distant fort, in a barbarous country, shares in some measure the fate of an exile. Yet, though the only motive of Barreto was, in this unpleasant situation, to retain the conversation of Camoens at his table, it was his least care to render the life of his guest agreeable. Chagrined with his treatment, and a considerable time having elapsed in vain dependence upon Barreto, Camoens resolved to return to his native country. A ship, on the homeward voyage, at this time touched at Sofala, and several gentlemen who were on board were desirous that Camoens should accompany them. But this the governor ungenerously endeavoured to prevent, and charged him with a debt for board. Anthony de Cabra, however, and Hector de Sylveyra, paid the demand; and Camoens, says Faria, and the honour of Barreto, were sold together.

After an absence of 16 years, Camoens, in 1569, returned to Lisbon, unhappy even in his arrival, for the pestilence then raged in that city, and prevented his publication for three years. At last, in 1572, he printed his Lusiad, which, in the opening of the first book, in a most elegant turn of compliment, he addressed to his prince, king Sebastian, then in his 18th year. The king, says the French translator, was so pleased with his merit, that he gave the author a pension of 4000 reals, on condition that he should reside at court. But this salary, says the same writer, was withdrawn by cardinal Henry, who succeeded to the crown of Portugal, lost by Sebastian at the battle of Alcazar.

Though the great patron of one species of literature, a species the reverse of that of Camoens, certain it is, that the author of the Lusiad was utterly neglected by Henry, under whose inglorious reign he died in all the misery of poverty. By some, it is said, he died in an alms-house. It appears, however, that he had not even the certainty of subsistence which these houses provide. He had a black servant, who had grown old with him, and who had long experienced his master's humanity. This grateful Indian, a native of Java, who, according to some writers, saved his master's life in the unhappy shipwreck where he lost his effects, begged in the streets of Lisbon for the only man in Portugal on whom God had bestowed those talents which have a tendency to erect the spirit of a downward age. To the eye of a careful observer, the fate of Camoens throws great light on that of his country, and will appear strictly connected with it. The same ignorance, the same degenerated spirit, which suffered Camoens to depend on his share of the alms begged in the streets by his old hoary servant,

Camoens.

vant, the same spirit which caused this, sunk the kingdom of Portugal into the most abject vassalage ever experienced by a conquered nation. While the grandees of Portugal were blind to the ruin which impended over them, Camoens beheld it with a pungency of grief which hastened his exit. In one of his letters he has these remarkable words: *Em fim accaberey a vida, e verram todos que fuy afeiçoada a minha patria,* &c. "I am ending the course of my life, the world will witness how I have loved my country. I have returned, not only to die in her bosom, but to die with her."

In this unhappy situation, in 1579, in his 62d year, the year after the fatal defeat of Don Sebastian, died Louis de Camoens, the greatest literary genius ever produced by Portugal; in martial courage and spirit of honour, nothing inferior to her greatest heroes. And in a manner suitable to the poverty in which he died, was he buried.

CAMOMILE, in botany. See ANTHEMIS.

CAMP, the ground on which an army pitch their tents. It is marked out by the quarter-master general, who appoints every regiment their ground.

The chief advantages to be minded in chusing a camp for an army, are, to have it near the water, in a country of forage, where the soldiers may find wood for dressing their victuals; that it have a free communication with garrisons, and with a country from whence it may be supplied with provisions; and, if possible, that it be situated on a rising ground, in a dry gravelly soil. Besides, the advantages of the ground ought to be considered, as marshes, woods, rivers, and inclosures; and if the camp be near the enemy, with no river or marsh to cover it, the army ought to be intrenched. An army always encamps fronting the enemy; and generally in two lines, running parallel about 500 yards distance; the horse and dragoons, on the wings, and the foot, in the centre: sometimes a body of two, three, or four brigades is encamped behind the two lines, and is called the *body of reserve*. The artillery and bread-waggons are generally encamped in the rear of the two lines. A battalion of foot is allowed 80 or 100 paces for its camp; and 30 or 40 for an interval betwixt one battalion and another. A squadron of horse is allowed 30 for its camp, and 10 for an interval, and more if the ground will allow it.

Where the grounds are equally dry, those camps are always the most healthful that are pitched on the banks of large rivers; because, in the hot season, situations of this kind have a stream of fresh air from the water, serving to carry off the moist and putrid exhalations. On the other hand, next to marshes, the worst encampments are on low grounds close beset with trees; for then the air is not only moist and hurtful in itself, but by stagnating becomes more susceptible of corruption. However, let the situation of camps be ever so good, they are frequently rendered infectious by the putrid effluvia of rotten straw, and the privies of the army; more especially if the bloody flux prevails, in which case the best method of preventing a general infection, is to leave the ground with the privies, foul straw, and other filth of the camp, behind. This must be frequently done, if consistent with the military operations: but when these render it improper to change the ground often, the privies should be made deeper than usual, and once a day a thick layer of earth thrown into them till the pits are near full; and then they are to be well covered, and supplied by others. It may also be a proper caution to order the pits to be made either in the front or the rear, as the then stationary winds may best carry off their effluvia from the camp. Moreover, it will be necessary to change the straw frequently, as being not only apt to rot, but to retain the infectious steams of the sick. But if fresh straw cannot be procured, more care must be taken in airing the tents, as well as the old straw.

The disposition of the Hebrew encampment was at first laid out by God himself. Their camp was of a quadrangular form, surrounded with an inclosure of the height of 10 hands-breadth. It made a square of 12 miles in compass about the tabernacle; and within this was another, called the *Levites camp*.

The Greeks had also their camps, fortified with gates and ditches. The Lacedemonians made their camp of a round figure, looking upon that as the most perfect and defensible of any form: we are not, however, to imagine, that they thought this form so essential to a camp, as never to be dispensed with when the circumstances of the place require it. Of the rest of the Grecian camps, it may be observed, that the most valiant of the soldiers were placed at the extremities, the rest in the middle. Thus we learn from Homer, that Achilles and Ajax were posted at the ends of the camp before Troy, as bulwarks on each side of the rest of the princes.

The figure of the Roman camp was a square divided into two principal parts: in the upper parts were the general's pavilion, or prætorium, and the tent of the chief officers; in the lower, those of inferior degree were placed. On one side of the prætorium stood the quæstorium, or apartment of the treasurer of the army; and near this the forum, both for a market-place and the assembling of councils. On the other side of the prætorium were lodged the legati; and below it the tribunes had their quarters, opposite to their respective legions. Aside of the tribunes were the præfecti of the foreign troops, over against their respective wings; and behind these were the lodgments of the evocati, then those of the extraordinarii and ablecti equites, which concluded the higher part of the camp. Between the two partitions was a spot of ground called *principia*, for the altars and images of the gods, and probably also for the chief ensigns. The middle of the lower partition was assigned to the Roman horse; next to them were quartered the triarii, then the principes, and close by them the hastati; afterwards the foreign horse, and lastly the foreign foot. They fortified their camp with a ditch and parapet, which they termed *fossa* and *vallum*; in the latter some distinguish two parts, viz. the *agger* or earth, and the *sudes* or wooden stakes driven in to secure it. The camps were sometimes surrounded by walls made of hewn stone; and the tents themselves formed of the same matter.

In the front of the Turkish camp are quartered the janizaries and other foot, whose tents encompass their aga; in the rear are the quarters of the spahis and other horsemen. The body of the camp is possessed by the stately tents or pavilions of the vizier or general, reis effendi or chancellor, kahija or steward, the testerdar bashaw or lord treasurer, and capiclar kahiasse or master

master of the ceremonies. In the middle of these tents is a spacious field, wherein are erected a building for the divan, and a hasne or treasury. When the ground is marked out for a camp, all wait for the pitching of the tent *tallar*, the place where the courts of justice are held; it being the disposition of this that is to regulate all the rest.

The Arabs still live in camps, as the ancient Scenites did. The camp of the Assyne Emir, or king of the country about Tadmor, is described by a traveller who viewed it, as spread over a very large plain, and possessing so vast a space, that though he had the advantage of a rising ground, he could not see the utmost extent of it. His own tent was near the middle; scarce distinguishable from the rest, except that it was bigger, being made, like the others, of a sort of hair-cloth.

Camp, is also used by the Siamese, and some other nations in the East Indies, as the name of the quarters which they assign to foreigners who come to trade with them. In these camps, every nation forms, as it were, a particular town, where they carry on all their trade, not only keeping all their warehouses and shops there, but also live in these camps with their whole families. The Europeans, however, are so far indulged, that at Siam, and almost every where else, they may live either in the cities or suburbs, as they shall judge most convenient.

Camp fight, or *Kamp fight*, in law writers, denotes the trial of a cause by duel, or a legal combat of two champions in the field, for decision of some controversy.

In the trial by camp fight, the accuser was, with the peril of his own body, to prove the accused guilty; and by offering him his glove, to challenge him to this trial, which the other must either accept of, or acknowledge himself guilty of the crime whereof he was accused.

If it were a crime deserving death, the camp fight was for life and death: if the offence deserved only imprisonment, the camp fight was accomplished when one combatant had subdued the other, so as either to make him yield or take him prisoner. The accused had liberty to choose another to fight in his stead, but the accuser was obliged to perform it in his own person, and with equality of weapons. No women were permitted to be spectators, nor men under the age of thirteen. The priest and the people who looked on, were engaged silently in prayer, that the victory might fall to him who had right. None might cry, shriek, or give the least sign; which in some places was executed with so much strictness, that the executioner stood ready with an axe to cut off the right hand or foot of the party that should offend herein.

He that, being wounded, yielded himself, was at the other's mercy either to be killed or suffered to live. But if life were granted him, he was declared infamous by the judge, and disabled from ever bearing arms, or riding on horseback.

CAMPAGNA. See Campania.

CAMPAIGN, in the art of war, denotes the space of time that an army keeps the field, or is encamped.— The beginning of every campaign is considerably more unhealthy than if the men were to remain in quarters. After the first fortnight or three weeks encampment, the sickness decreases daily; the most infirm being by that time in the hospitals, and the weather daily growing warmer. This healthy state continues throughout the summer, unless the men get wet clothes or wet beds; in which case, a greater or less degree of the dysentery will appear in proportion to the preceding heats. But the most sickly part of the campaign begins about the middle or end of August, whilst the days are still hot, but the nights cool and damp, with fogs and dews: then, and not sooner, the dysentery prevails; and though its violence is over by the beginning of October, yet the remitting fever gaining ground, continues throughout the rest of the campaign, and never entirely ceases, even in winter quarters, till the frosts begin. At the beginning of a campaign the sickness is so uniform, that the number may be nearly predicted; but for the rest of the season, as the diseases are then of a contagious nature, and depend so much upon the heats of summer, it is impossible to foresee how many may fall sick from the beginning to the end of autumn. It is also observed, that the last fortnight of a campaign, if protracted till the beginning of a campaign, is attended with more sickness than the first two months encampment: so that it is better to take the field a fortnight sooner, in order to return into winter-quarters so much the earlier. As to winter expeditions, though severe in appearance, they are attended with little sickness, if the men have strong shoes, quarters, fuel, and provisions. Long marches in summer are not without danger, unless made in the night, or so early in the morning as to be over before the heat of the day.

CAMPANACEÆ, in botany, an order of plants in the *Fragmenta methodi naturalis* of Linnæus, in which are the following genera, viz. convolvulus, ipomea, polemonium, campanula, roella, viola, &c.*

* See Botany, p. 462.

CAMPANELLA (Thomas,) a famous Italian philosopher, born at Stilo in Calabria, in 1568. He distinguished himself by his early proficiency in learning; for at the age of 13 he was a perfect master of the ancient orators and poets. His peculiar inclination was to philosophy, to which he at last confined his whole time and study. In order to arrive at truth, he shook off the yoke of authority: by which means the novelty of some of his opinions exposed him to many inconveniences; for at Naples he was thrown into prison, in which he remained 27 years, and during this confinement wrote his famous work entitled *Atheismus triumphatus*. Being at length set at liberty, he went to Paris, where he was graciously received by Louis XIII. and cardinal Richelieu; the latter procured him a pension of 2000 livres, and often consulted him on the affairs of Italy. Campanella passed the remainder of his days in a monastery of Dominicans at Paris, and died in 1639.

CAMPANI (Matthew) of Spoletto, curate at Rome, wrote a curious treatise on the art of cutting glasses for spectacles, and made several improvements in optics, assisted by his brother and pupil Joseph. He died after 1678.

CAMPANIA, a town of Italy, in the kingdom of Naples, and in the further principato, with a bishop's see. E. Long. 15. 30. N. Lat. 40. 42.

Campania or *Campagna di Roma*, anciently Latium, a province of Italy, bounded on the west by the

Tiber and the sea, on the south-west by the sea, on the south by Terra di Lavoro, on the east by Abruzzo, and on the north by Sabina. Though the soil is good, it produces little or nothing, on account of the heavy duties on corn; and though the waters are good, the air is unwholesome. It is subject to the Pope, and is about 60 miles in length on the Mediterranean sea.

It hath been generally thought that the air of this country hath something in it peculiarly noxious during the summer-time; but Mr Condamine is of opinion that it is not more unhealthy than any other marshy country. His account follows. "It was after the invasion of the Goths in the fifth and sixth centuries that this corruption of the air began to manifest itself. The bed of the Tiber being covered by the accumulated ruins of the edifices of ancient Rome, could not but raise itself considerably. But what permits us not to doubt of this fact is, that the ancient and well-preserved pavement of the Pantheon and its portico is overflowed every winter; that the water even rises there sometimes to the height of eight or ten feet; and that it is not possible to suppose that the ancient Romans should have built a temple in a place so low as to be covered with the waters of the Tiber on the least inundation. It is evident, then, that the level of the bed of this river is raised several feet; which could not have happened without forming there a kind of dikes or bars. The choaking up of its canal necessarily occasioned the overflow and reflux of its waters in such places as till then had not been subject to inundations: to these overflowings of the Tiber were added all the waters that escaped out of the ancient aqueducts, the ruins of which are still to be seen, and which were entirely broken and destroyed by Totila. What need, therefore, of any thing more to infect the air, in a hot climate, than the exhalations of such a mass of stagnating waters, deprived of any discharge, and become the receptacle of a thousand impurities, as well as the grave of several millions both of men and animals? The evil could not but increase from the same causes while Rome was exposed to the incursions and devastations of the Lombards, the Normans, and the Saracens, which lasted for several centuries. The air was become so infectious there at the beginning of the 13th century, that Pope Innocent III. wrote, that few people at Rome arrived to the age of forty years, and that nothing was more uncommon there than to see a person of sixty. A very short time after, the popes transferred the seat of their residence to Avignon: during the seventy-two years they remained there, Rome became a desert; the monasteries in it were converted into stables; and Gregory XI. on his return to Rome, in 1376, hardly counted there 30,000 inhabitants. At his death began the troubles of the great schism in the west, which continued for upwards of 50 years. Martin V. in whom this schism ended in the year 1429, and his first successors, were able to make but feeble efforts against so inveterate an evil. It was not till the beginning of the 16th century that Leo X. under whom Rome began to resume her wonted splendor, gave himself some trouble about re-establishing the salubrity of the air: but the city, being shortly after besieged twice successively by the emperor Charles V. saw itself plunged again into all its old calamities; and from 85,000 inhabitants, which it contained under Leo X. it was reduced under Clement VIII. to 32,000. In short, it is only since the time of Pius V. and Sixtus V. at the end of the 16th century, that the popes have constantly employed the necessary methods for purifying the air of Rome and its environs, by procuring proper discharges for the waters, drying up the humid and marshy grounds, and covering the banks of the Tiber and other places reputed uninhabitable with superb edifices. Since that time a person may dwell at Rome, and go in or out of it at all seasons of the year. At the beginning, however, of the present century, they were still afraid to lie out of the city in summer, when they had resided there; as they were also to return to it, when once they had quitted it. They never ventured to sleep at Rome, even in broad day, in any other house than their own. They are greatly relaxed at present from these ancient scruples: I have seen cardinals, in the months of July and August, go from Rome to lie at Frescati, Tivoli, Albano, &c. and return the next or the following days to the city, without any detriment to their health: I have myself tried all these experiments, without suffering the least inconvenience from them: we have even seen, in the last war in Italy, two armies encamped under the walls of Rome at the time when the heats were most violent. Yet, notwithstanding all this, the greater part of the country people dare not still venture to lie during that season of the year, nor even so much as sleep in a carriage, in any part of the territory comprehended under the name of the *Campagna of Rome*."

CAMPANIFORM, or CAMPANULATED, an appellation given to flowers resembling a bell.

CAMPANINI, a name given to an Italian marble dug out of the mountains of Carrara, because, when it is worked, it sounds like a bell.

CAMPANULA, or BELL-FLOWER: A genus of the monogynia order, belonging to the pentandria class of plants; and in the natural method ranking under the 29th order, *Campanaceæ*. The corolla is campanulated, with its fundus closed up by the valves that support the stamina; the stigma is trifid; the capsule inferior, or below the receptacle of the flower, opening and emitting the seeds by lateral pores.

Species. Of this genus there are no fewer than 41 species enumerated by botanical writers; but the following are the most worthy of attention. 1. The pyramidalis hath thick tuberous roots filled with a milky juice; it sends out strong, smooth, upright stalks, which rise to the height of four feet, garnished with smooth oblong leaves a little indented at the edges. The flowers are produced from the side of the stalks, and are regularly set on for more than half their length, forming a sort of pyramid; these are large, open, and shaped like a bell. The most common colour of the flowers is blue, though some are white, but the former are most esteemed. 2. The decurrens, or peach-leaved bell-flower, is a native of the northern parts of Europe: of this there are some with white, and some with blue flowers, and some with double flowers of both colours. These last have of late been propagated in such abundance as to have almost banished from the gardens those with single flowers. 3. The medium, commonly called *Canterbury bell-flower*, is a biennial plant, which perishes soon after it has ripened its seeds. It grows naturally in the woods of Italy and Austria; but is cul-

Campanula. cultivated in the Britiſh gardens for the beauty of its flowers, which are blue, purple, white, and ſtriped, with double flowers of all the colours. This ſpecies hath oblong, rough, hairy, leaves, ſerrated on their edges: from the centre of theſe riſes a ſtiff, hairy, furrowed ſtalk, about two feet high, ſending out ſeveral lateral branches, garniſhed with long, narrow, hairy leaves ſawed on their edges. From the ſetting on of theſe leaves proceed the foot-ſtalks of the flowers; thoſe which are on the lower part of the ſtalk and branches diminiſhing gradually in their length upward, and thereby forming a ſort of pyramid. The flowers of this kind are very large, ſo make a fine appearance. The ſeeds ripen in September, and the plants decay ſoon after. 4. The trachelium, with nettle leaves, hath a perennial root, which ſends up ſeveral ſtiff hairy ſtalks having two ribs or angles. Theſe put out a few ſhort ſide-branches, garniſhed with oblong hairy leaves deeply ſawed on their edges. Toward the upper part of the ſtalks, the flowers come out alternately upon ſhort trifid foot-ſtalks having hairy empalements. The colours of the flowers are a deep and a pale blue and white, with double flowers of the ſame; the double-flowered kind only merit a place in gardens. 5. The latifolia, or greateſt bell-flower, hath a perennial root, compoſed of many fleſhy fibres that abound with a milky juice. From theſe ariſe ſeveral ſtrong, round ſingle ſtalks, which never put out branches, but are garniſhed with oval ſpear-ſhaped leaves ſlightly indented on their edges. Towards the upper part of the ſtalk the flowers come out ſingly upon ſhort foot-ſtalks; their colours are blue, purple, and white. 6. The rapunculus, or rampion, hath roundiſh fleſhy roots, which are eatable, and much cultivated in France for ſallads; ſome years paſt it was cultivated in the Engliſh gardens for the ſame purpoſe, but is now generally neglected. It is a native of Britain; but the roots of the wild ſort never grow to half the ſize of thoſe which are cultivated. 7. The ſpeculum, with yellow eye-bright leaves, is an annual plant with ſlender ſtalks riſing a foot high, branching out on every ſide, and garniſhed with oblong leaves a little curled on their edges; from the wings of the leaves come out the flowers ſitting cloſe to the ſtalks, which are of a beautiful purple inclining to a violet colour. In the evening, they contract and fold into a pentagonal figure; from whence it is by ſome called *viola pentagonia*, or *five-cornered violet*. 8. The hybrida, or common Venus looking-glaſs. This ſeldom riſes more than ſix inches high, with a ſtalk branching from the bottom upward, and garniſhed with oval leaves ſitting cloſe to the ſtalks, from the baſe of which the branches are produced, which are terminated by flowers very like the former ſort. This was formerly cultivated in the gardens: but ſince the former kind hath been introduced, it hath almoſt ſupplanted this; for the other is a much taller plant, and the flowers larger, though of a leſs beautiful colour. 9. The canarienſis, with an orach leaf and tuberous root, is a native of the Canary iſlands. It hath a thick fleſhy root of an irregular form; ſometimes running downward like a parſnip, at other times dividing into ſeveral knobs near the top; and when any part of the root is broken, there iſſues out a milky juice at the wound. From the head or crown of the root ariſe one, two, three, or more ſtalks, in proportion to the ſize of the root; but that in the centre is Campanula. generally larger, and riſes higher, than the others. Theſe ſtalks are very tender, round, and of a pale green; their joints are far diſtant from each other; and when the roots are ſtrong, the ſtalks will riſe to ten feet high, ſending out ſeveral lateral branches. At each joint they are garniſhed with two, three, or four ſpear-ſhaped leaves, with a ſharp pointed beard on each ſide. They are of a ſea-green; and, when they firſt come out, are covered ſlightly with an aſh-coloured pounce. From the joints of the ſtalk the flowers are produced, which are of the perfect bell-ſhape, and hang downward; they are of a flame-colour, marked with ſtripes of a browniſh red: the flower is divided into five parts; at the bottom of each is ſeated a nectarium, covered with a white tranſparent ſkin, much reſembling thoſe of the crown imperial, but ſmaller. The flowers begin to open in the beginning of October, and there is often a ſucceſſion of them till March. The ſtalks decay to the root in June, and new ones ſpring up in Auguſt.

Culture, &c. The firſt ſort is cultivated to adorn halls, and to place before chimnies in the ſummer when it is in flower, for which purpoſe there is no plant more proper; for when the roots are ſtrong, they will ſend out four or five ſtalks which will riſe as many feet high, and are adorned with flowers a great part of their length. When the flowers begin to open, the pots are removed into the rooms, where, being ſhaded from the ſun and rain, the flowers will continue long in beauty; and if the pots are every night removed into a more airy ſituation, but not expoſed to heavy rains, the flowers will be fairer, and continue much longer in beauty. Thoſe plants which are thus treated, are ſeldom fit for the purpoſe the following ſeaſon; therefore a ſupply of young ones muſt be annually raiſed. The plant may be propagated either by dividing the roots or by ſeeds, but the latter produce the moſt vigorous and beſt flowering plants. The ſeeds muſt be ſown in autumn in boxes or pots filled with light undunged earth, and placed in the open air till the froſt or hard rains come on: then they muſt be placed under a hot-bed frame, where they may be ſheltered from both; but in mild weather the glaſſes ſhould be drawn off every day, that they may enjoy the free air: with this management the plants will come up early in the ſpring, and then they muſt be removed out of the frame, placing them firſt in a warm ſituation; but, when the ſeaſon becomes warm, they ſhould be ſo placed as to have the morning ſun only. In September the leaves of the plants will begin to decay, at which time they ſhould be tranſplanted; therefore there muſt be one or two beds prepared, in proportion to the number of plants. Theſe beds muſt be in a warm ſituation, and the earth light, ſandy, and without any mixture of dung. The plants muſt then be taken out of the pots or caſes very carefully, ſo as not to bruiſe their roots; for they are very tender, and on being broken the milky juice will flow out plentifully, which will greatly weaken them. Theſe ſhould be planted at about ſix inches diſtance each way, with the head or crown of the root half an inch below the ſurface. If the ſeaſon proves dry, they muſt be gently watered three or four days after they are planted: the beds ſhould alſo be covered with mats in the day time, but

Campanula. which should be taken off at night to let the dew fall on the plants. Towards the end of November the beds should be covered over with some old tanners bark to keep out the frost; and where there is not conveniency for covering them with frames, they should be arched over with hoops, that in severe weather they may be covered with mats. In the spring the mats must be removed, and, the following summer, the plants kept free from weeds. In autumn the earth should be stirred between them, some fresh earth spread over the beds, and the plants covered in winter as before. In these beds the plants may remain two years, during which time they are to be treated in the manner before directed. The roots will now be strong enough to flower; so, in September they should be carefully taken up, and some of the most promising carefully planted in pots; the others may be planted in warm borders, or in a fresh bed, at a greater distance than before, to allow them room to grow. Those plants which are potted should be sheltered in winter from great rains and hard frosts, otherwise they will be in danger of rotting, or at least will be so weakened as not to flower with any strength the following summer; and those which are planted in the full ground, should have some old tanners bark laid round them to prevent the frost from getting at the roots. The second, third, fourth, and fifth sorts are so easily propagated by parting the roots, or by seeds, that no particular directions for their culture need be given. The sixth sort, which is cultivated for its esculent roots, may be propagated by seeds, which are to be sown in a shady border; and when the plants are about an inch high, the ground shall be hoed as is practised for onions, to cut up the weeds, and thin the plants, to the distance of three or four inches; and when the weeds come up again they must be hoed over to destroy them: this, if well performed in dry weather, will make the ground clean for a long time; so that, being three times repeated, it will keep the plants clean till winter, which is the season for eating the roots, when they may be taken up for use as wanted. They will continue good till April, at which time they send out their stalks, when the roots become hard and unfit for use.—The seventh and eighth sorts are easily propagated by seeds, which they produce in plenty. If these, and the Venus navelwort, dwarf lychnis, candy-tuft, and other low annual flowers, are properly mixed in the border of the flower-garden, and sown at two or three different seasons, so as to have a succession of them in flower, they will make an agreeable variety. If these seeds are sown in autumn, the plants will flower early in the spring; but if sown in the spring, they will not flower till the middle of June; and if a third sowing is performed about the middle of May, the plants will flower in August; but from these, good seeds must not be expected.—The ninth sort is propagated by parting the roots, which must be done with caution: for if they are broken or wounded, the milky juice will flow out plentifully; and if planted before the wounds are skinned over, it occasions their rotting: therefore when any of them are broken, they should be laid in the green-house a few days to heal. These roots must not be too often parted, if they are expected to flower well; for by this means they are weakened. The best time for transplanting and parting their roots is in July, soon after the stalks are decayed. They must not be planted in rich earth, otherwise they will be very luxuriant in branches, and have but few flowers. They succeed best in a light sandy loam, mixed with a fourth part of screened lime-rubbish: when the roots are first planted the pots should be placed in the shade, and unless the season is very dry they should not be watered; for during the time they are inactive, wet is very injurious to them. About the middle of August, the roots will begin to put out fibres; at which time, if the pots are placed under a hot-bed frame, and, as the nights grow cool, covered with the glasses, but opened every day to enjoy the free air, it will greatly forward them for flowering, and increase their strength: when the stalks appear, they must be now and then refreshed with water; but it must not be given too often, nor in too great quantity. The plants thus managed, by the middle of September will have grown so tall as not to be kept any longer under the glass frame; they must, therefore, be removed into a dry airy glass-case, where they may enjoy the free air in mild weather, but screened from the cold. During the winter season they must be frequently refreshed with water, and guarded from frost; and, in the spring, when the stalks begin to decay, the pots should be set abroad in the shade, and not watered. Campbell.

CAMPBELL (Archibald), earl and marquis of Argyle, was the son of Archibald earl of Argyle, by the lady Anne Douglass, daughter of William earl of Morton. He was born in the year 1598; and educated in the profession of the Protestant religion, according to the strictest rules of the church of Scotland, as it was established immediately after the reformation. During the commonwealth he was induced to submit to its authority. Upon the restoration, he was tried for his compliance; a crime common to him with the whole nation, and such a one as the most loyal and affectionate subject might frequently by violence be induced to commit. To make this compliance appear the more voluntary and hearty, there were produced in court letters which he had wrote to Albemarle, while that general governed Scotland, and which contained expressions of the most cordial attachment to the established government. But, besides the general indignation excited by Albemarle's discovery of this private correspondence, men thought, that even the highest demonstrations of affection might, during jealous times, be exacted as a necessary mark of compliance from a person of such distinction as Argyle; and could not, by any equitable construction, imply the crime of treason. The parliament, however, scrupled not to pass sentence upon him, and he suffered with great constancy and courage.

Campbell (Archibald), earl of Argyle, son to the former, had from his youth distinguished himself by his loyalty and his attachment to the royal family. Tho' his father was head of the covenanters, he himself refused to concur in any of their measures; and when a commission of colonel was given him by the convention of states, he forbore to act upon it till it should be ratified by the king. By his respectful behaviour, as well as by his services, he made himself acceptable to Charles when that prince was in Scotland and even after the battle of Worcester, all the misfortunes which attended the royal cause could not engage him to desert it. Under

der Middleton he obstinately persevered to harass and infest the victorious English; and it was not till he received orders from that general, that he would submit to accept of a capitulation. Such jealousy of his loyal attachments was entertained by the commonwealth and protector, that a pretence was soon after fallen upon to commit him to prison; and his confinement was rigorously continued till the restoration. The king, sensible of his services, had remitted to him his father's forfeiture, and created him earl of Argyle; and when a most unjust sentence was passed upon him by the Scots parliament, Charles had anew remitted it. In the subsequent part of this reign Argyle behaved himself dutifully; and though he seemed not disposed to go all lengths with the court, he always appeared, even in his opposition, a man of mild dispositions and peaceable deportment.

A parliament was summoned at Edinburgh in summer 1681, and the duke was appointed commissioner. Besides granting money to the king, and voting the indefeasible right of succession, this parliament enacted a test, which all persons possessed of offices, civil, military, or ecclesiastical, were bound to take. In this test the king's supremacy was asserted, the covenant renounced, passive obedience assented to, and all obligations disclaimed of endeavouring any alteration in civil or ecclesiastical establishments. This was the state of the test as proposed by the courtiers; but the country party proposed also a clause of adherence to the Protestant religion, which could not with decency be rejected. The whole was of an enormous length, considered as an oath; and, what was worse, a confession of faith was there ratified which had been imposed a little after the reformation, and which contained many articles altogether forged by the parliament and nation. Among others, the doctrine of resistance was inculcated; so that the test being voted in a hurry, was found on examination to be a medley of absurdity and contradiction. Though the courtiers could not reject the clause of adhering to the Protestant religion, they proposed, as a requisite mark of respect, that all princes of the blood should be exempted from taking that oath. This exception was zealously opposed by Argyle; who observed that the sole danger to be dreaded for the Protestant religion must proceed from the perversion of the royal family. By insisting on such topics, he drew on himself the secret indignation of the duke of York, of which he soon felt the fatal consequences.

When Argyle took the test as a privy counsellor, he subjoined, in the duke's presence, an explanation which he had before hand communicated to that prince, and which he believed to have been approved by him. It was in these words. "I have considered the test, and am very desirous of giving obedience as far as I can. I am confident that the parliament never intended to impose contradictory oaths: therefore I think no man can explain it but for himself. Accordingly I take it as far as it is consistent with itself and the Protestant religion. And I do declare that I mean not to bind myself, in my station, and in a lawful way, from wishing and endeavouring any alteration, which I think to the advantage of church or state, and not repugnant to the Protestant religion and my loyalty: and this I understand as a part of my oath." The duke, as was natural, heard it with great tranquillity: no one took the least offence: Argyle was admitted to sit that day in council: and it was impossible to imagine that a capital offence had been committed where occasion seemed not to have been given so much as for a frown or reprimand.

Argyle was much surprised a few days after, to find that a warrant was issued for committing him to prison; that he was indicted for high treason, leasing-making, and perjury; and that from the innocent words abovementioned an accusation was extracted, by which he was to forfeit life, honours, and fortune. It is needless to enter into particulars, where the iniquity of the whole is so evidently apparent. Though the sword of justice was displayed, even her semblance was not put on; and the forms of law were preserved to sanctify, or rather aggravate, the oppression. Of five judges, three did not scruple to find the guilt of treason and leasing-making to be incurred by the prisoner; a jury of 15 noblemen gave verdict against him; and the king being consulted, ordered the sentence to be pronounced, but the execution of it to be suspended till further orders. Argyle, however, saw no reason to trust to the justice or mercy of such enemies: He made his escape from prison, and till he could find a ship for Holland he concealed himself during some time in London. The king heard of his lurking place, but would not suffer him to be arrested. All the parts, however, of his sentence, so far as the government in Scotland had power, were rigorously executed; his estate confiscated, his arms reversed and torn. Having got over to Holland, he remained there during the remaining part of the reign of Charles II. But thinking himself at liberty, before the coronation of James II. to exert himself in order to recover the constitution by force of arms, he concerted measures with the duke of Monmouth, and went into Scotland, to assemble his friends: but not meeting with the success he expected, he was taken prisoner; and being carried to Edinburgh, was beheaded upon his former unjust sentence, June 30, 1685. He showed great constancy and courage under his misfortunes: on the day of his death he ate his dinner very cheerfully: and, according to custom, slept after it a quarter of an hour or more, very soundly. At the place of execution, he made a short, grave, and religious speech; and, after solemnly declaring that he forgave all his enemies, submitted to death with great firmness.

Campbell (Archibald), first duke of Argyle, son to the preceding, was an active promoter of the revolution. He came over with the Prince of Orange; was admitted into the convention as Earl of Argyle, tho' his father's attainder was not reversed; and in the claim of rights the sentence against him was declared to be, what most certainly it was, a reproach upon the nation. The establishment of the crown upon the Prince and Princess of Orange being carried by a great majority in the Scottish convention, the earl was sent from the nobility, with Sir James Montgomery and Sir John Dalrymple from the barons and boroughs, to offer the crown, in the name of the convention, to their Majesties, and tendered them the coronation oath; for which, and many other eminent services, he was admitted a member of the privy council, and, in 1690, made one of the Lords of the Treasury. He was afterwards

terwards made a colonel of the Scots horse guards; and, in 1694, one of the extraordinary Lords of Session. He was likewise created Duke of Argyle, Marquis of Kintyre and Lorn, Earl of Campbell and Cowell, Viscount of Lochow and Glenyla, Lord Inverary, Mull, Morvern, and Terrey, by letters-patent, bearing date at Kensington the 23d of June 1701. He sent over a regiment to Flanders for king William's service, the officers of which were chiefly of his own name and family, who bravely distinguished themselves through the whole course of the war. He married Elisabeth, daughter of Sir Lionel Talmash of Helmingham in the county of Suffolk, by Elizabeth duchess of Lauderdale his wife, daughter and heir of William Murray earl of Dysart, by whom he left issue two sons and a daughter; namely, John duke of Argyle, the subject of the next article; Archibald, who succeeded his brother as Duke of Argyle; and Lady Anne, married to James Stuart, second earl of Bute, by whom she had the present earl.

Campbell (John), second duke of Argyle, and also duke of Greenwich and baron of Chatham, son to the subject of the preceding article, was born on the 10th of October 1680; and, on the very day when his grandfather suffered at Edinburgh, fell out of a window three pair of stairs high without receiving any hurt. At the age of 15, he had made a considerable progress in classical learning. His father then perceived and encouraged his military disposition, and introduced him to king William, who in the year 1694 gave him the command of a regiment. In this situation he remained till the death of his father in 1703; when, becoming duke of Argyle, he was soon after sworn of queen Anne's privy council, made captain of the Scotch horse guards, and appointed one of the extraordinary lords of session. In 1704, her Majesty reviving the Scottish order of the thistle, his grace was installed one of the knights of that order, and was soon after appointed high-commissioner to the Scotch parliament; where, being of great service in promoting the intended union, he was on his return created a peer of England, by the titles of *baron of Chatham* and *earl of Greenwich*, and in 1710 was made knight of the garter. His grace first distinguished himself in his military capacity at the battle of Oudenard; where he commanded as brigadier-general, with all the bravery of youth and the conduct of a veteran officer. He was present under the duke of Marlborough at the siege of Ghent, and took possession of the town. He had also a considerable share in the victory obtained over the French at the battle of Malplaquet, by dislodging them from the wood of Sart, and gaining a post of great consequence. In this sharp engagement, several musket-balls passed through the duke's clothes, hat, and peruke. Soon after this hot action, he was sent to take the command in Spain; and after the reduction of Port Mahon, he returned to England. His grace having now a seat in the house of lords, he censured the measures of the ministry with such freedom, that all his places were disposed of to other noblemen; but at the accession of George I. he recovered his influence. At the breaking out of the rebellion in 1715, he was made commander in chief of his majesty's forces in North Britain; and was the principal means and cause of the total extinction, at that time, of the rebellion in Scotland, without much bloodshed. In direct opposition to him, or that part of the army he commanded, at the head of all his Campbells was placed Campbell earl of Braidalbin, of the same family and kindred, by some fatal error that ever misguided and misled that unhappy family of the Stuarts and all its adherents. The consequence was, that both sets of Campbells, from family affection, refused to strike a stroke, and retired out of the battle. He arrived at London March 6th 1716, and was in high favour; but, to the surprise of people of all ranks, he was in a few months divested of all his employments; and from this period to the year 1718, he signalized himself in a civil capacity, by his uncorrupted patriotism and manly eloquence. In the beginning of the year 1719, he was again admitted into favour, appointed lord-steward of the household, and in April following was created duke of Greenwich. He continued in the administration during all the remaining part of that reign; and, after his late majesty's accession, till April 1740; when he delivered a speech with such warmth, that the ministry being highly offended, he was again dismissed from his employments. To these, however, on the change of the ministry, he was soon restored; but not approving of the measures of the new ministry more than those of the old, he gave up all his posts for the last time, and never after engaged in affairs of state. He now enjoyed privacy and retirement; and died of a paralytic disorder on the 4th of October 1743. To the memory of his grace a very noble monument was erected in Westminster-Abbey, executed by the ingenious Roubillac.

The duke of Argyle, though never first minister, was a very able statesman and politician, most steadily fixed in those principles he believed to be right, and not to be shaken or changed. His delicacy and honour were so great, that it hurt him to be even suspected; witness that application said to be made to him by one of the adherents of the Stuart family before the last rebellion in order to gain his interest, which was considerable both in Scotland and England. He immediately sent the letter to the secretary of state; and it vexed him much even to have an application made him, lest any person should think him capable of acting a double part. When he thought measures wrong or corrupt, he cared not who was the author, however great or powerful he might be; witness his boldly attacking the great duke of Marlborough in the house of lords, about his forage and army contracts in Flanders, in the very zenith of his power and popularity, though in all other respects he was the most able general of his time. The duke of Argyle, on all occasions, spoke well, with a firm, manly, and noble eloquence; and seems to deserve the character given of him by Pope:

> Argyle the state's whole thunder born to wield,
> And shake alike the senate and the field.

In private life, the duke's conduct was highly exemplary. He was an affectionate husband and an indulgent master. He seldom parted with his servants till age had rendered them incapable of their employments; and then he made provision for their subsistence. He was liberal to the poor, and particularly to persons of merit in distress: but though he was ready to patronise deserving persons, he was extremely cau-

tious

tions not to deceive any by laviſh promiſes, or leading them to form vain expectations. He was a ſtrict economiſt, and paid his tradeſmen punctually every month; and though he maintained the dignity of his rank, he took care that no part of his income ſhould be waſted in empty pomp or unneceſſary expences. He was twice married; and left five daughters, but no male iſſue. The titles of duke and earl of Greenwich and baron of Chatham became extinct at his death; but in his other titles he was ſucceeded by his brother Archibald earl of Ila, the ſubject of the next article.

CAMPBELL (Archibald), third Duke of Argyle, brother to the ſubject of the preceding article, was born at Hamhouſe, in England, in June 1682, and was educated at the Univerſity of Glaſgow. He afterwards applied himſelf to the ſtudy of the law at Utrecht; but, upon his father's being created a Duke, he betook himſelf to a military life, and ſerved ſome time under the duke of Marlborough. Upon quitting the army, in which he did not long remain, he applied to the acquiſition of that knowledge which would enable him to make a figure in the political world. In 1705, he was conſtituted treaſurer of Scotland, and made a conſiderable figure in Parliament, though he was not more than twenty-three years of age. In 1706, he was appointed one of the commiſſioners for treating of the Union; and the ſame year was created Lord Oranſay, Dunoon, and Arroſs, Viſcount and Earl of Ilay. In 1708, he was made an extraordinary Lord of Seſſion; and when the Union was effected, he was choſen one of the Sixteen Peers for Scotland, in the firſt Parliament of Great Britain; and was conſtantly elected to every future Parliament till his death, except the fourth. In 1710, he was made Juſtice-General of Scotland. In 1711, he was called to the privy council; and upon the acceſſion of George I. he was nominated lord regiſter of Scotland. When the rebellion broke out in 1715, he again betook himſelf to arms, in defence of the houſe of Hanover, and by his prudent conduct in the Weſt Highlands, he prevented General Gordon, at the head of three thouſand men, from penetrating into the country, and raiſing levies. He afterwards joined his brother at Stirling, and was wounded at the battle of Dumblain. In 1725, he was appointed keeper of the privy ſeal; and, from this time, he was entruſted with the management of Scottiſh affairs. In 1734, upon his reſigning the privy ſeal, he was made keeper of the great ſeal, which office he enjoyed till his death. Upon the deceaſe of his brother, he became duke of Argyle, hereditary juſtice general, lieutenant, ſheriff, and commiſſary of Argyleſhire and the Weſtern Iſles, hereditary great maſter of the houſhold, hereditary keeper of Dunſtaffnage, Carrick, and ſeveral other caſtles. He was alſo chancelor of the Univerſity of Aberdeen; and laboured to promote the intereſt of that, as well as of the other univerſities of Scotland. He particularly encouraged the ſchool of phyſic at Edinburgh, which has now acquired ſo high a reputation. Having the chief management of Scotch affairs, he was alſo extremely attentive to promote the trade, manufactures, and improvements of his country. It was by his advice that, after the rebellion in 1745, the Highlanders were employed in the royal army. He was a man of great endowments both natural and acquired, well verſed in the laws of his country, and poſſeſſed conſiderable parliamentary abilities. He was likewiſe eminent for his ſkill in human nature, had great talents for converſation, and had collected one of the moſt valuable private libraries in Great Britain. He built himſelf a very magnificent ſeat at Inverary. The faculties of his mind continued ſound and vigorous till his death, which happened ſuddenly on the 15th of April 1761, in the 79th year of his age. He was married, but had no iſſue; and was ſucceeded in his titles and the eſtates of the family by John Campbell, fourth duke of Argyle, ſon of the honourable John Campbell of Mamore, who was the ſecond ſon of Archibald the ninth earl of Argyle.

The family of Argyle was heritable juſtice-general for Scotland till aboliſhed by the juriſdiction act. They are ſtill heritable maſters of the king's houſhold in Scotland, and keepers of Dunſtaffnage and Carrick.

CAMPBELL (John), an eminent hiſtorical, biographical, and political writer, was born at Edinburgh, March 8, 1707-8. His father, Robert Campbell of Glenlyon, Eſq; was captain of horſe in a regiment commanded by the then earl of Hyndford; and his mother, Elizabeth, daughter of —— Smith, Eſq; of Windſor in Berkſhire, had the honour of claiming a deſcent from the poet Waller. Our author, their fourth ſon, was at the age of five years brought from Scotland to Windſor, where he received the firſt principles of his education; and at a proper age, he was placed out as clerk to an attorney, being intended for the law. This profeſſion, however, he never followed; but by a cloſe application to the acquiſition of knowledge of various kinds, became qualified to appear with great advantage in the literary world. In 1736, before he had completed his 29th year, he gave to the public, in two volumes folio, "The Military Hiſtory of Prince Eugene and the Duke of Marlborough," enriched with maps, plans, and cuts. The reputation hence acquired, occaſioned him ſoon after to be ſolicited to take a part in the "Ancient Univerſal Hiſtory." Whilſt employed in this capital work, Mr Campbell found leiſure to entertain the world with other productions. In 1739, he publiſhed the "Travels and Adventures of Edward Brown, Eſq;" 8vo. In the ſame year appeared his "Memoirs of the Baſhaw Duke de Ripperda," 8vo, reprinted, with improvements, in 1740. Theſe memoirs were followed, in 1741, by the "Conciſe Hiſtory of Spaniſh America," 8vo. In 1742, he was the author of "A Letter to a Friend in the Country, on the Publication of Thurloe's State Papers;" giving an account of their diſcovery, importance, and utility. The ſame year was diſtinguiſhed by the appearance of the 1ſt and 2d volumes of his "Lives of the Engliſh Admirals, and other eminent Britiſh Seamen." The two remaining volumes were completed in 1744; and the whole, not long after, was tranſlated into German. This was the firſt of Mr Campbell's works to which he prefixed his name; and it is a performance of great and acknowledged merit. In 1743, he publiſhed "Hermippus revived;" a ſecond edition of which, much improved and enlarged, came out in 1749, under the following title: "Hermippus Redivivus; or, the Sage's Triumph over old Age and the Grave. Wherein a method is laid down for prolonging the life and vigour of man. Including a Commentary upon an ancient Inſcription, in which this great ſecret is revealed; ſup-

2 ported

Campbell

ported by numerous authorities. The whole interspersed with a great variety of remarkable and well-attested relations." This extraordinary tract had its origin in a foreign publication; but it was wrought up to perfection by the additional ingenuity and learning of Mr Campbell. In 1744, he gave to the public in two volumes folio, his "Voyages and Travels," on Dr Harris's plan, being a very distinguished improvement of that collection which had appeared in 1705. The time and care employed by Mr Campbell in this important undertaking, did not prevent his engaging in another great work, the "Biographia Britannica," which began to be published in weekly numbers in 1745, and extended to seven volumes folio; but our author's articles were only in the first four volumes; of which, Dr Kippis observes, they constitute the prime merit.

When the late Mr Dodsley formed the design of "The Preceptor," which appeared in 1748, Mr Campbell was to assist in the undertaking; and the parts written by him were the Introduction to Chronology, and the Discourse on Trade and Commerce, both of which displayed an extensive fund of knowledge upon these subjects. In 1750, he published the first seperate edition of his "Present State of Europe;" a work which had been originally begun in 1746, in the "Museum," a very valuable periodical performance, printed for Dodsley. There is no production of our author's that hath met with a better reception. It has gone through six editions, and fully deserved this encouragement. The next great undertaking which called for the exertion of our author's abilities and learning, was "The Modern Universal History." This extensive work was published, from time to time, in detached parts, till it amounted to 16 volumes folio; and a second edition of it, in 8vo, began to make its appearance in 1759. The parts of it written by Mr Campbell were, the histories of the Portuguese, Dutch, Spanish, French, Swedish, Danish, and Ostend settlements in the East-Indies; and the Histories of the Kingdoms of Spain, Portugal, Algarve, Navarre, and that of France, from Clovis to 1656. As our author had thus distinguished himself in the literary world, the degree of LL.D. was very properly and honourably conferred upon him, June 18, 1754, by the university of Glasgow.

His principal and favourite work was, "A political survey of Great Britain," 2 vol. 4to, published a short time before his death; in which the extent of his knowledge, and his patriotic spirit, are equally conspicuous. Dr Campbell's reputation was not confined to his own country, but extended to the remotest parts of Europe. As a striking instance of this, it may be mentioned, that in the spring of 1774, the empress of Russia was pleased to honour him with the present of her picture, drawn in the robes worn in that country in the days of John Basiliowitz, grand duke of Muscovy, who was contemporary with queen Elizabeth. To manifest the doctor's sense of her imperial majesty's goodness, a sett of the "Political Survey of Britain," bound in Morocco, highly ornamented, and accompanied with a letter descriptive of the triumphs and felicities of her reign, was forwarded to St Petersburg, and conveyed into her hands by prince Orloff, who had resided some months in this kingdom.

Dr Campbell in 1736 married Elizabeth, daughter of Benjamine Vobe, of Leominster, in the county of Hereford, gentleman, with whom he lived nearly 40 years in the greatest conjugal harmony and happiness. So wholly did he dedicate his time to books, that he seldom went abroad: but to relieve himself as much as possible from the inconveniences incident to a sedentary life, it was his custom, when the weather would admit, to walk in his garden; or otherwise in some room of his house, by way of exercise. By this method, united with the strictest temperance in eating, and an equal abstemiousness in drinking, he enjoyed a good state of health, though his constitution was delicate. His domestic manner of living did not preclude him from a very extensive and honourable acquaintance. His house, especially on a Sunday evening, was the resort of the most distinguished persons of all ranks, and particularly of such as had rendered themselves eminent by their knowledge or love of literature. He received foreigners, who were fond of learning, with an affability and kindness which excited in them the highest respect and veneration; and his instructive and cheerful conversation made him the delight of his friends in general. He was, during the latter part of his life, agent for the province of Georgia in North America; and died at the close of the year 1775, in the 67th year of his age. The Doctor's literary knowledge was by no means confined to the subjects on which he more particularly treated as an author; he was well acquainted with the mathematics, and had read much in medicine. It hath been with great reason believed, that if he had dedicated his studies to the last science, he would have made a very conspicuous figure in the physical profession. He was eminently versed in the different parts of sacred literature; and his acquaintance with the languages extended not only to the Hebrew, Greek, and Latin among the ancients, and to the French, Italian, Spanish, Portuguese, and Dutch, among the moderns; but likewise to the Oriental tongues. He was particularly fond of the Greek language. His attainment of such a variety of knowledge was exceedingly assisted by a memory surprisingly retentive, and which indeed astonished every person with whom he was conversant. In communicating his ideas, he had an uncommon readiness and facility; and the style of his works, which had been formed upon the model of that of the celebrated bishop Sprat, was perspicuous, easy, flowing, and harmonious. To all these accomplishments of the understanding, Dr Campbell joined the more important virtues of a moral and pious character. His disposition was gentle and humane, and his manners kind and obliging. He was the tenderest of husbands, a most indulgent parent, a kind master, a firm and sincere friend. To his great Creator he paid the constant and ardent tribute of devotion, duty, and reverence; and in his correspondences he showed that a sense of piety was always nearest his heart.

Campbell || Campbelltown.

CAMPBELLTOWN, a parliament town of Argyle-shire in Scotland, seated on the lough of Kilkerran, on the eastern shore of Kintyre or Cantyre, of which it is the capital. It hath a good harbour; and is now a very considerable place, though within these 50 years only a petty fishing town. It has in fact been created by the fishery; for it was appointed the place of rendezvous for the bucses; and above 260 have been seen in the harbour at once. The inhabitants are reckoned to be upwards of 8000 in number. W. Long. 5. 10. N. Lat. 54.

CAMPDEN, a small town of Glocestershire in England, containing about 200 houses. It gives title of Viscount, by courtesy, to Earl of Gainsborough his son. W. Long. 1. 50. N. Lat. 52.

CAMPEACHY, a town of Mexico in South America, seated on the east coast of a bay of the same name, on the west of the province of Yucatan. It is defended by a good wall and strong forts; but is neither so rich, nor carries on such a trade, as formerly; it having been the port for the sale of logwood, the place where it is cut being about 30 miles distant. It was taken by the English in 1596; by the bucaneers in 1678; and by the Flibusters of St Domingo in 1685, who set it on fire and blew up the citadel. W. Long. 93. 7. N. Lat. 19. 20.

Campeachy-Wood, in botany. See HAEMATOXYLUM.

CAMPEN, a strong town of Overyssel in the United Provinces. It hath a citadel and a harbour; but the latter is almost choked up with sand. It was taken by the Dutch in 1578, and by the French in 1672; but they abandoned it the following year. It is seated near the mouth of the river Yssel and Zuider Sea. E. Long. 5. 15. N. Lat. 52. 38.

CAMPESTRE, in antiquity, a sort of cover for the privities, worn by the Roman soldiers in their field exercises; being girt under the navel, and hanging down to the knees. The name is supposed to be formed from *campus*, the field or place where the Roman soldiers performed their exercises.

CAMPHORA, or CAMPHIRE, a solid concrete juice extracted from the wood of the laurus camphora. See LAURUS, CHEMISTRY, and MATERIA MEDICA.

Pure camphire is very white, pellucid, somewhat unctuous to the touch; of a bitterish aromatic taste, yet accompanied with a sense of coolness; of a very fragrant smell, somewhat like that of rosemary, but much stronger. It has been very long esteemed one of the most efficacious diaphoretics; and has been celebrated in fevers, malignant and epidemical distempers. In deliria, also, where opiates could not procure sleep, but rather aggravated the symptoms, this medicine has often been observed to procure it. All these effects, however, Dr Cullen attributes to its sedative property, and denies that camphire has any other medicinal virtues than those of an antispasmodic and sedative. He allows it to be very powerful, and capable of doing much good or much harm. From experiments made on different brute creatures, camphire appears to be poisonous to every one of them. In some it produced sleep followed by death, without any other symptom. In others, before death, they were awakened into convulsions and rage. It seems, too, to act chiefly on the stomach; for an entire piece swallowed, produced the abovementioned effects with very little diminution of weight.

CAMPHUYSEN, (Dirk Theodore Raphael), an eminent painter, was born at Gorcum in 1586. He learned the art of painting from Diederic Govertze; and by a studious application to it, he very soon not only equalled, but far surpassed his master. He had an uncommon genius, and studied nature with care, judgement, and assiduity. His subjects were landscapes, mostly small, with ruinous buildings, huts of peasants, or views of villages on the banks of rivers, with boats and boys, and generally he represented them by moonlight. His pencil is remarkably tender and soft, his colouring true nature and very transparent, and his expertness in perspective is seen in the proportional distances of his objects, which are excellently contrived, and have a surprising degree of nature and truth. As he left off painting at an age when others are scarcely qualified to commence artists, few of his work are to be met with, and they bring considerable prices; as they cannot but give pleasure to the eye of every observer. He painted his pictures with a thin body of colour, but they are handled with singular neatness and spirit. He practised in his profession only till he was 18 years of age, and being then recommended as a tutor to the sons of the lord of Nieuport, he undertook the employment, and discharged it with so much credit, that he was appointed secretary to that nobleman. He excelled in drawing with a pen; and the designs which he finished in that manner are exceedingly valued.

CAMPIAN (Edmund), an English Jesuit, was born at London, of indigent parents, in the year 1540; and educated at Christ's hospital, where he had the honour to speak an oration before queen Mary on her accession to the throne. He was admitted a scholar of St John's college in Oxford at its foundation, and took the degree of master of arts in 1564. About the same time he was ordained by a bishop of the church of England, and became an eloquent Protestant preacher. In 1566, when queen Elizabeth was entertained by the university of Oxford, he spoke an elegant oration before her majesty, and was also respondent in the philosophy act in St Mary's church. In 1568, he was junior proctor of the university. In the following year, he went over to Ireland, where he wrote a history of that kingdom, and turned papist; but being found rather too assiduous in persuading others to follow his example, he was committed to prison. He soon, however, found means to make his escape. He landed in England in 1571; and thence proceeded to Doway in Flanders, where he publicly recanted his former heresy, and was created bachelor of divinity. He went soon after to Rome, where, in 1573, he was admitted of the society of Jesus, and was sent by the general of that order to Vienna, where he wrote his tragedy called *Nectar et ambrosia*, which was acted before the emperor with great applause.

From Vienna he went to Prague in Bohemia, where he resided in the Jesuits college about six years, and then returned to Rome. From thence, in 1580, he was sent by Pope Gregory XIII. with the celebrated Father Parsons, to convert the people of England. From Pitts we learn, that, some time before, several English priests, inspired by the Holy Ghost, had undertaken to convert their countrymen; that 80 of these foreign seminaries, besides several others who by God's grace had been converted in England, were actually engaged in the pious work with great success; that some of them had suffered imprisonment, chains, tortures, and ignominious death, with becoming constancy and resolution; but seeing at last that the labour was abundant and the labourers few, they solicited the assistance of the

Jesuits; requesting, that though not early in the morning, they would at least in the third, sixth, or ninth hour, send labourers into the Lord's vineyard. In consequence of this solicitation, the above two were sent to England. They arrived in an evil hour for Campian, at Dover; and were next day joyfully received by their friends at London. He had not been long in England, before Walsingham the secretary of state, being informed of his uncommon assiduity in the cause of the church of Rome, used every means in his power to have him apprehended, but for a long time without success. However, he was at last taken by one Elliot, a noted *priest-taker*, who found him in the house of Edward Yates, Esq; at Lyford in Berkshire, and conducted him in triumph to London, with a paper on his hat, on which was written *Campian the Jesuit*. He was imprisoned in the Tower; where, Wood says, "he did undergo many examinations, abuses, wrackings, tortures;" *exquisitissimis cruciatibus tortus*, says Pitts. It is hoped, for the credit of our reformers, this torturing part of the story is not true. The poor wretch, however, was condemned, on the statute 25 Ed. III. for high treason; and butchered at Tyburn, with two or three of his fraternity. Howsoever criminal in the eye of the law, or of the English gospel, might be the zeal of this Jesuit for the salvation of the poor heretics of this kingdom, biographers of each persuasion unite in giving him a great and amiable character. "All writers (says the Oxford antiquary), whether Protestants or Popish, say, that he was a man of admirable parts; an elegant orator, a subtile philosopher and disputant, and an exact preacher whether in English or the Latin tongue, of a sweet disposition, and a well-polished man." Fuller, in his church-history, says, "he was of a sweet nature, constantly carrying about him the charms of a plausible behaviour, of a fluent tongue, and good parts." His History of Ireland, in two books, was written in 1570; and published, by Sir James Ware, from a manuscript in the Cotton library, Dublin, 1633, folio. He wrote also *Chronologia universalis*, a very learned work; and various other tracts.

CAMPICURSIO, in the ancient military art, a march of armed men for several miles, from and back again to the camp, to instruct them in the military pace. This exercise was nearly akin to the *decursio*, from which it only differed, in that the latter was performed by horsemen, the former also by foot.

CAMPIDOCTORES, or CAMPIDUCTORES, in the Roman army, were officers who instructed the soldiery in the discipline and exercises of war, and the art of handling their weapons to advantage. These are also sometimes called *campigeni*, and *armiductores*.

CAMPIDUCTOR, in middle-age writers, signifies the leader or commander of an army, or party.

CAMPION, in botany, the English name of the LYCHNIS.

CAMPION a town of the kingdom of Tanguth in Tartary. It was formerly remarkable for being a place through which the caravans passed in the road from Bukharia to China. E. Long. 104. 53. N. Lat. 40. 25.

CAMPISTRON, a celebrated French dramatic author, was born in 1656. Racine directed his poetical talents to the theatre, and assisted him in his first pieces. He died in 1723.

CAMPITÆ, in church history, an appellation given to the donatists, on account of their assembling in the fields for want of churches. For a similar reason, they were also denominated *Montenses* and *Rupitani*.

CAMPLI, or CAMPOLI, a town of Italy, in the kingdom of Naples, and in the farther Abruzzo, situated in E. Long. 13. 35. N. Lat. 42. 38.

CAMPO MAJOR, a town of the province of Alentejo in Portugal. W. Long. 7. 24. N. Lat. 38. 50.

CAMPREDON, a town of Catalonia in Spain, seated at the foot of the Pyrenean mountains. The fortifications were demolished by the French in 1691. W. Long. 1. 56. N. Lat. 42. 20.

CAMPS (Francis de), abbot of Notre Dame at Sigi, was born at Amiens in 1643; and distinguished himself by his knowledge of medals, by writing an history of France, and several other works. He died at Paris in 1723.

CAMPVERE, See VEER.

CAMPUS, in antiquity, a field or vacant plain in a city, not built upon, left vacant on account of shows, combats, exercises, or other uses of the citizens.

Campus Maii, in ancient customs, an anniversary assembly of our ancestors held on May-day, when they confederated together for the defence of the kingdom against all its enemies.

Campus Martius, a large plain in the suburbs of ancient Rome, lying between the Quirinal and Capitoline mounts and the Tiber, thus called because consecrated to the god Mars, and set apart for military sports and exercises to which the Roman youth were trained, as the use and handling of arms, and all manner of feats of activity. Here were the races run, either with chariots or single horses; here also stood the villa publica, or palace for the reception of ambassadors, who were not permitted to enter the city. Many of the public comitia were held in the same field, part of which was for that purpose cantoned out. The place was also nobly decorated with statues, arches, columns, porticoes, and the like structures.

Campus Sceleratus, a place without the walls of ancient Rome, where the Vestals who had violated their vows of virginity were buried alive.

CAMUL, a town of Asia, on the eastern extremity of the kingdom of Cialis, on the frontiers of Tangut. E. Long. 98. 5. N. Lat. 37. 15.

CAMUS, a person with a low flat nose, hollowed in the middle.

The Tartars are great admirers of camus beauties. Rubruquis observes, that the wife of the great Jenghis Khan, a celebrated beauty, had only two holes for a nose.

CAMUS (John Peter), a French prelate born in 1582. He was author of a number of pious romances (the taste of his time), and other theological works, to the amount of 200 vols. His definition of politics is remarkable: *Ars non tam regendi, quam fallendi, homines*; "the art not so much of governing, as of deceiving mankind." He died in 1652.

CAN, in the sea-language, as can-pump, a vessel wherewith seamen pour water into the pump to make it go.

Can-Buoy. See BUOY.

Can-Hook, an instrument used to sling a cask by the ends of the staves: it is formed by fixing a broad and flat ſlat hook at each end of a ſhort rope; and the tackle by which the caſk ſo ſlung may be hoiſted or lowered, is hooked to the middle of the rope.

CANA (anc. geog.), a town on the confines of the Upper and Lower Galilee: memorable for the turning water into wine (John). The birth place of Simeon, called *Cananite* from this place, and of Nathaniel.

CANAAN, the fourth ſon of Ham. The irreverence of Ham towards his father Noah is recorded in Gen. ix. Upon that occaſion the patriarch curſed him in a branch of his poſterity: "Curſed," ſays he, "be Canaan; a ſervant of ſervants ſhall he be unto "his brethren." This curſe being pronounced, not againſt Ham the immediate tranſgreſſor, but againſt his ſon, who does not appear, from the words of Moſes, to have been any ways concerned in the crime, hath occaſioned ſeveral conjectures. Some have believed that Noah curſed Canaan, becauſe he could not well have curſed Ham himſelf, whom God had not long before bleſſed. Others think Moſes's chief intent in recording this prediction was to raiſe the ſpirits of the Iſraelites, then entering on a terrible war with the children of Canaan, by the aſſurance, that, in conſequence of the curſe, that people were deſtined by God to be ſubdued by them. For the opinion of thoſe who imagine all Ham's race were here accurſed, ſeems repugnant to the plain words of Scripture, which confines the malediction to Canaan and his poſterity; and is alſo contrary to fact. Indeed, the prophecy of Noah, that Canaan "ſhould be a ſervant of ſervants to his brethren," ſeems to have been wholly completed in him. It was completed with regard to Shem, not only in that a conſiderable part of the ſeven nations of the Canaanites were made ſlaves to the Iſraelites, when they took poſſeſſion of their land, as part of the remainder of them were afterwards enſlaved by Solomon; but alſo by the ſubſequent expeditions of the Aſſyrians and Perſians, who were both deſcended from Shem; and under whom the Canaanites ſuffered ſubjection, as well as the Iſraelites; not to mention the conqueſt of part of Canaan by the Elamites, or Perſians, under Chedorlaomer, prior to them all. With regard to Japhet, we find a completion of the prophecy, in the ſucceſſive conqueſts of the Greeks and Romans in Paleſtine and Phœnicia, where the Canaanites were ſettled; but eſpecially in the total ſubverſion of the Carthaginian power by the Romans; beſides ſome invaſions of the northern nations, as the poſterity of Thogarma and Magog; wherein many of them, probably, were carried away captive.

The poſterity of Canaan were very numerous. His eldeſt ſon was Sidon, who at leaſt founded and peopled the city of Sidon, and was the father of the Sidonians and Phœnicians. Canaan had beſides ten ſons, who were the fathers of ſo many people, dwelling in Paleſtine, and in part of Syria; namely, the Hittites, the Jebuſites, the Amorites, the Girgaſites, the Hivites, the Arkites, the Sinites, the Arvadites, the Zemarites, and Hamathites.

Land of CANAAN, the country ſo named from Canaan the ſon of Ham. It lies between the Mediterranean ſea and the mountains of Arabia, and extends from Egypt to Phœnicia. It is bounded to the eaſt by the mountains of Arabia; to the ſouth by the wilderneſs of Paran, Idumæa, and Egypt; to the weſt by the Mediterranean, called in Hebrew the Great Sea; to the north by the mountains of Libanus. Its length from the city of Dan (ſince called Cæſarea Philippi, or Paneadis, which ſtands at the foot of these mountains) to Beerſheba, is about 70 leagues; and its breadth from the Mediterranean ſea to the eaſtern borders, is in ſome places 30. This country, which was firſt called Canaan, from Canaan the ſon of Ham, whoſe poſterity poſſeſſed it, was afterwards called Paleſtine, from the people which the Hebrews call Philiſtines, and the Greeks and Romans corruptly Paleſtines, who inhabited the ſea coaſts, and were firſt known to them. It likewiſe had the name of the *Land of Promiſe*, from the promiſe God made Abraham of giving it to him; that of the *Land of Iſrael*, from the Iſraelites having made themſelves maſters of it; that of *Judah*, from the tribe of Judah, which was the moſt conſiderable of the twelve; and laſtly, the happineſs it had of being ſanctified by the preſence, actions, miracles, and death of Jeſus Chriſt, has given it the name of the *Holy Land*, which it retains to this day.

The firſt inhabitants of this land therefore were the Canaanites, who were deſcended from Canaan, and the eleven ſons of that patriarch. Here they multiplied extremely; trade and war were their firſt occupations; theſe gave riſe to their riches, and the ſeveral colonies ſcattered by them over almoſt all the iſlands and maritime provinces of the Mediterranean. The meaſure of their idolatry and abominations was completed, when God delivered their country into the hands of the Iſraelites. In St Athanaſius's time, the Africans ſtill ſaid they were deſcended from the Canaanites; and it is ſaid, that the Punic tongue was almoſt entirely the ſame with the Canaanitiſh and Hebrew language. The colonies which Cadmus carried into Thebes in Bœotia, and his brother Cilix into Cilicia, came from the ſtock of Canaan. The iſles of Sicily, Sardinia, Malta, Cyprus, Corfu, Majorca and Minorca, Gades and Ebuſus, are thought to have been peopled by the Canaanites. Bochart, in his large work entitled *Canaan*, has ſet all this matter in a good light.

Many of the old inhabitants of the north-weſt of the land of Canaan, however, particularly on the coaſt or territories of Tyre and Sidon, were not driven out by the children of Iſrael, whence this tract ſeems to have retained the name of Canaan a great while after thoſe other parts of the country, which were better inhabited by the Iſraelites, had loſt the ſaid name. The Greeks called this tract inhabited by the old Canaanites along the Mediterranean ſea, Phœnicia; the more inland parts, as being inhabited partly by Canaanites, and partly by Syrians, Syrophœnicia: and hence the woman ſaid by St Matthew (xv. 22.) to be a woman of Canaan, whoſe daughter Jeſus cured, is ſaid by St Mark (vii. 26.) to be a Syrophœnician by nation, as ſhe was a Greek by religion and language.

CANADA, or the province of Quebec, an extenſive country of North America, bounded on the north-eaſt by the gulph of St Lawrence, and St John's river; on the ſouth-weſt, by lands inhabited by the ſavage Indians, which are frequently included in this province: on the ſouth, by the provinces of Nova Scotia, New England, and New York; and on the

Canada.

north-west, by other Indian nations. Under the name of *Canada*, the French comprehended a very large territory; taking into their claim part of New Scotland, New England, and New York on the east; and extending it on the west as far as the Pacific Ocean. That part, however, which was reduced by the British arms in the last war, lies between 61 and 81 degrees of west longitude, and between 45 and 52 of north latitude. The climate is not very different from that of the northern British colonies; but as it is much farther from the sea, and more to the northward, than most of those provinces, it has a much severer winter, though the air is generally clear; and, like most of those American tracts that do not lie too far to the northward, the summers are very hot, and exceeding pleasant. The soil in general is very good, and in many parts extremely fertile; producing many different sorts of grains, fruits, and vegetables. The meadow grounds, which are well watered, yield excellent grass, and breed vast numbers of great and small cattle. The uncultivated parts are a continued wood, composed of prodigiously large and lofty trees, of which there is such a variety of species, that even of those who have taken most pains to know them, there is not perhaps one that can tell half the number. Canada produces, among others, two sorts of pines, the white and the red; four sorts of firs; two sorts of cedar and oak, the white and the red; the male and female maple; three sorts of ash-trees, the free, the mungrel, and the bastard; three sorts of walnut-trees, the hard, the soft, and the smooth; vast numbers of beech-trees and white wood; white and red elms, and poplars. The Indians hollow the red elms into canoes, some of which made out of one piece will contain 20 persons; others are made of the bark; the different pieces of which they sew together with the inner rind, and daub over the seams with pitch, or rather a bituminous matter resembling pitch, to prevent their leaking; the ribs of these canoes are made of boughs of trees. In the hollow elms, the bears and wild cats take up their lodging from November to April. The country produces also a vast variety of other vegetables, particularly tobacco, which thrives well. Near Quebec is a fine lead mine, and many excellent ones of iron have been discovered. It hath also been reported that silver is found in some of the mountains. The rivers are extremely numerous, and many of them very large and deep. The principal are, the Outtouais, St John's, Seguinay, Desprires, and Trois Rivieres; but all these are swallowed up by the great river St Laurence. This river issues from the lake Ontario; and, taking its course north-east, washes Montreal, where it receives the Outtauais, and forms many fertile islands. It continues the same course, and meets the tide upwards of 400 miles from the sea, where it is navigable for large vessels; and below Quebec, 320 miles from the sea, it becomes so broad and so deep, that ships of the line contributed in the last war to reduce that city. After receiving in its progress innumerable streams, it at last falls into the ocean at cape Rosiers, where it is 90 miles broad, and where the cold is intense and the sea boisterous. This river is the only one upon which any settlements of note are as yet formed; but it is very probable, that, in time to come, Canada, and those vast regions to the west, may be enabled of themselves to carry on a considerable trade upon the great lakes of fresh water which these countries environ. Here are five lakes, the least of which is of greater extent than the fresh-water lakes to be found in any other part of the world: these are the lake Ontario, which is not less than 200 leagues in circumference; Erie, or Oswego, longer, but not so broad, is about the same extent. That of the Huron spreads greatly in width, and is about 300 leagues in circuit; as also is that of Machigan, though like lake Erie it is rather long, and comparatively narrow. But the lake Superior is larger than any of these, being not less than 500 leagues in circumference. All these are navigable by any vessels, and they all communicate with each other; but the passage between *Erie* and *Ontario* is interrupted by a most stupendous fall or cataract, called the *falls of Niagara**. The river St Laurence, as already observed, is the outlet of these lakes, by which they discharge themselves into the ocean. The French built forts at these several straits, by which the lakes communicate with one another, and on that where the last of them communicates with the river. By these, while the country was in their possession, they effectually secured to themselves the trade of the lakes, and preserved an influence over all the Indian nations that lie near them.

Canada.

The most curious and interesting part of the natural history of Canada is the animals there produced. These are stags, elks, deer, bears, foxes, martins, wild cats, ferrets, weasels, large squirrels of a greyish hue, hares and rabbits. The southern parts, in particular, breed great numbers of wild bulls, divers sorts of roe bucks, goats, wolves, &c. The marshes, lakes, and pools, with which this country abounds, swarm with otters and beavers, of which the white are highly valued, as well as the right black kind. A vast variety of birds are also to be found in the woods; and the river St Lawrence abounds with such quantities of fish, that it is affirmed by some writers, this would be a more profitable article than even the fur-trade.—There are in Canada a multitude of different Indian tribes; but these are observed to decrease in number where the Europeans are most numerous; owing chiefly to the immoderate use of spirituous liquors, of which they are excessively fond. Their manners and way of living we have already particularly described†. The principal towns are Quebec, Trois Rivieres, and Montreal. The commodities required by the Canadians from Europe are, wine, or rather rum; cloths, chiefly coarse; linen; and wrought iron. The Indian trade requires rum, tobacco, a sort of duffil blankets, guns, powder, balls, and flints, kettles, hatchets, toys, and trinkets of all kinds. While the country was in possession of the French, the Indians supplied them with poultry; and the French had traders, who, like the original inhabitants, traversed the vast lakes and rivers in canoes, with incredible industry and patience, carrying their goods into the remotest parts of America, and among nations entirely unknown to us. These again brought the furs, &c. home to them, as the Indians were thereby habituated to trade with them. For this purpose, people from all parts, even from the distance of 1000 miles, came to the French fair at Montreal, which began in June, and sometimes lasted three months. On this occasion many solemnities were observed, guards

* See Niagara.

† See America, No [illegible] — [illegible]

3

were

Canada.

were placed, and the governor assisted to preserve order in so great and various a concourse of savage nations. But sometimes great disorders and tumults happened; and the Indians frequently gave for a dram all that they were possessed of. It is remarkable, that many of these nations actually passed by the English settlement of Albany in New York, and travelled 200 miles further to Montreal, though they could have purchased the goods they wanted cheaper at the former.

Since Britain became possessed of Canada, our trade with that country has generally employed 34 ships and 400 seamen; their exports, at an average of three years, in skins, furs, ginseng, snake-root, capillaire, and wheat, amount to 150,000*l*. Their imports from Great Britain are computed at nearly the same sum. It will, however, be always impossible to overcome certain inconveniences arising from the violence of the winter. This is so excessive from December to April, that the broadest rivers are frozen over, and the snow lies commonly from four to six feet deep on the ground, even in those parts of the country which lie three degrees south of London, and in the temperate latitude of Paris. Another inconvenience arises from the falls in the river St Lawrence below Montreal, which prevent ships from penetrating to that emporium of inland commerce. Our communication therefore with Canada, and the immense regions beyond it, will always be interrupted during the winter-season, until roads are formed that can be travelled without danger from the Indians. For these savage people often commit hostilities against us, without any previous notice; and frequently, without any provocation, they commit the most horrid ravages for a long time with impunity.

Canada was undoubtedly discovered by Sebastian Cabot, the famous Italian adventurer, who sailed under a commission from Henry VII. But though the English monarch did not think proper to make any use of this discovery, the French quickly attempted it; we have an account of their fishing for cod on the banks of Newfoundland, and along the sea-coast of Canada, in the beginning of the 16th century. About the year 1506, one Denys, a Frenchman, drew a map of the gulph of St Lawrence; and two years after, one Aubert, a ship-master of Dieppe, carried over to France some of the natives of Canada. As the new country, however, did not promise the same amazing quantities of gold and silver produced by Mexico and Peru, the French for some years neglected the discovery. At last, in the year 1523, Francis I. a sensible and enterprising prince, sent four ships, under the command of Verazani, a Florentine, to prosecute discoveries in that country. The particulars of this man's first expedition are not known. All we can learn is, that he returned to France, and next year he undertook a second. As he approached the coast, he met with a violent storm; however, he came so near as to perceive the natives on the shore, making friendly signs to him to land. This being found impracticable by reason of the surf upon the coast, one of the sailors threw himself into the sea; but, endeavouring to swim back to the ship, a surge threw him on shore without signs of life. He was, however, treated by the natives with such care and humanity, that he recovered his strength, and was allowed to swim back to the ship, which immediately returned to France. This is all we know of Verazani's second expedition. He undertook a third, but was no more heard of, and it is thought that he and all his company perished before he could form any colony. In 1534, one Jaques Cartier of St Maloes set sail under a commission from the French king, and on the 10th of May arrived at Cape Bonavista in Newfoundland. He had with him two small ships besides the one in which he sailed. He cruised along the coasts of that island, on which he discovered inhabitants, probably the Eskimaux. He landed in several places along the coast of the Gulf, and took possession of the country in the king's name. On his return, he was again sent out with a commission, and a pretty large force: he returned in 1535, and passed the winter at St Croix; but the season proved so severe, that he and his companions must have died of the scurvy, had they not, by the advice of the natives, made use of the decoction of the tops and bark of the white pine. As Cartier, however, could produce neither gold nor silver, all that he could say about the utility of the settlement was disregarded; and in 1540, he was obliged to become pilot to one M. Roberval, who was by the French king appointed viceroy of Canada, and who sailed from France with five vessels. Arriving at the gulph of St Lawrence, they built a fort; and Cartier was left to command the garrison in it, while Roberval returned to France for additional recruits to his new settlement. At last, having embarked in 1549, with a great number of adventurers, neither he nor any of his followers were heard of more.

This fatal accident so greatly discouraged the court of France, that, for 50 years, no measures were taken for supplying with necessaries the settlers that were left. At last, Henry IV. appointed the Marquis de la Roche lieutenant-general of Canada and the neighbouring countries. In 1598 he landed on the isle of Sable, which he absurdly thought to be a proper place for a settlement, though it was without any port, and without product except briars. Here he left about 40 malefactors, the refuse of the French jails. After cruising for some time on the coast of Nova Scotia, without being able to relieve these poor wretches, he returned to France, where he died of a broken heart. His colony must have perished, had not a French ship been wrecked on the island, and a few sheep driven upon it at the same time. With the boards of the ship they erected huts; and while the sheep lasted they lived on them, feeding afterwards on fish. Their clothes wearing out, they made coats of seal-skins; and in this miserable condition they spent seven years, when Henry ordered them to be brought to France. The king had the curiosity to see them in their seal-skin dresses, and was so moved with their appearance, that he forgave them all their offences, and gave each of them 50 crowns to begin the world anew.

In 1600, one Chauvin, a commander in the French navy, attended by a merchant of St Malo, called *Pontgrave*, made a voyage to Canada, from whence he returned with a very profitable quantity of furs. Next year he repeated the voyage with the same good fortune, but died while he was preparing for a third. The many specimens of profit to be made by the Canadian trade, at last induced the public to think favourably of it. An armament was equipped, and the command of it given to Pontgrave, with powers to extend his disco-

veries

veries up the river St Lawrence. He ſailed in 1603, having in his company Samuel Champlain, who had been a captain in the navy, and was a man of parts and ſpirit. It was not, however, till the year 1608, that the colony was fully eſtabliſhed. This was accompliſhed by founding the city of Quebec, which from that time commenced the capital of all the ſettlements in Canada. The colony, however, for many years continued in a low way, and was often in danger of being totally exterminated by the Indians. As the particulars of theſe wars, however, could neither be entertaining, nor indeed intelligible, to many of our readers, we chooſe to omit them, and in general obſerve, that the French not only concluded a permanent peace with the Indians, but ſo much ingratiated themſelves with them, that they could with the greateſt eaſe prevail upon them at any time to murder and ſcalp the Engliſh in their ſettlements. Theſe practices had a conſiderable ſhare in bringing about the laſt war with France, when the whole country was conquered by the Britiſh in 1761. The moſt remarkable tranſaction in this conqueſt was the ſiege of QUEBEC; for a particular account of which, ſee that article. And for the tranſactions here during the late American war, ſee AMERICA (United States of), n° 195, 200—207.

CANAL *of* COMMUNICATION, an artificial cut in the ground, ſupplied with water from rivers, ſprings, &c. in order to make a navigable communication betwixt one place and another.

The particular operations neceſſary for making artificial navigations depend upon a number of circumſtances. The ſituation of the ground; the vicinity or connection with rivers; the eaſe or difficulty with which a proper quantity of water can be obtained; theſe and many other circumſtances neceſſarily produce great variety in the ſtructure of artificial navigations, and augment or diminiſh the labour and expence of executing them. When the ground is naturally level, and unconnected with rivers, the execution is eaſy, and the navigation is not liable to be diſturbed by floods: but, when the ground riſes and falls, and cannot be reduced to a level, artificial methods of raiſing and lowering veſſels muſt be employed; which likewiſe vary according to circumſtances.

A kind of temporary ſluices are ſometimes employed for raiſing boats over falls or ſhoals in rivers by a very ſimple operation. Two poſts or pillars of maſon-work, with grooves, are fixed, one on each bank of the river, at ſome diſtance below the ſhoal. The boat having paſſed theſe poſts, planks are let down acroſs the river by pullies into the grooves, by which the water is dammed up to a proper height for allowing the boat to paſs up the river over the ſhoal.

The Dutch and Flemings at this day ſometimes, when obſtructed by caſcades, form an inclined plane or rolling-bridge upon dry land, along which their veſſels are drawn from the river below the caſcade into the river above it. This, it is ſaid, was the only method employed by the ancients, and is ſtill uſed by the Chineſe, who are ſaid to be entirely ignorant of the nature and utility of locks. Theſe rolling-bridges conſiſt of a number of cylindrical rollers which turn eaſily on pivots, and a mill is commonly built near by, ſo that the ſame machinery may ſerve the double purpoſe of working the mill and drawing up veſſels.

A LOCK is a baſon placed lengthwiſe in a river or canal, lined with walls of maſonry on each ſide, and terminated by two gates, placed where there is a caſcade or natural fall of the country; and ſo conſtructed, that the baſon being filled with water by an upper ſluice to the level of the waters above, a veſſel may aſcend thro' the upper gate; or the water in the lock being reduced to the level of the water at the bottom of the caſcade, the veſſel may deſcend through the lower gate; for when the waters are brought to a level on either ſide, the gate on that ſide may be eaſily opened. But as the lower gate is ſtrained in proportion to the depth of water it ſupports, when the perpendicular height of the water exceeds 12 or 13 feet, more locks than one become neceſſary. Thus, if the fall be 17 feet, two locks are required, each having 8½ feet fall; and if the fall be 26 feet, three locks are neceſſary, each having 8 feet 8 inches fall. The ſide-walls of a lock ought to be very ſtrong. Where the natural foundation is bad, they ſhould be founded on piles and platforms of wood: they ſhould likewiſe ſlope outwards, in order to reſiſt the preſſure of the earth from behind.

Plate CXIV. fig. 1. A perſpective view of part of a canal: the veſſel L, within the lock AC.—Fig. 2. Section of an open lock: the veſſel L about to enter.—Fig. 3: Section of a lock full of water; the veſſel L raiſed to a level with the water in the ſuperior canal.—Fig. 4. Ground ſection of a lock. L, a veſſel in the inferior canal. C, the under gate. A, the upper gate. GH, a ſubterraneous paſſage for letting water from the ſuperior canal run into the lock. KF, a ſubterraneous paſſage for water from the lock to the inferior canal.

X and Y (fig. 1.) are the two flood-gates, each of which conſiſts of two leaves, reſting upon one another, ſo as to form an obtuſe angle, in order the better to reſiſt the preſſure of the water. The firſt (X) prevents the water of the ſuperior canal from falling into the lock; and the ſecond (Y) dams up and ſuſtains the water in the lock. Theſe flood-gates ought to be very ſtrong, and to turn freely upon their hinges. In order to make them open and ſhut with eaſe, each leaf is furniſhed with a long lever A *b*, A *b*; C *b*, C *b*. They ſhould be made very tight and cloſe, that as little water as poſſible may be loſt.

By the ſubterraneous paſſage G H (fig. 2, 3, & 4) which deſcends obliquely, by opening the ſluice G, the water is let down from the ſuperior canal D into the lock, where it is ſtopt and retained by the gate C when ſhut, till the water on the lock comes to be on a level with the water in the ſuperior canal D; as repreſented, fig. 3. When, on the other hand, the water contained by the lock is to be let out, the paſſage G H muſt be ſhut by letting down the ſluice G, the gate A muſt be alſo ſhut, and the paſſage K F opened by raiſing the ſluice K: a free paſſage being thus given to the water, it deſcends through K F, into the inferior canal, until the water in the lock is on a level with the water in the inferior canal B; as repreſented, fig. 2.

Now, let it be required to raiſe the veſſel L (fig. 2) from the inferior canal B to the ſuperior one D; if the lock happens to be full of water, the ſluice G muſt be ſhut, and alſo the gate A, and the ſluice K opened, so that the water in the lock may run out till it is on a level with the water in the inferior canal B. When the water in the lock comes to be on a level with the water at B, the leaves of the gate C are opened by the levers C *b*, which is easily performed, the water on each side of the gate being in equilibrio; the vessel then sails into the lock. After this the gate C and the sluice K are shut, and the sluice G opened, in order to fill the lock, till the water in the lock, and consequently the vessel, be upon a level with the water in the superior canal D; as is represented in fig. 3. The gate A is then opened, and the vessel passes into the canal D.

Again, let it be required to make a vessel descend from the canal D into the inferior canal B. If the lock is empty, as in fig. 2. the gate C and sluice K must be shut, and the upper sluice G opened, so that the water in the lock may rise to a level with the water in the upper canal D. Then open the gate A, and let the vessel pass thro' into the lock. Shut the gate A and the sluice G; then open the sluice K, till the water in the lock be on a level with the water in the inferior canal; then the gate C is opened, and the vessel passes along into the canal B, as was required.

It is almost needless to spend time in enumerating the many advantages which necessarily result from artificial navigations. Their utility is now so apparent, that most nations in Europe give the highest encouragement to undertakings of this kind wherever they are practicable. The advantages of navigable canals did not escape the observation of the ancients. From the most early accounts of society we read of attempts to cut through large isthmuses, in order to make a communication by water, either betwixt different nations, or distant parts of the same nation, where land-carriage was long and expensive. Herodotus relates, that the Cnidians, a people of Caria in Asia Minor, designed to cut the isthmus which joins that peninsula to the continent; but were superstitious enough to give up the undertaking, because they were interdicted by an oracle. Several kings of Egypt attempted to join the Red-Sea to the Mediterranean. Cleopatra was exceedingly fond of this project. Soliman II. emperor of the Turks, employed 50,000 men in this great work. This canal was completed under the caliphate of Omar, but was afterwards allowed to fall into disrepair; so that it is now difficult to discover any traces of it. Both the Greeks and Romans intended to make a canal across the isthmus of Corinth, which joins the Morea and Achaia, in order to make a navigable passage by the Ionian sea into the Archipelago. Demetrius, Julius Cæsar, Caligula, and Nero, made several unsuccessful efforts to open this passage. But, as the ancients were entirely ignorant of the use of water-locks, their whole attention was employed in making level cuts, which is probably the principal reason why they so often failed in their attempts. Charlemagne formed a design of joining the Rhine and the Danube, in order to make a communication between the ocean and the Black Sea, by a canal from the river Almutz which discharges itself into the Danube, to the Rednitz, which falls into the Maine, and this last falls into the Rhine near Mayence: for this purpose he employed a prodigious number of workmen; but he met with so many obstacles from different quarters, that he was obliged to give up the attempt.

The French at present have many fine canals: that of Briare was begun under Henry IV. and finished under the direction of cardinal Richelieu in the reign of Louis XIII. This canal makes a communication betwixt the Loire and the Seine by the river Loing. It extends 11 French great leagues from Briare to Montargis. It enters the Loire a little above Briare, and terminates in the Loing at Cepoi. There are 42 locks on this canal.

The canal of Orleans, for making another communication between the Seine and the Loire, was begun in 1675, and finished by Philip of Orleans, regent of France, during the minority of Louis XV. and is furnished with 20 locks. It goes by the name of the *canal of Orleans*; but it begins at the village of Combleux, which is a short French league from the town of Orleans.

But the greatest and most useful work of this kind is the junction of the ocean with the Mediterranean by the canal of Languedoc. It was proposed in the reigns of Francis I. and Henry IV. and was undertaken and finished under Louis XIV. It begins with a large reservoir 4000 paces in circumference, and 24 feet deep; which receives many springs from the mountain Noire. This canal is about 64 leagues in length, is supplied by a number of rivulets, and is furnished with 104 locks, of about eight feet rise each. In some places it passes over bridges of vast height; and in others it cuts thro' solid rocks for 1000 paces. At one end it joins the river Garonne near Tholouse, and terminates at the other in the lake Tau, which extends to the port of Cette. It was planned by Francis Riquet in the 1666, and finished before his death, which happened in the 1680.

In the Dutch, Austrian, and French Netherlands, there is a very great number of canals; that from Bruges to Ostend carries vessels of 200 tons.

The Chinese have also a great number of canals; that which runs from Canton to Pekin extends about 825 miles in length, and was executed about 800 years ago.

It would be an endless task to describe the numberless canals in Holland, Russia, Germany, &c. We shall therefore confine ourselves to those that are either already finished, or at present executing, in our own country.

As the promoting of commerce is the principal intention of making canals, it is natural to expect that their frequency in any nation should bear some proportion to the trade carried on in it, providing the situation of the country will admit of them. The present state of England and Scotland confirms this observation. Though the Romans made a canal between the Nyne, a little below Peterborough, and the Witham, three miles below Lincoln, which is now almost entirely filled up, yet it is not long since canals were revived in England. They are now however become very numerous, particularly in the counties of York, Lincoln, and Cheshire. Most of the counties betwixt the mouth of the Thames and the Bristol channel are connected together either by natural or artificial navigations; those upon the Thames and Isis reaching within about

so

Canal.

90 miles of those upon the Severn. The duke of Bridgewater's canal in Cheshire runs 27 miles on a perfect level; but at Barton it is carried by a very high aqueduct bridge over the Irwell, a navigable river; so that it is common for vessels to be passing at the same time both under and above the bridge. It is likewise cut some miles into the hills, where the Duke's coal-mines are wrought.

A navigable canal betwixt the Forth and Clyde in Scotland, and which divides the kingdom in two parts, was first thought of by Charles II. for transports and small ships of war; the expence of which was to have been L. 500,000, a sum far beyond the abilities of his reign. It was again projected in the year 1722, and a survey made; but nothing more done till 1761, when the then Lord Napier, at his own expence, caused make a survey, plan, and estimate on a small scale. In 1764, the trustees for fisheries, &c. in Scotland caused make another survey, plan, and estimate of a canal five feet deep, which was to cost L. 79,000. In 1766, a subscription was obtained by a number of the most respectable merchants in Glasgow, for making a canal four feet deep and twenty-four feet in breadth; but when the bill was nearly obtained in Parliament, it was given up on account of the smallness of the scale, and a new subscription set on foot for a canal seven feet deep, estimated at L. 150,000. This obtained the sanction of Parliament; and the work was begun in 1768 by Mr Smeaton the engineer. The extreme length of the canal from the Forth to the Clyde is 35 miles, beginning at the mouth of the Carron, and ending at Dalmure Burnfoot on the Clyde, six miles below Glasgow, rising and falling 160 feet by means of 39 locks, 20 on the east side of the summit, and 19 on the west, as the tide does not ebb so low in Clyde as in the Forth by nine feet. Vessels drawing eight feet water, and not exceeding nineteen feet beam and seventy-three feet in length, pass with ease, the canal having afterwards been deepened to upwards of eight feet. The whole enterprise displays the art of man in a high degree. The carrying the canal through moss, quicksand, gravel, and rocks, up precipices and over valleys, was attended with inconceivable difficulties. There are eighteen draw-bridges and fifteen aqueduct bridges of note, besides small ones and tunnels. In the first three miles there are only six locks; but in the fourth mile there are no less than ten locks, and a very fine aqueduct bridge over the great road to the west of Falkirk. In the next six miles there are only four locks, which carry you to the summit. The canal then runs eighteen miles on a level, and terminates about a mile from Glasgow. In this course, for a considerable way the ground is banked above twenty feet high, and the water is sixteen feet deep, and two miles of it is made through a deep moss. At Kirkintulloch, the canal is carried over the water of Logie on an aqueduct arch of ninety feet broad. This arch was thrown over in three stretches, having only a centre of thirty feet, which was shifted on small rollers from one stretch to another; a thing new, and never attempted before with an arch of this size; yet the joinings are as fairly equal as any other part, and admired as a very fine piece of masonry. On each side there is a very considerable banking over the valley. The work was carried on till it came within six miles of its junction with the Clyde; when the subscription and a subsequent loan being exhausted, the work was stopt in 1775. The city of Glasgow, however, by means of a collateral branch, opened a communication with the Forth, which has produced a revenue of about L. 6000 annually; and, in order to finish the remaining six miles, the government in 1784 gave L. 50,000 out of the forfeited estates, the dividends arising from this sum to be applied to making and repairing roads in the Highlands of Scotland. Accordingly the work has been resumed; and by contract, under a high penalty, must be entirely completed in November 1789. The aqueduct bridge over the Kelvin (now finished, and supposed the greatest of the kind in the world) consists of four arches, and carries the canal over a valley 65 feet high and 420 in length, exhibiting a very singular effort of human ingenuity and labour. To supply the canal with water was of itself a very great work. There is one reservoir of 50 acres 24 feet deep, and another of 70 acres 22 feet deep, into which many rivers and springs terminate, which it is thought will afford sufficient supply of water at all times. This whole undertaking when finished will cost about L. 200,000. It is the greatest of the kind in Britain, and without doubt will be of great national utility; though it is to be regretted that it had not been executed on a still larger scale, the locks being too short for transporting large masts.

Canal, in anatomy, a duct or passage through which any of the juices flow.

Cananore Canara.

CANANOR, a large maritime town of Asia, on the coast of Malabar, in a kingdom of the same name, with a very large and safe harbour. It formerly belonged to the Portuguese, and had a strong fort to guard it; but in 1683, the Dutch, together with the natives, drove them away; and after they became masters of the town, enlarged the fortifications. They have but a very small trade; but there is a town at the bottom of the bay independent of the Dutch, whose prince can bring 20,000 men into the field. The Dutch fort is large, and the governor's lodgings are at a good distance from the gate; so that, when there was a skirmish between the factory and the natives, he knew nothing of it till it was over. E. Long. 78. 10. N. Lat. 12. 0.

Cananor, a small kingdom of Asia, on the coast of Malabar, whose king can raise a considerable army. The natives are generally Mahometans; and the country produces pepper, cardamoms, ginger, mirobolans, and tamarinds, in which they drive a considerable trade.

CANARA, a kingdom of Asia, on the coast of Malabar. The inhabitants are Gentoos, or Pagans; and there is a pagod, or temple, called *Ramtrut*, which is visited every year by a great number of pilgrims. Here the custom of burning the wives with their husbands had its beginning, and is practised to this day. The country is generally governed by a woman who keeps her court at a town called *Bednor*, two days journey from the sea. She may marry whom she pleases; and is not obliged to burn with her husband, like her female subjects. They are so good observers of their laws, that a robbery or murder is scarce ever heard of among them. The Canarans have forts built of earth along the coast, which are garrisoned with 200 or 300 soldiers, to guard against the robberies of their neighbours.

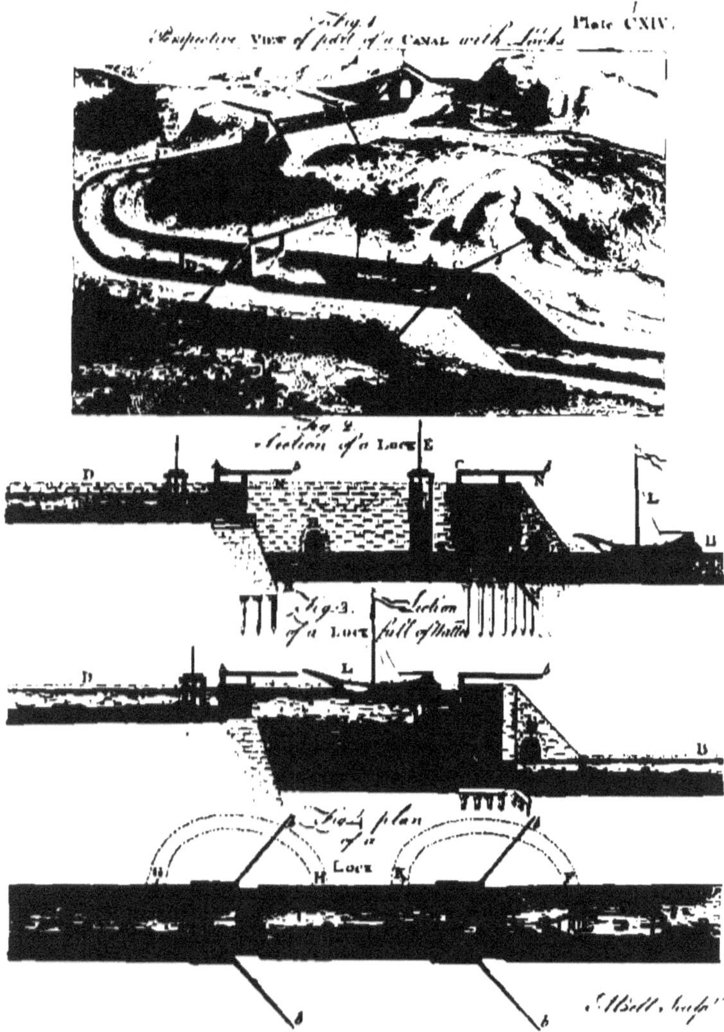
Plate CXIV.
Fig. 1
Perspective View of part of a Canal with Locks
Fig. 2
Section of a Lock
Fig. 3. Section
of a Lock full of Water
Fig. 4 plan
of a
Lock
J. Bell Sculp.

hours. The lower grounds yield every year two crops of corn or rice; and the higher produce pepper, betel nuts, fanders wood, iron, and fteel. The Portuguefe clergy here live very loofely, and make no fcruple of procuring women for ftrangers.

CANARIA (anc. geog.), one of the Fortunate iflands, a proof that thefe were what are now called the *Canaries*. Canaria had its name from its abounding with dogs of an enormous fize, two of which were brought to Juba king of Mauritania. See the following article.

CANARIA, or the GRAND CANARY, an ifland in the Atlantic Ocean, about 180 miles from the coaft of Africa. It is about 100 miles in circumference, and 33 in diameter. It is a fruitful ifland, and famous for the wine that bears its name. It alfo abounds with apples, melons, oranges, citrons, pomegranates, figs, olives, peaches, and plantains. The fir and palm trees are the moft common. The towns are, Canary the capital, Gualdera, and Genia.

CANARY, or CIUDAD DE PALMAS, is the capital of the ifland of Canaria, with an indifferent caftle, and a bifhop's fee. It has alfo a court of inquifition, and the fupreme council of the reft of the Canary-iflands; as alfo four convents, two for men and two for women. The town is about three miles in compafs, and contains 12,000 inhabitants. The houfes are only one ftory high, and flat at the top; but they are well built. The cathedral is a handfome ftructure. W. Long. 15. 20. N. Lat. 28. 4.

Canary-Iflands, are fituated in the Atlantic ocean, over againft the empire of Morocco in Africa. They were formerly called the *Fortunate Iflands*, on account of the temperate healthy air, and excellent fruits. The land is very fruitful, for both wheat and barley produce 130 for one. The cattle thrive well, and the woods are full of all forts of game. The Canary finging birds are well known all over Europe. There are here fugar-canes in great abundance; but the Spaniards firft planted vines here, from whence we have the wine called *Canary* or *Sack*.

Thefe iflands were not entirely unknown to the ancients; but they were a long while forgot, till John de Betencourt difcovered them in 1405. It is faid they were firft inhabited by the Phœnicians, or Carthaginians, but on no certain foundation; nor could the inhabitants themfelves tell from whence they were derived; on the contrary, they did not know there was any other country in the world. Their language, manners, and cuftoms, had no refemblance to thofe of their neighbours. However, they were like the people on the coaft of Barbary in complexion. They had no iron. After the difcovery, the Spaniards foon got poffeffion of them all, under whofe dominion they are to this day, except Madeira, which belongs to the Portuguefe. The inhabitants are chiefly Spaniards; though there are fome of the firft people remaining, whom they call *Guanches*, who are fomewhat civilized by their intercourfe with the Spaniards. They are a hardy, active, bold people, and live on the mountains. Their chief food is goat's milk. Their complexion is tawny, and their nofes flat. The Spanifh veffels, when they fail for the Weft Indies, always rendezvous at thefe iflands, going and coming. Their number is 12. 1. Alegranza; 2. Canaria; 3. Ferro; 4. Fuerteventura; 5. Gomera; 6. Graciofa; 7. Lancerota; 8. Madeira; 9. Palma; 10. Rocca; 11. Salvages; 12. Teneriff. Weft longitude from 12. to 21. north latitude from 27. 30. to 29. 50.

Canary-Bird. See FRINGILLA. Thefe birds are much admired for their finging, and take their name from the place from whence they originally came, viz. the Canary-iflands; but of late years there is a fort of birds brought from Germany, and efpecially from Tirol, and therefore called *German birds*, which are much better than the others; though both are fuppofed to have originally come from the fame place. The cocks never grow fat, and by fome country people cannot be diftinguifhed from common green-birds; though the Canary-birds are much luftier, have a longer tail, and differ much in the heaving of the paffages of the throat when they fing. Thefe birds being fo much efteemed for their fong, are fometimes fold at a high price, according to the goodnefs and excellency of their notes; fo that it will always be advifable to hear one fing before he is bought. In order to know whether he is in good health, take him out of the ftore-cage, and put him in a clean cage by himfelf; if he ftand up boldly, without crouching or fhrinking in his feathers, look with a brifk eye, and is not fubject to clap his head under his wing, it is a fign that he is in good health; but the greateft matter is to obferve his dungings: if he bolts his tail like a nightingale after he has dunged, it is a fign he is not in good health, or at leaft that he will foon be fick; but if his dung be very thin like water, or of a flimy white without any blacknefs in it, it is a fign of approaching death. When in perfect health, his dung lies round and hard, with a fine white on the outfide, dark within, and dries quickly; though a feed-bird feldom dungs fo hard, unlefs he is very young.

Canary-birds are fubject to many difeafes, particularly impofthumes, which affect the head, caufe them to fall fuddenly from the perch, and die in a fhort time, if not fpeedily cured. The moft approved medicine is an ointment made of frefh butter and capon's greafe melted together. With this the top of the bird's head is to be anointed for two or three days, and it will diffolve the impofthume: but if the medicine has been too long delayed, then, after three or four times anointing, fee whether the place of his head be foft; and if fo, open it gently, and let out the matter, which will be like the yolk of an egg; when this is done, anoint the place, and the bird will be cured. At the fame time he muft have figs with his other food, and in his water a flice or two of liquorice, with white fugar-candy.

Canary-birds are diftinguifhed by different names at different times and ages: fuch as are about three years old are called *runts*; thofe above two are named *eriffs*; thofe of the firft year under the care of the old ones, are termed *branchers*; thofe that are new-flown, and cannot feed themfelves, *pufhers*; and thofe brought up by hand, *neftlings*.

The Canary-birds may be bred with us; and, if treated with proper care, they will become as vigorous and healthful as in the country from whence they have their name. The cages in which thefe birds are kept are to be made either of walnut-tree or oak, with bars of wire; becaufe thefe, being woods of ftrength, do not require to be ufed in large pieces.

Canary-birds. The common shape of cages, which is cylindric, is very improper for these birds; for this allows little room to walk, and without that the birds usually become melancholy. The most proper of all shapes is the high and long, but narrow.

If these birds eat too much, they grow over-fat, lose their shape, and their singing is spoiled; or at least they become so idle, that they will scarce ever sing. In this case their victuals is to be given them in a much smaller quantity, and they will by this means be recovered by degrees to all their beauty, and will sing as at first.

At the time that they are about to build their nests, there must be put into their cages some hay, dried thoroughly in the sun; with this must be mixed some moss dried in the same manner, and some stag's hair; and great care is to be taken of breeding the young, in the article of food. As soon as the young birds are eight days old, or somewhat more, and are able to eat and pick up food of themselves, they are to be taken out of the cage in which they were hatched, and each put separately into another cage, and hung up in a room where it may never have an opportunity of hearing the voice of any other bird. After they have been kept thus about eight days, they are to be excited to sing by a bird-pipe; but this is not to be blowed too much, or in too shrill a manner, lest they sing themselves to death.

For the first fifteen days the cages are to be covered with a black cloth, and for the fifteen days following with a green one. Five lessons in a day from the pipe are sufficient for these young creatures; and they must not be disturbed with several sounds at the same time, lest they confound and puzzle them; two lessons should be given them early in the morning, one about the middle of the day, and two more at night.

The genius and temper of the several birds of this kind are very different. The males are almost always melancholy, and will not sing unless they are excited to it by hearing others continually singing about them. The male bird of this kind will often kill the female put to him for breeding; and when there are several females together with the males, they will often do the same to one another from jealousy. It is therefore not easy to manage the article of their breeding well in this particular, unless in this manner: let two female birds be put into one cage, and when they have lived together some time, they will have contracted a sort of love for one another, which will not easily be dissolved. Put a male bird into the cage with these two, and every thing will go well; their friendship will keep them from quarrelling about his favours, and from danger of his mischievous disposition; for if he attacks one of them, in order to kill her, the other will immediately take her part; and after a few of these battles, the male will find that they are together an over-match for him in fighting, and will then distribute his favours to them, and there will not fail of being a young breed or two, which are to be taken away from their parents, and educated as before directed. Some males watch the time of the female's laying, and devour the eggs as fast as she deposits them; and others take the young ones in their beak as soon as hatched, and crush them to death against the sides of the cage, or some other way destroy them. When a male has been known once to have been guilty of this, he is to be shut up in a small cage, in the middle of the large one in which the female is breeding her young, and thus he will often comfort her with singing all day long, while she sits upon the eggs or takes care of the young ones; and when the time of taking away, to put them into separate cages, is come, the male is to be let out, and he will always after this live in friendship with the female.

If the male become sick during the time of the female's sitting or bringing up her young, he must be removed immediately, and only brought to the side of her cage at certain times, that she may see him, till he is perfectly cured; and then he is to be shut up again in his cage in the middle.

Canary-birds are various in their notes; some having a sweet song, others a fewel note, others a long song, which is best, as having the greatest variety of notes; but they sing chiefly either the titlark or nightingale notes. *See* Song *of Birds*.

Cancalle || Cancer. CANCALLE, a town of France, in Upper Brittany, by the sea-side, where there is a road. Here the British landed in 1758, in their way to St Maloes, where they burnt a great number of ships in the harbour, and then retired without loss. This town was in their power; but they acted like generous enemies, and did no hurt to this nor any other on the coast. W. Long. 0. 13. N. Lat. 48. 41.

CANCELIER, in falconry, is when a light brown hawk, in her stooping, turns two or three times upon the wing, to recover herself before she seizes.

CANCELLI, a term used to denote lattice windows, or those made of cross bars disposed latticewise; it is also used for rails or ballusters inclosing the communion-table, a court of justice, or the like, and for the network in the inside of hollow bones.

CANCELLING, in the civil law, an act whereby a person consents that some former deed be rendered null and void. This is otherwise called *rescission*. The word comes from the Latin *cancellare* to encompass or pale a thing round. In the proper sense of the word, *to cancel*, is to deface an obligation, by passing the pen from top to bottom, or across it; which makes a kind of chequer lattice, which the Latins call *cancelli*.

CANCER, in zoology, a genus of insects belonging to the order of insecta aptera. The generic characters are these: they have eight legs, (seldom ten or six), besides the two large claws which answer the purpose of hands. They have two eyes at a considerable distance from each other, and for the most part supported by a kind of pedunculi or footstalks; the eyes are likewise elongated and moveable; they have two clawed palpi, and the tail is jointed. This genus includes the lobster, shrimp, &c. There are no less than 87 species of cancer, distinguished principally by the length of their tails and the margins of their breasts. The following are the most remarkable.

Common lobster. 1. The gammarus, or common lobster, with a smooth thorax, short serrated front; very long antennæ; and between them two shorter ones, bifid; claws and fangs large, the greater tuberculated, the lesser serrated on the inner edge; four pair of legs; six joints in the tail; tail-fins rounded. It inhabits all the rocky shores of our island, but chiefly where there is a depth of water. In Llyn in Caernarvonshire a certain small lob-

Cancer.

ster, nothing different except in size, borrows in the sand. They are brought in vast quantities from the Orkney isles, and many parts of the eastern coast of Scotland, to the London markets. Sixty or seventy thousand are annually brought from the neighbourhood of Montrose alone.—The lobster was well known to the ancients, and is well described by Aristotle under the name of ἀστακὸς. It is found as far as the Hellespont; and is called at Constantinople *lcavada* and *listipodo*.

Lobsters fear thunder, and are apt to cast their claws on a great clap; it is said that they will do the same on the firing of a great gun; and that, when men of war meet a lobster boat, a jocular threat is used, that, if the master does not sell them good lobsters, they will *salute him*.

The habitation of this species is in the clearest water, at the foot of rocks that impend over the sea. This has given opportunity of examining more closely into the natural history of the animal, than of many others who live in an element that prohibits most of the human researches, and limits the inquiries of the most inquisitive. Some lobsters are taken by hand; but the greater quantity in pots, a sort of trap formed of twigs, and baited with garbage; they are formed like a wire mouse-trap, so that when the lobster gets in, there is no return. These are fastened to a cord sunk in the sea, and their place marked by a buoy.—They begin to breed in the spring, and continue breeding most part of the summer. They propagate *more hominum*, and are extremely prolific. Dr Baster says he counted 12,444 eggs under the tail, besides those that remained in the body unprotruded. They deposit those eggs in the sand, where they are soon hatched.

Lobsters change their crust annually. Previous to their putting off their old one, they appear sick, languid, and restless. They totally acquire a new coat in a few days; but during the time that they remain defenceless, they seek some very lonely place, for fear of being devoured by such of their brethren as are not in the same situation. It is also remarkable, that lobsters and crabs will renew their claws, if by accident they are torn off; and it is certain they will grow again in a few weeks, though they never attain to the size of the first. They are very voracious animals, and feed on sea-weeds, garbage, and all sorts of dead bodies. The pincers of one of the lobsters large claws are furnished with knobs, and those of the other are always serrated. With the former it keeps firm hold of the stalks of submarine plants, and with the latter it cuts and minces its food very dexterously. The knobbed or *numb* claw, as the fishermen call it, is sometimes on the right and sometimes on the left side indifferently. It is more dangerous to be seized by them with the cutting claw than the other; but, in either case, the quickest way to get disengaged from the creature is to pull off its claw. The female or *hen* lobster does not cast her shell the same year that she deposits her ova, or, in the common phrase, is in *berry*. When the ova first appear under her tail, they are small, and extremely black; but they become in succession almost as large as ripe elder berries before they are deposited, and turn of a dark brown colour, especially towards the end of the time of her depositing them. They continue full, and depositing the ova in constant succession, as long as any of that black substance can be found in their body, which, when boiled, turns of a beautiful red colour, and is called their *coral*. Hen-lobsters are found in berry at all times of the year, but chiefly in winter. It is a common mistake, that a berried hen is always in perfection for the table. When her berries appear large and brownish, she will always be found exhausted, watery, and poor. Though the ova be cast at all times of the year, they seem only to come to life during the warm summer months of July and August. Great numbers of them may then be found, under the appearance of tadpoles, swimming about the little pools left by the tides among the rocks, and many also under their proper form from half an inch to four inches in length. In casting their shells, it is hard to conceive how the lobster is able to draw the fish of their large claws out, leaving the shells entire and attached to the shell of their body, in which state they are constantly found. The fishermen say, the lobster pines before casting, till the fish of its large claw is no thicker than the quill of a goose, which enables it to draw its parts through the joints and narrow passage near the trunk. The new shell is quite membranaceous at first, but hardens by degrees. Lobsters only grow in size while their shells are in their soft state. They are chosen for the table, by their being heavy in proportion to their size; and by the hardness of their shells on their sides, which, when in perfection, will not yield to moderate pressure. Barnacles and other small fish adhering to them are reckoned certain signs of superior goodness. Cock-lobsters are in general better than the hens in winter; they are distinguished by the narrowness of their tails, and by their having a strong spine upon the centre of each of the transverse processes beneath the tail, which support the four middle plates of their tails. The fish of a lobster's claw is more tender, delicate, and easy of digestion, than that of the tail. In summer, the lobsters are found near the shore, and thence to about six fathoms water; in winter, they are seldom taken in less than 12 or 15 fathoms. Like other insects, they are much more active and alert in warm weather than in cold. In the water, they can run nimbly upon their legs or small claws; and, if alarmed, can spring, tail foremost, to a surprising distance, as swift as a bird can fly. The fishermen can see them pass about 30 feet; and, by the swiftness of their motion, suppose they may go much farther. Athenæus remarks this circumstance, and says, that "the incurvated lobsters will spring with the activity of dolphins." Their eyes are raised upon moveable bases, which enables them to see readily every way. When frightened, they will spring from a considerable distance to their hold in the rock, and, what is not less surprising than true, will throw themselves into their hold in that manner through an entrance barely sufficient for their bodies to pass.

2. The strigosus, or plated lobster, with a pyramidal spiny snout; thorax elegantly plated, each plate marked near its junction with short striæ; claws much longer than the body, thick, echinated, and tuberculated; the upper fang trifid; only three legs spiny on their sides; tail broad. The largest of this species is about six inches long. It inhabits the coasts of Anglesea, under stones and fuci. It is very active; and, if taken, flaps its tail against the body with much violence and noise. Plate CXV.

3. The astacus, or craw-fish, with a projecting snout

slightly

Cancer. Craw-fish, prawn, shrimp, &c. slightly serrated on the sides; a smooth thorax; back smooth, with two small spines on each side; claws large, beset with small tubercles; two first pair of legs clawed, the two next subulated; tail consisting of five joints; the caudal fins rounded. It inhabits many of the rivers in England, lodged in holes which they form in the clayey banks. Cardan says, that this species indicates the goodness of water; for in the best water they are boiled into the reddest colour.

4. The serratus, or prawn, with a long serrated snout bending upwards; three pair of very long filiform feelers; claws small, furnished with two fangs; smooth thorax; five joints to the tail; middle caudal fin subulated, two outmost flat and rounded. It is frequent in several shores among loose stones; sometimes found at sea, and taken on the surface over 30 fathoms depth of water; cinereous when fresh, of a fine red when boiled.

5. The crangon, or shrimp, with long slender feelers, and between them two projecting laminæ; claws with a single, hooked, moveable fang; three pair of legs; seven joints in the tail; the middle caudal fin subulated, the four others rounded and fringed, a spine on the exterior side of each of the outmost. It inhabits the shores of Britain in vast quantities, and is the most delicious of the genus.

6. The squilla, with a snout like a prawn, but deeper and thinner; the feelers longer in proportion to the bulk; the sub-caudal fins rather larger; is, at full growth, not above half the bulk of the former.—It inhabits the coasts of Kent; and is sold in London under the name of the *white shrimp*, as it assumes that colour when boiled.

7. The atomos, or atom-lobster, with a slender body; filiform antennæ; three pair of legs near the head; behind which are two pair of oval vesiculæ; beyond are three pair of legs, and a slender tail between the last pair. It is very minute, and the help of the microscope is often necessary for its inspection.

8. The pulex, or flea lobster, with five pair of legs, and two claws, imperfect; with 12 joints of the body. It is very common in fountains and rivulets; swims very swiftly in an incurvated posture on its back; embraces and protects its young between the legs; does not leap.

9. The locusta, or locust-lobster, with four antennæ; two pair of imperfect claws; the first joint ovated; body consists of 14 joints, in which it differs from the former. It abounds, in summer, on the shores, beneath stones and algæ; leaps about with vast agility.

Hermit-crab. 10. The diogenes, soldier-crab, or hermit-crab, with rough claws; the left claw is the longest (this being the only difference between the *diogenes* and *bernardus*); the legs are subulated, and serrated along the upper ridge; the tail naked and tender, and furnished with a hook by which it secures itself in its lodging. This species is parasitic; and inhabits the empty cavities of turbinated shells, changing its habitation according to its increase of growth from the small *nerite* to the large *whelk*. Nature denies it the strong covering behind, which it hath given to others of this class; and therefore directs it to take refuge in the deserted cases of other animals. They crawl very fast with the shell on their back; and at the approach of danger draw themselves within the shell, and, thrusting out the larger claw, will pinch very hard whatever molests them. Aristotle describes it very exactly under the name of *καρκίνιον*. By the moderns it is called the *soldier*, from the idea of its dwelling in a tent; or the *hermit*, from retiring into a cell.

It is very diverting to observe this animal when wanting to change its shell. The little soldier is seen busily parading the shore along that line of pebbles and shells which is formed by the extremest wave; still, however, dragging its old incommodious habitation at its tail, unwilling to part with one shell, even though a troublesome appendage, till it can find another more convenient. It is seen stopping at one shell, turning it, and passing it by; going on to another, contemplating that for a while, and then slipping its tail from its old habitation to try on the new: this also is found to be inconvenient, and it quickly returns to its old shell again. In this manner it frequently changes, till at last it finds one light, roomy, and commodious; to this it adheres, though the shell be sometimes so large as to hide the body of the animal, claws and all. Yet it is not till after many trials, and many combats also, that the soldier is thus completely equipped; for there is often a contest between two of them for some well-looking favourite shell for which they are rivals. They both endeavour to take possession; they strike with their claws, they bite each other, till the weakest is obliged to yield by giving up the object of dispute. It is then that the victor immediately takes possession, and parades it in his new conquest three or four times back and forward upon the strand before his envious antagonist. When this animal is taken, it sends forth a feeble cry, endeavouring to seize the enemy with its nippers; which if it fastens upon, it will sooner die than quit the grasp.

The hermit-crabs frequent mostly those parts of the sea-shores which are covered with shrubs and trees, producing various wild fruits on which they subsist; though they will also feed on the fragments of fish and other animal substances cast on shore. When roasted in the shell, they are esteemed delicate. The hermit-crab, hung in the air, dissolves into a kind of oil, which speedily cures the rheumatism, if rubbed upon the part.

11. The vocans, or land-crab, is but of a small size; its colour light brown, or dusky white. It has eight legs, and two claws, one of which is double the size of the other: these claws serve both to defend and to feed themselves with. The head has two square holes, which are receptacles for its eyes; out of which it thrusts them, and draws them in again at pleasure. Their abode is only on the sandy shores of Ilathera, and many others of the Bahama islands. They run very fast, and retreat from danger into little holes they make in the sand.

12. The grapsus, or red mottled crab, hath a round body, the legs longer and larger than in other kinds; the claws red; except which, the whole is mottled in a beautiful manner with red and white. These crabs inhabit the rocks hanging over the sea; they are the nimblest of all others, and run with surprising agility along the upright side of a rock, and even under the rocks that hang horizontally below the water. This they are often necessitated to do for escaping the assaults of rapacious birds that pursue them. These crabs The [illegible]-crab.

never

Plate CXV.
Cancer.
Cancer.
Hermit Crab.
Hermit Crab.
Plated Lobster.

Cancer.

never go to land; but frequent mostly those parts of the promontories and islands of rocks in and near the sea, where, by the continual and violent agitation of the waves against the rocks, they are always wet, continually receiving the spray of the sea, which often washes them into it; but they instantly return to the rock again, not being able to live under water, and yet requiring more of that element than any of the crustaceous kinds that are not fish.

13. The granulatus, or rough-shelled crab: these crabs are pretty large, and are commonly taken from the bottom of the sea in shallow water; the legs are small in proportion to the body; the two claws are remarkably large and flat. The whole shell is covered over with innumerable little tubercles like shagreen: the colour is brown, variously stained with purple.

14. The cancer erythropus, or red-claw crab, is of a small size, and brown colour; it hath two claws of unequal bigness, red at the ends; and eight legs, which seem of less use to them than in other crabs; for when on the ground, they crawl with slow pace, dragging their bodies along; but they are mostly seen grasping with their claws, and hanging to some sea-plant, or other marine substance.

15. The pisum, or pea-crab, with rounded and smooth thorax, entire and blunt; with a tail of the size of the body, which commonly is the bulk of a pea. It inhabits the muscle, and has unjustly acquired the repute of being poisonous. The swelling after eating of muscles is wholly constitutional; for one that is affected by it, hundreds remain uninjured. Crabs either of this kind, or allied to them, the ancients believed to have been the consentaneous inmates of the Pinna, and other bivalves; which, being too stupid to perceive the approach of their prey, were warned of it by their vigilant friend. Oppian tells the fable prettily.

In clouded deeps below, the *pinna* hides,
And through the silent paths obscurely glides;
A stupid wretch, and void of thoughtful care,
He forms no bait, nor lays the tempting snare;
But the dull sluggard boasts a *crab* his friend,
Whose busy eyes the coming prey attend.
One room contains them, and the partners dwell
Beneath the convex of one sloping shell;
Deep in the watry vast the comrades rove,
And mutual interest binds their constant love;
That wiser friend the lucky juncture tells,
When in the circuit of his gaping shells
Fish wand'ring enter; then the bearded guide
Warns the dull mate, and pricks his tender side;
He knows the hint, nor at the treatment grieves,
But hugs th' advantage, and the pain forgives;
His closing shells the *pinna* sudden joins,
And 'twixt the pressing sides his prey confines:
Thus fed by mutual aid, the friendly pair
Divide their gains, and all the plunder share.

16. The mænas, or common crab, with three notches on the front; five serrated teeth on each side; claws ovated; next joint toothed; hind feet subulated; dirty green colour; red when boiled. It inhabits all our shores; and lurks under the *algæ*, or burrows under the sand. Is sold, and eaten by the poor of our capitals.

17. The pagurus, or black clawed crab, with a crenated thorax; smooth body; quinquedentated front; smooth claws and black tips; hind feet subulated. It inhabits the rocky coasts; is the most delicious meat of any; casts its shell between Christmas and Easter. The tips of the claws of this species are used in medicine; intended to absorb acidities in the stomach and bowels.

18. The velutinus, or velvet crab, with the thorax quinquedentated; body covered with short, brown, velvet-like pile; claws covered with minute tubercles; small spines round the top of the second joint; hind legs broadly ovated.—This is among the species taken notice of by Aristotle on account of the broad feet, which, he says, assist them in swimming; as web-feet do the water-fowl. It inhabits the western coast of Anglesea.

19. The horridus, or horrid-crab, with a projecting bifurcated snout, the end diverging; body heart-shaped; with the claws and legs covered with long and very sharp spines.—It is a large species, and inhabits the rocks on the eastern coasts of Scotland. It is common to Norway and Scotland, as many of the marine animals and birds are.

20. The ruricola, land-crab, or violet-crab, with a smooth entire thorax, and the two last joints of the feet armed with spines. It inhabits the Bahama islands, as well as most lands between the tropics; and feeds upon vegetables. — Violet-crab.

These animals live not only in a kind of orderly society in their retreats in the mountains, but regularly once a year march down to the sea-side in a body of some millions at a time. As they multiply in great numbers, they choose the month of April or May to begin their expedition; and then sally out by thousands from the stumps of hollow trees, from the clefts of rocks, and from the holes which they dig for themselves under the surface of the earth. At that time the whole ground is covered with this band of adventurers; there is no setting down one's foot without treading upon them. The sea is their place of destination, and to that they direct their march with right-lined precision. No geometrician could send them to their destined station by a shorter course; they neither turn to the right nor left, whatever obstacles intervene; and even if they meet with a house, they will attempt to scale the walls to keep the unbroken tenor of their way. But though this be the general order of their route, they, upon other occasions, are obliged to conform to the face of the country; and if it is intersected with rivers, they are then seen to wind along the course of the stream. The procession sets forward from the mountains with the regularity of an army under the guidance of an experienced commander. They are commonly divided into three battalions; of which the first consists of the strongest and boldest males, that, like pioneers, march forward to clear the route and face the greatest dangers. These are often obliged to halt for want of rain, and to go into the most convenient encampment till the weather changes. The main body of the army is composed of females, which never leave the mountains till the rain is set in for some time, and then descend in regular battalia, being formed into columns of 50 paces broad, and three miles deep, and so close that they almost cover the ground. Three or four days after this, the rear-guard follows, a straggling

Cancer.

gling undiſciplined tribe, conſiſting of males and females, but neither ſo robuſt nor ſo vigorous as the former. The night is their chief time of proceeding; but if it rains by day, they do not fail to profit by the occaſion; and they continue to move forward in their ſlow uniform manner. When the ſun ſhines and is hot upon the ſurface of the ground, they then make an univerſal halt, and wait till the cool of the evening. When they are terrified, they march back in a confuſed diſorderly manner, holding up their nippers, with which they ſometimes tear off a piece of the ſkin, and then leave the weapon where they inflicted the wound. They even try to intimidate their enemies; for they often clatter their nippers together, as if it were to threaten thoſe that come to diſturb them. But tho' they thus ſtrive to be formidable to man, they are much more ſo to each other; for they are poſſeſſed of one moſt unſocial property, which is, that if any of them by accident is maimed in ſuch a manner as to be incapable of proceeding, the reſt fall upon and devour it on the ſpot, and then purſue their journey.

When, after a fatiguing march, and eſcaping a thouſand dangers, (for they are ſometimes three months in getting to the ſhore), they have arrived at their deſtined port, they prepare to caſt their ſpawn. The peas are as yet within their bodies, and not excluded as is uſual in animals of this kind, under the tail; for the creature waits for the benefit of ſea-water to help the delivery. For this purpoſe the crab has no ſooner reached the ſhore, than it eagerly goes to the edge of the water, and lets the waves waſh over its body two or three times. This ſeems only a preparation for bringing their ſpawn to maturity; for, without farther delay, they withdraw to ſeek a lodging upon land: in the mean time the ſpawn grows larger, is excluded out of the body, and ſticks to the barbs under the flap, or more properly the tail. This bunch is ſeen as big as an hen's egg, and exactly reſembling the roes of herrings. In this ſtate of pregnancy they once more ſeek the ſhore for the laſt time; and ſhaking off their ſpawn into the water, leave accident to bring it to maturity. At this time whole ſhoals of hungry fiſh are at the ſhore in expectation of this annual ſupply; the ſea to a great diſtance ſeems black with them; and about two thirds of the crabs eggs are immediately devoured by theſe rapacious invaders. The eggs that eſcape are hatched under the ſand; and, ſoon after, millions at a time of theſe little crabs are ſeen quitting the ſhore, and ſlowly travelling up to the mountains. The old ones, however, are not ſo active to return; they have become ſo feeble and lean, that they can hardly creep along, and the fleſh at that time changes its colour. The moſt of them, therefore, are obliged to continue in the flat parts of the country till they recover, making holes in the earth, which they cover at the mouth with leaves and dirt, ſo that no air may enter. There they throw off their old ſhells, which they leave, as it were, quite whole; the place where they opened on the belly being unſeen. At that time they are quite naked, and almoſt without motion for ſix days together, when they become ſo fat as to be delicious food. They have then under their ſtomachs four large white ſtones, which gradually decreaſe in proportion as the ſhell hardens, and, when they come to perfection, are not to be found. It is at that time that the animal is ſeen ſlowly making its way back; and all this is moſt commonly performed in the ſpace of ſix weeks.

Cancer.

This animal, when poſſeſſed of its retreats in the mountains, is impregnable: for, only ſubſiſting upon vegetables, it ſeldom ventures out; and its habitation being in the moſt inacceſſible places, it remains for a great part of the ſeaſon in perfect ſecurity. It is only when impelled by the deſire of bringing forth its young, and when compelled to deſcend into the flat country, that it is taken. At that time the natives wait for its deſcent in eager expectation, and deſtroy thouſands; but, diſregarding their bodies, they only ſeek for that ſmall ſpawn which lies on each ſide of the ſtomach within the ſhell, of about the thickneſs of a man's thumb. They are much more valuable upon their return after they have caſt their ſhell; for, being covered with a ſkin reſembling ſoft parchment, almoſt every part except the ſtomach may be eaten. They are taken in the holes by feeling for them with an inſtrument; they are ſought after by night, when on their journey, by flambeaux. The inſtant the animal perceives itſelf attacked, it throws itſelf on its back, and with its claws pinches moſt terribly whatever it happens to faſten on. But the dexterous crab-catcher takes them by the hinder legs in ſuch a manner that the nippers cannot touch him, and thus he throws them into his bag. Sometimes alſo they are caught when they take refuge in the bottoms of holes in rocks by the ſea-ſide, by clapping a ſtick at the mouth of the hole, which prevents their getting out; and then ſoon after, the tide coming, enters the hole, and the animal is found, upon its retiring, drowned in its retreat.

Theſe crabs are of various ſizes, the largeſt about ſix inches wide; they walk ſide-ways like the ſea-crab, and are ſhaped like them; ſome are black, ſome yellow, ſome red, and others variegated with red, white, and yellow mixed. Some of theſe are poiſonous; and ſeveral people have died of eating of the crabs, particularly of the black kind. The light-coloured are reckoned beſt; and when full in fleſh, are very well taſted. In ſome of the ſugar iſlands they are eat without danger; and are no ſmall help to the negro ſlaves, who, on many of theſe iſlands, would fare very hard without them.

Cancer, in medicine, a roundiſh, unequal, hard, and livid tumour, generally ſeated in the glandulous parts of the body, ſuppoſed to be ſo called, becauſe it appears at length with turgid veins ſhooting out from it, ſo as to reſemble, as it is thought, the figure of a crab-fiſh; or, others ſay, becauſe, like that fiſh, where it has once got, it is ſcarce poſſible to drive it away. See (the *Index* ſubjoined to) Medicine.

Cancer, in aſtronomy, one of the twelve ſigns, repreſented on the globe in the form of a crab, and thus marked (♋) in books. It is the fourth conſtellation in the ſtarry zodiac, and that from which one quadrant of the ecliptic takes its denomination. The reaſon generally aſſigned for its name as well as figure, is a ſuppoſed reſemblance which the ſun's motion in this ſign bears to the crab-fiſh. As the latter walks backwards, ſo the former, in this part of his courſe, begins to go backwards, or recede from us; though the

diſpoſi-

disposition of stars in this sign is by others supposed to have given the first hint to the representation of a crab.

Tropic of Cancer, in astronomy, a lesser circle of the sphere parallel to the equator, and passing through the beginning of the sign Cancer.

CANCHERIZANTE, or Cancherizato, in the Italian music, a term signifying a piece of music that begins at the end, being the retrograde motion from the end of a song, &c. to the beginning.

CANCROMA, or Boat-bill, in ornithology, a genus of birds belonging to the order of *Grallæ*; the characters of which are: The bill is broad, with a keel along the middle: the nostrils are small, and lodged in a furrow; the tongue is small; and the toes are divided. There are two species:

1. The Cochlearia, or Crested Boat-bill, is of the size of a fowl; the length 22 inches. The bill is four inches long, and of a singular form, not unlike a boat with the keel uppermost, or, as some think, like the bowls of two spoons, placed with the hollow parts together; the upper mandible has a prominent ridge at the top, and on each side of this a long channel, at the bottom of which the nostrils are placed; these are oval, and situated obliquely; the general colour of the bill is dusky, or in some specimens dark brown; the skin between the under jaw capable of distension; from the hind head springs a long black crest, the feathers which compose it narrow, and end in a point; the middle ones are six inches in length, the others lessen by degrees, the outer ones being not more than one inch: between the bill and eye the skin is bare and dusky; the plumage on the forehead white; the rest of the bird of a pale bluish ash-colour; across the lower part of the neck behind is a transverse band of brownish black, which passes forwards on each side towards the breast, ending in a point, but does not encompass it: the fore part of the neck, and under parts, are bluish white, except the belly and thighs, which are rufous: the feathers which hang over the breast are loose, like those of the heron: the tail is three inches and a half long, and the wings, when closed, reach nearly to the end of it: the leg is three inches in length; and the thigh, from its insertion to the knee, four; the middle toe two inches and a half; the bare part above the knee one inch and a half; the colour of the bare parts yellowish brown; claws black: the toes are connected at the base by a membrane, which, as in the umbre, is deepest in the outer one.—It inhabits Cayenne, Guiana, and Brasil, and chiefly frequents such parts as are near the water: in such places it perches on the trees which hang over the streams, and, like the kings-fisher, drops down on the fish which swim beneath. It has been thought to live on crabs likewise, whence the Linnæan name

Plate CXVI. 2. The Cancrophaga, or Brown Boat-bill, a distinct species, according to Linnæus, but which Mr Latham considers as only a variety, is of the size of the former; the head and crest the same; the upper parts, instead of ash-colour, are of a pale rufous brown; the tail rufous-ish; and the under parts wholly of a cream colour; the bill and legs of a yellow brown. Its place and manners the same with those of the preceding.

CANDAHAR, a province of Persia, bounded on the north by the province of Balk; on the east, by that of Cabul; on the south, by Buchor and Sablestan; and on the west, by Sigestan. There have been bloody wars between the Indians and Persians on account of this province; but in 1650 it fell to the Persians. The inhabitants are known by the name of *Agwans*, or *Afghans*, who have often endeavoured to throw off the yoke. But, in 1737, they were severely punished for such an attempt. See Baskets.

Candahar, the capital of the above province, is seated on a mountain; and being a place of great trade, has a considerable fortress. The caravans that travel from Persia and the parts about the Caspian sea to the East Indies, choose to pass through Candahar, because there is no danger of being robbed on this road, and provisions are very reasonable. The religion is Mahometanism, but there are many Banians and Guebres. E. Long. 67. 5. N. Lat. 33. 0.

CANDAULES, the last king of Lydia, of the family of the Heraclidæ. See Lydia.

CANDELARES (from *candela* a candle), the name of an order in the former editions of Linnæus's Fragments of a natural method, consisting of these three genera, *rhizophora*, *nyssa*, and *mimusops*. They are removed, in the latter editions, into the order Holeraceæ; which see.

CANDIA, the modern name of the island of Crete (see Crete). The word is a variation of *Alhandak*, which was originally the Arabian name of the metropolis only, but in time came to be applied to the whole island.

Candia came into the possession of the Venetians by purchase in the year 1194, as related under the article Crete; and soon began to flourish under the laws of that wise republic. The inhabitants, living under the protection of a moderate government, and being encouraged by their masters, engaged in commerce and agriculture. The Venetian commandants readily afforded to those travellers who visited the island, that assistance which is necessary to enable them to extend and improve useful knowledge. Belon, the naturalist, is lavish in praise of their good offices, and describes, in an interesting manner, the flourishing state of that part of the island which he visited.

The seat of government was established at Candia. The magistrates and officers, who composed the council, resided there. The provisor-general was president. He possessed the chief authority; and his power extended over the whole principality. It continued in the possession of the Venetians for five centuries and an half. Cornaro held the chief command at the time when it was threatened with a storm, on the side of Constantinople. The Turks, for the space of a year, had been employed in preparing a vast armament. They deceived the Venetian, by assuring him that it was intended against Malta. In the year 1645, in the midst of a solemn peace, they appeared unexpectedly before Crete with a fleet of 400 sail, having on board 60,000 land forces, under the command of four pachas. The emperor Ibrahim, under whom this expedition was undertaken, had no fair pretext to offer in justification of his enterprize. He made use of all that perfidy which characterizes the people of the east, to impose on the Venetian senate. He loaded their ambassador with presents, directed his fleet to bear for Cape Matapan, as if they had been going beyond the

Archi-

Candia.

Archipelago; and caused the governors of Tina and Cerigua to be solemnly assured, that the republic had nothing to fear for her possessions. At the very instant when he was making those assurances, his naval armament entered the gulf of Canea; and, passing between that city and St Theodore, anchored at the mouth of Platania.

The Venetians, not expecting this sudden attack, had made no preparations to repel it. The Turks landed without opposition. The isle of St Theodore is but a league and an half from Canea. It is only three quarters of a league in compass. The Venetians had erected two forts there; one of which, standing on the summit of the highest eminence, on the coast of that little isle, was called Turluru; the other, on a lower situation, was named St Theodore. It was an important object to the Mussulmans to make themselves masters of that rock, which might annoy their ships. They immediately attacked it with ardour. The first of those fortresses, being destitute of soldiers and cannon, was taken without striking a blow. The garrison of the other consisted of no more than 60 men. They made a gallant defence, and stood out till the last extremity; and when the Turks at last prevailed, their number was diminished to ten, whom the captain-pacha cruelly caused to be beheaded.

Being now masters of that important post, as well as of Lazaret, an elevated rock, standing about half a league from Canea, the Turks invested the city by sea and land. General Cornaro was struck, as with a thunder-clap, when he learned the descent of the enemy. In the whole island there were no more than a body of 3500 infantry, and a small number of cavalry. The besieged city was defended only by 1000 regular troops, and a few citizens, who were able to bear arms. He made haste to give the republic notice of his distress; and posted himself off the road, that he might the more readily succour the besieged city. He threw a body of 250 men into the town, before the lines of the enemy were completed. He afterwards made several attempts to strengthen the besieged with other reinforcements; but in vain. The Turks had advanced in bodies close to the town, had carried a half-moon battery, which covered the gate of Retimo; and were battering the walls night and day with their numerous artillery. The besieged defended themselves with resolute valour, and the smallest advantage which the besiegers gained cost them dear. General Cornaro made an attempt to arm the Greeks, particularly the Spachiots, who boasted loudly of their valour. He formed a battalion of these. But the era of their valour was long past. When they beheld the enemy, and heard the thunder of the cannon, they took to flight; not one of them would stand fire.

While the senate of Venice were deliberating on the means to be used for relieving Canea, and endeavouring to equip a fleet, the Mahometan generals were sacrificing the lives of their soldiers to bring their enterprise to a glorious termination. In different engagements they had already lost 20,000 warriors; but, descending into the ditches, they had undermined the walls, and blown up the most impregnable forts with explosions of powder. They sprung one of those mines beneath the bastion of St Demetri. It overturned a considerable part of the wall, which crushed all the defenders of the bastion. That instant the besiegers sprung up with their sabres in their hands, and taking advantage of the general consternation of the besieged on that quarter, made themselves masters of the post. The besieged, recovering from their terror, attacked them with unequalled intrepidity. About 400 men assailed 2000 Turks already firmly posted on the wall, and pressed upon them with such obstinate and dauntless valour, that they killed a great number, and drove the rest down into the ditch. In this extremity, every person in the city was in arms. The Greek monks took up muskets; and the women, forgetting the delicacy of their sex, appeared on the walls among the defenders, either supplying the men with ammunition and arms, or fighting themselves; and several of those daring heroines lost their lives.

For 50 days the city held out against all the forces of the Turks. If, even at the end of that time, the Venetians had sent a naval armament to its relief, the kingdom of Candia might have been saved. Doubtless, they were not ignorant of this well known fact. The north wind blows straight into the harbour of Canea. When it blows a little briskly, the sea rages. It is then impossible for any squadron of ships, however numerous, to form in line of battle in the harbour, and to meet an enemy. If the Venetians had set out from Cerigo with a fair wind, they might have reached Canea in five hours, and might have entered the harbour with full sails, without being exposed to one cannon-shot; while none of the Turkish ships would have dared to appear before them: or if they had ventured, must have been driven back on the shore, and dashed in pieces among the rocks. But, instead of thus taking advantage of the natural circumstances of the place, they sent a few galleys, which, not daring to double Cape Spada, coasted along the southern shore of the island, and failed of accomplishing the design of their expedition.

At last, the Caneans, despairing of relief from Venice, seeing three breaches made in their walls, thro' which the infidels might easily advance upon them, exhausted with fatigue, and covered with wounds, and reduced to the number of 500 men, who were obliged to scatter themselves round the walls, which were half a league in extent, and undermined in all quarters, demanded a parley, and offered to capitulate. They obtained very honourable conditions; and after a glorious defence of two months, which cost the Turks 20,000 men, marched out of the city with the honours of war. Those citizens, who did not chuse to continue in the city, were permitted to remove; and the Ottomans, contrary to their usual practice, faithfully observed their stipulations.

The Venetians, after the loss of Canea, retired to Retimo. The captain-pacha laid siege to the citadel of the Sude, situated in the entrance of the bay, on an high rock, of about a quarter of a league in circumference. He raised earthen-batteries, and made an ineffectual attempt to level its ramparts. At last, despairing of taking it by assault, he left some forces to block it up from all communication, and advanced towards Retimo. That city, being unwalled, was defended by a citadel, standing on an eminence which overlooks the harbour. General Cornaro had retired thither. At the approach of the enemy, he advanced

Candia.

from the city, and waited for them in the open field. In the action, inattentive to his own safety, he encouraged the soldiers, by fighting in the ranks. A glorious death was the reward of his valour; but his fall determined the fate of Retimo.

The Turks having landed additional forces on the island, they introduced the plague, which was almost a constant attendant on their armies. This dreadful pest rapidly advanced, and, like a devouring fire, wasting all before it, destroyed most part of the inhabitants. The rest, fleeing in terror before its ravages, escaped into the Venetian territories, and the island was left almost desolate.

The siege of the capital commenced in 1646, and was protracted much longer than that of Troy. Till the year 1648, the Turks scarce gained any advantages before that city. They were often routed by the Venetians, and sometimes compelled to retire to Retimo. At that period Ibrahim was solemnly deposed, and his eldest son, at the age of nine years, was raised to the throne, under the name of Mahomet IV. Not satisfied with confining the sultan to the horrors and obscurity of a dungeon, the partisans of his son strangled him on the 19th of August, in the same year. That young prince, who mounted the throne by the death of his father, was afterwards expelled from it, and condemned to pass the remainder of his life in confinement.

In the year 1649, Ussein Pacha, who blockaded Candia, receiving no supplies from the Porte, was compelled to raise the siege, and retreat to Canea. The Venetians were then on the sea with a strong squadron. They attacked the Turkish fleet in the bay of Smyrna, burnt 12 of their ships and 2 gallies, and killed 6000 of their men. Some time after, the Mahometans having found means to land an army on Candia, renewed the siege of the city with greater vigour, and made themselves masters of an advanced fort that was very troublesome to the besieged; which obliged them to blow it up.

From the year 1650 till 1658, the Venetians, continuing masters of the sea, intercepted the Ottomans every year in the straits of the Dardanelles, and fought them in four naval engagements; in which they defeated their numerous fleets, sunk a number of their caravels, took others, and extended the terror of their arms even to the walls of Constantinople. That capital became a scene of tumult and disorder. The Grand Signior, alarmed, and trembling for his safety, left the city with precipitation.

Such glorious success revived the hopes of the Venetians, and depressed the courage of the Turks. They converted the siege of Candia into a blockade, and suffered considerable losses. The Sultan, in order to exclude the Venetian fleet from the Dardanelles, and to open to his own navy a free and safe passage, caused two fortresses to be built at the entrance of the straits. He gave orders to the Pacha of Canea to appear again before the walls of Candia, and to make every possible effort to gain the city. In the mean time, the republic of Venice, to improve the advantages which they had gained, made several attempts on Canea. In 1660, that city was about to surrender to their arms, when the Pacha of Rhodes, hastening to its relief, reinforced the defenders with a body of 2000 men. He happily

Candia.

doubled the extremity of Cape Melec, though within sight of the Venetian fleet, which was becalmed off Cape Spada, and could not advance one fathom to oppose an enemy considerably weaker than themselves.

Kiopruli, son and successor to the visir of that name, who had long been the support of the Ottoman empire, knowing that the murmurs of the people against the long continuance of the siege of Candia were rising to an height, and fearing a general revolt, which would be fatal to himself and his master, set out from Byzantium about the end of the year 1666 at the head of a formidable army. Having escaped the Venetian fleet, which was lying off Canea with a view to intercept him, he landed at *Paleo Castro*, and formed his lines around Candia. Under his command were four Pachas, and the flower of the Ottoman forces. Those troops, being encouraged by the presence and the promises of their chiefs, and supported by a great quantity of artillery, performed prodigies of valour. All the exterior forts were destroyed. Nothing now remained to the besieged but the bare line of the walls, unprotected by fortresses; and these being battered by an incessant discharge of artillery, soon gave way on all quarters. Still, however, what posterity may perhaps regard as incredible, the Candians held out three years against all the forces of the Ottoman empire. At last they were going to capitulate, when the hope of assistance from France reanimated their valour, and rendered them invincible. The expected succours arrived on the 26th of June 1669. They were conducted by the duke of Noailles. Under his command were a great number of French noblemen, who came to make trial of their skill in arms against the Turks.

Next day after their arrival, the ardour of the French prompted them to make a general sally. The duke of Beaufort, admiral of France, assumed the command of the forlorn hope. He was the first to advance against the Mussulmans, and was followed by a numerous body of infantry and cavalry. They advanced furiously upon the enemy, attacked them within their trenches, forced the trenches, and would have compelled them to abandon their lines and artillery, had not an unforeseen accident damped their courage. In the midst of the engagement a magazine of powder was set on fire; the foremost of the combatants lost their lives; the French ranks were broken; several of their leaders, among whom was the duke of Beaufort, disappeared for ever; the soldiers fled in disorder; and the duke of Noailles, with difficulty, effected a retreat within the walls of Candia. The French accused the Italians of having betrayed them; and on that pretext prepared to set off sooner than the time agreed upon. No intreaties of the commandant could prevail with them to delay their departure; so they reimbarked. Their departure determined the fate of the city. There were now no more than five hundred men to defend it. Morosini capitulated with Kiopruli, to whom he surrendered the kingdom of Crete, excepting only the Suda, Grabusa, and Spina-Longua. The grand visir made his entrance into Candia on the 4th of October 1670; and stayed eight months in that city, inspecting the reparation of its walls and fortresses.

The three fortresses left in the hands of the Vene-

Candia.

tions by the treaty of capitulation remained long after in their poſſeſſion. At laſt they were all taken, one after another. In ſhort, after a war of thirty years continuance, in the courſe of which more than two hundred thouſand men fell in the iſland, and it was deluged with ſtreams of Chriſtian and Mahometan blood, Candia was entirely ſubdued by the Turks, in whoſe hands it ſtill continues.

Of the climate of Candia travellers ſpeak with rapture. The heat is never exceſſive; and in the plains violent cold is never felt. In the warmeſt days of ſummer the atmoſphere is cooled by breezes from the ſea. Winter properly begins here with December and ends with January; and during that ſhort period ſnow never falls on the the lower grounds, and the ſurface of the water is rarely frozen over. Moſt frequently the weather is as fine then as it is in Britain at the beginning of June. Theſe two months have received the name of *winter*, becauſe in them there is a copious fall of rain, the ſky is obſcured with clouds, and the north winds blow violently; but the rains are favourable to agriculture, the winds chaſe the clouds towards the ſummits of the mountains, where a repoſitory is formed for thoſe waters which are to fertiliſe the fields; and the inhabitants of the plain ſuffer no inconvenience from theſe tranſient blaſts. In the month of February, the ground is overſpread with flowers and riſing crops. The reſt of the year is almoſt one continued fine day. The inhabitants of Crete never experience any of thoſe mortifying returns of piercing cold, which are ſo frequently felt in Britain and even more ſouthern countries; and which, ſucceeding ſuddenly after the cheriſhing heats of ſpring, nip the bloſſoming flowers, wither the open buds, deſtroy half the fruits of the year, and are fatal to delicate conſtitutions. The ſky is always unclouded and ſerene; the winds are mild and refreſhing breezes. The radiant ſun proceeds in ſmiling majeſty along the azure vault, and ripens the fruits on the lofty mountains, the riſing hills, and the plains. The nights are no leſs beautiful; their coolneſs is delicious. The atmoſphere not being overloaded with vapours, the ſky unfolds to the obſerver's view a countleſs profuſion of ſtars; theſe numerous ſtars ſparkle with the moſt vivid rays, and ſtrew the azure vault in which they appear fixed, with gold, with diamonds, and with rubies. Nothing can be more magnificent than this ſight, and the Cretans enjoy it for ſix months in the year.

To the charms of the climate other advantages are joined which augment their value: There are ſcarce any moraſſes in the iſland; the waters never ſtand here in a ſtate of ſtagnation; they flow in numberleſs ſtreams from the tops of the mountains, and form here and there large fountains or ſmall rivers that empty themſelves into the ſea; the elevated ſituation of their ſprings cauſes them to daſh down with ſuch rapidity, that they never loſe themſelves in pools or lakes; conſequently inſects cannot depoſit their eggs upon them, as they would be immediately hurried down into the ſea; and Crete is not infeſted like Egypt with thoſe clouds of inſects which ſwarm in the houſes, and whoſe ſting is inſufferably painful; nor is the atmoſphere here loaded with thoſe noxious vapours which riſe from marſhy grounds.

The mountains and hills are overſpread with various kinds of thyme, ſavoury, wild thyme, and with a multitude of odoriferous and balſamic plants; the rivulets which flow down the vallies are overhung with myrtles and laurel roſes; clumps of orange, citron, and almond trees, are plentifully ſcattered over the fields; the gardens are adorned with tufts of Arabian jaſmine. In ſpring, they are beſtrewed with beds of violets; ſome extenſive plains are arrayed in ſaffron; the cavities of the rocks are fringed with ſweet ſmelling dittany. In a word, from the hills, the vales, and the plains, on all hands, there ariſe clouds of exquiſite perfumes, which embalm the air, and render it a luxury to breathe it.

As to the inhabitants, the Mahometan men are generally from five feet and an half to ſix feet tall. They bear a ſtrong reſemblance to ancient ſtatues; and it muſt have been after ſuch models that the ancient artiſts wrought. The women alſo are generally beautiful. Their dreſs does not reſtrain the growth of any part of their bodies, and their ſhape therefore aſſumes thoſe admirable proportions with which the hand of the Creator has graced his faireſt workmanſhip on earth. They are not all handſome or charming; but ſome of them are beautiful, particularly the Turkiſh ladies. In general, the Cretan women have a riſing throat, a neck gracefully rounded, black eyes ſparkling with animation, a ſmall mouth, a fine noſe, and cheeks delicately coloured with the freſh vermilion of health. But the oval of their form is different from that of Europeans, and the character of their beauty is peculiar to their own nation.

The quadrupeds belonging to the iſland are not of a ferocious temper. There are no lions, tigers, bears, wolves, foxes, nor indeed any dangerous animal here. Wild goats are the only inhabitants of the foreſts that overſpread the lofty mountains; and theſe have nothing to fear but the ball of the hunter; hares inhabit the hills and the plain; ſheep graze in ſecurity on the thyme and the heath; they are *folded* every night, and the ſhepherd ſleeps ſoundly without being diſturbed with the fear that wild animals may invade and ravage his folds.

The Cretans are very happy in not being expoſed to the troubleſome bite of noxious inſects, the poiſon of ſerpents, and the rapacity of the wild beaſts of the deſert. The ancients believed that the iſland enjoyed theſe ſingular advantages, on account of its having been the birth-place of Jupiter. "The Cretans (ſay Ælian) celebrate in their ſongs the beneficence of Jupiter, and the favour which he conferred on their iſland, which was the place of his birth and education, by freeing it from every noxious animal, and even rendering it unfit for nouriſhing thoſe noxious animals that are introduced into it from foreign countries."

Dittany holds the firſt rank among the medicinal plants which are produced in Crete. The praiſes beſtowed on the virtues of this plant by the ancients are altogether extravagant; yet we perhaps treat the medicinal virtues of this plant with too much contempt. Its leaf is very balſamic, and its flower diffuſes around it a delicious odour. At preſent the inhabitants of the iſland apply it with ſucceſs on various occaſions. The leaf, when dried and taken in an infuſion with a little ſugar, makes a very pleaſant drink, of a finer flavour than tea. It is there an immediate cure for a

weak

Candia.

weak stomach, and enables it to recover its tone after a bad digestion.

Diseases are very rare in a country whose atmosphere is exceedingly pure; and in Candia, epidemical diseases are unknown. Fevers prevail here in summer, but are not dangerous; and the plague would be wholly unknown, had not the Turks destroyed the lazarets that were established by the Venetians, for strangers to do quarantine in. Since the period when these were demolished, it is occasionally introduced by ships from Smyrna and Constantinople. As no precautions are taken against it, it gains ground, and spreads over the island from one province to another; and as the colds and heats are never intemperate, it sometimes continues its ravages for six months at a time.

This fine country is infested with a disease somewhat less dangerous than the plague, but whose symptoms are somewhat more hideous; that disease is the leprosy. In ancient times, Syria was the focus in which it raged with most fury; and from Syria it was carried into several of the islands of the Archipelago. It is infectious, and is instantaneously communicated by contact. The victims who are attacked by it, are driven from society, and confined to little ruinous houses on the highway. They are strictly forbidden to leave these miserable dwellings, or hold intercourse with any person. These poor wretches have generally beside their huts a small garden producing pulse, and feeding poultry; and with that support, and what they obtain from passengers, they find means to drag out a painful life in circumstances of shocking bodily distress. Their bloated skin is covered with a scaly crust, speckled with red and white spots; which afflict them with intolerable itchings. A hoarse and tremulous voice issues from the bottom of their breasts. Their words are scarce articulated; because their distemper inwardly preys upon the organs of speech. These frightful spectres gradually lose the use of their limbs. They continue to breathe till such time as the whole mass of their blood is corrupted, and their bodies entirely in a state of putrefaction. The rich are not attacked by this distemper: it confines itself to the poor, chiefly to the Greeks. But these Greeks observe strictly their four lents; and eat nothing during that time but salt fish, bazargo, salted and smoked pickled olives, and cheese. They drink plentifully of the hot and muddy wines of the island. The natural tendency of such a regimen must be, to fire the blood, to thicken the fluid part of it, and thus at length to bring on a leprosy.

Candia is at present governed by three Pachas, who reside respectively at Candia, Canea, and Retimo. The first, who is always a Pacha of three tails, may be considered as viceroy of the island. He enjoys more extensive powers than the others. To him the inspection of the forts and arsenals is entrusted. He nominates to such military employments as fall vacant, as well as to the governments of the Selino, Girabusa, Spina Longua, and Gira-petra. The governors of these forts are denominated Beys. Each of them has a constable and three general officers under him; one of whom is commander of the artillery; another of the cavalry; and the third of the janissaries.

The council of the pacha consists of a kyaia, who is the channel through which all orders are issued, and all favours bestowed; an aga of the janissaries, colonel-general of the troops, who has the chief care of the regulation of the police; two topigi bachi; a desterdar, who is treasurer-general for the imperial revenues; a keeper of the imperial treasury; and the chief officers of the army. This government is entirely military, and the power of the pacha seraskier is absolute. The justice of his sentences is never called into question; they are instantly carried into execution.

The people of the law are the mufti, who is the religious head, and the cadi. The first interprets those laws which regard the division of the patrimony among the children of a family, successions, and marriages;—in a word, all that are contained in the Koran; and he also decides on every thing that relates to the ceremonies of the Mussulman religion. The cadi cannot pronounce sentence on affairs connected with these laws, without first taking the opinion of the mufti in writing, which is named *Fattsa*. It is his business to receive the declarations, complaints, and donations of private persons; and to decide on such differences as arise among them. The pacha is obliged to consult those judges when he puts a Turk legally to death; but the pacha, who is dignified with three tails, sets himself above all laws, condemns to death, and sees his sentence executed, of his own proper authority. All the mosques have their Iman, a kind of curate, whose duty is to perform the service. There are schoolmasters in the different quarters of the city. These persons are much respected in Turky, and are honoured with the title of Effendi.

The garrison of Candia consists of forty-six companies, composing a military force of about two thousand men. All these forces do not reside constantly in the city, but they may be mustered in a very short time. They are all regularly paid every three months, excepting the janissaries, none of whom but the officers receive pay. The different gradations of this military body do not depend on the pacha. The council of each company, consisting of veterans, and of officers in actual service, has the power of naming to them. A person can occupy the same post for no longer than two years; but the post of *Serdengi*, or captain, which is purchased at Constantinople, is held for life. The *aschi*, or cook, is also continued in his employment as long as the company to which he belongs is satisfied with him. Each company has its almoner, denominated *iman*.

The garrisons of Canea and Retimo, formed on a similar plan, are much less numerous. The first consists of about three thousand men, the other of five hundred; but as all the male children of the Turks are enrolled among the janissaries as soon as born, the number of these troops might be greatly augmented in time of war; but, to say the truth, they are far from formidable. Most of them have never seen fire, nor are they ever exercised in military evolutions.

The pachas of Canea and Retimo are no less absolute, within the bounds of their respective provinces, than the pacha of Candia. They enjoy the same privileges with him, and their council consists of the same officers. These governors chief object is to get rich as speedily as possible; and in order to accomplish that end, they practise all the arts and cruelties of oppression, to squeeze money from the Greeks. In truth, those poor wretches run to meet the chains with which they are loaded. Envy, which always preys upon them, continually prompts them to take up arms. If some one among them happen to enjoy a decent fortune, the rest assiduously seek some pretence for accusing him before the pacha, who takes advantage of these dissentions, to seize the property of both the parties. It is by no means astonishing, that under so barbarous a government, the number of the Greeks is daily diminished.

There are scarcely	150,000 Greeks
in the island, sixty-five thousand of whom pay the carach.	
The Turks have not possessed the island for more than one hundred and twenty years; yet, as they are not exposed to the same oppression, they have multiplied in it, and raised themselves upon the ruin of the ancient inhabitants. Their number amounts to	200,000 Turks.
The Jews, of whom there are not many in the island, amount only to	100.
Total is	350,100 souls.

This fertile country is in want of nothing but industrious husbandmen, secure of enjoying the fruit of their labours. It might maintain four times its present number of inhabitants.

Antiquity has celebrated the island of Crete as containing an hundred populous cities; and the industry of geographers has preserved their names and situations. Many of these cities contained no fewer than thirty thousand inhabitants;—and by reckoning them, on an average, at six thousand each, we shall in all probability be rather within than beyond the truth. This calculation gives for an hundred cities	600,000
By allowing the same number as inhabitants of the towns, villages, and all the rest of the island,	600,000
the whole number of the inhabitants of ancient Crete will amount to	1,200,000

This number cannot be exaggerated. When Candia was in the hands of the Venetians, it was reckoned to contain nine hundred fourscore and sixteen villages.

It appears, therefore, that when the island of Crete enjoyed the blessing of liberty, it maintained to the number of eight hundred and forty-nine thousand eight hundred more inhabitants than it does at present. But since those happier times, she has been deprived of her laws by the tyranny of the Romans; has groaned under the destructive sway of the monarchs of the lower empire; has been exposed for a period of an hundred and twenty years to the ravages of the Arabians; has next passed under the dominion of the Venetians; and has at last been subjected to the despotism of the Turks, who have produced a dreadful depopulation in all the countries which have been subdued by their arms.

The Turks allow the Greeks the free exercise of their religion, but forbid them to repair their churches or monasteries; and accordingly they cannot obtain permission to repair their places of worship, or religious houses, but by the powerful influence of gold. From this article the pachas derive very considerable sums. They have twelve bishops as formerly, the first of whom assumes the title of Archbishop of Gortynia. He resides at Candia; in which city the metropolitan church of the island stands. He is appointed by the patriarch of Constantinople; and has the right of nominating to all the other bishoprics of the island; the names of which are, Gortynia, Chosson, Miralella, Hyera, Gira-petra, Arcadia, Cherronese, Lambia, Milopotamo, Retimo, Canea, Cisamo. These bishoprics are nearly the same as under the reign of the Greek emperors. The patriarch wears a triple tiara, writes his signature in red ink, and answers for all the debts of the clergy. To enable him to fulfil his engagements, he lays impositions on the rest of the bishops, and particularly on the monasteries, from which he draws very handsome contributions. He is considered as the head of the Greeks, whom he protects, as far as his slender credit goes. The orders of government are directed to him on important occasions; and he is the only one of all the Greeks in the island who enjoys the privilege of entering the city on horseback.

Candia, is the capital of the above island, situated on its northern coast, in E. Long. 25. 0. N. Lat. 35. 30. It stands on the same situation which was formerly occupied by Heraclea, and is the seat of government under the Turks. Its walls, which are more than a league in compass, are in good repair, and defended by deep ditches, but not protected by any exterior fort. Towards the sea, it has no attacks to fear; because the shallowness of the harbour renders it inaccessible to ships of war.

The Porte generally commits the government of this island to a Pacha of three tails. The principal officers, and several bodies of the Ottoman soldiery, are stationed here. This city, when under the Venetians, was opulent, commercial, and populous; but it has now lost much of its former strength and grandeur. The harbour, naturally a fine bason, in which ships are securely sheltered from every storm, is every day becoming narrower and shallower. At present it admits only boats, and small ships after they have discharged a part of their freight. Those vessels, which the Turks freight at Candia, are obliged to go almost empty to the ports of Standie, whither their cargoes are conveyed to them in barks. Such inconveniences are highly unfavourable to commerce; and as government never thinks of removing them, the trade of Candia is therefore considerably decayed.

Candia, which was embellished by the Venetians with regular streets, handsome houses, a fine square, and a magnificent cistern, contains at present but a small number of inhabitants, notwithstanding the vast extent of the area inclosed within its walls. Several divisions of the city are void of inhabitants. That in which the market-place stands is the only one which discovers any stir of business, or show of affluence. The Mahometans have converted most of the Christian temples into mosques; yet they have left two churches to the Greeks, one to the Armenians, and a synagogue to the Jews. The Capuchins possess a small convent, with a chapel in which the vice-consul of France hears mass. At present he is the only Frenchman who attends it, as the French merchants have taken up their residence at Canea.

West of the city of Candia is an extensive range of

hills;

hills, which are a continuation of mount Ida, and of which the extremity forms the promontory of Dion. On the way to Dion, we find Palio Castro, on the shore; a name which the modern Greeks give indifferently to all remains of ancient cities. Its situation corresponds to that of the ancient Panormus, which stood north-west from Heraclea.

The river which runs west of Candia was anciently known by the name of Triton; near the source of which Minerva sprung from the brain of Jove. Loasus is a little farther distant. About a league east of that city, the river Ceratus flows through a delightful vale. According to Strabo, in one part of its course it runs near by Gnossus. A little beyond that, is another river supposed to be Therenus, on the banks of which, fable relates that Jupiter consummated his marriage with Juno. For the space of more than half a league round the walls of Candia there is not a single tree to be seen. The Turks cut them all down in the time of the siege, and laid waste the gardens and orchards. Beyond that extent, the country is plentifully covered with corn and fruit trees. The neighbouring hills are overspread with vineyards, which produce the malmsey of mount Ida,—worthy of preference at the table of the most exquisite connoisseur in wines. That species of wine, though little known, has a fine flavour, a very pleasant relish, and is highly esteemed in the island.

CANDIAC (John Lewis), a premature genius, born at Candiac in the diocese of Nismes in France, in 1719. In the cradle he distinguished his letters: at 13 months, he knew them perfectly: at three years of age, he read Latin, either printed or in manuscript: at four, he translated from that tongue: at six, he read Greek and Hebrew; was master of the principles of arithmetic, history, geography, heraldry, and the science of medals; and had read the best authors on almost every branch of literature. He died of a complication of disorders, at Paris, in 1726.

CANDIDATE, a person who aspires to some public office.

In the Roman commonwealth, they were obliged to wear a white gown during the two years of their soliciting a place. This garment, according to Plutarch, they wore without any other clothes, that the people might not suspect they concealed money for purchasing votes, and also that they might more easily show to the people the scars of those wounds they had received in fighting for the defence of the commonwealth. The candidates usually declared their pretensions a year before the time of election, which they spent in making interest and gaining friends. Various arts of popularity were practised for this purpose, and frequent circuits made round the city, and visits and compliments to all sorts of persons, the process of which was called *ambitus*. See AMBITUS.

CANDIDATI MILITES, an order of soldiers, among the Romans, who served as the emperor's body-guards to defend him in battle. They were the tallest and strongest of the whole troops, and most proper to inspire terror. They were called *candidati*, because clothed in white, either that they might be more conspicuous, or because they were considered in the way of preferment.

CANDISH, a considerable province of Asia, in the dominions of the Great Mogul, bounded by Chytor and Malva on the north, Orixa on the east, Decan on the south, and Guzarat on the west. It is populous and rich; and abounds in cotton, rice, and indigo. Brampore is the capital town.

CANDLE, a small taper of tallow, wax, or spermaceti; the wick of which is commonly of several threads of cotton, spun and twisted together.

A tallow-candle, to be good, must be half sheep's and half bullock's tallow; for hog's tallow makes the candle gutter, and always gives an offensive smell, with a thick black smoke. The wick ought to be pure, sufficiently dry, and properly twisted; otherwise the candle will emit an inconstant vibratory flame, which is both prejudicial to the eyes and insufficient for the distinct illumination of objects.

There are two sorts of tallow-candles; the one dipped, the other moulded: the former are the common candles; the others are the invention of the sieur le Brege at Paris.

As to the method of making candles in general: After the tallow has been weighed, and mixed in the due proportions, it is cut into very small pieces, that it may melt the sooner; for the tallow in lumps, as it comes from the butchers, would be in danger of burning or turning black, if it were left too long over the fire. Being perfectly melted and skimmed, they pour a certain quantity of water into it, proportionable to the quantity of tallow. This serves to precipitate to the bottom of the vessel the impurities of the tallow which may have escaped the skimmer. No water, however, must be thrown into the tallow designed for the three first dips; because the wick, being still quite dry, would imbibe the water, which makes the candles crackle in burning, and renders them of bad use. The tallow, thus melted, is poured into a tub, through a coarse sieve of horse-hair, to purify it still more, and may be used after having stood three hours. It will continue fit for use 24 hours in summer and 15 in winter. The wicks are made of spun cotton, which the tallow-chandlers buy in skains, and which they wind up into bottoms or clues. Whence they are cut out, with an instrument contrived on purpose, into pieces of the length of the candle required; then put on the sticks or broaches, or else placed in the moulds, as the candles are intended to be either dipped or moulded.

Wax-candles are made of a cotton or flaxen wick, slightly twisted, and covered with white or yellow wax. Of these, there are several kinds: some of a conical figure, used to illuminate churches, and in processions, funeral ceremonies, &c. (see TAPER); others of a cylindrical form, used on ordinary occasions. The first are either made with a ladle or the hand. 1. To make wax-candles with the ladle. The wicks being prepared, a dozen of them are tied by the neck, at equal distances, round an iron circle, suspended over a large bason of copper tinned, and full of melted wax: a large ladle full of this wax is poured gently on the tops of the wicks one after another, and this operation continued till the candle arrive at its destined bigness; with this precaution, that the three first ladles be poured on at the top of the wick, the fourth at the height of $\frac{3}{4}$, the fifth at $\frac{1}{2}$, and the sixth at $\frac{1}{4}$, in order to give the candle its pyramidal form. Then the candles are taken down, kept warm, and

and rolled and smoothed upon a walnut-tree table, with a long square instrument of box, smooth at the bottom. 2. As to the manner of making wax-candles by the hand, they begin to soften the wax, by working it several times in hot water, contained in a narrow but deep caldron. A piece of the wax is then taken out, and disposed by little and little around the wick, which is hung on a hook in the wall, by the extremity opposite to the neck; so that they begin with the big end, diminishing still as they descend towards the neck. In other respects the method is nearly the same as in the former case. However, it must be observed, that, in the former case, water is always used to moisten the several instruments, to prevent the wax from sticking; and in the latter, oil of olives, or lard, for the hands, &c. The cylindrical wax-candles are either made as the former, with a ladle, or drawn. Wax-candles drawn, are so called, because actually drawn in the manner of wire, by means of two large rollers of wood, turned by a handle, which, turning backwards and forwards several times, pass the wick through melted wax contained in a brass bason, and at the same time through the holes of an instrument like that used for drawing wire fastened at one side of the bason.

If any chandlers mix with their wares any thing deceitfully, &c. the candles shall be forfeited. Stat. 23 Eliz. and a tax or duty is granted on candles, by 8 and 9 Anne, cap. 6. made for sale, of one penny a pound, besides the duty upon tallow, by 8 Anne, cap. 9. And by 24 Geo. III. cap. 11. an additional duty of an halfpenny a pound; and by the same an additional duty of an halfpenny a pound is laid upon all candles imported (except those of wax and spermaceti, for which see *Wax-Candles*), subject also to the two additional 5 per cents. imposed by 19 and 22 Geo. III. besides the duty of 3¼d. formerly imposed by 2 W. sess. 1. cap. 4. 8 Anne, cap. 9. and 9 Anne, cap. 6. And every maker of candles, other than wax candles, for sale, shall annually take out a licence at L. 1. The maker of candles shall, in four weeks within the bills, and elsewhere in six weeks, after entry, clear off the duties on pain of double duty; nor sell any after default in payment on pain of double value; 8 Anne, cap. 9. The makers of candles are not to use melting houses, without making a true entry, on pain of L. 100, and to give notice of making candles to the excise officer for the duties; and of the number, &c. or shall forfeit L. 50, stat. 11. Geo. I. cap. 30. See also 23 Geo. II. cap. 21. and 26 Geo. II. cap. 32. No maker of candles for sale shall begin to make candles, without notice first given to the officer, unless from September 29th to March 25th yearly, between seven in the morning and five in the evening, and from March 25th to September 29th, between five in the morning and seven in the evening, on pain of L. 10, 10 Anne, cap. 26. The penalty of obstructing the officer is L. 20, and of removing candles before they are surveyed L. 20, 8 Anne, cap. 9. The penalty of privately making candles is the forfeiture of the same and utensils, and L. 100, 5 Geo. III. cap. 43. And the penalty of mingling weighed with unweighed candles, of removing them before they are weighed, or of concealing them, is the forfeiture of L. 100, 11 Geo. cap. 30. Candles, for which the duty hath been paid, may be exported, and the duty drawn back; but no draw-back shall be allowed on the exportation of any foreign candles imported. 8 Ann. cap. 9. 23 Geo. II. cap. 21.

The Roman candles were at first little strings dipt in pitch, or surrounded with wax; though afterwards they made them of the papyrus, covered likewise with wax; and sometimes also of rushes, by stripping off the outer rind, and only retaining the pith.—For religious offices, wax candles were used; for vulgar uses, those of tallow. Lord Bacon proposes candles of divers compositions and ingredients, as also of different sorts of wicks; with experiments of the degrees of duration, and light of each. Good housewives bury their candles in flour or bran, which it is said increases their lasting almost half.

Experiments to determine the real and comparative value of burning CANDLES *of different sorts and sizes.*

	Numb. of candles to one pound	Weight of one candle		The time one candle lasted		The time that one pound will last		The expence in 12 hours when candles are at 6s per dozen, which also shows the proportion of the expence at any price per dozen.
		Oz.	Dr.	Hr.	Min.	Hr.	Min.	Farthings and 100th parts.
Small wick.	18½	0	14	3	15	59	26	4.85
Large wick.	19	0	13½	2	40	50	34	5.70
	16½	0	15½	2	40	44	1	6.54
	12	1	5⅓	3	27	41	24	6.96
•	10½	1	8	3	36	34	24	7.50
•	7½	2	1	4	9	31	11	8.94
•	8	2	0	4	15	34	0	8.47
	5½	2	13	5	19	30	15	9.53
	Mould-candles							Mould-candl. at 7s per doz.
	5½	2	12	7	20	42	39	7.87
	4	4	0	9	3	36	20	9.18

N. B. The time that one candle lasted was taken from an average of several trials in each size.

It is observable, in optics, that the flame of two candles joined, give a much stronger light than both of them separate. The observation was suggested by Dr Franklin. Probably the union of the two flames produces a greater degree of heat, whereby the vapour is attenuated, and the particles of which light consists more copiously emitted.

Lighting a CANDLE *by a small spark of electricity.* This method, which is an invention of Dr Ingenhousz, is recorded in the Phil. Trans. vol. 68. It is done by a small phial, having eight or ten inches of metallic coating, or even less, charged with electricity, which may be done at any time of the night by a person who has an electric machine in his room. "When I have occasion to light a candle," says he, "I charge a small coated phial, whose knob is bent outwards, so as to hang a little over the body of the phial; then I wrap some loose cotton over the extremity of a long brass pin or a wire, so as to stick moderately fast to its substance. I next roll this extremity of the pin wrapped up with cotton in some fine powder of rosin, (which I always keep in readiness upon the table for this purpose, either in a wide-mouthed phial or in a loose paper); this being done, I apply the extremity of the pin or wire to the external coating of the charged phial, and bring as quickly as possible the other extremity wrapped round with cotton to the knob: the powder of resin takes fire, and communicates its flame to the cotton, and both together burn long enough to light a candle. As I do not want more than half a minute to light my candle in this way, I find it a readier method than kindling it by a flint and steel, or calling a servant. I have found, that powder of white or yellow resin lights easier than that of brown. The *farina lycopodii* may be used for the same purpose; but it is not so good as the powder of resin, because it does not take fire quite so readily, requiring a stronger spark not to miss: besides, it is soon burnt away. By dipping the cotton in oil of turpentine, the same effect may be as readily obtained, if you take a jar somewhat greater in size. This oil will inflame so much the readier if you strew a few fine particles of brass upon it. The pin dust is the best for this purpose; but as this oil is scattered about by the explosion, and when kindled fills the room with much more smoke than the powder of resin, I prefer the last."

Candle-Bombs, a name given to small glass bubbles, having a neck about an inch long, with a very slender bore, by means of which a small quantity of water is introduced into them, and the orifice afterwards closed up. This stalk being put through the wick of a burning candle, the vicinity of the flame soon rarifies the water into steam, by the elasticity of which the glass is broken with a loud crack.

Candle is also a term of medicine, and is reckoned among the instruments of surgery. Thus the *candela fumalis*, or the *candela pro suffitu odorata*, is a mass of an oblong form, consisting of odoriferous powders, mixed up with a third or more of the charcoal of willow or lime tree, and reduced to a proper consistence with a mucilage of gum tragacanth, labdanum, or turpentine. It is intended to excite a grateful smell without any flame, to correct the air, to fortify the brain, and to excite the spirits.

Medicated Candle, the same with Bougie.

Candle, Sale or auction by inch of candle, is when a small piece of candle, being lighted, the bystanders are allowed to bid for the merchandise that is selling; but the moment the candle is out, the commodity is adjudged to the last bidder.

There is also an excommunication by inch of candle; when the sinner is allowed to come to repentance while a candle continues burning; but after it is consumed, he remains excommunicated to all intents and purposes.

Rush-Candles, used in different parts of England, are made of the pith of a sort of rushes, peeled or stripped of the skin, except on one side, and dipped in melted grease.

Candle-Wood, slips of pine about the thickness of a finger, used in New England and other colonies to burn instead of candles, giving a very good light. The French inhabitants of Tortuga use slips of yellow sanctalwood for the same purpose, and under the same denomination, which yields a clear flame though of a green colour.

CANDLEBERRY tree, in botany, the English name of the Myrica.

CANDLEMAS, a feast of the church held on the second day of February, in honour of the purification of the Virgin Mary. It is borrowed from the practice of the ancient Christians, who on that day used abundance of lights both in their churches and processions, in memory, as is supposed, of our Saviour's being on that day declared by Simeon "to be a light to lighten the Gentiles." In imitation of this custom, the Roman-catholics on this day consecrate all the tapers and candles which they use in their churches during the whole year. At Rome, the Pope performs that ceremony himself; and distributes wax-candles to the cardinals and others, who carry them in procession through the great hall of the Pope's palace. This ceremony was prohibited in England by an order of council in 1548.

Candlemas, (2d Feb.) is made one of the four terms of the year for paying and receiving rents or borrowed money, &c.—In the courts of law, Candlemas terms begin 15th January, and ends 3d February.

CANDLESTICK, an instrument to hold a candle, made in different forms, and of all sorts of matter.

The golden candlestick was one of the sacred utensils made by Moses to be placed in the Jewish tabernacle. It was made of hammered gold, a talent in weight. It consisted of seven branches supported by a base or foot. These branches were adorned at equal distances with six flowers like lilies, and with as many bowls and knobs placed alternately. Upon the stock and six branches of the candlestick were the golden lamps, which were immoveable, wherein were put oil and cotton.

These seven lamps were lighted every evening, and extinguished every morning. The lamps had their tongs or snuffers to draw the cotton in or out, and dishes underneath them to receive the sparks or droppings of the oil. This candlestick was placed in the antichamber of the sanctuary on the south side, and served to illuminate the altar of perfume and the tabernacle of the shew-bread. When Solomon had built the temple of the Lord, he placed in it ten golden candlesticks of the same form as that described by Moses, five on the north and five on the south side of the holy place: But after the Babylonish captivity, the golden candlestick was again placed in the temple, as it had been before in the tabernacle by Moses. This sacred utensil, upon the destruction of the temple by the Romans, was lodged in the temple of peace built by Vespasian; and the representation of it is still to be seen on the triumphal arch at the foot of mount Palatine, on which Vespasian's triumph is delineated.

CANDY, a large kingdom of Asia, in the island of Ceylon. It contains about a quarter of the island; and as it is encompassed with high mountains, and covered with thick forests, through which the roads and paths are narrow and difficult, the king has them guarded to prevent his subjects from going into other countries. It is full of hills, from whence rivulets proceed which are full of fish; but as they run among the rocks, they are not fit for boats: however, the inhabitants are very dexterous in turning them to water their land, which is fruitful in rice, pulse, and hemp. The king is absolute, and his subjects are idolaters. The capital town is of the same name.

Candy, a town of Asia, and capital of a kingdom

Candy & Canea.

of the same name, in the island of Ceylon. It has been often burnt by the Portuguese, when they were masters of these coasts. The houses are very poor, low, and badly furnished. E. Long. 79. 12. N. Lat. 7. 35.

Candy, or *Sugar-Candy*, a preparation of sugar made by melting and crystallising it six or seven times over, to render it hard or transparent. It is of three kinds, white, yellow, and red. The white comes from the loaf-sugar, the yellow from the cassonado, and the red from the muscavado.

CANDYING, the act of preserving simples in substance, by boiling them in sugar. The performance of this originally belonged to the apothecaries, but is now become a part of the business of the confectioner.

CANE, in botany. See ARUNDO and CALAMUS.

CANE, denotes also a walking stick. It is customary to adorn it with a head of gold, silver, agate, &c. Some are without knots, and very smooth and even; others are full of knots about two inches distance from one another. These last have very little elasticity, and will not bend so well as the others.

Canes of Bengal are the most beautiful which the Europeans bring into Europe. Some of them are so fine, that people work them into bowls or vessels, which being varnished over in the inside, with black or yellow lacca, will hold liquors as well as glass or China ware does; and the Indians use them for that purpose.

CANE is also the name of a long measure, which differs according to the several countries where it is used. At Naples the cane is equal to 7 feet 3⅞ inches English measure: the cane of Tholouse and the Upper Languedoc, is equal to the varre of Arragon, and contains five feet 8¾ inches; at Mompellier, Provence, Dauphine, and the Lower Languedoc, to six English feet 5½ inches.

CANEA, a considerable town of the island of Candia, where a bashaw resides. It was built by the Venetians, and occupies part of the site of the ancient CYDONIA. It is but about two miles in compass; encircled on the land side with a single wall, extremely thick; and defended by a broad and deep ditch, cut through a bed of rock, which extends all around the wall. By cutting it still deeper, they might cause the sea to flow round its ramparts; on which they have raised high platforms, that their great guns might command a wider extent of the adjacent plain. The city has only one gate, the gate of Retimo, protected by an half-moon battery, which is the only exterior fort. The side which faces the sea is the best fortified. On the left of the harbour are four batteries, rising one above another, and planted with a number of large cannons of cast metal, marked with the arms of Venice. The first of these batteries stands close on the brink of the sea. The right side of the harbour is defended only by a strong wall, extending along a chain of pointed rocks which it is dangerous for ships to approach. At the extremity of this wall, there is an old castle, falling into ruins. Beneath that castle, the Venetians had immense arsenals, vaulted with stone. Each of these vaults was of sufficient length, breadth, and height, to serve as a work-shop for building a ship of the line. The ground is sloping, and the outermost part of these capacious arsenals is on a level with the sea; so that it was very easy to launch the ships built there into the water. The Turks are suffering that magnificent work to fall into ruins.

The city of Canea is laid out on a fine plan. The streets are large and straight; and the squares adorned with fountains. There are no remarkable buildings in it. Most of the houses are flat-roofed, and have only one story. Those contiguous to the harbour are adorned with galleries, from which you enjoy a delightful prospect. From the windows you discover the large bay formed between Cape Spada and Cape Meleć, and all the ships that are entering in or passing out. The harbour, at present, receives ships of 300 tons burden; and it might be enlarged so as to admit the largest frigates. Its mouth is exposed to the violence of the north winds, which sometimes swell the billows above the ramparts. But, as it is narrow, and the bottom is good, ships that are well moored run no danger. At the time when Tournefort visited Crete, Canea did not contain more than five or six thousand inhabitants. But, at present, when the gates of Gira-Petra, Candia, and Retimo are choaked up, the merchants have retired to Canea; and it is reckoned to contain 16,000 souls. The environs of the town are admirable; being adorned with forests of olive-trees mixed with fields, vineyards, gardens, and brooks bordered with myrtle-trees and laurel-roses. The chief revenue of this town consists in oil-olive. E. Long. 24. 15. N. Lat. 35. 18.

Canella.

CANELLA, in botany: A genus of the monogynia order belonging to the dodecandria class of plants; and in the natural method ranking under the 12th order, *Holeraceæ*. The calyx is three lobed; the petals are five; the antheræ 16, growing to an urceolated or bladder-shaped nectarium; and the fruit is a trilocular berry, with two seeds. There is but one species, the alba; which grows usually about 20 feet high, and eight or ten inches in thickness, in the thick woods of most of the Bahama islands. The leaves are narrow at the stalk, growing wider at their ends, which are broad and rounding, having a middle rib only; they are very smooth, and of a light shining green. In May and June the flowers, which are pentapetalous, come forth in clusters at the ends of the branches: they are red, and very fragrant, and are succeeded by round berries, of the size of large peas, green, and when ripe (which is in February) purple, containing two shining black seeds, flat on one side, otherwise not unlike in shape Pl. CXVI. to a kidney bean; these seeds in the berry are covelopеd in a slimy mucilage. The whole plant is very aromatic, the bark particularly, being more used in distilling, and in greater esteem, in the more northern parts of the world than in Britain.

The bark is the canella alba of the shops. It is brought to us rolled up into long quills, thicker than cinnamon, and both outwardly and inwardly of a whitish colour, lightly inclining to yellow. Infusions of it in water are of a yellowish colour, and smell of the canella; but they are rather bitter than aromatic. Tinctures in rectified spirit have the warmth of the bark, but little of its smell. Proof-spirit dissolves the aromatic as well as the bitter matter of the canella, and is therefore the best menstruum.

The canella is the interior bark freed from an outward

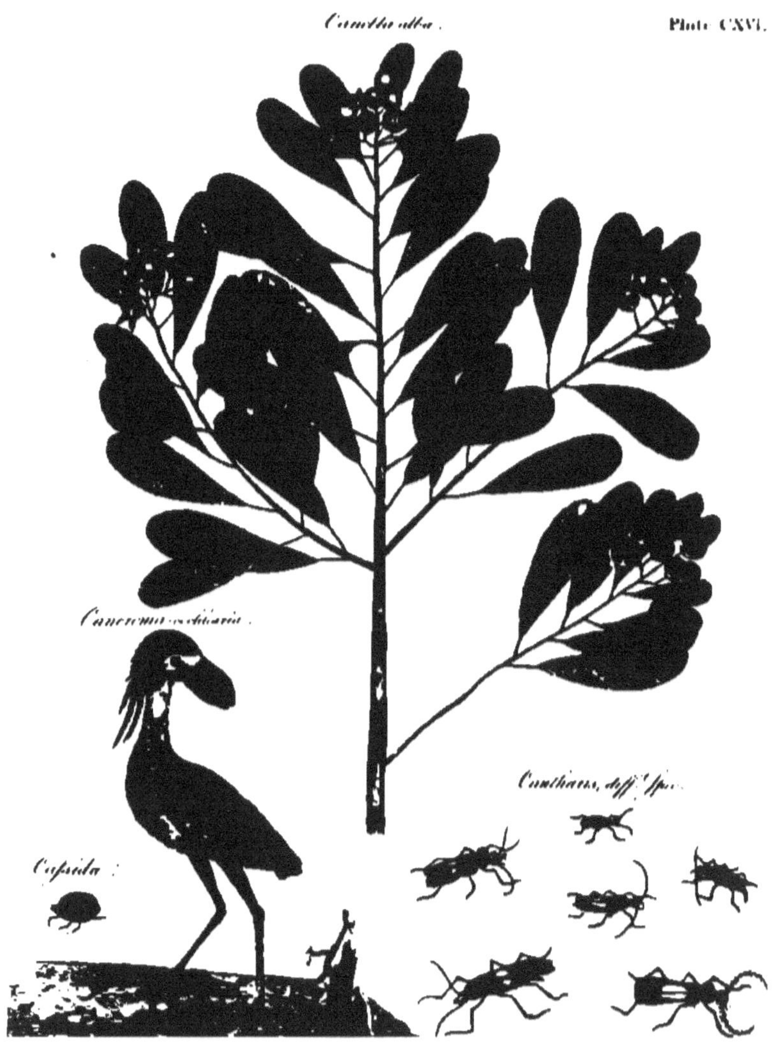
Canella alba.
Plate CXVI.
Cancroma cochlearia.
Cassida.
Cantharis, diff. Spe.

thin rough one, and dried in the shade. The shops distinguish two sorts of canella, differing from each other in the length and thickness of the quills; they are both the bark of the same tree; the thicker being taken from the trunk, and the thinner from the branches. This bark is a warm pungent aromatic, though not of the most agreeable kind: nor are any of the preparations of it very grateful.

Canella alba is often employed where a warm stimulant to the stomach is necessary, and as a corrigent of other articles. It is now, however, little used in composition by the London college; the only official formula which it enters being the pulvis aloeticus: but with the Edinburgh college it is an ingredient in the tinctura amara, vinum amarum, vinum rhei, &c. It is useful as covering the taste of some other articles.—This bark has been confounded with that called Winter's bark, which belongs to a very different tree. See WINTERA.

CANELLE, or CANE-LAND, a large country in the island of Ceylon, called formerly the *kingdom of Cota*. It contains a great number of cantons, the principal of which are occupied by the Dutch. The chief riches of this country consist in cinnamon, of which there are large forests. There are five towns on the coast, some forts, and a great number of harbours. The rest of the country is inhabited by the natives; and there are several rich mines, from whence they get rubies, sapphires, topazes, cats-eyes, and several other precious stones.

CANEPHORÆ, in Grecian antiquity, virgins who, when they became marriageable, presented certain baskets full of little curiosities to Diana, in order to get leave to depart out of her train, and change their state of life.

CANEPHORIA, in Grecian antiquity, a ceremony which made part of a feast, celebrated by the Athenian virgins on the eve of their marriage-day. At Athens the canephoria consisted in this; that the maid, conducted by her father and mother, went to the temple of Minerva, carrying with her a basket full of presents to engage the goddess to make the marriage-state happy; or, as the scholiast of Theocritus has it, the basket was intended as a kind of honourable amends made to that goddess, the protectrix of virginity, for abandoning her party; or as a ceremony to appease her wrath. Suidas calls it a festival in honour of Diana.

CANEPHORIA, is also the name of a festival in honour of Bacchus, celebrated particularly by the Athenians, on which the young maids carried golden baskets full of fruit, which baskets were covered, to conceal the mystery from the uninitiated.

CANES, in Egypt and other eastern countries, a poor sort of buildings for the reception of strangers and travellers. People are accommodated in these with a room at a small price, but with no other necessaries; so that, excepting the room, there are no greater accommodations in these houses than in the deserts, only that there is a market near.

Canes Venatici, in astronomy, the grey-hounds, two new constellations, first established by Hevelius, between the tail of the Great Bear and Bootes's arms, above the Coma Berenices. The first is called *asterion*, being that next the Bear's tail; the other *chara*. They comprehend 23 stars, of which Tycho only observed two. The longitudes and latitudes of each are given by Hevelius. In the British Catalogue they are 25.

CANETO, a strong town of Italy in the duchy of Mantua, seated on the river Oglio, which was taken by the Imperialists in 1701, by the French in 1702, afterwards by the Imperialists, and then by the French in 1705. E. Long. 10. 45. N. Lat. 40. 55.

CANOA, in the Chinese affairs, a wooden clog borne on the neck, by way of punishment for divers offences. The canga is composed of two pieces of wood notched, to receive the criminal's neck; the load lies on his shoulders, and is more or less heavy according to the quality of his offence. Some cangas weigh 200 lb; the generality from 50 to 60. The Mandarins condemn to the punishment of the canga. Sentence of death is sometimes changed for this kind of punishment.

CANGE (Charles du Fresne sieur du), one of the most learned writers of his time, was born at Amiens in 1610, and studied at the Jesuits college in that city. Afterwards he applied himself to the study of the law at Orleans, and gained great reputation by his works; among which are, 1. The history of the empire of Constantinople under the French emperors. 2. John Cinnamus's six books of the history of the affairs of John and Manuel Comnenus, in Greek and Latin, with historical and philological notes. 3. *Glossarium ad Scriptores mediæ & infimæ Latinitatis.*

CANGI, CEANGI, or *Cangani*, anciently a people of Britain, concerning whose situation antiquaries have been much perplexed. They are all the same people. Cambden discovered some traces of them in many different and distant places, as in Somersetshire, Wales, Derbyshire, and Cheshire; and he might have found as plain vestiges of them in Devonshire, Dorsetshire, Essex, Wiltshire, &c. Mr Horsley and others are no less perplexed and undetermined in their opinions on this subject. But Mr Baxter seems to have discovered the true cause of all this perplexity, by observing that the Cangi or Ceangi were not a distinct nation seated in one particular place, but such of the youth of many different nations as were employed in pasturage, in feeding the flocks and herds of their respective tribes. Almost all the ancient nations of Britain had their ceangi, their pastoritia pubes, the keepers of their flocks and herds, who ranged about the country in great numbers, as they were invited by the season and plenty of pasture for their cattle. This is the reason that vestiges of their name are to be found in so many different parts of Britain; but chiefly in those parts which are most fit for pasturage. These ceangi of the different British nations, naturally brave, and rendered still more hardy by their way of life, were constantly armed for the protection of their flocks from wild beasts; and these arms they occasionally employed in the defence of their country and their liberty.

CANGIAGIO, or CAMBIASI (Ludovico), one of the most eminent of the Genoese painters, was born in 1527. His works at Genoa are very numerous; and he was employed by the king of Spain to adorn part of the Escurial. It is remarked of him, that he was not only a most expeditious and rapid painter, but also that he worked equally well with both hands; and

and by that unusual power he executed more designs, and finished more grand works with his own pencil, in a much shorter time, than most other artists could do with several assistants. He died in 1585.

In the royal collection at Paris, there is a Sleeping Cupid, as large as life, and likewise Judith with her attendant; which are painted by Cangiagio, and are an honour to that master. And in the Pembroke collection at Wilton, is a picture, reputed the work of Cangiagio, representing Christ bearing his Cross.

CANICULA, is a name proper to one of the stars of the constellation *canis major*, called also simply the *dog-star*; by the Greeks σείριος, *sirius* *. Canicula is the tenth in order in the Britannic catalogue; in Tycho's and Ptolemy's it is the second. It is situated in the mouth of the constellation; and is of the first magnitude, being the largest and brightest of all the stars in the heavens. From the rising of this star not cosmically, or with the sun, but heliacally, that is, its emersion from the sun's rays, which now happens about the 15th day of August, the ancients reckoned their *dies caniculares*, or dog days. The Egyptians and Ethiopians began their year at the rising of the canicula, reckoning to its rise again the next year, which is called the *annus canarius*, or canicular year. This year consisted ordinarily of 365 days, and every fourth year of 366, by which it was accommodated to the civil year. The reason of their choice of the canicula before the other stars to compute their time by, was not only the superior brightness of that star, but because its heliacal rising was in Egypt a time of singular note, as falling on the greatest augmentation of the Nile, the reputed father of Egypt. Ephestion adds, that from the aspect and colour of canicula, the Egyptians drew prognostics concerning the rise of the Nile; and, according to Horus, predicted the future state of the year; so that the first rising of this star was annually observed with great attention.

* See Sirius.

CANICULUM, or CANICULUS, in the Byzantine antiquities, a golden standish or ink-vessel, decorated with precious stones, wherein was kept the sacred *encaustum*, or red ink, wherewith the emperors signed their decrees, letters, &c. The word is by some derived from *canis*, or *caniculus*; alluding to the figure of a dog which it represented, or rather because it was supported by the figures of dogs. The caniculum was under the care of a particular officer of state.

CANINA, the north part of the ancient Epirus, a province of Greece, which now belongs to the Turks, and lies off the entrance of the gulph of Venice. The principal town is of the same name, and is seated on the sea coast, at the foot of the mountains of Chimera. E. Long. 19. 25. N. Lat. 40. 55.

CANINANA, in zoology, the name of a species of serpent found in America, and esteemed one of the less poisonous kinds. It grows to about two feet long; and is green on the back, and yellow on the belly. It feeds on eggs and small birds; the natives cut off the head and tail, and eat the body as a delicate dish.

CANINE, whatever partakes of, or has any relation to, the nature of a dog.

Canine Appetite, amounts to much the same with BULIMY.

Canine Madness. See (the *Index* subjoined to) MEDICINE.

Canine Teeth, are two sharp edged teeth in each jaw; one on each side, placed between the incisores and molares.

CANINI (John Angelo and Marc Anthony,) brothers and Romans, celebrated for their love of antiquities. John excelled in designs for engraving on stones, particularly heads; Marc engraved them. They were encouraged by Colbert to publish a succession of heads of the heroes and great men of antiquity, designed from medals, antique stones, and other ancient remains; but John died at Rome soon after the work was begun: Marc Anthony, however, procured assistance, finished and published it in Italian in 1669. The cuts of this edition were engraved by Canini, Picard, and Valet; and a curious explanation is given, which discovers the skill of the Canini's in history and mythology. The French edition of Amsterdam, 1731, is spurious.

CANIS, or DOG, in zoology, a genus of quadrupeds, belonging to the order of feræ. The characters of the dog are these: he has six fore-teeth in the upper jaw, those in the sides being longer than the intermediate ones, which are lobated; in the under jaw there are likewise six fore teeth, those on the sides being lobated. He has six grinders in the upper, and seven in the lower jaw. The teeth called *dog-teeth* are four, one on each side, both in the lower and upper jaw; they are sharp-pointed, bent a little inward, and stand at a distance from any of the rest.

There are 14 species of this genus, viz.

Domestic Dog.

I. The FAMILIARIS, or Domestic Dog, is distinguished from the other species by having his tail bent to the left side; which mark is so singular, that perhaps the tail of no other quadruped is bent in this manner. Of this species there are a great number of varieties. Linnæus enumerates 11, and Buffon gives figures of no less than 17. The mastiff is about the size of a wolf, with the sides of the lips hanging down, and a full robust body. The large Danish dog differs only from the former in being fuller in the body, and generally of a larger size. The gre-hound is likewise the same with the mastiff; but its make is more slender and delicate. Indeed the difference betwixt these three dogs, although perfectly distinguishable at first sight, is not greater than that betwixt a Dutchman, a Frenchman, and an Italian. The shepherd's dog, the wolf-dog, and what is commonly called the *Siberian dog*, to which may be joined the Lapland dog, the Canada dog, and, in general, all those which have straight ears and a pointed snout, are all one kind, differing only in thickness, the roughness or smoothness of their skin, the length of their legs and tails. The hound or beagle, the terrier, the braque or harrier, and the spaniel, may be considered as the same kind; they have the same form and the same instincts; and differ only in the length of their legs, and size of their ears, which in each of them are long, soft, and pendulous. The bull-dog, the small Danish dog, the Turkish dog, and the Iceland dog, may likewise be considered as the same kind, all the varieties in their appearance taking their rise merely from climate. For instance, the Turkish dog, which has no hair, is nothing else but the small Danish dog transported to a warm climate, which makes the hair fall off. A dog of any kind loses its hair in very warm climates. But this is not the only change which arises from difference of climate. In some countries, the voice is changed;

See Plates CXVII, CXVIII, CXIX, and CXX.

ged; in others, dogs become altogether silent. In some climates they lose the faculty of barking, and howl like wolves, or yelp like foxes. Warm climates even change their form and instincts: they turn ill-shaped, and their ears become straight and pointed. It is only in temperate climes that dogs preserve their natural courage, ardour, and sagacity.

Dr Caius has left, among several other tracts relating to natural history, one written expressly on the species of British dogs; besides a description of the variety of dogs then existing in this country, he has added a systematic table of them, which we shall here insert, and explain by a brief account of each kind.

Synopsis of British Dogs.

- I. The most generous kinds.
  - Dogs of chace.
    - Hounds.
      - Terrier
      - Harrier
      - Blood-hound
    - Gaze-hound
    - Gre-hound
    - Leviner, or Lyemmer
    - Tumbler
  - Fowlers.
    - Spaniel
    - Setter
    - Water-spaniel, or finder
  - Lap Dogs.
    - Spaniel gentle, or comforter
- II. Farm Dogs.
  - Shepherd's dog
  - Mastiff, or ban dog.
- III. Mongrels.
  - Wappe
  - Turnspit
  - Dancer.

1. a. The first variety is the *terrarius* or terrier, which takes its name from its subterraneous employ; being a small kind of hound used to force the fox or other beasts of prey out of their holes; and, in former times, rabbits out of their burrows into nets.

b. The *leverarius*, or harrier, is a species well known at present; it derives its name from its use, that of hunting the hare; but under this head may be placed the fox hound, which is only a stronger and fleeter variety, applied to a different chace.

c. The *sanguinarius*, blood-hound, or *slot-hound* of the Scots, was a dog of great use, as already noticed under the article *Blood-Hound*.

The next subdivision of this species of dogs comprehends those that hunt by the eye; and whose success depends either upon the quickness of their sight, their swiftness, or their subtilty.

d. The *agasæus*, or gaze-hound, was the first: it chaced indifferently the fox, hare, or buck. It would select from the herd the fattest and fairest deer; pursue it by the eye; and, if lost for a time, recover it again by its singular distinguishing faculty; nay, should the beast rejoin the herd, this dog would fix unerringly on the same. This species is now lost, or at least unknown to us.

e. The next kind is the *leporarius*, or gre-hound. Dr Caius informs us, that it takes its name *quod præcipui gradus sit inter canes*, "the first in rank among dogs:" that it was formerly esteemed so, appears from the forest-laws of king Canute, who enacted that no one under the degree of a gentleman should presume to keep a gre-hound; and still more strongly from an old Welsh saying which signifies, that "you may know a gentleman by his hawk, his horse, and his gre-hound."

The variety called the *Highland gre-hound*, and now become very scarce, is of very great size, strong, deep-chested, and covered with long rough hair. This kind was much esteemed in former days, and used in great numbers by the powerful chieftains in their magnificent hunting-matches. It had as sagacious nostrils as the blood-hound, and was as fierce.

f. The third species is the *levinarius*, or lorarius; the leviner or lyemmer: the first name is derived from the lightness of the kind; the other from the old word *lyemme*, a thong; this species being used to be led in a thong, and slipped at the game. Our author says that this dog was a kind that hunted both by scent and sight; and in the form of its body observed a medium between the hound and the gre-hound. This probably is the kind now known among us by the name of the *Irish gre-hound*, a dog now extremely scarce in that kingdom, the late king of Poland having procured from them as many as possible. They were of the kind called by Buffon *le grand Danois*, and probably imported there by the Danes who long possessed that kingdom. Their use seems originally to have been for the chace of wolves with which Ireland swarmed till the latter end of the last century. As soon as these animals were extirpated, the numbers of the dogs decreased; for, from that period, they were kept only for state.

g. The *vertagus*, or tumbler, is a fourth species; which took its prey by mere subtilty, depending neither on the sagacity of its nose, nor its swiftness: if it came into a warren, it neither barked, nor ran on the rabbits; but by a seeming neglect of them, or attention to something else, deceived the object till it got within reach, so as to take it by a sudden spring. This dog was less than the hound, more scraggy, had prick'd up ears, and by Dr Caius's description seems to answer to the modern lurcher.

The third subdivision of the more generous dogs comprehends those which were used in fowling.

h. First, the *Hispaniolus*, or spaniel; from the name, it may be supposed that we were indebted to Spain for this breed. There were two varieties of this kind: the first used to spring the game, which are the same with our starters. The other variety was used only for the net, and was called *index* or the setter; a kind well known at present. This kingdom has been long remarkable for producing dogs of this sort, particular care having been taken to preserve the breed in the utmost purity. They are still distinguished by the name of *English Spaniels*; so that, notwithstanding the derivation of the name, it is probable they are natives of Great Britain.

i. The *aquaticus*, or finder, was another species used in fowling; was the same with our water-spaniel; and was used to find or recover the game that was shot.

k. The *Melitæus*, or *fotor*, the spaniel gentle or comforter of Dr Caius (the modern lap-dog), was the last of this division. The Maltese little dogs were as much esteemed by the fine ladies of past times as those of Bologna are among the modern. Old Hollingshed is ridiculously severe on the fair of his days for their

Canis.

excessive passion for these little animals; which is sufficient to prove that it was, in his time*, a novelty.

* The reign of Queen Elizabeth.

2. The second grand division of dogs comprehends the *rustici*, or those that were used in the country.

a. The first species is the *pastoralis*, or shepherd's dog; which is the same that is used at present, either in guarding our flocks, or in driving herds of cattle. This kind is so well trained for these purposes as to attend to every part of the herd, be it ever so large; confine them to the road; and force in every straggler, without doing it the least injury.

b. The next is the *villaticus*, or *catenarius*; the mastiff or ban dog; a species of great size and strength, and a very loud barker. Caius tells us that three of these were reckoned a match for a bear; and four for a lion: but from an experiment made in the Tower of London, that noble quadruped was found an unequal match to only three. Two of the dogs were disabled in the combat, but the third forced the lion to seek for safety by flight. The English bull-dog seems to belong to this species; and probably is the dog our author mentions under the title of *laniarius*. Great Britain was so noted for its mastiffs, that the Roman emperors appointed an officer in this island under the name of *procurator cynegii*, whose sole business was to breed, and transmit from hence to the amphitheatre, such as would prove equal to the combats of the place. Gratius speaks in high terms of the excellency of the British dog.

Cynegeticon, lin. 175.

Atque ipsos libeat penetrare Britannos?
O quanta est merces, et quantum impendia supra!
Si non ad speciem, mentiturosque decores
Protinus: haec una est catulis jactura Britannis.
At magnum cum venit opus, promendaque virtus,
Et vocat extremo praeceps discrimine Mavors,
Non tunc egregios tantum admirere Molossos.

If *Britain's* distant coast we dare explore,
How much beyond the cost the valued store?
If shape and beauty not alone we prize,
Which nature to the *British* hound denies:
But when the mighty toil the huntsman warms,
And all the soul is rous'd by fierce alarms,
When Mars calls furious to th' ensanguin'd field,
Even bold *Molossians* then to these must yield.

Strabo tells us that the mastiffs of Britain were trained to war, and were used by the Gauls in their battles; and it is certain a well trained mastiff might be of use in distressing such half-armed and irregular combatants as the adversaries of the Gauls seem generally to have been before the Romans conquered them.

3. The last division is that of the *degeneres*, or curs.

a. The first of these was the *wappe*, a name derived from its note; its only use was to alarm the family by barking, if any person approached the house.

b. Of this class was the *versator*, or turn-spit; and lastly the *saltator* or dancing-dog; or such as was taught variety of tricks, and carried about by idle people as a show. These *degeneres* were of no certain shape, being mongrels or mixtures of all kinds of dogs.

M. de Buffon has given a genealogical table of all the known dogs, in which he makes the *chien de berger*, or shepherd's dog, the origin of all, because it is naturally the most sensible. This table or tree is intended not only to exhibit the different kinds of dogs, but to give an idea of their varieties as arising from a degeneration in particular climates, and from a commixture of the different races. It is constructed in the form of a geographical chart, preserving as much as possible the position of the different climates to which each variety naturally belongs. The shepherd's dog, as already mentioned, is the root of the tree. This dog, when transported into Lapland, or other very cold climates, assumes an ugly appearance, and shrinks into a smaller size; but, in Russia, Iceland, and Siberia, where the climate is less rigorous, and the people a little more advanced in civilization, he seems to be better accomplished. These changes are occasioned solely by the influence of those climates, which produce no great alteration in the figure of this dog; for, in each of these climates, his ears are erect, his hair thick and long, his aspect wild, and he barks less frequently, and in a different manner, than in more favourable climates, where he acquires a finer polish. The Iceland dog is the only one that has not his ears entirely erect; for their extremities are a little inclined; and Iceland, of all the northern regions, has been longest inhabited by half civilized men.

Canis.

See Plate CXXXI.

The same shepherd's dog, when brought into temperate climates, and among a people perfectly civilized, as Britain, France, Germany, would, by the mere influence of the climate, lose his savage aspect, his erect ears, his rude, thick, long hair, and assume the figure of a bull dog, the hound, and the Irish gre-hound. The bull-dog and Irish grey-hound have their ears still partly erect, and very much resemble, both in their manners and sanguinary temper, the dog from which they derive their origin. The hound is farthest removed from the shepherd's dog; for his ears are long and entirely pendulous. The gentleness, docility, and even the timidity of the hound, are proofs of his great degeneration, or rather of the great perfection he has acquired by the long and careful education bestowed on him by man.

The hound, the harrier, and the terrier, constitute but one race; for, it has been remarked, that in the same litter, hounds, harriers, and terriers, have been brought forth, though the female hound had been covered by only one of these three dogs. I have joined the common harrier to the Dalmatian dog, or harrier of Bengal, because they differ only in having more or fewer spots on their coat. I have also linked the turnspit, or terrier with crooked legs, with the common terrier; because the defect in the legs of the former has originally proceeded from a disease similar to the rickets, with which some individuals had been affected, and transmitted the deformity to their descendants.

The hound, when transported into Spain and Barbary, where all animals have fine, long, bushy hair, would be converted into the spaniel and water-dog. The great and small spaniel, which differ only in size, when brought into Britain, have changed their white colour into black, and become, by the influence of climate, the great and little King Charles's dog: To these may be joined the pyrame, which is only a King Charles's dog, black like the others, but marked with red on the four legs, and a spot of the same colour above each eye, and on the muzzle.

The Irish gre-hound, transported to the north, is become the great Danish dog; and, when carried to the south, was converted into the common gre-hound. The

CANIS CXVII.

Canis.

The largeſt gre-hounds come from the Levant, thoſe of a ſmaller ſize from Italy; and thoſe Italian gre-hounds, carried into Britain, have been ſtill farther diminiſhed.

The great Daniſh dog, tranſported into Ireland, the Ukraine, Tartary, Epirus, and Albania, has been changed into the Iriſh gre-hound, which is the largeſt of all dogs.

The bull-dog, tranſported from Britain to Denmark, is become the little Daniſh dog; and the latter, brought into warm climates, has been converted into the Turkiſh dog. All theſe races, with their varieties, have been produced by the influence of climate, joined to the effects of ſhelter, food, and education. The other dogs are not pure races, but have proceeded from commixtures of thoſe already deſcribed. I have marked, in the table, by dotted lines, the double origin of theſe mongrels.

The gre-hound and Iriſh gre-hound have produced the mongrel gre-hound, called alſo the gre-hound with wolf's hair. The muzzle of this mongrel is leſs pointed than that of the true gre-hound, which is very rare in France.

The great Daniſh dog and the large ſpaniel have produced the Calabrian dog, which is a beautiful animal, with long buſhy hair, and larger than the Iriſh gre-hound.

The ſpaniel and terrier have produced the dog called *burgos*.

From the ſpaniel and little Daniſh dog has proceeded the lion-dog, which is now very rare.

The dogs with long, fine, criſped hair, called the *buffe dogs*, and which are larger than the water-dog, proceed from the ſpaniel and water-dog.

The little water-dog comes from the water-dog and ſmall ſpaniel.

From the bull-dog and Iriſh gre-hound proceeds a mongrel called the *maſtiff*, which is larger than the bull-dog, and reſembles the latter more than the Iriſh gre-hound.

The pug-dog proceeds from the bull-dog and ſmall Daniſh dog.

All theſe dogs are *ſimple* mongrels, and are produced by the commixture of two *pure races*. But there are other dogs, called *double mongrels*, becauſe they proceed from the junction of a pure race with a mongrel. The baſtard pug-dog is a double mongrel from a mixture of the pug-dog with the little Daniſh dog. The Alicant dog is alſo a double mongrel, proceeding from the pug-dog and ſmall ſpaniel. The Malteſe, or lap-dog, is a double mongrel, produced between the ſmall ſpaniel and little water-dog.

Laſtly, there are dogs which may be called *triple mongrels*, becauſe they are produced by two mixed races. Of this kind are the Artois and Iſſois dogs, which are produced by the pug-dog and the baſtard pug-dog; to which may be added the dogs called *ſtreet-dogs*, which reſemble no particular kind, becauſe they proceed from races which have previouſly been ſeveral times mixed.

The following is a ſyſtematic catalogue of all the known dogs, as arranged by Mr Pennant in his Hiſtory of Quadrupeds:

1. Shepherd's dog (*Canis domeſticus*, Lin. *Le Chien de Berger*, Buff.); ſo called, becauſe it becomes without diſcipline almoſt inſtantly the guardian of the flocks, keeps them within bounds, reduces the ſtragglers to their proper limits, and defends them from the attacks of the wolves. We have this variety in England; but it is ſmall and weak. It is the paſtoralis of Caius above mentioned. Thoſe of France and the Alps are very large and ſtrong; ſharp-noſed; erect and ſharp eared; very hairy, eſpecially about the neck; and have their tails turned up or curled; and by accident their faces often ſhow the marks of their combats with the wolf.

Its varieties or neareſt allies are: *a*, Pomeranian dog. *b*, Siberian dog. The other varieties in the inland parts of the empire and Siberia noticed by Buffon, are chiefly from the ſhepherd's dog; and there is a high-limbed taper-bodied kind, the common dog of the Calmuc and independent Tartars, excellent for the chace and all uſes.

2. The hound, or dog with long, ſmooth, and pendulous ears. This is the ſame with the blood-hound in Caius's Table, (*le Chien courant*, Buff. *Canis ſagax*, Lin.). It is the head of the other kinds with ſmooth and hanging ears: *a*, Harrier; *b*, Dalmatian, vulgarly the Daniſh, a beautiful ſpotted dog; *c*, Turnſpit; *d*, Water-dog, great and ſmall.

From this ſtock branches out another race with pendent ears, covered with long hairs, and leſs in ſize; which form,

3. The Spaniel; (*Canis avicularius*, Lin.). Thoſe of this kind vary in ſize from the ſetting dog to the ſpringing ſpaniels, and ſome of the little lap-dogs; as,

a, King Charles's. Charles II. never went out except attended by numbers of this kind. *b*, *Le pyrame* of Buffon. For this ſort, though common in Britain, there is no Engliſh name. It is black, marked on the legs with red, and having a ſpot of the ſame colour above each eye. *c*, The Shock-dog.

4. Dogs with ſhort pendent ears, and long legs and bodies; as,

a, Iriſh gre-hound; (*le Matin*, Buff.): a variety once very frequent in Ireland, and uſed in the chace of the wolf; now very ſcarce. Probably the ſame with the leviner in Caius's table, deſcribed above.

b, Common gre-hound, deſcribed above under Caius's table; (*le Levrier et Sebrder*, Buff. *Canis grajus*, Lin.) Its varieties are, 1. *Italian* gre-hound, ſmall and ſmooth; 2. *Oriental* gre-hound, tall, ſlender, with very pendulous ears, and very long hairs on the tail hanging down a great length.

c, Daniſh dog, of a ſtronger make than a gre-hound; the largeſt of dogs; (*le Grand Danois*, Buff.) Mr Pennant thinks it probable, that of this kind were the dogs of Epirus, mentioned by Ariſtotle, lib. iii. c. 21; or thoſe of Albania, the modern Schirwan or Eaſt Georgia, ſo beautifully deſcribed by Pliny, lib. viii. c. 40. Perhaps to this head may be referred the vaſt dogs of Thibet, ſaid by Marco Paulo to be as big as aſſes, and uſed in that country to take wild beaſts, and eſpecially the wild oxen called *Beyamini*.

d, Maſtiff, (*le Dogue de forte race*, Buff. *Canis moloſſus*, Lin.); Very ſtrong and thick made; the head large; the lips great, and hanging down on each ſide; a fine and noble countenance; grows to a great ſize: A Britiſh kind. See above under Dr Caius's table.

5. Dogs with ſhort pendent ears, ſhort compact bodies,

bodies, ſhort noſes, and generally ſhort legs. *a*, Bull-dog (*le Dogue*, Buff.), with a ſhort noſe, and under jaw longer than the upper: a cruel and very fierce kind, often biting before it barks; peculiar to England; the breed ſcarcer than it has been ſince the barbarous cuſtom of bull-baiting has declined. *b*, Pug-dog, (*le Doguin*, Buff.): A ſmall ſpecies; an innocent reſemblance of the laſt. *c*, Baſtard pug, (*le Roquet*, Buff.) *d*, Naked, (*le chien Turc*, Buff.): A degenerate ſpecies with naked bodies; having loſt their hair by the heat of climate.

Dogs are found in the Society iſlands, New Zealand, and the Low iſlands; there are alſo a few in New Holland. Of theſe are two varieties:

a, Reſembling the ſharp-noſed pricked-ear ſhepherd's cur. Thoſe of New Zeland are of the largeſt ſort. In the Society iſlands they are the common food, and are fattened with vegetables, which the natives cram down their throats as we ſerve turkeys when they will voluntarily eat no more. They are killed by ſtrangling, and the extravaſated blood is preſerved in cocoa-nut ſhells, and baked for the table. They grow very fat, and are allowed, even by Europeans who have got over their prejudices, to be very ſweet and palatable. But the taſte for the fleſh of theſe animals was not confined to the iſlanders of the Pacific ocean. The ancients reckoned a young and fat dog excellent food, eſpecially if it had been caſtrated: Hippocrates placed it on a footing with mutton and pork; and in another place ſays, that the fleſh of a grown dog is wholeſome and ſtrengthening, of puppies relaxing. The Romans admired ſucking puppies: they ſacrificed them alſo to their divinities, and thought them a ſupper in which the gods themſelves delighted.

b, The barbet, whoſe hair being long and ſilky, is greatly valued by the New Zelanders for trimming their ornamental dreſs. This variety is not eaten. The iſlanders never uſe their dogs for any purpoſes but what we mention; and take ſuch care of them as not to ſuffer them even to wet their feet. They are exceſſively ſtupid, have a very bad noſe for ſmelling, and ſeldom or never bark, only now and then howl. The New Zelanders feed their dogs entirely with fiſh.

The Marqueſas, Friendly Iſlands, New Hebrides, New Caledonia, and Eaſter Iſle, have not yet received thoſe animals.

Having thus traced the varieties of the Dog, and marked the peculiarities of each, we ſhall now give its general natural hiſtory.

From the ſtructure of the teeth, it might be concluded *à priori* that the dog is a carnivorous animal. He does not, however, eat indiſcriminately every kind of animal ſubſtance. There are ſome birds, as the colymbus arcticus, which the water-dog will lay hold of with keenneſs, but will not bring out of the water, becauſe its ſmell is exceedingly offenſive to him. He will not eat the bones of a gooſe, crow, or hawk: but he devours even the putrid fleſh of moſt other animals. He is poſſeſſed of ſuch ſtrong digeſtive powers, as to draw nouriſhment from the hardeſt bones. When fleſh cannot be procured, he will eat fiſh, fruits, ſucculent herbs, and bread of all kinds. When oppreſſed with ſickneſs, to which he is very ſubject, eſpecially in the beginning of ſummer, and before ill weather, in order to procure a puke, he eats the leaves of the quick-graſs, the bearded wheat-graſs, or the rough cock's-foot graſs, which gives him immediate relief. When he ſteals a piece of fleſh, as conſcious of the immorality of the action, he runs off with his tail hanging and bent in betwixt his feet.

His drink is water, which he takes in ſmall quantities at a time, by licking with his tongue. He is in ſome meaſure obliged to lick in this manner, otherwiſe his noſe would be immerſed in the water.

His excrements are generally hard ſcybals, which, eſpecially after eating bones, are white, and go by the name of *album græcum* among phyſicians. This album græcum was for a long time in great repute as a ſeptic; but it is now entirely diſregarded. He does not throw out his excrements promiſcuouſly upon every thing that happens to be in the way, but upon ſtones, trunks of trees, or barren places. This is a wiſe inſtitution of nature; for the excrements of a dog deſtroy almoſt every vegetable or animal ſubſtance. They are of ſuch a putrid nature, that if a man's ſkin touches them when recently expelled, that particular part will rot in a few days. He obſerves the ſame method in making his urine, which he throws out at a ſide. It is remarkable, that a dog will not paſs a ſtone or a wall againſt which any other dog has piſſed, without following his example, although a hundred ſhould occur in a few minutes, in ſo much that it is aſtoniſhing how ſuch a quantity can be ſecreted in ſo ſhort a time.

The dog is an animal not only of quick motion, but remarkable for travelling very long journeys. He can eaſily keep up with his maſter, either on foot or horſeback, for a whole day. When fatigued, he does not ſweat, but lolls out his tongue. Every kind of dog can ſwim; but the water-dog excels in this article.

The dog runs round when about to lie down, in order to diſcover the moſt proper ſituation. He lies generally on his breaſt, with his head turned to one ſide, and ſometimes with his head above his two fore-feet. He ſleeps little, and even that does not ſeem to be very quiet; for he often ſtarts, and ſeems to hear with more acuteneſs in ſleep than when awake. They have a tremulous motion in ſleep, frequently move their legs, and bark, which is an indication of dreaming.

Dogs are poſſeſſed of the ſenſation of ſmelling in a high degree. They can trace their maſter by the ſmell of his feet in a church, or in the ſtreets of a populous city. This ſenſation is not equally ſtrong in every kind. The hound can trace game, or his maſter's ſteps, 24 hours afterwards. He barks more ſeriouſly the nearer he approaches the fowls, unleſs he be beat and trained to ſilence.

The dog eats curiouſly, with oblique eyes; is an enemy to beggars; bites at a ſtone flung at it; is fond of licking wounds; howls at certain notes in muſic, and often urines on hearing them.

With regard to the propagation of dogs, the females admit the males before they are 12 months old. They remain in ſeaſon 10, 15, or even 25 days, during which time they will admit a variety of males. They come in ſeaſon generally twice in the year, and more frequently in the cold than in the hot months. The male diſcovers the condition of the female by the ſmell; but ſhe ſeldom admits him the firſt ſix or ſeven days. One

coitus

coitus will make her conceive a great number of young; but, when not restrained, she will admit several dogs every day: she seems to have no choice or predilection, except in favour of large dogs: from this circumstance it sometimes happens, that a small female, who has admitted a mastiff, perishes in bringing forth her young. During the time of copulation, these animals cannot separate themselves, but remain united so long as the erection subsists. This is owing to the structure of the parts. The dog has not only a bone in his penis, but in the middle of the corpus cavernosum there is a large hollow, which is blown up in the time of erection to a considerable bulk. The female, on the other hand, has a larger clitoris than perhaps any other animal; besides, a large firm protuberance rises in the time of copulation, and remains perhaps longer than that of the male, and prevents him from retiring till it subsides: accordingly, after the act of copulation is over, the male turns about in order to rest himself on his legs, and remains in that position till the parts turn flaccid. The female goes with young about nine weeks. They generally bring forth from six to twelve puppies. Those of a small size bring forth five, four, and sometimes but two. They continue to copulate and bring forth during life, which lasts generally about 14 or 15 years. The whelps are commonly blind, and cannot open their eyes till the 10th or 12th day: the males are like the dog, the females like the bitch. In the fourth month, they lose some of their teeth, which are soon succeeded by others.

The dog has such a strong resemblance to the wolf and the fox, that he is commonly supposed to be the production of one or other of these animals tamed and civilized. Buffon informs us, that he kept a young dog and a young wolf together till they were three years of age, without their discovering the least inclination to copulate. He made the same experiment upon a dog and a fox; but their antipathy was rather increased when the female was in season. From these experiments he concludes, that dogs, wolves, and foxes, are perfectly distinct genera of animals. There has, however, been lately an instance to the contrary: Mr Brooke, animal-merchant in Holborn, turned a wolf to a Pomeranian bitch in heat; the congress was immediate, and as usual between dog and bitch: she produced ten puppies. Mr Pennant saw one of them at Gordon Castle, that had very much the resemblance of a wolf, and also much of its nature; being slipped at a weak deer, it instantly caught at the animal's throat and killed it. "I could not learn (says Mr Pennant) whether this mongrel continued its species; but another of the same kind did, and stocked the neighbourhood of Fochabers, in the county of Moray (where it was kept), with a multitude of curs of a most wolfish aspect.—There was lately living a mongrel offspring of this kind. It greatly resembled its wolf parent. It was first the property of Sir Wolstein Dixey; afterwards of Sir Willoughby Aston. During day it was very tame; but at night sometimes relapsed into ferocity. It never barked, but rather howled; when it came into fields where sheep were it would feign lameness, but if no one was present would instantly attack them. It had been seen in copulation with a bitch, which afterwards pupped: the breed was imagined to resemble in many respects the supposed sire. It died between the age of five and six.—The bitch will also breed with the fox. The woodman of the manor of Mongewell, in Oxfordshire, has a bitch, which constantly follows him, the offspring of a tame dog-fox by a shepherd's cur; and she again has had puppies by a dog. Since there are such authentic proofs of the further continuance of the breed, we may surely add the wolf and fox to the other supposed stocks of these faithful domestics."

With regard to the natural disposition of the dog: in a savage state, he is fierce, cruel, and voracious; but, when civilized and accustomed to live with men, he is possessed of every amiable quality. He seems to have no other desire than to please and protect his master. He is gentle, obedient, submissive, and faithful. These dispositions, joined to his almost unbounded sagacity, justly claim the esteem of mankind. Accordingly no animal is so much caressed or respected: he is so ductile, and so much formed to please, that he assumes the very air and temper of the family in which he resides.

An animal endowed with such uncommon qualities must answer many useful purposes. His fidelity and vigilance are daily employed to protect our persons, our flocks, or our goods. The acuteness of his smell gains him employment in hunting: he is frequently employed as a turnspit; at Brussels and in Holland he is trained to draw little carts to the herb-market; and in the northern regions draws a sledge with his master in it, or loaden with provisions. The Kamtschatkans, Esquimaux, and Greenlanders, strangers to the softer virtues, treat these poor animals with great neglect. The former, during summer, the season in which they are useless, turn them loose to provide for themselves; and recall them in October into their usual confinement and labour: from that time till spring they are fed with fish-bones and opana, i. e. putrid fish preserved in pits, and served up to them mixed with hot water. Those used for draught are castrated; and four, yoked to the carriage, will draw five poods, or a hundred and ninety English pounds, besides the driver; and thus loaden, will travel 30 versts, or 20 miles a-day; or if unloaden, on hardened snow, on sledges of bone, a a hundred and fifty versts, or a hundred English miles.

It is pretty certain, Mr Pennant observes, that the Kamtschatkan dogs are of wolfish descent; for wolves abound in that country, in all parts of Siberia, and even under the arctic circle. If their master is flung out of his sledge, they want the affectionate fidelity of the European kind, and leave him to follow, never stopping till the sledge is overturned, or else stopped by some impediment. The great traveller of the 13th century, Marco Polo, had knowledge of this species of conveyance from the merchants who went far north to traffic for the precious furs. He describes the sledges; adds, that they were drawn by six great dogs; and that they changed them and the sledges on the road, as we do at present in going post. The Kamtschatkans make use of the skins of dogs for clothing, and the long hair for ornament: some nations are fond of them as a food; and reckon a fat dog a great delicacy. Both the Asiatic and American savages use these animals in sacrifices to their gods, to bespeak favour or avert evil. When the Koreki dread any infection, they kill a dog, wind the intestines round two poles, and pass between them.

Canis. The Greenlanders are not better maſters. They leave their dogs to feed on muſcles or berries; unleſs in a great capture of ſeals, when they treat them with the blood and garbage. Theſe people alſo ſometimes eat their dogs; uſe the ſkins for coverlets, for clothing, or to border and ſeam their habits; and their beſt thread is made of the guts. Theſe northern dogs in general are large; and in the frigid parts at leaſt have the appearance of wolves: are uſually white, with a black face; ſometimes varied with black and white, ſometimes all white; rarely brown or all black: have ſharp noſes, thick hair, and ſhort ears; and ſeldom bark, but ſet up a ſort of growl or ſavage howl. They ſleep abroad; and make a lodge in the ſnow, lying with only their noſes out. They ſwim moſt excellently; and will hunt in packs the ptarmigan, arctic fox, polar bear, and ſeals lying on the ice. The natives ſometimes uſe them in the chaſe of the bear. They are exceſſively fierce; and, like wolves, inſtantly fly on the few domeſtic animals introduced into Greenland. They will fight among themſelves even to death. Canine madneſs is unknown in Greenland. Being to the natives in the place of horſes, the Greenlanders faſten to their ſledges from four to ten; and thus make their viſits in ſavage ſtate, or bring home the animals they have killed. Egede ſays that they will travel over the ice 15 German miles in a day, or 60 Engliſh, with ſledges loaden with their maſters and five or ſix large ſeals.

Thoſe of the neighbouring iſland of Iceland have a great reſemblance to them. As to thoſe of Newfoundland, it is not certain that there is any diſtinct breed; moſt of them are curs, with a croſs of the maſtiff: ſome will, and others will not, take the water, abſolutely refuſing to go in. The country was found uninhabited, which makes it more probable that they were introduced by the Europeans; who uſe them, as the factory does in Hudſon's bay, to draw firing from the woods to the forts. The ſavages who trade to Hudſon's bay make uſe of the wolfiſh kind to draw their furs.

It is ſingular, that the race of European dogs ſhow as ſtrong an antipathy to this American ſpecies as they do to the wolf itſelf. They never meet with them, but they ſhow all poſſible ſigns of diſlike, and will fall on and worry them; while the wolfiſh breed, with every mark of timidity, puts its tail between its legs, and runs from the rage of the others. This averſion to the wolf is natural to all genuine dogs; for it is well known that a whelp, which has never ſeen a wolf, will at firſt ſight tremble, and run to its maſter for protection: an old dog will inſtantly attack it. Yet theſe animals may be made to breed with one another as above ſhown; and the following abſtract of a letter from Dr Pallas to Mr Pennant, dated October 5th 1781, affords a further confirmation of the fact. "I have ſeen at Moſcow about twenty ſpurious animals from dogs and black wolves. They are for the moſt part like wolves, except that ſome carry their tails higher, and have a kind of hoarſe barking. They multiply among themſelves: and ſome of the whelps are greyiſh, ruſty, or even of the whitiſh hue of the arctic wolves; and one of thoſe I ſaw, in ſhape, tail, and hair, and even in barking, ſo like a cur, that was it not for his head and ears, his ill-natured look, and fearfulneſs at the approach of man, I ſhould hardly have believed that it was of the ſame breed." Canis.

The dog is liable to many diſeaſes, as the ſcab, madneſs, &c. and he ſeldom wants the tænia or tape-worm in his guts, eſpecially if he drinks dirty water.

II. The ſecond ſpecies of this genus is the Lupus, or Wolf. He has a long head, pointed noſe, ears erect and ſharp, long legs well clothed with hair; tail buſhy and bending down, with the tip black; head and neck aſh-coloured; body generally pale brown tinged with yellow: ſometimes found white, and ſometimes entirely black. The wolf is larger and fiercer than a dog. His eyes ſparkle, and there is a great degree of fury and wildneſs in his looks. He draws up his claws when he walks, to prevent his tread from being heard. His neck is ſhort, but admits of very quick motion to either ſide. His teeth are large and ſharp; and his bite is terrible, as his ſtrength is great. The wolf, cruel, but cowardly and ſuſpicious, flies from man; and ſeldom ventures out of the woods, except preſſed by hunger: but when this becomes extreme, he braves danger, and will attack men, horſes, dogs, and cattle of all kinds; even the graves of the dead are not proof againſt his rapacity. Theſe circumſtances are finely deſcribed, in the following lines: The Wolf.

By wintry famine rous'd, ——————
Cruel as death, and hungry as the grave!
Burning for blood! bony, and ghaunt, and grim!
Aſſembling wolves in raging troops deſcend;
And, pouring o'er the country, bear along,
Keen as the north-wind ſweeps the gloſſy ſnow.
All is their prize. They faſten on the ſteed,
Preſs him to earth, and pierce his mighty heart.
Nor can the bull his awful front defend,
Or ſhake the murthering ſavages away.
Rapacious at the mother's throat they fly,
And tear the ſcreaming infant from her breaſt.
The god-like face of man avails him nought.
Even beauty, force divine! at whoſe bright glance
The generous lion ſtands in ſoften'd gaze,
Here bleeds, a hapleſs undiſtinguiſh'd prey.
But if, appriz'd of the ſevere attack,
The country be ſhut up, lur'd by the ſcent,
On church-yards drear (inhuman to relate!)
The diſappointed prowlers fall, and dig
The ſhrouded body from the grave; o'er which,
Mix'd with foul ſhades and frighted ghoſts, they howl.

Thomson's Winter.

The wolf, unlike the dog, is an enemy to all ſociety, and keeps no company even with thoſe of his own ſpecies. When ſeveral wolves appear together, it is not a ſociety of peace, but of war; it is attended with tumult and dreadful prowlings, and indicates an attack upon ſome large animal, as a ſtag, an ox, or a formidable maſtiff. This military expedition is no ſooner finiſhed, than they ſeparate, and each returns in ſilence to his ſolitude. There is even little intercourſe between the males and females: They feel the mutual attractions of love but once a-year, and never remain long together. The females come in ſeaſon in winter: many males follow the ſame female; and this aſſociation is more bloody than the former; for they growl, chaſe, fight, and tear one another, and often ſacrifice him

CANIS.
Plate CXVIII.
Spaniel.
Turnspits.
Hound.
Dalmatian D.
Small Water D.
Harrier.
Great Water D.
Bull Dog.
Mastiff.

Canis

him that is preferred by the female. The female commonly flies a long time, fatigues her admirers, and retires, while they sleep, with the most alert or most favourite male.

The season of love continues only twelve or fifteen days; it commences with the oldest females; the young ones are not so early disposed. The males have no marked period, but are equally ready at all times. They go from female to female, according as they are in a condition to receive them. They begin with the old females about the end of December, and finish with the young ones in the month of February or beginning of March. The time of gestation is about three months and a half; and young whelps are found from the end of April to the month of July. The wolves copulate like the dogs, and have an osseous penis, surrounded with a ring, which swells and hinders them from separating. When the females are about to bring forth, they search for a concealed place in the inmost recesses of the forest. After fixing on the spot, they make it smooth and plain for a considerable space, by cutting and tearing up with their teeth all the brambles and brush-wood. They then bring great quantities of moss, and prepare a commodious bed for their young, which are generally five or six, though sometimes they bring forth seven, eight, and even nine, but never less than three. They come into the world blind, like the dogs; the mother suckles them some weeks, and soon learns them to eat flesh, which she prepares for them by tearing it into small pieces. Some time after she brings them field-mice, young hares, partridges, and living fowls. The young wolves begin by playing with these animals, and at last worry them; then the mother pulls off the feathers, tears them in pieces, and gives a part to each of her young. They never leave their den till the end of six weeks or two months. They then follow their mother, who leads them to drink in the hollow trunk of a tree, or in some neighbouring pool. She conducts them back to the den, or, when any danger is apprehended, obliges them to conceal themselves elsewhere. Though, like other females, the she-wolf is naturally more timid than the male; yet when her young are attacked, she defends them with intrepidity; she loses all sense of danger, and becomes perfectly furious. She never leaves them till their education is finished, till they are so strong as to need no assistance or protection, and have acquired talents fit for rapine, which generally happens in ten or twelve months after their first teeth (which commonly fall out in the first month) are replaced.

Wolves acquire their full growth at the end of two or three years, and live 15 or 20 years. When old, they turn whitish, and their teeth are much worn. When full, or fatigued, they sleep, but more during the day than the night, and it is always a kind of slight slumber. They drink often; and, in the time of drought, when there is no water in the hollows, or in the trunks of old trees, they repair, several times in a day, to the brooks or rivulets. Though extremely voracious, if supplied with water, they can pass four or five days without meat.

The wolf has great strength, especially in the anterior parts of the body, in the muscles of the neck and jaws. He carries a sheep in his mouth, and, at the same time, outruns the shepherds; so that he can only be stopped or deprived of his prey by dogs. His bite is cruel, and always more obstinate in proportion to the smallness of the resistance; for when an animal can defend itself, he is cautious and circumspect. He never fights but from necessity, and not from motives of courage. When wounded with a ball, he cries; and yet, when dispatching him with bludgeons, he complains not. When he falls into a snare, he is so overcome with terror, that he may be either killed or taken alive without resistance; he allows himself to be chained, muzzled, and led where you please, without exhibiting the least symptom of resentment or discontent.

Canis

The senses of the wolf are excellent, but particularly his sense of smelling, which often extends farther than his eye. The odour of carrion strikes him at the distance of more than a league. He likewise scents live animals very far, and hunts them a long time by following their track. When he issues from the wood, he never loses the wind. He stops upon the borders of the forest, smells on all sides, and receives the emanations of living or dead animals brought to him from a distance by the wind. Though he prefers living to dead animals; yet he devours the most putrid carcases. He is fond of human flesh; and, if stronger, he would perhaps eat no other. Wolves have been known to follow armies, to come in troops to the field of battle, where bodies are carelessly interred, to tear them up, and to devour them with an insatiable avidity: And, when once accustomed to human flesh, these wolves ever after attack men, prefer the shepherd to the flock, devour women, and carry off children. Wolves of this vicious disposition are called *Loups garoux* by the French peasants, who suppose them to be possessed with some evil spirit; and of this nature were the *were wolfs* of the old Saxons.

The wolf inhabits the continents of Europe, Asia, Africa, and America; Kamtschatka, and even as high as the arctic circle. The wolves of North America are the smallest; and, when reclaimed, are the dogs of the natives: the wolves of Senegal the largest and fiercest; they prey in company with the lion. Those of the Cape are grey striped with black; others are black.—They are found in Africa as low as the Cape; and are believed to inhabit New Holland, animals resembling them having been seen there by the late circumnavigators. Dampier's people also saw some half-starved animals in the same country, which they supposed to be wolves. In the east, and particularly in Persia, wolves are exhibited as spectacles to the people. When young, they are learned to dance, or rather to perform a kind of wrestling with a number of men. Chardin tells us, that a wolf, well educated in dancing, is sold at 500 French crowns. This fact proves, that these animals, by time and restraint, are susceptible of some kind of education. M. Buffon brought up several of them: "When young, or during their first year (he informs us), they are very docile, and even caressing; and, if well fed, neither disturb the poultry nor any other animal: but, at the age of 18 months or two years, their natural ferocity appears, and they must be chained, to prevent them from running off and doing mischief. I brought up one till the age of 18 or 19 months, in a court along with fowls, none of which he ever attacked; but, for his first essay, he killed the whole in one night, with-

Canis. out eating any of them. Another, having broken his chain, ran off, after killing a dog with whom he had lived in great familiarity."

Whole countries are ſometimes obliged to arm, in order to deſtroy the wolves. Princes have particular equipages for this ſpecies of hunting, which is both uſeful and neceſſary. Hunters diſtinguiſh wolves into *young*, *old*, and *very old*. They know them by the tracks of their feet. The older the wolf, his feet is the larger. The ſhe-wolf's feet are longer and more ſlender; her heel is alſo ſmaller, and her toes thinner. A good blood-hound is neceſſary for hunting the wolf: and, when he falls into the ſcent, he muſt be coaxed and encouraged; for all dogs have an averſion from the wolf, and proceed with coldneſs in the chace. When the wolf is raiſed, the gre-hounds are let looſe in pairs, and one is kept for diſlodging him, if he gets under cover; the other dogs are led before as a reſerve. The firſt pair are let looſe after the wolf, and are ſupported by a man on horſe-back; then the ſecond pair are let looſe at the diſtance of ſeven or eight hundred paces; and, laſtly, the third pair, when the other dogs begin to join and to teaze the wolf. The whole together ſoon reduce him to the laſt extremity; and the hunters complete the buſineſs by ſtabbing him with a dagger. The dogs have ſuch a reluctance to the wolf's fleſh, that it muſt be prepared and ſeaſoned before they will eat it. The wolf may alſo be hunted with beagles or hounds; but as he darts always ſtraight forward, and runs for a whole day without ſtopping, the chace is irkſome, unleſs the beagles be ſupported by grey-hounds, to teaze him, and give the hounds time to come up.

Wolves are now ſo rare in the populated parts of America, that the inhabitants leave their ſheep the whole night unguarded: yet the governments of Penſylvania and New Jerſey did ſome years ago allow a reward of twenty ſhillings, and the laſt even thirty ſhillings, for the killing of every wolf. Tradition informed them what a ſcourge thoſe animals had been to the colonies; ſo they wiſely determined to prevent the like evil. In their infant ſtate, wolves came down in multitudes from the mountains, often attracted by the ſmell of the corpſes of hundreds of Indians who died of the ſmall-pox, brought among them by the Europeans: but the animals did not confine their inſults to the dead, but even devoured in their huts the ſick and dying ſavages.

Beſides being hunted, wolves are deſtroyed by pitfalls, traps, or poiſon. A peaſant in France who kills a wolf, carries its head from village to village, and collects ſome ſmall reward from the inhabitants: the Kirghis-Coſſacks take the wolves by the help of a large hawk called *berkut*, which is trained for the diverſion, and will faſten on them and tear out their eyes. Britain, a few centuries ago, was much infeſted by them. It was, as appears by Hollingſhed, very noxious to the flocks in Scotland in 1577; nor was it entirely extirpated till about 1680, when the laſt wolf fell by the hand of the famous Sir Ewen Cameron. We may therefore with confidence aſſert the non-exiſtence of theſe animals, notwithſtanding M. de Buffon maintains that the Engliſh pretend to the contrary. It has been a received opinion, that the other parts of theſe kingdoms were in early times delivered from this peſt by the care of king Edgar. In England he attempted to effect it, by commuting the puniſhments of certain crimes into the acceptance of a certain number of wolves tongues from each criminal; and in Wales by converting the tax of gold and ſilver into an annual tax of 300 wolves heads. But, notwithſtanding theſe his endeavours, and the aſſertions of ſome authors, his ſcheme proved abortive. We find, that ſome centuries after the reign of that Saxon monarch, theſe animals were again increaſed to ſuch a degree as to become again the object of royal attention: accordingly Edward I. iſſued out his royal mandate to Peter Corbet to ſuperintend and aſſiſt in the deſtruction of them in the ſeveral counties of Glouceſter, Worceſter, Hereford, Salop, and Stafford; and in the adjacent county of Derby (as Cambden, p. 602, informs us), certain perſons at Wormhill held their lands by the duty of hunting and taking the wolves that infeſted the country, whence they were ſtyled *wolve-hunt*. To look back into the Saxon times, we find, that in Athelſtan's reign wolves abounded ſo in Yorkſhire, that a retreat was built at Flixton in that county, "to defend paſſengers from the wolves, that they ſhould not be devoured by them:" and ſuch ravages did thoſe animals make during winter, particularly in January, when the cold was ſevereſt, that the Saxons diſtinguiſhed that month by the name of the *wolf-month*. They alſo called an outlaw *wolf's-head*, as being out of the protection of the law, proſcribed, and as liable to be killed as that deſtructive beaſt. Ireland was infeſted by wolves for many centuries after their extinction in England; for there are accounts of ſome being found there as late as the year 1710, the laſt preſentment for killing of wolves being made in the county of Cork about that time. Canis.

In many parts of Sweden the number of wolves has been conſiderably diminiſhed by placing poiſoned carcaſes in their way: but in other places they are found in great multitudes. Hunger ſometimes compels them to eat lichens: theſe vegetables were found in the body of one killed by a ſoldier; but it was ſo weak, that it could ſcarcely move. It probably had fed on the lichen vulpinus, which is a known poiſon to theſe animals. Madneſs, in certain years, is apt to ſeize the wolf. The conſequences are often very melancholy. Mad wolves will bite hogs and dogs, and the laſt again the human ſpecies. In a ſingle pariſh 14 perſons were victims to this dreadful malady. The ſymptoms are the ſame with thoſe attendant on the bite of a mad dog. Fury ſparkles in their eyes; a glutinous ſaliva diſtils from their mouths; they carry their tails low, and bite indifferently men and beaſts. It is remarkable that this diſeaſe happens in the depth of winter, ſo can never be attributed to the rage of the dog-days. Often, towards ſpring, wolves get upon the ice of the ſea, to prey on the young ſeals, which they catch aſleep: but this repaſt often proves fatal to them; for the ice, detached from the ſhore, carries them to a great diſtance from land, before they are ſenſible of it. In ſome years a large diſtrict is by this means delivered from theſe pernicious beaſts; which are heard howling in a moſt dreadful manner, far in the ſea. When wolves come to make their attack on cattle, they never fail attempting to frighten away the men by their cries; but the ſound of the horn makes them fly like lightning.

There is nothing valuable in the wolf but his ſkin,

whic

Canis.

which makes a warm durable fur. His flesh is so bad, that it is rejected with abhorrence by all other quadrupeds; and no animal but a wolf will voluntarily eat a wolf. The smell of his breath is exceedingly offensive. As, to appease hunger, he swallows indiscriminately every thing he can find, corrupted flesh, bones, hair, skins half tanned and covered with lime, he vomits frequently, and empties himself oftener than he fills. In fine, the wolf is consummately disagreeable; his aspect is base and savage, his voice dreadful, his odour insupportable, his disposition perverse, his manners ferocious; odious and destructive when living, and, when dead, he is perfectly useless.

Hyæna. III. The Hyæna has a straight jointed tail, with the hair of its neck erect, small naked ears, and four toes on each foot. It inhabits Asiatic Turky, Syria, Persia, and Barbary. Like the jackal, it violates the repositories of the dead, and greedily devours the putrid contents of the grave; like it, preys on the herds and flocks; yet, for want of other food, will eat the roots of plants, and the tender shoots of the palms: but, contrary to the nature of the former, it is an unsociable animal; is solitary, and inhabits the chasms of the rocks. The superstitious Arabs, when they kill one, carefully bury the head, lest it should be employed for magical purposes; as the neck was of old by the Thessalian sorceress.

Viscera non lyncis, non diræ nodus hyænæ
Defuit. Lucan, vi. 672.

The ancients were wild in their opinion of the hyæna; they believed that its neck consisted of one bone without any joint; that it changed its sex; imitated the human voice; had the power of charming the shepherds, and, as it were, rivetting them to the place they stood on: no wonder that an ignorant Arab should attribute preternatural powers to its remains. They are cruel, fierce, and untameable animals, of a most malevolent aspect; have a sort of obstinate courage, which will make them face stronger quadrupeds than themselves. Kæmpfer relates, that he saw one which had put two lions to flight, regarding them with the utmost contempt. Their voice is hoarse, a disagreeable mixture of growling and roaring.

Mr Pennant describes a variety of this species, undistinguished by former naturalists, which he calls the *spotted hyæna*. It has a large and flat head; some long hairs above each eye; very long whiskers on each side of the nose; a short black mane; hair on the body short and smooth; ears short and a little pointed, their outside black, inside cinereous; face and upper part of the head black; body and limbs reddish brown, marked with distinct black round spots; the hind legs with black transverse bars; the tail short, black, and full of hair. It inhabits Guinea, Ethiopia, and the Cape: lives in holes in the earth, or clifts of the rocks; preys by night; howls horribly; breaks into the folds, and kills two or three sheep; devours as much as it can, and carries away one for a future repast; will attack mankind, scrape open graves, and devour the dead. Bosman has given this creature the name of *jackal*; by which Buffon being misled, makes it synonymous with the common jackal. This hyæna is called the *tiger-wolf* by the colonists at the Cape, where it is a very common and formidable beast of prey. Of this animal, formerly but imperfectly known, the following account is given by Dr Sparmann in his voyage to the Cape.

Canis.

"The night, or the dark of the evening only, is the time in which these animals seek their prey, after which they are used to roam about both separately and in flocks. But one of the most unfortunate properties of this creature is, that it cannot keep its own counsel. The language of it cannot easily be taken down upon paper; however, with a view to make this species of wolf better known than it has been hitherto, I shall observe, that it is by means of a sound something like the following, *aoown*, and sometimes *euo*, yelled out with a tone of despair (at the interval of some minutes between each howl), that nature obliges this, the most voracious animal in all Africa, to discover itself, just as it does the most venomous of all the American serpents, by the rattle in its tail, itself, to warn every one to avoid its mortal bite. This same rattlesnake would seem, in consequence of thus betraying its own designs, and of its great inactivity (to be as it were nature's step-child), if, according to many credible accounts, it had not the wondrous property of charming its prey by fixing its eye upon it. The like is affirmed also of the tiger-wolf. This creature, it is true, is obliged to give information against itself; but, on the other hand, is actually possessed of the peculiar gift of being enabled, in some measure, to imitate the cries of other animals; by which means this arch-deceiver is sometimes lucky enough to beguile and attract calves, foals, lambs, and other animals. Near some of the larger farms, where there is a great deal of cattle, this ravenous beast is to be found almost every night; and at the same time frequently from one hour to another betraying itself by its howlings, gives the dogs the alarm. The peasants assured me, that the cunning of the wolves was so great (adding, that the trick had now and then even succeeded with some of them), that a party of them, half flying and half defending themselves, would decoy the whole pack of dogs to follow them to the distance of a gun-shot or two from the farm, with a view to give an opportunity to the rest of the wolves to come out from their ambuscade, and, without meeting with the least resistance, carry off booty sufficient for themselves and their fugitive brethren. As the tiger-wolf, though a much larger and stronger animal, does not venture, without being driven to the utmost necessity, to measure its strength with the common dog, this is certainly an evident proof of its cowardice. Neither does this same voracious beast dare openly to attack oxen, cows, horses, or any of the larger animals, while they make the least appearance as if they would defend themselves, or even as long as they do not betray any signs of fear. On the other hand, it has art enough to rush in upon them suddenly and unexpectedly, at the same time setting up a horrid and strange cry, so as to set them a running in consequence of the fright, that it may afterwards keep close to their heels with safety, till it has an opportunity with one bite or stroke to rip up the belly of its prey (even though it should be so large an animal as a draught-ox), or else give it some dangerous bite, and so at one single bout make itself master of its antagonist. On this account the peasants are obliged to drive their cattle home every evening before

Canis

it is dark, excepting the more confiderable droves of draught-oxen, which they let roam about day and night to feek their food unattended, by reafon that they are ufed both to the country and the artifices of the wolves, and can therefore the eafier depend upon and defend each other.

"Travellers, on the other hand, who are obliged to keep on in their journey, frequently fuffer great loffes by turning their cattle out at night; efpecially of the young ones, which are eafieft fcared. The Hottentots informed me that it was ftill within the memory of man, that the tiger-wolf was bold enough to fteal upon them and molest them in their huts, particularly by carrying off their children. This, however, is now no longer the cafe; a circumftance, perhaps, proceeding from the introduction of fire-arms into the country, a circumftance which, in thefe latter times, has caufed this, as well as other wild beafts, to ftand in greater awe of man than it did formerly. I have heard the following ftory of the tiger-wolf mentioned, as being related in a certain treatife on the Cape, of which I now cannot exactly remember the title. The tale is laughable enough, though perhaps not quite fo probable. 'At a feaft near the Cape one night, a trumpeter who had got his fill was carried out of doors, in order that he might cool himfelf, and get fober again. The fcent of him foon drew thither a tiger-wolf, which threw him on his back, and dragged him along with him as a corpfe, and confequently a fair prize, up towards Table-mountain. During this, however, our drunken mufician waked, enough in his fenfes to know the danger of his fituation, and to found the alarm with his trumpet, which he carried faftened to his fide. The wild beaft, as may eafily be fuppofed, was not lefs frightened in his turn.' Any other befides a trumpeter would, in fuch circumftances, have undoubtedly been no better than wolf's meat.

"In the mean while it is certain, that thefe wolves are to be found almoft every dark night about the fhambles at the Cape, where they devour the offals of bones, fkin, &c. which are thrown out there in great quantities, and drag away with them what they cannot eat. The inhabitants repay thefe good offices of the hyæna with a free and unlimited privilege of accefs and egrefs. The dogs too hereabouts, perfectly accuftomed to their company, are faid never to throw any impediment in their way; fo that the beaft, entertained and fed in the very heart of the town, has been feldom known to do any mifchief there. It is likewife a well-known fact, that thefe wolves, in different parts of Africa, exhibit different degrees of courage; this, however, may perhaps proceed from their being of different fpecies in different parts.

"Yet in this very greedinefs of the hyæna, and its difpofition to confume every thing it can get at, the provident economy of nature is abundantly evinced. The flowery fields at the Cape would certainly foon become hideous and disfigured with carcafes and fkeletons, the relicks of the great quantity of game of all forts which graze and die there in fucceffion, were not the tiger-wolf manifeftly fubfervient to nature in the regulation of her police, by clearing her theatre from them; nay, I had almoft faid the wolf alone: for lions and tigers, for example, never eat bones, and are not very fond of carcafes. Thefe are ferviceable in another way. They make the other animals vigilant and attentive to the functions for which nature has defigned them; and befides anfwering feveral other intentions of providence, they ferve, in conjunction with mankind, to keep in a juft equilibrium the increafe of the animal kingdom; fo that it may not exceed the fupplies afforded it by the vegetable part of the creation, and by this means prevent the neceffary renewal of the latter by feeds, &c. and thus, by defolating it and laying it wafte, in the end impoverifh and deftroy themfelves, and die moft wretched victims to want and hunger; fo that, notwithftanding the immenfe quantities of game exifting in this country, there are very feldom found any bones in the haunts they have left, and never after the tiger, lion, jackal, wild cat, and wild dog. Thefe latter animals, that they may not encumber and litter the ground which nature has ordained them to clear, never go out of their dens and caverns when they find themfelves weak and difabled; but there, oppreffed with hunger and difeafe, await the tranfitory moment, when they muft pay obedience to nature's laft law."

Canis.

IV. The MEXICANUS has a fmooth crooked tail. The body is afh-coloured, variegated with yellow fpots. It is a native of Mexico, and is called the mountain-cat by Seba. It agrees with the European wolf in its manners; attacks cattle, and fometimes men.

The Mexicanus.

V. The VULPES, or FOX, has a ftraight tail, white at the point. His body is yellowifh, or rather ftraw-coloured; his ears are fmall and erect; his lips are whitifh, and his forefeet black. From the bafe of the tail a ftrong fcent is emitted, which to fome people is very fragrant, and to others extremely difagreeable. The fox is a native of almoft every quarter of the globe, and is of fuch a wild and favage nature that it is impoffible fully to tame him. He is efteemed to be the moft fagacious and the moft crafty of all beafts of prey. The former quality he fhows in his method of providing himfelf with an afylum, where he retires from preffing dangers, where he dwells, and where he brings up his young; and his craftinefs is chiefly difcovered by the fchemes he falls upon in order to catch lambs, geefe, hens, and all kinds of fmall birds. The fox fixes his abode on the border of the wood, in the neighbourhood of cottages: he liftens to the crowing of the cocks and the cries of the poultry. He fcents them at a diftance; he choofes his time with judgment; he conceals his road as well as his defign; he flips forward with caution, fometimes even trailing his body, and feldom makes a fruitlefs expedition. If he can leap the wall, or get in underneath, he ravages the court-yard, puts all to death, and then retires foftly with his prey, which he either hides under the herbage, or carries off to his kennel. He returns in a few minutes for another, which he carries off, or conceals in the fame manner, but in a different place. In this way he proceeds till the progrefs of the fun, or fome movements perceived in the houfe, advertife him that it is time to fufpend his operations, and to retire to his den. He plays the fame game with the catchers of thrufhes, wood-cocks, &c. He vifits the nets and bird-lime very early in the morning, carries off fucceffively the birds which are entangled, and lays them in different places, efpecially near the fides of high-ways, in the furrows, under the herbage or brufhwood, where they fometimes lie

The Fox.

CANIS.
Plate CXIX.
King Charles's Dog.
Pyrame D.
Shock D.
Lion D.
Small Danish D.
Bastard Pug D.
Pug D.
Naked Turkish D.
Mongrel Turkish D.
The Wolf.
Mongrel Hound

Canis.

lie two or three days; but he knows perfectly where to find them when he is in need. He hunts the young hares in the plains, seizes old ones in their seats, never misses those which are wounded, digs out the rabbits in the warrens, discovers the nests of partridges and quails, seizes the mothers on the eggs, and destroys a vast quantity of game. The fox is exceedingly voracious; besides flesh of all kinds, he eats, with equal avidity, eggs, milk, cheese, fruits, and particularly grapes. When the young hares and partridges fail him, he makes war against rats, field-mice, serpents, lizards, toads, &c. Of these he destroys vast numbers; and this is the only service he does to mankind. He is so fond of honey, that he attacks the wild bees, wasps, and hornets. They at first put him to flight by a thousand stings; but he retires only for the purpose of rolling himself on the ground to crush them; and he returns so often to the charge, that he obliges them to abandon the hive, which he soon uncovers, and devours both the honey and wax. In a word, he eats fishes, lobsters, grass-hoppers, &c.

The fox is not easily, and never fully tamed: he languishes when deprived of liberty; and, if kept too long in a domestic state, he dies of chagrin. Foxes produce but once a year; and the litter commonly consists of four or five, seldom six, and never less than three. When the female is full, she retires, and seldom goes out of her hole, where she prepares a bed for her young. She comes in season in the winter; and young foxes are found in the month of April. When she perceives that her retreat is discovered, and that her young have been disturbed, she carries them off one by one, and goes in search of another habitation. The young are brought forth blind; like the dogs, they grow 18 months, or two years, and live 13 or 14 years.—The fox, as well as the congenerous wolf, will produce with the dog-kind, as noticed above.

The senses of the fox are equally good as those of the wolf; his sentiment is more delicate; and the organs of his voice are more pliant and perfect. The wolf sends forth only frightful howlings; but the fox barks, yelps, and utters a mournful cry like that of the peacock. He varies his tones according to the different sentiments with which he is affected: he has an accent peculiar to the chace, the tone of desire, of complaint, and of sorrow. He has another cry expressive of acute pain, which he utters only when he is shot, or has some of his members broken; for he never complains of any other wound, and, like the wolf, allows himself to be killed with a bludgeon without complaining; but he always defends himself to the last with great courage and bravery. His bite is obstinate and dangerous; and the severest blows will hardly make him quit his hold. His yelping is a species of barking, and consists of a quick succession of similar tones; at the end of which he generally raises his voice similar to the cry of the peacock. In winter, and particularly during frost and snow, he yelps perpetually; but, in summer, he is almost entirely silent, and, during this season, he casts his hair. He sleeps sound, and may be easily approached without wakening: he sleeps in a round form, like the dog; but, when he only reposes himself, he extends his hind legs, and lies on his belly. It is in this situation that he spies the birds along the hedges, and meditates schemes for their surprise. The fox flies when he hears the explosion of a gun, or smells gun powder. He is exceedingly fond of grapes, and does much mischief in vineyards. Various methods are daily employed to destroy foxes: they are hunted with dogs; iron traps are frequently set at their holes; and their holes are sometimes smoked to make them run out, that they may the more readily fall into the snares, or be killed by dogs or fire-arms.

The chace of the fox requires less apparatus, and is more amusing, than that of the wolf. To the latter every dog has great reluctance: but all dogs hunt the fox spontaneously and with pleasure; for, though his odour be strong, they often prefer him to the stag or the hare. He may be hunted with terriers, hounds, &c. Whenever he finds himself pursued, he runs to his hole; the terriers with crooked legs, or turnspits, go in with most ease. This mode answers very well when we want to carry off a whole litter of foxes, both mother and young. While the mother defends herself against the terriers, the hunters remove the earth above, and either kill or seize her alive. But, as the holes are often under rocks, the roots of trees, or sunk too deep in the ground, this method is frequently unsuccessful. The most certain and most common method of hunting foxes, is to begin with shutting up their holes, to place a man with a gun near the entrance, and then to search about with the dogs. When they fall in with him, he immediately makes for his hole; but, when he comes up to it, he is met with a discharge from the gun. If he escapes the shot, he runs with full speed, takes a large circuit, and returns again to the hole, where he is fired upon a second time; but, finding the entrance shut, he now endeavours to escape by darting straight forward, with the design of never revisiting his former habitation. He is then pursued by the hounds, whom he seldom fails to fatigue, because he purposely passes through the thickest parts of the forest or places of the most difficult access, where the dogs are hardly able to follow him; and, when he takes to the plains, he runs straight out, without stopping or doubling.

Of all animals the fox has the most significant eye, by which it expresses every passion of love, fear, hatred, &c. It is remarkably playful; but, like all savage creatures half reclaimed, will on the least offence bite those it is most familiar with. It is a great admirer of its bushy tail, with which it frequently amuses and exercises itself, by running in circles to catch its end, in cold weather, wraps it round its nose. The smell of this animal is in general very strong, but that of the urine is remarkably fetid. This seems so offensive even to itself, that it will take the trouble of digging a hole in the ground, stretching its body at full length over it; and there, after depositing its water, cover it over with the earth, as the cat does its dung. The smell is so obnoxious, that it has often proved the means of the fox's escape from the dogs; who have so strong an aversion at the filthy effluvia, as to avoid encountering the animal it came from. It is said that the fox makes use of its urine as an expedient to force the cleanly badger from its habitation: whether that is the means, is rather doubtful; but that the fox makes use of the badger's hole is certain: not through want of ability to form its own retreat, but to save itself some trouble; for after the ex-

pulsion

Canis.

Canis. possession of the first inhabitant, the fox improves as well as enlarges it considerably, adding several chambers, and providently making several entrances to secure a retreat from every quarter. In warm weather, it will quit its habitation for the sake of basking in the sun, or to enjoy the free air; but then it rarely lies exposed, but chuses some thick brake, that it may rest secure from surprise. Crows, magpies, and other birds, who consider the fox as their common enemy, will often, by their notes of anger, point out its retreat.—The skin of this animal is furnished with a warm soft fur, which in many parts of Europe is used to make muffs and to line clothes. Vast numbers are taken in Le Vallais, and the Alpine parts of Switzerland. At Lausanne there are furriers who are in possession of between 2000 and 3000 skins, all taken in one winter.

Of the fox there are several varieties, derived from colours; as,

1. The field-fox, or *alopex* of Linnæus, who makes it a distinct species; but it is every way the same with the common fox, except in the point of the tail, which is black.

2. The cross-fox, with a black mark passing transversely from shoulder to shoulder, with another along the back to the tail. It inhabits the coldest parts of Europe, Asia, and North-America: a valuable fur, thicker and softer than the common sort; great numbers of the skins are imported from Canada.

3. The black fox is the most cunning of any, and its skin the most valuable; a lining of it is, in Russia, esteemed preferable to the finest sables: a single skin will sell for 400 rubles. It inhabits the northern parts of Asia and North-America. The last is inferior in goodness.

4. The brant fox, as described by Gesner and Linnæus, is of a fiery redness; and called by the first *brand-fuchs*, by the last *brandrœf*; it is scarce half the size of the common fox: the nose is black, and much sharper: the space round the ears ferruginous; the forehead, back, shoulders, thighs, and sides black mixed with red, ash-colour, and black; the belly yellowish; the tail black above, red beneath, and cinereous on its side. It is a native of Pensylvania.

5. The corsac-fox, with upright ears, soft downy hair; tail bushy; colour in summer pale tawney, in winter grey: the base and tip of the tail black; a small kind. It inhabits the desarts beyond the Yaik: lives in holes: howls and barks: is caught by the Kirgis Cossacks with falcons and gre-hounds; 40 or 50,000 are annually taken, and sold to the Russians, at the rate of 40 kopeiks, or 20 pence, each: the former use their skins instead of money: great numbers are sent into Turky.

6. There are three varieties of foxes found in the mountainous parts of Britain, which differ a little in form, but not in colour, from each other. They are distinguished in Wales by as many different names. The *milgi*, or *gre-hound-fox*, is the largest, tallest, and boldest; and will attack a grown sheep or wedder: the *mastiff-fox* is less, but more strongly built: the *corgi*, or *cur-fox* is the least; lurks about hedges, out-houses, &c. and is the most pernicious of the three to the feathered tribe. The first of these varieties has a white tag or tip to the tail; the last a black. When hunted, they never run directly forward, but make a great many doublings and turnings; and when in danger of being taken, they emit such a smell from their posteriors that the hunters can hardly endure it. Canis.

VI. The Lagopus, or arctic fox, with a sharp nose; The arctic Fox. short rounded ears, almost hid in the fur; long and soft hair, somewhat woolly; short legs; toes covered on all parts, like that of a common hare, with fur; tail shorter and more bushy than that of the common fox, of a bluish grey or ash colour, sometimes white: the young of the grey are black before they come to maturity: the hair much longer in winter than summer, as is usual with animals of cold climates. It inhabits the countries bordering on the Frozen Sea; Khamschatka, the isles between it and America, and the opposite parts of America discovered in captain Bering's expedition, 1741; is again found in Greenland, Iceland, Spitzbergen, Nova Zembla, and Lapland. It burrows underground, forms holes many feet in length, and strews the bottom with moss. In Greenland and Spitzbergen it lives in the cliffs of rocks, not being able to burrow, by reason of the frost: two or three pair inhabit the same hole. They are in heat about Lady-day; and during that time, they continue in the open air, but afterwards take to their holes. They go with young nine weeks: like dogs, they continue united in copulation; they bark like that animal, for which reason the Russians call them *pesizi*, or dogs. They have all the cunning of the common fox; prey on geese, ducks, and other water-fowl, before they can fly; on grouse of the country, on hares, and the eggs of birds; and in Greenland (through necessity) on berries, shell-fish, or any thing the sea flings up. But their principal food in the north of Asia and in Lapland is the leming, or Lapland marmot: those of the countries last mentioned are very migratory, pursuing the leming which is a wandering animal: sometimes these foxes will desert the country for three or four years, probably in pursuit of their prey; for it is well known that the migrations of the leming are very inconstant, it appearing in some countries only once in several years. The people of Jenesea suspect they go to the banks of the Oby. Their chief rendezvous is on the banks of the Frozen Sea, and the rivers that flow into it, where they are found in great troops. The Greenlanders take them either in pitfalls dug in the snow, and baited with the capelin fish; or in springs made with whale-bone, laid over a hole made in the snow, strewed over at bottom with the same kind of fish; or in traps made like little huts, with flat stones, with a broad one by way of door, which falls down (by means of a string baited on the inside with a piece of flesh) whenever the fox enters and pulls at it. The Greenlanders preserve the skins for traffic; and in cases of necessity eat the flesh. They also make buttons of the skins; and split the tendons, and make use of them instead of thread. The blue furs are much more esteemed than the white.

VII. The Indica, or antarctic fox (the *coyotl* of The antarctic Fox. Fernandez, the *loup-renard* of Bougainville), has short pointed ears; irides hazel; head and body cinereous brown; hair more woolly than that of the common fox, resembling much that of the arctic; legs dashed with rust-colour; tail dusky, tipped with white; shorter and more bushy than that of the common fox, to which it is about one-third superior in size. It has much the habit of the wolf, in ears, tail, and strength of limbs.

The

Canis.

The French therefore call it *loup-renard*, or wolf-fox. It may be a wolf degenerated by climate. The largest are those of Senegal; the next are the European; those of North America are still smaller. The Mexican wolves, which Mr Pennant apprehends to be this species, are again less; and this, which inhabits the Falkland isles, near the extremity of South America, is dwindled to the size described. This is the only land animal of those distant isles; it has a fetid smell, and barks like a dog. It lives near the shores; kennels like a fox; and forms regular paths from bay to bay, probably for the conveniency of surprising the water-fowl, on which it lives. It is at times very meagre, from want of prey; and is extremely tame. The islands were probably stocked with those animals by means of masses of ice broken from the continent, and carried by the currents.

The grey-fox of Catesby.

VIII. The Grey-fox of Catesby, &c. has a sharp nose; sharp, long, upright ears; legs long; colour grey, except a little reddish about the ears.—It inhabits Carolina, and the warmer parts of North America: It differs from the arctic fox in form, and the nature of its dwelling; agrees with the common fox in the first, varies from it in the last: It never burrows, but lives in hollow trees; it gives no diversion to the sportsman; for after a mile's chace, it takes to its retreat; it has no strong smell; it feeds on poultry, birds, &c. These foxes are easily made tame; their skins, when in season, made use of for muffs.

The Silver Fox of Louisiana.

IX. The Silver fox of Louisiana. It resembles the common fox in form, but has a most beautiful coat. The short hairs are of a deep brown; and over them spring long silvery hairs, which give the animal a very elegant appearance. They live in forests abounding in game, and never attempt the poultry which run at large. The woody eminences in Louisiana are every where pierced with their holes.

The Barbary Fox.

X. The Barbary fox, (*le Chacal*, Buff.), or jackal-adive, has a long and slender nose, sharp upright ears, long bushy tail: colour, a very pale brown; space above and below the eyes, black; from behind each ear, there is a black line, which soon divides into two, which extend to the lower part of the neck; and the tail is surrounded with three broad rings. This species is of the size of the common fox, but the limbs are shorter, and the nose is more slender.—M. de Buffon informs us, that Mr Bruce told him this animal was common in Barbary, where it was called *thaleb*. But Mr Pennant observes, that Mr Bruce should have given it a more distinguishing name; for *thaleb*, or *taaleb*, is no more than the Arabic name for the common fox, which is also frequent in that country.

The Jackal.

XI. The Aureus, Schakal, or Jackal, as described by Mr Pennant, has yellowish brown irides; ears erect, formed like those of a fox, but shorter and less pointed: hairy and white within; brown without, tinged with dusky: head shorter than that of a fox, and nose blunter: lips black, and somewhat loose: neck and body very much resembling those of that animal, but the body more compressed: the legs have the same resemblance, but are longer: tail thickest in the middle, tapering to the point: five toes on the fore feet; the inner toe very short, and placed high: four toes on the hind feet; all are covered with hair even to the claws. The hairs are much stiffer than those of a fox, but scarcely so stiff as those of a wolf; short about the nose; on the back, three inches long; on the belly shorter. Those at the end of the tail four inches long. Colour of the upper part of the body a dirty tawny; on the back, mixed with black: lower part of the body of a yellowish white: tail tips with black; the rest of the same colour with the back: the legs of an unmixed tawny brown; the fore legs marked (but not always) with a black spot on the knees; but on no part are those vivid colours which could merit the title of *golden*, bestowed on it by Kæmpfer.—The length of this animal from the nose to the root of the tail is little more than twenty nine inches English: the tail, to the ends of the hairs, ten three quarters; the tip reaching to the top of the hind legs: the height, from the space between the shoulders to the ground, rather more than eighteen inches and a half; the hind parts a little higher.—This species inhabits all the hot and temperate parts of Asia, India, Persia, Arabia, Great Tartary, and about Mount Caucasus, Syria, and the Holy-land. It is found in most parts of Africa, from Barbary to the Cape of Good Hope.

Canis.

Professor Gueldenstaedt *, the able describer of this long-lost animal, remarks, that the cæcum entirely agrees in form with that of a dog, and differs from that of the wolf and fox. And Mr Pennant observes, that there is the same agreement in the teeth with those of a dog; and the same variation in them from those of the two other animals. These circumstances strengthen the opinion entertained by some writers, that the dogs of the old world did derive their origin from one or other of them. The jackals have indeed so much the nature of dogs, as to give reasonable cause to imagine that they are at least the *chief* stock from which is sprung the various races of those domestic animals. When taken young, they grow instantly tame; attach themselves to mankind; wag their tails; love to be stroked; distinguish their masters from others; will come on being called by the name given to them; will leap on the table, being encouraged to it: they drink, lapping; and make water sideways, with their leg held up. Their dung is hard: *odorat anum alterius, cohæret copula junctus*. When they see dogs, instead of flying, they seek them, and play with them. They will eat bread eagerly; notwithstanding they are in a wild state carnivorous. They have a great resemblance to some of the Calmuc dogs, which perhaps were but a few descents removed from the wild kinds. Our dogs are probably derived from those reclaimed in the first ages of the world; altered by numberless accidents into the many varieties which now appear among us.

* Nov. Com. Petrop. xx. 449.

The wild schakals go in packs of 40, 50, and even two hundred, and hunt like hounds in full cry from evening to morning. They destroy flocks and poultry, but in a less degree than the wolf or fox: ravage the streets of villages and gardens near towns, and will even destroy children, if left unprotected. They will enter stables and outhouses, and devour skins, or any thing made of that material. They will familiarly enter a tent, and steal whatsoever they can find from the sleeping traveller. In default of living prey, they will feed on roots and fruits; and even on the most infected carrion: they will greedily disinter the dead, and devour the putrid carcases; for which reason, in many countries the graves are made of a great depth. They at-

tend.

Canis. tend caravans, and follow armies, in hopes that death will provide them a banquet.

Their voice naturally is a howl. Barking, Mr Pennant observes, is latently inherent; and in their state of nature seldom exerted: but its different modifications are adventitious, and expressive of the new passions and affections gained by a domestic state. Their howlings and clamours in the night are dreadful, and so loud that people can scarcely hear one another speak. Dellon says, their voice is like the cries of a great many children of different ages mixed together; when one begins to howl, the whole pack join in the cry. Kempfer says, that every now and then a sort of bark is intermixed; which confirms what is above asserted by Mr Pennant. Dellon agrees in the account of their being tamed, and entertained as domestic animals. During day they are silent. They dig burrows in the earth, in which they lie all day, and come out at night to range for prey: they hunt by the nose, and are very quick of scent. The females breed only once a year; and go with young only four weeks; they bring from six to eight at a time. Both Mr Guldenstaedt and Mr Bell contradict the opinion of their being very fierce animals.

This animal is vulgarly called the *Lion's Provider*, from an opinion that it rouzes the prey for that bad-nosed quadruped. The fact is, every creature in the forest is set in motion by the fearful cries of the jackals; the lion, and other beasts of rapine, by a sort of instinct, attend to the chace, and seize such timid animals as betake themselves to flight at the noise of this nightly pack. The jackal is described by Oppian, under the name of [illegible], or *yellow wolf*; who mentions its horrible howl. It may, as M. de Buffon conjectures, be the *thos* of Aristotle, who mentions it with the wolf, and says that it has the same internal structure as the wolf, which is common with congenerous animals. The Thoes of Pliny may also be a variety of the same animal; for his account of it agrees with the modern history of the schakal, except in the last article: "Thoes, Luporum id genus est procerius longitudine, brevitate crurum dissimile, velox saltu, venatu vivens, innocuum homini;" lib. viii. c. 34.

The Mesomelas. XII. The Mesomelas, or *Capesch* of Schreber, the *tenlie* or *kenlie* of the Hottentots, has erect yellowish brown ears, mixed with a few scattered black hairs: the head is of a yellowish brown, mixed with black and white, growing darker towards the hind part: the sides are of a light brown, varied with dusky hairs: the body and also the back part of the legs are of a yellowish brown, lightest on the body; the throat, breast, and belly white. On the neck, shoulders, and back, is a bed of black; broad on the shoulders, and growing narrower to the tail: when the hairs are smooth, the part on the neck seems barred with white; that on the shoulders with white conoid marks, one within the other, the end pointing to the back: when the hairs are ruffled, these marks vanish, or grow less distinct, and a hoaryness appears in their stead. The tail is bushy, of a yellowish brown; marked on the upper part with a longitudinal stripe of black, and towards the end encircled with two rings of black, and is tipt with white. In length, the animal is two feet three quarters, to the origin of the tail: the tail is one foot. This species inhabits the countries about the Cape of Good Hope, and probably is found as high as the line. **Canis. Canis.**

The Thous. XIII. The Thous has a smooth crooked tail; the upper part of its body is grey, and its belly white. It is about the size of a large cat; and, according to Linnæus, is found at Surinam; it is mentioned by no other naturalist.

The Zerda. XIV. The Zerda. This animal has a very pointed visage; large bright black eyes; very large ears, of a bright rose-colour, internally lined with long hairs; the orifice so small as not to be visible, probably covered with a valve or membrane: the legs and feet are like those of a dog: the tail is taper: colour between a straw and pale brown. Length from nose to tail, ten inches; ears, three inches and a half long; tail, six: height, not five. It inhabits the vast desart of Sara, which extends beyond mount Atlas: It burrows in the sandy ground, which shows the necessity of the valves to the ears; and is so excessively swift, that it is very rarely taken alive. It feeds on insects, especially locusts: sits on its rump: is very vigilant: barks like a dog, but much shriller, and that chiefly in the night: never is observed to be sportive. We are indebted to Mr Eric Skioldebrand, the late Swedish consul at Algiers, for our knowledge of this singular animal. He never could procure but one alive, which escaped before he examined its teeth; the genus is very uncertain: the form of its head and legs, and some of its manners, determined Mr Pennant to rank it in this genus. That which was in possession of Mr Skioldebrand fed freely from the hand, and would eat bread or boiled meat. Buffon has given a figure of this animal; but from the authority of Mr Bruce ascribes to it a different place, and different manners. He says that it is found to the south of the Palus Tritonides, in Libya; that it has something of the nature of the hare, and something of the squirrel; and that it lives on the palm-trees, and feeds on the fruits.

Canis Major, the great dog in astronomy, a constellation of the southern hemisphere, below Orion's feet, though somewhat to the westward of him; whose stars Ptolemy makes 19; Tycho observed only 13; Hevelius 21; in the Britannic catalogue they are 31.

Canis Minor, the little dog, in astronomy, a constellation of the northern hemisphere; called also by the Greeks, *Procyon*, and by the Latins *Antecanis* and *Canicula*. The stars in the constellation canis minor, are in Ptolemy's catalogue 2; in Tycho's, 5; in Hevelius's, 13; and in the British catalogue, 14.

CANISIUS (Henry), a native of Nimeguen, and one of the most learned men of his time, was professor of canon law at Ingolstadt; and wrote a great number of books; the principal of which are, 1. *Summa Juris Canonici*. 2. *Antiquæ lectiones*, a very valuable work. He died in 1609.

CANITZ (the baron of), a German poet and statesman, was of an ancient and illustrious family in Brandenburg, and born at Berlin in 1654, five months after his father's death. After his early studies, he travelled to France, Italy, Holland, and England; and upon his return to his country, was charged with important negociations by Frederic II. Frederic III. employed him also. Canitz united the statesman with the poet; and was conversant in many languages, dead

CANIS.
Plate CXX.

as well as living. His German poems were published for the tenth time, 1750, in 8vo. He is said to have taken Horace for his model, and to have written purely and delicately. But he did not content himself with barely cultivating the fine arts in himself; he gave all the encouragement he could to them in others. He died at Berlin, in 1699, privy counsellor of state, aged 45.

CANKER, a disease incident to trees, proceeding chiefly from the nature of the soil. It makes the bark rot and fall. If the canker be in a bough, cut it off; in a large bough, at some distance from the stem; in a small one, close to it: but for over-hot strong ground, the ground is to be cooled about the roots with pond-mud and cow dung.

CANKER, among farriers. See FARRIERY, § aliv. 2.

CANNA, in botany: A genus of the monogynia order, belonging to the monandria class of plants; and in the natural method ranking under the eighth order, *Scitamineæ*. The corolla is erect, and divided into six parts, with a distinct lip bipartite and rolled back; the style lanceolate, and growing to the corolla; the calyx is triphyllous.

Species. 1. The indica, or common broad-leaved flowering cane, is a native of both Indies; the inhabitants of the British islands in America call it *Indian shot*, from the roundness and hardness of the seeds. It hath a thick, fleshy, tuberous root, which divides into many irregular knobs; it sends out many large oval leaves, without order. At their first appearance the leaves are like a twisted horn; but afterwards expand, and are near a foot long, and five inches broad in the middle; lessening gradually to both ends, and terminated in a point. The stalks are herbaceous, rising four feet high, and are encompassed by the broad leafy footstalks of the leaves; at the upper part of the stalk the flowers are produced in loose spikes, each being at first covered with a leafy hood, and turns to a brown colour. The flowers are succeeded by a fruit or capsule, oblong, rough, and crowned with the three-cornered empalement of the flower which remains. When the fruit is ripe, the capsule opens lengthwise into three cells, filled with round, shining, hard, and black seeds. 2. The latifolia, with a pale red flower, is a native of Carolina, and some other northern provinces of America. 3. The glauca, with a very large flower, is a native of South America. 4. The lutea, with obtuse oval leaves, is less common in America than the other sorts. 5. The coccinea, hath larger leaves than any of the other species, and the stalks rise much higher. The flowers are produced in large spikes; and are of a bright crimson, or rather scarlet colour.

Culture. These plants must always be kept in pots of rich earth, to be moved to shelter in winter. They are propagated by seeds sown on a hot-bed, in the spring; and in summer, when the plants are a little advanced in growth, prick them separately in small pots of rich earth, plunging them also in the hot-bed, giving shade, water, and fresh air; to which last harden them by degrees, till they bear it fully. In October they must be removed into a very good stove or green house.

CANNABIS, in botany: A genus of the pentandria order, belonging to the dioecia class of plants; and in the natural method ranking under the 53d order, *Scabridæ*. The calyx of the male is quinquepartite, with no corolla. In the female the calyx is monophyllous, entire, and gaping at the side; there is no corolla, but two styles; the fruit is a nut, bivalved, within the closed calyx. Of this there is but one species, viz. the sativa. This is propagated in the rich fenny parts of Lincolnshire in great quantities, for its bark, which is useful for cordage, cloth, &c. and the seeds abound with oil. Hemp is always sown on a deep, moist, rich, soil, such as is found in Holland, Lincolnshire, the fens of the island of Ely, where it is cultivated to great advantage, as it might be in many other parts of England where there is a soil of the same kind; but it will not thrive on clayey or stiff cold land. The ground on which hemp is designed to be sown, should be well ploughed, and made very fine by harrowing. About the middle of April the seed may be sown; three bushels is the usual allowance for an acre, but two are sufficient. In the choice of the seed, the heaviest and brightest coloured should be preferred; and particular care should be had to the kernel of the seed. For the greater certainty in this matter, some of the seeds should be cracked, to see whether they have the germ or future plant perfect: for, in some places, the male plants are drawn out too soon from the female, i. e. before they have impregnated the female plants with the farina; in which case, though the seeds produced by these females may seem fair to the eye, yet they will not grow*, according to the doctrine of Linnæus. When the plants are come up, they should be hoed out in the same manner as is practised for turnips, leaving them two feet apart; observe also to cut down all the weeds, which, if well performed, and in dry weather, will destroy them. This crop, however, will require a second hoeing, in about six weeks after the first; and, if this is well performed, the crop will require no further care. The first season for pulling hemp is usually about the middle of August, when they begin to pull what they call the *fimble hemp*, being that which is composed of the male plants; but it would be the much better method to defer this for a fortnight or three weeks longer, until those male plants have fully shed their farina or dust, without which the seeds will prove only empty husks. These male plants decay soon after they have shed their farina. The second pulling is a little after Michaelmas, when the seeds are ripe. This is usually called *karle hemp*, and consists of the female plants which were left. This karle hemp is bound in bundles of a yard compass, according to statute measure, which are laid in the sun for a few days to dry; and then it is stacked up, or housed, to keep it dry till the seed can be threshed out. An acre of hemp, on a rich soil, will produce near three quarters of seed, which, together with the unwrought hemp, is worth from six to eight pounds. Hemp is esteemed very effectual for destroying weeds; but this it accomplishes by impoverishing the ground, and thus robbing them of their nourishment; so that a crop of it must not be repeated on the same spot.

* See Botany, Sect. iii.

Some seeds of a large kind of hemp growing in China were lately sent by the East India Company to the Society for the encouragement of Arts, Manufactures, and Commerce, who distributed them to the members and other gentlemen who appeared likely to cultivate them; and from experiments made in consequence,

Cannabis, Cannæ. quarter, the plant has been found to succeed perfectly in this climate. The first trials were rather unpromising, the hemp produced from the foreign seeds proving of very little value. But the Reverend Dr Hinton of Northwold, who made the above trial in 1786, having accidentally saved some ripe seeds of that crop, sowed them in May 1787 on a spot of good land. They came up well, and attained as much perfection as ordinary hemp. The produce, when dressed, weighed at the rate of 95 stone 7 pounds and 12 ounces per acre, (being above 30 stone more, he says, than the usual crops of hemp in that neighbourhood); and at the rate of three bushels two pecks and half a pint of seed per acre were saved. Dr Hinton supposes that the seeds brought from China failed principally, if not entirely, by having been two years old, at which age hempseed seldom vegetates. Now that it is found to ripen with us, fresh seeds can always be obtained. It will yet, however, require a few years to determine whether this species will continue to retain its great size, or will degenerate and become the common hemp of Europe.

From the leaves of hemp pounded and boiled in water, the natives of the East Indies prepare an intoxicating liquor of which they are very fond. The plant, when fresh, has a rank narcotic smell; the water in which the stalks are soaked, in order to separate the tough rind for mechanic uses, is said to be violently poisonous, and to produce its effects almost as soon as drank. The seeds also have some smell of the herb, and their taste is unctuous and sweetish; they are recommended, boiled in milk, or triturated with water into an emulsion, against coughs, heat of urine, and the like. They are also said to be useful in incontinence of urine, and for restraining venereal appetites; but experience does not warrant their having any virtues of that kind.

CANNÆ, (anc. geog.) a town of Apulia in the Adriatic, at the mouth of the river Aufidus, rendered famous by a terrible overthrow which the Romans here received from the Carthaginians under Hannibal. The Roman consuls Æmilius Paulus and Terentius Varro, being authorized by the senate to quit the defensive plan, and stake the fortunes of the republic on the chance of a battle, marched from Canusium, and encamped a few miles east, in two unequal divisions, with the Aufidus between them. In this position they meant to wait for an opportunity of engaging to advantage; but Hannibal, whose critical situation in a desolated country, without refuge or allies, could admit of no delay, found means to inflame the vanity of Varro by some trivial advantages in skirmishes between the light horse. The Roman, elated with this success, determined to bring matters to a speedy conclusion; but, finding the ground on the south side too confined for the operations of so large an army, crossed the river; and Varro, resting his right wing upon the Aufidus, drew out his forces in the plain. Hannibal, whose head quarters were at Cannæ, no sooner perceived the enemy in motion, than he forded the water below, and marshalled his troops in a line opposite to that of his adversaries.

The Romans were vastly superior in number to the Carthaginians; but the latter were superior in cavalry. The army of the former, consisting of 87,000 men, was drawn up in the usual manner; the *hastati* in the first line, the *principes* in the second, and the *triarii* in the third. The cavalry were posted on the wings. On the right, the Roman knights flanked the legionaries; in the left, the cavalry of the allies covered their own infantry. The two consuls commanded the two wings, Emilius the right, and Terentius the left; and the two proconsuls Servilius and Attilius the main body. On the other hand, Hannibal, whose army consisted of 40,000 foot and 10,000 horse, placed his Gaulish and Spanish cavalry in his left wing, to face the Roman knights; and the Numidian horse in his right, over against the cavalry of the allies of Rome. As to his infantry, he divided the African battalions into two bodies; one of which he posted near the Gaulish and Spanish horse, the other near the Numidians. Between these two bodies were placed on one side the Gaulish, on the other the Spanish infantry, drawn up in such a manner as to form an obtuse angle projecting a considerable way beyond the two wings. Behind this line he drew up a second which had no projection. Asdrubal commanded the left wing; Maherbal the right; and Hannibal himself, with his brother Mago, the main body. He had also taken care to post himself in such a manner that the wind *Vulturnus*, which rises at certain stated times, should blow directly in the faces of the Romans during the fight, and cover them with dust. The onset was begun by the light-armed infantry; the Romans discharging their javelins, and the *Balears* their stones, with pretty equal success; nevertheless, the consul Emilius was wounded. Then the Roman cavalry in the right wing advanced against the Gaulish and Spanish in Hannibal's left. As they were shut in by the river Aufidus on one side, and by their infantry on the other, they did not fight, as usual, by charging and wheeling off, and then returning to the charge; but continued fighting each man against his adversary, till one of them was killed or retired. After they had made prodigious efforts on both sides to overbear each other, they all on a sudden dismounted, and fought on foot with great fury. In this attack the Gauls and Spaniards soon prevailed; put the Romans to the rout; and, pursuing them along the river, strewed the ground with their dead bodies, Asdrubal giving no quarter. This action was scarce over, when the infantry on both sides advanced. The Romans first fell upon the Spaniards and Gauls, who, as already observed, formed a kind of triangle projecting beyond the two wings. These gave ground, and, pursuant to Hannibal's directions, sunk into the void space in their rear; by which means they insensibly brought the Romans into the centre of the African infantry, and then the fugitives rallying, attacked them in front, while the Africans charged them in both flanks. The Romans, being by this artful retreat drawn into the snare and surrounded, no longer kept their ranks, but formed several platoons in order to face every way. Emilius, who was on the right wing, seeing the danger of the main body, at the head of his legionaries acted the part both of a soldier and general, penetrating into the heart of the enemy's battalions, and cutting great numbers of them in pieces. All the Roman cavalry that were left, attended the brave consul on foot; and, encouraged by his example, fought like men in despair. But, in the mean time, Asdrubal, at the head of a detachment of Gaulish and

Spanish

Spanish infantry brought from the centre, attacked Æmilius's legionaries with such fury, that they were forced to give ground and fly; the consul being all covered with wounds, was at last killed by some of the enemy who did not know him. In the main body, the Romans, though invested on all sides, continued to sell their lives dear; fighting in platoons, and making a great slaughter of the enemy. But being at length overpowered, and disheartened by the death of the two proconsuls Servilius and Attilius who headed them, they dispersed and fled, some to the right, and others to the left, as they could find opportunity; but the Numidian horse cut most of them in pieces: the whole plain was covered with heaps of dead bodies, insomuch that Hannibal himself, thinking the butchery too terrible, ordered his men to put a stop to it.—There is a great disagreement among authors as to the number of Romans killed and taken at the battle of Cannæ. According to Livy, the republic lost 50,000 men, including the auxiliaries. According to Polybius, of 6000 Roman horse, only 70 escaped to Venusia with Terentius Varro and 300 of the auxiliary horse. As to the infantry, that writer tells us, that 70,000 of the Roman foot died on the field of battle fighting like brave men; and that 13,000 were made prisoners. According to Dionysius of Halicarnassus, of 6000 horse, only 370 escaped the general slaughter, and of 80,000 foot, 3000 only were left. The most moderate computation makes the number of Romans killed to amount to 45,000. The scene of action is marked out to posterity, by the name of *Pezzo di Sangue*, "Field of Blood."

These plains have more than once, since the Punic war, afforded room for men to accomplish their mutual destruction. Melo of Bari, after raising the standard of revolt against the Greek emperors, and defeating their generals in several engagements, was at last routed here in 1019, by the Catapan Bolanus. Out of two hundred and fifty Norman adventurers, the flower of Melo's army, only ten escaped the slaughter of the day. In 1201, the archbishop of Palermo and his rebellious associates, who had taken advantage of the nonage of Frederic of Swabia, were cut to pieces at Cannæ by Walter de Brienne, sent by the pope to defend the young king's dominions.

The traces of the town of Cannæ are very faint, consisting of fragments of altars, cornices, gates, walls, vaults, and underground granaries. It was destroyed the year before the battle; but being rebuilt, became an episcopal see in the infancy of Christianity. It was again ruined in the sixth century, but seems to have subsisted in an humble state many ages later; for we read of its contending with Barletta for the territory, which till then had been enjoyed in common by them; and in 1284, Charles I. issued an edict for dividing the lands, to prevent all future litigation. The prosperity of the towns along the coast, which increased in wealth and population by embarkations for the Crusadoes and by traffic, proved the annihilation of the great inland cities; and Cannæ was probably abandoned entirely before the end of the thirteenth century.

CANNEQUINS, in commerce, white cotton cloths brought from the East Indies. They are a proper commodity for trading on the coast of Guinea, particularly about the rivers Senega and Gambia. These linens are folded square-wise, and are about eight ells long.

CANNEL Coal. See Ampelites.

CANNES, a town of France, in Provence, and in the viguerie of Grasse, seated on the coast of the Mediterranean sea, with a harbour and a castle. E. Long. 7. 7. N. Lat. 43. 34.

CANNIBAL, a modern term for an anthropophagus or man-eater, more especially in the West Indies. See Anthropophagi.

CANNON, a military engine for throwing balls, &c. by the help of Gunpowder.

The invention of brass cannon is by Larry ascribed to J. Owen: he says, that they were first known in England in the year 1353; but yet acknowledges, that, in 1346, there were four pieces of cannon in the English army at the battle of Cressy, and that these were the first that were known in France. And Mezeray relates, that king Edward, by five or six pieces of cannon, struck terror into the French army, it being the first time they had seen any of these thundering machines; though others affirm that cannon were known also in France at the same time; but that the French king, in his hurry to attack the English, and in confidence of victory, left all his cannon behind him as useless incumbrances (See Artillery). The Germans carry the invention farther back, and attribute it to Albertus Magnus, a Dominican monk, about the year 1250. Vossius rejects all these opinions, and finds cannon in China almost 1700 years ago. According to him, they were mounted by the emperor Kitey in the year of Christ 85. For further particulars of their history, &c. see Gun and Gunnery.

For the casting of cannon, see Foundery. For their different parts, proportions, management, operation, and effects, see Gunnery.

Cannon, with letter-founders and printers, the name of the largest size of letters they use.

CANNONADE, the application of artillery to the purposes of war, or the direction of its efforts against some distant object intended to be seized or destroyed, as a ship, battery, or fortress. See Gunnery.

Since a large ship of war may be considered as a combination of floating batteries, it is evident that the efforts of her artillery must be greatly superior to those of a fortress on the sea-coast; that is to say, in general; because, on some particular occasions, her situation may be extremely dangerous, and her cannonading ineffectual. Her superiority consists in several circumstances, as the power of bringing her different batteries to converge to one point; of shifting the line of her attack so as to do the greatest possible execution against the enemy, or to lie where she will be the least exposed to his fire; and chiefly because, by employing a much greater number of cannon against a fort than it can possibly return, the impression of her artillery against stone-walls soon becomes decisive and irresistible. Besides these advantages in the attack, she is also greatly superior in point of defence: because the cannon-shot, passing with rapidity through her sides, seldom do any execution out of the line of their flight, or occasion much mischief by their splinters; whereas they very soon shatter and destroy the faces of a parapet, and produce incredible havoc among the men by the fragments of the stones, &c. A ship may also retreat when ſhe finds it too dangerous to remain longer expoſed to the enemy's fire, or when her own fire cannot produce the deſired effect. Finally, the fluctuating ſituation of a ſhip, and of the element on which ſhe reſts, renders the effects of bombs very uncertain, and altogether deſtroys the effect of the *ricochet*, or rolling and bounding ſhot, which is ſo pernicious and deſtructive in a fortreſs or land engagement. The chief inconveniency to which a ſhip is expoſed, on the contrary, is, that the low-laid cannon in a fort near the brink of the ſea, may ſtrike her repeatedly on or under the ſurface of the water, ſo as to ſink her before her cannonade can have any conſiderable efficacy.

CANNULA, in ſurgery, a tube made of different metals, principally of ſilver and lead, but ſometimes of iron.

They are introduced into hollow ulcers, in order to facilitate a diſcharge of pus or any other ſubſtance; or into wounds, either accidental or artificial, of the large cavities, as the thorax or abdomen: they are uſed in the operation of bronchotomy; and, by ſome, after cutting for the ſtone, as a drain for urine.

Other cannulas are uſed for introducing cauteries, either actual or potential, into hollow parts, in order to guard the parts adjacent to that to be cauteriſed, from injury. They are of various figures; ſome being oval, ſome round, and others crooked.

CANO, a kingdom of Africa, in Negroland, with a town of the ſame name. It is bounded by Zaara on the north, by the river Niger on the ſouth, the kingdom of Agades on the weſt, and that of Caſſina on the eaſt. Some of the inhabitants are herdſmen, and others till the ground and dwell in villages. It produces corn, rice, and cotton. Here are alſo many deſerts, and mountains covered with woods, in which are wild citrons and lemon trees. The walls and houſes of the town are made of clay, and the principal inhabitants are merchants. E. Long. 16. 18. N. Lat. 11. 5.

CANOBIA, a town of Italy, in the duchy of Milan, ſeated on the weſtern bank of Lago Maggiore, or the Greater Lake. E. Long. 8. 47. N. Lat. 45. 55.

CANOE, a ſort of Indian boat or veſſel, formed of the trunk of a tree hollowed, and ſometimes of ſeveral pieces of the bark put together.

Canoes are of various ſizes, according to the uſe for which they may be deſigned, or the countries wherein they are formed. The largeſt are made of the cotton tree; ſome of them will carry between 20 and 30 hogſheads of ſugar or molaſſes. Some are made to carry ſail: and for this purpoſe are ſteeped in water till they become pliant; after which their ſides are extended, and ſtrong beams placed between them, on which a deck is afterwards laid that ſerves to ſupport their ſides. The other ſorts very rarely carry ſail, unleſs when going before the wind: their ſails are made of a ſort of ſhort ſilk graſs or ruſhes. They are commonly rowed with paddles, which are pieces of light wood ſomewhat reſembling a corn-ſhovel; and, inſtead of rowing with it horizontally like an oar, they manage it perpendicularly. The ſmall canoes are very narrow, having only room for one perſon in breadth, and ſeven or eight lengthwiſe. The rowers, who are generally American ſavages, are very expert in managing their paddles uniformly, and in balancing the canoes with their bodies; which would be difficult for a

ſtranger to do, how well accuſtomed ſoever to the conducting of European boats, becauſe the canoes are extremely light, and liable to be overturned. The American Indians, when they are under the neceſſity of landing to avoid a water-fall, or of croſſing the land from one river to another, carry their canoes on their heads, till they arrive at a place where they can launch them again. This is the general conſtruction of canoes, and method of managing them: but ſome nations have veſſels going under the name of canoes, which differ conſiderably from the above; as the inhabitants of Greenland, Hudſon's-bay, Otaheite, &c.

CANON, a perſon who poſſeſſes a prebend, or revenue allotted for the performance of divine ſervice, in a cathedral, or collegiate church.

Canons are of no great antiquity: Paſchier obſerves, that the name canon was not known before Charlemagne; at leaſt the firſt we hear of are in Gregory de Tours, who mentions a college of canons inſtituted by Baldwin XVI. archbiſhop of that city, in the time of Clotharius I. The common opinion attributes the inſtitution of this order to Chrodegangus, biſhop of Metz, about the middle of the eighth century.

Originally canons were only prieſts, or inferior eccleſiaſtics, who lived in community; reſiding by the cathedral church, to aſſiſt the biſhop; depending entirely on his will; ſupported by the revenues of the biſhopric; and living in the ſame houſe, as his domeſtics, or counſellors, &c. They even inherited his moveables, till the year 817, when this was prohibited by the council of Aix-la-Chapelle, and a new rule ſubſtituted in the place of that which had been appointed by Chrodegangus, and which was obſerved for the moſt part in the weſt till the twelfth century. By degrees, theſe communities of prieſts, ſhaking off their dependence, formed ſeparate bodies; whereof the biſhops, however, were ſtill heads. In the tenth century, there were communities or congregations of the ſame kind, eſtabliſhed even in cities where there were no biſhops: theſe were called collegiates, as they uſed the terms congregation and college indifferently: the name chapter, now given to theſe bodies, being much more modern. Under the ſecond race of the French kings, the canonical, or collegiate life, had ſpread itſelf all over the country; and each cathedral had its chapter, diſtinct from the reſt of the clergy. They had the name canon from the Greek κανων, which ſignifies three different things; a rule, a penſion, or fixed revenue to live on, and a catalogue or matricula; all which are applicable to them.

In time, the canons freed themſelves from their rules, the obſervance relaxed, and, at length, they ceaſed to live in community: yet they ſtill formed bodies; pretending to other functions beſides the celebration of the common office in the church; yet aſſuming the rights of the reſt of the clergy; making themſelves as a neceſſary council of the biſhop; taking upon them the adminiſtration of a ſee during a vacancy, and the election of a biſhop to ſupply it. There are even ſome chapters exempt from the juriſdiction of the biſhop, and owning no head but their dean. After the example of cathedral chapters, collegiate ones alſo continued to form bodies, after they had abandoned living in community.

CANONS are of various kinds; as,

Cardinal Canons, which are those attached, and, as the Latins call it, *incardinati* to a church, as a priest is to a parish.

Domicellary Canons, were young canons, who, not being in orders, had no right in any particular chapters.

Expectative Canons, were such as, without having any revenue or prebend, had the title and dignities of canons, a voice in the chapter, and a place in the choir; till such time as a prebend should fall.

Foreign Canons, were such as did not officiate in the canonries to which they belonged. To these were opposed mansionary canons, or canons residentiary.

Lay or honorary Canons, are such among the laity as have been admitted, out of honour and respect, into some chapter of canons.

Regular Canons, are canons that still live in community; and who, like religious, have, in process of time, to the practice of their rules, added the solemn profession of vows. They are called regulars, to distinguish them from those secular canons who abandon living in community, and at the same time the observance of the canons made as the rule of the clergy, for the maintenance of the ancient discipline. The canons subsisted in their simplicity till the eleventh, some say the twelfth century, when some of them, separating from the community, took with them the name of canons, or acephalous priests, because they declined to live in community with the bishop; and those who were left thenceforth acquired the denomination of canons regular, and adopted most of the professions of the rule of St Augustine. This order of regular canons of St Augustine was brought into England by Adelwald, confessor to Henry I. who erected a priory at Nodel in Yorkshire; and obtained for them the church of Carlisle as an episcopal see, with the privilege of choosing their own bishop. They were singularly protected and encouraged by Henry I. who gave them the priory of Dunstable in 1107, and by queen Maud, who, in the following year, gave them the priory of the Holy Trinity in London. It appears, that under the reign of Edward I. they had 53 priories.

Tertiary Canons, those who had only the third part of the revenues of the canonicate.

Canon, in an ecclesiastical sense, is a law or rule, either of doctrine or discipline, enacted especially by a council, and confirmed by the authority of the sovereign.

Canons are properly decisions of matters of religion; or regulations of the policy and discipline of a church, made by councils, either general, national, or provincial. Such are the canons of the council of Nice, or Trent, &c.

There have been various collections of the canons of the Eastern councils; but four principal ones, each ampler than the preceding. The first, according to Usher, A. D. 380, containing only those of the first oecumenical council, and the first provincial ones: they were but 164 in number. To these, Dionysius Exiguus, in the year 520, added the 50 canons of the apostles, and those of the other general councils. The Greek canons in this second collection end with those of the council of Chalcedon; to which are subjoined those of the council of Sardica, and the African councils. The fourth and last collection comes down as low as the second council of Nice; and it is on this that Balsamon and Zonaras have commented.

Apostolical Canons, are those which have been usually ascribed to St Clement. Bellarmin, Baronius, &c. will have them to be genuine canons of the apostles: Cotelerius observes, that they cannot be ascribed to the apostles or Clement, because they are not received with other books of scripture, are not quoted by the writers of the first ages, and contain many things not agreeable to the apostolical times: Hincmar, De Marca, Beveridge, &c. take them to be framed by the bishops who were the apostles disciples in the second or third century; S. Basnage is of opinion, that they were collected by an anonymous writer in the fifth century; but Daillé, &c. maintain them to have been forged by some heretic in the sixth century; and S. Basnage conjectures, that some of them are ancient, and others not older than the seventh century. The Greek church allow only 85 of them, and the Latins only 50; though there are 84 in the edition given of them in the Corpus Juris Canonici.

Canon is also used for the authorised catalogue of the sacred writings. See Bible.

The ancient canon, or catalogue of the books of the Old Testament, was made by the Jews, and is ordinarily attributed to Ezra; who is said to have distributed them into the law, the prophets, and the hagiographa, to which our Saviour refers, Luke, chap. xxiv. ver. 44. The same division is also mentioned by Josephus, cont. Appion.

This is the canon allowed to have been followed by the primitive church, till the council of Carthage; and, according to St Jerom, this consisted of no more than 22 books; answering to the number of the Hebrew alphabet; though at present they are classed into 24 divisions, containing Genesis, Exodus, Leviticus, Numbers, Deuteronomy, Joshua, Judges, Samuel, Kings, Isaiah, Jeremiah, Ezekiel, the twelve minor prophets, the Psalms, the Proverbs, Job, Canticles, Ruth, Lamentations, Ecclesiastes, Esther, Daniel, Ezra, comprehending the book of Nehemiah and the Chronicles. However, this order is not universally observed either among Jews or Christians: nor were all the books above enumerated admitted into the canon in Ezra's time. It is most likely, says Dr Prydeaux, that the two books of Chronicles, Ezra, Nehemiah, Esther, and Malachi, were added in the time of Simon the Just, when the canon was completed. But that council enlarged the canon very considerably, taking into it the books which we call apocryphal; which the council of Trent has farther enforced, enjoining all these to be received as books of Holy Scripture, upon pain of anathema, and being attainted of heresy. The Romanists, in defence of this canon, say, that it is the same with that of the council of Hippo, held in 393; and with that of the third council of Carthage, in 397, at which were present 46 bishops, and, among the rest, St Augustine; who declared that they received it from their fathers.

Their canon of the New Testament perfectly agrees with ours. It consists of books that are well known; some of which have been universally acknowledged; such are the four Gospels, the Acts of the Apostles, thirteen Epistles of St Paul, one Epistle of St Peter, and one Epistle of St John; and others, concerning which doubts were entertained, but which were afterwards received as genuine; such are the epistle to the Hebrews, that of James, the second of Peter, the second and third of John, that of Jude, and the Revelation. These books were written at different times, and they are authenticated, not by the decrees of councils, or infallible authority, but by such kind of evidence as is thought sufficient in the case of any other ancient writings. They were very extensively diffused; they were read in every Christian society; they were valued and preserved with care by the first Christians; they were cited by Christian writers of the second, third, and fourth century, as by Irenæus, Clement the Alexandrian, Tertullian, Origen, Eusebius, &c. and their genuineness is proved by the testimony of those who were contemporary with the apostles themselves, and by tradition. The four Gospels, and most of the other books of the New Testament, were collected either by one of the apostles, or some of their disciples and successors, before the end of the first century. The catalogue of canonical books furnished by the more ancient Christian writers, as Origen about the year 210, Eusebius and Athanasius in 315, Epiphanius in 370, Jerome in 382, Austin in 394, and many others, agrees with that which is now received among Christians. For the time of writing the several books of the New Testament, see the titles of the books themselves; as the Gospel of St Matthew, Mark, &c.

Some of the fathers distinguish the inspired writings into three classes; proto-canonical, deutero-canonical, and apocryphal.

Paschal Canon, a table of the moveable feasts, showing the day of Easter, and the other feasts depending on it, for a cycle of 19 years.

The paschal canon is supposed to be the calculation of Eusebius of Cæsarea, and to have been done by order of the council of Nice.

Canon, in monastic orders, a book wherein the religious of every convent have a fair transcript of the rules of their order, frequently read among them as their local statutes. This is also called *regula*, as containing the rule and institution of their order.

The canon differs from the missale, martyrologium, and necrologium.

Canon, again, is used for the catalogue of saints acknowledged and canonized in the Romish church.

Canon is also used, by way of excellence, in the Romish church, for the secret words of the mass, from the preface to the *parare*; in the middle of which the priest consecrates the host. The common opinion is, that the canon of the mass commences with *Te igitur*, &c. The people are to be on their knees, hearing the canon; and are to rehearse it to themselves, so as not to be heard.

Canon, in the ancient music, is a rule or method of determining the intervals of notes.

Ptolemy, rejecting the Aristoxenian way of measuring the intervals in music, by the magnitude of a tone (which was supposed to be formed by the difference between a diapente and a diatessaron), thought that musical intervals should be distinguished, according to the ratios or proportions which the sounds terminating those intervals bear to one another, when considered according to their degree of acuteness or gravity; which, before Aristoxenus, was the old Pythagorean way. He therefore made the diapason consist in a double ratio; the diapente, in a sesquialterate; the diatessaron, in a sesquitertian; and the tone itself, in a sesquioctave; and all the other intervals, according to the proportion of the sounds that terminate them: wherefore taking the canon (as it is called) for a determinate line of any length, he shows how this canon is to be cut accordingly, so that it may represent the respective intervals; and this method answers exactly to experiment, in the different lengths of musical chords. From this canon, Ptolemy and his followers have been called *Canonici*; as those of Aristoxenus were called *Musici*.

Canon, in modern music, is a kind of fugue, which they call a *perpetual fugue*, because the different parts beginning one after another, repeat incessantly the same air.

Formerly, says Zarlino, they placed, at the head of perpetual fugues, particular directions which showed how this kind of fugues was to be sung; and these directions being properly the rules by which perpetual fugues were composed were called *canoni*, *rules*, or *canons*. From this custom, others taking the title for the thing signified, by a metonimy, termed this kind of composition *canon*. Such canons as are composed with the greatest facility, and of consequence most generally used, begin the fugue either with the octave or the unison; that is to say, that every part repeats in the same tone the melody of the preceding. In order to form a canon of this kind, it is only necessary for the composer to make an air according to his taste; to add in score as many parts as he chooses, where the voices in octave or unison repeat the same melody; then forming a single air from all these parts successively executed, to try whether this succession may form an entire piece which will give pleasure, as well in the harmony as the melody.

In order to execute such a *canon*, he who sings the first part begins alone, and continues till the air is finished; then recommences immediately, without any suspence of sound or interruption of time: as soon as he has ended the first couplet, which ought to serve for the perpetual subject upon which the whole *canon* has been composed, the second part begins and repeats the same couplet, whilst the first who had begun pursues the second: others in succession begin, and proceed the same way, as soon as he who precedes has reached the end of the first couplet. Thus, by incessantly recommencing, an universal close can never be formed, and the *canon* may be repeated as long as the singers please.

A perpetual fugue may likewise consist of parts which begin with the intervals of a fourth or fifth; or, in other words, every part may repeat the melody of the first, a fourth or a fifth higher or lower. It is then necessary that the whole *canon* should be invented *di prima intenzione*, as the Italians say; and that sharps or flats should be added to the notes, whose natural gradations do not answer exactly, by a fourth or fifth, to the melody of the preceding part, and produce the same intervals with itself. Here the composer cannot pay the least regard to modulation; his only care is, that the melody may be the same, which renders the formation

Canon.

of a canon more difficult; for as every time when any part resumes the fugue, it takes a new key; it changes the tone almost at every note, and what is still worse, no part is at the same time found in the same tone with another; hence it is that this kind of canons, in other respects far from being easy to be pursued, never produces a pleasing effect, however good the harmony may be, and however properly it may be sung.

There is a third kind of *canon*, but very scarce, as well because it is extremely difficult, as because it is for the most part incapable of giving pleasure, and can boast no other merit but the pains which have been thrown away in its composition. This may be called a *double canon inverted*, as well by the inversions which are practised in it with respect to the melody of the parts, as by those which are found among the parts themselves, in singing. There is such an artifice in this kind of *canon*, that, whether the parts be sung in their natural order, or whether the paper in which they are set be turned the contrary way, to sing them backward from the end to the beginning, in such a manner that the bass becomes the upper part, and the rest undergo a similar change, still you have pretty harmony, and still a regular *canon*. The reader may consult Rousseau's Dictionary in this article, where he is referred to plate D fig. 11. for two examples of canons of this sort extracted from Bontempi, who likewise gives rules for their composition. But he adds, that the true principle from which this rule is deduced will be found at the word *Systeme*, in his account of the system of Tartini, to which we must likewise once more refer the reader; as a quotation of such length must have protracted our article to an enormous extent.

To form a *canon* in which the harmony may be a little varied, it is necessary that the parts should not follow each other in a succession too rapid, and that the one should only begin a considerable time after the other. When they follow one another so immediately as at the distance of a semibreve or a minim, the duration is not sufficient to admit a great number of chords, and the canon must of necessity exhibit a disagreeable monotony; but it is a method of composing, without much difficulty, a canon in as many parts as the composer chooses. For a *canon* of four bars only, will consist of eight parts if they follow each other at the distance of half a bar; and by each bar which is added, two parts will constantly be gained.

The emperor Charles VI. who was a great musician, and composed extremely well, took much pleasure in composing and singing *canons*. Italy is still replete with most beautiful *canons* composed for this prince, by the best masters in that country. To what has been said by Rousseau, we need only subjoin, that the English *catch* and the Italian *canon* are much the same; as any intelligent reader may perceive, from comparing the structure and execution of the English *catch* with the account of *canons* which has now been given.

Canon, in geometry and algebra, a general rule for the solution of all cases of a like nature with the present inquiry. Thus every last step of an equation is a canon; and, if turned into words, becomes a rule to solve all questions of the same nature with that proposed.

Canon-Law, a collection of ecclesiastical laws, serving as the rule and measure of church-government.

Canon ‖ Canonica.

The power of making laws was exercised by the church before the Roman empire became Christian. The canon-law that obtained throughout the West, till the 12th century, was the collection of canons made by Dionysius Exiguus in 520, the capitularies of Charlemagne, and the decrees of the popes from Siricius to Anastasius.

The canon-law, even when papal authority was at its height in England, was of no force when it was found to contradict the prerogative of the king, the laws, statutes, and customs of the realm, or the doctrine of the established church.

The ecclesiastical jurisdiction of the see of Rome in England was founded on the canon-law; and this created quarrels between kings and several archbishops and prelates who adhered to the papal usurpation.

Besides the foreign canons, there were several laws and constitutions made here for the government of the church: but all these received their force from the royal assent; and if, at any time, the ecclesiastical courts did, by their sentence, endeavour to enforce obedience to such canons, the courts at common law, upon complaints made, would grant prohibition. The authority vested in the church of England of making canons, was ascertained by a statute of Henry VIII. commonly called the *act of the clergy's submission*; by which they acknowledged, that the convocation had always been assembled by the king's writ; so that though the power of making canons resided in the clergy met in convocation, their force was derived from the authority of the king's assenting to and confirming them.

The old canons continued in full force till the reign of James I. when the clergy being assembled in convocation, the king gave them leave to treat and consult upon canons; which they did, and presented them to the king, who gave them the royal assent: these were a collection out of the several preceding canons and injunctions. Some of these canons are now obsolete. In the reign of Charles I. several canons were passed by the clergy in convocation.

CANONESS, in the Romish church, a woman who enjoys a prebend, affixed, by the foundation, to maids, without their being obliged to renounce the world or make any vows.

CANONICA, in philosophical history, an appellation given by Epicurus to his doctrine of logic. It was called *canonica*, as consisting of a few canons or rules for directing the understanding in the pursuit and knowledge of truth. Epicurus's *canonica* is represented as a very slight and insufficient logic by several of the ancients, who put a great value on his ethics and physics. Laertius even assures us, that the Epicureans rejected logic as a superfluous science; and Plutarch complains that Epicurus made an unskilful and preposterous use of syllogisms. But these censures seem too severe. Epicurus was not averse to the study of logic, but even gave better rules in this art than those philosophers who aimed at no glory but that of logics. He only seems to have rejected the dialectics of the stoics, as full of vain subtleties and deceits, and fitted rather for parade and disputation than real use. The stress of Epicurus's *canonica* consists in his doctrine of the criteria of truth. All questions in philosophy are either concerning words or things: concerning things,

Canonical | Canonry.

we ſeek their truth; concerning words, their ſignification: things are either natural or moral; and the former are either perceived by ſenſe or by the underſtanding. Hence, according to Epicurus, ariſe three criterions of truth, *viz.* ſenſe, anticipation or prenotion, and paſſion. The great canon or principle of Epicurus's logic is, that the ſenſes are never deceived; and therefore, that every ſenſation or perception of an appearance is true.

CANONICAL, ſomething that belongs to, or partakes of, the nature of a rule or canon.

Canonical Hours, are certain ſtated times of the day, conſigned, more eſpecially by the Romiſh church, to the offices of prayer and devotion. Such are *matins*, *lauds*, *ſixth*, *ninth*, *veſpers*. In our country the canonical hours are from eight to twelve in the forenoon, before or after which marriage cannot be legally performed in any pariſh-church.

Canonical Obedience, is that ſubmiſſion which, by the eccleſiaſtical laws, the inferior clergy are to pay to their biſhops, and religious to their ſuperiors.

Canonical Sins, in the ancient church, thoſe which were capital or mortal. Such eſpecially were idolatry, murder, adultery, hereſy, and ſchiſm.

Canonical Puniſhments, are thoſe which the church may inflict; ſuch as excommunication, degradation, and penance, in Roman Catholic countries, alſo faſting, alms, whipping, &c.

Canonical Life, the method or rule of living preſcribed by the ancient clergy who lived in community. The canonical life was a kind of medium between the monaſtic and clerical lives. Originally the orders of monks and clerks were entirely diſtinct; but pious perſons, in proceſs of time, inſtituted colleges of prieſts and canons, where clerks brought up for the miniſtry, as well as others already engaged therein, might live under a fixed rule, which, though ſomewhat more eaſy than the monaſtic, was yet more reſtrained than the ſecular. This was called the *canonical life*, and thoſe who embraced it *canons*.—Authors are divided about the founder of the canonical life. Some will have it to be founded by the apoſtles; others aſcribe it to pope Urban I. about the year 1230, who is ſaid to have ordered biſhops to provide ſuch of their clergy as were willing to live in community, with neceſſaries out of the revenues of their churches. The generality attribute it to St Auguſtin; who, having gathered a number of clerks to devote themſelves to religion, inſtituted a monaſtery within his epiſcopal palace, where he lived in community with them. Onuphrius Panvinius brings the inſtitution ſomewhat lower; according to him, pope Gelaſius I. about the year 495, placed the firſt regular canons of St Auguſtin in the Lateran church.

Canonical Letters, in the ancient church, were a ſort of teſtimonials of the orthodox faith, which the biſhops and clergy ſent each other to keep up the catholic communion, and diſtinguiſh orthodox Chriſtians from Arians and other heretics. They were denominated *canonical*, either as being compoſed according to a certain rule or form, or becauſe they were given to the *canonici*, that is, thoſe comprehended in the canon or catalogue of their church. When they had occaſion to travel into other dioceſes or countries, dimiſſory and recommendatory letters, alſo letters of peace, &c. were ſo many ſpecies of canonical letters.

Canonical is alſo an appellation given to thoſe epiſtles in the New Teſtament more frequently called *catholic or general* epiſtles.

CANONICUM, in a general ſenſe, denotes a tax or tribute.

Canonicum is more particularly uſed in the Greek church for a fee paid by the clergy to biſhops, archbiſhops, and metropolitans, for degrees and promotions.

Canonicum alſo denotes a due of firſt-fruits, paid by the Greek laity to their biſhops, or, according to Du-Cange, to their prieſts. The *canonicum* is aſſeſſed according to the number of houſes or chimnies in a place.

The emperor Iſaac Comnenus made a conſtitution for regulating the *canonicum* of biſhops, which was confirmed by another made in 1086, by his nephew Alexis Comnenus. A village containing thirty fires, was to pay for its *canonicum* one piece of gold, two of ſilver, one ſheep, ſix buſhels of barley, ſix of wheat flour, ſix meaſures of wine, and thirty hens.

CANONIST, a perſon ſkilled in or who makes profeſſion of the ſtudy and practice of the canon law. Canoniſts and civilians are uſually combined in the ſame perſons: and hence the title of *doctor juris utriuſque*, or *legum doctor*, uſually expreſſed in abbreviature, L. L. D. or J. U. D.

CANONIZATION, a ceremony in the Romiſh church, by which perſons deceaſed are ranked in the catalogue of the ſaints. It ſucceeds beatification.

Before a beatified perſon is canonized, the qualifications of the candidate are ſtrictly examined into, in ſome conſiſtories held for that purpoſe; after which, one of the conſiſtorial advocates, in the preſence of the pope and cardinals, makes the panegyric of the perſon who is to be proclaimed a ſaint, and gives a particular detail of his life and miracles: which done, the holy father decrees his canonization, and appoints the day.

On the day of canonization the pope officiates in white, and their eminences are dreſt in the ſame colour. St Peter's church is hung with rich tapeſtry, upon which the arms of the pope, and of the prince or ſtate requiring the canonization, are embroidered in gold and ſilver. An infinite number of lights blaze all round the church, which is crowded with pious ſouls, who wait with devout impatience till the new ſaint has made his public entry as it were into paradiſe, that they may offer up their petitions to him without danger of being rejected.

The following maxim with regard to canonization is now obſerved, though it has not been followed above a century, *viz.* not to enter into the inquiries prior to canonization, till 50 years, at leaſt, after the death of the perſon to be canonized. By the ceremony of canonization, it appears that this rite of the modern Romans has ſomething in it very like the apotheoſis or deification of the ancient Romans, and, in all probability, takes its riſe from it; at leaſt ſeveral ceremonies of the ſame nature are conſpicuous in both.

CANONRY, the benefice filled by a canon. It differs from a prebend, in that the prebend may ſubſiſt without

Canopus, Canosa.

without the canonicate: whereas the canonicate is inseparable from the prebend: again, the rights of suffrages, and other privileges, are annexed to the canonicate, and not to the prebend.

CANOPUS, in astronomy, a star of the first magnitude in the rudder of Argo, a constellation of the southern hemisphere.

Canopus, in Pagan mythology, one of the deities of the ancient Egyptians, and, according to some, the god of water. It is said, that the Chaldeans, who worshipped fire, carried their fancied deity thro' other countries to try its power, in order that, if it obtained the victory over the other gods, it might be acknowledged as the true object of worship; and it having easily subdued the gods of wood, stone, brass, silver, and gold, its priests declared, that all gods did it homage. This the priests of Canopus hearing, and finding that the Chaldeans had brought their god to contend with Canopus, they took a large earthen vessel, in which they bored several holes, which they afterwards stopped with wax, and having filled the vessel with water, painted it of several colours, and fitting the head of an idol to it, brought it out, in order to contend with the Chaldean deity. The Chaldeans accordingly kindled their fire all around it; but the heat having melted the wax, the water gushed out thro' the holes, and extinguished the fire; and thus Canopus conquered the god of the Chaldeans.

Canopus, or *Canobus*, according to Strabo, had been Menelaus's pilot, and had a temple erected to him in a town called *Canopus*, near one of the mouths of the Nile. Dionysius mentions it:

> [illegible]
> There stands Canobus' temple known to fame;
> The pilot who from fair Amyclae came.

Vossius remarks, on this occasion, the vanity of the Greeks, who, as he conjectures, hearing of an Egyptian deity named *Canopus*, took from thence an opportunity of deifying the pilot of Menelaus who bore the same name, and giving out that the Egyptian god Canopus had been a Greek. F. Montfaucon gives several representations of this deity. One, in allusion to the victory above mentioned, throws out water on every side through little holes.

Canopus, or *Canobus*, (anc. geog.) a town of the Lower Egypt, on the Mediterranean, an hundred and twenty stadia, or fifteen miles to the east of Alexandria; as old as the war of Troy, Canopus, or Canobus, Menelaus's steersman, being there buried. *Canopeni*, the gentilitious name; famous for their luxury and debauchery, (Strabo, Juvenal.) See Aboukir.

CANOPY, in architecture and sculpture, a magnificent kind of decoration, serving to cover and crown an altar, throne, tribunal, pulpit, chair, or the like. The word is formed from the barbarous Latin *conopeum*, of [illegible], *a net spread over a bed to keep off the gnats*, from [illegible] *a gnat*.

Canopies are also borne over the head in processions of state, after the manner of umbrellas. The canopy of an altar is more peculiarly called *Cibarium*.

The Roman grandees had their canopies, or spread veils, called *abaci*, over their chairs; the like were also in temples over the statues of the gods. The modern cardinals still retain the use of canopies.

CANOSA, a town of Puglia in Italy, occupying part of the site of the ancient Canusium. The old city was founded by Diomede, according to Strabo. It afterwards became a Roman colony, and one of the most considerable cities of this part of Italy for extent, population, and magnificence in building. The era of Trajan seems to have been that of its greatest splendour; but this pomp only served to mark it as a capital object for the avarice and fury of the Barbarians. Genseric, Totila, and Autharis, treated it with extreme cruelty. The deplorable state to which this province was reduced in 590 is concisely but strongly painted by Gregory the Great, in these terms: "On "every side we hear groans! on every side we behold "crowds of mourners, cities burnt, castles rased to the "ground, countries laid waste, provinces become de"serts, some citizens led away captives, and others in"humanly massacred." [*Swinburne's Travels in Sicily, page 428.*] No town in Puglia suffered more than Canosa from the outrages of the Saracens; the contests between the Greeks and Normans increased the measure of its woes, which was filled by a conflagration that happened when it was stormed by duke Robert. In 1090, it was assigned, by agreement, to Bohemund prince of Antioch, who died here in 1111. Under the reign of Ferdinand the Third, this estate belonged to the Grimaldis. On their forfeiture, the Affaitati acquired it, and still retain the title of marquis, though the Capeci are the proprietors of the fief.

Canosa, Cant.

The ancient city stood in a plain between the hills and the river Ofanto, and covered a large tract of ground. Many brick monuments, though degraded and stripped of their marble casing, still attest its ancient grandeur. Among them may be traced the fragments of aqueducts, tombs, amphitheatre baths, military columns, and two triumphal arches, which, by their position, seem to have been two city gates. The present town stands above, on the foundations of the old citadel, and is a most pitiful remnant of so great a city, not containing above three hundred houses. The church of St Sabinus, built, as is said, in the sixth century, is now without the inclosure. It is astonishing, that any part of this ancient cathedral should have withstood so many calamities. Its altars and pavements are rich in marbles; and in a small court adjoining, under an octagonal cupola, is the mausoleum of Bohemund, adorned in a minute Gothic style.

CANSO, a sea-port town of Acadia, or Nova Scotia, in North America, seated on a narrow strait which separates Nova Scotia from Cape Breton. Near this town is a fine fishery for cod. W. Long. 61. N. Lat. 46.

CANSTAT, a town of Swabia, in Germany, in the duchy of Wirtemberg, situated on the river Neckar, in E. Long. 9. 9. N. Lat. 48. 51.

CANT, a quaint affected manner of speaking, adapted chiefly to the lower sort. Skinner racks his invention for the origin of this word; which he successively deduces from the German, Flemish, and Saxon tongues. According to the general opinion, Cant is originally the proper name of a Cameronian preacher in Scotland, who by exercise had obtained the faculty of talking in the pulpit in such a tone and dialect as was understood by none but his own congregation: since Andrew Cant's time, the word has been extended to signify all sudden exclamations, and whining unmusical tones, especially in praying and preaching. But this origin of the word has been disputed by others; and perhaps the true derivation is from the Latin *cantare* "to beg."

Cant is also applied to words and phrases affected by particular persons or professions for low ends, and not authorised by the established language *. The difference between *cant* and *technical* seems to be this: the former is restrained to words introduced out of folly, affectation, or imposture; the latter is applied to such as are introduced for the sake of clearness, precision, and significancy.

* See Canting Language.

Cant is also used to denote a sale by auction. The origin of the word in this sense is dubious; it may come, according to some, from *quantum*, how much; according to others, from *cantare*, to sing or cry aloud; agreeably to which, we sometimes also call it an *outcry*.

Cant-Timbers, in ship-building, those timbers which are situated at the two ends of a ship. They derive their name from being *canted*, or raised obliquely from the keel; in contradistinction from those whose planes are perpendicular to it. The upper ends of those on the bow, or fore-part of the ship, are inclined to the stern; as those in the after, or hind part, incline to the stern-post above. See *Ship-Building*.

CANTABRIA, (anc. geog.), a district of Terraconensis, on the Oceanus Cantabricus or bay of Biscay; now Biscay. The inhabitants were famous for their warlike character. In conjunction with the Asturians †, they carried on desperate wars with the Romans; but were subdued by them about 25 years before Christ. Being impatient, however, of a foreign yoke, they in a few years revolted. Most of their youth had been already taken prisoners by the Romans, and sold for slaves to the neighbouring nations: but having found means to break their chains, they cut the throats of their masters; and returning into their own country, attacked the Roman garrisons with incredible fury. Agrippa marched against them with great expedition; but, on his arrival, met with so vigorous a resistance, that his soldiers began to despair of ever being able to reduce them. As the Cantabrians had waged war with the Romans for upwards of 200 years, they were well acquainted with their manner of fighting, no way inferior to them in courage, and were now become desperate; well knowing, that if they were conquered, after having so often attempted to recover their liberty, they must expect the most severe usage, and cruel slavery. Animated with this reflection, they fell upon the Romans with a fury hardly to be expressed, routed them in several engagements, and defended themselves when attacked by the enemy with such intrepidity, that Agrippa afterwards owned, that he had never, either by sea or land, been engaged in a more dangerous enterprise. That brave commander was obliged to use intreaties, menaces, and to brand some of his legionaries with ignominy, before he could bring them to enter the lists with such a formidable enemy. But having at last, with much ado, prevailed upon them to try the chance of an engagement in the open field, he so animated them by his example, that, after a most obstinate dispute, he gained a complete victory, which indeed cost him dear, but put an end to that destructive war. All the Cantabrians fit to bear arms were cut in pieces; their castles and strong holds taken and rased; and their women, children, and old men (none else being left alive), were obliged to abandon the mountainous places, and settle in the plain.

† See Asturia.

Dr Wallis seems to make the Cantabrian the ancient language of all Spain; which, according to him, like the Gaulish, gave way to a kind of broken Latin called *romance*, or *romanse*; which by degrees was refined into the Castilian or present Spanish. But we can hardly suppose, that so large a country, inhabited by such a variety of people, spoke all the same language. The ancient Cantabrian, in effect, is still found to subsist in the more barren and mountainous parts of the province of Biscay, Asturias, and Navarre, as far as Bayonne, much as the British does in Wales; but the people only talk it: for writing, they use either the Spanish or French, as they happen to live under the one or the other nation. Some attribute this to a jealousy of foreigners learning the mysteries of their language; others to a poverty of words and expressions. The Cantabrian does not appear to have any affinity with any other known language, abating that some Spanish words have been adopted in it for things whose use the Biscayers were anciently unacquainted with. Its pronunciation is not disagreeable. The Lord's prayer, in the Cantabrian tongue, runs thus: *Gure aita ceruetan aicena, santifica bedi hire icena, ethor bedi hire resumá, egin bedi hire vorondatea ceruan becala lurrean ere*, &c.

CANTABRICA, in botany: A synonime of a species of Convolvulus.

CANTABRUM, in antiquity, a large kind of flag used by the Roman emperors, distinguished by its peculiar colour, and bearing on it some words or motto of good omen, to encourage the soldiers.

CANTACUZENUS (Johannes), of Constantinople, a celebrated statesman, general, and historian, was born in that city, of a very ancient and noble family. He was bred to letters and to arms, and admitted to the highest offices of the state. The emperor Andronicus loaded him with wealth and honour; made him generalissimo of his forces; and was desirous of having him join him in the government, but this he refused. Andronicus dying in 1341, left to Cantacuzenus the care of the empire, till his son John Paleologus, who was then but nine years of age, should be fit to take it upon himself. This trust he faithfully discharged; till the empress dowager and her faction forming a party against him, declared him a traitor. On this the principal nobility and the army besought him to ascend the throne; and accordingly he was crowned on the 21st of May 1342. This was followed by a civil war, which lasted five years; when he admitted John a partner with him in the empire, and their union was confirmed by his giving him his daughter in marriage. Suspicions and enmities, however, soon arising, the war broke out again, and continued till John took Constantinople in 1355. A few days after, Cantacuzenus, unwilling to continue the effusion of blood, abdicated his share of the empire, and retiring to a monastery, took the habit of a monk, and the name of *Joasaphus*. His wife also retired to a nunnery, and changed her name of *Irene* for that of *Eugenia*. In this retirement he lived till the year 1411, when he was upwards of 100 years of age. Here he wrote a history of his own times, a Latin translation of which, from the Greek manuscript, was pub-

published by Pontanus at Ingolstadt, in 1603: and a splendid edition was printed at Paris in 1645, in three volumes folio, of the original Greek, and Pontanus's Latin version. He also wrote an apology for the Christian religion against that of Mahomet, under the name of *Christodulus*.

CANTALIVERS, in architecture, pieces of wood framed into the front or sides of a house, to suspend the mouldings and eves over it.

CANTAR, or CANTARO, an eastern weight, of different value in different places, equal at Acra in Turky to 603 pounds, at Tunis and Tripoli to 114 pounds.

CANTAR is also an Egyptian weight, which is denominated a *quintal*, and consists of an hundred or of an hundred and fifty rotolos, according to the goods they are to weigh.

CANTARO is also an Egyptian weight, which at Naples is equivalent to 25 pounds, at Genoa to 150 pounds. At Leghorn there are three kinds of *cantaros*, one weighing 150 pounds, another 151, and a third 160 pounds.

CANTARO is also a Spanish liquid measure, in use especially at Alicant, containing three gallons.

CANTARO is also a measure of capacity, used at Cochin, containing four rubies, the rubi 32 rotolos.

CANTARINI (Simon), a famous painter, called the *Pesarese*, from his being born at Pesaro, was the disciple of Guido; and copied the manner of his master so happily, that it is often difficult to distinguish between their works. He died at Verona in 1648.

CANTATA, in music, a song or composition, intermixed with recitatives, airs, and different movements, chiefly intended for a single voice, with a thorough bass, though sometimes for other instruments.

The cantata, when performed with judgement, has something in it very agreeable; the variety of the movements not clogging the ear, like other compositions. It was first used in Italy, then in France, whence it passed to us.

CANTAZARO, an episcopal city of Italy, in the kingdom of Naples, and in the territory of Calabria Ulterior. It is the residence of the governor of the province, and is seated near the sea, in E. Long. 17. 0. N. Lat. 38. 59.

CANTECROIX, a small territory of the Netherlands, in Brabant, and in the quarter of Antwerp, with the title of a principality; there is a small town of the same name, but Lire is the capital.

CANTEMIR (Demetrius), son of a prince of Moldavia. Disappointed by not succeeding his father in that dignity, held under the Ottoman Port, he went over with his army to the Czar Peter the great, against whom he had been sent by the Grand Signior: he signalized himself in the Czar's service; and in the republic of letters, by a Latin history of the origin and decline of the Ottoman empire, &c. Died in 1723.

CANTEMIR (Antiochus), esteemed the founder of the Russian poetry, was the youngest son of the preceding. Under the most ingenious professors, whom the czar had invited to Petersburgh, he learned mathematics, physic, history, moral philosophy, and polite literature; without neglecting the study of the Holy Scriptures, to which he had a great inclination. Scarce had he finished his academic course, when he printed a Concordance to the Psalms in the Russian language, and was elected member of the academy. The affairs of state in which he was soon after engaged, did not make him neglect his literary pursuits. In order to make himself useful to his fellow-citizens, he composed his satires, to ridicule certain prejudices which had got footing among them. When but 23 years of age, he was nominated minister at the court of Great Britain; and his dexterity in the management of public affairs was as much admired as his taste for the sciences. He had the same reputation in France, whither he went in 1738, in quality of minister plenipotentiary, and soon after was invested with the character of ambassador extraordinary. The wise and prudent manner in which he conducted himself during the different revolutions which happened in Russia during his absence, gained him the confidence and esteem of three successive princes. He died of a dropsy, at Paris, in 1744, aged 44. Besides the pieces already mentioned, he wrote, 1. Some fables and odes. 2. A translation of Horace's epistles into Russian verse. 3. A prose translation of Fontenelle's plurality of worlds; and, 4. Algarotti's dialogues on light. The abbe Guasco has written his life in French, and translated his satires into that language.

CANTERBURY, a city of England, and capital of the county of Kent, situated in E. Long. 1. 15. N. Lat. 51. 16. It had the names of *Durovernum* and *Darvernum* given it by the Romans, and *Dorobernia* by Bede, which are thought to be derived from *Durwhern*, signifying a rapid stream, such as the Stour, on which it stands, is. The Britons call it *Caer-Kent*, i. e. the city of Kent; and its present English name is of the same import, derived from the Saxon. Modern writers in Latin call it *Cantuaria*. Its great antiquity appears not only from Antoninus's itinerary, but from the military way which has been discovered here, and the causeways leading to Dover and Lymne, besides the coins and other curiosities found about it. The archiepiscopal and metropolitical dignity seems to have been settled here very early; and to prevent its being removed, an anathema was decreed against any who should attempt it. After that, the city flourished greatly; though it suffered in common with other towns during the Danish invasions, and at other times by the casualties of fire. The city was given entirely to the bishops by William Rufus, and was held in the utmost veneration in the Popish times, especially after the murder of Becket in the reign of Henry II. to whose shrine so great was the resort, and so rich were the offerings, that Erasmus, who was an eye-witness of its wealth, says the whole church and chapel in which he was interred glittered with jewels; and at the dissolution, the plate and jewels filled two great chests, each of which required eight strong men to carry out. The cathedral was granted by Ethelbert, king of Kent, upon his conversion, to Austin the monk, together with his palace, and the royalty of the city and its territories. This Austin founded a monastery for monks, called from him *Augustine*. After the cathedral had been several times destroyed by fire and rebuilt, the present was begun about the year 1174, and augmented and embellished by the succeeding archbishops, till it was completed in the reign of Henry V. It is a noble Gothic pile, and before the reformation had 37 altars. A great many kings, princes, cardinals, and archbishops, are buried in it. At the dissolution, Henry VIII. seized all the revenues both of the church and monastery, except what he allotted for the maintenance of a dean, 12 prebendaries, and six preachers, whom he established in place of the monks. During the grand rebellion, it suffered much; the usurper Cromwell having made a stable of it for his dragoons. After the restoration, it was repaired, and made what it now appears.

Besides the cathedral and other churches, as well as a monastery, the city had anciently a castle on the south-side, and strong walls, with towers, a ditch, and rampart; it had also a mint and an exchange. As to its government, it seems to have been entirely subject to the archbishop, both in spirituals and temporals; at least from the time that William Rufus gave it solely to bishop Anselm, till the reformation. It is now a county of itself; and the corporation consists of a mayor, recorder, 12 aldermen, a sheriff, 24 common-council-men, a mace-bearer, sword-bearer, and four serjeants at mace. Every Monday a court is held at Guildhall for civil and criminal causes; and every other Tuesday for the government of the city. Here were formerly 2000 or 3000 French Protestants employed in the silk manufacture; but this branch is now greatly decayed in the place, since Spitalfields became so flourishing. Besides the cathedral, it contains 15 parish-churches, seven hospitals, a free-school, a house of correction, a gaol for criminals, and a sumptuous conduit for supplying the inhabitants with water. It consists of four streets, disposed in the form of a cross, and divided into six wards, which are about three miles in circumference. It is surrounded on all hands with hop-grounds much to its advantage, and is famed for its excellent brawn.

The diocese of Canterbury contains 257 parishes, besides chapels, in Kent, and about 100 more in other dioceses. These are called *Peculiars*; it being an ancient privilege of this see, that, wheresoever the archbishops had either manors or advowsons, the place was exempted from the jurisdiction of the ordinary of the diocese where it was situated, and was deemed in the diocese of Canterbury. This see is valued in the king's books at L. 2816 : 17 : 9½, but is reckoned to produce a clear revenue of L. 8000 a-year. The clergy's tenths come to L. 651 : 18 : 2½. This see had many great privileges in the time of Popery, some of which it still retains. The archbishop is accounted primate and metropolitan of all England, and is the first peer in the realm; having the precedence of all dukes not of the blood-royal, and all the great officers of state. In common speech, he is styled *His Grace*, and he writes himself *Divina Providentia*; whereas other bishops style themselves *Divina Permissione*. At coronations, he places the crown on the king's head; and, wherever the court may be, the king and queen are the proper domestic parishioners of the archbishop of Canterbury. The bishop of London is accounted his provincial dean, the bishop of Winchester his sub-dean, the bishop of Lincoln his chancellor, and the bishop of Rochester his chaplain. This see hath yielded to the church 18 saints; to the church of Rome, 9 cardinals; to the civil state of England 12 lord chancellors, 4 lord treasurers, and 1 lord chief justice; and 9 chancellors to the University of Oxford. To this see belongs only one archdeacon, viz. of Canterbury. To the cathedral belongs an archbishop, a dean, a chancellor, an archdeacon, 12 prebends, 6 preachers, 6 minor canons, 6 substitutes, 12 lay clerks, 10 choristers, 2 masters, 50 scholars, and 12 almsmen.

Canterbury-Bell, in botany: The English name of a species of Campanula.

CANTERUS (William), an eminent linguist and philologer, was born at Utrecht, in 1542. He studied at Louvain and Paris; and gave surprising proofs of his progress in Greek and Latin literature. He afterwards visited the several universities of Germany and Italy; and died at Louvain, in 1575, aged 33. He understood six languages, besides that of his native country; and, notwithstanding his dying so young, wrote several philological and critical works, among which are, *Notæ, Scholia, Emendationes, et Explicationes, in Euripidem, Sophoclem, Æschylum, Ciceronem, Propertium, Ausonium*, &c. and many translations of Greek authors.

CANTHARIDES. See Cantharis and Meloe.

CANTHARIS, in zoology, a genus of insects belonging to the order of insecta coleoptera. The feelers of this genus are setaceous; the breast is marginated, and shorter than the head; the elytra, or wing-cases, are flexile; and the sides of the belly are plaited and papillous. Linnæus enumerates 27 species of the cantharis, most of them to be found in different parts of Europe. The cantharis used in making blistering plasters, is ranked under a different genus, viz. the Meloe.

CANTHI, in anatomy, cavities at the extremities of the eye-lids, commonly called the *corners of the eye*: the greater of them, or the greater canthus, is next the nose; the lesser of them, or the little canthus, lies towards the temple.

CANTICLES, a canonical book of the Old Testament, otherwise called the *Song of Solomon*; by the Jews the *Song of Songs, Canticum Canticorum*. The book of Canticles is usually supposed to be an epithalamium composed by Solomon, on occasion of his marriage with the king of Egypt's daughter. But those who penetrate further into the mystery, find in it the marriage of Jesus Christ with human nature, the church, and good men. On this principle the Canticles is held to be a continued allegory, wherein, under the terms of a common wedding, a divine and spiritual marriage is expressed. This song contains the adventures of seven days and seven nights; the exact time allowed for the celebration of marriage among the Hebrews. The Jews themselves, apprehending the book liable to be understood in a gross and carnal manner, prohibited the reading of it before the age of 30, and the same usage anciently obtained in the Christian church. Among the ancients, Theodore Mopsuestanus rejected the book of Canticles as not divine. Divers rabbins have also questioned its being written by inspiration. It is alleged, that the name of God is not once found in it. Mr Whiston has a discourse express to prove that the Canticles is not a sacred book of the Old Testament. He alleges it indeed to have been written by king Solomon the son of David; but asserts that it was composed at the time when that prince, blinded by his concubines, was sunk in lust and idolatry.

ry. This he chiefly infers from the general character of vanity and dissoluteness which reigns thro' the Canticles; in which there is not, according to Whiston, one thought that leads the mind towards religion, but all is worldly and carnal, to say no worse. For the mystic sense, he asserts it to be without foundation; and that the book is not cited as canonical by any writer before the destruction of Jerusalem. Mr Whiston will have it to have been taken into the canon between the years 77 and 118, when allegories came into vogue, and the rabbins began to corrupt the text of Scripture. Grotius, Nierembergius, the Dutch divines who criticised F. Simon, Menetrier, Basnage, and some others, seem also to take the Canticles for a profane composition, on a footing with the love-pieces of Catullus or Ovid. But this opinion is refuted by Michaelis, Majus, Witsius, Nat. Alexander, Outrein, Francius, and others. Mr Whiston's arguments have been particularly considered by Itchener, and also by Dr Gill. R. Akiba finds the book of Canticles more divine than the rest: the whole world, according to this rabbin, is not worth that day when the Canticles was given to Israel; for, whereas all the hagiographers are holy, the Canticles is the holy of holies.

CANTIMARONS, or Catimarons, a kind of floats or rafts, used by the inhabitants of the coast of Coromandel to go a fishing in, and to trade along the coast. They are made of three or four small canoes, or trunks of trees dug hollow, and tied together with cacao ropes, with a triangular sail in the middle, made of matts. The persons who manage them are almost half in the water, there being only a place in the middle a little raised to hold their merchandise; which last particular is only to be understood of the trading cantimarons, and not of those who go fishing.

CANTIN (Cape), a promontory of the coast of Morocco in Africa, situated in W. Long. 10. 2. N. Lat. 33. 9.

CANTING, a sea-phrase, denotes the act of turning any thing about.

Canting Language or *dialect*, is a mysterious sort of jargon used by gypsies, thieves, and strolling beggars, to express their sentiments to each other, without being understood by the rest of mankind. This dialect is not founded on any rules: yet, even out of that irregularity many words seem to retain something of scholarship; as *togeman* a gown, from *toga* in the Latin; *pannam*, bread, from *panis*; *caseum*, cheese, from *caseus*, &c. It is observable, that, even unknown to ourselves, we have adopted some of their terms into our vulgar language; as *bite* and *bilk*, to cheat; *bounce*, to vapour; *booze*, strong drink; *filch*, to steal; *flog*, to whip; *rig*, game or ridicule; *roast*, to rally; *rhino*, money. From the same source proceed the words *sham*, *banter*, *bubble*, *bully*, *sharper*, *cutting*, *shuffling*, *palming*, &c. An anonymous author has given a canting dictionary, comprehending all the terms used by the several tribes of gypsies, beggars, shoplifters, highwaymen, footpads, and other class of cheats and villains, with a collection of songs in the canting dialect; London, 1725, 8vo.

CANTIUM, (anc. geog.) a promontory of Britain, literally denoting a head land; giving name to a territory called Cantium, now Kent; and to a people called Cantii, (Cæsar), commended for their great humanity and politeness. The promontory now the North *Foreland*. It is supposed that this was the first district in Britain which received a colony from the continent; and that it had frequently changed its masters, by new colonies coming over from time to time, and driving the inhabitants further north. In the midst of all these revolutions it still retained its ancient name (which was so agreeable to its shape and situation), and gave the same name to all the successive tribes by which it was inhabited. Those who possessed it at the time of the first Roman invasion were evidently of Belgic origin, and had come over so lately, that they differed in nothing from their countrymen on the continent. "The inhabitants of Kent (says Cæsar) are the most civilized of all the Britons, and differ but very little in their manners from the Gauls." This great resemblance between the people of Kent and their neighbours on the continent, might be partly owing to the situation of their country, which being nearest to the continent, was most frequented by strangers from thence. It was this situation also which exposed them to the first assaults of the Romans. For Cæsar, in both his expeditions into this island, landed in Kent; and therefore we may conclude, that the Cantii had a great share in the vigorous opposition that was made to his landing, and in the several battles and skirmishes which were fought against him after his landing; particularly, they made a very bold, but unsuccessful attempt, upon his naval camp. The Cantii did not make the same vigorous resistance to the Romans on their next invasion in the reign of Claudius. For Aulus Plautius, the Roman general in that expedition, traversed their country without seeing an enemy; and as they now submitted to the power of Rome without a struggle, so they continued in a state of quiet submission to it to the very last. The situation of Cantium occasioned its being much frequented by the Romans, who generally took their way through it in their marches to and from the continent. Few places in Britain are more frequently mentioned by the Roman writers than Rutupium and Portus Rutupensis, most probably Richborough and Stonar. Rutupium was the same in those times that Dover is in ours; the usual place of embarking for, and landing from, the continent. Before the final departure of the Romans out of Britain, Portus Dubris, now Dover, had become a considerable place, and a well-frequented harbour, where the third iter of Antoninus ends, and from whence they often embarked for Gaul. Portus Lemanus, supposed to be Lime near West Hythe, was also a noted sea-port in these times, and the termination of the fourth iter of Antoninus. Durobrivæ and Durovernum, now Rochester and Canterbury, were both Roman towns and stations, and are often mentioned in the itinerary and other books. Besides these, there were several other Roman stations, towns, and ports in Cantium, which need not be particularly enumerated here. Cantium, in the most perfect state of the Roman government, made a part of the province which was called Flavia Cæsariensis.

CANTO denotes a part or division of a poem, answering to what is otherwise called a *book*. The word is Italian, where it properly signifies *song*. Tasso, Ariosto, and several other Italians, have divided their longer or heroic poems into cantos. In imitation of them,

Spencer

Canto.

Scarron has also divided his *Gigantomachia*, and Boileau his *Lutrin*, into chants or songs. The like usage has been adopted by some English writers, as Butler, who divides his Hudibras, and Dr Garth his Dispensary, into cantos. A late translator of part of Virgil's Æneid has even subdivided a book of Virgil into several cantos.

Canto, in the Italian music, signifies a *song*: hence *canto simplice* is where all the notes or figures are equal, and called also *canto fermo*; *canto figurato*, that where the figures are unequal, and express different motions.

Canto also signifies the treble part of a song: hence *canto concertante*, the treble of the little chorus; *canto ripieno*, the treble of the grand chorus, or that which sings only now and then in particular places. *Canto* signifies the first treble, unless some other word be added to it, as *secondo*; in which case it denotes the second treble.

CANTON, in geography, denotes a small district or country constituting a distinct government; such are the cantons of Switzerland.

Canton, *Quang-tong*, or Kouanton, one of the southern provinces of China; bounded on the north-east by Fokien, on the north by Kiang-si, on the west by Quang-si and the kingdom of Tonking, and every where else by the sea. The country is diversified with hills and plains, and the soil in general so fertile that it produces two crops annually. Besides many of the fruits of Europe, and those common in other parts of the Indies, the province of Canton produces some peculiar to itself. Abundance of valuable aromatic woods are also to be met with in this province, as well as eagle-wood, ebony, &c.; and in the mineral kingdom the province furnishes gold, precious stones, tin, quicksilver, and copper. Silk and sugar are also cultivated here, and pearls are fished up on the coasts; so that every thing which can contribute to the pleasure or convenience of life is to be met with in Canton. "One begins (says F. Premare) to have an idea of China, on entering the river Canton. Both sides of it present large fields of rice which resemble green meadows, and extend beyond the reach of sight. They are intersected by an infinite number of small canals, in such a manner that the barks which pass and repass in them seem at a distance, while the water which carries them is concealed, to glide along the grass. Farther inland the country appears covered with trees and cultivated along the valleys; and the whole scene is interspersed with villages, rural seats, and such a variety of delightful prospects, that one is never tired of viewing them, and regrets to be obliged to pass them so quickly.

All the coasts of this province abound with fish, and furnish vast numbers of crabs, oysters, and tortoises of an immense size. The inhabitants keep a prodigious number of tame ducks, which they hatch in ovens or dunghills, though it does not appear that they borrowed this custom from the Egyptians. The docility of these creatures exceeds what we should be apt at first to imagine. The inhabitants load a number of small barks with them, and carry them in flocks to feed on the sea-shore, where they find shrimps and other animals proper for their nourishment. But though the ducks from the different barks are thus unavoidably mixed together in the day-time, they are easily collected by only beating on a bason, on which they immediately collect themselves into different flocks, and each returns to its proper bark.

Canto, Canton.

In this province the Chinese have also a method of preserving not only the flesh of their ducks in such a manner that it loses nothing of its original flavour, but their eggs also. The latter operation is performed by covering the eggs with a coat of clay mixed with salt. When mixed in this manner, it seems that the salt has the property of penetrating through the pores of the shell, and thus impregnating the substance in the egg, which it could not do by simple solution of water.

Canton, though it suffered much in the Chinese wars, is at present one of the most flourishing provinces of the empire; and being at a great distance from court, its government is one of the most important. A great number of fortresses, many of which are cities provided with numerous garrisons, have been built along the coasts for the suppression of pirates and robbers; for which purpose also a certain number of troops are kept properly posted in different parts of the province. It is divided into tco districts, which contain as many cities of the first class, and 84 of the second and third. The air in general is warm but healthy, and the people are very industrious. They possess in an eminent degree the talent of imitation, so that if they are only shown any European work they can execute others like it with surprising exactness. The most remarkable cities in the province besides Canton the capital are, 1. Chao-tcheou-fou, chiefly noted for a monastery of the bonzes in its neighbourhood, to which the adjacent country belongs, and the origin of which is traced back for 8 or 900 years. It has under its jurisdiction six cities of the third class; near one of these grows a reed of which several instruments are made, which cannot be distinguished from real ebony. The air of Chao-tcheou-fou, however, is unhealthy; and great numbers of the inhabitants are carried off annually by contagious distempers, which prevail from the middle of October to the beginning of December. 2. Kao-tcheou-fou, situated in a delightful and plentiful country. In the neighbourhood is found a singular kind of stone much resembling marble, on which are natural representations of rivers, mountains, landscapes, and trees. These stones are cut into slabs, and made into tables, &c. Crabs are also caught on the coasts here, which very much resemble those of Europe; but, says M. Grosier, they have this singularity, that when taken out of the water, they become petrified without losing any thing of their natural figure. 3. Kiun-tcheou-fou, the capital of the island of Hai-nan. See Hai-nan.

Canton, a large, populous, and wealthy city of China, capital of the province of that name, stands on the banks of the river Ta, or great river, which, near the city, is wide and spacious. The wall of the city is pretty high, and about six or seven miles in circumference, though not more than one-third of the ground is occupied by buildings, the other parts being appropriated to pleasure grounds or to fish ponds. The country is extremely pleasant, and towards the east hilly, so as to command a beautiful prospect of the city and suburbs, the compass of which, together, is about ten miles.

The buildings of Canton are in general low, consisting of one story and a ground floor, which is covered with earth or red tiles in order to keep it cool; but the houses

Canton.

of the moſt reſpectable merchants and mandarins are comparatively lofty and well built. In different parts of the city and ſuburbs are joſs houſes or temples, in which are placed the images worſhipped by the Chineſe; before whom are placed, at particular ſeaſons, a vaſt variety of ſweetmeats, oranges, great plenty of food ready dreſſed, and alſo incenſe, which is kept perpetually burning.

The ſtreets of Canton are long and narrow, paved with flint ſtones, adorned at intervals with triumphal arches, which have a pleaſing effect, and much crowded with people. On both ſides are ſhops as in London, appropriated to the ſale of different commodities; and a kind of awning is extended from houſe to houſe, which prevents the ſun's rays from incommoding either inhabitants or paſſengers. At the end of every ſtreet is a barrier, which, with the gates of the city, are ſhut in the evening. In China Street, which is pretty long and conſiderably wider than the reſt, reſide merchants; whoſe trade, ſo far as reſpects China, lackered ware, fans, &c. is wholly confined to Europeans. Moſt of them ſpeak the foreign languages tolerably well, or at leaſt ſufficiently intelligible to tranſact buſineſs. Beſides theſe merchants, there is a company of twelve or thirteen, called the *Cohong*; who have an excluſive right by appointment from authority to purchaſe the cargoes from the different ſhips, and alſo to ſupply them with teas, raw ſilks, &c. in return. The eſtabliſhment of the Cohong, though injurious to private trade, is admirably well adapted for the ſecurity of the different companies with which they traffic; becauſe each individual becomes a guarantee for the whole; ſo that if one fail, the others conſider themſelves as reſponſible.

In Canton there are no carriages; all burdens are carried by porters acroſs their ſhoulders on bamboos; as are alſo the principal people in ſedan chairs, and the ladies always. The ſtreets of Canton may be traverſed from morning till evening without ſeeing a woman, thoſe excepted who are Tartars, and even theſe but very ſeldom.

On the wharf of the river, which is commodious and pleaſant, ſtand the factories of the different European nations, viz. the Dutch, French, Swedes, Danes, Engliſh, &c. In thoſe reſide the ſupercargoes belonging to their reſpective companies, who are appointed to diſpoſe of the cargoes brought to market; to ſupply the ſhips with others for Europe in return; and, during their abſence, to contract with the merchants for ſuch articles as may be judged neceſſary for the next fleet. Between the reſidents of the factories the moſt perfect cordiality ſubſiſts; in each a common and ſplendid table is kept at the company's expenſe, and viſits are reciprocally exchanged; ſo that nothing is wanting to make reſidence at Canton agreeable to an European, but the pleaſure naturally reſulting from the ſociety of women.

The ſide of the river next the city is covered with boats, which form a kind of town or ſtreets, in which live the poorer ſort of the Chineſe, or rather the deſcendants of the Tartars. Some of the men come on ſhore in the morning to their reſpective employments, and in thoſe tampans or boats which are not ſtationary, the women and alſo the men carry paſſengers from place to place in the ſame manner as is done by wherries on the Thames. On this river live many thouſand ſouls who never were permitted to come on ſhore; whoſe only habitation is their boat; in which they eat, drink, ſleep, carry on many occupations, keep ducks, &c. and occaſionally a hog.

Canton.

The manufactures of Canton are principally carried on in the ſuburbs; though it has been frequently ſuppoſed that they were confined to the city; and this, by ſome writers, has been given as a reaſon why Europeans are not permitted to enter within the gates. But this is a miſtake; and perhaps the true reaſon for this very ſingular reſtraint is, that the houſes in which they keep their women are chiefly within the city.

At Wampoa, a large commodious place for anchorage, and which is about 12 or 14 miles from Canton, the European veſſels lie and unload their cargoes, which are tranſmitted by lighters to the factories; and by the ſame conveyance receive their reſpective freights. Between this place and the city are three hoppo, or cuſtom-houſes, at which the boats paſſing and repaſſing are obliged to ſtop, and undergo with its paſſengers an examination, in order to prevent ſmuggling. The lighters juſt mentioned, and alſo the captain's pinnace, are, however, excepted; the former having proper officers on board for the purpoſe, and the latter being narrowly watched and examined at the landing.

The weather at Canton is, in ſummer, extremely hot; and in the months of December, January, and February, cold: the country is nevertheleſs pleaſant and healthful, abounding with all the neceſſaries and delicacies of life, which may be procured on terms much cheaper than in Europe. The number of inhabitants has been eſtimated at one million; but later calculations have made the number conſiderably leſs. N. Lat. 23. 30. E. Long. 113. 20.

Canton (John), an ingenious natural philoſopher, was born at Stroud, in Glouceſterſhire, in 1718; and was placed, when young, under the care of a Mr Davis, of the ſame place, a very able mathematician, with whom, before he had attained the age of nine years, he had gone through both vulgar and decimal arithmetic. He then proceeded to the mathematics, and particularly to algebra and aſtronomy, wherein he had made a conſiderable progreſs, when his father took him from ſchool, and put him to learn his own buſineſs, which was that of a broad cloth weaver. This circumſtance was not able to damp his zeal for the acquiſition of knowledge. All his leiſure time was devoted to the aſſiduous cultivation of aſtronomical ſcience; and, by the help of the Caroline tables, annexed to "Wing's Aſtronomy," he computed eclipſes of the moon and other phenomena. His acquaintance with that ſcience he applied likewiſe to the conſtructing of ſeveral kinds of dials. But the ſtudies of our young philoſopher being frequently purſued to very late hours, his father, fearing that they would injure his health, forbad him the uſe of a candle in his chamber any longer than for the purpoſe of going to bed, and would himſelf often ſee that his injunction was obeyed. The ſon's thirſt of knowledge was, however, ſo great, that it made him attempt to evade the prohibition, and to find means of ſecreting his light till the family had retired to reſt, when he roſe to proſecute undiſturbed his favourite purſuits. It was during this prohibition, and at theſe

Canton.

hours, that he computed, and cut upon stone, with no better an instrument than a common knife, the lines of a large upright sun-dial, on which, besides the hour of the day, was shown the rising of the sun, his place in the ecliptic, and some other particulars. When this was finished, and made known to his father, he permitted it to be placed against the front of his house, where it excited the admiration of several gentlemen in the neighbourhood, and introduced young Mr Canton to their acquaintance, which was followed by the offer of the use of their libraries. In the library of one of these gentlemen, he found "Martin's Philosophical Grammar," which was the first book that gave him a taste for natural philosophy. In the possession of another gentleman, a few miles from Stroud, he first saw a pair of globes; an object that afforded him uncommon pleasure, from the great ease with which he could solve those problems he had hitherto been accustomed to compute. The dial was beautified a few years ago at the expence of the gentlemen at Stroud, several of whom had been his school-fellows, and who continued still to regard it as a very distinguished performance. Among other persons with whom he became acquainted in early life, was the late reverend and ingenious Dr Henry Miles of Tooting, a learned and respectable member of the Royal Society, and of approved eminence in natural knowledge. This gentleman, perceiving that Mr Canton possessed abilities too promising to be confined within the narrow limits of a country town, prevailed on his father to permit him to come to London. Accordingly he arrived at the metropolis March 4. 1737, and resided with Dr Miles at Tooting till the 6th of May following; when he articled himself, for the term of five years, as a clerk to Mr Samuel Watkins, master of the academy in Spital-square. In this situation, his ingenuity, diligence, and good conduct, were so well displayed, that on the expiration of his clerkship in May 1742, he was taken into partnership with Mr Watkins for three years; which gentleman he afterwards succeeded in Spital-square, and there continued during his whole life. In 1744, he married Penelope, the eldest daughter of Mr Thomas Colbrooke, and niece to James Colbrooke, Esq; banker in London.

Towards the end of 1745, electricity, which seems early to have engaged Mr Canton's notice, received a very capital improvement by the discovery of the famous Leyden Phial. This event turned the thoughts of most of the philosophers of Europe to that branch of natural philosophy; and our author, who was one of the first to repeat and to pursue the experiment, found his assiduity and attention rewarded by many capital discoveries. Towards the end of 1749, he was concerned with his friend, the late Mr Benjamin Robins, in making experiments in order to determine to what height rockets may be made to ascend, and at what distance their light may be seen. In 1750 was read at the Royal Society, Mr Canton's "Method of making artificial magnets, without the use of, and yet far superior to, any natural ones." This paper procured him the honour of being elected a member of the Society, and the present of their gold medal. The same year he was complimented with the degree of M. A. by the university of Aberdeen; and, in 1751, was chosen one of the council of the Royal Society.

In 1752, our philosopher was so fortunate as to be the first person in England, who, by attracting the electric fire from the clouds during a thunder-storm, verified Dr Franklin's hypothesis of the similarity of lightning and electricity. Next year, his paper intitled, "Electrical Experiments, with an attempt to account for their several Phænomena," was read at the Royal Society. In the same paper Mr Canton mentioned his having discovered, by a great number of experiments, that some clouds were in a positive, and some in a negative, state of electricity. Dr Franklin, much about the same time, made the like discovery in America. This circumstance, together with our author's constant defence of the doctor's hypothesis, induced that excellent philosopher, immediately on his arrival in England, to pay Mr Canton a visit, and gave rise to a friendship which ever after continued without interruption or diminution. In the "Lady's Diary for 1756," our author answered the prize question that had been proposed in the preceding year. The question was, "How can what we call the shooting of stars be best accounted for; what is the substance of this phænomenon; and in what state of the atmosphere doth it most frequently show itself?" The solution, though anonymous, was so satisfactory to his friend, Mr Thomas Simpson, who then conducted that work, that he sent Mr Canton the prize, accompanied with a note, in which he said, he was sure that he was not mistaken in the author of it, as no one besides, that he knew of, could have answered the question. Our philosopher's next communication to the public, was a letter in the "Gentleman's Magazine for September 1759," on the electrical properties of the tourmalin, in which the laws of that wonderful stone are laid down in a very concise and elegant manner. On December 13th, in the same year, was read at the Royal Society, "An attempt to account for the regular diurnal variation of the Horizontal Magnetic Needle; and also for its irregular variation at the time of an Aurora Borealis." A complete year's observations of the diurnal variations of the needle are annexed to the paper. On Nov. 5. 1761, our author communicated to the Royal Society an account of the Transit of Venus, June 6. 1761, observed in Spital-square. Mr Canton's next communication to the Society, was a letter addressed to Dr Benjamin Franklin, and read Feb. 4. 1762, containing some remarks on Mr Delaval's electrical experiments. On Dec. 16. in the same year, another curious addition was made by him to philosophical knowledge, in a paper, intituled, "Experiments to prove that water is not incompressible." These experiments are a complete refutation of the famous Florentine experiment, which so many philosophers have mentioned as a proof of the incompressibility of water. On St Andrew's day 1763, our author was the third time elected one of the council of the Royal Society; and on Nov. 8. in the following year, were read, before that learned body, his farther "Experiments and observations on the compressibility of water, and some other fluids." The establishment of this fact, in opposition to the received opinion, formed on the hasty decision of the Florentine academy, was thought to be deserving of the Society's gold medal. It was accordingly moved for in the council of 1764; and after several invidious delays, which terminated much to the honour of Mr Canton, it was preſented to him Nov. 30. 1765.

The next communication of our ingenious author to the Royal Society, which we ſhall take notice of in this place, was on Dec. 22. 1768, being "An eaſy method of making a Phoſphorus that will imbibe and emit light like the Bolognian ſtone; with experiments and obſervations." When he firſt ſhowed to Dr Franklin the inſtantaneous light acquired by ſome of this phoſphorus from the near diſcharge of an electrified bottle, the doctor immediately exclaimed, "And God ſaid, let there be light, and there was light." The dean and chapter of St Paul's having, in a letter to the preſident, dated March 6. 1769, requeſted the opinion of the Royal Society relative to the beſt and moſt effectual method of fixing electrical conductors to preſerve that cathedral from damage by lightning, Mr Canton was one of the committee appointed to take the letter into conſideration, and to report their opinion upon it. The gentlemen joined with him in this buſineſs were, Dr Watſon, Dr Franklin, Mr Delaval, and Mr Wilſon. Their report was made on the 8th of June following; and the mode recommended by them has been carried into execution. The laſt paper of our author's, which was read before the Royal Society, was on Dec. 21. 1769; and contained "Experiments to prove that the Luminouſneſs of the Sea ariſes from the putrefaction of its animal ſubſtances." In the account now given of his communications to the public, we have chiefly confined ourſelves to ſuch as were the moſt important, and which threw new and diſtinguiſhed light on various objects in the philoſophical world. Beſides theſe, he wrote a number of papers, both in earlier and in later life, which appeared in ſeveral different publications, and particularly in the Gentleman's Magazine.

The cloſe and ſedentary life of Mr Canton, ariſing from an unremitted attention to the duties of his profeſſion, and to the proſecution of his philoſophical enquiries and experiments, probably contributed to ſhorten his days. The diſorder into which he fell, and which carried him off, was a dropſy. His death happened on March 22. 1772, in the 54th year of his age.

CANTONING, in the military art, is the allotting diſtinct and ſeparate quarters to each regiment; the town where they are quartered being divided into as many cantons as there are regiments.

CANTRED, or Cantref, ſignifies an hundred villages. It is a Britiſh word, compounded of the adjective *cant*, i. e. hundred; and *tref*, a town or village. In Wales ſome of the counties are divided into cantreds, as in England into hundreds.

CANTYRE, (from *Centierre*, ſignifying a "headland"); the ſouthern diviſion of the ſhire of Argyle in Scotland. It is a peninſula, ſtretching 37 miles from north to ſouth, and ſeven miles in breadth. It is moſtly plain, arable, and populous; inhabited promiſcuouſly by Highlanders and Lowlanders, the latter being invited to ſettle in this place by the Argyle family, that the lands might be the better cultivated. It gives the title of marquis to the duke, and is by *Lochfyn* divided from Argyle Proper. This loch is an inlet from the ſea, about 60 miles in length and four in breadth, affording heretofore an excellent herring-fiſhery. There are many paltry villages in this country, but no town of any conſequence except Campbeltown.

Cantyre was granted to the houſe of Argyle after a ſuppreſſion of a rebellion of the Macdonalds of the Iſles (and it is ſuppoſed of this peninſula) in the beginning of the laſt century, and the grant was afterwards ratified by parliament. The ancient inhabitants were the Mac-donalds, Mac-eachrans, Mac-kays, and Mac-maths.

Mull of Cantyre, the ſouth cape or promontory of the peninſula. There is here a light-houſe 235 feet above the ſea at high water, ſituated on the rocks called the *Merchants*, Lat. 55. 22. Long. 5. 42. weſt of London. The ſound of Iſla from the light-houſe bearing, by the compaſs, N. by E. diſtant 27 miles; the ſouth end of Iſla N. N. W. diſtant 25 miles; the north end of Rathlin iſland, N. W. by W. one half W.; the Maiden Rocks, S. by W. one half W. diſtant 14 miles; Copland light, S. by W. one half W. diſtant 31 miles. The lanthorn is ſeen from N. N. E. 1-4th E. from S. by W. 1-4th W. and intermediate points of the compaſs N. of theſe two points.

CANTZ, a town of Sileſia in Germany. E. Long. 16. 36. N. Lat. 51. 6.

CANVAS, in commerce, a very clear unbleached cloth of hemp, or flax, wove regularly in little ſquares. It is uſed for working tapeſtry with the needle, by paſſing the threads of gold, ſilver, ſilk, or wool, through the intervals or ſquares.

Canvas is alſo a coarſe cloth of hemp, unbleached, ſomewhat clear, which ſerves to cover womens ſtays, alſo to ſtiffen mens clothes, and to make ſome other of their wearing apparel, &c.

Canvas is alſo uſed among the French for the model or firſt words whereon an air or piece of muſic is compoſed, and given to a poet to regulate and finiſh. The canvas of a ſong contains certain notes of the compoſer, which ſhow the poet the meaſure of the verſes he is to make. Thus Du Lot ſays, he has canvas for ten ſonnets againſt the muſes.

Canvas is alſo the name of a cloth made of hemp, and uſed for ſhip-ſails.

Canvas, among painters, is the cloth on which they uſually draw their pictures; the canvas being ſmoothed over with a ſlick-ſtone, then ſized, and afterwards whited over, makes what the painters call their *primed cloth*, on which they draw their firſt ſketches with coal or chalk, and afterwards finiſh with colours.

CANUSIUM (anc. geog.), a town of Apulia, on the right or ſouth ſide of the Aufidus, to the weſt of Cannæ; whither the Romans fled after the defeat ſuſtained there. It was famous for its red ſhining wool; whence thoſe who wore clothes made of it were called *Canuſinati*. Now called Canosa; which ſee.

CANUTE, the firſt Daniſh king of England after Ironſide. He married Emma widow of king Ethelred; and put to death ſeveral perſons of quality who ſtood in his way to the crown. Having thus ſettled his power in England, he made a voyage to his other kingdom of Denmark, in order to reſiſt the attacks of the king of Sweden; and he carried along with him a great body of the Engliſh under the command of the earl of Godwin. This nobleman had here an opportunity of performing a ſervice by which he both reconciled the

Canute. king's mind to the English nation, and, gaining to himself the friendship of his sovereign, laid the foundation of that immense fortune which he acquired to his family. He was stationed near the Swedish camp; and, observing a favourable opportunity which he was obliged suddenly to seize, he attacked the enemy in the night, drove them suddenly from their trenches, threw them into disorder, pursued his advantage, and obtained a decisive victory over them. Next morning, Canute, seeing the English camp entirely abandoned, imagined that these disaffected troops had deserted to the enemy; and he was agreeably surprised to find that they were at that time engaged in pursuit of the discomfited Swedes. He was so pleased with this success, and the manner of obtaining it, that he bestowed his daughter in marriage upon Godwin, and treated him ever after with the most entire confidence and regard.

In another voyage which he afterwards made to Denmark, Canute attacked Norway, and expelled the just but unwarlike Olaus from his kingdom, of which he kept possession till the death of that prince. He had now by his conquests and valour attained the utmost height of his ambition; and having leisure from wars and intrigues, he felt the unsatisfactory nature of all human enjoyments; and, equally weary of the glory and turmoils of this life, he began to cast his view towards that future existence which is so natural for the human mind, whether satiated by prosperity or disgusted with adversity, to make the object of its attention. Unfortunately the spirit which prevailed in that age gave a wrong direction to his devotion; and, instead of making atonement to those whom he had formerly injured by his acts of violence, he entirely employed himself in those exercises of piety which the monks represented as most meritorious. He built churches; he endowed monasteries; he enriched ecclesiastics; and he bestowed revenues for the support of chantries at Assington and other places, where he appointed prayers to be said for the souls of those who had there fallen in battle against him. He even undertook a pilgrimage to Rome, where he sojourned a considerable time; and, besides obtaining from the Pope some privileges for the English school erected there, he engaged all the princes through whose dominions he was obliged to pass, to desist from those heavy impositions and tolls which they were accustomed to exact from the English pilgrims. By this spirit of devotion, no less than by his equitable and politic administration, he gained in a good measure the affections of his subjects.

Canute, who was the greatest and most powerful prince of his time, sovereign of Denmark and Norway as well as of England, could not fail to meet with adulation from his courtiers; a tribute which is liberally paid even to the meanest and weakest of princes. Some of his flatterers breaking out one day in admiration of his grandeur, exclaimed, that every thing was possible for him: upon which the monarch, it is said, ordered a chair to be set on the sea-shore while the tide was making; and, as the waters approached, he commanded them to retire, and to obey the voice of him who was lord of the ocean. He feigned to sit some time in expectation of their submission; but when the sea still advanced towards him, and began to wash him with its billows, he turned to his courtiers, and remarked to them, That every creature in the universe was feeble and impotent, and that power resided with one Being alone, in whose hands were all the elements of nature, who could say to the ocean, "Thus far shalt thou go, and no farther," and who could level with his nod the most towering piles of human pride and ambition. From that time, it is said, he never would wear a crown. He died in the 20th year of his reign; and was interred at Winchester, in the old monastery.

CANZONF., in music, signifies, in general, a song, where some little fugues are introduced: but it is sometimes used for a sort of Italian poem, usually pretty long, to which music may be composed in the style of a cantata. If this term be added to a piece of instrumental music, it signifies much the same as cantata: if placed in any part of a sonata, it implies the same meaning as *allegro*, and only denotes that the part to which it is prefixed is to be played or sung in a brisk and lively manner.

CANZONETTA, a diminutive of canzone, denoting a little short song. The canzonette neapolitane has two strains, each whereof is sung twice over, as the vaudevilles of the French: The canzonette siciliane is a species of Jigg, the measure whereof is usually twelve eighths, and six eighths, and sometimes both, as rondeaux.

CAORLO, a small island in the gulf of Venice, on the coast of Friuli, 20 miles south-west of Aquileia, subject to Venice. It has a town of the same name, with a bishop's see.

CAOUTCHOUC, Elastic Resin, or *India Rubber*, a substance produced from the syringe-tree of Cayenne and other parts of South America, and possessed of the most singular properties. No substance is yet known which is so pliable, and at the same time so elastic; and it is farther a matter of curiosity, as being capable of resisting the action of very powerful menstrua. From the account of M. de la Condamine, we learn, that this substance oozes out, under the form of a vegetable milk, from incisions made in the tree; and that it is gathered chiefly in time of rain, because, though it may be collected at all times, it flows then most abundantly. The means employed to inspissate and indurate it, M. de la Borde says, are kept a profound secret. M. Bancroft, and others, affirm, that it thickens and hardens gradually by being exposed to the air; and as soon as it acquires a solid consistence, it manifests a very extraordinary degree of flexibility and elasticity. Accordingly the Indians make boots of it, which water cannot penetrate, and which, when smoked, have the appearance of real leather. Bottles are also made of it, to the necks of which are fastened hollow reeds, so that the liquor contained in them may be squirted through the reeds or pipes by pressure. One of these filled with water is always presented to each of the guests at their entertainments, who never fail to make use of it before eating. This whimsical custom led the Portuguese in that country to call the tree that produces this resin *pao di xiringa*, and hence the name of *seringa* is given both to the tree and to its resinous production. Flambeaux, an inch and a half in diameter, and two feet long, are likewise made of this resin, which give a beautiful light, have no bad smell, and burn twelve hours. A kind of cloth is also prepared from it, which Caoutchouc.

Caout-chouc.

the inhabitants of Quito apply to the same purposes as our oil-cloth and sail-cloth. It is formed, in fine, by means of moulds, into a variety of figures for use and ornament; and the process is said to be thus:—The juice, which is obtained by incision, is spread over pieces of clay formed into the desired shape; and as fast as one layer is dry, another is added, till the vessel be of the proper thickness: the whole is then held over a strong smoke of vegetables on fire, whereby it hardens into the texture and appearance of leather; and before the finishing, while yet soft, is capable of having any impression made on the outside, which remains ever after. When the whole is done, the inside mould is picked out.

Ever since this resin has been known in Europe, its chemical qualities and other interesting properties have been very diligently investigated. In particular, it has been endeavoured to discover some method of dissolving it in such a manner that it would assume different figures with equal ease as when in its original state of milk. In the memoirs of the academy of sciences for 1768, we have an account of several attempts for this purpose, and how it may be effected. —The state of vegetable milk in which the caoutchouc resin is found when it comes from the tree, led Mr Macquer to imagine that it was composed of an oil and a watery matter. From its wanting aromatic flavour, from its little volatility, and from its being incapable of solution in spirit of wine, he concluded that the oil which entered its composition was not an essential, but a fatty, one. Hence he thought it probable that it passed from a fluid to a solid form by the evaporation of the watery part, and that the oily solvents would reduce it to a soft state. The first trials he made for dissolving it were with linseed oil, essence of turpentine, and several others. But all he could obtain by means of these menstrua was a viscid substance incapable of being hardened, and totally void of elasticity. The rectified essential oil of turpentine was employed seemingly with greater success. To separate from this menstruum the caoutchouc which it had dissolved, Mr Macquer added spirit of wine: but the consequence was, that part only of the oil united with the spirit; the rest remaining obstinately attached to the resin which it had dissolved, and thus preventing it from assuming a solid consistence. The author next endeavoured to dissolve it by means of heat in Papin's digester. But neither water, nor spirit of wine, although in this way capable of dissolving the hardest bones, could produce any other effect upon it than to render it more firm than before. After this, he tried what effect the milky juice of other vegetables would have upon it. He used several kinds, particularly that of the fig. But, in this way, he could obtain no solution. From the great volatility of ether, he was next induced to try it as a menstruum; and, for this purpose, he prepared some with great attention. The caoutchouc, cut into little bits, and put into a proper vessel with as much ether as was sufficient to cover it, was perfectly dissolved without any other heat than that of the atmosphere. This solution was transparent and of an amber colour. It still preserved the smell of ether, but mixed with the disagreeable odour of the caoutchouc, and it was a little less fluid than pure ether. Upon its being thrown into water, no milky liquor was produced; but there arose to the surface a solid membrane which possessed the great elasticity and other peculiar properties of the caoutchouc. He observes, however, that two pints of the best ether, obtained by rectifying eight or ten pints of the common ether by a gentle heat, must be used, in order to the success of the operation.—The distinguishing properties of this substance, viz. its solidity, flexibility, and elasticity, and its quality of resisting the action of aqueous, spirituous, saline, oily, and other common solvents, render it extremely fit for the construction of tubes, catheters, and other instruments, in which these properties are wanted. In order to form this resin into small tubes, M. Macquer prepared a solid cylindrical mould of wax, of the desired size and shape; and then dipping a pencil into the etherial solution of the resin, daubed the mould over with it, till he had covered it with a coat of resin of a sufficient thickness. The whole piece is then thrown into boiling water; by the heat of which the wax is soon melted, and rises to the surface, leaving the resinous tube completely formed behind.

A resin similar to this was some years ago discovered by M. Poivre, in the isle of France; and there are various milky juices extracted from trees in America and elsewhere, which by previous mixtures and preparations are formed into an elastic resin, but of so inferior quality to that of Cayenne: such, for instance, are the juices obtained from the *Cecropia peltata*, the *Ficus religiosa* and *indica*, &c.

Of the genuine trees, those growing along the banks of the river of the Amazons are described by M. Condamine as attaining a very great height, being at the same time perfectly straight, and having no branches except at top, which is but small, covering no more than a circumference of ten feet. Its leaves bear some resemblance to those of the *manioc*: they are green on the upper part, and white beneath. The seeds are three in number, and contained in a pod consisting of three cells, not unlike those of the *ricinus* or *palma Christi*; and in each of them there is a kernel, which being stripped and boiled in water produces a thick oil or fat, answering the purposes of butter in the cookery of that country.

A method of dissolving this elastic gum without ether, for the purposes of a varnish or the like, is as follows: Take one pound of the spirit of turpentine, and a pound of the gum cut into very small pieces; pour the turpentine into a long-necked matrass, which must be placed in a sand-bath; throw in the gum, not all at once, but by little and little according as it is perceived to dissolve: When it is entirely dissolved, pour into the matrass a pint of nut or linseed oil, or oil of poppies, rendered deficcative in the usual manner with litharge: Then let the whole boil for a quarter of an hour, and the preparation is finished. This would make an excellent varnish for air-balloons, were it not so expensive on account of the price of the gum.—Another method, invented by Mr Baldwin, is as follows. Take any quantity of the caoutchouc, as two ounces avoirdupois: cut it into small bits with a pair of scissars. Put a strong iron ladle (such as plumbers or glaziers melt their lead in) over a common pit-coal or other fire. The fire must be gentle, glowing, and without smoke. When the ladle is hot, much below a red heat, put a single bit into the ladle. If black smoke issues, it will presently flame and disappear: or it will evaporate without flame: the ladle is then too hot. When the ladle is less hot, put in a second bit, which will produce a white smoke. This white smoke will continue during the operation, and evaporate the caoutchouc: therefore no time is to be lost; but little bits are to be put in, a few at a time, till the whole are melted. It should be continually and gently stirred with an iron or brass spoon. Two pounds, or one quart, of the best drying oil (or of raw linseed oil which, together with a few drops of neats foot oil, has stood a month, or not so long, on a lamp of quicklime, to make it more or less drying) is to be put into the melted caoutchouc, and stirred till hot: and the whole poured into a glazed vessel, through a coarse gauze, or fine sieve. When settled and clear, which will be in a few minutes, it is fit for use, either hot or cold.

The Abbé Clavigero informs us, that the elastic gum is called by the Mexicans *Olin* or *Olli*, and by the Spaniards of that kingdom *Ule*: That it distils from the Olquahuitl, which is a tree of moderate size; the trunk of which is smooth and yellowish, the leaves pretty large, the flowers white, and the fruit yellow and rather round, but angular; within which there are kernels as large as filberds, and white, but covered with a yellowish pellicle: That the kernel has a bitter taste, and the fruit always grows attached to the bark of the tree: That when the trunk is cut, the Ule which distils from it is white, liquid, and viscous; afterwards it becomes yellow; and lastly of a leaden colour, though rather blacker, which it always retains. The tree, he adds, is very common in the kingdom of Guatimala.

As to the genus of this tree, it does not seem to be yet ascertained. Aublet, in his *Histoire des Plants de la Guiane* (p. 871.), describes the tree, the fruit, and manner of collecting the juice; but never saw the flower: he calls it, however, *Hevea Guianensis*. In Jacquin's America, it is called *Echites corymbosa*. The younger Linneus, in his *Supplementum Plantarum* (p. 422), names it *Jatropha elastica*; but acknowledges that he only gives it this name from the structure of the fruit having most resemblance to that genus, his dry species wanting the flowers.

Of the above gum, it is said, the Chinese make elastic rings for lascivious purposes.—Among us it is used by surgeons for injecting liquids, and by painters for rubbing out black-lead pencil marks, &c.

CAP, a part of dress made to cover the head, much in the figure thereof.

The use of caps and hats is referred to the year 1449, the first seen in these parts of the world being at the entry of Charles VII. into Rouen: from that time they began to take place of the hoods, or chaperoons, that had been used till then. When the cap was of velvet, they called it *mortier*; when of wool, simply *bonnet*. None but kings, princes, and knights, were allowed the use of the mortier. The cap was the head-dress of the clergy and graduates. Pasquier says, that it was anciently a part of the hood worn by the people of the robe; the skirts whereof being cut off as an incumbrance, left the *round* cap an easy commodious cover for the head; which round cap being afterwards assumed by the people, those of the gown changed it for a square one, first invented by a Frenchman, called Patrouillet: he adds, that the giving of the cap to the students in the universities, was to denote, that they had acquired full liberty, and were no longer subject to the rod of their superiors; in imitation of the ancient Romans, who gave a *pileus*, or cap, to their slaves, in the ceremony of making them free: whence the proverb, *Vocare servos ad pileum*. Hence, also, on medals, the cap is the symbol of liberty, whom they represent holding a cap in her right hand, by the point.

The Romans were many ages without any regular covering for the head: when either the rain or sun was troublesome, the lappet of the gown was thrown over the head; and hence it is that all the ancient statues appear bareheaded, excepting sometimes a wreath, or the like. And the same usage obtained among the Greeks, where, at least during the heroic age, no caps were known. The sort of caps or covers of the head in use among the Romans on divers occasions, were the *pitra*, *pileus*, *cucullus*, *galerus*, and *palliolum*; the differences between which are often confounded by ancient as well as modern writers.

The French clergy wear a shallow kind of cap, called *calotte*, which only covers the top of the head, made of leather, sattin, worsted, or other stuff. The red cap is a mark of dignity allowed only to those who are raised to the cardinalate. The secular clergy are distinguished by black leathern caps, the regulars by knit and worsted ones.

Churchmen, and the members of universities, students in law, physic, &c. as well as graduates, wear square caps. In most universities doctors are distinguished by peculiar caps, given them in assuming the doctorate. Wickliff calls the canons of his time *bifurcati*, from their caps. Pasquier observes, that, in his time, the caps worn by the churchmen, &c. were called square caps; though, in effect, they were round yellow caps.

The Chinese have not the use of the hat, like us; but wear a cap of a peculiar structure, which the laws of civility will not allow them to put off: it is different for the different seasons of the year: that used in summer is in form of a cone, ending at top in a point. It is made of a very beautiful kind of mat, much valued in that country, and lined with sattin: to this is added, at top, a large lock of red silk, which falls all round as low as the bottom; so that, in walking, the silk fluctuating regularly on all sides, makes a graceful appearance: sometimes, instead of silk, they use a kind of bright red hair, the lustre whereof no weather effaces. In winter they wear a plush cap, bordered with martlet's or fox's skin; as to the rest, like those for the summer. These caps are frequently sold for eight or ten crowns; but they are so short, that the ears are exposed.

The cap is sometimes used as a mark of infamy; in Italy the Jews are distinguished by a yellow cap; at Lucca by an orange one. In France, those who had been bankrupts were obliged ever after to wear a green cap, to prevent people from being imposed on in any future commerce. By several arrets in 1584, 1622, 1628, 1688, it was decreed, that if they were at any time found without their green cap, their protection should-

should be null, and their creditors impowered to cast them into prison; but the sentence is not now executed.

Cap of Maintenance, one of the regalia, or ornaments of state belonging to the kings of England, before whom it was carried at the coronation and other great solemnities. Caps of maintenance are also carried before the mayors of the several cities in England.

Cap, in ship building, a strong, thick, block of wood, used to confine two masts together, when one is erected at the head of the other in order to lengthen it. It is for this purpose furnished with two holes perpendicular to its length and breadth, and parallel to its thickness: one of these is square, and the other round; the former being solidly fixed upon the upper end of the lower mast, whilst the latter receives the mast employed to lengthen it, and secures it in this position.

CAPACIO, an episcopal town of Italy, in the kingdom of Naples, and in the hither Principato. E. Long. 15. 18. N. Lat. 40. 40.

CAPACITY, in a general sense, an aptitude or disposition to hold or retain any thing.

Capacity, in geometry, is the solid contents of any body; also our hollow measure for wine, beer, corn, salt, &c. are called *measures of capacity*.

Capacity, in law, the ability of a man, or body politic, to give or take lands or other things, or sue actions.

Our law allows the king two capacities; a natural, and a political: in the first, he may purchase lands to him and his heirs; in the second, to him and his successors. The clergy of the church of England have the like.

CAPARASON, or Caparison, the covering or clothing laid over a horse; especially a sumpter horse, or horse of state. The word is Spanish, being an augmentative of *capa*, *caput*, *head*.

Anciently the caparasons were a kind of iron armour, wherewith horses were covered in battle.

CAPE, in geography, an high land running out with a point into the sea, as Cape-Nord, Cape-Horn, the Cape of Good Hope, &c.

Cape-Elk. See Cervus.

Cape-Breton. See Breton.

Cape-Coast Castle. See Coast.

Cape of Good Hope. See Good Hope.

Cape-Verd. See Verd.

CAPELL (Edward), a gentleman well known by his indefatigable attention to the works of Shakespeare, was a native of the county of Suffolk, and received his education at the school of St Edmund's Bury. In the dedication of his edition of Shakespeare, in 1768, to the duke of Grafton, he observes, that "his father and the grandfather of his grace were friends, and to the patronage of the deceased nobleman he owed the leisure which enabled him to bestow the attention of 30 years on that work." The office which his grace bestowed on Mr Capell was that of deputy-inspector of the plays, to which a salary is annexed of 200l. a-year. So early as the year 1745, as Mr Capell himself informs us, shocked at the licentiousness of Hanmer's plan, he first projected an edition of Shakespeare, of the strictest accuracy, to be collated and published, in due time, *ex fide codicum*. He immediately proceeded to collect and compare the oldest and scarcest copies; noting the original excellencies and defects of the rarest quartos, and distinguishing the improvements or variations of the first, second, and third folios: and, after many years labour, produced a very beautiful small octavo, in 10 volumes, with "an Introduction." There is not, the authors of the Monthly Review observe, among the various publications of the present literary era, a more singular composition than that "Introduction." In style and manner, it is more obsolete and antique than the age of which it treats. It is Lord Herbert of Cherbury, walking the new pavement in all the trappings of romance; but, like Lord Herbert, it displays many valuable qualities accompanying this air of extravagance, much sound sense, and appropriate erudition. In the title-page of "Mr William Shakespeare his Comedies, Histories, and Tragedies," it was also announced and promulgated, "Whereunto will be added, in some other volumes, notes critical and explanatory, and a body of various readings entire." "The Introduction" likewise declared, that these "notes and various readings" would be accompanied with another work, disclosing the sources from which Shakespeare "drew the greater part of his knowledge in mythological and classical matters, his fable, his history, and even the seeming peculiarities of his language—to which," says Mr Capell, "we have given for title, The School of Shakespeare." Nothing surely could be more properly conceived than such designs, nor have we ever met with any thing better grounded on the subject of "the learning of Shakespeare" than what may be found in the long note to this part of Mr Capell's Introduction. It is more solid than even the popular "Essay" on this topic. Certain quaintnesses of style, and peculiarities of printing and punctuation, attended the whole of this publication. The outline, however, was correct; and the critic, with unremitting toil, proceeded in his undertaking. But while he was diving into the classics of Caxton (to continue the Reviewers account), and working his way underground, like the river Mole, in order to emerge with all his glories; while he was looking forward to his triumphs; certain other active spirits went to work upon his plan, and, digging out the promised treasures, laid them prematurely before the public, defeating the effect of our critic's discoveries by anticipation. Steevens, Malone, Farmer, Percy, Reed, and a whole host of literary ferrets, burrowed into every hole and corner of the warren of modern antiquity, and over-ran all the country, whose map had been delineated by Edward Capell. Such a contingency nearly staggered the steady and unshaken perseverance of our critic, at the very eve of the completion of his labours, and as his editor informs us—for, alas! at the end of near 40 years, the publication was posthumous, and the critic himself no more!—he was almost determined to lay the work wholly aside. He persevered, however, by the encouragement of some noble and worthy persons; and to such their encouragement, and his perseverance, the public was, in 1783, indebted for three large volumes in 4to, under the title of "Notes and various readings of Shakespeare; together with the School of Shakespeare, or Extracts from divers English Books,

Books, that were in print in the Author's time; evidently shewing from whence his several Fables were taken, and some parcel of his Dialogue. Also farther Extracts, which contribute to a due understanding of his Writings, or give a light to the History of his Life, or to the Dramatic History of his Time. By Edw. Capell."—Besides the works already mentioned, Mr Capell was the editor of a volume of ancient poems called "Prolusions;" and the alteration of "Antony and Cleopatra," as acted at Drury Lane in 1758. He died January 24. 1781.

CAPELLA, in astronomy, a bright fixed star in the left shoulder of the constellation Auriga.

CAPELLE, a town of France, in Picardy, and in the Tierache, eight miles from Guise. It was taken by the Spaniards in 1636; but retaken the year after. E. Long. 3. 59. N. Lat. 49. 58.

CAPELLETS, in farriery. See there, § xxxvi. 4.

CAPELLUS (Lewis), an eminent French Protestant divine, born at Sedan in Champagne about the year 1579. He was author of some learned works; but is chiefly known from the controversy he engaged in with the younger Buxtorf concerning the antiquity of Hebrew points, which Capellus undertook to disprove. His *Critica Sacra* was also an elaborate work, and excited some disputes. He died in 1658, having made an abridgement of his life in his work *De gente Capellori*.

CAPER, in botany. See CAPPARIS.

CAPER also denotes a vessel used by the Dutch for cruising and taking prizes from the enemy; in which sense, caper amounts to the same with privateer. Capers are commonly double-officered, and crowded with hands even beyond the rates of ships of war, because the thing chiefly in view is boarding the enemies.

CAPERNAUM, a city celebrated in the gospels, being the place where Jesus usually resided during the time of his ministry. This city is no where mentioned in the Old Testament under this or any other name like it; and therefore it is not improbable that it was one of those towns which the Jews built after their return from the Babylonish captivity. It stood on the sea-coast, *i. e.* on the coast of the sea of Galilee, in the borders of Zebulon and Nephthalim (Matt. iv. 15.), and consequently towards the upper part thereof. It took its name no doubt from an adjacent spring of great repute for its clear and limpid waters; and which, according to Josephus, was by the natives called *Capernaum*. As this spring might be some inducement to the building the town in the place where it stood, so its being a convenient wafting place from Galilee to any part on the other side of the sea, might be some motive to our Lord for his moving from Nazareth, and making this the place of his most constant residence. Upon this account Capernaum was highly honoured, and said by our Lord himself to be *exalted unto heaven*; but because it made no right use of this signal favour, it drew from him the severe denunciation, that it should *be brought down to hell* (Matt. xi. 23.), which has certainly been verified; for, as Dr Wells observes, so far is it from being the metropolis of all Galilee, as it once was, that it consisted long since of no more than six poor fishermens cottages, and may perhaps be now totally desolate.

CAPEROLANS, a congregation of religious in Italy, so called from Peter Caperole their founder, in the 15th century.

The Milanese and Venetians being at war, the enmity occasioned thereby spread itself to the very cloysters. The superiors of the province of Milan, of minor brothers, which extended itself as far as the territories of the republic of Venice, carried it so haughtily over the Venetians, that those of the convent of Brescia resolved to shake off a yoke which was grown insupportable to them. The superiors, informed of this, expelled out of the province those whom they considered as the authors of this design; the principal of whom were Peter Caperole, Matthew de Tharvilla and Bonaventure of Brescia. Peter Caperole, a man of an enterprising genius, found means to separate the convents of Brescia, Bergamo, and Cremona, from the province of Milan, and subject them to the conventuals. This occasioned a law-suit between the vicar-general and these convents, which was determined in favour of the latter; and these convents, in 1475, by the authority of Pope Sixtus IV. were erected into a distinct vicariate, under the title of that of *Brescia*. This not satisfying the ambition of Caperole, he obtained, by the interposition of the Doge of Venice, that this vicariate might be erected into a congregation, which was called from him *Caperolans*. This congregation still subsists in Italy, and is composed of 24 convents, situated in Brescia, Bergamo, and Cremona.

CAPERQUIN, a town of Ireland, in the county of Waterford, and province of Munster, situated on the river Blackwater. W. Long. 7. 50. N. Lat. 52. 5.

CAPESTAN, a town of France, in Lower Languedoc, in the diocese of Narbonne, and near the royal canal. E. Long. 3. 5. N. Lat. 43. 35.

CAPH, a Jewish measure of capacity for things estimated by Kimchi at the 30th part of the log, by Arbuthnot at the 16th part of the hin or 3d of the seah, amounting to five-eighths of an English pint. The caph does not occur in Scripture as the name of any measure.

CAPHAR, a duty which the Turks raise on the Christians who carry or send merchandises from Aleppo to Jerusalem and other places in Syria.

This duty of caphar was first imposed by the Christians themselves, when they were in possession of the Holy Land, for the maintenance of the troops which were planted in difficult passes to observe the Arabs and prevent their incursions. It is still continued, and much increased by the Turks, under pretence of defending the Christians against the Arabs; with whom, nevertheless, they keep a secret intelligence, favouring their excursions and plunders.

CAPHTOR (anc. geog.), a town or district of Higher Egypt; and hence the people called *Caphtorim* or *Caphtorasi*.—Caphtor is an island of Egypt, Ai Caphtor, (Jeremiah); probably one of those in the Nile. Dr Wells supposes it to be Copton, which stood in a small island. Thence came the *Caphtorim* or *Caphtorasi*, in Palestine; who with the Philistines conspired to extirpate the Hevari; and whose name was swallowed up in that of the Philistines.

CAPI-AGA, or *Capi-Agassi*, a Turkish officer who is governor of the gates of the seraglio, or grand master of the seraglio.

The capi-aga is the first dignity among the white

eunuchs; he is always near the person of the grand signior; he introduces ambassadors to their audience; nobody enters or goes out of the grand signior's apartment but by his means. His office gives him the privilege of wearing the turban in the seraglio, and of going every where on horseback. He accompanies the grand signior to the apartment of the sultanas, but stops at the door without entering. His appointment is very moderate; the grand signior bears the expence of his table, and allows him at the rate of about sixty French livres per day: but his office brings him in abundance of presents; no affair of consequence coming to the emperor's knowledge without passing through his hand. The capi-aga cannot be bashaw when he quits his post.

CAPIAS, in law, a writ of two sorts; one before judgment in an action, and the other after. That before judgment is called *capias ad respondendum*, where an original is issued out, to take the defendant, and make him answer the plaintiff. That after judgment is of divers kinds; as,

Capias ad Satisfaciendum, a writ of execution that issues on a judgment obtained, and lies where any person recovers in a personal action, as for debt, damages, &c. in which cases this writ issues to the sheriff, commanding him to take the body of him against whom the debt is recovered, who is to be kept in prison till he make satisfaction.

Capias pro Fine is a writ lying where a person is fined to the king, for some offence committed against a statute, and he does not discharge the fine according to the judgment; therefore his body shall be taken by this writ, and committed to goal till the fine is paid.

Capias Utlegatum, a writ which lies against any one outlawed, upon any action personal or criminal, by which the sheriff is ordered to apprehend the party outlawed, for not appearing on the exigent, and keep him in safe custody till the day of return, when he is ordered to present him to the court, to be there farther ordered for his contempt.

Capias in Withernam, a writ that lies for cattle in *withernam*; that is, where a distress taken is driven out of the county, so that the sheriff cannot make deliverance upon a replevin; then this writ issues, commanding the sheriff to take as many beasts of the distrainer, &c.

CAPIGI, a porter or door-keeper of the Turkish seraglio. There are about five hundred *capigis* or porters in the seraglio, divided into two companies; one consisting of three hundred, under a chief called *Capigi-Bassa*, who has a stipend of three ducats per day; the other consists of two hundred, distinguished by the name of *Cucicapigi*, and their chief *Cucicapigi-Bassa*, who has two ducats. The capigis have from seven to fifteen aspers per day; some more, others less. Their business is to assist the janizaries in the guard of the first and second gates of the seraglio; sometimes all together; as when the Turk holds a general council, receives an ambassador, or goes to the mosque; and sometimes only in part; being ranged on either side to prevent people entering with arms, any tumults being made, &c. The word, in its original, signifies *gate*.

CAPILLAMENT, in a general sense, signifies a hair: whence the word is applied to several things, which on account of their length or their fineness resemble hairs: as,

Capillaments of the Nerves, in anatomy, the fine fibres or filaments whereof the nerves are composed.

CAPILLARY, in a general sense, an appellation given to things on account of their extreme fineness or resembling hair.

Capillary Tubes, in physics, are small pipes of glass, whose canals are extremely narrow, their diameter being only a half, a third, or a fourth of a line.

The ascent of water, &c. in capillary tubes, is a phenomenon that has long embarrassed the philosophers: for let one end of a glass tube open at both extremities be immerged in water, the liquor within the tube will rise to a considerable height above the external surface: or if two or more tubes are immerged in the same fluid, one a capillary tube, and the other of a larger bore, the fluid will ascend higher in the former than in the latter; and this will be in a reciprocal ratio of the diameters of the tubes.

In order to account for this phenomenon, it will be necessary first to premise, that the attraction between the particles of glass and water is greater than the attraction between the particles of water themselves: for if a glass tube be placed in a position parallel to the horizon, and a drop of water be applied to the under side of the tube, it will adhere to it; nor will it fall from the glass till its bulk and gravity are so far increased, as to overcome the attraction of the glass. Hence it is easy to conceive how sensibly such a power must act on the surface of a fluid, not viscid, as water, contained within the small cavity or bore of a glass-tube; as also that it will be proportionably stronger as the diameter of the bore is smaller; for it will be evident that the efficacy of the power is in the inverse proportion of the diameter, when it is considered, that such particles only as are in contact with the fluid, and those immediately above the surface, can effect it.

Now these particles form a periphery contiguous to the surface, the upper part of which attracts and raises the surface, while the lower part, which is in contact with it, supports it; so that neither the thickness nor length of the tube is of any consequence here; the periphery of particles only, which is always proportionable to the diameter of the bore, is the only acting power. The quantity of the fluid raised will therefore be as the surface of the bore which it fills, that is, as the diameter; for otherwise the effect would not be proportional to the cause, since the quantities are always as the ratio of the diameters; the heights therefore to which the fluids will rise, in different tubes, will be inversely as the diameters.

Some doubt whether the law holds throughout, of the ascent of the fluid being always higher as the tube is smaller; Dr Hook's experiments, with tubes almost as fine as cobwebs, seem to show the contrary. The water in these, he observes, did not rise so high as one would have expected. The highest he ever found it, was at 21 inches above the level of the water in the bason; which is much short of what it ought to have been by the law above mentioned. See Cohesion.

Capillary Vessels. Many small vessels of animal bodies have been discovered by the modern invention of injecting the vessels of animals with a coloured fluid which

which upon cooling grows hard. But though most anatomists know the manner of filling the large trunks, few are acquainted with the art of filling the capillaries. Dr Monro, in the Medical Essays, has given what after many trials he has found most successful. See Injection.

CAPILLUS veneris. See Adianthum.

CAPILUPI, or Capilupus (Camillus), a native of Mantua in the 16th century. He wrote a book, entitled, *The Stratagem*; in which he relates not only what was perpetrated at Paris during the massacre on St Bartholomew's day, but also the artful preparations which preceded that horrid massacre. It is, however, blended with a great number of falsities.

Capilupi (Laelius), an Italian poet, brother to the former, made himself famous by some Centos of Virgil. The manner in which he applied Virgil's expressions to represent things which the poet never dreamt of, is admired. His Cento against women is very ingenious, but too satirical. The poems of Capilupi are inserted in the *Deliciae Poetarum Italorum*.

CAPISCOLUS, or Capischolus, in ecclesiastical writers, denotes a dignitary in certain cathedrals, who had the superintendency of the choir, or band of music, answering to what in other churches is called *chanter* or *precentor*. The word is also written *cabiscolus*, and *caputscholae*, q. d. the head of the school, or band of music.

The capiscolus is also called *scolasticus*, as having the instruction of the young clerks and choristers, how to perform their duty.

CAPITA, (distribution by), in law, signifies the appointing to every man an equal share of a personal estate; when all the claimants claim in their own rights, as in equal degrees of kindred, and not *jure representationis*.

Capita, (succession by), where the claimants are next in degree to the ancestor, in their own right, and not by right of representation.

CAPITAL, of the Latin *caput* "the head", is used on various occasions, to express the relation of a head, chief, or principal; thus,

Capital City, in geography, denotes the principal city of a kingdom, state, or province.

Capital Stock, among merchants, bankers, and traders, signifies, the sum of money which individuals bring to make up the common stock of a partnership when it is first formed. It is also said of the stock which a merchant at first puts into trade for his account. It likewise signifies the fund of a trading company or corporation, in which sense the word stock is generally added to it. Thus we say, the capital stock of the bank, &c. The word capital is opposed to that of profit or gain, though the profit often increases the capital, and becomes of itself part of the capital, when joined with the former.

Capital Crime, such a one as subjects the criminal to capital punishment, that is, to loss of life *.

* See *Crime and Punishment*.

Capital Picture, in painting, denotes one of the best and most excellent pieces of any celebrated master.

Capital Letters, in printing, large or initial letters, wherein titles, &c. are composed; with which all periods, verses, &c. commence; and wherewith also all proper names of men, kingdoms, nations, &c. begin. The practice which, for some time, obtained among our printers, of beginning every substantive with a capital, is now justly fallen into disrepute; being a manifest perversion of the design of capitals, as well as an offence against beauty and distinctness.

Capital, in architecture, the uppermost part of a column or pilaster, serving as the head or crowning, and placed immediately over the shaft, and under the entablature. See Architecture.

CAPITANA, or Captain *Galley*, the chief or principal galley of a state, not dignified with the title of a kingdom. The capitana was anciently the denomination of the chief galley of France, which the commander went on board of. But since the suppression of the office of captain general of the gallies in 1669, they have no capitana, but the first galley is called *reale*, and the second *patrone*.

CAPITANATA, one of the 12 provinces of the kingdom of Naples, in Italy, bounded on the north by the Gulph of Venice, on the east by the Terra di Barri, on the south by the Basilicata and the Farther Principato, and on the west by the county di Molise and a small part of Hither Abruzzo. It is a level country, without trees; the soil sandy, the air hot: the land, however, near the rivers, is fertile in pastures. The capital town is Manfredonia.

CAPITANEATE, in a general sense, the same with capitania. Capitaneates, in Prussia, are a kind of noble feuds, or estates, which, besides their revenue, raise their owners to the rank of nobility. They are otherwise called *starosties*.

CAPITANEI, or Catanei, in Italy, was a denomination given to all the dukes, marquisses, and counts, who were called *capitanei regis*. The same appellation was also given to persons of inferior rank who were invested with fees, formerly distinguished by the appellation *valvasores majores*.

CAPITANEUS, in ancient law writers, denotes a tenant in capite, or chief.

Capitaneus Ecclesiae, the same with advocate.

CAPITANIA, in geography, an appellation given to the 12 governments established by the Portuguese in the Brasils.

CAPITATION, a tax or imposition raised on each person, in proportion to his labour, industry, office, rank, &c. It is a very ancient kind of tribute. The Latins call it *tributum*, by which taxes on persons are distinguished from taxes on merchandise, which were called *vectigalia*.

Capitations are never practised among us but in exigencies of state. In France the capitation was introduced by Louis XIV. in 1695; and is a tax very different from the *taille*, being levied from all persons, whether they be subject to the taille or not. The clergy pay no capitation, but the princes of the blood are not exempted from it.

CAPITE, in law, (from *caput*, i. e. *rex*; whence *tenere in capite*, is to hold of the *king*, the *head* or lord paramount of all the lands in the kingdom); An ancient tenure of land, held immediately of the king, as of his crown, either by knight's service, or by soccage. It is now abolished. See Tenure.

Capite *Censi*, in antiquity, the lowest rank of Roman citizens, who in public taxes were rated the least of all, being such as never were worth above 365 asses. They were supposed to have been thus called, because

they

they were rather counted and marshalled by their heads than by their estates. The *capite censi* made part of the sixth class of citizens, being below the *proletarii*, who formed the other moiety of that class. They were not enrolled in the army, as being judged not able to support the expence of war; for in those days the soldiers maintained themselves. It does not appear, that before Caius Marius any of the Roman generals listed the *capite censi* in their armies.

CAPITOL, Capitolium, in antiquity, a famous fort or castle, on the Mons Capitolinus at Rome, wherein was a temple dedicated to Jupiter, thence also denominated *Capitolinus*, in which the senate anciently assembled; and which still serves as the city-hall, or town-house, for the meeting of the conservators of the Roman people.—It had its name *capitol*, from *caput*, a man's head, said to have been found fresh, and yet bleeding, upon digging the foundation of the temple built in honour of Jupiter. Arnobius adds, that the man's name was *Tolus*, whence *capitolium*.—The first foundations of the capitol were laid by Tarquin the Elder, in the year of Rome 139. His successor Servius raised the walls; and Tarquin the Proud finished it in the year 221. But it was not consecrated till the third year after the expulsion of the kings, and establishment of the consulate. The ceremony of the dedication of the temple was performed by the consul Horatius in 246.

The capitol consisted of three parts; a nave sacred to Jupiter; and two wings, the one consecrated to Juno, the other to Minerva: it was ascended to by stairs; the frontispiece and sides were surrounded with galleries, in which those who were honoured with triumphs entertained the senate at a magnificent banquet, after the sacrifices had been offered to the gods.

Both the inside and outside were enriched with an infinity of ornaments, the most distinguished of which was the statue of Jupiter, with his golden thunderbolt, his sceptre, and crown. In the capitol also were a temple to Jupiter the guardian, and another to Juno, with the mint; and on the descent of the hill was the temple of Concord. This beautiful edifice contained the most sacred deposits of religion, such as the ancylia, the books of the Sibyls, &c.

The capitol was burnt under Vitellius, and rebuilt under Vespasian. It was burnt a second time by lightning under Titus, and restored by Domitian.

Anciently the name *capitol* was likewise applied to all the principal temples, in most of the colonies throughout the Roman empire; as at Constantinople, Jerusalem, Carthage, Ravenna, Capua, &c.—That of Tholouse, has given the name of *capitouls* to its echevins or sheriffs.

CAPITOLINE games, annual games instituted by Camillus, in honour of Jupiter Capitolinus, and in commemoration of the capitol's not being taken by the Gauls. Plutarch tells us, that a part of the ceremony consisted in the public criers putting up the Hetrurians to sale by auction: they also took an old man, and tying a golden bulla about his neck, exposed him to the public derision. Festus says they also dressed him in a pretexta.—There was another kind of Capitoline games, instituted by Domitian, wherein there were rewards and crowns bestowed on the poets, champions, orators, historians, and musicians. These last Capitoline games were celebrated every five years, and became so famous, that, instead of calculating time by lustra, they began to count by Capitoline games, as the Greeks did by Olympiads. It appears, however, that this custom was not of long continuance.

CAPITOLINUS (Julius), an historian in the beginning of the fourth age under Dioclesian, to whom he inscribed the Lives of Verus, Antoninus Pius, Clodius Balbinus, Macrinus, the Maximins, and the Gordians. He wrote other lives, which are most of them lost.

CAPITOUL, or Capitol, an appellation given to the chief magistrates of Tholouse, who have the administration of justice and policy both civil and mercantile in the city. The capitouls at Tholouse are much the same with the echevins at Paris, and with the consuls, bailiffs, burger-masters, mayors, and aldermen, &c. in other cities. In ancient acts they are called *consules capitularii* or *capitolini*, and their body *capitulum*. From this last come the words *capitularii* and *capitouls*. The appellative *capitolini* arose hence, that they have the charge and custody of the town-house, which was anciently called *capitol*.

The office only lasts one year, and ennobles the bearers. In some ancient acts they are called *capitulum nobilium Tolosæ*. Those who have borne it, style themselves afterwards burgesses. They are called to all general councils, and have the *jus imaginum*; that is, when the year of their administration is expired, their pictures are drawn in the town-house; a custom which they have retained from the ancient Romans, as may be seen in Sigonius.

CAPITOULATE, an appellation given to the several quarters or districts of the city of Tholouse, each under the direction of a capitoul; much like the wards of London, under their aldermen. Tholouse is now divided into eight *capitoulates* or quarters, which are subdivided into *moulons*, each of which has its tithing-man, whose business is to inform the capitoul of what passes in his tithing, and to inform the inhabitants of the tithing of the orders of the capitoul.

CAPITULAR, or capitulary, denotes an act passed in a chapter, either of knights, canons, or religious.

The capitularia, or capitulars of Charlemagne, Charles the Bald, &c. are the laws, both ecclesiastical and civil, made by those emperors in the general councils or assemblies of the people; which was the way in which the constitutions of most of the ancient princes were made; each person present, though a plebeian, setting his hand to them.

Some distinguish these from laws; and say, they were only supplements to laws. They had their name, capitulars, because divided into capitula, chapters, or sections. In these capitulars did the whole French jurisprudence anciently consist. In process of time, the name was changed for that of ordonnances.

Some distinguish three kinds of capitulars, according to the difference of their subject-matter: those on ecclesiastical affairs, are really canons, extracted from councils; those on secular affairs, real laws; those relating to particular persons, or occasions, private regulations.

CAPITULATION, in military affairs, a treaty made between the inhabitants or garrison of a place besieged

beſieged and the beſiegers, for the delivering up the place on certain conditions. The moſt honourable and ordinary terms of capitulation are, To march out at the breach with arms and baggage, drums beating, colours flying, a match lighted at both ends, and ſome pieces of cannon, waggons and convoys for their baggage, and for their ſick and wounded.

CAPITULATION, in the German polity, a contract which the emperor makes with the electors, in the name of all the princes and ſtates in the empire, before he is declared emperor, and which he ratifies before he is raiſed to that ſovereign dignity. The principal points which the emperor undertakes to obſerve are, 1. To defend the church and empire. 2. To obſerve the fundamental laws of the empire. And, 3. To maintain and preſerve the rights, privileges, and immunities of the electors, princes, and other ſtates of the empire, ſpecified in the capitulation. Theſe articles and capitulations are preſented to the emperor by the electors only, without the concurrence of the other ſtates, who have complained from time to time of ſuch proceedings; and in the time of the Weſtphalian treaty, in 1648, it was propoſed to deliberate in the following diet, upon a way of making a perpetual capitulation; but the electors have always found means of eluding the execution of this article. In order, however, to give ſome ſatiſfaction to their adverſaries, they have inſerted in the capitulations of the emperors, and in that of Francis I. in particular, a promiſe to uſe all their influence to bring the affair of a perpetual capitulation to a concluſion. Some German authors own, that this capitulation limits the emperor's power; but maintain that it does not weaken his ſovereignty: though the moſt part maintain that he is not abſolute, becauſe he receives the empire under conditions, which ſets bounds to an abſolute authority.

CAPITULUM, in the ancient military art, was a tranſverſe beam, wherein were holes through which paſſed the ſtrings whereby the arms of huge engines, as baliſtæ, catapultæ, and ſcorpions, were played or worked.

CAPITULUM, in eccleſiaſtical writers, denoted part of a chapter of the bible read and explained. In which ſenſe they ſaid, *ire ad capitulum*, to go to ſuch a lecture. Afterwards the place or apartment where ſuch theological exerciſes were performed was denominated *domus capituli*.

CAPNICON, in antiquity, chimney-money, or a tax which the Roman emperors levied for ſmoke, and which of conſequence was due from all, even the pooreſt, who kept a fire. This was firſt invented by Nicephorus.

CAPNOMANCY, a kind of divination by means of ſmoke, uſed by the ancients in their ſacrifices. The word comes καπνος, *ſmoke*, and μαντεια, *divination*. The general rule was, when the ſmoke was thin, and light, and roſe ſtraight up, it was a good omen; if the contrary, it was an ill one. There was alſo another ſpecies of capnomancy, conſiſting in the obſervation of the ſmoke riſing from poppy and jeſſamin-ſeed, caſt upon lighted coals.

CAPO FINO, a large barren rock in the territory of the Genoeſe, which has a caſtle on its eaſtern peak. Near it is a ſmall harbour of the ſame name, 13 miles eaſt by ſouth of Genoa.

Capo d'Iſtria, a conſiderable town of Italy, in Iſtria, on the gulph of Trieſte, with a biſhop's ſee, and ſubject to the Venetians. The air is wholeſome and temperate; its principal revenue conſiſts in wine and ſalt. E. Long. 14. 0. N. Lat. 45. 48.

CAPON, a cock-chicken, gelded as ſoon as left by the dam, or as ſoon as he begins to crow. They are of uſe either to lead chickens, ducklings, pheaſants, &c. and defend them from the kites and buzzards; or to feed for the table, they being reckoned more delicate than either a cock or a hen.

CAPONIERE, or CAPPONIERE, in fortification, a covered lodgement, ſunk four or five feet into the ground, encompaſſed with a little parapet about two feet high, ſerving to ſupport ſeveral planks covered with earth. The caponiere is large enough to contain 15 or 20 ſoldiers; and is uſually placed in the glacis on the extremity of the counterſcarp, and in dry moats; having little embraſures for the ſoldiers to fire through.

CAPPADOCIA, an ancient kingdom of Aſia, comprehending all that country which lies between mount Taurus and the Euxine ſea. It was divided by the Perſians into two ſatrapies or governments; by the Macedonians into two kingdoms, the one called *Cappadocia ad Taurum*; the other, *Cappadocia ad Pontum*, and commonly *Pontus*; for the hiſtory, &c. of which laſt, ſee the article PONTUS.

CAPPADOCIA Magna, or *Cappadocia* properly ſo called, lies between the 38th and 41ſt degrees of north latitude. It was bounded by Pontus on the north, Lycaonia and part of Armenia Major on the ſouth, Galatia on the weſt, and by Euphrates and part of Armenia Minor on the eaſt. The firſt king of Cappadocia we read of in hiſtory was Pharnaces, who was preferred to the crown by Cyrus king of Perſia, who gave him his ſiſter Atoſſa in marriage. This is all we find recorded of him, except that he was killed in a war with the Hyrcanians. After him came a ſucceſſion of eight kings, of whom we know ſcarce any thing but that they continued faithful to the Perſian intereſt. In the time of Alexander the Great, Cappadocia was governed by Ariarathes II. who, notwithſtanding the vaſt conqueſts and fame of the Macedonian monarch, continued unſhaken in his fidelity to the Perſians. Alexander was prevented by death from invading his dominions; but Perdiccas marching againſt him with a powerful and well diſciplined army, diſperſed his forces, and having taken Ariarathes himſelf priſoner, crucified him, with all thoſe of the royal blood whom he could get into his power. Diodorus tells us that he was killed in the battle. He is ſaid to have reigned 82 years. His ſon Ariarathes III. having eſcaped the general ſlaughter of the royal family, fled into Armenia, where he lay concealed, till the civil diſſenſions which aroſe among the Macedonians gave him a fair opportunity of recovering his paternal kingdom. Amyntas, at that time the governor of Cappadocia, oppoſed him: but being defeated in a pitched battle, the Macedonians were obliged to abandon all the ſtrong holds. Ariarathes, after a long and peaceable reign, left his kingdom to his ſon Ariaramnes II. He applied himſelf more to the arts of peace than war, in conſequence of which Cappadocia flouriſhed greatly during his reign. He was ſucceeded by his ſon Ariarathes IV.

Cappadocia.

who proved a very warlike prince, and having overcome Arsaces, founder of the Parthian monarchy, considerably enlarged his own dominions.

He was succeeded by Ariarathes V. who marrying the daughter of Antiochus the Great, entered into an alliance with that prince against the Romans; but Antiochus being defeated, the king of Cappadocia was obliged to sue for peace, which he obtained, after having paid 200 talents by way of fine, for taking up arms against the people of Rome. He afterwards assisted the republic with men and money against Perseus king of Macedon, on which account he was by the senate honoured with the title of the *friend and ally of the Roman people*. He left the kingdom in a very flourishing condition to his son Mithridates, who on his accession took the name of Ariarathes VI.

This prince (surnamed *Philopater*, from the filial respect and love he showed his father from his very infancy) immediately renewed the alliance with Rome. Out of mere good-nature he restored Mithrobuzanes son to Ladriades king of the Lesser Armenia to his father's kingdom, though he foresaw that the Armenians would lay hold of that opportunity to join Artaxias, who was then on the point of invading Cappadocia. These differences, however, were settled before they came to an open rupture, by the Roman legates; and Ariarathes seeing himself thus delivered from an impending war by the mediation of the republic, presented the senate with a golden crown, and offered his service wherever they thought proper to employ him. The senate in return sent him a staff, and chair of ivory; which were presents usually bestowed on those only whom they looked upon as attached to their interest. Not long before this, Demetrius Soter king of Syria had offered Ariarathes his sister in marriage, the widow of Perseus king of Macedon; but this offer the king of Cappadocia was obliged to decline for fear of offending the Romans; and his so doing was in the highest degree acceptable to the republic, who reckoned him among the chief of her allies. Demetrius, however, being greatly incensed at the slight put upon his sister, set up a pretender to the throne, one Orophernes, a supposititious, or, as others call him, a natural son of the deceased king. The Romans ordered Eumenes king of Pergamus to assist Ariarathes with all his forces; which he did, but to no purpose; for the confederates were overthrown by Demetrius, and Ariarathes was obliged to abandon the kingdom to his rival. This happened about 159 years before Christ, and the usurper immediately dispatched ambassadors to Rome with a golden crown. The senate declined accepting the present, till they heard his pretensions to the kingdom; and this Orophernes, by suborned witnesses, made appear so plain, that the senate decreed that Ariarathes and he should reign as partners; but next year, Orophernes was driven out by Attalus brother to Eumenes, and his successor to the kingdom of Pergamus.

Ariarathes, being thus restored, immediately demanded of the Prienians 400 talents of gold which Orophernes had deposited with them. They honestly replied, that as they had been trusted with the money by Orophernes, they could deliver it to none but himself, or such as came in his name. Upon this, the king entered their territories with an army, destroying all with fire and sword. The Prienians, however, still persevered in their integrity; and though their city was besieged by the united forces of Ariarathes and Attalus, not only made an obstinate defence, but found means to restore the sum to Orophernes. At last they applied to the Romans for assistance, who enjoined the two kings to raise the siege, under pain of being declared enemies to the republic. Ariarathes immediately obeyed; and marching his army into Assyria, joined Alexander Epiphanes against Demetrius Soter, by whom he had been formerly driven out of his kingdom. In the very first engagement Demetrius was slain, and his army entirely dispersed, Ariarathes having on that occasion given uncommon proofs of his courage and conduct. Some years after, a war breaking out between the Romans and Aristonicus who claimed the kingdom of Pergamus in right of his father, Ariarathes joined the former, and was slain in the same battle in which P. Crassus proconsul of Asia was taken, and the Roman army cut in pieces. He left six sons by his wife Laodice, on whom the Romans bestowed Lycaonia and Cilicia. But Laodice, fearing lest her children, when they came of age, should take the government out of her hands, poisoned five of them, the youngest only having escaped her cruelty by being conveyed out of the kingdom. The queen herself was soon after put to death by her subjects, who could not bear her cruel and tyrannical government.

Laodice was succeeded by Ariarathes VII. who, soon after his accession, married another Laodice, daughter of Mithridates the Great, hoping to find in that prince a powerful friend to support him against Nicomedes king of Bithynia, who laid claim to part of Cappadocia. But Mithridates instead of assisting, procured one Gordius to poison his unhappy son-in-law; and, on his death, seized the kingdom, under pretence of maintaining the rights of the Cappadocians against Nicomedes, till the children of Ariarathes were in a condition to govern the kingdom. The Cappadocians at first fancied themselves obliged to their new protector; but, finding him unwilling to resign the kingdom to the lawful heir, they rose up in arms, and, driving out all the garrisons placed by Mithridates, placed on the throne Ariarathes VIII. eldest son of their deceased king.

The new prince found himself immediately engaged in a war with Nicomedes; but, being assisted by Mithridates, not only drove him out of Cappadocia, but stripped him of a great part of his hereditary dominions. On the conclusion of the peace, Mithridates, seeking for some pretence to quarrel with Ariarathes, insisted upon his recalling Gordius, who had murdered his father; which being rejected with abhorrence, a war ensued. Mithridates took the field first, in hopes of over-running Cappadocia before Ariarathes could be in a condition to make head against him; but, contrary to his expectation, he was met on the frontiers by the king of Cappadocia with an army no way inferior to his own. Hereupon he invited Ariarathes to a conference; and, in sight of both armies, stabbed him with a dagger, which he had concealed under his garment. This struck such terror into the Cappadocians, that they immediately dispersed, and gave Mithridates an opportunity of possessing himself of the kingdom without the least opposition. The Cappadocians, however, not able to endure the tyranny of his prefects, soon

Cappadocia.

shook off the yoke; and recalling the king's brother, who had fled into the province of Asia, proclaimed him king. He was scarce seated on the throne, however, before Mithridates invaded the kingdom at the head of a very numerous army, and having drawn Ariarathes to a battle, defeated his army with great slaughter, and obliged him to abandon the kingdom. The unhappy prince soon after died of grief; and Mithridates bestowed the kingdom on his son, who was then but eight years old, giving him also the name of *Ariarathes*. But Nicomedes Philopater king of Bithynia, fearing lest Mithridates, having now got possession of the whole kingdom of Cappadocia, should invade his territories, suborned a youth to pass himself for the third son of Ariarathes, and to present to them a petition in order to be restored to his father's kingdom. With him he sent to Rome Laodice, sister of Mithridates, whom he had married after the death of her former husband Ariarathes. Laodice declared before the senate, that she had three sons by Ariarathes, and that the petitioner was one of them; but that she had been obliged to keep him concealed, lest he should undergo the same fate with his brothers. The senate assured him that they would at all events reinstate him in his kingdom. But, in the mean time, Mithridates having notice of these transactions, dispatched Gordius to Rome, to undeceive the senate, and to persuade them that the youth to whom he had resigned the kingdom of Cappadocia was the lawful son of the late king, and grandson to Ariarathes who had lost his life in the service of the Romans against Aristonicus. This unexpected embassy put the senate upon enquiring more narrowly into the matter, whereby the whole plot was discovered; upon which Mithridates was ordered to resign Cappadocia, and the kingdom was declared free. The Cappadocians, however, in a short time sent ambassadors to Rome, acquainting the senate that they could not live without a king. This greatly surprised the Romans, who had such an aversion to royal authority; but they gave them leave to elect a king of their own nation. As the family of Pharnaces was now extinct, the Cappadocians chose Ariobarzanes; and their choice was approved by the senate, he having on all occasions shown himself a steady friend to the Romans.

Ariobarzanes had scarce taken possession of his kingdom when he was driven out by Tigranes king of Armenia; who resigned Cappadocia to the son of Mithridates, in pursuance of an alliance previously concluded between the two parties. Ariobarzanes fled to Rome; and, having engaged the senate in his cause, he returned into Asia with Sylla, who was enjoined to restore him to his kingdom. This was easily performed by Sylla, who, with a small body of troops, routed Gordius who came to meet him on the borders of Cappadocia at the head of a numerous army. Sylla, however, had scarce turned his back, when Ariobarzanes was again driven out by Ariarathes the son of Mithridates, on whom Tigranes had bestowed the kingdom of Cappadocia. This obliged Sylla to return into Asia, where he was attended with his usual success, and Ariobarzanes was again placed on the throne. After the death of Sylla, he was the third time forced by Mithridates to abandon his kingdom; but Pompey, having entirely defeated Mithridates near mount Stella, restored Ariobarzanes to his throne, and rewarded him for his services during the war, with the provinces of Sophene, Gordiene, and great part of Cilicia. The king, however, being now advanced in years, and desirous of spending the remainder of his life in ease, resigned the crown to his son Ariobarzanes, in presence of Pompey; and never afterwards troubled himself with affairs of state.

Ariobarzanes II. proved no less faithful to the Romans than his father had been. On the breaking out of the civil war between Cæsar and Pompey, he sided with the latter; but after the death of Pompey, he was received into favour by Cæsar, who even bestowed upon him great part of Armenia. While Cæsar was engaged in a war with the Egyptians, Pharnaces king of Pontus invaded Cappadocia, and stripped Ariobarzanes of all his dominions; but Cæsar, having defeated Pharnaces, restored the king of Cappadocia, and honoured him with new titles of friendship. After the murder of Cæsar, Ariobarzanes, having refused to join Brutus and Cassius, was by them declared an enemy to the republic, and soon after taken prisoner and put to death. He was succeeded by his brother Ariobarzanes III. who was by Marc Anthony deprived both of his kingdom and life; and in him ended the family of Ariobarzanes.

Archelaus, the grandson of that general of the same name who commanded against Sylla in the Mithridatic war, was by Marc Anthony placed on the throne of Cappadocia, though nowise related either to the family of Pharnaces or Ariobarzanes. His preferment was entirely owing to his mother Glaphyra, a woman of great beauty, but of a loose behaviour, who, in return for her compliance with the desires of Anthony, obtained the kingdom of Cappadocia for her son. In the war between Augustus and Anthony, he joined the latter; but at the intercession of the Cappadocians, was pardoned by the emperor. He afterwards received from him Armenia the Lesser, and Cilicia Trachea, for having assisted the Romans in clearing the seas of pirates who greatly infested the coasts of Asia. He contracted a strict friendship with Herod the Great, king of Judæa; and even married his daughter Glaphyra to Alexander, Herod's son. In the reign of Tiberius, Archelaus was summoned to appear before the senate; for he had always been hated by that emperor, because in his retirement at Rhodes he had paid him no sort of respect. This had proceeded from no aversion in him to Tiberius, but from the warning given Archelaus to his friends at Rome. For Caius Cæsar, the presumptive heir to the empire, was then alive, and had been sent to compose the differences of the east, whence the friendship of Tiberius was then looked upon as dangerous. But when he came to the empire, Tiberius, remembering the disrespect shown him by Archelaus, enticed the latter to Rome by means of letters from Livia, who promised him her son Tiberius's pardon, provided he came in person to implore it. Archelaus obeyed the summons, and hastened to Rome; where he was received by the emperor with great wrath and contempt, and soon after accused as a criminal in the senate. The crimes of which he was accused were mere fictions; but his concern at seeing himself treated as a malefactor was so great, that he died soon after of grief, or, as others say, laid vio-

6.

CAPRA. Plate CXXI.

Cappadocia. lent hands on himſelf. He is ſaid to have reigned 50 years.

On the death of Archelaus, the kingdom of Cappadocia was reduced to a Roman province, and governed by those of the equeſtrian order. It continued ſubject to the Romans till the invaſion of the eaſtern empire by the Turks, to whom it is now ſubject, but has no diſtinguiſhing modern name. In what was anciently called *Cappadocia*, however, the Turks have four Beglerbeglics, called *Sivas*, *Trebizond*, *Marasch*, and *Cogni*.

In the time of the Romans, the inhabitants of Cappadocia bore ſo bad a character, and were reputed ſo vicious and lewd, that, among the neighbouring nations, a wicked man was emphatically called a *Cappadocian*. In after ages, however, their lewd diſpoſition was ſo corrected and reſtrained by the pure doctrines of Chriſtianity, that no country whatever has produced greater champions of the Chriſtian religion, or given to the church prelates of more unblemiſhed characters.

We have now no ſyſtem of the Cappadocian laws, and ſcarce wherewithal to form any particular idea of them. As to their commerce, they carried on a conſiderable trade in horſes, great numbers of which were produced in their country; and we read of them in Scripture as frequenting the fairs of Tyre with this commodity. As Cappadocia abounded with mines of ſilver, braſs, iron, and alum, and afforded great ſtore of alabaſter, cryſtal, and jaſper, it is probable that they might ſupply the neighbouring countries with these commodities.

The religion of the ancient Cappadocians was much the ſame with that of the Perſians. At Comana there was a rich and ſtately temple dedicated to Bellona; whoſe battles the prieſts and their attendants uſed to repreſent on ſtated days, cutting and wounding each other as if ſeized with an enthuſiaſtic fury. No leſs famous and magnificent were the temples of Apollo Catanius, and of Jupiter; the laſt of which had 3000 ſacred ſervants, or religious votaries. The chief prieſt was next in rank to that of Comana; and, according to Strabo, had an yearly revenue of 15 talents. Diana Perſica was worſhipped in a city called *Caſtabella*, where women, devoted to the worſhip of that goddeſs, were reported to tread barefooted on burning coals, without receiving any hurt. The temples of Diana at Dioſpolis, and of Anias at Zela, were likewiſe held in great veneration both by the Cappadocians and Armenians, who flocked to them from all parts. In the latter were tendered all oaths in matters of conſequence; and the chief among the prieſts was no way inferior in dignity, power, and wealth, to any in the kingdom; having a royal attendance, and an unlimited authority over all the inferior ſervants and officers of the temple. The Romans, who willingly adopted all the ſuperſtitions and ſuperſtitious rites of the nations they conquered, greatly increaſed the revenues of this and other temples; conferring the prieſthood on ſuch as they thought moſt fit for carrying on their deſigns.—We are told that human ſacrifices were offered at Comana; and that this barbarous cuſtom was brought by Oreſtes and his ſiſter Iphigenia from Taurica Scythica, where men and women were immolated to Diana. But this cuſtom, if ever it obtained in Cappadocia, was aboliſhed in the times of the Romans.

Cappanus ‖ Capra.

CAPPANUS, a name given by ſome authors to a worm that adheres to and gnaws the bottoms of ſhips; to which it is extremely pernicious, eſpecially in the Eaſt and Weſt Indies: to prevent this, ſeveral ſhips have lately been ſheathed with copper; the firſt trial of which was made on his majeſty's frigate the Alarm.

CAPPARIS, in botany: A genus of the monogynia order, belonging to the polyandria claſs of plants; and in the natural method ranking under the 25th order, *Putamineae*. The calyx is tetraphyllous and coriaceous; there petals are four; the ſtamina are long; the fruit is a berry, carnous, unilocular, and pedunculated, or furniſhed with a foot-ſtalk.

There are ſeven ſpecies. The *ſpinoſa*, or common caper, is a low ſhrub, generally growing out of the joints of old walls, the fiſſures of rocks, and amongſt rubbiſh, in moſt of the warm parts of Europe: it hath woody ſtalks, which ſend out many lateral ſlender branches; under each of theſe are placed two ſhort crooked ſpines, between which and the branches come out the footſtalks of the leaves, which are ſingle, ſhort, and ſuſtain a round ſmooth entire leaf. At the intermediate joints, between the branches, come out the flowers on long footſtalks; before these expand, the bud with the empalement is gathered for pickling. Thoſe which are left expand in form of a ſingle roſe, having five large white petals, which are roundiſh and concave; in the middle are placed a great number of long ſtamina, ſurrounding a ſtyle which riſes above them, and crowned with an oval germen, which afterwards becomes a capſule filled with kidney-ſhaped ſeeds.

Culture. This plant is very difficultly preſerved in Britain: it delights to grow in crevices of rocks, old walls, &c. and always thrives beſt in an horizontal poſture; ſo that, when planted either in pots or in the full ground, they ſeldom thrive, though they may be kept alive for ſome years. They are propagated by ſeeds in the warm parts of Europe, but very ſeldom in Britain.

Uſes. The buds, pickled with vinegar, &c. are brought to Britain annually from Italy and the Mediterranean. They are ſuppoſed to excite appetite and aſſiſt digeſtion; and to be particularly uſeful as detergents and aperients in obſtructions of the liver and ſpleen.

CAPRA, or GOAT, a genus of quadrupeds belonging to the order of pecora. The horns are hollow, turned upwards, erect, and ſcabrous. There are eight fore-teeth in the under jaw, and none in the upper; and they have no dog-teeth. This genus conſiſts of 14 ſpecies, viz. Plates CXXI, CXXII, CXXIII, CXXIV.

I. The HIRCUS, or common goat, with arched carinated horns, and a long beard. It is a native of the eaſtern mountains.

The goat is an animal of more ſagacity than the ſheep. Inſtead of having an antipathy at mankind, they voluntarily mingle with them, and are eaſily tamed. Even in uninhabited countries, they betray no ſavage diſpoſitions. In the year 1698, an Engliſh veſſel having put in to the iſland of Bonavida, two negroes came aboard, and offered gratis to the captain as

Capra.

many goats as he pleased. The captain expressed his astonishment at this offer. But the negroes replied, that there were only 12 persons in the island; that the goats had multiplied to such a degree, that they were become extremely troublesome; and that, instead of having any difficulty in catching them, they followed the men wherever they went, and were so obstinately officious, that they could not get quit of them upon any account whatever.

Goats are sensible of caresses, and capable of a considerable degree of friendship. They are stronger, more agile, and less timid, than sheep. They have a lively, capricious, and wandering disposition; are fond of high and solitary places, and frequently sleep upon the very points of rocks. They are more easily supported than any other animal of the same size; for there is hardly an herb, or the bark of a tree, which they will not eat with pleasure. Neither are they liable to so many diseases as sheep: they can bear heat and cold with less inconvenience. The actions and movements of animals depend more upon the force and variety of their sensations than the structure of their bodies: the natural inconstancy or fancifulness of goats is accordingly expressed by the irregularity of their actions: they walk, stop short, run, jump, show and hide themselves, as it were by mere caprice, and without any other cause than what arises from the natural vivacity of their temper.

The buck will copulate when he is a year old, and the female when she is seven months. But as this is rather premature, they are generally restrained till they be 18 months or two years. The buck is bold, beautiful, and vigorous; one is sufficient to serve 150 females. A buck for propagation should be large, handsome, and about two years of age; his neck should be short and fleshy; his head slender; his ears pendent; his thighs thick; his limbs firm; his hair black, thick, and soft; and his beard should be long and bushy. The females are generally in season from September to the end of November. At that time the males drive whole flocks of the females continually from place to place, and fill the whole atmosphere around them with their strong disagreeable odour; which, though as disagreeable as asafoetida itself, yet may be conducive to prevent many distempers, and to cure nervous and hysterical ones. Horses are supposed to be much refreshed by it; on which account many people keep a he-goat in their studs or stables.

Goats go with young four months and an half, and bring forth from the latter end of February to the latter end of April: having only two teats, they generally bring forth but one or two young; sometimes three; and in good warm pastures there have been instances, tho' rare, of their bringing forth four at a time. They continue fruitful till they are seven years of age; but a buck goat is seldom kept after he is five. Both young and old are affected by the weather; a rainy season makes them thin, a dry sunny one makes them fat and blithe: their excessive venery prevents their longevity; for in our climate they seldom live above 11 or 12 years.

Though the food of this animal costs next to nothing, as it can support itself even upon the most barren mountains, their produce is valuable. The whitest wigs are made of their hair; for which purpose that of the he-goat is most in request: the whitest and clearest is selected from that which grows on the haunches, where it is longest and thickest: a good skin well haired is sold for a guinea; though a skin of bad hue, and so yellow as to baffle the barber's skill to bleach, will not fetch above 18d. or 2s. The Welsh goats are far superior in size, and in length and fineness of hair, to those of other mountainous countries. Their usual colour is white: those of France and the Alps are short-haired, reddish, and the horns small. Bolsters made from the hair of a goat were in use in the days of Saul, as appears from 1 Samuel xix. 13. The species very probably was the Angora goat, which is only found in the East, and whose soft and silky hair supplied a most luxurious couch.

The suet of the goat is in great esteem as well as the hair. Many of the inhabitants of Caernarvonshire suffer these animals to run wild on the rocks in winter as well as in summer; and kill them in October for the sake of their fat, either by shooting them with bullets, or by running them down with dogs like deer. The goats killed for this purpose are about four or five years old. Their suet will make candles far superior in whiteness and goodness to those made from that of the sheep or the ox, and accordingly brings a much greater price in the market; nor are the horns without their use, the country people making of them excellent handles for tucks and pen-knives. The skin is peculiarly well adapted for the glove manufactory, especially that of the kid: abroad it is dressed and made into stockings, bed-ticks, bed-hangings, sheets, and even shirts. In the army it covers the horseman's arms, and carries the foot-soldier's provisions. As it takes a dye better than any other skin, it was formerly much used for hangings in the houses of people of fortune, being susceptible of the richest colours, and when flowered and ornamented with gold and silver became an elegant and superb furniture.

The flesh is of great use to the inhabitants of those countries which abound with goats; and affords them a cheap and plentiful provision in the winter-months, when the kids are brought to market. The haunches of the goat are frequently salted and dried, and supply all the uses of bacon: this by the Welsh is called *coch yr wden*, or hung venison. The meat of a splayed goat of six or seven years old (which is called *hyfr*) is reckoned the best; being generally very fat and sweet. This makes an excellent pasty; goes under the name of *rock venison*; and is little inferior to that of the deer.

The milk of the goat is sweet, nourishing, and medicinal. It is an excellent succedaneum for ass's milk; and has (with a tea-spoonful of hartshorn drunk warm in bed in the morning, and at four in the afternoon, and repeated for some time) been a cure for phthisical people before they were gone too far. In some of the mountainous parts of Scotland and Ireland, the milk is made into whey, which has done wonders in this and other cases where coolers and restoratives are necessary; and to many of those places there is as great a resort of patients of all ranks, as there is in England to the Spas or baths. It is not surprising that the milk of this animal is so salutary, as it browses only on the tops, tendrils, and flowers, of the mountain shrubs, and medicinal herbs; rejecting the grosser parts. The blood

of

Capra.

of the he-goat, dried, was formerly reckoned a specific in pleurisies, and is even taken notice of by Dr Mead for this purpose; but is now deservedly neglected. Cheese made of goat's milk is much valued in some of our mountainous countries, when kept to a proper age; but has a peculiar taste and flavour.

a. The Angora goat is a variety that is found only in the tract that surrounds Angora and Beibazar, towns in Asiatic Turky, for the distance of three or four days journey. Strabo seems to have been acquainted with this kind; for speaking of the river Halys, he says, that there are goats found near it that are not known in other parts. In the form of their body they differ from the common goat, being shorter; their legs too are shorter, their sides broader and flatter, and their horns straighter; but the most valuable characteristic is their hair, which is soft as silk, of a glossy silvery whiteness, and curled in locks of eight or nine inches in length. This hair is the basis of our fine camlets, and imported to England in form of thread; for the Turks will not permit it to be exported raw, for a reason that does them honour; because it supports a multitude of poor, who live by spinning it. The goat-herds of Angora and Beibazar are extremely careful of their flocks, frequently combing and washing them. It is observed, that if they change their climate and pasture, they lose their beauty: we therefore suspect that the design of Baron Alstroemer, a patriotic Swede, turned out fruitless, who imported some into his own country, to propagate the breed for the sake of their hair.

b. The *Capricorn* of Buffon is another variety, having short horns, the ends turned forwards, their sides annulated, and the rings more prominent before than behind.

II. The IBEX, or wild-goat, is the stock from whence the tame species sprung. It has large knotty horns reclined upon its back, is of a yellowish colour, and its beard is black. The females are less, and have smaller horns, more like those of a common she-goat, and with few knobs on the upper surface: they bring one young one, seldom two, at a birth. They inhabit the highest Alps of the Grison's country and the Valais; are also found in Crete. They are very wild, and difficult to be shot, as they always keep on the highest points. Their chace is exceedingly dangerous: being very strong, they often tumble the incautious huntsman down the precipices, except he has time to lie down, and let the animals pass over him. They are said not to be long-lived.

III. The MAMBRINA, or Syrian goat, with reclined horns, pendant ears, and a beard. It is a native of the East. Their ears are of a vast length; from one to two feet; and sometimes so troublesome, that the owners cut off one to enable the animal to feed with more ease. These animals supply Aleppo with milk.

IV. The RUPICAPRA, or chamois-goat, has erect and hooked horns. The body is of a dusky red colour; but the front, top of the head, gullet, and inside of the ears, are white; the under part of the tail is blackish; and the upper lip is a little divided. It inhabits the Alps of Dauphine, Switzerland, and Italy; the Pyrenean mountains; Greece, and Crete: does not dwell so high in the hills as the ibex, and is found in greater numbers.

The chamois is of the size of a domestic goat, and his hair is as short as that of a hind. His vivacity is delightful, and his agility truly admirable. These animals are very social among themselves: We find them going in pairs, or in little flocks of from three to twenty; and sometimes we see from 60 to 100 of them dispersed in different flocks along the declivity of the same mountain. The large males keep at a distance from the rest, except in the rutting season, when they join the females, and beat off all the young. At this period, their ardour is still stronger than that of the wild bucks. They bleat often, and run from one mountain to another. Their season of love is in the months of October and November, and they bring forth in March and April. A young female takes the male at the age of 18 months. The females bring forth one, but rarely two, at a time. The young follow their mothers till October, if not dispersed by the hunters or the wolves. We are assured that they live between 20 and 30 years. Their flesh is very good. A fat chamois goat will yield from 10 to 12 pounds of suet, which is harder and better than that of the goat. The blood of the chamois is extremely hot, and it is said to have qualities and virtues nearly equal to those of the wild goat. The hunters sometimes mix the blood of the wild and chamois goats: At other times they sell the blood of the wild goat for that of the chamois. The voice of the chamois is a very low and almost imperceptible kind of bleating, resembling that of a hoarse domestic goat. It is by this bleating that they collect together, particularly the mothers and their young. But, when alarmed, or when they perceive their enemy, or any thing the nature of which they cannot distinguish, they advertise one another by a kind of whistling noise. The sight of the chamois is very penetrating, and his sense of smelling is acute. When he sees a man distinctly, he stops for some time, and flies off when he makes a nearer approach. His sense of hearing is equally acute as that of smelling; for he hears the smallest noise. When the wind blows in the direction between him and a man, he will perceive the scent at the distance of more than half a league. Hence, when he smells or hears any thing which he cannot see, he whistles or blows with such force, that the rocks and forests re-echo the sound. If there are many of them near, they all take the alarm. This whistling is as long as the animal can blow without taking breath. It is at first sharp, and turns flat at the end. The chamois then stops for a moment, looks round on all sides, and begins whistling afresh, which he continues from time to time. His agitation is extreme. He strikes the earth with his feet; he leaps upon the highest stones he can find; he again looks round, leaps from one eminence to another; and, when he discovers any thing, he flies off. The whistling of the male is sharper than that of the female. This whistling is performed through the nostrils, and consists of a strong blowing, similar to the sound which a man may make by fixing his tongue to the palate, with his teeth nearly shut, his lips open, and somewhat extended, and blowing long and with great force. The chamois feeds on the finest herbs. He selects the most delicate parts of plants, as the flowers and the tenderest buds. He is very fond of some aromatic herbs, particularly of the carline thistle and genipay, which

are

Capra.

are the hottest plants that grow in the Alps. When he eats green herbs, he drinks very little. He is very fond of the leaves and tender buds of shrubs. He ruminates like the common goat. The food he uses seems to announce the heat of his constitution. This animal is admired for his large round eyes, whose size corresponds with the vivacity of his disposition. His head is adorned with two small horns, from half a foot to nine inches in length. Their colour is a fine black, and they are placed on the front nearly between his eyes; and, instead of being reflected backward, like those of other animals, they advance forward above the eyes, and bend backward at the points, which are extremely sharp. He adjusts his ears most beautifully to the points of his horns. Two tufts of black hair descend from his horns to the sides of his face. The rest of the head is of a yellowish white colour, which never changes. The horns of the chamois are used for the heads of canes. Those of the female are smaller and less crooked. The skin of the chamois, when dressed, is very strong, nervous, and supple, and makes excellent riding-breeches, gloves, and vests. Garments of this kind last long, and are of great use to manufacturers. The chamois goats are so impatient of heat, that, in summer, they are only to be found under the shades of caverns in the rocks, among masses of congealed snow and ice, or in elevated forests on the northern declivities of the most scabrous mountains, where the rays of the sun seldom penetrate. They pasture in the mornings and evenings, and seldom during the day. They traverse the rocks and precipices with great facility, where the dogs dare not follow them. There is nothing more worthy of admiration than to see these animals climbing or descending inaccessible rocks. They neither mount nor descend perpendicularly, but in an oblique line. When descending, particularly, they throw themselves down across a rock which is nearly perpendicular, and of 20 or 30 feet in height, without having a single prop to support their feet. In descending, they strike their feet three or four times against the rock, till they arrive at a proper resting-place below. The spring of their tendons is so great, that, when leaping about among the precipices, one would imagine they had wings instead of limbs. It has been alleged by some, but without foundation, that the chamois, in climbing and descending rocks, supports himself by his horns. It is by the strength and agility of his limbs that the chamois is enabled to climb and descend rocks. His legs are very free and tall; those behind are somewhat longer, and always crooked, which favours their springing to a great distance; and, when they throw themselves from a height, the hind legs receive the shock, and perform the office of two springs in breaking the fall. In great snows, and during the rigour of winter, the chamois goats inhabit the lower forests, and live upon pine leaves, the buds of trees, bushes, and such green or dry herbs as they can find by scratching off the snow with their feet. The forests that delight them most, are those which are very full of rocks and precipices. The hunting of the chamois is very difficult and laborious. The mode most in use is to kill them by surprise. The hunters conceal themselves behind rocks or large stones, taking care that the wind blows opposite to them, and, when a favourable opportunity occurs, shoot them with musket-balls. They are likewise hunted in the same manner as stags and other animals, by posting some of the hunters in narrow passages, while others beat about to raise the game. Men are preferable for this purpose to dogs; for dogs too quickly disperse the animals, who fly off suddenly to the distance of four or five leagues.

Capra.

V. The DEPRESSA is an African goat, with small depressed horns, bent inwards, lying on the head. It is about the size of a kid; and the hair is long and pendulous.

VI. The REVERSA is likewise an African goat, with erect horns, and curved a little forwards. It is about the size of a kid of a year old. It inhabits Juda or Whidaw in Africa.

VII. The GAZELLA has long, erect, cylindrical horns, annulated near the base. It inhabits Egypt, the Cape, Arabia, the Levant, and India, dwelling in the plains.

VIII. The CERVICAPRA, with plated cylindrical horns, inhabits Barbary. The hair near the horns is longer than in any other part of the body. The females want horns. Mr Hasselquist gives the following account of this species: "The cervicapra is larger, swifter, and wilder, than the common rock-goat, and can scarcely be taken without a falcon. It is met with near Aleppo. I have seen a variety of this which is common in the East, and the horns appear different; perhaps it is a distinct species. This animal loves the smoke of tobacco; and, when caught alive, will approach the pipe of the huntsman, though otherwise more timid than any animal. This is perhaps the only creature, besides man, that delights in the smell of a poisonous and stinking plant. The Arabians hunt it with a falcon (*falco gentilis*, Lin.) I had an excellent opportunity of seeing this sport near Nazareth in Galilee. An Arab, mounted on a swift courser, held the falcon in his hand, as huntsmen commonly do: when he espied the rock-goat on the top of a mountain, he let loose the falcon, which flew in a direct line like an arrow, and attacked the animal; fixing the talons of one of his feet into the cheek of the creature, and the other into its throat, extending his wings obliquely over the animal; spreading one towards one of its ears, and the other to the opposite hip. The animal, thus attacked, made a leap twice the height of a man, and freed himself from the falcon: but being wounded, and losing his strength and speed, he was again attacked by the falcon; which fixed the talons of both its feet into the throat of the animal, and held it fast, till the huntsman coming up, took it alive, and cut its throat; the falcon drinking the blood as a reward for his labour. A young falcon, which was learning, was likewise set to the throat of the goat: by this means are young falcons taught to fix their talons in the throat of the animal, as being the properest part; for should the falcon fix them in the creature's hip, or some other part of the body, the huntsman would not only lose his game, but his falcon also: for the animal, roused by the wound, which could not prove mortal, would run to the deserts and the tops of the mountains, whither its enemy, keeping its hold, would be obliged to follow; and, being separated from its master, must of course perish."

IX. The

Buck of Juda.

Angora Goat.

IX. The BEZOARTICA, or bezoar goat, is bearded, and has cylindrical, arched, and wholly annulated horns. It is a native of Persia. The bezoar is found in one of its stomachs, called *abomasus*. See BEZOAR and ABOMASUS.

X. The TARTARICA, or saiga of Buffon, has cylindrical, straight, annulated horns; the points inclining inward, the ends smooth; the other part surrounded with very prominent annuli; of a pale yellow colour, and the greatest part semipellucid; the cutting teeth are placed so loose in their sockets, as to move with the least touch. The male is covered with rough hair like the he-goat, and has a very strong smell; the female is smoother. The hair on the bottom of the sides and the throat is long, and resembles wool; that on the sides of the neck and head is hoary; the back and sides of a dirty white; the breast, belly, and inside of the thighs, of a shining white. The females are destitute of horns. These animals inhabit all the deserts from the Danube and Dnieper to the river Irtish, but not beyond. Nor are they ever seen to the north of 54 or 55 degrees of latitude. They are found therefore in Poland, Moldavia, about Mount Caucasus, and the Caspian Sea, and Siberia, in the dreary open deserts, where salt-springs abound, feeding on the salt, the acrid and aromatic plants of those countries, and grow in the summer-time very fat: but their flesh acquires a taste disagreeable to many people, and is scarcely eatable, until it is suffered to grow cold after dressing. The females go with young the whole winter; and bring forth in the northern deserts in May. They have but one at a time; which is singular, as the numbers of these animals are prodigious. The young are covered with a soft fleece, like new-dropt lambs, curled and waved. They are regularly migratory. In the rutting-season, late in autumn, they collect in flocks of thousands, and retire into the southern deserts. In the spring they divide into little flocks, and return northward at the same time as the wandering Tartars change their quarters.

They very seldom feed alone; the males feeding promiscuously with the females and their young. They rarely lie down all at the same time: but, by a providential instinct, some are always keeping watch; and when they are tired, they seemingly give notice to such as have taken their rest, who arise instantly, and as it were relieve the centinels of the preceding hours. They thus often preserve themselves from the attack of wolves, and from the surprise of the huntsmen. They are excessively swift, and will outrun the fleetest horse or gre-hound; yet partly through fear (for they are the most timid of animals), and partly by the shortness of their breath, they are very soon taken. If they are but bit by a dog, they instantly fall down, nor will they even offer to rise. In running they seem to incline on one side, and their course is so rapid that their feet seem scarcely to touch the ground. In a wild state they seem to have no voice. When brought up tame, the young emit a short sort of bleating, like sheep.

The males are most libidinous animals: the Tartars, who have sufficient time to observe them, report that they will copulate twenty times together; and that this ability arises from their feeding on a certain herb, which has most invigorating powers. When taken young, they may easily be made tame; but if caught when at full age, are so wild and so obstinate as to refuse all food. When they die, their muscles are quite flaccid. Capra.

They are hunted for the sake of their flesh, horns, and skins, which are excellent for gloves, belts, &c. The huntsmen always approach them against the wind, least they should smell their enemy; they also avoid putting on red or white clothes, or any colours which might attract their notice. They are either shot, or taken by dogs; or by the black eagle, which is trained to this species of falconry. Their best season is in September: at other times, the skins are penetrated by worms. The fat resembles that of mutton; in taste, like that of a buck: the head is reckoned the most delicate part.

XI. The AMMON, has semicircular, plain, white horns, and no beard. It is about the size of a ram, and is a native of Siberia.

XII. The ÆGAGRUS of Pallas, or Caucasan goat, has smooth black horns, sharply ridged on their upper parts, and hollowed on their outward sides. No vestiges of knots or rings, but on the upper surface are some wavy risings; bend much back, and are much hooked at the end, approaching a little at the points. On the chin is a great beard, dusky, mixed with chesnut. The forepart of the head is black, the sides mixed with brown; the rest of the animal grey, or grey mixed with rust-colour. Along the middle of the back, from the neck to the tail, is a black list; and the tail is black.

The female is either destitute of horns, or has very short ones. In size it is superior to the largest he-goats, but in form and agility resembles a stag: yet Monardus compares it to the he-goat, and says that it has the feet of the goat. They inhabit the lower mountains of Caucasus and Taurus, all Asia Minor, and perhaps the mountains of India. They abound on the inhospitable hills of Laar and Khorazan in Persia; and according to Monardus are also found in Africa. It is an animal of vast agility. Monardus was witness to the manner of its saving itself from injury by falling on its horns; for he saw that which he describes leap from a high tower, precipitating itself on its horns; then springing on its legs, and leaping about, without receiving the least harm. This is one of the animals which yields the once-valued alexipharmic, the Bezoar-stone; which is a concretion formed of many coats, incrusting a nucleus of small pebble, stones of fruits, bits of straw, or buds of trees. The incrusting coats are created from the vegetable food of the animals, especially the rich, dry, and hot herbs of the Persian and Indian mountains. Its virtues are now exploded, and it is reckoned only an absorbent, and that of the weakest kind.

XIII. The GNOU, with scabrous horns, and thick at the base, bending forward close to the head, then suddenly reverting upwards. The mouth is square; the nostrils covered with broad flaps. From the nose, half way up the front, is a thick oblong-square brush of long stiff black hairs reflected upwards, on each side of which the other hairs are long, and point closely down the cheeks. Round the eyes are disposed in a radiated form several strong hairs. The neck is short, and a little arched. On the top a strong and upright mane, reaching from the horns beyond the shoulders. On the

Capra.

the chin is a long white beard; and on the gullet a very long pendulous bunch of hair. On the breast, and between the fore-legs, the hairs are very long and black. The tail reaches to the first joint of the legs, and is full of hair like that of a horse, and quite white. The body is thick; and covered with smooth short hair of a rust brown colour tipt with white. The legs are long, elegant, and slender, like those of a stag. On each foot is only a single spurious or hind hoof.—It is a strange compound of animals; having a rust head like that of an ox; body and tail, like a horse; legs like a stag; and the sinus lacrymalis of an antelope. The ordinary size of it is about that of a common galloway; the length of it being somewhat above five, and height of it rather more than four feet.—These animals inhabit in great numbers the fine plains of the great Namaquas, far north of the Cape of Good Hope, extending from S. lat. 25. to 28. 42. where Africa seems at once to open its vast treasures of hoofed quadrupeds. It is an exceedingly fierce animal; on the sight of any body it usually drops its head, and puts itself into an attitude of offence; and will dart with its horns against the pales of the inclosure towards the persons on the outside; yet it will afterwards take the bread which is offered. It will often go upon its knees, run swiftly in that singular posture, and furrow the ground with its horns and legs. The Hottentots call it *Gnu* from its voice. It has two notes, one resembling the bellowing of an ox, the other more clear. It is called an ox by the Europeans.

XIV. The Dorcas, or antelope, has cylindrical annulated horns, bent backward, contorted, and arising from the front between the eyes. It is a native of Africa and Mexico. These animals are of a most elegant and active make; of a restless and timid disposition; extremely watchful; of great vivacity; remarkably swift; exceedingly agile; and most of their boundings so light, so elastic, as to strike the spectator with astonishment. What is very singular, they will stop in the middle of their course, for a moment gaze at their pursuers, and then resume their flight.

As the chace of these animals is a favourite diversion with the eastern nations, from that may be collected proofs of the rapid speed of the antelope tribe. The gre-hound, the fleetest of dogs, is unequal in the course; and the sportsman is obliged to call in the aid of the falcon trained to the work, to seize on the animal and impede its motions, to give the dogs time to overtake it. In India and Persia a sort of leopard is made use of in the chace: this is an animal that takes its prey, not by swiftness of foot, but by the greatness of its springs, by motions similar to that of the antelope; but should the leopard fail in its first essay, the game escapes.

The fleetness of this animal was proverbial in the country it inhabited even in the earliest times: the speed of Asahel is beautifully compared to that of the tzebi; and the Gadites were said to be as swift as the roes upon the mountains. The sacred writers took their similes from such objects as were before the eyes of the people they addressed themselves to. There is another instance drawn from the same subject: the disciple raised to life at Joppa was supposed to have been called *Tabitha*, i. e. *Dorcas*, or the *Antelope*, from the beauty of her eyes; and this is still a common comparison in the east: *Aine el Czazel*, or, "You have eyes of an Antelope," is the greatest compliment that can be paid to a fine woman.

Some species of the antelopes form herds of 2000 or 3000, while others keep in small troops of five or six. They generally reside in hilly countries; though some inhabit plains: they often browse like the goat, and feed on the tender shoots of trees, which gives their flesh an excellent flavour. This is to be understood of those that are taken in the chase; for those that are fattened in houses are far less delicious. The flesh of some species are said to taste of musk, which perhaps depends on the qualities of the plants they feed on.

Mr Pennant makes the antelope a distinct genus of animals, forming a link between the goat and the deer; with the first of which they agree in the texture of the horns, which have a core in them, and they never cast them; with the last, in the elegance of their form, and great swiftness. He distinguishes several species, among which he ranks the *gazella*, the *cervicapra*, the *bubartica*, and the *tartarica* of Linnæus, described above, vii. viii. ix. x. with the *moschus grimmia* of the same author. See Moschus.

The other species of antelopes distinguished by zoologists are;

1. Kevella of Pallas, or flat-horned antelope, has horns twelve inches long, flattened on their sides, inclining first backwards, bending in the middle, and then reverting forwards at their ends, and annulated with from fourteen to eighteen rings: the upper side of the body is reddish brown; lower part and buttocks are white: the size equal to a small roebuck. They inhabit Senegal; where they live in great flocks, are easily tamed, and are excellent meat.

2. The corine antelope, with very slender horns, six inches long, surrounded with circular *rugæ*: on each side of the face is a white line; beneath that, is one of black: the neck, body, and flanks are tawny; belly and inside of the thighs white: on the knees is a tuft of hair. It is less than a roebuck, and inhabits Senegal.

3. The nagor, or red antelope, with horns 5½ inches long; one or two slight rings at the base: ears much longer than the horns: hair stiff and bright; in all parts of a reddish colour, palest on the chest: tail very short. Inhabits Senegal and the Cape; where it is very frequent, and is a common food.

4. The dama or swift antelope (*le Nanguer*, Buff.), with round horns, eight inches long, reverting at their ends. The general colour is tawny; but this species varies in that particular. It inhabits Senegal; and is easily tamed. It is very swift: Ælian compares its flight to the rapidity of a whirlwind.

5. The elk-antelope of Sparman (Indian antelope of Pennant), has thick straight horns, marked with two prominent spiral ribs near two thirds of their length, smooth towards their end; some above two feet long. The head is of a reddish colour, bounded on the cheeks by a dusky line. The forehead is broad; the nose pointed. On the forehead is a stripe of long loose hairs; and on the lower part of the dewlap, a large tuft of black hair. Along the neck and back, from head to tail, is a black short mane: the rest of the body is of a bluish grey, tinged with red. The tail does not reach to the first joint of the leg; is covered with short ci-

Capra.

cinereous hair; and the end tufted with long black hairs. The hoofs are short, surrounded at their junction with the legs by a circle of black hairs. The height to the shoulders is five feet. It is thick bodied and strongly made; but the legs are slender. It wants the *sinus lacrymales*. The females are horned like the males.—The Caffres call this species *empofos* and *pofo*. The Dutch of the Cape call it the *eland* or *elk*. M. de Buffon, by mistake, calls this the *condoma*, which he ought to have bestowed on his *condome*. It inhabits India, Congo, and the southern parts of Africa. They live in herds; but the old males are often solitary. They grow very fat, especially about the breast and heart; so that they are easily caught; and when pofured, will sometimes fall dead in the chace. They are slow runners; when roused, always go against the wind, nor can the hunters (even if they front the herd) divert them from their course. The flesh is fine-grained, very delicious, and juicy. The hide is tough: the Hottentots make tobacco-pipes of the horns.

6. The cervine antelope, or *antelope bubalis* of Pallas, with horns bending outward and backward, almost close at their base, and distant at their points; twisted and annulated; very strong and black: the head is large, and like that of an ox: the eyes are placed very high, and near to the horns: the form of the body is a mixture of the stag and heifer; height to the top of the shoulders four feet: the tail is rather more than a foot long, asinine, and terminated with a tuft of hair: the colour a reddish brown; white about the rump, the inner side of the thighs, and lower part of the belly: a dark space occupies the top of the back, the front of the upper part of the fore legs, and hinder part of the thighs. It inhabits Barbary, and probably other parts of Africa, being also found towards the Cape of Good Hope. It is the *bekker el wash* of the Arabs, according to Dr Shaw; who says, that its young quickly grow tame, and herd with other cattle. Mr Forskal mentions it among the Arabian animals of an uncertain genus, by the name of *bakar wahh*. This is the bubalus of the ancients; not the buffalo, as later writers have supposed. The Dutch of the Cape call this species *bonteboft*. They go in great herds; few only are solitary. They gallop seemingly with a heavy pace, yet go swiftly. They drop on their knees to fight like the white-footed antelope or nil-ghau, and the bosch-bok, after-described. The flesh is fine grained, but dry.—Mr Sparman informs us, that in this animal there is a pore one line in diameter, an inch or an inch and a half below and before the internal angle of the eye. From this pore, which is the aperture of a caruncle that lies below, there is secreted a matter almost like ear-wax, which he observed the Hottentots kept in a piece of skin as a rare and excellent medicine; on the dried skin of the animal, this pore is scarcely to be discerned. This Mr Sparman supposes is the reason why so great and accurate a zoologist as M. Pallas (who describes it in his *Spicilegia* under the denomination of *Antilope bubalis*) makes no mention of this pore, as he made his descriptions chiefly from the dried skins of this animal. The use of this pore, which is also found in the deer, is for affording freer respiration, a circumstance so essential to beasts of chase. See CERVUS.

7. The springer, with slender horns, annulated half way, and twice contorted. The ears very long and dusky. The face, cheeks, nose, chin, and throat, are white. The whole upper side of the neck, part of the lower, the back, sides, and outside of the limbs, are of a pale yellowish brown. The chest, belly, and inside of the limbs, are white; the sides and belly divided by a broad band of chesnut, which runs down part of the shoulders. The tail reaches to the first joint of the leg; the upper part white; the lower black, and furnished with long hair. The buttocks are white; and from the tail half way up the back is a stripe of white, expansible at pleasure. This elegant species weighs about fifty pounds, and is rather less than a roebuck. It inhabits the Cape of Good Hope, where it is called the *spring-bock*, from the prodigious leaps it takes on the sight of any body. When alarmed, it has the power of expanding the white space about the tail into the form of a circle, which returns to its linear form when the animal is tranquil. These animals migrate annually from the interior parts in small herds, and continue in the neighbourhood of the Cape for two or three months: then join companies, and go off in troops consisting of many thousands, covering the great plains for several hours in their passage. They are attended in their migrations by numbers of lions, hyaenas, and other wild beasts, which make great destruction among them. They are excellent eating, and with other antelopes are the venison of the Cape. Mr Mason* informs us, that they also make periodical migrations, in seven or eight years, in herds of many hundred thousands, from the north, as he supposes from the interior parts of *Terra de Natal*. They are compelled to it by the excessive drought which happens in that region, when sometimes there does not fall a drop of rain for two or three years. These animals in their course desolate Caffraria, spreading over the whole country, and not leaving a blade of grass. Lions attend them; where one of those beasts of prey are, his place is known by the vast void visible in the middle of the timorous herd.

8. The striped antelope, has smooth horns, twisted spirally, and compressed sideways, with a ridge on one side following the wreaths: they consist of three bends; and are sometimes four feet and a half long measured in a straight line. They are naturally of a dusky colour, and wrinkled; but are generally brought over highly polished. The females are destitute of horns. In the upper jaw is a hard horny substance, disposed in ridges. The length of the animal is nine feet; the legs are slender: the general colour is of a reddish cast, mixed with grey; and from the tail, along the top of the back, to the shoulders, is a white stripe; from which are seven others, four pointing towards the thighs, and three towards the belly; but they vary in number of stripes. On the upper part of the neck is a short mane; beneath the neck, from the throat to the breast, are some long hairs hanging down. It inhabits the Cape of Good Hope, where it is called *coedoes*, and is said to leap to a most astonishing height. This species wants the *sinus lacrymales*.

9. The bosch-bok, or wood-goat of the Cape, a species of antelope, according to Mr Sparman, unknown to all the cultivators of natural history, whether ancient or modern, till he described it in the memoirs of the Swedish academy for the year 1780, quarter 3d, by the name of *antilope sylvatica*. This animal has

* Phil. Trans. vol. lxvi. p. 303.

Capra.

has obtained the name it goes by, in conſequence of its being the only one among the gazels in Africa, which may be properly ſaid to live in the woods and groves. In fine, the boſch-bok is ſomewhat above two feet and a half high. The horns are ten inches and a half long; the ears half the length of the horns, or five inches.—The horns are black, in ſome meaſure triangular, and at the ſame time wreathed, ſo that both the ſides and angles have ſomewhat of a ſpiral turn. At bottom they are rather rough, in conſequence of a ſet of almoſt innumerable wavy-rings; which, however, are not elevated much above the ſurface. At top they are conical and ſharp-pointed, and in that part as ſmooth as though they had been poliſhed. The teeth of this animal are like thoſe of other antelopes. It has no fore teeth or *inciſores* except in the lower jaw, where it has eight.—There is no *porus ceriferus* in this, as there is in ſome other antelopes. The hairs on the head are very ſhort and fine; afterwards they become more rough and rugged, reſembling goats hair more than that of gazels or harts. Forwards on the neck, breaſt, ſides, and belly, they are an inch and a half or two inches long. On the ridge of the neck, and ſo on all along that of the back, they are three or four inches in length, ſo as to form a kind of mane there, terminating in a tail about a finger's breadth long. On the hind part of the thighs and buttocks likewiſe, the hairs are eight inches long; the legs and feet are ſlender, and covered with ſhort hairs; the fetlock-joints are ſmall; the noſe and under-lip are decorated with black whiſkers about an inch long. The predominant colour in this animal is dark-brown, which occupies the principal part of the ſides, the back, the upper part of the tail, the upper part of the cheſt and fore-ribs, and the fore-part of the belly. A ſtill darker brown, bordering upon black, is diſcoverable on the outſide of the ſhoulders, and ſome part of the fore-ribs. The fore-part of the noſe, from the eyes to the muzzle, is of a ſoot colour. The ears are likewiſe as black as ſoot on the outſide, but on the inſide grey; and both outwards and inwards covered with hairs ſtill ſhorter than thoſe on the head; excepting half the fore-part of the lower edge, where the hairs are white and half an inch long. Divers ſmall white ſpots, from nine to twelve in all, are ſeen on each of the haunches and on the ſides near them. A narrow line of long white hairs extends from the neck all along the back and tail, in the midſt of the long brown hairs already deſcribed. From the chine of the back to the ſides run five white parallel ſtreaks, which, however, are only diſcoverable by a cloſe inſpection.

This creature does much miſchief to the vineyards and kitchen-gardens of the Cape coloniſts; and it ſhows a great deal of craft and artifice in avoiding the ſnares and traps ſet for it, as well as the ambuſcades of the ſportſmen. As the *boſch-bok* runs but ſlowly, it ſometimes happens that he is caught by dogs. When he ſees there is no other reſource, he puts himſelf in a poſture of defence; and when he is going to butt, kneels down, like the white-footed antelope and the hartbeeſt. The coloniſts are not very fond of hunting him in this manner, as the beaſt on this occaſion generally ſells his life at a very dear rate, by goring and killing ſome of their beſt and moſt ſpirited hounds. This creature's horns, which are its chief defence, ſometimes alſo prove its bane, by being entangled in the buſhes and ſmall branches of trees, which thus ſtop the beaſt in its flight. In ſome meaſure to avoid this, it carries its noſe horizontally and ſtraight forward while it runs; ſo that its horns lie, as it were, directly on its neck: notwithſtanding which, their horns are generally worn away a little on the fore part, and thus acquire ſome degree of poliſh.—This ſpecies of antelope is monogamous, or keeps in pairs. It is ſwifter in woodlands than the dogs, which likewiſe ſooner loſe ſcent of him there. The female, which is without horns, and on that account runs about in the foreſt more free and unimpeded, does not ſuffer herſelf ſo eaſily to be hunted out of the woods, having there, as well as on the plains, a more certain defence againſt the dogs in her legs, than the male has in his horns, eſpecially as ſhe is not ſo bulky and heavy as the male. Her breaſt is ſaid to be very plump and fleſhy, but the fleſh in general is not very tender.

10. The leucoryx with the noſe thick and broad, like that of a cow; the ears ſomewhat ſlouching; body clumſy and thick: The horns long, very ſlightly incurvated, ſlender, annulated part of the way; black, pointed. The tail reaching to the firſt joint of the legs, and tufted. The colour is in all parts a ſnowy whiteneſs, except the middle of the face, ſides of the cheeks, and limbs, which are tinged with red.—This ſpecies is about the ſize of a Welch runt; and inhabits Gow Bahrein, an iſle in the gulph of Baſſora.

11. The picta, white-footed antelope, or nyl-ghau; with ſhort horns, bending a little forward; ears large, marked with two black ſtripes; a ſmall black mane on the neck, and half way down the back: a tuft of long black hairs on the fore-part of the neck; above that, a large ſpot of white; another between the fore-legs on the cheſt: one white ſpot on each fore-foot; two on each hind-foot; the tail is long, tufted with black hairs. The colour of the male is a dark grey. The female is of a pale brown colour; with a mane, tuft, and ſtriped ears, like the male; on each foot three tranſverſe bands of black and two of white: It is deſtitute of horns. The height to the top of the ſhoulders is four feet and an inch; the length from the bottom of the neck to the anus, four feet. The head is like that of a ſtag; the legs are delicate.—Theſe animals inhabit the diſtant and interior parts of India, remote from our ſettlements. They are brought down as curioſities to the Europeans, and have of late years been frequently imported into England. In the days of Aurenge Zebe, they abounded between Delhi and Lahor, on the way to Cachemire. They were called *nyl-ghau*, or *blue* or *grey bulls*; and were one of the objects of chace, with that mighty prince, during his journey. They were incloſed by his army of hunters within nets, which being drawn cloſer and cloſer, at length formed a ſmall precinct: into this the king, his omrahs, and hunters, entered, and killed the beaſts with arrows, ſpears, or muſkets; and ſometimes in ſuch numbers, that Aurenge Zebe uſed to ſend quarters as preſents to all his great people. They are uſually very gentle and tame, will feed readily, and lick the hands which give them food. In confinement they will eat oats, but prefer graſs and hay; are very fond of wheaten bread; and when thirſty, they will drink

two

The Swift Antilope
The Gnu
Elk Antilope

CAPRA.
Plate CXXIV.
The White footed Antilope.
Female.
Male.

two gallons at a time. They are faid to be at times very vicious and fierce. When the males fight, they drop on their knees at a diftance from one another, make their approaches in that attitude, and when they come near, fpring and dart at each other. They will often, in a ftate of confinement, fall into that pofture without doing any harm. They will, notwithftanding, attack mankind unprovoked. A labourer, who was looking over fome pales which inclofed a few of them, was alarmed by one of the males flying at him like lightning; but he was faved by the intervention of the woodwork, which it broke to pieces, and at the fame time one of its horns.—They have bred in England. They are fuppofed to go nine months with young, and have fometimes two at a birth.

11. The ftriped or harneffed antelope (*le guib*, Buff.), has ftraight horns nine inches long, pointing backwards, with two fpiral ribs. The general colour is a deep tawny; but the fides are moft fingularly marked with two tranfverfe bands of white, croffed by two others from the back to the belly; the rump with three white lines pointing downwards on each fide; and the thighs are fpotted with white. The tail is ten inches long, covered with long rough hairs.—It inhabits the plains and woods of Senegal, living in large herds. It is frequent at the Cape, where it is called the *bonte-bok*, or *fpotted goat*.

Capra-Saltans, in meteorology, a fiery meteor or exhalation fometimes feen in the atmofphere. It forms an inflected line, refembling in fome meafure the caperings of a goat; whence it has its name.

CAPRALA, an ifle of Italy, in the Tufcan fea, to the north-eaft of Corfica, on which it depends. It is pretty populous, and has a ftrong caftle for its defence. It is about 15 miles in circumference. E. Long. 11. 5. N. Lat. 43. 15.

CAPRARIA, in botany: A genus of the angiofpermia order, belonging to the didynamia clafs of plants; and in the natural method ranking under the 40th order, *Perfonatæ*. The calyx is quinquepartite; the corolla campanulated, quinquefid, with acute fegments; the capfule bivalved, bilocular, and polyfpermous. There is but one fpecies, the biflora, which is a native of the warm parts of America. Being a troublefome weed, and without beauty, it is never cultivated, except in botanic gardens for the fake of variety.

CAPRAROLA, one of the moft magnificent palaces in Italy, feated on a hill, in Ronciglione, whofe foot is watered by the river Tiveia. It was built by cardinal Farnefe; and has five fronts, in the middle of which is a round court, though all the rooms are fquare, and well proportioned. It is 27 miles north-weft of Rome.

CAPREÆ. See Capri.

CAPREOLUS (Elias), an excellent civilian, and learned hiftorian, born in Brefcia in Italy, wrote an hiftory of Brefcia, and other works: died in 1519.

CAPRI, (anciently *Capreæ*), a city and ifland at the entrance of the gulph of Naples, E. Long. 14. 50. N. Lat. 40. 45.—The ifland is only four miles long and one broad; the city is a bifhop's fee, fituated on a high rock at the weft end of the ifland. Capreæ was anciently famous for the retreat of the emperor Tiberius for feven years, during which he indulged himfelf in the moft fcandalous debaucheries*. Before Tiberius came hither, Capri had attracted the notice of Auguftus, as a moft eligible retreat, though in fight of populous cities, and almoft in the centre of the empire. His fucceffor preferred it to every other refidence; and in order to vary his pleafures, and enjoy the advantages as well as avoid the inconveniences of each revolving feafon, built twelve villas in different fituations, dedicated to the twelve greater gods: the ruins of fome of them are ftill to be feen: at Santa Maria are extenfive vaults and refervoirs; and on an adjoining brow are the remains of a light-houfe; two broken columns indicate the entrance of the principal court. According to Dion Caffius, this ifland was wild and barren before the Cæfars took it under their immediate protection: at this day a large portion of its furface is uncultivated and impracticable; but every fpot that will admit the hoe is induftrioufly tilled, and richly laden with the choiceft productions of agriculture. The odium attached to the memory of Tiberius proved fatal to his favourite abode; fcarce was his death proclaimed at Rome, when the fenate iffued orders for the demolition of every fabric he had raifed on the ifland, which by way of punifhment was thenceforward deftined to be a ftate prifon. The wife and fifter of Commodus were banifhed to its inhofpitable rocks, which were foon ftained with their blood. In the middle ages Capri became an appendage of the Amalfitan republic, and after the downfall of that ftate, belonged to the duchy of Naples. There ftood a pharos on this ifland, which, a few days before the death of Tiberius, was overthrown by an earthquake.

* See Tiberius.

CAPRIATA (Peter John), a civilian and hiftorian, was born at Genoa. He wrote, in Italian, the hiftory of the wars of Italy; an Englifh tranflation of which was printed in London in 1663.

CAPRICORN, in aftronomy, one of the 12 figns of the zodiac. See Astronomy, n° 404.

The ancients accounted Capricorn the tenth fign; and when the fun arrived thereat, it made the winter folftice with regard to our hemifphere: but the ftars having advanced a whole fign towards the eaft, Capricorn is now rather the 11th fign; and it is at the fun's entry into Sagittary that the folftice happens, though the ancient manner of fpeaking is ftill retained.

This fign is reprefented on ancient monuments, medals, &c. as having the forepart of a goat and the hindpart of a fifh, which is the form of an Ægipan; fometimes fimply under the form of a goat.

Tropic of Capricorn, a leffer circle of the fphere, which is parallel to the equinoctial, and at 23° 30′ diftance from it fouthwards; paffing through the beginning of Capricorn.

CAPRIFICATION, a method ufed in the Levant, for ripening the fruit of the domeftic fig-tree, by means of infects bred in that of the wild fig-tree.

The moft ample and fatisfactory accounts of this curious operation in gardening are thofe of Tournefort and Pontedera: the former, in his Voyage to the Levant, and in a Memoir delivered to the academy of fciences at Paris in 1705; the latter, in his *Anthologia*. The fubftance of Tournefort's account follows: "Of the thirty fpecies or varieties of the domeftic fig-tree which are cultivated in France, Spain, and Italy, there

are

Caprification.

are but two cultivated in the Archipelago. The first species is called *ornos*, from the old Greek *erinos*, which answers to *caprificus* in Latin, and signifies a wild fig-tree. The second is the domestic or garden fig-tree. The former bears successively, in the same year, three sorts of fruit, called *fornites*, *cratitires*, and *orni*; which, though not good to eat, are found absolutely necessary towards ripening those of the garden-fig. These fruits have a sleek even skin; are of a deep green colour; and contain in their dry and mealy inside several male and female flowers placed upon distinct foot-stalks, the former above the latter. The *fornites* appear in August, and continue to November without ripening: in these are bred small worms, which turn to a sort of gnats nowhere to be seen but about these trees. In October and November, these gnats of themselves make a puncture into the second fruit, which is called *cratitires*. These do not show themselves till towards the end of September. The *fornites* gradually fall away after the gnats are gone: the *cratitires*, on the contrary, remain on the tree till May, and inclose the eggs deposited by the gnats when they pricked them. In May, the third sort of fruit, called *orni*, begins to be produced by the wild fig-trees. This is much bigger than the other two; and when it grows to a certain size, and its bud begins to open, it is pricked in that part by the gnats of the *cratitires*, which are strong enough to go from one fruit to another to deposit their eggs. It sometimes happens that the gnats of the *cratitires* are slow to come forth in certain parts, while the *orni* in those very parts are disposed to receive them. In this case, the husbandman is obliged to look for the *cratitires* in another part, and fix them at the ends of the branches of those fig-trees whose *orni* are in a fit disposition to be pricked by the gnats. If they miss the opportunity, the *orni* fall, and the gnats of the *cratitires* fly away. None but those that are well acquainted with the culture know the critical moment of doing this; and in order to know it, their eye is perpetually fixed on the bud of the fig; for that part not only indicates the time that the prickers are to issue forth, but also when the fig is to be successfully pricked: if the bud is too hard and compact, the gnat cannot lay its eggs; and the fig drops when the bud is too open.

"The use of all these three sorts of fruit is to ripen the fruit of the garden fig-tree, in the following manner. During the months of June and July, the peasants take the *orni*, at the time their gnats are ready to break out, and carry them to the garden fig-trees: if they do not nick the moment, the *orni* fall; and the fruit of the domestic fig-tree, not ripening, will in a very little time fall in like manner. The peasants are so well acquainted with these precious moments, that, every morning, in making their inspection, they only transfer to their garden fig-trees such *orni* as are well conditioned, otherwise they lose their crop. In this case, however, they have one remedy, though an indifferent one; which is, to strew over the garden fig-trees another plant in whose fruit there is also a species of gnats which answer the purpose in some measure."

The caprification of the ancient Greeks and Romans, described by Theophrastus, Plutarch, Pliny, and other authors of antiquity, corresponds in every circumstance with what is practised at this day in the Archipelago and in Italy. These all agree in declaring, that the wild fig-tree, *caprificus*, never ripened its fruit; but was absolutely necessary for ripening that of the garden or domestic fig, over which the husbandmen suspended its branches. The reason of this success has been supposed to be, that by the punctures of these insects the vessels of the fruit are lacerated, and thereby a greater quantity of nutritious juice derived thither. Perhaps, too, in depositing their eggs, the gnats leave behind them some sort of liquor proper to ferment gently with the milk of the figs, and to make their flesh tender. The figs in Provence, and even at Paris, ripen much sooner for having their buds pricked with a straw dipped in olive-oil. Plums and pears likewise, pricked by some insects, ripen much the faster for it; and the flesh round such puncture is better tasted than the rest. It is not to be disputed, that considerable changes happen to the contexture of fruits so pricked, just the same as to parts of animals pierced with any sharp instrument. Others have supposed that these insects penetrated the fruit of the tree to which they were brought, and gave a more free admission to the air, and to the sun. Linnæus explained the operation, by supposing that the insects brought the farina from the wild fig, which contained male flowers only, to the domestic fig, which contained the female ones. Hasselquist, from what he saw in Palestine, seemed to doubt of this mode of fructification. M. Bernard, in the Memoirs of the Society of Agriculture, opposes it more decidedly. He could never find the insect in the cultivated fig; and, in reality, it appeared to leave the wild fig, after the stamina were mature, and their pollen dissipated: besides, he adds, what they may have brought on their wings must be rubbed away, in the little aperture which they would form for themselves. At Malta, where there are seven or eight varieties of the domestic fig, this operation is only performed on these which ripen latest: the former are of a proper size, fine flavour, and in great abundance without it; so that he thinks the caprification only hastens the ripening. He examined the parts of fructification of the fig; and he observes, if this examination be made previous to the ripening, that round the eye of the fig, and in the substance of its covering, may be seen triangular dentated leaves, pressed one against another; and under these leaves are the stamina, whose pollen is destined for the impregnation of the grains, which fill the rest of the fruit. These male organs are much more numerous in the wild fig than in the domestic; and the stamina are found to contain a yellow dust, which may be collected when it is ripe. The wild figs, when ripe, are not succulent, and have no taste, though the grains are disposed in the same manner as in the other kind. The pith of the grain of the wild fruit serves as food to a species of the cynips, whose larva is white, till the moment of its transformation; and it is by an opening, in the direction of the pistil, that the insect penetrates the grain. From this account it is thought probable that the insect is only communicated by accident to the domestic fig, and that the flowers of this genus are sometimes hermaphrodites. But the number of hermaphrodite flowers being fewer on the cultivated than on the wild fig, the seeds are fecundated more certainly and quickly by the caprification; and every botanist knows, that when the impregnation is completed, the flower soon withers; while, if by any accident it is delayed, it continues in bloom much longer. This view of the subject, therefore, explains very completely the reason why, in Malta, the caprification is practised on the late kind of figs, because it hastens the formation and maturity of the fruit.

CAPRIMULGUS, Goat-sucker, or *Fern-owl*, in ornithology, a genus of birds belonging to the order of passeres. The beak is incurvated, small, tapering, and depressed at the base; the mouth opens very wide.

1. The Europæus, with the tubes of the nostrils hardly visible. It feeds on moths, gnats, dorrs, or chaffers; from which Charleton calls it a *dorr-hawk*, its food being entirely of that species of beetle during the month of July, the period of that insect's flight in this country. This bird migrates. It makes but a short stay with us: appears the latter end of May; and disappears, in the northern parts of our island, the latter end of August; but, in the southern, stays above a month later. It inhabits all parts of Britain from Cornwall to the county of Ross. Mr Scopoli seems to credit the report of their sucking the teats of goats, an error delivered down from the days of Aristotle. Its notes are most singular. The loudest so much resembles that of a large spinning wheel, that the Welsh call this bird *aderyn y droell*, or the wheel-bird. It begins its song most punctually on the close of day, sitting usually on a bare bough, with the head lower than the tail, the lower jaw quivering with the efforts. The noise is so very violent, as to give a sensible vibration to any little building it chances to alight on and emit this species of note. The other is a sharp squeak, which it repeats often; this seems a note of love, as it is observed to reiterate it when in pursuit of the female among the trees. It lays its eggs on the bare ground; usually two: they are of a long form, of a whitish hue, prettily marbled with reddish brown. The length of this bird is 10½ inches; extent 22. Plumage, a beautiful mixture of white, black, ash-colour, and ferruginous, disposed in lines, bars, and spots. The male is distinguished from the female by a great oval white spot near the end of the three first quill-feathers, and another on the outmost feathers of the tail. This is the only one of the genus which is found in Europe. A variety less in size, being only eight inches in length, inhabits Virginia, in summer: arrives there towards the middle of April, and frequents the mountainous parts, but will frequently approach the houses in the evening, where it settles on a rail or post, and cries for several times together very loud, somewhat like the word *whipperiwhip*, or *whip-poor-will*, the first and last syllables pronounced the loudest. After continuing in one place for some time, it flies to another, and does the same; sometimes four or five cry all together: this noise it begins just after sun-set, and continues at intervals till just before sun-rise. It does not catch insects always on the wing; for it frequently sits upon a convenient place, and leaps up after them as they fly by, and returns to the same spot again. It makes no nest, but lays the eggs, which are two in number, and of a dull green with dusky spots and streaks, on the bare ground in the open fields. Kalm says that the flesh is good to eat. Another variety, larger, inhabits Virginia and Carolina; where it is called the *rain-bird*, because it never appears in the day-time, except when the sky, being obscured with clouds, betokens rain. It is said to lay the eggs on the ground, and that they are not unlike those of the Lapwing.

2. The Americanus, has the tubes of the nostrils very conspicuous. It is a night bird, and is found in America.

There are several other species or varieties inhabiting different countries, and differently marked, but all nearly similar in their manners.

CAPRIOLES, in the manege, leaps that a horse makes in the same place without advancing, in such a manner, that, when he is at the height of the leap, he jerks out with his hinder legs even and near. It is the most difficult of all the high manege. It differs from a croupade, in this, that, in a croupade, a horse does not show his shoes; and from a ballotade, because in this he does not jerk out. To make a horse work well at caprioles, he must be put between two pillars, and taught to raise first his fore-quarters, and then his hind-quarters while his fore ones are yet in the air; for which end you must give him the whip and the poinson.

CAPSA (anc. geog.), a large and strong town of Numidia, situated amidst vast deserts, waste, uncultivated, and full of serpents, where Jugurtha kept his treasure. In his time it was taken and rased by Marius the Roman general, who put to death all the citizens capable of bearing arms, and sold the rest for slaves. It was, however, afterwards rebuilt by the Romans, and strongly fortified; but, on the decline of their empire, was taken and demolished a second time, by Occuba a famous Arab general. The walls of the citadel are still remaining, and are monuments of the ancient glory and strength of Capsa. They are 25 fathoms in height, and five in thickness, built of large square stones, and have now acquired the solidity and firmness of a rock. The walls of the town were rebuilt by the inhabitants since their first demolition; but were afterwards destroyed by Jacob Almansor, who sent a governor and troops into the province. In Marmol's time Capsa was very populous, and abounded with stately mosques and other structures of superb and elegant workmanship: but at present it is occupied by a poor and indigent people, fleeced and oppressed by the Tunese government. In the very centre of the city stands an inclosed fountain, which both supplies the people with drink, and affords them an agreeable bath. The adjacent country is now cultivated, and produces several kinds of fruits; but the climate is unhealthy. The inhabitants are remarkable for their peevishness of temper. Both men and women dress handsomely except their feet, which they cover with coarse shoes of bungling workmanship, and made of the rough skins of wild beasts, equally inconvenient and unbecoming. E. Long. 9. 3. N. Lat. 33. 15.

CAPSARIUS, from *capsa*, satchel, in antiquity, a servant who attended the Roman youth to school, carrying a satchel with their books in it, sometimes also called librarius.

Capsarius was also an attendant at the baths, to whom persons committed the keeping of their clothes.

Capsarius (from *capsa*, "a chest,"), among the Roman bankers, was he who had the care of the money-chest or coffer.

CAPSICUM, or Guinea-pepper: A genus of the monogynia order, belonging to the pentandria class of plants; and in the natural method ranking under the 28th order, *Luridæ*. The corolla is verticillated, and the fruit a sapless berry.

Capsicum.

Species. 1. The annuum, with oblong fruit, is the common long-podded capsicum commonly cultivated in the gardens. Of this there is one kind with red, and another with yellow fruit; and of these there are several varieties, differing only in the size and figure of their fruit. 2. The tetragonum, commonly called *bell-pepper*. The fruit of this is red, and is the only kind proper for pickling, the skin being tender; whereas those of the other sorts are thin and tough. The pods are from an inch to an inch and half or two inches long; are very large, swelling, and wrinkled, flatted at the top, where they are angular, and sometimes stand erect, at others grow downward. 3. The cerasiforme, with a round smooth fruit, doth not grow so tall as the other sorts, but spreads near the ground; the leaves come out in clusters, are of a shining green, and stand on long footstalks. The fruit is of a beautiful red, and of the size of a cherry. 4. The pyramidale, is a native of Egypt, and hath much narrower leaves than the other sorts. The pods always grow erect, and are produced in great plenty, so that the plants make a good appearance for three months in the winter. 5. The minimum, commonly called *bird-pepper*, rises with a shrubby stalk four or five feet high; the leaves are of a lucid green; the fruit grows at the division of the branches, standing erect; these are small, oval, and of a bright red; they are much more sharp and biting than those of the other sorts. Besides these species, botanists describe as many more; viz. the cordiforme, with heart-shaped fruit; the angulosum, with angular heart-shaped fruit; the olivaeforme, with oval fruit; the conoide, commonly called *hen-pepper*, with a conical red fruit growing erect; and the fruitescens, with small pyramidal fruit growing erect; commonly called *Barbary pepper*. These, however, have no remarkable properties different from the others.

Culture. The three first species are annual plants, and must be propagated by seeds sown on a hot-bed in the spring, and treated in the same manner with other exotics; they will however bear the open air, after being inured to it by degrees. The plants of the second sort, whose fruit is used for pickling, should be taken from the hot-bed, and planted in a rich spot of ground in a warm situation about a foot and an half asunder. They must be shaded till they have taken root, and afterwards daily watered in dry weather, which will greatly promote their growth and cause them to be more fruitful, and likewise enlarge the size of the fruit. By this management, three or four crops of fruit for pickling may be obtained the same year. The other sorts are more tender; and therefore must be planted in pots plunged in a moderate hot-bed, and sheltered under a frame.

Uses, &c. The second sort, as already observed, produces fruit fit for pickling; for which purpose they must be gathered before they arrive at their full size, while their rind is tender. They must be slit down on one side to get out the seeds, after which they should be soaked two or three days in salt and water; when they are taken out of this and drained, boiling vinegar must be poured on them in a sufficient quantity to cover them, and closely stopped down for two months; then they should be boiled in the vinegar to make them green; but they want no addition of any spice, and are the wholesomest and best pickle in the world. The tenth species is used for making what is called *cayan-butter*, or *pepper-pots*, by the inhabitants of America, and which they esteem the best of all the spices. The following is a receipt for making of a pepper-pot: "Take of the ripe seeds of this sort of capsicum, and dry them well in the sun; then put them into an earthen or stone pot, mixing flour between every stratum of pods; and put them into an oven after the baking of bread, that they may be thoroughly dried: after which they must be well cleansed from the flour; and if any of the stalks remain adhering to the pods, they should be taken off, and the pods reduced to a fine powder: to every ounce of this add a pound of wheat-flour, and as much leaven as is sufficient for the quantity intended. After this has been properly mixed and wrought, it should be made into small cakes, and baked in the same manner as common cakes of the same size: then cut them into small parts, and bake them again, that they may be as dry and hard as biscuit; which being powdered and sifted, is to be kept for use." This is prodigiously hot and acrimonious, setting the mouth as it were on fire. It is by some recommended as a medicine for flatulencies; but it is greatly to be doubted whether all those hot irritating medicines are not productive of more harm than good, in this country at least. If the ripe pods of capsicum are thrown into the fire, they will raise strong and noisome vapours, which occasion vehement sneezing, coughing, and often vomiting, in those who are near the place, or in the room where they are burnt. Some persons have mixed the powder of the pods with snuff, to give to others for diversion: but where it is in quantity, there may be danger in using it; for it will occasion such violent fits of sneezing, as may break the blood-vessels of the head.

Capsicum | Capstan.

CAPSQUARES, strong plates of iron which come over the trunnions of a gun, and keep it in the carriage. They are fastened by a hinge to the prize-plate, that they may lift up and down, and form a part of an arch in the middle to receive a third part of the thickness of the trunnions: for two-thirds are let into the carriage, and the other end is fastened by two iron wedges called the *fore-locks* and *keys*.

CAPSTAN, or CAPSTERN, a strong massy column of timber, formed like a truncated cone, and having its upper extremity pierced with a number of holes to receive the bars or levers. It is let perpendicularly down through the decks of a ship; and is fixed in such a manner, that the men, by turning it horizontally with their bars, may perform any work which requires an extraordinary effort.

A capstern is composed of several parts, where A is the barrel, *b* the whelps, *c* the drum-head, and *d* the spindle. The whelps rise out from the main body of the capstern like buttresses, to enlarge the sweep, so that a greater quantity of cable, or whatever rope encircles the barrel, may be wound about it at one turn, without adding much to the weight of the capstern. The whelps reach downwards from the lower part of the drum-head to the deck. The drum-head is a broad, cylindrical piece of wood resembling a mill-stone, and fixed immediately above the barrel and whelps. On the outside of this piece are cut a number of square holes parallel to the deck to receive the bars. The spindle or pivot *d*, which is shod with iron, is the axis

Plate CXXVII.

or foot upon which the capſtern reſts, and turns round in the ſaucer, which is a ſort of iron ſocket let into a wooden ſtock or ſtandard called the *ſtep*, reſting upon and bolted to the beam.

Beſides the different parts of the capſtern above explained, it is furniſhed with ſeveral appurtenances, as the *bars*, the *pins*, the *pawls*, the *ſwifter*, and the *ſaucer*, already deſcribed. The bars are long pieces of wood or arms, thruſt into a number of ſquare holes in the drum-head all round, in which they are as the radii of a circle, or the ſpokes in the nave of a wheel. They are uſed to heave the capſtern round, which is done by the men ſetting their breaſts againſt them, and walking about, like the machinery of a horſe-mill, till the operation is finiſhed.—The pins *e*, are little bolts of iron thruſt perpendicularly through the holes of the drum-head, and through a correſpondent hole in the end of the bar, made to receive the pins when the bars are fixed. They are uſed to confine the bars, and to prevent them from working out as the men heave, or when the ſhip labours. Every pin is faſtened to the drum-head with a ſmall iron chain; and that the bars may exactly fit their reſpective holes, they are all numbered.—The pawls *f*, n° 1. are ſituated on each ſide the capſtern, being two ſhort bars of iron, bolted at one end through the deck to the beams cloſe to the lower part of the whelps; the other end, which occaſionally turns round on the deck, being placed in the intervals of the whelps, as the capſtern turns round, prevents it from recoiling or turning back by any ſudden jerk of the cable, as the ſhip riſes on the ſea, which might greatly endanger the men who heave. There are alſo hanging pawls *gg*, n° 3. uſed for the ſame purpoſes, reaching from the deck above to the drum-head immediately below it. The ſwifter is a rope paſſed horizontally through holes in the outer end of the bars, and drawn very tight; the intent of this is to keep the men ſteady as they walk round when the ſhip rocks, and to give room for a greater number to aſſiſt by pulling upon the ſwifter itſelf.

The moſt frequent uſe of the capſtern is to heave in the cable, and thereby remove the ſhip or draw up the anchor. It is alſo uſed to wind up any weighty body, as the maſts, artillery, &c. In merchant-ſhips it is likewiſe frequently employed to diſcharge or take in the cargo, particularly when conſiſting of weighty materials that require a great exertion of mechanical powers to be removed.

There are commonly two capſterns in a man of war, the *main* and the *jeer* capſtern; the former of which has two drum-heads, and may be called a *double one*. This is repreſented in n° 3. The latter is repreſented in n° 2.

Formerly the bars of the capſtern went entirely thro' the head of it, and conſequently were more than double the length of the preſent ones; the holes were therefore formed at different heights, as repreſented in n° 1. But this machine had ſeveral inconveniences, and has long been entirely diſuſed in the navy. Some of theſe ſort of capſterns, however, are ſtill retained in merchant-ſhips, and are uſually denominated *crabs*. The ſituation of the bars in a crab, as ready for heaving, is repreſented in n° 4.

To Rig the Capstern, is to fix the bars in their reſpective holes, and thruſt in the pins, in order to confine them.—*Surge the Capstern*, is the order to ſlacken the rope heaved round upon it, of which there are generally two turns and a half about the barrel at once, and ſometimes three turns.—*To Heave the Capstern*, is to go round with it heaving on the bars, and drawing in any rope of which the purchaſe is created.—*To Come up the Capstern*, is to let go the rope upon which they had been heaving.—*To Pawl the Capstern*, is to fix the pawls to prevent it from recoiling during any pauſe of heaving.

CAPSULE, in a general ſenſe, denotes a receptacle or cover in form of a bag.

Capsule, among botaniſts, a dry hollow ſeed-veſſel or pericarpium, that cleaves or ſplits in ſome determinate manner. See Pericarpium.

This ſpecies of ſeed-veſſel is frequently fleſhy and ſucculent, like a berry, before it has attained maturity; but, in ripening, becomes dry, and often ſo elaſtic as to dart the ſeeds from their departments with conſiderable velocity. This elaſticity is remarkably conſpicuous in wood-ſorrel; balſam, *impatiens*; African ſpiræa, *dioſma*; *fraxinella*; *juſticia*; *ruellia*; *barleria*; *lathræa*; and many others.—The general aptitude or diſpoſition of this ſpecies of ſeed-veſſel to cleave or ſeparate for the purpoſe of diſperſing its ſeeds, diſtinguiſhes it not leſs remarkably than its texture from the pulpy or ſucculent fruits of the apple, berry, and cherry kind. This opening of the capſule for diſcharging its ſeeds when the fruit is ripe, is either at the top, as in moſt plants; at the bottom, as in triglochin; at the ſide through a pore or ſmall hole, as in campanula and orchis; horizontally, as in plantain, amaranthus, and anagallis; or longitudinally, as in convolvulus. All fruit that is jointed opens at every one of the joints, each of which contains a ſingle ſeed. Capſules, in ſplitting, are divided, externally, into one or more pieces, called by Linnæus *valves*. The internal diviſions of the capſules are called *cells*, *loculamenta*: theſe, in point of number, are exceedingly diverſified; ſome having only one cell, as the primroſe; and others many, as the water-lily. Hence a capſule is termed *unilocular*, *bilocular*, *trilocular*, &c. according as it has one, two, three, &c. cells or cavities.

Capsulæ Atrabilariæ, called alſo *glandulæ renales*, and *renes ſuccenturiati*. See Anatomy, n° 100.

CAPTAIN, a military officer, whereof there are ſeveral kinds, according to their commands.

Captain of a Troop or Company, an inferior officer who commands a troop of horſe or a company of foot, under a colonel. The duty of this officer is to be careful to keep his company full of able-bodied ſoldiers; to viſit their tents and lodgings, to ſee what is wanting; to pay them well; to cauſe them keep themſelves neat and clean in their clothes, and their arms bright. He has power in his own company of making ſerjeants, corporals, and lanſpeſades.

In the horſe and foot guards, the captains have the rank of colonels.

Captain-General, he who commands in chief.

Captain-Lieutenant, he who with the rank of captain, but the pay of lieutenant, commands a troop or company in the name and place of ſome other perſon who is diſpenſed with on account of his quality from performing the functions of his poſt.

Thus the colonel being uſually captain of the firſt

company of his regiment, that company is commanded by his deputy under the title of *captain-lieutenant*.

So in England, as well as in France, the king, queen, dauphin, princes, &c. have usually the title of captain of the guards, *gens d'armes*, &c. the real duty of which offices is performed by captain-lieutenants.

Captain Reformed, one who, upon the reduction of the forces, has his commission and company suppressed; yet is continued captain, either as second to another, or without any post or command at all.

Captain of a Ship of War, the officer who commands a ship of the line of battle, or a frigate carrying 20 or more cannon. The charge of a captain in his majesty's navy is very comprehensive, in as much as he is not only answerable for any bad conduct in the military government, navigation, and equipment of the ship he commands, but also for any neglect of duty or ill management in his inferior officers, whose several charges he is appointed to superintend and regulate.

On his first receiving information of the condition and quality of the ship he is appointed to command, he must attend her constantly, and hasten the necessary preparations to fit her for sea. So strict, indeed, are the injunctions laid on him by the lord high admiral, or commissioners of the admiralty, that he is forbid to lie out of his ship, from his arrival on board to the day of his discharge, unless by particular leave from the admiralty or from his commander in chief. He is enjoined to show a laudable example of honour and virtue to the officers and men; and to discountenance all dissolute, immoral, and disorderly practices, and such as are contrary to the rules of subordination and discipline; as well as to correct those who are guilty of such offences as are punishable according to the usage of the sea. He is ordered particularly to survey all the military stores which are sent on board, and to return whatever is deemed unfit for service. His diligence and application are required to procure his complement of men; observing carefully to enter only such as are fit for the necessary duty, that the government may not be put to unnecessary expence. When his ship is fully manned, he is expected to keep the established number of men complete, and superintend the muster himself if there is no clerk of the check at the port. When his ship is employed on a cruising station, he is expected to keep the sea the whole length of time previously appointed; but if he is compelled by some unexpected accident to return to port sooner than the time limited, he ought to be very cautious in the choice of a good situation for anchoring, ordering the master or other careful officers to sound and discover the depths of water and dangers of the coast. Previous to any possibility of an engagement with the enemy, he is to quarter the officers and men to the necessary stations according to their office and abilities, and to exercise them in the management of the artillery, that they may be more expert in time of battle. His station in the time of an engagement is on the quarter-deck: at which time he is expected to take all opportunities of annoying his enemy, and improving every advantage over him; to exhibit an example of courage and fortitude to his officers and crew; and to place his ship opposite to his adversary in such a position as that every cannon shall do effectual execution. At the time of his arrival in port, after his return from abroad, he is to assemble his officers, and draw up a detail of the observations that have been made during the voyage, of the qualities of the ship as to her trim, ballast, stowage, manner of sailing, for the information and direction of those who may succeed him in the command; and this account is to be signed by himself and officers, and to be returned to the resident commissioner of the navy at the port where the ship is discharged.

Captain of a Merchant-ship, he who has the direction of the ship, her crew, and lading, &c. In small ships and short voyages, he is more ordinarily called the *master*. In the Mediterranean, he is called the *patron*. —The proprietor of the vessel appoints the captain or master; and he is to form the crew, and choose and hire the pilots, mates, and seamen; though, when the proprietor and master reside on the same spot, they generally act in concert together.

Captain Bashaw, or *Capoudan Bashaw*, in the polity of the Turks, signifies the Turkish high admiral. He possesses the third office of the empire, and is invested with the same power at sea that the vizir has on shore. Soliman II. instituted this office in favour of the famous Barbarossa, with absolute authority over the officers of the marine and arsenal, whom he may punish, cashier, or put to death, as soon as he is without the Dardanelles. He commands in chief in all the maritime countries, cities, castles, &c. and, at Constantinople, is the first magistrate of police in the villages on the side of the Porte, and the canal of the Black-Sea. The mark of his authority is a large Indian cane, which he carries in his hand, both in the arsenal and with the army.—The captain-bashaw enjoys two sorts of revenues; the one fixed, the other casual. The first arise from a capitation of the islands in the Archipelago, and certain governments in Natolia and Galipoli. The latter consist in the pay of the men who die during a campaign; in a fifth of all prizes made by the beys; in the profits accruing from the labour of the slaves, whom he hires as rowers to the grand signior; and in the contributions he exacts in all places where he passes.

CAPTION, in Scots law, a writ issuing under his majesty's signet, in his majesty's name, obtained at the instance of a creditor in a civil debt, commanding messengers at arms and other officers of the law to apprehend and imprison the person of the debtor until he pay the debt.—It is also the name of a writ issued by the court of Session against the agents of the court, to return papers belonging to processes or law-suits, or otherwise to go to prison.

CAPTIVE, a slave, or a person taken from the enemy.

Formerly captives in war became the slaves of those who took them; and though slavery, such as obtained among the ancients, is now abolished, some shadow of it still remains in respect of prisoners of war, who are accounted the property of their captors, and have no right to liberty but by concession from them. —The Romans used their captives with great severity; their necks were exposed to the soldiers to be trampled on, and their persons afterwards sold by public auction. Captives were frequently burnt in the funeral piles of the ancient warriors, as a sacrifice to the infernal feral gods. Those of royal or noble blood had their heads shaven, and their hair sent to Rome to serve as decorations for female toys, &c. They were led in triumph loaded with chains through Rome, in the emperor's train, at least as far as the foot of the Capitoline mount, for they were not permitted to ascend the sacred hill, but carried thence to prison. Those of the prime quality were honoured with golden chains on their hands and feet, and golden collars on their necks. If they made their escape, or killed themselves, to avoid the ignominy of being carried in triumph, their images or effigies were frequently carried in their place.

CAPTIVITY, in a general sense, the state or condition of a captive.

Captivity, in sacred history, a punishment which God inflicted upon his people for their vices and infidelities. The first of these captivities is that of Egypt, from which Moses delivered them; after which, are reckoned six during the government of the judges; but the greatest and most remarkable were those of Judah and Israel, which happened under the kings of each of these kingdoms. It is generally believed, that the ten tribes of Israel never came back again after their dispersion; and Josephus and St Jerom are of this opinion: nevertheless, when we examine the writings of the prophets, we find the return of Israel from captivity pointed out in a manner almost as clear as that of the tribes of Benjamin and Judah: See Hosea i. 10, 11. Amos ix. 14. The captivities of Judah are generally reckoned four; the fourth and last of which fell in the year of the world 3416, under Zedekiah: and from this period begins the 70 years captivity foretold by Jeremiah.

Since the destruction of the temple by the Romans, the Hebrews boast that they have always had their heads or particular princes, whom they call *princes of the captivity*, in the east and west. The princes of the captivity in the east governed the Jews that dwelt in Babylon, Assyria, and Persia; and the princes of the captivity in the west governed those who dwelt in Judæa, Egypt, Italy, and in other parts of the Roman empire. He who resided in Judæa commonly took up his abode at Tiberias, and assumed the name of *Rosch-abbot*, "head of the fathers or patriarchs." He presided in assemblies, decided in cases of conscience, levied taxes for the expences of his visits, and had officers under him who were dispatched through the provinces for the execution of his orders. As to the princes of the captivity at Babylon, or the east, we know neither the original nor succession of them. It only appears that they were not in being before the end of the second century.

CAPTURE, a prize, or prey; particularly that of a ship taken at sea. Captures made at sea were formerly held to be the property of the captors after a possession of twenty-four hours; but the modern authorities require, that before the property can be changed, the goods must have been brought into port, and have continued a night *intra præsidia*, in a place of safe custody, so that all hope of recovering them was lost.

Capture also denotes an arrest or seizure of a criminal, debtor, &c. at land.

CAPUA, (anc. geog.) a very ancient city of Italy, in Campania, and capital of that district. It is famous for the abode of Hannibal the Carthaginian general after the battle of Cannæ, and where Livy accuses him, but unjustly, of having enervated himself with pleasures*. It still retains the name, and is the see of an archbishop. It is seated on the river Vulturno, in E. Long. 15. 5. N. Lat. 41. 7. The history of Capua is thus shortly deduced by Mr Swinburne. "It was a settlement of the Osci known before the foundation of Rome; as the amazing fertility of the land and a lucrative commerce poured immense wealth upon its inhabitants, it became one of the most extensive and magnificent cities in the world. With riches excessive luxury crept in, and the Capuans grew insolent; but by their effeminacy they soon lost the power of repelling those neighbouring nations which their insolence had exasperated: For this reason Capua was continually exposed to the necessity of calling in foreign aid, and endangering its safety by the uncommon temptations it offered to needy auxiliaries. The Roman soldiers sent to defend Capua were on the point of making it their prey, and often the voice of the Roman people was loud for a removal from the barren unwholesome banks of the Tiber to the garden of Italy, near those of the Volturno. Through well-founded jealousy of the ambition of Rome, or, as Livy and other partial writers term it, natural inconstancy, the Capuans warmly espoused the quarrel of Carthage: Hannibal made Capua his winter-quarters after the campaign of Cannæ; and there, if we are to believe historians, his rough and hitherto invincible soldiers were enervated by pleasure and indulence.

* See Carthage.

"When through a failure of supplies from Carthage Hannibal was under a necessity of remaining in Brutium, and leaving the Capuans to defend themselves, this city, which had been long invested, was surrendered at discretion to the consuls Appius Claudius and Q. Fulvius Flaccus. The senators were put to death, the nobles imprisoned for life, and all the citizens sold and dispersed. Vibius, the chief of Hannibal's friends, avoided this ignominious fate, and escaped from the cruel vengeance of the Romans by a voluntary death. —When the mob insisted upon the gates being thrown open to the enemy, Vibius assembled his steady associates, and sat down with them to a superb banquet, after which each of the guests swallowed a poisonous draught, and expired in full possession of their freedom. The buildings were spared by the victors; and Capua was left to be merely a harbour for the husbandmen of the plain, a warehouse for goods, and a granary for corn; but so advantageous a situation could not long be neglected; colonies were sent to inhabit it, and in process of time it regained a degree of importance.

"Genseric the Vandal was more cruel than the Roman conquerors had been; for he massacred the inhabitants, and burnt the town to the ground. Narses rebuilt it; but in 841 it was totally destroyed by an army of Saracens, and the inhabitants driven into the mountains. Some time after the retreat of these savage invaders, the Lombards ventured down again into the plain, but not deeming their force adequate to the defence of so large a circuit as the old city, they built themselves a smaller one on the river, and called it Capua.—They chose the site of Casilinum, famous in the second Punic war for the resistance made by its garrison against Hannibal. Since the foundation of the new city, old Capua has remained in ruins.

"In 856 Landulph formed here an independent earldom dismembered from the duchy of Benevento, and in the course of a few generations Capua acquired the title of a principality. In the 11th century, the Normans of Aversa expelled the Lombard race of princes, and Richard their chief became prince of Capua; the grandson of Tancred of Hauteville drove out the descendants of Richard, and united this state to the rest of his possessions.

"Capua is at present a neat little city, fortified according to the rules of modern art, and may be considered as the key of the kingdom; though far removed from the frontier, it is the only fortification that really covers the approach to Naples."

CAPUCHINS, religious of the order of St Francis in its strictest observance; deriving their name from *capuce*, or *capuchon*, a stuff cap, or cowl, wherewith they cover their heads. They are clothed with brown or grey; always bare-footed; are never to go in a coach, nor ever shave their beard.—The capuchins are a reform made from the order of minors, commonly called *cordeliers*, set on foot in the 16th century by Matthew Baschi, a religious observant of the monastery of Montefiascone; who, being at Rome, was advertised several times from heaven, to practise the rule of St Francis to the letter. Upon this he made application to pope Clement in 1525; who gave him permission to retire into a solitude, with as many others as chose to embrace the strict observance. In 1528, they obtained the pope's bull. In 1529, the order was brought into complete form; Matthew was elected general, and the chapter made constitutions. In 1543, the right of preaching was taken from the capuchins by the pope: but in 1545 it was restored to them again with honour. In 1578, there were already 17 general chapters in the order of capuchins.

CAPUT, the head. See HEAD.

CAPUT *baroniae*, the head of the barony, in ancient customs, denotes the ancient or chief seat or castle of a nobleman, where he made his usual residence, and held his court; sometimes also called *caput honoris*, or the head of the honour. The caput baroniae could not be settled in dowry; nor could it be divided among the daughters, in case there were no son to inherit; but was to descend entire to the eldest daughter, *caeteris filiabus aliunde satisfactis*.

CAPUT *gallinaginis*, in anatomy, is a kind of septum, or spongious border, at the extremities or apertures of each of the *vesiculae seminales*; serving to prevent the seed coming from one side, from rushing upon, and so stopping, the discharge of the other.

CAPUT *lupinum*. Anciently an outlawed felon was said to have *caput lupinum*, and might be knocked on the head like a *wolf*, by any one that should meet him; because, having renounced all law, he was to be dealt with as in a state of nature, when every one that should find him might slay him: yet now, to avoid such inhumanity, it is holden that no man is intitled to kill him wantonly and wilfully; but in so doing he is guilty of murder, unless it is done in the endeavour to apprehend him.

CAPUT *Mortuum*, a Latin name given to fixed and exhausted residuums remaining in retorts after distillations. As these residuums are very different, according to the substances distilled, and the degree of heat employed, they are by the more accurate modern chemists particularly specified by adding a term denoting their qualities: as *earthy residuum*, *sharry residuum*, *saline residuum*, &c.

CARABINE, a fire-arm shorter than a musket, carrying a ball of 24 in the pound, borne by the light horse, hanging at a belt over the left shoulder. The barrel is two feet and an half long; and is sometimes furrowed spirally within, which is said to add to the range of the piece.

CARABINEERS, regiments of light horse, carrying longer carabines than the rest, and sometimes used on foot.

CARABUS, in zoology, a genus of insects belonging to the order of coleoptera, or the beetle kind. The feelers are bristly; the breast is shaped like a heart, and marginated; and the elytra are likewise marginated. There are 23 species of this genus, mostly distinguished by their colour. The most remarkable is the crepitans, or bombardier, with the breast, head, and legs, ferruginous or iron-coloured, and the elytra black. It keeps itself concealed among stones, and seems to make little use of its wings: when it moves, it is by a sort of jump; and whenever it is touched, one is surprised to hear a noise resembling the discharge of a musket, in miniature, during which a blue smoke may be perceived to proceed from its anus. The insect may be made at any time to play off its artillery, by scratching its back with a needle. If we may believe Rolander, who first made these observations, it can give 20 discharges successively. A bladder placed near the anus is the arsenal whence it derives its store, and this is its chief defence against an enemy, although the smoke emitted seems to be altogether inoffensive, except it be by causing a fright, or concealing its course. Its chief enemy is another species of the same genus, but four times larger: when pursued and fatigued, the bombardier has recourse to this stratagem, by lying down in the path of the large carabus, which advances with open mouth and claws to seize it; but, on the discharge of the artillery, suddenly draws back, and remains a while confused: during which the bombardier conceals himself in some neighbouring crevice; and if not happy enough to find one, the large carabus returns to the attack, takes the insect by the head, and tears it off. Plate CXXV.

CARACALLA (M. Antoninus Bassianus), emperor after his father Severus in 211, put the physicians to death for not dispatching his father as he would have had them. He killed his brother Geta; and put Papinianus to death, because he would not defend nor excuse his parricide. In short, it is said that 20,000 persons were massacred by his order. He married Julia, his father's widow. Going to Alexandria, he slew the inhabitants, and applied to the magicians and astrologers. At last, going from Edessa to Mesopotamia, one of his captains slew him, by order of Macrinus, who succeeded him. He died after he had reigned somewhat more than six years.

CARACALLA, in antiquity, a long garment, having a sort of capuchin, or hood a-top, and reaching to the heels; worn equally among the Romans by the men

and

and the women, in the city and the camp. Spartian and Xiphilian represent the emperor Caracalla as the inventor of this garment, and hence suppose the appellation *Caracalla* was first given him. Others, with more probability, make the caracalla originally a Gallic habit, and only brought to Rome by the emperor above mentioned, who first enjoined the soldiery to wear it. The people called it *antoniciana*, from the same prince, who had borrowed the name of Antoninus. The caracalla was a sort of cassock, or surtout. Salmasius, Scaliger, and after them Du-Cange, even take the name *casaque* to have been formed from that of *caracalla*, for *caracalla*. This is certain from St Jerom, that the caracalla, with a retrenchment of the capuchin, became an ecclesiastical garment. It is described as made of several pieces cut and sewed together, and hanging down to the feet; but it is more than probable there were some made shorter, especially out of Rome, otherwise we do not see how it could have fitted the soldiers purposes.

CARACCAS, a district of Terra Firma in South America, belonging to the Spaniards. The coast is rocky and mountainous, interspersed with small fertile valleys; subjected at certain seasons of the year to dry north-west winds, but blessed in general with a clear air and wholesome climate. A very great illicit trade is carried on by the English and Dutch with this province, notwithstanding all the vigilance of the Spaniards, who have scouts perpetually employed, and breast-works raised in all the valleys. A vast number of cacao-trees are cultivated in this province; and it is reckoned that the crop of cacao produced here amounts to more than 100,000 fanegas of 110 pounds each. The country of Santa Fe consumes 20,000; Mexico a little more; the Canaries a small cargo; and Europe from 50 to 60.000. The cultivation of the plant employs 10 or 12,000 negroes. Such of them as have obtained their liberty have built a little town called *Nirva*, into which they will not admit any white people. The chief town is likewise called *Caraccas*, and is situated in N. Lat. 10. 10. Dampier says it stands at a considerable distance from the sea; is large, wealthy, and populous; and extremely difficult of access, by reason of the steep and craggy hills over which an enemy must take his route. The commerce of this town, to which the bay of Guaira at two leagues distance serves for a harbour, was for a long time open to all the subjects of the Spanish monarchy, and is still so to the Americans; but the Europeans are not so well treated. In 1728 a company was formed at St Sebastian, which obtained an exclusive right of maintaining connections with this part of the new world. Four or five ships, which they dispatch every year, sail from thence, but they return to Cadiz.

CARACCI, (Lewis, Augustin, and Hannibal), three celebrated painters of the Lombard school, all of Bologna. Lewis was born in 1555; and was cousin-german to Augustin and Hannibal who were brothers, the sons of a taylor, who was yet careful to give them a liberal education. They were both disciples of their cousin Lewis. Augustin gained a knowledge of mathematics, natural philosophy, music, poetry, and most of the liberal arts; but, though painting was his principal pursuit, he learned the art of engraving from Cornelius Cort, and surpassed all the masters of his time. Hannibal, again, never deviated from his pencil. —These three painters, at length, having reaped all the advantages they could by contemplation and practice, formed a plan of association, continued always together, and laid the foundation of that celebrated school which has ever since been known by the name of *Caracci's academy*. Hither all the young students, who had a view of becoming masters, resorted to be instructed in the rudiments of painting; and here the Caracci taught freely, and without reserve, all that came. Lewis's charge was to make a collection of antique statues and bas-reliefs. They had designs of the best masters, and a collection of curious books on all subjects relating to their art; and they had a skilful anatomist always ready to teach what belonged to the knitting and motions of the muscles, *&c.* There were often disputations in the academy; and not only painters, but men of learned professions, proposed questions, which were always decided by Lewis. Every body was well received; and though stated hours were allotted to treat of different matters, yet improvements might be made at all hours by the antiquities and the designs which were to be seen.

The fame of the Caracci reaching Rome, the cardinal Farnese sent for Hannibal thither, to paint the gallery of his palace. Hannibal was the more willing to go, because he had a great desire to see Raphael's works, with the antique statues and bas-reliefs. The gusto which he took there from the ancient sculpture, made him change his Bolognian manner for one more learned but less natural in the design and in the colouring. Augustin followed Hannibal, to assist him in his undertaking of the Farnese gallery; but the brothers not rightly agreeing, Farnese sent Augustin to the court of the duke of Parma, where he died in the year 1602, being only 45 years of age. His most celebrated piece of painting is that of the communion of St Jerom, in Bologna.

In the mean while, Hannibal continued working in the Farnese gallery at Rome; and, after inconceivable pains and care, finished the paintings in the perfection in which they are now to be seen. He hoped that the cardinal would have rewarded him in some proportion to the excellence of his work, and the time it took him up, which was eight years; but he was disappointed. The cardinal, influenced by an ignorant Spaniard his domestic, gave him but a little above 200l. though it is certain he deserved more than twice as many thousands. When the money was brought him, he was so surprised at the injustice done him, that he could not speak a word to the person who brought it. This confirmed him in a melancholy to which his temper naturally inclined, and made him resolve never more to touch his pencil; which resolution he had undoubtedly kept, if his necessities had not compelled him to break it. It is said that his melancholy gained so much upon him, that at certain times it deprived him of the use of his senses. It did not, however, put a stop to his amours; and his debauches at Naples, whither he had retired for the recovery of his health, brought a distemper upon him of which he died in 1609, when he was 49 years of age. His veneration for Raphael was so great, that it was his deathbed request to be buried in the same tomb with him; which was accordingly done, in the pantheon or rotunda at Rome. There are extant se-

veral

veral prints of the bleffed Virgin, and fome other fubjects etched by the hand of this incomparable artift. He is faid to have been a friendly, plain, honeft, and open-hearted man; very communicative to his fcholars; and fo extremely kind to them, that he generally kept his money in the fame box with his colours, where they might have recourfe to either as they had occafion.

While Hannibal Caracci worked at Rome, Lewis was courted from all parts of Lombardy, efpecially by the clergy, to make pictures in their churches; and we may judge of his capacity and facility, by the great number of pictures he made, and by the preference that was given him to other painters. In the midft of thefe employments Hannibal folicited him to come and affift him in the Farnefe gallery; and fo earneftly, that he could not avoid complying with his requeft. He went to Rome; corrected feveral things in that gallery; painted a figure or two himfelf; and then returned to Bologna, where he died in 1619, aged 64.

CARACOL, in the manege, the half turn which an horfeman makes, either to the right or left.—In the army, the horfe always makes a caracol after each difcharge, in order to pafs the rear of the fquadron.

CARACOL, in architecture, denotes a ftair-cafe in a helix or fpiral form.

CARACOLI, a kind of metal of which the Caribbees, or natives of the Leffer Antilles, make a fort of ornament in the form of a crefcent, which they alfo call *caracoli*.—This metal comes from the main land; and the common opinion is, that it is a compound of filver, copper, and gold, fomething like the Corinthian brafs among the ancients. Thefe metals are fo perfectly mixed and incorporated together, that the compound which refults from them, it is faid, has a colour that never alters, how long foever it remains in the fea or under ground. It is fomewhat brittle; and they who work at it are obliged to mix a large proportion of gold with it, to make the compound more tough and malleable.

CARACT, or CARAT, the name of that weight which expreffes the degree of finenefs that gold is of. The word is alfo written, *carrall*, *carrat*, *karrall*, and *karrat*. Its origin is contefted: But the moft probable opinion is that of Kennet, who derives it from *caratta*, a term which anciently denoted any weight, and came not till of later days to be appropriated to that which expreffes the finenefs of gold and the gravity of diamonds.

Thefe carats are not real determinate weights, but only imaginary. The whole mafs, be the weight what it will, is conceived to be divided into 24 carats; and as many 24th parts as it contains of pure gold, it is called *gold of fo many carats*, or *fo many carats fine*. Thus, gold of 18 carats is a mixt, of which 18 parts is pure gold, and the other fix an inferior metal, &c. This is the common way of reckoning in Europe, and at the gold mines in the Spanifh Weft Indies, but with fome variation in the fubdivifion of the carat: among us, it is divided into four grains; among the Germans, into 12 parts; and by the French, according to Mr Helst, into 32. The Chinefe reckon by a different divifion called *touches*, of which the higheft number, or that which denotes pure gold, is 100; fo that 100 touches correfpond to our 24 carats, &c.

CARACT is alfo a certain weight which goldfmiths and jewellers ufe wherewith to weigh precious ftones and pearls.—In this fenfe, the word is by fome fuppofed to be derived from the Greek *ϰεϱάτιον*, a fruit which the Latins call *filiquas*, and we *carob beans*; each of which may weigh about four grains of wheat, whence the Latin *filiqua* has been ufed for a weight of four grains. This caract weighs four grains, but they are fomething lighter than the grains of other weights. Each of thefe grains is fubdivided in $\frac{1}{2}$, $\frac{1}{4}$, $\frac{1}{8}$, $\frac{1}{16}$, &c.

CARACTACUS, a renowned king of the ancient Britifh people called *Silures*, inhabiting South Wales. Having valiantly defended his country feven years againft the Romans, he was at length defeated; and flying to Cartifmanda, queen of the Brigantes (inhabitants of Yorkfhire), was by her treacheroufly delivered up to the Romans, and led in triumph to the emperor Claudius then at York; where his noble behaviour, and heroic but pathetic fpeech, obtained him not only his liberty, but the efteem of the emperor, A. D. 52.

CARAGROUTH, in commerce, a filver coin of the empire, weighing nine drachms. It goes at Conftantinople for 120 afpers. There are four forts of them, which are all equally current and of the fame value.

CARAITES, in the ecclefiaftical hiftory of the Jews, a religious fect among that people, whereof there are ftill fome fubfifting in Poland, Ruffia, Conftantinople, Cairo, and other places of the Levant; whofe diftinguifhing tenet and practice it is, to adhere clofely to the words and letter of the fcripture, exclufive of allegories, traditions, and the like.

Leo of Modena, a rabbin of Venice, obferves, that of all the herefies among that people, before the deftruction of the temple, there is none now left but that of the *Caraim*, a name derived from *Mikra*, which fignifies the pure text of the bible; becaufe of their keeping to the Pentateuch, obferving it to the letter, and rejecting all interpretations, paraphrafes, and conftitutions of the rabbins. Aben Ezra, and fome other rabbins, treat the Caraites as Sadducees; but Leo de Juda calls them, more accurately, Sadducees reformed; becaufe they believe the immortality of the foul, paradife, hell, refurrection, &c. which the ancient Sadducees denied. He adds, however, that they were doubtlefs originally real Sadducees, and fprung from among them.

M. Simon, with more probability, fuppofes them to have rifen hence; that the more knowing among the Jews oppofing the dreams and reveries of the rabbins, and ufing the pure texts of fcripture to refute their groundlefs traditions, had the name of *Caraim* given them; which fignifies as much as the barbarous Latin, *Scripturarii*; i. e. people attached to the text of fcripture. The other Jews give them the odious name Sadducees, from their agreement with thofe fectaries on the head of traditions. Scaliger, Voffius, and Spanheim, rank the Caraites among the Sabeans, Magi, Manichees, and Muffulmans, but by miftake: Wolfgang, Fabricius, &c. fay the Sadducees and Effeni were called Caraites, in oppofition to the Pharifees: others take them for the doctors of the law fo often mentioned in the gofpel: but thefe are all conjectures. Jofephus and Philo make no mention of them; which

fhows

shows them to be more modern than either of those authors. In all probability, this sect was not formed till after the collection of the second part of the Talmud, or the Gemara; perhaps not till after the compiling of the Mischna in the third century. The Caraites themselves pretend to be the remains of the ten tribes led captive by Shalmaneser. Wolfius, from the Memoirs of Mardochaeus, a Caraite, refers their origin to a massacre among the Jewish doctors, under Alexander Jannaeus, their king, about 100 years before Christ: because Simeon, son of Schetach, and the queen's brother, making his escape into Egypt, there forged his pretended traditions; and, at his return to Jerusalem, published his visions; interpolating the law after his own fancy, and supporting his novelties on the notices which God, he said, had communicated by the mouth of Moses, whose depositary he was: he gained many followers; and was opposed by others, who maintained, that all which God had revealed to Moses was written. Hence the Jews became divided into two sects, the Caraites and Traditionaries: among the first, Juda, son of Tabbai, distinguished himself; among the latter, Hillel. Wolfius reckons not only the Sadducees, but also the Scribes, in the number of Caraites. But the address of the Pharisees prevailed against them all; and the number of Caraites decreased: Anan, indeed, in the eighth century, retrieved their credit a little; and rabbi Schalomon in the ninth. They succeeded pretty well till the fourteenth; but since that time they have been declining.

The Caraites are but little known; their works coming only into very few hands, even among the greatest Hebraists. Buxtorf never saw more than one; Selden two; but Mr Trigland says, he has recovered enough to speak of them with assurance. He asserts, that soon after the prophets had ceased, the Jews became divided on the subject of works, and supererogation: some maintaining their necessity from tradition; whilst others keeping close to the written law, set them aside; and it was from these last that Caraitism commenced. He adds, that after the return from the Babylonish captivity, the observation of the law being to be re-established, there were several practices found proper for that end; and these once introduced, were looked upon as essential, and appointed by Moses; which was the origin of Pharisaism; as a contrary party, continuing to keep close to the letter, founded Caraitism.

The modern Caraites, Leo of Modena observes, have their synagogues and ceremonies; they pretend to be the sole proper Jews, or observers of the laws of Moses; calling the rest by the term *Rabbanim*, or *followers of the Rabbins*: these hate the Caraites mortally; refusing to ally or even converse with them, and treating them as *mamzerim*, or bastards; because of their rejecting the constitutions of the rabbins relating to marriages, repudiations, purifications of women, &c. This aversion is so great, that if a Caraite would become a rabbinist, he would never be received by the other Jews.

The Caraites, however, do not absolutely reject all kind of traditions; but only such as do not appear well-grounded. Selden, who is very express on this point, in his Uxor Hebraica, observes, that besides the mere text, they have certain interpretations, which they call hereditary, and which are proper traditions. Their theology only seems to differ from that of the other Jews, in that it is purer, and clearer of superstition: they give no credit to the explications of the Cabbalists, chimerical allegories, nor to any constitutions of the Talmud, but what are conformable to the scripture, and may be drawn from it by just and necessary consequences.

Peringer observes of the Caraites in Lithuania, that they are very different, both in aspect, language, and manners, from the rabbinists, wherewith that country abounds. Their mother tongue is the Turkish; and this they use in their schools and synagogues. In visage they resemble the Mahometan Tartars. Their synagogues are placed north and south; and the reason they give for it is, that Shalmaneser brought them northward: so that in praying, to look to Jerusalem, they must turn to the south. He adds, that they admit all the books of the Old Testament; contrary to the opinion of many of the learned, who hold that they reject all but the Pentateuch.

Caleb, a Caraite, reduces the difference between them and the rabbinists to three points: 1. In that they deny the oral law to come from Moses, and reject the Cabbala. 2. In that they abhor the Talmud. 3. In that they observe the feasts, as the sabbaths, &c. much more rigorously than the rabbins do. To this may be added, that they extend the degrees of affinity, wherein marriage is prohibited, almost to infinity.

CARAMANIA, a considerable province of Turky, in Asia, in the south part of Natolia. Bajazet united this province to his empire about the year 1488, and since that time it has continued in the possession of the Turks. Satalia was the capital city, but is now much decayed.

CARAMANTA, a town of South America, and capital of a province of the same name in Terra Firma, and in the audience of Santa Fe. W. Long. 72. 35. N. Lat. 5. 18. The province of Caramanta is extended on both sides the river Cauca; and is bounded on the north by the district of Carthagena, on the east by New Grenada, on the south by Popayan, and on the west by Popayan and by the audience of Panama. It is a valley surrounded on every side by very high mountains.

CARANGA, an inconsiderable island near Bombay in the East Indies. It affords nothing but some rice, fowls, and goats, for that market.

CARANNA, or KARANNA, a very scarce gum which comes from New Spain. It is said to possess many extraordinary medical virtues, but the present practice takes no notice of it.

CARANUS, the first king of Macedon, and the seventh of the race of the Heraclidae. See MACEDONIA.

CARARA, a weight at Leghorn, and in other parts of Italy, used in the sale of wool and cod-fish, equivalent to 60 pounds of that country.

CARAT. See CARACT.

CARAVAGGIO (Michael Angelo da). See ANGELO.

CARAVAN, or KARAVANNE, in the east, signifies a company or assembly of travellers and pilgrims, and more particularly of merchants, who, for their greater security, and in order to assist each other, march in a body through the deserts, and other dangerous places, which are infested with Arabs or robbers.

There are four regular caravans which go yearly to Mecca; the first from Damascus, composed of the pilgrims from Europe and Asia; the second from Cairo, for the Mahometans of Barbary; the third from Zibith, a place near the mouth of the Red Sea, where those of Arabia and India meet; the fourth from Babylon, where the Persians assemble. Most of the inland commerce of the East is carried on by caravans. The late czar Peter the Great established a trade between Russia and China by means of a caravan. M. Bourguon, geographer to the duke of Lorrain, has given a treatise of the caravans of merchants in Asia; wherein he shows of what they are composed, how many sorts there are, the several uses of the different sorts of animals in them; the prices given for them, the officers and men appointed to conduct them, and the pay of each, with their manner of marching, halting, fighting, retreating, &c. Caravans of this kind are large convoys of armed men, merchants, and travellers, with divers sorts of animals for the carriage of their provisions. There are commonly four chief officers of a caravan, viz. the caravan bachi, or chief; the captain-guide; captain of rest; and captain of distribution. The first has absolute command over all the rest; the second is absolute in the march: the office of the third only commences when the caravan stops and makes a stay: to the fourth it belongs to dispose of every part of the corps, in case of an attack or battle; he has also the inspection over the distribution of provisions, which is made under him by several distributors, who give security to the master of the caravan, and have each of them a certain number of persons, elephants, dromedaries, &c. to take care of at their own peril. The treasurer of the caravan makes a fifth officer, who has under him several agents and interpreters, who keep journals of all that passes, for the satisfaction of those concerned in fitting out the caravan.

Any dealer is at liberty to form a company, in order to make a caravan. He in whose name it is raised, is considered as the caravan bachi or chief of the caravan, unless he appoint some other in his place. If there are several merchants equally concerned, they elect a caravan bachi; after which, they appoint officers to conduct the caravan and decide all controversies that may arise during the journey.

There are also sea caravans; established on the same footing, and for the same purposes: such is the caravan of vessels from Constantinople to Alexandria.

CARAVANSERA, or KARAVANSERA, a place appointed for receiving and lodging the caravans.

It is commonly a large square building, in the middle of which there is a very spacious court; and under the arches or piazzas that surround it there runs a bank, raised some feet above the ground, where the merchants, and those who travel with them in any capacity, take up their lodgings as well as they can; the beasts of burden being tied to the foot of the bank. Over the gates that lead into the court, there are sometimes little rooms, which the keepers of the caravanseras let out at a very high price to such as have a mind to be private.

The caravanseras in the East are something of the nature of the inns in Europe; only that you meet with little accommodation either for man or beast, but are obliged to carry almost every thing with you; there is never a caravansera without a well, or spring of water. These buildings are chiefly owing to the charity of the Mahometans; they are esteemed sacred dwellings, where it is not permitted to insult any person, or to pillage any of the effects that are deposited there. There are also caravanseras where most things may be had for money; and as the profits of these are considerable, the magistrates of the cities to whose jurisdiction they belong, take care to store them well. There is an inspector, who, at the departure of each caravan, fixes the price of the night's lodging, from which there is no appeal.

CARAVANSERASKIER, the steward or keeper of a CARAVANSERA. He keeps an account of all the merchandises that are sold upon trust, and demands the payments of the sums due to the merchants for what has been sold in the caravansera, on the seller's paying two per cent.

CARAVEL; thus they call a small vessel on the coast of France, which goes to fish for herring on the banks. They are commonly from 25 to 30 tons burden. Those which are designed for the same fishery in the British channel are called by the French *traquarts*: these are from 12 to 15 tons burden.

CARAWAY, in botany. See CARUM.

CARBONADE, or CARBONADO, in cookery; flesh, fowl, or the like, seasoned and broiled on the coals.

CARBUNCLE, in natural history, a very elegant gem, whose colour is deep red, with an admixture of scarlet.

This gem was known among the ancients by the name of *anthrax*. It is usually found pure and faultless, and is of the same degree of hardness with the sapphire: it is naturally of an angular figure; and is found adhering, by its base, to a heavy and ferruginous stone of the emery kind; its usual size is near a quarter of an inch in length, and two thirds of that in diameter in its thickest parts: when held up against the sun, it loses its deep tinge, and becomes exactly of the colour of a burning charcoal, whence the propriety of the name which the ancients gave it. It bears the fire unaltered, not parting with its colour, nor becoming at all the paler by it. It is found only in the East Indies, so far as is yet known; and there but very rarely.

CARBUNCLE, or *Anthrax*, in medicine, an inflammation which arises, in time of the plague, with a vesicle or blister almost like that produced by burning.

CARBUNCLE, in heraldry, a charge or bearing, consisting of eight radii, four whereof make a common cross, and the other four a saltier.

Some call these radii *batons*, or staves, because round, and enriched with buttons, or pearled like pilgrim's staves, and frequently tipped or terminated with flower-de-luces; others blazon them, royal scepters, placed in saltier, pale and fesse.

CARCASSE, or CARCUS, in the art of war, an iron case, or hollow capacity, about the bigness of a bomb, of an oval figure, made of ribs of iron, filled with combustible matters, as meal-powder, saltpetre, sulphur, broken glass, shavings of horn, turpentine, tallow, &c. It has two or three apertures out of which the fire is to blaze; and the design of it is to be thrown out of a mortar, to set houses on fire, and do other execution. It has the name *carcass*, because the circles which pass from one ring or plate to the other seem to represent the ribs of a human carcase.

CARCASSONNE, an ancient city of France, in *Lower* Languedoc, with a bishop's see. It is divided into the upper and lower town. They are both surrounded with walls; and though their situations are different, they are both watered by the river Aude. The upper town is seated on a hill, with a castle that commands it, as well as the lower town. It is strong, not only by its situation on a craggy rock, but also by several large towers which are joined to its walls, and which render it of difficult access. The cathedral church is remarkable for nothing but its antiquity. The lower town is large, and built after the modern taste. The streets are very straight, and lead to a large square in the middle, from whence may be seen the four gates of the town. There is here a manufacture of cloth. The neighbouring country is full of olive-trees; and in the mountains there is a fine marble, commonly called *marble of Languedoc*. E. Long. 2. 25. N. Lat. 43. 11.

This place bore a considerable share in that celebrated crusade undertaken against the Albigenses in the beginning of the 13th century, and which forms one of the most astonishing instances of superstition and of atrocious barbarity to be found in the annals of the world. When the royal power was nearly annihilated, during the reigns of the last kings of the Carlovingian race in France, most of the cities of Languedoc erected themselves into little independent states, governed by their own princes. Carcassonne was then under the dominion of viscounts. At the time when Pope Innocent III. patronized and commanded the prosecution of hostilities against the Albigenses for the crime of heresy, Raymond the reigning viscount was included in that proscription. Simon de Montfort, general of the army of the church, invested the city of Carcassonne in 1209. The inhabitants, terrified at the fate of several other places where the most dreadful massacres had been committed, demanded leave to capitulate; but this act of mercy was only extended to them under a condition equally cruel, incredible, and unparalleled in history, if we were not compelled to believe it by the unanimous testimony of all the contemporary writers. The people found in the place were all obliged, without distinction of rank or sex, to evacuate it in a state of nudity; and Agnes the viscountess was not exempted, though young and beautiful, from this ignominious and shocking punishment. "On les fit sortir tous nuds de la ville de Carcassonne (says an ancient author) afin qu'ils recevssent de la honte, en montrant ces parties du corps que la pureté de la langue n'exprime point, desquelles ils avoient abusé, et s'en étoient servis dans des crimes execrables." It seems by this imputation that the Albigeois were accused by their enemies of some enormities, probably unjust, and similar to those which religious enmity and prejudice have attributed to the followers of Zinzendorf in the present century.

CARCERES, in the ancient Circensian games, were inclosures in the circus, wherein the horses were restrained till the signal was given for starting, when, by an admirable contrivance, they all at once flew open.

CARCHEMISH (anc. geog.), a town lying upon the Euphrates, and belonging to the Assyrians. Necho king of Egypt took it from the king of Assyria, 2 Chr. xxxv. 20. Necho left a garrison in it, which was taken and cut to pieces, in the fourth year of Jehoiachim king of Judah, by Nebuchadnezzar king of Babylon, 2 Kings xxiii. 29. Isaiah (x. 9.) speaks of Carchemish, and seems to say, that Tiglath pileser made a conquest of it, perhaps from the Egyptians. This is thought to be the same city with that called Circesium by the Greeks and Latins.

CARCINOMA, in medicine; the same with Cancer.

CARD, among artificers, an instrument consisting of a block of wood, beset with sharp teeth, serving to arrange the hairs of wool, flax, hemp, and the like: there are different kinds of them, as hand-cards, stock-cards, &c. They are made as follows:

A piece of thick leather, of the size intended for the card, is strained in a frame for that purpose; and then pricked full of holes, into which the teeth or pieces of iron wire are inserted. After which the leather is nailed by the edges to a flat piece of wood, in the form of an oblong square, about a foot in length and half a foot in breadth, with a handle placed in the middle of one of the longer sides.

The teeth are made in the following manner. The wire being drawn of the size intended, a skain or number of wires are cut into proper lengths by means of a gauge, and then doubled in a tool contrived for that purpose: after which they are bent into the proper direction by means of another tool; and then placed in the leather, as mentioned above.

CARDS, among gamesters, little pieces of fine thin pasteboard of an oblong figure, of several sizes; but most commonly, in Britain, three inches and an half long and two and an half broad, on which are painted several points and figures.

The moulds and blocks for making cards are exactly like those that were used for the first printed books. They lay a sheet of wet or moist paper on the block, which is first slightly done over with a sort of ink made of lamp-black diluted in water, and mixed with some starch to give it a body. They afterwards rub it off with a round list. The court-cards are coloured by means of several patterns, styled *stan-files*. These consist of papers cut through with a penknife; and in these apertures they apply severally the various colours, as red, black, &c. These patterns are painted with oil-colours, that the brushes may not wear them out; and when the pattern is laid on the pasteboard, they slightly pass over it a brush full of colour, which, leaving it within the openings, forms the face or figure of the card.

Among sharpers, divers sorts of false and fraudulent cards have been contrived; as, 1. *Marked* cards, where the aces, kings, queens, knaves, are marked on the corners of the backs with spots of different number and order, either with clear water or water tinged with pale Indian ink, that those in the secret may distinguish them. Aces are marked with single spots on two corners opposite diagonally; kings with two spots at the same corners; knaves with the same number transferred. 2. *Breef* cards, those which are longer or broader than the rest; chiefly used at whist and piquet. The broad cards are usually for kings, queens, knaves, and aces; the long for the rest. Their design is to direct the cutting, to enable him in the secret to cut the cards disadvantageously to his adversary, and draw the person unacquainted with the fraud to cut them favourably for the sharper. As the pack is placed either endwise or sidewise to him that is to cut, the long or broad cards naturally lead him to cut to them. Breef cards are sometimes made thus by the manufacturer; but, in defect of these, sharpers pare all but the breefs with a penknife or razor. 3. *Corner bend*, denotes four cards turned down slightly at one corner, to serve as a signal to cut by. 4. *Middle bend*, or Kingston-bridge, is where the tricks are bent two different ways, which causes an opening or arch in the middle, to direct likewise the cutting.

Cards were invented about the year 1390, to divert Charles VI. of France, who had fallen into a melancholy disposition. The inventor proposed, by the figures of the four suits or colours, as the French call them, to represent the four classes of men in the kingdom. By the *coeurs* (hearts) are meant the *gens de choeur*, choir-men, or ecclesiastics; and therefore the Spaniards, who certainly received the use of cards from the French, have *copas*, or chalices, instead of hearts. The nobility, or prime military part of the kingdom, are represented by the ends or points of lances or pikes; and our ignorance of the meaning or resemblance of the figure induced us to call them *spades*. The Spaniards have *espadas*, swords, in lieu of pikes, which are of similar import. By diamonds are designed the order of citizens, merchants, or tradesmen, *carreaux*, (square stones, tiles, or the like): The Spaniards have a coin, *dineros*, which answers to it; and the Dutch call the French word *carreaux* "*steenen*," stones and diamonds, from the form. *Trefle*, the trefoil-leaf, or clover-grass (corruptly called *clubs*), alludes to the husbandmen and peasants. But how this suit came to be called *clubs* is not easily explained; unless, borrowing the game from the Spaniards, who have *bastos* (staves or clubs) instead of the trefoil, we give the Spanish signification to the French figure.

The history of the four kings, which the French, in drollery, sometimes call the *cards*, are David, Alexander, Cæsar, and Charles; which names were then, and still are, on the French cards. These respectable names represent the four celebrated monarchies of the Jews, Greeks, Romans, and Franks under Charlemagne. By the queens are intended Argine, Esther, Judith, and Pallas (names retained in the French cards), typical of birth, piety, fortitude, and wisdom, the qualifications residing in each person. *Argine* is an anagram for *regina*, queen by descent. By the knaves were designed the servants to knights (for *knave* originally meant only *servant*); but French pages and valets, now indiscriminately used by various orders of persons, were formerly only allowed to persons of quality, esquires (*escuiers*), shield or armour bearers. Others fancy that the knights themselves were designed by those cards; because Hogier and Lahire, two names on the French cards, were famous knights at the time cards were supposed to have been invented.

Deceptions with Cards. See LEGERDEMAIN, sect. i.

CARDAMINE, in botany: A genus of the siliquosa order, belonging to the tetradynamia class of plants; and in the natural method ranking under the 39th order, *Siliquosæ*. The siliqua parts asunder with a spring, and the valves roll spirally backward; the stigma is entire, and the calyx a little gaping. Of this there are 15 species; but the most remarkable is the pratensis, with a large purplish flower. This grows naturally in many parts of Britain, and is also called *cuckow-flower*. There are four varieties, viz. the single, with purple and white flowers, which are frequently intermixed in the meadows; and the double, of both colours. The single sorts are not admitted into gardens; but the double deserve a place, as making a pretty appearance during the time they are in flower. They will thrive in a moist shady border; and are propagated by parting their roots, which is best performed in autumn. They delight in a soft loamy soil, not too stiff. By some the plant is reckoned antiscorbutic.

CARDAMOM, in the Materia Medica. See AMOMUM.

CARDAN (Jerom), one of the most extraordinary geniuses of his age, was born at Pavia on the 24th of September 1501. As his mother was not married, she tried every method to procure an abortion, but without effect. She was three days in labour, and they were at last obliged to cut the child from her. He was born with his head covered with black curled hair. When he was four years old, he was carried to Milan; his father being an advocate in that city. At the age of 20, he went to study in the university of that city; and two years afterwards he explained Euclid. In 1524, he went to Padua; and the same year he was admitted to the degree of master of arts: in the end of the following year, he took the degree of doctor of physic. He married about the year 1531. For ten years before, his impotency had hindered him from having knowledge of a woman; which was a great mortification to him. He attributed it to the evil influence of the planet under which he was born. When he enumerates, as he frequently does, the greatest misfortunes of his life, this ten years impotency is always one. At the age of 32, he became professor of mathematics at Milan. In 1539, he was admitted member of the college of physicians at Milan; in 1543, he read public lectures of medicine in that city, and at Pavia the year following; but discontinued them because he could not get payment of his salary, and returned to Milan. In 1552, he went into Scotland, having been sent for by the Archbishop of St Andrew's, who had in vain applied to the French king's physicians, and afterwards to those of the emperor of Germany. This prelate, then 40 years old, had for ten years been afflicted with a shortness of breath, which returned every eight days for the two last years. He began to recover from the moment that Cardan prescribed for him. Cardan took his leave of him at the end of six weeks and three days, leaving him prescriptions which in two years wrought a complete cure.

Cardan's journey to Scotland gave him an opportunity of visiting several countries. He crossed France in going thither; and returned through Germany, and the Low Countries, along the banks of the Rhine. It was on this occasion he went to London, and calculated king Edward's nativity. This tour took up about four months; after which, coming back to Milan, he continued there till the beginning of October 1552;

and

Cardan.

and then went to Pavia, from whence he was invited to Bologna in 1562. He taught in this last city till the year 1570; at which time he was thrown into prison; but some months after he was sent home to his own house. He left Bologna in 1571; and went to Rome, where he lived for some time without any public employment. He was, however, admitted a member of the college of physicians, and received a pension from the pope. He died at Rome on the 21st of September 1575, according to Thuanus. This account might be sufficient to show the reader that Cardan was of a very fickle temper; but he will have a much better idea of his singular and odd turn of mind by examining what he himself has written concerning his own good and bad qualities. He paid himself congratulatory compliments for not having a friend in this world; but that, in requital, he was attended by an aerial spirit, emaned partly from Saturn and partly from Mercury, who was the constant guide of his actions, and teacher of every duty to which he was bound. He declared, too, that he was so irregular in his manner of walking the streets, as induced all beholders to point at him as a fool. Sometimes he walked very slowly, like a man absorbed in profound meditation; then all on a sudden quickened his steps, accompanying them with very absurd attitudes. In Bologna his delight was to be drawn about in a mean vehicle with three wheels. When nature did not visit him with any pain, he would procure to himself that disagreeable sensation by biting his lips so wantonly, or pulling his fingers to such a vehement degree, as sometimes to force the tears from his eyes: and the reason he assigned for so doing, was to moderate certain impetuous sallies of the mind, the violence of which was to him by far more insupportable than pain itself; and that the sure consequence of such a severe discipline was the enjoying the pleasure of health. He says elsewhere, that, in his greatest tortures of soul, he used to whip his legs with rods, and bite his left arm; that it was a great relief to him to weep, but that very often he could not; that nothing gave him more pleasure than to talk of things which made the whole company uneasy; that he spoke on all subjects, in season and out of season; and he was so fond of games of chance, as to spend whole days in them, to the great prejudice of his family and reputation, for he even staked his furniture and his wife's jewels.

Cardanus makes no scruple of owning that he was revengeful, envious, treacherous, a dealer in the black art, a backbiter, a calumniator, and addicted to all the foul and detestable excesses that can be imagined: yet, notwithstanding (as one would think) so humbling a declaration, there was never perhaps a vainer mortal, or one that with less ceremony expressed the high opinion he had of himself, than Cardanus was known to do, as will appear by the following proofs. "I have been admired by many nations; an infinite number of panegyrics, both in prose and verse, have been composed to celebrate my fame. I was born to release the world from the manifold errors under which it groaned. What I have found out could not be discovered either by my predecessors or my contemporaries; and that is the reason why those authors who write any thing worthy of being remembered, scruple not to own that they are indebted to me for it. I have composed a book on the dialectic art, in which there is neither one superfluous letter nor one deficient. I finished it in seven days, which seems a prodigy. Yet where is there a person to be found, that can boast of his having become master of its doctrine in a year? And he that shall have comprehended it in that time, must appear to have been instructed by a familiar demon."

Cardan ‖ Carders.

The same capriciousness observable in his outward conduct is to be observed in the composition of his works. We have a multitude of his treatises in which the reader is stopped almost every moment by the obscurity of his text, or his digressions from the point in hand. In his arithmetical performances there are several discourses on the motions of the planets, on the creation, and on the tower of Babel. In his dialectic work, we find his judgment on historians and the writers of epistles. The only apology which he makes for the frequency of his digressions is, that they were purposely done for the sooner filling up of his sheet, his bargain with the bookseller being at so much per sheet; and that he worked as much for his daily support as for the acquisition of glory. The *Lyons* edition of his works, printed in 1663, consists of ten volumes in folio.

It was Cardanus who revived in latter times all the secret philosophy of the Cabbala or Cabbalists, which filled the world with spirits; a likeness to whom, he asserted, we might attain by purifying ourselves with philosophy. He chose for himself, however, notwithstanding such reveries, this fine device, *Tempus mea possessio, tempus meus ager*: "Time is my sole possession, and the only fund I have to improve."

In fact, when we consider the transcendent qualities of Cardan's mind, we cannot deny his having cultivated it with every species of knowledge, and his having made a greater progress in philosophy, in the medical art, in astronomy, in mathematics, &c. than the greatest part of his contemporaries who had applied their minds but to one of those sciences.

Scaliger affirms, that Cardan, having fixed the time of his death, abstained from food, that his prediction might be fulfilled, and that his continuance to live might not discredit his art. Cardan's father, who was a doctor of medicine, and a professor of civil and canon law, died in the same manner, in the year 1524, having abstained from all sustenance for nine days. He son tells us, that he had white eyes, and could see in the night-time.

CARDASS, a sort of card, proper for carding flocks of silk, to make cappadine of it. It is also the name which the French give to those flocks of silk.

Carrasses, is also the name which, in the cloth manufactories of Languedoc, they give to a sort of large card, which is used for carding the dyed wool, designed for making cloth of mixed colours.

CARDERS, in the woollen manufactory, are persons who prepare wool, &c. for spinning, &c.

Carders, spinners, weavers, fullers, shearmen, and dyers, not performing their duty in their occupations, shall yield to the party grieved double damages; to be committed until payment. One justice to hear and determine complaints.

Carders, combers, sorters, spinners, or weavers,

con-

Card & Cardigan.

conveying away, embezzling, or detaining any wool or yarn, delivered by the clothier, or any other perſon, ſhall give the party grieved ſuch ſatisfaction, as two juſtices, mayor, &c. ſhall think fit: if not able or willing to make ſatisfaction, for the firſt offence to be whipped, or ſet in the ſtocks in ſome market-town, or in any other town where the offence is committed: the ſecond offence to incur the like, or ſuch further puniſhment by whipping, &c. as juſtices ſhall think proper. Conviction by one witneſs on oath, or confeſſion.

CARDI (Lodovico). See Civoli.

CARDIAC, in a general ſenſe, ſignifies all medicines beneficial to the heart, whether internally or externally applied. The word comes from the Greek word *καρδια*, *cor*; the heart being reputed the immediate ſeat of their operation.

Cardiacs, in a more particular ſenſe, denote medicines which raiſe the ſpirits, and give preſent ſtrength and cheerfulneſs: theſe amount to the ſame with what are popularly called *cordials*. Cardiacs are medicines anciently ſuppoſed to exert themſelves immediately in comforting and ſtrengthening the heart; but the modern phyſicians rather ſuppoſe them to produce the effect by putting the blood into a gentle fermentation, whereby the ſprings, before decayed, are repaired and invigorated, and the tone and elaſticity of the fibres of the veſſels reſtored; the conſequence of which is a more eaſy and briſk circulation.

CARDIALGIA, in medicine, a violent ſenſation of heat or acrimony felt towards the upper or left orifice of the ſtomach, though ſeemingly at the heart; ſometimes accompanied with palpitations of the heart, fainting, and a propenſity to vomit: better known by the name of *cardiac paſſion*, or *heart-burn*. See (*Index ſubjoined to*) Medicine.

CARDIFF, a town of Glamorganſhire, in South Wales, ſeated on the river Tave, in a rich and fruitful ſoil. It is a large, compact, well built town, having a caſtle, a wall, and four gates, built by Robert Fitz-Hamon, a Norman, about the year 1100. It is governed by the conſtable of the caſtle, 12 aldermen, 12 burgeſſes, &c. and ſends one member to parliament. Here the aſſizes and ſeſſions are held, beſides ſeveral courts. There is a handſome bridge over the river, to which ſmall veſſels come to take in their lading. It has now only one church, St Mary's having been long ſince thrown down by the undermining of the river. The caſtle, though much decayed, makes a grand appearance even at this time; and the walls of the town are very ſtrong and thick. The church has a fine tower-ſteeple, and the town-hall is a good ſtructure. The magiſtrates are elected every year by the majority of the burgeſſes. W. Long. 3. 20. N. Lat. 51. 30. Cardiff gives title of Britiſh Baron to the family of Bute in Scotland.

CARDIGAN, the capital town of Cardiganſhire, in South Wales, is ſeated near the mouth of the river Teivy, on the Iriſh channel. It is indifferently large and well-built, containing three wards, one church, and the county-gaol. It is governed by a mayor, 13 aldermen, 13 common-council men, &c. Here are the ruins of a caſtle which was built by Gilbert de Clare, about the year 1160. It ſends one member to Parliament; and has two markets, held on Tueſdays and Saturdays. W. Long. 4. 38. N. Lat. 52. 15.

Cardiganſhire & Cardinal.

CARDIGANSHIRE, a county of South Wales, bounded on the north by Merionethſhire and Montgomeryſhire, on the eaſt by Radnorſhire and Brecknockſhire, on the weſt by the Iriſh Sea, and on the ſouth by Carmarthenſhire. Its length from north-weſt to ſouth-eaſt is about 44 miles, and its breadth near 20. The air, as in other parts of Wales, varies with the ſoil, which in the ſouthern and weſtern parts is more upon a level than this principality generally is, which renders the air mild and temperate. But as the northern and eaſtern parts are mountainous, they are conſequently more barren and bleak. However, there are cattle bred in all parts; but they have neither wood nor coals of their own for fuel: they have rich lead mines, and fiſh in plenty, with fowls both tame and wild. The principal rivers are the Teivy, the Ridol, and the Iſtwith. This county hath five market-towns, viz. Cardigan, Aberiſtwith, Llanbadarnvawr, Llanbedar, and Tregaron, with 75 pariſhes; and was formerly computed to have upward of 5000 houſes, and 520,000 acres of land. It ſends two members to parliament; one for the county, and one for Cardigan.

CARDINAL, in a general ſenſe, an appellation given to things on account of their pre-eminence. The word is formed of the Latin *cardo*, *a hinge*; it being on theſe fundamental points that all the reſt of the ſame kind are ſuppoſed to turn. Thus, juſtice, prudence, temperance, and fortitude, are called the four *cardinal virtues*, as being the baſis of all the reſt.

Cardinal Flower, in botany. See Lobelia.

Cardinal Points, in coſmography, are the four interſections of the horizon with the meridian, and the prime vertical circle. Of theſe, two, viz. the interſections of the horizon and meridian, are called *North* and *South*, with regard to the poles they are directed to. The other two, viz. the interſections of the horizon, and firſt vertical, are called *Eaſt* and *Weſt*.

The cardinal points, therefore, coincide with the four cardinal regions of the heavens; and are 90° diſtant from each other. The intermediate points are called *collateral points*.

Cardinal Points, in aſtrology, are the riſing and ſetting of the ſun, the zenith, and nadir.

Cardinal Signs, in aſtronomy, are Aries, Libra, Cancer, and Capricorn.

Cardinal Winds, are thoſe that blow from the cardinal points.

Cardinal Numbers, in grammar, are the numbers one, two, three, &c. which are indeclinable; in oppoſition to the ordinal numbers, firſt, ſecond, third, fourth, &c.

Cardinal, an eccleſiaſtical prince in the Romiſh church, being one who has a voice in the conclave at the election of a pope. Some ſay the cardinals were ſo called from the Latin *incardinatio*, which ſignifies the adoption in any church made of a prieſt of a foreign church, driven thence by misfortune; and add, that the uſe of the word commenced at Rome and Ravenna; the revenues of the churches of which cities being very great, they became the common refuge of the unhappy prieſts of all other churches.

The cardinals compoſe the pope's council or ſenate: in the Vatican is a conſtitution of pope John, which regulates the rights and titles of the *cardinals*; and which declares, that as the pope represents Moses, so the cardinals represent the seventy elders, who, under the pontifical authority, decide private and particular differences.

Cardinals, in their first institution, were only the principal priests, or incumbents of the parishes of Rome. In the primitive church, the chief priest of a parish, who immediately followed the bishop, was called *presbyter cardinalis*, to distinguish him from the other petty priests, who had no church nor preferment; the term was first applied to them in the year 150; others say, under pope Silvester, in the year 300. These cardinal priests were alone allowed to baptise, and administer the eucharist. When the cardinal priests became bishops, their cardinalate became vacant; they being then supposed to be raised to a higher dignity.—Under pope Gregory, cardinal priests, and cardinal deacons, were only such priests or deacons as had a church or chapel under their particular care: and this was the original use of the word. Leo IV. in the council of Rome, held in 853, calls them *presbyteros sui cardinis*; and their churches, *parochias cardinales*.

The cardinals continued on this footing till the eleventh century: but as the grandeur and state of his holiness became then exceedingly augmented, he would have his council of cardinals make a better figure than the ancient priests had done. It is true, they still preserved their ancient title; but the thing expressed by it was no more. It was a good while, however, before they had the precedence over bishops, or got the election of the pope into their hands; but when they were once possessed of those privileges, they soon had the red hat and purple; and growing still in authority, they became at length superior to the bishops, by the sole quality of being cardinals.

Du-Cange observes, that originally there were three kinds of churches: the first or genuine churches were properly called *parishes*; the second, *deaconries*, which were chapels joined to hospitals, and served by deacons; the third were simple *oratories*, where private masses were said, and were discharged by local and resident chaplains. He adds, that, to distinguish the principal or parish churches from the chapels and oratories, the name *cardinalis* was given to them. Accordingly, parish churches gave titles to cardinal priests; and some chapels also, at length, gave the title of *cardinal deacons*.

Others observe, that the term *cardinal* was given not only to priests, but also to bishops and deacons who were attached to certain churches, to distinguish them from those who only served them *in passant*, and by commission. Titular churches, or benefices, were a kind of parishes, i. e. churches assigned each to a cardinal priest; with some fixed district depending on it, and a font for administering of baptism, in cases where the bishop himself could not administer it. These cardinals were subordinate to the bishops; and accordingly, in councils, particularly that held at Rome in 868, subscribed after them.

It was not, however, only at Rome, that priests bore this name; for we find there were cardinal priests in France: thus, the curate of the parish of St John de Vignes is called in old charters the *cardinal priest* of that parish.

The title of *cardinal* is also given to some bishops, *quatenus* bishops; e. g. to those of Mentz and Milan: the archbishop of Bourges is also, in ancient writings, called *cardinal*; and the church of Bourges, a *cardinal church*. The abbot of Vendome calls himself *cardinalis natus*.

The cardinals are divided into three classes or orders; containing six bishops, fifty priests, and fourteen deacons; making in all seventy: which constitute what they call the *sacred college*. The cardinal bishops, who are, as it were, the pope's vicars, bear the titles of the bishopricks assigned to them; the rest take such titles as are given them: the number of cardinal bishops has been fixed; but that of cardinal priests and deacons, and consequently the sacred college itself, is always fluctuating. Till the year 1125, the college only consisted of fifty-two or fifty-three: the council of Constance reduced them to twenty-four; but Sixtus IV. without any regard to that restriction, raised them again to fifty-three, and Leo to sixty-five. Thus, as the number of cardinal priests was anciently fixed to twenty-eight, new titles were to be established, in proportion as new cardinals were created. As for the cardinal deacons, they were originally no more than seven for the fourteen quarters of Rome; but they were afterwards increased to nineteen, and after that were again diminished.

According to Onuphrius, it was pope Pius IV. who first enacted, in 1562, that the pope should be chosen only by the senate of cardinals; whereas, till that time, the election was by all the clergy of Rome. Some say, the election of the pope rested in the cardinals, exclusive of the clergy, in the time of Alexander III. in 1160. Others go higher still, and say, that Nicholas II. having been elected at Sienna, in 1058, by the cardinals alone, occasioned the right of election to be taken from the clergy and people of Rome; only leaving them that of confirming him by their consent; which was at length, however, taken from them. See his decree for this purpose, issued in the Roman council of 1059, in Harduin's Acta Conciliorum, tom. vi. pt. i. p. 1165. Whence it appears, that the cardinals who had the right of suffrage in the election of his successors, were divided by this pontiff into *cardinal bishops* and *cardinal clerks*: meaning by the former the seven bishops who belonged to the city and territory of Rome; and by the latter, the *cardinal presbyters* or ministers of the twenty-eight Roman parishes, or principal churches. To these were added, in process of time, under Alexander III. and other pontiffs, new members, in order to appease the tumults occasioned by the edict of Nicholas II.

At the creation of a new cardinal, the pope performs the ceremony of opening and shutting his mouth; which is done in a private consistory. The shutting his mouth implies the depriving him of the liberty of giving his opinion in congregations; and the opening his mouth, which is performed 15 days after, signifies the taking off this restraint. However, if the pope happens to die during the time a cardinal's mouth is shut, he can neither give his voice in the election of a new pope, nor be himself advanced to that dignity.

The dress of a cardinal is a red soutane, a rocket, a short purple mantle, and a red hat.

The

The cardinals began to wear the red hat at the council of Lyons, in 1243. The decree of pope Urban VIII. whereby it is appointed, that the cardinals be addressed under the title of *eminence*, is of the year 1630; till then, they were called *illustrissimi*.

When cardinals are sent to the courts of Princes, it is in quality of legates *a latere*; and when they are appointed governors of towns, their government is called by the name of *legation*.

Cardinal has also been applied to secular officers. Thus, the prime ministers in the court of the emperor Theodosius, are called *cardinales*. Cassiodorus, lib. vii. formul. 31. makes mention of the cardinal prince of the city of Rome; and in the list of officers of the duke of Bretagne, in 1447, we meet with one Raoul de Thorel, cardinal of Quillart, chancellor, and servant of the viscount de Rohan: which shows it to have been an inferior quality.

CARDIOID, in the higher geometry, an algebraical curve, so called from its resemblance to an heart.

CARDIOSPERMUM, in botany: A genus of the trigynia order, belonging to the octandria class of plants; and in the natural method ranking under the 39th order, *Trihilatæ*. The calyx is tetraphyllous, the petals four, the nectarium tetraphyllous and unequal; the capsules three, grown together, and inflated. There are two species, both natives of the East and West Indies; but have no great beauty, or any other remarkable property.

CARDIUM, or Cockle, in zoology, a genus of insects belonging to the order of vermes testaceæ. The shell consists of two equal valves, and the sides are equal. There are 21 species of this genus. Common on all sandy coasts, lodged a little beneath the sand; their place marked by a depressed spot. They are wholesome and delicious food.

CARDONA, a handsome town of Spain, in Catalonia, with a strong castle, and the title of a duchy. Near it is an inexhaustible mountain of salt of several colours, as red, white, carnation, and green; but when washed, it becomes white. There are also vineyards which produce excellent wine, and very lofty pine-trees. It is seated on an eminence, near the river Cardenero. E. Long. 1. 28. N. Lat. 41. 42.

CARDUUS, in botany: A genus of the polygamia æqualis order, belonging to the syngenesia class of plants; and in the natural method ranking under the 49th order, *Compositæ*. The calyx is ovate, imbricated with prickly scales, and the receptacle hairy. Of this genus there are 26 species, ten of which are natives of Britain, and being troublesome weeds require no description. Some few of the exotic kinds are propagated in gardens for the sake of variety; but even these have neither beauty nor any other property to recommend them.

Carduus Benedictus. See Cnicus.

CAREENING, in the sea-language, the bringing a ship to lie down on one side, in order to trim and caulk the other side.

A ship is said to be brought to the careen, when, the most of her lading being taken out, she is haled down on one side, by a small vessel, as low as necessary; and there kept by the weight of the ballast, ordnance, &c. as well as by ropes, lest her masts should be strained too much; in order that her sides and bottom may be trimmed, seams caulked, or any thing that is faulty under water mended. Hence, when a ship lies on one side when she sails, she is said to sail on the careen.

CAREER, in the manege, a place inclosed with a barrier, wherein they run the ring.

The word is also used for the race or course of the horse itself, provided it do not exceed 200 paces.

In the ancient circus, the career was the space the bigæ, or quadrigæ, were to run at full speed, to gain the prize. See Circus.

Career, in falconry, is a flight or tour of the bird, about 120 yards. If she mount more, it is called a *double career*; if less, a *semi-career*.

CARELIA, the eastern province of Finland; divided into Swedish Carelia, and Muscovite Carelia. The capital of the latter is Povenza, and of the former Weiburg.

CARELSCROON, a sea-port town of Sweden, in Blekingia, or Bleking, on the Baltic Sea, with a very good harbour defended by two forts. It was built in 1679; and is very populous, with arsenals for the marine; the house of the director-general of the admiralty is in this town, and here the Swedes lay up their royal navy. E. Long. 15. 5. N. Lat. 56. 15.

CARENTAN, a town of France in Lower Normandy, and in the Contentin, with an ancient castle. W. Long. 1. 14. N. Lat. 49. 10.

CARET, among grammarians, a character marked thus ^, signifying that something is added on the margin, or interlined, which ought to come in where the caret stands.

CAREW (George), born in Devonshire in 1557, an eminent commander in Ireland, was made president of Munster by queen Elizabeth; when, joining his forces with the earl of Thomond, he reduced the Irish insurgents, and brought the earl of Desmond to his trial. King James made him governor of Guernsey, and created him a baron. As he was a valiant commander, he was no less a polite scholar; and wrote *Pacata Hibernia*, a history of the late wars in Ireland, printed after his death, in 1633. He made several collections for a history of Henry V. which are digested into Speed's History of Great Britain. Besides these, he collected materials of Irish history in four large MSS. volumes, now in the Bodleian library, Oxford.

Carew (Thomas), descended from the family of Carew in Gloucestershire, was gentleman of the privy chamber to Charles I. who always esteemed him one of the most celebrated wits of his court. He was much respected by the poets of his time, particularly by Ben Johnson and Sir William Davenant; and left behind him several poems, and a masque called *Cœlum Britannicum*, performed at Whitehall on Shrove Tuesday night, 1633, by the king, and several of his nobles with their sons. Carew was assisted in the contrivance by Inigo Jones, and the music was set by Mr Henry Lawes of the king's chapel. He died in the prime of life, about the year 1639.

Carew (Richard), author of the "Survey of Cornwall," was the eldest son of Thomas Carew of East Anthony, and was born in 1551. When very young, he became a gentleman commoner of Christ-church college, Oxford; and at 14 years of age had the honour of disputing, extempore, with the afterwards famous Sir Philip Sydney, in the presence of the earls of Leicester, Warwick, and other nobility. After spending three years at the university, he removed to the Middle Temple, where he resided the same length of time, and then travelled into foreign parts. Not long after his return to England, he married, in 1577, Juliana Arundel, of Trerice. In 1581, Mr Carew was made justice of the peace, and in 1586 was appointed high-sheriff of the county of Cornwall; about which time he was likewise queen's deputy for the militia. In 1589. he was elected a member of the college of Antiquaries, a distinction to which he was intitled by his literary abilities and pursuits. What particularly engaged his attention was his native county, his "Survey" of which was published, in 4to, at London, in 1602. It hath been twice reprinted, first in 1723, and next in 1769. Of this work Cambden hath spoken in high terms, and acknowledges his obligations to the author. In the present improved state of topographical knowledge, and since Dr Borlase's excellent publications relative to the county of Cornwall, the value of Carew's "Survey" must have been greatly diminished. Mr Gough remarks, that the history and monuments of this county were faintly touched by Carew; but it is added, that he was a person extremely capable of describing them, if the infancy of those studies at that time had afforded light and materials. Another work of our author was a translation from the Italian, intituled, "The Examination of Men's Wits. In which, by discovering the variety of natures, is showed for what profession each one is apt, and how far he shall profit therein." This was published at London in 1594, and afterwards in 1604; and tho' Richard Carew's name is prefixed to it, hath been principally ascribed by some persons to his father. According to Wood, Carew wrote also, "The true and ready Way to learn the Latin Tongue," in answer to a query, whether the ordinary method of teaching the Latin by the rules of grammar be the best mode of instructing youths in that language? This tract is involved in Mr Hartlib's book upon the same subject, and with the same title. It is certain that Carew was a gentleman of considerable abilities and literature, and that he was held in great estimation by some of the most eminent scholars of his time. He was particularly intimate with Sir Henry Spelman, who extols him for his ingenuity, virtue, and learning.

Carew (George), brother to the subject of the last article, was educated in the university of Oxford, after which he studied the law in the inns of court, and then travelled to foreign countries for farther improvement. On his return to his native country, he was called to the bar, and after some time was appointed secretary to Sir Christopher Hatton lord chancellor of England. This was by the especial recommendation of queen Elizabeth herself, who gave him a prothonotaryship in the chancery, and conferred upon him the honour of knighthood. In 1597, Sir George Carew, who was then a master in chancery, was sent ambassador to the king of Poland. In the next reign, he was one of the commissioners for treating with the Scotch concerning an union between the two kingdoms; after which he was appointed ambassador to the court of France, where he continued from the latter end of the year 1605 till 1609. During his residence in that country, he formed an intimacy with Thuanus, to whom he communicated an account of the transactions in Poland whilst he was employed there, which was of great service to that admirable author in drawing up the 121st book of his history. After Sir George Carew's return from France, he was advanced to the important post of master of the court of Wards, which honourable situation he did not long live to enjoy; for it appears from a letter written by Thuanus to Cambden in the spring of 1613, that he was then lately deceased. Sir George Carew married Thomasine, daughter of Sir Francis Godolphin, great grandfather of the lord treasurer Godolphin, and had by her two sons and three daughters. When Sir George Carew returned, in 1609, from his French embassy, he drew up, and addressed to James I. "A Relation of the State of France, with the characters of Henry IV. and the principal Persons of that Court." The characters are drawn from personal knowledge and close observation, and might be of service to a general historian of that period. The composition is perspicuous and manly, and entirely free from the pedantry which prevailed in the reign of James I. but this is the less surprising, as Sir George Carew's taste had been formed in a better era, that of queen Elizabeth. The valuable tract we are speaking of lay for a long time in MS. till happily falling into the hands of the earl of Hardwicke, it was communicated by him to Dr Birch, who published it, in 1749, at the end of his "Historical View of the Negociations between the Courts of England, France, and Brussels, from 1592 to 1617." That intelligent and industrious writer justly observes, that it is a model upon which ambassadors may form and digest their notions and representations; and the late celebrated poet Mr Gray hath spoken of it as an excellent performance.

CAREY (Harry), a man distinguished by both poetry and music, but perhaps more so by a certain facetiousness, which made him agreeable to every body. He published in 1720 a little collection of poems; and in 1732, six cantatas, written and composed by himself. He also composed sundry songs for modern comedies, particularly those in the "Provoked Husband;" he wrote a farce called "The Contrivances," in which were several little songs to very pretty airs of his own composition; he also made two or three little dramas for Goodman's fields theatre, which were very favourably received. In 1729, he published by subscription his poems much enlarged; with the addition of one intituled "Namby Pamby," in which Ambrose Philips is ridiculed. Carey's talents, says his historian, lay in humour and unmalevolent satire; to ridicule the rant and bombast of modern tragedies he wrote one, to which he gave the strange title of "Chrononhotonthologos," acted in 1734. He also wrote a farce called "The Honest Yorkshireman." Carey was a thorough Englishman, and had an unsurmountable aversion to the Italian opera and the singers in it; he wrote a burlesque opera on the subject of the "Dragon of Wantley;" and afterwards a sequel to it, intituled, "The Dragoness;" both which were esteemed a true burlesque upon the Italian opera. His qualities being of the entertaining kind, he was led in-

to

to more expences than his finances could bear, and thus was frequently in diſtreſs. His friends however were always ready to aſſiſt him by their little ſubſcriptions to his works; and encouraged by theſe, he republiſhed, in 1740, all the ſongs he had ever compoſed, in a collection, intituled, "The Muſical Century, in 100 Engliſh Ballads, &c." and, in 1743, his dramatic works, in a ſmall volume, 4to. With all his mirth and good-humour, he ſeems to have been at times deeply affected with the malevolence of ſome of his own profeſſion, who, for reaſons that no one can gueſs at, were his enemies; and this, with the preſſure of his circumſtances, is ſuppoſed to have occaſioned his untimely end; for, about 1744, in a fit of deſperation, he laid violent hands on himſelf, and, at his houſe in Warner-ſtreet, Cold-bath Fields, put a period to a life, which, ſays Sir John Hawkins, had been led without reproach. It is to be noted, and it is ſomewhat ſingular in ſuch a character, that in all his ſongs and poems on wine, love, and ſuch kind of ſubjects, he ſeems to have manifeſted an inviolable regard for decency and good manners.

CARGADORS, a name which the Dutch give to thoſe brokers whoſe buſineſs is to find freight for ſhips outward bound, and to give notice to the merchants, who have commodities to ſend by ſea, of the ſhips that are ready to ſail, and of the places for which they are bound.

CARGAPOL, or KARGAPOL, the capital of a territory of the ſame name, in the province of Dwina, in Muſcovy: E. Long. 38°. N. Lat. 63°.

CARGO denotes all the merchandiſes and effects which are laden on board a ſhip.

Super-Cargo, a perſon employed by merchants to go a voyage, overſee the cargo, and diſpoſe of it to the beſt advantage.

CARIA (anc. geog.), a country of the Hither Aſia; whoſe limits are extended by ſome, while they are contracted by others. Mela, Pliny, extend the maritime Caria from Jaſus and Halicarnaſſus, to Calynda, and the borders of Lycia. The inland Caria Ptolemy extends to the Meander and beyond. *Car*, *Cariates*, *Cariatis*, *Cariſſi*, and *Caris*, and *Calra*, are the gentilitious names; *Carius* and *Caricus* the epithets. *In Care periculum*, was a proverbial ſaying on a thing expoſed to danger, but of no great value. The *Cares* being the Swiſs of thoſe days, were hired and placed in the front of the battle, (Cicero.) *Cum Core Cariſſe*, denoted the behaviour of clowns. The Cares came originally from the iſlands to the continent, being formerly ſubject to Minos, and called *Leleges*: this the Cretans affirm, and the Cares deny, making themſelves aborigines. They are of a common original with the Myſi and Lydi, having a common temple, of a very ancient ſtanding, at Melaſſa, a town of Caria, called *Jovis Carii Delubrum*, (Herodotus.) Homer calls the Carians, barbarians in language.

CARIATI, a town of Italy, in the kingdom of Naples, and province of Hither Calabria, with a biſhop's ſee, and the title of a principality. It is two miles from the gulf of Taranto, and 37 north-eaſt of Coſenza. E. Long. 17. 19. N. Lat. 30. 38.

CARIBBEE ISLANDS, a cluſter of iſlands ſituated in the Atlantic ocean between 59 and 63 degrees of weſt longitude, and between 11 and 18 degrees of north latitude. They lie in the form of a bow or ſemicircle, ſtretching almoſt from the coaſt of Florida north, to near the river Oroonoque. Thoſe that lie neareſt the eaſt have been called the *Windward Iſlands*, the others the *Leeward*, on account of the winds blowing generally from the eaſtern point in thoſe quarters. Abbé Raynal conjectures them to be the tops of very high mountains formerly belonging to the continent, which have been changed into iſlands by ſome revolution that has laid the flat country under water. The direction of the Caribbee iſlands, beginning from Tobago, is nearly north and N. N. W. This direction is continued forming a line ſomewhat curved towards the north-weſt, and ending at Antigua. In this place the line becomes at once curved; and extending itſelf in a ſtraight direction to the weſt and north-weſt, meets in its courſe with Porto-Rico, St Domingo, and Cuba, known by the name of the *Leeward Iſlands*, which are ſeparated from each other by channels of various breadths. Some of theſe are ſix, others 15 or 20 leagues broad; but in all of them the ſoundings are from 100 to 120 or 150 fathoms. Between Grenada and St Vincent's there is alſo a ſmall archipelago of 30 leagues, in which the ſoundings are not above ten fathom. The mountains in the Caribbee iſlands run in the ſame direction as the iſlands themſelves. The direction is ſo regular, that if we were to conſider the tops of theſe mountains only, independent of their baſes, they might be looked upon as a chain of hills belonging to the continent, of which Martinico would be the moſt north-weſterly promontory. The ſprings of water which flow from the mountains in the Windward Iſlands, run all in the weſtern parts of theſe iſlands. The whole eaſtern coaſt is without any running water. No ſprings come down there from the mountains: and indeed they would have there been uſeleſs; for after having run over a very ſhort tract of land, and with great rapidity, they would have fallen into the ſea. In Porto Rico, St Domingo, and Cuba, there are a few rivers that diſcharge themſelves on the northern ſide, and whoſe ſources riſe in the mountains running from eaſt to weſt, that is, thro' the whole length of theſe iſlands. From the other ſide of the mountains facing the ſouth, where the ſea, flowing with great impetuoſity, leaves behind it marks of its inundations, ſeveral rivers flow down, the mouths of which are capable of receiving the largeſt ſhips. The ſoil of the Caribbees conſiſts moſtly of a layer of clay or gravel of different thickneſs; under which is a bed of ſtone or rock. The nature of ſome of thoſe ſoils is better adapted to vegetables than others. In thoſe places where the clay is drier and more friable, and mixes with the leaves and remains of plants, a layer of earth is formed of greater depth than where the clay is moiſter. The ſand or gravel has different properties according to its peculiar nature; wherever it is leſs hard, leſs compact, and leſs porous, ſmall pieces ſeparate themſelves from it, which, though dry, preſerve a certain degree of coolneſs uſeful to vegetation. This ſoil is called in America a *pumice-ſtone* ſoil. Wherever the clay and gravel do not go through ſuch modifications, the ſoil becomes barren, as ſoon as the layer formed by the decompoſition of the original plants is deſtroyed.—By a treaty concluded in January 1660, between

Certhia Hook-billed.
Certhia Cardinal.
Carabus.

between the French and Engliſh, the Caribs were confined to the iſlands of St Vincent's and Dominica, where all the ſcattered body of this people were united, and at that time did not exceed in number 6000 men. See St Vincent's and Dominica.

As the Caribbee iſlands are all between the tropics, their inhabitants are expoſed, allowing for the varieties reſulting from difference of ſituation and ſoil, to a perpetual heat, which generally increaſes from the riſing of the ſun till an hour after noon, and then declines in proportion as the ſun declines. The variations of the temperature of the air ſeem to depend rather on the wind than on the changes of the ſeaſons. In thoſe places where the wind does not blow, the air is exceſſively hot, and none but the eaſterly winds contribute to temper and refreſh it: thoſe that blow from the ſouth and weſt afford little relief; but they are much leſs frequent and leſs regular than that which blows from the eaſt. The branches of the trees expoſed to the influence of the latter are forced round towards the weſt: but their roots are ſtronger, and more extended under the ground, towards the eaſt than towards the weſt; and hence they are eaſily thrown down by ſtrong weſt winds or hurricanes from that quarter. The eaſterly wind is ſcarce felt in the Caribbee iſlands before 9 or 10 o'clock in the morning, increaſes in proportion as the ſun riſes above the horizon, and decreaſes as it declines. Towards the evening it ceaſes entirely to blow on the coaſts, but not on the open ſea. It has alſo been obſerved, that it blows with more force, and more regularity, in the dog-days than at any other time of the year.

The rain alſo contributes to the temperature of the Caribbee iſlands, though not equally in them all. In thoſe places where the eaſterly wind meets with nothing to oppoſe its progreſs, it diſpels the clouds as they begin to riſe, and cauſes them to break either in the woods or upon the mountains. But whenever the ſtorms are too violent, or the blowing of the eaſterly wind is interrupted by the changeable and temporary effect of the ſoutherly and weſterly ones, it then begins to rain. In the other Caribbee iſlands, where this wind does not generally blow, the rains are ſo frequent and plentiful, eſpecially in the winter ſeaſon, which laſts from the middle of July to the middle of October, that, according to the moſt accurate obſervations, as much rain falls in one week as in our climates in a year. Inſtead of thoſe mild refreſhing ſhowers which fall in the European climates, the rains of the Caribbee iſlands are torrents, the ſound of which might be miſtaken for hail, were not that almoſt totally unknown under ſo burning a ſky. Theſe ſhowers indeed refreſh the air; but they occaſion a dampneſs, the effects of which are not leſs diſagreeable than fatal. The dead muſt be interred within a few hours after they have expired. Meat will not keep ſweet above 24 hours. The fruits decay, whether they are gathered ripe or before their maturity. The bread muſt be made up into biſcuits, to prevent its growing mouldy. Common wines turn ſour, and iron turns ruſty, in a day's time. The ſeeds can only be preſerved by conſtant attention and care, till the proper ſeaſon returns for ſowing them. When the Caribbee iſlands were firſt diſcovered, the corn that was conveyed there for the ſupport of the Europeans, was ſo ſoon damaged, that it became neceſſary to ſend it out in the ears. This neceſſary precaution ſo much enhanced the price of it, that few were able to purchaſe it. Flour was then ſubſtituted in lieu of corn; which lowered indeed the expences of tranſport, but had this inconvenience, that it was ſooner damaged. It was imagined by a merchant, that if the flour were entirely ſeparated from the bran, it would have the double advantage of being cheaper and keeping longer. He cauſed it therefore to be ſifted, and put the fineſt flour into ſtrong caſks, and beat it cloſe together with iron hammers, till it became ſo cloſe a body that the air could ſcarcely penetrate it. This method was found to anſwer the purpoſe; and if, by it, the flour cannot be preſerved as long as in our dry and temperate climates, it may be kept for ſix months, a year, or longer, according to the degree of care taken in the preparation.

However troubleſome theſe effects of the rain may be, it is attended with ſome others ſtill more formidable; namely, frequent and dreadful earthquakes. Theſe happening generally during the time or towards the end of the rainy ſeaſon, and when the tides are higheſt, ſome ingenious naturaliſts have ſuppoſed that there might be a connection between them. The waters of the ſky and of the ſea undermine, dig up, and ravage the earth in ſeveral different ways. Among the various ſhocks to which the Caribbee iſlands are expoſed from the fury of the boiſterous ocean, there is one diſtinguiſhed by the name of *raz de marée*, or *whirlpool*. It conſtantly happens once, twice, or thrice, from July to October, and always on the weſtern coaſts, becauſe it takes place after the time of the weſterly or ſoutherly winds, or while they blow. The waves, which at a diſtance ſeem to advance gently within 400 or 500 yards, ſuddenly ſwell againſt the ſhore, as if acted upon in an oblique direction by ſome ſuperior force, and break with the greateſt impetuoſity. The ſhips which are then upon the coaſt, or in the roads beyond it, unable either to keep their anchors or to put out to ſea, are daſhed to pieces againſt the land, and all on board moſt commonly periſh. The hurricane is another terrible phenomenon in theſe iſlands, by which incredible damage is occaſioned; but happily it occurs not often.

The produce of the Caribbee iſlands is exceedingly valuable to the Europeans, conſiſting of ſugar, rum, molaſſes, indigo, &c. a particular account of which is given under the names of the reſpective iſlands as they occur in the order of the alphabet.

CARIBBIANA, or Caribiana, the north eaſt coaſt of Terra Firma, in South America, otherwiſe called *New Andalusia*.

CARICA, the papaw; A genus of the decandria order, belonging to the diœcia claſs of plants; and in the natural method ranking under the 34th order, *Tricoccæ*. The calyx of the male almoſt none; the corolla is quinquefid and funnel-ſhaped; the filaments in the tube of the corolla, a longer and ſhorter one alternately. The calyx of the female quinquedentated; the corolla is pentapetalous, with five ſtigmata; the fruit an unilocular and polyſpermous berry.

Species. 1. The papaya riſes with a thick, ſoft, herbaceous ſtem, to the height of 18 or 20 feet, naked till within two or three feet of the top. The leaves come out on every ſide, upon very long footſtalks.

Carica. Those which are situated undermost are almost horizontal, but those on the top are erect: these leaves in full grown plants are very large, and divided into many lobes deeply sinuated. The stem of the plant, and also the footstalks of the leaves, are hollow. The flowers of the male plant are produced from between the leaves on the upper part of the plant. They have footstalks near two feet long; at the end of which the flowers stand in loose clusters, each having a separate short footstalk: these are of a pure white, and have an agreeable odour. The flowers of the female papaya also come out from between the leaves towards the upper part of the plant, upon very short footstalks, sitting close to the stem: they are large, and bell-shaped, composed of six petals, and are commonly yellow; when these fall away, the germen swells to a large fleshy fruit, of the size of a small melon. These fruits are of different forms: some angular, and compressed at both ends; others oval, or globular; and some pyramidal. The fruit, and all the other parts of the tree abound with a milky acrid juice, which is applied for killing of ring-worms. When the roundish fruit are nearly ripe, the inhabitants of India boil and eat them with their meat as we do turnips. They have somewhat the flavour of a pompion. Previous to boiling they soak them for some time in salt and water, to extract the corrosive juice; unless the meat they are to be boiled with should be very salt and old, and then this juice being in them will make it as tender as a chicken. But they mostly pickle the long fruit, and thus they make no bad succedaneum for mango. The buds of the female flowers are gathered, and made into a sweet-meat; and the inhabitants are such good managers of the produce of this tree, that they boil the shells of the ripe fruit into a repast, and the insides are eaten with sugar in the manner of melons.—The stem being hollow, has given birth to a proverb in the West-India islands; where, in speaking of a dissembling person, they say he is as hollow as a *Papa*.

2. The prosopasa, differs from the other in having a branching stalk, the lobes of the leaves entire, the flower of a rose colour, and the fruit shaped like a pear, and of a sweeter flavour than the papaya.

Culture, &c. These plants being natives of hot countries, cannot be preserved in Britain unless constantly kept in a warm stove, which should be of a proper height to contain them. They are easily propagated by seeds, which are annually brought in plenty from the West Indies, though the seeds of the European plants ripen well. The seeds should be sown in a hot-bed early in the spring: when the plants are near two inches high, they should be removed into separate small pots, and each plunged into a hot-bed of tanners bark, carefully shading them from the sun till they have taken root; after which, they are to be treated in the same manner as other tender exotics. When they are removed into other pots, care must be taken as much as possible to preserve the ball of earth about them, because wherever their roots are laid bare they fel om survive. When they are grown to a large size, they make a noble appearance with their strong upright stems, garnished on every side near the top with large shining leaves, spreading out near three feet all round the stem: the flowers of the male sort coming out in clusters on every side, and the fruit of the female growing round the stalks between the leaves, are so different from any thing of European production, as well to intitle these plants to a place in the gardens of the curious. The fruit of the first species is by the inhabitants of the Caribbee islands eaten with pepper and sugar as melons, but is much inferior to a melon in its native country; but those which have ripened in Britain were detestable: the only use to which Mr Miller says he has known them put was, when they were about half grown, to soak them in salt water to get out the acrid juice, and then pickle them for mangoes, to which they are a good substitute. Carica – Carina

CARICATURA, in painting, denotes the concealment of real beauties, and the exaggeration of blemishes, but still so as to preserve a resemblance of the object. The word is Italian; formed of *carica*, a load, burden, or the like.

CARICOUS, an epithet given to such tumors as resemble the figure of a fig. They are frequently found in the piles.

CARIES, the corruption or mortification of a bone. See MEDICINE and SURGERY, *Index*.

CARIGNAN, a fortified town of Piedmont, seated on the river Po, about seven miles south of Turin. E. Long. 7. 25. N. Lat. 44. 30. It was taken in 1544 by the French; who demolished the fortifications, but spared the castle. It was also taken, and retaken, in 1691.

CARILLONS, a species of chimes frequent in the low countries, particularly at Ghent and Antwerp, and played on a number of bells in a belfrey, forming a complete series or scale of tones and semitones, like those on the harpsichord and organ. There are petals communicating with the great bells, upon which the *carillonneur* with his feet plays the base to sprightly airs, performed with the two hands upon the upper species of keys. These keys are projecting sticks, wide enough asunder to be struck with violence and velocity by either of the hands edgeways, without the danger of hitting the neighbouring key. The player is provided with a thick leather covering for the little finger of each hand, to guard against the violence of the stroke. These carillons are heard through a large town.

CARINA, a Latin term, properly signifying the *keel* of a ship; or that long piece of timber running along the bottom of the ship from head to stern, upon which the whole structure is built or framed.

CARINA is also frequently used for the whole capacity or bulk of a ship; containing the hull or all the space below the deck. Hence the word is also sometimes used by a figure for the whole ship.

CARINA is also used in the ancient architecture. The Romans gave the name *carina* to all buildings in form of a ship, as we still give the name nave to the middle or principal vault of our Gothic churches; because it has that figure.

CARINA, among anatomists, is used to denote the *spina dorsi*; as likewise for the fibrous rudiments or embryo of a chick appearing in an incubated egg. The carina consists of the entire *vertebræ*, as they appear after ten or twelve days incubation. It is then called, because crooked in form of the keel of a ship.—Bota-

ni

nists also, for the like reason, use the word *carina*, to express the lower petalum of a papilionaceous flower.

CARINÆ were also weepers or women hired among the ancient Romans to weep at funerals: they were thus called from *Caria*, the country whence most of them came.

CARINOLA, an episcopal town of Italy, in the kingdom of Naples, and Terra di Lavoro. E. Long. 15. 5. N. Lat. 41. 15.

CARINTHIA, a duchy of Germany, in the circle of Austria, bounded by the archbishopric of Saltzburg on the north, and by Carniola and the Venetian territories on the south, on the west by Tyrol, and on the east by Stiria. A part of this country was anciently called *Carnia*, and the inhabitants *Carni*; but the former afterwards obtained the name of *Carinthia*, and the latter *Carantani* or *Carinthi*. The air of this country is cold, and the soil in general mountainous and barren; but there are some fruitful dales and valleys in it, which produce wheat and other grain. The lakes, brooks, and rivers, which are very numerous, abound with fish; and the mountains yield lead and iron, and in many places are covered with woods. The river Drave, which runs across the country, is the most considerable in Carinthia. The inhabitants are partly descendants of the ancient Germans, and partly of the Sclavonians or Wends. The states are constituted as in Austria, and their assemblies are held at Clagenfurt. The archbishop of Saltzburg and the bishop of Bamberg have considerable territories in this country. Christianity was planted here in the 7th century. The only profession tolerated at present is the Roman Catholic. The bishops are those of Gurk and Lavant, who are subject to the archbishop of Saltzburgh. This duchy was formerly a part of Bavaria. In the year 1282, the emperor Rodolph I. gave it to Maynad count of Tyrol, on condition that when his male issue failed, it should revert to the house of Austria; which happened in 1331. Carinthia has its particular governor or *land-captain*, as he is called; and contributes annually towards the expence of the military establishment 637,695 florins. Only one regiment of foot is usually quartered in it.

CARIPI, a kind of cavalry in the Turkish army. The caripi, to the number of about 1000, are not slaves, nor bred up in the seraglio, like the rest; but are generally Moors or renegado Christians, who having followed adventures, being poor, and having their fortune to seek by their dexterity and courage, have arrived at the rank of horse-guards to the Grand Signior.

CARISSA, in botany: A genus of the monogynia order, belonging to the pentandria class of plants; and in the natural method ranking under the 30th order, *Contortæ*. It has two many-seeded berries.

CARITAS.—The *poculum caritatis*, or grace-cup, was an extraordinary allowance of wine or other liquors, wherein the religious at festivals drank in commemoration of their founder and benefactors.

CARISBROOK-CASTLE, a castle situated in the middle of the isle of Wight, where king Charles I. was imprisoned. W. Long. 1. 30. N. Lat. 50. 40.

CARISTO, an episcopal city of Greece, in the eastern part of the island of Negropont, near Cape Loro. E. Long. 24. 15. N. Lat. 38. 6.

CARKE, denotes the 30th part of a SARPLAR of wool.

CARLE. See CHURL.

CARLETON (Sir Dudley), was born in Oxfordshire, 1573, and bred in Christ-church college. He went as secretary to Sir Ralph Winwood into the Low Countries, when king James resigned the cautionary towns to the states; and was afterwards employed for 20 years as ambassador to Venice, Savoy, and the United Provinces. King Charles created him viscount Dorchester, and appointed him one of his principal secretaries of state; in which office he died in 1631. He was esteemed a good statesman, though an honest man; and published several political works.

CARLINA, the CARLINA THISTLE: A genus of the polygamia æqualis order, belonging to the syngenesia class of plants; and in the natural method ranking under the 49th order, *Compositæ*. The calyx is radiated with long coloured marginal scales. There are seven species, only one of which is a native of Britain, viz. the vulgaris. The others are natives of the south of France or Italy; and are very easily propagated in this country by seeds, which must be sown on a bed of fresh undunged earth, where they are to remain, as they do not bear transplanting. When the plants appear above ground, they should be carefully weeded, and afterwards thinned, leaving them about ten inches or a foot asunder. The second year most of them will flower; but, unless the season proves dry, they rarely produce good seeds in this country, and some of the plants decay soon after they have flowered, so that it is pretty difficult to maintain them here. The roots are used in medicine, and for that purpose are imported from those countries where the plants grow naturally. As we receive them, they are about an inch thick, externally of a rusty brown colour, corroded as it were on the surface, and perforated with numerous small holes, appearing on the surface as if worm-eaten. They have a strong smell, and a subacrid, bitterish, weakly, aromatic taste. They are looked upon to be warm alexipharmics and diaphoretics. Frederic Hoffman the Elder relates that he has observed a decoction of them in broth to occasion vomiting. They have been for some time greatly esteemed among foreign physicians; but never were much in use in this country. The present practice has entirely rejected them, nor are they often to be met with in the shops.

CARLINE, or CAROLINA THISTLE. See CARLINA. It is said to have been discovered by an angel to Charlemagne, to cure his army of the plague; whence its denomination.

CARLINE, or *Carolin*, a silver coin current in the Neapolitan dominions, and worth about 4d. of our money.

CARLINES, or CARLINGS, in a ship, two pieces of timber lying fore and aft, along from one beam to another, directly over the keel; serving as a foundation for the whole body of the ship. On these the ledges rest, whereon the planks of the deck and other matters of carpentry are made fast. The carlines have their ends let into the beams called *culver-tail-wise*.

Carline-Knees, are timbers going athwart the ship,

 from

from the sides to the hatch-way, serving to sustain the deck on both sides.

CARLINGFORD, a port-town of Ireland, seated on Carlingford bay, in the county of Louth, and province of Leinster, 22 miles north of Drogheda. W. Long. 6. 24. N. Lat. 24. 5.

CARLISLE, the capital city of the county of Cumberland, seated on the south of the river Eden, and between the Petteril on the east, and the Caude on the west. It is surrounded by a strong stone-wall, and has a pretty large castle in the western part of it, as also a citadel in the eastern part, built by Henry VIII. It flourished in the time of the Romans, as appears from the antiquities that are to be met with here, and the Roman coins that have been dug up. At the departure of the Romans this city was ruined by the Scots and Picts; and was not rebuilt till the year 680, by Egfrid, who encompassed it with a wall, and repaired the church. In the 8th and 9th centuries, the whole country was again ruined, and the city laid desolate by the incursions of the Norwegians and Danes. In this condition it remained till the time of William Rufus, who repaired the walls and the castle, and caused the houses to be rebuilt. It was fortified by Henry I. as a barrier against Scotland; he also placed a garrison in it, and made it an episcopal see. It was twice taken by the Scots, and afterwards burnt accidentally in the reign of Richard II. The cathedral, the suburbs, and 1500 houses, were destroyed at that time. It is at present in a good condition; and has three gates, the English on the south, the Scotch on the north, and Irish on the west. It has two parishes, and as many churches, St Cuthbert and St Mary's, the last of which is the cathedral, and is separated from the town by a wall of its own. The eastern part, which is the newest, is a curious piece of workmanship. The choir with the aisles is 71 feet broad; and has a stately east window 48 feet high and 30 broad, adorned with curious pillars. The roof is elegantly vaulted with wood; and is embellished with the arms of England and France quartered; as also with Piercy's, Lucy's, Warren's, Mowbray's, and many others. In the choir are the monuments of three bishops who are buried there. The see was erected in 1133 by king Henry I. and made suffragan to the archbishop of York. The cathedral church here had been founded a short time before by Walter, deputy in these parts for king William Rufus, and by him dedicated to the Virgin Mary. He likewise built a monastery, and filled it with canons regular of St Augustine. This foundation continued till the dissolution of monasteries, when its lands were added to the see, and the maintenance of a dean, &c. placed here in their room. The church was almost ruined by the usurper Cromwell and his soldiers; and has never since recovered its former beauty, although repaired after the restoration. This diocese contains the greatest part of the counties of Cumberland and Westmoreland, in which are only 93 parishes; but these (as all the northern are) exceeding large; and of them 18 are impropriations. Here is one archdeacon, viz. of Carlisle. The see is valued in the king's books at L. 530 : 4 : 11½, but is computed to be worth annually L. 2800. The clergy's tenth amounts only to L. 16 : 11 : 7½. To this cathedral belong a bishop, a dean, a chancellor, an archdeacon, four prebendaries, eight minor canons, &c. and other inferior officers and servants.

The Picts wall, which was built across the country from Newcastle, terminates near this place. Carlisle was a fortified place, and still has its governor and lieutenant-governor, but no garrison. It was taken by the rebels, Nov. 15. 1745; and was retaken by the duke of Cumberland on the 10th of December following, and deprived of its gates. It is governed by a mayor, twelve aldermen, two bailiffs, &c. and has a considerable market on Saturdays. The manufactures of Carlisle are chiefly of printed linens, for which near 3000 *l.* per annum is paid in duties. It is also noted for a great manufacture of whips, in which a great number of children are employed.—Salmons appear in the Eden in numbers, so early as the months of December and January; and the London and even Newcastle markets are supplied with early fish from this river: but it is remarkable, that they do not visit the Esk in any quantity till April; notwithstanding the mouths of the two rivers are at a small distance from each other.—Carlisle sends two members to parliament, and gives title of Earl to a branch of the Howard family.

CARLOCK, in commerce, a sort of isinglass, made with the sturgeon's bladder, imported from Archangel. The chief use of it is for clarifying wine, but it is also used by the dyers. The best carlock comes from Astracan, where a great quantity of sturgeon is caught.

CARLOSTAD, or Carlstad, a town of Sweden in Wermeland, seated on the lake Wenner, in E. Long. 14. 4. N. Lat. 59. 18.

Carlstad, or *Carlstadt*, a town of Hungary, capital of Croatia, and the usual residence of the governors of the province. It is seated on the river Kulpa, in E. Long. 16. 5. N. Lat. 45. 34.

CARLOWITZ, a small town of Hungary, in Sclavonia, remarkable for a peace concluded here between the Turks and Christians in 1699. It is seated on the west side of the Danube, in E. Long. 19. 5. N. Lat. 45. 25.

CARLSCRONA, or Carlscroon, a sea-port town in the Baltic, belonging to Sweden. It derives its origin and name from Charles XI. who first laid the foundations of a new town in 1680, and removed the fleet from Stockholm to this place, on account of its advantageous situation in the centre of the Swedish seas, and the superior security of its harbour. The greatest part of Carlscrona stands upon a small rocky island, which rises gently in a bay of the Baltic; the suburbs extend over another small rock, and along the mole close to the bason where the fleet is moored. The way into the town from the main land is carried over a dyke to an island, and from thence along two long wooden bridges joined by a barren rock. The town is spacious, and contains about 18,000 inhabitants. It is adorned with one or two handsome churches, and a few tolerable houses of brick; but the generality of buildings are of wood. The suburbs are fortified towards the land by a stone-wall. The entrance into the harbour, which by nature is extremely difficult from a number of shoals and rocky islands, is still further secured from the attack of an enemy's fleet by two strong forts built on two islands, under the batteries of which all vessels must pass.

Formerly

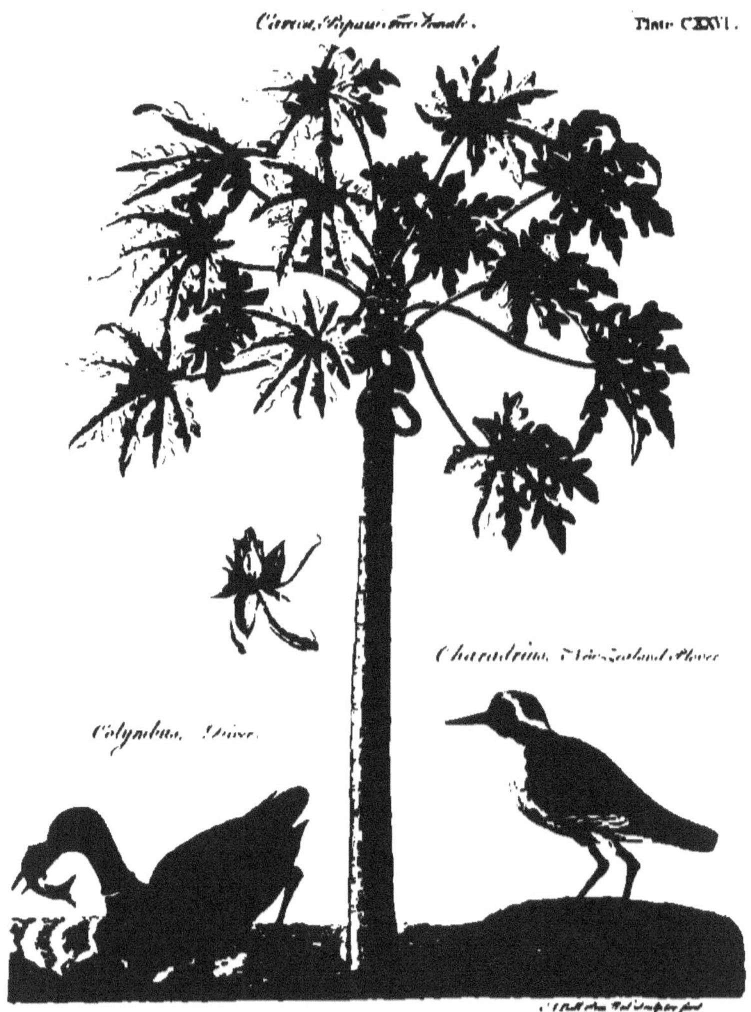
Carica, Papaw Tree Female.
Plate CXXVI.
Charadrius, New Zealand Plover
Colymbus, Diver.

Carlscrona || Carmel.

Formerly vessels in this port, when careened and repaired, were laid upon their sides in the open harbour, until a dock, according to a plan given by Polheim, was hollowed in the solid rock: it was begun in 1714, and finished in 1724; but as it was too small for the admission of men of war, it has lately been enlarged, and is now capable of receiving a ship of the first rate. But new docks have been began upon a stupendous plan worthy of the ancient Romans. According to the original scheme, it was intended to construct 30 docks, for building and laying up the largest ships, at the extremity of the harbour. A large bason, capable of admitting two men of war, is designed to communicate, by sluices, with two smaller basons, from each of which are to extend, like the radii of a circle, five rows of covered docks: each row is to be separated by walls of stone; and each dock to be provided with sluice-gates, so as to be filled or emptied by means of pumps. Close to the docks, magazines for naval stores are to be constructed, and the whole to be inclosed with a stone-wall. The project was begun in 1757; but was much neglected until the accession of his present majesty, who warmly patronized the arduous undertaking. At the commencement of the works, L.25,000 were annually expended upon them; which sum has been lessened to above L.6000 per annum, and the number of docks reduced to 20. The first dock was finished in 1779, and it was computed that the whole number would be executed in 20 years.

CARLSTADT, a town of Germany, in the circle of Franconia, and bishopric of Wurtsburg, seated on the river Maine, in E. Long. 9. 51. N. Lat. 50. 0.

CARLTON, a town in Norfolk held by this tenure, that they shall present 100 herrings baked in 24 pies to the king, wherever he shall be when they first come in season.

CARMAGNIOLA, a fortified town of Italy, in Piedmont, with a good castle. It was taken by the French in 1691, and retaken by prince Eugene the same year. It is seated in a country abounding in corn, flax, and silk, near the river Po, in E. Long. 7. 51. N. Lat. 44. 45.

CARMANIA (anc. geog.), a country of Asia, to the east of Persia, having Parthia to the north, Gedrosia to the east, to the south the Persian Gulf or Sea in part, and in part the Indian, called the *Carmanian Sea*, distinguished into *Carmania Deserta*, and *Carmania Propria*; the former lying to the south of Parthia; and to the south of that, the *Propria*, quite to the sea. Its name is from the Syriac, *Carma*, signifying a "vine," for which that country was famous, yielding clusters three feet long. Now KERMAN, or CARIMANIA, a province of modern Persia.

CARMEL, a high mountain of Palestine, standing on the skirts of the sea, and forming the most remarkable head-land on all that coast. It extends eastward from the sea as far as the plain of Jezreel, and from the city of that name quite to Cæsarea on the south. It seems to have had the name of *Carmel* from its great fertility; this word, according to the Hebrew import, signifying the *vine of God*, and is used in scripture to denote any fruitful spot, or any place planted with fruit trees. This mountain, we are assured, was very fertile. Mr Sandys acquaints us, that, when well cultivated, it abounds with olives, vines, and variety of fruits and herbs both medicinal and aromatic. Others, however, represent it as rather dry and barren; which perhaps may have happened from the neglect of agriculture so common in all parts of the Turkish empire, especially where they are exposed to the incursions of the Arabs. Carmel is the name of the mountain, and of a city built on it; as well as of a heathen deity worshipped in it, but without either temple or statue: though anciently there must have been a temple, as we are told that this mountain was a favourite retreat of Pythagoras, who spent a good deal of time in the temple, without any person with him. But what hath rendered mount Carmel most celebrated and revered both by Jews and Christians, is its having been the residence of the prophet Elijah, who is supposed to have lived there in a cave (which is there shown), before he was taken up into heaven.

Carmelites.

CARMELITES, an order of religious, making one of the four tribes of mendicants or begging friars; and taking its name from mount Carmel, formerly inhabited by Elias, Elisha, and the children of the prophets; from whom this order pretends to descend in an uninterrupted succession. The manner in which they make out their antiquity has something in it too ridiculous to be rehearsed. Some among them pretend they are descendants of Jesus Christ; others go further, and make Pythagoras a Carmelite, and the ancient druids regular branches of their order. Phocas, a Greek monk, speaks the most reasonably. He says, that in his time, 1585, Elias's cave was still extant on the mountain; near which were the remains of a building which intimated that there had been anciently a monastery; that, some years before, an old monk, a priest of Calabria, by revelation, as he pretended, from the prophet Elias, fixed there, and assembled ten brothers.—In 1209, Albert, patriarch of Jerusalem, gave the solitaries a rigid rule, which Papebroch has since printed. In 1217, or, according to others, 1226, pope Honorius III. approved and confirmed it. This rule contained 16 articles; one of which confined them to their cells, and enjoined them to continue day and night in prayer; another prohibited the brethren having any property; another enjoined fasting from the feast of the holy cross till Easter, except on Sundays; abstinence at all times from flesh was enjoined by another article; one obliged them to manual labour; another imposed a strict silence on them from vespers till the tierce the next day.

The peace concluded by the emperor Frederic II. with the Saracens, in the year 1229, so disadvantageous to Christendom, and so beneficial to the infidels, occasioned the Carmelites to quit the Holy Land, under Alan the sixth general of the order. He first sent some of the religious to Cyprus, who landed there in the year 1238, and founded a monastery in the forest of Fortania. Some Sicilians, at the same time, leaving mount Carmel, returned to their own country, where they founded a monastery in the suburbs of Messina. Some English departed out of Syria, in the year 1240, to found others in England. Others of Provence, in the year 1244, founded a monastery in the desart of Aigualates, a league from Marseilles: and thus, the number of their monasteries increasing, they held their European general chapter in the year 1215, at their monastery

aſtery of Aylesford in England.—This order is ſo much increaſed, that it has, at preſent, 38 provinces, beſides the congregation of Mantua, in which are 54 monaſteries, under a vicar-general; and the congregations of Barefooted Carmelites in Italy and Spain, which have their peculiar generals.

After the eſtabliſhment of the Carmelites in Europe, their rule was in ſome reſpects altered; the firſt time, by pope Innocent IV. who added to the firſt article a precept of chaſtity, and relaxed the 11th which enjoins abſtinence at all times from fleſh, permitting them, when they travelled, to eat boiled fleſh: this pope likewiſe gave them leave to eat in a common refectory, and to keep aſſes or mules for their uſe. Their rule was again mitigated by the popes Eugenius IV. and Pius II. Hence the order is divided into two branches, viz. *the Carmelites of the ancient obſervance*, called the *moderate or mitigated*; and thoſe *of the ſtrict obſervance*, who are the *barefooted Carmelites*; a reform ſet on foot in 1540, by S. Thereſa, a nun of the convent of Avila, in Caſtile: theſe laſt are divided into two congregations, that of Spain and that of Italy.

The habit of the Carmelites was at firſt white, and the cloak laced at the bottom with ſeveral liſts. But pope Honorius IV. commanded them to change it for that of the Minims. Their ſcapulary is a ſmall woollen habit of a brown colour, thrown over their ſhoulders. They wear no linen ſhirts; but inſtead of them linſey-wolſey, which they change twice a-week in the ſummer, and once a-week in the winter.

If a monk of this order lies with a woman, he is prohibited ſaying maſs for three or four years, is declared infamous, and obliged to diſcipline himſelf publicly once a-week. If he is again guilty of the ſame fault, his penance is doubled; and if a third time, he is expelled the order.

CARMEN, an ancient term among the Latins, uſed in a general ſenſe to ſignify a verſe; but more particularly to ſignify a ſpell, charm, form of expiation or execration, couched in a few words placed in a myſtic order, on which its efficacy depended. Pezron derives the word *carmen* from the Celtic *carm*, the ſhout of joy, or the verſes which the ancient bards ſung to encourage the ſoldiers before the combat.—*Carmen* was anciently a denomination given alſo to precepts, laws, prayers, imprecations, and all ſolemn formulæ couched in a few words placed in a certain order, though written in proſe. In which ſenſe it was that the elder Cato wrote a *Carmen de moribus*, which was not in verſe, but in proſe.

CARMENTALIA, a feaſt among the ancient Romans, celebrated annually upon the 11th of January, in honour of Carmenta, or Carmentis, a propheteſs of Arcadia, mother of Evander, with whom ſhe came into Italy 60 years before the Trojan war. The ſolemnity was alſo repeated on the 15th of January, which is marked in the old calendar by *Carmentalia rejata*. This feaſt was eſtabliſhed on occaſion of a great fecundity among the Roman dames, after a general reconciliation with their huſbands, with whom they had been at variance, in regard of the uſe of coaches being prohibited them by an edict of the ſenate. This feaſt was celebrated by the women: he who offered the ſacrifices was called *ſacerdos carmentalis*.

CARMINATIVES, medicines uſed in colics, or other flatulent diſorders, to diſpel the wind.

The word comes from the Latin *carminare*, to card or teaze wool, and figuratively to attenuate and diſcuſs wind or vapours, and promote their diſcharge by perſpiration. Though Dr Quincy makes it more myſterious: He ſays it comes from the word *carmen*, taking it in the ſenſe of an incantation or charm; and makes it to have been a general name for all medicines which operated like charms, *i. e.* in an extraordinary manner. Hence, as the moſt violent pains were frequently thoſe ariſing from pent-up wind, which immediately ceaſe upon diſperſion; the term *carminative* became in a peculiar ſenſe applied to medicines which gave relief in windy caſes, as if they cured by inchantment: but this interpretation ſeems a little too far ſtrained.

CARMINE, a powder of a very beautiful red colour, bordering upon purple; and uſed by painters in miniature, though rarely on account of its great price. The manner of preparing it is kept a ſecret by the colour-makers; neither do any of thoſe receipts which have for a long time been publiſhed concerning the preparation of this and other colours at all anſwer the purpoſe. See *Colour-Making*.

CARMONA, a town of Italy in Frioli, and in the county of Goritz, ſeated on a mountain near the river Iodri. It belongs to the houſe of Auſtria. E. Long. 5. 37. N. Lat. 46. 15.

Carmona, an ancient town of Spain in Andaluſia. The gate towards Seville is one of the moſt extraordinary pieces of antiquity in all Spain. It is ſeated in a fertile country, 15 miles eaſt of Seville. W. Long. 5. 37. N. Lat. 37. 24.

CARNATION, in botany. See Dianthus.

Carnation-Colour, among painters, is underſtood of all the parts of a picture, in general, which repreſent fleſh, or which are naked and without drapery. Titian and Corregio in Italy, and Rubens and Vandyke in Flanders, excelled in carnations.—In colouring for fleſh, there is ſo great a variety, that it is hard to lay down any general rules for inſtruction therein; neither are there any regarded by thoſe who have acquired a ſkill this way: the various colouring for carnations may be eaſily produced, by taking more or leſs red, blue, yellow, or biſtre, whether for the firſt colouring, or for the finiſhing: the colour for women ſhould be bluiſh, for children a little red, both freſh and gay; and for the men it ſhould incline to yellow, eſpecially if they are old.

Carnation, among dyers. To dye a carnation, or red roſe colour, it is directed to take liquor of wheat bran a ſufficient quantity, alum three pounds, tartar two ounces; boil them and enter twenty yards of broad cloth; after it has boiled three hours, cool and waſh it: take freſh clear bran liquor a ſufficient quantity, madder five pounds; boil and ſodden according to art.—The Bow dyers know that the ſolution of jupiter, or delved tin, being put in a kettle to the alum and tartar, in another proceſs, makes the cloth, &c. attract the colour into it, ſo that none of the cochineal is left, but the whole is abſorbed by the cloth.

CARNEADES, a celebrated Greek philoſopher, was a native of Cyrene in Africa, and founder of the third academy. He was ſo fond of ſtudy, that he not only avoided all entertainments, but forgot even to eat at his own table; his maid-ſervant Meliſſa was obliged to put the victuals into his hand. He was an antagoniſt of the Stoics; and applied himſelf with great eageness to refute the works of Chrysippus, one of the most celebrated philosophers of their sect. The power of his eloquence was dreaded even by a Roman senate. The Athenians being condemned by the Romans to pay a fine of 500 talents for plundering the city of Oropus, sent ambassadors to Rome, who got the fine mitigated to 100 talents. Carneades the academic, Diogenes the Stoic, and Critolaus the Peripatetic, were charged with this embassy. Before they had an audience of the senate, they harangued to great multitudes in different parts of the city. Carneades's eloquence was distinguished from that of the others by its strength and rapidity. Cato the elder made a motion in the senate, that these ambassadors should be immediately sent back, because it was very difficult to discern the truth thro' the arguments of Carneades. The Athenian ambassadors (said many of the senators) were sent rather to force us to comply with their demands, than to solicit them by persuasion; meaning, that it was impossible to resist the power of that eloquence with which Carneades addressed himself to them. According to Plutarch, the youth at Rome were so charmed by the fine orations of this philosopher, that they forsook their exercises and other diversions, and were carried with a kind of madness to philosophy; the humour of philosophising spreading like enthusiasm. This grieved Cato, who was particularly afraid of the subtility of wit and strength of argument with which Carneades maintained either side of a question. Carneades harangued in favour of justice one day, and the next day against it, to the admiration of all who heard him, among whom were Galba and Cato, the greatest orators of Rome. This was his element; he delighted in demolishing his own work; because it served in the end to confirm his grand principle, that there are only probabilities or resemblances of truth in the mind of man; so that of two things directly opposite, either may be chosen indifferently. Quintilian remarks, that though Carneades argued in favour of injustice, yet he himself acted according to the strict rules of justice. The following was a maxim of Carneades: "If a man privately knew that his enemy, or any other person whose death might be of advantage to him, would come to sit down on grass in which there lurked an asp, he ought to give him notice of it, though it were in the power of no person whatever to blame him for being silent." Carneades, according to some, lived to be 85 years old; others make him to be 90: his death is placed in the 4th year of the 162d Olympiad.

CARNEDDE, in British antiquity, denote heaps of stones supposed to be druidical remains, and thrown together on occasion of confirming and commemorating a covenant. Gen. xxxi. 46. They are very common in the isle of Anglesey, and were also used as sepulchral monuments, in the manner of *tumuli*; for Mr Rowland found a curious urn in one of these carnedde. Whence it may be inferred, that the Britons had the custom of throwing stones on the deceased. From this custom is derived the Welch proverb, *Karn ardyben*, "ill betide thee."

CARNEIA, in antiquity, a festival in honour of Apollo, surnamed Carneus, held in most cities of Greece, but especially at Sparta, where it was first instituted.

The reason of the name, as well as the occasion of the institution, is controverted. It lasted nine days, beginning on the 13th of the month Carneus. The ceremonies were an imitation of the method of living and discipline used in camps.

CARNEL.—The building of ships first with their timber and beams, and after bringing on their planks, is called *carnel-work*, to distinguish it from clinch-work.

Vessels also which go with mizzen-sails instead of main-sails are by some called carnels.

CARNELIAN, in natural history, a precious stone, of which there are three kinds, distinguished by three colours, a red, a yellow, and a white. The red is very well known among us; is found in roundish or oval masses, much like our common pebbles; and is generally met with between an inch and two or three inches in diameter: it is of a fine, compact, and close texture; of a glossy surface; and, in the several specimens, is of all the degrees of red, from the palest flesh-colour to the deepest blood-red. It is generally free from spots, clouds, or variegations: but sometimes it is veined very beautifully with an extremely pale red, or with white; the veins forming concentric circles, or other less regular figures, about a nucleus, in the manner of those of agates. The pieces of carnelian which are all of one colour, and perfectly free from veins, are those which our jewellers generally make use of for seals, though the variegated ones are much more beautiful. The carnelian is tolerably hard, and capable of a very good polish: it is not at all affected by acid menstruums: the fire divests it of a part of its colour, and leaves it of a pale red; and a strong and long continued heat will reduce it to a pale dirty gray.

The finest carnelians are those of the East Indies; but there are very beautiful ones found in the rivers of Silesia and Bohemia; and we have some not despicable ones in England.

Though the ancients have recommended the carnelian as astringent, and attributed a number of fanciful virtues to it, we know of no other use of the stone than the cutting seals on it; to which purpose it is excellently adapted, as being not too hard for cutting, and yet hard enough not to be liable to accidents, to take a good polish, and to separate easily from the wax.

CARNERO, in geography, a name given to that part of the gulph of Venice which extends from the western coast of Istria to the island of Grossa and the coast of Morlachia.

CARNERO is likewise the name of the cape to the west of the mouth of the bay of Gibraltar.

CARNIFEX, among the Romans, the common executioner. By reason of the odiousness of his office, the carnifex was expresly prohibited by the laws from having his dwelling-house within the city. In middle age writers carnifex also denotes a butcher.

Under the Anglo-Danish kings, the carnifex was an officer of great dignity; being ranked with the archbishop of York, earl Goodwin, and the lord steward. Flor. Wigorn. ann. 1040. *Rex Hardecnutus Alfricum Ebor. Archiep. Goodwinum comitem, Edricum dispensatorem, Throndum suum carnificem, & alios magnae dignitatis viros Londoniam misit.*

CARNIOLA, a duchy of Germany bounded on the south by the Adriatic sea, and that part of Istria possessed by the republic of Venice; on the north, by Carinthia and Stiria; on the east, by Sclavonia and Croatia; on the west, by Friuli, the county of Gorz or Goritz, and a part of the gulph of Venice; extending in length about 110 miles, and in breadth about 50. It had its ancient name *Carnia*, as well as the modern one *Carniola*, from its ancient inhabitants the *Carni*, a tribe of Scythians, otherwise called *Japides*, whence this and the adjacent countries were also called *Japidia*.

Carniola is full of mountains, some of which are cultivated and inhabited, some covered with wood, others naked and barren, and others continually buried in snow. The valleys are very fruitful. Here are likewise mines of iron, lead, and copper; but salt must be had from the sovereign's magazines. There are several rivers, besides many medicinal springs and inland lakes. The common people are very hardy, going barefooted in winter through the snow, with open breasts, and sleeping on a hard bench without bed or bolster. Their food is also very coarse and mean. In winter, when the snow lies deep on the ground, the mountaineers bind either small baskets, or long thin narrow boards, like the Laplanders, to their feet, on which, with the help of a stout staff or pole, they descend with great velocity from the mountains. When the snow is frozen, they make use of a sort of irons or skaits. In different parts of the country the inhabitants, especially the common sort, differ greatly in their dress, language, and manner of living. In Upper and Lower Carniola they wear long beards. The languages chiefly in use are the Sclavonian or Wendish, and German; the first by the commonalty, and the latter by people of fashion. The duchy is divided into the Upper, Lower, Middle, and Inner, Carniola. The principal commodities exported hence are, iron, steel, lead, quicksilver, white and red wine, oil of olives, cattle, sheep, cheese, linen, and a kind of woollen stuff called *mehalan*, Spanish leather, honey, walnuts, and timber; together with all manner of wood-work, as boxes, dishes, &c.—Christianity was first planted here in the eighth century.—Lutheranism made a considerable progress in it; but, excepting the Walachians or Uskokes, who are of the Greek church, and style themselves *Staroverci*, i. e. old believers, all the inhabitants at present are Roman Catholics. Carniola was long a marquisate or margraviate; but in the year 1231 was erected into a duchy. As its proportion towards the maintenance of the army, it pays annually 363,171 florins; but only two regiments of foot are quartered in it.

CARNIVAL, or CARNAVAL, a time of rejoicing, a season of mirth, observed with great solemnity by the Italians, particularly at Venice, holding from the twelfth day till Lent.

The word is formed from the Italian *Carnevale*; which Mr Du Cange derives from *Carn-a-val*, by reason the flesh then goes to pot, to make amends for the season of abstinence then ensuing. Accordingly, in the corrupt Latin, he observes, it was called *Carnelevamen*, and *Carnisprivium*; as the Spaniards still denominate it *carnes tollendas*.

Feasts, balls, operas, concerts of music, intrigues, marriages, &c. are chiefly held in carnival time. The carnival begins at Venice the second holiday in Christmas: Then it is they begin to wear masks, and open their play-houses and gaming houses; the place of St Mark is filled with mountebanks, jack-puddings, pedlars, whores, and such like mob, who flock thither from all parts. There have been no less than seven sovereign princes and 30,000 foreigners here to partake of these diversions.

CARNIVOROUS, an epithet applied to those animals which naturally seek and feed on flesh.

It has been a dispute among naturalists, whether man is naturally carnivorous. Those who take the negative side of the question, insist chiefly on the structure of our teeth, which are mostly incisores or molares; not such as *carnivorous* animals are furnished with, and which are proper to tear flesh in pieces: to which it may be added, that, even when we do feed on flesh, it is not without a preparatory alteration by boiling, roasting, &c. and even then that it is the hardest of digestion of all foods. To these arguments Dr Wallis subjoins another, which is that all quadrupeds which feed on herbs or plants have a long colon, with a coecum at the upper end of it, or somewhat equivalent, which conveys the food by a long and large progress, from the stomach downwards, in order to its slower passage and longer stay in the intestines; but that, in *carnivorous* animals, such coecum is wanting, and instead thereof there is a more short and slender gut, and a quicker passage through the intestines. Now, in man, the coecum is very visible: a strong presumption that nature, who is still consistent with herself, did not intend him for a *carnivorous* animal.—It is true, the coecum is but small in adults, and seems of little or no use; but in a foetus it is much larger in proportion: And it is probable, our customary change of diet, as we grow up, may occasion this shrinking. But to these arguments, Dr Tyson replies, that if man had been by nature designed not to be *carnivorous*, there would doubtless have been found, somewhere on the globe, people who do not feed on flesh; which is not the case. Neither are carnivorous animals always without a colon and coecum; nor are all animals carnivorous which have those parts: the opossum, for instance, hath both a colon and coecum, and yet feeds on poultry and other flesh; whereas the hedge-hog, which has neither colon nor coecum, and so ought to be carnivorous, feeds only on vegetables. Add to this, that hogs, which have both, will feed upon flesh when they can get it; and rats and mice, which have large coecums, will feed on bacon as well as bread and cheese. Lastly, the human race are furnished with teeth necessary for the preparation of all kinds of foods; from whence it would seem, that nature intended we should live on all. And as the alimentary duct in the human body is fitted for digesting all kinds of food, ought we not rather to conclude, that nature did not intend to deny us any?

It is no less disputed whether mankind were *carnivorous* before the flood. St Jerom, Chrysostom, Theodoret, and other ancients, maintain, that all animal food was then forbidden; which opinion is also strenuously supported among the moderns by Curcellæus, and refuted by Heidegger, Dausius, Bochhart, &c. See ANTEDILUVIANS.

CARNOSITY is used by some authors for a little

Caro. Carolina.

fleshy excrescence, tubercle, or wen, formed in the urethra, the neck of the bladder, or yard, which stops the passage of the urine.—Caruncles are very difficult of cure; they are not easily known but by introducing a probe into the passage, which there meets with resistance. They usually arise from some venereal malady ill managed.

CARO (Annibal), a celebrated Italian poet, was born at Civita Nuova in 1507. He became secretary to the Duke of Parma, and afterwards to Cardinal Farnese. He was also made a knight of Malta. He translated Virgil's Æneid into his own language with such propriety and elegance of expression, that he was allowed by the best judges to have equalled the original. He also translated Aristotle's rhetoric, two orations of Gregory Nazianzen, with a discourse of Cyprian. He wrote a comedy; and a miscellany of his poems was printed at Venice in 1584. He died at Rome in 1566.

CAROLINA, a province of North America, comprehending the most westerly part of Florida, and lying between 29 and 36 degrees of N. Lat. It is bounded on the east by the Atlantic, and on the west by the river Missisipi, on the north by Virginia, on the south by Georgia, and to the south of Georgia by the Floridas.

This country is seated between the extremities of heat and cold, though the heat is more troublesome in summer than the cold in winter; their winters being very short, and the frosty mornings frequently succeeded by warm days. The air is generally serene and clear the greatest part of the year; but in February and March the inhabitants have a custom of burning the woods, which causes such a smoke as to strangers would seem to proceed from a fog or thickness in the air. The smoke of the tar-kilns likewise deceives strangers, and gives them an ill opinion of the air of Carolina; to which also conduces a custom of the Indians of setting fire to the woods in their huntings, for many miles round. The great rains are in winter, though they are not without heavy showers at midsummer; add to these the constant dews that fall in the night, which refresh the ground and supply the plants with moisture. In North Carolina, the north-west winds in the winter occasion very pinching weather; but they are not of long continuance. Westerly winds bring very pleasant weather; but the southerly are hot and unwholesome, occasioning fevers and other disorders. But this must be understood of summer, for in winter they are very comfortable. The depth of winter is towards the latter end of February, and then the ice is not strong enough to bear a man's weight. In August and September there are sometimes great storms and squalls of wind, which are so violent as to make lanes of 100 feet wide, more or less, thro' the woods, tearing up the trees by the roots. These storms generally happen once in about seven years; and are attended with dreadful thunder, lightning, and heavy rains. They commonly happen about the time of the hurricanes which rage so fatally among the islands between the tropics; and seem to be occasioned by them, or to proceed from the same cause: but by the time they reach Carolina, their force is much abated; and the farther north they proceed, so much the more do they decrease in fury. The soil on the coast is sandy; but farther up, the country is so fruitful that they have not yet been at the trouble to manure their land. The grains most cultivated are Indian corn and rice, though any sort will thrive well enough; they have also pulse of several sorts, little known in England. All kinds of garden stuff usual in England are cultivated here, and may be had in great plenty. They export large quantities yearly of rice, pitch, tar, turpentine, deer-skins, and timber for building; cypress, cedar, sassafras, oak, walnut, and pine. Besides these they also send out beef, pork, tallow, hides, furs, wheat, peas, potatoes, honey, bees-wax, myrtle-wax, tobacco, snake-root, cotton, several sorts of gums and medicinal drugs. Indigo is also cultivated in this province, but of an inferior quality to that which comes from the Caribbee islands. It hath been attempted in vain to cultivate vines, and produce silk, in this country; for though the frosts here do not continue long without intervals of warmer weather, they are sufficient to check the growth of the vine, as well as olives, dates, oranges, &c. The furs are bought of the Indians with vermilion, lead, gunpowder, coarse cloth, iron, and spirituous liquors. As yet they have not a sufficient number of handicraftsmen; which renders labour very dear, and a supply of clothes from Europe necessary. The aspect of the country is very fine, being adorned with beautiful rivers and creeks, and the woods with lofty timber, which afford delightful and pleasant seats for the planters, and render the fencing their lands very easy. And as they have plenty of fish, wild fowl, and venison, besides other necessaries which this country produces naturally, they live easy and luxuriously.

Carolina. *Un. Hist.* xxvi. 84.

Their rivers are large, and navigable a great many miles up the country. They rise near the mountains, and abound with delicate fish, besides water-fowl of different kinds. In some there are islands which yield good pasture, without the annoyance of wild beasts. The chief mountains are the Cherokee or Allegany mountains, which are situated north and north-west, five or six hundred miles distant from the sea. They are very high; and abound with trees, plants, stones, and minerals, of different kinds.

This country is divided into North and South Carolina, and Georgia; each of which, before the late revolution, was under a particular governor. The North is subdivided into four counties, Granville, Colliton, Berkley, and Craven; and South Carolina into two, Clarendon and Albemarle. This last is also divided into 14 parishes or townships, each of which has a brick or timber church. The former likewise has the same number of parishes. Charlestown is the capital of the whole country.

Carolina was discovered by Sebastian Cabot, about the year 1500, in the reign of Henry VII. but the settling of it being neglected by the English, a colony of French Protestants, by the encouragement of Admiral Coligni, were transported thither; and named the place of their first settlement *Arx Carolina*, in honour of their prince, Charles IX. of France: but in a short time that colony was destroyed by the Spaniards; and no other attempt was made by any European power to settle there till the year 1664, when 800 English landed at Cape-Fear in North Carolina, and took possession of the country. In 1670 Cha. II. of

Carolina. of Britain granted Carolina to the Lords Berkley, Clarendon, Albemarle, Craven, and Aſhley, Sir George Carteret, Sir William Berkley, and Sir John Colliton. The plan of government for this new colony was drawn up by the famous Mr Locke, who very wiſely propoſed an univerſal toleration in religious matters. The only reſtriction in this reſpect was, that every perſon claiming the protection of that ſettlement, ſhould, at the age of 17, regiſter himſelf in ſome particular communion. To civil liberty, however, our philoſopher was not ſo favourable; the code of Carolina gave to the eight proprietors who founded the colony, and to their heirs, not only all the rights of a monarch, but all the powers of a legiſlation. The court, which was compoſed of this ſovereign body, and called the *Palatine Court*, was inveſted with the right of nominating to all employments and dignities, and even of conferring nobility; but with new and unprecedented titles. They were, for inſtance, to create in each county two *caſiques*, each of whom was to be poſſeſſed of 24,000 acres of land; and a *landgrave*, who was to have 80,000. The perſons on whom theſe honours ſhould be beſtowed were to compoſe the upper houſe, and their poſſeſſions were made unalienable. They had only the right of farming or letting out a third part of them at the moſt for three lives. The lower houſe was compoſed of the deputies from the ſeveral counties and towns. The number of this repreſentative body was to be increaſed as the colony grew more populous. No tenant was to pay more than about a ſhilling per acre, and even this rent was redeemable. All the inhabitants, however, both ſlaves and freemen, were under an obligation to take up arms upon the firſt order from the Palatine court.

It was not long before the defects of this conſtitution became apparent. The proprietary lords uſed every endeavour to eſtabliſh an arbitrary government; and, on the other hand, the coloniſts exerted themſelves with great zeal to avoid ſervitude. In conſequence of this ſtruggle, the whole province, diſtracted with tumults and diſſentions, became incapable of making any progreſs, though great things had been expected from its particular advantages of ſituation. Though a toleration in religious matters was a part of the original conſtitution, diſſentions aroſe likewiſe on that account. In 1705, Carteret, now Lord Granville, who, as the oldeſt of the proprietors, was ſole governor of the colony, formed a deſign of obliging all the non-conformiſts to embrace the ceremonies of the Church of England; and this act of violence, though diſavowed and rejected by the mother-country, inflamed the minds of the people. In 1720, while this animoſity was ſtill ſubſiſting, the province was attacked by ſeveral bands of ſavages, driven to deſpair by a continued courſe of the moſt atrocious violence and injuſtice. Theſe unfortunate wretches were all put to the ſword: but, in 1728, the lords proprietors having refuſed to contribute towards the expences of an expedition, of which they were to ſhare the immediate benefits, were deprived of their prerogative, except Lord Granville, who ſtill retained his eighth part. The reſt received a recompence of about 24,000l. The colony was taken under the immediate protection of the crown, and from that time began to flouriſh. The diviſion into North and South Carolina now took place, and the ſettlement of Georgia commenced in 1732. See Georgia. Carolina || Carp.

CAROLINE. See Carline.

Caroline-Books, the name of four books, compoſed by order of Charlemagne, to refute the ſecond council of Nice. Theſe books are couched in very harſh and ſevere terms, containing 120 heads of accuſation againſt the council of Nice, and condemning the worſhip of images.

CAROLOSTADIANS, or Carlostadians, an ancient ſect or branch of Lutherans, who denied the real preſence of Chriſt in the euchariſt.

They were thus denominated from their leader Andrew Caroloſtadius, who having originally been archdeacon of Wittemberg, was converted by Luther, and was the firſt of all the reformed clergy who took a wife; but diſagreeing afterwards with Luther, chiefly in the point of the ſacrament, founded a ſect apart. The Caroloſtadians are the ſame with what are otherwiſe denominated Sacramentarians, and agree in moſt things with the Zuinglians.

CAROLUS, an ancient Engliſh broad piece of gold ſtruck under Charles I. Its value has of late been at 23 ſhillings Sterling, though at the time it was coined it is ſaid to have been rated at 20 ſhillings.

Carolus, a ſmall copper coin, with a little ſilver mixed with it, ſtruck under Charles VIII. of France. The carolus was worth 12 deniers when it ceaſed to be current. Thoſe which are ſtill current in trade in Lorrain, or in ſome neighbouring provinces, go under the name of French ſols.

CAROTIDS, in anatomy, two arteries of the neck, which convey the blood from the aorta to the brain; one called the right, and the other the left, carotid.

CARP, in ichthyology, the Engliſh name of a ſpecies of cyprinus. See Cyprinus; alſo *Carp-Fishing*.

The carp is the moſt valuable of all kinds of fiſh for ſtocking of ponds. It is very quick in its growth, and brings forth the ſpawn three times a-year, ſo that the increaſe is very great. The female does not begin to breed till eight or nine years old; ſo that in breeding-ponds a ſupply muſt be kept of carp of that age. The beſt judges allow, that, in ſtocking a breeding-pond, four males ſhould be allowed to twelve females. The uſual growth of a carp is two or three inches in length in a year; but, in ponds which receive the fattening of common ſewers, they have been known to grow from five inches to 18 in one year. A feeding-pond of one acre extent will very well feed 300 carp of three years old, 300 of two years, and 400 of one year old. Carp delight greatly in ponds that have marley ſides; they love alſo clay-ponds well ſheltered from the winds, and grown with weeds and long graſs at the edges, which they feed on in the hot months. Carp and tench thrive very faſt in ponds and rivers near the ſea, where the water is a little brackiſh; but they are not ſo well taſted as thoſe which live in freſh water. Grains, blood, chicken-guts, and the like, may at times be thrown into carp-ponds, to help to fatten the fiſh. To make them grow large and fat, the growth of graſs under the water ſhould by all means poſſible be encouraged. For this purpoſe, as the water decreaſes in the ſummer, the ſides of the pond left naked and dry ſhould be well raked with an iron rake, to deſtroy all the weeds, and cut up the ſurface of the earth: hay-ſeed ſhould then be ſown plentifully in theſe places; and more ground prepared in the ſame manner, as the water falls more and more away. By this means there will be a fine and plentiful growth of young graſs along the ſides of the pond to the water's edge; and when the rains fill up the pond again, this will be all buried under the water, and will make a feeding-place for the fiſh, where they will come early in the morning, and will fatten greatly upon what they find there.

CARPATES, or ALPES BASTARNICAE, (anc. geog.) a range of mountains, running out between Poland, Hungary, and Tranſylvania. Now called the Carpathian Mountains.

CARPATHIUM (Mare, Horace, Ovid); the ſea that waſhes the iſland Carpathus.

CARPATHUS, an iſland on the coaſt of Aſia, two hundred ſtadia in compaſs, and an hundred in length. Its name is ſaid to be from its ſituation on the coaſt of Caria. It lies between Rhodes and Crete, in the ſea which, from this iſland, is called the Carpathian Sea, and has to the north the Ionian, to the ſouth the Egyptian, to the weſt the Cretan and Aſrican ſeas. It is two hundred furlongs in compaſs, and a hundred in length. It had anciently, according to Strabo, four cities; according to Sevlax only three. Ptolemy mentions but one, which he calls Poſidium. This iſland is now called Scarpanto.

CARPÆA, a kind of dance anciently in uſe among the Athenians and Magarſians, performed by two perſons, the one acting a labourer, the other a robber. The labourer, laying by his arms, goes to ploughing and ſowing, ſtill looking warily about him as if afraid of being ſurpriſed: the robber at length appears, and the labourer, quitting his plough, betakes himſelf to his arms, and fights in defence of his oxen. The whole was performed to the ſound of flutes, and in cadence. Sometimes the robber was overcome and ſometimes the labourer; the victor's reward being the oxen and plough. The deſign of the exerciſe was to teach and accuſtom the peaſants to defend themſelves againſt the attacks of ruffians.

CARPENTER, a perſon who practiſes CARPENTRY. The word is formed from the French *charpentier*, which ſignifies the ſame, formed of *charpente*, which denotes timber; or rather from the Latin *carpentarius*, a maker of *carpenta*, or carriages.

CARPENTER of a Ship, an officer appointed to examine and keep in order the frame of a ſhip, together with her maſts, yards, boats, and all other wooden machinery. It is his duty in particular to keep the ſhip *tight*; for which purpoſe he ought frequently to review the decks and ſides, and to caulk them when it is neceſſary. In the time of battle, he is to examine up and down, with all poſſible attention, in the lower apartments of the ſhip, to ſtop any holes that may have been made by ſhot, with wooden plugs provided of ſeveral ſizes.

CARPENTRAS, an epiſcopal town of Provence in France, and capital of Venaiſſin. It is ſubject to the pope; and is ſeated on the river Auſon, at the foot of a mountain. E. Long. 5. 6. N. Lat. 44. 4.

CARPENTRY, the art of cutting, framing, and joining large pieces of wood, for the uſes of building. It is one of the arts ſubſervient to architecture, and is divided into houſe-carpentry and ſhip-carpentry: the firſt is employed in raiſing roofing, flooring of houſes, &c. and the ſecond in the building of ſhips *, barges, &c. The rules in carpentry are much the ſame with thoſe of JOINERY; the only difference is, that carpentry is uſed in the larger and coarſer work, and joinery in the ſmaller and curious.

* See Ship-building.

CARPENTUM, in antiquity, a name common to divers ſorts of vehicles, anſwering to coaches as well as waggons, or even carts, among us. The carpentum was originally a kind of car or vehicle in which the Roman ladies were carried; though in after times it was alſo uſed in war. Some derive the word from *carro*; others from *Carmenta* the mother of Evander, by a converſion of the *m* into *p*.

CARPET, a ſort of covering of ſtuff, or other materials, wrought with the needle or on a loom, which is part of the furniture of a houſe, and commonly ſpread over tables, or laid upon the floor.

Perſian and Turkey carpets are thoſe moſt eſteemed; though at Paris there is a manufactory after the manner of Perſia, where they make them little inferior, not to ſay finer than the true Perſian carpets. They are velvety, and perfectly imitate the carpets which come from the Levant. There are alſo carpets of Germany, ſome of which are made of woollen ſtuffs, as ſerges, &c. and called ſquare carpets: others are made of wool alſo, but wrought with the needle, and pretty often embelliſhed with ſilk; and, laſtly, there are ſome made of dogs hair. We have likewiſe carpets made in Britain, which are uſed either as floor-carpets, or to cover chairs, &c. It is true, we are not arrived at the like perfection in this manufacture with our neighbours the French; but may not this be owing to the want of a like public encouragement?

Carpet-Knights, a denomination given to gown-men and others, of peaceable profeſſions, who, on account of their birth, office, or merits to the public, or the like, are, by the prince, raiſed to the dignity of knighthood.

They take the appellation *carpet*, becauſe they uſually receive their honours from the king's hands in the court, kneeling on a carpet. By which they are diſtinguiſhed from knights created in the camp, or field of battle, on account of their military proweſs. Carpet-knights poſſeſs a medium between thoſe called *truck*, or *dunghill-knights*, who only purchaſe or merit the honour by their wealth, and *knights-batchelors*, who are created for their ſervices in the war.

CARPI, a principality of Modena in Italy, lying about four leagues from that city. It formerly belonged to the houſe of Pio; the elder ſons of which bore the title of *Princes of St Gregory*. In the beginning of the 14th century *Manfrey* was the firſt prince of Carpi; but in the 16th, the emperor Cha. V. gave the principality to Alfonſo duke of Ferrara. This nobleman, in recompence, gave to Albert Pio, to whom the principality of Carpi belonged of right, the town of Saſſuolo and ſome other lands. Albert was, however, at laſt obliged to retire to Paris: where, being ſtripped of all his eſtates, he died in 1538, with the reputation of being one of the beſt and braveſt men of his age. The family of Pio is yet in being, and continues attached to the French court. Some of

Carpi, Carpinus.

there have even been raiſed to the purple, and ſtill make a figure in Europe.

Carpi, a town of Italy in the duchy of Modena, and capital of the laſt mentioned principality. It has a ſtrong caſtle, and is ſituated in E. Long. 11. 12. N. Lat. 44. 45.

Carpi, a town of the Veroneſe in Italy, memorable for a victory gained by the Imperialiſts over the French in 1701. It is ſubject to the Venetians; and is ſituated on the river Adige, in E. Long. 11. 59. N. Lat. 45. 10.

CARPI (Ugo da), an Italian painter, of no very conſiderable talents in that art, but remarkable for being the inventor of that ſpecies of engraving on wood, diſtinguiſhed by the name of chiaro-ſcuro, in imitation of drawing. This is performed by uſing more blocks than one; and Ugo da Carpi uſually had three; the firſt for the outline and dark ſhadows, the ſecond for the lighter ſhadows, and the third for the half tint. In that manner he ſtruck off prints after ſeveral deſigns, and cartons of Raphael; particularly one of the Sybil, a Deſcent from the Croſs, and the Hiſtory of Simon the Sorcerer. He died in 1500. This art was brought to a ſtill higher degree of perfection by Balthaſar Peruzzi of Siena, and Parmigiano, who publiſhed ſeveral excellent deſigns in that manner.

Carpi (Girolamo da), hiſtory and portrait painter, was born at Ferrara in 1501, and became a diſciple of Garofalo. When he quitted that maſter, he devoted his whole time, thoughts, and attention, to ſtudy the works of Correggio, and to copy them with a moſt critical care and obſervation; in which labour he ſpent ſeveral years at Parma, Modena, and other cities of Italy, where the beſt works of that exquiſite painter were preſerved. He acquired ſuch an excellence in the imitation of Correggio's ſtyle, and copying his pictures, that many paintings finiſhed by him were taken for originals, and not only admired, but were eagerly purchaſed by the connoiſſeurs of that time. Nor is it improbable that ſeveral of the paintings of Girolamo da Carpi paſs at this day for the genuine work of Correggio himſelf. He died in 1556.

CARPINUS, the horn-beam, in botany: A genus of the polyandria order, belonging to the monœcia claſs of plants; and in the natural method ranking under the 50th order, *Amentaceæ*. The calyx of the male is monophyllous and ciliated; there is no corolla, but 10 ſtamina. The calyx of the female is monophyllous and ciliated; no corolla; two germens, with two ſtyles on each. The fruit is an egg-ſhaped nut. There are two ſpecies, viz.

1. The betulus, or common hornbeam; a deciduous tree, native of Europe and America. Its leaves are of a darkiſh green, and about the the ſize of thoſe of the beech, but more pointed and deeply ſerrated. Its branches are long, flexible, and crooked; yet in their general appearance very much reſemble thoſe of the beech: indeed there is ſo great a likeneſs between thoſe two trees, eſpecially in the ſhrubby and underwood ſtate, that it would be difficult to diſtinguiſh them at the firſt glance, were it not for that gloſſy varniſh with which the leaves of the beech are ſtrongly marked. In the days of Evelyn, when topiary work was the gardener's idol, the hornbeam might be conſidered as deſerving of thoſe endearing expreſſions which that enthuſiaſtic writer has been pleaſed to laviſh upon it: nevertheleſs, as an ornamental in modern gardening it ſtands low; and its preſent uſes are few. As an underwood it affords ſtakes and edders, fuel and charcoal. Its timber ranks with that of the beech and the ſycamore; and the inner bark is ſaid to be much uſed in Scandinavia to dye yellow. The only ſuperior excellency of the hornbeam lies in its fitneſs for screen fences for ſheltering gardens, nurſeries, and young plantations from the ſeverities of the winter ſeaſon. It may be trained to almoſt any height, and by keeping it trimmed on the ſides it becomes thick of branches, and conſequently thick of leaves; which being by their nature retained upon the plant after they wither, a hornbeam hedge occaſions a degree of ſhelter nearly equal to that given by a brick wall. Indeed, being leſs reflective than that expenſive ſcreen, it affords a more uniform temperature of air to the plants which ſtand near it. In this point of view, too, the hornbeam is uſeful to be planted promiſcuouſly, or in alternate rows, amongſt more tender plants in expoſed ſituations, in the ſame manner as the birch; to which it has more than one preference: namely, it is warmer in winter,—and Hanbury ſays, the hornbeam is peculiarly grateful to hares and rabbits; conſequently it may prevent their injuring its more valuable neighbours: yet, like Evelyn, he ſeems to be of opinion that it is diſaffected by deer. If this be really the caſe, the hornbeam may upon many occaſions be introduced into deer-parks with ſingular propriety.

Of this ſpecies there are three varieties: The Eaſtern Hornbeam, Flowering Hornbeam, American Hornbeam. The eaſtern hornbeam arrives to the leaſt height of all the ſorts: about ten feet is the fartheſt of its growth, and it looks pretty enough with trees of the ſame growth. The leaves are by no means ſo large as the common ſort; and as the branches are always cloſer in proportion to the ſmallneſs of the leaves, where a low hedge is wanted of the deciduous kind, this would not be an improper tree for the purpoſe, either to be kept ſheered, or ſuffered to grow in its natural ſtate. The bark of this ſort is more ſpotted than that of the common. The flowering hornbeam is the moſt free ſhooter of any of the ſorts; and will arrive to be the higheſt, the common hornbeam only excepted. It will grow to be thirty or forty feet high. The branches of this tree are leſs ſpotted with greyiſh ſpots than any of the other ſorts. The leaves are very rough, of a dark-green colour, and are longer than the common ſort. The property which the common hornbeam is poſſeſſed of, of retaining its leaves all winter, does not belong to this ſort, the leaves of which conſtantly fall off in the autumn with other deciduous trees. American hornbeam is a more elegant tree than any of the former ſorts. The branches are ſlender, covered with a browniſh ſpeckled bark, and are more ſparingly ſent forth than from any of the others. The leaves are oblong, pointed, and of a paliſh green, and are not nearly ſo rough as the common hornbeam, though the flowers and fruit are produced in the ſame manner.

2. The oſtrya, or hop-hornbeam, a native of Italy and of Virginia. This is of taller growth than the eaſtern kind. It will arrive to the height of twenty feet, or more. The leaves are nearly the ſize of the

common

common ſort, and ſome people admire this tree on account of the ſingular appearance it makes with its ſeeds, before they begin to fall. There is a variety which grows to thirty feet high, ſhoots freely, has long rough leaves like thoſe of the elm, and longiſh yellow-coloured flowers, called the *Virginian flowering hop-hornbeam*.

Propagation. The common hornbeam may be propagated either by layering (at almoſt any time of the year), or from ſeeds in the following manner: In the autumn the ſeeds will be ripe; when, having gathered a ſufficient quantity for the purpoſe, let them be ſpread upon a mat a few days to dry. After this, they ſhould be ſown in the ſeminary-ground, in beds four feet wide, with an alley of about two feet, and from one to two inches deep. In this bed they muſt remain till the ſecond ſpring before they make their appearance; and all the ſummer they lie concealed, the weeds ſhould conſtantly be plucked up as ſoon as they peep; for if they are neglected, they will get ſo ſtrong, and the fibres of their roots will be ſo far ſtruck down among the ſeeds, as to endanger the drawing many ſeeds out with them, on weeding the ground. After the young plants appear, they ſhould conſtantly be kept clear of weeds during the next ſummer; and if they were to be now and then gently refreſhed with water in dry weather, it would prove ſerviceable to them. In the ſpring following they may be taken out of theſe beds, and planted in the nurſery, in which ſituation they may remain till they are of a ſufficient ſize to plant out for ſtandards.

The other ſorts are to be propagated by layers; for which purpoſe a few plants for ſtools muſt be procured. The ſtools of the eaſtern hornbeam ſhould be planted a yard, and the other ſorts a yard and a half or two yards aſunder. After theſe plants have made ſome young ſhoots, they ſhould be layered in the autumn, and by that time twelvemonth they will have ſtruck root; at which time, or any time in the winter, or early in the ſpring, they ſhould be taken off, and planted in the nurſery-way, obſerving always to bruſh up the ſtool, that it may afford fine young ſhoots for freſh layering by the autumn following. The diſtance the plants ſhould be allowed in the nurſery need be no more than one foot, in rows that are two feet aſunder; and here they may ſtand, with the uſual nurſery care of weeding and digging the rows in winter, until they are to be finally planted out; though the Virginian hornbeam will frequently ſend forth two ſhoots, which will ſeem to ſtrive for maſtery in the lead. When this is obſerved, the weakeſt ſhould always be taken away, otherwiſe the tree will grow forked.

CARPOBALSAM, in the Materia Medica, the fruit of the tree which yields the true oriental balſam. The carpobalſam is uſed in Egypt, according to Proſper Alpinus, in all the intentions in which the balſam itſelf is applied: but the only uſe the Europeans make of it is in Venice treacle and mithridate; and in theſe not a great deal, for cubebs and juniper-berries are generally ſubſtituted in its place.

CARPOCRATIANS, a branch of the ancient Gnoſtics, ſo called from *Carpocrates*, who in the ſecond century revived and improved upon the errors of Simon Magus, Menander, Saturninus, and other Gnoſtics. He owned, with them, one ſole principle and father of all things, whoſe name as well as nature was unknown. The world, he taught, was created by angels, vaſtly inferior to the firſt principle. He oppoſed the divinity of Jeſus Chriſt; making him a mere man, begotten carnally on the body of Mary by Joſeph, though poſſeſſed of uncommon gifts which ſet him above other creatures. He inculcated a community of women; and taught, that the ſoul could not be purified, till it had committed all kinds of abominations, making that a neceſſary condition of perfection.

CARPOLITHI, or Fruit-stone Rocks of the Germans, are compoſed of a kind of jaſper, of the nature of the amygdaloides, or almond-ſtones. Bertrand aſſerts that the latter are thoſe which appear to be compoſed of elliptical pieces like petrified almonds, though in truth they are only ſmall oblong pieces of calcareous ſtone rounded by attrition, and ſometimes ſmall muſcle-ſhells connected by a ſtony concretion. The name of carpolithi, however, is given in general by writers on foſſils to all ſorts of ſtony concretions that have any reſemblance to fruit of whatever kind.

CARPUS, the wriſt. See Anatomy, Nº 53.

CARR, a kind of rolling throne, uſed in triumphs, and at the ſplendid entries of princes. See Chariot.

The word is from the ancient Gauliſh, or Celtic, *Carr*; mentioned by Cæſar, in his commentaries, under the name *Carrus*. Plutarch relates, that Camillus having entered Rome in triumph, mounted on a carr drawn by four white horſes, it was looked on as too haughty an innovation.

Carr is alſo uſed for a kind of light open chariot. The carr, on medals, drawn either by horſes, lions, or elephants, uſually ſignifies either a triumph or an apotheoſis; ſometimes a proceſſion of the images of the gods at a ſolemn ſupplication, and ſometimes of thoſe of ſome illuſtrious family at a funeral. The carr covered, and drawn by mules, only ſignifies a conſecration, and the honour done any one of having his image carried at the games of the circus. See Consecration, &c.

CARRAC, or Carraca, a name given by the Portugueſe to the veſſels they ſend to Braſil and the Eaſt-Indies; being very large, round built, and fitted for fight as well as burden. Their capacity lies in their depth, which is very extraordinary. They are narrower above than underneath, and have ſometimes ſeven or eight floors; they carry about 2000 tons, and are capable of lodging 2000 men; but of late they are little uſed. Formerly they were alſo in uſe among the knights of Rhodes, as well as among the Genoeſe, and other Italians. It is a cuſtom among the Portugueſe, when the carracs returned from India, not to bring any boat or ſloop for the ſervice of the ſhip beyond the iſland of St Helena; at which place they ſink them on purpoſe, in order to take from the crew all hopes or poſſibility of ſaving themſelves, in caſe of ſhipwreck.

CARRARA marble, among our artificers, the name of a ſpecies of white marble, which is called *marmor lunenſe*, and *ligyſticum* by the ancients; it is diſtinguiſhed from the Parian, now called the ſtatuary marble, by being harder and leſs bright.

CARRAVEIRA, a town of Turkey in Europe, with a Greek archbishop's see. E. Long. 22. 25. N. Lat. 40. 37.

CARRIAGE, a vehicle serving to convey persons, goods, merchandizes, and other things, from one place to another.

For the construction and mechanical principles of wheel-carriages, see MECHANICS.

CARRIAGE of a cannon, the frame or timber work on which it is mounted, serving to point it for shooting, or to carry it from one place to another. It is made of two planks of wood, commonly of one-half the length of the gun, called the checks, and joined by three wooden transums, strengthened with three bolts of iron. It is mounted on two wheels, but on a march has two fore-wheels with limbers added. The principal parts of a carriage are the checks, transums, bolts, plates, train, bands, bridge, bed, hooks, trunnion holes, and capsquare.

Block-CARRIAGE, a cart made on purpose for carrying mortars and their beds from place to place.

Truck-CARRIAGE, two short planks of wood, supported on two axle-trees, having four trucks of solid wood for carrying mortars or guns upon battery, where their own carriages cannot go. They are drawn by men.

CARRICK, the southern division of the shire of Ayr in Scotland. It borders on Galloway; stretches 32 miles in length; and is a hilly country fit for pasturage. The chief rivers are the Stracher and Girven, both abounding with salmon; here are also several lakes and forests; and the people on the coast employ themselves in the herring-fishery, though they have no harbour of any consequence. The only towns of this district are Bargeny and Maybole, two inconsiderable villages, yet the first gave the title (now extinct) of baron to a branch of the Hamilton family. The prince of Wales, as prince of Scotland, is earl of Carrick.

CARRICK on the Sure, a town of Ireland, in the county of Tipperary and province of Munster. W. Long. 7. 14. N. Lat. 52. 16.

CARRICK-Fergus, a town of Ireland, in the county of Antrim and province of Ulster. It is a town and county in itself, and sends two members to parliament. It is very rich and populous, with a good harbour; and is governed by a mayor, recorder, and sheriffs.—It has, however, been of far greater consequence than at present, as appears from the mayor having been admiral of a considerable extent of coast in the counties of Down and Antrim, and the corporation enjoying the customs paid by all vessels within these bounds, the creeks of Belfast and Bangor excepted. This grant was repurchased, and the custom-house transferred to Belfast.—Here is the skeleton of a fine house built by Lord Chichester in the reign of James I. an old Gothic church with many family monuments, and a very large old castle. The town was formerly walled round, and some part of the walls is still remaining entire.—Carrick-fergus is seated on a bay of the same name in the Irish channel; and is noted for being the landing place of king William in 1690. Here also Thurot made a descent in 1759, took possession of the castle, and carried away hostages for the ransom of the town; but being soon after pursued by commodore Elliot, his three ships were taken, and he himself was killed.

CARRIER, is a person that carries goods for others for hire. A common carrier, having the charge and carriage of goods, is to answer for the same, or the value, to the owner. And where goods are delivered to a carrier, and he is robbed of them, he shall be charged and answer for them, because of the hire. If a common carrier who is offered his hire, and who has convenience, refuses to carry goods, he is liable to an action, in the same manner as an inn-keeper who refuses to entertain a guest. See ASSUMPSIT.

One brought a box to a carrier, with a large sum of money, and the carrier demanded of the owner what was in it; he answered, that it was filled with silks, and such like goods: upon which the carrier took it, and was robbed, and adjudged to make it good; but a special acceptance, *viz. provided there is no charge of money*, would have excused the carrier.—A person delivered to a carrier's book-keeper two bags of money sealed up, to be carried from London to Exeter, and told him that it was L. 200, and took his receipt for the same, with promise of delivery for 10 s *per cent.* carriage and risk: though it be proved that there was L. 400 in the bags, if the carrier be robbed, he shall answer only for L. 200, because there was a particular undertaking for that sum and no more; and his reward, which makes him answerable, extends no farther. If a common carrier loses goods which he is intrusted to carry, a special action on the case lies against him, on the custom of the realm, and not trover; and so of a common carrier by boat. An action will lie against a porter, carrier, or barge-man, upon his bare receipt of the goods, if they are lost through negligence. Also a lighter-man spoiling goods he is to carry, by letting water come to them, action of the case lies against him, on the common custom. *Jacob's Law Dict.*

CARRIER-Pigeon, or *courier-pigeon*, a sort of pigeon used, when properly trained, to be sent with letters from one place to another. See COLUMBA.

Though you carry these birds hood-winked, 20, 30, nay, 60 or 100 miles, they will find their way in a very little time to the place where they were bred. They are trained to this service in Turkey and Persia; and are carried first, while young, short flights of half a mile, afterwards more, till at length they will return from the farthest part of the kingdom. Every Bashaw has a basket of these pigeons bred in the seraglio, which, upon any emergent occasion, as an insurrection, or the like, he dispatches, with letters braced under their wings, to the seraglio; which proves a more speedy method, as well as a more safe one, than any other; he sends out more than one pigeon, however, for fear of accidents. Lithgow assures us, that one of these birds will carry a letter from Babylon to Aleppo, which is 30 days journey, in 48 hours. This is also a very ancient practice; Hirtius and Brutus, at the siege of Modena, held a correspondence with one another by means of pigeons. And Ovid tells us, that Taurosthenes, by a pigeon stained with purple, gave notice to his father of his victory at the Olympic Games, sending it to him at Ægina.

In modern times, the most noted were the pigeons of Aleppo,

Aleppo, which served as couriers at Alexandretta and Bagdad. But this use of them has been laid aside for the last 30 or 40 years, because the Curd robbers killed the pigeons. The manner of sending advice by them was this: they took pairs which had young ones, and carried them on horseback to the place from whence they wished them to return, taking care to let them have a full view. When the news arrived, the correspondent tied a billet to the pigeon's foot, and let her loose. The bird, impatient to see its young, flew off like lightning, and arrived at Aleppo in ten hours from Alexandretta, and in two days from Bagdad. It was not difficult for them to find their way back, since Aleppo may be discovered at an immense distance. This pigeon has nothing peculiar in its form, except its nostrils, which, instead of being smooth and even, are swelled and rough.

CARRON, a small but remarkable river in Scotland, rising about the middle of the isthmus between the friths of Forth and Clyde. Both its source, and the place where it empties itself into the sea, are within the shire of Stirling, which it divides into two nearly equal parts. The whole length of its course, which is from west to east, is not above 14 miles. It falls into the frith of Forth about three miles to the north-east of Falkirk. The stream thereof is but small, and scarce deserves the notice of a traveller; yet there is no river in Scotland, and few in the whole island of Britain, whose banks have been the scene of so many memorable transactions. When the Roman empire was in all its glory, and had its eastern frontiers upon the Euphrates, the banks of Carron were its boundaries upon the north-west; for the wall of Antoninus *, which was raised to mark the limits of that mighty empire, stood in the neighbourhood of this river, and ran parallel to it for several miles.

* See Antoninus's Wall.

Near the middle of its course, in a pleasant valley, stand two beautiful mounts, called the *Hills of Dunipace*, which are taken notice of by most of the Scottish historians as monuments of great antiquity. The whole structure of these mounts is of earth; but they are not both of the same form and dimensions. The more easterly one is perfectly round, resembling an oven, and about fifty feet in height: And that this is an artificial work does not admit of the least doubt; but we cannot affirm the same, with equal certainty, of the other, though it has been generally supposed to be so too. It bears no resemblance to the eastern one either in shape or size. At the foundation it is nearly of a triangular form; but the superstructure is quite irregular; nor does the height thereof bear any proportion to the extent of its base. These mounts are now planted with firs, which, with the parish-church of Dunipace standing in the middle between them, and the river running hard by, give this valley a very romantic appearance. The common account given of these mounts is, that they were erected as monuments of a peace concluded in that place between the Romans and the Caledonians, and that their name partakes of the language of both people; *Dun* signifying a hill in the old language of this island, and *Pax* "peace" in the language of Rome. The compound word, *Dunipace*, signifies "the hills of peace." And we find in history, that no less than three treaties of peace were, at different periods, entered into between the Romans and Caledonians; the first, by Severus, about the year 210; the second, soon after, by his son Caracalla; and the third, by the usurper Carausius, about the year 280; but of which of those treaties Dunipace is a monument, we do not pretend to determine. If the concurring testimony of historians and antiquaries did not agree in giving this original to these mounts, we would be tempted to conjecture that they are sepulchral monuments. Human bones and urns have been discovered in earthen fabrics of this kind in many parts of this island, and the little mounts or barrows, which are scattered in great numbers about Stonehenge in Salisbury plain are generally supposed to have been the sepulchres of the ancient Britons. See Barrows.

From the valley of Dunipace, the river runs for some time in a deep and hollow channel, with steep banks on both sides: here it passes by the foundations of the ancient Roman bridge; not far from which, as is generally thought, was the scene of the memorable conference betwixt the Scottish patriot William Wallace and Robert Bruce, father to the king of that name, which first opened the eyes of the latter to a just view, both of his own true interest and that of his country.

After the river has left the village and bridge of Larbert, it soon comes up to another small valley, through the midst of which it has now worn out to itself a straight channel; whereas, in former ages, it had taken a considerable compass, as appears by the tract of the old bed, which is still visible. The high and circling banks upon the south-side, give to this valley the appearance of a spacious bay; and, according to the tradition of the country, there was once an harbour here: nor does the tradition seem altogether groundless; pieces of broken anchors having been found here, and some of them within the memory of people yet alive. The stream-tides would still flow near the place, if they were not kept back by the dam-head built across the river at Stenhouse; and there is reason to believe, that the frith flowed considerably higher in former ages than it does at present. In the near neighbourhood of this valley, upon the south, stand the ruins of ancient Camelon; which, after it was abandoned by the Romans, was probably inhabited, for some ages, by the natives of the country.

Another ancient monument, called *Arthur's Oven*, once stood upon the banks of Carron; but was, with a spirit truly Gothic, entirely demolished about 40 years ago. The corner of a small inclosure between Stenhouse and the Carron iron-works, is pointed out as the place of its situation. This is generally supposed to have been a Roman work; though it is not easy to conceive what could be their motive for erecting such a fabric, at so great a distance from any other of their works, and in a spot which, at that time, must have been very remote and unfrequented. The form of it is said to have been perfectly round, and rising perpendicular for some yards at first, but afterwards gradually contracted, till it terminated in a narrow orifice at the top. Antiquaries are not agreed whether it had been a temple, or a trophy, or a mausoleum; but the most common opinion is, that it had been a temple,

and,

Carron.

and, Buchanan thinks, a temple of Terminus. Hector Boetius ſays, that there were benches of ſtone all around it, upon the inſide; and that there had been a large ſtone for ſacrificing upon, or an altar, upon the ſouth ſide.

As Carron extends over the half of the iſthmus, and runs ſo near the ancient boundaries of the Roman empire, the adjacent country fell naturally to be the ſcene of many battles and rencounters. Hiſtorians mention a bloody battle fought near this river between the Romans and the confederate army of the Scots and Picts in the beginning of the 5th century. The ſcenes of ſome of Oſſian's poems were, in the opinion of the tranſlator, upon the banks of this river. Here Fingal fought with Caracul, the ſon of the king of the world, ſuppoſed to have been the ſame with Caracalla the ſon of the Roman emperor Severus. Here alſo young Oſcar, the ſon of Oſſian, performed ſome of his heroic exploits. Hereabout was the ſtream of Crona, celebrated in the ancient compoſitions of the Gaelic bard; poſſibly that now called the water of Bonny, which runs in the neighbourhood of the Roman wall, and diſchargeth itſelf into Carron at Dunipace. In thoſe poems, mention is made of a green vale upon the banks of this river, with a tomb ſtanding in the middle of it, where young Oſcar's party and the warriors of Caros met. We only take notice of this as it ſtrengthens the conjecture hazarded above, that the mounts of Dunipace, eſpecially the more eaſterly of them, were ſepulchral monuments.—About the diſtance of half a mile from the river, and near the town of Falkirk, lies the field of that battle which was fought by William Wallace and the Engliſh in the beginning of the 14th century. It goes by the name of *Graham's muir*, from the valiant John Graham, who fell there, and whoſe grave-ſtone is ſtill to be ſeen in the church-yard of Falkirk.

The river Carron, though it hath long ſince ceaſed to roll its ſtream amidſt the din of arms, ſtill preſerves its fame, by lending its aid to trade and manufactures; (ſee the next article.)—The river is navigable for ſome miles near its mouth, and a conſiderable trade is carried on upon it by ſmall craft; for the convenience of which, its channel has of late years been ſtraightened and much ſhortened, and the great Canal * has its entrance from it.

* See the article Canal.

Carron-Works, a large iron-foundery, two miles north from Falkirk in Scotland. They are conveniently ſituated on the banks of the Carron, three miles above its entry into the frith of Forth. Above 100 acres of land have been converted into reſervoirs and pools, for water diverted from the river, by magnificent dams built about two miles above the works, which, after turning 18 large wheels for the ſeveral purpoſes of the manufacture, falls into a tide-navigation that conveys their caſtings to the ſea.

Theſe works are the greateſt of the kind in Europe, and were eſtabliſhed in 1760. At preſent, the buildings are of vaſt extent; and the machinery, conſtructed by Mr Smeaton, is the firſt in Britain, both in elegance and correctneſs: there are 1600 men employed, to whom is paid weekly above 650 l. Sterling; which has greatly enriched the adjoining country: 6500 tons of iron are ſmelted annually from the mineral with pit-coal, and caſt into cannon, cylinders, &c.—In the founding of cannon, theſe works have lately arrived at ſuch perfection, that they make above 5000 pieces a-year, many of which are exported to foreign ſtates; and their guns of *new conſtruction* are the lighteſt and neateſt now in uſe, not excepting braſs guns; the 32 pounder ſhip-gun weighing 42 hundred-weight, the 6 pounder 8 hundred-weight and one half, and the other calibers in proportion.

Carron
|
Carrucate.

The preſent proprietors are a chartered company, with a capital of 150,000 l. Sterling, a common ſeal, &c. but their ſtock is confined to a very few individuals.

CARRONADE, a ſhort kind of ordnance, capable of carrying a large ball, and uſeful in cloſe engagements at ſea. It takes its name from Carron, the place where this ſort of ordnance was firſt made, or the principle applied to an improved conſtruction. See the article Gunnery, n° 45, 46.

CARROT, in Botany. See Daucus.

Deadly-Carrot. See Thapsia.

CARROUSAL, a courſe of horſes and chariots, or a magnificent entertainment exhibited by princes on ſome public rejoicing. It conſiſts in a cavalcade of ſeveral gentlemen, richly dreſſed and equipped after the manner of ancient cavaliers, divided into ſquadrons, meeting in ſome public place, and practiſing juſts, tournaments, &c. The laſt carrouſals were in the reign of Louis XIV.—The word comes from the Italian word *carroſello*, a diminutive of *carro*, "chariot." Tertullian aſcribes the invention of carrouſals to Circe; and will have them inſtituted in honour of the Sun, her father; whence ſome derive the word from *carrus* or *carrus ſolis*. The Moors introduced cyphers, liveries, and other ornaments of their arms, with trappings, &c. for their horſes. The Goths added creſts, plumes, &c.

CARRUCA, in antiquity, a ſplendid kind of car, or chariot, mounted on four wheels, richly decorated with gold, ſilver, ivory, &c. in which the emperors, ſenators, and people of condition, were carried. The word comes from the Latin *carrus*, or Britiſh car, which is ſtill the Iriſh name for any wheel-carriage.

Carruca, or Caruca, is alſo uſed in middle-age writers for a plough.

Carruca was alſo ſometimes uſed for *carrucata*. See Carrucate.

CARUCAGE, (*carucagium*,) a kind of tax anciently impoſed on every plough, for the public ſervice. See Carrucate and Hidage.

Carrucage, Carucage, or Carvage, in huſbandry, denotes the ploughing of ground, either ordinary, as for grain, hemp, and flax; or extraordinary, as for woad, dyers weed, rape, and the like.

CARRUCATE, (*carrucata*,) in our ancient laws and hiſtory, denotes a plough-land, or as much arable ground as can be tilled in one year with one plough.

In Doomſday Inquiſitions, the arable land is eſtimated in carrucates, the paſture in hides, and meadow in acres. Skene makes the *carrucata* the ſame with *hilda*, or *hida terræ*; Littleton the ſame with *ſoc*.

The meaſure of a carrucate appears to have differed in reſpect of place as well as time. In the reign of Richard I. it was eſtimated at 60 acres, and in another

another charter of the same reign at 100 acres: in the time of Edward I. at 180 acres: and in the 23d of Edward III. a carucate of land in Bureester contained 112 acres, and in Middleton 150 acres.

By a statute under William III. for charging persons to the repair of the highways, a plough-land is rated at a fifty pounds *per annum*, and may contain houses, mills, wood, pasture, &c.

CARRYING, in falconry, signifies a hawk's flying away with the quarry. Carrying is one of the ill qualities of a hawk, which she acquires either by a dislike of the falconer, or not being sufficiently broke to the lure.

CARRYING, among huntsmen. When a hare runs on rotten ground (or even sometimes in a frost), and it sticks to her feet, they say she carries.

CARRYING, among riding-masters. A horse is said to carry low, when having naturally an ill-shaped neck, he lowers his head too much. All horses that arm themselves carry low, but a horse may carry low without arming. A French branch, or gigot, is prescribed as a remedy against carrying low.

A horse is said to carry well, when his neck is raised, or arched, and he holds his head high and firm, without constraint.

Carrying Wind, a term used by our dealers in horses to express such a one as frequently tosses his nose as high as his ears, and does not carry handsomely. This is called *carrying wind*; and the difference between carrying in the wind, and beating upon the hand, is this: that the horse who beats upon the hand, shakes the bridle and resists it, while he shakes his head; but the horse that carries in the wind puts up his head without shaking, and sometimes beats upon the hand. The opposite to carrying in the wind, is arming and carrying low; and even between these two there is a difference in wind.

CARS, or KARS, a considerable and strong town of Asia, in Armenia, seated on a river of the same name, with a castle almost impregnable. E. Long. 43. 50. N. Lat. 41. 30.

CARSE, or *Carse of Gowry*, a district of Perthshire in Scotland. It lies on the north side of the Tay, and extends 14 miles in length from Dundee to Perth, and is from two to four in breadth. It is a rich plain country, cultivated like a garden, and producing as good harvests of wheat as any in Great Britain. It abounds with all the necessaries of life; but from its low damp situation, the inhabitants are subject to agues, and the commonalty are in great want of firing. In this district, not far from the Tay, stands the house of Errol, which formerly belonged to the Earls of that name, the chiefs of the ancient family of Hay, hereditary constables of Scotland.

CARSTAIRS (William), an eminent Scots Divine, whose merit and good fortune called him to act in great scenes, and to associate with men to whose society and intercourse his birth gave him few pretensions to aspire. A small village, in the neighbourhood of Glasgow, was the place of his nativity. His father, of whom little is known, exercised the functions of a clergyman.

Young Carstairs turned his thoughts to the profession of theology; and the persecutions and oppressions of government, both in regard to civil and religious liberty, having excited his strongest indignation, it became a matter of prudence that he should prosecute his studies in a foreign university. He went accordingly to Utrecht; and his industry and attention being directed with skill, opened up and unfolded those faculties which he was about to employ with equal honour to his country and himself.

During his residence abroad, he became acquainted with Pensionary Fagel, and entered with warmth into the interest of the Prince of Orange. On his return to Scotland to procure a license to teach doctrines which he had studied with the greatest care, he became disgusted with the proud and insolent conduct of Archbishop Sharp, and prepared to revisit Holland; where he knew that religious liberty was respected, and where he hoped he might better his condition by the connections he had formed.

His expectations were not vain. His prudence, his reserve, and his political address, were strong recommendations of him to the Prince of Orange; and he was employed in personal negociations in Holland, England, and Scotland. Upon the elevation of his master to the English throne, he was appointed the King's chaplain for Scotland, and employed in settling the affairs of that kingdom. William, who carried politics into religion, was solicitous that episcopacy should prevail there as universally as in England. Carstairs, more versant in the affairs of his native country, saw all the impropriety of this project, and the danger that would arise from the enforcing of it. His reasonings, his remonstrances, his intreaties, overcame the firmness of king William. He yielded to considerations founded alike in policy and in prudence; and to Carstairs, Scotland is indebted for the full establishment of its church in the Presbyterian form of government.

The death of King William was a severe affliction to him; and it happened before that Prince had provided for him with the liberality he deserved. He was continued, however, in the office of chaplain for Scotland by Queen Anne; and he was invited to accept the Principality of the University of Edinburgh. He was one of the ministers of the city, and four times moderator of the general assembly. Placed at the head of the church, he prosecuted its interest with zeal and with integrity. Nor were his influence and activity confined to matters of religion. They were exerted with success in promoting the culture of the arts and sciences. The universities of Scotland owe him obligations of the highest kind. He procured, in particular, an augmentation of the salaries of their professors; a circumstance to which may be ascribed their reputation, as it enabled them to cultivate with spirit the different branches of knowledge.

A zeal for truth, a love of moderation and order, prudence and humanity, distinguished Principal Carstairs in an uncommon degree. His religion had no mixture of austerity; his secular transactions were attended with no imputation of artifice; and the versatility of his talents made him pass with ease from a court to a college. He was among the last who suffered torture before the privy-council, in order to make make him divulge the secrets intrusted to him, which he firmly resisted; and after the revolution, that inhuman instrument the thumb-screw was given to him in a present by the council.—This excellent person

died

died in 1715; and in 1774 his *State-papers and Letters*, with an account of his life, were published in one vol. 4to, by the Rev. Dr M'Cormick.

CARSUGHI (Rainier), a Jesuit, born at Citerna in Tuscany, in 1647, was the author of a Latin poem, entitled, *Ars bene scribendi*, which is esteemed both for the elegance of the style and for the excellent precepts it contains. He also wrote some good epigrams. He died in 1709.

CARTAMA, a town of Spain in the kingdom of Granada, formerly very considerable. It is seated at the foot of a mountain, near the river Guadala-Medina, in W. Long. 4. 28. N. Lat. 36. 40.

CART, a land-carriage with two wheels, drawn commonly by horses, to carry heavy goods, &c. from one place to another. The word seems formed from the French *charrette*, which signifies the same, or rather the Latin *carreta*, a diminutive of *carrus*. See CARR.

In London and Westminster carts shall not carry more than twelve sacks of meal, seven hundred and fifty bricks, one chaldron of coals, &c. on pain of forfeiting one of the horses, (6 Geo. I. cap. 6.) By the laws of the city, cart-men are forbidden to ride either on their carts or horses. They are to lead or drive them on foot through the streets on the forfeiture of ten shillings, (Stat. 1 Geo. I. cap. 57.) Criminals used to be drawn to execution in a cart. Bawds and other malefactors are whipped at the cart's tail.

Scripture makes mention of a sort of carts or drags used by the Jews to do the office of threshing. They were supported on low thick wheels, bound with iron, which were rolled up and down on the sheaves, to break them, and force out the corn. Something of the like kind also obtained among the Romans, under the denomination of *plaustra*, of which Virgil makes mention, (Georg. I.)

> *Tardaque Eleusinae matris volventia plaustra,*
> *Tribulaque, traheaeque.*——

On which Servius observes, that *trahea* denotes a cart without wheels, and *tribula* a sort of cart armed on all sides with teeth, used chiefly in Africa for threshing corn. The Septuagint and St Jerome represent these carts as furnished with saws, insomuch that their surface was beset with teeth. David having taken Rabbah, the capital of the Ammonites, ordered all the inhabitants to be crushed to pieces under such carts, moving on wheels set with iron teeth; and the king of Damascus is said to have treated the Israelites of the land of Gilead in the same manner.

Cart-Bote, in law, signifies wood to be employed in making and repairing instruments of husbandry.

Carts of War, a peculiar kind of artillery anciently in use among the Scots. They are thus described in an act of parliament, A. D. 1456: "It is thocht speidfull, that the King mak requeist to certain of the great burrows of the land that are of ony myght, to mak carts of weir, and in ilk cart twa gunnis, and ilk ane to have twa chalmers, with the remanent of the graith that effeirs thereto, and an cunnand man to shut thame." By another act, A. D. 1471, the prelates and barons are commanded to provide such carts of war against their old enemies the English.

CARTE (Thomas), the historian, was the son of Mr Samuel Carte prebendary of Litchfield, and born in 1686. When he was reader in the abbey-church at Bath, he took occasion, in a 30th of January sermon, 1714, to vindicate Charles I. with respect to the Irish massacre, which drew him into a controversy with Mr Chandler the dissenting minister; and on the accession of the present royal family he refused to take the oaths to government, and put on a lay habit. He is said to have acted as a kind of secretary to Bishop Atterbury before his troubles; and in the year 1722, being accused of high treason, a reward of 1000 *l.* was offered for apprehending him; but Queen Caroline, the great patroness of learned men, obtained leave for him to return home in security. He published, 1. An edition of Thuanus, in seven volumes folio. 2. The Life of the first Duke of Ormond, three volumes, folio. 3. The History of England, four volumes, folio. 4. A Collection of Original Letters and Papers concerning the affairs of England, two volumes octavo; and some other works. He died in April 1754.—His history of England ends in 1654. His design was to have brought it down to the Revolution; for which purpose he had taken great pains in copying every thing valuable that could be met with in England, Scotland, France, Ireland, &c.—He had (as he himself says, p. 43. of his Vindication of a full answer to a letter from a bystander), "read abundance of collections relating to the time of King Charles II. and had in his power a series of memoirs from the beginning to the end of that reign; in which all those intrigues and turns at court, at the latter end of that king's life, which bishop Burnet, with all his gout for tales of secret history, and all his genius for conjectures, does not pretend to account for, are laid open in the clearest and most convincing manner; by the person who was most affected by them, and had the best reason to know them."—At his death, all his papers came into the hands of his widow, who afterwards married Mr Jernegan, a member of the church of Rome. They are now deposited in the Bodleian library, having been delivered by Mr Jernegan to the university, 1778, for a valuable consideration. Whilst they were in this gentleman's possession, the earl of Hardwicke paid 200 *l.* for the perusal of them. For a consideration of 300 *l.* Mr Macpherson had the use of them; and from these and other materials compiled his history and state-papers. Mr Carte was a man of a strong constitution and indefatigable application. When the studies of the day were over, he would eat heartily; and in conversation was cheerful and entertaining.

Carte-Blanche, a sort of white paper, signed at the bottom with a person's name, and sometimes also sealed with his seal, giving another person power to superscribe what conditions he pleases. Much like this is the French *blanc signe*, a paper without writing, except a signature at the bottom, given by contending parties to arbitrators or friends, to fill up with the conditions they judge reasonable, in order to end the difference.

CARTEL, an agreement between two states for the exchange of their prisoners of war.

Cartel signifies also a letter of defiance or a challenge to decide a controversy either in a tournament or in a single combat. See Duel.

Cartel-Ship, a ship commissioned in time of war to exchange

Cartes. exchange the prisoners of any two hostile powers; also to carry any particular request or proposal from one to another: for this reason, the officer who commands her is particularly ordered to carry no cargo, ammunition, or implements of war, except a single gun for the purpose of firing signals.

CARTES (Rene des), descended of an ancient family in Touraine in France, was one of the most eminent philosophers and mathematicians in the 17th century. At the Jesuits College at la Fleche, he made a very great progress in the learned languages and polite literature, and became acquainted with Father Marsenne. His father designed him for the army; but his tender constitution then not permitting him to expose himself to such fatigues, he was sent to Paris, where he launched into gaming, in which he had prodigious success. Here Marsenne persuaded him to return to study; which he pursued till he went to Holland, in May 1616, where he engaged as a volunteer among the prince of Orange's troops. While he lay in garrison at Breda, he wrote *a treatise on music*, and laid the foundation of several of his works. He was at the siege of Rochelle in 1628; returned to Paris; and, a few days after his return, at an assembly of men of learning in the house of Monsignor Bagni the Pope's Nuncio, was prevailed upon to explain his sentiments with regard to philosophy, when the nuncio urged him to publish his system. Upon this he went to Amsterdam, and from thence to Franeker, where he began his *metaphysical meditations*, and drew up his *discourse on meteors*. He made a short tour to England; and not far from London, made some observations concerning the declination of the magnet. He returned to Holland, where he finished his *treatise on the world*.

His books made a great noise in France; and Holland thought of nothing but discarding the old philosophy, and following his. Voetius being chosen rector of the university of Utrecht, procured his philosophy to be prohibited, and wrote against him; but he immediately published a vindication of himself. In 1647, he took a journey into France, where the king settled a pension of 3000 livres upon him. Christina, queen of Sweden, having invited him into that kingdom, he went thither, where he was received with the greatest civility by her majesty, who engaged him to attend her every morning at five o'clock, to instruct her in philosophy, and desired him to revise and digest all his writings which were unpublished, and to form a complete body of philosophy from them. She likewise proposed to allow him a revenue, and to form an academy of which he was to be the director. But these designs were broken off by his death in 1650. His body was interred at Stockholm, and 17 years afterwards removed to Paris, where a magnificent monument was erected to him in the church of St Genevieve du Mont. The great Dr Halley, in a paper concerning optics, observes, that though some of the ancients mention refraction as an effect of transparent mediums, Des Cartes was the first who discovered the laws of refraction, and reduced dioptrics to a science. As to his philosophy, Dr Keil, in his introduction to his examination of Dr Burnet's theory of the earth, says, that Des Cartes was so far from applying geometry to natural philosophy, that his whole system is one continued blunder on account of his negligence in that point; the laws observed by the planets in their revolutions round the sun, not agreeing with his theory of vortices. His philosophy has accordingly given way to the more accurate discoveries and demonstrations of the Newtonian system.

Cartesians, Carthage.

CARTESIANS, a sect of philosophers, who adhered to the system of Des Cartes, founded on the two following principles, the one metaphysical, the other physical. The metaphysical one is, *I think, therefore I am*: the physical principle is, that *nothing exists but substance*. Substance he makes of two kinds; the one a substance that thinks, the other a substance extended; whence actual thought, and actual extension, are the essence of substance.

The essence of matter being thus fixed in extension, the Cartesians conclude that there is no vacuum, nor any possibility thereof in nature; but that the universe is absolutely full: mere space is excluded by this principle; because extension being implied in the idea of space, matter is so too. Upon these principles, the Cartesians explained mechanically how the world was formed, and how the present celestial phenomena came to take place. See ASTRONOMY, n° 391.

CARTHAGE, a famed city of antiquity, the capital of Africa Propria; and which, for many years, disputed with Rome the sovereignty of the world. According to Velleius Paterculus, this city was built 65, according to Justin and Trogus 72, according to others 100 or 140 years before the foundations of Rome were laid. It is on all hands agreed that the Phenicians were the founders. 7 When founded.

The beginning of the Carthaginian history, like that of all other nations, is obscure and uncertain. In the 7th year of Pygmalion king of Tyre, his sister Elissa, or Dido, is said to have fled, with some of her companions and vassals, from the cruelty and avarice of her brother Sichaeus. 8 Elissa, or Dido, escapes from her brother.

She first touched at the island of Cyprus, where she met with a priest of Jupiter, who was desirous of attending her; to which she readily consented, and fixed the priesthood in his family. At that time, it was a custom in the island of Cyprus, for the young women to go on certain stated days, before marriage, to the sea-side, there to look for strangers, that might possibly arrive on their coasts, in order to prostitute themselves for gain, that they might thereby acquire a dowry. Out of these, the Tyrians selected 80, whom they carried along with them. From Cyprus they sailed directly for the coast of Africa; and at last safely landed in the province called *Africa Propria*, not far from Utica, a Phenician city of great antiquity. The inhabitants received their countrymen with great demonstrations of joy, and invited them to settle among them. The common fable is, that the Phenicians imposed upon the Africans in the following manner: They desired, for their intended settlement, only as much ground as an ox's hide would encompass. This request the Africans laughed at; but were surprised, when, upon their granting it, they saw Elissa cut the hide into the smallest threads, by which means it surrounded a large territory; in which she built the citadel called *Byrsa*. The learned, however, are now unanimous 9 Builds the citadel Byrsa.

minions in exploding this fable; and it is certain that the Carthaginians for many years paid an annual tribute to the Africans for the ground they possessed.

The new city soon became populous and flourishing, by the accession of the neighbouring Africans, who came thither at first with a view of traffic. In a short time it became so considerable, that *Jarbas*, a neighbouring prince, thought of making himself master of it without any effusion of blood. In order to this, he desired that an embassy of ten of the most noble Carthaginians might be sent him; and, upon their arrival, proposed to them a marriage with Dido, threatening war in case of a refusal. The ambassadors, being afraid to deliver this message, told the queen that Jarbas desired some person might be sent him who was capable of civilising his Africans; but that there was no possibility of finding any of her subjects who would leave his relations for the conversation of such barbarians. For this they were reprimanded by the queen; who told them that they ought to be ashamed of refusing to live in any manner for the benefit of their country. Upon this, they informed her of the true nature of their message from Jarbas; and that, according to her own decision, she ought to sacrifice

4 She kills herself.

herself for the good of her country. The unhappy queen, rather than submit to be the wife of such a barbarian, caused a funeral pile to be erected, and put an end to her life with a dagger.

This is Justin's account of the death of Queen Dido, and is the most probable; Virgil's story of her amour with Æneas, being looked upon as fabulous, even in the days of Macrobius, as we are informed by that historian. How long monarchical government continued in Carthage, or what happened to this state in its infancy, we are altogether ignorant, by reason of the Punic Archives being destroyed by the Romans; so that there is a chasm in the Carthaginian history for above 300 years. It, however, appears, that from the very beginning, the Carthaginians applied themselves to maritime affairs, and were formidable by sea

5 Spanish mines of vast service to the Carthaginians.

in the time of Cyrus and Cambyses. From Diodorus Siculus and Justin, it appears, that the principal support of the Carthaginians were the mines of Spain, in which country they seem to have established themselves very early. By means of the riches drawn from these mines, they were enabled to equip such formidable fleets as we are told they fitted out in the time of Cyrus or Cambyses. Justin informs us, that the first Carthaginian settlement in Spain happened when the city of Gades, now Cadiz, was but of late standing, or even in its infancy. The Spaniards finding this new colony begin to flourish, attacked it with a numerous army, insomuch that the inhabitants were obliged to call in the Carthaginians to their aid. The latter very readily granted their request, and not only repulsed the Spaniards, but made themselves masters of almost the whole province in which their new city stood. By this success, they were encouraged to attempt the conquest of the whole country: but having to do with very warlike nations, they could not push their conquests to any great length at first; and it appears from the accounts of Livy and Polybius, that the greatest part of Spain remained unsubdued till the times of Hamilcar, Asdrubal, and Hannibal.

About 503 years before the birth of Christ, the Carthaginians entered into a treaty with the Romans. It related chiefly to matters of navigation and commerce. From it we learn, that the whole island of Sardinia, and part of Sicily, were then subject to

6 First treaty between Carthage and Rome.

Carthage; that they were very well acquainted with the coasts of Italy, and had made some attempts upon them before this time; and that, even at this early period, a spirit of jealousy had taken place between the two republics. Some time near this period, the Carthaginians had a mind to discontinue the tribute they had hitherto paid the Africans for the ground on which their city stood. But, notwithstanding all their power, they were at present unsuccessful; and at last were obliged to conclude a peace, one of the articles of which was, that the tribute should be continued.

7 Sicily invaded by the Carthaginians.

By degrees the Carthaginians extended their power over all the islands in the Mediterranean, Sicily excepted; and for the entire conquest of this, they made vast preparations, about 480 years before Christ. Their army consisted of 300,000 men; their fleet was composed of upwards of 2000 men of war, and 3000 transports; and with such an immense armament, they made no doubt of conquering the whole island in a single campaign. In this, however, they found themselves miserably deceived. Hamilcar their general having landed his numerous forces, invested Himera, a city of considerable importance. He carried on his attacks with the greatest assiduity; but was at last attacked in his trenches by Gelon and Theron, the tyrants of Syracuse and Agrigentum, who gave the Carthaginians one of the greatest overthrows mentioned in history. An hundred and fifty thousand were

8 They are utterly destroyed.

killed in the battle and pursuit, and all the rest taken prisoners; so that of so mighty an army, not a single person escaped. Of the 2000 ships of war and 3000 transports, of which the Carthaginian fleet consisted, eight ships only, which then happened to be out at sea, made their escape: these immediately set sail for Carthage; but were all cast away, and every soul perished, except a few who were saved in a small boat, and at last reached Carthage with the dismal news of the total loss of the fleet and army. No words can express the consternation of the Carthaginians upon receiving the news of so terrible a disaster. Ambassadors were immediately dispatched to Sicily, with orders to conclude a peace upon any terms. They put to sea without delay; and landing at Syracuse, threw themselves at the conqueror's feet. They beg-

9 Peace concluded.

ged Gelon, with many tears, to receive their city into favour, and grant them a peace on whatever terms he should choose to prescribe. He granted their request upon condition that Carthage should pay him 2000 talents of silver to defray the expences of the war; that they should build two temples, where the articles of the treaty should be lodged and kept as sacred; and that for the future they should abstain from human sacrifices. This was not thought a dear purchase of a peace for which there was such occasion; and to show their gratitude for Gelon's moderation, the Carthaginians complimented his wife Demarata with a crown of gold worth 100 talents.

From this time we find little mention of the Carthaginians for 70 years. Some time during this period, however, they had greatly extended their do-

Carthage. minions in Africa, and likewise shaken off the tribute which gave them so much uneasiness. They had
10 Disputes with the Cyreneans. warm disputes with the inhabitants of Cyrene the capital of Cyrenaica, about a regulation of the limits of their respective territories. The consequence of these disputes was a war, which reduced both nations so low, that they agreed first to a cessation of arms, and then to a peace. At last it was agreed, that each state should appoint two commissaries, who should set out from their respective cities on the same day, and that the spot on which they met should be
11 Story of the Philæni. the boundary of both states. In consequence of this, two brothers called *Philæni* were sent out from Carthage, who advanced with great celerity, while those from Cyrene were much more slow in their motions. Whether this proceeded from accident or design, or perfidy, we are not certainly informed; but, be this as it will, the Cyreneans finding themselves greatly outstripped by the Philæni, accused them of breach of faith, affirming that they had set out before the time appointed, and consequently that the convention between their principals was broken. The Philæni desired them to propose some expedient whereby their differences might be accommodated; promising to submit to it, whatever it might be. The Cyreneans then proposed, either that the Philæni should retire from the place where they were, or that they should be buried alive upon the spot. With this last condition the brothers immediately complied, and by their death gained a large extent of territory to their country. The Carthaginians ever after celebrated this as a most brave and heroic action; paid them divine honours; and endeavoured to immortalize their names by erecting two altars there, with suitable inscriptions upon them.

12 Sicily invaded anew. About the year before Christ 412, some disputes happening between the Egestines and Selinuntines, inhabitants of two cities in Sicily, the former called in the Carthaginians to their assistance; and this occasioned a new invasion of Sicily by that nation. Great preparations were made for this war; Hannibal, whom they had appointed general, was empowered to raise an army equal to the undertaking, and equip a suitable fleet. They also appointed certain funds for defraying all the expences of the war, intending to exert their whole force to reduce the island under their subjection.

13 Emporium and Selinus taken. The Carthaginian general having landed his forces, immediately marched for Selinus. In his way he took Emporium, a town situated on the river Mazara; and having arrived at Selinus, he immediately invested it. The besieged made a very vigorous defence; but at last the city was taken by storm, and the inhabitants were treated with the utmost cruelty. All were massacred by the savage conquerors, except the women who fled to the temples; and these escaped, not through the merciful disposition of the Carthaginians, but because they were afraid, that if driven to despair they would set fire to the temples, and by that means consume the treasure they expected to find in those places. Sixteen thousand were massacred; 2250 escaped to Agrigentum; and the women and children, about 5000 in number, were carried away captives. At the same time the temples were plundered, and the city rased to the ground.

After the reduction of Selinus, Hannibal laid siege to Himera; that city he desired above all things to become master of, that he might revenge the death of his grandfather Hamilcar, who had been slain before it by Gelon. His troops, flushed with their late success, behaved with undaunted courage; but finding his battering engines not to answer his purpose sufficiently, he undermined the wall, supporting it with large beams of timber, to which he afterwards set fire, and thus laid part of it flat on the ground. Notwithstanding this advantage, however, the Carthaginians were several times repulsed with great slaughter; but at last they became masters of the place, and treated it in the same manner as they had done Selinus. After this, Hannibal, dismissing his Sicilian and Italian allies, returned to Africa. 14 As likewise Himera.

The Carthaginians were now so much elated, that they meditated the reduction of the whole island. But as the age and infirmities of Hannibal rendered him incapable of commanding the forces alone, they joined in commission with him Imilcar the son of Hanno, one of the same family. On the landing of the Carthaginian army, all Sicily was alarmed, and the principal cities put themselves into the best state of defence they were able. The Carthaginians immediately marched to Agrigentum, and began to batter the walls with great fury. The besieged, however, defended themselves with incredible resolution, in a sally burnt all the machines raised against their city, and repulsed the enemy with great slaughter. The Syracusans in the mean time, being alarmed at the danger of Agrigentum, sent an army to its relief. On their approach they were immediately attacked by the Carthaginians; but after a sharp dispute the latter were defeated, and forced to fly to the very walls of Agrigentum, with the loss of 6000 men. Had the Agrigentine commanders now sallied out, and fallen upon the fugitives, in all probability the Carthaginian army must have been destroyed; but either through fear or corruption, they refused to stir out of the place, and this occasioned the loss of it. Immense booty was found in the city; and the Carthaginians behaved with their usual cruelty, putting all the inhabitants to the sword, not excepting even those who had fled to the temples. 15 Agrigentum besieged; 16 And taken.

The next attempt of the Carthaginians was designed against the city of Gela; but the Geleans, being greatly alarmed, implored the protection of Syracuse; and, at their request, Dionysius was sent to assist them with 2000 foot and 400 horse. The Geleans were so well satisfied with his conduct, that they treated him with the highest marks of distinction; they even sent ambassadors to Syracuse to return thanks for the important services done them by sending him thither; and soon after he was appointed generalissimo of the Syracusan forces and those of their allies against the Carthaginians. In the mean time Imilcar, having rased the city of Agrigentum, made an incursion into the territories of Gela and Camarina; which having ravaged in a dreadful manner, he carried off such immense quantity of plunder, as filled his whole camp. He then marched against the city; but though it was but indifferently fortified, he met with a very vigorous resistance; and the place held out for a long time without receiving any assistance from its allies. 17 Gela besieged.

4 As

Carthage.

At last Dionysius came to its assistance with an army of 50,000 foot and 1000 horse. With these he attacked the Carthaginian camp, but was repulsed with great loss; after which, he called a council of war, the result of whose deliberations was, that since the enemy was so much superior to them in strength, it would be highly imprudent to put all to the issue of a battle; and therefore, that the inhabitants should be persuaded to abandon the country, as the only means of saving their lives. In consequence of this, a trumpet was sent to Imilcar to desire a cessation of arms till the next day, in order, as was pretended, to bury the dead, but in reality to give the people of Gela an opportunity of
18 Abandoned by its inhabitants.
making their escape. Towards the beginning of the night the bulk of the citizens left the place; and he himself with the army followed them about midnight. To amuse the enemy, he left 2000 of his light armed troops behind him, commanding them to make fires all night, and set up loud shouts as though the army still remained in town. At day-break these took the same route as their companions, and pursued their march with great celerity. The Carthaginians finding the city deserted by the greatest part of its inhabitants, immediately entered it, putting to death all who had remained; after which, Imilcar having thoroughly plundered it, moved towards Camarina. The inhabitants of this city had been likewise drawn off by Dionysius, and it underwent the same fate with Gela.

19 Peace concluded.
Notwithstanding these successes, however, Imilcar finding his army greatly weakened, partly by the casualties of war, and partly by a plague which broke out in it, sent a herald to Syracuse to offer terms of peace. His unexpected arrival was very agreeable to the Syracusans, and a peace was immediately concluded upon the following terms, viz. That the Carthaginians, besides their ancient acquisitions in Sicily, should still possess the countries of the Silicani, the Selinuntines, the Himereans, and Agrigentines; that the people of Gela and Camarina should be permitted to reside in their respective cities, which yet should be dismantled, upon their paying an annual tribute to the Carthaginians; that all the other Sicilians should preserve their independency except the Syracusians, who should continue in subjection to Dionysius.

20 Dionysius breaks the treaty.
The tyrant of Syracuse, however, had concluded this peace with no other view than to gain time, and to put himself in a condition to attack the Carthaginian territories with greater force. Having accomplished this, he acquainted the Syracusians with his design, and they immediately approved of it; upon which he gave up to the fury of the populace the persons and possessions of the Carthaginians who resided in Syracuse, and traded there on the faith of treaties. As there were many of their ships at that time in the harbour, laden with cargoes of great value, the people immediately plundered them; and, not content with this, ransacked all their houses in a most outrageous manner. This example was followed throughout the whole island; and in the mean time Dionysius dispatched a herald to Carthage with a letter to the senate and people, telling them, that if they did not immediately withdraw their garrisons from all the Greek cities in Sicily, the people of Syracuse would treat them as enemies. With this demand, however, he did not allow them to comply; for without waiting for any answer from Carthage, he advanced with his army to Mount Eryx, near which stood the city of Motya, a Carthaginian colony of great importance, and this he immediately invested. But soon after, leaving his brother Leptines to carry on the attacks, he himself went with the greatest part of his forces to reduce the cities in alliance with the Carthaginians. He destroyed their territories with fire and sword, cut down all their trees; and then he sat down before Egesta and Entella, most of the other towns having opened their gates at his approach: but these baffling his utmost efforts, he returned to Motya, and pushed on the siege of that place with the utmost vigour.

The Carthaginians, in the mean time, though alarmed at the message sent them by Dionysius, and though reduced to a miserable situation by the plague which had broke out in their city, did not despond, but sent officers to Europe, with considerable sums, to raise troops with the utmost diligence. Ten gallies were also sent 21
from Carthage to destroy all the ships that were found in the harbour of Syracuse. The admiral, according to his orders, entered the harbour in the night, without being discerned by the enemy; and having sunk most of the ships he found there, returned without the loss of a man.
Syracusan fleet destroyed.

All this while the Motyans defended themselves with 22
incredible vigour; while their enemies, desirous of revenging the cruelties exercised upon their countrymen by the Carthaginians, fought like lions. At last the place was taken by storm, and the Greek soldiers began a general massacre. For some time Dionysius was not able to restrain their fury: but at last he proclaimed that the Motyans should fly to the Greek temples; which they accordingly did, and a stop was put to the slaughter; but the soldiers took care thoroughly to plunder the town, in which they found a great treasure.
Motya taken by the Greeks.

The following spring, Dionysius invaded the Carthaginian territories, and made an attempt upon Egesta; but here he was again disappointed. The Carthaginians were greatly alarmed at his progress; but, next year, notwithstanding a considerable loss sustained in a sea-fight with Leptines, Himilco their general landed a powerful army at Panormus, seized upon Eryx, and then advancing towards Motya, made himself master of it, before Dionysius could send any forces to its relief. He next advanced to Messana, which he likewise besieged and took; after which most of the Sicani revolted from Dionysius.

Notwithstanding this defection, Dionysius, finding 23
his forces still amount to 30,000 foot and 3000 horse, advanced against the enemy. At the same time, Leptines was sent with the Syracusan fleet against that of the Carthaginians, but with positive orders not to break the line of battle upon any account whatever. But, notwithstanding these orders, he thought proper to divide his fleet, and the consequence of this was a total defeat; above 100 of the Syracusan gallies being sunk or taken, and 20,000 of their men killed in the battle or in the pursuit. Dionysius disheartened by this 24
misfortune, returned with his army to Syracuse, being afraid that the Carthaginian fleet might become masters of that city, if he should advance to fight the land army. Himilco did not fail immediately to invest the
Greeks defeated by the Carthaginians.
Syracuse besieged by the Carthaginians.

6 capital;

capital; and had certainly become master of it, and consequently of the whole island, had not a most malignant pestilence obliged him to desist from all further operations. This dreadful malady made great havock among his forces both by sea and land; and to complete his misfortunes, Dionysius attacked him unexpectedly, totally ruined his fleet, and made himself master of his camp.

25 Himilco obliged to retire.

Himilco finding himself altogether unable to sustain another attack, was obliged to come to a private agreement with Dionysius: who for 300 talents consented to let him escape to Africa, with the shattered remains of his fleet and army. The unfortunate general arrived at Carthage, clad in mean and sordid attire, where he was met by a great number of people bewailing their sad and inauspicious fortune. Himilco joined them in their lamentations; and being unable to survive his misfortunes, put an end to his own life. He had left Mago in Sicily, to take care of the Carthaginian interests in the best manner he could. In order to this, Mago treated all the Sicilians subject to Carthage with the greatest humanity; and having received a considerable number of soldiers from Africa, he at last formed an army with which he ventured a battle: in this he was defeated, and driven out of the field, with the loss of 800 men; which obliged him to desist from further attempts of that nature.

26 Another invasion of Sicily.

Notwithstanding all these terrible disasters, the Carthaginians could not forbear making new attempts upon the island of Sicily; and about the year before Christ 392, Mago landed in it with an army of 80,000 men. This attempt, however, was attended with no better success than before; Dionysius found means to reduce him to such straits for want of provisions, that he was obliged to sue for peace. This continued for nine years, at the end of which the war was renewed with various success. It continued with little interruption till the year before Christ 367, when, the Syracusian state being rent by civil dissensions, the Carthaginians thought it a proper time to exert themselves, in order to become masters of the whole island. They fitted out a great fleet, and entered into alliance with Icetas, tyrant of Leontini, who pretended to have taken Syracuse under his protection. By this treaty, the two powers engaged to assist each other, in order to expel Dionysius II. after which they were to divide

27 Syracusans assisted by the Corinthians.

the island between them. The Syracusans applied for succours to the Corinthians; and they readily sent them a body of troops under the command of Timoleon an experienced general. By a stratagem, he got his forces landed at Tauromenium. The whole of them did not exceed 1200 in number: yet with these he marched against Icetas, who was at the head of 5000 men; his army he surprised at supper, put 300 of them to the sword, and took 600 prisoners. He then marched to Syracuse, and broke into one part of the town before the enemy had any notice of his approach: here he took post, and defended himself with such resolution, that he could not be dislodged by the united power of Icetas and the Carthaginians.

28 Foolish conduct of the Carthaginian admiral.

In this place he remained for some time, in expectation of a reinforcement from Corinth; till the arrival of which, he did not judge it practicable to extend his conquests.—The Carthaginians being apprised that the Corinthian succours were detained by tempestuous weather at Thurium, posted a strong squadron, under Hanno their admiral, to intercept them in their passage to Sicily. But that commander, not imagining the Corinthians would attempt a passage to Sicily in such a stormy season, left his station at Thurium, and ordering his seamen to crown themselves with garlands, and adorn their vessels with bucklers both of the Greek and Carthaginian form, sailed to Syracuse in a triumphant manner. Upon his arrival there, he gave the troops in the citadel to understand, that he had taken the succours Timoleon expected, thinking by this means to intimidate them to surrender. But, while he thus trifled away his time, the Corinthians marched with great expedition to Rhegium, and, taking the advantage of a gentle breeze, were easily wafted over into Sicily. Mago, the Carthaginian general, was no sooner informed of the arrival of this reinforcement, than he 29 Cowardice of Mago.
was struck with terror, though the whole Corinthian army did not exceed 4000 men; and, soon after, fearing a revolt of his mercenaries, he weighed anchor, in spite of all the remonstrances of Icetas, and set sail for Africa. Here he no sooner arrived, than, overcome with grief and shame for his unparalleled cowardice, he laid violent hands on himself. His body was hung upon a gallows or cross, in order to deter succeeding generals from forfeiting their honour in so flagrant a manner.

30 Exploits of Timoleon.

After the flight of Mago, Timoleon carried all before him. He obliged Icetas to renounce his alliance with the state of Carthage, and even deposed him, and continued his military preparations with the greatest vigour. On the other hand, the Carthaginians prepared for the ensuing campaign with the greatest alacrity. An army of 70,000 men was sent over, with a fleet of 200 ships of war, and 1000 transports laden with warlike engines, armed chariots, horses, and all other sorts of provisions. This immense multitude, however, was overthrown on the banks of the Crimesus by Timoleon: 10,000 were left dead on the field of battle; and of these, above 3000 were native Carthaginians of the best families in the city. Above 15,000 were taken prisoners; all their baggage and provisions, with 200 chariots, 1000 coats of mail, and 10,000 shields, fell into Timoleon's hands. The spoil, which consisted chiefly of gold and silver, was so immense, that the whole Sicilian army was three days in collecting it and stripping the slain. After this signal victory, he left his mercenary forces upon the frontiers of the enemy, to plunder and ravage the country; while he himself returned to Syracuse with the rest of his army, where he was received with the greatest demonstrations of joy. Soon after, Icetas, grown weary of his private station, concluded a new peace with the Carthaginians; and, having assembled an army, ventured an engagement with Timoleon: but in this he was utterly defeated; and himself, with Eupolemus his son, and Euthymus general of his horse, were brought bound to Timoleon by their own soldiers. The two first were immediately executed as tyrants and traitors, and the last murdered in cold blood; Icetas's wives and daughters were likewise cruelly put to death after a public trial. In a short time after, Mamercus, another of the Carthaginian confederates, was

over

Carthage.

overthrown by Timoleon, with the loss of 2000 men. These misfortunes induced the Carthaginians to conclude a peace on the following terms:

31 Peace concluded.

That all the Greek cities should be set free; that the river Halycus should be the boundary between the territories of both parties; that the natives of the cities subject to the Carthaginians should be allowed to withdraw, if they pleased, to Syracuse, or its dependencies, with their families and effects; and lastly, that Carthage should not, for the future, give any assistance to the remaining tyrants against Syracuse.

32 War renewed.

About 316 years before Christ, we find the Carthaginians engaged in another bloody war with the Sicilians, on the following occasion. Sosistratus, who had usurped the supreme authority at Syracuse, having been forced by Agathocles to raise the siege of Rhegium, returned with his shattered troops to Sicily. But soon after this unsuccessful expedition, he was obliged to abdicate the sovereignty and quit Syracuse. With him were expelled above 600 of the principal citizens, who were suspected of having formed a design to overturn the plan of government which then prevailed in the city. As Sosistratus and the exiles thought themselves ill treated, they had recourse to the Carthaginians, who readily espoused their cause. Hereupon the Syracusans having recalled Agathocles, who had before been banished by Sosistratus, appointed him commander in chief of all their forces, principally on account of the known aversion he bore that tyrant. The war, however, did not then continue long; for Sosistratus and the exiles were quickly received again into the city, and peace was concluded with Carthage; the people of Syracuse, however, finding that Agathocles wanted to make himself absolute, exacted an oath from him, that he would do nothing to the pre-

33 Agathocles raises himself to the throne of Syracuse.

judice of the democracy. But, notwithstanding this oath, Agathocles pursued his purpose, and by a general massacre of the principal citizens of Syracuse raised himself to the throne. For some time he was obliged to keep the peace he had concluded with Carthage; but at last finding his authority established, and that his subjects were ready to second his ambitious designs, he paid no regard to his treaties, but immediately made war on the neighbouring states, which he had expressly agreed not to do, and then carried his arms into the very heart of the island. In these expeditions he was attended with such success, that in two years time he brought into subjection all the Greek part of Sicily. This being accomplished, he committed great devastations in the Carthaginian territories, their general Hamilcar not offering to give him the least disturbance. This perfidious conduct greatly incensed the people of those districts against Hamilcar, whom they accused before the senate. He died, however, in Sicily; and Hamilcar the son of Gisco was appointed to succeed him in the command of the forces. The last place that held out against Agathocles was Messana, whither all the Syracusan exiles had retired. Pasiphilus, Agathocles's general, found means to cajole the inhabitants into a treaty; which Agathocles, according to custom, paid no regard to, but, as soon as he was in possession of the town, cut off all those who had opposed his government. For, as he intended to prosecute the war with the utmost vigour against Carthage, he thought it a point of good policy to destroy as many of his Sicilian enemies as possible.

Carthage.

34 Defeated by the Carthaginians and besieged in Syracuse.

The Carthaginians in the mean time having landed a powerful army in Sicily, an engagement soon ensued, in which Agathocles was defeated with the loss of 7000 men. After this defeat he was obliged to shut himself up in Syracuse, which the Carthaginians immediately invested, and most of the Greek states in the island submitted to them.

Agathocles seeing himself stripped of almost all his dominions, and his capital itself in danger of falling into the hands of the enemy, formed a design which, were it not attested by writers of undoubted authority, would seem absolutely incredible. This was no less

35 He invades Africa.

than to transfer the war into Africa, and lay siege to the enemy's capital, at a time when he himself was besieged, and only one city left to him in all Sicily. Before he departed, however, he made all the necessary preparations for the defence of the place, and appointed his brother Antandrus governor of it. He also gave permission to all who were not willing to stand the fatigues of a siege to retire out of the city. Many of the principal citizens, Justin says 1600, accepted of this offer; but they were no sooner got out of the place, than they were cut off by parties posted on the road for that purpose. Having seized upon their estates, Agathocles raised a considerable sum, which was intended in some measure to defray the expence of the expedition; however, he carried with him only 50 talents to supply his present wants, being well assured that he should find in the enemy's country whatever was necessary for his subsistence. As the Carthaginians had a much superior fleet, they for some time kept the mouth of the harbour blocked up; but at last a fair opportunity offered; and Agathocles hoisting sail, by the activity of his rowers soon got clear both of the port and city of Syracuse. The Carthaginians pursued him with all possible expedition; but, notwithstanding their utmost efforts, Agathocles got his troops landed with very little opposition.

36 He burns his fleet.

Soon after his forces were landed, Agathocles burnt his fleet, probably that his soldiers might behave with the greater resolution, as they saw no possibility of flying from their danger. He first advanced to a place called the Great City. This, after a feeble resistance, he took and plundered. From hence he marched to Tunis, which surrendered on the first summons; and Agathocles levelled both places with the ground.

The Carthaginians were at first thrown into the greatest consternation; but soon recovering themselves, the citizens took up arms with so much alacrity, that in a few days they had on foot an army of 40,000 foot and 1000 horse, with 2000 armed chariots. The

37 Carthaginians defeated.

command of this army they entrusted to Hanno and Bomilcar, two generals between whom there subsisted a great animosity. This occasioned the defeat of their whole army with the loss of their camp, though all the forces of Agathocles did not exceed 14,000 in number. Among other rich spoils the conqueror found many chariots of curious workmanship, which carried 20,000 pair of fetters and manacles that the enemy had provided for the Sicilian prisoners. After this de-

38 Their method of appeasing their deities.

feat, the Carthaginians, supposing themselves to have fallen under the displeasure of their deities on account of their neglecting to sacrifice children of noble fami-

lies

lies to them, resolved to expiate this guilt. Accordingly 200 children of the first rank were sacrificed to their bloody gods, besides 300 other persons who voluntarily offered themselves to pacify the wrath of these deities.

39 *Hamilcar makes an assault on Syracuse.* After these expiations, Hamilcar was recalled from Sicily. When the messengers arrived, Hamilcar commanded them not once to mention the victory of Agathocles; but, on the contrary, to give out among the troops that he had been entirely defeated, his forces all cut off, and his fleet destroyed by the Carthaginians. This threw the Syracusans into the utmost despair; however, one Eurymnon, an Etolian, prevailed upon Antandrus, not to consent to a capitulation, but to stand a general assault. Hamilcar being informed of this, prepared his battering engines, and made all the necessary preparations to storm the town without delay. But while matters remained in this situation, a galley, which Agathocles had caused to be built immediately after the battle, got into the harbour of Syracuse, and acquainted the inhabitants with the certainty of Agathocles's victory. Hamilcar observing that the garrison flocked down to the port on this occasion, and expecting to find the walls unguarded, ordered his soldiers to erect scaling-ladders, and begin the intended assault. The enemy having left the ramparts quite exposed, the Carthaginians mounted them without being discerned, and had almost possessed themselves of an entire part lying between two towers, when the patrol discovered them. Upon this a warm dispute
40 *He raises the siege.* ensued; but at last the Carthaginians were repulsed with loss. Hamilcar, therefore, finding it in vain to continue the siege after such glad tidings had restored life and soul to the Syracusans, drew off his forcet, and sent a detachment of 5000 men to reinforce the troops in Africa. He still entertained hopes, however, that he might oblige Agathocles to quit Africa, and return to the defence of his own dominions. He spent some time in making himself master of such cities as sided with the Syracusans; and after having brought all their allies under subjection, returned again
41 *Is defeated, and taken prisoner and put to death.* to Syracuse, hoping to surprise it by an attack in the night-time. But being attacked while advancing thro' narrow passes, where his numerous army had not room to act, he was defeated with great slaughter, and himself taken prisoner, carried into Syracuse, and put to death.

42 *Agrigentines attempt the sovereignty of Sicily.* In the mean time the Agrigentines, finding that the Carthaginians and Syracusans had greatly weakened each other by this war, thought it a proper opportunity to attempt the sovereignty of the whole island. They therefore commenced a war against both parties; and prosecuted it with such success, that in a short time they wrested many places of note both out of the hands of the Syracusans and Carthaginians.

43 *Success of Agathocles in Africa.* In Africa the tyrant carried every thing before him. He reduced most of the places of any note in the territory of Carthage; and hearing that Elymas king of Libya had declared against him, he immediately entered Libya Superior, and in a great battle overthrew that prince, putting to the sword a good part of his troops, and the general who commanded them; after which he advanced against the Carthaginians with such expedition, that he surprised and defeated them, with the loss of 2000 killed, and a great number taken prisoners. He next prepared for the siege of Carthage itself; and in order thereto advanced to a post within five miles of that city. On the other hand, notwithstanding the great losses they had already sustained, the Carthaginians, with a powerful army, encamped between him and their capital. In this situation Agathocles received advice of the defeat of the Carthaginian forces before Syracuse, and the head of Hamilcar their general. Upon this he immediately rode up to the enemy's camp, and showing them the head, gave them an account of the total destruction of their army before Syracuse. This threw them into such consternation, that in all human probability Agathocles would have made himself master of Carthage, had not an unexpected mutiny arisen in his camp, which gave the Carthaginians an opportunity of recovering from their terror.

The year following an engagement happened, in 44 *He makes an alliance with Ophellas;*
which neither party gained any great advantage: but soon after, the tyrant, notwithstanding all his victories, found himself unable to carry on the war alone; and therefore endeavoured to gain over to his interest Ophellas, one of the captains of Alexander the Great. In this he perfectly succeeded; and, to succour his new ally the more effectually, Ophellas sent to Athens for a body of troops. Having finished his military preparations, Ophellas found his army to consist of 10,000 foot and 600 horse, all regular troops, besides 100 chariots, and a body of 10,000 men, attended by their wives and children, as though he had been going to plant a new colony. At the head of these forces he continued his march towards Agathocles for 18 days; and then encamped at Automole, a city about 3000 stadia distant from the capital of his dominions. From thence he advanced through the Regio Syrtica; but found himself reduced to such extremities, that his army was in danger of perishing for want of bread, water, and other provisions. They were also greatly annoyed by serpents and wild beasts, with which that desert region abounded. The serpents made the greatest havock among the troops; for, being of the same colour with the earth, and extremely venomous, many soldiers, who trod upon them without seeing them, were stung to death. At last, after a very fatiguing march of two months, he approached Agathocles, and encamped at a small distance from him, to the no small terror of the Carthaginians, who apprehended the most fatal consequences from this
junction. Agathocles at first caressed him, and ad- 45 *Whom he treacherously murders.*
vised him to take all possible care of his troops that had undergone so many fatigues; but soon after cut him off by treachery, and then by fair words and promises persuaded his troops to serve under himself.

Agathocles now finding himself at the head of a numerous army, assumed the title of King of Africa, intending soon to complete his conquests by the reduction of Carthage. He began with the siege of Utica, which was taken by assault. After this he marched against Hippo Diarrhytus, the Biserta of the moderns, which was also taken by storm; and after this most of the people bordering upon the sea-coasts, and even those who inhabited the inland parts of the
country, submitted to him. But in the midst of this 46 *Is obliged*
career of success, the Sicilians formed an association in *to return home.*

Carthage.

ſavour of liberty; which obliged the tyrant to return home, leaving his ſon Archagathus to carry on the war in Africa.

47 Succeſs of Archagathus.

Archagathus, after his father's departure, greatly extended the African conqueſts. He ſent Eumachus at the head of a large detachment to invade ſome of the neighbouring provinces, while he himſelf, with the greateſt part of his army, obſerved the motions of the Carthaginians. Eumachus falling into Numidia, firſt took the great city of Toca, and conquered ſeveral of the Numidian cantons. Afterwards he beſieged and took Phellina; which was attended with the ſubmiſſion of the Aſphodelodians, a nation, according to Diodorus, as black as the Ethiopians. He then reduced ſeveral cities; and being at laſt elated with ſuch a run of good fortune, reſolved to penetrate into the more remote parts of Africa. Here he at firſt met with ſucceſs; but hearing that the barbarous nations were advancing in a formidable body to give him battle, he abandoned his conqueſts, and retreated with the utmoſt precipitation towards the ſea-coaſts, after having loſt abundance of men.

48 He is reduced to the utmoſt diſtreſs.

This unfortunate expedition made a great alteration for the worſe in the affairs of Archagathus. The Carthaginians being informed of Eumachus's bad ſucceſs, reſolved to exert themſelves in an extraordinary manner to repair their former loſſes. They divided their forces into three bodies: one of theſe they ſent to the ſea-coaſts, to keep the towns there in awe; another they diſpatched into the Mediterranean parts, to preſerve the allegiance of the inhabitants there; and the laſt body they ordered to the Upper Africa, to ſupport their confederates in that country. Archagathus being appriſed of the motions of the Carthaginians, divided his forces likewiſe into three bodies. One of theſe he ſent to obſerve the Carthaginian troops on the ſea-coaſts, with orders to advance afterwards into the Upper Africa; another, under the command of Æſchrion, one of his generals, he poſted at a proper diſtance in the heart of the country, to have an eye both on the enemy there and the barbarous nations; and with the laſt, which he led in perſon, he kept nearer Carthage, preſerving a communication with the other two, in order to ſend them ſuccours, or recal them, as the exigency of affairs ſhould require.—The Carthaginian troops ſent into the heart of the country, were commanded by Hanno, a general of great experience, who being informed of the approach of Æſchrion, laid an ambuſcade for him, into which he was drawn and cut off with 4000 foot and 200 horſe. Himilco, who commanded the Carthaginian forces in Upper Africa, having advice of Eumachus's march, immediately advanced againſt him. An engagement enſued, in which the Greeks were almoſt totally cut off, or periſhed with thirſt after the battle, out of 8000 foot only 30, and of 800 horſe only 40, having the good fortune to make their eſcape.

Archagathus receiving the melancholy news of theſe two defeats, immediately called in the detachments he had ſent out to haraſs the enemy, which would otherwiſe have been inſtantly cut off. He was, however, in a ſhort time hemmed in on all ſides in ſuch a manner as to be reduced to the laſt extremity for want of proviſions, and ready every moment to be ſwallowed up by the numerous forces which ſurrounded him. In this deplorable ſituation Agathocles received an expreſs from Archagathus, acquainting him of the loſſes he had ſuſtained and the ſcarcity of proviſions he laboured under. Upon this the tyrant, leaving the care of the Sicilian war to one Leptines, by a ſtratagem got 18 Etruſcan ſhips that came to his aſſiſtance out of the harbour; and then engaging the Carthaginian ſquadron which lay in its neighbourhood, took five of their ſhips, and made all their men priſoners. By this means he became maſter of the port, and ſecured a paſſage into it for the merchants of all nations, which ſoon reſtored plenty to that city, where the famine before had begun to make great havock. Supplying himſelf, therefore, with a ſufficient quantity of neceſſaries for the voyage he was going to undertake, he immediately ſet ſail for Africa.

Upon his arrival in this country, Agathocles reviewed his forces, and found them to conſiſt of 6000 Greeks, as many Samnites, Celtes, and Etruſcans; beſides 10,000 Africans, and 1500 horſe. As he found his troops almoſt in a ſtate of deſpair, he thought this a proper time for offering the enemy battle. The Carthaginians, however, did not think proper to accept the challenge; eſpecially as by keeping cloſe in their camp, where they had plenty of every thing, they could ſtarve the Greeks to a ſurrender without ſtriking a ſtroke. Upon this Agathocles attacked the Carthaginian camp with great bravery, made a conſiderable impreſſion upon it, and might perhaps have carried it, had not his mercenaries deſerted him almoſt at the firſt onſet. By this piece of cowardice he was forced to retire with precipitation to his camp, whither the Carthaginians purſued him very cloſely, doing great execution in the purſuit.

49 Agathocles arrives in Africa.

50 Attacks the camp of the enemy without ſucceſs.

51 Diſaſter in the Carthaginian camp.

The next night, the Carthaginians ſacrificed all the priſoners of diſtinction as a grateful acknowledgment to the gods for the victory they had gained. While they were employed in this inhuman work, the wind, ſuddenly riſing, carried the flames to the ſacred tabernacle near the altar, which was entirely conſumed, as well as the general's tent, and thoſe of the principal officers adjoining to it. A dreadful alarm took place through the whole camp, which was heightened by the great progreſs the fire made. For the ſoldiers tents conſiſting of very combuſtible materials, and the wind blowing in a moſt violent manner, the whole camp was almoſt entirely laid in aſhes; and many of the ſoldiers endeavouring to carry off their arms, and the rich baggage of their officers, periſhed in the flames. Some of thoſe who made their eſcape met with a fate equally unhappy: For, after Agathocles had received the laſt blow, the Africans deſerted him, and were in that inſtant coming over in a body to the Carthaginians. Theſe, the perſons who were flying from the flames took to be the whole Syracuſian army advancing in order of battle to attack their camp. Upon this a dreadful confuſion enſued. Some took to their heels; others fell down in heaps one upon another; and others engaged their comrades, miſtaking them for the enemy. Five thouſand men loſt their lives in this tumult, and the reſt thought proper to take refuge within the walls of Carthage; nor could the appearance of day-light, for ſome time, diſ-spate their terrible apprehensions. In the mean time, the African deserters, observing the great confusion the Carthaginians were in, and not knowing

52 *Another in that of Agathocles.*

the meaning of it, were so terrified, that they thought proper to return to the place from whence they came. The Syracusians seeing a body of troops advancing towards them in good order, concluded that the enemy were marching to attack them, and therefore immediately cried out "To arms." The flames ascending out of the Carthaginian camp into the air, and the lamentable outcries proceeding from thence, confirmed them in this opinion, and greatly heightened their confusion. The consequence was much the same as in the Carthaginian camp; for coming to blows with one another instead of the enemy, they scarce recovered their senses upon the return of light, and the intestine fray was so bloody, that it cost Agathocles 4000 men.

53 *He escapes privately.*

This last disaster so disheartened the tyrant, that he immediately set about contriving means for making his escape privately; and this he at last, though with great difficulty, effected. After his departure, his two sons were immediately put to death by the soldiers, who, choosing a leader from among themselves, made peace with the Carthaginians upon the following conditions: 1. That the Greeks should deliver up all the places they held in Africa, receiving from them 300 talents; 2. That such of them as were willing to serve in the Carthaginian army should be kindly treated, and receive the usual pay; and, 3. That the rest should be transported to Sicily, and have the city of Selinus for their habitation.

54 *Cause of the first Punic War.*

From this time, to that of their first war with the Romans, we find nothing remarkable in the history of the Carthaginians. The first Punic war, as it is commonly called, happened about 256 years before Christ. At that time, the Carthaginians were possessed of extensive dominions in Africa; they had made considerable progress in Spain; were masters of Sardinia, Corsica, and all the islands on the coast of Italy; and had extended their conquests to a great part of Sicily. The occasion of the first rupture between the two republics was as follows. The Mamertines being vanquished in battle, and reduced to great straits by Hiero king of Syracuse, had resolved to deliver up Messina, the only city they now possessed, to that prince, with whose mild government and strict probity they were well acquainted. Accordingly, Hiero was advancing at the head of his troops to take possession of the city, when Hannibal, who at that time commanded the Carthaginian army in Sicily, prevented him by a stratagem. He came to meet Hiero, as it were to congratulate him on his victory; and amused him, while some of the Carthaginian troops filed off towards Messina. Hereupon the Mamertines, seeing their city supported by a new reinforcement, were divided into several opinions. Some were for accepting the protection of Carthage; others were for surrendering to the king of Syracuse; but the greater part were for calling in the Romans to their assistance. Deputies were accordingly dispatched to Rome, offering the possession of the city to the Romans, and in the most moving terms imploring protection. This, after some debate, was agreed to; and the consul Appius Claudius received orders to attempt a passage to Sicily, at the head of a powerful army. Being obliged to stay some time at Rome, however, one Caius Claudius, a person of great intrepidity and resolution, was dispatched with a few vessels to Rhegium. On his arrival there, he observed the Carthaginian squadron to be so much superior to his own, that he thought it would be little better than madness to attempt at that time to transport forces to Sicily. He crossed the straits, however, and had a conference with the Mamertines, in which he prevailed upon them all to accept of the protection of Rome; and on this he made the necessary preparations for transporting his forces. The Carthaginians being informed of the resolutions of the Romans, sent a strong

squadron of gallies under the command of Hanno, to 55 *Hanno intercepts the Roman fleet.*

intercept the Roman fleet; and accordingly the Carthaginian admiral, coming up with them near the coast of Sicily, attacked them with great fury. During the engagement, a violent storm arose, which dashed many of the Roman vessels against the rocks, and did a vast deal of damage to their squadron; by which means Claudius was forced to retire to Rhegium, and this he accomplished with great difficulty. Hanno restored all the vessels he had taken; but ordered the deputies sent with them, to expostulate with the Roman general upon the infraction of the treaties subsisting between the two republics. This expostulation, however just, produced an open rupture; Claudius soon after possessing himself of Messina.

Such was the beginning of the first Punic war, 56 *Carthaginians and Syracusans defeated by the Romans.*

which is said to have lasted 24 years. The first year, the Carthaginians and Syracusans laid siege to Messina; but, not acting in concert as they ought to have done, were overthrown by the Consul Appius Claudius; and this defeat so much disgusted Hiero with the Carthaginians, that he soon after concluded an alliance with the Romans. After this treaty, having no enemy to contend with but the Carthaginians, the Romans made themselves masters of all the cities on the western coast of Sicily, and at the end of the campaign carried back most of their troops with them to take up their winter-quarters in Italy.

The second year, Hanno the Carthaginian general 57 *Agrigentum taken by the Romans.*

fixed his principal magazine at Agrigentum. This place was very strong by nature, had been rendered almost impregnable by the new fortifications raised by the Carthaginians during the preceding winter, and was defended by a numerous garrison commanded by one Hannibal, a general of great experience in war. For five months the Romans attempted to reduce the place by famine, and had actually brought the inhabitants to great distress, when a Carthaginian army of 50,000 foot, 6000 horse, and 60 elephants, landed at Lilybaeum, and from thence marched to Heraclea, within 20 miles of Agrigentum. There the general received a deputation from some of the inhabitants of Erbessa, where the Romans had their magazines, offering to put the town into his hands. It was accordingly delivered up; and by this means the Romans became so much distressed; that they had certainly been obliged to abandon their enterprise, had not Hiero supplied them with provisions. But all the assistance he was able to give could not long have supported

them,

Carthage. them, as their army was so much weakened by disorders occasioned by famine, that, out of 100,000 men of whom it originally consisted, scarce a fourth part remained fit for service, and could no longer subsist on such parsimonious supplies. But in the mean time Hannibal acquainted Hanno that the city was reduced to the utmost distress; upon which he resolved to venture an engagement, which he had before declined. In this the Romans were victorious, and the city surrendered at discretion, though Hannibal with the greatest part of the garrison made their escape. This ended the campaign; and the Carthaginians being greatly chagrined at their bad success, fined Hanno of an immense sum of money, and deprived him of his command, appointing Hamilcar to succeed him in the command of the land army, and Hannibal in that of the fleet.

The third year, Hannibal received orders to ravage the coasts of Italy; but the Romans had taken care to post detachments in such places as were most pro-
58 They build a fleet, per to prevent his landing, so that the Carthaginian found it impossible to execute his orders. At the same time, the Romans, perceiving the advantages of being masters of the sea, set about building 120 galleys. While this was doing, they made themselves masters of most of the inland cities, but the Carthaginians reduced or kept steady in their interest most of the maritime ones; so that both parties were equally successful during this campaign.

The fourth year, Hannibal by a stratagem made himself master of 17 Roman galleys; after which he committed great ravages on the coast of Italy, whither he had advanced to take a view of the Roman fleet.
59 And defeat the Carthaginians at sea. But he was afterwards attacked in his turn, lost the greatest part of his ships, and with great difficulty made his own escape. Soon after he was totally defeated by the consul Duillius, with the loss of 80 ships taken, thirteen sunk, 7000 men killed, and as many taken prisoners. After this victory Duillius landed in Sicily, put himself at the head of the land forces, relieved Segesta besieged by Hamilcar, and made himself master of Macella, though defended by a numerous garrison.

60 Sicilians defeated by the Carthaginians. The fifth year, a difference arose between the Romans and their Sicilian allies, which came to such an height, that they encamped separately. Of this Hamilcar availed himself, and attacking the Sicilians in their entrenchments, put 4000 of them to the sword. He then drove the Romans from their posts, took several cities from them, and over-ran the greatest part of the country. In the mean time, Hannibal, after his defeat, sailed with the shattered remains of his fleet to Carthage; but in order to secure himself from punishment, he sent one of his friends with all speed, before the event of the battle was known there, to acquaint the senate, that the Romans had put to sea with a good number of heavy ill-built vessels, each of them carrying some machine, the use of which the Carthaginians did not understand; and asked whether it was the opinion of the senate that Hannibal should attack them. These machines were the *corvi*, which were then newly invented, and by means of which, chiefly, Duillius had gained the victory. The senate were unanimous in their opinion, that the Romans should be attacked; upon which the messenger acquainted them with the unfortunate event of the battle. As the senators had already declared themselves for the engagement, they spared their general's life, and, according to Polybius, even continued him in the command of the fleet. In a short time, being reinforced by a good number of galleys, and attended by some officers of great merit, he sailed for the coast of Sardinia. He had not been long here, before he was surprised by the Romans, who carried off many of his ships, and took great numbers of his men prisoners. This so incensed the rest, that they seized their unfortunate admiral, and crucified him; but who was his immediate successor does not appear. 61

The sixth year, the Romans made themselves masters of the islands of Corsica and Sardinia. Hanno, who commanded the Carthaginian forces in the latter, defended himself at a city called Olbia with incredible bravery; but being at last killed in one of the attacks, the place was surrendered, and the Romans soon became masters of the whole island. Corsica and Sardinia reduced by the Romans.

The seventh year, the Romans took the town of Mytistratum, in Sicily, from whence they marched towards Camarina, but in their way were surrounded in a deep valley, and in the most imminent danger of being cut off by the Carthaginian army. In this extremity, a legionary tribune, by name *M. Calpurnius Flamma*, desired the general to give him 300 chosen men; promising, with this small company, to find the enemy such employment as should oblige them to leave a passage open for the Roman army. He performed his promise with a bravery truly heroic; for, having seized, in spite of all opposition, an eminence, and entrenched himself on it, the Carthaginians, jealous of his design, flocked from all quarters to drive him from his post. But the brave tribune kept their whole army in play, till the consul, taking advantage of the diversion, drew his army out of the bad situation in which he had imprudently brought it. The legions were no sooner out of danger, than they hastened to the relief of their brave companions: but all they could do was to save their bodies from the insults of their enemies; for they found them all dead on the spot, except Calpurnius, who lay under an heap of dead bodies all covered with wounds, but still breathing. His wounds were immediately dressed, and it fortunately happened that none of them proved mortal; and for this glorious enterprise he received a crown of *grass*. After this the Romans reduced several cities, and drove the enemy quite out of the territory of the Agrigentines; but were repulsed with great loss before Lipara. 62 The Roman army in great danger. 63 Rescued by the bravery of a legionary tribune.

The eighth year, Regulus, who commanded the Roman fleet, observing that of the Carthaginians lying along the coast in disorder, sailed with a squadron of ten galleys to observe their number and strength, ordering the rest of the fleet to follow him with all expedition. But as he drew too near the enemy, he was surrounded by a great number of Carthaginian galleys. The Romans fought with their usual bravery; but, being overpowered with numbers, were obliged to yield. The consul, however, found means to make his escape, and join the rest of the fleet; and then had his full revenge of the enemy, 18 of their ships being taken, and eight sunk. 64 Carthaginians defeated at sea by the Romans.

The ninth year, the Romans made preparations for invading

invading Africa. Their fleet for this purpose consisted of 330 galleys, each of them having on board 120 soldiers and 300 rowers. The Carthaginian fleet consisted of 360 sail, and was much better manned than that of the Romans. The two fleets met near Ecnomus, a promontory in Sicily; where, after a bloody engagement which lasted the greater part of the day, the Carthaginians were entirely defeated, with the loss of 30 galleys sunk, and 63 taken with all their men. The Romans lost only 24 galleys, which were all sunk.—After this victory, the Romans having refitted their fleet, set sail for the coast of Africa with all expedition. The first land they got sight of was Cape Hermea, where the fleet lay at anchor for some time waiting till the galleys and transports came up. From thence they coasted along till they arrived before Clupea, a city to the east of Carthage, where they made their first descent.

63. Regulus invades Africa.

64. Carthaginians in great consternation.

No words can express the consternation of the Carthaginians, on the arrival of the Romans in Africa. The inhabitants of Clupea were so terrified, that, according to Zonaras, they abandoned the place, which the Romans immediately took possession of. Having left there a strong garrison to secure their shipping, and keep the adjacent territory in awe, they moved nearer Carthage, taking a great number of towns; they likewise plundered a prodigious number of villages, laid vast numbers of noblemens seats in ashes, and took above 20,000 prisoners. In short, having plundered and ravaged the whole country, almost to the gates of Carthage, they returned to Clupea laden with the immense booty they had acquired in the expedition.

67 Success of Regulus.

The tenth year, Regulus pushed on his conquests with great rapidity. To oppose his progress, Hamilcar was recalled from Sicily, and with him Bostar and Asdrubal were joined in command. Hamilcar commanded an army just equal to that of Regulus. The other two commanded separate bodies, which were to join him or act apart as occasion required. But, before they were in a condition to take the field, Regulus, pursuing his conquests, arrived on the banks of the *Bragada*, a river which empties itself into the sea at a small distance from Carthage. Here he had a monstrous serpent to contend with, which, according to the accounts of those days, infected the waters of the river, poisoned the air, and killed all other animals with its breath alone. When the Romans went to draw water, this huge dragon attacked them; and, twisting itself round their bodies, either squeezed them to death, or swallowed them alive. As its hard and thick scales were proof against their darts and arrows, they were forced to have recourse to the balistæ, which they made use of in sieges to throw great stones, and to beat down the walls of besieged cities. With these they discharged showers of huge stones against this new enemy, and had the good luck, with one of them, to break his back-bone; which disabled him from twisting and winding his immense body, and by that means gave the Romans an opportunity of approaching and dispatching him with their darts. But his dead body corrupted the air and the water of the river; and spread so great an infection over the whole country, that the Romans were obliged to decamp. We are told that Regulus sent to Rome the skin of this monster, which was 120 feet long; and that it was hung up in a temple, where it was preserved to the time of the Numantine war.

68 He kills a monstrous serpent.

Having passed this river, he besieged *Adis*, or *Adda*, not far from Carthage, which the enemy attempted to relieve; but as they lay encamped among hills and rocks, where their elephants, in which the main strength of their army consisted, could be of no use, Regulus attacked them in their camp, killed 17,000 of them, and took 5000 prisoners, and 18 elephants. Upon the fame of this victory, deputations came from all quarters, insomuch that the conqueror in a few days became master of 80 towns; among which were the city and port of Utica. This increased the alarm at Carthage; which was reduced to despair, when Regulus laid siege to Tunis, a great city about nine miles from the capital. The place was taken in sight of the Carthaginians, who, from their walls, beheld all the operations of the siege, without making the least attempt to relieve it. And to complete their misfortunes, the Numidians, their neighbours, and implacable enemies, entered their territories, committing every where the most dreadful devastations, which soon occasioned a great scarcity of provisions in the city. The public magazines were soon exhausted: and, as the city was full of selfish merchants, who took advantage of the public distress, to sell provisions at an exorbitant price, a famine ensued, with all the evils which attend it.

69 Defeats the Carthaginians;

70 And reduces them to the utmost despair.

In this extremity Regulus advanced to the very gates of Carthage; and having encamped under the walls, sent deputies to treat of a peace with the senate. The deputies were received with inexpressible joy; but the conditions they proposed were such that the senate could not hear them without the greatest indignation. They were, 1. That the Carthaginians should relinquish all claims to Sardinia, Corsica, and Sicily. 2. That they should restore to the Romans all the prisoners they had taken from them since the beginning of the war. 3. That if they cared to redeem any of their own prisoners, they should pay so much a-head for them as Rome should judge reasonable. 4. That they should for ever pay the Romans an annual tribute. 5. That for the future they should fit out but one man of war for their own use, and 50 triremes to serve in the Roman fleet, at the expence of Carthage, when required by any of the future consuls. These extravagant demands provoked the senators, who loudly and unanimously rejected them; the Roman deputies, however, told them that Regulus would not alter a single letter of the proposals, and that they must either conquer the Romans or obey them.

71 His proposals of peace rejected.

In this extreme distress, some mercenaries arrived from Greece, among whom was a Lacedemonian, by name Xanthippus, a man of great valour and experience in war. This man, having informed himself of the circumstances of the late battle, declared publicly, that their overthrow was more owing to their own misconduct than to the superiority of the enemy. This discourse being spread abroad, came at last to the knowledge of the senate; and by them, and even by the desire of the Carthaginian generals themselves, Xanthippus was appointed commander in chief of their forces. His first care was to discipline his troops in a

72 Xanthippus appointed to command the Carthaginian army.

proper

Carthage.

proper manner. He taught them how to march, encamp, widen and close their ranks, and rally after the Lacedemonian manner under their proper colours. He then took the field with 12,000 foot, 4000 horse, and 100 elephants. The Romans were surprised at the sudden alteration they observed in the enemy's conduct; but Regulus, elated with his last success, came and encamped at a small distance from the Carthaginian army in a vast plain, where their elephants and horse had room to act. The two armies were parted by a river, which Regulus boldly passed, by which means he left no room for a retreat in case of

73 The Romans utterly defeated, and Regulus taken.

any misfortune. The engagement began with great fury; but ended in the total defeat of the Romans, who, except 1000 that escaped to Clupea, were all killed or taken prisoners, and among the latter was Regulus himself. The loss of the Carthaginians scarce exceeded 800 men.

74 He is cruelly used.

The Carthaginians remained on the field of battle till they had stripped the slain; and then entered their metropolis, which was almost the only place left them, in great triumph. They treated all their prisoners with great humanity, except Regulus; but as for him, he had so insulted them in his prosperity, that they could not forbear shewing the highest marks of their resentment. According to Zonaras and others, he was thrown into a dungeon, where he had only sustenance allowed him barely sufficient to keep him alive. Nay, his cruel masters, to heighten his other torments, ordered an huge elephant (at the sight of which animal, it seems, he was greatly terrified) to be constantly placed near him; which prevented him from enjoying any tranquillity or repose.

75 Carthaginians defeated by sea and land.

The eleventh year of this war, the Carthaginians, elated with their victory over Regulus, began to talk in a very high strain, threatening Italy itself with an invasion. To prevent this, the Romans took care to garrison all their maritime towns, and fitted out a new fleet. In the mean time, the Carthaginians besieged Clupea and Utica in vain, being obliged to abandon their enterprise, upon hearing that the Romans were equipping a fleet of 350 sail. The Carthaginians having with incredible expedition refitted their old vessels, and built a good number of new ones, met the Roman fleet off Cape Hermea. An engagement ensued, in which the Carthaginians were utterly defeated; 104 of their ships being sunk, 30 taken, and 15,000 of their soldiers and rowers killed in the action. The Romans pursued their course to Clupea, where they were no sooner landed, than they found themselves attacked by the Carthaginian army, under the two Hanno's, father and son. But, as the brave Xanthippus no longer commanded their army, notwithstanding the Lacedemonian discipline he had introduced among them, they were routed at the very first onset, with the loss of 9000 men, and among them many of their chief lords.

76 Romans obliged to abandon Africa.

Notwithstanding all their victories, however, the Romans found themselves now obliged, for want of provisions, to evacuate both Clupea and Utica, and abandon Africa altogether. Being desirous of signalizing the end of their consulate by some important conquest on Sicily, the consuls steered for that island, contrary to the advice of their pilots, who represented their danger, on account of the season being so far advanced. Their obstinacy proved the destruction of the whole fleet; for a violent storm arising, out of 370 vessels, only 80 escaped shipwreck, the rest being swallowed up by the sea, or dashed against the rocks. This was by far the greatest loss that Rome had ever sustained; for besides the ships that were cast away with their crews, a numerous army was destroyed, with all the riches of Africa, which had been by Regulus amassed and deposited in Clupea, and were now from thence transporting to Rome. The whole coast from Pachinum to Camerina was covered with dead bodies and wrecks of ships; so that history can scarce afford an example of such a dreadful disaster.

77 Their fleet totally destroyed by a storm.

The twelfth year, the Carthaginians hearing of this misfortune of the Romans, renewed the war in Sicily with fresh fury, hoping the whole island, which was now left defenceless, would fall into their hands. Carthalo, a Carthaginian commander, besieged and took Agrigentum. The town he laid in ashes and demolished the walls, obliging the inhabitants to fly to Olympium. Upon the news of this success, Asdrubal was sent to Sicily with a large reinforcement of troops, and 150 elephants. They likewise fitted out a squadron, with which they retook the island of Cosyra, and marched a strong body of forces into Mauritania and Numidia, to punish the people of those countries for shewing a disposition to join the Romans. In Sicily the Romans possessed themselves of Cephaloedium and Panormus, but were obliged by Carthalo to raise the siege of Drepanum with great loss.

78 Agrigentum taken and destroyed by the Carthaginians.

79 The Romans fit out a new fleet,

The 13th year, the Romans sent out a fleet of 260 galleys, which appeared off Lilybaeum in Sicily; but finding this place too strong, they steered from thence to the eastern coast of Africa, where they made several descents, surprised some cities, and plundered several towns and villages. They arrived safe at Panormus, and in a few days set sail for Italy, having a fair wind till they came off Cape Palinurus, where so violent a storm overtook them, that 160 of their galleys and a great number of their transports were lost; upon which the Roman senate made a decree, that, for the future, no more than 50 vessels should be equipped; and that these should be employed only in guarding the coast of Italy, and transporting the troops into Sicily.

80 Which is again destroyed.

The 14th year, the Romans made themselves masters of Himera and Lipara in Sicily; and the Carthaginians conceiving new hopes of conquering that island, began to make fresh levies in Gaul and Spain, and to equip a new fleet. But their treasures being exhausted, they applied to Ptolemy king of Egypt, intreating him to lend them 2000 talents; but he being resolved to stand neuter, refused to comply with their request; telling them, that he could not without breach of fidelity assist one friend against another. However, the republic of Carthage making an effort, equipped a fleet of 200 sail, and raised an army of 30,000 men, horse and foot, and 140 elephants, appointing Asdrubal commander in chief both of the fleet and army. The Romans then finding the great advantages of a fleet, resolved to equip one notwithstanding all former disasters; and while the vessels were building, two consuls were chosen, men of valour and experience, to supersede the acting ones in Sicily. Metellus, however, one of the former consuls, being continued with the title of proconsul, found means

81 They fit out another.

means to draw Asdrubal into a battle on disadvantageous terms near Panormus, and then sallying out

82 Carthaginians utterly defeated.

upon him, gave him a most terrible overthrow. Twenty thousand of the enemy were killed, and many elephants. An hundred and four elephants were taken with their leaders, and sent to Rome, where they were hunted and put to death in the circus.

83 Lilybæum besieged by the Romans.

The 15th year, the Romans besieged Lilybæum; and the siege continued during the rest of the first Punic war, and was the only thing remarkable that happened during that time*. The Carthaginians, on the first news of its being besieged, sent Regulus with some deputies to Rome to treat of a peace; but instead of forwarding the negociation, he hindered it; and notwithstanding he knew the torments prepared for him at Carthage, could not be prevailed upon to stay at Rome, but returning to his enemies country, was put to a most cruel death. During this siege,

* See *Lilybæum*.

84 They are defeated at sea by the Carthaginians.

the Roman fleet under Claudius Pulcher was utterly defeated by Adherbal the Carthaginian admiral. Ninety of the Roman galleys were lost in the action, 8000 of their men either killed or drowned, and 20,000 taken and sent prisoners to Carthage; and the Carthaginians gained this signal victory without the loss of a single

85 A Roman fleet utterly destroyed by a storm.

ship, or even a single man. Another Roman fleet met with a still severer fate. It consisted of 120 galleys, 800 transports, and was laden with all sorts of military stores and provisions. Every one of these vessels were lost by a storm, with all they contained, not a single plank being saved that could be used again; so that the Romans found themselves once more deprived of their whole naval force.

86 Hamilcar Barcas sent into Sicily.

In the mean time, the Carthaginian soldiery having shown a disposition to mutiny, the senate sent over Hamilcar Barcas, father of the famous Hannibal, to Sicily. He received a charte blanche from the senate to act as he thought proper; and by his excellent conduct and resolution, showed himself the greatest general of his age. He defended Eryx, which he had taken by surprise, with such vigour, that the Romans would never have been able to make themselves masters of it, had they not fitted out a new fleet at the expence of private citizens, which, having utterly defeated that of the Carthaginians, Hamilcar, notwithstanding all his valour, was obliged to yield up the place

87 Peace with the Romans.

which he had so long and so bravely defended. The following articles of a peace were immediately drawn up between the two commanders. 1. The Carthaginians shall evacuate all the places which they have in Sicily, and entirely quit that island. 2. They shall, in 20 years, pay the Romans, at equal payments every year, 2200 talents of silver, that is, L. 437,250 Sterling. 3. They shall restore the Roman captives and deserters without ransom, and redeem their own prisoners with money. 4. They shall not make war upon Hiero king of Syracuse, or his allies. These articles being agreed to, Hamilcar surrendered Eryx upon condition that all his soldiers should march out with him upon his paying for each of them 18 *Roman denarii*. Hostages were given on both sides, and deputies were sent to Rome to procure a ratification of the treaty by the senate. After the senators had thoroughly informed themselves of the state of affairs, two more articles were added, viz. 1. That 1000 talents should be paid immediately, and the 2200 in the space of 10 years at equal payments. 2. That the Carthaginians should quit all the little islands about Italy and Sicily, and never more come near them with ships of war, or raise mercenaries in those places. Necessity obliged Hamilcar to consent to these terms; but he returned to Carthage with an hatred to the Romans, which he did not even suffer to die with him, but transmitted to his son the great Hannibal.

88 Origin of the war with the mercenaries.

The Carthaginians were no sooner got out of this bloody and expensive war, than they found themselves engaged in another which was like to have proved fatal to them. It is called by ancient historians the *Libyan war*, or the *war with the mercenaries*. The principal occasion of it was, that when Hamilcar returned to Carthage, he found the republic so much impoverished, that, far from being able to give these troops the largesses and rewards promised them, it could not pay them their arrears. He had committed the care of transporting them to one *Gisco*, who, being an officer of great penetration, as though he had foreseen what would happen, did not ship them off all at once, but in small and separate parties, that those who came first might be paid off and sent home before the arrival of the rest. The Carthaginians at home, however, did not act with the same prudence. As the state was almost entirely exhausted by the last war, and the immense sum of money, in consequence of the peace, paid to the Romans, they judged it would be a laudable action to save something to the public. They did not therefore pay off the mercenaries in proportion as they arrived, thinking it more proper to wait till they all came together, with a view of obtaining some remission of their arrears. But being soon made sensible of their wrong conduct on this occasion, by the frequent disorders these barbarians committed in the city, they with some difficulty prevailed upon the officers to take up their quarters at Sicca, and canton their troops in that neighbourhood. To induce them to this, however, they gave them a sum of money for their present subsistence, and promised to comply with their pretensions when the remainder of their troops arrived from Sicily. Here, being wholly immersed in idleness, to which they had long been strangers, a neglect of discipline ensued, and of course a petulant and licentious spirit immediately took place. They were now determined not to acquiesce in receiving their bare pay, but to insist upon the rewards Hamilcar had promised them, and even to compel the state of Carthage to comply with their demands by force of arms. The senate being informed of the mutinous disposition of the soldiery, dispatched Hanno, one of the suffetes, to pacify them. Upon his arrival at Sicca, he expatiated largely upon the poverty of the state, and the heavy taxes with which the citizens of Carthage were loaded; and therefore, instead of answering their high expectations, he desired them to be satisfied with receiving part of their pay, and remit the remainder to serve the pressing exigencies of the republic. The mercenaries being highly provoked, that neither Hamilcar, nor any other of the principal officers who commanded them in Sicily, and were the best judges of their merit, made their appearance on this occasion, but only Hanno, a person utterly unknown, and above all others

89 Imprudent conduct of Hanno.

Carthage. others utterly disagreeable to them, immediately had recourse to arms. Assembling therefore in a body to the number of 20,000, they advanced to Tunis, and immediately encamped before that city.

The Carthaginians being greatly alarmed at the approach of so formidable a body to Tunis, made large concessions to the mercenaries, in order to bring them back to their duty; but, far from being softened, they grew more insolent upon these concessions, taking them for the effects of fear; and therefore were altogether averse to thoughts of accommodation. The Carthaginians, making a virtue of necessity, showed a disposition to satisfy them in all points, and agreed to refer themselves to the opinion of some general in Sicily, which they had all along desired; leaving the choice of such commander entirely to them. Gisco was accordingly pitched upon to mediate this affair, the mercenaries believing Hamilcar to have been a principal cause of the ill treatment they met with, since he never appeared among them, and, according to the general opinion, had voluntarily resigned his commission. Gisco soon arrived at Tunis with money to pay the troops; and after conferring with the officers of the several nations apart, he harangued them in such a manner, that a treaty was upon the point of being concluded, when Spendius and Mathos, two of the principal mutineers, occasioned a tumult in every part of the camp. Spendius was by nation a Campanian, who had been a slave at Rome, and had fled to the Carthaginians. The apprehensions he was under of being delivered to his old master, by whom he was sure to be hanged or crucified, prompted him to break off the accommodation. Mathos was an African, and free born; but as he had been active in raising the rebellion, and was well acquainted with the implacable disposition of the Carthaginians, he knew that a peace must infallibly prove his ruin. He therefore joined with Spendius, and insinuated to the Africans the danger of concluding a treaty at that juncture, but which could not leave them singly exposed to the rage of the Carthaginians. This so incensed the Africans, who were much more numerous than the troops of any other nation, that they immediately assembled in a tumultuous manner. The foreigners soon joined them, being inspired by Spendius with an equal degree of fury. Nothing was now to be heard but the most horrid oaths and imprecations against Gisco and the Carthaginians. Whoever offered to make any remonstrance, or lend an ear to temperate counsels, was stoned to death by the enraged multitude. Nay, many persons lost their lives barely for attempting to speak, before it could be known whether they were in the interest of Spendius or the Carthaginians.

In the midst of these commotions, Gisco behaved with great firmness and intrepidity. He left no methods untried to soften the officers and calm the minds of the soldiery; but the torrent of sedition was now so strong, that there was no possibility of keeping it within bounds. They therefore seized upon the military chest, dividing the money among themselves in part of their arrears, put the person of Gisco under an arrest, and treated him as well as his attendants with the utmost indignity. Mathos and Spendius, to destroy the remotest hopes of an accommodation with Carthage, applauded the courage and re- Carthage.
solution of their men, loaded the unhappy Gisco and
his followers with irons, and formally declared war 90
against the Carthaginians. All the cities of Africa The mercenaries declare war
to whom they had sent deputies to exhort them to recover their liberty, soon came over to them, except Utica and Hippo Diarhytus. By this means their army being greatly increased, they divided it into two parts, with one of which they moved towards Utica, whilst the other marched to Hippo, in order to besiege both places. The Carthaginians, in the mean time, found themselves ready to sink under the pressure of their misfortunes. After they had been harassed 24 years by a most cruel and destructive foreign war, they entertained some hopes of enjoying repose. The citizens of Carthage drew their particular subsistence from the rents or revenues of their lands, and the public expences from the tribute paid from Africa; all which they were not only deprived of at once, but, what was worse, had it directly turned against them. They were destitute of arms and forces either by sea or land; had made no preparations for the sustaining of a siege, or the equipping of a fleet. They suffered all the calamities incident to the most ruinous civil war; and, to complete their misery, had not the least prospect of receiving assistance from any foreign friend or ally. Notwithstanding their deplorable situation, however, they did not despond, but pursued all the measures necessary to put themselves into a posture of defence. Hanno was appointed commander in chief of all their forces; and the most strenuous efforts were made, not only to repel all the attempts of the mutineers, but even to reduce them by force of arms.

In the mean time Mathos and Spendius laid siege to Utica and Hippacra at once; but as they were carried on by detachments drawn from the army for that purpose, they remained with the main body of their forces at Tunis, and thereby cut off all communication betwixt Carthage and the continent of Africa. By this means the capital was kept in a kind of blockade. The Africans likewise harassed them by perpetual alarms, advancing to the very walls of Carthage by day as well as by night, and treating with the utmost cruelty every Carthaginian that fell into their hands.

Hanno was dispatched to the relief of Utica with a 91
good body of forces, 100 elephants, and a large They are defeated by Hanno.
train of battering engines. Having taken a view of the enemy, he immediately attacked their intrenchments, and, after an obstinate dispute, forced them. The mercenaries lost a vast number of men; and consequently the advantages gained by Hanno were so great, that they might have proved decisive, had he 92
made a proper use of them: But becoming secure af- He is afterwards defeated.
ter his victory, and his troops being every where off their duty, the mercenaries, having rallied their forces, fell upon him, cut off many of his men, forced the rest to fly into the town, retook and plundered the camp, and seized all the provisions, military stores, &c. brought to the relief of the besieged. Nor was this the only instance of Hanno's military incapacity. Notwithstanding he lay encamped in the most advantageous manner near a town called *Gorza*, at which place he twice overthrew the enemy, and had it in his

power to have totally ruined them, he yet neglected to improve those advantages, and even suffered the mercenaries to possess themselves of the isthmus which joined the peninsula on which Carthage stood, to the continent of Africa.

93
Hamilcar Barcas appointed to command against them.

These repeated mistakes induced the Carthagisians once more to place Hamilcar Barcas at the head of their forces. He marched against the enemy with 10,000 men, horse and foot; being all the troops the Carthaginians could then assemble for their defence; a full proof of the low state to which they were at that time reduced. As Mathos, after he had possessed himself of the isthmus, had posted proper detachments in two passes on two hills facing the continent, and guarded the bridge over the Bagrada, which through Hanno's neglect he had taken, Hamilcar saw little probability of engaging him upon equal terms, or indeed of coming at him. Observing, however, that on the blowing of certain winds the mouth of the river was choaked up with sand, so as to become passable, though with no small difficulty, as long as these winds continued; he halted for some time at the river's mouth, without communicating his design to any person. As soon as the wind favoured his intended project, he passed the river privately by night, and immediately after his passage he drew up the troops in order of battle, and advancing into the plain where his elephants were capable of acting, moved towards Mathos, who was posted at the village near the bridge. This daring action greatly surprised and intimidated the Africans. However, Spendius receiving intelligence of the enemy's motions, drew a body of 10,000 men out of Mathos's camp, with which he attended Hamilcar on one side, and ordered 15,000 from Utica to observe him on the other, thinking by this means to surround the Carthaginians, and cut

94
He defeats them.

them all off at one stroke. By feigning a retreat, Hamilcar found means to engage them at a disadvantage; and gave them a total overthrow, with the loss of 6000 killed and 2000 taken prisoners. The rest fled, some to the town at the bridge, and others to the camp at Utica. He did not give them time to recover from their defeat, but pursued them to the town near the bridge before mentioned; which he entered without opposition, the mercenaries flying in great confusion to Tunis; and upon this many towns submitted of their own accord to the Carthaginians, whilst others were reduced by force.

Notwithstanding these disasters, Mathos pushed on the siege of Hippo with great vigour, and appointed Spendius and Autaritus, commanders of the Gauls, with a strong body, to observe the motions of Hamilcar. These two commanders, therefore, at the head of a choice detachment of 6000 men drawn out of the camp at Tunis, and 2000 Gallic horse, attended the Carthaginian general, approaching him as near as they could with safety, and keeping close to the skirts of the mountains. At last Spendius, having received a strong reinforcement of Africans and Numidians, and possessing himself of all the heights surrounding the plain in which Hamilcar lay encamped, resolved not to let slip so favourable an opportunity of attacking him. Had a battle now ensued, Hamilcar and his army must in all probability have been cut off; but by the defection of one Naravasus, a young Numidian nobleman, with 2000 men, he found himself enabled to offer his enemies battle. The fight was

95
Mercenaries again defeated.

obstinate and bloody; but at last the mercenaries were entirely overthrown, with the loss of 10,000 men killed and 4000 taken prisoners. All the prisoners that were willing to inlist in the Carthaginian service, Hamilcar received among his troops, supplying them with the arms of the soldiers who had fallen in the engagement. To the rest he gave full liberty to go where they pleased; upon condition that they should never for the future bear arms against the Carthaginians; informing them at the same time, however, that as many violators of this agreement as fell into his hands must expect to find no mercy.

96
They put to death all the Carthaginian prisoners.

Mathos and his associates, fearing that this affected lenity of Hamilcar might occasion a defection among the troops, thought that the best expedient would be to put them upon some action so execrable in its nature that no hopes of reconciliation might remain. By their advice, therefore, Gisco and all the Carthaginian prisoners were put to death; and when Hamilcar sent to demand the remains of his countrymen, he received for answer, that whoever presumed hereafter to come upon that errand, should meet with Gisco's fate: after which they came to a resolution to treat with the same barbarity all such Carthaginians as should fall into their hands. In return for this enormity, Hamilcar threw all the prisoners that fell into his hands to be devoured by wild beasts; being convinced that compassion served only to make his enemies more fierce and untractable.

The war was now carried on generally to the advantage of the Carthaginians; nevertheless, the malecontents still found themselves in a capacity to take the field with an army of 50,000 men. They watched Hamilcar's motions, but kept on the hills, carefully avoiding to come down into the plains, on account of the Numidian horse and Carthaginian elephants. Hamilcar, being much superior in skill to any of their generals, at last shut them up in a post so situated that it was impossible to get out of it. Here he kept them strictly besieged; and the mercenaries, not daring to venture a battle, began to fortify their camp, and surround it with ditches and intrenchments.

97
They are besieged by Hamilcar.

They were soon pressed by famine so sorely, that they were obliged to eat one another: but they were driven desperate by the consciousness of their guilt, and therefore did not desire any terms of accommodation. At last, being reduced to the utmost extremity of misery, they insisted that Spendius, Autaritus, and Zarxas, their leaders, should in person have a conference with Hamilcar, and make proposals to him. Peace was accordingly concluded upon the following terms, viz. That ten of the ringleaders of the malecontents should be left entirely to the mercy of the Carthaginians; and that the troops should all be disarmed, every man retiring only in a single coat. The treaty was no sooner concluded, than Hamilcar, by virtue of the first article, seized upon the negociators themselves, and the army being informed that their chiefs were under arrest, had immediately recourse to arms, as suspecting they were

98
40,000 of them destroyed.

betrayed; but Hamilcar, drawing out his army in order of battle, surrounded them, and either cut them to pieces,

Carthage.

pieces, or trod them to death with his elephants. The number of wretches who perished on this occasion amounted to above 40,000.

After the destruction of this army, Hamilcar invested Tunis, whither Mathos had retired with all his remaining forces. Hamilcar had another general, named *Hannibal*, joined in the command with him. Hannibal's quarter was on the road leading to Carthage, and Hamilcar's on the opposite side. The army was no sooner encamped, than Hamilcar caused Spendius, and the rest of the prisoners, to be led out in the view of the besieged, and crucified near the walls. Mathos, however, observing that Hannibal did not keep so good a guard as he ought to have done, made a sally, attacked his quarters, killed many of his

99 Hannibal taken and crucified by Mathos.

men, took several prisoners, among whom was Hannibal himself, and plundered his camp. Taking the body of Spendius from the cross, Mathos immediately substituted Hannibal in its room; and 30 Carthaginian prisoners of distinction were crucified around him. Upon this disaster, Hamilcar immediately decamped, and posted himself along the sea-coast, near the mouth of the river Bagrada.

The senate, though greatly terrified by this unexpected blow, omitted no means necessary for their preservation. They sent 30 senators, with Hanno at their head, to consult with Hamilcar about the proper measures for putting an end to this unnatural war, conjuring, in the most pressing manner, Hanno to be reconciled to Hamilcar, and to sacrifice his private resentment to the public benefit. This, with some difficulty, was effected; and the two generals came to a full resolution to act in concert for the good of the public. The senate, at the same time, ordered all the youth capable of bearing arms to be pressed into the service: by which means a strong reinforcement being sent to Hamilcar, he soon found him-

100 Mathos entirely defeated and taken prisoner.

self in a condition to act offensively. He now defeated the enemy in all rencounters, drew Mathos into frequent ambuscades, and gave him one notable overthrow near Leptis. This reduced the rebels to the necessity of hazarding a decisive battle, which proved fatal to them. The mercenaries fled almost at the first onset; most of their army fell in the field of battle, and in the pursuit. Mathos, with a few, escaped to a neighbouring town, where he was taken alive, carried to Carthage, and executed; and then, by the reduction of the revolted cities, an end was put to this war, which, from the excesses of cruelty committed in it, according to Polybius, went among the Greeks by the name of the *inexpiable war*.

During the Lybian war, the Romans, upon some absurd pretences, wrested the island of Sardinia from the Carthaginians; which the latter, not being able to

101 Hamilcar's scheme to equal Carthage with Rome.

resist, were obliged to submit to. Hamilcar finding his country not in a condition to enter into an immediate war with Rome, formed a scheme to put it on a level with that haughty republic. This was by making an entire conquest of Spain, by which means the Carthaginians might have troops capable of coping with the Romans. In order to facilitate the execution of this scheme, he inspired both his son-in-law Asdrubal, and his son Hannibal, with an implacable aversion to the Romans, as the great opposers of his country's grandeur. Having completed all the necessary preparations, Hamilcar, after having greatly enlarged the Carthaginian dominions in Africa, entered Spain, where he commanded nine years, during which time he subdued many warlike nations, and amassed an immense quantity of treasure, which he distributed partly amongst his troops, and partly amongst the great men at Carthage; by which means he supported his interests with these two powerful bodies. At last, he was killed in a battle, and was succeeded by his son-in-law 102 His death.

Asdrubal. This general fully answered the expectations of his countrymen; greatly enlarged their dominions in Spain; and built the city of New Carthage, now Carthagena. He made such progress in his conquests, that the Romans began to grow jealous. They did not, however, choose at present to come to an open rupture, on account of the apprehensions they were under of an invasion from the Gauls. They judged it most proper, therefore, to have recourse to milder methods; and prevailed upon Asdrubal to conclude a 103 Asdrubal's

new treaty with them. The articles of it were, treaty with

1. That the Carthaginians should not pass the Iberus. the Romans.
2. That the Saguntines, a colony of Zacynthians, and a city situated between the Iberus and that part of Spain subject to the Carthaginians, as well as the other Greek colonies there, should enjoy their ancient rights and privileges.

Asdrubal, after having governed the Carthaginian 104 He is murdered.

dominions in Spain for eight years, was treacherously murdered by a Gaul whose master he had put to death. Three years before this happened, he had written to Carthage, to desire that young Hannibal, then twenty-two years of age, might be sent to him. This request was complied with, notwithstanding the opposition of Hanno: and from the first arrival of the young man in the camp, he became the darling of the whole army. The great resemblance he bore to Hamilcar, rendered him extremely agreeable to the troops. Every talent and qualification he seemed to possess that can contribute towards forming a great man. After the death of Asdrubal, he was saluted general by the 105 Succeeded by Hannibal, who makes vast conquests in Spain.

army with the highest demonstrations of joy. He immediately put himself in motion; and, in the first campaign, conquered the Olcades, a nation seated near the Iberus. The next year he subdued the Vaccæi, another nation in that neighbourhood. Soon after, the Carpetani, one of the most powerful nations in Spain, declared against the Carthaginians. Their army consisted of 100,000 men, with which they proposed to attack Hannibal on his return from the Vaccæi; but by a stratagem they were utterly defeated, and the whole nation obliged to submit.

Nothing now remained to oppose the progress of the Carthaginian arms but the city of Saguntum. Hannibal, however, for some time, did not think proper to come to a rupture with the Romans by attacking that place. At last he found means to embroil some of the neighbouring cantons, especially the Turdetani, or, as Appian calls them, the *Torbolæ*, with 106 He attacks Saguntum.

the Saguntines, and thus furnished himself with a pretence to attack their city. Upon the commencement of the siege, the Roman senate dispatched two ambassadors to Hannibal, with orders to proceed to Carthage in case the general refused to give them satisfaction. They were scarce landed, when Hannibal, who was carrying on the siege of Saguntum with great

Carthage. vigour, sent them word that he had something else to do than to give audience to ambassadors. At last, however, he admitted them; and, in answer to their remonstrances, told them, that the Saguntines had drawn their misfortunes upon themselves, by committing hostilities against the allies of Carthage; and at the same time desired the deputies, if they had any complaints to make of him, to carry them to the senate of Carthage. On their arrival in that capital, they demanded that Hannibal might be delivered up to the Romans to be punished according to his deserts; and this not being complied with, war was immediately declared between the two nations.

The Saguntines are said to have defended themselves for eight months with incredible bravery. At
207 And takes it. last, however, the city was taken, and the inhabitants were treated with the utmost cruelty. After this conquest, Hannibal put his African troops into winter-quarters at New Carthage; but in order to gain their affection, he permitted the Spaniards to retire to their respective homes.

The next campaign, having taken the necessary measures for securing Africa and Spain, he passed the Iberus, subdued all the nations betwixt that river and the Pyrenees, appointed Hanno commander of all the
208 He sets out for Italy. new conquered district, and immediately began his march for Italy. Upon mustering his forces, after they had been weakened by sieges, desertion, mortality, and a detachment of 10,000 foot and 1000 horse left with Hanno to support him in his new post, he found them to amount to 50,000 foot and 9000 horse, all veteran troops, and the best in the world. As they had left their heavy baggage with Hanno, and were all light armed, Hannibal easily crossed the Pyrenees; passed by Ruscino, a frontier town of the Gauls; and arrived on the banks of the Rhone without opposition. This river he passed, notwithstanding of some opposition from the Gauls; and was for some time in doubt whether he should advance to engage the Romans, who, under Scipio, were bending their march that way, or continue his march for Italy. But to the latter he was soon determined by the arrival of Magilus prince of the Boii, who brought rich presents with him, and offered to conduct the Carthaginian army over the Alps. Nothing could have happened more favourable to Hannibal's affairs than the arrival of this prince, since there was no room to doubt the sincerity of his intentions. For the Boii bore an implacable enmity to the Romans, and had even come to an open rupture with them upon the first news that Italy was threatened with an invasion from the Carthaginians.

209 He crosses the Alps. It is not known with certainty where Hannibal began to ascend the Alps. As soon as he began his march, the petty kings of the country assembled their forces in great numbers; and taking possession of the eminences over which the Carthaginians must necessarily pass, they continued harassing them, and were no sooner driven from one eminence than they seized on another, disputing every foot of land with the enemy, and destroying great numbers of them by the advantage they had of the ground. Hannibal, however, having found means to possess himself of an advantageous post, defeated and dispersed the enemy; and soon after took their capital city, where he found the prisoners, horses, &c. that had before fallen into the hands of the enemy, and likewise corn sufficient to serve the army for three days. At last, after a most fatiguing march of nine days, he arrived at the top of the mountains. Here he encamped, and halted two days, to give his wearied troops some repose, and to wait for the stragglers. As the snow was lately fallen in great plenty, and covered the ground, this sight terrified the Africans and Spaniards, who were much affected with the cold. In order therefore to encourage them, the Carthaginian general led them to the top of the highest rock on the side of Italy, and thence gave them a view of the large and fruitful plains of Insubria, acquainting them that the Gauls, whose country they saw, were ready to join them. He also pointed out to them the place whereabout Rome stood, telling them, that by climbing the Alps, they had scaled the walls of that rich metropolis; and having thus animated his troops, he decamped, and began to descend the mountains. The difficulties they met with in their descent were much greater than those that had occurred while they ascended. They had indeed no enemy to contend with, except some scattered parties that came to steal rather than to fight; but the deep snows, the mountains of ice, craggy rocks, and frightful precipices, proved more terrible than any enemy. After they had for some days marched through narrow, steep, and slippery ways, they came at last to a place which neither elephants, horses, nor men, could pass. The way which lay between two precipices was exceeding narrow; and the declivity, which was very steep, had become more dangerous by the falling away of the earth. Here the guides stopped; and the whole army being terrified, Hannibal proposed at first to march round about, and attempt some other way; but all places round him being covered with snow, he found himself reduced to the necessity of cutting a way into the rock itself, through which his men, horses, and elephants, might descend. This work was accomplished with incredible labour; and then Hannibal, having spent nine days in ascending, and six in descending, the Alps, gained at length Insubria; and, notwithstanding all the disasters he had met with by the way, entered the country with all the boldness of a conqueror.

Hannibal, on his entry into Insubria, reviewed his army, when he found that of the 50,000 foot with whom he set out from New Carthage five months and 15 days before, he had now but 20,000, and that his 9000 horse were reduced to 6000. His first care, after he entered Italy, was to refresh his troops; who after so long a march, and such inexpressible hardships, looked like so many skeletons raised from the dead, or savages born in a desert. He did not, however, suffer them to languish long in idleness; but, joining the Insubrians, who were at war with the 210 Taurinum taken.
Taurinians, laid siege to Taurinum, the only city in the country, and in three days time became master of it, putting all who resisted to the sword. This struck the neighbouring barbarians with such terror, that of their own accord they submitted to the conqueror, and supplied his army with all sorts of provisions.

Scipio, the Roman general, in the mean time, who had gone in quest of Hannibal on the banks of the Rhone, was surprised to find his antagonist had crossed

Carthage.

sed the Alps and entered Italy. He therefore returned with the utmost expedition. An engagement ensued near the river Ticinus, in which the Romans were defeated. The immediate consequence was, that Scipio repassed that river, and Hannibal continued his march to the banks of the Po. Here he staid two days, before he could cross that river over a bridge of boats. He then sent Mago in pursuit of the enemy, who having rallied their scattered forces, and repassed the Po, were encamped at Placentia. Afterwards having concluded a treaty with several of the Gallic cantons, he joined his brother with the rest of the army, and again offered battle to the Romans: but this they thought proper to decline; and at last the consul, being intimidated by the desertion of a body of Gauls, abandoned his camp, passed the Trebia, and posted himself on an eminence near that river. Here he drew lines round his camp, and waited the arrival of his colleague with the forces from Sicily.

111 The Romans defeated near the Ticinus.

Hannibal being apprised of the consul's departure, sent out the Numidian horse to harass him on his march; himself moving with the main body to support them in case of need. The Numidians arriving before the rear of the Roman army had quite passed the Trebia, put to the sword or made prisoners all the stragglers they found there. Soon after, Hannibal coming up, encamped in sight of the Roman army, on the opposite bank. Here having learned the character of the consul Sempronius lately arrived, he soon brought him to an engagement, and entirely defeated him. Ten thousand of the enemy retired to Placentia; but the rest were either killed or taken prisoners. The Carthaginians pursued the flying Romans as far as the Trebia, but did not think proper to repass that river on account of the excessive cold.

112 They are again defeated.

Hannibal, after this action upon the Trebia, ordered the Numidians, Celtiberians, and Lusitanians, to make incursions into the Roman territories, where they committed great devastations. During his state of inaction, he endeavoured to win the affections of the Gauls, and likewise of the allies of the Romans; declaring to the Gallic and Italian prisoners, that he had no intention of making war upon them, being determined to restore them to their liberty, and protect them against the Romans: and to confirm them in their good opinion of him, he dismissed them all without ransom.

113 They are utterly defeated near the lake Thrasymene.

Next year, having crossed the Apennines, and penetrated into Etruria, Hannibal received intelligence that the new consul Flaminius lay encamped with the Roman army under the walls of Arretium. Having learned the true character of this general, that he was of an haughty, fierce, and rash disposition, he doubted not of being soon able to bring him to a battle. To inflame the impetuous spirit of Flaminius, the Carthaginian general took the road to Rome, and, leaving the Roman army behind him, destroyed all the country through which he passed with fire and sword; and as that part of Italy abounded with all the elegancies as well as necessaries of life, the Romans and their allies suffered an incredible loss on this occasion. The rash consul was inflamed with the utmost rage on seeing the ravages committed by the Carthaginians; and therefore immediately approached them with great temerity, as if certain of victory. Hannibal in the mean time kept on, still advancing towards Rome, having Cortona on the left hand, and the lake Thrasymenus on the right; and at last, having drawn Flaminius into an ambuscade, entirely defeated him. The general himself, with 15,000 of his men, fell on the field of battle. A great number were likewise taken prisoners, and a body of 6000 men, who had fled to a town in Etruria, surrendered to Maherbal the next day. Hannibal lost only 1500 men on this occasion, most of whom were Gauls; though great numbers, both of his soldiers and of the Romans, died of their wounds. Being soon after informed that the consul Servilius had detached a body of 4000, or, according to Appian, 8000 horse from Ariminum, to reinforce his colleague in Etruria, Hannibal sent out Maherbal, with all the cavalry, and some of the infantry, to attack him. The Roman detachment consisted of chosen men, and was commanded by Centenius a Patrician. Maherbal had the good fortune to meet with him, and after a short dispute entirely defeated him. Two thousand of the Romans were laid dead on the spot; the rest, retiring to a neighbouring eminence, were surrounded by Maherbal's forces, and obliged next day to surrender at discretion; and this disaster, happening within a few days after the defeat at the lake Thrasymenus, almost gave the finishing stroke to the Roman affairs.

114 A Roman detachment cut to pieces or taken.

The Carthaginian army was now so much troubled with a scorbutic disorder, owing to the unwholesome encampments they had been obliged to make, and the morasses they had passed through, that Hannibal found it absolutely necessary to repose them for some time in the territory of Adria, a most pleasant and fertile country. In his various engagements with the Romans, he had taken a great number of their arms, with which he now armed his men after the Roman manner. Being now likewise master of that part of the country bordering on the sea, he found means to send an express to Carthage with the news of the glorious progress of his arms. The citizens received this news with the most joyful acclamations, at the same time coming to a resolution to reinforce their armies both in Italy and Spain with a proper number of troops.

The Romans being now in the utmost consternation, named a dictator, as was their custom in times of great danger. The person they chose to this office was Fabius Maximus, surnamed *Verrucosus*; a man as cool and cautious as Sempronius and Flaminius were warm and impetuous. He set out with a design not to engage Hannibal, but only to watch his motions, and cut off his provisions, which he knew was the most proper way to destroy him in a country so far from his own. Accordingly he followed him through Umbria and Picenum, into the territory of Adria, and then through the territories of the Marrucini and Frentani into Apulia. When the enemy marched, he followed them; when they encamped, he did the same; but for the most part on eminences, and at some distance from their camp, watching all their motions, cutting off their stragglers, and keeping them in a continual alarm. This cautious method of proceeding greatly distressed the Carthaginians, but at the same time raised discontents in his own army. But neither these

115 Fabius Maximus named dictator.

Carthage. these discontents, nor the ravages committed by Hannibal, could prevail upon Fabius to alter his measures. The former, therefore, entered Campania, one of the finest countries of Italy. The ravages he committed there, raised such complaints in the Roman army, that the dictator, for fear of irritating his soldiers, was obliged to pretend a desire of coming to an engagement. Accordingly he followed Hannibal with more expedition than usual; but at the same time avoided, under various pretences, an engagement with more care than the enemy sought it. Hannibal finding he could not by any means bring the dictator to a battle, resolved to quit Campania, which he found abounding more with fruit and wine than corn, and to return to Samnium through the pass called Eribanus. Fabius concluding from his march that this was his design, got there before him, and encamped on Mount Callicula, which commanded the pass, after having placed several bodies in all the avenues leading to it.

816 He is outwitted by Hannibal. Hannibal was for some time at a loss what to do; but at last contrived the following stratagem, which Fabius could not foresee nor guard against. Being encamped at the foot of Mount Callicula, he ordered Asdrubal to pick out of the cattle taken in the country, 2000 of the strongest and nimblest oxen, to tie faggots to their horns, and to have them and the herdsmen ready without the camp. After supper, when all was quiet, the cattle were brought in good order to the hill, where Fabius had placed some Roman parties in ambush to stop up the pass. Upon a signal given, the faggots on the horns of the oxen were set on fire; and the herdsmen, supported by some battalions armed with small javelins, drove them on quietly. The Romans seeing the light of the fires, imagined that the Carthaginians were marching by torch-light. However, Fabius kept close in his camp, depending on the troops he had placed in ambuscade; but when the oxen, feeling the fire on their heads, began to run up and down the hills, the Romans in ambush thinking themselves surrounded on all sides, and climbing the ways where they saw least light, returned to their camp leaving the pass open to Hannibal. Fabius, though rallied by his soldiers for being thus over-reached by the Carthaginian, still continued to pursue the same plan, marched directly after Hannibal, and encamped on some eminences near him.

Soon after this, the dictator was recalled to Rome; and as Hannibal, notwithstanding the terrible ravages he had committed, had all along spared the lands of Fabius, the latter was suspected of holding a secret correspondence with the enemy. In his absence, Minucius, the general of the horse, gained some advantages, which greatly tended to increase the discontent with the dictator, insomuch that before his return Minucius was put upon an equal footing with himself. The general of the horse proposed that each should command his day; but the dictator chose rather to divide the army, hoping by that means to save at least a part

817 Minucius in great danger, is rescued by Fabius. of it. Hannibal soon found means to draw Minucius to an engagement, and, by his masterly skill in laying ambushes, the Roman general was surrounded on every side, and would have been cut off with all his troops, had not Fabius hastened to his assistance, and relieved him. Then the two armies uniting, advanced in good order to renew the fight; but Hannibal, not caring to venture a second action, sounded a retreat, and retired to his camp; and Minucius, being ashamed of his rashness, resigned the command of the army to Fabius.

The year following, the Romans augmented their army to 87,000 men, horse and foot; and Hannibal being reduced to the greatest straits for want of provisions, resolved to leave Samnium, and penetrate into the heart of Apulia. Accordingly he decamped in the night; and by leaving fires burning, and tents standing in his camp, made the Romans believe for some time that his retreat was only feigned. When the truth was discovered, Æmilius was against pursuing him; but Terentius, contrary to the opinion of all the officers in the army, except the proconsul Servilius, was obstinately bent on following the enemy; and overtook them at Cannæ, till this time an obscure village in Apulia*. A battle ensued in this place, as memorable as any mentioned in history; in which the Romans, though almost double in number to the Carthaginians, were put to flight with most terrible slaughter; at least 45,000 of them being left dead on the field of battle, and 10,000 taken prisoners in the action or pursuit. The night was spent in Hannibal's camp in feasting and rejoicings, and next day in stripping the dead bodies of the unhappy Romans; after which the victorious general invested their two camps, where he found 4000 men.

818 The Romans terribly defeated at Cannæ.

* See Cannæ.

819 Consequences of this victory. The immediate consequence of this victory, as Hannibal had foreseen, was a disposition of that part of Italy called the Old province, Magna Græcia, Tarentum, and part of the territory of Capua, to submit to him. The neighbouring provinces likewise discovered an inclination to shake off the Roman yoke, but waited still to see whether Hannibal was able to protect them. His first march was into Samnium, being informed that the Hirpini and other neighbouring nations were disposed to enter into an alliance with the Carthaginians. He advanced to Compsa, which opened its gates to him. In this place he left his heavy baggage, as well as the immense plunder he had acquired. After which he ordered his brother Mago with a body of troops destined for that purpose to possess himself of all the fortresses in Campania, the most delicious province of Italy. The humanity Hannibal had all along shown the Italian prisoners, as well as the fame of the complete victory he had lately obtained, wrought so powerfully upon the Lucani, Brutii, and Apulians, that they expressed an eager desire of being taken under his protection. Nay, even the Campanians themselves, a nation more obliged to the Romans than any in Italy, except the Latins, discovered an inclination to abandon their natural friends.

820 Capua submits to Hannibal. Of this the Carthaginian general receiving intelligence, he bent his march towards Capua, not doubting, but that, by means of the popular faction there, he should easily make himself master of it; which accordingly happened. Soon after this place had made its submission, many cities of the Brutii opened their gates to Hannibal, who ordered his brother Mago to take possession of them. Mago was then dispatched to Carthage, with the important news of the victory at Cannæ, and the consequences attending it. Upon

his

Carthage.

111 Mago's account of Hannibal's success.

his arrival there, he acquainted the senate, that Hannibal had defeated six Roman generals, four of whom were consuls, one dictator, and the other general of horse to the dictator: that he had engaged six consular armies, killed two consuls, wounded one, and driven another out of the field with scarce 50 men to attend him: that he had routed the general of the horse, who was of equal power with the consuls; and that the dictator was esteemed the only general fit to command an army, merely because he had not the courage to engage him; and as a demonstrative proof of what he advanced, he produced, according to some authors, three bushels and an half of gold rings, taken from knights and senators who had been killed in the various engagements.

112 Hannibal superior to every other general mentioned in history.

Hitherto we have seen Hannibal surprisingly victorious; and, indeed, if we consider what he had already done, we shall find his exploits superior to those of any other general, either ancient or modern. Other commanders have been celebrated for victories gained over barbarous and uncivilized nations. Alexander the Great invaded and over-ran the empire of Persia; but that kingdom was then sunk in sloth and effeminacy, so as to be an easy conquest: but had the great commander turned his arms against the western nations, who were of a more martial disposition, it is more than probable he had not conquered so easily. Hannibal, on the other hand, lived at a time when the Romans were not only the most powerful, but the most warlike nation in the whole world. That nation he attacked with an army of only 26,000 men, without resources either for recruits, money, or provisions, except what he could procure in the enemies country. With these he had for three years resisted the Roman armies, which had been hitherto invincible by all other nations. Their armies had been commanded by generals of different tempers, dispositions, and abilities: the losses they sustained are by the Roman writers imputed to the faults of the generals themselves; but experience had abundantly shown, that these commanders, with all their faults, were able to conquer the most warlike nations, when commanded by another than Hannibal. In the battles fought with the Romans he had destroyed 200,000 of their men, and taken 50,000 prisoners; yet from the time of the battle of Cannæ, the affairs of this great man

113 Cause of the decline of his affairs.

totally declined. The reason of this is, by the Roman historians, said to be, that when he put his army into winter-quarters in Capua, he so enervated himself and his army by debaucheries in that place, that he became no longer capable of coping with the Roman forces. But this seems by no means to have been the case; for the Roman historians themselves own, that, after the battle of Cannæ, he gave their armies many and terrible defeats, and took a great number of towns in their sight.

The true reason of that reverse of fortune which Hannibal now experienced, was his not having sufficient resources for recruiting his army. On the first news, indeed, of his success at Carthage, a body of 4000 Numidian cavalry, 40 elephants, and 1000 talents of silver, were granted by the senate. A large detachment of Spanish forces was also appointed to follow them; and that these last might be ready in due time, Mago set out immediately for Spain to raise 20,000 foot and 4000 horse there. Had this ample supply been sent with proper expedition, it is by no means probable that the Romans would have had any occasion to reflect upon Hannibal's conduct at Capua. That general would undoubtedly have obliged the haughty republic to submit to the superior force of his arms the next campaign. But, notwithstanding the influence of the Barcinian faction at Carthage, Hanno and his adherents found means not only to retard the march of the supplies intended, but even to diminish their number. Mago, through the artifices of that infatuated party, could obtain an order for only 12,000 foot and 2500 horse, and even with this inconsiderable body of troops he was sent into Spain. Hannibal being thus deserted by his country, found himself obliged to act on the defensive; his army amounting to no more now than 26,000 foot and 9000 horse. But though obliged to act in this manner, he was only hindered from conquering; the utmost efforts of the whole Roman power not being able to drive this small army out of Italy for more than 14 years.

The Romans, though greatly reduced, were not yet exhausted. They were able still to send two consular armies into the field, fully recruited and in good order; and as neither the Gauls nor Italians were natural allies of the Carthaginians, they did not fail to abandon them on the first reverse of fortune. After the Romans had recovered from the consternation into which they were thrown by the defeat at Cannæ, they chose a dictator, and recalled Marcellus, the conqueror of Syracuse, from Sicily. All the young Romans, above 17 years of age, of what rank soever, were obliged to inlist themselves; as were also those who had already served their legal time. By this means four legions and 10,000 horse were soon raised in the city. The allies of Rome, the colonies, and the municipia, furnished the contingence as usual. To these were added 8000 of the youngest and strongest slaves in the city. The republic purchased them of their masters, but did not oblige them to serve without their own consent, which they gave, by answering *Volo*, "I am willing;" whence they were called *volones*, to distinguish them from the other troops. As the Romans, after the loss of so many battles, had no swords, darts, or bucklers, left in their magazines, the volones were supplied with the arms which had been formerly taken from the enemy, and hung up in the public temples and porticoes. The finances of Rome were no less exhausted; but this defect was supplied by the liberality of her citizens. The senators showing the example, were followed first by the knights, and afterwards by all the tribes; who stripping themselves of all the gold they had, brought it to the public treasury. The senators only reserved their rings, and the *bullæ* about their childrens necks. As for the silver coin, it was now, for the first time, alloyed with copper, and increased in its value. Thus the finances were put into a good condition, and a competent army raised.

114 Measures taken by the Romans.

This was plainly the last effort the Romans could make; and could Hannibal have procured a sufficient supply of men and money to enable him to cope with this army, and to break it as he had done the others before, there could have been no more resistance made on their part. He began, however, to be in want of

money;

Carthage.

money; and to procure it, gave the Roman prisoners leave to redeem themselves. These unhappy men agreed to send ten of their body to Rome to negociate their redemption; and Hannibal required no other security for their return but their oath. Carthalo was sent at the head of them to make proposals of peace; but upon the first news of his arrival, the dictator sent a lictor to him, commanding him immediately to depart the Roman territory; and it was resolved not to redeem the captives. Upon this Hannibal sent the most considerable of them to Carthage; and of the rest he made gladiators, obliging them to fight with one another, even relations with relations, for the entertainment of his troops.

125 They refuse to treat of peace.

126 Asdrubal defeated by the Romans in Spain.

All this time Cneius and Publius Scipio had carried on the war in Spain with great success against the Carthaginians. Asdrubal had been ordered to enter Italy with his army to assist Hannibal; but being defeated by the Romans, was prevented. The dictator and senate of Rome, encouraged by this news, carried on the preparations for the next campaign with the greatest vigour, whilst Hannibal remained inactive at Capua. This inaction, however, seems to have proceeded from his expectation of succours from Africa, which never came, and which delay occasioned his ruin. The Roman dictator now released from prison all criminals, and persons confined for debt, who were willing to inlist themselves. Of these he formed a body of 6000 foot, armed with the broad swords and bucklers formerly taken from the Gauls. Then the Roman army, to the number of about 25,000 men, marched out of the city, under the command of the dictator; while Marcellus kept the remains of Varro's army, amounting to about 15,000 men, at Casilinum, in readiness to march wherever there should be occasion.

Thus the Roman forces were still superior to those of Hannibal; and as they now saw the necessity of following the example of Fabius Maximus, no engagement of any consequence happened the first year after the battle of Cannæ. Hannibal made a fruitless attempt upon Nola, expecting it would be delivered up to him; but this was prevented by Marcellus, who had entered that city, and sallying unexpectedly from three gates upon the Carthaginians, obliged them to retire in great confusion, with the loss of 5000 men. This was the first advantage that had been gained by the Romans where Hannibal had commanded in person, and raised the spirits of the former not a little. They were, however, greatly dejected, on hearing that the consul Posthumius Albinus, with his whole army, had been cut off by the Boii, as he was crossing a forest. Upon this it was resolved to draw all the Roman forces out of Gaul and other countries, and turn them against Hannibal; so that the Carthaginians stood daily more and more in need of those supplies, which yet never arrived from Carthage. He reduced, however, the cities of Nuceria, Casilinum, Petelia, Consentia, Croton, Locri, and several others in Great Greece, before the Romans gained any advantage over him, except that before Nola already mentioned. The Campanians, who had espoused the Carthaginian interest, raised an army of 14,000 of their own nation in favour of Hannibal, and put one Marius Alfius at the head of it; but he was surprised by the consul Sempronius, who defeated and killed him, with 2000 of his men. It was now found, that Hannibal had concluded a treaty of alliance, offensive and defensive, with Philip king of Macedon; but to prevent any disturbance from that quarter, a Roman army was sent to Macedon. Soon after this Marcellus defeated Hannibal in a pitched battle, having armed his men with long pikes used generally at sea, and chiefly in boarding of ships; by which means the Carthaginians were pierced through, while they were totally unable to hurt their adversaries with the short javelins they carried. Marcellus pursued them close; and, before they got to their camp, killed 5000, and took 600 prisoners; losing himself about 1000 men, who were trod down by the Numidian horse, commanded by Hannibal in person. After this defeat the Carthaginian general found himself deserted by 1200 of his best horse, partly Spaniards, and partly Numidians, who had crossed the Alps with him. This touched him so sensibly, that he left Campania, and retired into Apulia.

127 Marcellus gains an advantage over Hannibal.

128 Hannibal takes several cities.

Carthage.

129 He is defeated by Marcellus.

130 He is deserted by a party of horse.

The Romans still continued to increase their forces; and Hannibal, not having the same resources, found it impossible to act against so many armies at once. Fabius Maximus advanced into Campania, whither Hannibal was obliged to return in order to save Capua. He ordered Hanno, however, at the head of 17,000 foot and 1700 horse, to seize Beneventum; but he was utterly defeated, scarce 2000 of his men being left alive. Hannibal himself, in the mean time, advanced to Nola, where he was again defeated by Marcellus. He now began to lose ground; the Romans retook Casilinum, Acerra in Apulia, Arpi, and Aternum; but the city of Tarentum was delivered up to him by its inhabitants. The Romans then entered Campania, and ravaged the whole country, threatening Capua with a siege. The inhabitants immediately acquainted Hannibal with their danger; but he was so intent upon reducing the citadel of Tarentum, that he could not be prevailed upon to come to their assistance. In the mean time Hanno was again utterly defeated by Fulvius, his camp taken, and he himself forced to fly into Brutium with a small body of horse. The consuls then advanced with a design to besiege Capua in form. But in their way, Sempronius Gracchus, a man of great bravery, and an excellent general, was betrayed by a Lucanian and killed, which proved a very great detriment to the republic. Capua, however, was soon after invested on all sides; and the besieged once more sent to Hannibal, who now came to their assistance with his horse, his light-armed infantry, and 33 elephants. He found means to inform the besieged of the time he designed to attack the Romans, ordering them to make a vigorous sally at the same time. The Roman generals, Appius and Fulvius, upon the first news of the enemy's approach, divided their troops, Appius taking upon him to make head against the garrison, and Fulvius to defend the intrenchments against Hannibal. The former found no difficulty in repulsing the garrison; and would have entered the city with them, had he not been wounded at the very gate, which prevented him from pursuing his design. Fulvius found it more difficult to withstand Hannibal, whose troops behaved themselves with extraordinary resolution. A body of Spaniards and Numidians

131 He is again defeated, and begins to lose ground.

132 Capua besieged by the Romans.

133 Hannibal, in vain, attempts to relieve it.

Carthage.

Numidians had even the boldness to pass the ditch, and, in spite of all opposition, climbing the ramparts, penetrated into the Roman camp; but not being properly seconded by the rest, they were all to a man cut in pieces. The Carthaginian general was so disheartened at this, especially after the garrison was repulsed, that he sounded a retreat, which was made in good
134 He marches to Rome. order. His next attempt for the relief of Capua was to march to Rome, where he hoped his approach would strike so much terror, that the armies would be called from before Capua; and that the Capuans might not be disheartened by his sudden departure, he found means to acquaint them with his design. The news of his approach caused great consternation in the metropolis. Some of the senators were for calling all the armies in Italy into the neighbourhood of Rome, as thinking nothing less was able to resist the terrible Carthaginian. But Fabius told them that Hannibal's design was not to take Rome, but relieve Capua; upon which Fulvius was recalled to Rome with 15,000 foot, and 1000 horse; and this obliged Hannibal again to
135 He surprises and defeats Appius. retire. He then returned before Capua so suddenly that he surprised Appius in his camp, drove him out of it with the loss of a great number of men, and obliged him to entrench himself on some eminences,
136 Capua submits to the Romans. where he expected to be soon joined by his colleague Fulvius. As Hannibal, however, now expected to have all the Roman forces upon him, he could do nothing more for the relief of Capua, which was, of consequence, obliged to submit to the Romans.

A little before the surrender of Capua, Hannibal
137 Centenius Penula defeated by Hannibal. came up with a Roman army commanded by one M. Centenius Penula, who had signalized himself on many occasions as a centurion. This rash man, being introduced to the senate, had the assurance to tell them, that if they would trust him with a body of only 5000 men, he would give a good account of Hannibal. They gave him 8000, and his army was soon increased to double that number. He engaged the Carthaginians on Hannibal's first offering him battle; but after an engagement of two hours, was defeated, himself and
138 As also the prætor Fulvius, all his men being slain, except about 1000. Soon after, having found means to draw the prætor Cnæius Fulvius into an ambuscade, Hannibal cut in pieces almost his whole army, consisting of 18,000 men. In the mean time Marcellus was making great progress in Samnium. The city of Salapia was betrayed to him; but he took other two by assault. In the last of these he found 3000 Carthaginians, whom he put to the sword; and carried off 240,000 bushels
139 And the proconsul Fulvius Centumalus. of wheat, and 110,000 of barley. This, however, was by no means a compensation for the defeat which Hannibal soon after gave the proconsul Fulvius Centumalus, whom he surprised and cut off, with 13,000 of his men.

After this defeat, the great Marcellus advanced with his army to oppose Hannibal. Various engagements happened without any thing decisive. In one of them the Romans are said to have been defeated, and in another Hannibal; but, notwithstanding these, it was
140 Marcellus drawn into an ambuscade and killed. neither in the power of Marcellus, nor any other Roman general, totally to defeat or disperse the army commanded by Hannibal in person. Nay, in the eleventh year of the war, Hannibal found means to decoy into an ambuscade, and cut off, the great Marcellus himself; the consequence of which was, that the Romans were obliged to raise the siege of Locri, with the loss of all their military engines.

Hitherto the Carthaginians, though no longer the 141 Carthaginian affairs totally ruined by the defeat of Asdrubal.
favourites of fortune, had lost but little ground; but now they met with a blow which totally ruined their affairs. This was the defeat of Asdrubal, Hannibal's brother, who had left Spain, and was marching to his assistance. He crossed the Pyrenees without any difficulty; and, as the silver mines had supplied him with a very considerable quantity of treasure, he not only prevailed upon the Gauls to grant him a passage through their territories, but likewise to furnish him with a considerable number of recruits. Meeting with many favourable circumstances to expedite his march, he arrived at Placentia sooner than the Romans, or even his brother Hannibal, expected. Had he continued to use the same expedition with which he set out, and hastened to join his brother, it would have been utterly impossible to have saved Rome; but, sitting down before Placentia, he gave the Romans an opportunity of assembling all their forces to attack him. At last he was obliged to raise the siege, and began his march for Umbria. He sent a letter to acquaint his brother of his intended motion; but the messenger was intercepted; and the two consuls, joining their armies, with united forces fell upon the Carthaginians. As the latter were inferior both in numbers and resolution, they were utterly defeated, and Asdrubal was killed. About the same time, Hannibal himself is said to have suffered several defeats, and was retired to Canusium; but, on the fatal news of his brother's defeat and death, he was filled with despair, and retired to the extremity of Brutium; where, assembling all his forces, he remained for a considerable time in a state of inaction, the Romans not daring to disturb him, so formidable did they esteem him alone, though every thing about him went to wreck, and the Carthaginian affairs seemed not far from the verge of destruction. Livy tells us, that it was difficult to determine whether his conduct was more wonderful in prosperity or in adversity. Notwithstanding which, Brutium being but a small province, and many of its inhabitants being either forced into the service, or forming themselves into parties of banditti, so that a great part of it remained uncultivated, he found it a difficult matter to subsist there, especially as no manner of supplies were sent him from Carthage. The people there were as solicitous about preserving their possessions in Spain, and as little concerned about the situation of affairs in Italy, as if Hannibal had met with an uninterrupted course of success, and no disaster befallen him since he first entered that country.

All their solicitude, however, about the affairs of 142 The great progress of Scipio Africanus.
Spain, was to no purpose; their generals, one after another, were defeated by the Romans. They had indeed cut off the two Scipios; but found a much more formidable enemy in the young Scipio, afterwards surnamed *Africanus*. He overthrew them in conjunction with Masinissa king of Numidia; and the latter, thereafter, abandoned their interest. Soon after, Syphax, king of the Masæsylii, was likewise persuaded to abandon their party. Scipio also gave the Spanish Reguli a great overthrow; and reduced the

Carthage.

cities of New Carthage. Gades, and many other important places. At last the Carthaginians began to open their eyes when it was too late. Mago was ordered to abandon Spain, and sail with all expedition
143 Mago lands in Italy. to Italy. He landed on the coast of Liguria with an army of 12,000 foot and 2000 horse; where he surprised Genoa, and also seized upon the town and port of Savo. A reinforcement was sent him to this place, and new levies went on very briskly in Liguria; but the opportunity was passed, and could not be recalled. Scipio having carried all before him in Spain, passed
144 Scipio lands in Africa. over into Africa, where he met with no enemy capable of opposing his progress. The Carthaginians then, seeing themselves on the brink of destruction, were obliged to recal their armies from Italy, in order to save their city. Mago, who had entered Insubria, was defeated by the Roman forces there; and having retreated into the maritime parts of Liguria,
145 Mago and Hannibal recalled. met a courier who brought him orders to return directly to Carthage. At the same time, Hannibal was likewise recalled. When the messengers acquainted him with the senate's pleasure, he expressed the utmost indignation and concern, groaning, gnashing his teeth, and scarce refraining from tears. Never banished man, according to Livy, showed so much regret in quitting his native country, as Hannibal did at going out of that of the enemy.

146 Hannibal's proceedings after his arrival in Africa. The Carthaginian general was no sooner landed in Africa, than he sent out parties to get provisions for the army, and buy horses to remount the cavalry. He entered into a league with the Regulus of the Areacidæ, one of the Numidian tribes. Four thousand of Syphax's horse came over in a body to him; but as he did not think proper to repose any confidence in them, he put them all to the sword, and distributed their horses among his troops. Vermina, one of Syphax's sons, and Masetulus, another Numidian prince, likewise joined him with a considerable body of horse. Most of the fortresses in Masinissa's kingdom either surrendered to him upon the first summons, or were taken by force. Narce, a city of considerable note there, he made himself master of by stratagem. Tychæus, a Numidian Regulus, and faithful ally of Syphax, whose territories were famous for an excellent breed of horses, reinforcing him also with 2000 of his best cavalry, Hannibal advanced to Zama, a town about five days journey distant from Carthage, where he encamped. He thence sent out spies to observe the posture of the Romans. These being brought to Scipio, he was so far from inflicting any punishment upon them, which he might have done by the laws of war, that he commanded them to be led about the camp, in order to take an exact survey of
147 He has an interview with Scipio. it, and then dismissed them. Hannibal, admiring the noble assurance of his rival, sent a messenger to desire an interview with him; which, by means of Masinissa, he obtained. The two generals, therefore, escorted by equal detachments of horse, met at Nadagara, where, by the assistance of two interpreters, they held a private conference. Hannibal flattered Scipio in the most refined and artful manner, and expatiated upon all those topics which he thought could influence that general to grant his nation a peace upon tolerable terms; amongst other things, that the Carthaginians would willingly confine themselves to Africa, since such was the will of the gods, in order to procure a lasting peace, whilst the Romans would be at liberty to extend their conquest to the remotest nations. Scipio answered, that the Romans were not prompted by ambition, or any sinister views, to undertake either the former or present war against the Carthaginians; but by justice, and a proper regard for their allies. He also observed, that the Carthaginians had, before his arrival in Africa, not only made him the same proposals, but likewise agreed to pay the Romans 5000 talents of silver, restore all the Roman prisoners without ransom, and deliver up all their galleys. He insisted on the perfidious conduct of the Carthaginians, who had broke a truce concluded with them; and told him, that, so far from granting them more favourable terms, they ought to expect more rigorous ones; which if Hannibal would submit to, a peace would ensue; if not, the decision of the dispute must be left to the sword.

This conference, betwixt two of the greatest gene- 148 The battle of Zama.
rals the world ever produced, ending without success, they both retired to their respective camps; where they informed their troops, that not only the fate of Rome and Carthage, but that of the whole world, was to be determined by them the next day. An engagement ensued *, in which, as Polybius informs us, the surprising military genius of Hannibal displayed itself in an extraordinary manner. Scipio likewise, according to Livy, passed an high encomium upon him, on account of his uncommon capacity in taking advantages, the excellent arrangement of his forces, and the manner in which he gave his orders during the engagement. The Roman general indeed, not only approved his conduct, but openly declared that it was superior to his own. Nevertheless, being vastly inferior to the enemy in horse, and the state of Carthage obliging him to hazard a battle with
the Romans at no small disadvantage, Hannibal was 149 Hannibal totally routed.
utterly routed, and his camp taken. He fled first to Thon, and afterwards to Adrumetum, from whence he was recalled to Carthage; where being arrived, he advised his countrymen to conclude a peace with Scipio on whatever terms he thought proper to prescribe.

Thus was the second war of the Carthaginians with 150 Peace concluded.
the Romans concluded. The conditions of peace were very humiliating to the Carthaginians. They were obliged to deliver up all the Romans deserters, fugitive slaves, prisoners of war, and all the Italians whom Hannibal had obliged to follow him. They also delivered up all their ships of war, except ten triremes, all their tame elephants, and were to train up no more of those animals for the service. They were not to engage in any war without the consent of the Romans. They engaged to pay to the Romans, in 50 years, 10,000 Euboic talents, at equal payments. They were to restore to Masinissa all they had usurped from him or his ancestors, and to enter into an alliance with him. They were also to assist the Romans both by sea and land, whenever they were called upon so to do, and never to make any levies either in Gaul or Liguria. These terms appeared so intolerable to the populace, that they threatened to plunder and burn the houses of the nobility; but Hannibal having assembled a body of 6000 foot and 500 horse at Marthama, prevented an infur-

* See Zama.

Carthage. insurrection, and by his influence completed the accommodation.

151 Carthaginians oppressed by Masinissa. The peace between Carthage and Rome was scarce signed, when Masinissa unjustly made himself master of part of the Carthaginian dominions in Africa, under pretence that these formerly belonged to his family. The Carthaginians, through the villainous mediation of the Romans, found themselves under a necessity of ceding these countries to that ambitious prince, and of entering into an alliance with him. The good understanding between the two powers continued for many years afterwards; but at last Masinissa violated the treaties subsisting betwixt him and the Carthaginian republic, and not a little contributed to its subversion.

After the conclusion of the peace, Hannibal still kept up his credit among his countrymen. He was intrusted with the command of an army against some neighbouring nations in Africa; but this being disagreeable to the Romans, he was removed from it, and raised to the dignity of prætor in Carthage. Here he continued for some time, reforming abuses, and putting the affairs of the republic into a better condition; but this likewise being disagreeable to the Romans, he was obliged to fly to Antiochus king of Syria.

152 Hannibal flies to Antiochus. After his flight, the Romans began to look upon the Carthaginians with a suspicious eye; though, to prevent every thing of this kind, the latter had ordered two ships to pursue Hannibal, had confiscated his effects, rased his house, and by a public decree declared him an exile. Soon after, disputes arising between the Carthaginians and Masinissa, the latter, notwithstanding the manifest iniquity of his proceedings, was supported by the Romans.

153 Iniquitous proceedings of Masinissa and the Romans. That prince, grasping at further conquests, endeavoured to embroil the Carthaginians with the Romans, by asserting that the former had received ambassadors from Perseus king of Macedon; that the senate assembled in the temple of Æsculapius in the night-time in order to confer with them; and that ambassadors had been dispatched from Carthage to Perseus, in order to conclude an alliance with him. Not long after this, Masinissa made an irruption into the province of Tysca, where he soon possessed himself of 70, or, as Appian will have it, 50 towns and castles. This obliged the Carthaginians to apply with great importunity to the Roman senate for redress, their hands being so tied up by an article in the last treaty, that they could not repel force by force, in case of an invasion, without their consent. Their ambassadors begged, that the Roman senate would settle once for all what dominions they were to have, that they might from thenceforth know what they had to depend upon; or if their state had any way offended the Romans, they begged that they would punish them themselves, rather than leave them exposed to the insults and vexations of so merciless a tyrant. Then prostrating themselves on the earth, they burst out into tears. But, notwithstanding the impression their speech made, the matter was left undecided; so that Masinissa had liberty to pursue his rapines as much as he pleased. But whatever villainous designs the Romans might have with regard to the republic of Carthage, they affected to show a great regard to the principles of justice and honour. They therefore sent Cato, a man famous for committing enormities under the specious pretence of public spirit, into Africa, to accommodate all differences betwixt Masinissa and the Carthaginians. The latter very well knew their fate, had they submitted to such a mediation; and therefore appealed to the treaty concluded with Scipio, as the only rule by which their conduct and that of their adversary ought to be examined. This *unreasonable* appeal so incensed the righteous Cato, that he pronounced them a devoted people, and from that time resolved upon their destruction. For some time he was opposed by Scipio Nasica; but the people of Carthage, knowing the Romans to be their inveterate enemies, and reflecting upon the iniquitous treatment they had met with from them ever since the commencement of their disputes with Masinissa, were under great apprehensions of a visit from them. To prevent a rupture as much as possible, by a decree of the senate, they impeached Asdrubal general of the army, and Carthalo commander of the auxiliary forces, together with their accomplices, as guilty of high treason, for being the authors of the war against the king of Numidia. They sent a deputation to Rome, to discover what sentiments were entertained there of their late conduct, and to know what satisfaction the Romans required. These messengers meeting with a cold reception, others were dispatched, who returned with the same success. This made the unhappy citizens of Carthage believe that their destruction was resolved upon; which threw them into the utmost despair. And indeed they had but too just grounds for such a melancholy apprehension, the Roman senate now discovering an inclination to fall in with Cato's measures. About the same time, the city of Utica, being the second in Africa, and famous for its immense riches, as well as its equally commodious and capacious port, submitted to the Romans. Upon the possession of so important a fortress, which, by reason of its vicinity to Carthage, might serve as a place of arms in the attack of that city, the Romans declared war against the Carthaginians without the least hesitation.

154 War declared by the Romans against Carthage. In consequence of this declaration, the consuls M. Manlius Nepos, and L. Marcius Censorinus, were dispatched with an army and fleet to begin hostilities with the utmost expedition. The land forces consisted of 80,000 foot and 4000 chosen horse; and the fleet of 50 quinqueremes, besides a vast number of transports. The consuls had secret orders from the senate not to conclude the operations but by the destruction of Carthage, without which, it was pretended, the republic could not but look upon all her possessions as insecure. Pursuant to the plan they had formed, the troops were first landed at Lilybæum in Sicily, from whence, after receiving a proper refreshment, it was proposed to transport them to Utica.

155 Ambassadors sent to Rome. The answer brought by the last ambassadors to Carthage had not a little alarmed the inhabitants of that city. But they were not yet acquainted with the resolutions taken at Rome. They therefore sent fresh ambassadors thither, whom they invested with full powers to act as they thought proper for the good of the republic, and even to submit themselves without reserve to the pleasure of the Romans. But the most sensible persons among them did not expect any great success from this condescension, since the early

Carthage. submission of the Uticans had rendered it infinitely less meritorious than it would have been before. However, the Romans seemed to be in some measure satisfied with it, since they promised them their liberty, the enjoyment of their laws, and in short every thing that was dear and valuable to them. This threw them into a transport of joy, and they wanted words to extol the moderation of the Romans. But the senate

156 The Romans demand 300 hostages,

immediately dashed all their hopes, by acquainting them, that this favour was granted upon condition that they would send 300 young Carthaginian noblemen of the first distinction to the prætor Fabius at Lilybæum, within the space of 30 days, and comply with all the orders of the consuls. These hard terms filled the whole city with inexpressible grief: but the hostages were delivered; and as they arrived at Lilybæum before the 30 days were expired, the ambassadors were not without hopes of softening their hard-hearted enemy. But the consuls only told them, that upon their arrival at Utica they should learn the farther orders of the republic.

The ministers no sooner received intelligence of the Roman fleet appearing off Utica, than they repaired thither, in order to know the fate of their city. The consuls, however, did not judge it expedient to communicate all the commands of their republic at once, lest they should appear so harsh and severe, that the Carthaginians would have refused to comply with them.

157 And all the Carthaginian arms, military machines, &c.

They first, therefore, demanded a sufficient supply of corn for the subsistence of their troops. Secondly, That they should deliver up into their hands all the triremes they were then masters of. Thirdly, That they should put them in possession of all their military machines. And fourthly, That they should immediately convey all their arms into the Roman camp.

As care was taken that there should be a convenient interval of time betwixt every one of these demands, the Carthaginians found themselves ensnared, and could not reject any one of them, though they submitted to the last with the utmost reluctance and concern. Censorinus now imagining them incapable

158 They command them to destroy their city.

of sustaining a siege, commanded them to abandon their city, or, as Zonaras will have it, to demolish it; permitting them to build another 80 stadia from the sea, but without walls or fortifications. This terrible decree threw the senate and every one else into despair; and the whole city became a scene of horror, madness, and confusion. The citizens cursed their ancestors for not dying gloriously in the defence of their country, rather than concluding such ignominious treaties of peace, that had been the cause of the deplorable condition to which their posterity was then reduced. At length, when the first commotion was a little abated, the senators assembled, and resolved to sustain a siege.

159 The Carthaginians resolve to sustain a siege.

They were stripped of their arms and destitute of provisions; but despair raised their courage, and made them find out expedients. They took care to shut the gates of the city; and gathered together on the ramparts great heaps of stones, to serve them instead of arms in case of a surprise. They took the malefactors out of prison, gave the slaves their liberty, and incorporated them in the militia. Asdrubal was recalled, who had been sentenced to die only to please the Romans; and he was invited to employ 20,000 men he had raised against his country, in defence of it. Another Asdrubal was appointed to command in Carthage; and all seemed resolute, either to save their city or perish in its ruins. They wanted arms; but, by

160 They make new arms.

order of the senate, the temples, porticoes, and all public buildings, were turned into workhouses, where men and women were continually employed in making arms. As they encouraged one another in their work, and lost no time in procuring to themselves the necessaries of life, which were brought to them at stated hours, they every day made 144 bucklers, 300 swords, 1000 darts, and 500 lances and javelins. As to balistæ and catapultæ, they wanted proper materials for them; but their industry supplied that defect. Where iron and brass were wanting, they made use of silver and gold, melting down the statues, vases, and even the utensils of private families; for, on this occasion, even the most covetous became liberal. As tow and flax were wanting to make cords for working the machines, the women, even those of the first rank, freely cut off their hair and dedicated it to that use. Without the walls, Asdrubal employed the troops in getting together provisions, and conveying them safe into Carthage; so that there was as great plenty there as in the Roman camp.

In the mean time the consuls delayed drawing near to Carthage, not doubting but the inhabitants, whom they imagined destitute of necessaries to sustain a siege, would, upon cool reflection, submit; but at length, finding themselves deceived in their expectation, they came before the place and invested it. As they were still persuaded that the Carthaginians had no arms, they flattered themselves that they should easily carry the city by assault. Accordingly they approached the walls in order to plant their scaling-ladders; but to their great surprise they discovered a prodigious multitude of men on the ramparts, shining in the armour they had newly made. The legionaries were so terrified at this unexpected sight, that they drew back, and would have retired, if the consuls had not led them on to the attack: which, however, proved unsuccessful; the Romans, in spite of their utmost efforts, being obliged to give over the enterprize, and lay aside all thoughts of taking Carthage by assault. 161

161 The city attacked by the Romans, who are repulsed.

In the mean time Asdrubal, having collected from all places subject to Carthage a prodigious number of troops, came and encamped within reach of the Romans, and soon reduced them to great straits for want of provisions. As Marcius, one of the Roman consuls, was posted near a marsh, the exhalations of the stagnating waters, and the heat of the season, infected the air, and caused a general sickness among his men. Marcius, therefore, ordered his fleet to draw as near the shore as possible, in order to transport his troops to an healthier place. Asdrubal being informed of this motion, ordered all the old barks in the harbour to be filled with faggots, tow, sulphur, bitumen, and other combustible materials; and then taking advantage of the wind, which blew towards the enemy, let them drive upon their ships, which were for the most part consumed. After this disaster, Marcius was called home to preside at the elections; and the Carthaginians looking upon the absence of one of the consuls to be a good omen, made a brisk sally in the night; and would have surprised the consul's camp, had not Æmilianus, with some squadrons, marched out of the gate

162 Part of the Roman fleet destroyed, &c.

Carthage.

gate opposite to the place where the attack was made, and, coming round, fell unexpectedly on their rear, and obliged them to return in disorder to the city.

Asdrubal had posted himself under the walls of a city named Nepheris, 14 miles distant from Carthage, and situated on an high mountain, which seemed inaccessible on all sides. From thence he made incursions into the neighbouring country, intercepted the Roman convoys, fell upon their detachments sent out to forage, and even ordered parties to insult the consular army in their camp. Hereupon the consul resolved to drive the Carthaginian from this advantageous post, and set out for Nepheris. As he drew near the hills, Asdrubal suddenly appeared at the head of his army in order of battle, and fell upon the Romans with incredible fury. The consular army sustained the attack with great resolution; and Asdrubal retired in good order to his post, hoping the Romans would attack him

163 The Roman army, in great danger, is saved by Scipio Æmilianus.

there. But the consul being now convinced of his danger, resolved to retire. This Asdrubal no sooner perceived, than he rushed down the hill, and falling upon the enemy's rear, cut a great number of them in pieces. The whole Roman army was now saved by the bravery of Scipio Æmilianus. At the head of 300 horse, he sustained the attack of all the forces commanded by Asdrubal, and covered the legions, while they passed a river in their retreat before the enemy. Then he and his companions threw themselves into the stream, and swam across it. When the army had crossed the river, it was perceived that four manipuli were wanting; and soon after they were informed that they had retired to an eminence, where they resolved to sell their lives as dear as possible. Upon this news Æmilianus, taking with him a chosen body of horse, and provisions for two days, crossed the river, and flew to the assistance of his countrymen. He seized an hill over against that on which the four manipuli were posted; and, after some short repose, marched against the Carthaginians who kept them invested, fell upon them at the head of his squadron with the boldness of a man determined to conquer or die, and in spite of all opposition opened a way for his fellow-soldiers to escape. On his return to the army, his companions, who had given him over for lost, carried him to his quarters in a kind of triumph; and the manipuli he had saved gave him a crown of *grass*. By these and some other exploits, Æmilianus gained such reputation, that Cato, who is said never to have commended any body before, could not refuse him the praises he deserved; and is said to have foretold that Carthage would never be reduced till Scipio Æmilianus was employed in that expedition.

The next year, the war in Africa fell by lot to the consul L. Calpurnius Piso; and he continued to employ Æmilianus in several important enterprises, in

164 He gains over the Carthaginian general of horse.

which he was attended with uncommon success. He took several castles; and in one of his excursions, found means to have a private conference with Phameas, general, under Asdrubal, of the Carthaginian cavalry, and brought him over, together with 2200 of his horse, to the Roman interest. Under the consul Calpurnius Piso himself, however, the Roman arms were unsuccessful. He invested Clupea; but was obliged to abandon the enterprise, with the loss of a great number of men killed by the enemy in their sallies. From this place he went to vent his rage on a city newly built, and thence called *Neapolis*, which professed a strict neutrality, and had even a safeguard from the Romans. The consul, however, plundered the place, and stripped the inhabitants of all their effects. After this he laid siege to *Hippagreta*, which employed the Roman fleet and army the whole summer; and, on the approach of winter, the consul retired to Utica, without performing a single action worth notice during the whole campaign.

Carthage.

The next year Scipio Æmilianus was chosen consul, 165 He is chosen consul.

and ordered to pass into Africa; and upon his arrival, the face of affairs was greatly changed. At the time of his entering the port of Utica, 3500 Romans were in great danger of being cut in pieces before Carthage. These had seized Megalia, one of the suburbs of the city; but as they had not furnished themselves with provisions to subsist there, and could not retire, being closely invested on all sides by the enemy's troops, the prætor Mancinus, who commanded this detachment, seeing the danger into which he had brought himself, dispatched a light boat to Utica, to acquaint the Romans there with his situation. Æmilianus received this letter a few hours after his landing; and immediately flew to the relief of the besieged Romans, obliged the Carthaginians to retire within their walls, and safely conveyed his countrymen to Utica. Having then drawn together all the troops, Æmilianus applied himself wholly to the siege of the capital.

His first attack was upon Megalia; which he carried by assault, the Carthaginian garrison retiring into the citadel of Byrsa. Asdrubal, who had commanded 166 Cruelty of Asdrubal.

the Carthaginian forces in the field, and was now governor of the city, was so enraged at the loss of Megalia, that he caused all the Roman captives taken in the two years the war lasted, to be brought upon the ramparts, and thrown headlong, in the sight of the Roman army, from the top of the wall; after having, with an excess of cruelty, commanded their hands and feet to be cut off, and their eyes and tongues to be torn out. He was of a temper remarkably inhuman, and it is said that he even took pleasure in seeing some of these unhappy men flayed alive. Æmilianus, in the mean time, was busy in drawing lines of circumvallation and contravallation cross the neck of land which joined the isthmus on which Carthage stood to the continent. By this means, all the avenues on the land- 167 Carthage blocked up by sea and land.

side of Carthage being shut up, the city could receive no provisions that way. His next care was to raise a mole in the sea, in order to block up the old port, the new one being already shut up by the Roman fleet; and this great work he effected with immense labour. The mole reached from the western neck of land, of which the Romans were masters, to the entrance of the port; and was 90 feet broad at the bottom and 80 at the top. The besieged, when the Romans first began this surprising work, laughed at the attempt; but were no less alarmed than surprised, when they beheld a vast mole appearing above water, and by that means the port rendered inaccessible to ships, and quite useless. Prompted by despair, however, the Carthagi- 168 The besieged dig a new bason.

nians, with incredible and almost miraculous industry, dug a new bason, and cut a passage into the sea, by which they could receive the provisions that were sent them by their troops in the field. With the same diligence

Carthage.

ligence and expedition, they fitted out a fleet of 50 triremes; which, to the great surprise of the Romans, appeared suddenly advancing into the sea through this new canal, and even ventured to give the enemy battle. The action lasted the whole day, with little advantage on either side. The day after, the consul endeavoured to make himself master of a terrace which covered the city on the side next the sea; and on this occasion the besieged signalized themselves in a most remarkable

169 They set fire to the Roman machines.

manner. Great numbers of them, naked and unarmed, went into the water in the dead of the night, with unlighted torches in their hands; and having, partly by swimming, partly by wading, got within reach of the Roman engines, they struck fire, lighted their torches, and threw them with fury against the machines. The sudden appearance of these naked men, who looked like so many monsters started up out of the sea, so terrified the Romans who guarded the machines, that they began to retire in the utmost confusion. The consul, who commanded the detachment in person, and had continued all night at the foot of the terrace, endeavoured to stop his men, and even ordered those who fled to be killed. But the Carthaginians, perceiving the confusion the Romans were in, threw themselves upon them like so many wild beasts; and having put them to flight only with their torches, they set fire to the machines, and entirely consumed them. This, however, did not discourage the consul: he renewed the attack a few days after, carried the terrace by assault, and lodged 4000 men upon it. As this was an important post, because it press in Carthage on the sea-side, Æmilianus took care to fortify and secure it against the sallies of the enemy; and then, winter approaching, he suspended all further attacks upon the place till the return of good weather. During the winter season, however, the consul was not inactive. The Carthaginians had a very numerous army under the command of one Diogenes, strongly encamped near Nepheris, whence convoys of provisions were sent by sea to the besieged, and brought into the new bason. To take Nepheris, therefore, was to deprive Carthage of her chief magazine. This Æmilianus undertook, and succeeded in the attempt. He

170 Vast slaughter of the Carthaginians.

first forced the enemy's entrenchments, put 70,000 of them to the sword, and made 10,000 prisoners; all the inhabitants of the country, who could not retire to Carthage, having taken refuge in this camp. After this, he laid siege to Nepheris, which was reduced in 22 days. Asdrubal being disheartened by the defeat of the army, and touched with the misery of the besieged now reduced to the utmost extremity for want of provisions, offered to submit to what conditions the Romans pleased, provided the city was spared; but this was absolutely refused.

171 Cotho taken.

Early in the spring, Æmilianus renewed the siege of Carthage; and in order to open himself a way into the city, he ordered Lælius to attempt the reduction of Cotho, a small island which divided the two ports. Æmilianus himself made a false attack on the citadel, in order to draw the enemy thither. This stratagem had the desired effect; for the citadel being a place of the greatest importance, most of the Carthaginians hastened thither, and made their utmost efforts to repulse their aggressors. But in the mean time Lælius having, with incredible expedition, built a wooden bridge over the channel which divided Cotho from the isthmus, entered the island, scaled the walls of the fortress which the Carthaginians had built there, and made himself master of that important post. The proconsul, who was engaged before Byrsa, no sooner understood, by the loud shouts of the troops of Lælius, that he had made himself master of Cotho, than he abandoned the false attack, and unexpectedly fell on the neighbouring gate of the city, which he broke

172 Romans enter the city.

down, notwithstanding the showers of darts that were incessantly discharged upon his men from the ramparts. As night coming on prevented him from proceeding farther, he made a lodgment within the gate, and waited there for the return of day, with a design to advance through the city to the citadel, and attack it on that side which was but indifferently fortified. Pursuant to this design, at day-break he ordered 4000 fresh troops to be sent from his camp, and, having solemnly devoted to the infernal gods the unhappy Carthaginians, he began to advance at the head of his men, through the streets of the city, in order to attack the citadel. Having advanced to the market-place, he found that the way to the citadel lay through three exceeding steep streets. The houses on both sides were very high, and filled with Carthaginians, who overwhelmed the Romans as they advanced with darts and stones; so that they could not proceed till they had cleared them. To this end Æmilianus in person, at the head of a detachment, attacked the first house, and made himself master of it sword in hand. His example was followed by the officers and soldiers, who went on from house to house, putting all they met with to the sword. As fast as the houses were cleared on both sides, the Romans advanced in order of battle towards the citadel; but met with a vigorous resistance from the Carthaginians, who on this occasion behaved with uncommon resolution. From the market-place to the citadel, two bodies of men fought their way every step, one above on the roofs of the houses, the other below in the streets. The slaughter was inexpressibly great and dreadful. The air rung with shrieks and lamentations. Some were cut in pieces, others threw themselves down from the tops of the houses; so that the streets were filled with dead and mangled bodies. But the destruction was yet greater,

173 Which is set on fire.

when the proconsul commanded fire to be set to that quarter of the town which lay next to the citadel. Incredible multitudes, who had escaped the swords of the enemy, perished in the flames, or by the fall of the houses. After the fire, which lasted six days, had demolished a sufficient number of houses, Æmilianus ordered the rubbish to be removed, and a large area to be made, where all his troops might have room to act. Then he appeared with his whole army before Byrsa; which so terrified the Carthaginians, who had fled thither for refuge, that first of all 25,000 women, and then 30,000 men, came out of the gates in such a condition as moved pity. They threw themselves prostrate before the Roman general, asking no favour but life. This was readily granted, not only to them, but to all that were in Byrsa, except the Roman deserters, whose number amounted to 900. Asdrubal's

174 Cruelty and cowardice of Asdrubal.

wife earnestly intreated her husband to suffer her to join the suppliants, and carry with her to the proconsul her two sons, who were as yet very young; but

but the barbarian denied her request, and rejected her remonstrances with menaces. The Roman deserters seeing themselves excluded from mercy, resolved to die sword in hand, rather than deliver themselves up to the vengeance of their countrymen. Then Asdrubal, finding them all resolved to defend themselves to the last breath, committed to their care his wife and children; after which he, in a most cowardly and mean-spirited manner, came and privately threw himself at the conqueror's feet. The Carthaginians in the citadel no sooner understood that their commander had abandoned the place, than they threw open the gates, and put the Romans in possession of Byrsa. They had now no enemy to contend with but the 900 deserters; who, being reduced to despair, retreated into the temple of Æsculapius, which was as a second temple within the first. There the proconsul attacked them; and these unhappy wretches, finding there was no way to escape, set fire to the temple. As the flames spread, they retreated from one part of the building to another, till

175 Asdrubal's wife destroys herself and two children.

they got to the roof. There Asdrubal's wife appeared in her best apparel, and having uttered the most bitter imprecations against her husband, whom she saw standing below with Æmilianus, "Base coward (said she), the mean things thou hast done to save thy life shall not avail thee: thou shalt die this instant, at least in thy two children." Having thus spoken, she stabbed both the infants with a dagger; and while they were yet struggling for life, threw them both from the top of the temple, and then leaped down after them into the flames.

176 Carthage plundered.

Æmilianus delivered up the city to be plundered, but in the manner prescribed by the Roman military law. The soldiers were allowed to appropriate to themselves all the furniture, utensils, and brass money, they should find in private houses; but all the gold and silver, the statues, pictures, &c. were reserved to be put into the hands of the quæstors. On this occasion the cities of Sicily, which had been often plundered by the Carthaginian armies, recovered a number of statues, pictures, and other valuable monuments: among the rest, the famous brazen bull, which Phalaris had ordered to be cast, and used as the chief instrument of his cruelty, was restored to the inhabitants of Agrigentum. As Æmilianus was greatly inclined to spare what remained of this stately metropolis, he wrote to the senate on the subject, from whom he received the following orders: 1. The city of Carthage, with Byrsa, and Megalia, shall be entirely destroyed, and no traces of them left. 2. All the cities that have lent Carthage any assistance shall be dismantled. 3. The territories of those cities which have declared for the Romans, shall be enlarged with lands taken from the enemy. 4. All the lands between Hippo and Carthage shall be divided among the inhabitants of Utica. 5. All the Africans of the Carthaginian state, both men and women, shall pay an annual tribute to the Romans at so much per head. 6. The whole country, which was subject to the Carthaginian state, shall be turned into a Roman province, and be governed by a prætor, in the same manner as Sicily. Lastly, Rome shall send commissioners into Africa, there to settle jointly with the proconsul the state of the new province. Before Æmilianus destroyed the city, he performed those religious ceremonies which were required on such occasions: he first sacrificed to the gods, and then caused a plough to be drawn round

177 and utterly destroyed.

the walls of the city. After this, the towers, ramparts, walls, and all the works which the Carthaginians had raised in the course of many ages, and at a vast expence, were levelled with the ground; and lastly, fire was set to the edifices of the proud metropolis, which consumed them all, not a single house escaping the flames. Though the fire began in all quarters at the same time, and burnt with incredible fury, it continued for 17 days before all the buildings were consumed.

Thus fell Carthage, about 146 years before the birth of Christ; a city whose destruction ought to be attributed more to the intrigues of an abandoned faction, composed of the most profligate part of its citizens, than to the power of its rival. The treasure Æmilianus carried off, even after the city had been delivered up to be plundered by the soldiers, was immense, Pliny making it to amount to 4,470,000 pounds weight of silver. The Romans ordered Carthage never to be inhabited again, denouncing dreadful imprecations against those who, contrary to this prohibition, should attempt to rebuild any part of it, especially Byrsa and Megalia. Notwithstanding this,

178 Rebuilt.

however, about 24 years after, C. Gracchus, tribune of the people, in order to ingratiate himself with them, undertook to rebuild it; and, to that end, conducted thither a colony of 6000 Roman citizens. The workmen, according to Plutarch, were terrified by many unlucky omens at the time they were tracing the limits and laying the foundations of the new city; which the senate being informed of, would have suspended the attempt. But the tribune, little affected with such presages, continued to carry on the work, and finished it in a few days. From hence it is probable that only a slight kind of huts were erected; but, whether Gracchus executed his design, or the work was entirely discontinued, it is certain, that Carthage was the first Roman colony ever sent out of Italy. According to some authors, Carthage was rebuilt by Julius Cæsar; and Strabo, who flourished in the reign of Tiberius, affirms it in his time to have been equal if not superior to any other city in Africa. It was looked upon as the capital of Africa for several centuries after the commencement of the Christian æra. Maxentius laid it in ashes about the sixth or seventh year of Constan-

179 Utterly destroyed by the Saracens.

tine's reign. Genseric, king of the Vandals, took it A. D. 439; but about a century afterwards it was re-annexed to the Roman empire by the renowned Belisarius. At last the Saracens, under Mohammed's successors, towards the close of the seventh century, so completely destroyed it, that there are now scarce any traces remaining.

180 Its former grandeur.

At the commencement of the third Punic war, Carthage appears to have been one of the first cities in the world.—It was seated on a peninsula 360 stadia or 45 miles in circumference, joined to the continent by an isthmus 25 stadia or three miles and a furlong in breadth. On the west side there projected from it a long tract of land half a stadium broad; which shooting out into the sea, separated it from a lake or morass, and was strongly fortified on all sides by rocks and a single wall. In the middle of the city stood the citadel of Byrsa, having on the top of it a temple sacred

to

Carthage. to Æsculapius, seated upon rocks on a very high hill, to which the ascent was by 60 steps. On the south side the city was surrounded by a triple wall, 30 cubits high; flanked all round by parapets and towers, placed at equal distances of 480 feet. Every tower had its foundation sunk 32 feet deep, and was four stories high, though the walls were but two: they were arched; and, in the lower part, corresponding in depth with the foundations above mentioned, were stalls large enough to hold 300 elephants with their fodder, &c. Over these were stalls and other conveniences for 4000 horses; and there was likewise room for lodging 20,000 foot and 4000 cavalry, without in the least incommoding the inhabitants. There were two harbours, so disposed as to have a communication with one another. They had one common entrance 70 feet broad, and shut up with chains. The first was appropriated to the merchants; and included in it a vast number of places of refreshment, and all kinds of accommodations for seamen. The second, as well as the island of Cothon, in the midst of it, was lined with large keys, in which were distinct receptacles for securing and sheltering from the weather 220 ships of war. Over these were magazines of all sorts of naval stores. The entrance into each of these receptacles was adorned with two marble pillars of the Ionic order; so that both the harbour and island represented on each side two magnificent galleries. Near this island was a temple of Apollo, in which was a statue of the god all of massy gold; and the inside of the temple all lined with plates of the same metal, weighing 1000 talents. The city was 23 miles in circumference, and at the time we speak of contained 700,000 inhabitants. Of their power we may have some idea, by the quantity of arms they delivered up to the Roman consuls. The whole army was astonished at the long train of carts loaded with them, which were thought sufficient to have armed all Africa. At least it is certain, that on this occasion were put into the hands of the Romans, 2000 catapultæ, 200,000 complete suits of armour, with an innumerable quantity of swords, darts, javelins, arrows, and beams armed with iron which were thrown from the ramparts by the balistæ.

The character transmitted of the Carthaginians is extremely bad; but we have it only on the authority of the Romans, who being their implacable enemies cannot be much relied upon. As to their religion, manners, &c. being much the same with the Phœnicians of which they were a colony, the reader is referred for an account of these things to the article Phoenicia.

On the ruins of Carthage there now stands only a small village called *Melcha*. The few remains of Carthage consist only of some fragments of walls and 17 cisterns for the reception of rain-water.

There are three eminences, which are so many masses of fine marble pounded together, and were in all probability the sites of temples and other distinguished buildings. The present ruins are by no means the remains of the ancient city destroyed by the Romans; who after taking it entirely erased it, and ploughed up the very foundations: so truly they adhered to the well-known advice perpetually inculcated by Cato the Elder, *Delenda est Carthago*. It was again rebuilt by the Gracchi family, who conducted a colony to re-people it; and continually increasing in splendour, it became at length the capital of Africa under the Roman emperors. It subsisted near 700 years after its first demolition, until it was entirely destroyed by the Saracens in the beginning of the 7th century.

It is a singular circumstance that the two cities of Carthage and Rome should have been built just opposite one to the other; the bay of Tunis and the mouth of the Tiber being in a direct line.

> *Littora littoribus contraria, fluctibus undas,*
> *Arma armis.* Virg. Æn. i. 4.

New Carthage. *New-Carthage*, a considerable town of Mexico, in the province of Costarica. It is a very rich trading place. W. Long. 86. 7. N. Lat. 9. 5.

Carthagena. CARTHAGENA, a province of South America, and one of the most considerable in New Castile, on account of the great trade carried on by the capital; for the country itself is neither fertile, rich, nor populous. The capital city, called likewise *Carthagena*, is situated in W. Long. 77. N. Lat. 11. on a sandy island, by most writers called a peninsula; which, forming a narrow passage on the south-west, opens a communication with that called *Tierra Bomba*, as far as *Bocca Chica*. The little island which now joins them was formerly the entrance of the bay; but it having been filled up by orders of the court, Bocca Chica became the only entrance: this, however, has been filled up since the attempt of Vernon and Wentworth, and the old passage again opened. On the north side the land is so narrow, that, before the wall was begun, the distance from sea to sea was only 35 toises; but afterwards enlarging, it forms another island on this side; so that, excepting these two places, the whole city is entirely surrounded by salt-water. To the eastward it has a communication, by means of a wooden bridge, with a large suburb called *Xemani*, built on another island, which is also joined to the continent by a bridge of the same materials. The fortifications both of the city and suburbs are built after the modern manner, and lined with free-stone; and, in time of peace, the garrison consists of ten companies of 77 men each, besides militia. The city and suburbs are well laid out, the streets straight, broad, uniform, and well paved. All the houses are built of stone or brick, only one story high, well contrived, neat, and furnished with balconies and lattices of wood, which is more durable in that climate than iron, the latter being soon corroded by the acrimonious quality of the atmosphere. The climate is exceedingly unhealthy. The Europeans are particularly subject to the terrible disease called the *black vomit*, which sweeps off multitudes annually on the arrival of the galleons. It seldom continues above three or four days; in which time the patient is either dead or out of danger, and if he recovers is never subject to a return of the same distemper. —This disease has hitherto foiled all the art of the Spanish physicians; as has also the leprosy, which is very common here. At Carthagena, likewise, that painful tumour in the legs, occasioned by the entrance of the *Dracunculus* or Guinea-worm, is very common and troublesome. Another disorder peculiar to this country, and to Peru, is occasioned by a little insect called *Nigua*, so extremely minute, as scarce to be visible to the naked eye. This insect breeds in the dust, insinuates itself into the soles of the feet and the legs, piercing the skin with such subtility, that there is no

being

being aware of it, before it has made its way to the flesh. If it is perceived in the beginning, it is extracted with little pain; but having once lodged its head, and pierced the skin, the patient must undergo the pain of an incision, without which a nodus would be formed, and a multitude of insects ingendered, which would soon overspread the foot and leg. One species of the *nigua* is venomous; and when it enters the toe, an inflammatory swelling, greatly resembling a venereal bubo, takes place in the groin.

Carthagena, a sea-port town of Spain in the kingdom of Murcia, and capital of a territory of the same name; built by Asdrubal, a Carthaginian general, and named after Carthage. It has the best harbour in all Spain, but nothing else very considerable; the bishop's see being transferred to Toledo. In 1706 it was taken by Sir John Leak; but the Duke of Berwick retook it afterwards. W. Long. 0. 58. N. Lat. 37. 36.

CARTHAMUS, in botany: A genus of the order of polygamia æqualis, belonging to the syngenesia class of plants, and in the natural method ranking under the 49th order, *Compositæ*. The calyx is ovate, imbricated with scales, close below, and augmented with subovate foliaceous appendices at top.—Of this genus there are nine species; but the only remarkable one is the tinctorius, with a saffron-coloured flower. This is a native of Egypt and some of the warm parts of Asia. It is at present cultivated in many parts of Europe, and also in the Levant, from whence great quantities of it are annually imported into Britain for the purposes of dyeing and painting. It is an annual plant, and rises with a stiff ligneous stalk, about two feet and a half or three feet in height, dividing upwards into many branches, garnished with oval pointed leaves sitting close to the branches. The flowers grow single at the extremity of each branch; the heads of the flowers are large, inclosed in a scaly empalement; each scale is broad at the base, flat, and formed like a leaf of the plant, terminating in a sharp spine. The lower part of the empalement spreads open; but the scales above closely embrace the florets, which are of a fine saffron colour, and are the part used for the purposes above mentioned. The good quality of this commodity is in the colour, which is of a bright saffron hue: and in this the British carthamus very often fails; for if there happens much rain during the time the plants are in flower, the flowers change to a dark or dirty yellow, as they likewise do if the flowers are gathered with any moisture remaining upon them.—The plants are propagated by seeds, which should be sown in drills, at two feet and a half distance from one another, in which the seeds should be scattered singly. The plants will appear in less than a month; and in three weeks or a month after, it will be proper to hoe the ground; at which time the plants should be left six inches distant: after this they will require a second hoeing; when they must be thinned to the distance at which they are to remain. If after this they are hoed a third time, they will require no farther care till they come to flower; when, if the safflower is intended for use, the florets should be cut off from the flowers as they come to perfection: but this must be performed when they are perfectly dry; and then they should be dried in a kiln with a moderate fire, in the same manner as the true saffron. But in those flowers which are propagated for seeds, the florets must be cut off, or the seeds will prove abortive.—The seeds of carthamus have been celebrated as a cathartic; but they operate very slowly, and for the most part disorder the stomach and bowels, especially when given in substance: triturated with distilled aromatic waters, they form an emulsion less offensive, yet inferior in efficacy to the more common purgatives. They are eaten by a species of Egyptian parrot, which is very fond of them; to other birds or beasts they would prove a mortal poison.

CARTHUSIANS, a religious order founded in the year 1080, by one Bruno. The Carthusians, so called from the desert of *Chartreux*, the place of their institution, are remarkable for the austerity of their rule. They are not to go out of their cells, except to church, without leave of their superior; nor speak to any person without leave. They must not keep any portion of their meat or drink till next day; their beds are of straw, covered with a felt; their clothing two hair-cloths, two cowls, two pair of hose, and a cloke, all coarse. In the refectory, they are to keep their eyes on the dish, their hands on the table, their attention on the reader, and their hearts fixed on God. Women are not allowed to come into their churches. It is computed that there are 172 houses of Carthusians; whereof five are of *Nuns*, who practise the same austerities as the Monks. They are divided into 16 provinces, each of which has two visitors. There have been several canonized saints of this order, four cardinals, 70 archbishops and bishops, and a great many very learned writers.

Carthusian-Powder, the same with kermes-mineral. See Kermes.

CARTILAGE, in anatomy, a body approaching to the nature of bones; but lubricous, flexible, and elastic. See Anatomy.

CARTILAGINOUS, in ichthyology, a title given to all fish whose muscles are supported by cartilages instead of bones; and comprehends the same genera of fish to which Linnæus has given the name of *amphibia nantes*; but the word *amphibia* ought properly to be confined to such animals as inhabit both elements; and can live, without any inconvenience, for a considerable time, either on land or in water; such as tortoises, frogs, and several species of lizards; and, among the quadrupeds, hippopotami, *&c. &c.* Brit. Zool. III 75.

Many of the cartilaginous fish are viviparous, being excluded from an egg, which is hatched within them. The egg consists of a white and a yolk; and is lodged in a case formed of a thick tough substance, not unlike softened horn: such are the eggs of the *ray* and *shark* kinds. Some again differ in this respect, and are oviparous; such is the *sturgeon*, and others.

They breathe either through certain apertures beneath, as in the *rays*; on their sides, as in the *sharks*, &c.; or on the top of the head, as in the *pipe-fish*; for they have not covers to their gills like the bony fish.

CARTMEL, a town of Lancashire in England. It is seated among the hills called Carmel-fells, not far from the sea, and near the river Kent; adorned with a very handsome church, built in the form of a cross like a cathedral. The market is well supplied with corn, sheep, and fish. W. Long. 2. 45. N. Lat. 54. 15.

CARTON, or Cartoon, in painting, a design drawn

drawn on strong paper, to be afterwards calked through, and transferred on the *fresh* plaster of a wall to be painted in fresco. It is also used for a design coloured, for working in mosaic, tapestry, &c. The word is from the Italian *Cartoni*, (*carta* "paper," and *oni* "large,") denoting many sheets of paper pasted on canvas, on which large designs are made, whether coloured or with chalks only. Of these many are to be seen at Rome, particularly by Domenichino. Those by Andrea Mantegna, which are at Hampton Court, were made for paintings in the old ducal palace at Mantua. But the most famous performances of this sort are,

The *Cartoons of Raphael*, so deservedly applauded throughout Europe by all authors of refined taste, and all true admirers of the art of design, for their various and matchless merit, particularly with regard to the invention, and to the great and noble expression of such a variety of characters, countenances, and most expressive attitudes, as they are differently affected and properly engaged, in every composition. These cartoons are seven in number, and form only a small part of the sacred historical designs executed by this great artist, while engaged in the chambers of the Vatican under the auspices of Popes Julius II. and Leo X. When finished, they were sent to Flanders, to be copied in tapestry, for adorning the pontifical apartments: which tapestries were not sent to Rome till several years after the decease of Raphael, and even in all probability were not finished and sent there before the terrible sack of that city in the time of Clement VII. when Raphael's scholars were fled from thence, and none left to enquire after the original Cartoons, which lay neglected in the store-rooms of the manufactory. The great revolution also which followed in the Low Countries prevented their being noticed amidst the entire neglect of the works of art. It was therefore a most fortunate circumstance that these seven escaped the wreck of the others, which were torn in pieces, and remain dispersed as fragments in different collections. These seven were purchased by Rubens for Charles I. and they have been so roughly handled from the first, that holes were pricked for the weavers to pounce the outlines, and other parts almost cut through in tracing also. In this state perhaps they as fortunately escaped the sale amongst the royal collection, by the disproportioned appraisement of these seven at 300 l. and the nine pieces, being the Triumph of Julius Cæsar, by Andrea Mantegna, appraised at 1000 l. They seem to have been taken small notice of till King William built a gallery, purposely to receive them, at Hampton Court; whence they were moved, on their suffering from damps, to the Queen's Palace. They are now at Windsor Castle, and open to public inspection.

CARTOUCHE, in architecture and sculpture, an ornament representing a scroll of paper. It is usually a flat member, with wavings, to represent some inscription, device, cipher, or ornament of armoury. They are, in architecture, much the same as modillions; only these are set under the cornice in wainscotting, and those under the cornice at the eaves of a house.

Cartouche, in the military art, a case of wood, about three inches thick at the bottom, girt with marlin, holding about four hundred musket-balls, besides six or eight balls of iron, of a pound weight, to be fired out of a hobit, for the defence of a pass, &c.

A cartouche is sometimes made of a globular form, and filled with a ball of a pound weight; and sometimes it is made for the guns, being of a ball of half or quarter a pound weight, according to the nature of the gun, tied in form of a bunch of grapes, on a tompion of wood, and coated over. These were made in the room of partridge-shot.

CARTRIDGE, in the military art, a case of pasteboard or parchment, holding the exact charge of a fire-arm. Those for muskets, carabines, and pistols, hold both the powder and ball for the charge; and those of cannon and mortars are usually in cases of pasteboard or tin, sometimes of wood, half a foot long, adapted to the caliber of the piece.

Cartridge-Box, a case of wood or turned iron, covered with leather, holding a dozen musket-cartridges. It is wore upon a belt, and hangs a little lower than the right pocket-hole.

CARTWRIGHT (William) an eminent divine and poet, born at Northway, near Tewksbury, in Gloucestershire, in September 1611. He finished his education at Oxford; afterwards went into holy orders, and became a most florid preacher in the university. In 1642, he had the place of succentor in the church of Salisbury; and, in 1643, was chosen junior proctor in the university. He was also metaphysical reader there. Wit, judgment, elocution, a graceful person and behaviour, occasioned that encomium of him from dean Fell, "That he was the utmost that "man could come to." He was an expert linguist; an excellent orator; and at the same time was esteemed an admirable poet. There are extant of his, four plays, and some poems. He died in 1643, aged 33.

CARVAGE, *carvagium*, the same with Carrucage.

Henry III. is said to have taken carvage, that is two marks of silver of every knight's fee, towards the marriage of his sister Isabella to the emperor. Carvage could only be imposed on the tenants *in capite*.

Carvage also denotes a privilege whereby a man is exempted from the service of carrucage.

CARUCATURIUS, in ancient law books, he that held land in soccage, or by plough tenure.

CARUCATE. See Carrucate.

CARVER, a cutter of figures or other devices in wood. See Carving.

Carvers answer to what the Romans called *sculptores*, who were different from *cælatores*, or engravers, as these last wrought in metal.

Carver is also an officer of the table, whose business is to cut up the meat, and distribute it to the guests. The word is formed from the Latin *carptor*, which signifies the same. The Romans also called him *carpus*, sometimes *scissor*, *scindendi magister*, and *structor*.

In the great families at Rome, the carver was an officer of some figure. There were masters to teach them the art regularly, by means of figures of animals cut in wood. The Greeks also had their carvers, called κρεωδαιται, q. d. *divisores*, or *distributores*. In the primitive times, the master of the feast carved for all his guests. Thus in Homer, when Agamemnon's ambassadors were entertained at Achilles's table, the hero himself

himself carved the meat. Of later times, the same office on solemn occasions was executed by some of the chief men of Sparta. Some derive the custom of distributing to every guest his portion, from those early ages when the Greeks first left off feeding on acorns, and learned the use of corn: The new diet was so great a delicacy, that to prevent the guests from quarrelling about it, it was found necessary to make a fair distribution.

In Scotland, the king has a hereditary carver in the family of Anstruther.

CARUI, or CARVI, in botany. See CARUM.

CARVING, in a general sense, the art or act of cutting or fashioning a hard body, by means of some sharp instrument, especially a chissel. In this sense carving includes statuary and engraving, as well as cutting in wood.

CARVING, in a more particular sense, is the art of engraving or cutting figures in wood. In this sense *carving*, according to Pliny, is prior both to statuary and painting.

To carve a figure or design, it must be first drawn or pasted on the wood; which done, the rest of the block, not covered by the lines of the design, are to be cut away with little narrow-pointed knives. The wood fitted for the use is that which is hard, tough, and close, as beech, but especially box: to prepare it for drawing the design on, they wash it over with white-lead tempered in water; which better enables it either to bear ink or the crayon, or even to take the impression by chalking. When the design is to be pasted on the wood, this whitening is omitted, and they content themselves with seeing the wood well planed. Then wiping over the printed side of the figure with gum tragacanth dissolved in water, they clap it smooth on the wood, and let it dry; which done, they wet it slightly over, and fret off the surface of the paper gently, till all the strokes of the figure appear distinctly. This done, they fall to cutting or carving, as above.

CARUM, in botany: A genus of the digynia order, belonging to the pentandria class of plants; and in the natural method ranking under the 45th order, *Umbellatae*. The fruit is ovate, oblong, and striated; the involucrum monophyllous; the petals are carinated or keel-shaped below, and emarginated by their inflection.

Species, &c. 1. The carui, or caraway of the shops, grows naturally in many places of Britain. It is a biennial plant, which rises from seeds one year, flowers the next, and perishes soon after the seeds are ripe. It hath a taper root like a parsnip, but much smaller, which runs deep into the ground, sending out many small fibres, and hath a strong aromatic taste. From the root arises one or two smooth, solid, channelled stalks, about two feet high, garnished with winged leaves, having long naked foot-stalks. 2. The hispanicum is also a biennial, and is a native of Spain. It rises with a stronger stalk than the former, which seldom grows more than a foot and half high; but is closely garnished with fine narrow leaves like those of dill. Both these plants are propagated by seeds, which ought to be sown in autumn. Sheep, goats, and swine, eat this plant; cows and horses are not fond of it. Parkinson says, the young roots of caraway are better eating than parsnips. The tender leaves may be boiled with pot herbs. The seeds have an aromatic smell, and a warm pungent taste. They are used in cakes, incrusted with sugar, as sweet-meats, and distilled with spirituous liquors, for the sake of the flavour they afford. They are in the number of the four greater hot seeds; and frequently employed, as a stomachic and carminative, in flatulent colics and the like.

CARUNCULA, or CARUNCLE, in anatomy, a term denoting a little piece of flesh, and applied to several parts of the human body. Thus,

CARUNCULAE *Myrtiformes*, in anatomy, fleshy knobs about the size of a myrtle berry, supposed to owe their origin to the breaking of the hymen. See ANATOMY, n° 108.

CARUNCLES in the urethra, proceeding from a gonorrhoea, or an ulceration of the urethra, may be reduced by introducing the bougies.

CARUS, a sudden deprivation of sense and motion, affecting the whole body. See (the *Index* subjoined to) MEDICINE.

CARUS (Marcus Aurelius), was raised from a low station, by his great merit, to be emperor of Rome in 282. He showed himself worthy of the empire; subdued its enemies; and gave the Romans a prospect of happy days, when he was unfortunately killed by lightning in 284.

CARWAR, a town of Asia, on the coast of Malabar in the East Indies, and where the East India company have a factory, fortified with two bastions. The valleys about it abound in corn and pepper, which last is the best in the East Indies. The woods on the mountains abound with quadrupeds, such as tygers, wolves, monkeys, wild hogs, deer, elks, and a sort of beeves of a prodigious size. The religion of the natives is Paganism; and they have a great many strange and superstitious customs. E. Long. 73. 7. N. Lat. 15. 0.

CARYA-AE, (Stephanus); *Carya*, *arum*, (Pausanias); a town of Laconia, between Sparta and the borders of Messenia: where stood a temple of Diana, thence called *Caryatis*, *idis*; whose annual festival, called *Carya*, *orum*, was celebrated by Spartan virgins with dances. An inhabitant, *Caryates*, and *Caryatis*; *Caryatis apis*, a Laconian bee, (Stephanus.)

CARYAE-*arum*, (anc. geog.), a place in Arcadia, towards the borders of Laconia. Whether from this of Arcadia, or that of Laconia, the *Columnae Caryatides* of Vitruvius and Pliny (which were statues of matrons in stoles or long robes) took the appellation, is disputed.

CARY (Lucius), Lord viscount Falkland, was born in Oxfordshire, about the year 1610; a young nobleman of great abilities and accomplishments. About the time of his father's death in 1633, he was made gentleman of the privy chamber to king Charles I. and afterwards secretary of state. Before the assembling of the long parliament, he had devoted himself to literature, and every pleasure which a fine genius, a generous disposition, and an opulent fortune, could afford: when called into public life, he stood foremost in all attacks on the high prerogatives of the crown; but when civil convulsions came to an extremity, and it was necessary to choose a side, he tempered his zeal,

and

Cary. Caryates.

and defended the limited powers that remained to monarchy. Still anxious however for his country, he seems to have dreaded equally the prosperity of the royal party, or that of the parliament; and among his intimate friends, often sadly reiterated the word *pax* [?]. This excellent nobleman freely exposed his person for the king in all hazardous enterprises, and was killed in the 34th year of his age at the battle of Newbery. In Welwood's memoirs we are told, that whilst he was with the king at Oxford, his majesty went one day to see the public library, where he was shown among other books a Virgil, nobly printed, and exquisitely bound. The lord Falkland, to divert the king, would have his majesty make a trial of his fortune by the Sortes Virgilianæ, an usual kind of divination in ages past, made by opening a Virgil. The king opening the book, the passage which happened to come up, was that part of Dido's imprecation against Æneas, iv. 615, &c. which is thus translated by Dryden.

"Oppress'd with numbers in th' unequal field,
"His men discourag'd, and himself expell'd;
"Let him for succour sue from place to place,
"Torn from his subjects and his son's embrace," &c.

King Charles seeming concerned at this accident, the lord Falkland, who observed it, would likewise try his own fortune in the same manner; hoping he might fall upon some passage that could have no relation to his case, and thereby divert the king's thoughts from any impression the other might make upon him; but the place lord Falkland stumbled upon was yet more suited to his destiny than the other had been to the king's; being the following expressions of Evander, upon the untimely death of his son Pallas, Æn. xi. 152.

"O Pallas! thou hast fail'd thy plighted word.
"To fight with caution, not to tempt the sword,
"I warn'd thee, but in vain; for well I knew
"What perils youthful ardour would pursue;
"That boiling blood would carry thee too far;
"Young as thou wert in dangers, raw to war.
"O curst essay of arms, disast'rous doom,
"Prelude of bloody fields and fights to come!"

He wrote several things, both poetical and political; and in some of the king's declarations, supposed to be penned by lord Falkland, we find the first regular definition of the English constitution that occurs in any composition published by authority. His predecessor, the first viscount Cary, was ennobled for being the first who gave king James an account of queen Elizabeth's death.

Cary (Robert), a learned English chronologer, born in Devonshire about the year 1615. On the restoration, he was preferred to the archdeaconry of Exeter; but on some pretext was ejected in 1664, and spent the rest of his days at his rectory of Portlemouth, where he died in 1688. He published *Palælogia Chronica*, a chronology of ancient times, in three parts, didactical, apodictical, and canonical; and translated the hymns of the church into Latin verse.

CARYATES, in antiquity, a festival in honour of Diana surnamed *Caryatis*, held at Caryum, a city of Laconia. The chief ceremony was a certain dance said to have been invented by Castor and Pollux, and performed by the virgins of the place. During Xerxes's invasion, the Laconians not daring to appear and celebrate the customary solemnity, to prevent incurring the anger of the goddess by such an intermission, the neighbouring swains are said to have assembled and sung pastorals or *bucolismi*, which is said to have been the origin of *bucolic* poetry.

Caryatides || Caryophyllæi.

CARYATIDES, or Caraites. See Architecture, n° 56.

CARYL (Joseph), a divine of the last century, bred at Oxford, and some time preacher to the society of Lincoln's inn, an employment he filled with much applause. He became a frequent preacher before the long parliament, a licenser of their books, one of the assembly of divines, and one of the triers for the approbation of ministers; in all which capacities he showed himself a man of considerable parts and learning, but with great zeal against the king's person and cause. On the restoration of Charles II. he was silenced by the act of uniformity, and lived privately in London, where, besides other works, he distinguished himself by a laborious *Exposition of the Book of Job*; and died in 1673.

CARYLL (John), a late English poet, was of the Roman Catholic persuasion, being secretary to queen Mary the wife of James II. and one who followed the fortunes of his abdicating master; who rewarded him, first with knighthood, and then with the honorary titles of earl Caryll and baron Dartford. How long he continued in that service is not known; but he was in England in the reign of queen Anne, and recommended the subject of the "Rape of the Lock" to Mr Pope, who at its publication addressed it to him. He was also the intimate friend of Pope's "Unfortunate Lady." He was the author of two plays: 1. "The English Princess, or the Death of Richard III. 1667," 4to.; 2. "Sir Salomon, or the Cautious Coxcomb, 1671," 4to.; and in 1700, he published "The Psalms of David, translated from the Vulgate," 12mo. In Tonson's edition of Ovid's Epistles, that of "Briseis to Achilles" is said to be by Sir John Caryll; and in Nichols's Select Collection of Miscellany Poems, vol. II. p. 1. the first Eclogue of Virgil is translated by the same ingenious poet. He was living in 1717, and at that time must have been a very old man. See three of his letters in the "Additions to Pope," vol. II. p. 114.

CARYOCAR, in botany: A genus of the tetragynia order, belonging to the polyandria class of plants. The calyx is quinquepartite, the petals five, the styles more frequently four. The fruit is a plum, with nucleusses, and four furrows netted.

CARYOPHYLLÆI, in botany, the name of a very numerous family or order in Linnæus's fragments of a natural method; containing, besides the class of the same name in Tournefort, many other plants, which from their general appearance seem pretty nearly allied to it. The following are the genera, viz. Agrostema, Cucubalus, Dianthus, Drypis, Gypsophila, Lychnis, Saponaria, Silene, Velezia, Alsine, Arenaria, Bufonia, Cerastium, Cherleria, Glinus, Holosteum, Loeflingia, Moehringia, Polycarpon, Sagina, Spergula, Stellaria, Minuartia, Mollugo, Ortegia, Pharnaceum, Queria. All the plants of this order are herbaceous,

and

and mostly annual. Some of the creeping kinds do not rise an inch, and the tallest exceed not seven or eight feet. See BOTANY, sect. vi. 22.

CARYOPHYLLUS, the PINK, in botany. See DIANTHUS.

CARYOPHYLLUS, the CLOVE TREE, in botany: A genus of the monogynia order, belonging to the polyandria class of plants; and in the natural method ranking under the 19th order, *Hesperideæ*. The corolla is tetrapetalous; the calyx tetraphyllous; the berry monospermous below the receptacle of the flower. Of this there is but one species, viz. the aromaticus, which is a native of the Molucca islands, particularly of Amboyna, where it is principally cultivated. The clove-tree resembles, in its bark, the olive; and is about the height of the laurel, which it also resembles in its leaves. No verdure is ever seen under it. It has a great number of branches, at the extremities of which are produced vast quantities of flowers, that are first white, then green, and at last pretty red and hard. When they arrive at this degree of maturity, they are, properly speaking, *cloves*. As they dry, they assume a dark yellowish cast; and, when gathered, become of a deep brown. The season for gathering the cloves is from October to February. The boughs of the trees are then strongly shaken, or the cloves beat down with long reeds. Large cloths are spread to receive them, and they are afterwards either dried in the sun or in the smoke of the bamboo-cane. The cloves which escape the notice of those who gather them, or are purposely left upon the tree, continue to grow till they are about an inch in thickness; and these falling off, produce new plants, which do not bear in less than eight or nine years. Those which are called *mother-cloves* are inferior to the common sort; but are preserved in sugar by the Dutch; and, in long voyages, eat after their meals, to promote digestion.

The clove, to be in perfection, must be full sized, heavy, oily, and easily broken; of a fine smell, and of a hot aromatic taste, so as almost to burn the throat. It should make the fingers smart when handled, and leave an oily moisture upon them when pressed. In the East Indies, and in some parts of Europe, it is so much admired as to be thought an indispensable ingredient in almost every dish. It is put into their food, liquors, wines, and enters likewise the composition of their perfumes. Considered as medicines, cloves are very hot, stimulating, aromatics; and possess in an eminent degree the general virtues of substances of this class. Their pungency resides in their resin; or rather in a combination of resin with essential oil: for the spirituous extract is very pungent; but if the oil and the resin contained in this extract are separated from each other by distillation, the oil will be very mild; and any pungency which it does retain, proceeds from some small portion of adhering resin, and the remaining resin will be insipid. No plant, or part of any plant, contains such a quantity of oil as cloves do. From 16 ounces Newman obtained by distillation two ounces and two drams, and Hoffman obtained an ounce and an half of oil from two ounces of the spice. The oil is specifically heavier than water. Cloves acquire weight by imbibing water; and this they will do at some considerable distance. The Dutch, who trade in cloves, make a considerable advantage by knowing this secret. They sell them always by weight; and when a bag of cloves is ordered, they hang it, for several hours before it is sent in, over a vessel of water, at about two feet distance from the surface. This will add many pounds to the weight, which the unwary purchaser pays for on the spot. This is sometimes practised in Europe, as well as in the spice islands: but the degree of moisture must be more carefully watched in the latter; for there a bag of cloves will, in one night's time, attract so much water, that it may be pressed out of them by squeezing them with the hand.

The clove tree is never cultivated in Europe. At Amboyna the company have allotted the inhabitants 4000 parcels of land, on each of which they were at first allowed, and about the year 1720 compelled, to plant about 125 trees, amounting in all to 500.000. Each of these trees produces annually on an average more than two pounds of cloves; and consequently the collective produce must weigh more than a million. The cultivator is paid with the specie that is constantly returned to the company, and receives some unbleached cottons which are brought from Coromandel.

CARYOTA, in botany: A genus belonging to the natural order of *Palmæ*. The male calyx is common, the corolla tripartite; the stamina very numerous: the female calyx the same; the corolla tripartite; one pistil, and a dispermous berry.

CASA, in ancient and middle-age writers, is used to denote a cottage or house.

Casa Santa, denotes the chapel of the holy virgin at Loretto.—The *Santa Casa* is properly the house, or rather chamber, in which the blessed virgin is said to have been born, where she was betrothed to her spouse Joseph, where the angel saluted her, the Holy Ghost overshadowed her, and by consequence where the Son of God was conceived or incarnated. Of this building the Catholics tell many wonderful stories too childish to transcribe. The *Santa Casa* or holy chamber consists of one room, forty-four spans long, eighteen broad, and twenty-three high. Over the chimney, in a niche, stands the image called the great *Madona* or Lady, four feet high, made of cedar, and, as they say, wrought by St Luke, who was a carver as well as a physician. The mantle or robe she has on, is covered with innumerable jewels of inestimable value. She has a crown, given her by Louis XIII. of France, and a little crown for her son.

CASAL, a strong town of Italy in Mountferrat, with a citadel and a bishop's see. It was taken by the French from the Spaniards in 1640; and the duke of Mantua sold it to the French in 1681. In 1695 it was taken by the allies, who demolished the fortifications; but the French retook it, and fortified it again. The king of Sardinia became master of it in 1706, from whom the French took it in 1745; however, the king of Sardinia got possession again in 1746. It is seated on the river Po, in E. Long. 8. 37. N. Lat. 54. 7.

Casal-Maggiore, a small strong town of Italy, in the duchy of Milan, seated on the river Po. E. Long. 11. 5. N. Lat. 45. 6.

CASA-NOVA (Marc Antony), a Latin poet, born

at Rome, succeeded particularly in epigrams. The poems he composed in honour of the illustrious men of Rome are also much esteemed. He died in 1527.

CASAN, a considerable town of Asia, and capital of a kingdom of the same name in the Russian empire, with a strong castle, a citadel, and an archbishop's see. The country about it is very fertile in all sorts of fruits, corn, and pulse. It carries on a great trade in furs, and furnishes wood for the building of ships. The kingdom of Casan is bounded on the north by Permia, on the east by Siberia, on the south by the river Wolga, and on the west by the province of Moscow. E. Long. 51. 25. N. Lat. 55. 38.

CASAS (Bartholomew de las), bishop of Chiapa, distinguished for his humanity and zeal for the conversion of the Indians, was born at Seville in 1474; and went with his father, who sailed to America with Christopher Columbus in 1493. At his return to Spain he embraced the state of an ecclesiastic, and obtained a curacy in the island of Cuba; but some time after quitted his cure in order to procure liberty for the Indians, whom he saw treated by the Spaniards in the most cruel and barbarous manner, which naturally gave them an unconquerable aversion to Christianity. Bartholomew exerted himself with extraordinary zeal, for 50 years together, in his endeavours to persuade the Spaniards that they ought to treat the Indians with equity and mildness; for which he suffered a number of persecutions from his countrymen. At last the court, moved by his continual remonstrances, made laws in favour of the Indians, and gave orders to the governors to observe them, and see them executed *. He died at Madrid in 1566, aged 92. He wrote several works, which breathe nothing but humanity and virtue. The principal of them are, 1. An account of the destruction of the Indies. 2. Several treatises in favour of the Indies, against Dr Sepulveda, who wrote a book to justify the inhuman barbarities committed by the Spaniards. 3. A very curious, and now scarce, work in Latin, on this question, "Whether kings or princes can, consistently with conscience, or in virtue of any right or title, alienate their subjects, and place them under the dominion of another sovereign?"

* See the article *Mexico*.

CASATI (Paul), a learned Jesuit, born at Placentia in 1617, entered early among the Jesuits; and, after having taught mathematics and divinity at Rome, was sent into Sweden to queen Christina, whom he prevailed on to embrace the popish religion. He wrote, 1. *Vacuum proscriptum.* 2. *Terra machinis mota.* 3. *Mechanicorum, libri octo.* 4. *De Igne Dissertationes*; which is much esteemed. 5. *De Angelis Disputatio Theolog.* 6. *Hydrostatice Dissertationes.* 7. *Optice Disputationes*: It is remarkable that he wrote this treatise on optics at 88 years of age, and after he was blind. He also wrote several books in Italian.

CASAURON (Isaac), was born at Geneva in 1559; and Henry IV. appointed him his library-keeper in 1603. After this prince's death, he went into England with Sir Henry Wotton, ambassador from King James I. where he was kindly received and engaged in writing against Baronius's annals: he died not long after this, in 1614; and was interred in Westminster-abbey, where a monument was erected to him. He was greatly skilled in the Greek, and in criticism; published several valuable commentaries; and received the highest elogiums from all his cotemporaries.

CASAUBON (Meric), son of the preceding, was born at Geneva in 1599. He was bred at Oxford, and took the degree of master of arts in 1621. The same year he published a book in defence of his father against the calumnies of certain Roman Catholics; which gained him the favour of King James I. and a considerable reputation abroad. He was made prebendary of Canterbury by archbishop Laud. In the beginning of the civil war he lost all his spiritual promotions, but still continued to publish excellent works. Oliver Cromwell, then lieutenant-general of the parliament's forces, would have employed his pen in writing the history of the late war; but he declined it, owning, that his subject would oblige him to make such reflections as would be ungrateful, if not injurious, to his lordship. Notwithstanding this answer, Cromwell, sensible of his worth, ordered three or four hundred pounds to be paid him by a bookseller in London whose name was Cromwell, on demand, without requiring from him any acknowledgment of his benefactor. But this offer he rejected, though his circumstances were then mean. At the same time it was proposed by his friend Mr Greaves, who belonged to the library at St James's, that, if Casaubon would gratify Cromwell in the request above mentioned, all his father's books which were then in the royal library, having been purchased by King James, should be restored to him, and a pension of 300 *l.* a-year paid to the family as long as the youngest son of Dr Casaubon should live; but this also was refused. He likewise refused handsome offers from Christina queen of Sweden, being determined to spend the remainder of his life in England. At the restoration he recovered all his preferments, and continued writing till his death in 1671. He was the author of an English translation of Marcus Aurelius Antoninus's meditations, and of Lucius Florus; editions of several of the classics, with notes; a treatise of use and custom; a treatise of enthusiasm; with many other works; and he left a number of MSS. to the university of Oxford.

CASAURINA, in botany: A genus of the monandria order, belonging to the monoecia class of plants. The male has the calyx of the amentum; the corolla a bipartite small scale. The female has a calyx of the amentum, no corolla; the style bipartite.

CASCADE, a steep fall of water from a higher into a lower place. The word is French, formed of the Italian *cascata*, which signifies the same; of *cascare*, *to fall*; and that from the Latin *cadere*.

Cascades are either natural, as that at Tivoli, &c. or artificial, as those of Versailles, &c. and either falling with gentle descent, as those of Sceaux; or in form of a buffet, as at Trianon; or down steps, in form of a perron, as at St Cloud; or from basin to basin, &c.

CASCAIS, a town of Estremadura in Portugal, situated at the mouth of the river Tagus, 17 miles east of Lisbon. W. Long. 10. 15. N. Lat. 38. 40.

CASCARILLA. See CLUTIA and CROTON.

CASE, among grammarians, implies the different

inflections

inflections or terminations of nouns, serving to express the different relations they bear to each other, and to the things they represent. See GRAMMAR.

CASE also denotes a receptacle for various articles; as a case of knives, of lancets, of pistols, &c.

CASE, in printing, a large flat oblong frame placed aslope, divided into several compartments or little square cells; in each of which are lodged a number of types or letters of the same kind, whence the compositor takes them out, each as he needs it, to compose his matter. See PRINTING.

CASE is also used for a certain numerous quantity of divers things. Thus a case of crown-glass contains usually 24 tables, each table being nearly circular, and about three feet six inches diameter; of Newcastle glass, 35 tables; of Normandy glass, 25.

Case-Hardening of Iron, is a superficial conversion of that metal into steel, by the ordinary method of conversion, namely by cementation with vegetable or animal coals. This operation is generally practised upon small pieces of iron wrought into tools and instruments to which a superficial conversion is sufficient; and it may be performed conveniently by putting the pieces of iron to be case-hardened, together with the cement, into an iron box, which is to be closely shut and exposed to a red heat during some hours. By this cementation a certain thickness from the surface of the iron will be converted into steel, and a proper hardness may be afterwards given by sudden extinction of the heated pieces of converted iron in a cold fluid. See STEEL.

Case-Shot, in the military art, musket-balls, stones, old iron, &c. put into cases, and shot out of great guns.

CASEMENT, or CASEMATE, in architecture, a hollow moulding, which some architects make one-sixth of a circle, and others one-fourth.

CASEMENT is also used in building, for a little moveable window, usually within a larger, being made to open or turn on hinges.

CASERN, in fortification, lodgings built in garrison-towns, generally near the rampart, or in the waste places of the town, for lodging soldiers of the garrison. There are usually two beds in each casern for six soldiers to lie, who mount the guard alternately; the third part being always on duty.

CASERTA, an episcopal town of Italy in the kingdom of Naples, and in the Terra di Lavoro, with the title of a duchy, seated at the foot of a mountain of the same name, in E. Long. 15. 5. N. Lat. 41. 5.

CASES (Peter-James), of Paris, the most eminent painter of the French school; the churches of Paris and of Versailles abound with his works. He died in 1754, aged 79.

CASH, in a commercial style, signifies the stock or ready money which a merchant or other person has in his present disposal to negociate; so called from the French term *caisse*, i. e. *chest* or *coffer* for the keeping of money.

M. Savary shows, that the management of the cash of a company is the most considerable article, and that whereon its good or ill success chiefly depends.

Cash-Book. See BOOK-KEEPING.

CASHEL, or CASSEL, a town of Ireland in the county of Tipperary, and province of Munster, with an archbishop's see. The ruins of the old cathedral testify its having been an extensive as well as handsome Gothic structure, boldly towering on the celebrated rock of Cashel, which taken together form a magnificent object, and bear honourable testimony to the labour and ingenuity, as well as the piety and zeal, of its former inhabitants. It is seen at a great distance, and in many directions. Adjoining it are the ruins of the chapel of Cormac M'Culinan, at once king and archbishop of Cashel, supposed to be the first stone building in Ireland; and seems, by its rude imitation of pillars and capitals, to have been copied after the Grecian architecture, and long to have preceded that which is usually called *Gothic*. Cormac M'Culinan was a prince greatly celebrated by the Irish historians for his learning, piety, and valour. He wrote, in his native language, a history of Ireland, commonly called the *Psalter of Cashel*, which is still extant, and contains the most authentic account we have of the annals of the country to that period, about the year 900. On the top of the rock of Cashel, and adjoining the cathedral, is a lofty round tower, which proudly defied the too successful attempts of archbishop Price, who in this century unroofed and thereby demolished the ancient cathedral founded by St Patrick. In the choir are the monuments of Myler Magrath, archbishop of this see, in the reign of queen Elisabeth, and some other curious remains of antiquity. Cashel was formerly the royal seat and metropolis of the kings of Munster; and on the ascent to the cathedral is a large stone on which every new king of Munster was, as the inhabitants report from tradition, solemnly proclaimed. Cashel is at present but small to what we may suppose it to have been in ancient days. The archbishop's palace is a fine building. Here is a very handsome market house, a sessions house, the county infirmary, a charter school for twenty boys and the same number of girls, and a very good barrack for two companies of foot. The present archbishop Dr Agar hath finished a very elegant church begun by his predecessor. W. Long. 7. 36. N. Lat. 52. 16.

CASHEW-NUT. See ANACARDIUM.

CASHIER, the cash-keeper; he who is charged with the receiving and paying the debts of a society.—In the generality of foundations, the cashier is called *treasurer*.

Cashiers of the Bank, are officers who sign the notes that are issued out, examine and mark them when returned for payment, &c.

CASHMIRE, a province of Asia in the dominions of the Mogul. It is situated at the extremity of Hindostan, northward of Lahore, and is bounded on the one side by a ridge of the great Caucasus, and on the other by the little Tartarian Thibet and Moultan. The extent of it is not very considerable; but being girt in by a zone of hills, and elevated very considerably above an arid plain, which stretches many miles around it, the scenes which it exhibits are wild and picturesque. Rivers, hills, and vallies, charmingly diversify the landscape. Here, Mr Sullivan† informs us, a cascade rushes from a foaming precipice; there a tranquil stream glides placidly along; the tinkling rill, too, sounds amidst the groves; and the feathered choristers sing the song of love, close sheltered in the glade.

† *Philosophical Rhapsodies.*

Cashmire ‖ Casing.

At what time Cashmire came under the dominion of the Mogul government, and how long, and in what manner it was independent, before it was annexed to the territories of the house of Timur, are points that are beyond our present purpose. Though inconsiderable as to its revenues, it was uniformly held in the highest estimation by the emperors of Hindostan. Thither they repaired, in the plenitude of their greatness, when the affairs of state would admit of their absence; and there they divested themselves of form and all the oppressive ceremony of state. The royal manner of travelling to Cashmire was grand, though tedious and unwieldy, and showed, in an eminent degree, the splendour and magnificence of an eastern potentate. Aurungzebe, we are told, seldom began his march to that country, for a march certainly it was to be called, without an escort of 80,000 or 100,000 fighting men, besides the gentlemen of his household, the attendants of his seraglio, and most of his officers of state. These all continued with him during the time he was on the road, which generally was a month: but no sooner was he arrived at the entrance of those aërial regions, than, with a select party of friends, he separated from the rest of his retinue, and with them ascended the defiles which led him to his Eden.

The temperature of the air of Cashmire, elevated as it is so much above the adjoining country, together with the streams which continually pour from its mountains, enables the husbandman to cultivate with success the soil he appropriates to agriculture; whilst the gardener's labour is amply repaid in the abundant produce of his fruit. In short, nature wears her gayest clothing in this enchanting spot. The rivers supply the inhabitants with almost every species of fish; the hills yield sweet herbage for the cattle; the plains are covered with grain of different denominations; and the woods are stored with variety of game. The Cashmirean, according to our author, seem a race distinct from all others in the East: their persons are more elegant, and their complexions more delicate and more tinged with red.

On the decadence of the Mogul power in Hindostan, Cashmire felt some of the ravages of war. It is now however in peace; and the inhabitants are desirous of keeping it so. They are sprightly and ingenious; and have several curious manufactures much valued in India. They are all Mahometans or Idolaters. Cashmire is the capital town.

CASIMIR, the name of several kings of Poland. See (*History of*) POLAND.

CASIMIR (Matthias Sarbiewski), a Polish Jesuit, born in 1597. He was a most excellent poet; and is, says M. Baillet, an exception to the general rule of Aristotle and the other ancients, which teaches us to expect nothing ingenious and delicate from northern climates. His odes, epodes, and epigrams, have been thought not inferior to those of the finest wits of Greece and Rome. Dr Watts has translated one or two of his small pieces, which are added to his Lyric Poems. He died at Warsaw in 1640, aged 43. There have been many editions of his poems, the best of which is that of Paris, 1759.

CASING *of* TIMBER-WORK, among builders, is the plastering the house all over the outside with mortar, and then striking it while wet by a ruler, with the corner of a trowel, to make it resemble the joints of free-stone. Some direct it to be done upon heart-laths, because the mortar would, in a little time, decay the sap-laths; and to lay on the mortar in two thicknesses, viz. a second before the first is dry.

Cask ‖ Caslon.

CASK, a piece of defensive armour wherewith to cover the head and neck; otherwise called the *head-piece* and *helmet**. The word is French, *casque*, from *cassicum* or *cassicus*, a diminutive of *cassis* a helmet. Le Gendre observes, that anciently, in France, the gens d'arms all wore *casks*. The king wore a *cask* gilt; the dukes and counts silvered; gentlemen of extraction polished steel; and the rest plain iron.

* See Helmet.

The cask is frequently seen on ancient medals, where we may observe great varieties in the form and fashion thereof; as the Greek fashion, the Roman fashion, &c. F. Joubert makes it the most ancient of all the coverings of the head, as well as the most universal. Kings, emperors, and even gods themselves, are seen therewith. That which covers the head of Rome has usually two wings like those of Mercury: and that of some kings is furnished with horns like those of Jupiter Ammon; and sometimes barely bulls or rams horns, to express uncommon force.

CASK, in heraldry, the same with helmet. See HERALDRY, n° 45.

CASK, a vessel of capacity, for preserving liquors of divers kinds; and sometimes also dry goods, as sugar, almonds, &c.—A cask of sugar is a barrel of that commodity, containing from eight to eleven hundred weight. A cask of almonds is about three hundred weight.

CASKET, in a general sense, a little coffer or cabinet. See CABINET.

CASKETS, in the sea language, are small ropes made of sinnet, and fastened to gromets, or little rings upon the yards: their use is to make fast the sail to the yard when it is to be furled.

CASLON (William), eminent in an art of the greatest consequence to literature, the art of letter-founding, was born in 1692, in that part of the town of Hales Owen which is situated in Shropshire. Tho' he justly attained the character of being the Coryphæus in that employment, he was not brought up to the business; and it is observed by Mr Mores, that this handy-work is so concealed among the artificers of it, that he could not discover that any one had taught it to another, but every person who had used it had learned it of his own genuine inclination. Mr Caslon served a regular apprenticeship to an engraver of ornaments on gun-barrels; and after the expiration of his term, carried on this trade in Vine-street, near the Minories. He did not, however, solely confine his ingenuity to that instrument; but employed himself likewise in making tools for the book-binders, and for the chasing of silver plate. Whilst he was engaged in this business, the elder Mr Bowyer accidentally saw, in a bookseller's shop, the lettering of a book uncommonly neat; and inquiring who the artist was by whom the letters were made, was hence induced to seek an acquaintance with Mr Caslon. Not long after, Mr Bowyer took Mr Caslon to Mr James's foundery, in Bartholomew-close. Caslon had never before that time seen any part of the business; and being asked by his friend, if he thought he could undertake to cut types,

Biog. Brit. and Anecdotes of Bowyer, by Nichols.

Caſlon, Caſpian. he requeſted a ſingle day to conſider the matter, and then replied that he had no doubt but he could. Upon this anſwer, Mr Bowyer, Mr Bettenham, and Mr Watts had ſuch a confidence in his abilities, that they lent him 500l. to begin the undertaking, and he applied himſelf to it with equal aſſiduity and ſucceſs. In 1720, the ſociety for promoting Chriſtian knowledge, in conſequence of a repreſentation from Mr Solomon Negri, a native of Damaſcus in Syria, who was well ſkilled in the Oriental tongues, and had been profeſſor of Arabic in places of note, deemed it expedient to print, for the uſe of the Eaſtern churches, the New Teſtament and Pſalter in the Arabic language. Theſe were intended for the benefit of the poor Chriſtians in Paleſtine, Syria, Meſopotamia, Arabia, and Egypt, the conſtitution of which countries did not permit the exerciſe of the art of printing. Upon this occaſion Mr Caſlon was pitched upon to cut the fount; in his ſpecimens of which he diſtinguiſhed it by the name of English Arabic. Under the farther encouragement of Mr Bowyer, Mr Bettenham, and Mr Watts, he proceeded with vigour in his employment; and he arrived at length to ſuch perfection, that he not only freed us from the neceſſity of importing types from Holland, but in the beauty and elegance of thoſe made by him he ſo far exceeded the productions of the beſt artificers, that his workmanſhip was frequently exported to the Continent. In ſhort, his foundery became, in proceſs of time, the moſt capital one that exiſts in this or in foreign countries. Having acquired opulence in the courſe of his employment, he was put into the commiſſion of the peace for the county of Middleſex. Towards the latter end of his life, his eldeſt ſon being in partnerſhip with him, he retired in a great meaſure from the active execution of buſineſs. His death happened in January 1766.

CASPIAN sea, a large lake of ſalt-water in Aſia, bounded by the province of Aſtrakan on the north, and by part of Perſia on the ſouth, eaſt, and weſt. It is upwards of 400 miles long from ſouth to north, and 300 broad from eaſt to weſt. This ſea forms ſeveral gulfs, and embraces between Aſtrakan and Aſtrabad an incredible number of ſmall iſlands. Its bottom is mud, but ſometimes mixed with ſhells. At the diſtance of ſome German miles from land it is 300 fathoms deep; but on approaching the ſhore it is every where ſo ſhallow, that the ſmalleſt veſſels, if loaded, are obliged to remain at a diſtance.

When we conſider that the Caſpian is incloſed on all ſides by land, and that its banks are in the neighbourhood of very high mountains, we eaſily ſee why the navigation in it ſhould be perfectly different from that in every other ſea. There are certain winds that domineer over it with ſuch abſolute ſway, that veſſels are often deprived of every reſource; and in the whole extent of it there is not a port that can truly be called ſafe. The north, north-eaſt, and eaſt winds, blow moſt frequently, and occaſion the moſt violent tempeſts. Along the eaſtern ſhore the eaſt winds prevail; for which reaſon veſſels bound from Perſia to Aſtrakan always direct their courſe along this ſhore.

Although the extent of the Caſpian Sea is immenſe, the variety of its productions is exceedingly ſmall. This undoubtedly proceeds from its want of communication with the ocean, which cannot impart to it any portion of its inexhauſtible ſtores. But the animals which this lake nouriſhes multiply to ſuch a degree, that the Ruſſians, who alone are in condition to make them turn to account, juſtly conſider them as a never failing ſource of profit and wealth. It will be underſtood that we ſpeak of the fiſh of the Caſpian and of its fiſheries, which make the ſole occupation and principal trade of the people inhabiting the banks of the Wolga and of the Jaik. This buſineſs is diſtinguiſhed into the great and leſſer fiſheries. The fiſh comprehended under the firſt diviſion, ſuch as the ſturgeon and others, abound in all parts of the Caſpian as well as in the rivers that communicate with it, and which they aſcend at ſpawning-time. The ſmall fiſhes, ſuch as the ſalmon and many others, obſerve the general law of quitting the ſalt waters for the freſh, nor is there an inſtance of one of them remaining conſtantly in the ſea.

Seals are the only quadrupeds that inhabit the Caſpian; but they are there in ſuch numbers as to afford the means of ſubſiſtence to many people in that country as well as in Greenland. The varieties of the ſpecies are numerous, diverſified, however, only by the colour. Some are quite black, others quite white; there are ſome whitiſh, ſome yellowiſh, ſome of a mouſe-colour, and ſome ſtreaked like a tiger. They crawl by means of their fore-feet upon the iſlands, where they become the prey of the fiſhermen, who kill them with long clubs. As ſoon as one is diſpatched, he is ſucceeded by ſeveral who come to the aſſiſtance of their unhappy companion, but come only to ſhare his fate. They are exceedingly tenacious of life, and endure more than thirty hard blows before they die. They will even live for ſeveral days after having received many mortal wounds. They are moſt terrified by fire and ſmoke; and as ſoon as they perceive them, retreat with the utmoſt expedition to the ſea. Theſe animals grow ſo very fat, that they look rather like oil-bags than animals. At Aſtrakan is made a ſort of grey ſoap with their fat mixed with pot-aſhes, which is much valued for its property of cleanſing and taking greaſe from woollen ſtuffs. The greateſt numbers of them are killed in ſpring and autumn. Many ſmall veſſels go from Aſtrakan merely to catch ſeals.

If the Caſpian has few quadrupeds, it has in proportion ſtill fewer of thoſe natural productions which are looked upon as proper only to the ſea. There have never been found in it any zoophytes, nor any animal of the order of moluſca. The ſame may almoſt be ſaid of ſhells; the only ones found being three or four ſpecies of cockle, the common muſcle, ſome ſpecies of ſnails, and one or two others.

But to compenſate this ſterility, it abounds in birds of different kinds. Of thoſe that frequent the ſhores there are many ſpecies of the gooſe and duck kind, of the ſtork and heron, and many others of the wader tribe. Of birds properly aquatic, it contains the grebe, the creſted diver, the pelican, the cormorant, and almoſt every ſpecies of gull. Crows are ſo fond of fiſh, that they haunt the ſhores of the Caſpian in prodigious multitudes.

The waters of this lake are very impure, the great number of rivers that run into it, and the nature of its bottom, affecting it greatly. It is true, that in general the waters are ſalt; but through the whole weſtern ſhore extends

extends from the 46th to the 55th degree of north latitude, and though one might conclude from analogy that these waters would contain a great deal of salt, yet experiments prove the contrary: and it is certain that the saltness of this sea is diminished by the north, north-east, and north-west winds; although we may with equal reason conclude, that it owes its saltness to the mines of salt which lie along its two banks, and which are either already known or will be known to posterity. The depth of these waters also diminishes gradually as you approach the shores, and their saltness in the same way grows less in proportion to their proximity to the land, the north winds not unfrequently causing the rivers to discharge into it vast quantities of troubled water impregnated with clay. These variations which the sea is exposed to are more or less considerable according to the nature of the winds; they affect the colour of the river waters to a certain distance from the shore, till these mixing with those of the sea, which then resume the ascendency, the fine green colour appears, which is natural to the ocean, and to all those bodies of water that communicate with it.

It is well known, that besides its salt taste, all sea-water has a sensible bitterness, which must be attributed not only to the salt itself, but to the mixture of different substances that unite with it, particularly to different sorts of alum, the ordinary effect of different combinations of acids. Besides this, the waters of the Caspian have another taste, bitter too, but quite distinct, which affects the tongue with an impression similar to that made by the bile of animals; a property which is peculiar to this sea, though not equally sensible at all seasons. When the north and north-west winds have raged for a considerable time, this bitter taste is sensibly felt; but when the wind has been south, very imperfectly. We shall endeavour to account for this phenomenon.

The Caspian is surrounded on its western side by the mountains of Caucasus, which extend from Derbent to the Black Sea. These mountains make a curve near Astrakan, and directing their course towards the eastern shore of the Caspian, lose themselves near the mouth of the Jaik, where they become secondary mountains, being disposed in strata. As Caucasus is an inexhaustible magazine of combustible substances, it consequently lodges an astonishing quantity of metals in its bowels. Accordingly, along the foot of this immense chain of mountains, we sometimes meet with warm springs, sometimes springs of naphtha of different quality; sometimes we find native sulphur, mines of vitriol, or lakes heated by internal fires. Now the foot of mount Caucasus forming the immediate western shore of the Caspian Sea, it is very easy to imagine that a great quantity of the constituent parts of the former must be communicated to the latter: but it is chiefly to the naphtha, which abounds so much in the countries which surround this sea, that we must attribute the true cause of the bitterness peculiar to its waters; for it is certain that this bitumen flows from the mountains, sometimes in all its purity, and sometimes mixed with other substances which it acquires in its passage through subterranean channels, from the most interior parts of these mountains to the sea, where it falls to the bottom by its specific gravity. It is certain too, that the north and north-west winds detach the greatest quantities of this naphtha; whence it is evident that the bitter taste must be most sensible when these winds prevail. We may also comprehend why this taste is not so strong at the surface or in the neighbourhood of the shore, the waters there being less impregnated with salt, and the naphtha which is united with the water by the salt, being then either carried to a distance by the winds or precipitated to the bottom.

But it is not a bitter taste alone that the naphtha communicates to the waters of the Caspian; these waters were analysed by M. Gmelion, and found to contain, besides the common sea-salt, a considerable proportion of Glauber-salt, intimately united with the former, and which is evidently a production of the naphtha.

As the waters of the Caspian have no outlet, they are discharged by subterraneous canals through the earth, where they deposit beds of salt; the surface of which corresponds with that of the level of the sea. The two great desarts which extend from it to the east and west are chiefly composed of a saline earth, in which the salt is formed by efflorescence into regular crystals; for which reason salt showers and dews are exceedingly common in that neighbourhood. The salt of the marshes at Astrakan, and that found in efflorescence in the desarts, is by no means pure sea-salt, but much debased by the bitter Glauber salt we mentioned above. In many places indeed it is found with crystals of a lozenge shape, which is peculiar to it, without any cubical appearance, the form peculiar to crystals of sea-salt.

A great deal has been written on the successive augmentation and decrease of the Caspian sea, but with little truth. There is indeed to be perceived in it a certain rise and fall of its waters; in which, however, no observation has ever discovered any regularity.

Many suppose (and there are strong presumptions in favour of the supposition), that the shores of the Caspian were much more extensive in ancient times than they are at present, and that it once communicated with the Black Sea. It is probable too, that the level of this last sea was once much higher than it is at present. If then it be allowed, that the waters of the Black Sea, before it procured an exit by the Straits of Constantinople, rose several fathoms above their present level, which from many concurring circumstances may easily be admitted; it will follow, that all the plains, of the Crimea, of the Kuman, of the Walga, and of the Jaik, and those of Great Tartary beyond the lake of Aral, in ancient times formed but one sea, which embraced the northern extremity of Caucasus by a narrow strait of little depth; the vestiges of which are still obvious in the river Mantysch.

CASSADA. See JATROPHA

CASSANA (Nicolo), called NICOLETTO, an eminent Italian painter, was born at Venice in 1659, and became a disciple of his father Giovanni Francesco Cassano, a Genoese, who had been taught the art of painting by Bernardino Strozzi. He so distinguished himself not only by the beauty of his colouring, but by the gracefulness of his figures in historical compositions, as well as in portrait. The most eminent personages solicited him to enrich their cabinets with some of his performances; and were more particularly desirous to obtain their portraits, because in that branch he excelled beyond competition. The Grand Duke of Tuscany, who was an excellent judge of merit in all professions, and as liberal an encourager of it, invited Nicoletto to his court; and he there painted the portraits of that prince and the princess Violante his consort. Those performances procured him uncommon applause, as well as a noble gratuity, and he was employed and caressed by the principal nobility of Florence. Beside several historical subjects painted by this master while he resided in that city, one was a very capital design: The subject of it was the *Conspiracy of Catiline*; it consisted of nine figures as large as life, down to the knees; and the two principal figures were represented as with one hand joined in the presence of their companions, and in their other hand holding a cup of blood. Some of the English nobility on their travels sat to him for their portraits; which being sent to London, and highly admired, Nicoletto was invited to England, with strong assurances of a generous reception; and on his arrival he experienced the kindness, the respect, and the liberality, so peculiar to the natives of that kingdom. He had the honour of being introduced to the presence of queen Anne, and to paint her portrait; in which he succeeded so happily, that the queen distinguished him by many marks of favour and honour; but he had not the happiness to enjoy his good fortune for any length of time, dying in London, universally regretted, in the year 1713.

Cassana (Giovanni Agostino), called *L'Abate Cassana*, was brother to the preceding, and born in 1664. He was educated along with him by their father Francesco Cassana; and he finished his studies at Venice, where his brother Niculo resided for some time. Although he composed and designed historical subjects with expertness, and with a correctness of outline equal to his brother; yet from prudence and fraternal affection, he declined to interfere with him, and chose therefore to design and paint all sorts of animals and fruits. In that style he arrived at a high degree of excellence, imitating nature with exactness, beauty, and truth; expressing the various plumage of his birds, and the hairs of the different animals with such tenderness and delicacy as rendered them estimable to all judges and lovers of the art. His works were admitted into the collections of those of the first rank, and accounted ornaments of those repositories of what is curious or valuable. He also painted fruits of those kinds which were the most uncommon, or naturally of odd and singular colours; and such fishes as seemed worthy to excite admiration by their unusual form, colour, or appearance. But besides those subjects, he sometimes painted the portraits of particular persons of distinction, which he designed, coloured, and touched, with the same degree of merit that was visible in all his other performances. At last he determined to visit Genoa, where his family had lived in esteem; and took with him several pictures which he had already finished. His intention was to display his generosity, and to appear as a person of more wealth and of greater consequence than he really was; and to support that character, he bestowed his pictures to several of the principal nobility of that city. But, unhappily, he experienced no grateful return for all that prodigal munificence: he reduced himself by that vain liberality to the most necessitous circumstances; was deprived of the means to procure for himself even the common necessaries of life; and wasted away the remainder of his days in the bitterness of poverty, misery, and neglect.

CASSANDER, king of Macedon after Alexander the Great, was the son of Antipater. He made several conquests in Greece, abolished democracy at Athens, and gave the government of that state to the orator Demetrius. Olympias, the mother of Alexander, having caused Aridæus and his wife Euridyce, with others of Cassander's party, to be put to death; he besieged Pydna, whither the queen had retired, took it by a stratagem, and caused her to be put to death. He married Thessalonica the sister of Alexander the Great; and killed Roxana and Alexander, the wife and son of that conqueror. At length he entered into an alliance with Seleucus and Lysimachus, against Antigonus and Demetrius; over whom he obtained a great victory near Ipsus in Phrygia, 301 years before the Christian era, and died three years after, in the 19th year of his reign.

CASSANDRA, in fabulous history, the daughter of Priam and Hecuba, was beloved of Apollo, who promised to bestow on her the spirit of prophecy, provided she would consent to his love. Cassandra seemed to accept the proposal; but had no sooner obtained that gift, than she laughed at the tempter, and broke her word. Apollo, being enraged, revenged himself by causing no credit be given to her predictions; hence she in vain prophesied the ruin of Troy. Ajax, the son of Oileus, having ravished her in the temple of Minerva, he was struck with thunder. She fell into the hands of Agamemnon, who loved her to distraction; but in vain did she predict that he would be assassinated in his own country. He was killed, with her, by the intrigues of Clytemnestra; but their death was avenged by Orestes.

CASSANO, a town of Italy in the duchy of Milan, rendered remarkable by an obstinate battle fought there between the Germans and French in 1705. It is subject to the House of Austria, and is seated on the river Adda, in E. Long. 10. 0. N. Lat. 45. 20.

CASSANO, a town of Italy in Calabria citerior, in the kingdom of Naples, with a bishop's see. E. Long. 16. 30. N. Lat. 39. 55.

CASSAVI, or Cassada. See Jatropha.

CASSEL, a town of French Flanders, and capital of a chatellany of the same name: It is seated on a mountain, where the terrace of the castle is still to be seen; and from whence there is one of the finest prospects in the world; for one may see no less than 32 towns, with a great extent of the sea, from whence it is distant 15 miles. E. Long. 2. 27. N. Lat. 50. 48.

Cassel, the capital city of the landgravate of Hesse-cassel, in the circle of the Upper Rhine in Germany; (see Hesse-cassel). It is divided into the Old, New, and High towns. The New Town is best built, the houses being of stone, and the streets broad. The houses of the Old Town, which is within the walls, are mostly of timber; but the streets are broad, and the market-places spacious. The place is strongly fortified, but the fortifications are not regular. It contains about 18,000 inhabitants, of whom a great proportion are French Protestants. These have establish-

ed

ed ſeveral manufactories in the place, particularly in the woollen branch. It is ſeated on the declivity of a hill near the river Fulva, in E. Long. 9. 10. N. Lat. 51. 20.

CASSIA, in botany: A genus of the monogynia order, belonging to the decandria claſs of plants; and in the natural method ranking under the 33d order, *Lomentaceæ*. The calyx is pentaphyllous; petals five; antheræ upper, three barren; lower, three-beaked: a leguminous plant. There are 30 ſpecies, all of them natives of warm climates. The moſt remarkable are,

1. The fiſtula or purging caſſia of Alexandria. It is a native of Egypt and both Indies, where it riſes to the height of 40 or 50 feet, with a large trunk, dividing into many branches, garniſhed with winged leaves, compoſed of five pair of ſpear-ſhaped lobes, which are ſmooth, having many tranſverſe nerves from the midrib to the border. The flowers are produced in long ſpikes at the end of the branches, each ſtanding upon a pretty long foot-ſtalk; theſe are compoſed, like the former, of five yellow concave petals, which are ſucceeded by cylindrical pods from one to two feet long, with a dark brown woody ſhell, having a longitudinal ſeam on one ſide, divided into many cells by tranſverſe partitions, each containing one or two oval, ſmooth, compreſſed ſeeds, lodged in a blackiſh pulp, which is uſed in medicine. There are two ſorts of this drug in the ſhops; one brought from the Eaſt Indies, the other from the Weſt: the canes or pods of the latter are generally large, rough, thick-rinded, and the pulp nauſeous; thoſe of the former are leſs, ſmoother, the pulp blacker, and of a ſweeter taſte; this ſort is preferred to the other. Such pods ſhould be choſen as are weighty, new, and do not make a rattling noiſe (from the ſeeds being looſe within them) when ſhaken. The pulp ſhould be of a bright ſhining black colour, and a ſweet taſte, not harſh, which happens from the fruit being gathered before it has grown fully ripe, or ſouriſh, which it is apt to turn upon keeping: it ſhould neither be very dry nor very moiſt, nor at all mouldy; which, from its being kept in damp cellars or moiſtened, in order to increaſe its weight, it is very ſubject to be. Greateſt part of the pulp diſſolves both in water and in rectified ſpirit; and may be extracted from the cane by either. The ſhops employ water, boiling the bruiſed pod therein, and afterwards evaporating the ſolution to a due conſiſtence. This pulp is a gentle laxative medicine, and frequently given, in a doſe of ſome drams, in coſtive habits. Some direct a doſe of two ounces or more as a cathartic, in inflammatory caſes, where the more acrid purgatives have no place; but in theſe large quantities it generally nauſeates the ſtomach, produces flatulencies, and ſometimes gripings of the bowels, eſpecially if the caſſia be not of a very good kind: theſe effects may be prevented by the addition of aromatics, and exhibiting it in a liquid form. Geoffroy ſays, it does excellent ſervice in the painful tenſion of the belly, which ſometimes follows the imprudent uſe of antimonials; and that it may be advantageouſly acuated with the more acrid purgatives, or antimonial emetics, or employed to abate their force. Valliſnieri relates, that the purgative virtue of this medicine is remarkably promoted by manna; that a mixture of four drams of caſſia and two of manna, purges as much as twelve drams of caſſia or thirty-two of manna alone. Senertus obſerves, that the urine is apt to be tinged of a green colour by the uſe of caſſia: and ſometimes, where a large quantity has been taken, blackiſh. This drug gives name to an officinal electuary, and is an ingredient alſo in another.

2. The caſſia ſenna is a ſhrubby plant cultivated in Perſia, Syria, and Arabia, for the leaves, which form a conſiderable article of commerce. They are of an oblong figure, ſharp-pointed at the ends, about a quarter of an inch broad, and not a full inch in length, of a lively yellowiſh green colour, a faint not very diſagreeable ſmell, and a ſubacrid, bitteriſh, nauſeous taſte. They are brought from the above places, dried and picked from the ſtalks, to Alexandria in Egypt, and thence imported into Europe. Some inferior ſorts are brought from Tripoli and other places; theſe may eaſily be diſtinguiſhed by their being either narrower, longer, and ſharper pointed; or larger, broader, and round pointed, with ſmall prominent veins; or large and obtuſe, of a freſh green colour, without any yellow caſt. Senna is a very uſeful cathartic, operating mildly, and yet effectually; and, if judiciouſly doſed and managed, rarely occaſioning the ill conſequences which too frequently follow the exhibition of the ſtronger purges. The only inconveniences complained of in this drug are, its being apt to gripe, and its nauſeous flavour. The griping quality depends upon a reſinous ſubſtance, which, like the other bodies of this claſs, is naturally diſpoſed to adhere to the coats of the inteſtines. The more this reſin is divided by ſuch matters as take off its tenacity, the leſs adheſive, and conſequently the leſs irritating and griping it will prove; and the leſs it is divided, the more griping: hence ſenna given by itſelf, or infuſions made in a very ſmall quantity of fluid, gripe ſeverely, and purge leſs than when diluted by a large portion of ſuitable menſtruum, or divided by mixing the infuſion with oily emulſions. The ill flavour of this drug is ſaid to be abated by the greater water-figwort: but we cannot conceive that this plant, whoſe ſmell is manifeſtly fetid and its taſte nauſeous and bitter, can at all improve thoſe of ſenna: others recommend bohea tea, though neither has this any conſiderable effect. The ſmell of ſenna reſides in its more volatile parts, and may be diſcharged by lightly boiling infuſions of it made in water: the liquor thus freed from the peculiar flavour of the ſenna, may be eaſily rendered grateful to the taſte, by the addition of any proper aromatic tincture or diſtilled water. The colleges both of London and Edinburgh have given ſeveral formulæ for the exhibition of this article, ſuch as thoſe of infuſion, powder, tincture, and electuary. The doſe of ſenna in ſubſtance, is from a ſcruple to a dram: in infuſion, from one to three or four drams. It has been cuſtomary to reject the pedicles of the leaves of ſenna as of little or no uſe; Geoffroy however obſerves, that they are not much inferior in efficacy to the leaves themſelves. The pods or ſeed-veſſels met with among the ſenna brought to us, are by the college of Bruſſels preferred to the leaves; they are leſs apt to gripe, but proportionably leſs purgative.

Caſſia-Lignea. See LAURUS.

CASSIDA, in botany. See SCUTELLARIA.

CASSIDA, in zoology, a genus of inſects belonging

Plate CXVI.

to the order of coleoptera. The feelers are like threads, but thicker on the outside; the elytra are marginated; and the head is hid under the thorax; from which last circumstance is derived the name of the genus. Foreign countries afford many fine species of them. Those we meet with in these parts have something singular. Their larva, by the help of the two prongs which are to be found at its hinder extremity, makes itself, with its own excrements, a kind of umbrella, that shelters it from the sun and rain. When this umbrella grows over-dry, it parts with it for a new one. This larva casts its slough several times. Thistles and verticillated plants are inhabited by these insects. There is one species, of which the remarkable chrysalis resembles an armorial escutcheon. It is that which produces our variegated cassida, and is a very singular one. Numbers of them are found on the side of ponds, upon the wild elecampane.

CASSIMER, or CASIMIR, the name of a thin twelled woollen cloth, much in fashion for summer use.

CASSIMIRE or CASHMIRE. See CASHMIRE.

CASSINE, in botany: A genus of the trigynia order, belonging to the pentandria class of plants; and in the natural method ranking under the 23d order, *Dumosæ*. The calyx is quinquepartite; the petals are five; and the fruit is a trispermous berry. There are three species, all of them natives of warm climates.

Of these the most remarkable is the *yapon*, which is a native of the maritime parts of Virginia and Carolina. It rises to the height of ten or twelve feet, sending out branches from the ground upward, garnished with spear-shaped leaves placed alternately, which continue green through the year. The flowers are produced in close whorls round the branches, at the footstalks of the leaves; they are white, and divided into five parts, almost to the bottom. The berries are of a beautiful red colour, and as they continue most part of the winter upon the plants without being touched by the birds, we may reasonably conclude that they are possessed of a poisonous quality; as few of the wholesome innocent fruits escape their depredations. The Indians, however, have a great veneration for this plant, and at certain seasons of the year come in great numbers to fetch away the leaves. On such occasions their usual custom, says Miller, is to make a fire upon the ground, and, putting on it a great kettle full of water, they throw in a large quantity of yapon leaves; and when the water has boiled sufficiently, they drink large draughts of the decoction out of the kettle; which seldom fails to vomit them very severely. In this manner, however, they continue drinking and vomiting for three days together, until they imagine themselves sufficiently cleansed; they then gather every one a bundle of the shrub, and carry it home with them.—In the operation of these leaves by vomiting, those who have tasted of them say, that there is no uneasy sensation or pain. The matter discharged comes away in a full stream by the mouth, without any violence, or so much as disposing the patient to reach, or decline his head. The Spaniards who live near the gold mines of Peru, are frequently obliged to drink an infusion of this herb in order to moisten their breasts; without which they are liable to a sort of suffocation, from the strong metallic exhalations that are continually proceeding from the mines. In Paraguay, the Jesuits make a great revenue by importing the leaves of this plant into many countries under the name of Paraguay or South-sea tea, which is there drank in the same manner as that of China or Japan is with us. It is with difficulty preserved in England.

CASSINI (Johannes Dominicus), a most excellent astronomer, born at Piedmont in 1635. His early proficiency in astronomy procured him an invitation to be mathematical professor at Bologna when he was no more than 25 years of age: and a comet appearing in 1652, he discovered that comets were not accidental meteors, but of the same nature, and probably governed by the same laws, as the planets. In the same year he solved a problem given up by Kepler and Bullialdus as insolvable, which was, to determine geometrically the apogee and eccentricity of a planet from its true and mean place. In 1663, he was appointed inspector-general of the fortifications of the castle of Urbino, and had afterwards the care of all the rivers in the ecclesiastical state: he still however prosecuted his astronomical studies, by discovering the revolution of Mars round his own axis; and, in 1666, published his theory of Jupiter's satellites. Cassini was invited into France by Louis XIV. in 1669, where he settled as the first professor in the royal observatory. In 1677 he demonstrated the line of Jupiter's diurnal rotation; and in 1684 discovered four more satellites belonging to Saturn, Huygens having found one before. He inhabited the royal observatory at Paris more than forty years; and when he died in 1712, was succeeded by his only son James Cassini.

CASSIODORUS (Marcus Aurelius), secretary of state to Theodoric king of the Goths, was born at Squillace, in the kingdom of Naples, about the year 470. He was consul in 514, and was in great credit under the reigns of Athalaric and Vitiges; but at seventy years of age retired into a monastery in Calabria, where he amused himself in making sun-dials, water hourglasses, and perpetual lamps. He also formed a library; and composed several works, the best edition of which is that of father Garet, printed at Rouen in 1679. Those most esteemed are his Divine Institutions, and his treatise on the Soul. He died about the year 562.

CASSIOPEIA, in fabulous history, wife to Cepheus king of Ethiopia, and mother of Andromeda. She thought herself more beautiful than the Nereides, who desired Neptune to revenge the affront; so that he sent a sea-monster into the country, which did much harm. To appease the god, her daughter Andromeda was exposed to the monster, but was rescued by Perseus; who obtained of Jupiter, that Cassiopeia might be placed after his death among the stars: hence the constellation of that name.

CASSIOPEIA, in astronomy, one of the constellations of the northern hemisphere, situated next to Cepheus. In 1572, there appeared a new star in this constellation, which at first surpassed in magnitude and brightness Jupiter himself; but it diminished by degrees, and at last disappeared, at the end of eighteen months. It alarmed all the astronomers of that age, many of whom wrote dissertations on it; among the rest Tycho Brahe, Kepler, Maurolycus, Lycetus, Gramineus, &c. Beza, the landgrave of Hesse, Rosa, &c. wrote to prove it a comet, and the same which appeared to the Magi at the

[Caſſio- ‖ Caſſumar.]

the birth of Jeſus Chriſt, and that it came to declare his ſecond coming: they were anſwered on this ſubject by Tycho. The ſtars in the conſtellation Caſſiopeia, in Ptolemy's Catalogue, are thirteen; in Hevelius's thirty-ſeven; in Tycho's, forty-ſix; but in the Britannic Catalogue, Mr Flamſtead makes them fifty-five.

CASSIS, in antiquity, a plated or metalline helmet; different from the *galea*, which was of leather.

CASSITERIA, in the hiſtory of foſſils, a genus of cryſtals, the figures of which are influenced by an admixture of ſome particles of tin.

The caſſiteria are of two kinds: the whitiſh pellucid caſſiterion, and the brown caſſiterion. The firſt is a tolerably bright and pellucid cryſtal, and ſeldom ſubject to the common blemiſhes of cryſtal: it is of a perfect and regular form, in the figure of a quadrilateral pyramid; and is found in Devonſhire and Cornwall principally. The brown caſſiterion is like the former in figure: it is of a very ſmooth and gloſſy ſurface, and is alſo found in great plenty in Devonſhire and Cornwall.

CASSITERIDES (anc. geog.), a cluſter of iſlands to the weſt of the Land's End; oppoſite to Celtiberia, (Pliny); famous for their tin, which he calls *candidum plumbum*; formerly open to none but the Phœnicians; who alone carried on this commerce from Gades, concealing the navigation from the reſt of the world, (Strabo). The appellation is from *Caſſiteros*, the name for tin in Greek. Now thought to be the Scilly Iſlands, or Sorlings. (Camden).

CASSIUS (Spurius), a renowned Roman general and conſul, whoſe enemies accuſing him of aſpiring to royalty, he was thrown down from the Tarpeian rock, 485 years before Chriſt; after having thrice enjoyed the conſular dignity, been once general of the horſe under the firſt dictator that was created at Rome, and twice received the honour of a triumph.

Cassius (Longinus), a celebrated Roman lawyer, flouriſhed 119 years before Chriſt. He was ſo inflexible a judge, that his tribunal was called the *Rock of the impeached*. It is from the judicial ſeverity of this Caſſius, that very ſevere judges have been called *Caſſiani*.

Cassius (Caius), one of the murderers of Julius Cæſar: after his defeat by Mark Anthony at the battle of Philippi, he ordered one of his freed-men to put him to death with his own ſword, 41 years before Chriſt. See Rome.

CASSOCK, or Cassula, a kind of robe or gown, wore over the reſt of the habit, particularly by the clergy. The word caſſock comes from the French *caſaque*, an horſeman's coat.

CASSONADE, in commerce, caſk ſugar, or ſugar put into caſks or cheſts, after the firſt purification, but which has not been refined. It is ſold either in powder or in lumps; the whiteſt, and that of which the lumps are largeſt, is the beſt. Many imagine it to ſweeten more than loaf ſugar; but it is certain that it yields a great deal more ſcum.

CASSOWARY, in ornithology. See Struthio.

CASSUMAR, in the Materia Medica, a root approaching to that of zedoary.

It is cardiac and ſudorific, and famous in nervous caſes; it is alſo an ingredient in many compoſitions, and is preſcribed in powders, boluſes, and infuſions. Its doſe is from five to fifteen grains.

[Caſſumbazar ‖ Caſtagno.]

CASSUMBAZAR, a town of India, in Aſia, ſituated on the river Ganges, in the province of Bengal. E. Long. 87. and N. Lat. 24.

CAST is peculiarly uſed to denote a figure or ſmall ſtatue of bronze. See Bronze.

Cast, among founders, is applied to tubes of wax fitted in divers parts of a mould of the ſame matter; by means of which, when the wax of the mould is removed, the melted metal is conveyed into all the parts which the wax before poſſeſſed.

Cast, alſo denotes a cylindrical piece of braſs or copper, ſlit in two, lengthwiſe, uſed by the founders in ſand, to form a canal or conduit in their moulds, whereby the metal may be conveyed to the different pieces intended to be caſt.

Cast, among plumbers, denotes a little braſen funnel at one end of a mould, for caſting pipes without ſoldering, by means of which the melted metal is poured into the mould.

Cast, or *Caſte*, in ſpeaking of the eaſtern affairs, denotes a tribe, or number of families, of the ſame rank and profeſſion. The diviſion of a nation into caſts chiefly obtains in the dominions of the Great Mogul, kingdom of Bengal, iſland of Ceylon, and the great peninſula oppoſite thereto. In each of theſe there are, according to father Martin, four principal caſts, viz. the caſt of the *bramins*, which is the firſt and moſt noble; the caſt of the *rajas*, or princes, who pretend to be deſcended from divers royal families; the caſt of the *choutres*, which comprehends all the artificers; and that of the *parias*, the loweſt and moſt contemptible of all: though Henry Lord, it muſt be obſerved, divides the Indians about Surat into four caſts, ſomewhat differently from Martin, viz. into *bramins*, or prieſts; *cuttery*, or ſoldiers; *ſhuddery*, which we call banians, or merchants; and *wyſe*, the mechanics or artificers. Every art and trade is confined to its proper *caſt*, nor is allowed to be exerciſed by any but thoſe whoſe fathers profeſſed the ſame. So that a taylor's ſon can never riſe to be a painter, nor a painter's ſon fall to be a taylor; though there are ſome employments that are proper to all the caſts, *e. g.* every body may be a ſoldier, or a merchant. There are alſo divers caſts which are allowed to till the ground, but not all. The caſt of *parias* is held infamous, in ſo much that it is a diſgrace to have any dealings or converſation with them; and there are ſome trades in the caſt of *choutres*, which debaſe their profeſſors almoſt to the ſame rank. Thus ſhoemakers, and all artificers in leather, as alſo fiſhermen, and even ſhepherds, are reputed no better than *parias*.

CASTAGNO (Andrea Dal), hiſtorical painter, was born at a ſmall village called Caſtagno, belonging to the territory of Tuſcany, in 1409; and being deprived of his parents, was employed by his uncle to attend the herds of cattle in the fields; but, having accidentally ſeen an ordinary painter at work in the country, he obſerved him for ſome time with ſurpriſe and attention, and afterwards made ſuch efforts to imitate him, as aſtoniſhed all who ſaw his productions. The extraordinary genius of Andrea became at laſt a common topic of diſcourſe in Florence; and ſo far excited the curioſity of Bernardetto de Medici, that he ſent for Andrea; and perceiving that he had promiſing talents, he placed him under the care of the

Castagno, Castalio.

best masters who were at that time in Florence. Andrea diligently pursued his studies, devoted himself entirely to practice under the direction of his instructors, became particularly eminent in design, and in a few years made so great a progress, that he found as much employment as he could possibly execute. He painted only in distemper, and fresco, with a manner of colouring that was not very agreeable, being rather dry and hard; till he learned the secret of painting in oil from Domenico Venetiano, who had derived his knowledge of that new discovery from Antonello da Messina. Andrea was the first of the Florentine artists who painted in oil; but although he was in the highest degree indebted to Domenico for disclosing the secret, yet he secretly envied the merit of the man who taught him the art; and because his own works seemed to be much less admired than those of Domenico, he determined to assassinate his friend and benefactor. He executed his design with the utmost ingratitude and treachery (for Domenico at that time lived with him, and painted in partnership with him), and he stabbed him at a corner of a street so secretly, that he escaped unobserved, and unsuspected, to his own house, where he compusedly sat down to work; and thither Domenico was soon after conveyed, to die in the arms of his murderer. The real author of so inhuman a transaction was never discovered, till Andrea, through remorse of conscience, disclosed it on his death-bed, in 1480. He finished several considerable works at Florence, by which he gained great riches, and as great a reputation; but when his villanous misconduct became public, his memory was ever after held in the utmost detestation. The most noted work of this master is in the hall of justice at Florence, representing the execution of the conspirators against the house of Medici.

CASTALIO (Sebastian), was born at Chatillon, on the Rhone, in the year 1515. Calvin conceived such an esteem and friendship for him, during the stay he made at Strasburg in 1540 and 1541, that he lodged him some days at his house, and procured him a regent's place in the college of Geneva. Castalio, after continuing in this office near three years, was forced to quit it in the year 1544, on account of some particular opinions which he held concerning Solomon's song, and Christ's descent into hell. He retired to Basil, where he was made Greek professor, and died in that place in 1563, aged 48. He incurred the high displeasure of Calvin and Theodore Beza, for differing with them concerning predestination and the punishment of heretics. His works are very considerable, both on account of their quality and number. In 1545, he printed at Basil four books of dialogues, containing the principal histories of the bible in elegant Latin; so that youth might thereby make a proficiency in piety and in the Latin tongue at the same time. But his principal work is a Latin and French translation of the scriptures. He began the Latin translation at Geneva in 1542, and finished it at Basil in 1550. It was printed at Basil in 1551, and dedicated by the author to Edward VI. king of England. The French version was dedicated to Henry II. of France, and printed at Basil in 1555. The fault which has been most generally condemned in his Latin translation, is the affectation of using only classical terms.

Castalia ‖ Castelfolit.

CASTALIUS FONS, (Strabo, Pausanias); *Castalia*, (Pindar, Virgil): A fountain at the foot of mount Parnassus, in Phocis, near the temple of Apollo, or near Delphi; sacred to the Muses, thence called *Castalides*. Its murmurs were thought prophetic, (Nonnus, Lucian.)

CASTANEA, in botany. See FAGUS.

CASTANETS, CASTAGNETTES, or CASTANETTAS, a kind of musical instrument, wherewith the Moors, Spaniards, and Bohemians, accompany their dances, sarabands, and guittars. It consists of two little round pieces of wood dried, and hollowed in manner of a spoon, the concavities whereof are placed on one another, fastened to the thumb, and beat from time to time with the middle finger, to direct their motion and cadences. The *castanets* may be beat eight or nine times in the space of one measure, or second of a minute.

CASTANOVITZ, a town of Croatia, situated on the river Vans, which divides Christendom from Turkey. E. Long. 17. 20. N. Lat. 45. 40. It is subject to the House of Austria.

CASTEL (Lewis Betrand), a learned Jesuit, was born at Montpellier in 1688, and entered among the Jesuits in 1703. He studied polite literature in his youth; and at length applied himself entirely to the study of mathematics and natural philosophy. He distinguished himself by writing on gravity; the mathematics; and on the music of colours, a very whimsical idea, which he took great pains to reduce to practice. His piece on gravity, entitled *Traité de la Pesanteur universelle*, was printed at Paris, in 1724. He afterwards published his *Mathematique universelle*; which occasioned his being unanimously chosen a fellow of the Royal Society of London, without the least solicitation. He was also a member of the academies of Bourdeaux and Rouen: but his *Clavecin oculaire* made the most noise; and he spent much time and expence in making an harpsichord for the eye, but without success. He also wrote for and against Sir Isaac Newton, and published several other works; the principal of which are, *Le Plan du Mathematique abregée*, and a treatise entitled *Optique des Colours*. He led a very exemplary life, and died in 1757.

CASTELAMARA, a town of Italy, in the kingdom of Naples, and in the hither Principato, with a bishop's see, and a good harbour. E. Long. 14. 25. N. Lat. 41. 40.

CASTEL-ARAGONESE, a strong town of Italy, in the island of Sardinia, with a bishop's see, and a good harbour. It is seated on the N. W. coast of the island, in E. Long. 8. 57. N. Lat. 40. 56.

Castel-Branco, a town of Portugal, and capital of the province of Beira; seated on the river Lyra, 35 miles N. W. of Alcantara. W. Long. 8. 0. N. Lat. 39. 35.

Castel-Franco, a very small, but well-fortified frontier town of the Bolognese, in Italy, belonging to the Pope.

Castel-de-Vide, a small strong town of Alentejo. It was taken by Philip V. W. Long. 6. 25. N. Lat. 39. 15.

Castel-Folit, a town of Spain, in Catalonia, seated on an inaccessible eminence, between Gironne and Campredon,

Campredon, about 15 miles from each, and near the river Fulva.

Castel-Gandolpho, a town of Italy, in the territory of the church, with a castle, to which the Pope retires in the summer season; 10 miles S. by E. of Rome. E. Long. 12. 46. N. Lat. 41. 44.

Castel-Novo, a strong town of Dalmatia, subject to the Venetians; seated on the gulph of Cataro, in E. Long. 18. 45. N. Lat. 42. 25.

Castel-Rodrigo, a town of Portugal, in the province of Tra-los-Montes, in W. Long. 7. 1. N. 41. 0.

Castel-Novo-di-Carfagnana, a town of Italy, in the Modenese, with a strong fortress. It is the capital of the valley of Carfagnana; and seated on the river Serchio, 17 miles above Lucca.

Castel del Ovo, a small island in the Tuscan Sea, in the gulph of Naples, near a town of that name, to which it is joined by a stone bridge. The fortress is called Castel del Ovo, in which there is always a good garrison.

CASTELBAR, a town of Ireland, in the county of Mayo, and province of Connaught, 35 miles N. of Galway. W. Long. 9. 25. N. Lat. 53. 45.

CASTELL (Edmund) D. D. a learned English divine of the 17th century, distinguished by his skill in the eastern languages. He was educated at Cambridge; where he was master of Catharine hall, and Arabic professor; and was at length canon of Canterbury. He had the greatest share in the Polyglott bible of London; and wrote the *Heptaglotton pro septem Orientalibus*, &c. On this excellent work, which occupied a great part of his life, he bestowed incredible pains and expence, even to the breaking of his constitution, and exhausting of his fortune, having expended no less than 12,000*l.* upon that work. At length, when it was printed, the copies remained unsold upon his hands. He died in 1685; and lies buried in the church-yard of Higham Gobyon in Bedfordshire, of which he was rector. It appears from the inscription on his monument, which he erected in his lifetime, that he was chaplain to Charles II. He bequeathed all his oriental manuscripts to the university of Cambridge, on condition that his name should be written on every copy in the collection.

CASTELLA, a town of the Mantuan, in Italy, about five miles north-east of the city of Mantua. E. Long. 11. 15. N. Lat. 45. 30.

CASTELLAN, the name of a dignity or charge in Poland: The castellans are senators of the kingdom, but senators only of the lower class, who, in diets, sit on low seats, behind the palatines, or great senators. They are a kind of lieutenants of provinces, and command a part of the palatinate under the palatine.

CASTELLANY, the territory belonging to any city or town, chiefly used in France and Flanders: Thus we say, the castellany of Lisle, Ypres, &c.

CASTELLARIUS, the keeper, or curator, of a castellum. Gruter gives an ancient sepulchral inscription in memory of a *castellarius*.

CASTELLATIO, in middle age writers, the act of building a castle, or of fortifying a house, and rendering it a castle.—By the ancient English laws, castellation was prohibited without the king's especial licence.

CASTELLI (Bernard), an Italian painter, was born at Genoa in 1557; and excelled in colouring and in portraits. He was the intimate friend of Tasso, and took upon himself the task of designing and etching the figures of his Jerusalem Delivered. He died at Genoa in 1629.

Valerio Castelli, one of his sons, was born at Genoa in 1625, and surpassed his father. He particularly excelled in painting battles; which he composed with spirit, and executed them with so pleasing a variety, and so great freedom of hand, as gained him universal applause. His horses are admirably drawn, thrown into attitudes that are natural and becoming, full of motion, action, and life. In that style of painting he showed all the fire of Tintoretto, united with the fine taste of composition of Paolo Veronese. He died in 1659. The works of this master are not very frequent; but they are deservedly held in very high esteem. It is believed that a greater number of his easel pictures are in the collections of the nobility and gentry of England, than in any other part of Europe.

CASTELLORUM OPERATIO, castle-work, or service and labour done by inferior tenants for the building and upholding of castles of defence; toward which some gave personal assistance, and others paid their contributions. This was one of the three necessary charges to which all lands among the Anglo-Saxons were expressly subject.

CASTELVETRO (Lewis), a native of Modena, of the 16th century, famous for his *Comment on Aristotle's Poetics*. He was prosecuted by the inquisition for a certain book of Melancthon, which he had translated into Italian. He retired to Basil, where he died.

CASTIGATION, among the Romans, the punishment of an offender by blows, or beating with a wand or switch. Castigation was chiefly a military punishment; the power of inflicting which on the soldiery was given to the tribunes. Some make it of two kinds; one with a stick or cane called *fustigatio*; the other with rods, called *flagellatio*: the latter was the most dishonourable.

CASTIGATORY *for* Scolds. A woman indicted for being a common scold, if convicted, shall be placed in a certain engine of correction, called the *trebucket*, *castigatory*, or *cucking-stool*; which, in the Saxon language, signifies the *scolding-stool*; though now it is frequently corrupted into the *ducking-stool*; because the residue of the judgment is, that, when she is placed therein, she shall be plunged in water for her punishment.

CASTIGLIONE (Giovanni Benedetto), a celebrated painter, was born at Genoa in 1616. His first master was Gio-Battista Paggi. Afterwards he studied under Andrea Ferrari; and lastly perfected himself from the instructions of Anthony Vandyck, who at that time resided at Genoa. He painted portraits, historical pieces, landscapes, and cattle: in the latter of which he is said chiefly to have excelled; as also in fairs, markets, and all kinds of rural scenes. By this master we have also a great number of etchings, which are all spirited, free, and full of taste. The effect is, in general, powerful and pleasing; and many of them have a more harmonized and finished appearance, than is usual from the

the point, fo little affifted by the graver. His drawing of the naked figure, though by no means correct, is notwithftanding managed in a ftyle that indicates the hand of the mafter.

His fon, *Francefco*, was bred under himfelf, and excelled in the fame fubjects; and it is thought that many good paintings which are afcribed to Benedetto, and are frequently feen at fales, or in modern collections, are copies after him by his fon Francefco, or perhaps originals of the younger Caftiglione.

Castiglioni, a fmall, but ftrong town of Italy, in Mantua, with a caftle. It was taken by the Germans in 1701, and the French defeated the Imperialifts near it in 1706. E. Long. 10. 19. N. Lat. 45. 23.

CASTIGLIONI (Balthazar), an eminent Italian nobleman, defcended from an illuftrious and ancient family, and born at his own villa at Cafatico in the dutchy of Milan in 1478. He ftudied painting, fculpture, and architecture, as appears from a book he wrote in favour of thefe arts; and excelled fo much in them, that Raphael Urbino, and Buonaroti, though incomparable artifts, never thought their works complete without the approbation of Count Caftiglioni. When he was 26 years of age, Guido Ubaldo, Duke of Urbino, fent him ambaffador to Pope Julius II. He was fent upon a fecond embaffy to Louis XII. of France, and upon a third to Henry VII. of England. After he had difpatched his bufinefs here, he returned, and began his celebrated work intitled *the Courtier*; which he completed at Rome in 1516. This work is full of moral and political inftruction; and if we feek for the Italian tongue in perfection, it is faid to be nowhere better found than in this performance. A verfion of this work, together with the original Italian, was publifhed at London in 1727, by A. P. Caftiglioni, a gentleman of the fame family, who refided there under the patronage of Dr Gibfon bifhop of London. Count Caftiglioni was fent by Clement VII. to the court of the Emperor Charles V. in quality of legate, and died at Toledo in 1529.

CASTILE (New), or The Kingdom of Toledo, a province of Spain, bounded on the north by Old Caftile, on the eaft by the kingdoms of Arragon and Valencia, on the fouth by that of Murcia and Andalufia, and on the weft by the kingdom of Leon. It is divided into three parts; Algaria to the north, Mancha to the eaft, and Sierra to the fouth. Madrid is the capital. Both thefe provinces are very well watered with rivers, and the air is generally pure and healthy; but the land is mountainous, dry, and uncultivated, through the lazinefs of the inhabitants. The north part produces fruits and wine, and the fouth good paftures and fine wool. Thefe provinces are divided by a long chain of mountains, which run from eaft to weft.

Castile (Old), a province of Spain, with the title of a kingdom. It is about 192 miles in length, and 115 in breadth; bounded on the fouth by New Caftile, on the eaft by Arragon and Navarre, on the north by Bifcay and Afturia, and on the weft by the kingdom of Leon. Burgos is the capital town.

Castile-de-Oro, a large and fertile country in South America, lying to the weft of Oronoko. It comprehends eight governments; viz. Terra Firma, Proper Carthagena, St Martha, Rio de la Hacha, Venezuela, New Andalufia, Popayan, and the new kingdom of Granada.

CASTILLAN, or Castellany, a gold coin, current in Spain, and worth fourteen rials and fixteen deniers.

Castillan is alfo a weight ufed in Spain for weighing gold. It is the hundredth part of a pound Spanifh weight. What they commonly call a weight of gold in Spain, is always underftood of the caftillan.

CASTILLARA, a town of the Mantuan in Italy, feated fix miles north-eaft of the city of Mantua. E. Long. 11. 25. N. Lat. 45. 20.

CASTILLON, a town of Perigort, in the province of Guienne in France, feated on the river Dordonne, 16 miles eaft of Bourdeaux. W. Long. 2. 40. N. Lat. 44. 50.

CASTING, in foundery, the running a metal into a mould, prepared for that purpofe.

Casting of Metals, of Letters, Bells, &c. See the article Foundery.

Casting in Sand or Earth is the running of metals between two frames, or molds, filled with fand or earth, wherein the figure that the metal is to take has been impreffed *en creux*, by means of the pattern.

Casting, among fculptors, implies the taking of cafts and impreffions of figures, bufts, medals, leaves, &c.

The method of taking of cafts of figures and bufts is moft generally by the ufe of plafter of Paris, *i. e.* alabafter calcined by a gentle heat. The advantage of ufing this fubftance preferably to others, is, that notwithftanding a flight calcination reduces it to a pulverine ftate, it becomes again a tenacious and cohering body, by being moiftened with water, and afterwards fuffered to dry; by which means either a concave or a convex figure may be given by a proper mold or model to it when wet, and retained by the hardnefs it acquires when dry: and from thefe qualities, it is fitted for the double purpofe of making both cafts, and molds for forming thofe cafts. The particular manner of making cafts depends on the form of the fubject to be taken. Where there are no projecting parts, it is very fimple and eafy; as likewife where there are fuch as form only a right or any greater angle with the principal furface of the body; but where parts project in leffer angles, or form a curve inclined towards the principal furface of the body, the work is more difficult.

The firft ftep to be taken is the forming the mold. In order to this, if the original or model be a bafs relief, or any other piece of a flat form, having its furface firft well greafed, it muft be placed on a proper table, and furrounded by a frame, the fides of which muft be at fuch a diftance from it as will allow a proper thicknefs for the fides of the mold. As much plafter as will be fufficient to cover and rife to fuch a thicknefs as may give fufficient ftrength to the mold, as alfo to fill the hollow betwixt the frame and the model, muft be moiftened with water, till it be just of fuch confiftence as will allow it to be poured upon the model. This muft be done as foon as poffible; or the plafter would concrete or fet, fo as to become more troublefome in the working, or unfit to be ufed. The whole muft then be fuffered to remain in this condition, till the plafter has attained its hardnefs; and then the frame being taken away, the preparatory

Casting.

caft or mold thus formed may be taken off from the fubject entire.

Where the model or original fubject is of a round or erect figure, a different method muft be purfued; and the mold muft be divided into feveral pieces: or if the fubject confifts of detached and projecting parts, it is frequently moft expedient to caft fuch parts feparately, and afterwards join them together.

Where the original fubject or mold forms a round, or fpheroid, or any part of fuch round or fpheroid, more than one half the plafter muft be ufed without any frame to keep it round the model; and muft be tempered with water to fuch a confiftence, that it may be wrought with the hand like very foft pafte; but though it muft not be fo fluid as when prepared for flat figured models, it muft yet be as moift as is compatible with its cohering fufficiently to hold together: and being thus prepared, it muft be put upon the model, and compreffed with the hand, or any flat inftrument, that the parts of it may adapt themfelves, in the moft perfect manner, to thofe of the fubject, as well as be compact with refpect to themfelves. When the model is fo covered to a convenient thicknefs, the whole muft be left at reft till the plafter be fet and firm, fo as to bear dividing without falling to pieces, or being liable to be put out of its form by flight violence; and it muft then be divided into pieces, in order to its being taken off from the model, by cutting it with a knife with a very thin blade; and being divided, muft be cautioufly taken off, and kept till dry: but it muft be always carefully obferved, before the feparation of the parts be made, to notch them crofs the joints, or lines of the divifion, at proper diftances, that they may with eafe and certainty be properly conjoined again; which would be much more precarious and troublefome without fuch directive marks. The art of properly dividing the molds, in order to make them feparate from the model, requires more dexterity and fkill than any other thing in the art of cafting; and does not admit of rules for the moft advantageous conduct of it in every cafe. Where the fubject is of a round or fpheroidal form, it is beft to divide the mold into three parts, which will then eafily come off from the model; and the fame will hold good of a cylinder or any regular curve figure.

The mold being thus formed, and dry, and the parts put together, it muft be firft greafed, and placed in fuch a pofition that the hollow may lie upwards, and then filled with plafter mixed with water, in the fame proportion and manner as was directed for the cafting the mold: and when the caft is perfectly fet and dry, it muft be taken out of the mold, and repaired where it is neceffary; which finifhes the operation.

This is all that is required with refpect to fubjects where the furfaces have the regularity above mentioned: but where they form curves which interfect each other, the conduct of the operation muft be varied with refpect to the manner of taking the caft of the mold from off the fubject or model; and where there are long projecting parts, fuch as legs or arms, they fhould be wrought in feparate cafts. The operator may eafily judge from the original fubjects, what parts will come off together, and what require to be feparated; the principle of the whole confifts only in this, that where under-workings, as they are called, occur, that is, wherever a ftraight line drawn from the bafe or infertion of any projection, would be cut or croffed by any part of fuch projection, fuch part cannot be taken off without a divifion; which muft be made either in the place where the projection would crofs the ftraight line; or, as that is frequently difficult, the whole projection muft be feparated from the main body, and divided alfo lengthwife into two parts: and where there are no projections from the principal furfaces, but the body is fo formed as to render the furface a compofition of fuch curves, that a ftraight line being drawn parallel to the furface of one part would be cut by the outline, in one or more places, of another part, a divifion of the whole fhould be made, fo as to reduce the parts of it into regular curves, which muft then be treated as fuch.

In larger maffes, where there would otherwife be a great thicknefs of the plafter, a corps or body may be put within the mold, in order to produce a hollow in the caft; which both faves the expence of the plafter, and renders the caft lighter.

This corps may be of wood, where the forming a hollow of a ftraight figure, or a conical one with the bafe outward, will anfwer the end: but if the cavity require to be round, or of any curve figure, the corps cannot be then drawn while entire; and confequently fhould be of fuch matter as may be taken out piecemeal. In this cafe, the corps is beft formed of clay; which muft be worked upon wires to give it tenacity, and fufpended in the hollow of the mold, by crofs wires lying over the mouth; and when the plafter is fufficiently fet to bear handling, the clay muft be picked out by a proper inftrument.

Where it is defired to render the plafter harder, the water with which it is tempered fhould be mixed with parchment fize properly prepared, which will make it very firm and tenacious.

In the fame manner, figures, bufts, &c. may be caft of lead, or any other metal, in the molds of plafter: only the expence of plafter, and the tedioufnefs of its becoming fufficiently dry, when in a very large mafs, to bear the heat of melted metal, render the ufe of clay, compounded with fome other proper materials, preferable where large fubjects are in queftion. The clay, in this cafe, fhould be wafhed over till it be perfectly free from gravel or ftones; and then mixed with a third or more of fine fand to prevent its cracking; or, inftead of fand, coal-afhes fifted fine may be ufed. Whether plafter or clay be employed for the cafting in metal, it is extremely neceffary to have the mold perfectly dry; otherwife the moifture, being rarified, will make an explofion that will blow the metal out of the mold, and endanger the operator, or at leaft crack the mold in fuch a manner as to fruftrate the operation. Where the parts of a mold are larger, or project much, and confequently require a greater tenacity of the matter they are formed of to keep them together, flocks of cloth, prepared like thofe defigned for paper-hangings, or fine cotton plucked or cut till it is very fhort, fhould be mixed with the afhes or fand before they are added to the clay to make the compofition for the mold. The proportion fhould be according to the degree of cohefion required; but a fmall quantity will anfwer the end, if the other ingredients

of

Casting.

of the compoſition be good, and the parts of the mold properly linked together by means of the wires above directed.

There is a method of taking caſts in metals from ſmall animals, and the parts of vegetables, which may be practiſed for ſome purpoſes with advantage; particularly for the decorating grottoes or rock-work, where nature is imitated. The proper kinds of animals are lizards, ſnakes, frogs, birds, or inſects; the caſts of which, if properly coloured, will be exact repreſentations of the originals.

This is to be performed by the following method. A coffin or proper cheſt for forming the mold being prepared of clay, or four pieces of boards fixed together, the animal or parts of vegetables muſt be ſuſpended in it by a ſtring; and the leaves, tendrils, or other detached parts of the vegetables, or the legs, wings, &c. of the animals, properly ſeparated and adjuſted in their right poſition by a ſmall pair of pincers: a due quantity of plaſter of Paris and calcined talc, in equal quantities, with ſome alumen plumoſum, muſt then be tempered with water to the proper conſiſtence for caſting; and the ſubject from whence the caſt is to be taken, as alſo the ſides of the coffin, moiſtened with ſpirit of wine. The coffin or cheſt muſt then be filled with the tempered compoſition of the plaſter and talc, putting at the ſame time a piece of ſtraight ſtick or wood to the principal part of the body of the ſubject, and pieces of thick wire to the extremities of the other parts, in order that they may form, when drawn out after the matter of the mold is properly ſet and firm, a channel for pouring in the melted metal, and vents for the air; which otherwiſe, by the rarefaction it would undergo from the heat of the metal, would blow it out or burſt the mold. In a ſhort time the plaſter and talc will ſet and become hard, when the ſtick and wires may be drawn out, and the frame or coffin in which the mold was caſt taken away: and the mold muſt then be put firſt into a moderate heat, and afterwards, when it is as dry as can be rendered by that degree, removed into a greater; which may be gradually increaſed till the whole be red-hot. The animal, or part of any vegetable, which was included in the mold, will then be burnt to a coal; and may be totally calcined to aſhes, by blowing for ſome time gently into the channel and paſſages made for pouring in the metal, and giving vent to the air, which will, at the ſame time that it deſtroys the remainder of the animal or vegetable matter, blow out the aſhes. The mold muſt then be ſuffered to cool gently; and will be perfect; the deſtruction of the ſubſtance of the animal or vegetable having produced a hollow of a figure correſpondent to it; but it may be nevertheleſs proper to ſhake the mold, and turn it upſide down, as alſo to blow with the bellows into each of the air-vents, in order to free it wholly from any remainder of the aſhes; or, where there may be an opportunity of filling the hollow with quickſilver without expence, it will be found a very effectual method of clearing the cavity, as all duſt, aſhes, or ſmall detached bodies will neceſſarily riſe to the ſurface of the quickſilver, and be poured out with it. The mold being thus prepared, it muſt be heated very hot when uſed, if the caſt be made with copper or braſs: but a leſs degree will ſerve for lead or tin: and the matter being poured in, the mold muſt be gently ſtruck; and then ſuffered to reſt till it be cold; at which time it muſt be carefully taken from the caſt, but without the leaſt force; for ſuch parts of the matter as appear to adhere more ſtrongly, muſt be ſoftened by ſoaking in water, till they be entirely looſened, that none of the more delicate parts of the caſt may be broken off or bent.

Where the alumen plumoſum, or talc, cannot eaſily be procured, the plaſter may be uſed alone; but it is apt to be calcined by the heat uſed in burning the animal or vegetable from whence the caſt is taken, and to become of too incohering and crumbly a texture: or, for cheapneſs, Sturbridge or any other good clay, waſhed over till it be perfectly fine, and mixed with an equal part of ſand, and ſome flocks cut ſmall, may be employed. Pounded pumice-ſtone and plaſter of Paris, taken in equal quantities, and mixed with waſhed clay in the ſame proportion, is ſaid to make excellent moulds for this and parallel uſes.

Caſts of metals, or ſuch ſmall pieces as are of a ſimilar form, may be made in plaſter by the method directed for baſs relievos.

Indeed there is nothing more required than to form a mold by laying them on a proper board; and having ſurrounded them by a rim made of a piece of a card, or any other paſteboard, to fill the rim with ſoft tempered plaſter of Paris; which mold, when dry, will ſerve for ſeveral caſts. It is nevertheleſs a better method to form the mold of melted ſulphur; which will produce a ſharper impreſſion in the caſt, and be more durable than thoſe made of plaſter.

The caſts are likewiſe frequently made of ſulphur, which being melted muſt be treated exactly in the ſame manner as the plaſter.

For taking caſts from medals, Dr Lewis recommends a mixture of flowers of brimſtone and red lead: equal parts of theſe are to be put over the fire in a laddle, till they ſoften to the conſiſtence of pap; then they are kindled with a piece of paper, and ſtirred for ſome time. The veſſel being afterwards covered cloſe, and continued on the fire, the mixture grows fluid in a few minutes. It is then to be poured on the metal, previouſly oiled and wiped clean. The caſts are very neat; their colour ſometimes a pretty deep black, ſometimes a dark grey: they are very durable; and when ſoiled, may be waſhed clean in ſpirits of wine. *Philoſoph. Commerce of Arts.*

Dr Leſom recommends tin-foil for taking off caſts from medals. The thinneſt kind is to be uſed. It ſhould be laid over the ſubject from which the impreſſion is to be taken, and then rubbed with a bruſh, the point of a ſkewer, or a pin, till it has perfectly received the impreſſion. The tin-foil ſhould now be pared cloſe to the edge of the medal, till it is brought to the ſame circumference: the medal muſt then be reverſed, and the tin-foil will drop off into a chip-box or mold placed ready to receive it. Thus the concave ſide of the foil will be uppermoſt, and upon this plaſter of Pairs, prepared in the uſual manner, may be poured. When dry, the whole is to be taken out, and the tin-foil ſticking on the plaſter will give a perfect repreſentation of the medal, almoſt equal in beauty to ſilver. If the box or mold is a little larger than the medal, the plaſter running round the tin-foil will give the appearance of a white frame or circular border; *Naturaliſt's Companion.*

border; whence the new made medal will appear more neat and beautiful.

Casts may be made likewise with iron, prepared in the following manner: "Take any iron-bar, or piece of a similar form; and having heated it red-hot, hold it over a vessel containing water, and touch it very slightly with a roll of sulphur, which will immediately dissolve it, and make it fall in drops into the water. As much iron as may be wanted being thus dissolved, pour the water out of the vessel; and pick out the drops formed by the melted iron from those of the sulphur, which contain little or no iron, and will be distinguishable from the other by their colour and weight." The iron will, by this means, be rendered so fusible, that it will run with less heat than is required to melt lead; and may be employed for making casts of medals, and many other such purposes, with great convenience and advantage.

Impressions of medals, having the same effect as casts, may be made also of isinglass glue, by the following means. Melt the isinglass, beaten, as when commonly used, in an earthen pipkin, with the addition of as much water as will cover it, stirring it gently till the whole is dissolved; then with a brush of camel's hair, cover the medal, which should be previously well cleansed and warmed, and then laid horizontally on a board or table, greased in the part around the medal. Let them rest afterwards till the glue be properly hardened; and then, with a pin, raise the edge of it; and separate it carefully from the medal: the cast will be thus formed by the glue as hard as horn; and so light, that a thousand will scarcely weigh an ounce. In order to render the relief of the medal more apparent, a small quantity of carmine may be mixed with the melted isinglass; or the medal may be previously coated with leaf-gold by breathing on it, and then laying it on the leaf, which will by that means adhere to it: but the use of leaf-gold is apt to impair a little the sharpness of the impression.

Impressions of medals may be likewise taken in putty; but it should be the true kind made of calx of tin, and drying oil. These may be formed in the molds, previously taken in plaster or sulphur; or molds may be made in its own substance, in the manner directed for those of the plaster. These impressions will be very sharp and hard; but the greatest disadvantage that attends them, is their drying very slowly, and being liable in the mean time to be damaged.

Impressions of prints, or other engravings, may be taken from copper-plates, by cleansing them thoroughly, and pouring plaster upon them: but the effect in this way is not strong enough for the eye; and therefore the following method is preferable, where such impressions on plaster are desired.

Take vermilion, or any other coloured pigment, finely powdered, and rub it over the plate: then pass a folded piece of paper, or the flat part of the hand, over the plate, to take off the colour from the lights or parts where there is no engraving: the proceeding must then be the same as where no colour is used. This last method is also applicable to the making of impressions of copper-plates on paper with dry colours: for the plate being prepared as here directed, and laid on the paper properly moistened, and either passed under the rolling-press, or any other way strongly forced down on the paper, an impression of the engraving will be obtained.

Impressions may be likewise taken from copper-plates, either on plaster or paper, by means of the smoke of a candle or lamp: if, instead of rubbing them with any colour, the plate be held over the candle or lamp till the whole surface become black, and then wiped off by the flat of the hand, or paper.

These methods are not, however, of great use in the case of copper-plates, except where impressions may be desired on occasions where printing-ink cannot be procured: but as they may be applied likewise to the taking impressions from snuff-boxes, or other engraved subjects, by which means designs may be instantly borrowed by artists or curious persons, they may in such instances be very useful.

The expedient of taking impressions by the smoke of a candle or lamp may be employed also for botanical purposes in the case of leaves, as a perfect and durable representation of not only the general figure, but the contexture and disposition of the larger fibres, may be extemporaneously obtained at any time. The same may be nevertheless done in a more perfect manner, by the use of linseed oil, either alone, or mixed with a small proportion of colour, where the oil can be conveniently procured: but the other method is valuable on account of its being practicable at almost all seasons, and in all places, within the time that the leaves will keep fresh and plump. In taking these impressions, it is proper to bruise the leaves, so as to take off the projections of the large ribs, which might prevent the other parts from plying to the paper.

Leaves, as also the petals, or flower-leaves, of plants, may themselves be preserved on paper, with their original appearance, for a considerable length of time, by the following means.—Take a piece of paper, and rub it over with isinglass glue treated as above directed for taking impressions from medals; and then lay the leaves in a proper position on the paper. The glue laid on the paper being set, brush over the leaves with more of the same; and that being dry likewise, the operation will be finished, and the leaves so secured from the air and moisture, that they will retain their figure and colour much longer than by any other treatment.

Butterflies, or other small animals of a flat figure, may also be preserved in the same manner.

Casting is also sometimes used for the quitting, laying, or throwing aside any thing; thus deer cast their horns, snakes their skins, lobsters their shells, hawks their feathers, &c. annually.

Casting of feathers is more properly called *moulting* or *mewing*.

A horse *casts* his hair, or coat, at least once a-year, viz. in the spring when he casts his winter coat; and sometimes, at the close of autumn, he casts his summer coat, in case he has been ill kept. Horses also sometimes *cast* their hoofs, which happens frequently to coach-horses brought from Holland: these, being bred in a moist marshy country, have their hoofs too flabby: so that coming into a drier soil, and less juicy provender,

der, their hoofs fall off, and others that are firmer succeed.

Casting a Colt, denotes a mare's proving abortive.

Casting-Net, a sort of fishing-net so called, because it is to be *cast*, or thrown out; which, when exactly done, nothing escapes it, but weeds and every thing within its extent are brought away.

CASTLE, a fortress, or place rendered defensible either by nature or art. It frequently signifies with us the principal mansion of noblemen. In the time of Henry II. there were no less than 1115 castles in England, each of which contained a manor.

Castles, walled with stone, and designed for residence as well as defence, are, for the most part, according to Mr Grose, of no higher antiquity than the conquest: for although the Saxons, Romans, and even, according to some writers on antiquity, the ancient Britons, had castles built with stone; yet these were both few in number, and, at that period, through neglect or invasions, either destroyed, or so much decayed, that little more than their ruins were remaining. This is asserted by many of our historians and antiquaries, and assigned as a reason for the facility with which William made himself master of this country.

Grose's Antiquities of England and Wales, Vol. I. Preface.

This circumstance was not overlooked by so good a general as the Conqueror; who, effectually to guard against invasions from without, as well as to awe his newly acquired subjects, immediately began to erect castles all over the kingdom, and likewise to repair and augment the old ones. Besides, as he had parcelled out the lands of the English amongst his followers, they, to protect themselves from the resentment of those so despoiled, built strong-holds and castles on their estates. This likewise caused a considerable increase of these fortresses; and the turbulent and unsettled state of the kingdom in the succeeding reigns, served to multiply them prodigiously, every baron or leader of a party building castles; insomuch, that towards the latter end of the reign of king Stephen, they amounted to the almost incredible number of 1115.

As the feudal system gathered strength, these castles became the heads of baronies. Each castle was a manor: and its castelain, owner, or governor, the lord of that manor. Markets and fairs were directed to be held there; not only to prevent frauds in the king's duties or customs, but also as they were esteemed places where the laws of the land were observed, and as such had a very particular privilege. But this good order did not long last: for the lords of castles began to arrogate to themselves a royal power, not only within their castles, but likewise its environs; exercising judicature both civil and criminal, coining of money, and arbitrarily seising forage and provision for the subsistence of their garrisons, which they afterwards demanded as a right: at length their insolence and oppression grew to such a pitch, that, according to William of Newbury, "there were in England as many kings, or rather tyrants, as lords of castles;" and Matthew Paris styles them, very nests of devils and dens of thieves. Castles were not solely in the possession of the crown and the lay barons, but even bishops had these fortresses; though it seems to have been contrary to the canons, from a plea made use of in a general council, in favour of king Stephen, who had seized upon the strong castles of the bishops of Lincoln and Salisbury. This prohibition (if such existed) was however very little regarded; as in the following reigns many strong places were held, and even defended, by the ecclesiastics: neither was more obedience afterwards paid to a decree made by the Pope at Viterbo, the sixth of the kalends of June 1220, wherein it was ordained, that no person in England should keep in his hands more than two of the king's castles.

The licentious behaviour of the garrisons of these places becoming intolerable, in the treaty between king Stephen and Henry II. when only duke of Normandy, it was agreed, that all the castles built within a certain period should be demolished; in consequence of which many were actually razed, but not the number stipulated.

The few castles in being under the Saxon government, were probably, on occasion of war or invasions, garrisoned by the national militia, and at other times slightly guarded by the domestics of the princes or great personages who resided therein; but after the conquest, when all the estates were converted into baronies held by knight's service, castle-guard coming under that denomination, was among the duties to which particular tenants were liable. From these services the bishops and abbots, who till the time of the Normans had held their lands in *frank almoign*, or free alms, were, by this new regulation, not exempted; they were not indeed, like the laity, obliged to personal service, it being sufficient that they provided fit and able persons to officiate in their stead. This was however at first stoutly opposed by Anselm archbishop of Canterbury; who being obliged to find some knights to attend king William Rufus in his wars in Wales, complained of it as an innovation and infringement of the rights and immunities of the church.

It was no uncommon thing for the Conqueror and the kings of those days, to grant estates to men of approved fidelity and valour, on condition that they should perform castle-guard in the royal castles, with a certain number of men, for some specified time; and sometimes they were likewise bound by their tenures to keep in repair and guard some particular tower or bulwark, as was the case at Dover castle.

In process of time these services were commuted for annual rents, sometimes styled *ward-penny*, and waytefee, but commonly *castle-guard* rents, payable on fixed days, under prodigious penalties called *surfises*. At Rochester, if a man failed in the payment of his rent of castle-guard on the feast of St Andrew, his debt was doubled every tide during the time for which the payment was delayed. These were afterwards restrained by an act of parliament made in the reign of king Henry VIII. and finally annihilated, with the tenures by knight's service, in the time of Charles II. Such castles as were private property were guarded either by mercenary soldiers, or the tenants of the lord or owner.

Castles which belonged to the crown, or fell to it either by forfeiture or escheat (circumstances that frequently happened in the distracted reigns of the feudal times), were generally committed to the custody of some trusty person, who seems to have been indifferently styled governor and constable. Sometimes also they were put into the possession of the sheriff of the county, who often

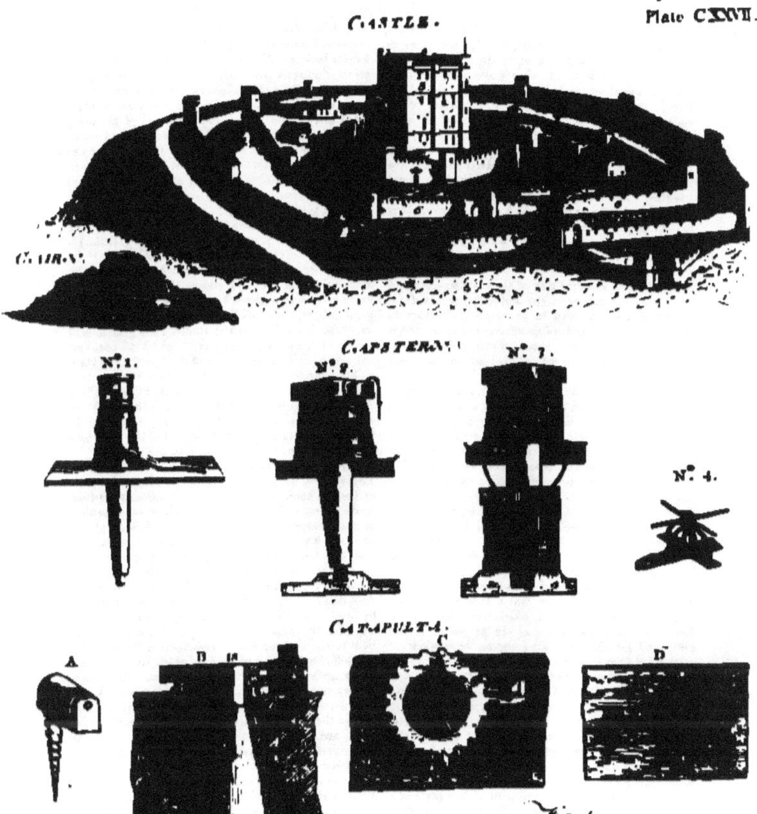
CASTLE.
Plate CXXVII.
CAIRN.
CAPSTERN.
No. 1.
No. 2.
No. 3.
No. 4.
CATAPULTA.
A
B
C
D
Fig. 1.

often converted them into priſons. That officer was then accountable at the exchequer, for the farms or produce of the lands belonging to the places entruſted to his care, as well as all other profits: he was likewiſe, in caſe of war or invaſion, obliged to victual and furniſh them with munition out of the iſſues of his county; to which he was directed by writ of privy ſeal.

The materials of which caſtles were built, varied according to the places of their erection; but the manner of their conſtruction ſeems to have been pretty uniform. The outſides of the walls were generally built with the ſtones neareſt at hand, laid as regularly as their ſhapes would admit; the inſides were filled up with the like materials, mixed with a great quantity of fluid mortar, which was called by the workmen grout-work.

The general ſhape or plan of theſe caſtles depended entirely on the caprice of the architects, or the form of the ground intended to be occupied: neither do they ſeem to have confined themſelves to any particular figure in their towers; ſquare, round, and poligonal, oftentimes occurring in the original parts of the ſame building.

The ſituation of the caſtles of the Anglo-Norman kings and barons, was moſt commonly on an eminence, and near a river; a ſituation on ſeveral accounts eligible. The whole ſite of the caſtle (which was frequently of great extent and irregular figure) was ſurrounded by a deep and broad ditch, ſometimes filled with water, and ſometimes dry, called the *foſſe*. Before the great gate was an outwork, called a *barbacan*, or *antemural*, which was a ſtrong and high wall, with turrets upon it, deſigned for the defence of the gate and draw-bridge. On the inſide of the ditch ſtood the wall of the caſtle, about eight or ten feet thick, and between 20 and 30 feet high, with a parapet, and a kind of embraſures, called *crenaels*, on the top. On this wall at proper diſtances ſquare towers of two or three ſtories high were built, which ſerved for lodging ſome of the principal officers of the proprietor of the caſtle, and for other purpoſes; and on the inſide were erected lodgings for the common ſervants or retainers, granaries, ſtorehouſes, and other neceſſary offices. On the top of this wall, and on the flat roofs of theſe buildings, ſtood the defenders of the caſtle, when it was beſieged, and from thence diſcharged arrows, darts, and ſtones, on the beſiegers. The great gate of the caſtle ſtood in the courſe of this wall, and was ſtrongly fortified with a tower on each ſide, and rooms over the paſſage, which was cloſed with thick folding-doors of oak, often plated with iron, and with an iron portcullis or grate let down from above. Within this outward wall was a large open ſpace or court, called, in the largeſt and moſt perfect caſtles, the *outer bayle*, or *ballium*, in which ſtood commonly a church or chapel. On the inſide of this outer bayle was another ditch, wall, gate, and towers, incloſing the inner bayle or court, within which the chief tower or *keep* was built. This was a very large ſquare fabric, four or five ſtories high, having ſmall windows in prodigious thick walls, which rendered the apartments within it dark and gloomy. This great tower was the palace of the prince, prelate, or baron, to whom the caſtle belonged, and the reſidence of the conſtable or governor. Under ground were diſmal dark vaults, for the confinement of priſoners, which made it ſometimes be called the *dungeon*. In this building alſo was the great hall, in which the owner diſplayed his hoſpitality, by entertaining his numerous friends and followers. At one end of the great halls of caſtles, palaces, and monaſteries, there was a place raiſed a little above the reſt of the floor, called the *deis*, where the chief table ſtood, at which perſons of the higheſt rank dined. Though there was unqueſtionably great variations in the ſtructure of caſtles, yet the moſt perfect and magnificent of them ſeem to have been conſtructed nearly on the above plan. Such, to give one example, was the famous caſtle of Bedford, as appears from the following account of the manner in which it was taken by Henry III. A. D. 1224. The caſtle was taken by four aſſaults. "In the firſt was taken the barbican; in the ſecond the outer ballia; at the third attack, the wall by the old tower was thrown down by the miners, where, with great danger, they poſſeſſed themſelves of the inner ballia, through a chink; at the fourth aſſault the miners ſet fire to the tower, ſo that the ſmoke burſt out, and the tower itſelf was cloven to that degree, as to ſhow viſibly ſome broad chinks: whereupon the enemy ſurrendered." See a repreſentation of a caſtle in Plate CXXVII. where 1 is the barbacan, 2 the ditch or moat, 3 the wall of the outer ballium, 4 the outer ballium, 5 the artificial mount, 6 the wall of the inner ballium, 7 the inner ballium, 8 the keep or dungeon.

Before the acceſſion of James VI. to the throne of England, the ſituation of Scotland was ſuch, that every baron's houſe was more or leſs fortified, according to the power and conſequence of its lord, or according to the ſituation of the caſtle. Near Edinburgh or Stirling, where the inhabitants were more poliſhed in their manners, and overawed by the ſeat of government, no more was neceſſary than towers capable of reſiſting the curſory attack of robbers and thieves, who never durſt ſtop to make a regular inveſtment, but plundered by ſurpriſe, and, if repulſed, inſtantly fled away. Such was Melville Caſtle. It anciently conſiſted of a ſtrong built tower of three ſtories, embattled at the top, and was ſufficiently ſtrong to reſiſt a ſudden attack, unaided by artillery, or other engines of war. But, when further removed, as in Perthſhire, Inverneſsſhire, or Aberdeenſhire, then it was neceſſary to be better defended, and the aids of a peel or dungeon, with outer walls, moat, and wet ditch, barmkin, &c. added to enable the powerful lord to reſiſt the formidable attack of his powerful adverſary. The hiſtory of Scotland, ſo late as the reign of the Stuart family, affords a number of melancholy inſtances of inveterate feuds among the greater and leſſer barons of that period; by which every mode of fortification then in uſe was ſeldom adequate to the defence of the caſtle againſt the ſtorm or blockade of the enraged chieftain. The caſtle of Doun ſeems to anſwer this deſcription of fortification, and has made ſeveral gallant defences, in the annals of Scotland. The third kind of fortreſſes we meet with in Scotland are thoſe ſituated on the borders of England, or on the ſea-coaſts of the kingdom, and in the weſtern iſles, and very remote places. Many of the old caſtles in Scotland were ſituated on an iſland, in a deep lake, or on a peninſula, which by a broad deep cut was made an iſland. Of this kind was Lochmaben, in the

ſtewartry

ſtewartry of Annandale, the caſtle of Cloſeburn in the ſhire of Nithſdale, the caſtle of the Rive, ſituated on the river Dee, in the ſhire of Galloway, Lochleven caſtle, and many others.

This kind of fortreſs was only acceſſible in a hard froſt, or by boats which were not eaſily tranſported, by a people deſtitute of good roads and wheel-carriages. In fact, they could only be taken by ſurpriſe or blockade; the firſt very difficult, the ſecond very tedious; ſo that, before the uſe of artillery, they might be deemed almoſt impregnable. On that account, their ſituation was very deſirable in the inland parts of Scotland.

On the ſea-coaſts of Scotland we generally find the ſtrongeſt and moſt ancient, as well as the moſt impregnable caſtles. Theſe had to defend themſelves from the invaſion of the foreign enemy, as well as the attacks of the domeſtic foe. Thus we find the barons, whoſe lands extended to the ſea-coaſt, perched, like the eagle, on the moſt inacceſſible rocks that lay within their poſſeſſions. Of this kind were Slains caſtle, Tantallon, and Dunotter on the eaſt coaſt, and Dunvegan in the iſle of Sky, with Dunolly on the weſt coaſt. Theſe muſt have been moſt uncomfortable retreats, except to a barbarous people, or when a preſſing danger forced the baron to ſeek his ſafety in the only poſſible retreat left him.

Castle, in ancient writers, denotes a town or village ſurrounded with a ditch and wall, furniſhed with towers at intervals, and guarded by a body of troops. The word is originally Latin, *caſtellum*, a diminutive from *caſtrum*. *Caſtellum* originally ſeems to have ſignified a ſmaller fort for a little garriſon; though Suetonius uſes the word where the fortification was large enough to contain a cohort. The *caſtella*, according to Vegetius, were often like towns, built on the borders of the empire, and where there were conſtant guards and fences againſt the enemy. Horſley takes them for much the ſame with what were otherwiſe denominated *ſtationes*.

Castle, or *Caſtle-ſteed*, is alſo an appellation given by the country-people in the north to the Roman *caſtella*, as diſtinguiſhed from the *caſtra ſtativa* which they uſually call *cheſters*. Horſley repreſents this as an uſeful criterion, whereby to diſcover or diſtinguiſh a Roman camp or ſtation. There are ſeveral of theſe caſtles on Severus's wall: they are generally 60 feet ſquare; their north ſide is formed by the wall itſelf which falls in with them; the intervals between them are from ſix furlongs and an half to ſeven; they ſeem to have ſtood cloſeſt where the ſtations are wideſt. The neighbouring people call them *caſtles* or *caſtle-ſteeds*, by which it ſeems probable that their ancient Latin name had been *caſtellum*. Some modern writers call them *mile-caſtles*, or military *caſtella*: Horſley ſometimes *exploratory caſtles*. In theſe *caſtella* the *areani* had their ſtations, who were an order of men whoſe buſineſs was to make incurſions into the enemies country, and give intelligence of their motions.

Castle, in the ſea language, is a part of the ſhip, of which there are two: the forecaſtle, being the elevation at the prow, or the uppermoſt deck towards the mizen, the place where the kitchens are. Hindcaſtle is the elevation which reigns on the ſtern, over the laſt deck, where the officers cabins and places of aſſembly are.

6

Castle (Edmund). See Castel.

Castle-Bar, a borough and market-town, capital of the county of Mayo in Ireland, is a well-inhabited place, and carries on a briſk trade: it has a barrack for a troop of horſe; and there is here a charter-ſchool capable of receiving fifty children, and endowed with two acres of land, rent-free, by the Right Honourable Lord Lucan, who has alſo granted a leaſe of twenty acres more at a pepper-corn yearly.

Castle-Cary, a remarkable Roman ſtation about four miles weſt from Falkirk on the borders of Stirlingſhire in Scotland. It comprehends ſeveral acres of ground, is of a ſquare form, and is ſurrounded with a wall of ſtone and mortar: all the ſpace within the walls has been occupied by buildings, the ruins of which have raiſed the earth eight or ten feet above its natural ſurface; ſo that the fort now ſeems like an hill-top ſurrounded with a ſunk fence. In 1770, ſome workmen employed in ſearching for ſtones for the great canal which paſſes very near it, diſcovered ſeveral apartments of ſtone; and in one of them a great number of ſtones about two feet in length, and ſtanding erect, with marks of fire upon them, as if they had been employed in ſupporting ſome veſſel under which fire was put. In a hollow of the rock near this place, in 1771, a conſiderable quantity of wheat quite black with age was found, with ſome wedges and hammers ſuppoſed to be Roman.

Castle-Riſing, a borough-town of Norfolk in England, which ſends two members to parliament. E. Long. 0. 40. N. Lat. 52. 46.

Castle-ward, ſervice or labour done by inferior tenants, for the building and upholding caſtles of defence, toward which ſome gave their perſonal aſſiſtance, and others paid their contributions. This was one of the three neceſſary charges to which the Anglo-Saxons were expreſsly ſubject.

CASTLETOWN, the capital of the iſle of Man, ſeated on the ſouth-weſt part of the iſland. It has a ſtrong caſtle; but of no great importance, on account of its diſtance from the rocky and ſhallow harbour. W. Long. 4. 39. N. Lat. 53. 50.

CASTOR, the Beaver, in zoology, a genus of quadrupeds belonging to the order of glires. The fore-teeth of the upper jaw are truncated, and hollowed in a tranſverſe angular direction. The tips of the fore-teeth of the lower jaw lie in a tranſverſe direction; and the tail is depreſſed. There are three ſpecies of caſtor, viz.

1. The fiber, or common beaver, with a plain ovated tail, is found on the banks of the rivers in Europe, Aſia, and America. It has ſhort ears hid in the fur; a blunt noſe; the fore-feet ſmall, the hinder large: its length from noſe to tail about three feet, tail about one foot. It is from the inguinal glands of this animal that the caſtor is obtained; it is contained in cods or pouches reſembling a dog's teſticles. Nothing equals the art with which theſe animals conſtruct their dwellings. They chooſe a level piece of ground, with a ſmall rivulet running through it. This they form into a pond, by making a dam acroſs; firſt by driving into the ground ſtakes of five or ſix feet in length, placed in rows, wattling each row with pliant twigs, and filling the interſtices with clay, ramming it down cloſe. The ſide next the water is ſloped, the other perpendicular;

Plate CXXVI.

Castor.

cular; the bottom is from ten to twelve feet thick; but the thickness gradually diminishes to the top, which is about two or three: the length of these dams is sometimes not less than 100 feet.

Their houses are made in the water collected by means of the dam, and are placed near the edge of the shore. They are built on piles; are either round or oval; but their tops are vaulted, so that their inside resembles an oven, the top a dome. The walls are two feet thick, made of earth, stones, and sticks, most artificially laid together; and the walls within as neatly plastered as if with a trowel. In each house are two openings, the one into the water, the other towards the land. The height of these houses above the water is eight feet. They often make two or three stories in each dwelling, for the conveniency of change in case of floods. Each house contains from 20 to 30 beavers; and the number of houses in each pond is from 10 to 25. Each beaver forms its bed of moss; and each family forms its magazine of winter provisions, which consist of bark and boughs of trees. Those they lodge under water, and fetch into their apartments as occasion requires. Lawson says, they are fondest of the sassafras, ash, and sweet gum. Their summer food is leaves, fruits, and sometimes crabs and craw fish; but they are not fond of fish.

To effect these works, a community of two or three hundred assembles; each bears his share in the labour; some fall to gnawing with their teeth trees of great size, to form beams or piles; others roll the pieces along to the water; others dive, and with their feet scrape holes in order to place them in; while others exert their efforts to rear them in their proper places: another party is employed in collecting twigs to wattle the piles with; a third in collecting earth, stones, and clay; a fourth is busied in beating and tempering the mortar; others in carrying it on their broad tails to proper places, and with the same instrument ram it between the piles, or plaster the inside of their houses. A certain number of smart strokes given with their tails, is a signal made by the overseer for repairing to such and such places, either for mending any defects, or at the approach of an enemy; and the whole society attend to it with the utmost assiduity. Their time of building is early in summer; for in winter they never stir but to their magazines of provisions, and during that season are very fat. They breed once a-year, and bring forth at the latter end of the winter two or three young at a birth.

Besides these associated beavers, is another sort called *terriers*, which either want industry or sagacity to form houses like the others. They burrow in the banks of rivers, making their holes beneath the freezing depth of the water, and work up for a great number of feet. These also form their winter stock of provision.

Beavers vary in their colours; the finest are black, but the general colour is a chesnut brown, more or less dark: some have been found, but very rarely, white. The skins are a prodigious article of trade, being the foundation of the hat-manufactory. In 1763 were sold, in a single sale of the Hudson's bay company, 54,670 skins. They are distinguished by different names. *Coat-beaver* is what has been worn as coverlets by the Indians: *Parchment-beaver*, because the lower side resembles it: *Stage-beaver* is the worst, and is that which the Indians kill out of season, on their stages or journeys.

In hunting the beavers, the savages sometimes shoot them, always getting on the contrary side of the wind; for they are very shy, quick in hearing, and of a keen scent. This is generally done when the beavers are at work, or on shore feeding on poplar bark. If they hear any noise when at work, they immediately jump into the water, and continue there some time; and when they rise, it is at a distance from the place where they went in.

They sometimes are taken with traps: these are nothing but poplar sticks laid in a path near the water; which when the beaver begins to feed upon, they cause a large log of wood to fall upon their necks, which is put in motion by their moving of the sticks, and consequently requires an ingenious contrivance. The savages generally prefer this way of taking them, because it does not damage their skins.

In the winter-time they break the ice in two places at a distance from the house, the one behind the other. Then they take away the broken ice with a kind of racket, the better to see where to place their stakes. They fasten their nets to these, which have large meshes, and sometimes are eighteen or twenty yards in length. When these are fixed, they proceed to demolish the house, and turn a dog therein; which terrifying the beaver, he immediately leaves it, and takes to the water; after which, he is soon entangled by the net.

2. The moschatus, with a long, compressed, lanceolated tail, and palmated feet. It has a long slender nose like that of a shrew-mouse; no external ears, and very small eyes. Length from nose to tail, seven inches; of the tail, eight. It is the water-rat of Clusius; and inhabits Lapland, Russia, the banks of the rivers Wolga and the Yaick. It never wanders far from the sides; is very slow in its pace; makes holes in the cliffs, with the entrance far beneath the lowest fall of the water; works upwards, but never to the surface, only high enough to be beyond the highest flow of the river: feeds on fish; is devoured by the pikes and *siluri*, and gives those fish so strong a flavour of musk as to render them not eatable; has the same scent as the former, especially about the tail, out of which is expressed a sort of musk very much resembling the genuine kind. The skins are put into chests among clothes, to drive away moths. At Orenburgh the skins and tails sell for 15 or 20 copecs *per* hundred. They are so common near Nisney Nowogorod, that the peasants bring 500 a-piece to market, where they are sold for one ruble *per* hundred. The German name for these animals is *bisem-ratze*; the Russian, *wychuchol*.

3. The zibethicus, or musk-rat, with a long, compressed, lanceolated tail, and the toes of the feet separated from each other. Length from nose to tail, one foot; of the tail, nine inches. This species inhabits North America, breeds three or four times in a year, and brings from three to six young ones at a time: during summer the male and female consort together: at the approach of winter they unite in families, and retire into small round edifices covered with a dome, formed of herbs and reeds cemented

with

Castor. with clays at the bottom are several pipes through which they pass in search of food; for they do not form magazines like the beavers: during winter their habitations are covered many feet deep with snow and ice; but they creep out and feed on the roots beneath: they quit their old habitations annually, and form new ones: the fur is soft and much esteemed: the whole animal, during summer, has a most exquisite smell of musk, which it loses in winter: perhaps the scent is derived from the calamus aromaticus, a favourite food of this animal. Lescarbot says they are very good to eat.

CASTOR, in astronomy, a moiety of the constellation GEMINI; called also APOLLO. Its latitude northwards, for the year 1700, according to Hevelius, was 10° 4′ 23″; and its longitude, of Cancer, 16° 4′ 14″. It is also called Rasalgeuse, Apollo, Aphellan, Avellar, and Anelar.

Castor and Pollux, in Pagan mythology. Jupiter having an amour with Leda, the wife of Tyndarus king of Sparta, in the form of a swan, she brought forth two eggs, each containing twins. From that impregnated by Jupiter proceeded Pollux and Helena, who were both immortal; from the other Castor and Clytemnestra, who being begot by Tyndarus were both mortal. They were all, however, called by the common name of *Tyndaridae*. These two brothers entered into an inviolable friendship: they went with the other noble youths of Greece in the expedition to Colchis, and, on several occasions, signalized themselves by their courage; but Castor being at length killed, Pollux obtained leave to share his own immortality with him; so that they are said to live and die alternately every day: for, being translated into the skies, they form the constellation of gemini, one of which stars rises as the other sets.

A martial dance, called the *Pyrrhic* or *Castorian* dance, was invented in honour of these deities whom the Cephelenses placed among the Dii Magni, and offered to them white lambs. The Romans also paid them particular honours on account of the assistance they are said to have given them in an engagement against the Latins; in which, appearing mounted on white horses, they turned the scale of victory in their favour, for which a temple was erected to them in the forum.

Castor and *Pollux*, a fiery meteor, which at sea appears sometimes sticking to a part of the ship, in form of one, two, or even three or four fire-balls: when one is seen alone, it is more properly called *Helena*; two are denominated Castor and Pollux, and sometimes Tyndaridae. Castor and Pollux are called by the Spaniards, San Elmo; by the French, St Elme, St Nicholas, St Clare, St Helene; by the Italians, Hermo; by the Dutch, Vree Vuuren.

Castor and Pollux are commonly judged to portend a cessation of the storm, and a future calm; being rarely seen till the tempest is nigh spent. Helena alone portends ill, and witnesses the severest part of the storm yet behind. When the meteor sticks to the masts, yards, &c. they conclude, from the air's not having motion enough to dissipate this flame, that a profound calm is at hand; if it flutter about, it indicates a storm.

Castoreum. CASTOREUM, in the Materia Medica, castor; the inguinal glands of the beaver. The ancients had a notion that it was lodged in the testicles; and that the animals, when hard pressed, would bite them off, and leave them to its pursuers, as if conscious of what they wanted to destroy him for. The best sort of castor is what comes from Russia. So much is Russian castor superior to the American, that two guineas per pound is paid for the former, and only 8s. 6d. for the latter. The Russian castor is in large hard round cods, which appear, when cut, full of a brittle, red, liver-coloured substance, interspersed with membranes and fibres exquisitely interwoven. An inferior sort is brought from Danzic, and is generally fat and moist. The American castor, which is the worst of all, is in longish thin cods. Russia castor has a strong disagreeable smell; and an acrid, bitterish, and nauseous taste. Water extracts the nauseous part, with little of the finer bitter; rectified spirit extracts this last without much of the nauseous; proof-spirit both: water elevates the whole of its flavour in distillation; rectified spirit brings over nothing. Castor is looked upon as one of the capital nervine and antihysteric medicines: some celebrated practitioners, nevertheless, have doubted its virtues; and Newman and Stahl declare it insignificant. Experience, however, has shown that the virtues of castor are considerable, tho' less than they have been generally supposed.

Castration. CASTRATION, in surgery, the operation of gelding, i. e. of cutting off the testicles, and putting a male animal out of a capacity of generation.

Castration is much in use in Asia, especially among the Turks, who practise it on their slaves, to prevent any commerce with their women. The Turks often make a general amputation.

Castration also obtains in Italy, where it is used with a view to preserve the voice for singing. See EUNUCH.

The Persians, and other eastern nations, have divers methods of making eunuchs, different from those which obtain in Europe: we say, of making eunuchs, for it is not always done among them by cutting, or even collision. Cicuta and other poisonous herbs do the same office, as is shewn by Paulus Aegineta. Those eunuchised in this manner are called *thlibiae*. Besides which there is another sort named *thlasiae*, in whom the genitals are left entire, and only the vessels which should feed them are cut; by which means the parts do indeed remain, but so lax and weak, as to be of no use.

Castration was for some time the punishment of adultery. By the laws of the Visigoths, sodomites underwent the same punishment.

By the civil law, it is made penal in physicians and surgeons to castrate, even with consent of the party, who is himself included in the same penalty, and his effects forfeited. The offence of Mayhem by castration is, according to all our old writers, felony; tho' committed upon the highest provocation. See a record to this purpose of Henry III. transcribed by Sir Edward Coke, 3 Inst. 62. or Blackstone's Com. vol. iv. p. 206.

Castration is sometimes found necessary on medicinal considerations, as in mortifications, and some other diseases of the testicles, especially the *sarcocele* and *varicocele*. Some have also used it in maniac cases.

Caſtration
Caſtruccio.

Castration is alſo in ſome ſort practiſed on women. Athenæus mentions, that king Andramytes was the firſt who caſtrated women. Heſychius and Suidas ſay Gyges did the ſame thing. Galen obſerves, that women cannot be caſtrated without danger of life; and Dalechampius, on the forementioned paſſage of Athenæus, holds, that it is only to be underſtood of ſimple pudlocking.

Castration, in reſpect of brutes, is called Gelding and Spaying.

Castration alſo denotes the art of retrenching, or cutting away any part of a thing from its whole.—*Caſtrating* a book, among bookſellers, is the taking out ſome leaf, ſheet, or the like, which renders it imperfect and unfit for ſale. The term is alſo applied to the taking away particular paſſages, on account of their obſcenity, too great freedom with reſpect to government, &c.

Castration, among botaniſts, a term derived from the fancied analogy betwixt plants and animals. The caſtration of plants conſiſts in cutting off the *anthera*, or tops of the ſtamina, before they have attained maturity, and diſperſed the pollen or fine duſt contained within their ſubſtance. This operation has been frequently practiſed by the moderns, with a view to eſtabliſh or confute the doctrine of the ſexes of plants; the antheræ or tops being conſidered by the ſexualiſts as the male organs of generation. The experiment of caſtration ſucceeds principally on plants which, like the melon, have their male flowers detached from the female. In ſuch as have both male and female flowers contained within the ſame covers, this operation cannot be eaſily performed without endangering the neighbouring organs. The reſult of experiments on this ſubject by Linnæus, Alſton, and other eminent botaniſts, may be ſeen under the article Botany, ſect. iii.

CASTREL, a kind of hawk reſembling the lanner in ſhape, but the hobby in ſize. The caſtrel is alſo called keſtrel, and is of a ſlow and cowardly kind; her game is the grous, though ſhe will kill a partridge.

CASTRES, a city of Languedoc in France, about 35 miles eaſt of Thoulouſe. E. Long. 2. and N. Lat. 43. 40. It is a biſhop's ſee.

CASTRO, the capital of the iſland of Chiloe, on the coaſt of Chili in South America. W. Long. 82. S. Lat. 43.

Castro is alſo the capital of a duchy of the ſame name in the Pope's territories in Italy, ſituated on the confines of Tuſcany. E. Long. 12. 35. N. Lat. 42. 30.

Castro (*Pietro de*), a celebrated painter, who flouriſhed about the middle of the 17th century. The ſubjects which this great artiſt choſe to paint, were what "are diſtinguiſhed by the name of ſtill life; vaſes, ſhells, muſical inſtruments, gems, veſſels of gold, ſilver, and cryſtal, books, and rich bracelets; and in thoſe ſubjects his choice and diſpoſition were elegant, and his execution admirable."

CASTRUCCIO (Caſtracani), a celebrated Italian general, was born (nobody knows of whom) at Lucca in Florence in 1284, and left in a vineyard covered with leaves, where he was found by Dianora a widow lady, the ſiſter of Antonio, a canon of St Michael in Lucca, who was deſcended from the illuſtrious family of the Caſtracani. The lady having no children, they reſolved to bring him up, and educated him as carefully as he had been their own. They intended him for a prieſt; but he was ſcarcely 14 years old when he began to devote himſelf to military ſports, and thoſe violent exerciſes which ſuited his great ſtrength of body. The factions named the *Guelfs* and *Gibelines* then ſhared all Italy between them; divided the popes and the emperors; and engaged in their different intereſts not only the members of the ſame town, but even thoſe of the ſame family. Franciſco, a conſiderable perſon on the ſide of the Gibelines, obſerving Caſtruccio's uncommon ſpirit and great qualities, prevailed with Antonio to let him turn ſoldier; on which Caſtruccio ſoon became acquainted with every thing belonging to that profeſſion, and was made a lieutenant of a company of foot by Franciſco Guinigi. In his firſt campaign he gave ſuch proofs of his courage and conduct as ſpread his fame all over Lombardy; and Guinigi, dying ſoon after, committed to him the care of his ſon and the management of his eſtate. Still diſtinguiſhing himſelf by his exploits, he filled his commander in chief with ſuch jealouſy and envy, that he was impriſoned by ſtratagem in order to be put to death. But the people of Lucca ſoon releaſed him, and afterwards choſe him for their ſovereign prince. The Gibelines conſidered him as the chief of their party; and thoſe who had been baniſhed from their country fled to him for protection, and unanimouſly promiſed, that if he could reſtore them to their eſtates, they would ſerve him ſo effectually that the ſovereignty of their country ſhould be his reward. Flattered by theſe promiſes, he entered into a league with the prince of Milan. He kept his army conſtantly on foot, employing it as beſt ſuited his own deſigns. For ſervices he had done the pope, he was made ſenator of Rome with more than ordinary ceremony; but while there, received news which obliged him to haſten back to Lucca. The Florentines entered into a war with him, but Caſtruccio fought his way through them; and the ſupreme authority of Tuſcany was ready to fall into his hands, when a period was put to his life. In May 1328, he gained a complete victory over his enemies, who amounted to 30,000 foot and 10,000 horſe; in which 22,000 of them were ſlain, with the loſs of not quite 16,000 of his own men: but as he was returning from the field of battle, tired with the action, and covered with ſweat, he halted a little, in order to thank and careſs his ſoldiers as they paſſed; when, the north wind blowing upon him, he was immediately ſeized with an ague, which he at firſt neglected, but it carried him off in a few days, in the 44th year of his age.

Machiavel, who has written the life of Caſtruccio, ſays, that he was not only an extraordinary man in his own age, but would have been ſo in any other. He was of a noble aſpect, and of the moſt winning addreſs. He had all the qualities that make a man great; was grateful to his friends, juſt to his ſubjects, terrible to his enemies. No man was more forward to encounter dangers; no man more careful to eſcape them. He had an uncommon preſence of mind, and often made repartees with great ſmartneſs. Some of them are recorded, which diſcover a ſingular turn of humour;

and, for a specimen, we shall mention three or four of them.—Passing one day through a street where there was a house of bad fame, he surprised a young man, who was just coming out, and who, upon seeing him, was all over blushes and confusion: "Friend, you should not be ashamed when you come out, but when you go in."—One asking a favour of him with a thousand impertinent and superfluous words: "Hark you, friend; when you would have any thing with me for the future, send another man to ask it."—Another great talker having tired him with a tedious discourse, excused himself at last, by saying, he was afraid he had been troublesome. "No indeed, (replied he), for I did not mind one word you said."—He was forced to put a citizen of Lucca to death, who had formerly been a great instrument of his advancement; and being reproached by somebody for having dealt so severely with an old friend, replied, "No, you are mistaken, it was with a new foe."—One of his courtiers, desirous to regale him, made a ball and invited him to it. Castruccio came, entertained himself among the ladies, danced, and did other things which did not seem to comport with the dignity of his rank. One of his friends intimating that such freedoms might diminish the reverence that ought to be paid him: "I thank you for your caution; but he who is reckoned wise all the day, will never be reckoned a fool at night."

CASTRUM DOLORIS, in middle-aged writers, denotes a catafalco, or a lofty tomb of state, erected in honour of some person of eminence, usually in the church where his body is interred; and decorated with arms, emblems, lights, and the like.

Ecclesiastical writers speak of a ceremony of consecrating a *castrum doloris*; the edifice was to be made to represent the body of the deceased, and the priest and deacon were to take their posts, and say the prayers after the same manner as if the corpse were actually present.

CASTS. See CASTING.

CASU CONSIMILI, in law, a writ of entry granted where a tenant, by courtesy or for life, aliens either in fee, in tail, or for the term of another's life. It is brought by him in reversion against the person to whom such tenant does so alien to the prejudice of the reversioner in the tenant's life-time.

Casu-Proviso, in law, a writ of entry founded on the statute of Gloucester, where a tenant in dower aliens the lands she so holds in fee, or for life; and lies for the party in reversion against the alienee.

CASUAL, something that happens fortuitously, without any design, or any measures taken to bring it to pass.

Casual-Revenues, are those which arise from forfeitures, confiscations, deaths, attainders, &c.

Casual-Theology, a denomination given to what is more frequently called CASUISTRY.

CASUALTY, in a general sense, denotes an accident, or a thing happening by chance, not design. It is particularly used for an accident producing unnatural death.

CASUALTY, in Scot's law. *Casualties of a superior*, are those duties and emoluments which a superior has right to demand out of his vassal's estate, over and besides the constant yearly duties established by the *reddendo* of his charter upon certain casual events.

CASUALTY, in Metallurgy. See CAUSALTY.

CASUIST, a person who proposes to resolve cases of conscience. Escobar has made a collection of the opinions of all the casuists before him. M. Le Fevre, preceptor of Louis XIII. called the books of the casuists the art of quibbling with God; which does not seem far from truth, by reason of the multitude of distinctions and subtleties they abound withal. Mayer has published a bibliotheca of casuists, containing an account of all the writers on cases of conscience, ranged under three heads, the first comprehending the Lutheran, the second the Calvinist, and the third the Romish, casuists.

CASUISTRY, the doctrine and science of conscience and its cases, with the rules and principles of resolving the same; drawn partly from natural reason or equity; partly from authority of scripture, the canon law, councils, fathers, &c. To casuistry belongs the decision of all difficulties arising about what a man may lawfully do or not do; what is sin or not sin; what things a man is obliged to do in order to discharge his duty, and what he may let alone without breach of it.

CASUS AMISSIONIS, in Scots law, in actions proving the tenor of obligations inextinguishable by the debtors retiring or cancelling them, it is necessary for the pursuer, before he is allowed a proof of the tenor, to condescend upon such a *casus amissionis*, or accident by which the writing was destroyed, as shews it was lost while in the writer's possession.

CAT, in zoology. See FELIS.

CAT, in sea-affairs, a ship employed in the coal-trade, formed from the Norwegian model. It is distinguished by a narrow stern, projecting quarters, a deep waist, and by having no ornamental figures on the prow. These vessels are generally built remarkably strong, and carry from four to six hundred tons, or, in the language of their own mariners, from 20 to 30 keels of coals.

CAT, is also a sort of strong tackle, or combination of pullies, to hook and draw the anchor perpendicularly up to the *cat-head*. See *CAT-Heads*.

Cat's Eye, or *Sun-stone* of the Turks, a kind of gem found chiefly in Siberia. Cat's-eye is by the Latins called *oculus cati*, and sometimes *asteropodus*, as having white zones or rings like the onyx; and its colours variable like OPAL, from which last it differs chiefly by its superior hardness. It is very hard, and semitransparent, and has different points, from whence the light is reflected with a kind of yellowish radiation somewhat similar to the eyes of cats, from whence it had its name. The best of them are very scarce, and jewellers cut them round to the greatest advantage. One of these stones, an inch in diameter, was in the possession of the duke of Tuscany.

Cat-Fish, in ichthyology. See SQUALUS.

Cat-Gut, a denomination given to small strings for fiddles, and other instruments, made of the intestines of sheep or lambs, dried and twisted together, either singly, or several together. These are sometimes coloured red, sometimes blue, but are commonly left whitish or brownish, the natural colour of the gut.

They

They are also used by watch-makers, cutlers, turners, and other artificers. Great quantities are imported into England, and other northern countries, from Lyons and Italy.

Cat-Harpings, a purchase of ropes employed to brace in the shrowds of the lower masts behind their yards, for the double purpose of making the shrowds more tight, and of affording room to draw in the yards more obliquely, to *trim* the sails for a side-wind, when they are said to be close hauled.

Cat-Heads, two strong short beams of timber, which project almost horizontally over the ship's bows on each side of the bow-sprit; being like two radii which extend from a centre taken in the direction of the bow-sprit. That part of the cat-head which rests upon the forecastle, is securely bolted to the beams: the other part projects like a crane as above described, and carries in its extremity two or three small wheels or *sheaves* of brass or strong wood, about which a rope called the *cat-fall* passes, and communicates with the cat-block, which also contains three sheaves. The machine formed by this combination of pullies is called the *Cat*, which serves to pull the anchor up to the cat-head, without tearing the ship's sides with its flukes. The cat-head also serves to suspend the anchor clear of the bow, when it is necessary to let it go: it is supported by a sort of knee, which is generally ornamented with sculpture. See Plate CXXVIII.

The cat-block is filled with a large and strong hook, which catches the ring of the anchor when it is to be drawn up.

Cat-Mint, See Mentha.

Cat-Salt, a name given by our salt-workers to a very beautifully granulated kind of common salt. It is formed out of the bittern, or leach-brine, which runs from the salt when taken out of the pan. When they draw out the common salt from the boiling pans, they put it into long wooden troughs, with holes bored at the bottom for the brine to drain out; under these troughs are placed vessels to receive this brine, and across them small sticks to which the cat-salt affixes itself in very large and beautiful crystals. This salt contains some portion of the bitter purging salt, is very sharp and pungent, and is white when powdered, though pellucid in the mass. It is used by some for the table, but the greatest part of what is made of it is used by the makers of hard-soap.

Cat-Silver. See Mica.

CATACAUSTIC curves, in the higher geometry, that species of caustic curves which are formed by reflection. See Fluxions.

CATACHRESIS, in rhetoric, a trope which borrows the name of one thing to express another. Thus Milton, describing Raphael's descent from the empyreal heaven to paradise, says,

" Down thither prone in flight,
" He speeds, and through the vast etherial sky
" Sails between worlds and worlds."

CATACOMB, a grotto, or subterraneous place for the burial of the dead.

Some derive the word *catacomb* from the place where ships are laid up, which the modern Latins and Greeks call *cumbe*. Others say, that *cata* was used for *ad*, and *catacumbas* for *adtumbas*: accordingly, Dadin says, they anciently wrote *catatumbas*. Others fetch the word from the Greek [illegible], and [illegible], a hollow, cavity, or the like.

Anciently the word *catacomb* was only understood of the tombs of St Peter and St Paul; and M. Chastelain observes, that, among the more knowing of the people of Rome, the word *catacomb* is never applied to the subterraneous burying-places hereafter mentioned, but only to a chapel in St Sebastian, one of the seven stational churches; where the ancient Roman kalendars say the body of St Peter was deposited, under the consulate of Tuscus and Bassus, in 354.

Catacombs of Italy; a vast assemblage of subterraneous sepulchres about Rome, chiefly at about three miles from that city in the Via Appia; supposed to be the sepulchres of the martyrs; and which are visited accordingly out of devotion, and relics thence taken and dispersed throughout the catholic countries, after having been first baptized by the pope under the name of some saint. These *catacombs* are said by many to be caves or cells wherein the primitive Christians hid and assembled themselves together, and where they interred such among them as were martyred. Each *catacomb* is three feet broad, and eight or ten high; running in form of an alley or gallery, and communicating with others: in many places they extend within a league of Rome. There is no masonry or vaulting therein, but each supports itself: the two sides, which we may look on as the *parietes* or walls, were the places where the dead were deposited; which were laid lengthwise, three or four rows over one another, in the same *catacomb*, parallel to the alley. They were commonly closed with large thick tyles, and sometimes pieces of marble, cemented in a manner inimitable by the moderns. Sometimes, though very rarely, the name of the deceased is found on the tyle: frequently a palm is seen, painted or engraven, or the cipher Xp, which is commonly read *pro Christo*. The opinion held by many Protestant authors is, that the *catacombs* are heathen sepulchres, and the same with the puticuli mentioned by Festus Pompeius; maintaining, that whereas it was the practice of the ancient Romans to burn their dead, the custom was, to avoid expence, to throw the bodies of their slaves to rot in holes of the ground; and that the Roman Christians, observing, at length, the great veneration paid to relics, resolved to have a stock of their own; entering therefore the *catacombs*, they added what ciphers and inscriptions they pleased; and then shut them up again, to be opened on a favourable occasion. Those in the secret, add they, dying or removing, the contrivance was forgot, till chance opened them at last. But this opinion has even less of probability than the former. Mr Monro, in the *Philosophical Transactions*, supposes the *catacombs* to have been originally the common sepulchres of the first Romans, and dug in consequence of these two opinions, viz. That shades hate the light; and that they love to hover about the places where the bodies are laid.

Though the catacombs of Rome have made the greatest noise of any in the world, there are such belonging to many other cities. Those of Naples, according to bishop Burnet, are much more noble and spacious than the catacombs of Rome. Catacombs have also been discovered at Syracuse, and Catanea in Sicily, and in the island of Malta. The Roman catacombs take particular names from the churches in their neighbourhood, and seem to divide the circumference of the city without the walls between them, extending their galleries every where under, and a vast way from it; so that all the ground under Rome, and for many miles about it, some say 20, is hollow. The largest, and those commonly shown to strangers, are the catacombs of San Sebastiano, those of Saint Agnese, and the others in the fields a little off Saint Agnese. Women are only allowed to go into the catacombs in the church-yard of the Vatican on Whitsun-Monday, under pain of excommunication. There are men kept constantly at work in the *catacombs*. As soon as these labourers discover a grave with any of the supposed marks of a saint upon it, intimation is given to the cardinal Camerlingo, who immediately sends men of reputation to the place, where finding the palm, the monogram, the coloured glass, *&c.* the remains of the body are taken up with great respect, and translated to Rome. After the labourers have examined a gallery, they stop up the entry that leads to it; so that most of them remain thus closed up; only a few being left open to keep up the trade of showing them to strangers. This they say is done to prevent people from losing themselves in these subterraneous labyrinths, which indeed has often happened; but more probably to deprive the public of the means of knowing whither and how far the catacombs are carried.

The method of preserving the dead in catacombs seems to have been common to a number of the ancient nations. The catacombs of Egypt are still extant about nine leagues from the city of Grand Cairo, and two miles from the city of Zaccara. They extend from thence to the pyramids of Pharaoh, which are about eight miles distant. They lie in a field covered with a fine running sand, of a yellowish colour. The country is dry and hilly; the entrance of the tomb is choaked up with sand; there are many open, but more that are still concealed.

The bodies found in catacombs, especially those of Egypt, are called *mummies*; and as their flesh was formerly reckoned an efficacious medicine, they were much sought after. In this work the labourers were often obliged to clear away the sand for weeks together, without finding what they wanted. Upon coming to a little square opening of about 18 feet in depth, they descend into it by holes for the feet, placed at proper intervals; and there they are sure of finding a mummy. These caves, or *wells* as they call them there, are hollowed out of a white free-stone, which is found in all this country a few feet below the covering of sand. When one gets to the bottom of these, which are sometimes 40 feet below the surface, there are several square openings on each side into passages of 10 or 15 feet wide; and these lead to chambers of 15 or 20 feet square. These are all hewn out in the rock; and in each of the catacombs are to be found several of these apartments communicating with one another. They extend a great way under ground, so as to be under the city of Memphis, and in a manner to undermine its invirons. In some of the chambers the walls are adorned with figures and hieroglyphics; in others the mummies are found in tombs, round the apartment hollowed out in the rock.

The Egyptians seem to have excelled in the art of embalming and preserving their dead bodies; as the mummies found in the Egyptian catacombs are in a better state than the bodies found either in the Italian catacombs or those of any other part of the world. See Embalming and Mummy.

Laying up the bodies in caves, is certainly the original way of disposing of the dead; and appears to have been propagated by the Phœnicians throughout the countries to which they sent colonies: the interring as we now do in the open air or in temples was first introduced by the Christians. When an ancient hero died or was killed in a foreign expedition, as his body was liable to corruption, and for that reason unfit to be transported entire, they fell on the expedient of burning, in order to bring home the ashes, to oblige the manes to follow; that so his country might not be destitute of the benefit of his tutelage. It was thus burning seems to have had its original; and by degrees it became common to all who could bear the expences of it, and took place of the ancient burying: thus *catacombs* became disused among the Romans, after they had borrowed the manner of burning from the Greeks, and then none but slaves were laid in the ground. See Burial, *&c.*

CATALAUNI, called also *Durocatalauni*, a town of Gallia Belgica: *Catalauni*, the people. A name rather of the lower age than of classical antiquity. Now *Chalons sur Marne*, in Champaign. E. Long. 4. 35. N. Lat. 48. 55.

CATADROMUS (from κατα and δρεμω, *I run*), in antiquity, a stretched sloping rope in the theatres, down which the *funambuli* walked to show their skill.

Some have taken the word to signify the hippodrome or decursorium wherein the Roman knights used to exercise themselves in running and fighting on horseback. But the most natural meaning is that of a rope fastened at one end to the top of the theatre, and at the other to the bottom, to walk or run down, which was the highest glory of the ancient *schœnobatæ* or *funambuli*. Elephants were also taught to run down the *catadromus*. Suetonius speaks of the exploit of a Roman knight, who passed down the *catadromus* mounted on an elephant's back.

CATAGOGION, a heathen festival at Ephesus, celebrated on the 22d of January, in which the devotees ran about the streets, dressed in divers antic and unseemly manners, with huge cudgels in their hands, and carrying with them the images of their gods; in which guise they ravished the women they met with, abused and often killed the men, and committed many other disorders, to which the religion of the day gave a sanction.

CATAGRAPHA, in antiquity, denote oblique figures or views of mens faces; answering to what the moderns call *profiles*.

Catagrapha are said to be the invention of Simon Cleonæus, who first taught painters to vary the looks of their figures, and sometimes direct them upwards, sometimes downwards, and sometimes sidewards or backwards.

CATALEPSIS, or Catalepsy, in medicine, a kind

Catalogue.

kind of apoplexy or a drowsy disease wherein the patient is taken speechless, senseless, and fixed in the same posture wherein the disease first seized him; his eyes open, without seeing or understanding. See MEDICINE-*Index*.

CATALOGUE, a list or enumeration of the names of several books, men, or other things, disposed according to a certain order.

Catalogues of books are digested in different manners, some according to the order of the times when the books were printed, as that of Mattaire; others according to their form and size, as the common booksellers-catalogues; others according to the alphabetical order of the authors names, as Hyde's catalogue of the Bodleian library; others according to the alphabetical order of matters or subjects, which are called *real* or *classical catalogues*, as those of Lipenius and Draudius; lastly, others are digested in a mixed method, partaking of several of the former, as de Seine's catalogue of cardinal Slusius's library, which is first divided according to the subjects or sciences, and afterwards the books in each are recited alphabetically.

The most applauded of all catalogues is that of Thuanus's library, in which are united the advantages of all the rest. It was first drawn up by the two Puteani in the alphabetical order, then digested according to the sciences and subjects by Ismael Bullialdus, and published by F. Quesnel at Paris in 1679; and reprinted, though incorrectly, at Hamburg, in 1704. The books are here ranged with justness under their several sciences and subjects, regard being still had to the nation, sect, age, &c. of every writer. Add, that only the best and choicest books in every subject are found here, and the most valuable editions. Yet the catalogue of M. le Tellier's archbishop of Rheim's library, made by M. Clement, is not inferior to any published in our age, either on account of the number and choice of the books, or the method of its disposition. One advantage peculiar to this catalogue is, the multitude of anonymous and pseudonymous authors detected in it, scarce to be met with elsewhere. Some even prefer it to Thuanus's catalogue, as containing a greater variety of classes and books on particular subjects.

The conditions required in a catalogue are, that it indicate at the same time the order of the authors and of the matters, the form of the book, the number of volumes, the chronological order of the editions, the language it is written in, and its place in the library; so as that all these circumstances may appear at once in the shortest, clearest, and exactest manner possible. In this view, all the catalogues yet made will be found to be defective.

An anonymous French writer has laid down a new plan of a catalogue, which shall unite all the advantages, and avoid all the inconveniences of the rest.

The Jesuits of Antwerp has given us a catalogue of the popes; which makes what they call their *Propylæum*.

CATALOGUE *of the Stars*, is a list of the fixed stars, disposed in their several constellations; with the longitudes, latitudes, &c. of each.

The first who undertook to reduce the fixed stars into a catalogue was Hipparchus Rhodius, about 120 years before Christ; in which he made use of the observations of Timocharis and Aristyllus for about 180 years before him. Ptolemy retained Hipparchus's catalogue, containing 1026 fixed stars; though he himself made abundance of observations, with a view to a new catalogue, A. D. 140. About the year of Christ 880, Albategni, a Syrian, brought down the same to his time. Anno 1437, Ulugh Beigh, king of Parthia and India, made a new catalogue of 1022 fixed stars, since translated out of Persian into Latin by Dr Hyde. The third who made a catalogue from his own observations was Tycho Brahe, who determined the places of 777 stars for the year 1600, which Kepler from other observations of Tycho afterwards increased to the number of 1000 in the Rudolphine tables; adding those of Ptolemy omitted by Tycho, and of other authors, so that his catalogue amounts to above 1160. At the same time, William landgrave of Hesse, with his mathematicians Christopher Rothmannus and Justus Byrgius, determined the places of 400 fixed stars by his own observations, with their places rectified for the year 1593: which Hevelius prefers to those of Tycho's. Ricciolus, in his *Astronomia Reformata*, determined the places of 101 stars for the year 1700, from his own observations: for the rest he followed Tycho's catalogue; altering it where he thought fit. Anno 1667, Dr Halley, in the island of St Helena, observed 350 southern stars not visible in our horizon. The same labour was repeated by F. Noel in 1710, who published a new catalogue of the same stars constructed for the year 1687.

Bayer, in his *Uranometria*, published a catalogue of 1160 stars, compiled chiefly from Ptolemy and Tycho, in which every star is marked with some letter of the Greek alphabet; the biggest star in any constellation being denoted by the first letter, the next by the second, &c. and if the number exceeds the Greek alphabet, the remaining stars are marked by letters of the Roman alphabet, which letters are preserved by Flamstead, and by Senex on his globes. The celebrated Hevelius composed a catalogue of 1888 stars, 1553 of which were observed by himself; and their places were computed for the year 1660.

The last and greatest is the Britannic catalogue, compiled from the observations of the accurate Mr Flamstead; who for a long series of years devoted himself wholly thereto. As there was nothing wanting either in the observer or apparatus, we may look on this as a perfect work so far as it goes. It is to be regretted the impression had not passed through his own hands: that now extant, was published by authority, but without the author's consent: it contains 2734 stars. There was another published in 1725, pursuant to his testament; containing no less than 3000 stars, with their places rectified for the year 1689: to which is added Mr Sharp's catalogue of the southern stars not visible in our hemisphere, adapted to the year 1726.

Catalogue, Catalonia.

CATALONIA, a province of Spain, bounded on the north by the Pyrenean mountains, which divide it from France; by the kingdom of Arragon and Valencia on the west; and by the Mediterranean sea on the south and east. It is 155 miles in length, and 100 in breadth. It is watered by a great number of rivers; the principal of which are the *Lobregat*, the Ter, and the

the Segra. The air is temperate and healthy; but the land is mountainous, except in a few places. It produces, however, corn, wine, oil, pulse, flax, and hemp, sufficient for the inhabitants. The mountains are covered with large forests of tall trees, such as the oak, the ever-green oak, the beech, the pine, the fir, the chesnut, and many others; with cork-trees, shrubs, and medicinal plants. There are several quarries of marble of all colours, crystal, alabaster, amethysts, and lapis lazuli. Gold dust has been found among the sands of one or two of the rivers; and there are mines of tin, iron, lead, alum, vitriol, and salt. They likewise fish for coral on the eastern coast. The inhabitants are hardy, courageous, active, vigorous, and good soldiers, but apt to be discontented. The miquelets are a sort of soldiers which guard the passes over the mountains, and ought to protect travellers; but if they are not paid to their minds, they seldom fail to pay themselves. The river Lobregat divides Catalonia into two parts, the east and west, according to their situation. This province comprehends 17 vigueries or territories; two of which are in Rousillon, and belong to the French. The rest are subject to the Spaniards. The principal towns are Barcelona the capital, Tarragona, Tortosa, Lerida, Solsona, Cardona Vich, Girona, Seu d'Urgel, Pui Cerda, and Cervera. Catalonia was the last province in Spain which submitted to Philip in the succession-war.

CATAMENIA, in medicine. See MENSES.

CATAMITE, a boy kept for sodomitical practices.

CATANA, or CATINA (anc. geog.), a town of Sicily, situated opposite to Ætna, to the south-east; one of the five Roman colonies: anciently built by the people of Naxos seven years after the building of Syracuse, 718 years before Christ. It was the country of Charondas, the famous lawgiver. The town is still called *Catania*. See CATANEA.

CATANANCHE, CANDIA LION'S-FOOT: A genus of the polygamia æqualis order, belonging to the syngenesia class of plants; and in the natural method ranking under the 49th order, *Compositæ*. The receptacle is paleaceous; the calyx imbricated; the pappus furnished with awns by a caliculus of five stiff hairs. There are three species, of which the cerulea is the most remarkable. This sends out many long, narrow, hairy leaves, which are jagged on their edges like those of the buckshorn plantain, but broader; the jags are deeper, and at greater distances: these lie flat on the ground, turning their points upwards. Between the leaves come out the flower stalks, which are in number proportionable to the size of the plants; for, from an old thriving root, there are frequently eight or ten, while young plants do not send out above two or three. These stalks rise near two feet high, dividing into many small branches upward, garnished with leaves like those below, but smaller, and without jags on their edges; each of these smaller branches are terminated by single heads of flowers, of a fine blue colour. This is a perennial plant, and may be propagated by seeds or slips. The seeds may be sown in the spring on a bed of common earth; and in the autumn following the plants may be removed to the places where they are to remain. The seeds ripen in August. This plant is a pretty ornament in gardens, and is easily kept within bounds.

CATANEA, or CATANIA, a city of Sicily, seated on a gulph of the same name, near the foot of Mount Ætna or Gibel. It was founded by the Chalcidians soon after the settlement of Syracuse, and enjoyed great tranquillity till Hiero I. expelled the whole body of citizens; and after replenishing the town with a new stock of inhabitants, gave it the name of *Ætna*: immediately after his decease, it regained its ancient name, and its citizens returned to their abodes. Catania fell into the hands of the Romans, among their earliest acquisitions in Sicily, and became the residence of a pretor. To make it worthy of such an honour, it was adorned with sumptuous buildings of all kinds, and every convenience was procured to supply the natural and artificial wants of life. It was destroyed by Pompey's son, but restored with superior magnificence by Augustus. The reign of Decius is famous in the history of this city for the martyrdom of its patroness St Agatha. On every emergency her intercession is implored. She is piously believed to have preserved Catania from being overwhelmed by torrents of lava, or shaken to pieces by earthquakes; yet its ancient edifices are covered by repeated streams of volcanic matter; and almost every house, even her own church, has been thrown to the ground. In the reign of William the Good, 20,000 Catanians, with their pastor at their head, were destroyed before the sacred veil could be properly placed to check the flames. In the last century the eruptions and earthquakes raged with redoubled violence, and Catania was twice demolished. See ÆTNA.

The present prince of Biscari has been at infinite pains, and spent a large sum of money, in working down to the ancient town, which on account of the numerous torrents of lava that have flowed out of Mount Ætna for these last thousand years, is now to be sought for in dark caverns many feet below the present surface of the earth. Mr Swinburne informs us that he descended into baths, sepulchres, an amphitheatre, and a theatre, all very much injured by the various catastrophes that have befallen them. They were erected upon old beds of lava, and even built with square pieces of the same substance, which in no instance appears to have been fused by the contact of new lavas: The sciarra or stones of cold lava, have constantly proved as strong a barrier against the flowing torrent of fire as any other stone could have been, though some authors were of opinion that the hot matter would melt the old mass and incorporate with it.

This city has been frequently defended from the burning streams by the solid mass of its own ramparts, and by the air compressed between them and the lava; as appears by the torrent having stopt within a small distance of the walls, and taken another direction. But when the walls were broken or low, the lava collected itself till it rose to a great height, and then poured over in a curve. A similar instance is seen at the Torre del Greco near Naples, where the stream of liquid fire from Vesuvius divided itself into two branches, and left a church untouched in the middle. There is a well at the foot of the old walls of Catania, where the lava, after running along the parapet, and then

]

falling

falling forwards, has produced a very complete lofty arch over the spring.

The church here is a noble fabric. It is accounted the largest in Sicily, though neither a porch nor cupola has been erected, from a doubt of the solidity of the foundations, which are no other than the bed of lava that ran out of Ætna in 1669, and is supposed to be full of cavities. The organ is much esteemed by connoisseurs in musical instruments.

Catania, according to Mr Swinburne's account, is reviving with great splendor. "It has already (he says) much more the features of a metropolis and royal residence than Palermo; the principal streets are wide, straight, and well paved with lava. An obelisk of red granite, placed on the back of an antique elephant of touchstone stands in the centre of the great square, which is formed by the town-hall, seminary, and cathedral. The cathedral erected by the abbot Angerius in the year 1094, was endowed by earl Roger with the territories of Catania and Ætna, for the small acknowledgment of a glass of wine and a loaf of bread offered once a-year. It has suffered so much by earthquakes, that little of the original structure remains, and the modern parts have hardly any thing except their materials to recommend them. The other religious edifices of the city are profusely ornamented, but in a bad taste. The spirit of building seems to have seized upon this people, and the prince of Biscari's example adds fresh vigour. It were natural to suppose men would be backward in erecting new habitations, especially with any degree of luxury, on ground so often shaken to its centre, and so often buried under the ashes of a volcano; but such is their attachment to their native soil, and their contempt of dangers they are habituated to, that they rebuild their houses on the warm cinders of Vesuvius, the quaking plains of Calabria, and the black mountains of Sciarra at Catania; it is however surprising to see such embellishments lavished in so dangerous a situation. There is a great deal of activity in the disposition of this people: they know by tradition that their ancestors carried on a flourishing commerce; and that, before the fiery river filled it up, they had a spacious convenient harbour, where they now have scarce a creek for a felucca: they therefore wish to restore those advantages to Catania, and have often applied to government for assistance towards forming a mole and port, an undertaking their strength alone is unequal to; but whether the refusal originates in the deficiencies of the public treasury or the jealousy of other cities, all their projects have ended in fruitless applications. The number of inhabitants dwelling in Catania amounts to 30,000; the Catanians make it double: A considerable portion of this number appertains to the university, the only one in the island, and the nursery of all the lawyers." E. Long. 15. 19. N. Lat. 37. 30.

CATANZARO, a city in the kingdom of Naples, the capital of Calabria Ulterior, with a bishop's see. It is the usual residence of the governor of the province, and is seated on a mountain, in E. Long. 18. 20. N. Lat. 38. 58.

CATAPHONICS, the science which considers the properties of reflected sounds. See ACOUSTICS.

CATAPHORA, in medicine, the same as COMA.

CATAPHRACTA (from κατα, and φρασσω, *I fortify or arm*), in the ancient military art, a piece of heavy defensive armour, formed of cloth or leather, fortified with iron scales or links, wherewith sometimes only the breast, sometimes the whole body, and sometimes the horse too, was covered. It was in use among the Sarmatians, Persians, and other Barbarians. The Romans also adopted it early for their foot; and, according to Vegetius, kept to it till the time of Gratian, when the military discipline growing remiss, and field exercises and labour discontinued, the Roman foot thought the cataphracta as well as the helmet too great a load to bear, and therefore threw both by, choosing rather to march against the enemy barebreasted; by which, in the war with the Goths, multitudes were destroyed.

CATAPHRACTÆ *Naves*, ships armed and covered in fight, so that they could not be easily damaged by the enemy. They were covered over with boards or planks, on which the soldiers were placed to defend them; the rowers sitting underneath, thus screened from the enemy's weapons.

CATAPHRACTUS, denotes a thing defended or covered on all sides with armour.

CATAPHRACTUS, or *Cataphractarius*, more particularly denotes a horseman, or even horse, armed with a cataphracta. The *cataphracti equites* were a sort of cuirassiers, not only fortified with armour themselves, but having their horses guarded with solid plates of brass or other metals, usually lined with skins and wrought into plumes or other forms. Their use was to bear down all before them, to break in upon the enemies ranks, and spread terror and havock wherever they came, as being themselves invulnerable and secure from danger. But their disadvantage was their unwieldiness, by which, if once unhorsed or on the ground, they were unable to rise, and thus fell a prey to the enemy.

CATAPHRYGIANS, a *sect* in the second century, so called as being of the country of Phrygia. They were orthodox in every thing, setting aside this, that they took Montanus for a prophet, and Priscilla and Maximilla for true prophetesses, to be consulted in every thing relating to religion; as supposing the Holy spirit had abandoned the church. See MONTANIST.

CATAPLASMA, a poultice; from καταπλασσω, *illino*, to spread like a plaster. Cataplasms take their name sometimes from the part to which they are applied, or effects they produce; so are called *anacollema*, *frontale*, *epicarpium*, *epispasticum*, *vesicatorium*; and when mustard is an ingredient, they are called *sinapisms*.

These kind of applications are softer and more easy than plasters or ointments. They are formed of some vegetable substances, and applied of such a consistence as neither to adhere nor run; they are also more useful when the intention is effected by the perpetuity of the heat or cold which they contain, for they retain them longer than any other kind of composition.

When designed to *relax*, or to promote suppuration, they should be applied warm. Their warmth, moisture, and the obstruction they give to perspiration, is the method of their answering that end. The proper heat, when applied warm, is no more than to promote a kindly pleasant sensation; for great heat prevents the design for which they are used. They should be renewed as often as they cool. For relaxing and

and ſuppurating, none excel the white-bread poultice, made with the crumb of an old loaf, a ſufficient quantity of milk to boil the bread in until it is ſoft, and a little oil; which laſt ingredient, beſides preventing the poultice from drying and ſticking to the ſkin, alſo retains the heat longer than the bread and milk alone would do. To preſerve the heat longer, the poultice, when applied, may be covered with a ſtrong ox's bladder.

When deſigned to *repel*, they ſhould be applied cold, and ought to be renewed as oft as they become warm. A proper compoſition for this end is a mixture of oatmeal and vinegar.

CATAPULTA, in antiquity, a military engine contrived for the throwing of arrows, darts, and ſtones upon the enemy.—Some of theſe engines were of ſuch force that they would throw ſtones of an hundred weight. Joſephus takes notice of the ſurpriſing effects of theſe engines, and ſays, that the ſtones thrown out of them beat down the battlements, knocked off the angles of the towers, and would level a whole file of men from one end to the other, was the phalanx ever ſo deep. This was called the

Battering Catapulta, and is repreſented on Plate CXXVII. This catapulta is ſuppoſed to carry a ſtone, *&c.* of an hundred weight, and therefore a deſcription of it will be ſufficient to explain the doctrine of all the reſt; for ſuch as threw ſtones of 300 and upwards were conſtructed on the ſame principles.

The baſe is compoſed of two large beams 2, 3. The length of theſe beams is fifteen diameters of the bore of the capitals 9. At the two extremities of each beam, two double mortiſes are cut to receive the eight tenons of two croſs beams, each of them four of the diameters in length. In the centre of each of the beams of the baſe, and near two thirds of their length, a hole, perfectly round, and 16 inches in diameter, ſhould be bored: theſe holes muſt be exactly oppoſite to each other, and ſhould increaſe gradually to the inſide of the beams, ſo that each of them, being 16 inches on the outſide towards the capitals 9, ſhould be 17½ at the opening on the inſide, and the edges carefully rounded off. The capitals 9 are, in a manner, the ſoul of the machine, and ſerve to twiſt and ſtrain the cordage, which forms its principle or power of motion.

The capitals are either of caſt braſs or iron; each conſiſting of a wheel with teeth, C 10, of 2½ inches thick. The hollow or bore of theſe wheels ſhould be 11½ inches in diameter, perfectly round, and the edges ſmoothed down. As the friction would be too great, if the capitals rubbed againſt the beams, by the extreme ſtraining of the cordage, which draws them towards theſe beams, that inconvenience is remedied by the means of eight friction-wheels, or cylinders of braſs, about the 13th of an inch in diameter, and an inch and one ſixth in length, placed circularly, and turning upon axes, as repreſented at D 13, B 12. One of theſe friction-wheels at large with its ſcrew, by which it is faſtened into the beam, is repreſented at A.

Upon this number of cylindrical wheels the capitals 9 muſt be placed in the beams, 2, 3, ſo that the cylinders do not extend to the teeth of the wheels, which muſt receive a ſtrong pinion 14. By the means of this pinion the wheel of the capital is made to turn for ſtraining the cordage with the key 15. The capital wheel has a ſtrong catch 16, and another of the ſame kind may be added to prevent any thing from giving way through the extreme and violent force of the ſtrained cordage.

The capital-piece of the machine is a nut or eſſeopin of iron, 17, ſeen at C, and hammered cold into its form. It divides the bore of the capitals exactly in two equal parts, and fixed in groves about an inch deep. This piece, or nut, ought to be about two inches and one third thick at the top 18, as repreſented in the ſection at B; and rounded off and poliſhed as much as poſſible, that the cords folded over it may not be hurt or cut by the roughneſs or edges of the iron. Its height ought to be eight inches, decreaſing gradually in thickneſs to the bottom, where it ought to be only one inch. It muſt be very exactly inſerted in the capitals.

After placing the two capitals in the holes of the two beams in a right line with each other, and fixing the two croſs diametrical unte or pieces over which the cordage is to wind, one end of the cord is feeved through a hole in one of the capitals in the baſe, and made faſt to a nail within-ſide of the beam. The other ſide of the cord is then carried through the hole in the oppoſite beam and capital, and ſo wound over the croſs pieces of iron in the centre of the two capitals, till they are full, the cordage forming a large ſkain. The tenſion or ſtraining of the cordage ought to be exactly equal, that is, the ſeveral foldings of the cord over the capital-pieces ſhould be equally ſtrained, and ſo near each other as not to leave the leaſt ſpace between them. As ſoon as the firſt folding or ſkain of cord has filled up one whole ſpace or breadth of the capital pieces, another muſt be carried over it; and ſo on, always equally ſtraining the end till no more will paſs through the capitals, and the ſkain of cordage entirely fills them, obſerving to rub it from time to time with ſoap.

At three or four inches behind the cordage, thus wound over the capital pieces, two very ſtrong upright beams 21 are raiſed: theſe are poſts of oak 14 inches thick, croſſed over at top by another of the ſame ſolidity. The height of the upright beams is 9½ diameters; each ſupported behind with very ſtrong props 25, fixed at bottom in the extremities of the baſe 2, 3. The croſs beam 24 is ſupported in the ſame manner by a prop in the centre.

The tree, arm, or ſtylus 22, ſhould be of ſound aſh. Its length is from 15 to 16 diameters of the bore of the capitals. The end at the bottom, or that fixed in the middle of the ſkain, is 10 inches thick, and 14 broad. To ſtrengthen the arm or tree, it ſhould be wrapped round with a cloth dipped in ſtrong glue like the tree of a ſaddle, and bound very hard with waxed thread of the ſixth of an inch in diameter from the large end at bottom, almoſt to the top, as repreſented in the figure.

At the top of the arm, juſt under the iron-hand or receiver 27, a ſtrong cord is faſtened, with two loops twiſted one within another, for the greater ſtrength. Into theſe two loops the hook of a braſs pulley 28 is put. The cord 29 is then reeved through the pulley, and faſtened to the roll 30. The cock or trigger 31, which

which serves as a stay, is then brought to it, and made fast by its hook to the extremity of the band 27, in which the body to be discharged is placed. The pulley at the neck of the arm is then unhooked; and when the trigger is to let it off, a stroke must be given upon it with an iron-bar or crow of about an inch in diameter; on which the arm flies up with a force almost equal to that of a modern mortar. The cushion or stomacher 25, placed exactly in the middle of the cross beam 24, should be covered with turned ox-hide, and stuffed with hair, the arm striking against it with inconceivable force. It is to be observed, that the tree or arm 22 describes an angle of 90 degrees, beginning at the catch, and ending at the stomacher or cushion.

Catapulta for Arrows, Spears, or Darts. Some of the spears, *&c.* thrown by these engines, are said to have been 18 feet long, and to have been thrown with such velocity as to take fire in their course.

Fig. 1. ABCD is the frame that holds the darts or arrows, which may be of different numbers, and placed in different directions. EF is a large and strong iron spring, which is bent by a rope that goes over three pullies, I, K, L; and is drawn by one or several men; this rope may be fastened to a pin at M. The rope, therefore, being set at liberty, the spring must strike the darts with great violence, and send them, with surprising velocity, to a great distance. This instrument differs in some particulars from the description we have of that of the ancients; principally in the throwing of several darts at the same time, one only being thrown by theirs.

CATARACT, in hydrography, a precipice in the channel of a river, caused by rocks, or other obstacles, stopping the course of the stream, from whence the water falls with a greater noise and impetuosity. The word comes from , "I tumble down with violence;" compounded of , "down," and , *dejicio*, "I throw down."—Such are the cataracts of the Nile, the Danube, Rhine, &c. In that of Niagara, the perpendicular fall of the water is 137 feet; and in that of Pistill Rhaiadr, in North Wales, the fall of water is near 240 feet from the mountain to the lower pool.

Strabo calls that a *cataract* which we call a *cascade*; and what we call a *cataract*, the ancients usually called a *catadupa*. Herminius has an express dissertation, "De admirandis mundi Cataractis supra et subterraneis;" where he uses the word in a new sense; signifying, by cataract, any violent motion of the elements.

Cataract, in medicine and surgery, a disorder of the humours of the eye, by which the pupilla, that ought to appear transparent and black, looks opaque, blue, grey, brown, &c. by which vision is variously impeded, or totally destroyed. See Surgery.

CATARO, a town of Dalmatia, and capital of the territory of the same name, with a strong castle, and a bishop's see. It is subject to Venice, and seated on a gulph of the same name. E. Long. 19. 19. N. Lat. 42. 25.

CATARACTES, in ornithology, the trivial name of a species of Larus.

CATARRH, in medicine, a distillation or defluxion from the head upon the mouth and aspera arteria, and through them upon the lungs. See (the *Index* subjoined to) Medicine.

CATASTASIS, in poetry, the third part of the ancient drama; being that wherein the intrigue, or action, set forth in the epitasis, is supported, carried on, and heightened, till it be ripe for the unravelling in the catastrophe. Scaliger defines it, the full growth of the fable, while things are at a stand in that confusion to which the poet has brought them.

CATASTROPHE, in dramatic poetry, the fourth and last part in the ancient drama; or that immediately succeeding the catastasis: or, according to others, the third only; the whole drama being divided into protasis, epitasis, and catastrophe; or in the terms of Aristotle, prologue, epilogue, and exode.

The catastrophe clears up every thing, and is nothing else but the discovery or winding up of the plot. It has its peculiar place; for it ought entirely to be contained, not only in the last act, but in the very conclusion of it; and when the plot is finished, the play should be so also. The catastrophe ought to turn upon a single point, or start up on a sudden.

The great art in the catastrophe is, that the clearing up of all difficulties may appear wonderful, and yet easy, simple, and natural.

It is a very preposterous artifice of some writers to show the catastrophe in the very title of the play. Mr Dryden thinks that a catastrophe resulting from a mere change in the sentiments and resolutions of a person, without any other machinery, may be so managed as to be exceedingly beautiful.

It is a dispute among the critics, whether the catastrophe should always fall out favourably on the side of virtue or not. The reasons on the negative side seem the strongest. Aristotle prefers a shocking catastrophe to a happy one.—The catastrophe is either simple or complex. The first is that in which there is no change in the state of the principal persons, nor any discovery or unravelling, the plot being only a mere passage out of agitation into quiet repose. In the second, the principal persons undergo a change of fortune, in the manner already defined.

CATCH, in the musical sense of the word, a fugue in the unison, wherein, to humour some conceit in the words, the melody is broken, and the sense interrupted in one part, and caught again or supported by another; as in the catch in Shakespeare's play of the Twelfth-night, where there is a catch sung by three persons, in which the humour is, that each who sings, calls and is called *knave* in turn. Or, as defined by Mr Jackson, "a catch is a piece for three or more voices, one of which leads, and the others follow in the same notes. It must be so contrived, that rests (which are made for that purpose) in the music of one line be filled up with a word or two from another line; these form a cross purpose, or catch, from whence the name."

Catch-Fly, in botany. See Lychnis.

Catch-Pole, (quasi one that *catches* by the *pole*), a term used, by way of reproach, for the bailiff's follower or assistant.

Catch-Word, among printers, that placed at the bottom of each page, being always the first word of the following page.

CATECHESIS, in a general sense, denotes an instruction

struction given any person in the first rudiments of an art or science; but more particularly of the Christian religion. In the ancient church, catechesis was an instruction given *viva voce*, either to children, or adult heathens, preparatory to their receiving of baptism. In this sense, *catechesis* stands contradistinguished from *mystagogics*, which were a higher part of instruction given to those already initiated, and containing the mysteries of faith. Those who give such instructions are called *catechists*; and those who receive them, *catechumens*.

CATECHETIC, or CATECHETICAL, something that relates to oral instruction in the rudiments of Christianity.—Catechetic schools were buildings appointed for the office of the catechist, adjoining to the church, and called *catechumena*; such was that in which Origen and many other famous men read catechetical lectures at Alexandria. See CATECHUMEN.

CATECHISM, in its primary sense, an instruction, or institution, in the principles of the Christian religion, delivered *viva voce*, and so as to require frequent repetitions, from the disciple or hearer, of what has been said. The word is formed from κατηχεω, a compound of κατα and ηχεω, q. d. *circumsono*, alluding to the noise or din made in this sort of exercise, or to the zeal and earnestness wherewith things are to be inculcated over and over on the learners.—Anciently the candidates for baptism were only to be instructed in the secrets of their religion by tradition *viva voce*, without writing; as had also been the case among the Egyptian priests, and the British and Gaulish druids, who only communicated the mysteries of their theology by word of mouth.

CATECHISM is more frequently used in modern times for an elementary book, wherein the principal articles of religion are summarily delivered in the way of question and answer.

CATECHIST, κατηχιστης, *catechista*, he that catechises, *i. e.* he that instructs novices in the principles of religion.

CATECHIST more particularly denotes a person appointed by the church to *instruct* those intended for baptism, by word of mouth, in the fundamental articles of the Christian faith.—The catechists of churches were ministers usually distinct from the bishops and presbyters, and had their auditories or *catechumena* apart. Their business was to instruct the catechumens, and prepare them for the reception of baptism. But the catechists did not constitute any distinct order of the clergy, but were chosen out of any other order. The bishop himself sometimes performed the office; at other times presbyters, or even readers or deacons, were the catechists. Origen seems to have had no higher degree in the church than reader, when he was made catechist at Alexandria, being only 18 years of age, and consequently incapable of the deaconship.

CATECHU, in the materia medica, the name of a troche consisting of Japan earth and gum arabic, each two ounces, and of sugar of roses sixteen ounces, beat together with a little water. It is recommended as a mild restringent, &c.

CATECHUMEN, a candidate for baptism, or one who prepares himself for the receiving thereof.

The catechumens, in church-history, were the lowest order of Christians in the primitive church. They had some title to the common name of Christian, being a degree above pagans and heretics, though not consummated by baptism. They were admitted to the state of catechumens by the imposition of hands, and the sign of the cross. The children of believing parents were admitted catechumens, as soon as ever they were capable of instruction; but at what age those of heathen parents might be admitted, is not so clear. As to the time of their continuance in this state, there were no general rules fixed about it; but the practice varied according to the difference of times and places, and the readiness and proficiency of the catechumens themselves.

There were four orders or degrees of catechumens; the first were those instructed privately without the church, and kept at a distance for some time from the privilege of entering the church, to make them the more eager and desirous of it. The next degree were the *audientes*, so called from their being admitted to hear sermons, and the scriptures read in the church, but were not allowed to partake of the prayers. The third sort of catechumens were the *genuflectentes*, so called because they received imposition of hands kneeling. The fourth order was the *competentes & electi*, denoting the immediate candidates for baptism, or such as were appointed to be baptized the next approaching festival; before which, strict examination was made into their proficiency under the several stages of catechetical exercises.

After examination, they were exercised for twenty days together, and were obliged to fasting and confession: some days before baptism they went veiled; and it was customary to touch their ears, saying, *Ephatha*, i. e. Be opened; as also to anoint their eyes with clay; both ceremonies being in imitation of our Saviour's practice, and intended to shadow out to the catechumens their condition both before and after their admission into the Christian church.

CATEGORICAL, in a general sense, is applied to those things ranged under a CATEGORY.

CATEGORICAL also imports a thing to be absolute, and not relative; in which sense it stands opposed to *hypothetical*. We say, a *categorical* proposition, a *categorical* syllogism, &c.

A *categorical* answer denotes an express and pertinent answer made to any question or objection proposed.

CATEGORY, in logic, a series or order of all the predicates or attributes contained under any genus.

The school-philosophers distribute all the objects of our thoughts and ideas into certain *genera* or classes, not so much, say they, to learn what they do not know, as to communicate a distinct notion of what they do know; and these classes the Greeks called *categories*, and the Latins *prædicaments*.

Aristotle made ten categories, viz. quantity, quality, relation, action, passion, time, place, situation, and habit, which are usually expressed by the following technical distich:

Arbor, sex, servos, ardore, refrigerat, ustos,
Ruri cras stabo, nec tunicatus ero.

CATEK. See BENGAL, n° 15.

CATENARIA, in the higher geometry, the name of a curve-line formed by a rope hanging freely from two points of suspension, whether the points be horizontal or not. See FLUXIONS.

CATERPILLAR, in zoology, the name of all winged insects when in their reptile or worm-state. See ERUCA.

Method of Destroying CATERPILLARS *on Trees.*— Take a chafing dish with lighted charcoal, and placing it under the branches that are loaded with caterpillars, throw some pinches of brimstone upon the coals. The vapour of the sulphur, which is mortal to these insects, will not only destroy all that are on the tree, but prevent it from being infected with them afterwards. A pound of sulphur will clear as many trees as grow on several acres. This method has been successfully tried in France. In the *Journal Oeconomique*, the following is said to be infallible against the caterpillars feeding on cabbage, and perhaps may be equally serviceable against those that infest other vegetables. Sow with hemp all the borders of the ground where you mean to plant your cabbage; and, although the neighbourhood is infested with caterpillars, the space inclosed by the hemp will be perfectly free, not one of the vermin will approach it.

Caterpillar-Eaters, a name given by some authors to a species of worms bred in the body of the caterpillar, and which eat its flesh: these are owing to a certain kind of fly that lodges her eggs in the body of this animal, and they, after their proper changes, become flies like their parents.

Mr Reaumur has given us, in his history of insects, some very curious particulars in regard to these little worms. Every one of them, he observes, spins itself a very beautiful case of a cylindric figure, made of a very strong sort of silk; these are the cases in which this animal spends its state of chrysalis; and they have a mark by which they may be known from all other animal productions of this kind, which is, that they have always a broad stripe or band surrounding their middle, which is black when the rest of the case is white, and white when that is black. Mr Reaumur has had the pains and patience to find out the reason of this singularity, which is this: the whole shell is spun of a silk produced out of the creature's body: this at first runs all white, and towards the end of the spinning turns black. The outside of the case must necessarily be formed first, as the creature works from within: consequently this is truly white all over, but it is transparent, and shows the last spun or black silk through it. It might be supposed that the whole inside of the shell should be black; but this is not the case: the whole is fashioned before this black silk comes; and this is employed by the creature, not to line the whole, but to fortify certain parts only; and therefore is all applied either to the middle, or to the two ends omitting the middle; and so gives either a black band in the middle, or a black case at both ends, leaving the white in the middle to appear. It is not unfrequent to find a sort of small cases, lying about garden-walks, which move of themselves; when these are opened, they are found to contain a small living worm. This is one of the species of these caterpillar-eaters; which, as soon as it comes out of the body of that animal, spins itself a case for its transformation long before that happens, and lives in it without food till that change comes on; and it becomes a fly like that to which it owed its birth.

CATERVA, in ancient military writers, a term used in speaking of the Gaulish or Celtiberian armies, denoting a body of 6000 armed men. The word *caterva*, or *catervarius*, is also frequently used by ancient writers to denote a party or corps of soldiers in disorder or disarray: by which it stands distinguished from cohort or turma, which were in good order.

CATESBÆA, the LILY-THORN: A genus of the monogynia order, belonging to the tetrandria class of plants; and in the natural method ranking under the 48th order, *Luridæ*. The corolla is monopetalous, funnel-shaped, very long above the receptacle of the fruit; the stamina are within its throat; the fruit a polyspermous berry. There is only one species, viz. the spinosa, which was discovered in the island of Providence by Mr Catesby, who gathered the seeds, and brought them to England. It rises to the height of ten or twelve feet, and is covered with a pale russet bark; the branches come out alternately, and are garnished with small leaves resembling those of the box-tree, coming out in clusters all round the branches at certain distances; the flowers hang downward, and come out from the side of the branches: they are tubulous and near six inches long, very narrow at their base, but widening upwards towards the top, where it is divided into four parts which spread open, and are reflexed backward. They are of a dull yellow colour. This plant is propagated by seeds which must be procured from the country where it grows. The seeds must be sown on a hot-bed, and are to be treated in the same manner as other tender exotics.

CATHÆRETICS, in pharmacy, medicines of a caustic nature, serving to eat off proud flesh.

CATHARINE, *Knights of St* CATHARINE *of Mount Sinai*, an ancient military order, erected for the assistance and protection of pilgrims going to pay their devotions to the body of St Catharine, a virgin of Alexandria, distinguished for her learning, and said to have suffered martyrdom under Maximin. The body of the martyr having been discovered on mount Sinai, caused a great concourse of pilgrims; and travelling being very dangerous, by reason of the Arabs, an order of knighthood was erected in 1063, on the model of that of the holy sepulchre, and under the patronage of St Catharine: the knights of which obliged themselves by oath to guard the body of the saint, keep the roads secure, observe the rule of St Basil, and obey their grand master. Their habit was white, and on it were represented the instruments of martyrdom whereby the saint had suffered; viz. a half-wheel armed with spikes, and traversed with a sword stained with blood.

CATHARINE, *Fraternity of St Catharine at Sienna*, a sort of religious society instituted in that city, in honour of St Catharine, a saint famous for her revelations, and for her marriage with Jesus Christ, whose wedding ring is still preserved as a valuable relick. This fraternity yearly endows a certain number of destitute virgins, and has the privilege of redeeming annually two criminals condemned for murder, and the same number of debtors, by paying their debts.

CATHARTICS, in medicine, remedies which pro-more evacuation by stool. See Materia Medica.

CATHECU, in botany. See Areca.

CATHEDRA, in a general sense, a chair.—The word is more particularly used for a professor's chair, and a preacher's pulpit.

Cathedra is also used for the bishop's see, or throne, in a church.

CATHEDRAL, a church wherein is a bishop's see or seat: See Church, and Bishop. The word comes from the Greek καθεδρα, "chair," of καθεζομαι, *sedeo*, "I sit." The denomination *cathedral* seems to have taken its rise from the manner of sitting in the ancient churches, or assemblies of primitive Christians: in these, the council, i.e. the elders and priests, was called *Presbyterium*; at their head was the bishop, who held the place of chairman, *Cathedralis*, or *Cathedraticus*; and the presbyters, who sat on either side, were also called by the ancient fathers, *Assessores Episcoporum*. The episcopal authority did not reside in the bishop alone; but in all the presbyters, whereof the bishop was president. A *cathedral* therefore, originally, was different from what it is now; the Christians, till the time of Constantine, having no liberty to build any temple: by their churches they only meant their assemblies; and by *cathedrals*, nothing more than consistories.

CATHERINE Parr. See Parr.

Catherine I. *Empress of Russia*, a most extraordinary personage, whose history deserves to be given in detail. She was the natural daughter of a country girl; and was born at Ringen, a small village upon the lake Virtcherve, near Dorpt, in Livonia. The year of her birth is uncertain; but, according to her own account, she came into the world on the 5th of April, 1687. Her original name was Martha, which she changed for Catherine when she embraced the Greek religion. Count Rosen, a lieutenant-colonel in the Swedish service, who owned the village of Ringen, supported, according to the custom of the country, both the mother and the child; and was, for that reason, supposed by many persons to have been her father. She lost her mother when she was but three years old; and, as count Rosen died about the same time, she was left in so destitute a situation, that the parish-clerk of the village received her into his house. Soon afterwards Gluck, Lutheran minister of Marienburgh, happening, in a journey through those parts, to see the foundling, took her under his protection, brought her up in his family, and employed her in attending his children. In 1701, and about the 14th year of her age, she espoused a dragoon of the Swedish garrison of Marienburgh. Many different accounts are given of this transaction: one author of great credit affirms that the bride and bridegroom remained together eight days after their marriage; another, of no less authority, asserts, on the contrary, that on the morning of the nuptials her husband being sent with a detachment for Riga, the marriage was never consummated. Thus much is certain, that the dragoon was absent when Marienburgh surrendered to the Russians; and Catherine, who was reserved for a higher fortune, never saw him more.

General Bauer, upon the taking of Marienburgh, saw Catherine among the prisoners; and, being smitten with her youth and beauty, took her to his house, where she superintended his domestic affairs, and was supposed to be his mistress. Soon afterwards she was removed into the family of prince Menzikof, who was no less struck with the attractions of the fair captive. With him she lived until 1704; when, in the 17th year of her age, she became the mistress of Peter the Great, and won so much upon his affections, that he espoused her on the 29th of May 1711. The ceremony was secretly performed at Jawerof in Poland, in the presence of General Bruce; and on the 20th of February 1712, it was publicly solemnized with great pomp at Petersburgh.

Catherine, by the most unwearied assiduity and unremitted attention, by the softness and complacency of her disposition, but above all by an extraordinary liveliness and gaiety of temper, acquired a wonderful ascendency over the mind of Peter. The latter was subject to occasional horrors, which at times rendered him gloomy and suspicious, and raised his passions to such an height as to produce a temporary madness. In these dreadful moments Catherine was the only person who durst venture to approach him; and such was the kind of fascination she had acquired over his senses, that her presence had an instantaneous effect, and the first sound of her voice composed his mind and calmed his agonies. From these circumstances she seemed necessary, not only to his comfort, but even to his very existence; she became his inseparable companion on his journeys into foreign countries, and even in all his military expeditions.

The peace of Pruth, by which the Russian army was rescued from certain destruction, has been wholly attributed to Catherine, though she was little more than an instrument in procuring the consent of Peter. The latter, in his campaign of 1711 against the Turks, having imprudently led his troops into a disadvantageous situation, took the desperate resolution of cutting his way through the Turkish army in the night. With this resolution he retired to his tent in an agony of despair, and gave positive orders that no one should be admitted under pain of death. In this important juncture the principal officers and the vice-chancellor Shaffirof assembled in the presence of Catherine, and drew up certain preliminaries in order to obtain a truce from the grand vizir. In consequence of this determination, plenipotentiaries were immediately dispatched, without the knowledge of Peter, to the grand vizir, and a peace obtained upon more reasonable conditions than could have been expected. With these conditions Catherine, notwithstanding the orders issued by Peter, entered his tent, and prevailed upon him to sign them. Catherine, by her conduct on this occasion, acquired great popularity; and the emperor particularly specifies her behaviour at Pruth as one of the reasons which induced him to crown her publicly at Moscow with his own hand. This ceremony was performed in 1724; and although designed by Peter only as a proof of his affection, was the principal cause of her subsequent elevation.

Her influence continued undiminished until a short time before the death of the emperor, when some circumstances happened which occasioned such a coolness between them as would probably have ended in a total rupture, if his death had not fortunately intervened. The

original

original cause of this misunderstanding arose from the following discovery of a fecret connection between Catherine and her first chamberlain, whofe name was Mons. The emperor, who was fufpicious of this connection, quitted Peterfburgh under pretence of removing to a villa for a few days, but privately returned to his winter palace in the capital. From thence he occafionally fent one of his confidential pages with a complimentary meffage to the emprefs, as if he had been in the country, and with fecret orders to obferve her motions. From the page's information the emperor, on the third night, furprifed Catherine in an arbour of the garden with her favourite Mons; while his fifter, Madame Balke, who was firft lady of the bed-chamber to the emprefs, was, in company with a page, upon the watch without the arbour.

Peter, whofe violent temper was inflamed by this difcovery, ftruck Catherine with his cane, as well as the page, who endeavoured to prevent him from entering the arbour, and then retired without uttering a fingle word either to Mons or his fifter. A few days after this tranfaction thefe perfons were taken into cuftody, and Mons was carried to the winter palace, where no one had admiffion to him but Peter, who himfelf brought him his provifions. A report was at the fame time circulated, that they were imprifoned for having received bribes, and making their influence over the emprefs fubfervient to their own mercenary views. Mons being examined by Peter, in the prefence of major-general Ufchakof, and threatened with the torture, confeffed the corruption which was laid to his charge. He was beheaded; his fifter received five ftrokes of the knout, and was banifhed into Siberia; two of her fons, who were chamberlains, were alfo degraded, and fent as common foldiers among the Ruffian troops in Perfia. On the day fubfequent to the execution of the fentence, Peter conveyed Catherine in an open carriage under the gallows, to which was nailed the head of Mons. The emprefs, without changing colour at this dreadful fight, exclaimed, "What a pity it is that there is fo much corruption among courtiers!"

This event happened in the latter end of the year 1724; and as it was foon followed by Peter's death, and Catherine upon her acceffion recalled Madame Balke, it has been fufpected that fhe fhortened the days of her hufband by poifon. But notwithftanding the critical fituation for Catherine in which he died, and her fubfequent elevation, this charge is totally deftitute of the leaft fhadow of proof: for the circumftances of Peter's diforder were too well known, and the peculiar fymptoms of his laft illnefs fufficiently account for his death, without the neceffity of recurring to poifon.

While Peter was yet lying in the agonies of death, feveral oppofite parties were caballing to difpofe of the crown. At a confiderable meeting of many among the principal nobility, it was fecretly determined, on the moment of his diffolution, to arreft Catherine, and to place Peter Alexievitch upon the throne. Baffevitz, apprized of this refolution, repaired in perfon to the emprefs, although it was already night. "My grief and confternation," replied Catherine, "render me incapable of acting myfelf; do you and prince Menzikof confult together, and I will embrace the meafures which you fhall approve in my name." Baffevitz, finding Menzikof afleep, awakened and informed him of the preffing danger which threatened the emprefs and her party. As no time remained for long deliberation, the prince inftantly feized the treafure, fecured the fortrefs, gained the officers of the guards by bribes and promifes, alfo a few of the nobility, and the principal clergy. Thefe partizans being convened in the palace, Catherine made her appearance: fhe claimed the throne in right of her coronation at Mofcow; fhe expofed the ill effects of a minority; and promifed, that, "fo far from depriving the great-duke of the crown, fhe would receive it only as a facred depofit, to be reftored to him when fhe fhould be united, in another world, to an adored hufband, whom fhe was now upon the point of lofing."

The pathetic manner with which fhe uttered this addrefs, and the tears which accompanied it, added to the previous diftribution of large fums of money and jewels, produced the defired effect: at the clofe of this meeting the remainder of the night was employed in making the neceffary preparations to infure her acceffion in cafe of the emperor's death.

Peter at length expired in the morning of the 28th of January 1725. This event being made known, the fenate, the generals, the principal nobility and clergy, haftened to the palace to proclaim the new fovereign. The adherents of the great-duke feemed fecure of fuccefs, and the friends of Catherine were avoided as perfons doomed to deftruction. At this juncture Baffevitz whifpered one of the oppofite party, "The emprefs is miftrefs of the treafure and the fortrefs; fhe has gained over the guards and the fynod, and many of the chief nobility; even here fhe has more followers than you imagine; advife therefore your friends to make no oppofition as they value their heads." This information being rapidly circulated, Baffevitz gave the appointed fignal, and the two regiments of guards, who had been gained by a largefs to declare for Catherine, and had already furrounded the palace, beat to arms. "Who has dared (exclaimed prince Repnin, the commander in chief) to order out the troops without my knowledge?" "I, (returned general Butterlin), without pretending to difpute your authority, in obedience to the commands of my moft gracious miftrefs." This fhort reply was followed by a dead filence. In this moment of fufpence and anxiety Menzikof entered, preceding Catherine, fupported by the duke of Holftein. She attempted to fpeak, but was prevented by fighs and tears from giving utterance to her words: at length, recovering herfelf, "I come (fhe faid), notwithftanding the grief which now overwhelms me, to affure you, that, fubmiffive to the will of my departed hufband, whofe memory will be ever dear to me, I am ready to devote my days to the painful occupations of government until Providence fhall fummon me to follow him." Then, after a fhort paufe, fhe artfully added, "If the great-duke will profit by my inftructions, perhaps I fhall have the confolation, during my wretched widowhood, of forming for you an emperor worthy of the blood and the name of him whom you have now irretrievably loft." "As this crifis (replied Menzikof) is a moment of fuch importance to the good of the empire, and requires the moft mature deliberation, your ma-

Catherine. jesty will permit us to confer, without restraint, that this whole affair may be transacted without reproach, as well in the opinion of the present age as in that of posterity." "Acting as I do (answered Catherine), more for the public good than for my own advantage, I am not afraid to submit all my concerns to the judgment of such an enlightened assembly: you have not only my permission to confer with freedom; but I lay my commands upon you all to deliberate maturely on this important subject, and I promise to adopt whatever may be the result of your decisions." At the conclusion of these words the assembly retired into another apartment, and the doors were locked.

It was previously settled by Menzikof and his party that Catherine should be empress; and the guards, who surrounded the palace with drums beating and colours flying, effectually vanquished all opposition. The only circumstance, therefore, which remained, was to give a just colour to her title, by persuading the assembly that Peter intended to have named her his successor. For this purpose Menzikof demanded of that emperor's secretary, whether his late master had left any written declaration of his intentions? The secretary replied, "That a little before his last journey to Moscow he had destroyed a will; and that he had frequently expressed his design of making another, but had always been prevented by the reflection, that if he thought his people, whom he had raised from a state of barbarism to an high degree of power and glory, could be ungrateful, he would not expose his final inclinations to the insult of a refusal; and that if they recollected what they owed to his labours, they would regulate their conduct by his intentions, which he had disclosed with more solemnity than could be manifested by any writing." An altercation now began in the assembly; and some of the nobles having the courage to oppose the accession of Catherine, Theophanes archbishop of Plescof called to their recollection the oath which they had all taken in 1722 to acknowledge the successor appointed by Peter; and added, that the sentiments of that emperor delivered by the secretary were in effect an appointment of Catherine. The opposite party, however, denied these sentiments to be so clear as the secretary chose to insinuate; and insisted, that as their late monarch had failed to nominate his heir, the election of the new sovereign should revert to the state. Upon this the archbishop farther testified, that the evening before the coronation of the empress at Moscow, Peter had declared, in the house of an English merchant, that he should place the crown upon her head with no other view than to leave her mistress of the empire after his decease. This attestation being confirmed by many persons present, Menzikof cried out, "What need have we of any testament! A refusal to conform to the inclination of our great sovereign, thus authenticated, would be both unjust and criminal. Long live the empress Catherine!" These words being instantaneously repeated by the greatest part of those who were present, Menzikof, saluting Catherine by the title of empress, paid his first obeisance by kissing her hand; and his example was followed by the whole assembly. She next presented herself at the window to the guards, and to the people, who shouted acclamations of "Long live Catherine!" while Menzikof scattered amongst them handfuls of money. Thus (says a contemporary) the empress was raised to the throne by the guards, in the same manner as the Roman emperors by the pretorian cohorts, without either the appointment of the people or of the legions. Catherine.

The reign of Catherine may be considered as the reign of Menzikof, that empress having neither inclination or abilities to direct the helm of government; and she placed the most implicit confidence in a man who had been the original author of her good fortune, and the sole instrument of her elevation to the throne.

During her short reign her life was very irregular; she was extremely averse to business; would frequently, when the weather was fine, pass whole nights in the open air; and was particularly intemperate in the use of tokay-wine. These irregularities, joined to a cancer and a dropsy, hastened her end; and she expired on the 17th of May 1727, a little more than two years after her accession to the throne, and in about the 40th year of her age.

As the deaths of sovereigns in despotic countries are seldom imputed to natural causes, that of Catherine has also been attributed to poison; as if the disorders which preyed upon her frame were not sufficient to bring her to her grave. Some assert, that she was poisoned in a glass of spirituous liquor; others, by a pear given her by general Diever. Suspicions also fell upon prince Menzikof, who, a short time before her decease, had a trifling misunderstanding with her, and who was accused of hastening her death, that he might reign with still more absolute power during the minority of Peter II. But these reports deserve not the least credit, and were merely dictated by the spirit of party or by popular rumour.

Catherine was in her person under the middle-size, and in her youth delicate and well-formed, but inclined to corpulency as she advanced in years. She had a fair complexion, dark eyes, and light hair, which she was always accustomed to dye with a black colour. She could neither read nor write: her daughter Elizabeth usually signed her name for her, and particularly to her last will and testament; and count Osterman generally put her signature to the public decrees and dispatches. Her abilities have been greatly exaggerated by her panegyrists. Gordon, who had frequently seen her, seems, of all writers, to have represented her character with the greatest justness, when he says, "She was a very pretty well-look'd woman, of good sense, but not of that sublimity of wit, or rather that quickness of imagination, which some people have believed. The great reason why the czar was so fond of her, was her exceeding good temper; she never was seen peevish or out of humour; obliging and civil to all, and never forgetful of her former condition; withal, mighty grateful." Catherine maintained the pomp of majesty with an air of ease and grandeur united; and Peter used frequently to express his admiration at the propriety with which she supported her high station, without forgetting that she was not born to that dignity.

The following anecdotes will prove that she bore her elevation meekly; and, as Gordon asserts, was never forgetful of her former condition. When Wurmb, who had been tutor to Gluck's children at the

the time that Catherine was a domestic in that clergyman's family, presented himself before her after her marriage with Peter had been publicly solemnized, she recollected and addressed him with great complacency, "What, thou good man, art thou still alive! I will provide for thee." And she accordingly settled upon him a pension. She was no less attentive to the family of her benefactor Gluck, who died a prisoner at Moscow: she pensioned his widow; made his son a page; portioned the two eldest daughters; and advanced the youngest to be one of her maids of honour. If we may believe Weber, she frequently enquired after her first husband; and, when she lived with prince Menzikof, used secretly to send him small sums of money, until, in 1705, he was killed in a skirmish with the enemy.

But the most noble part of her character was her peculiar humanity and compassion for the unfortunate. Motraye has paid no handsome tribute to this excellence. "She had, in some sort, the government of all his (Peter's) passions; and even saved the lives of a great many more persons than Le Fort was able to do: she inspired him with that humanity, which, in the opinion of his subjects, nature seemed to have denied him. A word from her mouth in favour of a wretch, just going to be sacrificed to his anger, would disarm him; but if he was fully resolved to satisfy that passion, he would give orders for the execution when she was absent, for fear she should plead for the victim." In a word, to use the expression of the celebrated Munich, "*Elle etoit proprement la mediatrice entre le monarque et ses sujets.*"

Catherine (Order of St), in modern history, belongs to ladies of the first quality in the Russian court. It was instituted in 1714 by Catherine wife of Peter the Great, in memory of his signal escape from the Turks in 1711. The emblems of this order are a red cross, supported by a figure of St Catherine, and fastened to a scarlet string edged with silver, on which are inscribed the name of St Catherine, and the motto, *Pro fide et patria.*

CATHERLOUGH, a town of Ireland, in the county of Catherlough, and province of Leinster; seated on the river Barrow, 16 miles N. E. of Kilkenny. W. Long. 7. 1. N. Lat. 52. 45.

Catherlough, a county of Ireland, about 28 miles in length, and eight in breadth; bounded on the east by Wicklow and Wexford, on the west by Queen's-county, on the north by Kildare, and on the south and south-west by Wexford. It contains 5600 houses, 42 parishes, five baronies or boroughs, and sends six members to parliament, viz. two for the county, two for Catherlough, and two for Old Leighlin.

CATHETER, in surgery, a fistulous instrument, usually made of silver, to be introduced into the bladder, in order to search for the stone, or discharge the urine when suppressed. See Surgery.

CATHETUS, in geometry, a line or radius falling perpendicularly on another line or surface; thus the catheti of a right-angled triangle, are the two sides that include the right angle.

Cathetus of Incidence, in catoptrics, a right line drawn from a point of the object, perpendicular to the reflecting line.

Cathetus of Reflexion, or of the Eye, a right line drawn from the eye perpendicular to the reflecting plane.

Cathetus of Obliquation, a right line drawn perpendicular to the speculum, in the point of incidence or reflexion.

Cathetus, in architecture, a perpendicular line, supposed to pass through the middle of a cylindrical body, as a ballaster, column, &c.

CATHNESS. See Caithness.

CATHOLIC, in a general sense, denotes any thing that is universal or general.

Catholic Church. The rise of heresies induced the primitive Christian church to assume to itself the appellation of *catholic*, being a characteristic to distinguish itself from all sects, who, though they had party names, sometimes sheltered themselves under the name of Christians.

The Romish church distinguishes itself now by the name of *catholic*, in opposition to all those who have separated from her communion, and whom she considers as heretics and schismatics, and herself only as the true and Christian church. In the strict sense of the word, there is no catholic church in being, that is, no universal Christian communion.

Catholic King, is a title which has been long hereditary to the king of Spain. Mariana pretends, that Reccarede first received this title after he had destroyed Arianism in his kingdom, and that it is found in the council of Toledo for the year 589. Vaseé ascribes the origin of it to Alphonsus in 738. Some allege that it has been used only since the time of Ferdinand and Isabella. Colombiere says, it was given them on occasion of the expulsion of the Moors. The Bollandists pretend it had been borne by their predecessors the Visigoth kings of Spain; and that Alexander VI. only renewed it to Ferdinand and Isabella. Others say, that Philip de Valois first bore the title; which was given him after his death by the ecclesiastics, on account of his favouring their interests.

In some epistles of the ancient popes, the title *catholic* is given to the kings of France and of Jerusalem, as well as to several patriarchs and primates.

CATHOLICON, in pharmacy, a kind of soft purgative electuary, so called, as being supposed an universal purger of all humours.

CATILINE (*Lucius*), a Roman of a noble family, who having spent his whole fortune in debauchery, formed the design of oppressing his country, destroying the senate, seizing the public treasury, setting Rome on fire, and usurping a sovereign power over his fellow-citizens. In order to succeed in this design, he drew some young noblemen into his plot; whom he prevailed upon, it is said, to drink human blood as a pledge of their union. His conspiracy, however, was discovered by the vigilance of Cicero, who was then consul. Upon which, retiring from Rome, he put himself at the head of an army, with several of the conspirators, and fought with incredible valour against Petreius, lieutenant to Anthony, who was colleague with Cicero in the consulship; but was defeated and killed in battle. See *(History of)* Rome.—Sallust has given an excellent history of this conspiracy.

CATO (*Marcus Portius*), the Censor, one of the greatest men among the ancients, was born at Tusculum in the year of Rome 519, about the 232d before Christ.

Cat.

Christ. He began to bear arms at 17; and, on all occasions, showed extraordinary courage. He was a man of great sobriety, and reckoned no bodily exercise unworthy of him. He had but one horse for himself and his baggage, and he looked after and dressed it himself. At his return from his campaigns, he betook himself to plough his ground; not that he was without slaves to do it, but it was his inclination. He dressed also like his slaves, sat down at the same table with them, and partook of the same fare. He did not in the mean while neglect to cultivate his mind, especially in regard to the art of speaking; and he employed his talents, which were very great, in generously pleading causes in the neighbouring cities without fee or reward. Valerius Flaccus, who had a country-seat near Cato, conceiving an esteem for him, persuaded him to come to Rome; where Cato, by his own merit, and the influence of so powerful a patron, was soon taken notice of, and promoted. He was first of all elected tribune of the soldiers for the province of Sicily. He was next made questor in Africa under Scipio. Having in this last office reproved him for his profuseness to his soldiers, the general answered, that "he did not want so exact a questor, but would make war at what expence he pleased; nor was he to give an account to the Roman people of the money he spent, but of his enterprises, and the execution of them." Cato, provoked at this answer, left Sicily, and returned to Rome.

Afterwards Cato was made pretor, when he fulfilled the duties of his office with the strictest justice. He conquered Sardinia, governed with admirable moderation, and was created consul. Being tribune in the war of Syria, he gave distinguished proofs of his valour against Antiochus the Great; and at his return stood candidate for the office of censor. But the nobles, who not only envied him as a new man, but dreaded his severity, set up against him seven powerful competitors. Valerius Flaccus, who had introduced him into public life, and had been his colleague in the consulship, was a ninth candidate, and these two united their interests. On this occasion Cato, far from employing soft words to the people, or giving hopes of gentleness or complaisance in the execution of his office, loudly declared from the rostra, with a threatening look and voice, "That the times required firm and vigorous magistrates to put a stop to that growing luxury which menaced the republic with ruin; censors who would cut up the evil by the roots, and restore the rigour of ancient discipline." It is to the honour of the people of Rome, that, notwithstanding these terrible intimations, they preferred him to all his competitors, who courted them by promises of a mild and easy administration: the comitia also appointed his friend Valerius to be his colleague, without whom he had declared that he could not hope to compass the reformations he had in view. Cato's merit, upon the whole, was superior to that of any of the great men who stood against him. He was temperate, brave, and indefatigable; frugal of the public money, and not to be corrupted. There is scarce any talent requisite for public or private life which he had not received from nature, or acquired by industry. He was a great soldier, an able statesman, an eloquent orator, a learned historian, and very knowing in rural affairs. Yet, with all these accomplishments, he had very great faults. His ambition being poisoned with envy, disturbed both his own peace and that of the whole city as long as he lived. Though he would not take bribes, he was unmerciful and unconscionable in amassing wealth by all such means as the law did not punish.

The first act of Cato in his new office, was naming his colleague to be prince of the senate: after which the censors struck out of the list of the senators the names of seven persons; among whom was Lucius the brother of T. Flaminius. Lucius, when consul, and commanding in Gaul, had with his own hand murdered a Boian of distinction, a deserter to the Romans; and he had committed this murder purely to gratify the curiosity of his public, a young Carthaginian, who longing to see some body die a violent death, had reproached the general for bringing him away from Rome just when there was going to be a fight of gladiators. Titus Flaminius, full of indignation at the dishonour done to his brother, brought the affair before the people; and insisted upon Cato's giving the reason of his proceeding. The censor related the story; and when Lucius denied the fact, put him to his oath. The accused, refusing to swear, was deemed guilty; and Cato's censure was approved. But no part of the censor's conduct seemed so cruel to the nobles and their wives as the taxes he laid upon luxury in all its branches; dress, household furniture, womens toilets, chariots, slaves, and equipage. These articles were all taxed at three *per cent*. of the real value. The people, however, in general, were pleased with his regulations; insomuch that they ordered a statue to be erected to his honour in the temple of *Health*, with an inscription that mentioned nothing of his victories or triumph, but imported only that by his wise ordinances in his censorship he had reformed the manners of the republic. Plutarch relates, that before this, upon some of Cato's friends expressing their surprise, that while many persons without merit or reputation had statues, he had none; he answered, "I had much rather it should be asked why the people have not erected a statue to Cato, than why they have." Cato was the occasion of the third Punic war. Being dispatched to Africa to terminate a difference between the Carthaginians and the king of Numidia, on his return to Rome he reported, that Carthage was grown excessively rich and populous, and he warmly exhorted the senate to destroy a city and republic, during the existence of which, Rome could never be safe. Having brought from Africa some very large figs, he showed them to the conscript fathers in one of the lappets of his gown. "The country (says he) where this fine fruit grows, is but a three days voyage from Rome." We are told, that from this time he never spoke in the senate upon any subject, without concluding with these words, "I am also of opinion, that Carthage ought to be destroyed." He judged, that, for a people debauched by prosperity, nothing was more to be feared than a rival state, always powerful, and now from its misfortunes grown wise and circumspect. He held it necessary to remove all dangers that could be apprehended from *without*, when the republic had *within* so many distempers threatening her destruction.

From the censor dignified and severe, the reader will

Cat.

Cato.

will not perhaps be displeased to turn his view upon Cato sociable and relaxed. For we should have a false notion of him, if we imagined that nothing but a sad austerity prevailed in his speech and behaviour. On the contrary, he was extremely free; and often with his friends at table intermixed the conversation with lively discourses and witty sayings. Of these Plutarch has collected a pretty large number; we shall relate but one, and make use of Balzac's paraphrase, and the preface with which he introduces it. "The very censors, though sadness seemed to be one of the functions of their office, did not altogether lay aside raillery. They were not always bent upon severity; and the first Cato, that troublesome and intolerable honest man, ceased sometimes to be troublesome and intolerable. He had some glimpses of mirth, and some intervals of good humour. He dropped now and then some words that were not unpleasant, and you may judge of the rest by this. He had married a very handsome wife; and history tells us that she was extremely afraid of the thunder, and loved her husband well. These two passions prompted her to the same thing; she always pitched upon her husband as a sanctuary against thunder, and threw herself into his arms at the first noise she fancied she heard in the sky. Cato, who was well pleased with the storm, and very willing to be caressed, could not conceal his joy. He revealed that domestic secret to his friends; and told them one day, speaking of his wife, "that she had found out a way to make him love bad weather; and that he never was so happy as when Jupiter was angry." It is worth observing, that this was during his censorship; when he degraded the senator Manlius, who would probably have been consul the year after, only for giving a kiss to his wife in the day-time, and in the presence of his daughter.

Oeuvres diverses, p. 69.

Cato died in the year of Rome 604, aged 85. He wrote several works. 1. A Roman History. 2. Concerning the art of war. 3. Of rhetoric. 4. A treatise of husbandry. Of these, the last only is extant.

Cato (Marcus Portius), commonly called Cato *Minor*, or Cato of *Utica*, was great grandson of Cato *the Censor*. It is said, that from his infancy he discovered by his speech, by his countenance, and even his childish sports and recreations, an inflexibility of mind; for he would force himself to go through with whatever he had undertaken, though the task was ill suited to his strength. He was rough towards those that flattered him, and quite intractable when threatened; was rarely seen to laugh, or even to smile; was not easily provoked to anger; but if once incensed, hard to be pacified. Sylla having had a friendship for the father of Cato, sent often for him and his brother, and talked familiarly with them. Cato, who was then about 14 years of age, seeing the heads of great men brought there, and observing the sighs of those that were present, asked his preceptor, "Why does no body kill this man?" Because, said the other, he is more feared than he is hated. The boy replied, Why then did you not give me a sword when you brought me hither, that I might have stabbed him, and freed my country from this slavery?

He learned the principles of the Stoic philosophy, which so well suited his character, under Antipater of Tyre, and applied himself diligently to the study of it. Eloquence he likewise studied, as a necessary means to defend the cause of justice, and he made a very considerable proficiency in that science. To increase his bodily strength, he inured himself to suffer the extremes of heat and cold; and used to make journeys on foot, and bare-headed in all seasons. When he was sick, patience and abstinence were his only remedies; he shut himself up, and would see no body till he was well. Though remarkably sober in the beginning of his life, making it a rule to drink but once after supper, and then retire, he insensibly contracted a habit of drinking more freely, and of sitting at table till morning. His friends endeavoured to excuse this, by saying that the affairs of the public engrossed his attention all the day; and that, being ambitious of knowledge, he passed the night in the conversation of philosophers. Cæsar wrote that Cato was once found dead drunk at the corner of a street, early in the morning, by a great number of people who were going to the levee of some great man; and that when, by uncovering his face, they perceived who it was, they blushed for shame: "You would have thought (added Cæsar), that Cato had found them drunk, not they him." Pliny observes, that by this reflection Cæsar praises his enemy at the same time that he blames him. And Seneca, his extravagant panegyrist, ventures to assert, that it is easier to prove drunkenness to be a virtue, than Cato to be vicious. He affected singularity, and, in things indifferent, to act directly contrary to the taste and fashions of the age. Magnanimity and constancy are generally ascribed to him; and Seneca would fain make that haughtiness and contempt for others which, in Cato, accompanied those virtues, a matter of praise. Cato, says Seneca, having received a blow in the face, neither took revenge nor was angry; he did not even *pardon the affront*, but *denied that he had received it*. His virtue raised him so high, that injury could not reach him. He is reputed to have been chaste in his youth. His first love was Lepida; but when the marriage was upon the point of being concluded, Metellus Scipio, to whom she had been promised, interfered, and the preference was given to him. This affront extremely exasperated our Stoic. He was for going to law with Scipio; and when his friends had diverted him from that design, by showing him the ridicule of it, he revenged himself by making verses upon his rival. When this first flame subsided, he married Attilia the daughter of Serranus, had two children by her, and afterwards divorced her for her very indiscreet conduct.

Cato.

He served as a volunteer under Gellius in the war of Spartacus; and when military rewards were offered him by the commander, he refused them, because he thought he had no right to them. Some years after, he went a legionary tribune into Macedonia under the prætor Rubrius: in which station he appeared, in his dress, and during a march, more like a private soldier than an officer: but the dignity of his manners, the elevation of his sentiments, and the superiority of his views, set him far above those who bore the titles of generals and proconsuls. It is said, that Cato's design in all his behaviour was to engage the soldiers to the love of virtue; whose affections he engaged thereby to himself, without his having that in his intention. "For the sincere love of virtue, (adds Plutarch), implies

Cato. plies an affection for the virtuous. Those who praise the worthy without loving them, pay homage to their glory; but are neither admirers nor imitators of their virtues." When the time of his service expired, and he was leaving the army, the soldiers were all in tears; so effectually had he gained their hearts by his condescending manners, and sharing in their labours. After his return home, he was chosen to the questorship; and had scarce entered on his charge, when he made a great reformation in the questor's office, and particularly with regard to the registers. These registers, whose places were for life, and through whose hands passed incessantly all the public accounts, being to act under young magistrates unexperienced in business, assumed an air of importance; and, instead of asking orders from the questors, pretended to direct and govern as if they themselves were the questors. Cato reduced them to their proper sphere.

One thing by which Cato extremely pleased the people, was his making the assassins to whom Sylla had given considerable rewards out of the treasury, for murdering the proscribed, disgorge their gains. Plutarch tells us, that Cato was so exact in discharging the duties of a senator, as to be always the first who came to the house, and the last who left it; and that he never quitted Rome during those days when the senate was to sit. Nor did he fail to be present at every assembly of the people, that he might awe those who, by an ill-judged facility, bestowed the public money in largesses, and frequently, through mere favour, granted remission of debts due to the state. At first his austerity and stiffness displeased his colleagues; but afterwards they were glad to have his name to oppose to all the unjust solicitations, against which they would have found it difficult to defend themselves. Cato very readily took upon him the task of refusing.

Cato, to keep out a very bad man, put in for the tribuneship. He sided with Cicero against Catiline, and opposed Cæsar on that occasion. His enemies sent him to recover Cyprus, which Ptolemy had forfeited, thinking to hurt his reputation by so difficult an undertaking; yet none could find fault with his conduct.

Cato laboured to bring about an agreement between Cæsar and Pompey; but seeing it in vain, he sided with the latter. When Pompey was slain, he fled to Utica; and being pursued by Cæsar, advised his friends to be gone, and throw themselves on Cæsar's clemency. His son, however, remained with him; and Statilius, a young man, remarkable for his hatred to Cæsar.

The evening before the execution of the purpose he had formed with regard to himself, after bathing, he supped with his friends and the magistrates of the city. They sat late at table, and the conversation was lively. The discourse falling upon this maxim of the Stoics, that "the wise man alone is free, and that the vicious are slaves;" Demetrius, who was a Peripatetic, undertook to confute it from the maxims of his school. Cato, in answer, treated the matter very amply; and with so much earnestness and vehemence of voice, that he betrayed himself, and confirmed the suspicions of his friends, that he designed to kill himself. When he had done speaking, a melancholy silence ensued; and Cato perceiving it, turned the discourse to the present situation of affairs, expressing his concern for those who had been obliged to put to sea, as well as for those who had determined to make their escape by land, and had a dry and sandy desart to pass. After supper, the company being dismissed, he walked for some time with a few friends, and gave his orders to the officers of the guard; and going into his chamber, he embraced his son and his friends with more than usual tenderness, which farther confirmed the suspicions of the resolution he had taken. Then laying himself down on his bed, he took up Plato's Dialogue on the immortality of the Soul. Having read for some time, he looked up, and missing his sword, which his son had removed while he was at supper, he called a slave, and asked who had taken it away; and receiving no pertinent answer, he resumed his reading. Some time after, he asked again for his sword; and, without showing any impatience, ordered it to be brought to him: but, having read out the book, and finding nobody had brought him his sword, he called for all his servants, fell into a rage, and struck one of them on the mouth with so much violence, that he very much hurt his own hand, crying out in a passionate manner, "What! do my own son and family conspire to betray me, and deliver me up naked and unarmed to the enemy!" Immediately his son and friends rushed into the room; and began to lament, and to beseech him to change his resolution. Cato raising himself, and looking fiercely at them, "How long is it," said he, "since I have lost my senses, and my son is become my keeper? Brave and generous son, why do you not bind your father's hands, that when Cæsar comes, he may find me unable to defend myself? Do you imagine that without a sword I cannot end my life? Cannot I destroy myself by holding my breath for some moments, or by striking my head against the wall?" His son answered with his tears, and retired. Apollonides and Demetrius remained with him, and to them he addressed himself in the following words: "Is it to watch over me that ye sit silent here? Do you pretend to force a man of my years to live? or can you bring any reason to prove, that it is not base and unworthy of Cato to beg his safety of an enemy? or why do you not persuade me to unlearn what I have been taught, that, rejecting all the opinions I have hitherto defended, I may now, by Cæsar's means, grow wiser, and be yet more obliged to him than for life alone? Not that I have determined any thing concerning myself; but I would have it in my power to perform what I shall think fit to resolve upon: and I shall not fail to ask your counsel, when I have occasion to act up to the principles which your philosophy teaches. Go tell my son, that he should not compel his father to what he cannot persuade him." They withdrew, and the sword was brought by a young slave. Cato drew it, and finding the point to be sharp; "Now, (said he), I am my own master:" And, laying it down, he took up his book again, which, it is reported, he read twice over. After this he slept so soundly that he was heard to snore by those who were near him. About midnight he called two of his freedmen, Cleanthes his physician, and Butas whom he chiefly employed in the management of his affairs. The last he sent to the port, to see whether all the

Romans

Romans were gone; to the physician he gave his hand to be dressed, which was swelled by the blow he had given his slave. This being an intimation that he intended to live, gave great joy to his family. Butas soon returned, and brought word that they were all gone except Crassus, who had staid upon some business, but was just ready to depart. He added, that the wind was high, and the sea rough. These words drew a sigh from Cato. He sent Butas again to the port, to know whether there might not be some one, who, in the hurry of embarkation, had forgot some necessary provisions, and had been obliged to put back to Utica. It was now break of day, and Cato slept yet a little more, till Butas returned to tell him, that all was perfectly quiet. He then ordered him to shut his door; and he flung himself upon his bed, as if he meant to finish his night's rest; but immediately he took his sword, and stabbed himself a little below his chest; yet not being able to use his hand so well by reason of the swelling, the blow did not kill him. It threw him into a convulsion, in which he fell from his bed, and overturned a table near it. The noise gave the alarm; and his son, and the rest of the family, entering the room, found him weltering in his blood, and his bowels half out of his body. The surgeon, upon examination, found that his bowels were not cut; and was preparing to replace them, and bind up the wound, when Cato, recovering his senses, thrust the surgeon from him, and, tearing out his bowels, immediately expired, in the 48th year of his age.

By this rash act, independent of all moral or religious considerations, he carried his patriotism to the highest degree of political frenzy: for Cato, dead, could be of no use to his country; but had he preserved his life, his counsel might have moderated Cæsar's ambition, and (as Montesquieu observes) have given a different turn to public affairs.

CATOCHE, or CATOCHUS, a disease, by which the patient is rendered in an instant as immoveable as a statue, without either sense or motion, and continues in the same posture he was in at the moment of his being seized. See (the *Index* subjoined to) MEDICINE.

CATOPTRICS.

CATOPTRICS is that part of optics which explains the properties of reflected light, and particularly that which is reflected from mirrors.

As this and the other branches of OPTICS are fully treated under the collective word, we shall, in the present article, *1st*, Just give a summary of the principles of the branch, in a few plain aphorisms, with some preliminary definitions; and, *2dly*, Insert a set of entertaining experiments founded upon them.

SECT. I. *Definitions.*

1 Definitions. 1. Every polished body that reflects the rays of light is called a mirror, whether its surface be plane, spherical, conical, cylindric, or of any other form whatever.

Plate CXXVIII. 2. Of mirrors there are three principally used in optical experiments: The plane mirror, G H I, (fig. 1.); the spherical convex mirror, GHI, (fig. 2.); and the spherical concave mirror, G H I, (fig. 3.)

3. The point K, (fig. 2, 3.) round which the reflecting surface of a spherical mirror is described, is called its centre. The line KH, drawn from its centre perpendicular to its two surfaces, is the axis of the mirror; and the point H, to which that line is drawn, is its vertex.

4. The distance between the lines AG and BG, (fig. 1.) is called the angle of incidence, and the distance between BG and CG is the angle of reflection.

SECT. II. *Aphorisms.*

2 I. In a plain mirror. 1. The image DF, (fig. 1.) will appear as far behind the mirror, as the object AC is before it.

2. The image will appear of the same size, and in the same position as the object.

3. Every such mirror will reflect the image of an object of twice its own length and breadth.

4. If the object be an opaque body, and its rays fall on the mirror nearly in direct lines, there will be only one image visible, which will be reflected by the inner surface of the glass. But,

5. If the object be a luminous body, and its rays fall very obliquely on the mirror, there will appear, to an eye placed in a proper position, several images; the first of which, reflected from the outer surface of the glass, will not be so bright as the second, reflected from the inner surface. The following images, that are produced by the repeated reflections of the rays between the two surfaces of the glass, will be in proportion less vivid, to the eighth or tenth, which will be scarce visible.

1. The image DF, (fig. 2.) will always appear behind it. 3 II. In a spherical convex mirror.

2. The image will be in the same position as the object.

3. It will be less than the object.

4. It will be curved, but not, as the mirror, spherical.

5. Parallel rays falling on this mirror will have the focus or image at half the distance of the centre K, from the mirror.

6. In converging rays, the distance of the object must be equal to half the distance of the centre, to make the image appear behind the mirror.

7. Diverging rays will have their image at less than half the distance of the centre. If the object be placed in the centre of the mirror, its image will appear at one-eighth of that distance behind it.

1. That point where the image appears of the same dimensions as the object, is the centre of that mirror. 4 III. In a spherical concave mirror.

2. Parallel rays will have their focus at one half the distance of the centre.

3. Converging rays will form an image before the mirror.

4. In diverging rays, if the object be at less than one half the distance of the centre, the image will be behind the mirror, erect, curved, and magnified, as

DEF, (fig. 3.) but if the distance of the object be greater, the image will be before the mirror, inverted and diminished, as DEF, (fig. 4.)

5. The sun's rays falling on a concave mirror, and being parallel, will be collected in a focus at half the distance of its centre, where their heat will be augmented in proportion of the surface of the mirror to that of the focal spot.

6. If a luminous body be placed in the focus of a concave mirror, its rays being reflected in parallel lines will strongly enlighten a space of the same dimension with the mirror, at a great distance. If the luminous object be placed nearer than the focus, its rays will diverge, and consequently enlighten a larger space. It is on this principle that reverberators are constructed.

IV. In all plane and spherical mirrors the angle of incidence is equal to the angle of reflection.

Sect. III. *Entertaining Experiments.*

5 I. Catoptrical illusions.

I. Of all our senses the sight is certainly subject to the greatest illusion. The various writers on optics have described a great number of instances in which it deceives us, and have constantly endeavoured to investigate the causes, to explain their effects, and to reconcile appearance with reality. We every day discover new phenomena, and doubtless many more are reserved for posterity. It frequently happens, moreover, that a discovery which at first seemed of little consequence, has led to matters of the highest importance.

Take a glass bottle A (fig. 14.) and fill it with water to the point B; leave the upper part BC empty, and cork it in the common manner. Place this bottle opposite a concave mirror, and beyond its focus, that it may appear reversed, and before the mirror (see sect. ii. aphor. 4. of a spher. concave mirror,) place yourself still further distant from the bottle, and it will appear to you in the situation, *a*, *b*, *c*, (fig. 15.)

Now it is remarkable in this apparent bottle, that the water, which, according to all the laws of catoptrics, and all the experiments made on other objects, should appear at *a b*, appears on the contrary at *b c*, and consequently the part *a b* appears empty.

If the bottle be inverted and placed before the mirror (as in fig. 16.), its image will appear in its natural, erect position; and the water, which is in reality at BC, will appear at *a b*.

If while the bottle is inverted it be uncorked, and the water run gently out, it will appear, that while the part BC is emptying, that of *a b* in the image is filling; and what is likewise very remarkable, as soon as the bottle is empty the illusion ceases, the image also appearing entirely empty. If the bottle likewise be quite full there is no illusion.

If while the bottle is held inverted, and partly empty, some drops of water fall from the bottom A towards BC, it seems in the image as if there were formed at the bottom of the part *a b*, bubbles of air that rose from *a* to *b*; which is the part that seems full of water. All these phenomena constantly appear.

The remarkable circumstances in this experiment, are, first, not only to see an object where it is not, but also where its image is not; and secondly, that of two objects which are really in the same place, as the surface of the bottle and the water it contains, the one is seen at one place, and the other at another; and to see the bottle in the place of its image, and the water where neither it nor its image are.

II. Construct a box AB, of about a foot long, eight inches wide, and six high; or what other dimension you shall think fit, provided it does not greatly vary from these proportions. 6 II. Appearance of a boundless vista. fig. 5.

On the inside of this box, and against each of its opposite ends A and B, place a mirror of the same size. Take off the quicksilver from the mirror that you place at B, for about an inch and an half, at the part C, where you are to make a hole in the box of the same size, by which you may easily view its inside. Cover the top of the box with a frame, in which must be placed a transparent glass, covered with gauze, on the side next the inner part of the box. Let there be two grooves at the parts E and F to receive the two painted scenes hereafter mentioned. On two pieces of cut pasteboard let there be skilfully painted on both sides (see fig. 6. and 7.) any subject you think proper; as woods, gardens, bowers, colonnades, &c. and on two other pasteboards, the same subjects on one side only; observing that there ought to be on one of them some object relative to the subject placed at A, that the mirror placed at D may not reflect the hole at C on the opposite side.

Place the two boards painted on both sides in the grooves E and F; and those that are painted on one side only, against the opposite mirrors C and D; and then cover the box with its transparent top. This box should be placed in a strong light to have a good effect.

When the eye is placed at C, and views the objects on the inside of the box, of which some, as we have said, are painted on both sides, they are successively reflected from one mirror to the other; and if, for example, the painting consists of trees, they will appear like a very long vista, of which the eye cannot discern the end; for each of the mirrors repeating the objects, continually more faintly, contribute greatly to augment the illusion.

III. Take a square box ABCD, of about six inches long, and twelve high; cover the inside of it with four plane mirrors, which must be placed perpendicular to the bottom of the box CHFD. 7 III. Of a boundless [illegible] of armed men, fig. 8.

Place certain objects in relief on the bottom of this box; suppose, for example, a piece of fortification, (as fig. 9.) with tents, soldiers, &c. or any other subject that you judge will produce an agreeable effect by its disposition when repeatedly reflected by the mirrors.

On the top of this box place a frame of glass, in form of the bottom part of a pyramid, whose base AGEB is equal to the size of the box; its top ILN, must form a square of six inches, and should not be more than four or five inches higher than the box. Cover the four sides of this frame with a gauze, that the inside may not be visible but at the top ILN, which should be covered with a transparent glass.

When you look into this box through the glass ILN, the mirrors that are diametrically opposite each other, mutually reflecting the figures inclosed, the eye beholds a boundless extent, completely covered with these

these objects; and if they are properly disposed, the illusion will occasion no small surprise, and afford great entertainment.

Note, The nearer the opening ILN is to the top of the box, the greater will be the apparent extent of the subject. The same will happen if the four mirrors placed on the sides of the box be more elevated. The objects, by either of these dispositions will appear to be repeated nine, twenty-five, forty-nine times, &c. by taking always the square of the odd numbers of the arithmetical progression 3, 5, 7, 9, &c. as is very easy to conceive, if we remember that the subject enclosed in the box is always in the centre of a square, composed of several others, equal to that which forms the bottom of the box.

Other pieces of the same kind (that is viewed from above) may be contrived, in which mirrors may be placed perpendicular on a triangular, pentagon, or hexagon, (that is, a three, five, or six-sided) plane. All these different dispositions, properly directed, as well with regard to the choice as position of the objects, will constantly produce very remarkable and pleasing illusions.

If instead of placing the mirrors perpendicular, they were to incline equally, so as to form part of a reversed pyramid, the subject placed in the box would then have the appearance of a very extensive globular or many-sided figure.

8 IV. Surprising multiplication of objects, fig. 10.

IV. On the hexagonal or six-sided plane ABCDEF draw six semi-diameters GA, GB, GC, GD, GE, GF; and on each of these place perpendicularly two plane mirrors, which must join exactly at the centre G, and which placed back to back must be as thin as possible. Decorate the exterior boundary of this piece (which is at the extremity of the angles of the hexagon) with six columns, that at the same time serve to support the mirrors, by grooves formed on their inner sides. (See the profile H). Add to these columns their entablatures, and cover the edifice in such manner as you shall think proper.

In each one of these six triangular spaces, contained between two mirrors, place little figures of pasteboard, in relief, representing such objects as when seen in an hexagonal form will produce an agreeable effect. To these add small figures of enamel; and take particular care to conceal, by some object that has relation to the subject, the place where the mirrors join, which, as we have said before, all meet in the common centre G.

When you look into any one of the six openings of this palace, the objects there contained being repeated six times, will seem entirely to fill up the whole of the building. This illusion will appear very remarkable; especially if the objects made choice of are properly adapted to the effect that is to be produced by the mirrors.

Note, if you place between two of these mirrors part of a fortification, as a curtain and two demi-bastions, you will see an entire citadel, with its six bastions. Or if you place part of a ball-room, ornamented with chandeliers and figures in enamel, all those objects being here multiplied, will afford a very pleasing prospect.

9 V. Opaque bodies seemingly rendered transparent, fig. 11.

V. Within the case ABCD, place four mirrors, O, P, Q, R, so disposed that they may each of them make an angle of forty-five degrees, that is, that they may be half way inclined from the perpendicular, as in the figure. In each of the two extremities AB, make a circular overture, in one of which fix the tube GL, in the other the tube MF, and observe that in each of these is to be inserted another tube, at H and I (A).

Furnish the first of these tubes with an object-glass at G, and a concave eye-glass at F. You are to observe, that in regulating the focus of these glasses, with regard to the length of the tube, you are to suppose it equal to the line G, or visual pointed ray, which entering at the overture G, is reflected by the four mirrors, and goes out at the other overture F, where the ocular glass is placed. Put any glass you will into the two ends of the moveable tubes H and I; and lastly place the machine on a stand E, moveable at the point S, that it may be elevated or depressed at pleasure.

When the eye is placed at F, and you look through the tube, the rays of light that proceed from the object T, passing through the glass G, are successively reflected by the mirrors, O, P, Q, and R, to the eye at F, and there paint the object T, in its proper situation, and these rays appear to proceed directly from that object.

The two moveable tubes H and I, at the extremities of each of which a glass is placed, serve only the more to disguise the illusion, for they have no communication with the interior part of the machine. This instrument being moveable on the stand E, may be directed to any object; and if furnished with proper glasses will answer the purpose of a common perspective.

The two moveable tubes H and I being brought together, the machine is directed toward any object, and desiring a person to look in at the end F, you ask him if he see distinctly that object. You then separate the two moveable tubes, and leaving a space between them sufficient to place your hand, or any other solid body, you tell him that the machine has the power of making objects visible through the most opaque body; and as a proof you desire him then to look at the same object, when, to his great surprise, he will see it as distinct as when there was no solid body placed between the tubes.

Note, This experiment is the more extraordinary, as it is very difficult to conceive how the effect is produced. The two arms of the case appearing to be made to support the perspective glass; and to whatever object it is directed, the effect is still the same.

VI.

(A) These four tubes must terminate in the substance of the case, and not enter the inside, that they may not hinder the effect of the mirrors. The fourfold reflection of the rays of light from the mirrors, darkens in some degree the brightness of the object; some light is also lost by the magnifying power of the perspective: If, therefore, instead of the object-glass at G, and concave eye-glass at F, plain glasses were substituted; the magnifying power of the perspective will be taken away, and the object will appear brighter.

10 VI. The magician's mirror, fig. 12.

VI. In the partition AB, make two overtures, CD, and EF, of a foot high, and ten inches wide, and about a foot distant from each other. Let them be at the common height of a man's head; and in each of them place a transparent glass, surrounded with a frame, like a common mirror.

Behind this partition place two mirrors H and I, inclined to it in an angle of forty-five degrees: that is, half-way between a line drawn perpendicular to the ground and its surface: let them be both 18 inches square: let all the space between them be inclosed by boards or pasteboard painted black, and well closed, that no light may enter: let there be also two curtains to cover them, which may be drawn aside at pleasure.

When a person looks into one of these supposed mirrors, instead of seeing his own face, he will perceive the object that is in front of the other: so that if two persons present themselves at the same time before these mirrors, instead of each one seeing himself, they will reciprocally see each other.

Note, There should be a sconce with a candle placed on each side of the two glasses in the wainscot, to enlighten the faces of the persons who look in them, otherwise this experiment will have no remarkable effect.

This experiment may be considerably improved by placing the two glasses in the partition in adjoining rooms, and a number of persons being previously placed in one room, when a stranger enters the other, you may tell him his face is dirty; and desire him to look in the glass, which he will naturally do; and on seeing a strange face he will draw back: but returning to it, and seeing another, another, and another, like the phantom kings in Macbeth, what his surprize will be is more easy to conceive than express. After this, a real mirror may be privately let down on the back of the glass; and if he can be prevailed to look in it once more, he will then, to his further astonishment, see his own face; and may be told, perhaps persuaded, that all he thought he saw before was mere imagination.

How many tricks, less artful than this, have passed in former times for sorcery; and pass at this time, in some countries, for apparitions!

Note, When a man looks in a mirror that is placed perpendicular to another, his face will appear entirely deformed. If the mirror be a little inclined, so as to make an angle of 80 degrees (that is, one-ninth parts from the perpendicular), he will then see all the parts of his face, except the nose and forehead. If it be inclined to 60 degrees (that is, one-third part), he will appear with three noses and six eyes: in short, the apparent deformity will vary at each degree of inclination; and when the glass comes to 45 degrees (that is, half way down), the face will vanish. If, instead of placing the two mirrors in this situation, they are so disposed that their junction may be vertical, their different inclinations will produce other effects; as the situation of the object relative to these mirrors is quite different. The effects of these mirrors, though remarkable enough, occasions but little surprise, as there is no method of concealing the cause by which they are produced.

Fig. 13. VII. Make a box of wood, of a cubical figure, ABCD, of about 15 inches every way. Let it be fixed on the pedestal P, at the usual height of a man's head. In each side of this box let there be an opening of an oval form, of ten inches high, and seven wide.

In this box place two mirrors A, D, with their backs against each other; let them cross the box in a diagonal line, and in a vertical position. Decorate the openings in the sides of this box with four oval frames and transparent glasses, and cover each of them with a curtain, so contrived that they may all draw up together.

Place four persons in front of the four sides, and at equal distances from the box, and then draw up the curtains that they may see themselves in the mirrors; when each of them, instead of his own figure, will see that of the person who is next him, and who, at the same time, will seem to him to be placed on the opposite side. Their confusion will be the greater, as it will be very difficult for them to discover the mirrors concealed in the box. The reason of this phenomenon is evident; for though the rays of light may be turned aside by a mirror, yet, as we have before said, they always appear to proceed in right lines.

VIII. Provide a box ABCD of about two feet long, 15 inches wide, and 12 inches high. At the end AC place a concave mirror, the focus of whose parallel rays is at 18 inches from the reflecting surface. At IL place a pasteboard blacked, in which a hole is cut sufficiently large to see on the mirror H the object placed at BEFD. 11 VIII. The perspective mirror, fig. 17.

Cover the top of the box, from A to I, close, that the mirror H may be entirely darkened. The other part IB, must be covered with a glass, under which is placed a gauze.

Make an aperture at G, near the top of the side E B; beneath which, on the inside, place, in succession, paintings of different subjects, as vistas, landscapes, &c. so that they may be in front of the mirror H. Let the box be so placed that the object may be strongly illuminated by the sun, or by wax lights placed under the enclosed part of the box AI.

By this simple construction the objects placed at GD will be thrown into their natural perspective; and if the subjects be properly chosen, the appearance will be altogether as pleasing as in optical machines of a much more complicated form.

Note, A glass mirror should be always here used, as those of metal do not represent the objects with equal vivacity, and are beside subject to tarnish. It is also necessary that the box be sufficiently large, that you may not be obliged to use a mirror whose focus is too short; for in that case, the right lines near the border of the picture will appear bent in the mirror, which will have a disagreeable effect, and cannot be avoided.

IX. The rays of a luminous body placed in the focus of a concave mirror being reflected in parallel lines, if a second mirror be placed diametrically opposite the first, it will, by collecting those rays in its focus, set fire to a combustible body. 12 IX. To set fire to a combustible body by the reflection of two concave mirrors, fig. 18.

Place two concave mirrors, A and B, at about 12 or 15 feet distance from each other, and let the axis of each of them be in the same line. In the focus C of one of them, place a live coal, and in the focus D of the other, some gun-powder. With a pair of double bellows, which make a continual blast, keep constantly blowing the coal, and notwithstanding the distance between them, the powder will presently take fire.

It is not necessary that these mirrors be of metal or brass, those made of wood or pasteboard, gilded, will produce the explosion, which has sometimes taken effect at the distance of 50 feet, when mirrors of 18 inches, or two feet diameter, have been used.

This experiment succeeds with more difficulty at great distances; which may proceed from the moisture in a large quantity of air. It would doubtless take effect more readily, if a tin tube, of an equal diameter with the mirrors, were to be placed between them.

10 The reflecting partition, fig. 19. X. Behind the partition AB, place, in a position something oblique, the concave mirror EF, which must be at least ten inches in diameter, and its distance from the partition equal to three-fourths of the distance of its centre.

In the partition make an opening of seven or eight inches, either square or circular: it must face the mirror, and be of the same height with it. Behind this partition place a strong light, so disposed that it may not be seen at the opening, and may illumine an object placed at C, without throwing any light on the mirror.

Beneath the aperture in the partition place the object C, that you intend shall appear on the outside of the partition, in an inverted position; and which we will suppose to be a flower. Before the partition, and beneath the aperture, place a little flower-pot D, the top of which should be even with the bottom of the aperture, that the eye, placed at G, may see the flower in the same position as if its stalk came out of the pot.

Take care to paint the space between the back part of the partition and the mirror black, to prevent any reflections of light from being thrown on the mirror; in a word, so dispose the whole that it may be as little enlightened as possible.

When a person is placed at the point G, he will perceive the flower that is behind the partition, at the top of the pot at D, but on putting out his hand to pluck it, he will find that he attempts to grasp a shadow.

If in the opening of the partition a large double convex lens of a short focus be placed, or, which is not quite so well, a bottle of clear water, the image of the flower reflected thereon will appear much more vivid and distinct.

Observation. The phenomena that may be produced by means of concave mirrors are highly curious and astonishing. By their aid, spectres of various kinds may be exhibited. Suppose, for example, a person with a drawn sword places himself before a large concave mirror, but farther from it than its focus; he will then see an inverted image of himself in the air, between him and the mirror, of a less size than himself. If he steadily present the sword towards the centre of the mirror, an image of the sword will come out therefrom towards the sword in his hand, point to point, as it were to fence with him; and by his pushing the sword nearer, the image will appear to come nearer him, and almost to touch his breast, having a striking effect upon him. If the mirror be turned 45 degrees, or one eighth round, the reflected image will go out perpendicular to the direction of the sword presented, and apparently come to another person placed in the direction of the motion of the image. If that person is unacquainted with the experiment, and does not see the original sword, he will be much surprised and alarmed.—This experiment may be another way diversified, by telling any person, that at such an hour, and in such a place, he should see the apparition of an absent or deceased friend (of whose portrait you are in possession). In order to produce this phantom, instead of the hole in the partition AB in the last figure, there must be a door which opens into an apartment to which there is a considerable descent. Under that door you are to place the portrait, which must be inverted and strongly illuminated, that it may be lively reflected by the mirror, which must be large and well polished. Then having introduced the incredulous spectator at another door, and placed him in the proper point of view, you suddenly throw open the door at AB, when, to his great astonishment, he will immediately see the apparition of his friend.

It will be objected, perhaps, that this is not a perfect apparition, because it is only visible at one point of view, and by one person. But it should be remembered, that it was an established maxim in the last centuries, that a spectre might be visible to one person and not to others. So Shakespeare makes both Hamlet and Macbeth see apparitions that were not visible to others, present at the same time. It is not unlikely, moreover, that this maxim took its rise from certain apparitions of this kind that were raised by the monks, to serve some purposes they called religious; as they alone were in possession of what little learning there then was in the world.

Opticians sometimes grind a glass mirror concave in one direction only, as it is said longitudinally; it is in fact a concave portion of a cylinder, the breadth of which may be considered that of the mirror. A person looking at his face in this mirror, in the direction of its concavity, will see it curiously distorted in a very lengthened appearance; and by turning the cylindrical mirror a quarter round, his visage will appear distorted another way, by an apparent increase in width only. Another curious and singular property attends this sort of mirrors: If in a very near situation before it, you put your finger on the right-hand side of your nose, it will appear the same in the mirror; but if in a distant situation, somewhat beyond the centre of concavity, you again look at your face in the mirror, your finger will appear to be removed to the other or left-hand side of your nose. This, though something extraordinary, will in its cause appear very evident from a small consideration of the properties of spherical concave mirrors.

CATOPTROMANCY, [illegible], a kind of divination among the ancients; so called, because consisting in the application of a mirror. The word is formed from [illegible], *speculum*, "mirror," and [illegible], *divinatio*, "divination." Pausanias says, it was in use among the Achaians; where those who were sick, and in danger of death, let down a mirror, or looking glass fastened by a thread, into a fountain before the temple of Ceres; then, looking in the glass, if they saw a ghastly disfigured face, they took it as a sure sign of death; on the contrary, if the flesh appeared fresh and healthy, it was a token of recovery. Sometimes glasses were used without water, and the images of things future represented in them. See Gastromancy.

CATROU (Francis), a famous Jesuit, born at Paris in 1659. He was engaged for 12 years in the *Journal de Trevous*, and applied himself at the same time to other works, which distinguished him among the learned. He wrote a general History of the Mogul empire, and a Roman history, in which he was assisted by Father Rouille a brother Jesuit. Catrou died in 1737; and this last history was continued by Rouille, who died in 1740.

CATTERTHUN, a remarkable Caledonian post, a few miles north of the town of Brechin in the county of Angus in Scotland. Mr Pennant describes it as of uncommon strength. "It is (says he) of an oval form, made of a stupendous dike of loose white stones, whose convexity, from the base within to that without, is 122 feet. On the outside a hollow, made by the disposition of the stones, surrounds the whole. Round the base is a deep ditch, and below that about 100 yards, are vestiges of another, that went round the hill. The area within the stony mound is flat; the axis, or length of the oval, is 436 feet, the transverse diameter 200. Near the east side is the foundation of a rectangular building; and on most parts are the foundations of others small and circular; all which had once their superstructures, the shelter of the possessors of the post: there is also a hollow, now almost filled with stones, the well of the place." There is another fortification, but of inferior strength, in the neighbourhood. It is called the *Brown Catterthun*, from the colour of the ramparts which are composed only of earth. It is of a circular form, and consists of various concentric dikes. On one side of this rises a small rill, which, running down the hill, has formed a deep gully. From the side of the fortress is another rampart, which extends parallel to the rill, and then reverts, forming an additional post or retreat. The meaning of the word *Catter-thun* is *Camp-town*; and Mr Pennant thinks these might probably be the posts occupied by the Caledonians before their engagement at the foot of the Grampian Mountains with the celebrated Agricola. See (*History of*) Scotland.

CATTI, a people of Germany, very widely spread, on the east reaching to the river Sala, on the north to Westphalia; occupying, besides Hesse, the Wetterau, and part of the tract on the Rhine, and on the banks of the river Lohne. The Hercynian forest began and ended in their country.

CATTIVELLAUNI, anciently a people of Britain, seated in the country which is now divided into the counties of Hertford, Bedford, and Bucks. The name of this ancient British people is written in several different ways by Greek and Roman authors, being sometimes called Catti, Cassii, Catticuclani, Cattidudani, Cattiduclani, &c. That they were of Belgic origin cannot be doubted, and it is not improbable, that they derived their name of Catti from the Belgic word Katten, which signifies illustrious or noble, and that the addition of Vellauni, which means on the banks of rivers, might be given them after their arrival in Britain, as descriptive of the situation of their country. However this may be, the Cattivellauni formed one of the most brave and warlike of the ancient British nations when Cæsar invaded Britain, and long after. Cassibelanus, their prince, was made commander in chief of the confederated Britons, not only on account of his own personal qualities, but also because he was at the head of one of their bravest and most powerful tribes. In the interval between the departure of Cæsar and the next invasion under Claudius, the Cattivellauni had reduced several of the neighbouring states under their obedience; and they again took the lead in the opposition to the Romans at their second invasion, under their brave but unfortunate prince Caractacus. The country of the Cattivellauni was much frequented and improved by the Romans, after it came under their obedience. Verulamium, their capital, which stood near where St Alban's now stands, became a place of great consideration, was honoured with the name and privileges of a municipium or free city, and had magistrates after the model of the city of Rome. This place was taken and almost destroyed by the insurgents under Boadicia; but it was afterwards rebuilt, restored to its former splendor, and surrounded with a strong wall, some vestiges of which are still remaining. Durocobrivæ and Magiovinium, in the second iter of Antoninus, were probably Dunstable and Fenny-Stratford, at which places there appear to have been Roman stations. The Salenæ of Ptolemy, a town in the country of the Cattivellauni, was perhaps situated at Salndy, in Bedfordshire, where several Roman antiquities have been found. There were, besides these, several other Roman forts, stations, and towns in this country, which it would be tedious to enumerate. The territories of the Cattivellauni made a part of the Roman province called Britannia Prima.

CATTLE, a collective word, which signifies the four-footed animals, which serve either for tilling the ground, or for food to man. They are distinguished into large, or black cattle; and into small cattle: of the former are horses, bulls, oxen, cows, and even calves and heifers; amongst the latter are rams, ewes, sheep, lambs, goats, kids, &c. Cattle are the chief stock of a farm: they who deal in cattle are styled graziers.

CATULLUS (Caius Valerius), a Latin poet, born at Verona, in the year of Rome 666. The harmony of his numbers acquired him the esteem and friendship of Cicero, and other great men of his time. Many of his poems, however, abound with gross obscenities. He wrote satirical verses against Cæsar, under the name of Marmorra. He spent his whole life in a state of poverty; and died in the flower of his age, and the height of his reputation. Joseph Scaliger, Passerat, Muret, and Isaac Vossius, have written learned notes on this poet.

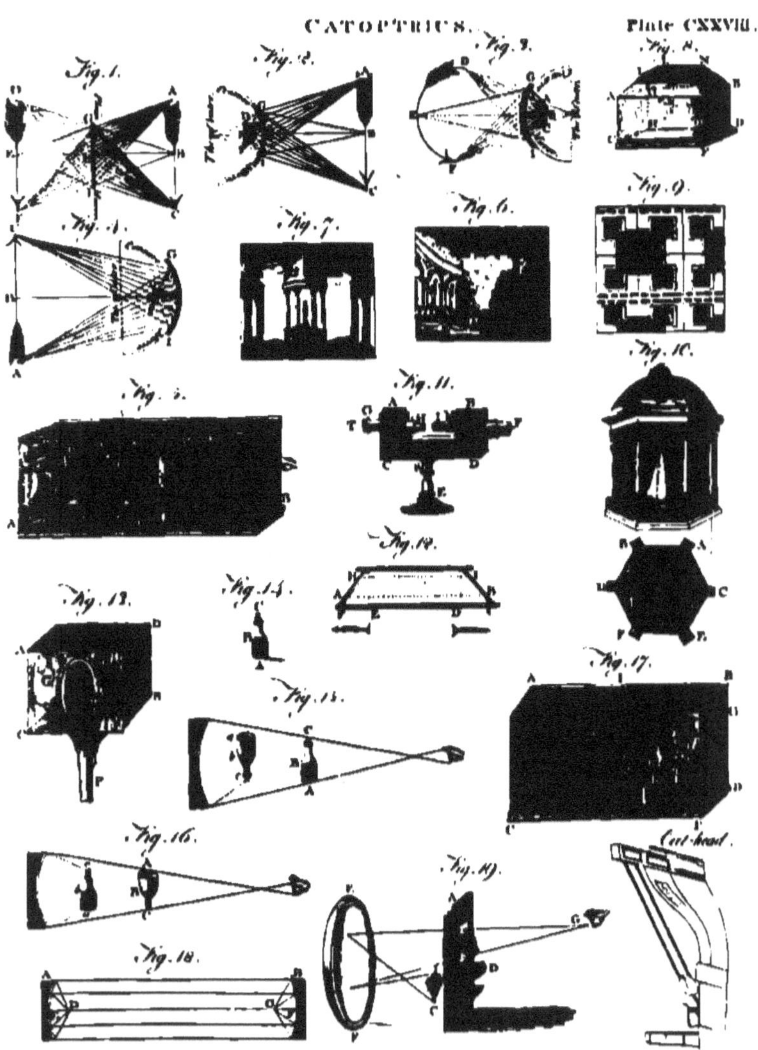
CATOPTRICS.
Plate CXXVIII.
Fig. 1.
Fig. 2.
Fig. 7.
Fig. 6.
Fig. 9.
Fig. 11.
Fig. 10.
Fig. 12.
Fig. 14.
Fig. 17.
Fig. 16.
Fig. 18.
Cat-head.

CATZ (James), a great civilian, politician, and Dutch poet, was born at Browershaven, in Zealand, in the year 1577. After having made several voyages, he fixed at Middleburg; and acquired by his pleadings such reputation, that the city of Dort chose him for its pensionary; as did also, some time after, that of Middleburg. In 1634, he was nominated pensionary of Holland and West Friesland; and in 1648, he was elected keeper of the seal of the same state, and stadtholder of the fiefs: but some time after, he resigned these employments, to enjoy the repose which his advanced age demanded. As the post of grand pensionary had been fatal to almost all those who had enjoyed it, from the beginning of the republic till that time, Catz delivered up his charge on his knees, before the whole assembly of the states, weeping for joy, and thanking God for having preserved him from the inconveniences that seemed attached to the duties of that office. But though he was resolved to spend the rest of his days in repose, the love of his country engaged him to comply with the desires of the state, who importuned him to go on an embassy to England, in the delicate conjuncture in which the republic found itself during the protectorate of Cromwell. At his return, he retired to his fine country seat at Sorgvliet, where he lived in tranquillity till the year 1660, in which he died. He wrote a great number of poems in Dutch; most of which are on moral subjects, and so esteemed, that they have been often printed in all the different sizes; and next to the Bible, there is no work so highly valued by the Dutch.

CATZENELLIBOGEN, a town of Germany, in the lower part of the upper circle of the Rhine, with a strong castle. It is capital of a county of the same name. E. Long. 7. 58. N. Lat. 50. 20.

CAVA, in anatomy, the name of a vein, the largest in the body, terminating in the right ventricle of the heart. See ANATOMY, p. 751. col. 2.

CAVA, a considerable and populous town of Italy, in the kingdom of Naples, and in the Hither Principato, with a bishop's see. It is situated at the foot of Mount Metelian, in E. Long. 15. 5. N. Lat. 40. 42.

CAVAILLAN, a town of France in Comtal Venaissin, with a bishop's see. It is situated on the river Durance, in a fertile and pleasant country. E. Long. 4. 17. N. Lat. 43. 52.

CAVALCADE, a formal pompous march or procession of horsemen, equipages, &c. by way of parade, or ceremony, as a grace to a triumph, public entry, or the like.

CAVALCADOUR, or CAVALCADIUR, anciently denoted a riding-master; but at present is disused in that sense, and only employed to denote a sort of equerries or officers who have the direction of princes stables. The French say, *ecuyer cavalcadour* of the king, the duke of Orleans, &c. Menage writes it *cavalcadour*, and derives it from the Spanish *cavalgador*, a horseman.

CAVALCANTE (Guido), a nobleman of Florence in the 13th century, who having followed the party of the Guelfes, experienced the changeableness of fortune. He showed great strength of mind in his misfortunes, and never neglected to improve his talents. He wrote a treatise in Italian concerning style, and some verses which are esteemed. His poem on the love of this world, has been commented on by several learned men.

CAVALIER, a horseman, or person mounted on horseback; especially if he be armed withal, and have a military appearance.

Anciently, the word was restrained to a knight, or *miles*. The French still use *Chevalier* in the same sense.

CAVALIER, considered as a faction. See BRITAIN, n° 109.

CAVALIER, in fortification, an elevation of earth of different shapes, situated ordinarily in the gorge of a bastion, bordered with a parapet, and cut into more or less embrasures, according to the capacity of the cavalier. Cavaliers are a double defence for the faces of the opposite bastion: they defend the ditch, break the besiegers galleries, command the traverses in dry moats, scour the saliant angle of the counterscarp, where the besiegers have their counter-batteries, and enfilade the enemies trenches, or oblige them to multiply their parallels: they are likewise very serviceable in defending the breach and the retrenchments of the besieged, and can very much incommode the entrenchments which the enemy make, being lodged in the bastion.

CAVALIER, in the manege, one that understands horses, and is practised in the art of riding them.

CAVALIERI (Bonaventure), an eminent mathematician in the 17th century, a native of Milan, and a friar of the order of the Jesuati of St Jerome, was professor of mathematics at Bologna, where he published several mathematical books, particularly the *Method of Indivisibles*. He was a scholar of Galileo. His *Directorium generale Uranometricum* contains great variety of most useful practices in trigonometry and astronomy. His trigonometrical tables in that work are excellent.

CAVALRY, a body of soldiers that charge on horseback. The word comes from the French, *cavalerie*, and that from the corrupt Latin, *caballus*, a horse.

The Roman cavalry consisted wholly of those called *equites*, or knights, who were a distinct order in the distribution of citizens.—The Grecian cavalry were divided into *cataphractæ* and *non cataphractæ*, i. e. into heavy and light armed.—Of all the Greeks, the Thessalians excelled most in cavalry. The Lacedemonians, inhabiting a mountainous country, were but meanly furnished with cavalry, till, carrying their arms into other countries, they found great occasion for horses to support and cover their foot. The Athenian cavalry, for a considerable time, consisted only of 96 horsemen: after expelling the Persians out of Greece, they increased the number to 300; and afterwards to 1200, which was the highest pitch of the Athenian cavalry. The Turkish cavalry consists partly of Spahis, and partly of horsemen raised and maintained by the Zaims and Timariots.

The chief use of the cavalry is to make frequent excursions to disturb the enemy, intercept his convoys, and destroy the country: in battle to support and cover the foot, and to break through and disorder the enemy; also to secure the retreat of the foot. Formerly, the manner of the fighting of the cavalry was

was, after firing their pistols or carabines, to wheel off, to give opportunity for loading again. Gustavus Adolphus is said to have first taught the cavalry to charge through, to march straight up to the enemy, with the sword drawn in the bridlehand, and each man having fired his piece, at the proper distance, to betake himself to his sword, and charge the enemy as was found most advantageous.

CAVAN, a town of Ireland, and capital of a county of the same name, in the province of Ulster, seated in W. Long. 7. 31. N. Lat. 5. 04.

Cavan, a county of Ireland, 47 miles in length, and 23 in breadth; is bounded on the east by Monaghan, and on the south by Longford, West-Meath, and East-Meath. It has but two towns of any note, viz. Cavan and Kilmore. It sends five members to parliament; two for the county, two for Cavan, and one for Kilmore. It contains upwards of 8000 houses, 37 parishes, seven baronies, and two boroughs.

CAUCASUS, the name of a very high mountain of Asia, being one of that great ridge which runs between the Black and Caspian seas. Sir John Chardin describes this as the highest mountain, and the most difficult to pass, of any he had seen. It has frightful precipices, and in many places the roads are cut out of the solid rock. At the time he passed it, the mountain was entirely covered with snow; so that, in many places, his guides behoved to clear the way with shovels. The mountain is 36 leagues over, and the summit of it eight leagues in breadth. The top is perpetually covered with snow; and our traveller relates, that the two last days he seemed to be in the clouds, and was not able to see 20 paces before him. Excepting the very top, however, all the parts of Mount Caucasus are extremely fruitful; abounding in honey, corn, fruits, hogs, and large cattle. The vines twine about the trees, and rise so high, that the inhabitants cannot gather the fruit from the uppermost branches. There are many streams of excellent water, and a vast number of villages. The inhabitants are for the most part Christians of the Georgian Church. They have fine complexions, and the women are very beautiful.—In the winter they wear snow-shoes in the form of rackets, which prevent their sinking in the snow, and enable them to run upon it with great swiftness.

CAUDEBEC, a rich, populous, and trading town in Normandy, and capital of the territory of Caux. It is seated at the foot of a mountain near the river Seine, in E. Long. 0. 46. N. Lat. 40. 30.

CAUDEX, by Malphigi and other botanists, is used to signify the stem or trunk of a tree: by Linnæus, the stock or body of the root, part of which ascends, part descends. The ascending part raises itself gradually above ground, serving frequently for a trunk, and corresponds in some measure to the *caudex* of former writers: the descending part strikes gradually downward into the ground, and puts forth radicles or small fibres, which are the principal and essential part of every root. The descending caudex therefore corresponds to the radix of other botanists. Agreeably to this idea, Linnæus considers trees and shrubs as roots above ground; an opinion which is confirmed by a well-known fact, that trees, when inverted, put forth leaves from the descending caudex, and radicles or roots from the ascending. For the varieties in the descending caudex, see the article Radix.

CAUDIUM (anc. geog.), a town of Samnium, on the Via Appia, between Calatia and Beneventum: *Caudinus*, the epithet. The *Caudinæ Furcæ*, or *Furculæ*, were memorable by the disgrace of the Romans; being spears disposed in the form of a gallows under which prisoners of war were made to pass, and gave name to a defile or narrow pass near *Caudium*, Livy; where the Samnites obliged the Roman army and the two consuls to lay down their arms and pass under the gallows, or yoke, as a token of subjection.

CAVE, any large subterraneous hollow. These were undoubtedly the primitive habitations, before men began to build edifices above ground. The primitive method of burial was also to reposite the bodies in caves, which seems to have been the origin of catacombs. They long continued the proper habitations of shepherds. Among the Romans, *caves (antra)* used to be consecrated to nymphs, who were worshipped in caves, as other gods were in temples. The Persians also worshipped their god Mithras in a natural cave consecrated for the purpose by Zoroaster. The cave of the nymph Egeria is still shown at Rome. Kircher, after Gaffarellus, enumerates divers species of caves; as divine, natural, &c.—Of natural caves some are possessed of a medicinal virtue, as the Grotto de Serpente; others are poisonous or mephitical; some are replete with metalline exhalations, and others with waters. Divine caves were those said to affect the human mind and passions in various ways, and even to inspire with a knowledge of future events. Such were the sacred caverns at Delphi which inspired the Pythia; the Sibyl's cave at Cumæ, still shown near the lake Avernus; the cave of Trophonius, &c.

Cave (Dr William), a learned English divine born in 1637, educated in St John's college Cambridge; and successively minister of Hasely in Oxfordshire, Allhallows the Great in London, and of Islington. He became chaplain to Charles II. and in 1684 was installed a canon of Windsor. He compiled *the Lives of the Primitive Fathers in the three first centuries of the church*, which is esteemed a very useful work; and *Historia Literaria*, &c. in which he gives an exact account of all who had written for or against Christianity, from the time of Christ to the 14th century: which works produced a warm controversy between Dr Cave and M. Le Clerc, who was then writing his *Bibliotheque Universelle* in Holland, and who charged the doctor with partiality. Dr Cave died in 1713.

CAVE (Edward), printer, celebrated as the projector of the *Gentleman's Magazine*,—the first publication of the species, and since

The fruitful mother of a thousand more,

was born in 1691. His father being disappointed of some small family-expectations, was reduced to follow the trade of a shoemaker at Rugby in Warwickshire. The free school of this place, in which his son had, by the rules of its foundation, a right to be instructed, was then in high reputation, under the Rev. Mr Holyock, to whose care most of the neighbouring families, even of the highest rank, entrusted their sons. He had judgment to diſcover, and for ſome time generoſity to encourage, the genius of young Cave; and was ſo well pleaſed with his quick progreſs in the ſchool, that he declared his reſolution to breed him for the univerſity, and recommend him as a ſervitor to ſome of his ſcholars of high rank. But proſperity which depends upon the caprice of others, is of ſhort duration. Cave's ſuperiority in literature exalted him to an invidious familiarity with boys who were far above him in rank and expectations; and, as in unequal aſſociations it always happens, whatever unlucky prank was played was imputed to Cave. When any miſchief, great or ſmall, was done, though perhaps others boaſted of the ſtratagem when it was ſucceſsful, yet upon detection or miſcarriage, the fault was ſure to fall upon poor Cave. The harſh treatment he experienced from this ſource, and which he bore for a while, made him at laſt leave the ſchool, and the hope of a literary education, to ſeek ſome other means of gaining a livelihood.

He was firſt placed with a collector of the exciſe: but the inſolence of his miſtreſs, who employed him in ſervile drudgery, quickly diſguſted him, and he went up to London in queſt of more ſuitable employment. He was recommended to a timber-merchant at the Bankſide: and while he was there on liking, is ſaid to have given hopes of great mercantile abilities: but this place he ſoon left, and was bound apprentice to Mr Collins, a printer of ſome reputation, and deputy alderman. This was a trade for which men were formerly qualified by a literary education, and which was pleaſing to Cave, becauſe it furniſhed ſome employment for his ſcholaſtic attainments. Here, therefore, he reſolved to ſettle, though his maſter and miſtreſs lived in perpetual diſcord, and their houſe was therefore no comfortable habitation. From the inconveniences of theſe domeſtic tumults he was ſoon releaſed, having in only two years attained ſo much ſkill in his art, and gained ſo much the confidence of his maſter, that he was ſent without any ſuperintendant to conduct a printing-houſe at Norwich, and publiſh a weekly paper. In this undertaking he met with ſome oppoſition, which produced a public controverſy, and procured young Cave the reputation of a writer.

His maſter died before his apprenticeſhip was expired, and he was not able to bear the perverſeneſs of his miſtreſs. He therefore quitted her houſe upon a ſtipulated allowance, and married a young widow with whom he lived at Bow. When his apprenticeſhip was over, he worked as a journeyman at the printing-houſe of Mr Barber, a man much diſtinguiſhed and employed by the Tories, whoſe principles had at that time ſo much prevalence with Cave, that he was for ſome years a writer in Miſt's Journal. He afterwards obtained by his wife's intereſt a ſmall place in the poſt-office; but ſtill continued, at his intervals of attendance, to exerciſe his trade or to employ himſelf with ſome typographical buſineſs. He corrected the *Gradus ad Parnaſſum*; and was liberally rewarded by the company of Stationers. He wrote an Account of the Criminals, which had for ſome time a conſiderable ſale; and publiſhed many little pamphlets that accident brought into his hands, of which it would be very difficult to recover the memory. By the correſpondence which his place in the poſt-office facilitated, he procured a country news-paper, and ſold their intelligence to a journaliſt in London for a guinea a week. He was afterwards raiſed to the office of clerk of the franks, in which he acted with great ſpirit and firmneſs; and often ſtopped franks which were given by members of parliament to their friends, becauſe he thought ſuch extenſion of a peculiar right illegal. This raiſed many complaints; and the influence that was exerted againſt him procured his ejectment from office. He had now, however, collected a ſum ſufficient for the purchaſe of a ſmall printing-office, and began the Gentleman's Magazine; an undertaking to which he owed the affluence in which he paſſed the laſt 20 years of his life, and the large fortune which he left behind him. When he formed the project, he was far from expecting the ſucceſs which he found; and others had ſo little proſpect of its conſequence, that though he had for ſeveral years talked of his plan among printers and bookſellers, none of them thought it worth the trial. That they were not (ſays Dr Johnſon) reſtrained by their virtue from the execution of another man's deſign, was ſufficiently apparent as ſoon as that deſign began to be gainful; for in a few years a multitude of magazines aroſe, and periſhed: only the London Magazine, ſupported by a powerful aſſociation of bookſellers, and circulated with all the art and all the cunning of trade, exempted itſelf from the general fate of Cave's invaders, and obtained though not an equal yet a conſiderable ſale.

Cave now began to aſpire to popularity; and being a greater lover of poetry than any other art, he ſometimes offered ſubjects for poems, and propoſed prizes for the beſt performers. The firſt prize was 50 l. for which, being but newly acquainted with wealth, and thinking the influence of 50 l. extremely great, he expected the firſt authors of the kingdom to appear as competitors; and offered the allotment of the prize to the univerſities. But when the time came, no name was ſeen among the writers that had been ever ſeen before; the univerſities and ſeveral private men rejected the province of aſſigning the prize. The determination was then left to Dr Cromwell Mortimer and Dr Birch; and by the latter the award was made, which may be ſeen in Gent. Mag. Vol. VI. p. 59.

Mr Cave continued to improve his Magazine, and had the ſatiſfaction of ſeeing its ſucceſs proportionate to his diligence, till in 1751 his wife died of an aſthma. He ſeemed not at firſt much affected by her death, but in a few days loſt his ſleep and his appetite, which he never recovered. After having lingered about two years, with many viciſſitudes of amendment and relapſe, he fell by drinking acid liquors into a diarrhœa, and afterwards into a kind of lethargic inſenſibility; and died Jan. 10. 1754, having juſt concluded the 23d annual collection.

CAVEARE. See CAVIARE.

CAVEAT, in law, a kind of proceſs in the ſpiritual courts, to ſtop the proving of a will, the granting letters of adminiſtration, &c. to the prejudice of another. It is alſo uſed to ſtop the inſtitution of a clerk to a benefice.

CAVEATING, in fencing, is the ſhifting the ſword from one ſide of that of your adverſary to the other.

Cavedo, Cavendish.

CAVEDO, in commerce, a Portuguese long measure, equal to $27\frac{7}{35}$ English inches.

CAVENDISH (Thomas), of Suffolk, the second Englishman that sailed round the globe, was descended from a noble family in Devonshire. Having dissipated his fortune, he resolved to repair it at the expence of the Spaniards. He sailed from Plymouth with two small ships in July 1586; passed through the straits of Magellan; took many rich prizes along the coasts of Chili and Peru; and near California possessed himself of the St Ann, an Acapulco ship, with a cargo of immense value. He completed the circumnavigation of the globe, by returning home round the Cape of Good Hope, and reached Plymouth again in September 1588. On his arrival, it is said, that his soldiers and sailors were clothed in silk, his sails were damask, and his topmast was covered with cloth of gold. His acquired riches did not last long: he reduced himself, in 1591, to the expedient of another voyage; which was far from being so successful as the former; he went no farther than the straits of Magellan, where the weather obliging him to return, he died of grief on the coast of Brazil.

Cavendish (Sir William), descended of an ancient and honourable family, was born about the year 1505, the second son of Thomas Cavendish, of Cavendish in Suffolk, clerk of the pipe in the reign of Henry VIII. Having had a liberal education, he was taken into the family of the great cardinal Woolsey, whom he served in the capacity of gentleman-usher of the chamber, when that superb prelate maintained the dignity of a prince. In 1527, he attended his master on his splendid embassy to France, returned with him to England, and was one of the few who continued faithful to him in his disgrace. Mr Cavendish was with him when he died, and delayed going to court till he had performed the last duty of a faithful servant by seeing his body decently interred. The king was so far from disapproving of his conduct, that he immediately took him into his houshold, made him treasurer of his chamber, a privy-counsellor, and afterwards conferred on him the order of knighthood. He was also appointed one of the commissioners for taking the surrender of religious houses. In 1540 he was nominated one of the auditors of the court of augmentations, and soon after obtained a grant of several considerable lordships in Hertfordshire. In the reign of Edward VI. his estates were much increased by royal grants in seven different counties; and he appears to have continued in high favour at court during the reign of queen Mary. He died in the year 1557. He was the founder of Chatsworth, and ancestor of the dukes of Devonshire. He wrote "The life and death of cardinal Woolsey;" printed at London 1667; reprinted in 1706, under the title of "Memoirs of the great favourite cardinal Woolsey."

Cavendish (William), duke of Newcastle, grandson of Sir William Cavendish, was born in 1592. In 1610, he was made knight of the bath; in 1620, raised to the dignity of a peer, by the title of baron Ogle, and viscount Mansfield; and in the third year of king Charles I. created earl of Newcastle upon Tyne, and baron Cavendish of Bolsover. He was after this made governor to the prince of Wales, afterwards Charles II. When the first troubles broke out in Scotland, and the king's treasury was but indifferently provided, he contributed ten thousand pounds; and also raised a troop of horse, consisting of about two hundred knights and gentlemen, who served at their own charge, were commanded by the earl, and honoured with the title of *the prince's troop*. He had after this the command of the northern counties; and was constituted general and commander in chief of all the forces that might be raised north of Trent, and of several counties south of that river. He afterwards raised an army of eight thousand horse, foot, and dragoons; with which he took some towns, and gained several important victories. On this he was advanced to the dignity of marquis of Newcastle; but his majesty's affairs being totally ruined by the rashness of prince Rupert, he, with a few of the principal officers of the army, went abroad, and staid for some time at Paris; where, notwithstanding the vast estate he had when the civil war broke out, his circumstances were now so bad, that himself and wife were reduced to the necessity of pawning their clothes for a dinner. He afterwards removed to Antwerp, that he might be nearer his own country; and there, though under great difficulties, resided for several years: but, notwithstanding his distresses, he was treated, during an exile of eighteen years, with extraordinary marks of distinction. On his return to England at the restoration, he was advanced to the dignity of earl of Ogle and duke of Newcastle. He spent his time in a country retirement, and was the patron of men of merit. His grace died in 1679, aged 84. He wrote a treatise on horsemanship, which is esteemed; and some comedies, which are not.

Cavendish.

Mr Granger observes, that he was master of many accomplishments, and was much better qualified for a court than a camp: that he understood horsemanship, music, and poetry; but was a better horseman than musician, and a better musician than poet.

Cavendish (Margaret), duchess of Newcastle, famous for her voluminous productions, was born about the latter end of the reign of James I. and was the youngest sister of Lord Lucas of Colchester. She married the duke of Newcastle abroad in 1645; and on their return after the restoration, spent the remainder of her life in writing plays, poems, with the life of her husband, to the amount of about a dozen of folios. "What gives the best idea of her unbounded passion for scribbling (says Mr Walpole), was her seldom revising the copies of her works, lest, as she said, it should disturb her following conceptions." She died in 1673.

Cavendish (William), the first duke of Devonshire, and one of the most distinguished patriots in the British annals, was born in 1640. In 1677, being then member for Derby, he vigorously opposed the venal measures of the court; and, the following year, was one of the committee appointed to draw up articles of impeachment against the lord treasurer Danby. In 1679, being re-elected to serve for Derby in a new parliament, Charles II. thought fit to make him a privy counsellor; but he soon withdrew from the board, with his friend lord Russel, when he found that popish interest prevailed. He carried up the articles of impeachment to the house of lords, against lord chief-justice Scroggs, for his arbitrary and illegal proceedings

ings in the court of king's bench; and when the king declared his resolution not to sign the bill for excluding the Duke of York (afterwards James II.), he moved the house of commons, that a bill might be brought in for the association of all his majesty's protestant subjects. He also openly named the king's evil counsellors, and voted for an address to remove them from his presence and councils for ever. He nobly appeared at lord Russel's trial, in defence of that great man, at a time when it was scarce more criminal to be an accomplice than a witness for him. The same fortitude, activity, and love of his country, animated this illustrious patriot to oppose the arbitrary proceedings of James II.; and when he saw there was no other method of saving the nation from impending slavery, he was the foremost in the association for inviting over the prince of Orange, and the first nobleman who appeared in arms to receive him at his landing. He was created Duke of Devonshire in 1694, by William and Mary. His last public service was in the union with Scotland, for concluding of which he was appointed a commissioner by queen Anne. He died in 1707, and ordered the following inscription to be put on his monument.

Willielmus Dux Devon,
Bonorum Principum Fidelis Subditus,
Inimicus et Invisus Tyrannis.
William Duke of Devonshire,
Of good Princes the faithful Subject,
The Enemy and Aversion of Tyrants.

Besides being thus estimable for public virtues, his grace was distinguished by his literary accomplishments. He had a poetical genius, which showed itself particularly in two pieces, written with equal spirit, dignity, and delicacy: these are, an ode on the death of queen Mary; and an allusion to the archbishop of Cambray's supplement to Homer. He had great knowledge in the languages, was a true judge in history, and a critic in poetry; he had a fine hand in music, an elegant taste in painting, and in architecture had a skill equal to any person of the age in which he lived. His predecessor, Sir John Cavendish, was the person who killed the famous Wat Tyler in 1381.

CAVETTO, in architecture, a hollow member, or round concave moulding, containing a quadrant of a circle, and having a quite contrary effect to that of a quarter round: it is used as an ornament in cornices.

CAVEZON, in the manege, a sort of nose-band, either of iron, leather, or wood, sometimes flat, and at other times hollow or twisted, clapt upon the nose of a horse to wring it, and so forward the suppling and breaking of the horse.

CAVIARE, a kind of food lately introduced into Britain. It is made of the hard roes of sturgeon*, formed into small cakes, about an inch thick and three or four inches broad. The method of making it is, by taking out of the spawn all the nerves or strings, then washing it in white-wine or vinegar, and spreading it on a table. It is then salted and pressed in a fine bag; after which it is cased up in a vessel with a hole at the bottom, that if any moisture is left it may run out. This kind of food is in great request among the Moscovites, on account of their three lents, which they keep with a superstitious exactness; wherefore the Italians settled at Moscow drive a very great trade in this commodity throughout that empire, there being a prodigious quantity of sturgeon taken at the mouth of the Wolga and other rivers which fall into the Caspian sea. A pretty large quantity of the commodity is also consumed in Italy and France. They get the caviare from Archangel, but commonly buy it at second hand of the English and Dutch.—According to Savary, the best caviare brought from Muscovy is prepared from the belluga, a fish eight or ten feet long, caught in the Caspian sea, which is much preferable to that made of the spawn of sturgeon. A kind of caviare, or rather sausage, is also made from the spawn of some other fishes; particularly a sort of mullet caught in the Mediterranean. See Mooil and Botargo.

* See *Acipenser*.

Insect Caviare. See Axayacatl.

CAVIDOS. See Cabidos.

CAVIL, (*cavillatio*), is defined by some a fallacious kind of reason, carrying some resemblance of truth, which a person, knowing its falsehood, advances in dispute for the sake of victory. The art of framing sophisms or fallacies is called by Boethius *cavillatoria*.

CAUK, or Cawk. See Terra Ponderosa, and Chemistry, *Index*.

CAUKING, or Caulking, *of a ship*, is driving a quantity of oakum, or old ropes untwisted and drawn asunder, into the seams of the planks, or into the intervals where the planks are joined together in the ship's decks or sides, in order to prevent the entrance of water. After the oakum is driven very hard into these seams, it is covered with hot melted pitch or rosin, to keep the water from rotting it.

Among the ancients, the first who made use of pitch in caulking, were the inhabitants of Phæacia, afterwards called Corsica. Wax and rosin appear to have been commonly used previous to that period; and the Poles at this time use a sort of unctuous clay for the same purpose, on their navigable rivers.

Caulking-Irons, are iron chissels for that purpose. Some of these irons are broad, some round, and others grooved. After the seams are stopped with oakum, it is done over with a mixture of tallow, pitch, and tar, as low as the ship draws water.

CAUL, in anatomy, a membrane in the abdomen, covering the greatest part of the guts; called, from its structure, *Reticulum*, but most frequently *Omentum*. See Anatomy, n° 90.

Caul is likewise a little membrane, found on some children, encompassing the head when born.

Drelincourt takes the *caul* to be only a fragment of the membranes of the fœtus; which ordinarily break at the birth of the child. Lampridius tells us, that the midwives sold this *caul* at a good price to the advocates and pleaders of his time; it being an opinion, that while they had this about them, they should carry with them a force of persuasion which no judge could withstand: the canons forbid the use of it; because some witches and sorcerers, it seems, had abused it.

CAULIFLOWERS, in gardening, a much esteemed species of cabbage. See Brassica.

CAURIS, in natural history, a name given by some to the genus of shells called, by the generality of writers, *porcellana*, and *concha venerea*. It is from a false pronunciation of this word *cauris* that we call these shells *gowries*. See *Porcelain-Shell*.

CAURSINES, (*Caorsini*), were Italians that came into England about the year 1235, terming themselves

Cauſa & Cauſe.

the Pope's merchants, but driving no other trade than letting out money; and having great banks in England, they differed little from Jews, ſave (as hiſtory ſays) they were rather more merciless to their debtors. Some will have them called *Caurſini*, quaſi *Cauſa Urſini*, bearish and cruel in their cauſes; others *Corſini* or *Corſini*, as coming from the iſle of Corſica; but Cowel ſays, they have their name from *Caurſium*, *Caorſi*, a town in Lombardy, where they firſt practiſed their arts of uſury and extortion; from whence, ſpreading themſelves, they carried their infamous trade through moſt parts of Europe, and were a common plague to every nation where they came. The then biſhop of London excommunicated them; and king Henry III. baniſhed them from this kingdom in the year 1240. But, being the pope's ſolicitors and money-changers, they were permitted to return in the year 1250; tho' in a very ſhort time they were again driven out of the kingdom on account of their intolerable exactions.

CAUSA MATRIMONII PRÆLOCUTI, in common law, a writ that lies where a woman gives land to a man in fee to the intent he ſhall marry her, and he refuſes to do it in a reaſonable time, being thereunto required by the woman; and in ſuch caſe, for not performing the condition, the entry of the woman into the lands again has been adjudged lawful.

The huſband and wife may ſue this writ againſt another who ought to have married her.

CAUSALITY, among metaphyſicians, the action or power of a cauſe in producing its effect.

CAUSALTY, among miners, denotes the lighter, ſulphureous, earthy parts of ores, carried off in the operation of waſhing. This, in the mines, they throw in heaps upon banks, which in ſix or ſeven years they find it worth their while to work over again.

CAUSE, that from whence any thing proceeds, or by virtue of which any thing is done: it ſtands oppoſed to effect. We get the ideas of cauſe and effect from our obſervation of the viciſſitude of things, while we perceive ſome qualities or ſubſtances begin to exiſt, and that they receive their exiſtence from the due application and operation of other beings. That which produces, is the cauſe; and that which is produced, the effect: thus, fluidity in wax is the effect of a certain degree of heat, which we obſerve to be conſtantly produced by the application of ſuch heat.

Reid on the Active Powers of Man.

Ariſtotle, and the ſchoolmen after him, diſtinguiſhed four kinds of cauſes; the efficient, the material, the formal, and the final. This, like many of Ariſtotle's diſtinctions, is only a diſtinction of the various meanings of an ambiguous word; for the efficient, the matter, the form and the end, have nothing common in their nature, by which they may be accounted ſpecies of the ſame *genus*; but the Greek word, which we tranſlate *cauſe*, had theſe four different meanings in Ariſtotle's days, and we have added other meanings. We do not indeed call the matter or the form of a thing its cauſe; but we have final cauſes, inſtrumental cauſes, occaſional cauſes, and many others. Thus the word *cauſe* has been ſo hackneyed, and made to have ſo many different meanings in the writings of philoſophers, and in the diſcourſe of the vulgar, that its original and proper meaning is loſt in the crowd.

With regard to the phenomena of nature, the important end of knowing their cauſes, beſides gratifying our curioſity, is, that we may know when to expect them, or how to bring them about. This is very often of real importance in life; and this purpoſe is ſerved, by knowing what, by the courſe of nature, goes before them and is connected with them; and this, therefore, we call the *cauſe* of ſuch a phenomenon.

Cauſe.

If a magnet be brought near to a mariner's compaſs, the needle, which was before at reſt, immediately begins to move, and bends its courſe towards the magnet, or perhaps the contrary way. If an unlearned ſailor is aſked the cauſe of this motion of the needle, he is at no loſs for an anſwer. He tells you it is the magnet; and the proof is clear; for, remove the magnet, and the effect ceaſes; bring it near, and the effect is again produced. It is, therefore, evident to ſenſe, that the magnet is the cauſe of this effect.

A Carteſian philoſopher enters deeper into the cauſe of this phenomenon. He obſerves, that the magnet does not touch the needle, and therefore can give it no impulſe. He pities the ignorance of the ſailor. The effect is produced, ſays he, by magnetic effluvia, or ſubtile matter, which paſſes from the magnet to the needle, and forces it from its place. He can even ſhow you, in a figure, where theſe magnetic effluvia iſſue from the magnet, what round they take, and what way they return home again. And thus he thinks he comprehends perfectly how, and by what cauſe, the motion of the needle is produced.

A Newtonian philoſopher inquires what proof can be offered for the exiſtence of magnetic effluvia, and can find none. He therefore holds it as a fiction, a hypotheſis; and he has learned that hypotheſes ought to have no place in the philoſophy of nature. He confeſſes his ignorance of the real cauſe of this motion, and thinks that his buſineſs as a philoſopher is only to find from experiment the laws by which it is regulated in all caſes.

Theſe three perſons differ much in their ſentiments with regard to the real cauſe of this phenomenon; and the man who knows moſt is he who is ſenſible that he knows nothing of the matter. Yet all the three ſpeak the ſame language, and acknowledge that the cauſe of this motion is the attractive or repulſive power of the magnet.

What has been ſaid of this, may be applied to every phenomenon that falls within the compaſs of natural philoſophy. We deceive ourſelves, if we conceive that we can point out the real efficient cauſe of any one of them.

The grandeſt diſcovery ever made in natural philoſophy, was that of the law of gravitation, which opens ſuch a view of our planetary ſyſtem, that it looks like ſomething divine. But the author of this diſcovery was perfectly aware that he diſcovered no real cauſe, but only the law or rule according to which the unknown cauſe operates.

Natural philoſophers, who think accurately, have a precise meaning to the terms they uſe in the ſcience; and when they pretend to ſhow the cauſe of any phenomenon of nature, they mean by the cauſe, a law of nature of which that phenomenon is a neceſſary conſequence.

The whole object of natural philoſophy, as Newton expreſsly teaches, is reducible to theſe two heads: firſt, by juſt induction from experiment and obſervation, to discover the laws of nature; and then to apply those laws to the solution of the phenomena of nature. This was all that this great philosopher attempted, and all that he thought attainable. And this indeed he attained in a great measure, with regard to the motions of our planetary system, and with regard to the rays of light.

But supposing that all the phenomena which fall within the reach of our senses were accounted for from general laws of nature justly deduced from experience; that is, supposing natural philosophy brought to its utmost perfection; it does not discover the efficient cause of any one phenomenon in nature.

The laws of nature are the rules according to which the effects are produced; but there must be a cause which operates according to these rules. The rules of navigation never navigated a ship. The rules of architecture never built a house.

Natural philosophers, by great attention to the course of nature, have discovered many of her laws, and have very happily applied them to account for many phenomena: but they have never discovered the efficient cause of any one phenomenon; nor do those who have distinct notions of the principles of the science make any such pretence.

Upon the theatre of nature we see innumerable effects, which require an agent endowed with active power; but the agent is behind the scene. Whether it be the Supreme Cause alone, or a subordinate cause or causes; and if subordinate causes be employed by the Almighty, what their nature, their number, and their different offices may be; are things hid, for wise reasons, without doubt, from the human eye.

Cause, among civilians, the same with action. See Action.

Cause, among physicians. The cause of a disease is defined by Galen to be that during the presence of which we are ill, and which being removed the disorder immediately ceases. The doctrine of the causes of diseases is called Etiology.

Physicians divide causes into procatarctic, antecedent, and continent.

Procatarctic Cause, [illegible], called also *primitive* and *incipient cause*, is either an occasion which of its own nature does not beget a disease, but, happening on a body inclined to diseases, breeds a fever, gout, &c. (such as are watching, fasting, and the like); or an evident and manifest cause, which immediately produces the disease, as being sufficient thereto, such as is a sword in respect of a wound.

Antecedent Cause, [illegible], a latent disposition of the body, from whence some disease may arise; such as a plethora in respect of a fever, a cacochymia in respect of a scurvy.

Continent, Conjunct, or *Proximate Cause*, that principle in the body, which immediately adheres to the disease, and which being present, the disease is also present; or, which being removed, the disease is taken away: such is the stone in a nephritic patient.

CAUSEWAY, or Causey, a massive construction of stone, stakes, and fascines; or an elevation of fat, viscous earth, well beaten; serving either as a road in wet marshy places, or as a mole to retain the waters of a pond, or prevent a river from overflowing the lower grounds. See Road.—The word comes from the French *Chaussée*, anciently wrote *Chaulsée*; and that from the Latin *Calceata*, or *Calceta*; according to Sommer and Spelman, *a calcando*. Bergier rather takes the word to have had its rise *à pedum calcis, quibus teruntur*. Some derive it from the Latin *calx*, or French *chaux*, as supposing it primarily to denote a way paved with chalk-stones.

Causeway, *calcetum*, or *calcea*, more usually denotes a common hard raised way, maintained and repaired with stones and rubbish.

Devil's Causeway, a famous work of this kind, which ranges through the county of Northumberland, commonly supposed to be Roman, though Mr Horsley suspects it to be of later times.

Giant's Causeway, is a denomination given to a huge pile of stony columns in the district of Coleraine in Ireland. See *Giant's Causeway*.

CAUSSIN (Nicholas), surnamed the Just, a French Jesuit, was born at Troyes in Champagne, in the year 1580; and entered into the Jesuits order when he was 26 years of age. He taught rhetoric in several of their colleges, and afterwards began to preach, by which he gained very great reputation. He increased this reputation by publishing books, and in time was preferred to be confessor to the king. But he did not discharge this office to the satisfaction of Cardinal Richelieu, though he discharged it to the satisfaction of every honest man; and therefore, it is not to be wondered at that he came at length to be removed. He died in the Jesuits convent at Paris in 1651. None of his works did him more honour than that which he entitled *La Cour Sainte*. It has been printed a great many times; and translated into Latin, Italian, Spanish, Portuguese, German, and English. He published several other books both in Latin and French.

CAUSTICITY, a quality belonging to several substances, by the acrimony of which the parts of living animals may be corroded and destroyed. Bodies which have this quality, when taken internally, are true poisons. The causticity of some of these, as of arsenic, is so deadly, that even their external use is proscribed by prudent physicians. Several others, as nitrous acid, lapis infernalis or lunar caustic, common caustic, butter of antimony, are daily and successfully used to consume fungous flesh, to open issues, &c. They succeed very well when properly employed and skilfully managed.

The causticity of bodies depends entirely on the state of the saline, and chiefly of the acid, matters they contain. When these acids happen to be at the same time much concentrated, and slightly attached to the matters with which they are combined, they are then capable of acting, and are corrosive or caustic. Thus fixed and volatile alkalies, although they are themselves caustic, become much more so by being treated with quicklime; because this substance deprives them of much fat and inflammable matter, and all their fixed air, which binds and restrains the action of their saline principle. By this treatment, then, the saline principle is more disengaged, and rendered more capable of action. Also all combinations of metallic matters with acids form salts more or less corrosive, because these acids are deprived of all their superabundant water, and are besides but imperfectly saturated with the metallic matters. Nevertheless, some other circumstance is necessary to constitute the causticity of these saline

Causticity. metalline matters. For the same quantity of marine acid, which, when pure and diluted with a certain quantity of water, would be productive of no harm, shall, however, produce all the effects of a corrosive poison, when it is united with mercury in *corrosive sublimate*, although the sublimate shall be dissolved in so much water that its causticity cannot be attributed to the concentration of its acid. This effect is, by some chemists, attributed to the great weight of the metallic matters with which the acid is united; and this opinion is very probable, seeing its causticity is nothing but its dissolving power, or its disposition to combine with other bodies; and this disposition is nothing else than attraction.

On this subject Dr Black observes, that the compounds produced by the union of the metals with acids are in general corrosive. Many of them applied to the skin destroy it almost as fast as the mineral acids; and some of the most powerful potential cauteries are made in this way. Some are reckoned more acrid than the pure acids themselves; and they have more powerful effects when taken internally, or at least seem to have. Thus we can take 10 or 12 drops of a fossil acid, diluted with water, without being disturbed by it; but the same quantity of acid previously combined with silver, quicksilver, copper, or regulus of antimony, will throw the body into violent disorders, or even prove a poison, if taken all at once.

This increased activity was, by the mechanical philosophers, supposed to arise from the weight of the metallic particles. They imagined that the acid was composed of minute particles of the shape of needles or wedges; by which means they were capable of entering the pores of other bodies, separating their atoms from each other, and thus dissolving them. To these acid spiculæ the metallic particles gave more force; and the momentum of each particular needle or wedge was increased in proportion to its increase of gravity by the additional weight of the metallic particle. But this theory is entirely fanciful, and does not correspond with facts. The activity of the compound is not in proportion to the weight of the metal; nor are the compounds always possessed of any great degree of acrimony: neither is it true that any of them have a greater power of destroying animal substances than the pure acids have.

There is a material difference between the powers called *stimuli* and *corrosives*. Let a person apply to any part of the skin a small quantity of lunar caustic, and likewise a drop of strong nitrous acid, and he will find that the acid acts with more violence than the caustic; and the disorders that are occasioned by the compounds of metals and acids do not proceed from a *causticity* in them, but from the metal affecting and proving a stimulus to the nerves: and that this is the case, appears from their affecting some particular nerves of the body. Thus the compounds of regulus of antimony and mercury with the vegetable acids, do not show the smallest degree of acrimony; but, taken internally, they produce violent convulsive motions over the whole body, which are occasioned by the metallic matter having a power of producing this effect; and the acid is only the means of bringing it into a dissolved state, and making it capable of acting on the nervous system. In general, however, the compounds of metallic substances with acids may be considered as milder than the acids in a separate state; but the acid is not so much neutralized as in other compounds, for it is less powerfully attracted by the metal; so that alkaline salts, absorbent earths, or even heat alone, will decompound them; and some of the inflammable substances, as spirit of wine, aromatic oils, &c. will attract the acid, and precipitate the metal in its metallic form; and the metals can be employed to precipitate one another in their metallic form; so that the cohesion of these compounds is much weaker than those formed of the same acids with alkaline salts or earths.

Caustics || Caxa.

CAUSTICS, in physics, an appellation given to medicines of so hot and fiery a nature, that, being applied, consume, and as it were burn, the texture of the parts, like hot iron.

Caustics are generally divided into four sorts; the common stronger caustic, the common milder caustic, the antimonial caustic, and the lunar caustic. See PHARMACY and CHEMISTRY.

Caustic Curve, in the higher geometry, a curve formed by the concourse or coincidence of the rays of light reflected from some other curve.

CAUSUS, or BURNING FEVER, a species of continual fever, accompanied with a remarkable inflammation of the blood.

CAUTERIZATION, the act of burning or searing some morbid part, by the application of fire either actual or potential. In some places they cauterize with burning tow, in others with cotton or moxa, in others with live coals; some use Spanish wax, others pyramidal pieces of linen, others gold or silver; Severinus recommends flame blown through a pipe; but what is usually preferred among us is a hot iron.

Cauterizing irons are of various figures; some flat, others round, some curved, *&c.* of all which we find draughts in Albucasis, Scultetus, Ferrara, and others. Sometimes a cautery is applied through a capsula, to prevent any terror from the sight of it. This method was invented by Placentinus, and is described by Scultetus. In the use of all cauteries, care is to be taken to defend the neighbouring parts, either by a lamina, defensive plaster, or lint moistened in oxycrate. Sometimes the hot iron is transmitted through a copper cannula, for the greater safety of the adjoining parts. The degrees and manners of cauterizing are varied according to the nature of the disease and the part affected.

CAUTERY, in surgery, a medicine for burning, eating, or corroding any solid part of the body.

Cauteries are distinguished into two classes; actual and potential: by actual cauteries are understood red hot instruments, usually of iron; and by potential cauteries are understood certain kinds of corroding medicines. See PHARMACY.

CAUTION, in the civil and Scots law, denotes much the same with what, in the law of England, is called BAIL.

CAUTIONER, in Scots law, that person who becomes bound for another to the performance of any deed or obligation. As to the different kinds and effects of Cautionary, see LAW, Part III. Nº clxxv. 17.

CAWK. See CAUK.

CAXA, a little coin made of lead mixed with some

fervis of copper, ftruck in China, but current chiefly at Bantam in the ifland of Java, and fome of the neighbouring iflands. See (the *Table* fubjoined to) Money.

CAXAMALCA, the name of a town and diftrict of Peru in South America, where there was a moft fumptuous palace belonging to the Incas, and a magnificent temple dedicated to the fun.

CAXTON (William), a mercer of London, eminent by the works he publifhed, and for being *reputed* the firft who introduced and practifed the art of printing in England: as to which, fee (*the Hiftory of*) Printing.

CAVENNE, a rich town and ifland of South America, and capital of the French fettlements there, is bounded on the north by the Dutch colonies of Surinam, and fituated in W. Long. 53. 10. N. Lat. 5o.

This fettlement was begun in 1635. A report had prevailed for fome time before, that, in the interior parts of Guiana, there was a country known by the name of *del Dorado*, which contained immenfe riches in gold and precious ftones; more than ever Cortez and Pizarro had found in Mexico and Peru; and this fable had fired the imagination of every nation in Europe. It is fuppofed that this was the country in queft of which Sir Walter Raleigh went on his laft voyage; and, as the French were not behind their neighbours in their endeavours to find out fo defirable a country, fome attempts, for this purpofe, were likewife made by that nation much about the fame time; which at laft coming to nothing, the adventurers took up their refidence on the ifland of Cayenne. In 1643, fome merchants of Rouen united their ftock, with a defign to fupport the new colony; but, committing their affairs to one Poncet de Bretigny, a man of a ferocious difpofition, he declared war both againft the colonifts and favages, in confequence of which he was foon maffacred. This cataftrophe entirely extinguifhed the ardour of thefe affociates; and in 1651 a new company was eftablifhed. This promifed to be much more confiderable than the former; and they fet out with fuch a capital as enabled them to collect 700 or 800 colonifts in the city of Paris itfelf. Thefe embarked on the Seine, in order to fail down to Havre de Grace; but unfortunately the Abbé de Marivault, a man of great virtue, and the principal promoter of the undertaking, was drowned as he was ftepping into his boat. Another gentleman, who was to have acted as general, was affaffinated on his paffage; and 12 of the principal adventurers, who had promifed to put the colony into a flourifhing fituation, not only were the principal perpetrators of this fact, but uniformly behaved in the fame atrocious manner. At laft they hanged one of their own number; two died; three were banifhed to a defert ifland; and the reft abandoned themfelves to every kind of excefs. The commandant of the citadel deferted to the Dutch with part of his garrifon. The favages, roufed by numberlefs provocations, fell upon the remainder; fo that the few who were left thought themfelves happy in efcaping to the Leeward Iflands in a boat and two canoes, abandoning the fort, ammunition, arms, and merchandife, fifteen months after they had landed on the ifland.

In 1663, a new company was formed, whofe capital amounted only to L. 8750. By the affiftance of the miniftry they expelled the Dutch, who had taken poffeffion of the ifland, and fettled themfelves much more comfortably than their predeceffors. In 1667 the ifland was taken by the Englifh, and in 1676 by the Dutch, but afterwards reftored to the French; and fince that time it has never been attacked. Soon after fome pirates, laden with the fpoils they had gathered in the South Seas, came and fixed their refidence at Cayenne; refolving to employ the treafures they had acquired in the cultivation of the lands. In 1688, Ducaffe, an able feaman, arrived with fome fhips from France, and propofed to them the plundering of Surinam. This propofal exciting their natural turn for plunder, the pirates betook themfelves to their old trade, and almoft all the reft followed their example. The expedition, however, proved unfortunate. Many of the affailants were killed, and all the reft taken prifoners and fent to the Caribbee Iflands. This lofs the colony has never yet recovered.

The ifland of Cayenne is about 16 leagues in circumference, and is only parted from the continent by two rivers. By a particular formation, uncommon in iflands, the land is higheft near the water fide, and low in the middle. Hence the land is fo full of moraffes, that all communication between the different parts of it is impoffible, without taking a great circuit. There are fome fmall tracts of an excellent foil to be found here and there; but the generality is dry, fandy, and foon exhaufted. The only town in the colony is defended by a covert way, a large ditch, a very good mud rampart, and five baftions. In the middle of the town is a pretty confiderable eminence, of which a redoubt has been made that is called the *fort*. The entrance into the harbour is through a narrow channel; and fhips can only get in at high water through the rocks and reefs that are fcattered about this pafs.

The firft produce of Cayenne was the arnotto; from the produce of which, the colonifts proceeded to that of cotton, indigo, and laftly fugar. It was the firft of all the French colonies that attempted to cultivate coffee. The coffee-tree was brought from Surinam in 1721, by fome deferters from Cayenne, who purchafed their pardon by fo doing. Ten or twelve years after they planted cocoa. In the year 1752, there were exported from Cayenne 260,541 pounds of arnotto, 80,365 pounds of fugar, 17,919 pounds of cotton, 26,881 pounds of coffee, 91,916 pounds of cocoa, 618 trees for timber, and 104 planks.

CAYLUS (Count de), Marquis de Sternay, Baron de Branfac, was born at Paris in 1692. He was the eldeft of the two fons of John count de Caylus, lieutenant-general of the armies of the king of France, and of the Marchionefs de Villete. The count and countefs his father and mother, were very careful of the education of their fon. The former inftructed him in the profeffion of arms, and in bodily exercifes; the latter watched over and foftered the virtues of his mind; and this delicate tafk fhe difcharged with fingular fuccefs. The countefs was the niece of Madam de Maintenon, and was remarkable both for the folidity of her underftanding and the charms of her wit. She was the author of that agreeable book intitled, "The Recollections of Madam de Caylus," of which Voltaire lately publifhed an elegant edition. The amiable qualities of the mother appeared in the fon; but they appeared with a bold and military

Caylus.

tary air. In his natural temper he was gay and sprightly, had a taste for pleasure, a strong passion for independence, and an invincible aversion to the servitude of a court. Such were the instructors of the Count de Caylus. He was only twelve years of age when his father died at Brussels in 1704. After finishing his exercises, he entered into the corps of the *Mousquetaires*; and in his first campaign in the year 1709, he distinguished himself by his valour in such a manner, that Louis XIV. commended him before all the court, and rewarded him with an ensigncy in the *Gendarmerie*. In 1711 he commanded a regiment of dragoons, which was called by his own name; and he signalized himself at the head of it in Catalonia. In 1713, he was at the siege of Fribourg, where he was exposed to imminent danger in the bloody attack of the covered way. The peace of Radstadt having left him in a state of inactivity ill-suited to his natural temper, his vivacity soon carried him to travel into Italy; and his curiosity was greatly excited by the wonders of that country, where antiquity is still fruitful, and produces so many objects to improve taste and to excite admiration. The eyes of the count were not yet learned; but he was struck with the sight of so many beauties, and soon became acquainted with them. After a year's absence, he returned to Paris with so strong a passion for travelling, and for antiquities, as induced him to quit the army.

He had no sooner quitted the service of Louis, than he sought for an opportunity to set out for the Levant. When he arrived at Smyrna, he visited the ruins of Ephesus. From the Levant he was recalled in February 1717 by the tenderness of his mother. From that time he left not France, but to make two excursions to London. The academy of painting and sculpture adopted him an honorary member in the year 1731; and the count, who loved to realize titles, spared neither his labour, nor his credit, nor his fortune, to instruct, assist, and animate the artists. He wrote the lives of the most celebrated painters and engravers that have done honour to this illustrious academy; and, in order to extend the limits of the art, which seemed to him to move in too narrow a circle, he collected, in three different works, new subjects for the painter, which he had met with in the works of the ancients.

Such was his passion for antiquity, that he wished to have had it in his power to bring the whole of it to life again. He saw with regret, that the works of the ancient painters, which have been discovered in our times, are effaced and destroyed almost as soon as they are drawn from the subterraneous mansions where they were buried. A fortunate accident furnished him with the means of showing us the composition and the colouring of the pictures of ancient Rome. The coloured drawings which the famous Pietro Sante Bartoli had taken there from antique pictures, fell into his hands. He had them engraved; and, before he enriched the king of France's cabinet with them, he gave an edition of them at his own expence. It is perhaps the most extraordinary book of antiquities that ever will appear. The whole is painted with a purity and a precision that are inimitable; we see the liveliness and the freshness of the colouring that charmed the Cæsars. There were only 30 copies published; and there is no reason to expect that there will hereafter be any more.

Caylus.

Count de Caylus was engaged at the same time in an enterprise still more favourable to Roman grandeur, and more interesting to the French nation. Colbert had framed the design of engraving the Roman antiquities that are still to be seen in the southern provinces of France. By his orders Mignard the architect had made drawings of them, which count de Caylus had the good fortune to recover. He resolved to finish the work begun by Colbert, and to dedicate it to that great minister; and so much had he this enterprise at heart, that he was employed in it during his last illness, and warmly recommended it to M. Mariette.

In 1742, Count Caylus was admitted honorary member of the academy of belles lettres; and then it was that he seemed to have found the place for which nature designed him. The study of literature now became his ruling passion; he consecrated to it his time and his fortune; he even renounced his pleasures to give himself wholly up to that of making some discovery in the field of antiquity. But amidst the fruits of his research and invention, nothing seemed more flattering to him than his discovery of encaustic painting. A description of Pliny's, but too concise a one to give him a clear view of the matter, suggested the idea of it. He availed himself of the friendship and skill of M. Magaudt, a physician in Paris, and an excellent chemist; and by repeated experiments found out the secret of incorporating wax with divers tints and colours, and of making it obedient to the pencil. Pliny has made mention of two kinds of encaustic painting practised by the ancients; one of which was performed with wax, and the other upon ivory, with hot punches of iron. It was the former that Count Caylus had the merit of reviving; and M. Muntz afterwards made many experiments to carry it to perfection.

In the hands of Count Caylus, literature and the arts lent each other a mutual aid. But it would be endless to give an account of all his works. He published above 40 dissertations in the Memoirs of the Academy of Belles Lettres. The artists he was particularly attentive to; and to prevent their falling into mistakes from an ignorance of costume, which the ablest of them have sometimes done, he founded a prize of 500 livres, the object of which is to explain, by means of authors and monuments, the usages of ancient nations. In order that he might enjoy with the whole world the treasures he had collected, he caused them to be engraved, and gave a learned description of them in a work which he embellished with 800 copperplates.

The strength of his constitution seemed to give him hopes of a long life: but a humour settling in one of his legs, which entirely destroyed his health, he expired on the 5th of September 1765, and by his death his family is extinct. The tomb erected to the honour of Count Caylus is to be seen in the chapel of St Germain-l'Auxerrois, and deserves to be remarked. It is perfectly the tomb of an antiquary. This monument was an ancient sepulchral antique, of the most beautiful porphyry, with ornaments in the Egyptian taste. From the moment he procured it, he

had

had destined it to grace the place of his interment. While he awaited the fatal hour, he placed it in his garden, where he used to look upon it with a tranquil but thoughtful eye, and pointed it out to the inspection of his friends.

The character of Count Caylus is to be traced in the different occupations which divided his cares and his life. In society, he had all the frankness of a soldier, and a politeness which had nothing in it of deceit or circumvention. Born independent, he applied to studies which suited his taste. His heart was yet better than his abilities. In his walks he used frequently to try the honesty of the poor, by sending them with a piece of money to get change for him. In these cases he enjoyed their confusion at not finding him; and then presenting himself, used to commend their honesty, and give them double the sum. He said frequently to his friends, "I have this day lost a crown; but I was sorry that I had not an opportunity of giving a second. The beggar ought not to want integrity."

CAYSTER, or CAYSTRUS, (anc. geog.), a river of Ionia, whose mouth Ptolemy places between Colophon and Ephesus; commended by the poets for its swans, which it had in great numbers. Its source was in the Montes Cilbiani, (Pliny). *Caystrius Campus* was a part of the territory of Ephesus. *Campi Caystriani* of Lydia, were plains lying in the middle between the inland parts and mount Tmolus.

CAZEROM, or CAZERON, a city of Asia in Persia, situated in E. Long. 70. N. Lat. 29. 15.

CAZIC, or CAZIQUE, a title given by the Spaniards to the petty kings, princes, and chiefs, of the several countries of America, excepting those of Peru, which are called *curacas*. The French call them *casiques*, a denomination which they always give to the Tartarian hords.—The cazics, in some places, do the office of physicians, and in others of priests, as well as of captains. The dignity of cazic among the Chiites, a people of South America, does not descend to children, but must be acquired by valour and merit. One of the prerogatives annexed to it is, that the cazic may have three wives, while the other people are allowed only one. Mexico comprehended a great number of provinces and islands, which were governed by lords called *caziques*, dependent on and tributary to the emperor. Thirty of these vassals are said to have been so powerful, that they were able, each of them, to bring an army of 100,000 men into the field.

CAZIMIR, a handsome town of Poland, in the palatinate of Lublin, situated on a hill covered with trees, in E. Long. 3. 10. N. Lat. 51. 5.

CEA. See CEOS.

CEANOTHUS, NEW-JERSEY TEA, in botany; A genus of the monogynia order, belonging to the pentandria class of plants; and in the natural method ranking under the 43d order, *Dumosæ*. There are five petals, pouched and arched. The fruit is a dry, trilocular and trispermous berry. There are three species, of which the most remarkable is the Americanus, a native of most parts of North America, from whence great plenty of the seeds have been imported into Europe. In England, this plant seldom rises more than three feet high. The stem, which is of a pale-brown colour, sends out branches from the bottom. These are thin, flexible, and of a reddish colour, which may have occasioned this tree to go by the name of *Red Twig*. The leaves which ornament these branches stand on reddish pedicles, about half an inch in length. They are oval, serrated, pointed, about two inches and a half long, are proportionably broad, and have three nerves running lengthwise. From the footstalk to the point they are of a light green colour, grow irregularly on the branches, and not opposite by pairs, as has been asserted. They are late in the spring before they shoot. The flowers grow at the ends of the twigs in clusters: They are of a white colour, and when in blow give the shrub a most beautiful appearance. Indeed, it seems to be almost covered with them, as there is usually a cluster at the end of nearly every twig; and the leaves which appear among them serve as ornaments only, like myrtle in a distant nosegay: nature however has denied them smell. This tree will be in blow in July; and the flowers are succeeded by small brownish fruit, in which the seeds will sometimes ripen in England.

This plant is propagated by layering; or from seeds sown in pots of compost, consisting of two parts virgin earth well tempered and one part sand, about a quarter of an inch deep; being equally careful to defend the young seedlings from an extremity of cold in winter, as from the parching droughts of the summer months. The best time of layering them is in the summer, just before they begin to flower: At that time lay the tender twigs of the spring shoots in the earth, and nip off the end which would produce the flowers. By the autumn twelvemonth some of them will be rooted. At the stools, however, the plants should remain until the spring, when they should be taken off, and the best rooted and the strongest may be planted in the nursery-way, or in a dry soil and well sheltered place, where they are to remain; while the bad-rooted ones and the weakest should be planted in pots; and if these are plunged into a moderate warmth of dung, it will promote their growth, and make them good plants before autumn. In the winter they should be guarded against the frosts; and in the spring they may be planted out where they are to remain.

CEBES, of Thebes, a Socratic philosopher, author of the admired *Table of Cebes*; or "Dialogues on the birth, life, and death of Mankind." He flourished about 405 years before Christ.—The above piece is mentioned by some of the ancient writers, by Lucian, D. Laertius, Tertullian, and Suidas; but of Cebes himself we have no account, save that he is once mentioned by Plato, and once by Xenophon. The former says of him, in his "Phædo," that he was a sagacious investigator of truth, and never assented without the most convincing reasons: the latter, in his "Memorabilia," ranks him among the few intimates of Socrates, who excelled the rest in the innocency of their lives. Cebes's *Tabula* is usually printed with Epictetus's *Manuale*.

CECIL (William), Lord Burleigh, treasurer of England in the reign of queen Elizabeth, was the son of Richard Cecil, Esq; master of the robes to king Henry VIII. He was born in the house of his grandfather, David Cecil, Esq; at Bourn in Lincolnshire, in the year 1520; and received the rudiments of his education in the grammar-school at Grantham. From

Cecil.

thence he was removed to Stamford; and about the year 1535, was entered of St John's College, Cambridge. Here he began his ſtudies with a degree of enthuſiaſtic application very uncommon in young gentlemen of family. At the age of 16 he read a ſophiſtry lecture, and at 19 a voluntary Greek lecture; which was the more extraordinary as being at a time when the Greek language was by no means univerſally underſtood. In 1541 he went to London, and became a member of the ſociety of Gray's-Inn, with an intention to ſtudy the law; but he had not been long in that ſituation, before an accident introduced him to king Henry, and gave a new bias to his purſuits. O'Neil, a famous Iriſh chief, coming to court, had brought with him two Iriſh chaplains, violent bigots to the Romiſh faith; with theſe Mr Cecil, viſiting his father, happened to have a warm diſpute in Latin, in which he diſplayed uncommon abilities. The king, being informed of it, ordered the young man into his preſence, and was ſo pleaſed with his converſation, that he commanded his father to find a place for him. He accordingly requeſted the reverſion of the *cuſtos brevium*, which Mr Cecil afterwards poſſeſſed. About this time he married the ſiſter of Sir John Cheke, by whom he was recommended to the earl of Hertford, afterwards duke of Somerſet and protector.

Soon after king Edward's acceſſion, Mr Cecil came into the poſſeſſion of his office of *cuſtos brevium*, worth about L. 240 a-year. His firſt lady dying in 1543, he married the daughter of Sir Anthony Cook, director of the king's ſtudies. In 1547, he was appointed by the protector, maſter of requeſts; and ſoon after, attended his noble patron on his expedition againſt the Scots, and was preſent at the battle of Muſſelburgh. In this battle, which was fought on the 10th of September 1547, Mr Cecil's life was miraculouſly preſerved by a friend, who in puſhing him out of the level of a cannon, had his arm ſhattered to pieces. The ſight and judgment of his friend muſt have been as extraordinary as his friendſhip, to perceive the preciſe direction of a cannon ſhot; unleſs we ſuppoſe, that the ball was almoſt quite ſpent; in which caſe the thing is not impoſſible. The ſtory is told in his life by a domeſtic. In the year 1548, Mr Cecil was made ſecretary of ſtate; but in the following year, the duke of Northumberland's faction prevailing, he ſuffered in the diſgrace of the protector Somerſet, and was ſent priſoner to the Tower. After three months confinement he was releaſed; in 1551 reſtored to his office; and ſoon after knighted, and ſworn of the privy council. In 1553 he was made chancellor of the Order of the Garter, with an annual fee of 100 marks.

On the death of Edward VI. Mr Cecil prudently refuſed to have any concern in Northumberland's attempt in favour of the unfortunate Lady Jane Grey; and when queen Mary acceded to the throne, he was graciouſly received at Court; but, not chooſing to change his religion, was diſmiſſed from his employments. During this reign, he was twice elected knight of the ſhire for the county of Lincoln; and often ſpoke in the houſe of commons, with great freedom and firmneſs, in oppoſition to the miniſtry. Nevertheleſs, though a proteſtant and a *patriot* (that is, a courtier out of place), he had the addreſs to ſteer through a very dangerous ſea without ſhipwreck.

Queen Elizabeth's acceſſion in the year 1558 immediately diſpelled the cloud which had obſcured his fortunes and miniſterial capacity. During the horrid reign of her ſiſter, he had conſtantly correſponded with the princeſs Elizabeth. On the very day of her acceſſion, he preſented her with a paper containing twelve articles neceſſary for her immediate diſpatch; and, in a few days after, was ſworn of the privy-council, and made ſecretary of ſtate. His firſt advice to the queen was, to call a parliament; and the firſt buſineſs he propoſed after it was aſſembled, was the eſtabliſhment of a national church. A plan of reformation was accordingly drawn up under his immediate inſpection, and the legal eſtabliſhment of the church of England was the conſequence. Sir William Cecil's next important concern, was to reſtore the value of the coin, which had in the preceding reigns been conſiderably debaſed. In 1561, he was appointed maſter of the wards; and, in 1571, created baron of Burleigh, as a reward for his ſervices, particularly in having lately ſtifled a formidable rebellion in the north. The following year he was honoured with the garter, and raiſed to the office of Lord High Treaſurer of England. From this period we find him the *primum mobile* of every material tranſaction during the glorious reign of Queen Elizabeth. Notwithſtanding the temporary influence of other favourites, Lord Burleigh was, in fact, her prime miniſter, and the perſon in whom ſhe chiefly confided in matters of real importance. Having filled the higheſt and moſt important offices of the ſtate for 40 years, and guided the helm of government during the moſt glorious period of Engliſh hiſtory, he departed this life on the 4th of Auguſt 1598, in the 78th year of his age. His body was removed to Stamford, and there depoſited in the family vault, where a magnificent tomb was erected to his memory.—Notwithſtanding his long enjoyment of ſuch lucrative employments, he left only an eſtate of L. 4000 *per annum*, L. 11,000 in money, and effects worth about L. 14,000. He lived, indeed, in a manner ſuitable to his high rank and importance. He had four places of reſidence, viz. his lodgings at court, his houſe in the Strand, his ſeat at Burleigh-Park near Stamford, and his ſeat at Theobalds. The laſt of theſe was his favourite place of retirement, where he frequently entertained the queen at a vaſt expence.

Lord Burleigh was doubtleſs a man of ſingular abilities and prudence; amiable in his private character, and one of the moſt able, upright, and indefatigable miniſters ever recorded in the annals of this kingdom. His principal works are, 1. *La Complainte de l'ame pechereſſe*, or the Complaint of a ſinful Soul, in French verſe, in the king's library. 2. Materials for Patten's *Diarium expedi. Scotica*, London 1541, 12mo. 3. Slanders and lies maliciouſly, groſsly, and impudently vomited out, in certain traiterous books and pamphlets, againſt two counſellors, Sir Francis Bacon and Sir William Cecil. 4. A ſpeech in parliament, 1562, Strype's Mem. vol. iv. p. 107. 5. Precepts or directions for the well ordering of a man's life, 1637, Harl. Cat. vol. ii. p. 755. 6. Meditations on the death of his lady, Ballard's Mem. p. 184. 7.

Meditations

Meditations on the state of England during the reign of queen Elisabeth, manuscript. 8. The execution of justice in England for the maintenance of public and Christian peace, &c. Lond. 1581, 1583, Somer's tracts, 4th collect. vol. i. p. 5. 9. Advice to queen Elisabeth in matters of religion and state, ib. p. 101. 16. 10. A great number of letters. See Peck's *Desiderata Curiosa*, Howard's collections, &c. 11. Several pedigrees, some of which are preserved in the archbishop of Canterbury's library at Lambeth, n° 299. 747.

CECILIA (St), the patroness of music, has been honoured as a martyr ever since the fifth century. Her story as delivered by the notaries of the Roman church, and from them transcribed into the Golden Legend and other books of the like kind, says, that she was a Roman lady born of noble parents, about the year 225. That, notwithstanding she had been converted to Christianity, her parents married her to a young pagan nobleman named Valerianus; who going to bed to her on the wedding night, *as the custom is*, says the book, was given to understand by his spouse, that she was nightly visited by an angel, and that he must forbear to approach her, otherwise the angel would destroy him. Valerianus, somewhat troubled at these words, desired that he might see his rival the angel; but his spouse told him that was impossible, unless he would consent to be baptized and become a Christian. This he consented to; after which, returning to his wife, he found her in her closet at prayer, and by her side, in the shape of a beautiful young man, the angel clothed with brightness. After some conversation with the angel, Valerianus told him that he had a brother named Tiburtius, whom he greatly wished to see a partaker of the grace which he himself had received. The angel told him that his desire was granted, and that they should be both crowned with martyrdom in a short time. Upon this the angel vanished, and was not long in showing himself as good as his word; Tiburtius was converted, and both he and his brother Valerianus were beheaded. Cecilia was offered her life upon condition that she would sacrifice to the deities of the Romans; but she refused: upon which she was thrown into a caldron of boiling water, and scalded to death: others say that she was stifled in a dry bath, i. e. an inclosure, from whence the air was excluded, having a slow fire underneath it; which kind of death was sometimes inflicted by the Romans upon women of quality who were criminals. Upon the spot where her house stood, is a church said to have been built by pope Urban I. who administered baptism to her husband and his brother: it is the church of St Cecilia at Trastevere; within is a most curious painting of the saint, as also a stately monument with a cumbent statue of her with her face downwards. There is a tradition of St Cecilia, that she excelled in music; and that the angel who was thus enamoured of her, was drawn from the celestial regions by the charms of her melody: this has been deemed authority sufficient for making her the patroness of music and musicians. The legend of St Cecilia has given frequent occasion to painters and sculptors to exercise their genius in representations of her, playing on the organ, and sometimes on the harp. Raphael has painted her singing with a regal in her hands; and Domenichino and Mignard, singing and playing on the harp.

CECROPS, the founder and first king of Athens, about the time of Moses the lawgiver of the Hebrews. He was the first who established civil government, religious rites, and marriage among the Greeks; and died after a reign of 50 years. See ATTICA, n° 4.

CEDAR, in botany. See JUNIPERUS and PINUS.

The species of cedar famous for its duration, is that popularly called by us the cedar of Lebanon (*Pinus cedrus*), by the ancients *cedrus magna*, or the great cedar; also *cedrelate*, [illegible]. See the article PINUS.

CEDRENUS (George), a Grecian monk, lived in the 11th age, and wrote "Annals, or an abridged History, from the Beginning of the World to the Reign of Isaac Comnenus, emperor of Constantinople, who succeeded Michael IV. in 1057." This work is no more than an extract from several historians. There is an edition of it, printed at Paris in 1647, with the Latin version of Xylander, and the notes of father Goar a Dominican.

CEDRUS, the CEDAR-TREE, MAHOGANY, &c. See JUNIPERUS, PINUS, and SWIETENIA.

CEILING, in architecture, the top or roof of a lower room; or a covering of plaster, over laths nailed on the bottom of the joists that bear the floor of the upper room; or where there is no upper room, on joists for the purpose; hence called *ceiling joists*. The word *ceiling* answers pretty accurately to the Latin *lacunar*, "every thing over head."

Plastered ceilings are much used in Britain, more than in any other country: nor are they without their advantages, as they make the room lightsome; are good in case of fire; stop the passage of the dust; lessen the noise over head; and, in summer, make the air cooler.

CEILING, in sea-language, denotes the inside planks of a ship.

CEIMELIA, from [illegible], "to be laid up," in antiquity, denotes choice or precious pieces of furniture or ornaments, reserved or laid up for extraordinary occasions and uses: in which sense, sacred garments, vessels, and the like, are reputed of the ceimelia of a church. Medals, antique stones, figures, manuscripts, records, &c. are the ceimelia of men of letters.

CEIMELIARCHIUM, the repository or place where ceimelia are preserved.

CEIMELIOPHYLAX, (from [illegible] and [illegible], *I keep*), the keeper or curator of a collection of ceimelia; sometimes also denominated *ceimeliarcha*. The ceimeliarcha, or ceimeliophylax, was an officer in the ancient churches or monasteries, answering to what was otherwise denominated *chartophylax*, and *custos archivorum*.

CELÆNÆ (anc. geog.), the capital of Phrygia Magna, situated on a cognominal mountain, at the common sources of the Mæander and Marsyas. The king of Persia had a strong palace beneath the citadel, by the springs of the Marsyas, which rose in the market-place, not less in size than the Mæander, and flowed through the city. Cyrus the younger had also a palace there, but by the springs of the Mæander, which river passed likewise through the city. He

Led,

had, moreover, an extenſive paradiſe or park, full of wild beaſts, which he hunted on horſeback for exerciſe or amuſement; and watered by the Mæander, which ran through the middle. Xerxes was ſaid to have built theſe palaces and the citadel after his return from his expedition into Greece.

Antiochus Soter removed the inhabitants of Celænæ into a city, which he named from his mother, Apamea; and which became afterwards a mart inferior only to Epheſus. See Apamea.

CELANDINE, in botany. See Chelidonium.

CELANO, a town of Italy, in the kingdom of Naples, in Farther Abruzzo. It is ſeated a mile from the lake Celano, anciently called Fucinus. E. Lon. 13. 39. N. Lat. 41. 55.

CELARENT, among logicians, a mode of ſyllogiſm, wherein the major and concluſion are univerſal negative propoſitions, and the minor an univerſal affirmative.

E. gr. *cE* None whoſe underſtanding is limited can be omniſcient.

lA Every man's underſtanding is limited.

rEnt Therefore no man is omniſcient.

CELASTRUS, in botany: A genus of the monogynia order, belonging to the pentandria claſs of plants; and in the natural method ranking under the 43d order, *Dumoſæ*. The corolla is pentapetalous and patent; the capſule quinquangular and trilocular; the ſeeds veiled. There are 11 ſpecies; two of which are counted to our climate.

1. The bullatus, an uncertain deciduous ſhrub, is a native of Virginia. It is about four feet in growth, riſing from the ground with ſeveral ſtalks, which divide into many branches, and are covered with a browniſh bark. The leaves are of a fine green colour, and grow alternately on the branches. They are of an oval figure, and have their edges undivided. The flowers are produced in July, at the ends of the branches, in looſe ſpikes. They are of a white colour, and in their native countries are ſucceeded by very ornamental ſcarlet fruit; but with us this ſeldom happens. It is eaſily propagated from ſeeds ſown, about an inch deep, in beds of good freſh mould made fine. They ſeldom come up until the ſecond, and ſometimes not before the third ſpring. It is alſo propagated by layers; which work muſt be performed on the young wood, in the autumn, by a ſlit at the joint. Theſe layers may be expected to ſtrike root by the autumn following; when they may be taken up and planted in the nurſery-ground. This ſhrub muſt have a well-ſheltered ſituation, otherwiſe the leaves are apt to fall off at the approach of froſty weather. And Miller ſays, that, growing naturally in moiſt places, it will not thrive well in a dry ſoil.

2. The ſcandens, or baſtard euonymus, with woody, twining ſtalks, riſing by the help of neighbouring trees or buſhes to the height of 12 feet. The leaves are oblong, ſerrated, of a pleaſant green colour, pale, and veined underneath, and grow alternately on the branches. The flowers are produced in ſmall bunches, from the ſides of the branches, near the ends. They are of a greeniſh colour, appear in June; and are ſucceeded by roundiſh, red, three-cornered capſules, containing ripe ſeeds, in the autumn. This ſpecies is exceeding hardy, and makes a beautiful appearance among other trees in the autumn, by their beautiful red berries, which much reſemble thoſe of the ſpindle-tree, and will be produced in vaſt profuſion on the tops of other trees, to the heights of which theſe plants by their twiſting property aſpire. They ſhould not be planted near weak or tender trees, to climb on; for they embrace the ſtalks ſo cloſely as to bring on death to any but the hardieſt trees and ſhrubs. It is propagated, 1. By laying down the young ſhoots in the ſpring. By the autumn they will have ſtruck root, and may then be taken off and ſet in the places where they are deſigned to remain. 2. By ſeeds; which ſhould be ſoon ſown after they are ripe, otherwiſe they will be two and ſometimes three years before they come up. When they make their appearance, nothing more need be done than keeping them clear from weeds all ſummer and the winter following; and in the ſpring the ſtrongeſt plants may be drawn out, and ſet in the nurſery for a year, and then removed to the places where they are deſigned to remain; whilſt the weakeſt, being left in the ſeed-bed one year more, may undergo the ſame diſcipline.

In Senegal the negroes uſe the powder of the root as a ſpecific againſt gonorrhœas, which it is ſaid to cure in eight or ſometimes in three days. An infuſion of the bark of a ſpecies of ſtaff-tree, which grows in the Iſle of France, is ſaid to poſſeſs the ſame virtues.

CELEBES, an iſland in the Indian ſea, ſeated under the equator, and called by ſome *Macaſſar*. The length and breadth has not been accurately computed; but the circumference, at a medium, is about 800 miles. It had formerly ſix kingdoms, which are reduced to one. The air is hot and moiſt; and ſubject to great rains during the north-weſt winds, which blow from November to March, at which time the country is overflowed, and for this reaſon they build their houſes on piles of wood 10 feet high. The moſt healthful time is during the northern monſoons, which ſeldom fail blowing regularly in one part of the year. The chief vegetables are rice and cocoas; but they have ebony, ſanders, &c. Their fruits and flowers are much the ſame as in the neighbouring parts of the Indies. They have pepper, ſugar, betel, areca, the ſmall cotton, and opium. The natives have bright olive complexions, and the women have ſhining black hair. They are thought to be very handſome by the Dutch and Chineſe, who often purchaſe them for bedfellows. The men are induſtrious, robuſt, and make excellent ſoldiers. Their arms are ſabres, and trunks, from whence they blow poiſoned darts, which are pointed with the tooth of a ſea-fiſh. Some likewiſe uſe poiſoned daggers. They were the laſt of the Indian nations that were enſlaved by the Dutch, which could not be effected till after a long war. They teach their children to read and write, and their characters have ſome reſemblance of the Arabic. Their religion being Mahometan, the men indulge themſelves in many wives and concubines. The employment of the women is ſpinning, cookery, and making their own and their huſbands cloaths. The men wear jewels in their ears, and the women gold chains about their necks. The inhabitants in general go half naked, without any thing on their head, legs, or feet, and ſome have nothing but a cloth about their middle. The ſtreets of the town Macassar are spacious, and planted with trees on every side. It stands by the side of the only large river they have in the island. The Dutch have a fort here, mounted with 40 guns, and garrisoned with 700 men. There is only one other town of note, called Jampandam, where they also have a fort. The island is not near so populous as when the Dutch conquered it; the men being hired for soldiers in most of the neighbouring countries.

The religion of these islands was formerly idolatry. They worshipped the sun and moon. They sacrificed to them in the public squares, having no materials which they thought valuable enough to be employed in raising temples. About two centuries ago, some Christians and Mahometans having brought their opinions to Celebes, the principal king of the country took a dislike to the national worship. Having convened a general assembly, he ascended an eminence, when, spreading out his hands towards heaven, he told the Deity, that he would acknowledge for truth that doctrine whose ministers should first arrive in his dominions, and, as the winds and waves were at his command, the Almighty would have himself to blame if he embraced a falsehood. The assembly broke up, determined to wait the orders of heaven, and to obey the first missionaries that should arrive. The mahometans were the most active, and their religion accordingly prevailed.

CELERES, in Roman antiquity, a regiment of body-guards belonging to the Roman kings, established by Romulus, and composed of 300 young men, chosen out of the most illustrious Roman families, and approved by the suffrages of the curiæ of the people, each of which furnished ten. The name comes from *celer*, "quick, ready;" and was given them because of their promptness to obey the king.

The celeres always attended near the king's person, to guard him, to be ready to carry his orders, and to execute them. In war, they made the van-guard in the engagement, which they always began first; in retreats, they made the rear-guard.

Though the celeres were a body of horse, yet they usually dismounted, and fought on foot; their commander was called tribune, or prefect of the celeres. They were divided into three troops, of 100 each, commanded by a captain called centurio: their tribune was the second person in the kingdom.

Plutarch says, Numa broke the celeres; if this be true, they were soon re-established; for we find them under most of the succeeding kings: witness the great Brutus, who expelled the Tarquins, and who was the tribune of the celeres.

CELERI, in botany, the English name of a variety of the APIUM GRAVEOLENS.

The seed of celeri should be sown at two or three different times, the better to continue it for use thro' the whole season without running up to seed. The first sowing should be in the beginning of March, upon a gentle hot-bed; the second may be at the end of the same month, which ought to be in an open spot of light earth, where it may enjoy the benefit of the sun; the third time of sowing should be in the latter end of April, or beginning of May, on a moist soil; and if exposed to the morning-sun only, it will be so much the better, but it should not be under the drip of trees. The middle of May, some of the plants of the first sowing will be fit to transplant for blanching.

The manner of transplanting it is as follows: after having cleared the ground of weeds, you must dig a trench by a line about 10 inches wide, and 8 or 9 inches deep, loosening the earth in the bottom, and laying it level; and the earth that comes out of the trench should be equally laid on each side the trench, to be ready to draw in again to earth the celeri as it advances in height. These trenches should be made at three feet distance from each other; then plant your plants in the middle of the trench, at about four or five inches distance, in one straight row, having before trimmed the plants, and cut off the tops of the long leaves: and as they are planted, you must observe to close the earth well to their roots with your feet, and to water them plentifully until they have taken new root. As these plants advance in height, you must observe to draw the earth on each side close to them, being careful not to bury their hearts, nor ever to do it but in dry weather; otherwise the plants will rot. When your plants have advanced a considerable height above the trenches, and all the earth, which was laid on the sides thereof, hath been employed in earthing them up, you must then make use of a spade to dig up the earth between the trenches, which must also be made use of for the same purpose, continuing from time to time to earth it up until it is fit for use. The last crop should be planted in a drier soil, to prevent its being rotted with too much wet in the winter. You will do well to cover your ridges of celeri with some pease-haulm, or some such light covering, when the frost is very hard, which will admit the air to the plants; for if they are covered too close, they will be very subject to rot: by this means you will preserve your celeri till spring; but you must remember to take off the covering whenever the weather will permit, otherwise it will be apt to cause the celeri to pipe, and run to seed. The celeri, when full blanched, will not continue good above three weeks or a month before it will rot or pipe; therefore, in order to continue it good, you should have, at least, six or seven different seasons of planting, proportioned to the consumption.

The other sort of celeri, which is commonly called celeriac, is to be managed in the same manner; excepting that this should be planted on the level ground, or in very shallow drills: for this plant seldom grows above eight or ten inches high, so requires but little earthing up; the great excellency of this being in the size of the root, which is often as large as ordinary turnips.

The best method to save the seed of celeri, is to make choice of some long good roots of the upright celeri, which have not been too much blanched, and plant them out, at about a foot asunder, in a moist soil, early in the spring; and when they run up to seed, keep them supported with stakes, to prevent their being broken down with the wind: and in July, when the seed begins to be formed, if the season should prove very dry, it will be proper to give some water to the plants, which will greatly help its producing good seeds. In August these seeds will be ripe, at which time it should be cut up, in a dry time, and

spread

spread upon cloths in the sun to dry; then beat out the seeds, and preserve it in bags for use.

Celeri, wild, (*Apium antarcticum*), was found in considerable quantities by Mr Banks and Dr Solander, on the coast of Terra del Fuego. It is like the garden celeri in the colour and disposition of the flowers, but the leaves are of a deeper green. The taste is between that of celeri and parsley. It is a very useful ingredient in the soup for seamen, because of its antiscorbutic quality.

CELERITY, in mechanics, the swiftness of any body in motion. It is also defined to be an affection of motion, by which any moveable body runs through a given space in a given time.

CELESTINS, a religious order so called from their founder Peter de Meuron, afterwards raised to the pontificate under the name of Celestin V. This Peter, who was born at Isernia, a little town in the kingdom of Naples, in the year 1215, of but mean parents, retired, while very young, to a solitary mountain, in order to dedicate himself wholly to prayer and mortification. The fame of his piety brought several, out of curiosity, to see him; some of whom, charmed with his virtues, renounced the world to accompany him in his solitude. With these he formed a kind of community in the year 1254; which was approved by Pope Urban IV. in 1264, and erected into a distinct order, called the *hermits of St Damien*. Peter de Meuron governed this order till 1286, when his love of solitude and retirement induced him to quit the charge. In July 1294, the great reputation of his sanctity raised him, though much against his will, to the pontificate. He then took the name of Celestin V. and his order that of *Celestins* from him. By his bull he approved their constitutions, and confirmed all their monasteries to the number of 20. But he sat too short time in the chair of St Peter to do many great things for his order; for having governed the church five months and a few days, and considering the great burden he had taken upon him, to which he thought himself unequal, he solemnly renounced the pontificate in a consistory held at Naples.

After his death, which happened in 1296, his order made great progress not only in Italy, but in France likewise; whither the then general Peter of Tivoli sent 12 religious, at the request of king Philip the Fair, who gave them two monasteries; one in the forest of Orleans, and the other in the forest of Compeigne at mount Chartres. This order likewise passed into several provinces of Germany. They have about 96 convents in Italy, and 21 in France, under the title of priories.

The Celestins rise two hours after midnight, to say matins. They eat no flesh at any time, except when they are sick. They fast every Wednesday and Friday, from Easter to the feast of the exaltation of the holy cross; and, from that feast to Easter, every day. As to their habit, it consists of a white gown, a capuche, and a black scapulary. In the choir, and when they go out of the monastery, they wear a black cowl with the capuche: their shirts are of serge.

CELETES, or CELETAE, (from [illegible], *a race-horse*,) in antiquity, denote single or saddle-horses; by way of contradistinction from those yoked or harnessed together, called *bigarii, quadrigarii*, &c. The same denomination is also given to the cavaliers or riders on horseback; and hence some deduce celeres, the name of Romulus's guard.

CELEUSMA, or CELEUMA, in antiquity, the shout or cry of the seamen, whereby they animated each other in their work of rowing. The word is formed from [illegible], *to call, to give the signal*.

CELEUSMA was also a kind of song or formula, rehearsed or played by the master, or others, to direct the strokes and movements of the mariners, as well as to encourage them to labour. See CELEUSTES.

CELEUSTES, in ancient navigation, the boatswain or officer appointed to give the rowers the signal, when they were to pull, and when to stop. He was also denominated *epopeus*, and by the Romans *portisculus*; sometimes simply *hortator*.

CELIBACY, the state of unmarried persons. Scaliger derives the word from the Greek [illegible], "bed," and [illegible], *linquo*, "I leave:" others say it is formed from *coeli beatitudo*; q. d. *the blessedness of heaven*.

The ancient Romans used all means imaginable to discourage celibacy. Nothing was more usual than for the censors to impose a fine on bachelors. Dionysius Halicarnassensis mentions an ancient constitution whereby all persons of full age were obliged to marry. But the first law of that kind, of which we have any certainty, is that under Augustus, called *lex Julia de maritandis ordinibus*. It was afterwards denominated *Papia Poppea*, and more usually *Julia Papia*, in regard of some new sanction and amendments made to it under the consuls Papius and Poppaeus. By this law, divers prerogatives were given to persons who had many children; penalties imposed on those who lived a single life, as that they should be incapable of receiving legacies, and not exceeding a certain proportion.

CELIBATE, the same with celibacy; but it is chiefly used in speaking of the single life of the Popish clergy, or the obligation they are under to abstain from marriage. In this sense we say the law of *celibate*. Monks and religious take a vow of celibate; and what is more, of chastity.

The church of Rome imposes an universal celibacy on all its clergy, from the pope to the lowest deacon and subdeacon. The advocates for this usage pretend, that a vow of perpetual celibacy was required in the ancient church as a condition of ordination, even from the earliest apostolic ages. But the contrary is evident from numerous examples of bishops and archbishops, who lived in a state of matrimony, without any prejudice to their ordination or their function. It is generally agreed that most of the apostles were married. Some say all of them, except St Paul and St John. Others say St Paul himself was married, because he writes to his *yoke-fellow*, whom they interpret his wife. Be this as it will, in the next ages after the apostles, we have accounts of divers married bishops, presbyters, and deacons, without any reproof or mark of dishonour set on them; *e. g.* Valens, presbyter of Philippi, mentioned by Polycarp; and Chaeremon, bishop of Nilus. Novatus was a married presbyter of Carthage, as we learn from Cyprian; who himself was also a married man, as Pagi confesses; and so was Caecilius the presbyter who converted him; and Numidicus another presbyter of Carthage. The reply which the Romanists give to this is, that all married persons, when they came to be ordained, promised to lived separate from their wives by consent, which answered the vow of celibacy in other persons. But this is not only said without proof, but against it. For Novatus presbyter of Carthage, was certainly allowed to cohabit with his wife after ordination; as appears from the charge that Cyprian brings against him, that he had struck and abused his wife, and thereby caused her to miscarry. There seems indeed to have been, in some cases, a tendency towards the introduction of such a law, by one or two zealots; but the motion was no sooner made, than it was quashed by the authority of wiser men. Thus Eusebius observes, that Pinytus, bishop of Gnossus in Crete, was for laying the law of celibacy upon his brethren; but Dionysius bishop of Corinth wrote to him, that he should consider the weakness of men, and not impose that heavy burden on them. In the council of Nice, *anno* 325, the motion was renewed for a law to oblige the clergy to abstain from all conjugal society with their wives, whom they had married before their ordination: but Paphnutius, a famous Egyptian bishop, and one who himself never was married, vigorously declaimed against it, upon which it was unanimously rejected. So Socrates and Sozomen tell the story; to which all that Valesius, after Bellarmin, has to say, is, that he suspects the truth of it. The council in Trullo, held in 692, made a difference in this respect between bishops and presbyters; allowing presbyters, deacons, and all the inferior orders, to cohabit with their wives after ordination; and giving the Roman church a smart rebuke for the contrary prohibition, but at the same time laying an injunction upon bishops to live separate from their wives, and appointing the wives to betake themselves to a monastic life, or become deaconesses in the church. And thus was a total celibate established in the Greek church, as to bishops, but not any others. In the Latin church, the like establishment was also made, but by slow steps in many places. For in Africa, even bishops themselves cohabited with their wives at the time of the council of Trullo. The celibacy of the clergy, however, appears of an ancient standing, if not of command and necessity, yet as of counsel and choice. But as it is clearly neither of divine nor apostolical institution, it is, at first, hard to conceive from what motive the court of Rome persisted so very obstinately to impose this institution on the clergy. But we are to observe that this was a leading step to the execution of the project formed of making the clergy independent of princes, and rendering them a separate body to be governed by their own laws. In effect, while priests had children, it was very difficult to prevent their dependence on princes, whose favours have such an influence on private men; but having no family, they were more at liberty to adhere to the Pope.

CELIDOGRAPHIA, the description of the spots which appear on the surfaces of the sun and planets. See ASTRONOMY, n° 56, &c.

CELL, CELLA, in ancient writers, denotes a place or apartment usually under ground, and vaulted, in which were stored up some sort of necessaries, as wine, honey, and the like; and according to which it was called *Cella Vinaria*, *Olearia*, *Mellaria*, &c. The word is formed from the Latin *celare*, to conceal.

CELLA was also used for the lodge or habitation of a common prostitute, as being anciently under ground, hence also denominated *fornix*.

> *Intravit calidum veteri centone lupanar,*
> *Et cellam vacuam.* Juv. Sat. vi. ver. 121.

On which place an ancient scholiast remarks, that the names of the whores were written on the doors of their several cells; by which we learn the meaning of *inscripta cella* in Martial, lib. xi. ep. 46.

CELLA was also applied to the bed-chambers of domestics and servants; probably as being low and narrow.—Cicero, inveighing against the luxury of Antony, says, the beds in the very *cellæ* of his servants were spread with pompous purple coverlets.

CELLA is also applied to the members or apartments of baths. Of these there were three principal, called *frigidaria*, *tepidaria*, and *caldaria*; to which may be added a fourth, called *cella assa*, and sometimes *sudatoria*.

CELLA likewise signified the *adytum*, or inmost and most retired parts of temples, wherein the images of the gods to whom the edifices were consecrated were preserved. In this sense we meet with *cella Jovis*, *cella Concordiæ*, &c.

CELL is also used for a lesser or subordinate sort of minister dependent on a great one, by which it was erected, and continues still to be governed. The great abbeys in England had most of them *cells* in places distant from the mother abbey, to which they were accountable, and from which they received their superiors. The alien priories in England were cells to abbeys in Normandy, France, Italy, &c. The name *cell* was also given to rich and considerable monasteries not dependent on any other.

CELL signifies also a little apartment or chamber, such as those wherein the ancient monks, solitaries, and hermits, lived in retirement. Some derive the word from the Hebrew כלא, *i. e.* "a prison, or place where any thing is shut up."

The same name is still retained in divers monasteries. The dormitory is frequently divided into so many cells or lodges. The Carthusians have each a separate house, which serves them as a cell. The hall wherein the Roman conclave is held, is divided, by partitions, into divers cells, for the several cardinals to lodge in.

CELL is also a name given to the little divisions in honey-combs, which are always regular hexagons. See BEE.

CELL, in botany, is applied to the hollow places between the partitions in the pods, husks, and other seed-vessels of plants; according as there is one, two, three, &c. of these cells, the vessel is said to be unilocular, bilocular, trilocular, &c.

CELLS, in anatomy, little bags, or bladders, where fluids or other matters are lodged; called *loculi*, *cellulæ*, &c. Thus the *cellulæ adiposæ* are the little cells where the fat is contained; *cellulæ* in the *colon*, are spaces wherein the excrements are detained till voided, &c.

CELLAR (*Cellarium*), in ancient writers, denotes the same with cella, viz. a conservatory of eatables, or drinkables.

Cellar differs from vault, as the latter is supposed to be deeper, the former being frequently little below the surface of the ground. In which sense, *cellarium* only differed from *penus*, as the former was only a store-house for several days, the latter for a long time. Thus it is, the bactroperatæ, a sect of ancient Cynics, are said by St Jerome to carry cellar about with them.

Cellarium also denoted an allowance of bread, wine, oil, or other provision, furnished out of the cellar, to the use of the governor of the province and his officers, &c. In which sense, the word amounts to much the same with *annona*.

CELLARS, in modern building, are the lowest rooms in a house, the ceilings of which usually lie level with the surface of the ground on which the house is built; or they are situated under the pavement before the house, especially in streets and squares.

Cellars, and other places vaulted under ground, were called by the Greeks *hypogea*: the Italians still call them *fondi delle case*.

CELLARER, or CELLERER, (*Cellerarius* or *Cellarius*), an officer in monasteries, to whom belong the care and procurement of provisions for the convent. The denomination is said to be borrowed from the Roman law, where *cellarius* denotes an examiner of accounts and expences. Ulpian defines it thus: "Cellarius, id est, ideo præpositus ut rationes salvæ sint."

The *cellerarius* was one of the four *obedientiarii*, or great officers of monasteries: under his ordering was the *pistrinum* or bakehouse, and the *bracinum*, or brewhouse. In the richer houses there were particular lands set apart for the maintenance of his office, called in ancient writings *ad cibum monachorum*. The *cellerarius* was a great man in the convent. His whole office in ancient times had a respect to that origin: he was to see his lord's corn got in, and laid up in granaries; and his appointment consisted in a certain proportion thereof, usually fixed at a thirteenth part of the whole together with a furred gown. The office of cellarer then only differed in name from those of bailiff and minstrel; excepting that the cellarer had the receipt of his lord's rents through the whole extent of his jurisdiction.

CELLARER was also an officer in chapters, to whom belonged the care of the temporals, and particularly the distributing of bread, wine, and money to canons, on account of their attendance in the choir. In some places he was called *cellerer*, in others *burser*, and in others *currier*.

CELLARIUS (Christopher), was born in 1638, at Smalcade in Franconia, of which town his father was minister. He was successively rector of the colleges at Weymar, Zeits, and Mersbourg; and the king of Prussia having founded an university at Hall in 1693, he was prevailed on to be professor of eloquence and history there, where he composed the greatest part of his works. His great application to study hastened the infirmities of old age; for it is said, he would spend whole days and nights together at his books, without any attention to his health, or even the calls of nature. His works relate to grammar, geography, history, and the oriental languages, and the number of them is amazing. He died in 1707.

CELLINI (Benvenuto), an eminent statuary, who was bred a jeweller and goldsmith, but seems to have had an extraordinary genius for the fine arts in general. He was cotemporary with Michael Angelo, and Julio Romano, and was employed by popes, kings, and other princely patrons of sciences and arts, so highly cultivated in the days of Leo X. and Charles V. some of his productions being esteemed most exquisite. He lived to a very considerable old age; and his life, almost to the last, was a continued scene of adventure, persecution, and misfortune, truly wonderful. He wrote his own history, which was not, however, published till the year 1730, probably on account of the excessive freedom with which he therein treated many distinguished personages of Italy and other countries. It was translated into English by Dr Nugent in 1771, to which the reader is referred, as it will not admit of an abridgement suitable to the design of this work.

CELLULAR, in a general sense, is applied to any thing consisting of single cells.

CELLULAR *Membrane*. See ANATOMY, n° 8 *et seq.*

CELOSIA, COCKS-COMB: A genus of the monogynia order, belonging to the pentandria class of plants; and in the natural method ranking under the 54th order, *Miscellaneæ*. The calyx is triphyllous; the corolla is five-petalled in appearance; the stamina are conjoined at the base to the plaited nectarium; the capsule gaping horizontally. There are eight species, of which the most worthy of notice is the *cristata*, or common cockscomb, so called on account of its crested head of flowers, resembling a cock's comb; of these there are a great variety of species. The principal colours of their flowers are red, purple, yellow, and white; but there are some whose heads are variegated with two or three colours. The heads are sometimes divided like a plume of feathers, and are of a beautiful scarlet colour. These plants are very tender exotics, and require a great deal of care to cultivate them in this country. Three hot-beds must be prepared; a small one in March, on which to raise the plants an inch or two in height; a second in April, of larger dimensions, in which to transplant them when proper; and a third in May for a large frame, to receive them transplanted into pots, to remain till the end of June or beginning of July to grow to full size: all of which hot-beds must be covered with frames and glasses, and have five or six inches depth of fine rich light earth for the reception of the seed and plants; and in the second and third hot-bed, the frames must occasionally be raised or augmented, according as the plants shall rise in height.

CELSIA, in botany: A genus of the angiospermia order, belonging to the tridynamia class of plants; and in the natural method ranking under the 28th order, *Luridæ*. The calyx is quinquepartite: the corolla wheel-shaped; the filaments bearded or woolly; the capsule bilocular.

CELSUS (Aurelius Cornelius), a celebrated physician of the first century, who wrote eight books on medicine, in elegant Latin. He was the Hippocrates of the Latins, and Quintilian gives him a high eulogium. The great Boerhaave tells us, that Celsus is one of the best authors of antiquity for letting us into the true meaning and opinions of Hippocrates; and that, without him, the writings of this father in phy-

be

he would be often unintelligible, often misunderstood by us. He shows us also how the ancients cured distempers by friction, bathing, &c. His eight books *de Medicina* have been several times printed. The Elzivir edition, in the year 1650, by Vander Linden, is the best, as being entirely corrected from his manuscripts.

Celsus, an Epicurean philosopher, in the second century. He wrote a work against the Christians, entitled, *The true Discourse;* to which Origen, at the desire of Ambrose his friend, wrote a learned answer. To this philosopher Lucian dedicated his *Pseudomantis*.

CELTÆ, or Celtes, an ancient nation, by which most of the countries of Europe are thought to have been peopled. The compilers of the Universal History are of opinion, that they are descended from Gomer the eldest son of Japhet, the son of Noah. They think that Gomer settled in the province of Phrygia in Asia: Ashkenaz his eldest son, or Togarmah his youngest, or both, in Armenia, and Riphath the second son in Cappadocia. When they spread themselves wider, they seem to have moved regularly in columns without interfering with or disturbing their neighbours. The descendants of Gomer, or the Celtes, took the left hand, insensibly spreading themselves westward towards Poland, Hungary, Germany, France, and Spain; while the descendants of Magog, Gomer's brother, moving eastward, peopled Tartary.

In this large European tract, the Celtes began to appear a powerful nation under a regular monarchy, or rather under several considerable kingdoms. Mention is made of them indeed in so many parts of Europe, by ancient geographers and historians, that Ortelius took *Celtica* to be a general name for the continent of Europe, and made a map of it bearing this title. In those parts of Asia, which they possessed, as well as in the different parts of Europe, the Celtes went by various names. In Lesser Asia they were known by the names of *Titans* and *Sacks;* in the northern parts of Europe, by those of *Cymmerians*, *Cymbrians*, &c.; and in the southern parts they were called *Celtes*, *Gauls*, or *Galatians*.

With respect to the government of the Celtes we are entirely in the dark. All we know is, that the curetes, and afterwards druids and bards, were the interpreters of their laws; judged all causes whether criminal or civil; and their sentence was reckoned so sacred, that whoever refused to abide by it was by them excluded from assisting at their sacred rites; after which no man dared converse with him; so that this punishment was reckoned the most severe of all, even severer than death itself.

They neither reared temples nor statues to the deity, but destroyed them wherever they could find them, planting in their stead large spacious groves; which being open on the top and sides, were, in their opinion, more acceptable to the divine Being, who is absolutely unconfined. In this their religion seems to have resembled that of the Persees and disciples of Zoroaster. The Celtes only differed from them in making the oak instead of the fire the emblem of the deity; in choosing that tree above all others to plant their groves with, and attributing several supernatural virtues both to its wood, leaves, fruit, and misletoe; all which were made use of in their sacrifices and other parts of their worship. But after they had adopted the idolatrous superstition of the Romans and other nations, and the apotheosis of their heroes and princes, they came to worship them much in the same manner: as Jupiter under the name of *Taran*, which in the Celtic signifies thunder: Mercury, whom some authors call *Hesus* or *Hesus*, probably, from the Celtic *hundh*, which signifies a dog, and might be the *Anubis latrans* of the Egyptians. But Mars was held in the greatest veneration by the warlike, and Mercury by the trading part of the nation. The care of religion was immediately under their curetes, since known by the name of druids and bards. These were, as Cæsar tells us, the performers of sacrifices and all religious rites, and expounders of religion to the people. They also instructed youth in all kinds of learning, such as philosophy, astronomy, astrology, &c. Their doctrines were taught only by word of mouth, esteeming them too sacred to be committed to writing. Other more common subjects, such as their hymns to their gods, the exploits of princes and generals in time of war, and especially before a battle, were couched in elegant verse, and recited, or rather sung, on all proper occasions; though even these were also kept from vulgar eyes, and either committed to memory, or if to writing, the whole was a secret to all the laity. The latter indeed seems the most probable, if what Cæsar hints be true; namely, that these poetic records were increased in his time to such a bulk, that it took up a young bard near 20 years to learn them by heart. Diodorus tells us farther, that these poets used to accompany their songs with instrumental music, such as that of organs, harps, and the like; and that they were held in such veneration, that if, in the time of an engagement between two armies, one of these bards appeared, both sides immediately ceased fighting. The reason of this was, that they were universally believed to be prophets as well as poets; so that it was thought dangerous as well as injurious to disobey what they supposed came from their gods. These prophetic philosophers kept academies, which were resorted to not only by a great number of their own youth, but also of those from other countries, insomuch that Aristotle says, their philosophy passed from thence into Greece, and not from Greece thither. Diodorus likewise quotes a passage from Hecateus, which is greatly in their praise; viz. that the druids had some kind of instruments by which they could draw distant objects nearer, and make them appear larger and plainer; and by which they could discover even seas, mountains, and valleys, in the moon. But whatever might be their learning, it is certain, that in process of time they adopted several very barbarous customs, such as sacrificing human victims to their gods as more acceptable to them than those of any other animals. And Diodorus tells us of another inhuman custom they used in their divinations, especially in great matters, which was done by killing some of their slaves, or some prisoners of war, if any they had, with a scimetar, to draw their augury from the running of his blood from his mangled limbs.

For the history, &c. of the different Celtic nations, see the article Gaul, &c.

Celtes, certain ancient instruments of a wedge-like form, of which several have been discovered in

different

different parts of Great Britain. Antiquarians have generally attributed them to the Celtæ; but, not agreeing as to their use, distinguished them by the above unmeaning appellation. But Mr Whittaker makes it probable that they were British battle-axes. See *Battle-Ax*.

CELTIBERIA (anc. geog.), a county of the Hither Spain, lying the right or south-west side of the river Iberus; though sometimes the greatest part of Spain was called by the name of *Celtiberia*. The people were denominated *Celtiberi*, or the Celtæ seated on the Iberus. They were very brave and warlike, their cavalry in particular was excellent. They wore a black and rough cloak, the shag of which was like goats hair. Some of them had light bucklers like the Gauls; other hollow and round ones like those of other nations. They all wore boots made of hair, and iron helmets adorned with crests of a purple colour. They used swords which cut on both sides, and poinards of a foot long. Their arms were of an admirable temper, and are said to have been prepared in the following manner: they buried plates of iron under ground, where they let them remain till the rust had eaten the weakest part of the metal, and the rest was consequently hard and firm. Of this excellent iron they made their swords, which were so strong and well tempered, that there was neither buckler nor helmet that could resist their edge. The Celtiberians were very cruel towards their enemies and malefactors, but showed the greatest humanity to their guests. They not only cheerfully granted their hospitality to strangers who travelled in their country, but were desirous that they should seek protection under their roof.

CELTIS, in botany: A genus of the monœcia order, belonging to the polygamia class of plants; and in the natural method ranking under the 53d order, *Scabridæ*. It is an hermaphrodite plant: The female calyx is quinquepartite; there is no corolla; there are five stamina, and two styles. The fruit is a monospermous plum. In the male, there is no calyx: the corolla is hexapetalous; there are six stamina, and an embryo of a pistillum. There are three species, all of them deciduous, viz.

1. The Australis or Southern Celtis, a deciduous tree, native of Africa and the South of Europe. 2. The Occidentalis or Western Celtis, a native of Virginia. And 3. The Orientalis or Eastern Celtis, a native of Armenia. The two first species grow with large, fair, straight stems; their branches are numerous and diffuse; their bark is of a darkish grey colour; their leaves are of a pleasant green; three or four inches long, deeply serrated, end in a narrow point, nearly resemble the leaves of the common stinging-nettle, and continue on the trees till late in the autumn: So that one may easily conceive what an agreeable variety these trees would make. Add to this, their shade is admirable. The leaves are late in the spring before they show themselves; but they make amends for this, by retaining their verdure till near the close of autumn, and then do not resemble most deciduous trees, whose leaves show their approaching fall by the change of their colour; but continue to exhibit themselves of a pleasant green even to the last. Hanbury speaks highly of the celtis as a timber-tree: he says, "The wood of the Lote-tree is extremely durable. In Italy they make their flutes, pipes, and other wind-instruments of it. With us the coach-makers use it for the frames of their vehicles." Millar mentions also the wood of the Occidentalis being used by the coach-makers. The third species will grow to about twelve feet; and the branches are numerous, smooth, and of a greenish colour. The leaves are smaller than those of the other sorts, though they are of a thicker texture, and of a lighter green. The flowers come out from the wings of the leaves, on slender footstalks: They are yellowish, appear early in the spring, and are succeeded by large yellow fruit.

Propagation, &c. All the species are propagated from seeds, which ripen in England, if they have a favourable autumn; but the foreign seeds are the most certain of producing a crop. These seeds should be sown, soon after they are ripe, either in boxes, or in a fine warm border of rich earth, a quarter of an inch deep; and in the following spring many of the young plants will appear; though a great part often lie till the second spring before they show their heads. If the seeds in the beds shoot early in the spring, they should be hooped, and protected by mats from the frosts, which would nip them in the bud. When all danger from frosts is over, the mats should be laid aside till the parching beams of the sun get powerful; when, in the day-time, they may be laid over the hoops again, to screen the plants from injury. The mats should be constantly taken off every night, and the young plants should never be covered either in rainy or cloudy weather. During the whole summer, these seedlings should be frequently watered in dry weather, and the beds kept clean of weeds, &c. In the autumn, they must be protected from the frosts, which often come early in that season, and would not fail to destroy their tops. The like care should be continued all winter to defend them from the same enemies. In this seminary they may remain, being kept clean of weeds and watered in dry weather, till the end of June, when they should be taken out of their beds, and planted in others at six inches distance. And here let no one (continues Hanbury) be startled at my recommending the month of June for this work; for I have found by repeated experience, that the plants will be then almost certain of growing, and will continue their shoots till the autumn; whereas I have ever perceived, that many of those planted in March have frequently perished, and that those which did grow made hardly any shoot that year, and showed the early figure of a stunted tree. In June, therefore, let the ground be well dug, and prepared for this work; and let the mould be rich and good: But the operation of removing must be deferred till rain comes; and if the season should be dry, this work may be postponed till the middle of July. After a shower, therefore, or a night's rain, let the plants be taken out of their beds, and pricked out at six inches distance from each other. After this, the beds in which they are planted should be hooped, and covered with mats when the sun shines; but these must always be taken away at night, as well as in rainy or cloudy weather. With this management, they will have shot to a good height by the autumn, and have acquired so much hardiness and strength as to need no farther care than to be kept clear

Cement.

clear of weeds for two or three years; when they may be planted out in places where they are to remain, or fet in the nurfery, to be trained up for large ftandards. The beft feafon for planting out thefe ftandard trees is the latter end of October, or beginning of November; and in performing that operation, the ufual rules muft be obferved with care. The foil for the lote-tree fhould be light, and in good heart; and the fituation ought to be well defended, the young fhoots being very liable to be deftroyed by the winter's frofts.

CEMENT, in a general fenfe, any glutinous fubftance capable of uniting and keeping things together in clofe cohefion. In this fenfe the word *cement* comprehends mortar, folder, glue, *&c.* but has been generally reftrained to the compofitions ufed for holding together broken glaffes, china, and earthen ware. For this purpofe the juice of garlic is recommended as exceedingly proper, being both very ftrong, and, if the operation is performed with care, leaving little or no mark. Quicklime and the white of an egg mixed together, and expeditioufly ufed, are alfo very proper for this purpofe. Dr Lewis recommends a mixture of quicklime and cheefe, in the following manner: "Sweet cheefe fhaved thin and ftirred with boiling hot water, changes into a tenacious flime which does not mingle with the water. Worked with frefh parcels of hot water, and then mixed upon a hot ftone with a proper quantity of unflaked lime, into the confiftence of a pafte, it proves a ftrong and durable cement for wood, ftone, earthen-ware, and glafs. When thoroughly dry, which will be in two or three days, it is not in the leaft acted upon by water. Cheefe barely beat with quicklime, as directed by fome of the chemifts for luting cracked glaffes, is not near fo efficacious." A compofition of the drying oil of linfeed and white-lead is alfo ufed for the fame purpofes, but is greatly inferior.

Cement in building, is ufed to denote any kind of mortar of a ftronger kind than ordinary. The cement commonly ufed is of two kinds; hot, and cold. The hot cement is made of rofin, bees wax, brick-duft, and chalk, boiled together. The bricks to be cemented are heated, and rubbed one upon another, with cement between them. The cold cement is that above defcribed for cementing china, *&c.* which is fometimes, though rarely, employed in building.

The ruins of the ancient Roman buildings are found to cohere fo ftrongly, that moft people have imagined the ancients were acquainted with fome kind of mortar, which, in comparifon of ours, might juftly be called *cement*; and that to our want of knowledge of the materials they ufed, is owing the great inferiority of modern buildings in their durability. In 1770, one M. Loriot, a Frenchman, pretended to have difcovered the fecret of the ancient cement, which, according to him, was no more than a mixture of powdered quick-lime with lime which had been long flaked and kept under water. The flaked lime was firft to be made up with fand, earth, brick-duft, *&c.* into mortar after the common method, and then about a third part of quick-lime in powder was added to the mixture. This produced an almoft inftantaneous petrification, fomething like what is called the *fetting* of alabafter, but in a much ftronger degree; and was poffeffed of many wonderful qualities needlefs here to relate, feeing it has never been known to fucceed with any other perfon who tried it. Mr Anderfon, in his effays on agriculture, has difcuffed this fubject at confiderable length, and feemingly with great judgment. He is the only perfon we know, who has given any rational theory of the ufes of lime in building, and why it comes to be the proper bafis of all cements. His account is in fubftance as follows:

Lime which has been flaked and mixed with fand, becomes hard and confiftent when dry, by a procefs fimilar to that which produces the natural *ftalactites* in caverns. Thefe are always formed by water dropping from the roof. By fome unknown and inexplicable procefs of nature, this water has diffolved in it a fmall portion of calcareous matter in a *cauftic* ftate. As long as the water continues covered from the air, it keeps the earth diffolved in it; it being the natural property of calcareous earths, when deprived of their fixed air, to diffolve in water. But when the fmall drop of water comes to be expofed to the air, the calcareous matter contained in it begins to attract the fixable part of the atmofphere. In proportion as it does fo, it alfo begins to feparate from the water, and to reaffume its native form of limeftone or marble. This procefs Mr Anderfon calls a *cryftallization*; and when the calcareous matter is perfectly *cryftallized* in this manner, he affirms that it is to all intents and purpofes limeftone or marble of the fame confiftence as before; and "in this manner (fays he), within the memory of man, have huge rocks of marble been formed near Matlock in Derbyfhire." If lime in a cauftic ftate is mixed with water, part of the lime will be diffolved, and will alfo begin to cryftallize. The water which parted with the cryftallized lime, will then begin to act upon the remainder, which it could not diffolve before; and thus the procefs will continue, either till the lime be all reduced to an *effete*, or (as he calls it) *cryftalline* ftate, or fomething hinders the action of the water upon it. It is this cryftallization which is obferved by the workmen when a heap of lime is mixed with water, and left for fome time to macerate. A hard cruft is formed upon the furface, which is ignorantly called *frofting*, though it takes place in fummer as well as in winter. If therefore the hardnefs of the lime, or its becoming a cement, depends entirely on the formation of its cryftals, it is evident, that the perfection of the cement muft depend on the perfection of the cryftals, and the hardnefs of the matters which are entangled among them. The additional fubftances ufed in making of mortar, fuch as fand, brick-duft, or the like, according to Mr Anderfon, ferve only for a purpofe fimilar to what is anfwered by fticks put into a veffel full of any faline folution, namely, to afford the cryftals an opportunity of faftening themfelves upon it. If therefore the matter interpofed between the cryftals of the lime is of a friable, brittle nature, fuch as brick duft or chalk, the mortar will be of a weak and imperfect kind; but when the particles are hard, angular, and very difficult to be broken, fuch as thofe of river or pit-fand, the mortar turns out exceedingly good and ftrong. Sea-fand is found to be an improper material for mortar, which Mr Anderfon afcribes to its being lefs angular than the other kinds. That the cryftallization may be the more perfect, he alfo recommends a large quantity of water, that the ingredients

Cement.

be

be perfectly mixed together, and that the drying be as slow as possible. An attention to these circumstances, he thinks, would make the buildings of the moderns equally durable with those of the ancients; and from what remains of the ancient Roman works, he thinks a very strong proof of his hypothesis might be adduced. The great thickness of their walls necessarily required a vast length of time to dry. The middle of them was composed of pebbles thrown in at random, and which have evidently had mortar so thin as to be *poured* in among them. By this means, a great quantity of the lime would be dissolved, and the crystallization performed in the most perfect manner; and the indefatigable pains and perseverance for which the Romans were so remarkable in all their undertakings, leave no room to doubt that they would take care to have the ingredients mixed together as well as possible. The consequence of all this is, that the buildings formed in this manner are all as firm as if cut out of a solid rock; the mortar being equally hard, if not more so, than the stones themselves.

Notwithstanding the bad success of those who have attempted to repeat M. Loriot's experiments, however, Dr Black informs us, that a cement of this kind is certainly practicable. It is done, he says, by powdering the lime while hot from the kiln, and throwing it into a thin paste of sand and water; which, not slaking immediately, absorbs the water from the mortar by degrees, and forms a very hard mass. "It is plain (he adds) that the strength of this mortar depends on using the lime hot or fresh from the kiln."

By mixing together gypsum and quick-lime, and then adding water, we may form a cement of tolerable hardness, and which apparently might be used to advantage in making troughs for holding water, or lining small canals for it to run in. Mr Wiegleb says, that a good mortar or cement, which will not crack, may be obtained by mixing three parts of a thin magma of slaked lime with one of powdered gypsum; but adds, that it is used only in a dry situation. A mixture of terras with slaked lime acquires in time a stony hardness, and may be used for preventing water from entering. See MORTAR and STUCCO.

CEMENT, among engravers, jewellers, *&c.* is the same with the hot cement used in building*; and is used for keeping the metals to be engraven firm to the block, and also for filling up what is to be chisseled.

* See the foregoing article.

CEMENT, in chemistry, is used to signify all those powders and pastes with which any body is surrounded in pots or crucibles, and which are capable by the help of fire of producing changes upon that body. They are made of various materials; and are used for different purposes, as for parting gold from silver, converting iron into steel, copper into brass: and by cementation more considerable changes can be effected upon bodies, than by applying to them liquids of any kind; because the active matters are then in a state of vapour, and assisted by a very considerable degree of heat.

Cement which quickly hardens in Water. This is described in the posthumous works of Mr Hooke, and is recommended for gilding live craw-fish, carps, *&c.* without injuring the fish. The cement for this purpose is prepared, by putting some Burgundy pitch into a new earthen pot, and warming the vessel till it receives so much of the pitch as will stick round it; then strewing some finely powdered umbar over the pitch when growing cold, adding a mixture of three pounds of linseed oil, and one of oil of turpentine, covering the vessel and boiling them for an hour over a gentle fire, and grinding the mixture as it is wanted with as much pumice-stone in fine powder as will reduce it to the consistence of paint. The fish being wiped dry, the mixture is spread upon it; and the gold leaf being then laid on, the fish may be immediately put into water again, without any danger of the gold coming off, for the matter quickly grows hard in the water.

Cement-Pots, are those earthen pots used in the cementation of metals.

CEMENTATION, the act of corroding or otherwise changing a metal by means of a CEMENT.

CEMETERY (Κοιμητήριον, from κοιμάω to "*sleep*;") a place set apart or consecrated for the burial of the dead.

Anciently none were buried in churches or church-yards: it was even unlawful to inter in cities, and the cemeteries were without the walls. Among the primitive Christians these were held in great veneration. It even appears from Eusebius and Tertullian, that, in the early ages, they assembled for divine worship in the cemeteries. Valerian seems to have confiscated the cemeteries and other places of divine worship, but they were restored again by Gallienus. As the martyrs were buried in these places, the Christians chose them for building churches on, when Constantine established their religion; and hence some derive the rule which still obtains in the church of Rome, never to consecrate an altar without putting under it the relics of some saint. The practice of consecrating cemeteries is of some antiquity. The bishop walked round it in procession, with the crosier or pastoral staff in his hand, the holy water-pot being carried before, out of which the aspersions were made.

CENCHRUS, in botany: A genus of the monoecia order, belonging to the polygamia class of plants; and in the natural method ranking under the 4th order, *Gramina*. The involucrum is laciniated, and echinated, or beset with small prickles, and bifurous. The calyx is a biflorous glume, with one floret-male, and the other hermaphrodite. The hermaphrodite corolla is a pointless glume; there are three stamina; one seed: the male corolla a pointless glume; with three stamina.

CENEGILD, in the Saxon Antiquities, an expiatory mulct, paid by one who had killed a man, to the kindred of the deceased. The word is compounded of the Saxon *cene*, i. e. *cognatio*, "relation", and *gild*, *solutio*, "payment".

CENOBITE. See COENOBITE.

CENOTAPH, in antiquity, an empty tomb, erected by way of honour to the deceased. It is distinguished from a sepulchre, in which a corpse was deposited. Of these there were two sorts; one for those who had, and another for those who had not, been honoured with funeral rites in another place.

The sign whereby honorary sepulchres were distinguished from others, was commonly the wreck of a ship, to denote the decease of the person in some foreign country.

CENSER, in antiquity, a vase containing incense to be used in sacrifices. Censer is chiefly used in speaking of the Jewish worship. Among the Greeks and Romans it is more frequently called *thuribulum*, *thymiaterion*, and *acerra*.

The Jewish censer was a small sort of chafing-dish, covered with a dome, and suspended by a chain. Josephus tells us, that Solomon made twenty thousand gold censers for the temple of Jerusalem, to offer perfumes in, and fifty thousand others to carry fire in.

CENSIO, in antiquity, the act or office of the censor. See CENSUS.

Censio included both the rating or valuing a man's estate, and the imposing mulcts and penalties.

Censio hastaria, a punishment inflicted on a Roman soldier for some offence, as laziness or luxury, whereby his *hasta* or spear was taken from him, and consequently his wages and hopes of preferment stopped.

CENSITUS, a person censed, or entered in the censual tables. See CENSUS.

In an ancient monument found at Ancyra, containing the actions of the emperor Octavius, we read,

Quo lustro civium Romanorum
Censita sunt capita quadragies
Centum millia & sexaginta tria.

CENSITUS is also used in the civil law for a servile sort of tenant, who pays capitation to his lord for the land he holds of him, and is entered as such in the lord's rent-roll. In which sense, the word amounts to the same with *capite census*, or *capite censitus*. See CAPITE Censi.

CENSOR, (from *censere* to "see" or "perceive"), one of the prime magistrates in ancient Rome.—Their business was to register the effects of the Roman citizens, to impose taxes in proportion to what each man possessed, and to take cognizance or inspection of the manners of the citizens. In consequence of this last part of their office, they had a power to censure vice or immorality by inflicting some public mark of ignominy on the offender. They had even a power to create the *princeps senatus*, and to expel from the senate such as they deemed unworthy of that office. This power they sometimes exercised without sufficient grounds; and therefore a law was at length passed, that no senator should be degraded or disgraced in any manner, until he had been formally accused and found guilty by both the censors. It was also a part of the censorian jurisdiction, to fill up the vacancies in the senate, upon any remarkable deficiency in their number; to let out to farm all the lands, revenues, and customs, of the republic; and to contract with artificers for the charge of building and repairing all the public works and edifices both in Rome and the colonies of Italy. In all parts of their office, however, they were subject to the jurisdiction of the people; and an appeal always lay from the sentence of the censors to that of an assembly of the people.

The first two censors were created in the year of Rome 311, upon the senate's observing that the consuls were so much taken up with war, as not to have time to look into other matters. The office continued to the time of the emperors, who assumed the censorial power, calling themselves *morum praefecti*; though Vespasian and his sons took the title of censors. Decius attempted to restore the dignity to a particular magistrate. After this we hear no more of it, till Constantine's time, who made his brother censor, and he seems to have been the last that enjoyed the office.

The office of censor was so considerable, that for a long time none aspired to it till they had passed all the rest; so that it was thought surprising that Crassus should be admitted censor, without having been either consul or pretor. At first the censors enjoyed their dignity for five years, but in 420 the dictator Mamercus made a law restraining it to a year and an half, which was afterwards observed very strictly. At first one of the censors was elected out of a patrician, and the other out of a plebeian family; and upon the death of either, the other was discharged from his office, and two new ones elected, but not till the next lustrum. In the year of Rome 622, both censors were chosen from among the plebeians; and after that time the office was shared between the senate and people. —After their election in the Comitia Centuriata, the censors proceeded to the capitol, where they took an oath not to manage either by favour or disaffection, but to act equitably and impartially throughout the whole course of their administration.

The republic of Venice still has a censor of the manners of their people, whose office lasts six months.

Censors of Books, are a body of doctors or others established in divers countries, to examine all books before they go to the press, and to see they contain nothing contrary to faith and good manners.

At Paris, the faculty of theology claim this privilege, as granted to them by the pope; but, in 1624, new commissions of four doctors were created, by letters-patent, the sole censors of all books, and answerable for every thing contained therein.

In England, we had formerly an officer of this kind, under the title of licenser of the press: but, since the revolution, our press has been laid under no such restraint.

CENSORINUS, a celebrated writer in the third century, well known by his treatise *De Die Natali*. This treatise, which was written about the year 238, Gerard Vossius calls a little book of gold; and declares it to be a most learned work of the highest use and importance to chronologers, since it connects and determines, with great exactness, some of the principal eras in pagan history. It was printed at Cambridge, with the notes of Lindenbrokius, in 1695.

CENSURE, a judgment which condemns some book, person, or action, or, more particularly, a reprimand from a superior. Ecclesiastical censures are penalties by which, for some remarkable misbehaviour, Christians are deprived of the communion of the church, or prohibited to execute the sacerdotal office.

CENSUS, in Roman antiquity, an authentic declaration made before the censors, by the several subjects of the empire, of their respective names and places of abode. This declaration was registered by the censors; and contained an enumeration, in writing, of all the estates, lands, and inheritances they possessed; their quantity, quality, place, wives, children, domestics, tenants, slaves. In the provinces the census served not only to discover the substance of each person, but where, and in what manner and proportion, taxes might be best imposed. The census at Rome is commonly

Census, Cent.

ly thought to have been held every five years; but Dr Middleton hath shown, that both census and lustrum were held irregularly and uncertainly at various intervals. The census was an excellent expedient for discovering the strength of the state: for by it they discovered the number of the citizens, how many were fit for war, and how many for offices of other kinds; how much each was able to pay of taxes, &c. It went through all ranks of people, though under different names; that of the common people was called *census*; that of the knights, *census, recensio, recognitio*; that of the senators, *lectio, relectio*.—Hence also *censu* came to signify a person who had made such a declaration; in which sense it was opposed to *incensus*, a person who had not given in his estate, or name, to be registered.

The census, according to Salmasius, was peculiar to the city of Rome. That in the provinces was properly called *professio* and [illegible]. But this distinction is not every where observed by the ancients themselves.

Census was also used for the book or register wherein the professions of the people were entered: in which sense, the census was frequently cited and appealed to, as evidence in the courts of justice.

Census is also used to denote a man's whole substance or estate.

Census Senatorius, the patrimony of a senator, which was limited to a certain value; being at first rated at eight hundred thousand sesterces, but afterwards, under Augustus, enlarged to twelve hundred thousand.

Census Equester, the estate or patrimony of a knight, rated at four hundred thousand sesterces, which was required to qualify a person for that order, and without which no virtue or merit was available.

Census was also used for a person worth an hundred thousand sesterces, or who was entered as such in the censual tables, on his own declaration. In which sense, census amounts to the same with *classicus*, or a man of the first class; though Gellius limits the estate of those of this class to an hundred and twenty-five thousand asses. By the Voconian law, no census was allowed to give by his will above a fourth part of what he was worth to a woman.

Census was also used to denote a tax or tribute imposed on persons, and called also capitation. See *Capita Census*.

Census Dominicatus, in writers of the lower age, denotes a rent due to the lord.

Census Duplicatus, a double rent or tax, paid by vassals to their lord on extraordinary or urgent occasions; as expeditions to the Holy Land, &c.

Census Ecclesiae Romanae, was an annual contribution voluntarily paid to the see of Rome by the several princes of Europe.

CENT, signifies properly an hundred, being an abridgement of the word *centum*; but is often used in commerce to express the profit or loss arising from the sale of any commodity: so that when we say there is 10 *per cent.* profit, or 10 *per cent.* loss, upon any merchandise that has been sold, it is to be understood, that the seller has either gained or lost ten pounds on every hundred pounds of the price at which he bought that merchandize; which is $\frac{1}{11}$ of profit, or $\frac{1}{10}$ of loss, upon the total of the sale.

Centaurea, Centella.

CENTAUREA, in botany: A genus of the polygamia frustanea order, belonging to the syngenesia class of plants; and in the natural method ranking under the 49th order, *Compositae*. The receptacle is bristly; the pappus simple; the corollulae of the radius funnel-shaped, longer than those of the disk, and irregular.

CENTAUR, in astronomy, a part or moiety of a southern constellation, in form half-man half-horse; usually joined with the wolf. The word comes from [illegible], formed of [illegible], *pungo*; and [illegible], *bull*; q. d. *bull-pricker*. The stars of this constellation, in Ptolemy's Catalogue are 37; in Tycho's 4; and in the Britannic Catalogue, with Sharp's Appendix, 35.

CENTAURS, in mythology, a kind of fabulous monsters, half men and half horses.—The poets pretend that the centaurs were the sons of Ixion and a cloud; the reason of which fancy is, that they retired to a castle called [illegible], which signifies a "cloud."—This fable is differently interpreted: some will have the centaurs to have been a body of shepherds and herdsmen, rich in cattle, who inhabited the mountains of Arcadia, and to whom is attributed the invention of bucolic poetry. Palaephatus, in his book of incredibles, relates, that under the reign of Ixion, king of Thessaly, a herd of bulls on mount Thessaly ran mad, and ravaged the whole country, rendering the mountains inaccessible; that some young men who had found the art of taming and mounting horses, undertook to clear the mountains of these animals, which they pursued on horseback, and thence obtained the appellation of *Centaurs*. This success rendering them insolent, they insulted the Lapithae, a people of Thessaly: and because when attacked they fled with great rapidity, it was supposed they were half horses and half men.—The Centaurs in reality were a tribe of Lapithae, who inhabited the city Pelethronium adjoining to mount Pelion, and first invented the art of breaking horses, as is intimated by Virgil.

CENTAUREA, greater centaury: A genus of the polygamia frustanea order, belonging to the syngenesia class of plants; and in the natural method ranking under the 49th order, *Compositae*. The receptacle is bristly, the pappus simple, the corollulae of the radius funnel-shaped, longer than those of the disk, and irregular. There are 61 species. The root of one of them called *glastifolia*, is an article in the materia medica. It has a rough, somewhat acrid taste, and abounds with a red viscid juice. Its rough taste has gained it some esteem as an astringent; its acrimony as an aperient; and its glutinous quality as a vulnerary: but the present practice takes very little notice of it in any intention. Another of the species is the cyanus or blue bottle, which grows commonly among corn. The expressed juice of this flower stains linen of a beautiful blue colour, but is not permanent. Mr Boyle says, that the juice of the inner petals, with a little alum, makes a beautiful permanent colour, equal to ultramarine.

Lesser Centaury. See Gentiana.

CENTELLA, in botany: A genus of the tetrandria order, belonging to the monoecia class of plants; and in the natural method ranking under the 11th order, *Sarmentaceae*. The male involucrum is tetraphyllous and quinqueflorous, with four petals; the female in-

involucrum is diphyllous and uniflorous; the petals four; the germen inferior; two ſtyles; and a bilocular ſeed-caſe.

CENTENARIUS, or CENTENARII, in the middle age, an officer who had the government or command, with the adminiſtration of juſtice, in a village. The centenarii as well as vicarii were under the juriſdiction and command of the court. We find them among the Franks, Germans, Lombards, Goths, &c.

CENTENARIUS was alſo uſed for an officer who had the command of 100 men; moſt frequently called a CENTURION.

CENTENARIUS, in monaſteries, was an officer who had the command of 100 monks.

CENTENINUM ovum, among naturaliſts, denotes a ſort of hen's egg much ſmaller than ordinary, vulgarly called a *cock's egg*; from which it has been fabulouſly held that the cockatrice or baſiliſk is produced. The name is taken from an opinion, that theſe are the laſt eggs which hens lay, having laid 100 before; whence *centeninum*, q. d. the hundredth egg.—Theſe eggs have no yolks, but in other reſpects differ not from common ones; having the albumen, chalazes, membranes, &c. in common with others. In the place of the yolk is found a little body like a ſerpent coiled up, which doubtleſs gave riſe to the fable of the baſiliſk's origin from thence. Their origin is with probability aſcribed by Harvey to this, that the yolks in the vitellary of the hen are exhauſted before the albumina.

CENTER, or CENTRE, in a general ſenſe, ſignifies a point equally diſtant from the extremities of a line, figure, or body. The word is formed from the Greek κεντρον, *a point*.

CENTRE of Gravity, in mechanics, that point about which all the parts of a body do in any ſituation exactly balance each other.

CENTRE of Motion, that point which remains at reſt, while all the other parts of a body move about it.

CENTRE of a Sphere, a point in the middle, from which all lines drawn to the ſurface are equal.

Hermes Triſmegiſtus defines God an intellectual ſphere, whoſe center is every where, and circumference no where.

CENTESIMA USURA, that wherein the intereſt in an hundred months became equal to the principal; *i. e.* where the money is laid out at one *per cent.* per month; anſwering to what in our ſtyle would be called 12 *per cent.* for the Romans reckoned their intereſt not by the year, but by the month.

CENTESIMATION, a milder kind of military puniſhment, in caſes of deſertion, mutiny, and the like, when only every hundredth man is executed.

CENTILOQUIUM, denotes a collection of 100 ſentences, opinions, or ſayings.

The centiloquium of Hermes, contains 100 aphoriſms, or aſtrological ſentences, ſuppoſed to have been written by ſome Arab, falſely fathered on Hermes Triſmegiſtus. It is only extant in Latin, in which it has ſeveral times been printed.—The centiloquium of Ptolomy is a famous aſtrological piece, frequently confounded with the former, conſiſting likewiſe of 100 ſentences, or doctrines, divided into ſhort aphoriſms, intitled alſo in Greek καρπος, as being the fruit or reſult of the former writings of that celebrated aſtronomer, viz. his *quadripartitum* and *almageſtum*; or rather, by reaſon that herein is ſhown the uſe of aſtrological calculations.

CENTIPES, in zoology. See SCOLOPENDRA.

CENTIPED WORM, a term uſed for ſuch worms as have a great many feet, though the number does not amount to 100, as the term ſeems to import.—M. Maloet relates the hiſtory of a man, who, for three years, had a violent pain in the lower part of the forehead near the root of the noſe: at length he felt an itching, and afterwards ſomething moving within his noſtril, which he brought away with his finger; it was a worm of the centiped kind, an inch and an half long, which ran ſwiftly. It lived five or ſix days among tobacco. The patient was free of his pain ever after. Mr Littre mentioned a like caſe in 1708, of a larger centiped voided at the noſe, after it had thrown the woman, in whoſe frontal ſinus it was, into convulſions, and had almoſt deprived her of her reaſon.

CENTLIVRE (Suſanna), a celebrated comic writer, was the daughter of Mr Freeman of Holbeach, in Lincolnſhire; and had ſuch an early turn for poetry, that it is ſaid ſhe wrote a ſong before ſhe was ſeven years old. Before ſhe was twelve years of age, ſhe could not only read Moliere in French, but enter into the ſpirit of all the characters. Her father dying, left her to the care of a ſtep-mother; whoſe treatment not being agreeable to her, ſhe determined, though almoſt deſtitute of money and every other neceſſary, to go up to London to ſeek a better fortune than what ſhe had hitherto experienced. As ſhe was proceeding on her journey on foot, ſhe was met by a young gentleman from the univerſity of Cambridge, the afterwards well-known Anthony Hammond, Eſq; who was ſo extremely ſtruck with her youth and beauty, that he fell inſtantly in love with her; and inquiring into the particulars of her ſtory, ſoon prevailed upon her unexperienced innocence to ſeize on the protection he offered her, and go with him to Cambridge. After ſome months cohabitation, he perſuaded her to come to London; where, in a ſhort time, ſhe was married to a nephew of Sir Stephen Fox. But that gentleman not living with her above a twelvemonth, her wit and beauty ſoon procured her a ſecond huſband, whoſe name was Carrol, and who was an officer in the army; but he having the misfortune to be killed in a duel about a year and an half after their marriage, ſhe became a ſecond time a widow. For the ſake of ſupport ſhe now applied to her pen, and became a votary of the muſes; and it is under this name of Carrol that ſome of her earlier pieces were publiſhed. Her firſt attempt was in tragedy, in a play called the *Perjured Huſband*; yet her natural vivacity leading her afterwards to comedy, we find but one more attempt in the buſkin, among 18 dramatic pieces which ſhe afterwards wrote.

In 1706, ſhe wounded the heart of one Mr Joſeph Centlivre, yeoman of the mouth, or in other words principal cook to her Majeſty, who married her; and, after paſſing ſeveral years happily together, ſhe died at his houſe in Spring-Garden, Charing-Croſs, in December 1723.

This lady for many years enjoyed the intimacy and eſteem of the moſt eminent wits of the times, viz. Sir Richard Steele, Mr Rowe, Budgell, Farquhar, Dr Sewell, &c. and very few authors received more tokens of eſteem and patronage from the great. With regard to her merit as a writer, it muſt be allowed that her plays do not abound with wit, and that the language of them is ſometimes even poor, enervate, incorrect, puerile; but then her plots are buſy and well conducted, and her characters in general natural and well marked.

CENTNER, or Docimastic Hundred, in metallurgy and aſſaying, is a weight diviſible, firſt into an hundred, and thence into a greater number of other ſmaller parts; but though the word is the ſame both with the aſſayers and metallurgiſts, yet it is to be underſtood as expreſſing a very different quantity in their different acceptation of it. The weights of the metallurgiſts are eaſily underſtood, as being of the common proportion, but thoſe of the aſſayers are a thouſand times ſmaller than theſe, as the portions of metals or ores examined by the aſſayers are uſually very ſmall.

The metallurgiſts, who extract metals out of their ores, uſe a weight divided into an hundred equal parts, each part a pound; the whole they call a *centner* or *hundred weight*; the pound is divided into thirty-two parts, or half ounces: and the half ounce into two quarters of ounces, and theſe each into two drams.

Theſe diviſions and denominations of the metallurgiſts are eaſily underſtood; but the ſame words, tho' they are equally uſed by aſſayers, with them expreſs very different quantities; for as the centner of the metallurgiſts contains an hundred pounds, the centner of the aſſayers is really no more than one dram, to which the other parts are proportioned.

As the aſſayers weights are divided into ſuch an extreme degree of minuteneſs, and are ſo very different from all the common weights, the aſſayers uſually make them themſelves in the following manner, out of ſmall ſilver, or fine ſolder plates, of ſuch a ſize, that the mark of their weight, according to the diviſion of the dram, which is the *docimaſtic* or *aſſaying centner*, may be put upon them. They firſt take for a baſis one weight, being about two-thirds of a common dram: this they mark (64lb.) Then having at hand ſome granulated lead, waſhed clean, well dried, and ſifted very fine, they put as much of it into one of the ſmall diſhes of a fine balance as will equipoiſe the (64lb.) as it is called, juſt mentioned: then dividing this granulated lead into very nice halves, in the two ſcales, after taking out the firſt ſilver weight, they obtain a perfect equilibrium between the two ſcales; they then pour the granulated lead out of one diſh of the ſcales, and inſtead of it put in another ſilver weight, which they make exactly equiponderant with the lead in the other ſcale, and mark it (32lb.) If this ſecond weight, when firſt put into the ſcale, exceed by much the weight of the lead, they take a little from it by a very fine file; but when it comes very near, they uſe only a whetſtone to wear off an extremely ſmall portion at a time. When it is brought to be perfectly even and equal to the lead, they change the ſcales to ſee that no error has been committed, and then go on in the ſame manner till they have made all the diviſions, and all the ſmall weights. Then to have an entire centner or hundred weight, they add to the (64lb.) as they call it, a 32lb. and a 4lb. and weighing againſt them one ſmall weight, they make it equal to them, and mark it (100.) This is the docimaſtical, or aſſaying centner, and is really one dram.

CENTO, in poetry, a work wholly compoſed of verſes or paſſages promiſcuouſly taken from other authors, only diſpoſed in a new form and order.—Proba Falconia has written the life of Jeſus Chriſt in centos taken from Virgil. Alexander Roſs has done the like in his Chriſtiados, and Stephen de Pleure the ſame.

CENTONARII, in antiquity, certain of the Roman army, who provided different ſorts of ſtuff called centones, made uſe of to quench the fire which the enemies engines threw into the camp.

Theſe centonarii kept with the carpenters and other officers of artillery.

CENTRAL forces, the powers which cauſe a moving body to tend towards, or recede from, the center of motion. See Mechanics.

Central Rule, a rule diſcovered by Mr Thomas Baker, whereby to find the centre of a circle deſigned to cut the parabola in as many points as an equation to be conſtructed hath real roots. Its principal uſe is in the conſtruction of equations, and he hath applied it with good ſucceſs as far as biquadratics.

The central rule is chiefly founded on this property of the parabola, that, if a line be inſcribed in that curve perpendicular to any diameter, a rectangle formed of the ſegments of the inſcript is equal to the rectangle of the intercepted diameter and parameter of the axis.

The central rule has the advantage over Cartes and Dr Lalere's methods of conſtructing equations, in that both theſe are ſubject to the trouble of preparing the equation by taking away the ſecond term.

CENTRIFUGAL force, that force by which all bodies that move round any other body in a curve endeavour to fly off from the axis of their motion in a tangent to the periphery of the curve, and that in every part of it. See Mechanics.

Centrifugal-Machine, a very curious machine, invented by Mr Erſkine, for raiſing water by means of a centrifugal force combined with the preſſure of the atmoſphere.

It conſiſts of a large tube of copper, &c. in the form of a croſs, which is placed perpendicular in the water, and reſts at the bottom on a pivot. At the upper part of the tube is a horizontal cog-wheel, which touches the cogs of another in a vertical poſition; ſo that by the help of a double winch, the whole machine is moved round with very great velocity.

Near the bottom of the perpendicular part of the tube is a valve opening upwards; and near the two extremities, but on the contrary ſides of the arms, or croſs part of the tube, are two other valves opening outwards. Theſe two valves are, by the aſſiſtance of ſprings, kept ſhut till the machine is put in motion, when the centrifugal velocity of the water forces them open, and diſcharges itſelf into a ciſtern or reſervoir placed there for that purpoſe.

On the upper part of the arms are two holes, which

are closed by pieces screwing into the metal of the tube. Before the machine can work, these holes must be opened, and water poured in through them, till the whole tube be full: by this means all the air will be forced out of the machine, and the water supported in the tube by means of the valve at the bottom.

The tube being thus filled with water, and the holes closed by their screw caps, it is turned round by means of the winch, when the water in the arms of the tube acquires a centrifugal force, opens the valves near the extremities of the arms, and flies out with a velocity nearly equal to that of the extremities of the said arms.

The above description will be very easily understood by the figure we have added on Plate CXXXVI. which is a perspective view of the centrifugal machine, erected on board a ship. ABC is the copper tube. D, a horizontal cog-wheel, furnished with twelve cogs. E, a vertical cog-wheel, furnished with thirty-six cogs. F, F, the double winch. *a*, the valve near the bottom of the tube. *b*, *b*, the two pivots on which the machine turns. *c*, one of the valves in the cross-piece; the other at *d*, cannot be seen in this figure, being on the other side of the tube. *e*, *e*, the two holes through which the water is poured into the machine. GH, the cistern or reservoir. I, I, part of the ship's deck. The distance between the two valves, *c*, *d*, is six feet. The diameter of these valves is about three inches; and that of the perpendicular tube about seven inches.

If we suppose the men who work the machine can turn the winch round in three seconds, the machine will move round its axis in one second; and consequently each extremity of the arms will move with a velocity of 18.8 feet in a second. Therefore a column of water of three inches diameter will issue through each of the valves with a velocity of 18.8 feet in a second: but the area of the aperture of each of the valves is 7.14 inches; which being multiplied by the velocity in inches = 225.6, gives 1610.784 cubic inches, the quantity of water discharged through one of the apertures in one second; so that the whole quantity discharged in that space of time through both the apertures is = 3221.568 inches; or 193294.08 cubic inches in one minute. But 60812 cubic inches make a tun, beer-measure; consequently, if we suppose the centrifugal machine revolves round its axis in one second, it will raise nearly 3 tuns 44 gallons in one minute: but this velocity is certainly too great, at least to be held for any considerable time; so that, when this and other deficiencies in the machine are allowed for, two tuns is nearly the quantity that can be raised by it in one minute.

It will perhaps be unnecessary to observe, that as the water is forced up the perpendicular tube by the pressure of the atmosphere, this machine cannot raise water above 32 feet high.

An attempt was made to substitute this machine in place of the pumps commonly used on ship-board, but the labour of working was found to be so great as to render the machine inferior to the chain-pump. A considerable improvement, we apprehend, would be, to load with a weight of lead the ends of the tubes thro' which the water issues, which would make the machine turn with a great deal more ease, as the centrifugal force of the lead would in some measure act the part of a fly.

CENTRIPETAL FORCE, that force by which a body is every where impelled, or any how tends, towards some point as a centre. See MECHANICS.

CENTRISCUS, in ichthyology, a genus of fishes belonging to the order of amphibia nantes. The head gradually ends in a narrow snout, the aperture is broad and flat; the belly is carinated; and the belly-fins united. There are two species, viz. 1. The scutatus has its back covered with a smooth bony shell, which ends in a sharp spine under which is the tail; but the back fins are between the tail and the spine. It is a native of the East Indies. 2. The scolopax has a rough scabrous body, and a straight extended tail. It has two belly-fins, with four rays in each, and has no teeth. It is found in the Mediterranean.

CENTRONIA, in natural history, a name by which the echini marini have been lately distinguished. Dr Hill makes them a distinct class of animals living under the defence of shelly coverings formed of one piece, and furnished with a vast number of spines moveable at the creature's pleasure.

CENTUMCELLÆ, (anc. geog.), Trajan's villa in Tuscany, on the coast, three miles from Abrè; with an excellent port, called *Trajanus Portus*, (Tujano); and a factitious island at the mouth of the port, made with a huge block of stone, on which two turrets rose, with two entrances into the bason or harbour, Rutilius. Now *Civita Vecchia*. E. Long. 12. 30. N. Lat. 42.

CENTUMVIRI, in Roman antiquity, judges appointed to decide common causes among the people: they were chosen, three out of each tribe; and though five more than an hundred, were nevertheless called *centumviri*, from the round number *centum*, an hundred.

CENTUNCULUS, in botany: A genus of the monogynia order, belonging to the tetrandria class of plants; and in the natural method ranking under the 20th order, *Rotaceæ*. The calyx is quadrifid; the corolla quadrifid, and patent; the stamina are short; the capsule is unilocular, cut round, or parting horizontally.

CENTURION, among the Romans, an officer in the infantry, who commanded a century, or an hundred men.

In order to have a proper notion of the centurions, it must be remembered, that every one of the thirty manipuli* in a legion was divided into two *ordines*, or ranks; and consequently the three bodies of the hastati, principes, and triarii, into 20 orders a piece, as into 10 manipuli. Now, every manipulus was allowed two centurions, or captains, one to each order or century: and, to determine the point of priority between them, they were created at two different elections. The 30 who were made first always took the precedency of their fellows; and therefore commanded the right-hand orders, as the others did the left. The triarii, or *pilani*, so called from their weapon the *pilum*, being esteemed the most honourable, had their centurions elected first, next to them the principes, and afterwards the hastati; whence they were called *primus et secundus pilus*, *primus et secundus princeps*, *primus et secundus hastatus*; and so on. Here it may be observed, that *primi ordines* is sometimes used in historians for the centu-

* See Manipulus.

rions of these orders; and the centurions are sometimes styled *principes ordinum*, and *principes centurionum*. We may take notice too what a large field there lay for promotion: sill through all the orders of the hastati; then quite through the principes; and afterwards from the last order of the triarii to the primipilus, the most honourable of the centurions, and who deserves to be particularly described. This officer, besides his title of primipilus, went under the several titles of *dux legionis*, *praefectus legionis*, *primus centurionum*, and *primus centurio*; and was the first centurion of the triarii in every legion. He presided over all the other centurions, and generally gave the word of command by order of the tribunes. Besides this, he had the care of the eagle, or chief standard, of the legion: hence, *aquilae praeesse*, is to bear the dignity of primipilus; and hence *aquila* is taken by Pliny for the said office. Nor was this station only honourable, but very profitable too; for he had a special stipend allowed him, probably as much as a knight's estate; and, when he left that charge, was reputed equal to the members of the equestrian order, bearing the title of *primipilarius*, in the same manner as those who had discharged the greatest civil offices were styled ever after, *consulares*, *censorii*, &c.

CENTURIPÆ, Centoripa, or Centuripa, (anc. geog.), a town in the south-west of the territory of Etna, on the river Cyamosorus: Now *Centorbi*, or *Centurippi*. It was a democratical city, which, like Syracuse, received its liberty from Timoleon. Its inhabitants cultivated the fine arts, particularly sculpture and engraving. In digging for the remains of antiquities, cameos are no where found in such abundance as at Centurippi and its environs. The situation of the place is romantic: it is built on the summit of a vast group of rocks, which was probably chosen as the most difficult of access, and consequently the properest in times of civil commotion. The remains still existing of its ancient bridge are a proof of its having been a considerable city. Cicero speaks of it as such. It was taken by the Romans, plundered and oppressed by Verres, destroyed by Pompey, and restored by Octavius, who made it the residence of a Roman colony.

CENTURY, in a general sense, any thing divided into, or consisting of, an hundred parts.

The marquis of Worcester published a *Century* of inventions, (for a specimen of which, see Acoustics, n° 27.); and Dr Hooke has given a *decimate* of inventions, as part of a *Century*, of which he affirmed himself master. It is remarkable, that both in the century of the former, and the decimate of the latter, we find the principle on which Savary's fire or steam engine is founded. See *Steam-Engine*.

Century in antiquity. The Roman people, when they were assembled for the electing of magistrates, enacting of laws, or deliberating upon any public affair, were always divided into centuries, and voted by centuries, in order that their votes might be the more easily collected, whence these assemblies were called *comitia centuriata*. The Roman cohorts were also divided into centuries. See Centurion and Cohort.

Century, in chronology, the space of one hundred years. This method of computing by centuries is generally observed in church history, commencing from the time of our Saviour's incarnation; in which sense we say the first century, the second century, &c.

Centuries of Magdeburg, a famous ecclesiastical history, ranged into 13 centuries, carried down to the year 1298, compiled by several hundred protestants of Magdeburg, the chief of whom was Flacius Illyricus.

CENTUSSIS, in Roman antiquity, a coin containing 100 asses.

CENTZONTLI, in ornithology, the Mexican name of the *Turdus polyglottus*. See Turdus.

CEODES, in botany: A genus of the dioecia order, belonging to the polygamia class of plants. There is no calyx; the corolla is monopetalous, with a short turbinated tube; the stamina are ten subulated filaments; the antherae roundish.

CEORLES, the name of one of the classes or orders into which the people were distinguished among the Anglo-Saxons. The ceorles, who were persons completely free, and descended from a long race of freemen, constituted a middle class between the labourers and mechanics (who were generally slaves, or descended from slaves) on the one hand, and the nobility on the other. They might go where they pleased, and pursue any way of life that was most agreeable to their humour; but so many of them applied to agriculture, and farming the lands of the nobility, that a ceorl was the most common name for a husbandman or farmer in the Anglo-Saxon times. These ceorls, however, seem in general to have been a kind of gentlemen farmers; and if any one of them prospered so well as to acquire the property of five hydes of land, upon which he had a church, a kitchen, a bell-house, and great gate, and obtained a seat and office in the king's court, he was esteemed a nobleman or thane. If a ceorl applied to learning, and attained to priest's orders, he was also considered as a thane; his weregild, or price of his life, was the same, and his testimony had the same weight in a court of justice. When he applied to trade, and made three voyages beyond sea, in a ship of his own, and with a cargo belonging to himself, he was also advanced to the dignity of a thane. But if a ceorl had a greater propensity to arms than to learning, trade, or agriculture, he then became the sithcundman, or military retainer, to some potent and warlike earl, and was called the *huscarle* of such an earl. If one of these huscarles acquitted himself so well as to obtain from his patron either five hydes of land, or a gilt sword, helmet, and breastplate, as a reward of his valour, he was likewise considered as a thane. Thus the temple of honour stood open to these ceorls, whether they applied themselves to agriculture, commerce, letters, or arms, which were then the only professions esteemed worthy of a freeman.

CEOS, Cea, Cia, or Cos, (anc. geog.); one of the Cyclades, lies opposite to the promontory of Attica called Sunium, and is 50 miles in compass. This island is commended by the ancients for its fertility and richness of its pastures. The first silk stuffs, if Pliny and Solinus are to be credited, were wrought here. Ceos was particularly famous for the excellent figs it produced. It was first peopled by Aristaeus, the son of Apollo and Cyrene, who, being grieved for the death of his son Actaeon, retired from Thebes, at the persuasion of his mother, and went over with some Thebans

bans to Ceus, at that time uninhabited. Diodorus Siculus tells us, that he retired to the island of Cos; but the ancients, as Servius observes, called both these islands by the name of Cos. Be that as it will, the island of Ceos became so populous, that a law prevailed there, commanding all persons upwards of sixty to be poisoned, that others might be able to subsist; so that none above sixty were to be seen in the island, being obliged, after they arrived at that age, either to submit to the law, or abandon the country, together with their effects. Ceos had, in former times, four famous cities, viz. Julis, Carthæa, Coressus, and Pœeessa. The two latter were, according to Pliny, swallowed up by an earthquake. The other two flourished in Strabo's time. Carthæa stood on a rising ground, at the end of a valley, about three miles from the sea. The situation of it agrees with that of the present town of Zia, which gives name to the whole island. The ruins both of Carthæa and Julis are still remaining; those of the latter take up a whole mountain, and are called by the modern inhabitants Polis, that is, *the city*. Near this place are the ruins of a stately temple, with many pieces of broken pillars, and statues of most exquisite workmanship. The walls of the city were of marble, and some pieces are still remaining above 12 feet in length. Julis was, according to Strabo, the birth-place of Simonides, Bacchylides, Erasistratus, and Aristo. The Oxford marbles tell us, that Simonides, the son of Leoprepis, invented a sort of artificial memory, the principles of which he explained at Athens, and add, that he was descended of another Simonides, who was a poet no less renowned than himself. One of these two poets invented those melancholy verses which were sung at funerals, and are called by the Latins *nenia*. Strabo says, that the Athenians, having besieged the city of Julis, raised the siege, upon advice that the inhabitants had resolved to murder all the children under a certain age, that useful persons might not be employed in looking after them. Ceos was, with the other Greek islands, subdued by the Romans, and bestowed upon the Athenians by Marc Antony the triumvir, together with Ægina, Tinos, and some other adjoining islands, which were all reduced to one Roman province by Vespasian. The island is now called *Zea*.

CEPA, the onion. See Allium.

CEPHALANTHUS, button-wood: A genus of the monogynia order, belonging to the tetrandria class of plants; and in the natural method ranking under the 48th order, *Aggregatæ*. There is no common calyx; the proper one is superior, and funnel-shaped; the receptacle globose and naked, with one downy seed. There is only one species, the *Occidentalis*; a deciduous shrub, native of north America. It grows to about five or six feet high; and is not a very bushy plant, as the branches are always placed thinly in proportion to the size of the leaves, which will grow more than three inches long, and one and a half broad, if the trees are planted in a soil they like. The leaves stand opposite by pairs on the twigs, and also sometimes by threes, and are of a light-green colour: Their upper surface is smooth; they have a strong nerve running from the footstalk to the point, and several others from that on each side to the borders: These, as well as the footstalks, in the autumn dye to a reddish colour. The flowers, which are aggregate flowers, properly so called, are produced at the ends of the branches, in globular heads, in July. The florets which compose these heads are funnel-shaped, of a yellow colour, and fastened to an axis which is in the middle.—The cephalanthus is propagated from seeds, which we receive from America. These should be sown as soon as they arrive, and there will be a chance of their coming up the first spring; though they often lie till the spring after before they make their appearance. They may be sown in good garden mould of almost any soil, if somewhat moist the better, and should be covered about a quarter of an inch deep. This shrub is also propagated by layers. If the young shoots are laid in autumn, they will have struck good root by the autumn following, and may be then taken up, and set in the places where they are designed to remain. Cuttings of this tree, also, planted in the autumn in a rich, light, moist soil, will grow: and by that means also plenty of these plants may be soon obtained.

CEPHALIC, in a general meaning, signifies any thing belonging to the head.

Cephalic Medicines, are remedies for disorders of the head. Cordials are comprehended herein, as are also whatever promotes a free circulation of the blood through the brain.

Except when the disorder arises from excess of heat, or an inflammatory disposition in the head, moist topicals should never be used; but always dry ones.

To rub the head after it is shaved proves an instantaneous cure for a cephalalgia, a stuffing of the head, and a weakness of the eyes, arising from a weak and relaxed state of the fibres. And as by every fresh evacuation of the humours their quantity is not only lessened, but also their recrementitious parts derived thither, the more frequently the head is shaved, the larger quantity of humour is discharged; so that the frequent shaving of the head and beard is likewise a perpetual blister; and in as much as it is useful, it is a cephalic.

Cephalic Vein, in anatomy, creeps along the arm between the skin and the muscles, and divides it into two branches: the external goes down to the wrist, where it joins the basilica, and turns up to the back of the hand; the internal branch, together with a small one of the basilica, makes the mediana.

The ancients used to open this vein for disorders of the head, for which reason it bears this name; but a better acquaintance with the circulation of the blood informs us, that there is no foundation for such a notion.

CEPHALENIA, or Cephallenia, an island of the Ionian sea between Ithaca and Zacynthus, known in Homer's time by the names of Samus and Epirus Melæna, is about eighty miles in length, forty in breadth, and a hundred and thirty in compass. It had anciently four cities, one of which bore the name of the island. Strabo tell us, that in his time there were only two cities remaining; but Pliny speaks of three; adding, that the ruins of Same, which had been destroyed by the Romans, were still in being. Same was the metropolis of the island, and is supposed to have stood in the place which the Italians call Porto Guiscardo. The names of the four cities were, according to Thucydides, Same, Prome, Cranii, and Pale. This iſland was ſubdued by the Thebans, under the conduct of Amphitryo, who is ſaid to have killed Pterelas, who then reigned here. While Amphitryo was carrying on the war in Cephalenia, then called Samos, one Cephalus, a man of great diſtinction at Athens, having accidentally killed his wife Procris in ſhooting at a deer, fled to Amphitryo, who, pitying his caſe, not only received him kindly, but made him governor of the iſland, which thenceforth was called Cephalenia. After it had been long in ſubjection to the Thebans, it fell under the power of the Macedonians, and was taken from them by the Ætolians, who held it till it was reduced by M. Fulvius Nobilior, who, having gained the metropolis after a four months ſiege, ſold all the citizens for ſlaves, adding the whole iſland to the dominions of his republic. Now called Cephalonia.

CEPHALONIA, the capital of an iſland of the ſame name, ſituated in the Mediterranean, near the coaſt of Epirus, and ſubject to the Venetians. E. Long. 21. N. Lat. 30. 30.

CEPHEUS, in fabulous hiſtory, a king of Arcadia, on whoſe head Minerva faſtening one of Meduſa's hairs, he was rendered invincible.

Cepheus, in aſtronomy, a conſtellation of the northern hemiſphere. See Astronomy, n° 406.

CERAM, an iſland in the Indian ocean, between the Molucca iſlands on the north, and thoſe of Amboina and Banda on the ſouth, lying between E. Long. 126. and 129. in S. Lat. 3. It is about 150 miles long, and 60 broad; and here the Dutch have a fortreſs, which keeps the natives in ſubjection.

CERAMBYX, in zoology, a genus of inſects of the beetle kind, belonging to the order of inſecta coleoptera. The antennæ are long and ſmall; the breaſt is ſpinous or gibbous; and the elytra are linear. There are no leſs than 83 ſpecies enumerated by Linnæus, principally diſtinguiſhed by the figure of the breaſt.

CERASTES, in zoology, the trival name of a ſpecies of Anguis and Coluber.

CERASTIUM, mouse-ear: A genus of the pentagynia order, belonging to the decandria claſs of plants; and in the natural method ranking under the 22d order, *Caryophyllei*. The calyx is pentaphyllous; the petals are bifid; the capſule is unilocular, and opening at the top. There are 16 ſpecies, but none of them poſſeſſed of any remarkable property.

CERASUS, in botany. See Prunus.

CERATE, in pharmacy, a thickiſh kind of ointment, applied to ulcerations, excoriations, &c. See Pharmacy, *Index*.

CERATION, the name given by the ancients to the ſmall ſeeds of Ceratonia, uſed by the Arabian phyſicians as a weight to adjuſt the doſes of medicines; as the grain weight with us took its riſe from a grain of barley.

Ceraton, or *ceration*, was alſo a ſilver coin, equal to one third of an obolus.

CERATOCARPUS, in botany: A genus of the monandria order, belonging to the monœcia claſs of plants; and in the natural method ranking under the 12th order, *Holoraceæ*. The male calyx is bipartite; there is no corolla; the filament is long: The female calyx is diphyllous, and grows to the germen; there is no corolla; the ſtyles are two; the ſeed is two-horned and compreſſed.

CERATONIA, the Carob Tree, or *St John's-bread*: A genus of the polyœcia order, belonging to the polygamia claſs of plants; and in the natural method ranking under the 33d order, *Lomentaceæ*. The calyx is hermaphrodite and quinquepartite; there is no corolla; the ſtamina are five; the ſtyle is filiform; the legumen coriaceous and polyſpermous. It is alſo diœcious, or male and female diſtinct on different plants. There is but one ſpecies, the ſiliqua, a native of Spain, of ſome parts of Italy, and the Levant. It is an ever-green; and, in the countries where it is native, grows in the hedges. It produces a quantity of long, flat, brown-coloured pods, which are thick, mealy, and of a ſweetiſh taſte. Theſe pods are many times eaten by the poorer ſort of inhabitants when there is a ſcarcity of other food; but they are apt to looſen the belly, and cauſe gripings of the bowels. They are called *St John's-bread*, from an ill-founded aſſertion of ſome writers on Scripture, that theſe pods were the locuſts St John eat with his honey in the wilderneſs. The tree may be propagated in this country from ſeeds, which are to be ſown in a moderate hot-bed, and the plants inured to the open air by degrees.

CERATOPHYLLUM, in botany: A genus of the polyandria order, belonging to the monœcia claſs of plants; and in the natural method ranking under the 15th order, *Inundatæ*. The male calyx is multipartite; no corolla; ſtamina from 16 to 20: The female calyx is multipartite; no corolla; one piſtil; no ſtyle; one naked ſeed.

CERAUNIA, Ceraunias, or Ceraunius *Lapis*, in natural hiſtory, a ſort of flinty ſtone, of no certain colour, but of a pyramidal or wedge-like figure; popularly ſuppoſed to fall from the clouds in the time of thunder-ſtorms, and to be poſſeſſed of divers outside virtues, as promoting ſleep, preſerving from lightning, &c. The word is from the Greek κεραυνὸς, *thunderbolt*. The ceraunia is the ſame with what is otherwiſe called the thunder-ſtone, or thunder-bolt; and alſo ſometimes *ſagitta*, or arrow's-head, on account of its ſhape. The ceraunia are frequently confounded with the ombriæ and brontiæ, as being all ſuppoſed to have the ſame origin. The generality of naturaliſts take the ceraunia for a native ſtone, formed among the Pyrites, of a ſaline, concrete, mineral juice. Mercatus and Dr Woodward aſſert it to be artificial, and to have been faſhioned thus by tools. The ceraunia, according to theſe authors, are the heads of the ancient weapons of war, in uſe before the invention of iron; which, upon the introduction of that metal, growing into diſuſe, were diſperſed in the fields through this and that neighbouring country. Some of them had poſſibly ſerved in the early ages for axes, others for wedges, others for chiſſels; but the greater part for arrow-heads, darts, and lances. The ceraunia is alſo held by Pliny for a white or cryſtal-coloured gem, that attracted lightning to itſelf. What this was, is hard to ſay. Prudentius alſo ſpeaks of a yellow ceraunia; by which he is ſuppoſed to mean the carbuncle or pyropus.

CERBERA, in botany: A genus of the monogynia

Cerbera ‖ Cercis — Cercis

nia order, belonging to the pentandria class of plants; and in the natural method ranking under the 30th order, *Contortæ*. The fruit is a monospermous plum. The most remarkable species is the *arvensis*, a native of the warm parts of America. It rises with an irregular stem to the height of eight or ten feet, sending out many crooked diffused branches, which towards their tops are garnished with thick succulent leaves of a lucid green, smooth, and very full of a milky juice. The flowers come out in loose bunches at the end of the branches; they are of a cream colour, having long narrow tubes, and at the top are cut into five obtuse segments, which seem twisted, so as to stand oblique to the tube. The wood of this tree stinks most abominably, and the kernels of the nuts are a deadly poison to which there is no antidote; so that the Indians will not even use the wood for fuel.

CERBERUS, in fabulous history, a dreadful three-headed mastiff, born of Typhon and Echidna, and placed to guard the gates of hell. He fawned upon those who entered, but devoured all who attempted to get back. He was, however, mastered by Hercules, who dragged him up to the earth, when, in struggling, a foam dropped from his mouth, which produced the poisonous herb called *aconite or wolf's-bane*.

Some have supposed that Cerberus is the symbol of the earth, or of all-devouring time; and that its three mouths represent the present, past, and future. The victory obtained by Hercules over this monster, denotes the conquest which this hero acquired over his passions. Dr Bryant supposes that Cerberus was the name of a place, and that it signified the temple of the Sun; deriving it from *Kir-Abor, the place of light*. This temple was also called *Tor-Caph-El*, which was changed to [illegible]; and hence Cerberus was supposed to have had three heads. It was likewise called *Tor-Keren, Turris Regia*; whence [illegible], from [illegible], *three*, and [illegible], *head*.

CERCELE, in heraldry: a *cross cercele* is a cross which, opening at the ends, turns round both ways like a ram's horn. See CROSS.

CERCIS, the JUDAS-TREE: A genus of the monogynia order, belonging to the decandria class of plants; and in the natural method ranking under the 33d order, *Lomentaceæ*. The calyx is quinquedentated, and gibbous below; the corolla papilionaceous, with a short vexillum or flag-petal under the wings or side-petals; a leguminous plant. There are only two species, both deciduous.

1. The Siliquastrum, common Judas-tree, or Italian cercis, a native of Italy and other parts of the south of Europe.—These differ in the height of their growth in different places: In some they will arrive to be fine trees, of near twenty feet high; whilst in others they will not rise to more than ten or twelve feet, sending forth young branches irregularly from the very bottom. The stem of this tree is of a dark-greyish colour, and the branches, which are few and irregular, have a purplish cast. The leaves are smooth, heart-shaped, and roundish, of a pleasant green on their upper surface, hoary underneath, and grow alternately on long footstalks. The flowers are of a fine purple: They come out early in the spring, in clusters, from the side of the branches, growing upon short footstalks; and in some situations they are succeeded by long flat pods, containing the seeds, which, in very favourable seasons, ripen in England. Some people are fond of eating these flowers in sallads, on which account alone in some parts this tree is propagated. The varieties of this species are, 1. The Flesh-coloured; 2. The White-flowered; and, 3. The Broad-podded Judas-tree.

2. The Canadensis, or Canadian cercis, will grow to the size of the first sort in some places. The branches are also irregular. The leaves are cordated, downy, and placed alternately. The flowers usually are of a palish red colour, and show themselves likewise in the spring, before the leaves are grown to their size. These too are often eaten in sallads, and afford an excellent pickle. There is a variety of this with deep red, and another with purple flowers. The pleasure which these trees will afford in a plantation may be easily conceived, not only as they exhibit their flowers in clusters, in different colours, early in the spring, before the leaves are grown to such a size as to hide them; but from the difference of the upper and lower surface of the leaves; the one being of a fine green, the other of a hoary cast; so that on the same tree, even in this respect, is shown variety; an improvement whereof is made by the waving winds, which will present them alternately to view.

Propagation. As these species will not take root by layers, they must be propagated by seeds, which may be had from abroad. They are generally brought us sound and good, and may be sown in the months of February or March. Making any particular compost for their reception is unnecessary; common garden mould, of almost every sort, will do very well: And this being well dug, and cleared of all roots, weeds, &c. lines may be drawn for the beds. The mould being fine, part of it should be taken out, and sifted over the seeds, after they are sown, about half an inch thick. Part of the seeds will come up in the spring, and the others will remain until the spring following; so that whoever is desirous of drawing the seedlings of a year old to plant out, must not destroy the bed, but draw them carefully out, and after that there will be a succeeding crop. However, be this as it will, the seeds being come up, they must be weeded, and encouraged by watering in the dry season; and they will require no farther care during the first summer. In the winter also they may be left to themselves, for they are very hardy; though not so much but that the ends of the branches will be killed by the frost, nay, sometimes to the very bottom of the young plant, where it will shoot out again afresh in the spring. Whoever, therefore, is desirous of securing his seedling-plants from this evil, should have his beds hooped, in order to throw mats over them during the hard frosts. Toward the latter end of March, or beginning of April, the plants having been in the seed-bed one or two years, they should be taken out, and planted in the nursery: The distance of one foot asunder, and two feet in the rows, should be given them. Hoeing the weeds down in the summer must also be allowed, as well as digging between the rows in the winter. Here they may stand until they are to be removed finally; but they must be gone over in the winter with the knife, and such irregular branches taken off

as

ts are produced near the root; by which management the tree may be trained up to a regular ſtem. Such, continues Hanbury, is the culture of the ſpecies of cercis; ſorts that are not to be omitted where there are any pretenſions to a collection. Beſides, the wood itſelf is of great value; for it poliſhes exceedingly well, and is admirably veined with black and green.

CERCOPITHECI, in natural hiſtory, the name given by Mr Ray to monkeys, or the claſs of apes with long tails. See Ape and Simia.

CERDA (*John Lewis de la*), a learned Jeſuit of Toledo, wrote large commentaries on Virgil, which have been much eſteemed; alſo ſeveral other works. He died in 1643, aged 80.

CERDONIANS, ancient heretics, who maintained moſt of the errors of Simon Magus, Saturnians, and the Manichees. They took their name from their leader *Cerdon*, a Syrian, who came to Rome in the time of pope Hyginus, and there abjured his errors; but in appearance only; for he was afterwards convicted of perſiſting in them, and accordingly caſt out of the church again. Cerdon aſſerted two principles, the one good and the other evil: this laſt, according to him, was the creator of the world, and the god that appeared under the old law. The firſt, whom he called *unknown*, was the father of Jeſus Chriſt; who, he taught, was incarnate only in appearance, and was not born of a virgin; nor did he ſuffer death but in appearance. He denied the reſurrection; and rejected all the books of the Old Teſtament, as coming from an evil principle. Marcion, his diſciple, ſucceeded him in his errors.

CEREALIA, in antiquity, feaſts of Ceres, inſtituted by Triptolemus, ſon of Celeus king of Eleuſine in Attica, in gratitude for his having been inſtructed by Ceres, who was ſuppoſed to have been his nurſe, in the art of cultivating corn and making bread.

There were two feaſts of this kind at Athens; the one called *Eleuſinia*, the other *Theſmophoria*. See the article Eleusinia. What both agreed in, and was common to all the *cerealia*, was, that they were celebrated with a world of religion and purity; ſo that it was eſteemed a great pollution to meddle, on thoſe days, in conjugal matters. It was not Ceres alone that was honoured here, but alſo Bacchus. The victims offered were hogs, by reaſon of the waſte they make in the products of the earth: whether there was any wine offered or not, is matter of much debate among the critics. Plautus and Macrobius ſeem to countenance the negative ſide; Cato and Virgil the poſitive. Macrobius ſays, indeed, they did not offer wine to Ceres, but *mulſum*, which was a compoſition of wine and honey boiled up together: that the ſacrifice made on the 21ſt of December to that goddeſs and Hercules, was a pregnant ſow, together with cakes and mulſum; and that this is what Virgil means by *Miti Baccho*. The *cerealia* paſſed from the Greeks to the Romans, who held them for eight days ſucceſſively; commencing, as generally held, on the fifth of the ides of April. It was the women alone who were concerned in the celebration, all dreſſed in white; the men, likewiſe in white, were only ſpectators. They eat nothing till after ſun-ſet; in memory of Ceres, who in her ſearch after her daughter took no repaſt but in the evening.

After the battle of Cannæ, the deſolation was ſo great at Rome, that there were no women to celebrate the feaſt, by reaſon they were all in mourning; ſo that it was omitted that year.

Cerealia, in botany, from *Ceres* the goddeſs of corn; Linnæus's name for the larger eſculent ſeeds of the graſſes: theſe are rice, wheat, rye, barley, oats, millet, panic graſs, Indian millet, holcus, zizania, and maize. To this head may be likewiſe referred darnel, (*lolium*), which, by preparation, is rendered eſculent.

CEREBELLUM, the hinder part of the head. See Anatomy, nº 133.

CEREBRUM, the brain. Its ſtructure and uſe are not ſo fully known as ſome other parts of the body, and different authors conſider it in various manners. However, according to the obſervations of thoſe moſt famed for their accuracy and dexterity in anatomical inquiries, its general ſtructure is as given in Anatomy, nº 132.

Dr Hunter obſerves, that the principal parts of the medullary ſubſtance of the brain in ideots and madmen, ſuch as the *thalami nervorum opticorum*, and *medulla oblongata*, are found entirely changed from a medullary to a hard, tough, dark-coloured ſubſtance, ſometimes reſembling white leather.

CEREMONIAL (*ceremoniale*), a book in which is preſcribed the order of the ceremonies to be obſerved in certain actions and occaſions of ſolemnity and pomp. The ceremonial of the Roman church is called *ordo Romanus*. It was publiſhed in 1516 by the biſhop of Corcyra; at which the college of cardinals were ſo ſcandalized, that ſome of them voted to have the author as well as book burnt, for his temerity in expoſing the ſacred ceremonies to the eyes of profane people.

Ceremonial is alſo uſed for the ſet or ſyſtem of rules and ceremonies which cuſtom has introduced for regulating our behaviour, and which perſons practiſe towards each other, either out of duty, decency, or civility.

Ceremonial, in a more particular ſenſe, denotes the manner in which princes and ambaſſadors uſe to receive and to treat one another. There are endleſs diſputes among ſovereigns about the *ceremonial*; ſome endeavouring to be on a level, and others to be ſuperior; inſomuch that numerous ſchemes have been propoſed for ſettling them. The chief are, 1. to accommodate the difference by compromiſe or alternation, ſo that one ſhall precede now, the other the next time; or one in one place, and the other in another: 2. By ſeniority; ſo that an elder prince in years ſhall precede a younger, without any other diſtinction. Theſe expedients, however, have not yet been accepted of by any, except ſome *alternate princes*, as they are called, in Germany.

Ceremonial is more particularly uſed in ſpeaking of the laws and regulations given by Moſes relating to the worſhip of God among the ancient Jews. In this ſenſe it amounts to much the ſame with what is called the *Levitical law*, and ſtands contradiſtinguiſhed from the moral as well as judicial law.

CEREMONY, an aſſemblage of ſeveral actions, forms, and circumſtances, ſerving to render a thing more magnificent and ſolemn.

In 1646, M. Ponce publiſhed a hiſtory of ancient ceremonies, tracing the riſe, growth, and introduction of such rite into the church, and its gradual advancement to superstition therein. Many of them were borrowed from Judaism; but more seemingly from Paganism. Dr Middleton has given a fine discourse on the conformity between the pagan and popish ceremonies, which he exemplifies in the use of incense, holy water, lamps, and candles, before the shrines of saints, votive gifts or offerings round the shrines of the deceased, &c. In effect, the altars, images, crosses, processions, miracles, and legends; nay, even the very hierarchy, pontificate, religious orders, &c. of the present Romans, he shows, are all copied from their heathen ancestors.—We have an ample and magnificent account of the religious ceremonies and customs of all nations in the world, represented in figures designed by Picart, with historical explanations, and many curious dissertations.

Master of the Ceremonies, an officer instituted by king James I. for the more honourable reception of ambassadors and strangers of quality. He wears about his neck a chain of gold, with a medal under the crown of Great Britain, having on one side an emblem of peace, with this motto, *Beati pacifici*; and on the other, an emblem of war, with *Dieu et mon droit*: his salary is 300 *l. per annum*.

Assistant Master of the Ceremonies, is to execute the employment in all points, whensoever the master of the ceremonies is absent. His salary is 142 *l.* 13 *s.* and 4 *d. per annum*.

Marshall of the Ceremonies is their officer, being subordinate to them both. His salary is 100 *l. per annum*.

CERENZA, a town of Italy in the kingdom of Naples, and in the Hither Calabria, with a bishop's see. It is seated on a rock, in E. Long. 17. 5. N. Lat. 39. 23.

CERES, a Pagan deity, the inventor or goddess of corn; in like manner as Bacchus was of wine.

According to the poets, she was the daughter of Saturn and Ops, and the mother of Proserpine, whom she had by Jupiter. Pluto having stolen away Proserpine, Ceres travelled all over the world in quest of her daughter, by the help of a torch, which she had lighted in Mount Ætna.

As Ceres was thus travelling in search of her daughter, she came to Celeus king of Eleusis, and undertook to bring up his infant son Triptolemus. Being desirous to render her charge immortal, she fed him in the day-time with divine milk, and in the night covered him with fire. Celeus observing an unusual improvement in his son, resolved to watch his nurse, to which end he hid himself in that part of the house where she used to cover the child with fire; but when he saw her put the infant under the embers, he cried out and discovered himself. Ceres punished the curiosity and indiscretion of the father with death. Afterwards she taught the youth the art of sowing corn and other fruits, and mounted him in a chariot drawn by winged dragons, that he might traverse the world, and teach mankind the use of corn and fruits. After this, having discovered, by means of the nymph Arethusa, that Proserpine was in the infernal regions, she applied to Jupiter, and obtained of him that Proserpine should be restored, on condition that she had tasted nothing during her stay in that place: but it being discovered, by the information of Ascalaphus, that, as she was walking in Pluto's orchard, she had gathered an apple, and had tasted of some of the seeds, she was for ever forbidden to return. Ceres, out of revenge, turned Ascalaphus into an owl. At length, Jupiter, to mitigate her grief, permitted that Proserpine should pass one half of the year in the infernal regions with Pluto, and the other half with her mother on earth.

Cicero speaks of a temple of Ceres at Catanea in Sicily, where was a very ancient statue of that goddess, but entirely concealed from the sight of men, every thing being performed by matrons and virgins.

CERET, a town of France in Roussillon, with a magnificent bridge of a single arch. It is seated near the river Tec, in E. Long. 2. 46. N. Lat. 42. 23.

CEREUS, in botany. See CACTUS.

CERIGO, an island in the Archipelago, anciently called *Cytherea*; noted for being the birth-place of Helen, and, as the poets say, of Venus. At present, there is nothing very delightful in the place; for the country is mountainous, and the soil dry. It abounds in hares, quails, turtles, and excellent falcons. It is about 50 miles in circumference, and had formerly good towns; but there is now none remaining but that which gives name to the island. This is strong both by art and nature, it being seated on a craggy rock. The inhabitants are Christian Greeks, and subject to the Venetians, who keep a governor there, whom they change every two years.

CERINES, a town in the island of Cyprus, with a good castle, an harbour, and a bishop's see. E. Long. 33. 35. N. Lat. 35. 28.

CERINTHE, HONEYWORT: A genus of the monogynia order, belonging to the pentandria class of plants; and in the natural method ranking under the 41st order, *Asperifoliæ*. The limb of the corolla is a ventricose tube with the throat pervious; and there are two bilocular seeds. There are three species, natives of Germany, Italy, and the Alps. They are low annual plants with purple, yellow, and red flowers, which may be propagated by seed sown in autumn, in a warm situation.

CERINTHIANS, ancient heretics, who denied the deity of Jesus Christ.—They took their name from Cerinthus, one of the first heresiarchs in the church, being cotemporary with St John. See CERINTHUS.

They believed that Jesus Christ was a mere man, born of Joseph and Mary; but that, in his baptism, a celestial virtue descended on him in form of a dove; by means whereof he was consecrated by the holy spirit, and made Christ. It was by means of this celestial virtue, therefore, that he wrought so many miracles; which, as he received it from heaven, quitted him after his passion, and returned to the place whence it came; so that Jesus, whom they called a *pure man*, really died and rose again; but that Christ, who was distinguished from Jesus, did not suffer at all. It was partly to refute this sect, that St John wrote his gospel. They received the gospel of St Matthew, to countenance their doctrine of circumcision, from Christ's being circumcised; but they omitted the genealogy. They discarded the epistles of St Paul, because that apostle held circumcision abolished.

CERINTHUS, a heresiarch, cotemporary with the apostles,

Ceropegia, Certhia.

apoſtles, aſcribed the creation not to God, but to angels. He taught that Jeſus Chriſt was the ſon of Joſeph; and that circumciſion ought to be retained under the goſpel. He is looked upon as the head of the converted Jews, who raiſed in the church of Antioch the tumult of which St Luke has given the hiſtory in the 15th chapter of the Acts. Some authors aſcribe the book of the apocalypſe to Cerinthus; adding, that he put it off under the name of St John, the better to authoriſe his reveries touching Chriſt's reign upon earth: and it is even certain that he publiſhed ſome works of this kind under the title of *Apocalypſe*. See APOCALYPSE.

CEROPEGIA, in botany: A genus of the monogynia order, belonging to the pentandria claſs of plants; and in the natural method ranking under the 30th order, *Contortæ*. There are two erect follicles; the ſeeds plumoſe or covered with a feathered pappus; the limb of the corolla connivent or cloſing at top.

Plate CXLV.

CERTHIA, in ornithology, the CREEPER or OX-EYE, a genus belonging to the order of picæ. The beak is arched, ſlender, ſharp, and triangular; the tongue is ſharp at the point; and the feet are of the walking kind, *i. e.* having the toes open and unconnected. Of this genus near 50 ſpecies have been enumerated by ornithologiſts; but Mr Latham ſuppoſes that many now deſcribed as ſpecies, will be found hereafter to be mere varieties; which, he adds, is no wonder, ſince many creepers do not gain their full plumage till the third year's moult. The following are a few of the moſt remarkable:

1. The familiaris, or common ox-eye, is grey above, and white underneath, with brown wings and ten white ſpots on the ten prime feathers. This bird is found in moſt parts of Europe, though it is believed no where ſo common as in Britain. It may be thought more ſcarce than it really is by the leſs attentive obſerver; for, ſuppoſing it on the body or branch of any tree, the moment it obſerves any one, it gets to the oppoſite ſide, and ſo on, let a perſon walk round the tree ever ſo often. The facility of its running on the bark of a tree, in all directions, is wonderful: This it does with as much eaſe as a fly on a glaſs window. Its food is principally, if not wholly, inſects, which it finds in the chinks and among the moſs of trees. It builds its neſt in ſome hole of a tree, and lays generally five eggs, very rarely more than ſeven: theſe are aſh-coloured, marked at the end with ſpots and ſtreaks of a deeper colour; and the ſhell is obſerved to be pretty hard. It remains in the places which it frequents during the winter, and builds its neſt early in the ſpring.

2. The hook-billed green creeper has a bill an inch and three quarters long, and bent quite in the ſhape of a ſemicircle; the plumage in general is olive green, paleſt beneath, and ſomewhat inclined to yellow: the quills and tail are duſky; the legs duſky brown; and the feathers juſt above the knee, or garter, white. It inhabits the Sandwich Iſlands in general, and is one of the birds whoſe plumage the natives make uſe of in conſtructing their feathered garments; which, having theſe olive-green feathers intermixed with the beautiful ſcarlet and yellow ones belonging to the next ſpecies, and yellow-tufted Bee-eater*, make ſome of the moſt beautiful coverings of theſe iſlanders.

* See Merops.

3. The hook-billed red creeper has the bill ſomewhat leſs hooked than the laſt ſpecies; the general colour of the plumage is ſcarlet; wings and tail black. In ſome birds the forehead is of a buff-colour; and the parts about the head and neck have both a mixture of buff and duſky black, which are ſuſpected to be the birds not yet arrived at their full plumage.

Certhia.

4. The puſilla, or brown and white creeper, according to Edwards, is not above half the ſize of our European creeper. The upper part of the body is brown, with a changeable gloſs of copper: the under parts are white; the quills brown, edged with gloſſy copper; the tail blackiſh, the outer feather tipped with white. The bird from which Edwards drew his figure had a label tied to it, by the name of Honey-thief. And that they are fond of honey is manifeſt, from thoſe who keep birds at the Cape of Good Hope having many ſorts in large cages, and ſupplying them with only honey and water; but beſides this, they catch a great many flies, which come within the reach of their confinement; and theſe two make up their whole ſubſiſtence; indeed, it has been attempted to tranſport them further, but the want of flies on board a ſhip prevented them living more than three weeks; ſo neceſſary are inſects to their ſubſiſtence.

5. The Loteni, or Loten's creeper, has the head, neck, back, rump, ſcapulars, and upper tail-coverts, of green gold: beneath, from the breaſt to the vent, of velvet black, which is ſeparated from the green on the neck by a tranſverſe bright violet band, a line and half in breadth: the leſſer wing coverts are of this laſt colour; the middle coverts are green gold; and the greater coverts are very fine black, edged with green gold on the outer edge: the quills are of the ſame colour, as are alſo the tail feathers. The female differs in having the breaſt, belly, ſides, thighs, under wing and tail coverts, of a dirty white, ſpotted with black; and the wings and tail not of ſo fine a black. It inhabits Ceylon, and Madagaſcar; and is called Angaladian.

Buffon tells us, that it makes its neſt of the down of plants, in form of a cup, like that of a chaffinch, the female laying generally five or ſix eggs; and that it is ſometimes chaſed by a ſpider as large as itſelf, and very voracious, which ſeizes on the whole brood, and ſucks the blood of the young birds.

6. The cærulea, or blue creeper, has the head of a moſt elegant blue; but on each ſide there is a ſtripe of black like velvet, in which the eye is placed; the chin and throat are marked with black in the ſame manner; the reſt of the body violet blue. It inhabits Cayenne. Seba ſays, that it makes its neſt with great art. The outſide is compoſed of dry ſtalks of graſs, or ſuch like; but within of very downy ſoft materials, in the ſhape of a retort, which it ſuſpends from ſome weak twig, at the end of a branch of a tree; the opening or mouth downwards, facing the ground: the neck is a foot in length, but the real neſt is quite at the top, ſo that the bird has to climb up this funnel-like opening to get at the neſt. Thus it is ſecure from every harm; neither monkey, ſnake, nor lizard, daring to venture at the end of the branch, as it would not ſteadily ſupport them.

7. The cardinal creeper, (*Lev. Muſ.*), has the head, neck, and breaſt, of crimſon colour; down the middle

cf

of the back is a stripe of the same colour to the rump: the rest of the body is black; and the wings and tail are black. It inhabits the cultivated parts of the island of Tanna; is there called Kuyameta, and lives by sucking the nectar of flowers.

8. The mocking creeper is of the size of the lesser thrush. On the cheeks is a narrow white spot: the head, especially on the crown, is inclined to violet: the plumage in general is olive green, inclining to yellow on the under parts: the quills are brown; the secondaries edged with olive: the colour of the tail is like that of the secondaries, and somewhat forked: the legs are dusky blue, and the claws black. It inhabits both the islands of New Zealand. It has an agreeable note in general; but at times so varies and modulates the voice, that it seems to imitate the notes of all other birds; hence it was called by the English the Mocking-bird. This bird being fond of thrusting its head into the bosom of flowers which have a purplish-coloured farina, much of it adheres to the feathers about the head and bill, and in course gives the appearance above mentioned; but this in time rubs off, and the colour of the head appears the same with the rest of the plumage.

CERTIFICATE *(Trial by)*, in the law of England, a species of trial allowed in such cases where the evidence of the person certifying is the only proper criterion of the point in dispute.*. For when the fact in question lies out of the cognizance of the court, the judges must rely on the solemn averment or information of persons in such a station as affords them the most clear and competent knowledge of the truth. As therefore such evidence, if given to a jury, must have been conclusive, the law, to save trouble and circuity, permits the fact to be determined upon such certificate merely. Thus, 1. If the issue be whether A was absent with the king in his army out of the realm in time of war, this shall be tried by the certificate of the mareschal of the king's host in writing under his seal, which shall be sent to the justices. 2. If, in order to avoid an outlawry, or the like, it was alleged that the defendant was in prison, *ultra mare*, at Bourdeaux, or in the service of the mayor of Bourdeaux, this should have been tried by the certificate of the mayor; and the like of the captain of Calais. But when this was law, those towns were under the dominion of the crown of England. And therefore, by a parity of reason, it should now hold, that in similar cases arising at Jamaica or Minorca, the trial should be by certificate from the governor of those islands. We also find that the certificate of the queen's messenger, sent to summon home a peeress of the realm, was formerly held a sufficient trial of the contempt in refusing to obey such summons. 3. For matters within the realm; the customs of the city of London shall be tried by the certificate of the mayor and aldermen, certified by the mouth of their recorder; upon a surmise from the party alleging it, that the custom ought to be thus tried: else it must be tried by the country. As, the custom of distributing the effects of freemen deceased; of enrolling apprentices; or that he who is free of one trade may use another; if any of these, or other similar points come in issue. 4. The trial of all customs and practice of the courts shall be by certificate from the proper officers of those courts respectively; and what return was made on a writ by the sheriff or under-sheriff, shall be only tried by his own certificate.

* See Trial.

Black's Comment.

CERTIORARI, in law, a writ which issues out of the chancery, directed to an inferior court, to call up the records of a cause there depending, in order that justice may be done. And this writ is obtained upon complaint, that the party who seeks it has received hard usage, or is not like to have an impartial trial in the inferior court. A certiorari is made returnable either in the king's bench, common pleas, or in chancery.

It is not only issued out of the court of chancery, but likewise out of the king's bench, in which last mentioned court it lies where the king would be certified of a record. Indictments from inferior courts, and proceedings of the quarter-sessions of the peace, may also be removed into the king's bench by a certiorari; and here the very record must be returned, and not a transcript of it; though usually in chancery, if a certiorari be returnable there, it removes only the tenor of the record.

CERTITUDE, considered in the things or ideas which are the objects of our understanding, is a necessary agreement or disagreement of one part of our knowledge with another: as applied to the mind, it is the perception of such agreement or disagreement; or such a firm well-grounded assent, as excludes not only all manner of doubt, but all conceivable possibility of a mistake.

There are three sorts of certitude, or assurance, according to the different natures and circumstances of things. 1. A physical or natural certitude, which depends upon the evidence of sense; as that I see such or such a colour, or hear such or such a sound; no body questions the truth of this, where the organs, the medium, and the object, are rightly disposed. 2. Mathematical certitude is that arising from mathematical evidence; such is, that the three angles of a triangle are equal to two right ones. 3. Moral certitude is that founded on moral evidence, and is frequently equivalent to a mathematical one; as that there was formerly such an emperor as Julius Cæsar, and that he wrote the commentaries which pass under his name; because the historians of those times have recorded it, and no man has ever disproved it since: this affords a moral certitude, in common sense so great, that one would be thought a fool or a madman for denying it.

CERTOSA, a celebrated Carthusian monastery, in the territory of the Pavese, in the duchy of Milan, four miles from Pavia; its park is surrounded with a wall 20 miles in circumference; but there are several small towns and villages therein.

CERVANTES. See SAAVEDRA.

CERVERA, a town of Spain, in Catalonia, seated on a small river of the same name, in E. Long. 1. 9. N. Lat. 41. 18.

CERVIA, a sea-port town of Italy, in Romagna, with a bishop's see, seated on the gulph of Venice, in E. Long. 13. 5. N. Lat. 44. 16.

CERVICAL NERVES, are seven pair of nerves, so called, as having their origin in the *cervix*, or neck.

Cervical Vessels, among anatomists, denote the arteries, veins, &c. which pass through the *vertebræ* and muscles of the neck, up to the skull.

Cervix ‖ Cervus.

CERVIX, in anatomy, properly denotes the hind part of the neck; as contradistinguished from the fore part, which is called *jugulum*, or the throat.

Cervix of the *Scapula*, denotes the head of the shoulder-blade, or that upper process whose *sinus* receives the head of the *humerus*.

Cervix of the *Uterus*, the neck of the *uterus*, or that oblong canal, or passage between the internal and external orifices, which receives and includes the *penis* like a sheath, whence it is also called Vagina.

CERUMEN, a thick, viscous, bitter, excrementitious humour, separated from the blood by proper glands placed in the *meatus auditorius*, or outer passage of the ear.

CERUSS, white-lead, a sort of calx of lead, made by exposing plates of that metal to the vapour of vinegar. See Chemistry-*Index*.

Ceruss, as a medicine, is used externally either mixed in ointments, or by sprinkling it on old gleeting and watery ulcers, and in many diseases of the skin. If, when it is reduced into a fine powder, it is received in with the breath in inspiration, and carried down into the lungs, it causes incurable asthmas. Instances of the very pernicious effects of this metal are too often seen among those persons who work lead in any form, but particularly among the workers in white-lead.

The painters use it in great quantities; and that it may be afforded cheap to them, it is generally adulterated with common whiting.

Plate CXXIX, CXXX, and CXXXI. **CERVUS**, or Deer, in zoology, a genus of quadrupeds belonging to the order of Pecora. The horns are solid, brittle, covered with a hairy skin, and growing from the top; they likewise fall off and are renewed annually. There are eight fore-teeth in the under jaw, and they have no dog-teeth. The species of this genus enumerated by Linnæus are seven, viz.

1. The Camelopardalis, or Giraffe, with simple or unbranched horns, straight, about six inches long, covered with hair, and truncated at the end and tufted; in the forehead a tubercle, about two inches high, resembling a third horn. The fore legs are not much longer than the hind legs; but the shoulders are of a vast length, which gives the disproportionate height between the fore and hind parts: the head is like that of a stag: the neck is slender and elegant, and on the upper side is a short mane; the ears are large: tail is long, with strong hairs at the end: the colour of the whole animal a dirty white, marked with large broad rusty spots. This is an uncommon animal, few of them having been ever seen in Europe. It inhabits the forests of Ethiopia, and other interior parts of Africa, almost as high as Senegal; but is not found in Guinea, or any of the western parts; nor farther south than about lat. 28. 10. It is very timid, but not swift; and has been represented as living only by browsing the trees, being unable from the disproportionate length of its fore legs to graze or feed from the ground. When it would leap, it lifts up its fore legs and then its hind, like a horse whose fore legs are tied. It runs very badly and awkwardly, and is very easily taken. The latest and best description of this extraordinary quadruped is given in the 16th number of a work entitled, "A Description of the uncommon Animals and remarkable Productions in the Cabinet and *Museum* of his Serene Highness the Prince of Orange;" by M. Vosmaer, Director of his Highness's Collections of Natural History. His account of the giraffe is composed partly from the notices of M. Vaillant and Mr Gordon of the Cape of Good Hope, and partly from his own observations on the skins of four of these animals, together with a complete skeleton, in the cabinet of curiosities under his care.

All the accounts we have of the giraffe, agree in representing its hind quarters as about 1½ feet lower than its withers: but from observations made by the late professor Camper on the above mentioned skeleton, it would appear that naturalists have been greatly mistaken in this particular. That its fore legs are longer than its hind legs, is indeed true; but the difference is not more than seven inches, which, in a height of seven feet, is no great matter. It may, however (the professor observes), be rendered apparently more considerable by the obliquity of the thigh-bone with respect to the tibia, when compared with that of the humerus to the radius.

The giraffe has always been celebrated for the gentleness of its disposition. Antonius Constantius, a writer of the 15th century, in a letter to Galeas Manfredi, Prince of Faenza, dated Fano, 16th December 1486, gives an account of a giraffe which he saw there. He says it was so gentle, that it would eat bread, hay, or fruit, out of the hand of a child; and that, when led through the street, it would take whatever food of this kind was offered to it by the spectators at the windows, as it passed along. This character is confirmed by Mr Gordon, who relates, that a giraffe, which he had wounded, suffered him to approach it as it lay on the ground, without offering to strike with its horns, or showing any inclination to revenge itself: he even stroked it over its eyes several times, when it only closed them, without any signs of resentment. Its throat was afterwards cut for the sake of its skin; and when in the pangs of death, it struck the ground with its feet with a force much exceeding that of any other animal, and these seem to be its principal means of defence. M. Vosmaer observes, that both the male and female are furnished with horns, which, from their size and form, seem intended merely for ornament: they appear to be excrescences of the *os frontis*, and therefore are probably not deciduous. The notion of some writers, that the giraffe cannot feed from the ground, is confuted by the testimony of M. Vaillant, who asserts, that it can even drink from a river, the surface of which is lower than the bank on which it stands. M. Vosmaer observes, that this account is confirmed by considering the structure of the neck, the vertebræ of which are connected with those of the back by a very strong ligament.

The giraffe here described, which Mr Gordon, who dissected it, says was the largest he had ever seen, was 15 feet 4 inches Rhinland measure (about 15 feet 10 inches English) from the ground to the top of its head; the length of the body, from the chest to the rump, was 5 feet 7 inches Rhinland measure. M. Vaillant asserts, that he has seen several which were at least 17 feet high; and M. Vosmaer declares, that he has been assured by some very respectable inhabitants of the Cape, that they had seen and killed giraffes,

which,

CERVUS. Plate CXXIX.

Camelopardalis.

Cervus.

which, including the horns, were 22 Rhinland feet in height.

The giraffe was known to the Romans in early times. It appears among the figures in the assemblage of eastern animals on the celebrated Prænestine Pavement, made by the direction of Sylla; and is represented both grazing and browsing, in its natural attitudes. It was exhibited at Rome by the popular Cæsar, among other animals in the Circæan games.

2. The Alces, Elk, or Moose Deer, has palmated horns, without any proper stem, and a fleshy protuberance on the throat. The neck is much shorter than the head, with a short, thick, upright mane, of a light brown colour. The eyes are small; the ears a foot long, very broad and slouching; nostrils very large; the upper lip square, hangs greatly over the lower, and has a deep sulcus in the middle, so as to appear almost bifid. This is the bulkiest animal of the deer kind, being sometimes 17 hands high, and weighing above 1200 pounds. The female is less than the male, and wants horns. The elks inhabit the isle of Cape Breton, Nova Scotia, and the western side of the bay of Fundy; Canada, and the country round the great lakes, almost as far south as the river Ohio. These are its present northern and southern limits. In all ages it affected the cold and woody regions in Europe, Asia, and America. They are found in all the woody tracts of the temperate parts of Russia, but not on the Arctic flats, nor yet in Kamtschatka. In Siberia they are of a monstrous size, particularly among the mountains. The elk and the moose, according to Mr Pennant, are the same species; the last derived from *musu*, which in the Algonkin language signifies that animal. The English used to call it the black moose, to distinguish it from the stag, which they named the grey moose. The French call it *Orignal*.

These animals reside amidst forests, for the conveniency of browsing the boughs of trees, because they are prevented from grazing with any kind of ease, by reason of the shortness of their necks and length of their legs. They often have recourse to water-plants, which they can readily get at by wading. M. Sarrasin says, that they are very fond of the anagyris fœtida, or stinking bean trefoil, and will uncover the snow with their feet in order to get at it. In passing through the woods, they raise their heads to a horizontal position, to prevent their horns from being entangled in the branches. They have a singular gait; their pace is a shambling trot, but they go with great swiftness. In their common walk they lift their feet very high, and will without any difficulty step over a gate five feet high. They feed principally in the night. If they graze, it is always against an ascent; an advantage they use for the reason above assigned. They ruminate like the ox. They go to rut in autumn; are at that time very furious, seeking the female by swimming from isle to isle. They bring two young at a birth, in the month of April, which follow the dam a whole year. During the summer they keep in families. In deep snows they collect in numbers in the forests of pines, for protection from the inclemency of the weather under the shelter of those evergreens. They are very inoffensive, except in the rutting-season; or except they are wounded, when they will turn on the assailant, and attack him with their horns, or trample him to death beneath their great hoofs.

Cervus.

The flesh of the moose is extremely sweet and nourishing. The Indians say, that they can travel three times farther after a meal of moose, than after any other animal food. The tongues are excellent; but the nose is perfect marrow, and esteemed the greatest delicacy in Canada. The skin makes excellent buff; being strong, soft, and light. The Indians dress the hide, and, after soaking it for some time, stretch and render it supple by a lather of the brains in hot water. They not only make their snow-shoes of the skin, but after a chase form the canoes with it; they sew the skins neatly together, cover the seams with an unctuous earth, and embark in them with their spoils to return home. The hair on the neck, withers, and hams of a full-grown elk, is of much use in making mattresses and saddles; being by its great length well adapted for those purposes. The palmated parts of the horns are farther excavated by the savages, and converted into ladles, which will hold a pint.

It is not strange that so useful an animal should be a principal object of chase. The savages perform it in different ways. The first, and the more simple, is before the lakes or rivers are frozen. Multitudes assemble in their canoes, and form with them a vast crescent, each horn touching the shore. Another party perform their share of the chase among the woods; they surround an extensive tract, let loose their dogs, and press towards the water with loud cries. The animals, alarmed with the noise, fly before the hunters, and plunge into the lake, where they are killed by the persons in the canoes, prepared for their reception, with lances or clubs. The other method is more artful. The savages inclose a large space with stakes hedged with branches of trees, forming two sides of a triangle; the bottom opens into a second inclosure, completely triangular. At the opening are hung numbers of snares, made of slips of raw hides. The Indians, as before, assemble in great troops, and with all kinds of noises drive into the first inclosure not only the mooses, but the other species of deer which abound in that country: some, in forcing their way into the farthest triangle, are caught in the snares by the neck or horns; and those which escape the snares, and pass the little opening, find their fate from the arrows of the hunters, directed at them from all quarters. They are often killed with the gun. When they are first unharboured, they squat with their hind parts and make water, at which instant the sportsman fires; if he misses, the moose sets off in a most rapid trot, making, like the rein-deer, a prodigious rattling with its hoofs, and will run for 20 or 30 miles before it comes to bay or takes the water. But the usual time for this diversion is the winter. The hunters avoid entering on the chase till the sun is strong enough to melt the frozen crust with which the snow is covered, otherwise the animal can run over the firm surface: they wait till it becomes soft enough to impede the flight of the moose; which sinks up to the shoulders, flounders, and gets on with great difficulty. The sportsman pursues at his ease on his broad rackets, or

snow-

Cervus. snow-shoes, and makes a ready prey of the distressed animals.

As weak against the mountain heaps they push
Their beating breast in vain, and piteous bray,
He lays them quivering on th' ensanguin'd snows,
And with loud shouts rejoicing bears them home.

THOMPSON.

The opinion of this animal's being subject to the epilepsy seems to have been universal, as well as the cure it finds by scratching its ear with the hind hoof till it draws blood. That hoof has been used in Indian medicine for the falling-sickness; they apply it to the heart of the afflicted, make him hold it in his left hand, and rub his ear with it. They use it also in the colic, pleurisy, vertigo, and purple fever; pulverising the hoof, and drinking it in water. The Algonkins pretend that the flesh imparts the disease; but it is notorious that the hunters in a manner live on it with impunity. The savages esteem the moose a beast of good omen; and are persuaded that those who dream often of it may flatter themselves with long life.

The elk was known to the Romans by the name of *Alce* and *Machlis*: they believed that it had no joints in its legs; and, from the great size of the upper lip, imagined it could not feed without going backward as it grazed.

3. The Elaphus, or Stag, with long cylindrical ramified horns bent backwards, and slender sharp brow antlers. The colour is generally a reddish brown with some black about the face, and a black list down the hind part of the neck and between the shoulders. Stags are common to Europe, Barbary, the north of Asia, and America. In spring, they shed their horns, which fall off spontaneously, or by rubbing them gently against the branches of trees. It is seldom that both horns fall off at the same time, the one generally preceding the other a day or two. The old stags cast their horns first, which happens about the end of February or beginning of March. An aged stag, or one in his seventh year or upwards, does not cast his horns before the middle of March; a stag of six years sheds his horns in April: young stags, or those from three to five years old, shed their horns in the beginning, and those which are in their second year, not till the middle or end of May. But in all this there is much variety; for old stags sometimes cast their horns sooner than those which are younger. Besides, the shedding of the horns is advanced by a mild, and retarded by a severe and long winter.

As soon as the stags cast their horns, they separate from each other, the young ones only keeping together. They no longer haunt the deepest recesses of the forest, but advance into the cultivated country, and remain among brushwood during the summer, till their horns are renewed. In this season, they walk with their heads low to prevent their horns from rubbing against the branches; for they continue to have sensibility till they acquire their full growth. The horns of the oldest stags are not half completed in the middle of May, and acquire their full length and hardness before the end of July. Those of the younger stags are proportionally later both in shedding and being renewed. But as soon as they have acquired their full dimensions and solidity, the stags rub them against the trees, in order to clear them of a skin with which they are covered. Cerv.

Soon after the stags have polished their horns, they begin to feel the impressions of love. Towards the end of August or beginning of September, they leave the coppice, return to the forests, and search for the hinds. They cry with a loud voice; their neck and throat swell; they become perfectly restless, and traverse in open day the fields and the fallow grounds; they strike their horns against trees and hedges; in a word, they seem to be transported with fury, and run from country to country till they find the hinds or females, whom they pursue and compel into compliance; for the female at first avoids and flies from the male, and never submits to his embraces till she be fatigued with the pursuit. The old hinds likewise come in season before the younger ones. When two stags approach the same hind, they must fight before they enjoy. If nearly equal in strength, they threaten, paw the ground, set up terrible cries, and attack each other with such fury, that they often inflict mortal wounds with the strokes of their horns. The combat never terminates but in the defeat or flight of one of the rivals. The conqueror loses not a moment in enjoying his victory, unless another rival approaches, whom he is again obliged to attack and repel. The oldest stags are always masters of the field; because they are stronger and more furious than the young ones, who must wait patiently till their superiors tire, and quit their mistresses. Sometimes, however, the young stags accomplish their purposes when the old ones are fighting, and, after a hasty gratification, fly off. The hinds prefer the old stags, not because they are most courageous, but because they are much more ardent. They are likewise more inconstant, having often several females at a time; and when a stag has but one hind, his attachment to her does not continue above a few days: He then leaves her, goes in quest of another, with whom he remains a still shorter time; and in this manner passes from one to another till he is perfectly exhausted.

This ardour of love lasts only three weeks, during which the stags take very little food, and neither sleep nor rest. Night and day, they are either walking, running, fighting, or enjoying the hinds. Hence, at the end of the rutting season, they are so meagre and exhausted, that they recover not their strength for a considerable time. They generally retire to the borders of the forests, feed upon the cultivated fields, where they find plenty of nourishment, and remain there till their strength is re-established. The rutting season of old stags commences about the beginning, and ends about the 20th day of September. In those of six or seven years old, it begins about the 10th of September, and concludes in the beginning of October. In young stags, or those in their third, fourth, or fifth year, it begins about the 20th of September, and terminates about the 15th of October; and at the end of October, the rutting is all over, excepting among the *prickets*, or those which have entered into their second year; because they, like the young hinds, are latest of coming into season. Hence, at the beginning of November, the season of love is entirely finished; and the stags, during this period of weakness and lassitude, are easily hunted down. In seasons when acorns and

Cervus.

and other nuts are plentiful, the stags soon recover their strength, and a second rutting frequently happens at the end of October; but it is of much shorter duration than the first.

In climates warmer than that of France, the rutting time, like the seasons, is more forward. Aristotle informs us, that, in Greece, it commences in the beginning of August, and terminates about the end of September. The hinds go with young eight months and some days, and seldom produce more than one fawn. They bring forth in May or the beginning of June, and so anxiously conceal their fawns, that they often expose themselves to be chased, with a view to draw off the dogs, and afterwards return to take care of their young. All hinds are not fertile; for some of them never conceive. These barren hinds are grosser and fatter than those which are prolific, and also come soonest in season. The young are not called *fawns* or *calves* after the sixth month: The knobs of their horns then begin to appear, and they take the name of *knobbers* till their horns lengthen into *spears*, and then they are called *brocks* or *staggards*. During the first season, they never leave their mothers. In winter, the stags and hinds, of all ages, keep together in flocks, which are always more numerous in proportion to the rigour of the season. They separate in spring: The hinds retire to bring forth; and, during this period, the flocks consist only of knobbers and young stags. In general, the stags are inclined to associate, and nothing but fear or necessity obliges them to disperse.

The life of the stag is spent in alternate plenty and want, vigour and debility, health and sickness, without having any change introduced into his constitution by these opposite extremes. He lives as long as other animals which are not subjected to such vicissitudes. As he grows five or six years, he lives seven times that number, or from 35 to 40 years. What has been reported concerning the longevity of the stag merits no credit. It is only a popular prejudice which prevailed in the days of Aristotle, and which that philosopher considered as improbable, because neither the time of gestation, nor of the growth of the young stag, indicated long life. This authority ought to have abolished the prejudice; but it has been renewed, in the ages of ignorance, by a fabulous account of a stag taken by Charles VI. in the forest of Senlis, with a collar upon which was written this inscription, *Cæsar hoc me donavit*. The love of the marvellous inclined men to believe that this animal had lived 1000 years, and had his collar from a Roman emperor, rather than to suppose that he came from Germany, where all the emperors take the name of *Cæsar*.

The stag appears to have a fine eye, an acute smell, and an excellent ear. When listening, he raises his head, erects his ears, and hears from a great distance. When he is going into a coppice, or other half covered place, he stops to look round him on all sides, and scents the wind, to discover if any object is near that might disturb him. He is a simple, and yet a curious and crafty animal. When hissed or called to from a distance, he stops short, and looks stedfastly, and with a kind of admiration, at carriages, cattle, or men; and if they have neither arms nor dogs, he moves on unconcernedly, and without flying. He appears to listen, with great tranquillity and delight, to the shepherd's pipe; and the hunters sometimes employ this artifice to encourage and deceive him. In general, he is less afraid of men than of dogs, and is never suspicious, or uses any arts of concealment, but in proportion to the disturbances he has received. He eats slow, and has a choice in his aliment; and after his stomach is full, he lies down, and ruminates at leisure. He seems to ruminate with less facility than the ox. It is only by violent shakes that the stag can make the food rise from his first stomach. This difficulty proceeds from the length and direction of the passage through which the aliment has to go. The neck of the ox is short and straight, but that of the stag is long and arched; and therefore greater efforts are necessary to raise the food. These efforts are made by a kind of hiccup, the movement of which is apparent, and continues during the time of rumination. His voice is stronger, and more quivering, in proportion as he advances in years. The voice of the hind is shorter and more feeble. She never bellows from love, but from fear. The stag, during the rutting season, bellows in a frightful manner: He is then so transported, that nothing disturbs or terrifies him. He is therefore easily surprised; as he is loaded with fat, he cannot keep long before the dogs. But he is dangerous when at bay, and attacks the dogs with a species of fury. He drinks none in winter nor in spring, the dews and tender herbage being then sufficient to extinguish his thirst; but, during the parching heats of summer, to obtain drink, he frequents the brooks, the marshes, and the fountains; and in the season of love, he is so over-heated, that he searches every where for water, not only to satisfy his immoderate thirst, but to bathe and refresh his body. He then swims easier than at any other times on account of his fatness. He has been observed crossing very large rivers. It has even been alleged, that, attracted by the odour of the hinds, the stags, in the rutting season, throw themselves into the sea, and pass from one island to another at the distance of several leagues. They leap still more nimbly than they swim; for, when pursued, they easily clear a hedge or a pale fence of six feet high. Their food varies in different seasons. In autumn, after rutting, they search for the buds of green shrubs, the flowers of broom or heath, the leaves of brambles, &c. During the snows of winter, they feed upon the bark, moss, &c. of trees; and in mild weather, they browse in the wheat-fields. In the beginning of spring, they go in quest of the catkins of the trembling poplar, willow, and hazel-trees, the flowers and buds of the cornel tree, &c. In summer, when they have great choice, they prefer rye to all other grain, and the black berry-bearing alder to all other wood. The flesh of the fawn is very good; that of the hind and knobber not absolutely bad; but that of the stag has always a strong and disagreeable taste. The skin and the horns are the most useful parts of this animal. The skin makes a pliable and very durable leather. The horns are used by cutlers, sword-slippers, &c. and a volatile spirit, much employed in medicine, is extracted from them by the chymists.

In America, stags feed eagerly on the broad-leaved kalmia; yet that plant is a poison to all other horned animals: their intestines are found filled with it during winter. If their entrails are given to dogs, they become stupified, and as if drunk, and often are so ill

Cervus. as hardly to escape with life. The American stags grow very fat; their tallow is much esteemed for making of candles. The Indians shoot them. As they are very shy animals, the natives cover themselves with a hide, leaving the horns erect; under shelter of which they walk within reach of the herd. De Brie, in the 25th plate of the History of Florida, gives a very curious representation of this artful method of chase, when it was visited by the French in 1564. Their skins are an article of commerce imported by the Hudson's Bay company; but brought from the distant parts far inland by the Indians, who bring them from the neighbourhood of the lakes. In most parts of North America they are called the grey moose, and the elk; this has given occasion to the mistaken notion of that great animal being found in Virginia and other southern provinces.

In Britain the stag is become less common than formerly; its excessive viciousness during the rutting season, and the badness of its flesh, induce most people to part with the species. Stags are still found wild in the Highlands of Scotland, in herds of four or five hundred together, ranging at full liberty over the vast hills of the north. Formerly the great Highland chieftains used to hunt with the magnificence of an eastern monarch, assembling four or five thousand of their clan, who drove the deer into the toils or to the stations the lairds had placed themselves in; but as this pretence was frequently used to collect their vassals for rebellious purposes, an act was passed prohibiting any assemblies of this nature. Stags are likewise met with on the moors that border on Cornwal and Devonshire; and in Ireland on the mountains of Kerry, where they add greatly to the magnificence of the romantic scenery to the lake of Killarny. The stags of Ireland during its uncultivated state, and while it remained an almost boundless tract of forest, had an exact agreement in habit with those that range at present through the wilds of America. They were less in body, but very fat; and their horns of a size far superior to those of Europe, but in form agreed in all points.

The chace of the stag has been formed into an art, and requires a species of knowledge which can only be learned by experience: It implies a royal assemblage of men, horses, and dogs, all so trained, practised, and disciplined, that their movements, their researches, and their skill, must concur in producing one common end. The huntsman should know the age and the sex of the animal; he should be able to distinguish with precision, whether the stag he has harboured with his hound be a knobber, a young stag, in his sixth or seventh year, or an old stag. The chief marks which convey this intelligence is derived from the foot, and the excrement. The foot of the stag is better formed than that of the hind, or female. Her leg is more gross and nearer the heel. The impressions of his feet are rounder, and farther removed from each other. He moves more regularly, and brings the hind foot into the impression made by the fore-foot. But the distance between the steps of the hind are shorter, and her hind-feet strike not so regularly the track of the fore feet. As soon as the stag acquires his fourth horns, he is easily distinguished; but to know the foot of a young stag from that of a hind, requires repeated experience. Stags of six, seven, &c. years, are still more easily known; for their fore foot is much larger than the hind foot; the older they are, the sides of their feet are the more worn; the distance of their steps are more regular than those of young stags; they always place their hind-foot exactly in the track of the fore-foot, excepting, when they shed their horns, the old stags misplace, at this season, nearly as often as the young ones; but in this they are more regular than the hind or young stag, placing the hind foot always at the side of the fore-foot, and never beyond or within it. When the huntsman, from the dryness of the season, or other circumstances, cannot judge by the foot, he is obliged to trace the animal backwards, and endeavour to find his dung. This mark requires, perhaps, greater experience than the knowledge of the foot; but without it the huntsman would be unable to give a proper report to the company. After the report of the huntsman, and the dogs are led to the refuge of the stag, he ought to encourage his hound, and make him rest upon the track of the stag, till the animal be unharboured. Instantly the alarm is given to uncouple the dogs, which ought to be enlivened by the voice and the horn of the huntsman. He should also diligently observe the foot of the stag, in order to discover whether the animal has started, and substituted another in his place. But it is then the business of the hunters to separate also, and to recal the dogs which have gone astray after false game. The huntsman should always accompany his dogs, and encourage, without pressing them too hard. He should assist them in detecting all the arts of escape used by the stag; for this animal has remarkable address in deceiving the dogs. With this view, he often returns twice or thrice upon his former steps; he endeavours to raise hinds or younger stags to accompany him, and draw off the dogs from the object of their pursuit: he then flies with redoubled speed, or springs off at side, lies down on his belly, and conceals himself. In this case, when the dogs have lost his foot, the huntsmen, by going backwards and forwards, assist them in recovering it. But if they cannot find it, they suppose that he is resting within the circuit they have made, and go in quest of him. But if they are still unable to discover him, there is no other method left, but, from viewing the country, to conjecture where he may have taken refuge, and repair to the place. As soon as they have recovered his foot, and put the dogs upon the track, they pursue with more advantage, because they perceive that the stag is fatigued. Their ardour augments in proportion to his feebleness; and their scent becomes more distinct as the animal grows warm. Hence they redouble their cries and their speed; and though the stag practises still more arts of escape than formerly, as his swiftness is diminished, his arts and doublings become gradually less effectual. He has now no other resource but to fly from the earth which he treads, and get into the waters, in order to cut off the scent from the dogs. The huntsmen go round these waters, and again put the dogs on the track of his foot. The stag, after taking to the water, is incapable of running far, and is soon at bay. But he still attempts to defend his life, and often wounds the dogs, and even the huntsmen when too forward, by blows with his horns, till one of them cuts his hams

CERVUS. Plate CXXX.

horns to make him fall, and then puts an end to his life by a blow of a hanger. They now celebrate the death of the stag by a flourish of their horns; the dogs are allowed to trample upon him, and at last partake richly of the victory by devouring his flesh.

4. The Tarandus, or Rein-deer, is a native of Lapland, and the northern parts of Europe, Asia, and America. The horns are large, cylindrical, branched, and palmated at the tops. Two of the branches hang over the face. He is about the size of a buck, of a dirty whitish colour; the hairs of his skin are thick and strong. To the Laplanders this animal is the substitute of the horse, the cow, the goat, and the sheep; and is their only wealth: the milk affords them cheese; the flesh, food; the skin, clothing; the tendons, bow-strings; and when split, thread; the horns, glue; the bones, spoons. During the winter it supplies the want of a horse, and draws their sledges with amazing swiftness over the frozen lakes and rivers, or over the snow, which at that time covers the whole country. A rich Laplander is possessed of a herd of 1000 rein deer. In autumn they seek the highest hills, to avoid the Lapland gad-fly, which at that time deposits its eggs in their skin; it is the pest of these animals, and numbers die that are thus visited. The moment a single fly appears, the whole herd instantly perceives it; they fling up their heads, toss about their horns, and at once attempt to fly for shelter amidst the snows of the loftiest Alps. In summer they feed on several plants; but during winter on the rein-liverwort, which lies far beneath the snow, which they remove with their feet and palmated brow antlers, in order to get at their beloved food.

The Samoieds, less intelligent than the Laplanders, consider them in no other view than as animals of draught, to convey them to the chase of the wild reins; which they kill for the sake of the skins, either to clothe themselves, or to cover their tents. They know not the cleanly delicacy of the milk or cheese; but prefer for their repast the intestines of beasts, or the half-putrid flesh of a horse, ox, or sheep, which they find dead on the high road.—The Koreki, a nation of Kamtschatka, may be placed on a level with the Samoieds. They keep immense herds of reins; some of the richest to the amount of 10 or 20 thousand; yet so sordid are they as to eat none except such as they kill for the sake of the skins; an article of commerce with their neighbours the Kamtschatkans; otherwise they content themselves with the flesh of those which die by disease or chance. They train them in the sledge, but neglect them for every domestic purpose. Their historian says, they couple two to each carriage; and that the deer will travel 150 versts in a day, that is, 112 English miles. They castrate the males by piercing the spermatic arteries, and tying the scrotum tight with a thong.—The savage and uninformed Eskimaux and Greenlanders, who possess, amidst their snows, these beautiful animals, neglect not only the domestic uses, but even are ignorant of their advantage in the sledge. Their element is properly the water; their game the seals. They seem to want powers to domesticate any animals except dogs. They are at enmity with all; consider them as an object of chase, and of no utility till deprived of life. The flesh of the rein is the most coveted part of their food; they eat it raw, dressed, and dried and smoked with the snow lichen. The wearied hunters will drink the raw blood; but it is usually dressed with the berries of the heath; they eagerly devour the contents of the stomach, but use the intestines boiled. They are very fond of the fat, and will not lose the least bit. The skin, sometimes a part of their cloathing, dressed with the hair on, is soft and pliant; it forms also the inner lining of their tents, and most excellent blankets. The tendons are their bow-strings, and when split are the threads with which they sew their jackets.

The Greenlanders, before they acquired the knowledge of the gun, caught them by what was called the *clapper-hunt*. The women and children surrounded a large space, and, where people were wanting, set up poles capped with a turf in certain intervals, to terrify the animals; they then with great noise drove the reins into the narrow defiles, where the men lay in wait and killed them with harpoons or darts. But they are now become very scarce.

The rein-deers are found in the neighbourhood of Hudson's Bay, in most amazing numbers, columns of eight or ten thousand are seen annually passing from north to south in the months of March and April, driven out of the woods by the musketoes, seeking refreshment on the shore, and a quiet place to drop their young. They go to rut in September, and the males soon after shed their horns; they are at that season very fat, but so rank and musky as not to be eatable. The females drop their young in June, in the most sequestered spots they can find; and then they likewise lose their horns. Beasts of prey follow the herds: first, the wolves, who single out the stragglers (for they fear to attack the drove), destroy and hunt them down; the foxes attend at a distance, to pick up the offals left by the former. In autumn the deer with the fawns remigrate northward. The Indians are very attentive to their motions; for the rein forms the chief part not only of their dress but of their food. They often kill multitudes for the sake of their tongues only; but generally they separate the flesh from the bones, and preserve it by drying it in the smoke; they also save the fat, and sell it to the English in bladders, who use it in frying instead of butter. The skins are also an article of commerce, and used in London by the Breeches-makers. The Indians shoot them in the winter. The English make hedges with stakes and boughs of trees along the woods for five miles in length, leaving openings at proper intervals beset with snares, in which multitudes are taken. The Indians also kill great numbers during the season of migration, watching in their canoes, and spearing them while passing over the rivers of the country, or from island to island; for they swim most admirably well.

5. The Dama or Fallow-deer, Buck and Doe; with horns branched, compressed, and palmated at the top. The colour is various; reddish, deep brown, white or spotted. This species is not so universal as the stag: rare in France and Germany. It is found in Greece, the Holy Land, and the north of China. They are very numerous in England; but, except on a few chases, confined in parks. None originally in America. They are easily tamed; and their flesh, which goes by the name of venison, is in high esteem among the luxurious. During rutting-time they will contend

Cervus.

with each other for their mistress, but are less fierce than the stag; during that season, the male will form a hole in the ground, make the female lie down in it, and then often walk round and smell at her. Moore speaks of a species found on the banks of the Gambia, in the interior parts of Africa, near Barracunda, called *Tangceag*, which he says differed not in form from the English fallow-deer; only that its size was equal to that of a small horse, and weighed 300 lb. It had also on its neck an erect black mane, four or five inches long.—Mr White, in his Natural History of Selborne, mentions, as a piece of information to naturalists, that if some curious gentleman would procure the head of a fallow deer, and have it dissected, he would find it furnished with two *spiracula*, or breathing-places, besides the nostrils; probably analogous to the *puncta lachrymalia* in the human head. When deer are thirsty they plunge their noses, like some horses, very deep under water, while in the act of drinking, and continue them in that situation for a considerable time; but, to obviate any inconveniency, they can open two vents, one at the inner corner of each eye, having a communication with the nose. This seems, as our author observes, to be an extraordinary provision of nature; for it looks as if these creatures could not be suffocated, though their mouths and nostrils were both stopped. This curious formation of the head, he farther remarks, may be of singular service to beasts of chase, by affording them free respiration; and no doubt these additional nostrils are thrown open when they are hard run. Mr Pennant has observed the same curious organization in the antelope. See CAPRA.

6. The Capreolus, or Roe-buck, has erect, cylindrical, branched horns, and forked at the top. His size is only three feet nine inches long, two feet three inches high before, and two feet seven inches high behind: weight from 50 to 60 lb. Though the least of the deer-kind, his figure is most elegant and handsome. His eyes are more brilliant and animated than those of the stag. His limbs are more nimble, his movements quicker, and he bounds, seemingly without effort, with equal vigour and agility. His coat, or hair, is always clean, smooth, and glossy. He never wallows in the mire like the stag. He delights in dry and elevated situations, where the air is purest. He is likewise more crafty, conceals himself with greater address, is more difficult to trace, and derives superior resources from instinct: for though he has the misfortune to leave behind him a stronger scent than the stag, which redoubles the ardour and appetite of the dogs, he knows how to withdraw himself from their pursuit, by the rapidity with which he begins his flight, and by his numerous doublings. He delays not his arts of defence till his strength fails him; but, as soon as he finds that the first efforts of a rapid chace have been unsuccessful, he repeatedly returns on his former steps; and after confounding, by these opposite movements, the direction he has taken, after intermixing the present with the past emanations from his body, he rises from the earth by a great bound, and, retiring to a side, he lies down flat on his belly; and in this immoveable situation, he allows the whole troop of his deceived enemies to pass very near him.

The roe-deer differs from the stag and fallow-deer in disposition, temperament, manners, and almost every natural habit. Instead of associating in herds, they live in separate families. The father, mother, and young, go together, and never mix with strangers. They are constant in their amours, and never unfaithful like the stag. As the females generally produce two fawns, the one male and the other female, these young animals, brought up and nourished together, acquire so strong a mutual affection, that they never quit each other, unless one of them meets with a misfortune, which never ought to separate lovers. This attachment is more than love; for though always together, they feel the ardour of the rut but once a year, and it continues only fifteen days, commencing at the end of October, and ending before the fifteenth day of November. They are not then, like the stag, over-loaded with fat; they have no strong smell, no fury, in a word, nothing that can change the state of their bodies. During this period, they indeed suffer not their fawns to remain with them. The father drives them off, as if he meant to oblige them to yield their place to those which are to succeed, and to form new families for themselves. However, after the rutting season is past, the fawns return to their mother, and remain with her some time; after which they separate for ever, and remove to a distance from the place which gave them birth.

The female goes with young five months and a half, and brings forth about the end of April or beginning of May. She produces two at a time, which she is obliged to conceal from the buck while very young. In 10 or 12 days they acquire strength sufficient to enable them to follow her. When threatened with danger, she hides them in a close thicket, and, to preserve them, presents herself to be chaced. But notwithstanding all her care and anxiety, the young are sometimes carried off by men, dogs, or wolves.

Roe-bucks prefer a mountainous woody country to a plain one. They were formerly very common in Wales, in the north of England, and in Scotland; but at present the species nowhere exists in Great Britain except in the Scottish highlands. In France they are more frequent; they are also found in Italy, Sweden, and Norway; and in Asia they are met with in Siberia. The first that are met with in Great Britain are in the woods on the south side of Loch-Rannoch, in Perthshire: the last in those of Longwal, on the southern borders of Caithness; but they are most numerous in the beautiful forests of Invercauld, in the midst of the Grampian hills. They are unknown in Ireland. Wild roes, during summer, feed on grass; and are very fond of the *rubus saxatilis*, called in the Highlands the roe-buck berry; but in the winter time, when the ground is covered with snow, they browse on the tender branches of the fir and birch.

7. The Guineensis, about the size of a cat, is of a grayish colour, and black underneath. It is a native of Guinea, and the size and figure of its horns have not been hitherto described with any precision.

8. The Axis, or Speckled Deer, has slender trifurcated horns; the first branch near the base, the second near the top, each pointing upwards. This species is about the size of the fallow-deer; of a light red colour; the body beautifully marked with white spots; along

Cervus. along the lower part of the sides, near the belly, is a line of white; the tail long, as that of a fallow-deer; red above, white beneath.—They are common on the banks of the Ganges, and in the isle of Ceylon. Pliny describes them well among the animals of India, and adds that they were sacred to Bacchus. They will bear our climate; and have bred in the prince of Orange's menagery near the Hague. They are very tame, and have the sense of smelling in an exquisite degree. They readily eat bread, but will refuse a piece that has been breathed on; many other animals of this, the antelope and goat kind, will do the same.

9. The Porcine or Hog Deer, has slender trifurcated horns, 13 inches long: His body is thick and clumsy; his legs are fine and slender: The upper part of the neck, body, and sides, are brown; belly and rump, of a lighter colour.—They are found in Bengal; and called, from the thickness of their body, *hog-deer*. The same species is also found in Borneo. They are taken in square pit-falls, about four feet deep, covered with some slight materials. Of their feet, as well as those of the lesser species of musks and antelopes, are made tobacco stoppers.

10. The Virginiana, or Virginian Deer, has slender horns, bending very much forward; numerous branches on the interior sides; no brow antlers. It is about the size of the English fallow-deer; of a light colour, cinereous brown. A quite distinct species, and peculiar to America. It inhabits all the provinces south of Canada, but in greatest abundance in the southern; but especially the vast savannas contiguous to the Missisippi, and the great rivers which flow into it. They graze in herds innumerable, along with the stags and buffaloes. This species probably extends to Guiana, and is the *biche* of that country, which is said to be about the size of a European buck, with short horns, bending at their ends. They are capable of being made tame; and when properly trained, are used by the Indians to decoy the wild deer (especially in the rutting season) within shot. Both bucks and does herd from September to March; after that they separate, and the does secrete themselves to bring forth, and are found with difficulty. The bucks from this time keep separate till the amorous season of September revolves. The deer begin to feed as soon as night begins; and sometimes, in the rainy season, in the day; otherwise they seldom or never quit their haunts. An old American sportsman has remarked, that the bucks will keep in the thickets for a year, or even two.

These animals are very restless, and always in motion, coming and going continually. Those which live near the shores are lean and bad, subject to worms in their heads and throats, generated from the eggs deposited in those parts. Those that frequent the hills and savannas are in better case, but the venison is dry. In hard winters they will feed on the long moss which hangs from the trees in the northern parts.

These and other cloven-footed quadrupeds of America are very fond of salt, and resort eagerly to the places impregnated with it. They are always seen in great numbers in the spots where the ground has been torn by torrents or other accidents, where they are seen licking the earth. Such spots are called *licking-places*. The huntsmen are sure of finding the game there; for notwithstanding they are often disturbed, the buffaloes and deer are so passionately fond of the savoury regale, as to bid defiance to all danger, and return in droves to their favourite haunts.

The deer are of the first importance to the savages. The skins form the greatest branch of their traffick, by which they procure from the colonists, by way of exchange, many of the articles of life. To all of them the flesh is the principal food throughout the year; for drying it over a gentle but clear fire, after cutting it into small pieces, it is not only capable of long preservation, but is very portable in their sudden excursions, especially when reduced to powder, which is frequently done.

Hunting is more than an amusement to these people. They give themselves up to it not only for the sake of subsistence, but to fit themselves for war, by habituating themselves to fatigue. A good huntsman is an able warrior. Those who fail in the sports of the field are never supposed to be capable of supporting the hardships of a campaign; they are degraded to ignoble offices, such as dressing the skins of deer, and other employs allotted only to slaves and women. When a large party meditates a hunting match, which is usually at the beginning of winter, they agree on a place of rendezvous, often 500 miles distant from their homes, and a place perhaps that many of them had never been at. They have no other method of fixing on the spot than by pointing with their finger. The preference is given to the eldest, as the most experienced. When this matter is settled, they separate into small parties, travel and hunt for subsistence all the day, and rest at night; but the women have no certain resting-places. The savages have their particular hunting countries; but if they invade the limits of those belonging to other nations, feuds ensue, fatal as those between Percy and Douglas in the famed Chevy Chace. As soon as they arrive on the borders of the hunting country (which they never fail doing to a man, be their respective routes ever so distant or so various), the captain of the band delineates on the bark of a tree his own figure, with a rattlesnake twined round him with distended mouth; and in his hand a bloody tomahawk. By this he implies a destructive menace to any who are bold enough to invade their territories, or to interrupt their diversion.—The chase is carried on in different ways. Some surprise the deer by using the skin of the head, horns, and hide; but the general method is performed by the whole body. Several hundreds disperse in a line, encompassing a vast space of country, fire the woods, and drive the animals into some strait or peninsula, where they become an easy prey. The deer alone are not the object; foxes, raccoons, bears, and all beasts of fur, are thought worthy of attention, and form articles of commerce with the Europeans.

The number of deer destroyed in some parts of America is incredible; as is pretended, from an absurd idea which the savages have, that the more they destroy, the more they shall find in succeeding years. Certain it is that multitudes are destroyed; the tongues only preserved, and the carcases left a prey to wild beasts. But the motive is much more political. The savages well discern, that should they overstock the market, they would certainly be over-reached by the European dealers, who take care never to produce more goods than are barely sufficient for the demand of the season, establishing their prices according to the quantity of furs brought by the natives.

Cervus Volans, in natural history, a name given by authors to the stag-fly, or horned beetle, a very large species of beetle with horns shaped, and something like those of the stag.

CERYX, in antiquity. The ceryces were a sort of public criers appointed to proclaim or publish things aloud in assemblies. The *ceryx* among the Greeks answered to the *præco* among the Romans. Our criers have only a small part of their office and authority.

There were two kinds of ceryces, *civil* and *sacred*. The former were those appointed to call assemblies and make silence therein; also to go on messages, and do the office of our heralds, &c. The sacred ceryces were a sort of priests, whose office was to proclaim silence in the public games and sacrifices, publish the names of the conquerors, proclaim feasts, and the like. The priesthood of the ceryces was annexed to a particular family, the descendants of Ceryx, son of Eumolphus. To them it also belonged to lead solemn victims to slaughter. Before the ceremonies began, they called silence in the assembly, by the formula, [illegible]; answering to the *favete linguis* of the Romans. When the service was over, they dismissed the people with this formula, [illegible], *Ite missa est*.

CESARE, among logicians, one of the modes of the second figure of syllogisms; the minor proposition of which is an universal affirmative, and the other two universal negatives: thus,

CE No immoral books ought to be read;
SA But every obscene book is immoral;
RE Therefore no obscene books ought to be read.

CECENA, a town of Romagna in Italy, with a bishop's see, subject to the pope, and seated on the river Savio, in E. Long. 12. 46. N. Lat. 44. 8.

CESPITOSÆ PLANTÆ (from *cespes*, turf or sod), are those plants which produce many stems from one root, and thence form a close thick carpet on the surface of the earth.

Cespitosæ Paludes, turf bogs.

CESSATION, the act of intermitting, discontinuing or interrupting the course of any thing, work, action, or the like.

Cessation of Arms, an armistice or occasional truce. See Truce.

When the commander of a place finds things reduced to an extremity, so that he must either surrender, or sacrifice the garrison and inhabitants to the mercy of the enemy, he plants a white flag on the breach, or beats the chamade; on which a cessation of arms and hostilities commences, to give room for a capitulation.

CESSIO BONORUM, in Scots law, the name of that action by which an insolvent debtor may apply for liberation from prison, upon making over his whole real and personal estate to his creditors.

CESSION, in law, an act by which a person surrenders and transmits to another person a right which belonged to himself. Cession is more particularly used in the civil law for a voluntary surrender of a person's effects to his creditors, to avoid imprisonment. See the article Bankrupt.

In several places the cession carried with it a mark of infamy, and obliged the person to wear a green cap or bonnet; at Lucca, an orange one: to neglect this was to forfeit the privileges of the cession. This was originally intended to signify that the cessionary was become poor through his own folly. The Italian lawyers describe the ceremony of cession to consist in striking the bare breech three times against a stone, called *Lapis Vituperii*, in presence of the judge. Formerly it consisted in giving up the girdles and keys in court; the ancients using to carry at their girdles the chief utensils wherewith they got their living; as the scrivener his escritoire, the merchant his bag, &c. The form of cession among the ancient Gauls and Romans was as follows: The cessionary gathered up dust in his left hand from the four corners of the house, and standing on the threshold, holding the door-post in his right hand, threw the dust back over his shoulders; then stripping to his shirt, and quitting his girdle and bags, he jumped with a pole over a hedge; hereby letting the world know, that he had nothing left, and that when he jumped all he was worth was in the air with him. This was the cession in criminal matters. In civil cases, it was sufficient to lay a broom, a switch, or a broken straw, on the threshold: this was called *chrenecruda per durpillum et festucam*.

Cession, in the ecclesiastical law, is when an ecclesiastical person is created a bishop, or when a parson of a parish takes another benefice, without dispensation, or being otherwise qualified. In both these cases their first benefices became void by cession, without any resignation; and to those livings that the person had, who was created bishop, the king may present for that time, whosoever is patron of them; and in the other case the patron may present: but by dispensation of retainder, a bishop may retain some or all the preferments he was intitled to before he was made bishop.

CESTRUM, BASTARD JASMINE: A genus of the monogynia order, belonging to the pentandria class of plants; and in the natural method ranking under the 28th order, *Luridæ*. The corolla is funnel-shaped; the stamina each sending out a little tooth about the middle of the infide. There are six species, all of them natives of the warmest parts of America; so cannot be preserved in this country without artificial heat. They are flowering shrubs, rising in height from five to twelve feet, with flowers of a white, herbaceous, or pale yellow colour. The flowers of one species commonly called *Bockingtom Jessamine*, have the property of sending out a strong scent after sunset. They may be propagated either by seeds or cuttings.

CESTUI, a French word, signifying *he* or *him*, frequently used in the English law writings. Thus, *Cestui que trust*, a person who has lands, &c. committed to him for the benefit of another; and if such person does not perform his trust, he is compellable to it in chancery. *Cestui que vie*, one for whose life any lands, &c. are granted. *Cestui que use*, a person to whose use any one is infeoffed of lands or tenements. Formerly the feoffees to uses were deemed owners of the

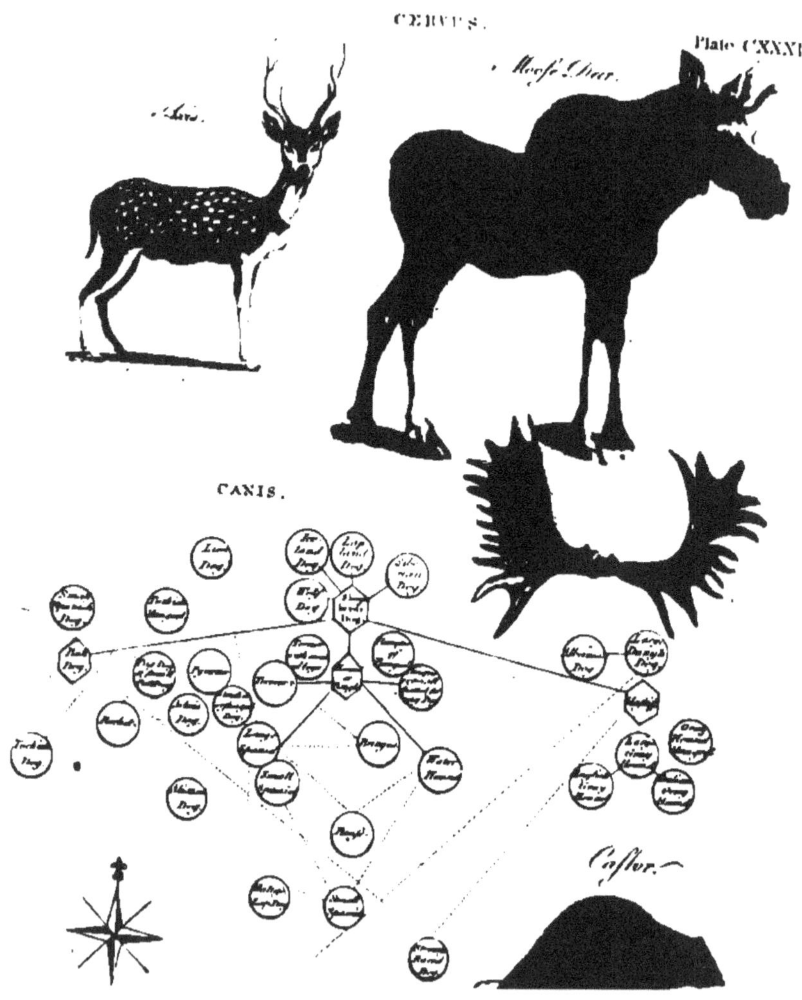
CERVUS.
Plate CXXXI.
Moose Deer.
Axis.
CANIS.
Castor.

the land, but now the possession is adjudged in *cestui qui est*.

CESTUS, among ancient poets, a fine embroidered girdle said to be worn by Venus, to which Homer ascribes the power of charming and conciliating love. The word is also written *cestum* and *cestos*: it comes from κεστος, *a girdle*, or other thing embroidered or wrought with a needle; derived, according to Servius, from κεντειν, *pungere*; whence also *incestus*, a term used at first for any indecency by undoing the girdle, &c. but now restrained to that between persons near skin. See INCEST.

CETACEOUS, an appellation given to the fishes of the whale kind; the characters of which are: they have no gills; there is an orifice on the top of the head, through which they breathe and eject water; and they have a flat or horizontal tail.

Nature on this tribe hath bestowed an internal structure in all respects agreeing with that of quadrupeds; and in a few others the external parts in both are similar. Cetaceous fish, like land animals, breathe by means of lungs, being destitute of gills. This obliges them to rise frequently on the surface of the water to respire, to sleep on the surface, as well as to perform several other functions. They have the power of uttering sounds, such as bellowing and making other noises denied to genuine fish. Like land animals they have warm blood, are furnished with organs of generation, copulate, bring forth, and suckle their young, showing a strong attachment to them. Their bodies beneath the skin are entirely surrounded with a thick layer of fat (blubber), analogous to the lard on hogs. The number of their fins never exceed three, viz. two pectoral fins, and one back fin; but in some species the last is wanting. Their tails are placed horizontally, or flat in respect to their bodies; contrary to the direction of those of all other fish, which have them in a perpendicular site. This situation of the tail enables them to force themselves suddenly to the surface of the water to breathe, which they are so frequently constrained to do. Many of these circumstances induced Linnæus to place this tribe among his *mammalia*, or what other writers call *quadrupeds* *. To have preserved the chain of beings entire, he should in this case have made the genus of *phoca* or *seals*, and that of the *trichecus* or *manati*, immediately precede the whale, those being the links that connect the mammalia or quadrupeds with the fish: for the seal is, in respect to its legs, the most imperfect of the former class; and in the manati the hind feet coalesce, assuming the form of a broad horizontal tail.

* See Zoology.

Notwithstanding the many parts and properties which cetaceous fish have in common with land animals, yet there still remain others which render it more natural to place them, with Ray, in the rank of fish: the form of their bodies agrees with that of fish; they are entirely naked, or covered only with a smooth skin; they live constantly in the water, and have all the actions of fish.

CETE, the name of Linnæus's seventh order of mammalia, comprehending the MONODON, BALÆNA, PHYSETER, and DELPHINUS.

CETERACH, in botany, the trivial name of a species of ASPLENIUM.

CETTE, a maritime town of France, in Languedoc, seated at the place where the canal of Languedoc begins, between Montpellier and Agde, on the bay of Maguelona in the Mediterranean sea. E. Long. 3. 15. N. Lat. 43. 25.

CETUS, in astronomy, the whale; a large constellation of the southern hemisphere, under Pisces, and near the water of Aquarius. The stars in the constellation Cetus, in Ptolemy's catalogue, are twenty-two; in Tycho's twenty-one; in Hevelius's forty-five; in the Britannic catalogue ninety-seven.

Cetus is represented by the poets, as the sea-monster which Neptune, at the suit of the nymphs, sent to devour Andromeda for the pride of her mother, and which was killed by Perseus. In the mandible of cetus is a variable star which appears and disappears periodically, passing through the several degrees of magnitude both increasing and diminishing, in about 333 days. See ASTRONOMY, n° 45.

CEVA, a strong town of Piedmont in Italy, seated on the river Tanero, with a strong fort, in E. Long. 8. 8. N. Lat. 44. 20.

CEVENNES, mountains of Languedoc in France, remarkable for the frequent meetings of the Protestants there as a place of security against the tyranny of their governors. In queen Anne's reign there was an attempt made to assist them by an English fleet in the Mediterranean; but to no purpose, for the French had occupied the passages.

CEUTA, a maritime town of Barbary in Africa, and in the kindom of Fez, seated on the straits of Gibraltar, opposite that place, in W. Long. 6. 25. N. Lat. 36. 35. John king of Portugal took it from the Moors in 1415, but it now belongs to Spain. In 1697, it sustained a vigorous siege by the Moors.

CEYLON, a large island in the East Indies, about 250 miles in length and 200 in breadth. It abounds in trees and shrubs, valuable both on account of their timber and the gums or spices they produce. Among these Mr Ives enumerates the euphorbium, tulip-tree, ebony, red-wood, cassia, cocoa-nut, cotton, lime, mangoe, citron, coffee; the trees producing balsam of capivi, gum gamboge, lac, and *cinquenomah*. This last is as yet unknown in Europe; but, according to the information of a Dutch surgeon, an oil or balsam is produced from it by distillation, which is of great use in paralytic complaints. There is also another gum named *hedale*, which has been but lately discovered, and of which the use is as yet unknown. Here is also the black and yellow *wood*, the wood of which is of a most beautiful grain, but so hard that the cutting of it proves very destructive to the carpenters tools. But the most remarkable, as well as the most useful, of the vegetable productions of Ceylon, is the cinnamon-tree, which grows wild in every wood on the south-west part of the island. The very young trees are not fit for rinding, and the old ones are cut down for firewood. The common flowering shrubs, of which the whole island is full, send forth a most agreeable fragrance every morning and evening. It abounds with high hills, between which the soil is a fat red earth; and the valleys are extremely pleasant, having a clear rivulet running thro' almost every one of them. Thus the finest fruits grow in vast plenty, and may be had at the most trifling rates; a pine-apple being bought for less than a penny, and so of the rest. Other provisions are almost equally

cheap;

Ceylon

cheap; a dozen of fowls or five ducks being ſold for a rupee, not quite half-a-crown of Engliſh money. Here the Dutch ſhow a poiſonous fruit called by them *Adam's apple*. In ſhape it reſembles the quarter of an apple cut out, with the two inſides a little convex, and a continued ridge along the outer edges; and is of a beautiful orange colour. Pepper, ginger, and cardamoms, are alſo produced here; as well as five kinds of rice, which ripen one after another.

Ceylon produces alſo topazes, garnets, rubies, and other precious ſtones, which are diſcovered by waſhing the ſoil wherein they grow. It has likewiſe ores of copper, iron, and probably of tin, with veins of black cryſtal.

Common deer are found in this iſland in great abundance, as well as Guinea-deer; but the horned cattle are both very ſmall and ſcarce, ſix of them weighed, all together, but 714 pounds, and one of theſe weighed only 70 pounds. They have, however, the largeſt and beſt elephants in the world; and their woods are infeſted by tygers, the moſt terrible of all ravenous beaſts. They abound alſo with ſnakes of a monſtrous ſize, one of which has been known to deſtroy a tyger and devour him at one meal. Mr Ives ſaw one 15 feet long and 30 inches in circumference. Spiders, centipedes, and ſcorpions, alſo grow here to an enormous ſize. Our author ſaw a ſpider here as large as a toad, with brown hair upon it, and legs as thick as the ſhank of a large tobacco-pipe. A ſcorpion, taken out of a piece of wood, was eight inches long, from head to tail, excluſive of the claws; the ſhell was as hard as that of a crab: and our author killed a centipede more than ſeven inches long. Here the *mantis* or creeping leaf is met with; which our author ſuppoſes to be a ſpecies of graſshopers, having every member we ſee in common inſects, though in ſhape and appearance it greatly reſembles a leaf. It is of a green colour. The ſea-coaſts abound with fiſh, which are to be had very cheap. Neither harp-ſhells nor ventle-traps are to be met with here; but there are abundance of painted cockles, and others commonly called *pomana ſhells*.

"The natives of this iſland (ſays our author) are the ſtouteſt Indians I ever ſaw. Mr Knox in his hiſtory reports many ſtrange things of their religion and cuſtoms, none of which I had any opportunity of ſeeing. He ſays 'that they have various ways of treating their dead. Some burn them, which is not uncommon in India; while others throw their limbs up into the forks of trees.' This may be true, becauſe when our wood-cutters were once hewing down a ſtick of timber, there fell from it the ſkull and many bones of a human body; and I alſo ſaw here a human body hanging on a tree. Other hiſtorians relate, that the natives of Ceylon feed on human fleſh; nay, that they eat the bodies of their deceaſed parents, imagining that no other ſepulchre is ſo fit for them as their own bowels, ſince thereby they think they are changed into their own ſubſtance, and live again in themſelves. This ſhocking cuſtom is reported of the ancient Scythians, and poſſibly might have been uſed by the inhabitants of Ceylon, but is now in both countries entirely aboliſhed; and yet even at this day theſe iſlanders are ſaid to make cups of their parents ſkulls, with a view, that in midſt of their mirth and jollity they may be ſure to preſerve a reſpectful remembrance of them."

The Ceyloneſe make uſe of boats hollowed out of the trunks of trees, which are about 12 or 14 feet long, but only as many inches broad within. The tree part in the bottom is much larger; but when the boat, on account of the ſize of the tree, is too ſmall, they make a trough on the top of it ſquare at both ends. Some boats, however, are much larger, being built between two trees; and with theſe they coaſt along ſhore; the others are for fiſhermen. It lies from E. Long. 78° to 82°, and from N. Lat. 6° to 10.

The conqueſt of this iſland was the firſt attempt of Albuquerque the celebrated Portugueſe admiral. He found it well peopled, and inhabited by two different nations, the *Bedas* inhabiting the northern, and the *Cinglaſſes* who dwelt in the ſouthern parts. The former were very barbarous, but the latter a good deal more poliſhed. Beſides the advantages already mentioned, which theſe nations derived from their mines of precious ſtones, they carried on the greateſt pearl-fiſhery in the Eaſt. Theſe nations the Portugueſe conquered, and tyrannized over in ſuch a manner, that they aſſiſted the Dutch in expelling them from the iſland; and by their united efforts this was accompliſhed in 1658, after a bloody and obſtinate war. All the Portugueſe ſettlements fell into the hands of the Dutch Eaſt India company, who ſtill keep poſſeſſion of them, excepting a ſmall diſtrict on the eaſtern coaſt without any port, from whence the ſovereign of the country had his ſalt. Theſe ſettlements formed a regular track, extending from two to twelve leagues into the inland parts of the iſland. The company have appropriated all the productions of the iſland. The ſeveral articles of trade are, 1. Amethyſts, ſapphires, topazes, and rubies; the laſt are very ſmall, and very indifferent. The Moors who come from the coaſt of Coromandel buy them, paying a moderate taxe and when they are cut, ſell them at a low price in the different countries of India. 2. Pepper, which the company buy for about 4d. *per* pound: coffee, for which they only pay 2d. and cardamom, which has no fixed price. Theſe articles are all of an inferior quality, and through the indolence of the inhabitants will never turn to any account. 3. An hundred bales of handkerchiefs, pagnes, and ginghams, of a fine red colour, which are fabricated by the Malabars at Jaffanapatan. 4. A ſmall quantity of ivory, and about 50 elephants, which are carried to the coaſt of Coromandel. 5. Areca, which the company buys at about 8s. 9d. the amunonan, and ſells on the ſpot at L. 1, 13s. to the merchants of Bengal, Coromandel, and the Maldives; who give in return rice, coarſe linen, and cowries. 6. The pearl-fiſhery, which was formerly of great conſequence; but is now ſo much exhauſted as not to bring in more than L. 8,750 *per annum*. 7. After all, the great object of the company is cinnamon. They purchaſe the greateſt part of their cinnamon of the Indians who are ſubject to them, and, all expences deducted, it does not coſt them above 6d. *per* pound. The annual expences of the colony may amount to about L. 96,250; their revenues and ſmall branches of commerce produce only about L. 87,500. —This deficiency muſt be ſupplied out of the profits

Ceylon

site arising from the cinnamon trade; and they are obliged to provide for the expences of the wars in which they are frequently engaged with the king of Candy, who is at present the sole sovereign of the island. These are very detrimental to the interests of the Hollanders; for which reason they endeavoured to engage the good will of this monarch by showing him all imaginable civilities. The harmony, however, has been often interrupted. In a bloody war which terminated on the 14th of February 1766, the Ceylonese monarch was driven from his capital, so that the Dutch made a very advantageous treaty. Their sovereignty was acknowledged over all that part of the country they possessed before the troubles broke out; and that part of the coasts held by the natives was ceded to them. They were allowed to gather cinnamon in all the plains; and the court was to sell them the best sort, which is produced in the mountains, at the rate of l. 1:16:1, for 18 lb. The government engaged to have no connection with any foreign power; and even to deliver up any Europeans who might happen to stray into the island. In return for so many concessions, the king was to receive annually the value of the produce of the ceded coasts; and from thence his subjects were to be furnished gratis with as much salt as they had occasion for. The Ceylonese are in the most miserable situation: they are in a state of total inactivity; live in huts without any furniture; and subsist upon fruits: those who are the most affluent have no other covering than a piece of coarse linen wrapt about their waist.

CHACE. See CHASE.

CHACO, a large country of South America situated between 19 and 37° S. Lat. It belongs to the Spaniards, by whom it was conquered in 1536. It is not naturally fruitful, but abounds in gold mines, which are so much the more valuable that they are easily worked. The works are carried on by about 8000 blacks, who deliver every day to their masters a certain quantity of gold; and what they can collect above this, belongs to themselves; as well as what they find on those days that are consecrated to religion and rest, upon condition that during the festival they maintain themselves. This enables many of them to purchase their liberty; after which they intermarry with the Spaniards.

CHADCHOD, in Jewish antiquity. Ezekiel mentions *chadchod* among the several merchandises which were brought to Tyre. The old interpreters, not very well knowing the meaning of this term, continued it in their translation. St Jerom acknowledges that he could not discover the interpretation of it. The Chaldee interprets it pearls; others think that the onyx, ruby, carbuncle, crystal, or diamond is meant by it.

CHÆRONEA, (anc. geog.), the last town, or rather the last village, of Bœotia, towards Phocis; the birthplace of Plutarch: famous for the fatal defeat of the confederate Greeks by Philip of Macedon. This place was considered by Philip as well adapted to the operations of the Macedonian phalanx; and the ground for his encampment, and afterwards the field of battle, were chosen with equal sagacity; having in view on one side a temple of Hercules, whom the Macedonians regarded as the author of their royal house, and the high protector of their fortune; and on the other the banks of the Thermodon, a small river flowing into the Cephissus, announced by the oracles of Greece as the destined scene of desolation and woe to their unhappy country. The generals of the confederate Greeks had been much less careful to avail themselves of the powerful sanctions of superstition. Unrestrained by inauspicious sacrifices, the Athenians had left their city at the exhortation of Demosthenes, to wait no other omen but the cause of their country. Regardless of oracles, they afterwards advanced to the ill-fated Thermodon, accompanied by the Thebans, and the scanty reinforcements raised by the islands and states of Peloponnesus which had joined their alliance. Their army amounted to 30,000 men, animated by the noblest cause for which men can fight, but commanded by the Athenians Lysicles and Chares; the first but little, and the second unfavourably, known; and by Theagenes the Theban, a person strongly suspected of treachery: all three creatures of cabal and tools of faction, slaves of interest or voluptuousness, whose characters (especially as they had been appointed to command the only states whose shame, rather than virtue, yet opposed the public enemy) are alone sufficient to prove that Greece was ripe for ruin.

When the day approached for abolishing the tottering independence of those turbulent republics, which their own internal vices, and the arms and intrigues of Philip, had been gradually undermining for 22 years, both armies formed in battle array before the rising of the sun. The right wing of the Macedonians was headed by Philip, who judged proper to oppose in person the dangerous fury of the Athenians. His son Alexander, only 19 years of age, but surrounded by experienced officers, commanded the left wing, which faced the Sacred Band of the Thebans. The auxiliaries of either army were posted in the centre. In the beginning of the action, the Athenians charged with impetuosity, and repelled the opposing divisions of the enemy; but the youthful ardour of Alexander obliged the Thebans to retire, the Sacred Band being cut down to a man. The activity of the young prince completed their disorder, and pursued the scattered multitude with his Thessalian cavalry.

Meantime the Athenian generals, too much elated by their first advantage, lost the opportunity to improve it; for having repelled the centre and right wing of the Macedonians, except the phalanx, which was composed of chosen men, and immediately commanded by the king, they, instead of attempting to break this formidable body by attacking it in flank, pressed forward against the fugitives, the insolent Lysicles exclaiming in vain triumph, "Pursue, my brave countrymen! let us drive the cowards to Macedon." Philip observed this rash folly with contempt; and saying to those around him, "Our enemies know not how to conquer," commanded his phalanx, by a rapid evolution, to gain an adjacent eminence, from which they poured down, firm and collected, on the advancing Athenians, whose confidence of success had rendered them totally insensible to danger. But the irresistible shock of the Macedonian spear converted their fury into despair. Above a thousand fell, two thousand were taken prisoners;

Chæronea. tanen; the rest escaped by a precipitate and shameful flight. Of the Thebans more were killed than taken. Few of the confederates perished, as they had little share in the action, and as Philip, perceiving his victory to be complete, gave orders to spare the vanquished, with a clemency unusual in that age, and not less honourable to his understanding than his heart; since his humanity thus subdued the minds, and gained the affections, of his conquered enemies.

According to the Grecian custom, the battle was followed by an entertainment, at which the king presiding in person, received the congratulations of his friends, and the humble supplications of the Athenian deputies, who craved the bodies of their slain. Their request, which served as an acknowledgment of their defeat, was readily granted; but before they availed themselves of the permission to carry off their dead, Philip, who with his natural intemperance had protracted the entertainment till morning, issued forth with his licentious companions to visit the field of battle; their heads crowned with festive garlands, their minds intoxicated with the insolence of wine and victory; yet the sight of the slaughtered Thebans, which first presented itself to their eyes, and particularly the sacred band of friends and lovers, who lay covered with honourable wounds on the spot where they had been drawn up to fight, brought back these insolent spectators to the sentiments of reason and humanity. Philip beheld the awful scene with a mixture of admiration and pity; and, after an affecting silence, denounced a solemn curse against those who basely suspected the friendship of such brave men to be tainted with criminal and infamous passions.

But this serious temper of mind did not last long; for having proceeded to that quarter of the field where the Athenians had fought and fallen, the king abandoned himself to all the levity and littleness of the most petulant joy. Instead of being impressed with a deep sense of his recent danger, and with dutiful gratitude to Heaven for the happiness of his escape and the importance of his victory, Philip only compared the boastful pretensions with the mean performances of his Athenian enemies; and, struck by this contrast, rehearsed, with the insolent mockery of a buffoon, the pompous declaration of war lately drawn up by the ardent patriotism and too sanguine hopes of Demosthenes. It was on this occasion that the orator Demades at once rebuked the folly, and flattered the ambition, of Philip, by asking him, Why he assumed the character of Thersites when fortune assigned him the part of Agamemnon?

Whatever might be the effect of this sharp reprimand, it is certain that the king of Macedon indulged not, on any future occasion, a vain triumph over vanquished. When advised by his generals to advance into Attica, and to render himself master of Athens, he only replied, "Have I done so much for glory, and shall I destroy the theatre of that glory?" His subsequent conduct corresponded with the moderation of this sentiment. He restored without ransom the Athenian prisoners; who, at departing, having demanded their baggage, were also gratified in this particular; the king pleasantly observing, that the Athenians seemed to think he had not conquered them in earnest. Soon afterwards he dispatched his son Alexander, and Antipater, the most trusted of his ministers, to offer them peace on such favourable terms as they had little reason to expect. They were required to send deputies to the Isthmus of Corinth, where, to adjust their respective contingents of troops for the Persian expedition, Philip purposed assembling early in the spring a general convention of all the Grecian states: they were ordered to surrender the isle of Samos, which actually formed the principal station of their fleet, and the main bulwark and defence of all their maritime or insular possessions; but they were allowed to enjoy, unmolested, the Attic territory, with their hereditary form of government.

Chærophyllum || Chaff-cutter.

CHÆROPHYLLUM, Chervil: A genus of the digynia order, belonging to the pentandria class of plants; and in the natural method ranking under the 45th order, *Umbellatæ*. The involucrum is reflexed-concave; the petals inflexed-cordate; the fruit oblong and smooth. There are seven species, two of which, called cow-weed and wild chervil, are weeds common in many places of Britain. The roots of the first have been found poisonous when used as parsnips: the rundles afford an indifferent yellow dye; the leaves and stalks a beautiful green. Its presence indicates a fertile and grateful soil. It ought to be rooted out from all pastures early in the spring, as no animal but the ass will eat it. It is one of the most early plants in shooting, so that by the beginning of April the leaves are near two feet high. The leaves are recommended by Geoffroy as aperient and diuretic, and at the same time grateful to the palate and stomach. He even asserts, that dropsies which do not yield to this medicine can scarcely be cured by any other. He directs the juice to be given in the dose of three or four ounces every fourth hour, and continued for some time either alone, or in conjunction with nitre and syrup of the five opening roots.—The other species of chærophyllum are not possessed of any remarkable property.

CHÆTODON, in ichthyology, a genus of fishes belonging to the order of thoracic. The teeth are very numerous, thick, setaceous, and flexile; the rays of the gills are six. The back-fin and the fin at the anus are fleshy and squamous. There are 29 species, distinguished from each other principally by the figure of the tail, and the number of spines in the back-fin. The most remarkable is the rostratus, or shooting-fish, having a hollow, cylindrical beak. It is a native of the East Indies, where it frequents the sides of the sea and rivers in search of food, from its singular manner of obtaining which it receives its name. When it spies a fly sitting on the plants that grow in shallow water, it swims on to the distance of four, five, or six feet; and then, with a surprising dexterity, it ejects out of its tubular mouth a single drop of water, which never fails striking the fly into the water, where it soon becomes its prey.

CHAFF, in husbandry, the husks of the corn, separated by screening or winnowing it. It signifies also the rind of corn, and straw cut small for the use of cattle.

Chaff-Cutter, a machine for making chaff to feed horses.—The advantages of an easy and expeditious method of cutting straw into chaff by an engine which could be used by common labourers have been long

long acknowledged, and various attempts have been made to bring such an engine to perfection. But the objections to most of them have been their complicated structure, their great price, and the noise they make in working; all which inconveniences seem to have been lately removed by an invention of Mr James Pike watchmaker of Newton Abbot in Devonshire. Of his engine, which is of a simple and cheap construction, the following description, and figure referred to, are extracted from the Transactions of the Society of Arts for 1787.

The engine is fixed on a wood frame, which is supported with four legs, and on this frame is a box for containing the straw, four feet six inches long, and about ten inches broad; at one end is fixed across the box two rollers inlaid with iron, in a diagonal line about an eighth of an inch above the surface; on the ends of these rollers are fixed two strong brass wheels, which takes one into the other. On one of these wheels is a contrate wheel, whose teeth take in a worm on a large arbour; on the end of this arbour is fixed a wooden wheel, two feet five inches diameter and three inches thick; on the inside-part of this wheel is fixed a knife, and every revolution of the wheel the knife passes before the end of the box and cuts the chaff, which is brought forward between the rollers, which are about two inches and a half asunder; the straw is brought on by the worm taking one tooth of the wheel every round of the knife; the straw being so hard pressed between the rollers, the knife cuts off the chaff with so great ease, that twenty-two bushels can be cut within the hour, and makes no more noise than is caused by the knife passing through the chaff.

Plate CXXXVI.

A is the box into which the straw is put. *B*, the upper roller, with its diagonal projecting ribs of iron, the whole moving by the revolution of the brass wheel *C* on the axis of which it is fixed. *D*, a brass wheel, having upon it a face wheel, whose teeth take into the endless screw on the arbor *E*, while the teeth on the edge of this wheel enter between those on the edge of the wheel *C*. On the axis of the wheel *D* is a roller, with iron ribs similar to *B*, but hid within the box. *E*, the arbor, one of the ends of which being made square and passing through a mortise in the centre of the wooden wheel *F*, is fastened by a strong screw and nut; the other end of this arbor moves round in a hole within the wooden block *G*. *H*, the knife, made fast by screws to the wooden wheel *F*, and kept at the distance of nearly three quarters of an inch from it by means of a strip of wood of that thickness, of the form of the blade, and reaching to within an inch of the edge. *I*, the handle mortised into the outside of the wooden wheel *F*.

CHAFFER, in zoology, a species of beetle. See Scarabæus.

CHAFFERCONNERS, in commerce, printed linens manufactured in the Great Mogul's dominions. They are imported by the way of Surat; and are of the number of those linens prohibited in France.

CHAFFERY, in the iron-works, the name of one of the two principal forges. The other is called the *finery*. When the iron has been brought at the finery into what is called an ancony, or square mass, hammered into a bar in its middle, but with its two ends rough, the business to be done at the chaffery is the reducing the whole to the same shape, by hammering down these rough ends to the shape of the middle part.

CHAFFINCH, in ornithology, the English name of a species of Fringilla.

CHAGRE, a fort of America in the province of Darien at the mouth of a river of the same name. It has been taken several times by the buccaneers, and last of all by Admiral Vernon in 1740. W. Long. 82. 7. N. Lat. 9. 50.

CHAIN (*Catena*), a series of several rings, or links, fitted into one another.

There are chains of divers matters, sizes, forms, and for divers uses.—Ports, rivers, streets, &c. are closed with iron chains: rebellious cities are punished by taking away their chains and barriers.

The arms of the kingdom of Navarre are, *Chains Or, in a field Gules*. The occasion hereof is referred to the kings of Spain leagued against the Moors; who having gained a celebrated victory against them in 1212, in the distribution of the spoils the magnificent tent of Miralmumin fell to the king of Navarre, as being the first that broke and forced the chains thereof.

A gold Chain, is one of the ornaments or badges of the dignity of the chief magistrates of a city, as the mayor of London, the provost and bailies of Edinburgh, &c.—Something like this obtained among the ancient Gauls: the principal ornament of their persons in power and authority was a gold chain, which they wore on all occasions and even in battle, to distinguish them from the common soldiers.

Chain also denotes a kind of string, of twisted wire; serving to hang watches, tweezer-cases, and other valuable toys upon. The invention of this piece of curious work is owing to the English; whence, in foreign countries, it is denominated the *English chain*. These chains are usually either of silver or gold, some of gilt copper; the thread or wire of each kind to be very fine.—For the fabric, or making of these chains: a part of the wire is folded into little links of an oval form; the longest diameter about three lines; the shortest, one. These, after they have been exactly soldered, are again folded into two; and then bound together or interwove, by means of several other little threads of the same thickness; some whereof, which pass from one end to the other, imitate the warp of a stuff; and the others, which pass transverse, the woof. There are at least four thousand little links in a chain of four pendants; which are by this means bound so equally, and withal so firmly together, that the eye is deceived, and takes the whole to consist of one entire piece.

Chain is also a kind of measure in France, in the trade of wood for fuel. There are chains for wood by tale, for wood by the rope, for faggots, for cleft wood, and for round sticks. There are also chains for measuring the sheaves of all sorts of corn, particularly with regard to the payment of tithes; for measuring pottles of hay, and for measuring horses. All these are divided into feet, inches, hands, &c. according to the use they are designed for.

Chain, in surveying, is a measure, consisting of a certain number of links of iron wire, usually a hundred; serving to take the dimensions of fields, &c.

Chain.

This is what Mersenne takes to be the arvipendium of the ancients.

The chain is of various dimensions, as the length or number of links varies: that commonly used in measuring land, called Gunter's chain, is in length four poles or perches, or sixty-six feet, or a hundred links; each link being seven inches $\frac{92}{100}$. Whence it is easy to reduce any number of those links to feet, or any number of feet to links.

This chain is entirely adapted to English measures; and its chief convenience is in finding readily the numbers contained in a given field. Where the proportions of square feet and acres differ, the chain, to have the same advantages as Gunter's chain, must also be varied. Thus in Scotland, the chain ought to be of 74 feet, or 24 Scotch ells, if no regard be had to the difference between the Scotch and English foot; but if regard be had to this difference, the Scotch chain ought to consist of 74⅖ English feet, or 74 feet 4 inches and ⅘ of an inch. This chain being divided into an hundred links, each of these will be $8\frac{928}{1000}$ inches.

That ordinarily used for large distances, is in length a hundred feet; each link one foot. For small parcels, as gardens, &c. is sometimes used a small chain of one pole, or fifteen feet and a half length; each link one inch $\frac{86}{100}$.

Some in lieu of chains use ropes; but these are liable to several irregularities; both from the different degrees of moisture, and of the force which stretches them. Schwenterus, in his Practical Geometry, tells us, he has observed a rope sixteen feet long, reduced to fifteen in an hour's time, by the mere falling of a hoar frost. To obviate these inconveniences, Wolfius directs, that the little strands whereof the rope consists be twisted contrary ways, and the rope dipped in boiling hot oil; and when dry, drawn through melted wax. A rope thus prepared, will not get or lose any thing in length, even though kept under water all day.

Chain-Pump. See Pump.

Chain-Shot, two bullets with a chain between them. They are used at sea to shoot down yards or masts, and to cut the shrouds or rigging of a ship.

Top-Chain, on board a ship, a chain to sling the sail-yards in time of battle, in order to prevent them from falling down when the ropes by which they are hung happen to be shot away or rendered incapable of service.

Plate CXXXVI

Chain-Wales, or *Channels*, of a ship, *porteboissoirs*, are broad and thick planks projecting horizontally from the ship's outside, abreast of and somewhat behind the masts. They are formed to extend the shrouds from each other, and from the axis or middle line of the ship, so as to give a greater security and support to the masts, as well as to prevent the shrouds from damaging the gunwale, or being hurt by rubbing against it. Every mast has its chain-wales, which are either built above or below the second deck-ports in a ship of the line: they are strongly connected to the side by knees, bolts, and standards, besides being confined thereto by the chains whose upper ends pass through notches on the outer edge of the chain-wales, so as to unite with the shrouds above.

Chains, in ship-building, are strong links or plates of iron, the lower ends of which are bolted through the ship-side to the timbers.

Chain | Chairman.

Hanging in Chains, a kind of punishment inflicted on murderers. By stat. 25. Geo. II. c. 37. the judge shall direct such to be executed on the next day but one, unless Sunday intervene; and their bodies to be delivered to the surgeons to be dissected and anatomized: and he may direct them afterwards to be hung in chains. During the interval between sentence and execution, the prisoner shall be kept alone, and sustained only with bread and water. The judge, however, hath power to respite the execution, and relax the other restraints of the act.

Chain-Island, an island lately discovered by captain Wallis in the South-sea. It seemed to be about five miles long and as much broad, lying in the direction of north-west and south-east. It appeared to be a double range of woody islands joined together by reefs, so as to compose one island of an oval figure, with a lake in the middle. The trees are large; and from the smoke that issued from the woods, it appeared to be inhabited. W. Long. 145.54. S. Lat. 17.23.

CHAJOTLI, or Chayote, a Mexican fruit of a round shape, and similar in the husk with which it is covered to the chesnut, but four or five times larger, and of a much deeper green colour. Its kernel is of a greenish white, and has a large stone in the middle, which is white, and like it in substance. It is boiled, and the stone eat with it. This fruit is produced by a twining perennial plant, the root of which is also good to eat. See Plate CXXXVIII.

CHAIR, *(Cathedra)*, was anciently used for the pulpit, or suggestum, whence the priest spoke to the people.

It is still applied to the place whence professors and regents in universities deliver their lectures, and teach the sciences to their pupils: thus, we say, the professor's chair, the doctor's chair, &c.

Curule Chair, was an ivory seat placed on a car, wherein were seated the prime magistrates of Rome, and those to whom the honour of a triumph had been granted.

Sedan Chair, a vehicle supported by poles, wherein persons are carried; borne by two men. There are two hundred chairs allowed by act of parliament; and no person is obliged to pay for a hackney-chair more than the rate allowed by the act for a hackney-coach driven two third parts of the said distance. 9 Ann. c. 23. § 8. Their number is since increased, by 10 Ann. c. 19. and 12 Geo. I. c. 12. to four hundred. See *Hackney-Coaches*.

Chair is also applied by the Romanists to certain feasts, held anciently in commemoration of the translation of the see, or seat of the vicarage of Christ, by St Peter.

The perforated chair, wherein the new-elected pope is placed, F. Mabillon observes, is to be seen at Rome: but the origin thereof he does not attribute, as is commonly done, to the adventure of Pope Joan; but says there is a mystery in it; and it is intended, forsooth, to explain to the pope those words of scripture, that *God draws the poor from out of the dust and mire*.

CHAIRMAN, the president, or speaker of an assembly,

assembly, company, &c. We say, the chairman of a committee, &c.

CHAISE, a sort of light open chariot, or calash. Aurelius Victor relates, that Trajan first introduced the use of post-chaises: but the invention is generally ascribed to Augustus; and was probably only improved by Trajan, and succeeding emperors.

CHALAZA, among naturalists, a white knotty sort of string at each end of an egg, formed of a plexus of the fibres of the membranes, whereby the yolk and white are connected together. See Egg.

CHALCAS, in botany: A genus of the monogynia order, belonging to the pentandria class of plants. The calyx is quinquepartite; the corolla campanulated, with the petals keeled; the stigma round-headed and warty.

CHALCEDON, or Calcedon, anciently known by the names of *Procerastis* and *Colpusa*; a city of Bithynia, situated at the mouth of the Euxine, on the north extremity of the Thracian Bosphorus, over against Byzantium. Pliny, Strabo, and Tacitus, call it *The City of the Blind*; alluding to the answer which the Pythian Apollo gave to the founders of Byzantium, who, consulting the oracle relative to a place where to build a city, were directed to choose that spot which lay opposite "to the habitation of the blind;" that is, as was then understood, to Chalcedon; the Chalcedonians well deserving that epithet for having built their city in a barren and sandy soil, without seeing that advantageous and pleasant spot on the opposite shore, which the Byzantines afterwards chose.—Chalcedon, in the Christian times, became famous on account of the council which was held there against Eutyches. The emperor Valens caused the walls of this city to be levelled with the ground for siding with Procopius, and the materials to be conveyed to Constantinople, where they were employed in building the famous Valentinian aqueduct. Chalcedon is at present a poor place, known to the Greeks by its ancient name, and to the Turks by that of *Cadiaci*, or "the judges town."

CHALCEDONY, in natural history, a genus of the semipellucid gems. They are of an even and regular, not tabulated structure; of a semi-opaque crystalline basis; and variegated with different colours, but those ever disposed in form of mists or clouds, and, if nicely examined, found to be owing to an admixture of various coloured earths, but imperfectly blended in the mass, and often visible in distinct molecules.—It has been doubted by some whether the ancients were at all acquainted with the stone we call *chalcedony*; they having described a Chalcedonian carbuncle and emerald, neither of which can at all agree with the characters of our stone; but we are to consider that they have also described a Chalcedonian jasper which seems to have been the very same stone as they describe by the word *turbida*, which extremely well agrees with our chalcedony.

There are four known species of the chalcedony. 1. A bluish white one. This is the most common of all, and is found in the shape of our flints and pebbles, in masses of two or three inches or more in diameter. It is of a whitish colour, with a faint cloud of blue diffused all over it, but always in the greatest degree near the surface. This is a little less hard than the oriental onyx. The oriental chalcedonies are the only ones of any value; they are found in vast abundance on the shores of rivers in all parts of the East Indies, and frequently come over among the ballast of the East India ships. They are common in Silesia and Bohemia, and other parts of Europe also; but with us are less hard, more opaque, and of very little value. 2. The dull milky-veined chalcedony. This is a stone of little value; and is sometimes met with among our lapidaries, who mistake it for a kind of nephritic stone. It is of a somewhat yellowish white or cream colour, with a few milk-white veins. This is principally found in New Spain. 3. The third is a brownish, black, dull, and cloudy one, known to the ancients by the name of smoky jasper, or jaspis capnitis. This is the least beautiful stone of all the class: it is of a pale brownish white, clouded all over with a blackish mist, as the common chalcedony is with a blue. It is common both in the East and West Indies, and in Germany; but is very little valued, and is seldom worked into any thing better than the handles of knives. 4. The yellow and red chalcedony is greatly superior to all the rest in beauty; and is in great repute in Italy, though very little known among us. It is naturally composed of an admixture of red and yellow only, on a clouded crystalline basis; but is sometimes found blended with the matter of common chalcedony, and then is mixed with blue. It is all over of the misty hue of the common chalcedony. This is found only in the East Indies, and there not plentifully. The Italians make it into beads, and call these *cassidonies*; but they are not determinate in the use of the word, but call beads of several of the agates by the same name.—All the chalcedonies readily give fire with steel, and make no effervescence with aqua-fortis.

CHALCIDENE, or Chalcidice, (anc. geog.) an inland country of Syria, having Antiochia or Seleucis to the west, Cyrrhestica to the north, to the south Apamene and Coelesyria, and to the east Chalybonitis; being so called from its principal city Chalcis. This province, one of the most fruitful in Syria, was seized by Ptolemy the son of Mennaeus during the troubles of Syria, and by him made a separate kingdom. Ptolemy himself is styled by Josephus and Hegesippus only Prince of Chalcis, but his son Lysanias is honoured both by Josephus and Dio with the title of King. Upon the death of Antiochus Dionysius king of Syria, Ptolemy attempted to make himself master of Damascus and all Coelesyria; but the inhabitants, having an utter aversion to him on account of his cruelty and wickedness, chose rather to submit to Aretas king of Arabia, by whom Antiochus and his whole army had been cut off. He opposed Pompey on his entering Syria; but was by him defeated, taken prisoner, and sentenced to death; which, however, he escaped by paying a thousand talents, and was left also in the possession of his kingdom. After Aristobulus king of Judea had been poisoned by the friends of Pompey, and Alexander his son beheaded at Antioch, he sent Philippion his son to Ascalon, whither the widow of Aristobulus had retired with her other children, to bring them all to Chalcis; proposing, as he was in love with one of the daughters named Alexandria, to maintain them in his own kingdom in a manner suitable to their rank: but Philippion likewife being in love with Alexandria, married her on the way; for which presumption Ptolemy put him to death on his return, and then took her to wife. On account of this affinity, he supported to the utmost of his power Antigonus the younger son of Aristobulus, who took the field at the head of a considerable army, but on his entering Judæa was entirely defeated by Herod. Ptolemy soon after died, and was succeeded by his son Lysanias; who, espousing the cause of the Asmonæan family with great warmth, promised to Barzapharnes who commanded the Parthian troops in Syria, and to Pacorus the king's son, a thousand talents and five hundred women, provided they should put Antigonus in possession of the kingdom of Judæa, and depose Hyrcanus. He was not long after put to death by Marc Antony, at the instigation of Cleopatra; who, in order to have his dominions, accused him falsely of having entered into an alliance with the Parthians.

CHALCIDIC, Chalcidicum, or Chalcedonicon, in the ancient architecture, a large magnificent hall belonging to a tribunal or court of justice.—Festus says, it took its name from the city Chalcis; but he does not give the reason. Philander will have it to be the court or tribunal where affairs of money and coinage were regulated; so called from χαλκος *brass*, and δικη *justice*. Others say, the money was struck in it; and derive the word from χαλκος, and οικος, *house*. In Vitruvius, it is used for the auditory of a basilica; in other of the ancient writers for a hall or apartment where the heathens imagined their gods to eat.

CHALCIDICE, (anc. geog.) an eastern district of Macedonia, stretching northwards between the Sinus Toronæus and Singiticus. Formerly a part of Thrace, but invaded by Philip of Macedon. Named from the city Chalcis near Olynthus.

CHALCIDIUS, a famous platonic philosopher in the third century, who wrote a commentary, which is esteemed, on the Timæus of Plato. This work has been translated from the Greek into Latin.

CHALCIS, a city of Chalcidice. See Chalcidice. (anc. geog.)—Another of Ætolia, near the mouth of the river Evenus, on the Ionian Sea, at the foot of a cognominal mountain; and therefore called by some *Hypochalcis*.—Another of Eubœa (Strabo), on the Euripus, the country of Lycophron the poet, one of the seven which formed the constellation Pleiades. Now *Negropont*. E. Long. 24. 30 Lat. 38. 30.—A fourth, the capital of Chalcidene in Syria; distinguished by the surnames *ad Belum*, a mountain or a river; and *ad Libanum*, from its situation (Pliny).

CHALCITIS, one of the divisions or districts of Mesopotamia, to the south of Anthemusia, the most northern district, next to Armenia, and situated between Edessa and Carræ. *Chalcitis* (Pliny), an island opposite to Chalcedon.

CHALCONDYLAS (Demetrius), a learned Greek, born at Constantinople, left that city after its being taken by the Turks, and afterwards taught Greek in several cities in Italy. He composed a Greek grammar; and died at Milan in 1513.

Chalcondylas (Laonicus), a famous Greek historian of the 15th century, was born at Athens; and wrote an excellent history of the Turks, from Ottoman, who reigned about the year 1300, to Mahomet II. in 1463.

CHALDEA (anc. geog.), taken in a larger sense, included Babylonia; as in the prophecies of Jeremiah and Ezekiel. In a restricted sense, it denoted a province of Babylonia, towards Arabia Deserta; called in Scripture *The land of the Chaldeans*. Named from Chesed the fourth son of Nahor. See Babylonia.

CHALDEE language, that spoken by the Chaldeans, or people of Chaldea. It is a dialect of the Hebrew.

Chaldee Paraphrase, in the rabbinical style, is called Targum. There are three Chaldee paraphrases in Walton's Polyglot; viz. that of Onkelos, that of Jonathan son of Uziel, and that of Jerusalem.

CHALDRON, a dry English measure, consisting of thirty six bushels, heaped up according to the sealed bushel kept at Guildhall, London: but on shipboard, twenty-one chaldrons of coals are allowed to the score. The chaldron should weigh two thousand pounds.

CHALICE, the cup or vessel used to administer the wine in the sacrament, and by the Roman Catholics in the mass.

The use of the chalice, or communicating in both kinds, is by the church of Rome denied to the laity, who communicate only in one kind, the clergy alone being allowed the privilege of communicating in both kinds.

CHALK, *Creta*, is a white earth found plentifully in Britain, France, Norway, and other parts of Europe, said to have been anciently dug chiefly in the island of Crete, and thence to have received its name of *Creta*. They have a very easy way of digging chalk in the county of Kent in England. It is there found on the sides of hills; and the workmen undermine it so far as appears proper; then digging a trench at the top as far distant from the edge as the undermining goes at bottom, they fill this with water, which soaks through in the space of a night, upon which the whole flake falls down at once. In other parts of the kingdom, chalk generally lies deeper, and they are forced to dig for it at considerable depths, and draw it up in buckets.

Chalk is of two kinds; hard, dry, and firm, or soft and unctuous; both of which are adapted to various purposes. The hard and dry kind is much the properest for burning into lime; but the soft and unctuous chalk is best for using as a manure for lands. Chalk, whether burnt into lime or not, is in some cases an excellent manure. Its mode of operating on the soil is explained under the article Agriculture, n° 20, 25, &c.

Pure chalk melts easily with alkali and flint into a transparent colourless glass. With alkaline salts it melts somewhat more difficultly, and with borax somewhat more easily, than with flint or sand. It requires about half its weight of borax, and its whole weight of alkali, to fuse it. Sal mirabile, and sandiver, which do not vitrify at all with the crystalline earths, form, with half their weight of chalk, the first a yellowish black, the latter a greenish, glass. Nitre, on the other hand, one of the most active fluxes for flint, does not perfectly vitrify with chalk. This earth notably promotes the vitrification of flint; a mixture of the two requiring less alkali than either of them separately. If glass made from flint and alkali is further saturated with the flint, so as to be incapable of bearing any further addition of that earth without becoming opaque and milky, it will still in a strong fire take up a considerable proportion, one-third or one-fourth of its weight, of chalk, without injury to its transparency; hence chalk is sometimes made use of in compositions for glass, as a part of the salt may then be spared. Chalk likewise has a great effect in melting the stony matters intermixed with metallic ores, and hence might be of use in smelting ores; as indeed limestone is used for that purpose. But it is remarkable, that chalk, when deprived of its fixed air, and converted into limestone, loses much of its disposition to vitrify. It is then found to melt very difficultly and imperfectly, and to render the glass opaque and milky.

Chalk readily imbibes water; and hence masses of it are employed for drying precipitates, lakes, earthy powders that have been levigated with water, and other moist preparations. Its economical uses in cleaning and polishing metalline or glass utensils are well known. In this case it is powdered and washed from any gritty matter it may contain, and is then called *whiting*.— In medicine it is one of the most useful absorbents, and is to be looked upon simply as such. The astringent virtues which some have attributed to it have no foundation, unless in so far as the earth is saturated with an acid, with which it composes a saline concrete manifestly sub-astringent. For the further properties of chalk, see Chemistry, *Index*.

Black Chalk, a name given by painters to a species of earth with which they draw on blue paper, &c. It is found in pieces from two to ten feet long, and from four inches to twenty in breadth, generally flat, but somewhat rising in the middle, and thinner towards the edges, commonly lying in large quantities together. While in the earth, it is moist and flaky; but being dried, it becomes considerably hard and very light; but always breaks in some particular direction; and if attentively examined when fresh broken, appears of a striated texture. To the touch it is soft and smooth, stains very freely, and by virtue of its smoothness makes very neat marks. It is easily reduced into an impalpable soft powder without any diminution of its blackness. In this state it mixes easily with oil into a smooth paste; and being diffused through water, it slowly settles in a black slimy or muddy form; properties which make its use very convenient to the painters both in oil and water colours. It appears to be an earth quite different from common chalk, and rather of the slaty bituminous kind. In the fire it becomes white with a reddish cast, and very friable, retaining its flaky structure, and looking much like the white flaky masses which some sorts of pit-coal leave in burning. Neither the chalk nor these ashes are at all affected by acids.

The colour-shops are supplied with this earth from Italy or Germany; though some parts of England afford substances nearly, if not entirely, of the same quality, and which are found to be equally serviceable both for marking and as black paints. Such particularly is the black earth called *kellow*, said by Dr Merret in his *Pinax Rerum Britannicarum* to be found in Lancashire; and by Mr Da Costa, in his history of fossils, to be plentiful near the top of Cay-Avon, an high hill in Merionethshire.

Red Chalk, an earth much used by painters and artificers, and common in the colour-shops. It is properly an indurated clayey ochre; and is dug in Germany, Italy, Spain, and France, but in greatest quantity in Flanders. It is of a fine, even, and firm texture; very heavy, and very hard; of a pale red on the outside, but of a deep dusky chocolate colour within. It adheres firmly to the tongue, is perfectly insipid to the taste, and makes no effervescence with acids.

Chalk-Land. Barley and wheat will succeed very well on the better sort of chalky land, and oats generally do well on any kind of it. The natural produce of this sort of land in weeds, is that sort of small vetch called the *tine-tare*, with poppies, may-weed, &c. Sainfoin and hop-clover will generally succeed tolerably well on these lands; and, where they are of the better sort, the great clover will do. The best manure is dung, old rags, and the sheep-dung left after folding them.

Chalk-Stones, in medicine, signify the concretions of calcareous matter in the hands and feet of people violently afflicted with the gout. Leeuwenhoek has been at the pains of examining these by the microscope. He divides them into three parts. The first is composed of various small parcels of matter looking like white grains of sand; this is harder and drier, and also whiter, than the rest. When examined with large magnifiers, these are found to be composed of oblong particles laid closely and evenly together; though the whole small stones are opaque, these component parts of them are pellucid, and resemble pieces of horse-hair cut short, only that they are somewhat pointed at both ends. These are so extremely thin, that Mr Leeuwenhoek computes that 1000 of them placed together would not amount to the size of one hair of our heads. The whole stones in this harder part of the chalk are not composed of these particles, but there are confusedly thrown in among them some broken parts of other substances, and in a few places some globules of blood and small remains of other juices. The second kind of chalky matter is less hard and less white than the former, and is composed of fragments or irregular parts of those oblong bodies which compose the first or hardest kind, and these are mixed among tough and clear matter, interspersed with the small broken globules of blood discoverable in the former, but in much greater quantity. The third kind appears red to the naked eye; and, when examined with glasses, is found to be a most tough and clammy white matter, in which a great number of globules of blood are interspersed; these give it the red appearance it has.

CHALLENGE, a cartel or invitation to a duel or other combat *. A challenge either by word or letter, or to be the bearer of such a challenge, is punishable by fine and imprisonment on indictment or information.

Challenge, among hunters. When hounds or beagles, at first finding the scent of their game, presently open and cry, they are said to challenge.

Challenge, in the law of England, is an exception made to jurors †; and is either in civil or criminal cases.

* See Duel.

† See the article Trial.

I. In

I. In *civil* cases challenges are of two sorts; challenges to the *array*, and challenges to the *poll*.

1. Challenges to the array are at once an exception to the whole panel, in which the jury are arrayed, or set in order by the sheriff in his return; and they may be made upon account of partiality or some default in the sheriff or his under officer who arrayed the panel. Also, though there be no personal objection against the sheriff, yet if he arrays the panel at the nomination, or under the direction of either party, this is good cause of challenge to the array. Formerly, if a lord of parliament had a cause to be tried, and no knight was returned upon the jury, it was a cause of challenge to the array: also by the policy of the ancient law, the jury was to come *de vicineto*, from the neighbourhood of the vill or place where the cause of action was laid in the declaration; and therefore some of the jury were obliged to be returned from the hundred in which such vill lay; and, if none were returned, the array might be challenged from defect of hundredors. For, living in the neighbourhood, these were supposed to know beforehand the characters of the parties and witnesses; and therefore they better knew what credit to give to the facts alleged in evidence. But this *convenience* was overbalanced by another very natural and almost unavoidable inconvenience; that jurors coming out of the immediate neighbourhood, would be apt to intermix their prejudices and partialities in the trial of right. And this the law was so sensible of, that it for a long time has been gradually relinquishing this practice; the number of necessary hundredors in the whole panel, which in the reign of Edward III. were constantly six, being in the time of Fortescue reduced to four; afterwards by statute 27 Eliz. c. 6. to two; and at length, by statute 4 and 5 Anne, c. 16. it was entirely abolished upon all civil actions, except upon penal statutes; and upon those also by the 24 Geo. II. c. 18. the jury being now only to come *de corpore comitatus*, from the body of the country at large, and not *de vicineto*, or from the particular neighbourhood. The array by the ancient law may also be challenged, if an alien be party to the suit, and, upon a rule obtained by his motion to the court for a jury *de medietate linguæ*, such a one be not returned by the sheriff pursuant to the statute 28 Edward III. c. 13. enforced by 8 Hen. VI. c. 29. which enacts, that where either party is an alien born, the jury shall be one half denizens and the other aliens (if so many be forthcoming in the place), for the more impartial trial: A privilege indulged to strangers in no other country in the world; but which is as ancient in England as the time of King Ethelred, in whose statute *de malefactoribus Wallia* (then aliens to the crown of England), c. 3. it is ordained, that "duodeni legales homines, quorum sex Walli et sex Angli erunt, Anglis et Wallis jus dicunto."

2. Challenges to the polls, *in capita*, are exceptions to particular jurors; and seem to answer the *recusatio judicis* in the civil and canon laws; by the constitutions of which, a judge might be refused upon any suspicion of partiality. By the laws of England also, in the times of Bracton and Fleta, a judge might be refused for good cause; but now the law is otherwise, and it is held that judges or justices cannot be challenged. For the law will not suppose a possibility of bias or favour in a judge who is already sworn to administer impartial justice, and whose authority greatly depends on that presumption and idea. And, should the fact at any time prove flagrantly such, as the delicacy of the law will not presume beforehand, there is no doubt but that such misbehaviour would draw down a heavy censure from those to whom the judge is accountable for his conduct. But challenges to the polls of the jury (who are judges of fact) are reduced to four heads by Sir Edward Coke: *propter honoris respectum*; *propter defectum*; *propter affectum*; and *propter delictum*. 1. *Propter honoris respectum*: as, if a lord of parliament be impanelled on a jury, he may be challenged by either party, or he may challenge himself. 2. *Propter defectum*: as, if a juryman be an alien born, this is defect of birth; if he be a slave or bondman, this is defect of liberty, and he cannot be a *liber et legalis homo*. Under the word *homo* also, though a name common to both sexes, the female is however excluded, *propter defectum sexus*: except when a widow feigns herself with child in order to exclude the next heir, and a supposititious birth is suspected to be intended; then, upon the writ *de ventre inspiciendo*, a jury of women is to be impanelled to try the question whether with child or not. But the principal deficiency is defect of estate sufficient to qualify him to be a juror, which depends upon a variety of statutes*. 3. Jurors may be challenged *propter affectum*, for suspicion of bias or partiality. This may be either a principal challenge, or to the favour. A *principal* challenge is such, where the cause assigned carries with it, *prima facie*, evident marks of suspicion either of malice or favour: as, that a juror is of kin to either party within the ninth degree; that he has an interest in the cause; that there is an action depending between him and the party; that he has taken money for his verdict, *&c.* which, if true, cannot be overruled, for jurors must be *omni exceptione majores*. Challenges *to the favour*, are where the party hath no principal challenge; but objects only some probable circumstances of suspicion, as acquaintance, and the like; the validity of which must be left to the determination of *triors*, whose office is to decide whether the juror be favourable or unfavourable. 4. Challenges *propter delictum*, are for some crime or misdemeanour that affects the juror's credit, and renders him infamous: As for a conviction of treason, felony, perjury, or conspiracy; or if, for some infamous offence, he hath received judgment of the pillory or the like.

* See Blackstone's Com. III. 362.

II. In *criminal* cases, challenges may be made either on the part of the king, or on that of the prisoner; and either to the whole array, or to the separate polls, for the very same reasons that they may be in civil causes. For it is here at least as necessary as there, that the sheriff or returning officer be totally indifferent; that, where an alien is indicted, the jury should be *de medietate*, or half foreigners, if so many are found in the place (which does not indeed hold in treasons, aliens being very improper judges of the breach of allegiance; nor yet in the case of Egyptians under the statute 22 Hen. VIII. c. 10.); that on every panel there should be a competent number of hundredors; and that the particular jurors should be *omni exceptione majores*, not liable to objections either *propter honoris respectum*, *fectum, propter defectum, propter affectum, or propter delictum.*

Challenges on any of the foregoing accounts are styled challenges *for cause*; which may be without stint in both civil and criminal trials. But in criminal cases, or at least in capital ones, there is, *in favorem vitae*, allowed to the prisoner an arbitrary and capricious species of challenge to a certain number of jurors, without showing any cause at all; which is called a peremptory challenge: a provision full of that tenderness and humanity to prisoners for which our laws are justly famous. This is grounded on two reasons: 1. As every one must be sensible what sudden impressions and unaccountable prejudices we are apt to conceive upon the bare looks and gestures of another; and how necessary it is, that a prisoner, when put to defend his life, should have a good opinion of his jury, the want of which might totally disconcert him; the law wills not that he should be tried by any one man against whom he has conceived a prejudice even without being able to assign a reason for such his dislike. 2. Because upon challenges for cause shown, if the reason assigned prove insufficient to set aside the juror, perhaps the bare questioning his indifference may sometimes provoke a resentment; to prevent all ill consequences from which, the prisoner is still at liberty, if he pleases, peremptorily to set him aside.

This privilege of peremptory challenges, though granted to the prisoner, is denied to the king by the statute 33 Edward I. stat. 4. which enacts, that the king shall challenge no jurors without assigning a cause certain to be tried and approved by the court. However, it is held that the king need not assign his cause of challenge till all the panel is gone through, and unless there cannot be a full jury without the persons so challenged. And then, and not sooner, the king's counsel must show the cause: otherwise the juror shall be sworn.

The peremptory challenges of the prisoner must, however, have some reasonable boundary; otherwise he might never be tried. This reasonable boundary is settled by the common law to the number of 35; that is, one under the number of three full juries. For the law judges, that 35 are fully sufficient to allow the most timorous man to challenge through mere caprice; and that he who peremptorily challenges a greater number, or three full juries, has no intention to be tried at all. And therefore it deals with one who peremptorily challenges above 35, and will not retract his challenge, as with one who stands mute or refuses his trial; by sentencing him to the *peine forte et dure* in felony, and by attainting him in treason. And so the law stands at this day with regard to treason of any kind. But by statute 22 Hen. VIII. c. 14. (which, with regard to felonies, stands unrepealed), no person arraigned for felony can be admitted to make more than 20 peremptory challenges.

CHALLON-sur-Saone, an ancient town of France, in Burgundy, and capital of the Challonnois, with a citadel and bishop's see. It is seated on the river Saone, in E. Long. 5. 7. N. Lat. 46. 47.

Challons-Sur-Marne, a large episcopal town of France, in Champagne. It carries on a considerable trade in shalloons, and other woollen stuffs. It is seated between two fine meadows on the rivers Marne, Man, and Nau, in E. Long. 4. 37. N. Lat. 48. 57.

CHALONER (Sir Thomas), a statesman, soldier, and poet, descended from a good family in Denbigh in Wales, was born at London about the year 1515. Having been educated in both universities, but chiefly at Cambridge, he was introduced at the court of Henry VIII. who sent him abroad in the retinue of Sir Henry Knevet ambassador to Charles V. and he had the honour to attend that monarch on his fatal expedition against Algiers in 1541. Soon after the fleet left that place, he was shipwrecked on the coast of Barbary in a very dark night: and having exhausted his strength by swimming, he chanced to strike his head against a cable, which he had the presence of mind to catch hold of with his teeth; and, with the loss of several of them, was drawn up by it into the ship to which he belonged. Mr Chaloner returned soon after to England, and was appointed first clerk of the council, which office he held during the rest of that reign. On the accession of Edward VI. he became a favourite of the Duke of Somerset, whom he attended to Scotland, and was knighted by that nobleman after the battle of Musselburgh, in 1547. The protector's fall put a stop to Sir Thomas Chaloner's expectations, and involved him in difficulties. During the reign of queen Mary, being a determined protestant, he was in some danger; but having many powerful friends, he had the good fortune to escape. On the accession of queen Elizabeth, he appeared again at Court; and was so immediately distinguished by her Majesty, that she appointed him ambassador to the emperor Ferdinand I. being the first ambassador she nominated. His commission was of great importance; and the queen was so well satisfied with his conduct, that, soon after his return, she sent him in the same capacity to Spain: but Sir Thomas was by no means satisfied with this instance of her majesty's confidence: the courts of England and Spain being at this time extremely dissatisfied with each other, he foresaw that his situation would be very disagreeable; and so it proved; but Elizabeth must be obeyed. He embarked for Spain in 1561, and returned to London in 1564, in consequence of a request to his sovereign, in an elegy written in imitation of Ovid. After his return, he resided in a house built by himself in Clerkenwell-close, where he died in the year 1565, and was buried in St Paul's. Sir William Cecil assisted as chief mourner at his funeral.

So various were the talents of Sir Thomas Chaloner, that he excelled in every thing to which he applied himself. He made a considerable figure as a poet. His poetical works were published by William Malim, master of St Paul's school, in 1579. His capital work was that "Of restoring the English republic, in ten books," which he wrote when he was ambassador in Spain. It is remarkable, that this great man, who knew how to transact as well as write upon the most important affairs of states and kingdoms, could descend to compose a *dictionary for children*, and to translate from the Latin a book *Of the office of Servants*, merely for the utility of the subjects.

Chaloner (Sir Thomas) the younger, though inconsiderable as an author, deserves to be recorded as a skilful naturalist, in an age wherein natural history was

2 very

very little underſtood in this or any other country; and particularly as the founder of the alum-works in Yorkſhire, which have ſince proved ſo exceedingly advantageous to the commerce of this kingdom. He was the only ſon of Sir Thomas Chaloner mentioned in the laſt article, and was born in the year 1559. Being very young at the time of his father's death, the lord treaſurer Burleigh taking charge of his education, ſent him to St Paul's ſchool, and afterwards to Magdalen college in Oxford, where, like his father, he diſcovered extraordinary talents for Latin and Engliſh poetry. About the year 1580, he made the tour of Europe, and returned to England before 1584; for, in that year, we find him a frequent attendant in the court of queen Elizabeth. About this time he married the daughter of Sir William Fleetwood, recorder of London. In 1591 he was knighted; and, ſome time after, diſcovered the alum-mines on his eſtate at Giſborough, near the river Tees in Yorkſhire (A).

Towards the latter end of the queen's reign, Sir Thomas viſited Scotland; and returning to England in the retinue of king James I. found ſuch favour in the ſight of his majeſty, that he was immediately appointed governor to prince Henry, whom he conſtantly attended, and, when his royal pupil viſited Oxford, was honoured with the degree of maſter of arts. How he was employed after the death of the prince is not known. Some years before that event, he married a ſecond wife, the daughter of Mr William Blount of London, by whom he had ſome children. He died in the year 1615, and was buried at Chiſwick in Middleſex. His eldeſt ſon William was created a baronet in the 18th of James anno 1620. The title was extinct in 1681. He wrote, 1. Dedication to Lord Burleigh of his father's poetical works, dated 1579. 2. The virtue of nitre, wherein is declared the ſundry cures by the ſame effected. Lond. 1584, 4to.

CHALYBEAT, in medicine, an appellation given to any liquid, as wine or water, impregnated with particles of iron or ſteel. See Mineral Waters.

CHALYBES (anc. geog.), an ancient people of the Hither Aſia. Their ſituation is differently aſſigned; Strabo placing them in Paphlagonia, to the eaſt of Synope; Apollonius Rhodius and Stephanus on the eaſt of the Thermodon, in Pontus; called *Halizones* by Homer. They either gave their name to, or took it from, their iron manufactures, (Xenophon, Val. Flaccus), their only ſupport, their ſoil being barren and ungrateful, (Dionyſius Periegetes).

CHAM, or Khan, the title given to the ſovereign princes of Tartary.

The word, in the Perſian, ſignifies *mighty lords*; in the Sclavonic, *emperor*. Sperlingius, in his Diſſertation on the Daniſh term of *Majeſty, koning, king*, thinks the Tartarian *cham* may be well derived from it; adding, that in the north they ſay *kan, kanon, konge, koning*, &c. The term *cham* is alſo applied, among the Perſians, to the great lords of the court, and the governors of provinces.

Cham, in geography, a town of the Bavarian palatinate, ſituated on a river of the ſame name, about 25 miles north-eaſt of Ratiſbon; E. Long. 13. N. Lat. 49. 15.

CHAMA, in zoology, a genus of ſhell-fiſh belonging to the order of vermes teſtacea. The ſhell is thick, and has two valves; it is an animal of the oyſter kind. Linnæus enumerates 14 ſpecies, principally diſtinguiſhed by the figure of their ſhells.

CHAMADE, in war, a certain beat of a drum, or ſound of a trumpet, which is given the enemy as a ſignal to inform them of ſome propoſition to be made to the commander, either to capitulate, to have leave to bury their dead, make a truce, or the like.—Menage derives the word from the Italian *chiamata*, of *chiamare* to "cry."

CHAMÆDRYS, in botany. See Veronica.

CHAMÆLEON, in zoology, the trivial name of a ſpecies of Lacerta.

CHAMÆPITYS, in botany. See Teucrium.

CHAMÆROPS, in botany: A genus of the natural order of palmæ. The hermaphrodite calyx is tripartite; the corolla tripetalous; there are ſix ſtamina, three piſtils, and three monoſpermous plums. The male, in a diſtinct plant, the ſame as the hermaphrodite. There are two ſpecies, the moſt remarkable of which is the glabra, a native of the Weſt Indies, and warm parts of America, alſo of the correſponding latitudes of Aſia and Africa. It never riſes with a tall ſtem; but when the plants are old, their leaves are five or ſix feet long, and upwards of two feet broad; theſe ſpread open like a fan, having many foldings, and at the top are deeply divided like the fingers of a hand. This plant the Americans call *thatch*, from the uſe to which the leaves are applied.—Under the name of palmetto, however, Mr Adanſon deſcribes a ſpecies of palm which grows naturally at Senegal, whoſe trunk riſes from 50 to 60 feet in height: from the upper end of the trunk iſſues a bundle of leaves, which, in turning off, form a round head; each leaf repreſents a fan of five or ſix feet in expanſion, ſupported by a tail of the ſame length. Of theſe trees, ſome produce male flowers, which are conſequently barren; others are female, and loaded with fruit, which ſucceed each other uninterruptedly almoſt the whole year round. The fruit of the large palmettos, Mr Adanſon affirms to be of the bigneſs of an ordinary melon, but rounder: it is inveloped in two ſkins as tough as leather, and as thick as ſtrong parchment; within the fruit is yellowiſh, and full of filaments faſtened to three large kernels in the middle. The negroes are very fond of this fruit, which,

(A) Sir Thomas, during his reſidence in Italy, being particularly fond of natural hiſtory, ſpent ſome time at Puzzoli, where he was very attentive to the art of producing alum. This attention proved infinitely ſerviceable to his country, though of no great benefit to himſelf or his family, his attempt being attended with much difficulty and expence. It was begun about the year 1600, in the reign of queen Elizabeth; but was not brought to any degree of perfection till ſome time in the reign of Charles I. by the aſſiſtance of one Ruſſel a Walloon, and two other workmen brought from the alum works at Rochelle. By one of the arbitrary acts of Charles, it was then deemed a mine-royal, and granted to Sir Paul Pindar. The long parliament adjudged it a monopoly, and juſtly reſtored it to the original proprietors.

Chamænia ‖ Chamber.

which, when baked under the aſhes, is faid to taſte like a quince.

The little palmetto may be eafily raifed in this country from feeds brought from America; but, as the plants are tender, they muſt be conſtantly kept in a bark-ſtove.

CHAMANIM, in the Jewiſh antiquities, is the Hebrew name for that which the Greeks call *Pyreia* or *Pyrateria*; and St Jerom in Leviticus has tranflated *Simulachra*, in Iſaiah, *delubra*. Theſe chamanim were, according to Rabbi Solomon, idols expofed to the fun upon the tops of houſes. Abenezra fays they were portable chapels or temples made in the *form* of chariots, in honour of the fun. What the Greeks call Pyreia, were temples confecrated to the fun and fire, wherein a perpetual fire was kept up. They were built upon eminences; and were large incloſures without covering, where the fun was worſhipped. The Guebres, or worſhippers of fire, in Perſia and the Eaſt Indies, have ſtill their Pyreia. The word *chamanim* is derived from *Chaman*, which ſignifies to warm, or burn.

CHAMARIM, a word which occurs in ſeveral places of the Hebrew bible, and is generally tranſlated the *prieſts of the idols*, or the *prieſts clothed in black*, becauſe *chamar* ſignifies "black," or "blackneſs." St Jerom, in the ſecond book of Kings, renders it *aruſpices*. In Hoſea and Zephaniah, he tranſlates it *æditui* or church-wardens. But the beſt commentators are of opinion, that by this word we are to underſtand the prieſts of the falſe gods, and in particular the worſhippers of fire; becauſe they were, as they ſay, dreſſed in black; or perhaps the Hebrews gave them this name in deriſion, becauſe, as they were continually employed in taking care about the fuel, and keeping up the fire, they were always as black as ſmiths or colliers. We find prieſts, among thoſe of Iſis, called *melanephori*, that is to ſay, that wear black; but whether this may be by reaſon of their dreſſing in black, or whether it were becauſe they wore a certain ſhining black veil in the proceſſions of this goddeſs, is not certain. *Camar*, in Arabic, ſignifies the "moon." Iſis is the ſame deity. Grotius thinks the Roman prieſts, called *camilli*, came from the Hebrew *chamarim*. Thoſe among the heathens who ſacrificed to the infernal gods were dreſſed in black.

CHAMBER, in building, a member of a lodging, or piece of an apartment, ordinarily intended for ſleeping in; and called by the Latins *cubiculum*. The word comes from the Latin *camera*; and that, according to *Nicod*, from the Greek καμαρα, *vault* or *curve*; the term *chamber* being originally confined to places arched over.

A complete apartment is to conſiſt of a hall, antichamber, *chamber*, and cabinet.

Privy-Chamber. Gentlemen of the privy-chamber, are ſervants of the king, who are to wait and attend on him and the queen at court, in their diverſions, *&c.* Their number is forty-eight, under the lord-chamberlain, twelve of whom are in quarterly waiting, and two of theſe lie in the privy-chamber.

In the abſence of the lord-chamberlain, or vice-chamberlain, they execute the king's orders: at coronations, two of them perſonate the dukes of Aquitain and Normandy; and ſix of them, appointed by the lord-chamberlain, attend ambaſſadors from crowned heads to their audiences, and in public entries. The gentlemen of the privy-chamber were inſtituted by Henry VII.

Chamber, in policy, the place where certain aſſemblies are held, alſo the aſſemblies themſelves. Of theſe ſome are eſtabliſhed for the adminiſtration of juſtice, others for commercial affairs.

Of the firſt kind are, 1. Star-chamber, ſo called, becauſe the roof was painted with ſtars; the authority, power, and juriſdiction of which, are abſolutely aboliſhed by the ſtatute 17 Car. I. 2. Imperial chamber of Spire, the ſupreme court of judicatory in the empire, erected by Maximilian I. This chamber has a right of judging by appeal; and is the laſt reſort of all civil affairs of the ſtates and ſubjects of the empire, in the ſame manner as the aulic council of Vienna. Nevertheleſs it is reſtrained in ſeveral caſes: it takes no notice of matrimonial cauſes, theſe being left to the pope; nor of criminal cauſes, which either belong to particular princes or towns in their reſpective territories, or are cognizable by all the ſtates of the empire in a diet. By the treaty of Oſnaburg, in 1648, fifty aſſeſſors were appointed for this chamber, whereof 24 were to be Proteſtants, and 26 Catholics; beſides five preſidents, two of them Proteſtants, and the reſt Catholics. 3. Chamber accounts, a ſovereign court in France, where accounts are rendered of all the king's revenues, inventories, and avowals thereof regiſtered; oaths of fidelity taken, and other things relating to the finances tranſacted. There are nine in France, that of Paris is the chief; it regiſters proclamations, treaties of peace, naturalizations, titles of nobility, *&c.* All the members wear long black gowns of velvet, of ſattin, or damaſk, according to their places. 4. Eccleſiaſtical chambers in France, which judge by appeal of differences about collecting the tythes. 5. Chamber of audience, or grand chamber, a juriſdiction in each parliament of France, the counſellors of which are called *jugeurs*, or judges, as thoſe of the chamber of inqueſts are called *rapporteurs*, reporters of proceſſes by writing. 6. Chamber of the edict, or miparty, a court eſtabliſhed by virtue of the edict of pacification in favour of thoſe of the reformed religion. This chamber is now ſuppreſſed. 7. Apoſtolical chamber of Rome, that wherein affairs relating to the revenues of the church and the pope are tranſacted. This council conſiſts of the cardinal-camerlingo, the governor of the rota, a treaſurer, an auditor, a preſident, one advocate-general, a ſolicitor-general, a commiſſary, and 12 clerks. 8. Chamber of London, an apartment in Guildhall, where the city money is depoſited.

Of the laſt ſort are, the chambers of commerce; the chambers of aſſurance; and the royal or ſyndical chamber of bookſellers in France.

1. The chamber of commerce is an aſſembly of merchants and traders, where the affairs relating to trade are treated of. There are ſeveral eſtabliſhed in moſt of the chief cities of France; and in our own country, we have lately ſeen chambers of this kind erected, particularly in London, Edinburgh, and Glaſgow. 2. Chamber of aſſurance in France, denotes a ſociety of merchants and others for carrying on the buſineſs of inſuring: but in Holland, it ſignifies a court of juſtice, where cauſes relating to inſurances are tried.

Chamber, Chamberlain.

3. Chamber of booksellers in Paris, an assembly consisting of a syndic and assistants, elected by four delegates from the printers, and twelve from the booksellers, to visit the books imported from abroad, and to search the houses of sellers of marbled paper, printsellers, and dealers in printed paper for hangings, who are prohibited from keeping any letters proper for printing-books. In the visitation of books, which ought to be performed by three persons at least from among the syndic and assistants, all libels against the honour of God and the welfare of the state, and all books printed either within or without the kingdom in breach of their regulations and privileges, are stopt, even with the merchandises that may happen to be in the bales with such libels or other prohibited books. The days appointed for this chamber to meet, are Tuesdays and Fridays, at two o'clock in the afternoon.

Chamber, in military affairs. 1. Powder-chamber, or bomb-chamber; a place sunk under ground for holding the powder, or bombs, where they may be out of danger, and secured from the rain. 2. Chamber of a mine; the place, most commonly of a cubical form, where the powder is confined. 3. Chamber of a mortar; that part of the chase, much narrower than the rest of the cylinder, where the powder lies. It is of different forms; sometimes like a reversed cone; sometimes globular, with a neck for its communication with the cylinder, whence it is called a bottled chamber; but most commonly cylindrical, that being the form which is found by experience to carry the ball to the greatest distance.

CHAMBERLAIN, an officer charged with the management and direction of a chamber. See Chamber, *in policy*.

There are almost as many kinds of chamberlains as chambers, the principal whereof are as follows.

Lord Chamberlain of Great Britain, the sixth great officer of the crown; to whom belongs livery and lodging in the king's court; and there are certain fees due to him from each archbishop or bishop when they perform their homage to the king, and from all peers at their creation or doing their homage. At the coronation of every king, he is to have forty ells of crimson velvet for his own robes. This officer, on the coronation-day, is to bring the king his shirt, coif, and wearing clothes; and after the king is dressed, he claims his bed, and all the furniture of his chamber, for his fees: he also carries, at the coronation, the coif, gloves, and linen, to be used by the king on that occasion; also the sword and scabbard, the gold to be offered by the king, and the robes-royal and crown: he dresses and undresses the king on that day, waits on him before and after dinner, *&c.* To this officer belongs the care of providing all things in the house of lords, in the time of parliament; to him also belongs the government of the palace of Westminster: he disposes likewise of the sword of state, to be carried before the king, to what lord he pleases.

The great chamberlain of Scotland was ranked by King Malcolm as the third great officer of the crown, and was called *Camerarius Domini Regis*. Before there was a treasurer appointed, it was his duty to collect the revenue of the crown, and he disbursed the money necessary for the king's expences, and the maintenance of the king's household. From the time that a treasurer was appointed, his province was limited to the boroughs throughout the kingdom, where he was a sort of justice-general, as he had a power for judging of all crimes committed within the borough, and of the crime of forestalling. He was to hold chamberlain-ayres every year. He was supreme judge; nor could any of his decrees be questioned by any inferior judicatory. His sentences were put in execution by the magistrates of the boroughs. He also regulated the prices of provisions within the borough, and the fees of the workmen in the mint-house. His salary was only L. 200 a-year. The smallness of his salary, and his great powers, had no doubt been the causes of much oppression in this officer, and the chamberlain-ayre was called rather a legal robbery than a court of justice; and when the combined lords seized king James VI. August 24, 1582, and carried him to Ruthven Castle, they issued a proclamation in the king's name, discharging the chamberlain-ayres to be kept. The chamberlain had great fees arising from the profits of escheats, fines, tolls, and customs. This office was granted heritably to the family of Stuart, duke of Lenox; and when their male line failed, king Charles II. conferred it in like manner upon his natural son, whom he created duke of Monmouth, and on his forfeiture it went to the duke of Lenox; but that family surrendered the office to the crown in 1703.

Lord Chamberlain of the Household, an officer who has the oversight and direction of all officers belonging to the king's chambers, except the precinct of the king's bed-chamber.

He has the oversight of the officers of the wardrobe at all his majesty's houses, and of the removing wardrobes, or of beds, tents, revels, music, comedians, hunting, messengers, *&c.* retained in the king's service. He moreover has the oversight and direction of the serjeants at arms, of all physicians, apothecaries, surgeons, barbers, the king's chaplains, *&c.* and administers the oath to all officers above stairs.

Other chamberlains are those of the king's court of exchequer, of North Wales, of Chester, of the city of London, &c. in which cases this officer is generally the receiver of all rents and revenues belonging to the place whereof he is chamberlain.

In the exchequer there are two chamberlains, who keep a controlment of the pells of receipts and exitus, and have certain keys of the treasury, records, *&c.*

Chamberlain of London keeps the city money, which is laid up in the chamber of London: he also presides over the affairs of masters and apprentices, and makes free of the city, *&c.*

His office lasts only a year; but the custom usually obtains to re-chuse the same person, unless charged with any misdemeanor in his office.

Chamberlain, Chamberlayne.

CHAMBERLAYNE (Edward), descended from an ancient family, was born in Gloucestershire 1616, and made the tour of Europe during the distractions of the civil war. After the restoration, he went as secretary with the earl of Carlisle, who carried the order of the Garter to the king of Sweden; was appointed tutor to the duke of Grafton, natural son of Charles II. and was afterwards pitched on to instruct prince George of Denark in the English tongue. He died in 1703, and was buried in a vault in Chelsea church.

Chamberlayne ‖ Chambers.

church-yard; his monumental inſcription mentions ſix books of his writing; and that he was deſirous of doing ſervice to poſterity, that he ordered ſome copies of his books to be covered with wax, and buried with him. That work by which he is beſt known, is his *Angliæ Notitia*, or *the preſent ſtate of England*, which has been often ſince printed.

Chamberlayne (John), ſon to the author of *The Preſent State of England*," and continuator of that uſeful work, was admitted into Trinity College, Oxford, 1685; but it doth not appear that he took any degree. Beſide the *Continuation* juſt mentioned, he was author of "Diſſertations hiſtorical, critical, theological, and moral, on the moſt memorable events of the Old and New Teſtaments, with Chronological Tables;" one vol. folio; and tranſlated a variety of works from the French, Dutch, and other languages. He likewiſe was F. R. S. and communicated ſome pieces, inſerted in the Philoſophical Tranſactions. It was ſaid of him that he underſtood ſixteen languages; but it is certain that he was maſter of the Greek, Latin, French, High and Low Dutch, Portugueſe, and Italian. Though he was qualified for employment, he had none but that of Gentleman-Uſher to George Prince of Denmark. After a uſeful and well-ſpent life, he died in the year 1724. He was a very pious and good man, and zealous in promoting the advancement of religion, and the intereſt of true Chriſtianity; for which purpoſe he kept a large correſpondence abroad.

CHAMBERRY, a conſiderable and populous town of Italy, in Savoy, with a caſtle. It is capital of the duchy, and well built, but has no fortifications. It is watered by ſeveral ſtreams, which have their ſources in St Martin's-hill, and run through ſeveral of the ſtreets. There are piazzas under moſt part of the houſes, where people may walk dry in the worſt weather. It hath large and handſome ſuburbs; and in the centre of the town is the royal palace. The parliament meet here, which is compoſed of four preſidents, and a pretty large number of ſenators, being the ſupreme tribunal of the whole duchy. The principal church is St Leger, and the Jeſuits college is the moſt magnificent of all the monaſteries. E. Long. 5. 50. N. Lat. 45. 35.

CHAMBERS (David), a Scots hiſtorian, prieſt, and lawyer, was born in the ſhire of Roſs, about the year 1530, and educated in the univerſity of Aberdeen. From thence he went to France and Italy, where he continued ſome time, particularly at Boulogne, where, in 1556, he was a pupil of Marianus Sozenus.

After his return to Scotland, he was appointed, by queen Mary, parſon of Suddy and chancellor of Roſs. He was ſoon after employed in digeſting the laws of Scotland, and was principally concerned in publiſhing the acts of parliament of that kingdom by authority in 1566. He was alſo appointed one of the lords of ſeſſion, and continued her majeſty's faithful ſervant till her declining fortune obliged her adherents to ſeek for refuge in other kingdoms. Chambers went firſt to Spain, where he was graciouſly received by king Philip; and thence he travelled to Paris, where he was no leſs kindly received by Charles IX. of that kingdom, to whom, in 1572, he preſented his hiſtory of Scotland, &c. He died at Paris in the year 1592, much regretted (ſays Mackenzie) by all who knew him. His writings were chiefly calculated to aſſiſt his royal miſtreſs, and to extol the wiſdom of the Scots nation.

Chambers.

Chambers (Ephraim), author of the ſcientific Dictionary which goes under his name, was born at Milton, in the county of Weſtmoreland. His parents were diſſenters of the Preſbyterian perſuaſion; and his education no other than that common one which is intended to qualify a youth for trade and commerce. When he became of a proper age, he was put apprentice to Mr Senex the globe-maker, a buſineſs which is connected with literature, and eſpecially with aſtronomy and geography. It was during Mr Chambers's reſidence with this ſkilful mechanic, that he contracted that taſte for ſcience and learning which accompanied him through life, and directed all his purſuits. It was even at this time that he formed the deſign of his grand work, the "Cyclopædia;" and ſome of the firſt articles of it were written behind the counter. Having conceived the idea of ſo great an undertaking, he juſtly concluded that the execution of it would not conſiſt with the avocations of trade; and therefore he quitted Mr Senex, and took chambers at Gray's-Inn, where he chiefly reſided during the reſt of his days. The firſt edition of the *Cyclopædia*, which was the reſult of many years intenſe application, appeared in 1728, in two vols. fol. It was publiſhed by ſubſcription, the price being 4l. 4 s. and the liſt of ſubſcribers was very reſpectable. The dedication, which was to the king, is dated October 15. 1727. The reputation that Mr Chambers acquired by his execution of this undertaking, procured him the honour of being elected F. R. S. Nov. 6. 1729. In leſs than ten years time, a ſecond edition became neceſſary; which accordingly was printed, with corrections and additions, in 1738; and was followed by a third the very next year.

Although the Cyclopædia was the grand buſineſs of Mr Chambers's life, and may be regarded as almoſt the ſole foundation of his fame, his attention was not wholly confined to this undertaking. He was concerned in a periodical publication, intituled, "The Literary Magazine," which was begun in 1735. In this work he wrote a variety of articles, and particularly a review of Morgan's "Moral Philoſopher." He was engaged, likewiſe, in conjunction with Mr John Martyn, F. R. S. and profeſſor of botany at Cambridge, in preparing for the preſs a tranſlation and abridgment of the "Philoſophical Hiſtory and Memoirs of the Royal Academy of Sciences at Paris, or an Abridgment of all the Papers relating to Natural Philoſophy which have been publiſhed by the Members of that illuſtrious Society." This undertaking, when completed, was compriſed in five volumes 8vo, which did not appear till 1742, ſome time after our author's deceaſe, when they were publiſhed in the joint names of Mr Martyn and Mr Chambers. Mr Martyn, in a ſubſequent publication, hath paſſed a ſevere cenſure, upon the ſhare which his fellow-labourer had in the abridgment of the Pariſian papers. The only work beſides, that we find aſcribed to Mr Chambers, is a tranſlation of the *Jeſuit's Perſpective*, from the French; which was printed in 4to, and hath gone through ſeveral editions. Mr Chambers's cloſe and unremitting attention to his ſtudies at length impaired his health, and obliged him occaſionally to take a lodging at Canonbury-houſe, Iſlington. This air having greatly contributed to his recovery, he made an excurſion to the ſouth of France, but did not reap that benefit from it which he had himſelf hoped, and his friends wiſhed. Returning to England, he died at Canonbury-houſe, and was buried at Weſtminſter; where the following inſcription, written by himſelf, is placed on the north ſide of the cloyſters of the Abbey:

Multis pervulgatus,
Paucis notus;
Qui vitam, inter lucem & umbram,
Nec eruditus, nec idiota,
Literis deditus, tranſegit; ſed ut homo
Qui humani nihil a ſe alienum putat.
Vita ſimul, & laboribus functus,
Hic requieſcere voluit,
EPHRAIM CHAMBERS, R. S. S.
Obiit xv Maii, MDCCXL.

After the author's death, two more editions of his Cyclopædia were publiſhed. The proprietors afterwards procured a ſupplement to be compiled, which extended to two volumes more: And in the year 1778 began to be publiſhed in weekly numbers, an edition of both, improved, and incorporated into one alphabet, by Dr Rees, which has been lately completed in four volumes folio, and forms a very valuable work.

CHAMBRE (Martin Cureau de la), phyſician in ordinary to the French king, was diſtinguiſhed by his knowledge in medicine, philoſophy, and polite learning. He was born at Mans; and was received into the French academy in 1635, and afterwards into the academy of ſciences. He wrote a great number of works, the principal of which are, 1. The characters of the paſſions. 2. The art of knowing men. 3. On the knowledge of brutes, &c. He died at Paris in 1669.

CHAMELEON. See LACERTA.

CHAMFERING, in architecture, a phraſe uſed for cutting any thing aſlope on the under ſide.

CHAMIER (Daniel), an eminent proteſtant divine, born in Dauphine. He was many years preacher at Montelimart; from whence he went in 1612 to Montauban, to be profeſſor of divinity in that city, and was killed by a cannon-ball during the ſiege in 1621. The moſt conſiderable of his works is his *Panſtratia Catholica*, or "Wars of the Lord," in four volumes folio; in which he treats very learnedly of the controverſies between the Proteſtants and Roman Catholics.

CHAMOIS, or CHAMOIS-GOAT, in zoology. See CAPRA.

CHAMOMILE. See ANTHEMIS.

CHAMOS, or CHEMOSH, the idol or god of the Moabites.

The name of *chamos* comes from a root which, in Arabic, ſignifies to *make haſte*; for which reaſon many believe chamos to be the ſun, whoſe precipitate courſe might well procure it the name of ſwift or ſpeedy. Others have confounded chamos with the god *Hammon*, adored not only in Libya and Egypt, but alſo in Arabia, Ethiopia, and the Indies. Macrobius ſhows that Hammon was the ſun; and the horns, with which he was repreſented, denoted his rays. Calmet is of opinion, that the god Hamonus, and Apollo Chomeus, mentioned by Strabo and Ammianus Marcellinus, was the very ſame as chamos or the ſun. Theſe deities were worſhipped in many of the eaſtern provinces. Some who go upon the reſemblance of the Hebrew term *chamos*, to that of the Greek *comos*, have believed chamos to ſignify the god Bacchus the god of drunkenneſs, according to the ſignification of the Greek *comos*. St Jerom, and with him moſt other interpreters, take Chamos and Peor for the ſame deity. But it ſeems that Baal-Peor was the ſame as Tammuz or Adonis; ſo that Chamos muſt be the god whom the heathens call the Sun.

CHAMOUNI, one of the elevated valleys of the Alps, ſituated at the foot of Mount Blanc. See ALPS and BLANC.

The firſt ſtrangers whom a curioſity to viſit the glaciers drew to Chamouni (M. Saſſure obſerves), certainly conſidered this valley as a den of robbers; for they came armed cap-a-pee, attended with a troop of domeſtics armed in the ſame manner: they would not venture into any houſe; they lived in tents which they had brought along with them; fires were kept burning, and centinels on guard the whole night over. It was in the year 1741 that the celebrated traveller Pocock, and another Engliſh gentleman called Wyndham, undertook this intereſting journey. It is remembered by the old men of Chamouni, and they ſtill laugh at the fears of the travellers, and at their unneceſſary precautions. For 20 or 25 years after this period, the journey was made but ſeldom, and then chiefly by Engliſhmen, who lodged with the curate: for, when I was there in 1760, and even for four or five years afterwards, there was no habitable houſe except one or two miſerable inns, like thoſe in villages that are little frequented. But now that this expedition has gradually become ſo faſhionable, three large and good inns, which have been ſucceſſively built, are hardly ſufficient to contain the travellers that come during the ſummer from all quarters.

This concourſe of ſtrangers, and the money they leave behind them at Chamouni, have ſomewhat affected the ancient ſimplicity of the inhabitants, and even the purity of their manners. Nobody, however, has any thing to fear from them: the moſt inviolable fidelity is obſerved with reſpect to travellers; they are only expoſed to a few importunate ſolicitations, and ſome ſmall artifices, dictated by the extreme eagerneſs with which the inhabitants offer their ſervices as guides.

The hope of obtaining this employment brings together, round a traveller, almoſt all the men in every village through which he paſſes, and makes him believe that there are a great many in the valley; but there are very few at Chamouni in ſummer. Curioſity, or the hope of making money, draws many to Paris and into Germany: beſides, as the ſhepherds of Chamouni have the reputation of excelling in the making of cheeſe, they are in great requeſt in the Tarentaiſe, in the valley of Aoſte, and even at greater diſtances; and they receive there, for four or five months in ſummer, very conſiderable wages. Thus the labours of the field devolve almoſt entirely on the women, even ſuch as in other countries fall ſolely on the men; as mowing, cutting of wood, and threſhing: even the animals of the ſame ſex are not ſpared, for the cows there are yoked in the plough.

Chamouni.

The only labours that belong exclusively to the men are the seeking for rock crystal, and the chace. Happily they are now less employed than formerly in the first of these occupations. I say happily, for many of them perished in this pursuit. The hope of enriching themselves quickly by the discovery of a cavern filled with fine crystals, was so powerful a motive, that they exposed themselves in the search to the most alarming dangers; and hardly a year passed without some of them perishing in the snows, or among the precipices.

The principal indication of the grottes, or crystal scene, as they are here called, are veins of quartz, which appear on the outside of the rocks of granite, or of the laminated rock. These white veins are seen at a distance, and often at great heights, on vertical and inaccessible places. The adventurers endeavour to arrive at these, either by fabricating a road across the rocks, or by letting themselves down from above suspended by ropes. When they reach the place, they gently strike the rock; and if the stone returns a hollow sound, they endeavour to open it with a hammer, or to blow it up with powder. This is the principal method of searching: but young people, and even children, often go in quest of these crystals over the glaciers, where the rocks have lately fallen down. But whether they consider these mountains as nearly exhausted, or that the quantity of crystal found at Madagascar has too much lowered the price of this fossil, there are now but few people that go in search of it, and perhaps there is not a single person at Chamouni that makes it his only occupation. They go however occasionally, as to a party of pleasure.

But the chace of the Chamois goat, as dangerous, and perhaps more so than the seeking for crystal, still occupies many inhabitants of the mountains, and carries off, in the flower of their age, many men whose lives are most valuable to their families. And when we are informed how this chace is carried on, we will be astonished that a course of life, at once so laborious and perilous, should have irresistible attractions for those who have been accustomed to it.

The Chamois hunter generally sets out in the night, that he may reach by break of day the most elevated pastures where the goats come to feed, before they arrive. As soon as he discovers the place where he hopes to find them, he surveys it with his glass. If he finds none of them there, he proceeds always ascending: whenever he descries any, he endeavours to get above them, either by stealing along some gully, or getting behind some rock or eminence. When he is near enough to distinguish their horns, which is the mark by which he judges of the distance, he rests his piece on a rock, takes his aim with great composure, and rarely misses. This piece is a rifle-barrelled carabine, into which the ball is thrust, and these carabines often contain two charges, though they have but one barrel; the charges are put one above another, and are fired in succession. If he has wounded the chamois, he runs to his prey, and for security he hamstrings it; then he considers his way home: if the road is difficult, he skins the chamois, and leaves the carcase; but, if it is practicable, he throws the animal on his shoulders, and bears him to his village, though at a great distance, and often over frightful precipices: he feeds his family with the flesh, which is excellent, especially when the creature is young, and he dries the skins for sale.

Chamouni.

But if, as is the most common case, the vigilant chamois perceives the approach of the hunter, he immediately takes flight among the glaciers, through the snows, and over the most precipitous rocks. It is particularly difficult to get near these animals when there are several together; for then one of them, while the rest are feeding, stands as a centinel on the point of some rock that commands a view of the avenues leading to the pasture; and as soon as he perceives any object of alarm, he utters a sort of hiss, at which the others instantly gather round him to judge for themselves of the nature of the danger: if it is a wild beast, or a hunter, the most experienced puts himself at the head of the flock; and away they fly, ranged in a line, to the most inaccessible retreats.

It is here that the fatigues of the hunter begin: instigated by his passion for the chace, he is insensible to danger; he passes over snows, without thinking of the horrid precipices they conceal; he intangles himself among the most dangerous paths, and bounds from rock to rock, without knowing how he is to return. Night often surprises him in the midst of his pursuit; but he does not for that reason abandon it; he hopes that the same cause will arrest the flight of the chamois, and that he will next morning overtake them. Thas he passes the night, not at the foot of a tree, like the hunter of the plain; not in a grotto, softly reclined on a bed of moss, but at the foot of a rock, and often on the bare points of shattered fragments, without the smallest shelter. There, all alone, without fire, without light, he draws from his bag a bit of cheese, with a morsel of oaten bread, which make his common food; bread so dry, that he is sometimes obliged to break it between two stones, or with the hatchet he carries with him to cut out steps in the ice. Having thus made his solitary and frugal repast, he puts a stone below his head for a pillow, and goes to sleep, dreaming on the road which the chamois may have taken. But soon he is awakened by the freshness of the morning; he gets up, benumbed with cold; surveys the precipices which he must traverse in order to overtake his game; drinks a little brandy, of which he is always provided with a small portion, and sets out to encounter new dangers. Hunters sometimes remain in these solitudes for several days together, during which time their families, their unhappy wives in particular, experience a state of the most dreadful anxiety: they dare not go to rest for fear of seeing their husbands appear to them in a dream; for it is a received opinion in the country, that when a man has perished, either in the snow, or on some unknown rock, he appears by night to the person he held most dear, describes the place that proved fatal to him, and requests the performance of the last duties to his corpse.

"After this picture of the life which the chamois hunters lead, could one imagine that this chace would be the object of a passion absolutely unsurmountable? I knew a well-made, handsome man, who had just married a beautiful woman:—'My grandfather, said he to me, lost his life in the chace; so did my father; and I am persuaded, that I too shall die in the same manner: this bag which I carry with me when I hunt I call my grave-clothes, for I am sure I will

Voyage dans les Alpes, par M. Saussure, tom. II.

will have no other; yet if you ſhould offer to make my fortune on condition of abandoning the chace of the chamois, I could not conſent. I made ſome excurſions on the Alps with this man: his ſtrength and addreſs were aſtoniſhing; but his temerity was greater than his ſtrength; and I have heard, that, two years afterwards, he miſſed a ſtep on the brink of a precipice, and met with the fate he had expected.

"The few who have grown old in this employment bear upon their faces the marks of the life they have led. A ſavage look, ſomething in it haggard and wild, makes them be known in the midſt of a crowd, even when they are not in their hunting dreſs. And undoubtedly it is this ill look which makes ſome ſuperſtitious peaſants believe that they are ſorcerers, that they have dealings with the devil in their ſolitudes, and that it is he who throws them down the rocks. What then can be the paſſionate inducement to this courſe of life? It is not avarice, at leaſt it is not avarice conſiſtent with reaſon: the moſt beautiful chamois is never worth more to the perſon that kills it than a dozen of franks, even including the value of its fleſh; and now that the number is ſo much diminiſhed, the time loſt before one can be taken is much more than its value. But it is the very dangers that attend the purſuit, thoſe alternations of hope and fear, the continual agitation and exerciſe which theſe emotions produce in the mind, that inſtigate the hunter: they animate him as they do the gameſter, the warrior, the ſailor, and even to a certain degree, the naturaliſt of the Alps; whoſe life, in ſome meaſure, pretty much reſembles that of the hunter whoſe manners we have deſcribed."

But there is another kind of hunting, which is neither dangerous nor laborious, nor fatal to any one but to the poor animals that are the objects of it.—Theſe are the marmots, animals that inhabit the high mountains; where in ſummer they ſcoop out holes, which they line with hay, and retire to at the beginning of autumn: here they grow torpid with the cold, and remain in a ſort of lethargy, till the warmth of the ſpring returns to quicken their languid blood, and to recal them to life. When it is ſuppoſed that they have retired to their winter abode, and before the ſnow has covered the high paſtures where their holes are made, people go to unharbour them. They are found from 10 to 12 in the ſame hole, heaped upon one another, and buried in the hay. Their ſleep is ſo profound, that the hunter often puts them into his bag, and carries them home without their awaking. The fleſh of the young is good, though it taſtes of oil, and ſmells ſomewhat of muſk; the fat is uſed in the cure of rheumatiſms and pains, being rubbed on the parts affected; but the ſkin is of little value, and is ſold for no more than five or ſix ſols. Notwithſtanding the little benefit they reap from it, the people of Chamouni go in queſt of this animal with great eagerneſs, and its numbers accordingly diminiſh very ſenſibly.

It has been ſaid, that marmots, in order to tranſport the hay into their holes, uſe one of their number laid on his back as a cart; but this is fabulous, for they are ſeen carrying the hay in their mouths. Nor is it for food that they gather it, but for a bed, and in order to ſhut out the cold, and to guard the avenues of their retreat from enemies. When they are taken in autumn, their bowels are quite empty, and even as clean as if they had been waſhed with water; which proves that their torpidity is preceded by a faſt, and even by an evacuation; a wiſe contrivance of Nature for preventing their accumulated fæces from growing putrid, or too dry, in the long lethargy they are expoſed to. They alſo continue a few days after their revival without eating, probably to allow the circulation and digeſtive power to recover their activity. At firſt, leaving their holes, they appear ſtupid and dazzled with the light: they are at this time killed with ſticks, as they do not endeavour to fly, and their bowels are then alſo quite empty. They are not very lean when they awake, but grow more ſo for a few days after they firſt come abroad. Their blood is never congealed, however profound their ſleep may be; for at the time that it is deepeſt, if they are bled, the blood flows as if they were awake.

In theſe countries the period is ſo ſhort between the diſſolution of the ſnow and its return, that grain has hardly time to come to maturity. Mr Sauſſure mentions a very uſeful and ingenious practice, invented by mountaineers of the Argentiere, for enlarging this period. "I obſerved (ſays he), in the middle of the valley, ſeveral large ſpaces where the ſurface of the ſnow exhibited a ſingular appearance, ſomewhat reſembling a piece of white cloth ſpotted with black. While I was endeavouring to divine the cauſe of this phenomenon, I diſcovered ſeveral women walking with meaſured pace, and ſowing ſomething in handfuls that was black; and which being ſcattered, regularly diverging, on the ſurface of the ſnow, formed that ſpotted appearance that I had been admiring. I could not conceive what ſeed ſhould be ſown on ſnow ſix feet deep; but my guide, aſtoniſhed at my ignorance, informed me, that it was black earth ſpread upon the ſnow to accelerate its melting; and thus to anticipate, by a fortnight or three weeks, the time of labouring the fields and ſowing. I was ſtruck with the elegant ſimplicity of a practice ſo uſeful, the effects of which I already ſaw very evidently in places which had not been thus treated above three days.

"As to the inhabitants of Chamouni, the men, like thoſe of moſt high valleys, are neither well-made nor tall: but they are nervous and ſtrong, as are alſo the women. They do not attain to a great age; men of 80 are very rare. Inflammatory diſeaſes are the moſt fatal to them; proceeding, no doubt, from obſtructed perſpiration, to which the inconſtant temperature of the climate expoſes them.

"They are in general honeſt, faithful, and diligent in the practice of religious duties. It would, for inſtance, be in vain to perſuade them to go any where on a holiday before hearing maſs. They are economical, but charitable. There are among them neither hoſpitals nor foundations for the poor; but orphans and old people, who have no means of ſubſiſtence, are entertained by every inhabitant of a pariſh in his turn. If a man is prevented by age or infirmities from taking charge of his affairs, his neighbours join among themſelves and do it for him.

"Their mind is active and lively, their temper gay, with an inclination to raillery: they obſerve, with ſingular acuteneſs, the ridiculous in ſtrangers, and turn it it into a fund of very facetious merriment among themselves; yet they are capable of serious thinking: many of them have attacked me on religious and metaphysical subjects; not as professing a different faith from theirs, but on general questions, which showed they had ideas independent of those they were taught."

CHAMPAGNE, a considerable province of France, about 162 miles in length, and 112 in breadth, bounded on the north by Hainhalt and Luxemburg, on the east by Lorrain and the Franche-Comté, on the south by Burgundy, and on the west by the isle of France and Soissonnois. It has a great number of rivers, the principal of which are the Meuse, the Seine, the Marne, the Aube, and the Aine. Its principal trade consists in excellent wine, all sorts of corn, linen cloth, woollen stuffs, cattle, and sheep. It is also divided into the higher and lower, and Troys is the capital town. Its sub-divisions are Champagne Proper, and Rhemois, the Retelois, the Pertois, the Vallage, Baligni, the Senonois, and the Brie Champenois.

Champagne Proper, is one of the eight parts of Champagne, which comprehend the towns of Troys, Chalons, St Menehold, Eperney, and Vertus.

CHAMPAIN, or *Point Champain*, in heraldry, a mark of dishonour in the coat of arms of him who kills a prisoner of war after he has cried quarter.

CHAMPERTRY, in law, a species of MAINTENANCE, and punished in the same manner: being a bargain with the plaintiff or defendant *campum partire*, "to divide the land," or other matter sued for between them, if they prevail at law; whereupon the champertror is to carry on the party's suit at his own expence. Thus *Champart*, in the French law, signifies a similar division of profits, being a part of the crop annually due to the landlord by bargain or custom. In our sense of the word, it signifies the purchasing of a suit, or right of suing: a practice so much abhorred by our law, that it is one main reason why a *chose* in action, or thing of which one hath the right but not the possession, is not assignable in common law; because no man should purchase any pretence to sue in another's right. These pests of civil society, that are perpetually endeavouring to disturb the repose of their neighbours, and officiously interfering in other mens quarrels, even at the hazard of their own fortunes, were severally animadverted on by the Roman law; and were punished by the forfeiture of a third part of their goods and perpetual infamy. Hitherto also must be referred the provision of the statute 32 Henry VIII. c. 9. that no one shall sell or purchase any pretended right or title to land, unless the vendor hath received the profits thereof for one whole year before such grant, or hath been in actual possession of the land, or of the reversion or remainder; on pain that both purchaser and vendor shall each forfeit the value of such land to the king and the prosecutor.

CHAMPION, a person who undertakes a combat in the place or quarrel of another; and sometimes the word is used for him who fights in his own cause.

It appears that champions, in the just sense of the word, were persons who fought instead of those that, by custom, were obliged to accept the duel, but had a just excuse for dispensing with it, as being too old, infirm, or being ecclesiastics, and the like. Such causes as could not be decided by the course of common law, were often tried by single combat; and he who had the good fortune to conquer, was always reputed to have justice on his side. See the article BATTEL.

Champion of the King, (*campio regis*), is an ancient officer, whose office is, at the coronation of our kings, when the king is at dinner, to ride armed cap-a-pee, into Westminster-Hall, and by the proclamation of an herald make a challenge, "That if any man shall deny the king's title to the crown, he is there ready to defend it in single combat, &c." which being done, the king drinks to him, and sends him a gilt cup with a cover full of wine, which the champion drinks, and hath the cup for his fee. This office, at the coronation of king Richard II. when Baldwin Freville exhibited his petition for it, was adjudged from him to his competitor Sir John Dymocke (both claiming from Marmion), and hath continued ever since in the family of the Dymockes; who hold the manor of Sievelsby in Lincolnshire, hereditary from the Marmions by grand serjeantry, viz. that the lord thereof shall be the king's champion as aforesaid. Accordingly Sir Edward Dymocke performed this office at the coronation of king Charles II. a person of the name of Dymocke performed at the coronation of his present majesty George the third.

CHAMPLAIN (Samuel de), a celebrated French navigator, the founder of the colony of New France, or Canada. He built Quebec; and was the first governor of the colony in 1603. Died after 1649. See QUEBEC.

CHANANAEI (anc. geog.) the name of the ancient inhabitants of Canaan in general, descendants of Canaan; but peculiarly appropriated to some one branch; though uncertain which branch or son of Canaan it was, or how it happened that they preferred the common gentilitious name to one more appropriated as descendants of one of the sons of Canaan; unless from their course of life, as being in the mercantile way, the import of the name *Canaan*; and for which their situation was greatly adapted. they living on the sea and about Jordan, and thus occupying the greater part of the Land of Promise.

CHANCE, a term we apply to events, to denote that they happen without any necessary or foreknown cause. See CAUSE.

Our aim is, to ascribe those things to *chance*, which are not necessarily produced as the natural effects of any proper cause; but our ignorance and precipitancy lead us to attribute effects to *chance*, which have a necessary and determinate cause.

When we say a thing happens *by chance*, we really mean no more than that its cause is unknown to us: not, as some vainly imagine, that *chance* itself can be the cause of any thing.

The case of the painter, who, unable to express the foam at the mouth of a horse he had painted, threw his sponge in despair at the piece, and, *by chance*, did that which he could not before do by design, is an eminent instance of the force of *chance*: yet, it is obvious, all we here mean by *chance*, is, that the painter was not aware of the effect; or that he did not throw the sponge with such a view: not but that he actually did every thing necessary to produce the effect; insomuch, that, considering the direction

wherein

Chance.

wherein he threw his ſpunge, together with its form, ſpecific gravity, the colours wherewith it was ſmeared, and the diſtance of the hand from the piece, it was impoſſible, on the preſent ſyſtem of things, the effect ſhould not follow.

Chance is frequently perſonified, and erected into a chimerical being, whom we conceive as acting arbitrarily, and producing all the effects whoſe real cauſes do not appear to us: in which ſenſe the word coincides with the τυχη, *fortuna*, of the ancients.

Chance is alſo uſed for the manner of deciding things, the conduct or direction whereof is left at large, and not reducible to any determinate rules or meaſures; or where there is no ground for preference: as at cards, dice, lotteries, &c.

For the Laws of Chance, *or the Proportion of Hazard in Gaming*, ſee Game.

The ancient *ſortilege*, or *chance*, M. Placette obſerves, was inſtituted by God himſelf: and in the Old Teſtament we find ſeveral ſtanding laws and expreſs commands which preſcribed its uſe on certain occaſions: hence the Scripture ſays, "The *lot*, or *chance*, fell on Matthias," when it was in queſtion who ſhould fill Judas's place in the apoſtolate.

Hence alſo aroſe the *ſortes ſanctorum*; or method of determining things, among the ancient Chriſtians, by opening ſome of the ſacred books, and pitching on the firſt verſe they caſt their eye on, as a ſure prognoſtic of what was to befal them. The *ſortes Homericæ*, *Virgilianæ*, *Prœneſtinæ*, &c. uſed by the heathens, were with the ſame view, and in the ſame manner. See Sortes.

St Auguſtin ſeems to approve of this method of determining things future, and owns that he had practiſed it himſelf; grounded on this ſuppoſition, that God preſides over *chance*; and on Prov. xvi. 33.

Many among the modern divines hold *chance* to be conducted in a particular manner by Providence; and eſteem it an extraordinary way which God uſes to declare his will, and a kind of immediate revelation.

Chance-Medley, in law, is where one is doing a lawful act, and a perſon is killed by chance thereby: for if the act be unlawful, it is felony. If a perſon caſt, not intending harm, a ſtone, which happens to hit one, whereof he dies; or ſhoots an arrow in an highway, and another that paſſeth by is killed therewith; or if a workman, in throwing down rubbiſh from a houſe after warning to take care, kills a perſon; or a ſchoolmaſter in correcting his ſcholar, a maſter his ſervant, or an officer in whipping a criminal in a reaſonable manner, happens to occaſion his death; it is chance-medley and miſadventure. But if a man throw ſtones in a highway where perſons uſually paſs; or ſhoot an arrow, &c. in a market-place among a great many people; or if a workman caſt down rubbiſh from a houſe in cities and towns where people are continually paſſing; or a ſchoolmaſter, &c. correct his ſervant or ſcholar, &c. exceeding the bounds of moderation; it is manſlaughter: and if with an improper inſtrument of correction, as with a ſword or iron bar, or by kicking, ſtamping, &c. in a cruel manner, it is murder. If a man whips his horſe in a ſtreet to make him gallop, and the horſe runs over a child and kills it, it is manſlaughter: but if another whips the horſe, it is manſlaughter in him, and chance-medley in the rider. And if two are fighting, and a third perſon coming to part them is killed by one of them without any evil intent, yet this is murder in him, and not manſlaughter by chance medley or miſadventure. In chance-medley, the offender forfeits his goods; but hath a pardon of courſe.

Chancel, Chancellor.

CHANCEL, is properly that part of the choir of a church, between the altar or communion-table and the baluſtrade or rail that incloſes it, where the miniſter is placed at the celebration of the communion. The word comes from the Latin *cancellus*, which in the lower Latin is uſed in the ſame ſenſe, from *cancelli*, "lattices or croſs bars," wherewith the chancels were anciently encompaſſed, as they now are with rails. The right of a ſeat and a ſepulchre in the chancels is one of the privileges of founders.

CHANCELLOR, was at firſt only a chief notary or ſcribe under the emperors; and was called *cancellarius*, becauſe he ſat behind a lattice (in Latin *cancellus*) to avoid being crowded by the people: though ſome derive the word from *cancellare*, "to cancel" (See Chancery). This officer was afterwards inveſted with ſeveral judicial powers, and a general ſuperintendency over the reſt of the officers of the prince. From the Roman empire it paſſed to the Roman church, ever emulous of imperial ſtate; and hence every biſhop has to this day his chancellor, the principal judge of his conſiſtory. And when the modern kingdoms of Europe were eſtabliſhed upon the ruins of the empire, almoſt every ſtate preſerved its chancellor with different juriſdictions and dignities, according to their different conſtitutions. But in all of them he ſeems to have had the ſupervifion of all charters, letters, and ſuch other public inſtruments of the crown as were authenticated in the moſt ſolemn manner; and therefore, when ſeals came in uſe, he had always the cuſtody of the king's great ſeal.

Lord High Chancellor *of Great Britain*, or *Lord Keeper of the Great Seal*, is the higheſt honour of the long robe, being created by the mere delivery of the king's great ſeal into his cuſtody: whereby he becomes, without writ or patent, an officer of the greateſt weight and power of any now ſubſiſting in the kingdom. He is a privy counſellor by his office; and, according to Lord Chancellor Elleſmere, prolocutor of the houſe of lords by preſcription. To him belongs the appointment of all the juſtices of the peace throughout the kingdom. Being in former times commonly an eccleſiaſtic (for none elſe were then capable of an office ſo converſant in writing), and preſiding over the royal chapel, he became keeper of the king's conſcience; viſitor, in right of the king, of all hoſpitals and colleges of the king's foundation; and patron of all the king's livings under the value of L. 20 *per annum* in the king's books. He is the general guardian of all infants, idiots, and lunatics; and has the general ſuperintendance of all charitable uſes in the kingdom. And all this over and above the vaſt extenſive juriſdiction which he exerciſes in his judicial capacity in the court of chancery. He takes precedence of every temporal lord except the royal family, and of all others except the archbiſhop of Canterbury. See Chancery.

Chancellor, in Scotland, was the chief in matters of juſtice. In the laws of King Malcolm II. he is placed

Chancellor. placed before all other officers; and from thefe it appears, that he had the principal direction of the Chancery, or Chancellary as it is called, which is his proper office. He had the cuftody of the king's feal; and he was the king's moft intimate counfellor, as appears by an old law cited by Sir James Balfour; "The chanceller fall at al tymes affift the king, in giving him counfall mair fecretly nor the reft of the nobility, to quais ordinances all officiaris, als weill of the realme as of the kingis hous, fould anfwer and obey. The chanceller fall be ludgit neir unto the kingis grace, for keiping of his bodie, and the feill; and that he may be readie baith day and nicht at the kingis command." By having the cuftody of the great feal, he had an opportunity of examining the king's grants and other deeds which were to pafs under it, and to cancel them if they appeared againft law, and were obtained furreptitioufly or by falfe fuggeftions.

King James VI. ordained the chancellor to have the firft place and rank in the nation, *ratione officii*; by virtue whereof he prefided in the parliament, and in all courts of judicature. After the reftoration of King Charles II. by a particular declaratory law, parliament firft, the lord chancellor was declared, by virtue and right of his office, prefident in all the meetings of parliament, or other public judicatures of the kingdom. Although this act was made to declare the chancellor prefident of the exchequer as well as other courts, yet in 1663 the king declared the treafurer to be prefident of that court.

The office of lord chancellor was abolifhed by the Union, there being no farther ufe for the judicial part of this office; and, to anfwer all the other parts of the chancellor's office, a lord keeper of the great feal was erected, with a falary of L. 3000 a-year.

Chancellor of a Cathedral, an officer that hears leffons and lectures read in the church, either by himfelf or his vicar; to correct and fet right the reader when he reads amifs; to infpect fchools; to hear caufes; apply the feal; write and difpatch the letters of the chapter; keep the books; take care that there be frequent preachings, both in the church and out of it; and affign the office of preaching to whom he pleafes.

Chancellor of the Duchy of Lancafter, an officer appointed chiefly to determine controverfies between the king and his tenants of the duchy-land, and otherwife to direct all the king's affairs belonging to that court. See *Duchy-Court*.

Chancellor of the Exchequer, an officer who prefides in that court, and takes care of the intereft of the crown. He is always in commiffion with the lord-treafurer, for the letting of crown-lands, &c. and has power, with others, to compound for forfeitures of lands upon penal ftatutes. He has alfo great authority in managing the royal revenues, and in matters relating to the firft-fruits.

Chancellor of the Order of the Garter, and other Military Orders, is an officer who feals the commiffions and mandates of the chapter and affembly of the knights, keeps the regifter of their proceedings, and delivers acts thereof under the feal of their order.

Chancellor of an Univerfity, is he who feals the diplomas, or letters of degrees, provifion, &c. given in the univerfity.

The chancellor of Oxford is ufually one of the prime nobility, chofen by the ftudents themfelves in convocation. He is their chief magiftrate; his office is, *durante vita*, to govern the univerfity, preferve and defend its rights and privileges, convoke affemblies, and do juftice among the members under his jurifdiction. Chancellor ‖ Chancery.

Under the chancellor is the vice-chancellor, who is chofen annually, being nominated by the chancellor, and elected by the univerfity in convocation. He is always the head of fome college, and in holy orders. His proper office is to execute the chancellor's power, to govern the univerfity according to her ftatutes, to fee that officers and ftudents do their duty, that courts be duly called, &c. When he enters upon his office, he chofes four pro-vice-chancellors out of the heads of the colleges, to execute his power in his abfence.

The chancellor of Cambridge is alfo ufually one of the prime nobility, and in moft refpects the fame as that in Oxford; only he does not hold his office *durante vita*, but may be elected every three years. Under the chancellor there is a commiffary, who holds a court of record for all privileged perfons and fcholars under the degree of mafter of arts, where all caufes are tried and determined by the civil and ftatute law, and by the cuftom of the univerfity.

The vice-chancellor of Cambridge is chofen annually by the fenate, out of two perfons nominated by the heads of the feveral colleges and halls.

Chancellor's Court. See *University-Courts*.

CHANCERON, in natural hiftory, a name given by the French writers to the fmall caterpillar that eats the corn, and does vaft mifchief in their granaries. See the article *Corn-Butterfly*.

CHANCERY, the higheft court of juftice in Britain next to the parliament, and of very ancient inftitution. It has its name chancery (*cancellaria*) from the judge who prefides here, the lord chancellor, or *cancellarius*; who, according to Sir Edward Coke, is fo termed a *cancellando*, from cancelling the king's letters patent when granted contrary to law, which is the higheft point of his jurifdiction. In chancery there are two diftinct tribunals: the one ordinary, being a court of common law; the other extraordinary, being a court of equity.

1. The *ordinary* legal court holds pleas of recognizances acknowledged in the chancery, writs of *fcire facias*, for repeal of letters patent, writs of partition, &c. and alfo of all perfonal actions by or againft any officer of the court. Sometimes a *fuperfedeas*, or writ of privilege, hath been here granted to difcharge a perfon out of prifon; one from hence may have a *habeas corpus* prohibition, &c. in the vacation; and here a *fubpœna* may be had to force witneffes to appear in other courts, when they have no power to call them. But, in profecuting caufes, if the parties defcend to iffue, this court cannot try it by jury; but the lord chancellor delivers the record into the king's bench to be tried there; and after trial had, it is to be remanded into the chancery, and there judgment given: tho' if there be a demurrer in law, it fhall be argued in this court. Blackft. Comment.

In this court is alfo kept the *officina juftitiæ*; out of which all original writs that pafs under the great feal, all commiffions of charitable ufes, fewers, bankruptcy,

idiocy,

Chancery. idiocy, lunacy, and the like, do issue; and for which it is always open to the subject, who may there at any time demand and have, *ex debito justitiæ*, any writ that his occasions may call for. These writs, relating to the business of the subject, and the returns of them, were, according to the simplicity of ancient times, originally kept in a hamper, *in hanaperio*; and the others (relating to such matters wherein the crown is mediately or immediately concerned) were preserved in a little sack or bag, *in parva baga*: and hence hath arisen the distinction of the *hanaper* office, and the *petty-bag* office, which both belong to the common law-court in chancery.

2. The *extraordinary* court, or court of equity, proceeds by the rules of equity and conscience; and moderates the rigour of the common law, considering the *intention* rather than the *words* of the law. It gives relief for and against infants notwithstanding their minority, and for and against married women notwithstanding their coverture. All frauds and deceits for which there is no redress at common law; all breaches of trust and confidence; and accidents, as to relieve obligors, mortgagers, &c. against penalties and forfeitures, where the intent was to pay the debt, are here remedied: for in chancery, a forfeiture, &c. shall not bind, where a thing may be done after or compensation made for it. Also this court will give relief against the extremity of unreasonable engagements entered into without consideration; oblige creditors that are unreasonable to compound with an unfortunate debtor; and make executors, &c. give security and pay interest for money that is to lie long in their hands. This court may confirm title to lands, though one hath lost his writings; and render conveyances, defective through mistake, &c. good and perfect. In chancery, copy-holders may be relieved against the ill usage of their lords; inclosures of lands that are common be decreed; and this court may decree money or lands given to charitable uses, oblige men to account with each other, &c. But in all cases where the plaintiff can have his remedy at law, he ought not to be relieved in chancery; and a thing which may be tried by a jury is not triable in this court.

The proceedings in chancery are, first to file the bill of complaint, signed by some counsel, setting forth the fraud or injury done, or wrong sustained, and praying relief: after the bill is filed, process of *subpœna* issues to compel the defendant to appear; and when the defendant appears, he puts in his answer to the bill of complaint, if there be no cause for the plea to the jurisdiction of the court, in disability of the person, or in bar, &c. Then the plaintiff brings his replication, unless he files exceptions against the answer as insufficient, referring it to a master to report whether it be sufficient or not; to which report exceptions may also be made. The answer, replication, rejoinder, &c. being settled, and the parties come to issue, witnesses are to be examined upon interrogatories, either in court or by commission in the country, wherein the parties usually join; and when the plaintiff and defendant have examined their witnesses, publication is to be made of the depositions, and the cause is to be set down for hearing; after which follows the decree. But it is now usual to appeal to the house of lords; which appeals are to be signed by two noted counsel, and exhibited by way of petition; the petition or appeal is lodged with the clerk of the house of lords, and read in the house, whereon the appellee is ordered to put in his answer, and a day fixed for hearing the cause; and after counsel heard, and evidence given on both sides, the lords will affirm or reverse the decree of the chancery, and finally determine the cause by a majority of votes, &c.

CHANDELIER, in fortification, a kind of moveable parapet, consisting of a wooden frame, made of two upright stakes, about six feet high, with cross planks between them; serving to support fascines to cover the pioneers.

CHANDERNAGORE, a French settlement in the kingdom of Bengal in the East Indies. It lies on the river Ganges, two leagues and a half above Calcutta. The district is hardly a league in circumference, and has the disadvantage of being somewhat exposed on the western side; but its harbour is excellent, and the air is as pure as it can be on the banks of the Ganges. Whenever any building is undertaken that requires strength, it must here, as well as in all other parts of Bengal, be built upon piles; it being impossible to dig three or four feet without coming at water.

CHANDLER (Mary), distinguished by her talent for poetry, was the daughter of a dissenting minister at Bath; and was born at Malmsbury in Wiltshire in 1687. She was bred a milliner; but from her childhood had a turn for poetry, and in her riper years applied herself to the study of the poets. Her poems, for which she was complimented by Mr Pope, breathe the spirit of piety and philosophy. She had the misfortune to be deformed, which determined her to live single; though she had great sweetness of countenance, and was solicited to marry. She died in 1745, aged 58.

CHANDLER (Dr Samuel), a learned and respectable dissenting minister, descended from ancestors heartily engaged in the cause of religious liberty, and sufferers for the sake of conscience and nonconformity; was born at Hungerford in Berks, where his father was a minister of considerable worth and abilities. Being by his literary turn destined to the ministry, he was first placed at an academy at Bridgewater, and from thence removed to Gloucester under Mr Samuel Jones. Among the pupils of Mr Jones were Mr Joseph Butler, afterwards bishop of Durham, and Mr Thomas Secker, afterwards archbishop of Canterbury. With these eminent persons he contracted a friendship that continued to the end of their lives, notwithstanding the different views by which their conduct was afterwards directed, and the different situations in which they were placed.

Mr Chandler having finished his academical studies, began to preach about July 1714; and being soon distinguished by his talents in the pulpit, he was chosen in 1716 minister of the Presbyterian congregation at Peckham near London, in which station he continued some years. Here he entered in the matrimonial state, and began to have an increasing family, when, by the fatal South-sea scheme of 1720, he unfortunately lost the whole fortune which he had received with his wife. His circumstances being thereby embarrassed, and his income as a minister being inadequate to his expences, he engaged in the trade of a bookseller, and kept a shop in the Poultry, London, for about two or three

years,

years, still continuing to discharge the duties of the pastoral office. He also officiated as joint preacher with the learned Dr Lardner of a winter weekly evening lecture at the meeting-house in the Old Jewry, London; in which meeting he was established assistant preacher about the year 1725, and then as the pastor. Here he ministered to the religious improvement of a very respectable congregation for 40 years with the greatest applause; and with what diligence and application he improved the vacancies of time from his pastoral duties, for improving himself and benefiting the world, will appear from his many writings on a variety of important subjects. While he was thus laudably employed, not only the universities of Edinburgh and Aberdeen gave him, without any application, testimonies of their esteem in diplomas, conferring on him the degree of D. D. but he also received offers of preferment from some of the governors of the established church, which he nobly declined. He had likewise the honour of being afterwards elected F. R. and A. SS.

On the death of George II. in 1760, Dr Chandler published a sermon on that event, in which he compared that prince to King David. This gave rise to a pamphlet, which was printed in the year 1761, intitled "The History of the Man after God's own Heart;" wherein the author ventured to exhibit King David as an example of perfidy, lust, and cruelty, fit only to be ranked with a Nero or a Caligula; and complained of the insult that had been offered to the memory of the late British monarch by Dr Chandler's parallel between him and the king of Israel. This attack occasioned Dr Chandler to publish in the following year "A Review of the History of the Man after God's own Heart; in which the Falsehoods and Misrepresentations of the Historian are exposed and corrected." He also prepared for the press a more elaborate work, which was afterwards published in two volumes 8vo, under the following title: "A Critical History of the Life of David: in which the principal Events are ranged in Order of time; the chief Objections of Mr Bayle and others against the Character of this Prince, and the Scripture Account of him, and the Occurrences of his Reign, are examined and refuted; and the Psalms which refer to him explained." As this was the last, it was likewise one of the best, of Dr Chandler's productions. The greatest part of this work was printed off at the time of our author's death, which happened May 8th 1766, aged 73. During the last year of his life, he was visited with frequent returns of a very painful disorder, which he endured with great resignation and Christian fortitude. He was interred in the burying-ground at Bunhill-fields on the 16th of the month; and his funeral was very honourably attended by ministers and other gentlemen. He expressly desired, by his last will, that no delineation of his character might be given in his funeral sermon, which was preached by Dr Amory. He had several children; two sons and a daughter who died before him, and three daughters who survived him; two of whom are yet living, and both married, one of them to the Rev. Dr Harwood.

Dr Chandler was a man of very extensive learning and eminent abilities; his apprehension was quick and his judgment penetrating; he had a warm and vigorous imagination; he was a very instructive and animated preacher; and his talents in the pulpit and as a writer procured him very great and general esteem, not only among the dissenters, but among large numbers of the established church. He was principally instrumental in the establishment of the fund for relieving the widows and orphans of poor Protestant dissenting ministers: the plan of it was first formed by him; and it was by his interest and application to his friends that many of the subscriptions for its support were procured.

In 1768, four volumes of our author's sermons were published by Dr Amory, according to his own directions in his last will; to which was prefixed a neat engraving of him, from an excellent portrait by Mr Chamberlin. He also expressed a desire to have some of his principal pieces reprinted in four volumes 8vo; proposals were accordingly published for that purpose, but did not meet with sufficient encouragement. But in 1777, another work of our author was published in one volume 4to, under the following title: "A Paraphrase and Notes on the Epistles of St Paul to the Galatians and Ephesians, with doctrinal and practical Observations; together with a critical and practical Commentary on the two Epistles of St Paul to the Thessalonians." Dr Chandler also left, in his interleaved Bible, a large number of critical notes, chiefly in Latin, which are now the property of Dr Kippis, Mr Farmer, Dr Price, and Dr Savage, and which have been intended to be published; but the design has not yet been executed. A complete list of Dr Chandler's works is given in the Biographia Britannica, vol. III. p. 435.

CHANG-TONG, a province of China, bounded on the east by Petcheli and part of Honan, on the south by Kiang-nan, on the east by the sea, and on the north by the sea and part of Petcheli. The country is well watered by lakes, streams, and rivers; but is nevertheless liable to suffer from drought, as rain falls here but seldom. The locusts also sometimes make great devastation. However, it abounds greatly in game; and there is perhaps no country where quails, partridges, and pheasants, are sold cheaper, the inhabitants of this province being reckoned the keenest sportsmen in the empire. The province is greatly enriched by the river Yun, called the *Grand Imperial Canal*, through which all the barks bound to Pekin must pass in their way thither. The duties on this canal alone amount to more than L. 450,000 annually. The canal itself is greatly admired by European travellers on account of its strong and long dikes, the banks decorated with cut stone, the ingenious mechanism of its locks, and the great number of natural obstacles which have been overcome in the execution of the work.—The province produces silk of the ordinary kind; and, besides this, another from a sort of insect resembling our caterpillar. It is coarser than the ordinary silk, but much stronger and more durable; so that the stuffs made from it have a very extensive sale throughout the empire.

Chang-tong is remarkable for being the birth-place of the celebrated philosopher and lawgiver Confucius. His native city is called *Kio-feou*, where there are several monuments erected in honour of this great man. The province is divided into six districts, which contain six cities of the first class, and 114 of the second

Chang-tong ‖ Changes.

and third. Along the coast, also, are 15 or 16 villages of considerable importance on account of their commerce; there are likewise a number of small islands, most of which have harbours very convenient for the Chinese junks which pass from thence to Corea or Leatong. The most remarkable cities are, 1. Tsi-nan-fou, the capital, which stands south of the river Tsingho or Tsi. It is large and populous; but chiefly celebrated for having been the residence of a long series of kings, whose tombs, rising on the neighbouring mountains, afford a beautiful prospect. 2. Yen-tcheu-fou, the second city of the province, situated between two rivers, and in a mild and temperate climate. Great quantities of gold are said to have been formerly collected in its neighbourhood. 3. Lin-tçin-tcheu, situated on the great canal, is much frequented by ships, and may be called a general magazine for every kind of merchandise. Here is an octagonal tower, divided into eight stories, the walls of which are covered on the outside with porcelain loaded with various figures neatly executed, and encrusted on the inside with variously coloured marble. A staircase, constructed in the wall, conducts to all the stories, from which there are passages that lead into magnificent galleries ornamented with gilt balustrades. All the cornices and projections of the tower are furnished with little bells; which, says Mr Grosier, when agitated by the wind, form a very agreeable harmony. In the highest story is an idol of gilt copper, to which the tower is dedicated. In the neighbourhood are some other temples, the architecture of which is exceedingly beautiful.

CHANGER, an officer belonging to the king's mint, who changes money for gold or silver bullion. See MINT.

Money-CHANGER, is a banker who deals in the exchange, receipt, and payment, of moneys. See BANKER.

CHANGES, in arithmetic, &c. the permutations or variations of any number of quantities; with regard to their position, order, &c. See COMBINATION.

To find all the possible CHANGES of any Number of Quantities, or how oft their Order may be varied.] Suppose two quantities *a* and *b*. Since they may be either wrote *a b* or *b a*, it is evident their *changes* are 2=2.1. Suppose three quantities *a b c*; their *changes* will be as in the margin; as is evident by combining *c* first with *a b*, then with *b a*; and hence the number of *changes* arises 3. 2. 1=6. If the quantities be 4, each may be combined four ways with each order of the other three; whence the number of changes arises 6. 4=4. 3. 2. 1.=24. Wherefore, if the number of quantities be supposed *n*, the number of *changes* will be *n.n*−1.*n*−2.*n*−3.*n*−4.&c. If the same quantity occur twice, the *changes* of two will be found *b b*; of three, *b a b*, *a b b*, *b b c*; of four, *c b a b*, *b c a b*, *b a b c*. And thus the number of *changes* in the first case will be 1=(2.1): 2.1; in the second, 3=(3.2.1): 2.1; in the third, 12=(4.3.2.1): 2.1.

c a b
a c b
a b c
——
c b a
b c a
b a c

If a fifth letter be added, in each series of four quantities, it will beget five *changes*, whence the number of all the *changes* will be 60=(5.4.3.2.1): 1.2.1. Hence if the number of quantities be *n*, the number of *changes* will be (*n.n*−1.*n*−2.*n*−3.*n*−4. &c.): 2.1.

From these special formulæ may be collected a general one, viz. if *n* be the number of quantities, and *m* the number which shows how oft the same quantity occurs; we shall have (*n.n*−1.*n*−2.*n*−3.*n*−4.*n*−5.*n*−6.*n*−7.*n*−8.*n*−9. &c.): *m.m*−1.*m*−2.*m*−3.*m*−4. &c.) the series being to be continued, till the continued subtraction of unity from *n* and *m* leave 0. After the same manner we may proceed further, till putting *n* for the number of quantities, and *l*, *m*, *r*, &c. for the number that shows how oft any of them is repeated, we arrive at an universal form. (*n.n*−1.*n*−2.*n*−3.*n*−4.*n*−5.*n*−6.*n*−7.*n*−8. &c.): (*l.l*−1.*l*−2.*l*−3.*l*−4.*l*−5. &c. *m.m*−1.*m*−2.*m*−3. &c. *r.r*−1.*r*−2.*r*−3.*r*−4.*r*−5. &c.

Suppose, for instance, *n*=6, *l*=3, *r*=0. The number of *changes* will be (6.5.4.3.2.1.): (3.2.1.3.2.1.) =(6.5.4.): (3.2=2.3.2=20).

Hence, suppose thirteen persons at a table, if it be required how oft they may *change* places; we shall find the number 13.12.11.10.9.8.7.6.5.4.3.2.1. =6227020800.

In this manner may all the possible anagrams of any word be found in all languages, and that without any study; suppose *v. g.* it were required to find the anagrams of the word *amor*, the number of *changes* will be

a	*oam*	*rmoa*	*maro*	*orom*
——	*aom*	*mroa*	*maor*	*aorm*
ma	*amo*	*mora*	——	*aomr*
am	——	*moar*	*raom*	——
——	*roma*	——	*oram*	*ramo*
oma	*orma*	*rmao*	*oarm*	*armo*
moa	*omra*	*mrao*	*oamr*	*amro*
mao	*omar*		——	*amor*
			raom	

The anagrams therefore of the word *amor*, in the Latin tongue, are *roma*, *mora*, *maro*, *ramo*, *oram*. See ANAGRAM.

Whether this new method of anagrammatising be like to prove of much service to that art, is left to the poets.

CHANNA, in zoology, the name of a fish caught in great plenty in the Mediterranean, and brought to market in Italy and elsewhere, among the sea-perch, which it so nearly resembles, that it would not be distinguishable from it, but that the sea-perch is bigger, and has only broad transverse lines on its back, whereas the channa has them both transverse and longitudinal. It has a very wide mouth, and its lower jaw is longer than its upper; so that its mouth naturally falls open. Its eyes are small, and its teeth very sharp; its back is of a blackish red; it has several longitudinal lines of a reddish hue, and its tail is marked with reddish spots. There is an observation, that in all the fish of this kind which have been examined by naturalists, there have been found none but females. This is as old as the days of Aristotle. Whether this be true in fact, would require many observations. If it should prove so, the whole seems to end in this, that the channa is no distinct species, but only the female of some other fish. There is another fish not unlike this, called *cannadella*, or rather *channadella*, which at Marseilles is known by the name of *cherino*.

Changes ‖ Channel.

CHANNEL, in geography, an arm of the sea, or a narrow sea between two continents, or between a continent

continent and an island. Such are the British channel, St George's channel, the channel of Constantinople, &c.

Channel of a Ship. See *Chain-Wales.*

CHAN-si, a province of China, and one of the smallest in the empire, is bounded on the east by Pet-cheli, on the south by Honan, on the west by Chen-si, and on the north by the great wall. The climate is healthful and agreeable, and the soil generally fertile, though the country is full of mountains. Some of these last are rough, wild, and uninhabited; but others are cultivated with the greatest care from top to bottom, and cut into terraces, forming a very agreeable prospect; while some have on their tops vast plains no less fertile than the richest low-lands. These mountains abound with coal, which the inhabitants pound and make into cakes with water; a kind of fuel which, though not very inflammable, affords a strong and lasting fuel when once kindled. It is principally used for heating their stoves, which are constructed with brick as in Germany; but the inhabitants of this province give them the form of small beds, and sleep upon them. The best grapes to be met with in this part of Asia grow in the province of Chan-si; so that good wine might be made, but the people choose rather to dry and sell them to the neighbouring provinces. The country abounds with musk, porphyry, marble, lapis lazuli, and jasper of various colours; and iron mines as well as salt-pits and crystal are very common. Here are five cities of the first class, and eighty-five of the second and third; the most remarkable are, 1. Tai-youen-fou the capital, an ancient city about three leagues circumference, but much decayed in consequence of being no longer the residence of the princes of the blood as it was formerly. Nothing now remains of the palaces of those princes but a few ruins; but their tombs are still to be seen on a neighbouring mountain. The burying-place is magnificently ornamented; and all the tombs are of marble or cut stone, having near them triumphal arches, statues of heroes, figures of lions and different animals, especially horses, and which are disposed in very elegant order. An awful and melancholy gloom is preserved around these tombs by groves of aged cypresses, which have never felt the stroke of an axe, placed chequer-wise. The principal articles of trade here are, hard-ware, stuffs of different kinds, particularly carpets in imitation of those of Turky. 2. Ngan-y is situated near a lake as salt as the ocean, from which a great quantity of salt is extracted. 3. Fuen-tcheou-fou, an ancient and commercial city, built on the banks of the river Fuenho; it has baths and springs almost boiling hot, which by drawing hither a great number of strangers, add greatly to its opulence. 4. Tai-tong-fou, situated near the wall, is a place of great strength, and important by reason of its situation, as being the only one exposed to the incursions of the Tartars. Its territories abound with lapis lazuli, medicinal herbs, and a particular kind of jasper called *pietsu*, which is as white and beautiful as agate; marble and porphyry are also common; and a great revenue is produced from the skins which are dressed here.

CHANT, (*cantus*), is used for the vocal music of churches.

In church-history we meet with divers kinds of chant or song. The first is the *Ambrosian*, established by St Ambrose. The second, the *Gregorian chant*, introduced by Pope Gregory the great, who established schools of chantors, and corrected the church-song. This is still retained in the church under the name of *plain song*: at first it was called the *Roman song*. The *plain* or *Gregorian chant*, is where the choir and people sing in unison, or all together in the same manner.

CHANTILLY, a village in France, about seven leagues from Paris, where there is a magnificent palace and fine forest belonging to the duke of Bourbon.

CHANTOR, a singer of a choir in a cathedral. The word is almost grown obsolete, *chorister* or *singing-man* being commonly used instead of it. All great chapters have chantors and chaplains to assist the canons, and officiate in their absence.

Chantor is used by way of excellence for the precentor or master of the choir, which is one of the first dignities of the chapter. At St David's in Wales, where there is no dean, he is next in dignity to the bishop. The ancients called the chantor *primicerius cantorum*. To him belonged the direction of the deacons and other inferior officers.

Chantors, in the temple of Jerusalem, were a number of Levites employed in singing the praises of God, and playing upon instruments before his altar. They had no habits distinct from the rest of the people; yet in the ceremony of removing the ark to Solomon's temple, the chantors appeared dressed in tunics of byssus or fine linen. 2 Chron. v. 12.

CHANTRY, or Chauntry, was anciently a church or chapel endowed with lands, or other yearly revenue, for the maintenance of one or more priests, daily saying or singing mass for the souls of the donors, and such others as they appointed. Hence *chauntry-rents* are rents paid to the crown by the tenants or purchasers of *chauntry lands*.

CHAOLOGY, the history or description of the chaos. See Chaos.

Orpheus, in his chaology, sets forth the different alterations, secretions, and divers forms which matter went through till it became inhabitable, which amounts to the same with what we otherwise call *cosmogony*. Dr Burnet, in his theory of the earth, represents the chaos as it was at first, entire, undivided, and universally rude and deformed; or the *tohu bohu*; then shows how it came to be divided into its respective regions; how the homogeneous matter gathered itself apart from all of a contrary principle; and lastly, how it hardened, and became a solid habitable globe. See Earth.

CHAOS, that confusion in which matter lay when newly produced out of nothing at the beginning of the world, before God, by his almighty word, had put it into the order and condition wherein it was after the six days creation. See Earth.

Chaos is represented by the ancients as the first principle, ovum, or seed of nature and the world. All the sophists, sages, naturalists, philosophers, theologues, and poets, held that chaos was the eldest and first principle, το αρχαιον χαος. The Barbarians, Phœnicians, Egyptians, Persians, &c. all refer the origin of the world to a rude, mixed, confused mass of matter. The Greeks, Orpheus, Hesiod, Menander, Aristophanes, Euripides, and the writers of the Cyclic Poems, all speak

ſpeak of the firſt chaos: the Ionic and Platonic philoſophers build the world out of it. The Stoics hold, that as the world was firſt made of a chaos, it ſhall at laſt be reduced to a chaos; and that its periods and revolutions in the mean time are only tranſitions from one chaos to another. Laſtly, the Latins, as Ennius, Varro, Ovid, Lucretius, Statius, &c. are all of the ſame opinion. Nor is there any ſect or nation whatever, that does not derive their [illegible], *the ſtructure of the world*, from a chaos.

The opinion firſt aroſe among the Barbarians, whence it ſpread to the Greeks, and from the Greeks to the Romans and other nations. Dr Burnet obſerves, that beſides Ariſtotle and a few other pſeudo-Pythagoreans, nobody ever aſſerted that our world was always from eternity of the ſame nature, form, and ſtructure, as at preſent; but that it had been the ſtanding opinion of the wiſe men of all ages, that what we now call the *terreſtrial globe*, was originally an unformed, indigeſted maſs of heterogeneous matter, called *chaos*; and no more than the rudiments and materials of the preſent world.

It does not appear who firſt broached the notion of a chaos. Moſes, the eldeſt of all writers, derives the origin of this world from a confuſion of matter, dark, void, deep, without form, which he calls *tohu bohu*; which is preciſely the chaos of the Greek and Barbarian philoſophers. Moſes goes no further than the chaos; nor tells us whence it took its origin, or whence its confuſed ſtate; and where Moſes ſtops, there, preciſely, do all the reſt. Dr Burnet endeavours to ſhow, that as the ancient philoſophers, &c. who wrote of the coſmogony, acknowledged a chaos for the principle of their world; ſo the divines, or writers of the theogony, derive the origin or generation of their fabled gods from the ſame principle.

Mr Whiſton ſuppoſes the ancient chaos, the origin of our earth, to have been the atmoſphere of a comet; which, though new, yet, all things conſidered, is not the moſt improbable aſſertion. He endeavours to make it out by many arguments, drawn from the agreement which appears to be between them. So that, according to him, every planet is a comet, formed into a regular and laſting conſtitution, and placed at a proper diſtance from the ſun, revolving in a nearly circular orbit; and a comet is a planet either beginning to be deſtroyed or re-made; that is, a chaos or planet unformed or in its primeval ſtate, and placed as yet in an orbit very eccentrical.

Chaos, in the phraſe of Paracelſus, imports the air. It has alſo ſome other ſignifications amongſt the alchemiſts.

Chaos, in zoology, a genus of inſects belonging to the order of vermes zoophyta. The body has no ſhell or covering, and is capable of reviving after being dead to appearance for a long time: it has no joints or external organs of ſenſation. There are five ſpecies, moſtly obtained by infuſions of different vegetables in water, and only diſcoverable by the microſcope. See Animalcule.

CHAPEAU, in heraldry, an ancient cap of dignity worn by dukes, being ſcarlet-coloured velvet on the outſide, and lined with a fur. It is frequently borne above an helmet inſtead of a wreath, under gentlemens creſts.

CHAPEL, a place of divine worſhip, ſo called. The word is derived from the Latin *capella*. In former times, when the kings of France were engaged in war, they always carried St Martin's hat into the field, which was kept in a tent as a precious relic; from whence the place was called *capella*; and the prieſts, who had the cuſtody of the tent, *capellani*. Afterwards the word *capella* became applied to private oratories.

In Britain there are ſeveral ſorts of chapels. 1. Parochial chapels: theſe differ from pariſh-churches only in name; they are generally ſmall, and the inhabitants within the diſtrict few. If there be a preſentation *ad eccleſiam*, inſtead of *capellam*, and an admiſſion and inſtitution upon it, it is no longer a chapel, but a church. 2. Chapels, which adjoin to, and are part of the church: ſuch were formerly built by honourable perſons, as burying-places for themſelves and their families. 3. Chapels of eaſe: theſe are uſually built in very large pariſhes, where all the people cannot conveniently repair to the mother-church. 4. Free chapels; ſuch as were founded by kings of England. They are free from all epiſcopal juriſdiction, and only to be viſited by the founder and his ſucceſſors; which is done by the lord chancellor: yet the king may licenſe any ſubject to build and endow a chapel, and by letters patent exempt it from the viſitation of the ordinary. 5. Chapels in the univerſities, belonging to particular colleges. 6. Domeſtic chapels, built by noblemen or gentlemen for the private ſervice of God in their families. See Chaplain.

Chapel is alſo a name given to a printer's workhouſe; becauſe, according to ſome authors, printing was firſt actually performed in chapels or churches; or, according to others, becauſe Caxton, an early printer, exerciſed the art in one of the chapels in Weſtminſter Abbey. In this ſenſe they ſay, *the orders or laws of the chapel, the ſecrets of the chapel*, &c.

Knights of the Chapel, called alſo *Poor knights of Windſor*, were inſtituted by Henry VIII. in his teſtament. Their number was at firſt thirteen, but has been ſince augmented to twenty-ſix. They aſſiſt in the funeral ſervices of the kings of England: they are ſubject to the office of the canons of Windſor, and live on penſions aſſigned them by the order of the garter. They wear a blue or red cloak, with the arms of St George on the left ſhoulder.

CHAPELAIN (James), an eminent French poet born at Paris in 1595, and often mentioned in the works of Balzac, Menage, and other learned men. He wrote ſeveral works, and at length diſtinguiſhed himſelf by an heroic poem called *La Pucelle, ou France Delivrée*, which employed him ſeveral years; and which, raiſing the expectation of the public, was as much decried by ſome as extolled by others. He was one of the king's counſellors; and died in 1674, very rich, but was very covetous and ſordid.

CHAPELET, in the manege, a couple of ſtirrup-leathers, mounted each of them with a ſtirrup, and joined at top in a ſort of leather buckle, called the *head of the chapelet*, by which they are made faſt to the pommel of the ſaddle, after being adjuſted to the rider's length and bore. They are uſed both to avoid the trouble of taking up or letting down the ſtirrups every time that the gentleman mounts on a different horſe and

and saddle, and to supply the place of the academy saddles, which have no stirrups to them.

CHAPELLE (Claudius Emanuel Luillier), the natural son of Francis Luillier, took the name of *Chapelle* from a village between Paris and St Denys, where he was born. He distinguished himself by writing small pieces of poetry, in which he discovered great delicacy, an easy turn, and an admirable facility of expression. He was the friend of Gassendi and Moliere; and died in 1686.

CHAPERON, CHAPERONNE, or CHAPEROON, properly signifies a sort of hood or covering of the head anciently worn both by men and women, the nobles and the populace, and afterwards appropriated to the doctors, and licentiates in colleges, &c. Hence the name passed to certain little shields, and other funeral devices, placed on the foreheads of the horses that drew the hearses in pompous funerals, and which are still called *chaperonnes*, or *shaffroons*; because such devices were originally fastened on the *chaperonnes*, or hoods, worn by those horses with their other coverings of state.

Chaperon of a bit-mouth, in the manege, is only used for scatch-mouths, and all others that are not cannon-mouths, signifying the end of the bit that joins to the branch just by the banquet. In scatch-mouths the chaperon is round, but in others it is oval; and the same part that in scatch and other mouths is called *chaperon*, is in cannon-mouths called *fronteau*.

CHAPITERS, in architecture, the same with CAPITALS.

CHAPITERS, in law, formerly signified a summary of such matters as were inquired of, or presented before justices in eyre, justices of assize, or of the peace in their sessions.

Chapiters, at this time, denote such articles as are delivered by the mouth of the justice in his charge to the inquest.

CHAPLAIN properly signifies a person provided with a chapel; or who discharges the duty thereof.

CHAPLAIN is also used for an ecclesiastical person, in the house of a prince, or a person of quality, who officiates in their chapels, &c.

In England there are 48 chaplains to the king, who wait four each month, preach in the chapel, read the service to the family, and to the king in his private oratory, and say grace in the absence of the clerk of the closet. While in waiting they have a table, and attendance, but no salary. In Scotland the king has six chaplains, with a salary of L. 50 each, three of them having in addition the deanery of the chapel-royal divided between them, making up above L. 100 to each. Their only duty at present is to say prayers at the election of peers for Scotland to sit in parliament.——According to a statute of Henry VIII. the persons vested with a power of retaining chaplains, together with the number each is allowed to qualify, is as follows: An archbishop, eight; a duke or bishop, six; marquis or earl, five; viscount, four; baron, knight of the garter, or lord chancellor, three; a duchess, marchioness, countess, baroness, the treasurer and comptroller of the king's house, clerk of the closet, the king's secretary, dean of the chapel, almoner, and master of the rolls, each of them two; chief justice of the king's bench, and warden of the cinque-ports, each one. All these chaplains may purchase a licence or dispensation, and take two benefices with cure of souls. A chaplain must be retained by letters testimonial under hand and seal; for it is not sufficient that he serve as chaplain in the family.

The first chaplains are said to have been those instituted by the ancient kings of France, for preserving the chape, or cape, with the other relics of St Martin, which the kings kept in their palace, and carried out with them to the war. The first chaplain is said to have been Gul. de Mesmes, chaplain to St Louis.

Chaplain in the order of Malta, is used for the second rank, or class, in that order; otherwise called *diaco*.

The knights make the first class, and the chaplains the second.

Chaplains of the Pope, are the auditors, or judges of causes in the sacred palace; so called, because the pope anciently gave audience in his chapel, for the decision of cases sent from the several parts of Christendom. He hither summoned as assessors the most learned lawyers of his time; and they hence acquired the appellation of *capellani*, chaplains. It is from the decrees formerly given by these, that the body of decretals is composed: their number pope Sixtus IV. reduced to twelve.

Some say, the shrines of relics were covered with a kind of tent, cape, or *capella*, i. e. little cape; and that hence the priests, who had the care of them, were called chaplains. In time these relics were reposited in a little church, either contiguous to a larger, or separate from it; and the same name, *capella*, which was given to the cover, was also given to the place where it was lodged: and hence the priest who superintended it came to be called chaplain.

CHAPLET, an ancient ornament for the head, like a garland or wreath; but this word is frequently used to signify the circle of a crown. There are instances of its being borne in a coat of arms, as well as for crests; the paternal arms for Lascelles are argent, three chaplets, gules.

CHAPLET also denotes a string of beads used by the Roman Catholics, to count the number of their prayers. The invention of it is ascribed to Peter the hermit, who probably learned it of the Turks, as they owe it to the East-Indians.

Chaplets are sometimes called *pater-nosters*; and are made of coral, of diamonds, of wood, *&c.* The common chaplet contains fifty ave-marias, and five paternosters. There is also a chaplet of our Saviour, consisting of 33 beads, in honour of his 33 years living on earth, instituted by father Michael the Camaldulian.

The Orientals have a kind of chaplets which they call *chains*, and which they use in their prayers, rehearsing one of the perfections of God on each link or bead. The Great Mogul is said to have 18 of these chains, all precious stones; some diamonds, others rubies, pearls, &c. The Turks have likewise chaplets, which they bear in the hand, or hang at the girdle: but father Dandini observes, they differ from those used by the Romanists, in that they are all of the same bigness, and have not that distinction into decads; though they consist of six decads, or 60 beads. He adds, that the mussulmans run over the chaplet almost in an instant, the prayers being extremely short, as containing only these words, "praise to God," or "glory

"glory to God," for each bead. Besides the common chaplet they have likewise a larger one consisting of 100 beads, where there is some distinction, as being divided by little threads into three parts; on one of which they repeat 30 times *soubhan Allah*, i. e. "God is worthy to be praised;" on another, *elhamd Allah*, "glory be to God;" and on the third, *Allah acbar*, "God is great." These thrice thirty times making only 90; to complete the number 100, they add other prayers for the beginning of the chaplet.—He adds, that the Mahometan chaplet appears to have had its rise from the *mea beracoth*, or "hundred benedictions;" which the Jews are obliged to repeat daily, and which we find in their prayer-books; the Jews and Mahometans having this in common, that they scarce do any thing without pronouncing some laud or benediction.

Menage derives the word *chaplet* from *chapeau*, "hat." The modern Latins call it *chapellina*, the Italians more frequently *corona*.

Chaplet, or *Chapelet*, in architecture, a little moulding, cut, or carved into round beads, pearls, olives, or the like.

CHAPMAN (George), born in 1557, a man highly esteemed in his time for his dramatic and poetic works. He wrote 17 plays; translated Homer and some other ancient poets; and was thought no mean genius. He died in 1634; and was buried in St Giles's in the fields, where his friend Inigo Jones erected a monument to him.

CHAPPE', in heraldry, the dividing an escutcheon by lines drawn from the centre of the upper edge to the angles below, into three parts, the sections on the sides being of different metal or colour from the rest.

CHAPPEL in frith, a market-town of Derbyshire, about 26 miles north-west of Derby; W. Long. 1. 50. N. Lat. 53. 22.

Chappel (William) a learned and pious bishop of Cork, Cloyne, and Ross, in Ireland, born in Nottinghamshire in 1582. When the troubles began under Charles I. he was prosecuted by the puritan party in parliament, and retired to Derby, where he devoted himself to study until his death in 1649. He wrote *Methodus Concionandi*, i. e. "the method of preaching;" and he is one of those to whom the *Whole Duty of Man* has been attributed. He left behind him also his own life written by himself in Latin, which has been twice printed.

CHAPTER, in ecclesiastical polity, a society or community of clergymen belonging to the cathedrals and collegiate churches.

It was in the eighth century that the body of canons began to be called a chapter. The chapter of the canons of a cathedral were a standing council to the bishop, and, during the vacancy of the see, had the jurisdiction of the diocese. In the earlier ages, the bishop was head of the chapter; afterwards abbots and other dignitaries, as deans, provosts, treasurers, &c. were preferred to this distinction. The deans and chapters had the privilege of choosing the bishops in England; but Henry VIII. got this power vested in the crown: and as the same prince expelled the monks from the cathedrals, and placed secular canons in their room, those he thus regulated were called deans and chapters of the new foundation; such are Canterbury, Winchester, Ely, Carlisle, &c. See Dean.

Chapter, in matters in literature, a division in a book for keeping the subject treated of more clear and distinct.

CHAR, in ichthyology, a species of Salmo.

CHARA, in botany; A genus of the monandria order, belonging to the monoecia class of plants. There is neither male calyx nor corolla; and the anthera is placed under the germen. The female calyx is tetraphyllous; no corolla; the stigma quinquefid, with one roundish seed.

CHARABON, a sea-port town on the northern coast of the island of Java in the East Indies; E. Long. 10. 8. S. Lat. 6.

CHARACENE, the most southern part of Susiana, a province of Persia, lying on the Persian gulph, between the Tigris and the Eulaeus. It was so named from the city of Charax, called first Alexandria, from its founder Alexander the Great; afterwards Antiochia, from Antiochus V. king of Syria, who repaired and beautified it; and lastly, Charax Spasinae, or Pasinae, that is the Mole of the Spasines, an Arabian king of that name having secured it against the overflowing of the Tigris, by a high bank or mole, extending three miles, which served as a fence to all that country. Dionysius Periegetes, and Isidorus, author of the Parthian Mansions, were both natives of this city. The small district of Characene was seized by Pasines, the son of Sogdonacus, king of the neighbouring Arabs, during the troubles of Syria, and erected into a kingdom. Lucian calls him Hyspasines, and adds, that he ruled over the Characeni and the neighbouring people: he died in the 85th year of his age. The other kings of this country we find mentioned by the ancients are, Tiraeus, who died in the 92d year of his age, and after him Artabazus the seventh, as Lucian informs us, who was driven from the throne by his own subjects, but restored by the Parthians. And this is all we find in the ancients relating to the kings of Characene.

CHARACTER, in a general sense, signifies a mark or figure, drawn on paper, metal, stone, or other matter, with a pen, graver, chissel, or other instrument, to signify or denote any thing. The word is Greek, χαρακτηρ, formed from the verb χαρασσειν, *insculpere*, "to ingrave, impress," &c.

The various kinds of characters may be reduced to three heads, viz. *Literal Characters*, *Numeral Characters*, and *Abbreviations*.

I. *Literal Character*, is a letter of the alphabet, serving to indicate some articulate sound, expressive of some idea or conception of the mind. See Alphabet.

1. These may be divided, with regard to their nature and use, into *Nominal Characters*, or those we properly call *letters*; which serve to express the names of things: See Letter. *Real Characters*; those that instead of names express things and ideas: See Idea, &c. *Emblematical* or *Symbolical Characters*; which have this in common with real ones, that they express the things themselves; but have this further, that they in some measure personate them, and exhibit their forms: such are the hieroglyphics of the ancient Egyptians. See Hieroglyphic, Symbol, &c.

2. *Literal Characters* may be again divided, with regard

Characters regard to their invention and use, into *particular* and *general* or *universal*.

Particular CHARACTERS, are those peculiar to this or that nation. Such are the Roman, Italic, Greek, Hebrew, Arabic, Gothic, Chinese, &c. *characters*. See HEBREW, GOTHIC, CHINESE, &c.

Universal CHARACTERS, are also *real characters*, and make what some authors call a *Philosophical Language*.

That diversity of *characters* used by the several nations to express the same idea, is found the chief obstacle to the advancement of learning: to remove this, several authors have taken occasion to propose plans of *characters* that should be universal, and which each people should read in their own language. The *character* here is to be real, not nominal: to express things and notions; not, as the common ones, letters or sounds: yet to be mute, like letters, and arbitrary; not emblematical, like hieroglyphics.

Thus, every nation should retain its own language, yet every one understand that of each other, without learning it; only by seeing a real or universal *character*, which should signify the same thing to all people, by what sounds soever each express it in their particular idiom. For instance, by seeing the *character* destined to signify *to drink*, an Englishman should read *to drink*; a Frenchman, *boire*; a Latin, *bibere*; a Greek, [illegible]; a Jew, [illegible]; a German, *trincken*; and so of the rest: in the same manner as seeing a horse, each people express it after their own manner; but all mean the same animal.

This real *character* is no chimera; the Chinese and Japonese have already something like it. They have a common *character* which each of those nations understand alike in their several languages; though they pronounce them with such different sounds, that they do not understand one another in speaking.

The first and most considerable attempts for a *real character*, or philosophical language, in Europe, are those of bishop Wilkins and Dalgarme: but these, with how much art soever they were contrived, have yet proved ineffectual.

M. Leibnitz had some thoughts the same way; he thinks those great men did not hit the right method. It was probable, indeed, that by their means, people, who do not understand one another, might easily have a commerce together; but they have not hit on true *real characters*.

According to him, the *characters* should resemble those used in Algebra: which, in effect, are very simple, yet very expressive; without any thing superfluous or equivocal; and contain all the varieties required.

The *real character* of bishop Wilkins has its just applause: Dr Hook recommends it on his own knowledge and experience, as a most excellent scheme; and to engage the world to the study thereof, publishes some fine inventions of his own therein.

M. Leibnitz tells us, he had under consideration an *alphabet of human thoughts*; in order to a new philosophical language, on his own scheme: but his death prevented its being brought to maturity.

M. Lodwic, in the *philosophical transactions*, gives us a plan of an *universal alphabet* or *character* of another kind: this was to contain an enumeration of all such single sounds, or letters, as are used in any language; by means whereof, people should be enabled to pronounce truly and readily any language; to describe the pronunciation of any language that shall be pronounced in their hearing, so as others accustomed to this language, though they had never heard the language pronounced, shall at first be able truly to pronounce it: and, lastly, this *character* to serve as a standard to perpetuate the sounds of any language. In the Journal Literaire, an. 1720, we have a very ingenious project for an universal *character*. The author, after obviating the objections that might be made against the feasibleness of such schemes in the general, proposes his own: his *characters* are to be the common Arabic, or numeral figures. The combinations of these nine are sufficient to express distinctly an incredible quantity of numbers, much more than we shall need terms to signify our actions, goods, evils, duties, passions, &c. Thus is all the trouble of framing and learning any new *character* at once saved; the Arabic figures having already all the universality required.

The advantages are immense. For, 1mo, We have here a stable, faithful interpreter; never to be corrupted or changed, as the popular languages continually are. 2do, Whereas the difficulty of pronouncing a foreign language is such as usually gives the learner the greatest trouble, and there are even some sounds which foreigners never attain to; in the *character* here proposed, this difficulty has no place: every nation is to pronounce them according to the particular pronunciation that already obtains among them. All the difficulty is, the accustoming the pen and the eye to affix certain notions to *characters* that do not, at first sight, exhibit them. But this trouble is no more than we find in the study of any language whatever.

The inflexions of words are here to be expressed by the common letters. For instance, the same *character* shall express a *filly* or a *colt*, a *horse* or a *mare*, an *old horse* or an *old mare*, as accompanied with this or that distinctive letter, which shall show the sex, youth, maturity, or old age: a letter also to express the bigness or *size* of things; thus v. g. a man with this or that letter, to signify a *great man*, or a *little man*, &c.

The use of these letters belongs to the grammar; which, once well understood, would abridge the vocabulary exceedingly. An advantage of this grammar is, that it would only have one declension and one conjugation: those numerous anomalies of grammarians are exceeding troublesome; and arise hence, that the common languages are governed by the populace, who never reason on what is best: but in the *character* here proposed, men of sense having the introduction of it, would have a new ground, whereon to build regularly.

But the difficulty is not in inventing the most simple, easy, and commodious *character*, but in engaging the several nations to use it; there being nothing they agree less in, than the understanding and pursuing their common interest.

3. Literal characters may again be divided, with respect to the nations among whom they have been invented, into Greek characters, Roman characters, Hebrew characters, &c. The Latin character now used through all Europe, was formed from the Greek, as the Greek was from the Phœnician; and the Phœnician,

Characters. as well as the Chaldee, Syriac, and Arabic characters, were formed from the ancient Hebrew, which subsisted till the Babylonish captivity; for after that event the character of the Assyrians, which is the square Hebrew now in use, prevailed, the ancient being only found on some Hebrew medals, commonly called Samaritan medals. It was in 1091 that the Gothic characters, invented by Ulfilas, were abolished, and the Latin ones established in their room.

Medallists observe, that the Greek character, consisting only of majuscule letters, has preserved its uniformity on all medals, as low as the time of Gallienus, from which time it appears somewhat weaker and rounder: from the time of Constantine to Michael we find only Latin characters: after Michael, the Greek characters recommence; but from that time they began to alter with the language, which was a mixture of Greek and Latin. The Latin medals preserve both their character and language as low as the translation of the seat of the empire to Constantinople: towards the time of Decius the character began to lose its roundness and beauty; some time after, it retrieved, and subsisted tolerably till the time of Justin, when it degenerated gradually into the Gothic. The rounder, then, and better formed a character is upon a medal, the fairer pretence it has to antiquity.

II. *Numeral* CHARACTERS, or characters used to express numbers, are either letters or figures.

The Arabic character, called also the common one, because it is used almost throughout Europe in all sorts of calculations, consists of these ten digits 1, 2, 3, 4, 5, 6, 7, 8, 9, 0.

The Roman numeral character consists of seven majuscule letters of the Roman alphabet, *viz.* I, V, X, L, C, D, M. The I denotes one, V five, X ten, L fifty, C a hundred, D five hundred, and M a thousand. The I repeated twice makes two, II; thrice, three, III; four is expressed thus IV, as I before V or X takes an unit from the number expressed by these letters. To express six, an I is added to a V, VI; for seven, two, VII; and for eight, three, VIII. nine is expressed by an I before X, thus IX. The same remark may be made of the X before L or C, except that the diminution is by tens; thus, XL denotes forty, XC ninety, and LX sixty. The C before D or M diminishes each by a hundred. The number five hundred is sometimes expressed by an I before a C inverted, thus, IↃ; and instead of M, which signifies a thousand, an I is sometimes used between two C's, the one direct, and the other inverted, thus CIↃ. The addition of C and Ↄ before or after raises CIↃ by tens, thus, CCIↃↃ expresses ten thousand, CCCIↃↃↃ, a hundred thousand. The Romans also expressed any number of thousands by a line drawn over any numeral less than a thousand; thus V̄ denotes five thousand, L̄X̄, sixty thousand: so likewise M̄ is one million, M̄M̄ is two millions, &c.

The Greeks had three ways of expressing numbers: 1. Every letter, according to its place in the alphabet, denoted a number, from α, one, to ω, twenty-four. 2. The alphabet was divided into eight units, α one, β two, three, &c.; into eight tens, ι ten, κ twenty λ thirty, &c.; and eight hundreds, ρ one hundred, σ two hundred, τ three hundred, &c. 3. I stood for one, Π five, Δ ten, Η a hundred, Χ a thousand, Μ ten thousand; and when the letter Π included any of these, except I, it showed the included letter to be five times its value; as |Δ| fifty, |Η| five hundred, |Χ| five thousand, |Μ| fifty thousand.

The French CHARACTER used in the chamber of accounts, and by persons concerned in the management of the revenue, is, properly speaking, nothing else than the Roman numerals, in letters that are not majuscule; thus, instead of expressing fifty-six by LVI, they denote it by smaller characters lvj.

III. CHARACTERS of Abbreviations, &c. in several of the arts, are symbols contrived for the more concise and immediate conveyance of the knowledge of things. For the

CHARACTERS *used in Algebra.* See ALGEBRA, Introduction.

CHARACTERS *used in Astronomy, viz.*

Of the Planets. See Plate LXII. fig. 19.

Of the Signs. Plate LXXVI. fig. 158. & LXXXV. fig. 204.

Of the aspects.

☌ or S Conjunction	△ Trine
SS Semisextile	Bq Biquintile
* Sextile	Vc Quincunx
Q Quintile	☍ Opposition
□ Quartile	☊ Dragon's head
Td Tredecile	☋ Dragon's tail

Of time.

A. M. *ante meridiem*, before the sun comes upon the meridian.

O. or N. noon.

P. M. *post meridiem*, when the sun is past the meridian.

CHARACTERS *in Commerce.*

D° *ditto*, the same	R° *recto* } *folio*
N° *numero*, or number	V° *verso* }
F° *folio*, or page	
C or ℔ hundred weight, or 112 pounds	£ or *L* pounds sterling
	p^r *per*, or by, as p^r *ann.* by the year, p^r *cent.*
q^{rs} quarters	R^x rixdollar
S or *s* shillings	D^t ducat
d pence or deniers	P. S. postscript; &c.
℔ pound weight.	

CHARACTERS *in Chemistry.* See Pl. chemil. & chemistry.

CHARACTERS *in Geometry and Trigonometry.*

∥ the character of parallelism	∼ equiangular, or similar
△ triangle	≐ equilateral
□ square	∠ an angle
▯ ▭ rectangle	∟ right angle
⊙ circle	⊥ perpendicular

° denotes a degree; thus 45° implies 45 degrees.

′ Denotes a minute; thus 50′, is 50 minutes. ″, ‴, ⁗, Denote seconds, thirds, and fourths: and the same characters are used where the progressions are by tens, as it is here by sixties.

CHARACTERS *in Grammar, Rhetoric, Poetry, &c.*

( ) parenthesis	D. D. doctor in divinity
[ ] crotchets	V. D. M. minister of the word of God.
- hyphen	
' apostrophe	LL. D. doctor of laws
' emphasis or accent	J. V. D. doctor of civil and canon law
˘ breve	
¨ dialysis	
^ caret and circumflex.	" quotation
† ‡ and * references	M. D. doctor in physic

Characters.

§ section or division — A. M. master of arts
¶ paragraph — A. B. bachelor of arts
F. R. S. fellow of the royal society.

For the other characters used in grammar, see Comma, Colon, Semicolon, &c.

Characters among the ancient Lawyers, and in ancient Inscriptions.

§ paragraph	P. P. pater patriæ
ff digests	C. code
Scto. senatus consulto	C. C. consules
E. extra	T. titulus
S. P. Q. R. senatus populusque Romanus	P. P. D. D. propria pecunia dedicavit
	D. D. M. dono dedit monumentum.

Characters in Medicine and Pharmacy.

℞ recipe	M. manipulus, a handful
ā, āā, or ana, of each alike	P. a pugil
℔ a pound, or a pint	P. Æ. equal quantities
℥ an ounce	S. A. according to art
ʒ a drachm	q. s. a sufficient quantity
℈ a scruple	q. pl. as much as you please
gr. grains	P. P. pulvis patrum, the Jesuit's bark.
ß or ss half of any thing	
cong. congius, a gallon,	
coch. cochleare, a spoonful	

Characters upon Tombstones.

S. V. Siste viator, *i. e.* Stop traveller.

M. S. Memoriæ sacrum, *i. e.* Sacred to the memory.

D. M. Diis manibus.

J. H. S. Jesus.

X. P. a character found in the catacombs, about the meaning of which authors are not agreed.

Characters used in Music, and of Musical Notes with their proportions, are as follows.

character of a large	8		crotchet	$\frac{1}{4}$
a long	4		quaver	$\frac{1}{8}$
a breve	2		semiquaver	$\frac{1}{16}$
a semibreve	1		demisemiquaver	$\frac{1}{32}$
a minim	$\frac{1}{2}$			

♯ character of a sharp note: this character at the beginning of a line or space, denotes that all the notes in that line are to be taken a semitone higher than in the natural series; and the same affects all the octaves above and below, though not marked: but when prefixed to any particular note, it shows that note alone to be taken a semitone higher than it would be without such character.

♭ or *b*, character of a flat note: this is the contrary to the other above; that is, a semitone lower.

♮ character of a natural note: when in a line or series of artificial notes, marked at the beginning *b* or ♯, the natural note happens to be required, it is denoted by this character.

𝄞 character of the treble cliff.

𝄡 character of the mean cliff.

𝄢 bass cliff.

$\frac{2}{4}$, or $\frac{4}{8}$ characters of common duple time, signifying the measure of two crotchets to be equal to two notes, of which four make a semibreve.

C, ₵, Ɔ, characters that distinguish the movements of common time, the first implying slow, the second quick, and the third very quick.

$\frac{3}{1}$, $\frac{3}{2}$, $\frac{3}{4}$, $\frac{3}{8}$, $\frac{3}{16}$, characters of simple triple time, the measure of which is equal to three semibreves, or to three minims.

$\frac{6}{4}$, $\frac{6}{8}$, or $\frac{6}{16}$, characters of a mixed triple time, where the measure is equal to six crotchets, or six quavers.

$\frac{9}{4}$, or $\frac{9}{8}$, or $\frac{9}{16}$, or $\frac{9}{1}$, or $\frac{9}{2}$, characters of compound triple time.

$\frac{12}{4}$, $\frac{12}{8}$, $\frac{12}{16}$, or $\frac{12}{1}$, or $\frac{12}{2}$, characters of that species of triple time called the measure of twelve times.

Character, in human life, that which is peculiar in the manners of any person, and distinguishes him from all others.

Good Character is particularly applied to that conduct which is regulated by virtue and religion; in an inferior but very common sense, it is understood of mere honesty of dealing between man and man. The importance of a good character in the commerce of life seems to be universally acknowledged.—To those who are to make their own way either to wealth or honours, a good character is usually no less necessary than address and abilities. To transcribe the observation of an elegant moralist: Though human nature is degenerate, and corrupts itself still more by its own inventions; yet it usually retains to the last an esteem for excellence. But even if we are arrived at such an extreme degree of depravity as to have lost our native reverence for virtue; yet a regard to our own interest and safety, which we seldom lose, will lead us to apply for aid, in all important transactions, to men whose integrity is unimpeached. When we choose an assistant, a partner, a servant, our first enquiry is concerning his character. When we have occasion for a counsellor or attorney, a physician or apothecary, whatever we may be ourselves, we always choose to trust our property and persons to men of the best character. When we fix on the tradesmen who are to supply us with necessaries, we are not determined by the sign of the lamb, or the wolf, or the fox; nor by a shop fitted up in the most elegant taste, but by the fairest reputation. Look into a daily newspaper, and you will see, from the highest to the lowest rank, how important the characters of the employed appear to the employers. After the advertisement has enumerated the qualities required in the person wanted, there constantly follows, that none need apply who cannot bring an undeniable character. Offer yourself as a candidate for a seat in parliament, be promoted to honour and emolument, or in any respect attract the attention of mankind upon yourself, and, if you are vulnerable in your character, you will be deeply wounded. This is a general testimony in favour of honesty, which no writings and no practices can possibly refute.

Young men, therefore, whose characters are yet unfixed, and who, consequently, may render them just such as they wish, ought to pay great attention to the first steps which they take on entrance into life. They are usually careless and inattentive to this object. They pursue their own plans with ardour, and neglect the opinions which others entertain of them. By some thoughtless action or expression, they suffer a mark to be impressed upon them, which scarcely any subsequent merit can entirely erase. Every man will find some per-

Character. som, who, though they are not professed enemies, yet view him with an envious or a jealous eye, and who will gladly revive any tale to which truth has given the slightest foundation.

In this turbulent and censorious scene, where our words and actions are often misunderstood, and oftener misrepresented, it is indeed difficult even for innocence and integrity to avoid reproach, abuse, contempt, and hatred. These not only hurt our interest and impede our advancement in life, but sorely afflict the feelings of a tender and delicate mind. It is then the part of wisdom first to do every thing in our power to preserve an irreproachable character, and then to let our happiness depend chiefly on the approbation of our own consciences, and on the advancement of our interest in a world where liars shall not be believed, and where slanderers shall receive countenance from none but him who, in Greek, is called, by way of eminence, *Diabolus*, or the calumniator.

Character, in poetry, particularly the epopee and drama, is the result of the manners or peculiarities by which each person is distinguished from others.

The poetical character, says Mr Bossu, is not properly any particular virtue or quality, but a composition of several which are mixed together, in a different degree, according to the necessity of the fable and the unity of the action: there must be one, however, to reign over all the rest; and this must be found, in some degree, in every part. The first quality in Achilles, is wrath; in Ulysses, dissimulation; and in Æneas, mildness: but as these characters cannot be alone, they must be accompanied with others to embellish them, as far as they are capable, either by hiding their defects, as in the anger of Achilles, which is palliated by extraordinary valour; or by making them centre in some solid virtue, as in Ulysses, whose dissimulation makes a part of his prudence; and in Æneas, whose mildness is employed in a submission to the will of the gods. In the making up of which union, it is to be observed, the poets have joined together such qualities as are by nature the most compatible; valour with anger, piety with mildness, and prudence with dissimulation. The fable required prudence in Ulysses, and piety in Æneas; in this, therefore, the poets were not left to their choice: but Homer might have made Achilles a coward without abating any thing from the justness of his fable: so that it was the necessity of adorning his character that obliged him to make him valiant: the character, then, of a hero in the epic poem, is compounded of three sorts of qualities; the first essential to the fable; the second, embellishments of the first; and valour, which sustains the other two, makes the third.

Unity of character is as necessary as the unity of the fable. For this purpose a person should be the same from the beginning to the end: not that he is always to betray the same sentiments, or one passion; but that he should never speak nor act inconsistently with his fundamental character. For instance, the weak may sometimes sally into a warmth, and the breast of the passionate be calm, a change which often introduces in the drama a very affecting variety; but if the natural disposition of the former was to be represented as boisterous, and that of the latter mild and soft, they would both act out of character, and contradict their persons.

True characters are such as we truly and really see in men, or may exist without any contradiction to nature; no man questions but there have been men as generous and as good as Æneas, as passionate and as violent as Achilles, as prudent and wise as Ulysses, as impious and atheistical as Mezentius, and as amorous and passionate as Dido; all these characters, therefore, are true, and nothing but just imitations of nature. On the contrary, a character is false when an author so feigns it, that one can see nothing like it in the order of nature wherein he designs it shall stand: these characters should be wholly excluded from a poem, because transgressing the bounds of probability and reason, they meet with no belief from the readers; they are fictions of the poet's brain, not imitations of nature; and yet all poetry consists in an imitation of nature. Characte | Charade.

Character is also used for certain visible qualities, which claim respect or reverence to those vested therewith.—The majesty of kings gives them a character which procures respect from the people. A bishop should sustain his character by learning and solid piety, rather than by worldly lustre, &c. The law of nations secures the character of an ambassador from all insults.

Character, among naturalists, is synonymous with the definition of the genera of animals, plants, &c.

CHARACTERISTIC, in the general, is that which characterises a thing or person, i. e. constitutes its character, whereby it is distinguished. See Character.

Characteristic, is peculiarly used in grammar, for the principal letter of a word: which is preserved in most of its tenses and moods, its derivatives and compounds.

Characteristic of a Logarithm, is its index or exponent. See Logarithm.

Characteristic Triangle of a Curve, in the higher geometry, is a rectilinear right-angled triangle, whose hypothenuse makes a part of the curve, not sensibly different from a right line. It is so called, because curve lines are used to be distinguished hereby. See Curve.

CHARADE, the name of a new species of composition or literary amusement. It owes its name to the idler who invented it. Its subject must be a word of two syllables, each forming a distinct word; and these two syllables are to be concealed in an enigmatical description, first separately, and then together. The exercise of charades, if not greatly instructive, is at least innocent and amusing. At all events, as it has made its way into every fashionable circle, and has employed even Garrick, it will scarcely be deemed unworthy of attention. The silliness indeed of most that have appeared in the papers under this title, are not only destitute of all pleasantry in the stating, but are formed in general of words utterly unfit for the purpose. They have therefore been treated with the contempt they deserved. In trifles of this nature, inaccuracy is without excuse. The following examples therefore are at least free from this blemish.

I.

My *first*, however here abused,
Designs the fex alone;
In Cambria, such is custom's pow'r,
'Tis Jenkin, John, or Jone.

My

Charade, Charadrius.

My *second* oft is loudly call'd,
When men prepare to fish it;
Its name delights the female ear;
Its force, may none resist it!
It binds the weak, it binds the strong,
The wealthy and the poor;
Still 'tis to joy a passport deem'd,
For sullied fame a cure.
It may insure an age of bliss,
Yet mis'ries oft attend it;
To fingers, ears, and noses too,
Its various lords commend it.
My *whole* may chance to make one drink,
Though vended in a fish-shop;
'Tis now the monarch of the seas,
And has been an archbishop. *Her-ring.*

II.

My *first*, when a Frenchman is learning English, serves him to swear by. My *second*, is either hay or corn. My *whole*, is the delight of the present age, and will be the admiration of posterity. *Gar-rick.*

III.

My *first*, is plowed for various reasons, and grain is frequently buried in it to little purpose. My *second*, is neither riches nor honours; yet the former would generally be given for it, and the latter is often tasteless without it. My *whole* applies equally to spring, summer, autumn, and winter; and both fish and flesh, praise and censure, mirth and melancholy, are the better for being in it. *Sea-son.*

IV.

My *first*, with the most rooted antipathy to a Frenchman, prides himself, whenever they meet, upon sticking close to his jacket. My *second* has many virtues, nor is it its least that it gives name to my first. My *whole*, may I never catch! *Tar-tar.*

V.

My *first* is one of England's prime boasts; it rejoices the ear of a horse, and anguishes the toe of a man. My *second*, when brick, is good; when stone, better; when wooden, best of all. My *whole* is famous alike for rottenness and tin. *Corn-wall.*

VI.

My *first* is called bad or good,
May pleasure or offend ye;
My *second*, in a thirsty mood,
May very much befriend ye.
My *whole*, tho' styled a "cruel word,"
May yet appear a kind one;
It often may with joy be heard,
With tears may often blind one. *Fare-well.*

VII.

My *first* is equally friendly to the thief and the lover, the toper and the student. My *second* is light's opposite: yet they are frequently seen hand in hand; and their union, if judicious, gives much pleasure. My *whole*, is tempting to the touch, grateful to the sight, fatal to the taste. *Night-shade.*

CHARADRIUS, in ornithology, a genus belonging to the order of grallæ. The beak is cylindrical and blunt; the nostrils are linear; and the feet have three toes.

1. The Hiaticula, or Sea-lark of Ray, has a black breast; a white streak along the front; the top of the head is brown; and the legs and beak are reddish. It is found on the shores of Europe and America. They frequent our shores in the summer, but are not numerous. They lay four eggs, of a dull whitish colour, sparingly sprinkled with black: at the approach of winter they disappear.

2. The Alexandrinus, or Alexandrian Dotterel, is of a brownish colour, with the forehead, collar, and belly white; the prime tail-feathers on both sides are white; and the legs are black. It is about the size of a lark, and lives upon insects.

3. The Vociferus, or Noisy Plover of Catesby, has black streaks on the breast, neck, forehead, and cheeks; and the feet are yellow. It is a native of North America.

4. The Ægyptius has a black streak on the breast, white eye-brows, the prime tail-feathers streaked with black at the points, and bluish legs. It is found in the plains of Egypt, and feeds on insects.

5. The Morinellus has an iron-coloured breast, a small white streak on the breast and eye-brows, and black legs. It is the Dotterel of Ray, and a native of Europe. They are found in Cambridgeshire, Lincolnshire, and Derbyshire; on Lincoln-heath, and on the moors of Derbyshire, they are migratory; appearing there in small flocks of eight or ten only in the latter end of April, and stay there all May and part of June, during which time they are very fat, and much esteemed for their delicate flavour. In the months of April and September, they are taken on the Wiltshire and Berkshire downs: they are also found in the beginning of the former month on the sea-side at Meales in Lancashire, and continue there about three weeks, attending the barley fallows: from thence they remove northward to a place called *Leyton Haws*, and stay there about a fortnight; but where they breed, or where they reside during the winter, we have not been able to discover. They are reckoned very foolish birds, so that a dull fellow is proverbially styled a *dotterel.* They were also believed to mimic the action of the fowler, stretching out a wing when he stretches out an arm, &c. continuing their imitation, regardless of the net that is spreading for them.

6. The Apricarius has a black belly; the body is brown, and variegated with white and yellow spots; and the legs are ash-coloured. It is the spotted Plover of Edwards, and a native of Canada.

7. The Pluvialis is black above, with green spots, white underneath, and the feet are ash-coloured. It is the green plover of Ray, and is a native of Europe. They lay four eggs, sharply pointed at the lesser end, of a dirty white colour, and irregularly marked, especially at the thicker end, with blotches and spots. It breeds on several of our unfrequented mountains; and is very common on those of the isle of Rum, and others of the loftier Hebrides. They make a shrill whistling noise; and may be enticed within a shot by a skilful imitator of the note.

8. The Torquatus has a black breast, and a white front; the top of the head and the collar is black; and the beak and feet are bluish. It is a native of St Domingo.

9. The Calidris has black feet, and a black bill; the rump is greyish; and the body is pure white below. It frequents the shores of Europe.

10. The Œdicnemus or Stone-curlew of Ray, is of a grey colour, with two of the prime wing-feathers black, but white in the middle: it has a sharp bill,

and aſh-coloured feet; and is about the ſize of a crow. In Hampſhire, Norfolk, and on Lincoln-heath, it is called the ſtone-curlew, from a ſimilarity of colours to the curlew. It breeds in ſome places in rabbit-burrows; alſo among ſtones on the bare ground, laying two eggs of a copper-colour ſpotted with a darker red. The young run ſoon after they are hatched. Theſe birds feed in the night on worms and caterpillars: they will alſo eat toads, and will catch mice. They inhabit fallow lands and downs; affect dry places, never being ſeen near any waters. When they fly, they extend their legs ſtraight out behind: are very ſhy birds; run far before they take to wing; and often ſquat: are generally ſeen ſingle; and are eſteemed very delicate food.—Haſſelquiſt informs us, that this bird is alſo met with in Lower Egypt, in the Acacia groves, near the villages Abuſir and Sackhara, near the ſepulchres of the ancient Egyptians, and in the deſarts. The Arabians call it Kervan. It has a ſhrill voice, ſomewhat reſembling that of the black woodpecker, which it raiſes and lowers ſucceſſively, uttering agreeable notes. The Turks and Egyptians value it much, if they can get it alive; and keep it in a cage for the ſake of its ſinging. Its fleſh is hard, and of a very good taſte, inclined to aromatic. It is a very voracious bird, catching and devouring rats and mice, which abound in Egypt. It ſeldom drinks; and when taken young, and kept in a cage in Egypt, they give it no water for ſeveral months, but feed it with freſh meat macerated in water, which it devours very greedily. It is found in deſarts, and is therefore accuſtomed to be without water.

11. The Himantopus is white below, with a black back, and a long black bill; the feet are red, and very long. It is the autumnal dotterel of the Engliſh authors, and frequents the ſea-ſhores of Europe. It is alſo found in the lakes of Egypt in the month of October.

12. The Spinoſus, armed Dotterel, or Lapwing, has black breaſt, legs, and wings; it has a creſt on the hinder part of the head. It is of the ſize of a pigeon; the French call it *dominicanus*, from the reſemblance it has to the dreſs of a Dominican monk. It is a native of Egypt.

13. The New-Zealand plover, has the forepart of the head, taking in the eye, chin, and throat, black, paſſing backwards in a collar at the hind head; all the back part of the head, behind the eye, greeniſh aſh-colour; theſe two colours divided by white: the plumage on the upper parts of the body is the ſame colour as the back of the head: the quills and tail are duſky: the laſt order of coverts is white for ſome part of their length, forming a bar on the wing: the under parts of the body are white; and the legs red. It inhabits Queen Charlotte's ſound; where it is known by the name of *Doodooroo-attoo*. See Plate CXXII. There are 12 or 13 more ſpecies.

CHARAG, the tribute which Chriſtians and Jews pay to the grand ſignior.

It conſiſts of ten, twelve, or fifteen francs *per annum*, according to the eſtate of the party. Men begin to pay it at nine or at ſixteen years old; women are diſpenſed with, as alſo prieſts, rabbins, and religious.

CHARAIMS, a ſect of the Jews in Egypt. They live by themſelves, and have a ſeparate ſynagogue; and as the other Jews are remarkable for their eyes, ſo are thoſe for their large noſes, which run through all the families of this ſect. Theſe are the ancient Eſſenes. They ſtrictly obſerve the five books of Moſes, according to the letter; and receive no written traditions. It is ſaid that the other Jews would join the *Charaims*; but thoſe not having obſerved the exact rules of the law with regard to divorces, theſe think they live in adultery.

CHARANTIA, in botany. See MOMORDICA.

CHARBON, in the manege, that little black ſpot or mark which remains after a large ſpot in the cavity of the corner teeth of a horſe: about the ſeventh or eighth year, when the cavity fills up, the tooth being ſmooth and equal, it is ſaid to be raſed.

CHARCAS, the ſouthern diviſion of Peru in South America, remarkable for the ſilver mines of Potoſi.

CHARCOAL, a ſort of artificial coal, or fuel, conſiſting of wood half burnt; chiefly uſed where a clear ſtrong fire, without ſmoke, is required; the humidity of the wood being here mostly diſſipated, and exhaled in the fire wherein it is prepared.

The microſcope diſcovers a ſurpriſing number of pores in charcoal: they are diſpoſed in order, and traverſe it lengthwiſe; ſo that there is no piece of charcoal, how long ſoever, but may be eaſily blown through. If a piece be broken pretty ſhort, it may be ſeen through with a microſcope. In a range the 18th part of an inch long, Dr Hook reckoned 150 pores; whence he concludes, that in a charcoal of an inch diameter, there are not leſs than 5,724,000 pores. It is to this prodigious number of pores, that the blackneſs of charcoal is owing: for the rays of light ſtriking on the charcoal, are received and abſorbed in its pores, inſtead of being reflected; whence the body muſt of neceſſity appear black, blackneſs in a body being no more than a want of reflection. Charcoal was anciently uſed to diſtinguiſh the bounds of eſtates and inheritances; as being incorruptible, when let very deep within ground. In effect, it preſerves itſelf ſo long, that there are many pieces found entire in the ancient tombs of the northern nations. M. Dodart ſays, there is charcoal made of corn, probably as old as the days of Cæſar: he adds, that it has kept ſo well, that the wheat may be ſtill diſtinguiſhed from the rye; which he looks on as proof of its incorruptibility.

The operation of charring wood, is performed in the following manner: The wood intended for this purpoſe is cut into proper lengths, and piled up in heaps near the place where the charcoal is intended to be made: when a ſufficient quantity of wood is thus prepared, they begin conſtructing their ſtacks, for which there are three methods. The firſt is this: They level a proper ſpot of ground, of about twelve or fifteen feet in diameter, near the piles of wood; in the centre of this area a large billet of wood, ſplit acroſs at one end and pointed at the other, is fixed with its pointed extremity in the earth, and two pieces of wood inſerted through the clefts of the other end, forming four right-angles; againſt theſe croſs pieces four other billets of wood are placed, one end on the ground, and the other leaning againſt the angles. This being finiſhed, a number of large and ſtraight

billets

billets are laid on the ground to form a floor, each being as it were the radius of the circular area; on this floor a proper quantity of brush or small wood is strewed, in order to fill up the interstices, when the floor will be compleat; and in order to keep the billets in the same order and position in which they were first arranged, pegs or stumps are driven into the ground in the circumference of the circle, about a foot distant from one another: upon this floor a stage is built with billets set upon one end, but something inclining towards the central billet; and on the tops of these another floor is laid in a horizontal direction, but of shorter billets, as the whole is, when finished, to form a cone.

The second method of building the stacks for making charcoal is performed in this manner: A long pole is erected in the centre of the area above described, and several small billets ranged round the pole on their ends: the interstices between these billets and the pole is filled with dry brush-wood, then a floor is laid, on that a stage in a reclining position, and on that a second floor, &c. in the same manner as described above; but in the lower floor there is a billet larger and longer than the rest, extending from the central pole to some distance beyond the circumference of the circle.

The third method is this: A chimney, or aperture of a square form, is built with billets in the centre, from the bottom to the top; and round these, floors and inclined stages are erected, in the same manner as in the stacks above described, except that the base of this, instead of being circular like the others, is square; and the whole stack, when compleated, forms a pyramid.

The stack of either form being thus finished, is covered over with turf, and the surface plastered with a mixture of earth and charcoal-dust well tempered together.

The next operation is the setting the stack on fire. In order to this, if it be formed according to the first construction, the central billet in the upper stage is drawn out, and some pieces of very dry and combustible wood are placed in the void space, called, by workmen, the chimney, and fire set to these pieces. If the stack be built according to the second construction, the central pole is drawn out, together with the large horizontal billet above described; and the void space occupied by the latter being filled with pieces of very dry combustible wood, the fire is applied to it at the base of the stack. With regard to the third construction, the square aperture or chimney is filled with small pieces of very dry wood, and the fire applied to it at the top or apex of the pyramidal stack. When the stack is set on fire, either at the top or bottom, the greatest attention is necessary in the workman; for in the proper management of the fire the chief difficulty attending the art of making good charcoal consists. In order to this, care is taken, as soon as the flame begins to issue some height above the chimney, that the aperture be covered with a piece of turf, but not so close as to hinder the smoke from passing out: and whenever the smoke appears to issue very thick from any part of the pile, the aperture must be covered with a mixture of earth and charcoal dust. At the same time, as it is necessary that every part of the stack should be equally burnt, it will be requisite for the workman to open vents in one part and shut them in another. In this manner the fire must be kept up till the charcoal be sufficiently burnt, which will happen in about two days and a half, if the wood be dry; but if green, the operation will not be finished in less than three days. When the charcoal is thought to be sufficiently burnt, which is easily known from the appearance of the smoke, and the flames no longer issuing with impetuosity through the vents; all the apertures are to be closed up very carefully with a mixture of earth and charcoal-dust, which, by excluding all access of the external air, prevents the coals from being any further consumed, and the fire goes out of itself. In this condition it is suffered to remain, till the whole is sufficiently cooled; when the cover is removed, and the charcoal is taken away. If the whole process is skilfully managed, the coals will exactly retain the figure of the pieces of wood: some are said to have been so dexterous as to char an arrow without altering even the figure of the feather.

There are considerable differences in the coals of different vegetables, in regard to their habitude to fire: the very light coals of linen, cotton, some fungi, &c. readily catch fire from a spark, and soon burn out; the more dense ones of woods and roots are set on fire more difficultly, and burn more slowly: the coals of the black berry-bearing alder, of the hazel, the willow, and the lime-tree, are said to answer best for the making of gunpowder and other pyrotechnical compositions, perhaps from their being easily inflammable: for the reduction of metallic calces those of the heavier woods, as the oak and the beech, are preferable, these seeming to contain a larger proportion of the phlogistic principle, and that, perhaps, in a more fixed state: considered as common fuel, those of the heavy woods give the greatest heat, and require the most plentiful supply of air to keep them burning; those of the light woods preserve a glowing heat, without much draught of air, till the coals themselves are consumed; the bark commonly crackles and flies about in burning, which the coal of the wood itself very seldom does.

Mathematical-instrument makers, engravers, &c. find charcoal of great use to polish their brass and copper-plates after they have been rubbed clean with powdered pumice-stone. Plates of horn are polishable in the same way, and a gloss may be afterwards given with tripoli.

The coals of different substances are also used as pigments; hence the bone-black, ivory-black, &c. of the shops. Most of the paints of this kind, besides their incorruptibility, have the advantage of a full colour, and work freely in all the forms in which powdery pigments are applied; provided they have been carefully prepared, by thoroughly burning the subject in a close vessel, and afterwards grinding the coal into a powder of due fineness. Pieces of charcoal are used also in their entire state for tracing the outlines of drawings, &c.; in which intention they have an excellence, that their mark is easily wiped out. For these purposes, either the finer pieces of common charcoal are picked out and cut to a proper shape; or the pencils are formed of wood, and afterwards burnt into charcoal in a proper vessel well covered. The artists commonly make choice of the smaller branches of the tree freed from the bark and pith; and the willow and

vine

Charcoal.

Philoſoph. Commerce of Arts.

vine are preferred to all others. This choice is confirmed by the experiments of Dr *Lewis*, who has found that the wood of the trunks of trees produces charcoal of a harder nature than their ſmall twigs or branches; and the hard woods, ſuch as box and guaiacum, produced coals very ſenſibly harder than the ſofter woods. Willow he prefers to all others. The ſhells and ſtones of fruits yielded coals ſo hard that they would ſcarce mark on paper at all; while the coals of the kernels of fruits were quite ſoft and mellow. The ſeveral coals produced by the doctor's experiments were levigated into fine powder, mixed both with gum-water and oil, and applied as paints both thin and thick, and diluted with different degrees of white. All of them, when laid on thick, appeared of a ſtrong full black, nor could it be judged that one was of a finer colour than another; diluted with white, or when ſpread thin, they had all ſomewhat of a bluiſh caſt.

Horns and the bones both of fiſhes and land animals, gave coals rather gloſſier and deeper-coloured than vegetables; and which, in general, were very hard, ſo as difficultly, or not at all, to ſtain paper. Here alſo the hardneſs of the coal ſeemed to depend on that of the ſubject from whence it was prepared; for ſilk, woollen, leather, blood, and the fleſhy parts of animals, yielded ſoft coals. Some of theſe differed from others very ſenſibly in colour: that of ivory is ſuperior to all the reſt, and indiſputably the fineſt of all the charcoal blacks. The animal coals had much leſs of the bluiſh caſt in them than the vegetable, many of them inclining rather to a brown. Charred pit-coal, on the other hand, ſeemed to have this blueneſs in a greater degree.

Charcoal is not ſoluble in any of the acids; but may be diſſolved in conſiderable quantities by a ſolution of *hepar ſulphuris*, to which it communicates a green colour. Melted with colourleſs frits or glaſſes, it gives a pale yellow, dark yellow, reddiſh, browniſh, or blackiſh colour, according as the inflammable matter is in greater or leſs proportion; the phlogiſton, or inflammable matter of the coal ſeeming to be the direct tinging ſubſtance. When the phlogiſtic matter is thus diffuſed through glaſs, it is no more affected by continued ſtrong fire than charcoal is when excluded from the air.

The vapour of burning charcoal is found to be highly noxious, being no other than *fixed air*. How this affects the animal ſyſtem is explained under the article Blood.

From ſome late experiments it appears, that charcoal poſſeſſes many extraordinary properties altogether unſuſpected by former chemiſts. It has particularly a great attraction for what is called the *phlogiſton*, or rather for any kind of oily matter with which other ſubſtances may be ſullied; ſo that it now promiſes to be very uſeful in the arts in various ways never thought of before. M. Lowitz has found that it is uſeful in preparing cryſtals of tartar of a very white colour; and that the marine and nitrous acids are decompoſed by being diſtilled upon it: the red juices of vegetable fruits are diſcoloured, without loſing any of their acidity; brown rancid oils are rendered ſweet and clear by agitating them for ſome days with charcoal in powder; it changes the ſmell of putrid vegetables to that of a pure volatile alkali, and it produces the ſame effect on freſh meat. On boiling coals in powder with honey, the pure ſaccharine parts of the latter are ſaid to be ſeparated, and the honey to become a well-taſted ſugar; the purification of raw ſugar is alſo ſaid to be facilitated by the ſame method. Thus alſo the mother-water of the Pruſſian alkali and of the tartareous acid are made to cryſtalliſe eaſily; terra folíata tartari may be made white without calcination, by previouſly diſtilling the vinegar from coals. Vinegar concentrated by freezing, and diſtilled from a large proportion of powdered coal, is extremely ſtrong, pure, and fragrant. Corn ſpirit merely ſhaken with coal loſes its bad flavour; and if honey is added, it becomes a ſweet and pleaſant liquor. Even when ardent ſpirits are impregnated with any vegetable oils, the flavour is deſtroyed in this way; and if the ſpirit be diſtilled, the reſiduum is ſaid not to be brown; ſo that if the diſtillation is carried too far, no inconvenience enſues. With Peruvian bark a clear decoction was formed, and the reſiduum was a ſalt, in taſte like digeſtive ſalt. Theſe effects were produced by every kind of coal, whether foſſil or charred vegetable ſubſtances.

Charcoal.

Charcoal has lately been ſeparated from the pureſt ſpirit of wine in the proceſs for making ether*; and by M. Lavoiſier is ſuppoſed to be one of the conſtituent parts or elements of that very volatile liquid. But the moſt extraordinary modern diſcovery concerning this ſubſtance is that of Dr Prieſtley, who has found that ſeveral of the metals may be converted into charcoal by paſſing the ſteam of ſpirit of wine over them when red-hot; and this, by way of diſtinction, he calls the *charcoal of metals*.

* See Chemiſtry, Index.

This ſurpriſing diſcovery was made accidentally, while the Doctor was repeating the experiments by which M. Lavoiſier imagined water might be converted into air. Having tranſmitted the ſteam of water thro' a copper tube, on which it had no effect, he was willing to try the effects of that of other fluids; and for this purpoſe made choice of ſpirit of wine, having before procured inflammable air by ſending the ſame ſteam through a red-hot tobacco pipe. No ſooner had the vapour of this fluid, however, touched the red-hot copper, than he was aſtoniſhed at the rapid production of air from it, which reſembled the blowing of a pair of bellows; and before four ounces of the ſpirit were expended, the tube was found to be perforated in two or three places. In a moment afterwards it was ſo far deſtroyed, that it fell to pieces on attempting to remove it from the fire; the inſide being filled with a black matter reſembling lamp-black. Having now recourſe to earthen tubes, the Doctor found that, by melting copper and other metals in them, and tranſmitting the vapour of ſpirit of wine in contact with them while in a ſtate of ignition, different ſubſtances were formed according to the metals employed. On ſending three ounce-meaſures of ſpirit of wine over two ounces of copper, the metal loſt 28 grains of its weight, and 446 grains of charcoal were procured, chiefly in the form of powder, though ſome of it was in large flakes ſeveral inches long; having ſeparated at once from the ſurface of the melted metal. Theſe pieces were almoſt quite black, and bore handling without any danger of being broken. In another experiment, 308 grains of charcoal were obtained from 19 grains of copper; but here the metal had been previouſly reduced

Charcoal.

duced to this places, and they were not all converted into charcoal, being ſomething harder, and therefore partially metallic in the middle.

Silver was found to be affected very much as copper had been; but the larger maſſes of charcoal procured from this metal were much whiter than thoſe from copper. Only a ſmall quantity of charcoal could be procured from lead. Three ounce-meaſures of ſpirit of wine and near four ounces of lead, gave only a ſmall quantity of whitiſh powdery ſubſtance, though 58 grains of the lead were miſſing; but the inſide of the glaſs-tube through which the air was tranſmitted became very black. The like quantity of ſpirit of wine ſent over 360 grains of melted tin, and produced 26 grains of black duſt, the metal not being diminiſhed quite four grains. The vapour of two ounce-meaſures of ſpirit of wine, ſent over 960 grains of iron-ſhavings, diminiſhed the metal only two grains; but no charcoal could be collected, though the air was loaded with black particles. The iron had acquired a dark blue colour. Gold was not ſenſibly changed or diminiſhed in weight; and it not only remained unalterable by the proceſs itſelf, but effectually protected a tenth-part of its weight of copper from the action of the ſteam.

Spirit of turpentine was found to anſwer for the production of this charcoal, as well as ſpirit of wine; 120 grains of the former being obtained from five of copper by means of the turpentine, notwithſtanding a very denſe black ſmoke which iſſued from the end of the tube during the whole time of the operation. The Doctor obſerves, indeed, that in all thoſe experiments, where the heat is very great, the minute diviſion and volatility of this charcoal is very extraordinary. Seeing it iſſue from the end of a tube in a denſe black cloud, he endeavoured to collect it in a large glaſs receiver; but after having given the glaſs a very thin black coating, not diſtinguiſhable in appearance from ſoot, it iſſued from the orifice like denſe ſmoke, and appeared to be altogether incoercible, even when ſeveral adopters were connected with the receiver, and a tube, from whence it finally iſſued, plunged deep into water.

It is obſerved, that charcoal of wood, when freſh made, has a ſtrong attraction for air, and will continue to abſorb it for a conſiderable time; a property which it has in common with ſeveral other ſubſtances. Dr Prieſtley made ſome experiments to aſcertain the quantity abſorbed. For this purpoſe, he left in an open diſh, on the fourth of September, ſome charcoal freſh made from dry oak, and weighing 364 grains. Two or three days after it weighed 390 grains; on the 24th of October, 419; and on the 25th of April following it weighed 421 grains. By diſtillation in an earthen retort it yielded a quantity of air conſiderably phlogiſticated, and then weighed 312 grains, but the retort appeared to have been cracked. On expoſing it again to the open air for a whole year, it weighed 371 grains. In another experiment, a quantity of charcoal which had yielded by a ſtrong heat 336 ounce-meaſures of air, and weighed immediately afterwards 756 grains, increaſed in three days to 817; and on expelling the air from it was reduced to 781 grains. In all theſe experiments the air was worſe than that of the atmoſphere, and a part was fixed air.

It has been generally ſuppoſed by chemiſts, that charcoal was indeſtructible by any other means than burning in an open fire, though of late it is found totally diſſipable and convertible into inflammable air, by the heat of a burning lens *in vacuo*, at leaſt with the aſſiſtance of a ſmall quantity of water. By burning in dephlogiſticated air, it is found to convert almoſt the whole of it into fixed air. See AEROLOGY, n° 110—113, 129, 131. From the experiments there related, it is now evident, that charcoal as ſuch, and without any decompoſition, is an ingredient in both theſe aerial fluids, and is indeed the phlogiſton of Stahl ſo long ſought in vain. This diſcovery, however, has not by any means put an end to the diſputes betwixt the *Phlogiſtians* and *Antiphlogiſtians*, though it certainly ought to have done ſo, and muſt aſſuredly do ſo in a ſhort time. The experiments of Dr Prieſtley are not doubted; and charcoal, the gravitating matter of light inflammable air, and *phlogiſton*, are allowed to be the ſame by the Antiphlogiſtians as well as by the oppoſite party. "The preſent controverſy (ſays Mr Higgins) amongſt philoſophers depends upon the following queſtions: 1. Whether water be or be not compoſed of dephlogiſticated and light inflammable air? 2. Whether or no the condenſation of dephlogiſticated air, or its union to different bodies, does not depend upon one principle, common to all combuſtible bodies? or, in other words, whether or no all bodies which burn or calcine, ſuch as ſulphur, phoſphorus, charcoal, oils, metals, phlogiſticated air, &c. contain the matter of light inflammable air as one of their conſtituent principles? One ſhould ſuppoſe, if theſe ſubſtances were compoſed of two principles, namely a peculiar baſis, and the matter of light inflammable air or phlogiſton, that it would be poſſible to reſolve them into theſe principles; more eſpecially when we conſider the great attraction of the matter of light inflammable air to fire; but the maintainers of phlogiſton have not as yet been able to do this," &c.

Higgins's Comparative View, Pref. p. 5.

The limits of this work will not allow us to enter on a full diſcuſſion of this controverſy, nor can we pretend to be able to ſettle the diſputes on the ſubject. It nevertheleſs ſeems ſomewhat unnatural to call iron, lead, copper, ſulphur, phoſphorus, &c. ſimple and unchangeable bodies, or if we pleaſe *elements*; as thus the number of elementary bodies might be increaſed without number, and *water*, which has generally been reckoned a ſimple one, ſuppoſed to be almoſt the only compound body in nature. It is alſo certain, that Dr Prieſtley has made ſome very ſtriking and apparently deciſive experiments on the ſubject of metals, to which no proper reply has ever been made. In order to ſee the force of theſe experiments, however, we muſt ſtill obſerve, that, according to the Phlogiſtians, the calces of metals are reduced, on the addition of charcoal, not only by emitting the dephlogiſticated air which adheres to them when in the form of calces, but by the admiſſion of a quantity of the charcoal itſelf into their ſubſtance. This the Antiphlogiſtians deny; and though they admit the neceſſity of charcoal in the operation, yet they affirm that it acts only by attracting the dephlogiſticated air contained in the calx, with which it forms fixed air; and hence they muſt ſay, that in all metallic reductions a quantity of fixed air is produced, equivalent not only to the weight of the charcoal employed, but alſo to that of the dephlogiſticated air con-

Charcoal

contained in the calx. The decisive experiment therefore would be, to expel from a metallic calx all the air it contained, to weigh it exactly in that state, and then observe whether it gained any thing in weight by being restored to a metal. This, however, has not been done; and the Antiphlogistians complain that their adversaries have not been able to produce a pure metallic calx free from all kind of aerial vapour. But though it is not pretended that any such calx has yet been produced, if the Phlogistians can show the possibility of reducing a calx without the production of fixed air, it would seem to be equally destructive of the antiphlogistic doctrine. This appears to have been done by Dr P[rie]stley in the experiments above alluded to; and it is even doubtful whether he did not obtain the so much desired calx, viz. one perfectly free from air altogether. "I put (says he) upon a piece of broken crucible, which could yield no air, a quantity of minium, *out of which all air* had been extracted; and placing it upon a convenient stand, introduced it into a large receiver filled with inflammable air confined by water. As soon as the minium was dry, by means of the heat thrown upon it, I observed that it became black, and then ran in the form of perfect lead, at the same time that the air diminished at a great rate the water ascending within the receiver. Before this first experiment was concluded, I perceived, that if the phlogiston in inflammable air had any base, it must be very inconsiderable; for the process went on till there was no more room to operate without endangering the receiver; and examining the air that remained, I found that it could not be distinguished from that in which I began the experiment, which was air extracted from iron by oil of vitriol.

"I afterwards carefully expelled, from a quantity of minium, all the phlogiston, and every thing else that could have assumed the form of air, by giving it a red heat when mixed with spirit of nitre; and immediately using it in the manner mentioned above, I reduced 101 ounce-measures of inflammable air to two. To judge of its degree of inflammability, I presented the flame of a small candle to the mouth of a vial filled with it, and observed, that it made 13 separate explosions, though weak ones (stopping the mouth of the phial with my finger after each explosion); when fresh made inflammable air, in the same circumstances, made only 14 explosions, though stronger ones. In this experiment, however, I overlooked one obvious consideration, viz. that water, or any thing soluble in water, might be the basis of inflammable air. All that could be absolutely inferred from the experiment was, that this basis could not be any thing that was capable of subsisting in the form of air. It will be seen, that I afterwards made the experiment with air confined by mercury."

In this experiment it is to be regretted that the Doctor did not inform us whether the weight of his calces was on the whole increased or diminished by the operation. As it stands, though sufficient to overthrow the doctrine of the Antiphlogistians, it is not altogether sufficient to establish that of their adversaries. Mr Higgins, however, though he does not reply to this experiment, gives an account of another from Dr Higgins, which he considers as absolutely decisive against the Phlogistians. "Dr Higgins (says he) introduced some pieces of well-burned charcoal into a deep crucible, and covered them over an inch deep with powdered charcoal. Having luted on a cover, he exposed them for two hours to heat sufficient to melt silver; he then placed the crucible in such a manner that the powder might remain red hot for some time after the pieces next the bottom had cooled. This he had done, as the charcoal must imbibe something on cooling, both to supply it with inflammable air, and to prevent a communication with the external air, which the charcoal would otherwise have imbibed.

Charcoal

"One hundred and twenty grains of this charcoal quickly powdered, were well mixed with 7680 grains of litharge, which had been previously fused to separate any uncalcined lead it might contain. This mixture was charged into a coated retort just large enough to contain it; so that the common air must have been nearly secluded. Being then placed in a reverberating furnace, and heat duly applied, it yielded by estimation, after cooling to the mean temperature of the atmosphere, 384 grains of fixable air, at the rate of 0.57 grains to a cubic inch, 8.704 of phlogisticated air, and 0.911 grains of dephlogisticated air, besides 49 grains of water. On breaking the retort, 3888 grains of revived lead were found, besides some vitrified litharge; but not an atom of charcoal was left, nor was there a particle of inflammable air produced. Now, let my reader consider the weight that 3888 grains of lead acquire by its conversion to litharge, and the quantity of inflammable air that 120 grains of charcoal will afford (which, according to Dr Priestley, is about 360 ounce-measures), and he will find, making allowance for the phlogisticated air, that these nearly correspond with the proportion of heavy inflammable air and dephlogisticated air necessary to the formation of fixable air by the electric spark. Hence we may conclude, that not a particle of charcoal entered into the constitution of the revived lead, but must have been wholly converted into fixable air."

To this experiment, however, the Phlogistians will reply, that so far from being decisive on the subject, no conclusion whatever can be drawn from it, on account of its *enormous* inaccuracy. The quantity of matter put into the retort was 7680+120, or 7800 grains, and the whole produce was 3888+384+8.704+0.911+49=4330.615 grains: a deficiency therefore of no less than 3469.385 grains is to be accounted for; and of this we hear not one word; so that we are at liberty to suppose that the vitrified litharge had perforated the retort in such a manner as to admit the fixed and phlogisticated air from without, as Dr Priestley found earthen retorts pervious to air from without; and this, though coated, might by a corrosion of the glass (if it was a glass one) be reduced to a similar situation.

We do not mean that this should be reckoned a formal answer to Dr Higgins's experiment; all we intend here, is to state the arguments fairly on both sides, so that the reader who has not an opportunity of making experiments himself, may be able to judge on which side the truth lies. Dr Priestley informs us, that in his experiment, the calx of lead absorbed a quantity of inflammable air without the extrication of fixed air, or any thing else that could be perceived. Whether or not have we reason to conclude from thence,

Charcoal.

that the gravitating, solid, or coally, part of the inflammable air was received into the calx, and became part of the revived metal? In Dr Higgins's experiment a quantity of elastic fluid was produced, and a quantity of lead revived; but we neither know how much of the calx went to this lead, how much the litharge had originally attracted from the air, nor whether the elastic fluids were certainly produced; or indeed whether any of them, the small quantity of dephlogisticated air alone excepted, came from the materials or not. From such a state of the case then, have we reason to "conclude, that not a particle of charcoal entered into the constitution of the lead?"

We shall next consider an experiment made by Mr Higgins himself, and which he likewise considers as decisive against the Phlogistians. "I introduced (says he) some iron nails, free from rust, into strong volatile vitriolic acid; when it stood for a few minutes, it acquired a milky appearance, and the solution went on without ebullition or extrication of air. On standing for a few hours, the solution acquired a darkish colour, and a black powder was precipitated. This powder, when collected and washed, put on red hot iron, burned partly like sulphur and partly like charcoal dust, and the incombustible residuum was of a purplish colour. The filtered solution was perfectly neutralised, and free from the least sulphureous pungency. Its taste was strongly chalybeate, but not so disagreeable as that of the solution of iron in the perfect vitriolic acid, or in any of the mineral acids. Nitrous acid dropped into the solution instantly produced a cloudiness, which immediately disappeared without ebullition, though volatile sulphureous acid was extricated in its utmost degree of pungency. The vitriolic, marine, and acetous acids, decomposed this solution, but caused no turbidness, nor was any inflammable air produced.

Higgins's Comparative View, p. 49

"In order to know whether the sulphur was disengaged from the volatile sulphureous acid or the iron, I poured marine acid on the same nails, when light inflammable air and hepatic air were copiously produced, and likewise sulphur was deposited in its crude state. When I used vitriolic, or the nitrous acid, no sulphur was produced. I tried different nails, and likewise iron-filings, with the same result. These facts convinced me that the sulphur came from the iron; but that all sorts of iron contain sulphur is what I cannot pretend to know, as I have not tried steel, or varieties enough of malleable iron. However, I have strong reason to suspect, that sulphur has more to do in the different properties of iron than we are aware of. That iron should contain sulphur, notwithstanding the different processes it must necessarily undergo before it acquires malleability, considering the volatility of sulphur, points out the force of their attraction to one another; and the separation of this again by volatile sulphureous acid, shows likewise the greater attraction of iron to sulphur and dephlogisticated air jointly. That volatile sulphureous acid should dissolve iron without the extrication of inflammable air or phlogiston, is a very strong instance of the fallacy of the phlogistic doctrine. A small quantity of inflammable air is produced, but it is so trifling comparatively to what should be produced from the quantity of iron dissolved, that it is hardly worth noticing; and in my opinion proceeds from a portion of perfect vitriolic acid, which is generally inseparable from the volatile acid. If volatile vitriolic acid were a compound of phlogiston, a certain basis, and dephlogisticated air, a greater quantity of inflammable air should have been disengaged during the solution of iron in this acid than when the perfect vitriolic acid is used. Let us even suppose volatile sulphureous acid to be composed of the basis of sulphur, phlogiston, and dephlogisticated air, which is the opinion of all the Phlogistians, though they differ with respect to the modification of these three principles; and likewise iron to be composed of a certain basis and phlogiston; I would ask the Phlogistians, What becomes of the phlogiston of the iron during its solution?"

Charcoal.

But however much Mr Higgins may be convinced, from this experiment, of the fallacy of the phlogistic doctrine, his adversaries, instead of being silenced, will urge his own experiment against himself. He owns, that during the solution something was separated of a black colour, and which burned like charcoal dust. Unless therefore Mr Higgins shall prove the contrary, they will say, that this was the real *phlogiston* or *charcoal* which entered into the substance of the metal; and that it appeared in its native form, because the volatile vitriolic acid had not specific or latent heat sufficient to convert it into inflammable air. At any rate, it was incumbent on Mr Higgins to have accounted for the coally part of his residuum as well as the sulphureous one; yet he has been at considerable pains to deduce the latter from the iron, without speaking a word about the former. Indeed, whether he deduced this from the iron or the vitriolic acid, it will make equally against him; for his principles do not allow that the volatile vitriolic acid contains any charcoal. That the latter really does so, however, appears from an experiment of Dr Priestley, in which he reduced a calx of lead by means of vitriolic acid air, the same with the vitriolic or volatile sulphureous acid. It is true, that only a small quantity of metal was thus procured; but however small this was, the Antiphlogistians do not pretend that metals can be reduced to their metallic state in any quantity, except by the mediation of charcoal.

Thus it appears, that with regard to metals the dispute is as yet far enough from being decided in favour of the Antiphlogistians. Their cause is equally doubtful with regard to sulphur and phosphorus, both of which Dr Priestley has produced by heating vitriolic and phosphoric acid in inflammable air. Indeed, by some experiments on sulphur, the matter seems to be decided against them. "Perhaps (says Dr Priestley) as decisive a proof as any, of the real production of fixed air from phlogiston and dephlogisticated air, may be drawn from the experiments in which I always found a quantity of it when I burned sulphur in dephlogisticated air. In one of these experiments to which I gave more particular attention, six ounce-measures and an half of the dephlogisticated air were reduced to about two ounce-measures, and one-fifth of this was fixed air." Now, though the Doctor inferred from this, that fixed air was composed of phlogiston and dephlogisticated air, on the supposition of sulphur containing phlogiston; yet, admitting from other proofs, that fixed air is composed of these two principles, the experiment

Charcoal.

riment unanswerably proves, that sulphur contains phlogiston or charcoal, though indeed in a very small quantity: but if the sulphur contained none at all, and the dephlogisticated air as little, as the Antiphlogistians would have it, how is it possible that a compound, of which phlogiston makes a part, should result from an union of the two *? Another experiment equally decisive, even with regard to metals, is that quoted from Dr Priestley in the place just referred to (a), where he obtained pure fixed air from a mixture of red precipitate and iron-filings. Now, according to the antiphlogistic doctrine, neither of these materials contained an atom of charcoal or phlogiston; whence then came the phlogiston in the fixed air which issued from the mixture?

* See Aerology, n° 111.

Thus the Antiphlogistians seem to be unanswerably refuted with regard to sulphur and metallic substances; for if the two experiments just related be accurate, it is impossible to invalidate them by any argumentation whatever. Their last resource therefore is the decomposition of water: and even here it is evident they have little reason to boast. On this subject, however, we are sorry to observe, that the opinions have been so many, so various, and so fluctuating, that it is not only impossible to say what are the prevailing ones, but even difficult to ascertain what are the sentiments of any individual on the subject. Under the article AEROLOGY, n° 81. we have quoted Dr Priestley as favouring the doctrine of the decomposition of water; and in Mr Higgins's work we find him quoted as opposing it. "Dr Priestley (says he) supposes that the water produced by the condensation of inflammable and dephlogisticated air, is only what was suspended and attached to them in their elastic state, and that their respective gravitating particles form a different compound, namely, the nitrous acid. To ascertain this, he confined his mixture of airs with dry fixed alkali over mercury, in order to abstract from it as much water as possible. Having thus prepared his mixture of airs, he found, after exploding them, that the product of water fell far short of the weight of both airs; and he observed a dense vapour after every explosion, which soon condensed, and adhered in a solid state to the sides of the vessel, which he found afterwards to be the nitrous acid." To this Mr Higgins answers, that the airs ought to have been accurately weighed after abstracting the water from them, when (he supposes) the weight of water produced would have equalled them. This indeed ought to have been done; but Mr Higgins, or some Antiphlogistian, ought to have done so before he decided positively in favour of the opposite doctrine. At any rate, it cannot be pretended, that in any experiment, let the circumstances of it be what they would, the quantity of water produced ever equalled that of the two airs. It is evident therefore, that till this shall some how or other be cleared up, the matter must remain uncertain. That the purest water we can obtain always contains phlogiston, is what no Phlogistian denies; that it essentially belongs to it is doubtful, though indeed it must be probable, that it does so until experiments show the contrary. Mr Cavendish supposes that *dephlogisticated* air and *dephlogisticated water* may be the same; and indeed this would seem to be almost certain, were it not for a circumstance taken notice of by Mr Higgins, viz. that in the firing of iron in dephlogisticated air the latter appears to be totally absorbed; though it is certain, that a quantity of undecomposed water enters into its composition.

Comparative View, p. 3.

How far this circumstance throws any obscurity on the matter the reader must determine. For a more full investigation of the subject, however, we must refer to the article WATER; and in the mean time shall dismiss the article with a few observations on the composition of charcoal.

From the days of Stahl till very lately, the component parts of this substance have been reckoned a certain kind of earth combined with what was called phlogiston. The late experiments of Dr Priestley have shown, that this doctrine is erroneous, and that charcoal is wholly dissipable into vapour. "On the whole (says the translator of Wiegleb's Chemistry), charcoal appears, from the experiments of Lavoisier and Bertholet, to be an oil deprived of its inflammable gas. But coal of wood (or common charcoal) likewise contains fixed alkali, which the soot (or the coal of oil) does not, but instead of this exhibits volatile alkali. The fixed alkali of the former proceeds from the plant itself, and this, in the case of soot, is joined with inflammable gas, and forms volatile alkali, the earthy part being left behind, as happens when this latter is prepared from fixed alkali. Genuine charcoal, therefore, consists of this vegetable principle, united with a little fixed alkali and part of the phlogiston that constituted the oil of the plant of which it is made: for some of this principle is carried off, together with the *hydrophlogy* (b), in the form of inflammable gas, if distilled in close vessels; but if burned in the open air, the hydrophloge unites with the pure part of the air, and forms water. From these considerations, as well as from the experiments and observations of M. Berthollet, in the Mem. de l'Acad. des Sciences pour 1786, p. 33. *et seq.* it appears, that common charcoal consists of the vegetable principle, some phlogiston, fixed alkali, and no inflammable gas."

On all this, however, we must observe, that it is entirely disproved by the experiments of Dr Priestley, so often quoted, in which it was totally dissipated into inflammable air *. On this occasion indeed he acknowledges, that some very minute particles of ashes were observed, which could not have amounted to a single grain from many pounds of wood. Even these, according to what he observes in the same place, may be supposed to have come from the small quantity of air in the receiver; and it is to be wished that the Doctor would repeat the experiment in one of those perfect vacuums through which the electric fluid cannot be made to pass. From undoubted experiments, however, it appears, that charcoal cannot be decomposed by mere heat; as *in vacuo* it is dissipated into inflammable air; and

* See Aerology, n° 119, 130.

(a) See *Encycl.* Vol. I. p. 169. col. 1. where, in lines 18, 19 from the top, read *precipitate* for *charcoal*.

(b) A word used by Mr Wiegleb, as far as we can comprehend the author's meaning, for one of the component parts of water. See his General System of Chemistry, translated by Hopson, p. 59.

Charcoal.

and this, on preſenting a proper ſubſtance to attract the ſolid part, again diſcovers itſelf, by its blackneſs, to be real charcoal. As little does it appear deſtructible by burning in the open air; for though ſome aſhes are left, it appears probable that theſe differ from the coal itſelf in nothing but having a quantity of air attached to them. By far the greateſt part of it, even in the common way of burning, is converted into fixed air; and from this it may again be ſeparated by taking the electric ſpark in that fluid, when it is reſolved into very pure dephlogiſticated and inflammable air. The ſame ſeparation may be effected by merely heating iron in fixed air, in which caſe the dephlogiſticated part will unite to the iron, and the coaly part, together with part of the phlogiſton of the metal, be converted into inflammable air. From all theſe, and other conſiderations, a ſuſpicion is induced, that the matter of charcoal is not different from the element of earth itſelf; and that, according to the different modifications of this ſubſtance, it either appears as coal, aſhes, earth of various kinds, or even metals. This receives ſome confirmation from the following experiments of Mr Watt, related in the 74th volume of the Philoſophical Tranſactions: "I diſſolved (ſays he) magneſia alba, calcareous earth, and minium, in nitrous acid dephlogiſticated by boiling, and diluted with proper proportions of water. I made uſe of glaſs-retorts coated with clay; and I received the air in glaſs-veſſels, whoſe mouths were immerſed in a glazed earthen baſon containing the ſmalleſt quantity of water that could be uſed for the purpoſe. As ſoon as the retort was heated a little above the degree of boiling water, the ſolutions began to diſtil watery vapours containing nitrous acid. Soon after theſe vapours ceaſed, yellow fumes, and, in ſome of the caſes, dark red fumes, began to appear in the neck of the retort; and, at the ſame time, there was a production of dephlogiſticated air, which was greater in quantity from ſome of theſe mixtures than from others, but continued in all of them until the ſubſtances were reduced to dryneſs. I found in the receiving water, &c. very nearly the whole of the nitrous acid uſed for their ſolution, but highly phlogiſticated, ſo as to emit nitrous air by the application of heat; and there is reaſon to believe, that with more precaution the whole might have been obtained. As the quantity of dephlogiſticated air produced by theſe proceſſes did not form a ſufficient part of the whole weight to enable me to judge whether any of the real acid entered into the compoſition of the air I obtained, I ceaſed to purſue them further, having learned from them the fact, that however much the acid and the earths were dephlogiſticated before the ſolution, the acid always became highly phlogiſticated in the proceſs.

"In order to examine whether this phlogiſton was furniſhed by the earths, ſome dephlogiſticated nitrous acid was diſtilled from minium till no more air or acid came over. More of the ſame acid was added to the minium as ſoon as it was cold, and the diſtillation repeated, which produced the ſame appearances of red fumes and dephlogiſticated air. This operation was repeated a third time on the ſame minium, without any ſenſible variation in the phenomena. The proceſs ſhould have been ſtill farther repeated, but the retort broke about the end of the third diſtillation; the quantity of minium uſed was 180 grains, and the quantity of nitrous acid added each time was 240 grains, of ſuch ſtrength that it could diſſolve half its weight of mercury by means of heat. It appears from this experiment, that unleſs minium be ſuppoſed principally to conſiſt of phlogiſton, the ſource of the phlogiſton thus obtained, was either the nitrous acid itſelf, or the water with which it was diluted; or elſe that it came through the retort with the light; for the retort was in this caſe red hot before any air was produced. Yet this latter concluſion does not appear very ſatiſfactory, when it is conſidered, that in the proceſs wherein the earth made uſe of was magneſia, the retort was not red hot, or very obſcurely ſo, in any part of the proceſs, and by no means luminous when the yellow and red fumes firſt made their appearance."

To theſe experiments, however, the Antiphlogiſtians will no doubt reply, that there was no phlogiſton in the caſe, and that the nitrous acid was only decompoſed; and indeed the deciſive experiment here would be, the entire diſſipation of a quantity of earth into ſome kind of air, as may be done with charcoal; but to do this in the way of diſtillation muſt be attended with incredible labour, though, as finally deciding this point, it ſeems to be well worth purſuing.

A pretty ſtrong proof of the identity of metallic calces with charcoal, is their converſion into it in the manner already related. Experiments, however, are yet wanting on the ſubject; though it ſeems probable from what Dr Prieſtley has already done, that they may thus be entirely diſſipated into air as well as common charcoal.

Chardin || Charge.

CHARDIN (Sir John), a celebrated traveller, was born at Paris in 1643. His father, who was a jeweller, had him educated in the Proteſtant religion; after which he travelled into Perſia and India. He traded in jewels, and died at London in 1713. The account he wrote of his travels is much eſteemed.

CHARENTON, the name of two towns of France, the one upon the Marmande in the Bourbonnois; the other in the iſle of France, near the confluence of the Marne with the Seine.

CHARES the Lydian, a celebrated ſtatuary, was the diſciple of Lyſippus; and made the famous Coloſſus of the ſun in the city of Rhodes. Flouriſhed 288 years before Chriſt.

CHARGE, in gunnery, the quantity of powder and ball wherewith a gun is loaded for execution.

The rules for charging large pieces in war are, That the piece be firſt cleaned or ſcoured withinſide; that the proper quantity of powder be next driven in and rammed down; care, however, being taken, that the powder, in ramming, be not bruiſed, becauſe that weakens its effect: that a little quantity of paper, hay, lint, or the like, be rammed over it; and that the ball or ſhot be intruded. If the ball be red-hot, a tompion, or trencher of green wood, is to be driven in before it. The common allowance for a charge of powder of a piece of ordnance, is half the weight of the ball. In the Britiſh Navy, the allowance for 32 pounders is but ſeven-ſixteenths of the weight of the bullet. But a late author is of opinion, that if the powder in all ſhip-cannon whatever was reduced to one-third weight of the ball, or even leſs, it would be of conſiderable advantage, not only by ſaving ammunition, but by keeping

Robins's Propoſal for increaſing the Strength of the Navy.

ing the guns cooler and quieter, and at the ſame time more effectually injuring the veſſels of the enemy. With the preſent allowance of powder the guns are heated, and their tackle and furniture ſtrained; and this only to render the bullets leſs efficacious: for a bullet which can but juſt paſs through a piece of timber, and loſes almoſt all its motion thereby, has a much better chance of rending and fracturing it, than if it paſſes through with a much greater velocity.

Charge, in heraldry, is applied to the figures repreſented on the eſcutcheon, by which the bearers are diſtinguiſhed from one another; and it is to be obſerved, that too many charges are not ſo honourable as fewer.

Charge of Lead, denotes a quantity of 36 pigs. See Pig.

To Charge in the military language, is to attack the enemy either with horſe or foot.

Charge, in law, denotes the inſtructions given to the grand jury, with reſpect to the articles of their inquiry, by the judge who preſides on the bench.

Charge, in law, alſo ſignifies a thing done that bindeth him who doth it; and diſcharge is the removal of that charge. Lands may be charged in various ways; as, by grant of rent out of it, by ſtatutes, judgments, conditions, warranties, &c.

Charge of horning, in Scots law. See Horning.

Charge to enter Heir, in Scots law, a writing paſſing under the ſignet, obtained at the inſtance of a creditor, either againſt the heir of his debtor, for fixing upon him the debt as repreſenting the debtor, which is called a general charge: or, againſt the debtor himſelf, or his heir, for the purpoſe of veſting him in the right of any heritable ſubject to which he has made up no title, in order the creditor may attach that ſubject for payment of his debt, in the ſame manner as if his debtor or his heir were legally veſted in it by ſervice or otherwiſe. This laſt kind is called a *ſpecial charge*.

Charge, or rather *Overcharge*, in painting, is an exaggerated repreſentation of any perſon; wherein the likeneſs is preſerved, but at the ſame time ridiculed.

Few painters have the genius neceſſary to ſucceed in theſe charges: the method is, to ſelect and heighten ſomething already amiſs in the face, whether by way of defect, or redundancy: thus, *e. g.* if Nature have given a man a noſe a little larger than ordinary, the painter falls in with her, and makes the noſe extravagantly long: or if the noſe be naturally too ſhort, in the painting it will be a mere ſtump; and thus of the other parts.

CHARGED, in heraldry, a ſhield carrying ſome impreſs or figure, is ſaid to be charged therewith; ſo alſo, when one bearing, or charge, has another figure added upon it, it is properly ſaid to be charged.

Charged, in electrical experiments, is when a vial, pane of glaſs, or other electric ſubſtance, properly coated on both ſides, has a quantity of electricity communicated to it; in which caſe the one ſide is always electrified poſitively, and the other negatively.

CHARIOT, a half coach, having only a ſeat behind, with a ſtool before. See Coach.

The chariots of the ancients, chiefly uſed in war, were called by the ſeveral names *bigæ*, *trigæ*, &c. according to the number of horſes applied to draw them.

Every chariot carried two men, who were probably the warrior and the charioteer; and we read of ſeveral men of note and valour employed in driving the chariot. When the warriors came to encounter in cloſe fight, they alighted out of the chariot, and fought on foot; but when they were weary, which often happened by reaſon of their armour, they retired into their chariots, and thence annoyed their enemies with darts and miſſive weapons. Theſe chariots were made ſo ſtrong, that they laſted for ſeveral generations.

Beſides this ſort, we find frequent mention of the *currus falcati*, or thoſe chariots armed with hooks, or ſcythes, with which whole ranks of ſoldiers were cut off together, if they had not the art of avoiding the danger; theſe were not only uſed by the Perſians, Syrians, Egyptians, *&c.* but we had them among the ancient Britons; and notwithſtanding the imperfect ſtate of ſome of the moſt neceſſary arts among that nation before the invaſion of the Romans, it is certain that they had war-chariots in great abundance. By the Greek and Roman hiſtorians, theſe chariots are deſcribed by the ſix following names; viz. Benna, Petoritum, Currus or Carrus, Covinus, Eſſedum, and Rheda. The benna ſeems to have been a chariot deſigned rather for travelling than war. It contained two perſons, who were called *combennones*, from their ſitting together in the ſame machine. The petoritum ſeems to have been a larger kind of chariot than the benna; and is thought to have derived its name from the British word *pedwar*, ſignifying *four*; this kind of cariage having four wheels. The carrus or currus was the common cart or waggon. This kind of chariot was uſed by the ancient Britons, in times of peace, for the purpoſes of agriculture and merchandiſe; and, in time of war, for carrying their baggage, and wives and children, who commonly followed the armies of all the Celtic nations. The covinus was a war-chariot, and a very terrible inſtrument of deſtruction; being armed with ſharp ſcythes and hooks for cutting and tearing all who were ſo unhappy as to come within its reach. This kind of chariot was made very light, and had few or no men in it beſides the charioteer; being deſigned to drive with great force and rapidity, and to do execution chiefly with its hooks and ſcythes. The eſſedum and rheda were alſo war-chariots, probably of a large ſize, and ſtronger made than the covinus, deſigned for containing a charioteer for driving it, and one or two warriors for fighting. The far greateſt number of the British war-chariots ſeem to have been of this kind. Theſe chariots, as already obſerved, were to be found in great numbers among the Britons; inſomuch that Cæſar relates that Caſſibelanus, after diſmiſſing all his other forces, retained no fewer than 4000 of theſe war-chariots about his perſon. The ſame author relates, that, by continual experience, they had at laſt arrived at ſuch perfection in the management of their chariots, that "in the moſt ſteep and difficult places they could ſtop their horſes upon full ſtretch, turn them which way they pleaſed, run along the pole, reſt on the harneſs, and throw themſelves back into their chariots, with incredible dexterity."

Chariots, in the heathen mythology, were ſometimes conſecrated to the ſun; and the ſcripture obſerves, that Joſiah burnt thoſe which had been offered to the ſun by the king's predeceſſors. This ſuperſti-

tion

those custom was an imitation of the heathens, and principally of the Persians, who had horses and chariots consecrated in honour of the sun. Herodotus, Xenophon, and Quintus Curtius, speak of white chariots crowned, which were consecrated to the sun, among the Persians, which in their ceremonies were drawn by white horses consecrated to the same luminary.

Triumphal CHARIOT, was one of the principal ornaments of the Roman celebration of a victory.

The Roman triumphal chariot was generally made of ivory, round like a tower, or rather of a cylindrical figure; it was sometimes gilt at the top, and ornamented with crowns; and to represent a victory more naturally, they used to stain it with blood. It was usually drawn by four white horses; but oftentimes by lions, elephants, tygers, bears, leopards, dogs, &c.

CHARISIA, in the heathen theology, a wake, or night-festival, instituted in honour of the graces. It continued the whole night, most of which time was spent in dancing; after which, cakes made of yellow flour mixed with honey, and other sweetmeats, were distributed among the assistants.—Charisia is also sometimes used to signify the sweetmeats used on such occasions.

CHARISIUS, in the heathen theology, a surname given to Jupiter. The word is derived from χαρις, *gratia*, "grace" or "favour;" he being the God by whose influence men obtain the favour and affection of one another. On which account the Greeks used at their meals to make a libation of a cup to Jupiter Charisius.

CHARISTIA, a festival of the ancient Romans, celebrated in the month of February, wherein the relations by blood and marriage met, in order to preserve a good correspondence; and that if there happened to be any difference among them, it might be the more easily accommodated, by the good humour and mirth of the entertainment. *Ovid. Fast.* i. 617.

CHARISTICARY, commendatary, or donatory, a person to whom is given the enjoyment of the revenues of a monastery, hospital, or benefice.

The charisticaries among the Greeks, were a kind of donataries, or commendataries, who enjoyed all the revenues of hospitals and monasteries, without giving an account thereof to any person.—The original of this abuse is referred to the Iconoclastæ, particularly Constantine Copronymus, the avowed enemy of the monks, whose monasteries he gave away to strangers. In after times, the emperors and patriarchs gave many to people of quality, not by way of gift, to reap any temporal advantage from them; but to repair, beautify, and patronize them. At length avarice crept in, and those in good condition were given away, especially such as were rich; and at last they were all given away, rich and poor, those of men and of women, and that to laymen and married men.

CHARITY, among divines, one of the three grand theological virtues, consisting in the love of God and of our neighbour, or the habit and disposition of loving God with all our heart, and our neighbour as ourselves.

CHARITY is also used for the effect of a moral virtue, which consists in supplying the necessities of others, whether with money, counsel, assistance, or the like.

As pecuniary relief is generally the most efficacious, and at the same time that from which we are most apt to excuse ourselves, this branch of the duty merits particular illustration; and a better cannot be offered than what is contained in the following extracts (if we may be permitted to make them) from the elegant *Moral System* of Archdeacon *Paley*.

Whether pity be an instinct or a habit, it is in fact a property of our nature, which God appointed: and the final cause for which it was appointed, is to afford to the miserable, in the compassion of their fellow creatures, a remedy for those inequalities and distresses which God foresaw that many must be exposed to, under every general rule for the distribution of property.

The Christian scriptures are more copious and explicit upon this duty than almost any other. The description which Christ hath left us of the proceedings of the last day, establishes the obligation of bounty beyond controversy. "When the Son of man shall come in his glory, and all the holy angels with him, then shall he sit upon the throne of his glory, and before him shall be gathered all nations; and he shall separate them one from another. Then shall the king say unto them on his right hand, Come ye blessed of my father, inherit the kingdom prepared for you from the foundation of the world: For I was an hungered, and ye gave me meat; I was thirsty, and ye gave me drink; I was a stranger, and ye took me in; naked, and ye clothed me; I was sick, and ye visited me; I was in prison, and ye came unto me. And inasmuch as ye have done it to one of the least of these my brethren, ye have done it unto me." It is not necessary to understand this passage as a literal account of what will actually pass on that day. Supposing it only a scenical description of the rules and principles by which the Supreme Arbiter of our destiny will regulate his decisions, it conveys the same lesson to us; it equally demonstrates of how great value and importance these duties in the sight of God are, and what stress will be laid upon them. The apostles also describe this virtue as propitiating the divine favour in an eminent degree. And these recommendations have produced their effect. It does not appear that, before the times of Christianity, an infirmary, hospital, or public charity of any kind, existed in the world; whereas most countries in Christendom have long abounded with these institutions. To which may be added, that a spirit of private liberality seems to flourish amidst the decay of many other virtues: not to mention the legal provision for the poor, which obtains in this country, and which was unknown and unthought of by the most polished nations of antiquity.

St Paul adds upon the subject an excellent direction; and which is practicable by all who have any thing to give. "Upon the first day of the week (or any other stated time) let every one of you lay by in store, as God hath prospered him." By which the apostle may be understood to recommend what is the very thing wanting with most men, *the being charitable upon a plan*; that is, from a deliberate comparison of our fortunes with the reasonable expences and expectations of our families, to compute what we can spare, and to lay by so much for charitable purposes, in some mode or other. The mode will be a consideration afterwards.

Charity.

The effect, which Christianity produced upon some of its converts, was such as might be looked for from a divine religion coming with full force and miraculous evidence upon the consciences of mankind. It overwhelmed all worldly considerations in the expectation of a more important existence. "And the multitude of them that believed were of one heart and of one soul; neither said any of them that aught of the things, which he possessed, was his own; but they had all things in common.—Neither was there any among them that lacked; for as many as were possessors of lands or houses sold them, and brought the prices of the things that were sold, and laid them down at the apostles' feet; and distribution was made unto every man, according as he had need." Acts iv. 32.

Nevertheless, this community of goods, however it manifested the sincere zeal of the primitive Christians, is no precedent for our imitation. It was confined to the church at Jerusalem; continued not long there; was never enjoined upon any (Acts v. 4.); and, although it might suit with the particular circumstances of a small and select society, is altogether impracticable in a large and mixed community.

The conduct of the apostles upon the occasion deserves to be noticed. Their followers laid down their fortunes at their feet: but so far were they from taking advantage of this unlimited confidence to enrich themselves or establish their authority, that they soon after got rid of this business as inconsistent with the main object of their mission, and transferred the custody and management of the public fund to deacons, elected to that office by the people at large. (Acts vi.)

There are three kinds of charity, our author observes, which prefer a claim to attention.

1. The first, and apparently one of the best, is to give stated and considerable sums, by way of pension or annuity to individuals or families, with whose behaviour and distress we ourselves are acquainted. In speaking of considerable sums, it is meant only, that five pounds, or any other sum, given at once, or divided amongst five or fewer families, will do more good than the same sum distributed amongst a greater number in shillings or half crowns; and that, because it is more likely to be properly applied by the persons who receive it. A poor fellow, who can find no better use for a shilling than to drink his benefactor's health, and purchase half an hour's recreation for himself, would hardly break into a guinea for any such purpose, or be so improvident as not to lay it by for an occasion of importance, for his rent, his clothing, fuel, or stock of winter's provision. It is a still greater recommendation of this kind of charity, that pensions and annuities, which are paid regularly, and can be expected at the time, are the only way by which we can prevent one part of a poor man's sufferings, the dread of want.

2. But as this kind of charity supposes that proper objects of such expensive benefactions fall within our private knowledge and observation, which does not happen to all, a second method of doing good, which is in every one's power who has the money to spare, is by subscription to public charities. Public charities admit of this argument in their favour, that your money goes farther towards attaining the end for which it is given, than it can do by any private and separate beneficence. A guinea, for example, contributed to an infirmary, becomes the means of providing one patient, at least, with a physician, surgeon, apothecary; with medicine, diet, lodging, and suitable attendance; which is not the tenth part of what the same assistance, if it could be procured at all, would cost to a sick person or family in any other situation.

Charity.

3. The last, and, compared with the former, the lowest exertion of benevolence, is in the relief of beggars. Nevertheless, the indiscriminate rejection of all who implore our alms in this way, is by no means approved. Some may perish by such a conduct. Men are sometimes overtaken by distress, for which all other relief would come too late. Besides which, resolutions of this kind compel us to offer such violence to our humanity, as may go near, in a little while, to suffocate the principle itself; which is a very serious consideration. A good man, if he do not surrender himself to his feelings without reserve, will at least lend an ear to importunities which come accompanied with outward attestations of distress; and after a patient hearing of the complaint, will direct himself by the circumstances and credibility of the account that he receives.

There are other species of charity well contrived to make the money expended *go far*; such as keeping down the price of fuel or provision in case of a monopoly or temporary scarcity, by purchasing the articles at the best market, and retailing them at prime cost, or at a small loss; or the adding a bounty to a particular species of labour, when the price is accidentally depressed.

The proprietors of large estates have it in their power to facilitate the maintenance, and thereby encourage the establishment of families (which is one of the noblest purposes to which the rich and great can convert their endeavours), by building cottages, splitting farms, erecting manufactures, cultivating wastes, embanking the sea, draining marshes, and other expedients, which the situation of each estate points out. If the profits of these undertakings do not repay the expence, let the authors of them place the difference to the account of charity. It is true of almost all such projects, that the public is a gainer by them, whatever the owner be. And where the loss can be spared, this consideration is sufficient.

It is become a question of some importance, Under what circumstances works of charity ought to be done in private, and when they may be made public without detracting from the merit of the action; if indeed they ever may: the Author of our religion having delivered a rule upon this subject, which seems to enjoin universal secrecy. "When thou doest alms, let not thy left hand know what thy right hand doth; that thy alms may be in secret, and thy Father which seeth in secret, himself shall reward thee openly." (Matth. vi. 3. 4.) From the preamble to this prohibition, it is plain, that our Saviour's sole design was to forbid *ostentation*, and all publishing of good works which proceeds from that motive. "Take heed that ye do not your alms before men, *to be seen of them*; otherwise ye have no reward of your Father, which is in heaven: therefore, when thou doest thine alms, do not sound a trumpet before thee, as the hypocrites do, in the synagogues and in the streets, *that they may have glory of*

Charity. men. Verily I say unto thee, they have their reward," v. 2. There are motives for the doing our alms in public beside those of ostentation; with which therefore our Saviour's rule has no concern: such as to testify our approbation of some particular species of charity, and to recommend it to others; to take off the prejudice which the want, or, which is the same thing, the suppression, of our name in the list of contributors, might excite against the charity or against ourselves. And, so long as these motives are free from any mixture of vanity, they are in no danger of invading our Saviour's prohibition; they rather seem to comply with another direction which he has left us: "Let your light so shine before men, that they may see your good works, and glorify your father which is in heaven." If it be necessary to propose a precise distinction upon the subject, there can be none better than the following: When our bounty is beyond our fortune or station, that is, when it is more than could be expected from us, our charity should be private, if privacy be practicable; when it is not more than might be expected, it may be public: for we cannot hope to influence others to the imitation of extraordinary generosity, and therefore want, in the former case, the only justifiable reason for making it public.

The pretences by which men excuse themselves from giving to the poor, are various; as,

1. "That they have nothing to spare;" i. e. nothing, for which they have not some other use; nothing, which their plan of expence, together with the savings they have resolved to lay by, will not exhaust: never reflecting whether it be in their power, or that it is their duty, to retrench their expences, and contract their plan, "that they may have to give to them that need;" or rather that this ought to have been part of their plan originally.

2. "That they have families of their own, and that charity begins at home." A father is no doubt bound to adjust his economy with a view to the reasonable demands of his family upon his fortune; and until a sufficiency for these is acquired, or in due time probably will be acquired (for in human affairs probability is enough), he is justified in declining *expensive* liberality; for to take from those who want, in order to give to those who want, adds nothing to the stock of public happiness. Thus far, therefore, and no farther, the plea in question is an excuse for parsimony, and an answer to those who solicit our bounty.

3. "That charity does not consist in giving money, but in benevolence, philanthropy, love to all mankind, goodness of heart," &c. Hear St James. "If a brother or sister be naked, and destitute of daily food, and one of you say unto them, depart in peace, be ye warmed and filled, notwithstanding *ye give them not those things which are needful to the body*, what doth it profit?" (James ii. 15, 16.)

4. "That giving to the poor is not mentioned in St Paul's description of charity, in the 13th chapter of his first epistle to the Corinthians." This is not a description of charity, but of good nature; and it is not necessary that every duty be mentioned in every place.

5. "That they pay the poor-rates." They might as well allege that they pay their debts; for the poor have the same right to that portion of a man's property, which the laws assign them, that the man himself has to the remainder. Charity.

6. "That they employ many poor persons:"—for their own sake, not the poor's—otherwise it is a good plea.

7. "That the poor do not suffer so much as we imagine; that education and habit have reconciled them to the evils of their condition, and make them easy under it." Habit can never reconcile human nature to the extremities of cold, hunger, and thirst, any more than it can reconcile the hand to the touch of a red-hot iron: besides, the question is not, how unhappy any one is, but how much more happy we can make him.

8. "That these people, give them what you will, will never thank you, or think of you for it." In the first place, this is not true: in the second place, it was not for the sake of their thanks that you relieved them.

9. "That we are so liable to be imposed upon." If a due enquiry be made, our motive and merit is the same: beside that, the distress is generally real, whatever has been the cause of it.

10. "That they should apply to their parishes." This is not always practicable: to which we may add, that there are many requisites to a comfortable subsistence, which parish-relief does not always supply; and that there are some who would suffer almost as much from receiving parish-relief as by the want of it: and lastly, that there are many modes of charity, to which this answer does not relate at all.

11. "That giving money encourages idleness and vagrancy." This is true only of injudicious and indiscriminate generosity.

12. "That we have too many objects of charity at home to bestow any thing upon strangers; or that there are other charities which are more useful, or stand in greater need." The value of this excuse depends entirely upon the *fact*, whether we actually relieve those neighbouring objects, and contribute to those other charities.

Beside all these excuses, pride, or prudery, or delicacy, or love of ease, keep one half of the world out of the way of observing what the other half suffer.

Charity Schools, are schools erected and maintained in various parishes by the voluntary contributions of the inhabitants, for teaching poor children to read, write, and other necessary parts of education. See School.

Brothers of Charity, a sort of religious hospitallers, founded about the year 1297, since denominated *Billetins*. They took the third order of St Francis, and the scapulary, making three usual vows, but without begging.

Brothers of Charity also denote an order of hospitallers still subsisting in Romish countries, whose business is to attend the sick poor, and minister to them both spiritual and temporal succour.

They are all laymen, except a few priests, for administering the sacraments to the sick in their hospitals. The brothers of charity usually cultivate botany, pharmacy, surgery, and chemistry, which they practise with success.

They were first founded at Granada, by St John de

Dieu; and a second establishment was made at Madrid in the year 1553: the order was confirmed by Gregory XIII. in 1572: Gregory XIV. forbad them to take holy orders; but by leave of Paul V. in 1609, a few of the brothers might be admitted to orders. In 1619 they were exempted from the jurisdiction of the bishop. Those of Spain are separated from the rest; and they, as well as the brothers of France, Germany, Poland, and Italy, have their distinct generals, who reside at Rome. They were first introduced into France by Mary of Medicis in 1601, and have since built a fine hospital in the Fauxbourg St Germain.

Charity of St Hippolitus, a religious congregation founded about the end of the 14th century, by one Bernardin Alvarez, a Mexican, in honour of St Hippolitus the martyr, patron of the city of Mexico; and approved by Pope Gregory XIII.

Charity of our Lady, in church-history, a religious order in France, which, though charity was the principal motive of their union, grew in length of time so disorderly and irregular, that their order dwindled, and at last became extinct.

There is still at Paris a religious order of women, called *nuns hospitallers of the charity of our lady*. The religious of this hospital are by vow obliged to administer to the necessities of the poor and the sick, but those only women.

CHARLATAN, or Charletan, signifies an empiric or quack, who retails his medicines on a public stage, and draws people about him with his buffooneries, feats of activity, &c. The word, according to Calepine, comes from the Italian *cerritano*; of *Cerreto*, a town near Spoletto in Italy, where these impostors are said to have first risen. Menage derives it from *ciarlatano*, and that from *circulatorius*, of *circulator*, a quack.

CHARLEMAGNE, or Charles I. king of France by succession, and emperor of the west by conquest in 800, (which laid the foundation of the dynasty of the western Franks, who ruled the empire 472 years till the time of Rodolphus Auspurgensis, the founder of the house of Austria). Charlemagne was as illustrious in the cabinet as in the field; and, though he could not write his name, was the patron of men of letters, the restorer of learning, and a wise legislator; he wanted only the virtue of humanity to render him the most accomplished of men; but when we read of his beheading 4500 Saxons, solely for their loyalty to their prince, in opposing his conquests, we cannot think he merits the extravagant encomiums bestowed on him by some historians. He died in 814, in the 74th year of his age, and 47th of his reign.

France had nine sovereigns of this name, of whom Charles V. merited the title of *the wise*, (crowned in 1364, died in 1380); and Charles VIII. signalised himself in the field by rapid victories in Italy; crowned 1483, died in 1498. The rest do not deserve particular mention in this place. See *(History of)* France.

CHARLEMONT, a town of the province of Namur in the Austrian Netherlands, about 18 miles south of Namur. E. Long. 4. 40. N. Lat. 50. 10.

Charlemont is also the name of a town of Ireland, situated on the river Blackwater, in the county of Armagh, and province of Ulster, about six miles south-east of Dungannon. W. Long. 6. 50. N. Lat. 50. 16.

CHARLEROY, a strong town in the province of Namur, in the Austrian Netherlands, situated on the river Sambre, about 19 miles west of Namur. E. Long. 4. 20. N. Lat. 50. 30.

CHARLES Martel, a renowned conqueror in the early annals of France. He deposed and restored Chilperic king of France; and had the entire government of the kingdom, once with the title of *mayor of the palace*, and afterwards as *duke of France*; but he would not accept the crown. He died, regretted, in 741.

Charles le Gros, emperor of the west in 881, king of Italy and Suabia, memorable for his reverse of fortune; being dethroned at a diet held near Mentz, by the French, the Italians, and the Germans, in 887; after which he was obliged to subsist on the bounty of the archbishop of Mentz. He died in 888.

Charles V. (emperor and king of Spain), was son of Philip I. archduke of Austria, and of Jane queen of Castile. He was born at Ghent, February 24. 1500, and succeeded to the crown of Spain in 1517. Two years afterwards he was chosen emperor at Francfort after the death of Maximilian his grandfather. He was a great warrior and politician; and his ambition was not satisfied with the many kingdoms and provinces he possessed; for he is supposed, with reason, to have aspired at universal empire. He is said to have fought 60 battles, in most of which he was victorious. He took the king of France (Francis I.) prisoner, and sold him his liberty on very hard terms; yet afterwards, when the people of Ghent revolted, he asked leave to pass through his dominions; and though the generous king thus had him in his power, and had an opportunity of revenging his ill-treatment, yet he received and attended him with all pomp and magnificence. He sacked Rome, and took the Pope prisoner; and the cruelties which his army exercised there are said to have exceeded those of the northern barbarians. Yet the pious emperor went into mourning on account of this conquest; forbad the ringing of bells; commanded processions to be made, and prayers to be offered up for the deliverance of the Pope his prisoner; yet did not inflict the least punishment on those who treated the holy father and the holy see with such inhumanity. He is accused by some Romish writers of favouring the Lutheran principles, which he might easily have extirpated. But the truth is, he found his account in the divisions which that sect occasioned; and he for ever made his advantage of them, sometimes against the Pope, sometimes against France, and at other times against the empire itself. He was a great traveller, and made 50 different journeys into Germany, Spain, Italy, Flanders, France, England, and Africa. Though he had been successful in many unjust enterprizes, yet his last attempt on Metz, which he besieged with an army of 100,000 men, was very just and very unsuccessful.

Vexed at the reverse of fortune which seemed to attend his latter days, and oppressed by sickness, which unfitted him any longer from holding the reins of government with steadiness, or to guide them with address,

Charles.

dress, he resigned his dominions to his brother Ferdinand and his son Philip; and retreated to the monastery of St Justus near Placentia in Estramadura.

When Charles entered this retreat, he formed such a plan of life for himself as would have suited a private gentleman of moderate fortune. His table was neat, but plain; his domestics few; his intercourse with them familiar; all the cumbersome and ceremonious forms of attendance on his person were entirely abolished, as destructive of that social ease and tranquillity which he courted in order to sooth the remainder of his days. As the mildness of the climate, together with his deliverance from the burdens and cares of government, procured him at first a considerable remission from the acute pains of the gout, with which he had been long tormented, he enjoyed perhaps more complete satisfaction in this humble solitude than all his grandeur had ever yielded him. The ambitious thoughts and projects which had so long engrossed and disquieted him, were quite effaced from his mind. Far from taking any part in the political transactions of the princes of Europe, he restrained his curiosity even from an inquiry concerning them; and he seemed to view the busy scene which he had abandoned with all the contempt and indifference arising from his thorough experience of its vanity, as well as from the pleasing reflection of having disentangled himself from its cares.

Other amusements, and other objects, now occupied him. Sometimes he cultivated the plants in his garden with his own hand; sometimes he rode out to the neighbouring wood on a little horse, the only one that he kept, attended by a single servant on foot. When his infirmities confined him to his apartment, which often happened, and deprived him of these more active recreations, he either admitted a few gentlemen who resided near the monastery to visit him, and entertained them familiarly at his table; or he employed himself in studying mechanical principles, and in forming curious works of mechanism, of which he had always been remarkably fond, and to which his genius was peculiarly turned. With this view he had engaged Turriano, one of the most ingenious artists of that age, to accompany him in his retreat. He laboured together with him in framing models of the most useful machines, as well as in making experiments with regard to their respective powers; and it was not seldom that the ideas of the monarch assisted or perfected the inventions of the artist. He relieved his mind at intervals with slighter and more fantastic works of mechanism, in fashioning puppets, which, by the structure of internal springs, mimicked the gestures and actions of men, to the no small astonishment of the ignorant monks, who, beholding movements which they could not comprehend, sometimes distrusted their own senses, and sometimes suspected Charles and Torriano of being in compact with invisible powers. He was particularly curious with regard to the construction of clocks and watches; and having found, after repeated trials, that he could not bring any two of them to go exactly alike, he reflected, it is said, with a mixture of surprise as well as regret on his own folly, in having bestowed so much time and labour in the more vain attempt of bringing mankind to a precise uniformity of sentiment concerning the intricate and mysterious doctrines of religion.

But in what manner soever Charles disposed of the rest of his time, he constantly reserved a considerable portion of it for religious exercises. He regularly attended divine service in the chapel of the monastery every morning and evening; he took great pleasure in reading books of devotion, particularly the works of St Augustine and St Bernard; and conversed much with his confessor, and the prior of the monastery, on pious subjects. Thus did Charles pass the first year of his retreat in a manner not unbecoming a man perfectly disengaged from the affairs of this present life, and standing on the confines of a future world, either in innocent amusements which soothed his pains, and relieved a mind worn out with excessive application to business; or in devout occupations, which he deemed necessary in preparing for another state.

But, about six months before his death, the gout, after a longer intermission than usual, returned with a proportional increase of violence. His shattered constitution had not strength enough remaining to withstand such a shock. It enfeebled his mind as much as his body; and from this period we hardly discern any traces of that sound and masculine understanding which distinguished Charles among his contemporaries. An illiberal and timid superstition depressed his spirit. He had no relish for amusements of any kind. He endeavoured to conform, in his manner of living, to all the rigour of monastic austerity. He desired no other society than that of monks, and was almost continually employed in chanting with them the hymns of the missal. As an expiation for his sins, he gave himself the discipline in secret with such severity, that the whip of cords which he employed as the instrument of his punishment, was found, after his decease, tinged with his blood. Nor was he satisfied with these acts of mortification, which, however severe, were not unexampled. The timorous and distrustful solicitude which always accompanies superstition, still continued to disquiet him, and depreciating all that he had done, prompted him to aim at something extraordinary, at some new and singular act of piety, that would display his zeal, and merit the favour of heaven. The act on which he fixed was as wild and uncommon as any that superstition ever suggested to a disordered fancy. He resolved to celebrate his own obsequies before his death. He ordered his tomb to be erected in the chapel of the monastery. His domestics marched thither in funeral procession, with black tapers in their hands. He himself followed in his shroud. He was laid in his coffin with much solemnity. The service for the dead was chanted; and Charles joined in the prayers which were offered up for the rest of his soul, mingled his tears with those which his attendants shed, as if they had been celebrating a real funeral. The ceremony closed with sprinkling holy water on the coffin in the usual form, and, all the assistants retiring, the doors of the chapel were shut. Then Charles rose out of the coffin, and withdrew to his apartment, full of those awful sentiments which such a singular solemnity was calculated to inspire. But either the fatiguing length of the ceremony, or the impreſſion which this image of death left on his mind, affected him ſo much, that next day he was ſeized with a fever. His feeble frame could not long reſiſt its violence; and he expired on the 21ſt of September, after a life of 58 years ſix months and 21 days.

CHARLES I. } Kings of Britain. See BRITAIN,
CHARLES II. } n° 49. — 154.

CHARLES XII. king of Sweden, was born in 1682. By his father's will, the adminiſtration was lodged in the hands of the queen-dowager Eleonora with five ſenators, till the young prince was 18: but he was declared major at 15, by the ſtates convened at Stockholm. The beginning of his adminiſtration raiſed no favourable ideas of him, as he was thought both by Swedes and foreigners to be a perſon of mean capacity. But the difficulties that gathered round him, ſoon afforded him an opportunity to diſplay his real character. Three powerful princes, Frederic king of Denmark, Auguſtus king of Poland and elector of Saxony, and Peter the Great czar of Muſcovy, preſuming on his youth, conſpired his ruin almoſt at the ſame inſtant. Their meaſures alarming the council, they were for diverting the ſtorm by negociations; but Charles, with a grave reſolution that aſtoniſhed them, ſaid, "I am reſolved never to enter upon an unjuſt "war, nor to put an end to a juſt one but by the "deſtruction of my enemies. My reſolution is fixed: I will attack the firſt who ſhall declare againſt "me; and when I have conquered him, I may hope "to ſtrike a terror into the reſt." The old counſellors received his orders with admiration; and were ſtill more ſurpriſed when they ſaw him on a ſudden renounce all the enjoyments of a court, reduce his table to the utmoſt frugality, dreſs like a common ſoldier, and, full of the ideas of Alexander and Cæſar, propoſe thoſe two conquerors for his models in every thing but their vices. The king of Denmark began by ravaging the territories of the duke of Holſtein. Upon this Charles carried the war into the heart of Denmark; and made ſuch a progreſs, that the king of Denmark thought it beſt to accept of peace, which was concluded in 1700. He next reſolved to advance againſt the king of Poland, who had blocked up Riga. He had no ſooner given orders for his troops to go into winter-quarters, than he received advice that Narva, where count Horne was governor, was beſieged by an army of 100,000 Muſcovites. This made him alter his meaſures, and move toward the Czar; and at Narva he gained a ſurpriſing victory, which coſt him not above 2000 men killed and wounded. The Muſcovites were forced to retire from the provinces they had invaded. He purſued his conqueſts, till he penetrated as far as where the diet of Poland was ſitting; when he made them declare the throne of Poland vacant, and elect Staniſlaus their king: then making himſelf maſter of Saxony, he obliged Auguſtus himſelf to renounce the crown of Poland, and acknowledge Staniſlaus by a letter of congratulation on his acceſſion. All Europe was ſurpriſed with the expeditious finiſhing of this great negociation, but more at the diſintereſtedneſs of the king of Sweden, who ſatisfied himſelf with the bare reputation of this victory, without demanding an inch of ground for enlarging his dominions. After thus reducing the king of Denmark to peace, placing a new king on the throne of Poland, having humbled the emperor of Germany, and protected the Lutheran religion, Charles prepared to penetrate into Muſcovy in order to dethrone the Czar. He quickly obliged the Muſcovites to abandon Poland, purſued them into their own country, and won ſeveral battles over them. The Czar, diſpoſed to peace, ventured to make ſome propoſals; Charles only anſwered, "I will treat with "the Czar at Moſcow." When this haughty anſwer was brought to Peter, he ſaid, "My brother Charles "ſtill affects to act the Alexander, but I flatter myſelf he will not in me find a Darius." The event juſtified him: for the Muſcovites, already beaten into diſcipline, and under a prince of ſuch talents as Peter, entirely deſtroyed the Swediſh army at the memorable battle of Pultowa, July 8. 1709; on which deciſive day, Charles loſt the fruits of nine years labour, and of almoſt 100 battles! The king, with a ſmall troop, purſued by the Muſcovites, paſſed the Boriſthenes to Oczakow in the Turkiſh territories; and from thence, through deſert countries, arrived at Bender; where the Sultan, when informed of his arrival, ſent orders for accommodating him in the beſt manner, and appointed him a guard. Near Bender Charles built a houſe, and intrenched himſelf; and had with him 1800 men, who were all clothed and fed, with their horſes, at the expence of the Grand Signior. Here he formed a deſign of turning the Ottoman arms upon his enemies; and is ſaid to have had a promiſe from the Vizir of being ſent into Muſcovy with 200,000 men. While he remained here, he inſenſibly acquired a taſte for books; he read the tragedies of Corneille and Racine, with the works of Deſpreaux, whoſe ſatires he reliſhed, but did not much admire his other works. When he read that paſſage in which the author repreſents Alexander as a fool and a madman, he tore out the leaf. He would ſometimes play at cheſs: but when he recovered of his wounds, he renewed his fatigues in exerciſing his men; he tired three horſes a day; and thoſe who courted his favour were all day in their boots. To diſpoſe the Ottoman Porte to this war, he detached about 800 Poles and Coſaques of his retinue, with orders to paſs the Neiſter, that runs by Bender, and to obſerve what paſſed on the frontiers of Poland. The Muſcovite troops, diſperſed in thoſe quarters, fell immediately upon this little company, and purſued them even to the territories of the Grand Signior. This was what the king expected. His miniſters at the Porte excited the Turks to vengeance; but the Czar's money removed all difficulties, and Charles found himſelf in a manner priſoner among the Tartars. He imagined the Sultan was ignorant of the intrigues of his Grand Vizir. Poniatoſky undertook to make his complaints to the Grand Signior. The ſultan, in anſwer, ſome days after, ſent Charles five Arabian horſes, one of which was covered with a ſaddle and houſing of great riches; with an obliging letter, but conceived in ſuch general terms, as gave reaſon to ſuſpect that the miniſter had done nothing without the ſultan's conſent: Charles therefore refuſed them. Poniatoſky had the courage to form a deſign of depoſing the Grand Vizir; who

Charles. who accordingly was deprived of his dignity and wealth, and banished. The seal of the empire was given to Numan Cuprouglhy; who persuaded his master, that the law forbid him to invade the Czar, who had done him no injury; but to succour the king of Sweden as an unfortunate prince in his dominions. He sent his majesty 800 purses, every one of which amounted to 500 crowns, and advised him to return peaceably to his own dominions. Charles rejected this advice, threatening to hang up the bashaws, and shave the beards of any Janisaries who brought him such messages; and sent word that he should depend upon the Grand Signior's promise, and hoped to re-enter Poland as a conqueror with an army of Turks. After various intrigues at the Porte, an order was sent to attack this *head of iron*, as he was called, and to take him either alive or dead. He stood a siege in his house, with forty domestics, against the Turkish army; killed no less than 20 Janisaries with his own hand; and performed prodigies of valour on a very unnecessary and unwarrantable occasion. But the house being set on fire, and himself wounded, he was at last taken prisoner, and sent to Adrianople; where the Grand Signior gave him audience, and promised to make good all the damages he had sustained. At last, after a stay of above five years, he left Turkey; and, having disguised himself, traversed Wallachia, Transylvania, Hungary, and Germany, attended only by one person; and in 16 days riding, during which time he never went to bed, came to Stralsund at midnight, November 21. 1714. His boots were cut from his swollen legs, and he was put to bed; where when he had slept some hours, the first thing he did was to review his troops, and examine the state of the fortifications. He sent out orders that very day, to renew the war with more vigour than ever. But affairs were now much changed: Augustus had recovered the throne of Poland; Sweden had lost many of its provinces, and was without money, trade, credit, or troops. The kings of Denmark and Prussia seized the island of Rugen; and besieged him in Stralsund, which surrendered; but Charles escaped to Carelscroon. When his country was threatened with invasion by so many princes, he, to the surprise of all Europe, marched into Norway with 20,000 men. A very few Danes might have stopped the Swedish army; but such a quick invasion they could not foresee. Europe was yet more at a loss to find the Czar so quiet, and not making a descent upon Sweden, as he had before agreed with his allies. This inaction was the consequence of one of the greatest designs, and at the same time the most difficult of any that were ever formed by the imagination of man. In short, a scheme was set on foot for a reconciliation with the Czar; for replacing Stanislaus on the throne of Poland; and setting James the second's son upon that of England, beside restoring the duke of Holstein to his dominions. Charles was pleased with these grand ideas, though without building much upon them, and gave his minister leave to act at large. In the mean time, Charles was going to make a second attempt upon Norway in 1718; and he flattered himself with being master of that kingdom in six months: but while he was examining the works at Frederickshall, a place of great strength and importance, which is reckoned to be the key of that kingdom, he was killed by a shot from the enemy, as has been generally believed; though it has been also reported that he fell by the treachery of one of his own officers, who had been bribed for that purpose. Charles.

This prince experienced the extremes of prosperity and of adversity, without being softened by the one, or disturbed for a moment at the other; but was a man rather extraordinary than great, and fitter to be admired than imitated. He was honoured by the Turks for his rigid abstinence from wine, and his regularity in attending public devotion.

As to his person, he was tall and of a noble mien, had a fine open forehead, large blue eyes, flaxen hair, fair complexion, an handsome nose, but little beard, and a laugh not agreeable. His manners were harsh and austere, not to say savage: and as to religion, he was indifferent towards all, though exteriously a Lutheran, and a strong believer in predestination. A few anecdotes will illustrate his character. No dangers, however great, made the least impression upon him. When a horse or two were killed under him at the battle of Narva in 1700, he leaped nimbly upon fresh ones, saying, "these people find me exercise." One day, when he was dictating letters to a secretary, a bomb fell through the roof into the next room of the house, where they were sitting. The secretary, terrified lest the house should come down upon them, let his pen drop out of his hand: "What is the matter," says the king calmly. The secretary could only reply, "Ah, Sir, the bomb." "The bomb (says the king)! what has the bomb to do with what I am dictating to you? Go on."

He preserved more humanity than is usually found among conquerors. Once, in the middle of an action, finding a young Swedish officer wounded and unable to march, he obliged the officer to take his horse, and continued to command his infantry on foot. The princess Lubomirski, who was very much in the interest and good graces of Augustus, falling by accident into the hands of one of his officers, he ordered her to be set at liberty; saying, "that he did not make war with women." One day, near Leipsic, a peasant threw himself at his feet, with a complaint against a grenadier, that he had robbed him of certain eatables provided for himself and his family. "Is it true (said Charles sternly), that you have robbed this man?" The soldier replied, "Sir, I have not done near so much harm to this man as your majesty has done to his master; for you have taken from Augustus a kingdom, whereas I have only taken from this poor scoundrel a dinner." Charles made the peasant amends, and pardoned the soldier for his firmness: "However, my friend (says he to him), you will do well to recollect, that if I took a kingdom from Augustus, I did not take it for myself."

Though Charles lived hardily himself, a soldier did not fear to remonstrate to him against some bread, which was very black and mouldy, and which yet was the only provision the troops had. Charles called for a piece of it, and calmly eat it up; saying, "that it was indeed not good, but that it might be eaten." From the danger he was in in Poland, when he beat the Saxon troops in 1708, a comedy was exhibited at Marienburg, where the combat was represented to the disadvantage of the Swedes. "Oh, (says Charles, hearing of it), I am far from envying them in this pleasure. Let them beat me upon the theatres as long as they will, provided I do but beat them in the field." He wrote some observations on war, and on his own campaigns from 1700 to 1709; but the MS. was lost at the unfortunate battle of Pultowa.

CHARLES's-CAPE, a promontory of Virginia, in North America, forming the northern head-land of the strait that enters the bay of Chesapeak.

Charles's-Fort, a fortress in the county of Cork, and province of Munster, in Ireland, situated at the mouth of Kinsale harbour. W. Long. 8. 10. and N. Lat. 51. 21.

Charles's-Town, or *Charlestown*, the capital of South Carolina, in North America, situated on a peninsula formed by Ashley and Cooper rivers, the former of which is navigable for ships twenty miles above the town. W. Long. 79. 0. and N. Lat. 32. 30.

Charles's-Wain, in astronomy, seven stars in the constellation called *ursa major* or the Great Bear.

CHARLETON, an island at the bottom of Hudson's-bay, in North America, subject to Great Britain. W. Long. 82. 0. and N. Lat. 52. 30.

CHARLETON (Walter), a learned English physician born in 1619, was physician in ordinary to Charles I. and Charles II. one of the first members of the royal society, and president of the college of physicians. He wrote on various subjects; but at last his narrow circumstances obliged him to retire to the island of Jersey, were he died in 1707.

CHARLOCK, the English name of the RAPHANUS; it is a very troublesome weed among corn, being more frequent than almost any other. There are two principal kinds of it; the one with a yellow flower, the other with a white. Some fields are particularly subject to be over-run with it, especially those which have been manured with cow-dung alone, that being a manure very favourable to the growth of it. The farmers in some places are so sensible of this, that they always mix horse-dung with their cow-dung, when they use it for arable land. When barley, as is often the case, is infested with this weed to such a degree as to endanger the crop, it is a very good method to mow down the charlock in May, when it is in flower, cutting it so low as just to take off the tops of the leaves of barley with it: by this means the barley will get up above the weed; and people have got four quarters of grain from an acre of such land as would have scarce yielded any thing without this expedient. Where any land is particularly subject to this weed, the best method is to sow it with grass-seed, and make a pasture of it; for then the plant will not be troublesome, it never growing where there is a coat of grass upon the ground.

Queen CHARLOTTE's ISLAND, an island in the South Sea, first discovered by captain Wallis in the Dolphin, in 1767, who took possession of it in the name of King George III. Here is good water, and plenty of cocoa-nuts, palm-nuts, and scurvy-grass. The inhabitants are of a middle stature, and dark complexion, with long hair hanging over their shoulders; the men are well made, and the women handsome; their cloathing is a kind of coarse cloth, or matting, which they fasten about their middle.

Queen Charlotte's Islands, a cluster of South-sea islands discovered in 1767 by captain Carteret. He counted seven, and there were supposed to be many more. The inhabitants of these islands are described as extremely nimble and vigorous, and almost as well qualified to live in the water as upon land: they are very warlike; and, on a quarrel with some of captain Carteret's people, they attacked them with great resolution; mortally wounded the master and three of the sailors; were not at all intimidated by the fire-arms; and at last, notwithstanding the aversion of captain Carteret to shed blood, he was obliged to secure the watering places by firing grape-shot into the woods, which destroyed many of the inhabitants. These islands lie in S. Lat. 11°. E. Long. 164°. They are supposed to be the Santa Cruz of Mendana, who [illegible] there in 1595.

CHARM, a term derived from the Latin [illegible], a "verse;" and used to denote a magic power, or spell, by which, with the assistance of the devil, sorcerers and witches were supposed to do wonderful things, far surpassing the power of nature.

CHARNEL, or CHARNEL-HOUSE, a kind of portico or gallery, usually in or near a church-yard, over which were anciently laid the bones of the dead, after the flesh was wholly consumed. Charnel-houses are now usually adjoining to the church.

CHARON, in fabulous history, the son of Erebus and Nox, whose office was to ferry the souls of the deceased over the waters of Acheron, for which each soul was to pay a piece of money. For this reason the Pagans had a custom of putting a piece of money into the mouth of the dead, in order that they might have something to pay Charon for their passage.

CHARONDAS, a celebrated legislator of the Thurians, and a native of Catanea in Sicily, flourished 446 before Christ. He forbad any person's appearing armed in the public assemblies of the nation; but one day going thither in haste, without thinking of his sword, he was no sooner made to observe his mistake than he ran it through his body.

CHAROST, a town of France, in Berry, with the title of a duchy. It is seated on the river Arnon, E. Long. 2. 15. N. Lat. 46. 56.

CHAROUX, a town of France, in the Bourbonnois, seated on an eminence, near the river Sioulle. It has two parishes, which are in different dioceses. E. Long. 3. 25. N. Lat. 46. 10.

CHARPENTIER (Francis), dean of the French academy, was born in 1620. His early capacity inclined his friends to educate him for the bar; but he was much more delighted with the study of languages and antiquity than of the law; and preferred repose to tumult. M. Colbert made use of him in establishing his new academy of medals and inscriptions; and no person of that learned society contributed more than himself toward that noble series of medals which were struck on the considerable events that distinguished the reign of Louis XIV. He published several works, which were all well received; and died in 1702.

CHARR,

CHARR, in ichthyology. See Salmo.

CHARRON (Peter), the author of a book intitled *Of Wisdom*, which gained him great reputation, was born at Paris in the year 1541. After being advocate in the parliament of Paris for five or six years, he applied himself to divinity; and became so great a preacher, that the bishops of several dioceses offered him the highest dignities in their gift. He died at Paris, suddenly in the street, November 16. 1603.

CHART, or Sea-chart, an hydrographical map, or a projection of some part of the earth's superficies *in plano*, for the use of navigators.

Charts differ very considerably from geographical or land-maps, which are of no use in navigation. Nor are sea-charts all of the same kind, some being what we call plane-charts, others mercator-charts, and others globular charts.

Plane Chart, is a representation of some part of the superficies of the terraqueous globe, in which the meridians are supposed parallel to each other, the parallels of latitude at equal distances, and consequently the degrees of latitude and longitude every where equal to each other. See *Plane Chart*.

Mercator's Chart, is that where the meridians are straight lines, parallel to each other, and equidistant; the parallels are also straight lines, and parallel to each other: but the distance between them increases from the equinoctial towards either pole, in the ratio of the secant of the latitude to the radius. See Navigation.

Globular Chart, a meridional projection, wherein the distance of the eye from the plane of the meridian, upon which the projection is made, is supposed to be equal to the sine of the angle 45°. This projection comes the nearest of all to the nature of the globe, because the meridians therein are placed at equal distances; the parallels also are nearly equidistant, and consequently the several parts of the earth have their proper proportion of magnitude, distance, and situation, nearly the same as on the globe itself. See *Globular Projection*.

Hydrographic Charts, sheets of large paper, whereon several parts of the land and sea are described, with their respective coasts, harbours, sounds, flats, rocks, shelves, sands, &c. together with the longitude and latitude of each place, and the points of the compass. See *Mercator's Chart*.

Selenographic Charts, particular descriptions of the spots, appearances, and maculæ of the moon. See Astronomy, n° 63. and 140.

Topographic Charts, draughts of some small parts of the earth only, or of some particular places, without regard to its relative situation, as London, York, &c.

CHARTA, or Carta, primarily signifies a sort of paper made of the plant *papyrus* or *biblus*. See Papyrus, and Charter.

Charta Emporetica, in pharmacy, &c. a kind of paper made very soft and porous, used to filter withal. See Filtration, &c.

Charta is also used in our ancient customs for a charter, or deed in writing. See Charter.

Magna Charta, the great charter of the liberties of Britain, and the basis of our laws and privileges.

This charter may be said to derive its origin from king Edward the Confessor, who granted several privileges to the church and state by charter: these liberties and privileges were also granted and confirmed by king Henry I. by a celebrated great charter now lost; but which was confirmed or re-enacted by king Henry II. and king John. Henry III. the successor of this last prince, after having caused 12 men make inquiry into the liberties of England in the reign of Henry I. granted a new charter; which was the same as the present magna charta. This he several times confirmed, and as often broke; till, in the 37th year of his reign, he went to Westminster-hall, and there, in presence of the nobility and bishops, who held lighted candles in their hands, magna charta was read, the king all the time holding his hand to his breast, and at last solemnly swearing faithfully and inviolably to observe all the things therein contained, &c. Then the bishops extinguishing the candles, and throwing them on the ground, they all cried out, "Thus let him be extinguished, and sink in hell, who violates this charter." It is observed, that, notwithstanding the solemnity of this confirmation, king Henry, the very next year, again invaded the rights of his people, till the barons entered into a war against him; when, after various success, he confirmed this charter, and the charter of the forest, in the 52d year of his reign.

This charter confirmed many liberties of the church, and redressed many grievances incident to feodal tenures, of no small moment at the time; tho' now, unless considered attentively and with this retrospect, they seem but of trifling concern. But, besides these feodal provisions, care was also taken therein to protect the subject against other oppressions, then frequently arising from unreasonable amercements, from illegal distresses or other process for debts or services due to the crown, and from the tyrannical abuse of the prerogative of purveyance and pre-emption. It fixed the forfeiture of lands for felony in the same manner as it still remains; prohibited for the future the grants of exclusive fisheries; and the erection of new bridges so as to oppress the neighbourhood. With respect to private rights, it established the testamentary power of the subject over part of his personal estate, the rest being distributed among his wife and children; it laid down the law of dower, as it hath continued ever since; and prohibited the appeals of women, unless after the death of their husbands. In matters of public police and national concern, it enjoined an uniformity of weights and measures; gave new encouragements to commerce, by the protection of merchant-strangers; and forbad the alienation of lands in mortmain. With regard to the administration of justice: besides prohibiting all denials or delays of it, it fixed the court of common-pleas at Westminster, that the suitors might no longer be harassed with following the king's person in all his progresses; and at the same time brought the trial of issues home to the very doors of the freeholders, by directing assizes to be taken in the proper counties, and establishing annual circuits: it also corrected some abuses then incident to the trials by wager of law and of battle; directed the regular awarding of inquests for life or member; prohibited the king's inferior ministers from holding pleas of the crown, or trying any criminal charge, whereby many hu-

forfeitures might otherwise have unjustly accrued to the exchequer; and regulated the time and place of holding the inferior tribunals of justice, the county-court, sheriff's torn, and court-leet. It confirmed and established the liberties of the city of London, and all other cities, boroughs, towns, and ports of the kingdom. And lastly (which alone would have merited the title that it bears, of the *great charter*), it protected every individual of the nation in the free enjoyment of his life, his liberty, and his property, unless declared to be *forfeited* by the judgment of his peers or the law of the land.

This excellent charter, so equitable, and beneficial to the subject, is the most ancient written law in the kingdom. By the 25th Edward I. it is ordained, that it shall be taken as the common law; and by the 43d Edward III. all statutes made against it are declared to be void.

CHARTER, in law, a written instrument, or evidence of things acted between one person and another. The word charter comes from the Latin *charta*, anciently used for a public and authentic act, a donation, contract, or the like; from the Greek χαρτης, "thick paper" or "pasteboard," whereon public acts were wont to be written. Britton divides charters into those of the king, and those of private persons. 1. Charters of the king, are those whereby the king passeth any grant to any person or body politic, as a *charter of exemption* of privilege, &c.; *charter of pardon*, whereby a man is forgiven a felony, or other offence committed against the king's crown and dignity; *charter of the forest*, wherein the laws of the forest are comprised, such as the charter of Canutus, &c. 2. Charters of private persons, are deeds and instruments for the conveyance of lands, &c. And the purchaser of lands shall have all the charters, deeds, and evidences, as incident to the same, and for the maintenance of his title.

Charter-Governments in America. See Colony.

Charter-Land, such land as a person holds by charter; that is, by evidence in writing, otherwise called freehold.

CHARTERPARTY, in commerce, denotes the instrument of freightage, or articles of agreement for the hire of a vessel. See Freight, &c.

The charterparty is to be in writing; and to be signed both by the proprietor or the master of the ship, and the merchant who freights it. It is to contain the name and the burden of the vessel; the names of the master and the freighter; the price or rate of freight; and the time of loading and unloading; and the other conditions agreed on. It is properly a deed, or policy, whereby the master or proprietor of the vessel engages to furnish immediately a tight sound vessel, well equipped, caulked, and stopped, provided with anchors, sails, cordage, and all other furniture to make the voyage required, as equipage, hands, victuals, and other munitions; in consideration of a certain sum to be paid by the merchant for the freight. Lastly, the ship with all its furniture, and the cargo, are respectively subjected to the conditions of the *charterparty*. The *charterparty* differs from a *bill of lading*, in that the first is for the entire freight, or lading, and that both for going and returning; whereas the latter is only for a part of the freight, or at most only for the voyage one way.

The present Boyer says, the word comes from hence, that *per medium charta incidebatur, et sic fiebat charta partita*; because, in the time when notaries were less common, there was only one instrument made for both parties: this they cut in two, and gave each his portion; joining them together at their return, to know if each had done his part. This he observes to have seen practised in his time; agreeable to the method of the Romans, who, in their stipulations, used to break a staff, each party retaining a moiety thereof as a mark.

CHARTOHPYLAX, the name of an officer of the church of Constantinople, who attends at the door of the rails when the sacrament is administered, and gives notice to the priests to come to the holy table. He represents the patriarch upon the bench, tries all ecclesiastical causes, keeps all the marriage registers, assists at the consecration of bishops, and presents the bishop elect at the solemnity, and likewise all other subordinate clergy. This office resembles in some shape that of the *Bibliothecarius* at Rome.

CHARTRES, a large city of France, in the province of Orleannois, situated on the river Eure, in E. Long. 1. 30. N. Lat. 48. 47. It is a bishop's see.

CHARTREUSE, or Chartreuse-grand, a celebrated monastery, the capital of all the convents of the Carthusian monks, situated on a steep rock in the middle of a large forest of fir-trees, about seven miles north-east of Grenoble, in the province of Dauphine in France: E. Long. 5. 5. N. Lat. 45. 10. See Carthusians.

From this mother-convent, all the others of the same order take their name; among which was the Chartreuse of London, corruptly called the charterhouse, now converted into an hospital, and endowed with a revenue of 600 l. *per ann.*

Here are maintained 80 decayed gentlemen, not under 50 years of age: also 40 boys are educated and fitted either for the university or trades. Those sent to the university, have an exhibition of 20 l. a-year for eight years; and have an immediate title to nine church-livings in the gift of the governors of the hospital, who are fifteen in number, all persons of the first distinction, and take their turns in the nomination of pensioners and scholars.

CHARTULARY, Chartularius, a title given to an ancient officer in the Latin church, who had the care of charters and papers relating to public affairs. The chartulary presided in ecclesiastical judgments, in lieu of the pope. In the Greek church the chartulary was called *chartophylax*; but his office was there much more considerable; and some even distinguish the chartulary from the chartophylax in the Greek church. See Chartophylax.

CHARYBDIS, (anc. geog.) a whirlpool in the straits of Messina, according to the poets; near Sicily, and opposite to Scylla, a rock on the coast of Italy. Thucydides makes it to be only a strong flux and reflux in the strait, or a violent reciprocation of the tide, especially if the wind sets south. But on diving into the Charybdis, there are found vast gulphs and whirl-

pools

Chase.

pools below, which produce all the commotion on the surface of the water.

Charybdis is used by Horace to denote a rapacious prostitute.

CHASE, or CHACE, in law, is used for a driving of cattle to or from any place; as to a distress, or fortlet, *&c.*

CHASE, or *Chace*, is also a place of retreat for deer and wild beasts; of a middle kind between a forest and a park, being usually less than a forest, and not possessed of so many privileges; but wanting, e. g. courts of attachment, swainmote, and justice-seat *. Yet it is of a large extent, and stocked both with a greater diversity of wild beasts or game, and more keepers than a park. Crompton observes, that a forest cannot be in the hands of a subject, but it forthwith loses it name, and becomes a *chase*; in regard all those courts lose their nature when they come into the hands of a subject; and that none but a king can make a lord chief justice in eyre of the forest. See JUSTICE *in Eyre*.

* See Forest.

The following history of the English chases is given by Mr Pennant. "At first the beasts of chase had this whole island for their range; they knew no other limits than the ocean, nor confessed any particular master. When the Saxons had established themselves in the heptarchy, they were reserved by each sovereign for his own particular diversion; hunting and war, in those uncivilized ages, were the only employ of the great; their active, but uncultivated minds, being susceptible of no pleasures but those of a violent kind, such as gave exercise to their bodies, and prevented the pain of thinking.

British Zool. i. 42.

"But as the Saxon kings only appropriated those lands to the use of forests which were unoccupied, so no individuals received any injury; but when the conquest had settled the Norman line on the throne, this passion for the chace was carried to an excess, which involved every civil right in a general ruin: it superseded the consideration of religion even in a superstitious age: the village-communities, nay even the most sacred edifices, were turned into one vast waste, to make room for animals, the objects of a lawless tyrant's pleasure. The new forest in Hampshire is too trite an instance to be dwelt on; sanguinary laws were enacted to preserve the game; and in the reigns of William Rufus, and Henry I. it was less criminal to destroy one of the human species than a beast of chase. Thus it continued while the Norman line filled the throne; but when the Saxon line was restored under Henry II. the rigour of the forest laws was immediately softened.

"When our barons began to form a power, they claimed a vast, but more limited, tract for a diversion that the English were always fond of. They were very jealous of any encroachments on their respective bounds, which were often the cause of deadly feuds; such a one gave cause to the fatal day of *Chevy-chace*; a fact which, though recorded only in a ballad, may, from what we know of the manners of the times, be founded on truth; not that it was attended with all the circumstances which the author of that natural but heroic composition hath given it; for, on that day, neither a *Percy* nor a *Douglas* fell: here the poet seems to have claimed his privilege, and mixed with this fray some of the events of the battle of *Otterbourne*.

"When property became happily more divided by the relaxation of the feodal tenures, these extensive hunting-grounds became more limited; and as tillage and husbandry increased, the beasts of chace were obliged to give way to others more useful to the community. The vast tracts of land, before dedicated to hunting, were then contracted; and, in proportion as the useful arts gained ground, either lost their original destination, or gave rise to the invention of *parks*. Liberty and the arts seem coeval; for when once the latter got footing, the former protected the labours of the industrious from being ruined by the licentious sportsman, or being devoured by the objects of his diversion: for this reason, the subjects of a despotic government still experience the inconveniences of vast wastes and forests, the terrors of the neighbouring husbandmen; while in our well regulated monarchy very few chaces remain. The English still indulge themselves in the pleasures of hunting; but confine the deer kind to parks, of which England boasts of more than any other kingdom in Europe. The laws allow every man his pleasure; but confine them in such bounds as prevent them from being injurious to the meanest of the community. Before the reformation, the prelates seem to have guarded sufficiently against this want of amusement, the see of Norwich, in particular, being possessed, about that time, of thirteen parks."

CHASE, in the sea-language, is to pursue a ship; which is also called *giving chase*.

Stern CHASE, is when the chaser follows the chased astern directly upon the same point of the compass.

To lie with a ship's fore-foot in a CHASE, is to sail and meet with her by the nearest distance; and so to cross her in her way, or to come across her fore-foot.

A ship is said to have a *good chase*, when she is so built forward on, or a-stern, that she can carry many guns to shoot forwards or backwards; according to which she is said to have a *good forward*, or *good stern chase*.

CHASE-Guns, are such whose ports are either in the head (and then they are used in chasing of others); or in the stern, which are only useful when they are pursued or chased by any other ship.

CHASE of a Gun, is the whole bore or length of a piece taken within-side.

Wild-goose CHACE, a term used to express a sort of racing on horseback used formerly, which resembled the flying of wild-geese; those birds generally going in a train one after another, not in confused flocks as other birds do. In this sort of race the two horses, after running twelve score yards, had liberty, which horse soever could take the leading, to ride what ground the jocky pleased, the hindmost horse being bound to follow him within a certain distance agreed on by the articles, or else to be whipped in by the tryers and judges who rode by; and whichever horse could distance the other, won the race. This sort of racing was not long in common use; for it was found inhuman, and destructive to good horses, when two such were matched together. For in this case neither

was

Chaſing | Chaſtity

was able to diſtance the other till they were both ready to ſink under their riders; and often two very good horſes were both ſpoiled, and the wagers forced to be drawn at laſt. The miſchief of this ſort of racing ſoon brought in the method now in uſe, of running only for a certain quantity of ground, and determining the plate or wager by the coming in firſt at the poſt.

Chasing of Gold, Silver, &c. See Enchasing.

CHASTE-tree. See Vitex.

CHASTITY; purity of the body, or freedom from obſcenity.—The Roman law juſtifies homicide in defence of the chaſtity either of one's ſelf or relations; and ſo alſo, according to Selden, ſtood the law in the Jewiſh republic. Our law likewiſe juſtifies a woman for killing a man who attempts to raviſh her. So the huſband or father may juſtify killing a man who attempts a rape upon his wife or daughter; but not if he takes them in adultery by conſent: for the one is forcible and felonious, but not the other.

Chaſtity is a virtue univerſally celebrated. There is indeed no charm in the female ſex that can ſupply its place. Without it, beauty is unlovely, and rank is contemptible; good breeding degenerates into wantonneſs, and wit into impudence. Out of the numerous inſtances of eminent chaſtity recorded by authors, the two following are ſelected on account of the leſſon afforded by the different modes of conduct which they exhibit.

Lucretia was a lady of great beauty and noble extraction; ſhe married Collatinus, a relation of Tarquinius Superbus, king of Rome. During the ſiege of Ardea, which laſted much longer than was expected, the young princes paſſed their time in entertainments and diverſions. One day as they were at ſupper *, at Sextus Tarquin's the king's eldeſt ſon, with Collatinus, Lucretia's huſband, the converſation turned on the merit of their wives: every one gave his own the preference. "What ſignify ſo many words!" ſays Collatinus; "you may in a few hours, if you pleaſe, be convinced by your own eyes, how much my Lucretia excels the reſt. We are young: let us mount our horſes, and go and ſurpriſe them. Nothing can better decide our diſpute than the ſtate we ſhall find them in at a time when moſt certainly they will not expect us." They were a little warmed with wine: "Come on, let us go," they all cried together. They quickly galloped to Rome, which was about twenty miles from Ardea, where they find the princeſſes, wives of the young Tarquins, ſurrounded with company, and every circumſtance of the higheſt mirth and pleaſure. From thence they rode to Collatia, where they ſaw Lucretia in a very different ſituation. With her maids about her, ſhe was at work in the inner part of her houſe, talking on the dangers to which her huſband was expoſed. The victory was adjudged to her unanimouſly. She received her gueſts with all poſſible politeneſs and civility. Lucretia's virtue, which ſhould have commanded reſpect, was the very thing which kindled in the breaſt of Sextus Tarquin a ſtrong and deteſtable paſſion. Within a few days he returned to Collatia; and upon the plauſible excuſe he made for his viſit, he was received with all the politeneſs due to a near relation, and the eldeſt ſon of a king. Watching the fitteſt opportunity, he declares the paſſion ſhe had excited at his laſt viſit, and employed the moſt tender intreaties, and all the artifices poſſible, to touch a woman's heart; but all to no purpoſe. He then endeavoured to extort her compliance by the moſt terrible threatenings. It was in vain. She ſtill perſiſted in her reſolution; nor could ſhe be moved, even by the fear of death. But when the monſter told her that he would firſt diſpatch her, and then having murdered a ſlave, would lay him by her ſide, after which he would ſpread a report, that having caught them in the act of adultery, he had puniſhed them as they deſerved; this ſeemed to ſhake her reſolution. She heſitated, not knowing which of theſe dreadful alternatives to take, whether, by conſenting, to diſhonour the bed of her huſband, whom ſhe tenderly loved; or, by refuſing, to die under the odious character of having proſtituted her perſon to the luſt of a ſlave. He ſaw the ſtruggle of her ſoul; and ſeizing the unlucky moment, obtained an inglorious conqueſt. Thus Lucretia's virtue, which had been proof againſt the *fear of death*, could not hold out againſt the *fear of infamy*. The young prince, having gratified his paſſion, returned home as in triumph. On the morrow, Lucretia, overwhelmed with grief and deſpair, ſent early in the morning to deſire her father and her huſband to come to her, and bring with them each a truſty friend, aſſuring them there was no time to loſe. They came with all ſpeed, the one accompanied with Valerius (ſo famous after under the name of Publicola), and the other with Brutus. The moment ſhe ſaw them come, ſhe could not command her tears; and when her huſband aſked her if all was well? "By no means," ſaid ſhe, "it cannot be well with a woman after ſhe has loſt her honour. Yes, Collatinus, thy bed has been defiled by a ſtranger; but my body only is polluted; my mind is innocent, as my death ſhall witneſs. Promiſe me only not to ſuffer the adulterer to go unpuniſhed: it is Sextus Tarquinius, who laſt night, treacherous gueſt, or rather cruel foe, offered me violence, and reaped a joy fatal to me; but, if you are men, it will be ſtill more fatal to him." All promiſed to revenge her; and, at the ſame time, tried to comfort her with repreſenting, "That the mind only ſins, not the body; and where the conſent is wanting, there can be no guilt." "What Sextus deſerves," replies Lucretia, "I leave you to judge; but for me, though I declare myſelf innocent of the crime, I exempt not myſelf from puniſhment. No immodeſt woman ſhall plead Lucretia's example to outlive her diſhonour." Thus ſaying, ſhe plunged into her breaſt a dagger ſhe had concealed under her robe, and expired at their feet. Lucretia's tragical death has been praiſed and extolled by Pagan writers, as the higheſt and moſt noble act of heroiſm. The goſpel thinks not ſo: it is murder, even according to Lucretia's own principles, ſince ſhe puniſhed with death an innocent perſon, at leaſt acknowledged as ſuch by herſelf. She was ignorant that our life is not in our own power, but in his diſpoſal from whom we receive it. St Auſtin, who carefully examines, in his book *De Civitate Dei*, what we are to think of Lucretia's death, conſiders it not as a courageous action, flowing from a true love of chaſtity, but as an infirmity of a woman too ſenſible of worldly fame and glory; and who, from

* *Liv.* l. i. c. 57—60. *Dionyſ.* l. iv. p. 261—277. *Flor.* l. i. 9.

a-

Chastity. Chateau-Briant.

a dread of appearing in the eyes of men an accomplice of the violence she abhorred, and of a crime to which she was entirely a stranger, commits a real crime upon herself voluntarily and designedly. But what cannot be sufficiently admired in this Roman lady is her abhorrence of adultery, which she seems to hold so detestable as not to bear the thoughts of it. In this sense, she is a noble example for all her sex.

Chiomara, the wife of Ortiagon, a Gaulish prince, was equally admirable for her beauty and chastity. During the war between the Romans and the Gauls, A. R. 563, the latter were totally defeated on Mount Olympus. Chiomara, among many other ladies, was taken prisoner, and committed to the care of a centurion, no less passionate for money than women. He, at first, endeavoured to gain her consent to his infamous desires; but not being able to prevail upon her, and subvert her constancy, he thought he might employ force with a woman whom misfortune had reduced to slavery. Afterwards, to make her amends for that treatment, he offered to restore her liberty; but not without ransom. He agreed with her for a certain sum, and to conceal this design from the other Romans, he permitted her to send any of the prisoners she should choose to her relations, and assigned a place near the river where the lady should be exchanged for gold. By accident there was one of her own slaves amongst the prisoners. Upon him she fixed; and the centurion soon after carried her beyond the advanced posts, under cover of a dark night. The next evening two of the relations of the princess came to the place appointed, whither the centurion also carried his captive. When they had delivered him the Attic talent they had brought, which was the sum they had agreed on, the lady, in her own language, ordered those who came to receive her to draw their swords and kill the centurion, who was then amusing himself with weighing the gold. Then, charmed with having revenged the injury done her chastity, she took the head of the officer, which she had cut off with her own hands, and hiding it under her robe, went to her husband Ortiagon, who had returned home after the defeat of his troops. As soon as she came into his presence, she threw the centurion's head at his feet. He was strangely surprised at such a sight; and asked her whose head it was, and what had induced her to do an act so uncommon to her sex? With a face covered with a sudden blush, and at the same time expressing her fierce indignation, she declared the outrage which had been done her, and the revenge she had taken for it. During the rest of her life, she stedfastly retained the same attachment for the purity of manners which constitutes the principal glory of the sex, and nobly sustained the honour of so glorious, bold, and heroic an action.—This lady was much more prudent than Lucretia, in revenging her injured honour by the death of her ravisher, rather than by her own. Plutarch celebrates this fact, in his treatise upon the virtue and great actions of women; and it is from him we have the name of this, which is well worthy of being transmitted to posterity.

The above virtue in men is termed *continence*. See Continence.

CHATEAU-BRIANT, a town of France in Bretany, with an old castle. W. Long. 1. 10. N. Lat. 47. 40.

Chateau || Chatelle-rault.

Chateau-Chinon, a town of France in Nivernois, and capital of Morvant, with a considerable manufacture of cloth. E. Long. 3. 48. N. Lat. 47. 2.

Chateau-Dauphin, a very strong castle of Piedmont in Italy, and in the marquisate of Saluces, belonging to the king of Sardinia. It was taken by the combined army of France and Spain in 1744, and was restored by the treaty of Aix-la-Chapelle.

Chateau-du-Loir, a town of France in the Maine, famous for sustaining a siege of seven years against the Count of Mans. It is seated on the river Loir, in E. Long. 0. 25. N. Lat. 47. 40.

Chateau-Dun, an ancient town of France, and capital of the Dunois, with a castle and rich monastery; seated on an eminence near the river Loir, in E. Long. 1. 26. N. Lat. 48. 4.

Chateau-Neuf, the name of several towns of France, viz. one in Perche; another in Angumois, on the river Charente, near Angoulesme; a third in Berry, seated on the river Cher; and several other small places.

Chateau-Portien, a town of France, in Champagne, and in a district called Portien, with a castle built on a rock, near the river Aisne. E. Long. 4. 13. N. Lat. 49. 35.

Chateau-Renaud, a town of France, in the Gatenois, where clothes are made for the army, and where there is a trade in saffron. E. Long. 2. 25. N. Lat. 48. 0. This is also the name of a town of Touraine, in France, with the title of a marquisate. E. Long. 2. 41. N. Lat. 47. 22.

Chateau-Roux, a town of France, in Berry, with the title of a duchy. It has a cloth-manufacture, and is seated in a very large pleasant plain on the river Indre, in E. Long. 1. 47. N. Lat. 46. 49.

Chateau-Thierry, a town of France, in Champagne, with the title of a duchy, and a handsome castle on an eminence, seated on the river Maine, in E. Long. 3. 23. N. Lat. 49. 12.

Chateau-Vilain, a town of France, in Champagne, with a castle, and the title of a duchy; seated on the river Anjou. E. Long. 2. 59. N. Lat. 48. 0.

CHATEL, or Chate, a town of Lorrain, in the Vosque, seated on the river Moselle, eight miles from Mirecourt.

Chatel-Aillon, a maritime town of France, in Saintonge, five miles from Rochelle; formerly very considerable, but is now greatly decayed.

Chatel-Chalon, a town of France, in Franche Comte, remarkable for its abbey of benedictine nuns. E. Long. 5. 25. N. Lat. 46. 50.

CHATELET, a town of the Netherlands, in Namur, seated on the Sambre, in the bishoprick of Liege. E. Long. 4. 28. N. Lat. 50. 25.

Chatelet, the name of certain courts of justice established in several cities in France. The grand chatelet at Paris, is the place where the presidial or ordinary court of justice of the provost of Paris is kept; consisting of a presidial, a civil chamber, a criminal chamber, and a chamber of policy. The little chatelet is an old fort, now serving as a prison.

CHATELLERAULT, a town of France, in Poiton, with the title of a duchy; ſeated in a fertile and pleaſant country, on the river Vienne, over which there is a handſome ſtone-bridge. E. Long. 0. 40. N. Lat. 46. 34.

CHATHAM, a town of Kent, adjoining to Rocheſter, and ſeated on the river Medway. It is the principal ſtation of the royal navy; and the yards and magazines are furniſhed with all kinds of naval ſtores, as well as materials for building and rigging the largeſt men of war. The entrance into the river Medway is defended by Sheerneſs and other forts; notwithſtanding which, the Dutch fleet burnt ſeveral ſhips of war here in the reign of Charles II. after the peace of Breda had been agreed upon. In the year 1757, by direction of the Duke of Cumberland, ſeveral additional fortifications were begun at Chatham; ſo that now the ſhips are in no danger of an inſult either by land or water. It has a church, a chapel of eaſe, and a ſhip uſed as a church for the ſailors. It has likewiſe about 500 houſes, moſtly low, and built with brick; the ſtreets are narrow, and paved; and it contains about 3000 inhabitants. The principal employment of the labouring hands is ſhip-building in the king's yard and private docks. This town gave title of Earl to that great ſtateſman William Pitt in the reigns of George II. and III. E. Long. 0. 40. N. Lat. 51. 20.

CHATIGAN, a town of Aſia, in the kingdom of Bengal, on the moſt eaſterly branch of the river Ganges. It is but a poor place, though it was the firſt the Portugueſe ſettled at in theſe parts, and who ſtill keep a ſort of poſſeſſion. It has but a few cotton manufactures; but affords the beſt timber for building of any place about it. The inhabitants are ſo ſuſpicious of each other, that they always go armed with a ſword, piſtol, and blunderbuſs, not excepting the prieſts. It is ſubject to the Great Mogul. E. Long. 91. 10. N. Lat. 23. 0.

CHATILLON sur-Seine, a town of France, in Burgundy, divided into two by the river Seine. It is 91 miles from Langres, and 40 from Dijon; and has iron works in its neighbourhood. E. Long. 4. 33. N. Lat. 47. 45.

CHATRE, a town of France, in Berry, ſeated on the river Indre, 37 miles from Bourges. It carries on a conſiderable trade in cattle. E. Long. 1. 55. N. Lat. 46. 35.

CHATTELS, a Norman term, under which were anciently comprehended all moveable goods; thoſe immoveable being termed *fief*, or *fee*.

Chattels, in the modern ſenſe of the word, are all ſorts of goods, moveable or immoveable, except ſuch as are in the nature of freehold.

CHATTERER, in ornithology. See Ampelis.

CHATTERTON (Thomas), a late unfortunate poet, whoſe fate and performances have excited in no ſmall degree the public attention, as well as given riſe to much literary controverſy. He was born at Briſtol, Nov. 20. 1752; and educated at a charity-ſchool on St Auguſtin's Back, where nothing more was taught than reading, writing, and accounts. At 14 years of age, he was articled clerk to an attorney at Briſtol, with whom he continued about three years; yet, though his education was thus confined, he diſcovered an early turn towards poetry and Engliſh antiquities, and particularly towards heraldry. How ſoon he began to be an author is not known. In the Town and Country Magazine for March 1769, are two letters, probably from him, as they are dated from Briſtol, and ſubſcribed with his uſual ſignature, D. B. that is, *Dunhelmus Briſtolienſis*. The former contains ſhort extracts from two MSS. "written 300 years ago by one Rowley a monk," concerning dreſs in the age of Henry II.; the latter, "Ethelgar, a Saxon poem," in bombaſt proſe. In the ſame magazine for May 1769, are three communications from Briſtol, with the ſame ſignature D. B. one of them intitled "Obſervations upon Saxon Heraldry, with drawings of Saxon Atchievements;" and in the ſubſequent months of 1769 and 1770, there are ſeveral other pieces in the ſame magazine, which are undoubtedly of his compoſition.

In April 1770, he left Briſtol, diſguſted with his profeſſion, and irreconcileable to the line of life in which he was placed; and coming to London in hopes of advancing his fortune by his pen, he ſunk at once from the ſublimity of his views to an abſolute dependence on the patronage of bookſellers. Things, however, ſeem ſoon to have brightened up a little with him; for, May 14. he writes to his mother, in high ſpirits, upon the change of his ſituation, with the following ſarcaſtic reflection upon his former patrons at Briſtol. "As to Mr ——, Mr ——, Mr ——, &c. &c. they rate literary lumber ſo low, that I believe an author, in their eſtimation, muſt be poor indeed; but here matters are otherwiſe. Had Rowley been a Londoner inſtead of a Briſtowyan, I could have lived by copying his works." In a letter to his ſiſter, May 30, he informs her that he is to be employed in writing a voluminous Hiſtory of London, to appear in numbers the beginning of next winter. Meanwhile, he had written ſomething in praiſe of Beckford, then lord mayor, which had procured him the honour of being preſented to his lordſhip; and, in the letter juſt mentioned, he gives the following account of his reception, with certain obſervations upon political writing. "The lord mayor received me as politely as a citizen could; but the devil of the matter is, there is no money to be got on this ſide of the queſtion.—However, he is a poor author who cannot write on both ſides.—Eſſays on the patriotic ſide will fetch no more than what the copy is ſold for. As the patriots themſelves are ſearching for places, they have no gratuity to ſpare.—On the other hand, unpopular eſſays will not even be accepted, and you muſt pay to have them printed; but then you ſeldom loſe by it, as courtiers are ſo ſenſible of their deficiency in merit, that they generouſly reward all who know how to daub them with the appearance of it."

He continued to write inceſſantly in various periodical publications. July 11th, he tells his ſiſter that he had pieces laſt month in ſeveral magazines; in The Goſpel Magazine, The Town and Country, The Court and City, The London, The Political Regiſter, &c. But all theſe exertions of his genius brought in ſo little profit, that he was ſoon reduced to the extremeſt indigence; ſo that at laſt, oppreſſed with poverty and alſo diſeaſe, in a fit of deſpair he put an end to his exiſtence, Aug. 1770, with a doſe of poiſon. This unfortunate perſon, though certainly a moſt extraordinary genius, ſeems yet to have been a moſt ungracious compoſition. He was violent and impetuous to a ſtrange

degree.

Chatterton. degree. From the firft of the above-cited letters he feems to have had a portion of ill-humour and fpleen more than enough for a lad of 17; and the editor of his Mifcellanies records, "that he poffeffed all the vices and irregularities of youth, and that his profligacy was at leaft as confpicuous as his abilities."

In 1777 were publifhed, in one volume 8vo, "Poems, fuppofed to have been written at Briftol, by Thomas Rowley and others, in the 15th century; the greateft part now firft publifhed from the moft authentic copies, with an engraved fpecimen of one of the MSS. To which are added, a Preface, an introductory Account of the feveral Pieces, and a Gloffary." And, in 1778, were publifhed, in one volume 8vo, "Mifcellanies in Profe and Verfe, by Thomas Chatterton, the fuppofed author of the Poems publifhed under the names of Rowley, &c."

Of Rowley's Poems, we have the following account in the preface, given in the words of Mr George Catcot of Briftol, to whom, it is faid, the public is indebted for them. "The firft difcovery of certain MSS. having been depofited in Redclift church above three centuries ago, was made in the year 1768, at the time of opening the new bridge at Briftol; and was owing to a publication in Farley's Weekly Journal, Oct. 1ft, containing an account of the ceremonies obferved at the opening of the old bridge, taken, as it was faid, from a very ancient MS. This excited the curiofity of fome perfons to enquire after the original. The printer, Mr Farley, could give no account of it, or of the perfon who brought the copy; but after much inquiry it was difcovered, that this perfon was a youth between 15 and 16 years of age, whofe name was Thomas Chatterton, and whofe family had been fextons of Redclift church for near 150 years. His father, who was now dead, had alfo been mafter of the free-fchool in Pile-ftreet. The young man was at firft very unwilling to difcover from whence he had the original; but, after many promifes made to him, was at laft prevailed on to acknowledge that he had received this, together with many other MSS. from his father, who had found them in a large cheft in an upper room over the chapel, on the north fide of Redclift church." It is added, that foon after this Mr Catcot commenced an acquaintance with Chatterton, and partly as prefents, partly as purchafes, procured from him copies of many of his MSS. in profe and verfe; as other copies were difpofed of in like manner to others. It is concluded, however, that whatever may have been Chatterton's part in this very extraordinary tranfaction, whether he was the author, or only (as he conftantly afferted) the copier of all thefe productions, he appears to have kept the fecret entirely himfelf, and not to have put it in any one's power to bear certain teftimony either of his fraud or of his veracity.

This affair, however, hath fince become the foundation of a mighty controverfy among the critics, which hath yet fcarcely fubfided. The poems in queftion, publifhed in 1777, were republifhed in 1778, with an "Appendix, containing fome obfervations upon their language; tending to prove that they were written, not by any ancient author, but entirely by Chatterton." Mr Warton, in the third volume of his Hiftory of Englifh poetry, hath efpoufed the fame fide of the queftion. Mr Walpole alfo obliged the world with a Letter on Chatterton, from his prefs at Strawberry-hill. On the other hand have appeared, "Obfervations" upon thefe poems, "in which their authenticity is afcertained," by Jacob Bryant, Efq. 1781, 2 vols 8vo; and another edition of the "Poems, with a Comment, in which their Antiquity is confidered and defended, by Jeremiah Milles, D. D. Dean of Exeter, 1782," 4to. In anfwer to thefe two works, we have had three pamphlets: 1. "Curfory Obfervations on the Poems, and Remarks on the Commentaries of Mr Bryant and Dr Milles; with a falutary propofal addreffed to the friends of thofe gentlemen." 2. "An Archæological Epiftle to Dean Milles, editor of a fuperb edition of Rowley's Poems, &c." 3. "An Inquiry into the Authenticity of the Poems attributed to Thomas Rowley, in which the Arguments of the Dean of Exeter and Mr Bryant are examined, by Thomas Warton;" and other pieces in the public prints and magazines: All preparatory to the complete fettlement of the bufinefs in "A Vindication of the Appendix to the Poems called Rowley's, in reply to the Anfwers of the Dean of Exeter, Jacob Bryant, Efq; and a third Anonymous Writer; with fome further Obfervations upon thofe Poems, and an Examination of the Evidence which has been produced in fupport of their Authenticity. By Thomas Tyrwhitt, 1782," 8vo.

Chaucer. CHAUCER (Sir Geofrey), an eminent Englifh poet in the 14th century, born at London in 1328. After he left the univerfity, he travelled into Holland, France, and other countries. Upon his return he entered himfelf in the Inner-temple, where he ftudied the municipal laws of England. His firft ftation at court was page to Edward III. and he had a penfion granted him by that prince till he could otherwife provide for him. Soon after we find him gentleman of the king's privy chamber; next year, fhield-bearer to the king. Efteemed and honoured, he fpent his younger days in a conftant attendance at court, or for the moft part living near it, in a fquare ftone-houfe near the park-gate at Woodftock, ftill called *Chaucer's Houfe*.

Soon after, having got the Duke of Lancafter for his patron, Chaucer began every day to rife in greatnefs. In 1373, he was fent, with other perfons, to the republic of Genoa to hire fhips for the king's navy (our want of fhipping in thofe times being ufually fupplied by fuch means); and the king was fo well fatiffied with his negociation, that, on his return, he obtained a grant of a pitcher of wine daily in the port of London, to be delivered by the butler of England; and foon after was made comptroller of the cuftoms for wool, wool-fells, and hides; an office which he difcharged with great diligence and integrity. At this period, Chaucer's income was about L. 1000 a-year; a fum which in thofe days might well enable him to live, as he fays he did, with dignity in office, and hofpitality among his friends. It was in this meridian blaze of profperity, in perfect health of body and peace of mind, that he wrote his moft humorous poems. His fatires againft the priefts were probably written to oblige his patron the Duke of Lancafter, who favoured the caufe of Wickliff, and endeavoured to expofe the clergy to the indignation of the people. In the laft year of Edward III. our poet was employed in a commiffion miſſion to treat with the French; and in the beginning of King Richard's reign, he was in ſome degree of favour at court.

The Duke of Lancaſter at laſt finding his views checked, began to abandon Wickliff's party: upon which Chaucer likewiſe, how much ſoever he had eſpouſed that divine's opinions, thought it prudent to conceal them more than he had done. With the Duke's intereſt that of Chaucer entirely ſunk; and the former paſſing over ſea, his friends felt all the malice of the oppoſite party. Theſe misfortunes occaſioned his writing that excellent treatiſe *The Teſtament of Love*, in imitation of Boethius on the conſolation of philoſophy. Being much reduced, he retired to Woodſtock, to comfort himſelf with ſtudy, which produced his admirable treatiſe of the *Aſtrolabe*.

The Duke of Lancaſter at laſt ſurmounting his troubles, married Lady Catharine Swynford, ſiſter to Chaucer's wife; ſo that Thomas Chaucer, our poet's ſon, became allied to moſt of the nobility, and to ſeveral of the kings of England. Now the ſun began to ſhine upon Chaucer with an evening ray; for by the influence of the Duke's marriage, he again grew to a conſiderable ſhare of wealth. But being now 70, he retired to Dunnington-caſtle near Newbury. He had not enjoyed this retirement long before Henry IV. ſon of the Duke of Lancaſter, aſſumed the crown, and in the firſt year of his reign gave our poet marks of his favour. But however pleaſing the change of affairs might be to him at firſt, he afterwards found no ſmall inconveniences from it. The meaſures and grants of the late king were annulled; and Chaucer, in order to procure freſh grants of his penſions, left his retirement, and applied to court: where, though he gained a confirmation of ſome grants, yet the fatigue of attendance, and his great age, prevented him from enjoying them. He fell ſick at London; and ended his days in the 72d year of his age, leaving the world as though he deſpiſed it, as appears from his ſong of *Flie from the Preſe*. The year before his death he had the happineſs, if at his time of life it might be ſo called, to ſee the ſon of his brother-in-law (Hen. IV.) ſeated on the throne. He was interred in Weſtminſter abbey; and in 1556, Mr Nicholas Bingham, a gentleman of Oxford, at his own charge, erected a handſome monument for him there. Caxton firſt printed the Canterbury Tales; but his works were firſt collected and publiſhed in one volume folio, by William Thynne, London, 1542. They were afterwards reprinted in 1561, 1598, 1602. Oxford, 1721.

Chaucer was not only the firſt, but one of the beſt poets which theſe kingdoms ever produced. He was equally great in every ſpecies of poetry which he attempted; and his poems in general poſſeſs every kind of excellence, even to a modern reader, except melody and accuracy of meaſure; defects which are to be attributed to the imperfect ſtate of our language, and the infancy of the art in this kingdom at the time when he wrote. "As he is the father of Engliſh poetry (ſays Mr Dryden), ſo I hold him in the ſame degree of veneration as the Grecians held Homer, or the Romans Virgil. He is a perpetual fountain of good ſenſe, learned in all ſciences, and therefore ſpeaks properly on all ſubjects. As he knew what to ſay, ſo he knows alſo when to leave off; a continence which is practiſed by few writers, and ſcarcely by any of the ancients, except Virgil and Horace." This character Chaucer certainly deſerved. He had read a great deal; and was a man of the world, and of ſound judgment. He was the firſt Engliſh poet who wrote *poetically*, as Dr Johnſon obſerves in the preface to his Dictionary, and (he might have added) who wrote like a gentleman. He had alſo the merit of improving our language conſiderably, by the introduction and naturalization of words from the Provençal, at that time the moſt poliſhed dialect in Europe.

CHAUCIS (anc. geog.), the country of the Chauci, a people of Germany; divided into the *Minores*, now *Eaſt Frieſland* and the county of *Oldenburg*; and into the *Majores*, now the duchy of *Bremen* and a part of *Lunenburg*.

CHAUD-MEDLEY, in law, is of much the ſame import with *Chance-Medley*. The former in its etymology ſignifies an affray in the heat of blood or paſſion; the latter, a caſual affray. The latter is in common ſpeech too often erroneouſly applied to any manner of homicide by miſadventure; whereas it appears by the ſtat. 24 Hen. VIII. c. 5. and ancient books (Staundf. P.C. 16.), that it is properly applied to ſuch killing as happens in ſelf-defence upon ſudden encounter.

CHAUL, a town of the Eaſt Indies, on the coaſt of Malabar, in the province of Blagana, and kingdom of Viſapour. Its river affords a good harbour for ſmall veſſels. The town is fortified, and ſo is the iſland on the ſouth ſide of the harbour. It had formerly a good trade, but is now miſerably poor. It was taken by the Portugueſe in 1507, to whom it ſtill belongs. It is 15 miles ſouth of Bombay, and five miles from the ſea. E. Long. 72. 45. N. Lat. 18. 30.

CHAULIEU (William Amfrye de), abbé d'Amale, one of the moſt polite and ingenious of the French poets, was born in 1639, and died at the age of 84. The moſt complete edition of his poems is that printed in 2 vols 8vo in 1733.

CHAUMONT, a town of France, in Champagne, and in the diſtrict of Baſſigni, of which it is the capital. It is ſeated on a mountain near the river Marne. E. Long. 5. 15. N. Lat. 48. 6.

CHAUNE, a town of France, in Picardy, and in the diſtrict of Sanſterre, with the title of a duchy. E. Long. 2. 55. N. Lat. 49. 45.

CHAUNTRY. See CHANTRY.

CHAUNY, a town of France, in Picardy, ſeated on the river Oiſe, in Chantry. E. Long. 3. 17. N. Lat. 49. 37.

CHAUVIN (Stephen), a celebrated miniſter of the reformed religion, born at Niſmes, left France at the revocation of the edict of Nantz, and retired to Rotterdam, where he began a new *Journal des Sçavans*; and afterwards removing to Berlin, continued it there three years. At this laſt place, he was made profeſſor of philoſophy, and diſcharged that office with much honour and reputation. His principal work is a philoſophical dictionary, in Latin, which he publiſhed at Rotterdam in 1692; and gave a new edition of it much augmented, at Lewarden, in 1713, folio. He died in 1725, aged 85.

CHAVEZ, a ſtrong town of Tralos-Montes in Portugal, is ſeated at the foot of a mountain on the river Tamega. It has two ſuburbs, and as many forts; one

one of which looks like a citadel. Between the town and suburb of Magdalena, is an old Roman stone-bridge about 92 geometrical paces long. W. Long. 7. 1. N. Lat. 41. 42.

CHAZELLES (John Matthew), a celebrated French mathematician and engineer, was born at Lyons in 1657. M. du Hamel, with whom he got acquainted, finding his genius incline towards astronomy, presented him to M. Cassini, who employed him in his observatory. In 1684, the Duke of Mortemar made use of Chazelles to teach him mathematics; and, the year after, procured him the preferment of hydrography professor for the galleys of Marseilles, where he set up a school for young pilots designed to serve aboard the galleys. In 1686, the galleys made four little campaigns, or rather four courses, purely for exercise. Chazelles went on board every time with them; kept his school upon the sea, and showed the practice of what he taught. In the year 1687 and 1688, he made two other sea-campaigns, in which he drew a great many plans of ports, roads, towns, and forts, which were lodged with the ministers of state. At the beginning of the war, which ended with the peace of Ryswick, some marine officers, and Chazelles among the rest, fancied the galleys might be so contrived as to live upon the ocean; that they might serve to tow the men of war when the wind failed or proved contrary, and also help to secure the coast of France upon the ocean. Chazelles was sent to the west coasts in July 1689, to examine the practicableness of this scheme; and in 1690, fifteen galleys new built set sail from Rochefort, and cruised as far as Torbay in England, and proved serviceable at the descent upon Tinmouth. After this, he digested into order the observations he had made on the coasts of the ocean; and drew distinct maps with a portulan to them, viz. a large description of every haven, of the depth, the tides, the dangers and advantages discovered, &c. These maps were inserted in the *Neptune François*, published in 1692, in which year Chazelles was engineer at the descent at Oneille. In 1693, Monsieur de Pontchartrain, then secretary of state for the marine, and afterwards chancellor of France, resolved to get the *Neptune François* carried on to a second volume, which was also to take in the Mediterranean. Chazelles desired that he might have a year's voyage on this sea, for making astronomical observations; and the request being granted, he passed by Greece, Egypt, and the other parts of Turky, with his quadrant and telescope in his hand. When he was in Egypt he measured the pyramids; and finding the sides of the largest precisely facing the four cardinal points, naturally concluded this position to have been intended, and also that the poles of the earth and meridians had not since deviated. Chazelles likewise made a report of his voyage in the Levant, and gave the academy all the satisfaction they wanted concerning the position of Alexandria: upon which he was made a member of the academy in 1695. He died in 1710.

CHAZINZARIANS, a sect of heretics who rose in Armenia in the seventh century. The word is formed of the Armenian *chazus*, "cross." They are also called *staurolatrae*, which in Greek signifies the same as *Chazinzarians* in Armenian, viz. *adorers of the cross*; they being charged with paying adoration to the cross alone. In other respects they were Nestorians; and admitted two persons in Jesus Christ. Nicephorus ascribes other singularities to them; particularly their holding an annual feast in memory of the dog of their false prophet Sergius, which they called *artziburtzi*.

CHEASAPEAK bay, in North America, the entrance between Cape Henry and Cape Charles, running up 300 miles between Virginia and Maryland. It is navigable almost all the way for large ships, and has several navigable rivers that fall into it, by means of which ships go up to the very doors of the planters, to take in their lading of goods.—Here was a sea-engagement in 1781 between the British fleet under Admiral Graves consisting of 19 ships of the line, and the French fleet of 24 line-of-battle ships under the Count de Grasse, which ended in the Count's keeping possession of the Bay, by which Lord Cornwallis and his whole army were made prisoners of war at York-town, being invested both by sea and land by very superior numbers.

CHEATS, are deceitful practices in defrauding, or endeavouring to defraud, another of his known right, by means of some artful device, contrary to the plain rules of common honesty: as by playing with false dice, or by causing an illiterate person to execute a deed to his prejudice, by reading it over to him in words different from those in which it was written, &c.—If any person deceitfully get into his hands or possession any money or other things of any other person's by colour of any false token, &c. being convicted, he shall have such punishment by imprisonment, setting upon the pillory, or by any corporeal pain except pain of death, as shall be adjudged by the persons before whom he shall be convicted.—As there are frauds which may be relieved civilly, and not punished criminally; so there are other frauds which in a special case may not be helped civilly, and yet shall be punished criminally. Thus if a minor goes about the town, and, pretending to be of age, defrauds many persons by taking credit for a considerable quantity of goods, and then insisting on his nonage, the persons injured cannot recover the value of their goods, but they may indict and punish him for a common cheat. Persons convicted of obtaining money or goods by false pretences, or of sending threatening letters in order to extort money or goods, may be punished with fine or imprisonment, or by pillory, whipping, or transportation.

CHEBRECHIN, a town of Poland, in the province of Russia and palatinate of Belikow. It is seated on the declivity of a hill, and the river Wierpi waters its walls, and afterwards falls into the river Bog. The Jews there are very rich. E. Long. 23. 51. N. Lat. 50. 35.

CHECAYA, in Turkish affairs, the second officer of the Janizaries, who commands them under the aga, and is otherwise called *protogero*.

There is also a checaya of the treasury, stables, kitchen, &c. the word signifying as much as lieutenant, or the second in any office.

CHECK, or *Check-Roll*, a roll or book, wherein are contained the names of such persons as are attendants and in the pay of the king, or other great personages, as their houshold servants.

Clerk of the Check in the king's houfehold, has the check and controlment of the yeomen of the guard, and all the ufhers belonging to the royal family, allowing their abfence or defects in attendance, or diminifhing their wages for the fame, &c. He alfo, by himfelf or deputy, takes the view of thofe that are to watch in the court, and has the fetting of the watch, &c.

Clerk of the Check in the royal dock-yards, an officer who keeps a mufter or regifter of all the men employed aboard his majefty's fhips and veffels, and alfo of all the artificers and others in the fervice of the navy at the port where he is fettled.

Check, in falconry, a term ufed of a hawk, when fhe forfakes her proper game, to fly at pyes, crows, rooks, or the like, that crofs her in her flight.

CHECKY, in heraldry, is when the fhield, or a bordure, &c. is chequered, or divided into chequers or fquares, in the manner of a chefs-board.

This is one of the moft noble and moft ancient figures ufed in armoury; and a certain author faith, that it ought to be given to none but great warriors, in token of their bravery: for the chefs-board reprefents a field of battle; and the pawns placed on both fides reprefent the foldiers of the two armies, which move, attack, advance, or retire, according to the will of the gamefters, who are the generals.

This figure is always compofed of metal and colour. But fome authors would have it reckoned among the feveral forts of furs.

CHEEK, in anatomy, that part of the face fituated below the eyes on each fide.

Cheeks, a general name among mechanics, for almoft all thofe pieces of their machines and inftruments, that are double, and perfectly alike. Thus, the cheeks of a printing-prefs are its two principal pieces: they are placed perpendicular, and parallel to each other; ferving to fuftain the three fummers, viz. the head, fhelves, and winter, which bear the fpindle, and other parts of the machine. See Printing-Prefs.

The *cheeks of a turner's lathe*, are two long pieces of wood, between which are placed the puppets, which are either pointed or otherwife, ferving to fupport the work and the mandrils of the workman. Thefe two pieces are placed parallel to the horizon, feparated from one another by the thicknefs of the tail of the puppets, and joined with tenons to two other pieces of wood placed perpendicularly, called the *legs of the lathe*.

Cheeks of the glazier's vice, are two pieces of iron joined parallel at top and bottom; in which are the axis, or fpindles, little wheel, cufhions, &c. whereof the machine is compofed.

The cheeks of a mortar, or the *brackets*, in artillery, are made of ftrong planks of wood, bound with thick plates of iron, and are fixed to the bed by four bolts; they rife on each fide of the mortar, and to ferve to keep her at what elevation is given her, by the help of ftrong bolts of iron which go through both cheeks, both under and behind the mortar, betwixt which are driven coins of wood; thefe bolts are called the *bracket-bolts*, and the bolts which are put one in each end of the bed, are the traverfe-bolts, becaufe with handfpikes the mortar is by thefe traverfed to the right or left.

Cheeks, in fhip-building, are two pieces of timber, fitted on each fide of the maft at the top, ferving to ftrengthen the mafts there. The uppermoft rail or piece of timber in the beak of a fhip, is called the *cheek*. The knees which faften the beak-head to the fhip, are called *cheeks*; and the fides of any block, or the fides of a fhip's carriage of a gun, are called *cheeks*.

CHEESE, a fort of food prepared of curdled milk purged from the ferum or whey, and afterwards dried for ufe.

Cheefe differs in quality according as it is made from new or fkimmed milk, from the curd which feparates fpontaneoufly upon ftanding, or that which is more fpeedily produced by the addition of runnet. Cream alfo affords a kind of cheefe, but quite fat and butyraceous, and which does not keep long. Analyzed chemically, cheefe appears to partake much more of an animal nature than butter, or the milk from which it was made. It is infoluble in every liquid except fpirit of nitre, and cauftic alkaline ley. Shaved thin, and properly treated with hot water, it forms a very ftrong cement if mixed with quicklime *. When prepared with the hot water, it is recommended in the Swedifh memoirs to be ufed by anglers as a bait; it may be made into any form, is not foftened by the cold water, and the fifhes are fond of it. As a food, phyficians condemn the too free ufe of cheefe. When new, it is extremely difficult of digeftion; when old, it becomes acrid and hot; and, from Dr Percival's experiments, is evidently of a feptic nature. It is a common opinion that old cheefe digefts every thing, yet is left undigefted itfelf; but this is without any folid foundation. Cheefe made from the milk of fheep digefts fooner than that from the milk of cows, but is lefs nourifhing; that from the milk of goats digefts fooner than either, but is alfo the leaft nourifhing. In general, it is a kind of food fit only for the laborious, or thofe whofe organs of digeftion are ftrong.

* See Cement.

Every country has places noted for this commodity: thus Chefter and Gloucefter cheefe are famous in England; and the Parmefan cheefe is in no lefs repute abroad, efpecially in France. This fort of cheefe is entirely made of fweet cow-milk; but at Rochefort in Languedoc, they make it of ewe's milk; and in other places it is ufual to add goat or ewe's milk in a certain proportion to that of the cow. There is likewife a kind of medicated cheefe made by intimately mixing the expreffed juice of certain herbs, as fage, baum, mint, &c. with the curd before it is fafhioned into a cheefe.—The Laplanders make a fort of cheefe of the milk of their rein-deer; which is not only of great fervice to them as food, but on many other occafions. It is a very common thing in thefe climates to have a limb numbed and frozen with the cold: their remedy for this is the heating an iron red hot, and thrufting it through the middle of one of thefe cheefes: they catch what drops out, and with this anoint the limb, which foon recovers. They are fubject alfo to coughs and difeafes of the lungs, and thefe they cure by the fame fort of medicine: they boil a large quantity of the cheefe in the frefh deer's milk, and drink the decoction in large draughts warm feveral times a-day. They make a lefs ftrong decoction of the fame kind alfo, which they ufe as their common drink, for three or four days together, at feveral times of the year. They

Cheese. do this to prevent the mischiefs they are liable to from their water, which is otherwise their constant drink, and is not good.

The hundred weight of cheese pays on importation 1s. 3 7/20d. and draws back on exportation 1s. 1 1/2d. at the rate of 6s. 8d.

Best methods of making Cheese in England. The double Gloucester is a cheese that pleases almost every palate. The best of this kind is made from new, or (as it is called in that and the adjoining counties) *covered milk.* An inferior sort is made from what is called *half-covered milk*; though when any of these cheeses turn out to be good, people are deceived, and often purchase them for the best *covered milk cheese*: but farmers who are honest have them stamped with a piece of wood made in the shape of a heart, so that any person may know them.

It will be every farmer's interest (if he has a sufficient number of cows) to make a large cheese from one meal's milk. This, when brought in warm, will be easily changed or turned with the rennet; but if the morning or night's milk be to be mixed with that which is fresh from the cow, it will be a longer time before it turns, nor will it change sometimes without being heated over the fire, by which it often gets dust or soot, or smoke, which will give the cheese a very disagreeable flavour.

When the milk is turned, the whey should be carefully strained from the curd. The curd should be broken small with the hands; and when it is equally broken, it must be put by little at a time into the vat, carefully breaking it as it is put in. The vat should be filled an inch or more above the brim, that when the whey is pressed out it may not shrink below the brim; if it does, the cheese will be worth very little. But first, before the curd is put in, a cheese-cloth or strainer should be laid at the bottom of the vat; and this should be so large, that when the vat is filled with the curd, the ends of the cloth may turn again over the top of it. When this is done, it should be taken to the press, and there remain for the space of two hours; when it should be turned and have a clean cloth put under it, and turned over as before. It must then be pressed again, and remain in the press six or eight hours; when it should again be turned and rubbed on each side with salt. After this it must be pressed again for the space of 12 or 14 hours more; when, if any of the edges project, they should be pared off: it may then be put on a dry board, where it should be regularly turned every day. It is a good way to have three or four holes bored round the lower part of the vat, that the whey may drain so perfectly from the cheese as not the least particle of it may remain.

The prevailing opinion of the people of Gloucestershire and the neighbouring counties is, that the cheeses will spoil if they do not scrape and wash them when they are found to be mouldy. But others think that suffering the mould to remain, mellows them, provided they are turned every day. Those, however, who will have the mould off, should cause it to be removed with a clean dry flannel, as the washing the cheeses is only a means of making the mould (which is a species of fungus rooted in the coat) grow again immediately.

Some people scald the curd: but this is a bad and mercenary practice; it robs the cheese of its fatness, and can only be done with a view to raise a greater quantity of whey butter, or to bring the cheeses forward for sale, by making them appear older than they really are.

As most people like to purchase high-coloured cheese, it may be right to mix a little anatto with the milk before it is turned. No cheese will look yellow without it; and though it does not in the least add to the goodness, it is perfectly innocent in its nature and effects.

It is not in the power of any person to make good cheese with bad rennet; therefore the following receipt should be attended to. Let the *vell, maw, rennet-bag* (or by whatever name it is called), be perfectly sweet; for if it be the least tainted, the cheese will never be good. When this is fit for the purpose, three pints or two quarts of soft water (clean and sweet) should be mixed with salt, wherein should be put sweet-briar, rose leaves and flowers, cinnamon, mace, cloves, and, in short, almost every sort of spice and aromatic that can be procured; and if these are put into two quarts of water, they must boil gently till the liquor is reduced to three pints, and care should be taken that this liquor is not smoked. It should be strained clean from the spices, &c. and when found to be not warmer than milk from the cow, it should be poured upon the vell or maw. A lemon may then be sliced into it; when it may remain a day or two: After which it should be strained again, and put in a bottle; where, if well corked, it will keep good for twelve months or more. It will smell like a perfume; and a small quantity of it will turn the milk, and give the cheese a pleasing flavour. After this, if the vell be salted, and dried for a week or two near the fire, it will do for the purpose again almost as well as before.

Cheddar cheese is held in high esteem; but its goodness is said to be chiefly owing to the land whereon the cows feed, as the method of making it is the same as is pursued throughout Somersetshire, and the adjoining counties.

Cheshire cheese is much admired; yet no people take less pains with the rennet than the Cheshire farmers. But their cheeses are so large as often to exceed one hundred pounds weight each; to this (and the age they are kept, the richness of the land, and the keeping such a number of cows as to make such a cheese without adding a second meal's milk) their excellence may be attributed. Indeed they salt the curd (which may make a difference), and keep the cheeses in a damp place after they are made, and are very careful to turn them daily.

But of all the cheese this kingdom produces, none is more highly esteemed than the Stilton, which is called the *Parmesan* of England, and (except faulty) is never sold for less than 1s. or 1s. 2d. per pound.

The Stilton cheeses are usually made in square vats, and weigh from six to twelve pounds each cheese. Immediately after they are made, it is necessary to put them into square boxes made exactly to fit them; they being so extremely rich, that except this precaution be taken they are apt to bulge out, and break asunder. They should be continually and daily turned in these boxes, and must be kept two years before they are properly mellowed for sale.

Some make them in a net, somewhat like a cabbage net; so that they appear, when made, not unlike an a-

Cheese. corn. But these are never so good as the other, having a thicker coat, and wanting all that rich flavour and mellowness which make them so pleasing.

It is proper to mention that the making of these cheeses is not confined to the Stilton farmers, as many others in Huntingdonshire (not forgetting Rutland and Northamptonshires) make a similar sort, sell them for the same price, and give all of them the name of *Stilton cheeses.*

Though these farmers are remarked for cleanliness, they take very little pains with the rennet, as they in general only cut pieces from the vell or maw, which they put into the milk, and move gently about with the hand, by which means it breaks or turns it so, that they easily obtain the curd. But if the method above described for making rennet were put in practice, they would make their cheese still better; at least they would not have so many faulty and unsound cheeses; for notwithstanding their cheeses bear such a name and price, they often find them so bad as not to be saleable; which is probably owing to their being so careless about the rennet.

It has been alleged, that as good cheese might be made in other counties, if people would adhere to the Stilton plan, which is this—They make a cheese every morning; and to this meal of new milk they add the cream taken from that which is milked the night before. This, and the age of their cheeses, have been supposed the only reasons why they are preferred to others; for from the nicest observation, it does not appear that their land is in any respect superior to that of other counties.

Excellent cream cheeses are made in Lincolnshire, by adding the cream of one meal's milk to milk which comes immediately from the cow; these are pressed gently two or three times, turned for a few days, and are then disposed of at the rate of 1s. per pound, to be eaten while new with radishes, sallad, &c.

Many people give skimmed milk to pigs, but the whey will do equally as well after cheeses are made from this milk; such cheeses will always sell for at least 2d. per pound, which will amount to a large sum annually where they make much butter. The peasants and many of the farmers in the north of England never eat any better cheese; and though they appear harder, experience hath proved them to be much easier of digestion than any new milk cheeses. A good market may always be found for the sale of them at Bristol.

Account of the making of Parmesan Cheese: by Mr Zappa of Milan, in answer to queries from Arthur Young, Esq.

"Are the cows regularly fed in stables?"—From the middle of April, or sooner if possible, the cows are sent to pasture in the meadows till the end of November usually.

"Or only fed in stables in winter?"—When the season is past, and snow comes, they are put into stables for the whole winter, and fed with hay.

"Do they remain in the pasture from morning till night? or only in hot weather?"—Between nine and ten in the morning the cows are sent to water, and then to the pastures, where they remain four or five hours at most, and at three or four o'clock are driven to the stables if the season is fresh, or under porticos if hot; where, for the night, a convenient quantity of hay is given them. Cheese

"In what months are they kept at pasture the whole day?"—Mostly answered already; but it might be said, that no owner will leave his cattle, without great cause, in uncovered places at night. It happens only to the shepherds from the Alps, when they pass, because it is impossible to find stables for all their cattle.

"What is the opinion in the Lodesan, on the best conduct for profit in the management of meadows?"—For a dairy farm of 100 cows, which yields daily a cheese weighing 70 to 75 lb. of 28 ounces, are wanted 1000 pertices of land. Of these about 800 are standing meadows, the other 200 are in cultivation for corn and grass fields in rotation.

"Do they milk the cows morning and evening?"—Those that are in milk are milked morning and evening, with exception of such as are near calving.

"One hundred cows being wanted to make a Lodesan each day, it is supposed that it is made with the milk of the evening and the following morning; or of the morning and evening of the same day: how is it?"—The 100 cows form a dairy farm of a good large cheese; it is reckoned that 80 are in milk, and 20 with calves sucking, or near calving. They reckon one with the other about 32 boccalis of 32 oz. of milk. Such is the quantity for a cheese of about 70 lb. of 28 ounces. They join the evening with the morning milk, because so it is fresher than if it was that of the morning and evening of the same day. The morning milk would be 24 hours old when the next morning the cheese should be made.

"Do they skim or not the milk to make butter before they make the cheese?"—From the evening milk all the cream possible is taken away for butter, mascarponi (cream-cheese), &c. The milk of the morning ought to be skimmed slightly; but every one skims as much cream as he can. The butter is sold on the spot immediately at 24 sous; the cheese at about 28 sous. The butter loses nothing in weight; the cheese loses one-third of it, is subject to hurt, and requires expences of service, attention, warehouses, &c. before it is sold; and a man in two hours makes 45 to 50 lb. of butter that is sold directly. However, it is not possible to leave much cream in the milk to make Lodesan cheese, called *grained cheese*; because if it is too rich, it does not last long, and it is necessary to consume it while young and sound.

"Is Parmesan or Lodesan cheese made every day in the year or not?"—With 100 cows it is. In winter, however, the milk being less in quantity, the cheese is of lesser weight, but certainly more delicate.

"After gathering or uniting the milk, either skimmed or not, what is exactly the whole operation?"—The morning of the 3d of March 1786, I have seen the whole operation, having gone on purpose to the spot to see the whole work from beginning to end. At 16 Italian hours, or ten in the morning, according to the northern way to account hours, the skimming of that morning's milk, gathered only two hours before, was finished. I did, meanwhile, examine the boiler or pot. At the top it was eight feet (English) diameter, or thereabout; and about five feet three inches deep,

made

Cheese.

made like a bell, and narrowing towards the bottom to about two one-half feet. They joined the cream produced that morning with the other produced by the milk of the evening before. That produced by this last milk was double in quantity to that of the morning milk, because it had the whole night to unite, and that of the morning had only two hours to do it, in which it could not separate much. Of the cream some was destined to make mascarponics (cream-cheese), and they put the rest into the machine for making butter. Out of the milk of the evening before and of that morning that was all put together after skimming, they took and put into the boiler 272 boccali, and they put under it two faggots of wood; which being burnt, were sufficient to give the milk a warmth a little superior to lukewarm. Then the boiler being withdrawn from the fire, the foreman put into it the rennet, which they prepare in small balls of one ounce each, turning the ball in his hand always kept in the milk entirely covered; and after it was perfectly dissolved, he covered the boiler to keep the milk defended, that it might not suffer from the coldness of the season, in particular as it was a windy day. I went then to look on the man that was making mascarponics, &c. and then we went twice to examine if the milk was sufficiently coagulated. At the 18 hours, according to the Italian clocks, or noon, the true manufactory of cheese began. The milk was coagulated in a manner to be taken from the boiler in pieces from the surface. The foreman, with a stick that had 18 points, or rather nine small pieces of wood fixed by their middle in the end of it, and forming nine points to each side, began to break exactly all the coagulated milk, and did continue to do so for more than half an hour, from time to time examining it to see its state. He ordered to renew the fire, and four faggots of willow branches were used all at once: he turned the boiler that the fire might act; and then the underman began to work in the milk with a stick like the above, but with only four smaller sticks at the top, forming eight points, four at each side, a span long each point. In a quarter of an hour the foreman mixed in the boiler the proper quantity of saffron, and the milk was all in knobs, and finer grained than before, by the effect of turning and breaking the coagulation, or curd, continually. Every moment the fire was renewed or fed; but with a faggot only at a time, to continue it regular. The milk was never heated much, nor does it hinder to keep the hand in it to know the fineness of the grain, which refines continually by the stick-work of the underman. It is of the greatest consequence to mind when the grain begins to take a consistence. When it comes to this state, the boiler is turned from the fire, and the underman immediately takes out the whey, putting it into proper receivers. In that manner the grain subsides to the bottom of the boiler; and leaving only in it whey enough to keep the grain covered a little, the foreman extending himself as much as he can over and in the boiler, unites with his hands the grained milk, making like a body of paste of it. Then a large piece of linen is run by him under that paste, while another man keeps the four corners of it, and the whey is directly put again into the boiler, by which is facilitated the means of raising that paste that is taken out of the boiler, and put for one quarter of an hour into the receiver where the whey was put before, in the same linen it was taken from the boiler; which boiler is turned again directly on the fire, to extract the mascarpa (whey-cheese); and is a second product, eaten by poor people. After the paste remained for a quarter of an hour in that receiver, it was taken out and turned into the wooden form called fassera, without any thing else made than the rotundity, having neither top or bottom. Immediately after having turned it into that round wooden form, they put a piece of wood like a cheese on it, putting and increasing gradually weights on it, which serve to force out the remnant of whey; and in the evening the cheese so formed is carried into the warehouse, where, after 24 hours, they begin to give the salt. It remains in that warehouse for 15 or 20 days; but in summer only from 8 to 12 days. Meanwhile the air and salt form the crust to it; and then it is carried into another warehouse for a different service. In the second warehouse they turn every day all the cheeses that are not older than six months; and afterwards it is enough if they are only turned every 48 or 60 hours, keeping them clean, in particular of that bloom which is inevitable to them, and which, if neglected, turns musty, and causes the cheese to acquire a bad smell. The Lodesan, because it is a province watered, has a great deal of meadows, and abounds with cows, its product being mostly in cheese, butter, &c. However, the province of Pavia makes a great deal of that cheese; and we Milanese do likewise the same from the side of Porte Tosa, Romana, Ticinese, and Vercellina, because we have fine meadows and dairy farms.

Cheese-Rennet. See Gallium and Rennet.

CHEGOE, or Nigua, the Indian name of an insect common in Mexico, and also found in other hot countries where it is called *pique*, is an exceeding small animal, not very unlike a flea, and is bred in the dust. It fixes upon the feet, and breaking insensibly the cuticle, it nestles betwixt that and the true skin, which also, unless it is immediately taken out, it breaks, and pierces at last to the flesh, multiplying with a rapidity almost incredible. It is seldom discovered until it pierces the true skin, when it causes an intolerable itching. These insects, with their astonishing multiplication, would soon dispeople those countries, were it less easy to avoid them, or were the inhabitants less dexterous in getting them out before they begin to spread. On the other hand, nature, in order to lessen the evil, has not only denied them wings, but even that conformation of the legs and those strong muscles which are given to the flea for leaping. The poor, however, who are in some measure doomed to live in the dust, and to a habitual neglect of their persons, suffer these insects sometimes to multiply so far as to make large holes in their flesh, and even to occasion dangerous wounds.

Cheese ‖ Cheiranthus.

CHEIRANTHUS, stock-gilliflower, or *Wall-flower*: A genus of the 39th natural order, *Siliquosæ*; and belonging to the tetradynamia class of plants. The germen is marked with a glandulous denticle on each side; the calyx is close, with two of its leaves gibbous at the base; the seeds plane. The species are 13; but the following three are most worthy of notice. 1. The cheiri, or common wall-flower, with ligneous, long, tough roots; an upright, woody, abiding stalk, divided into many erect angular branches, forming a bushy head from one to two feet high, closely garnished with spear-shaped, acute, smooth leaves, and all the branches terminating in long erect spikes of numerous flowers, which in different varieties are yellow, bloody, white, &c. 2. The incanus, or hoary cheiranthus, with ligneous, long, naked, white roots; and upright, strong, woody, abiding stem, from one to three feet high, branchy at top, adorned with long, spear-shaped, obtuse, hoary leaves; and the top of the stalk and all the branches terminated by erect spikes of flowers from one to two or three feet long, of different colours in different varieties. 3. The annuus, or ten-weeks-stock, with an upright, woody, smooth stalk, divided into a branchy head, 12 or 15 inches high, garnished with spear-shaped, blunt, hoary leaves, a little indented, and all the branches terminated by long erect spikes of numerous flowers of different colours in different varieties.—The two first sorts are very hardy evergreen biennials or perennials; but the last is an annual plant, so must be continued by seed sown every year; and even the two first, notwithstanding their being perennial, degenerate so much in their flowers after the first year, that it will be proper also to raise an annual supply of them. The seeds are to be saved only from the plants with single flowers; for the double ones bring no seeds to perfection. The seeds are to be chosen from such flowers as have five, six, or more petals, or from such as grow near to the double ones. They may be sown in the full ground in the spring, and may be afterwards transplanted. When fine doubles of the two first kinds are obtained, they may be multiplied by slips from the old plants.

CHEKAO, in natural history, the name of an earth found in many parts of the East Indies, and sometimes used by the Chinese in their porcelain manufacture. It is a hard and stony earth; and the manner of using it is this: they first calcine it in an open furnace, and then beat it to a fine powder. This powder they mix with large quantities of water: then stirring the whole together, they let the coarser part subside; and pouring off the rest yet thick as cream, they leave it to settle, and use the matter which is found at the bottom in form of a soft paste, and will retain that humidity a long time. This supplies the place of the earth called *hoache*, in the making of that elegant sort of china-ware which is all white, and has flowers which seem formed by a mere vapour within its surface. The manner of their using it is this: they first make the vessel of the common matter of the manufacture; when this is almost dry, they paint upon it the flowers, or whatever other figures they please, with a pencil dipt in this preparation of the chekao; when this is thoroughly dry, they cover the whole vessel with the varnish in the common way, and bake it as usual. The consequence is, that the whole is white; but the body of the vessel, the figures, and the varnish, being three different substances, each has its own particular white; and the flowers being painted in the finest white of all, are distinctly seen through the varnish upon the vessel, and seem as if traced by a vapour only. The hoache does this as well as the chekao; and has besides this the quality of serving for making the porcelain ware either alone, or in the place of kaolin: the chekao has not this property, nor any other substance besides this hoache, which appears to be the same with our steatites or soap-rock.

CHEKE (Sir John), a celebrated statesman, grammarian, and divine, of an ancient family in the isle of Wight, was born at Cambridge in the year 1514, and educated at St John's college in that university; where, after taking his degrees in arts, he was first chosen Greek lecturer, and in 1540 professor of that language, with a stipend of 40 l. a-year. In this station he was principally instrumental in reforming the pronunciation of the Greek language, which, having been much neglected, was imperfectly understood. About the year 1543 he was incorporated master of arts at Oxford, where, we are told, he had studied for some time. In the following year he was sent to the court of king Henry VIII. and appointed tutor for the Latin language, jointly with Sir Anthony Cooke, to prince Edward, about which time he was made canon of the college newly founded in Oxford; wherefore he must have now been in orders. On the accession of his royal pupil to the crown, Mr Cheke was first rewarded with a pension of 100 marks, and afterwards obtained several considerable grants from the crown. In 1550 he was made chief gentleman of the privy-chamber, and was knighted the following year; in 1551, chamberlain of the exchequer for life; in 1553, clerk of the council; and soon after secretary of state and privy-counsellor. But these honours were of short duration. Having concurred in the measures of the duke of Northumberland for settling the crown on the unfortunate Jane Grey, and acted as her secretary during the nine days of her reign, on the accession of queen Mary, Sir John Cheke was sent to the tower, and stript of the greatest part of his possessions. In September 1554 he obtained his liberty, and a licence from her majesty to travel abroad. He went first to Basil, thence to Italy, and afterwards returned to Strasburg, where he was reduced to the necessity of reading Greek lectures for subsistence. In 1556 he set out in an evil hour to meet his wife at Brussels; but, before he reached that city, he was seized by order of king Philip II. hoodwinked, and thrown into a waggon; and thus ignominiously conducted to a ship, which brought him to the tower of London. He soon found that religion was the cause of his imprisonment; for he was immediately visited by two Romish priests, who piously endeavoured to convert him, but without success. However, he was at last visited by Fleckenham; who told him from the queen, that he must either comply or burn. This powerful argument had the desired effect; and Sir John Cheke accordingly complied in form, and his lands, upon certain conditions, were restored: but his remorse soon put an end to his life. He died in September 1557, at the house of his friend Mr Peter Osborne in Wood-street, London, and was buried in St Alban's church. He left three sons, the eldest of whom, Henry, was knighted by queen Elizabeth. He wrote 1. A Latin translation of two of St Chrysostom's homilies. Lond. 1543, 4to. 2. The Hurt of Sedition. Lond. 1549, 1576, 1641. 3. Latin Translation of the English Communion Service. Printed among Bucer's opuscula. 4. De pronunciatione Græcæ. Basil, 1555, 8vo. 5. Several letters published in his life by Strype; and a great number of other books.

CHE-KYANG, or Tche-kiang, a maritime province of China, and one of the most considerable in the empire; is bounded on the south by Fo-kien; on the north and west by Kiang-nan and Kiang-si; and on the east by the sea. The air is pure and healthful, and the soil fertile, being watered by a number of rivers and canals, as well as springs and lakes. The chief produce is silk; a vast quantity of which is cultivated here, and for which the whole country is covered with mulberry trees. These are purposely checked in their growth by the natives, experience having taught them, that the leaves of the smallest trees produce the best silk. The stuffs made in this province, which are embroidered with gold and silver, are reckoned the best in the empire; and notwithstanding a vast exportation to the Japan and Philippine islands, as well as to every part of China, and to Europe, such an abundance is left in the province, that a complete suit of silk may be bought here as cheap as one of the coarsest woollen in France.

This province is also remarkable for a particular species of mushrooms, which is exported to every part of the empire. They are pickled, and then dried; when they will keep good for a whole year. When used they must be soaked in water, which renders them as fresh as at first. Here also the tallow tree is met with; and the province affords excellent hams, and those small gold-fishes with which the ponds are usually stocked.

Che kyang contains 11 cities of the first class, 72 of the third, and 18 fortresses, which, in Europe, would be accounted large cities. The principal of these are, 1. Hang-tcheou-fou, the metropolis, accounted by the Chinese to be the paradise of the earth. It is four leagues in circumference, exclusive of the suburbs; and the number of its inhabitants are computed at more than a million, and 10,000 workmen are supposed to be employed within its walls in manufacturing of silk. Its principal beauty is a small lake, close to the walls on the western side, the water of which is pure and limpid, and the banks almost every where covered with flowers. Its banks are likewise adorned with halls and open galleries supported by pillars, and paved with large flag-stones for the convenience of those who are fond of walking; and the lake itself is intersected with causeways cased with cut-stone, openings covered with bridges being left in them for the passage of boats. In the middle are two islands with a temple and several pleasure-houses, and the emperor has a small palace in the neighbourhood. The city is garrisoned by 3000 Chinese and as many Tartars, and has under its jurisdiction seven cities of the third class. 2. Hou-tcheou-fou is also situated on a lake, and manufactures an incredible quantity of silk, insomuch, that the tribute of a city under its jurisdiction amounts to more than 500,000 ounces of silver. 3. Ning-po-fou, by Europeans called Liampo, is an excellent port, opposite to Japan. Eighteen or twenty leagues from it is an island called Tcheou-chan, where the English first landed on their arrival at China. 4. Ning-po is remarkable for the silk manufactured there, which is much esteemed in foreign countries, especially Japan, where it is exchanged for gold, silver, and copper. 5. Chau-hing-fou, situated in an extensive and fertile plain, is remarkable for a tomb about half a league distant, which is said to be that of *Yu*. The people of this province are said to be the most versed in chicanery of any in China. 6. Tcho-tcheou-fou, remarkable for having in its neighbourhood pines of an extraordinary size, capable of containing 40 men in their trunks. The inhabitants are ingenious, polite, and courteous to strangers, but very superstitious.

CHELIDONIAS, according to Pliny, an anniversary wind, blowing at the appearance of the swallows; otherwise the Favonius, or Zephyrus.

CHELIDONIUM, CELANDINE, and HORNED or PRICKLY POPPY: A genus of the monogynia order, belonging to the pentandria class of plants; and in the natural method ranking under the 27th order, *Rhoeadeae*. The corolla is tetrapetalous, the calyx diphyllous, the siliqua unilocular and linear. There are six species, none of which are remarkable for their beauty; but one of them, viz. the majus, is an article in the materia medica. It grows on old walls, among rubbish, and in waste shady places. The herb is of a bluish green colour; the root of a deep red; and both contain a gold-coloured juice: their smell is disagreeable, the taste somewhat bitterish, very acrid, burning and biting the mouth; the root is the most acrid. The juice takes off warts; cures tetters, ring-worms, and the itch; and, diluted with milk, it consumes opaque white spots on the eye.—Horses, cows, goats, and swine, refuse to eat the herb.

CHELIDONIUS LAPIS, in natural history, a stone said by the ancients to be found in the stomachs of young swallows, and greatly cried up for its virtues in the falling-sickness; but, from their description, it appears to be only a species of lycodnotes, or bufonita. See LYCODONTES, and BUFONITA.

CHELM, a town of *Poland*, capital of a palatinate of the same name. It is situated in the province of Red Russia. E. Long. 23. 30. N. Lat. 51. 25.

CHELMSFORD, the county town of Essex, situated on the river Chelmer, in E. Long. 0. 30. N. Lat. 51. 40. It sends two members to parliament.

CHELONE, in botany: A genus of the angiospermia order, belonging to the didynamia class of plants; and in the natural method ranking under the 40th order, *Personatae*. The calyx is quinquepartite; the rudiment of a fifth filament among the highest stamina, the capsule bilocular. There are three species, viz. the Glabra, the Hirsuta, and the Pentstemon. They are natives of North America; and are herbaceous flowery perennials, with upright stalks two feet high, decorated with spear-shaped leaves, and beautiful spikes of monopetalous, ringent flowers, red, rose-coloured, blue, and purple. They flower from September to November, and are sometimes succeeded by ripe seeds in this country. They are very hardy plants, and may be propagated by seeds sown in any soil or situation; but the two first multiply so fast by their creeping roots, that the seeds are seldom regarded.

CHELSEA, a fine village situated on the northern bank of the river Thames, a mile westward of Westminster, remarkable for a magnificent hospital of invalids and old decrepit soldiers; and a pleasure house, called Ranelagh, to which a great deal of fine company resort in summer; and a noble botanic garden belonging to the company of apothecaries. The royal hospital of invalids was begun by Charles II. carried on by James II. and finished by king William. It consists of a vast range of buildings, that form three large squares, in which there is an uncommon air of neatness and elegance observed. It is under the direction of commissioners, who consist generally of the

Chelſea. officers of ſtate and of war. There is a governor with 500l. ſalary, a lieutenant governor with 400l. and a major, with 250l. beſides inferior officers, ſerjeants, corporals and drums, with about 400 men, who all do garriſon duty; and there are above 10,000 out penſioners who receive an annuity of 7l. 12s. 6d. each; all which expence is defrayed by a poundage deducted from the army, deficiences being made good by parliament.—The botanic garden is very extenſive, enriched with a vaſt variety of domeſtic and exotic plants, the original ſtock of which was given to the apothecaries of London by Sir Hans Sloane.—At Ranelagh Garden and amphitheatre the entertainment is a fine band of muſic, with an organ and ſome of the beſt voices, and the regale is tea and coffee.

CHELTENHAM, or Chiltenham, a market town of Glouceſterſhire, ſeven miles north-eaſt of Glouceſter. W. Long. 2. 10. N. Lat. 51. 50. It is chiefly remarkable for its mineral waters, of the ſame kind with thoſe of Scarborough. See Scarborough. Chelten-ham. Chemiſe.

CHEMISE, in fortification, the wall with which a baſtion, or any other bulwark of earth, is lined for its greater ſupport and ſtrength: or it is the ſolidity of the wall from the talus to the ſtone-row.

Fire-Chemise, a piece of linen cloth, ſteeped in a compoſition of oil of petrol, camphor, and other combuſtible matters, uſed at ſea, to ſet fire to an enemy's veſſel.

CHEMISTRY

1 Definition. MAY be defined, The ſtudy of ſuch phenomena or properties of bodies as are diſcovered by variouſly mixing them together, and by expoſing them to different degrees of heat, alone, or in mixture, with a view to the enlargement of our knowledge in nature, and to the improvement of the uſeful arts: or, It is the ſtudy of the effects of heat and mixture upon all bodies, whether natural or artificial, with a view to the improvement of arts and natural knowledge.

2 Antiquity. The ſcience of chemiſtry is undoubtedly of very high antiquity; and, like moſt other ſciences, its origin cannot be traced. In ſcripture, Tubal Cain, the 8th from Adam, is mentioned as the father or inſtructor of every artificer in braſs or iron. This, however, does not conſtitute him a chemiſt, any more than a founder or blackſmith among us has a right to that title. The name of chemiſt could only belong to him, whoever he was, who firſt diſcovered the method of extracting metals from their ores; and this perſon muſt neceſſarily have lived before Tubal Cain, as every blackſmith or founder muſt have metals ready prepared to his hand. Nevertheleſs, as Tubal Cain lived before the flood, and the ſcience of chemiſtry muſt have exiſted before his time, ſome have conjectured, that the metallurgic part, on account of its [illegible]e uſefulneſs to mankind, was revealed to Adam by God himſelf.

3 Science founded. Be this as it will, *Siphoas*, an Egyptian, is conſidered by the chemiſts as the founder of their ſcience. He was known by the Greeks under the name of *Hermes*, or *Mercurius Triſmegiſtus*; and is ſuppoſed to have lived more than 1900 years before the Chriſtian era. A numerous liſt of this philoſopher's works is given by Clemens Alexandrinus; but none of them are now to be found, nor do any of them appear to have been written profeſſedly on chemiſtry.

Two illuſtrious Egyptians, of the name of Hermes, are recorded by ancient authors. The elder ſuppoſed to be the ſame with *Mizraim*, the grandſon of Noah, the *Hermes* of the Greeks, and *Mercury* of the Romans. The younger Hermes lived a thouſand years afterwards; and is ſuppoſed to have reſtored the ſciences after they had fallen into oblivion, in conſequence of an inundation of the Nile. No leſs than 36,000 books are ſaid to have been written under the name of Hermes; but, according to Jamblichus, a cuſtom prevailed of inſcribing all books of ſcience with the name of Hermes. Some authors deny the exiſtence of Hermes, and maintain that his hiſtory is allegorical.

As the ſcience of chemiſtry is ſuppoſed to have been well known to the Egyptians, Moſes, who was ſkilled in their wiſdom, is thence ranked among the number of chemiſts; a proof of whoſe ſkill in this ſcience is thought to be, his diſſolving the golden calf made by the Iſraelites, ſo as to render it potable. 4 Moſes ſuppoſed to be ſkilled in chemiſtry.

Of all the Greeks who travelled into Egypt in order to acquire knowledge, Democritus alone was admitted into their myſteries. The Egyptian prieſts are ſaid to have taught him many chemical operations; among which were the art of ſoftening ivory, of vitrifying flints, and of imitating precious ſtones. Dr Black, however, is of opinion, that Democritus knew nothing more of theſe arts than that of making a coarſe kind of glaſs, as no mention is particularly made of his imitating any other precious ſtone than the emerald, whoſe colour is green; and the coarſer the glaſs the greener it is.

After the time of Democritus, we may know that conſiderable improvements were made in chemiſtry, as phyſicians began to make uſe of metallic preparations, as ceruſe, verdegris, litharge, &c. Dioſcorides deſcribes the diſtillation of mercury from cinnabar by means of an *ambix*, from which, by adding the Arabic *Al*, 5 Derivation of the word Alembic. comes the term *Alembic*. The art of diſtillation, however, at that time, was in a very rude ſtate; the operation being performed chiefly by ſeparating the air, and more ſubtile part of tar, from the reſt of the matter. This was done by putting the matter to be diſtilled into a veſſel, the mouth of which was covered with a wet cloth; and by this the ſteams of aſcending vapour were condenſed, which were afterwards procured by wringing out the cloth. 6 Original method of diſtilling. No other diſtillation, beſides this kind, is mentioned by Galen, Oribaſius, Ætius, or Paulus Ægineta.

The preciſe time is not known when the three mineral acids were firſt diſcovered; though, as no mention is made of them by Geber, Avicenna, or Roger Bacon, it is probable that they were not known in the 12th century.

6

tury. Raymond Lully gives some hints of his being acquainted with the marine ... ds; whence it is probable, that it was discovered towards the end of the 13th, or beginning of the 14th, century.

7 Pliny's account of the origin of glass-making.

Several chemical facts are related by Pliny, particularly the making of glass, which he ascribes to the following accident. "Some merchants in the Levant, who had nitre on board their ship, having occasion to land, lighted a fire on the sand in order to prepare their food. To support their vessels they took some of the lumps of nitre with which their ship was loaded; and the fire acting on these, melted part of them along with the sand, and thus formed the transparent substance called glass, to the great surprise of the beholders." But it is probable, that the art of glass-making was known long before; and it is by no means likely that it took its rise from such an accident.

The next traces we find of chemistry are to be extracted from the extravagant pursuits of the *Alchemists*, who imagined it possible to convert the baser metals

8 Alchemy first mentioned by Firmicus Maternus.

into gold or silver. The first mention we find of this study is by Julius Firmicus Maternus, who lived in the beginning of the fourth century, and speaks of it as a well known pursuit in his time. Æneas Gaza, who lived in the fifth century, likewise speaks of it; and Suidas explains the term by telling us, that it is the art of making gold and silver. He tells us, that Dioclesian, when persecuting the Christians, forbad all chemical operations, lest his subjects should discover the art of making gold, and thus be induced to rebel against

9 Origin of the fable of the Argonauts.

him. He supposes also, that the Argonautic expedition was only an attempt to procure a skin or parchment, on which was written the recipe for making gold. It is a common practice, however, in some places where gold is washed down in small particles by brooks and rivulets from the mountains, to suspend in the water the skins of animals having wool or hair upon them, in order to detain the heavier particles which contain the gold; and this probably gave rise to the fable of the golden fleece. Suidas, however, who lived as late as the tenth century, deserves very little credit, especially as alchemy is not mentioned by any ancient author.—The Arabian physicians afford the most clear and distinct evidence concerning alchemy. Avicenna, who lived in the tenth century, is said by a disciple of his to have wrote upon alchemy; he mentions also rose-water, and some other chemical preparations; and in the 18th century we find physicians advised to cultivate an acquaintance with the chemists; and another

10 Alchemy first supposed to be derived from the Arabians.

of the Arbian writers say, that the method of preparing rose-water, &c. was then well known.—From this evidence of the existence of alchemy among the Arabians, with the prefatory article *Al*, to denote the greatness of the science, it has been conjectured, that the doctrine of the transmutation of metals first took its rise among the Arabians, and was introduced into Europe by means of the Crusades, and by the rapid conquests of the Arabians themselves in Europe as well as in Asia and Africa. Europe at that time had been in a state of the greatest barbarity from the incursions of the northern nations; but the Arabians contributed to revive some of the sciences, and introduced alchemy among the rest, which continued till the middle of the 17th century; at which time the extravagance of its professors rose to the greatest height.

Though the pretensions of the alchemists are now universally refuted, yet from some of the discoveries which have been made in chemistry, we are even yet in danger of giving some credit to the possibility of the process of transmutation. 11 No credit due to the doctrine of transmutation.

When we consider that the metals are bodies compounded of parts which we can take away and restore, and that they are closely allied to one another in their external appearance, we may be inclined to think favourably even of the projects of the alchemists. The very separation of the metals from their ores, the depriving them of their ductility and malleability, and the restoration of these properties to them at pleasure, will appear very surprising to those who are unacquainted with chemistry. There are also processes of the more difficult kind, by which quicksilver may be produced from metals that are commonly solid, as from lead. 12 Quicksilver produced from lead.

Some of these we find in Boerhaave, Boyle, &c. authors of the greatest credit, who both speak of the operation and product as realities of which they were convinced by their own experience. These have been urged, not without some plausibility, in favour of the transmutation of the imperfect metals into gold; and hence the delusions of alchemy were not confined to the vain, the ignorant, and the ambitious part of mankind; but many ingenious and learned men, who took pleasure in the study of nature, have been seduced into this unhappy pursuit. This happened chiefly in Germany, where the variety of mines naturally turned the thoughts of chemists principally towards the metals, though the numerous failures of those who had attempted this art ought to have taught them better.

About the beginning of the 16th century, the pretenders to alchemy were very numerous, and a multitude of knaves, who had beggared themselves in the attempt, now went about to ensnare others, performing legerdemain tricks, and causing people believe that they could actually make gold and silver. A number of the tricks they made use of are to be met with in Lemery. Many books, with the same design of imposing upon mankind, were written upon the subject of alchemy. They assumed fictitious names of the greatest antiquity, and contained rules for preparing the philosopher's stone; a small quantity of which thrown into a base metal should convert the whole into gold. They are wrote in a mysterious style, without any distinct meaning; and though sometimes processes are clearly enough described, they are found to be false and deceitful upon trial, the products not answering the pretensions of the authors. Their excuse was, that it was vain to expect plain accounts of these matters, or that the books on these subjects should be written distinctly and clearly; that the value of gold was in proportion to its scarcity, and that it might be employed to bad purposes; they wrote only for the laborious and judicious chemists, who would understand them provided they made themselves acquainted with the metals by study and experience. But in fact, no distinct meaning has ever been obtained, and the books have only served to delude and betray a great number of others into the loss of their *lives*.

But though the alchemists failed in the execution of their

13 *Chemistry derived some advantages from the labours of the alchemists.*

their grand project, we must still own ourselves indebted to them for many discoveries brought to light during the time they vainly spent their labour in the expectation of making gold. Some of these are the methods of preparing spirit of wine, aquafortis, volatile alkali, vitriolic acid, and gun-powder. Medicine too was indebted to them for several valuable remedies; whence also it appears that many, who had wasted their time in the vain pursuit of the philosopher's stone, thought of trying some of their most elaborate preparations in the cure of diseases; and meeting with some success, they presumed that diseases were only to be cured by the assistance of chemistry; and that the most elaborate of all its preparations, the philosopher's stone, would cure all diseases. Some cures they performed did indeed awaken the attention of physicians; and they introduced the use of opium, which had formerly been accounted poisonous. They succeeded also in the cure of the venereal disease, which had lately made its appearance, and baffled the regular physicians; but the chemists, by giving mercury, put a stop to its ravages, and thus introduced this valuable article into the materia medica.

14 *Account of Paracelsus.*

The most famous of the chemical professors was Paracelsus, well known for his arrogance, absurdity, and profligacy. He was bred to the study of medicine; but becoming acquainted with the alchemists, travelled about in the character of a physician, and was at great pains to collect powerful medicines from all quarters. These he used with great freedom and boldness. His success in some cases operated so upon the natural arrogance and self-sufficiency of his disposition, that he formed a design of overturning the whole system of medicine, and supplying a new one from chemistry; and indeed he found but very weak adversaries in the subtle theories of Galen with the refinements of the Arabian physicians, which only prevailed in his time; and he no doubt had some share in banishing that veneration which had been so long entertained for these celebrated personages.

15 *History of chemistry since the time of Paracelsus.*

From the time of Paracelsus, chemistry began every where to assume a new face. In our own country, Lord Verulam amused himself at his leisure hours with forming plans for promoting the sciences in general, especially those which related to the study of nature.

16 *The science studied by Lord Verulam;*

He soon found that chemistry might turn out one of the most useful and comprehensive branches of natural philosophy, and pointed out the means of its improvement. A number of experiments were proposed by him; but he observed, that the views of chemists were as yet only adapted to explain their particular operations on metals; and he observed, that, instead of the abstruse and barren philosophy of the times, it was necessary to make a very large collection of facts, and to compare them with each other very maturely and cautiously, in order to discover the common causes and circumstances of connection upon which they all depend. He did not, however, make any considerable discoveries, and his works are tedious and disagreeable to the reader.

17 *And by Mr Boyle.*

A superior genius to Lord Verulam was Mr Boyle, who was born the very day that the former died. His circumstances were opulent, his manners agreeable; he was endowed by nature with a goodness of heart; and his inclination led him entirely to the study of nature, which he was best pleased with cultivating in the way of experiment. He considered the weight, spring, and qualities of the air; and wrote on hydrostatics and other subjects; and was possessed of that happy penetration and ingenuity so well suited to the making of experiments in philosophy, which serves to deduce the most useful truths from the most simple and seemingly insignificant facts. As chemistry was his favourite science, he spared no pains to procure from chemists of greatest note the knowledge of curious experiments, and entertained a number of operators constantly about him. His discoveries are related in an easy style; and though rather copious, suited to the taste of the times in which he lived, and free from that absurd and mysterious air which formerly prevailed in chemical writings; nor does he betray a design of concealing any thing except some particulars which were communicated to him under the notion of secrecy, or the knowledge of which might do more harm than good. It is objected indeed, that he betrays a good deal of credulity with regard to facts which are given on the faith of others, and which may seem incredible; but this proceeded from his candour, and his being little disposed to suspect others. He showed the necessary connection between philosophy and the arts; and said, that by attending the shop of a workman, he learned more philosophy than he had done in the schools for a long time. Thus his writings showed an universal taste for the study of nature, which had now made some advances in the other parts of the world.

18 *Chemistry [illegible]*

Agricola is one of the first and best authors on the subject of metallurgy. Being born in a village in Misnia, a country abounding in mines and metallurgic works, he described them exactly and copiously. He was a physician, and cotemporary with Paracelsus, but of a character very different. His writings are clear and instructive, as those of Paracelsus are obscure and useless. Lazarus Erker, Schinder, Schlutter, Henkel, &c. have also written on metallurgy, and described the art of assaying metals. Anthony Neri, Dr Merret, and the famous Kunkel (who discovered the phosphorus of urine), have described very fully the arts of making glass, enamels, imitations of precious stones, &c.: but their writings, as well as those of succeeding chemists, are not free from the illusions of alchemy; so true it is, that an obstinate and inveterate malady never disappears at once, without leaving traces behind. In a short time, however, the alchemical phrensy was attacked by many powerful antagonists, who contributed to rescue the science of chemistry from an evil which at once disgraced it and retarded its progress. Among these, the most distinguished are Kircher a Jesuit, and Conringius a physician, who wrote with much success and reputation.

19 *Royal Society [illegible] London.*

About the year 1650 the Royal Society was formed by a number of gentlemen who were unwilling to engage in the civil wars; and being struck with the extensive views of Lord Verulam and Mr Boyle, contributed to the expence of costly experiments. This example appeared so noble, and the design so good, that it has been followed by all the civilized states of Europe, and has met with the protection of their respective sovereigns; and from these chemistry has received considerable improvements. In France, Geoffroy, Lemery, Reaumur, &c. came to be distinguish-

ed;

ed; and in Germany Margraaf, Pott, and others, have made a considerable figure in those societies. Kunckel, Beger, Stahl, and Hoffman, &c. have done great service to society, by introducing new arts, and the numerous improvements they have made.

10 Of the improvements made by different nations in chemistry. The chemists who have made a figure in Germany and France are more in number than those whom our island has produced. In France, the society was encouraged by the sovereign; and in it they have divested themselves of that mysterious air which was affected in former ages. In Germany, the richness of the country, and the great variety of mines, by turning the attention of chemists to the metals, have given that alchymistical air to their writings which we observe in them. The number of those who have applied themselves to chemistry is very small in England, owing to the great improvements made by Sir Isaac Newton in the sciences of astronomy and optics; which, by turning the general attention that way, has occasioned what may be called a neglect of chemistry. But if their number be inconsiderable, they are by no means inferior in merit and fame. The name of Boyle has always been held in the highest esteem, as well as that of Hales, for the analysis he has made of the air. Sir Isaac Newton alone has done more to the establishing a rational chemical theory than ever was done before. Of late, the taste for the study has become more general, and many useful books have appeared; so that it is to be hoped we shall soon excel in this branch of science, as we have done in all the rest.

Part I. THEORY of CHEMISTRY.

11 Perfect Theory, what. According to the definition we have given of this science, the theory of it ought to consist in a thorough knowledge of all the phenomena which result from every possible combination of its objects with one another, or from exposing them in all possible ways to those substances which chemists have found to be the most active in producing a change. So various, however, and so widely extended are the objects of chemistry (comprehending all terrestrial bodies whatever), that a knowledge of this kind is utterly unattainable by man. The utmost that can be done in this case is, to give some account of the phenomena which accompany the mixtures of particular substances, or the appearances they put on when exposed to heat; and these have been already so well ascertained, that they may now be laid down as rules, whereby we may, with a good deal of certainty, judge of the event of our experiments, even before they are made.

12 Objects of Chemistry, what. Here we must observe, that though the objects of chemistry are as various as there are different substances in the whole system of nature, yet they cannot all be examined with equal ease. Some of these substances act upon others with great violence; and the greater their activity, the more difficultly are they themselves subjected to a chemical examination. Thus, fire, which is the most active body in nature, is so little the subject of examination, that it hath hitherto baffled the ingenuity of the greatest philosophers to understand its composition. This substance, therefore, though it be the principal if not the only *agent* in chemistry, is not properly an *object* of it, because it cannot be made a subject of any chemical operation.

13 Supposition of elements the origin of alchemy. It hath been customary to consider all bodies as composed of certain permanent and unchangeable parts called *elements*; and that the end of chemistry was to resolve bodies into these elements, and to recompose them again by a proper mixture of the elements when so separated. Upon this supposition the alchemists went; who, supposing that all bodies were composed of salt, sulphur, and mercury, endeavoured to find out the proportions in which these existed in gold, and then to form that metal by combining them in a similar manner. Had they taken care to ascertain the real existence of their elements, and, by mixing them together, composed any one metal whatever, though but a grain of lead, the least valuable of them all; their pretensions would have been very rational and well founded; but as they never ascertained the existence of such elementary bodies, it is no wonder that their labours were never attended with success.

Another set of elements which were as generally received, and indeed continue to be so in some measure to this day, are fire, air, earth, and water.— 14 Mr Boyle's opinion.
This doctrine of elements was strenuously opposed by Mr Boyle; who endeavoured to prove, that fire was not an element *per se*, but generated merely from the motion of the particles of terrestrial bodies among one another; that air was generally produced from the substance of solid bodies; and that water, by a great number of distillations, was converted into earth. His arguments, however, concerning fire were not at all conclusive; nor does the expulsion of air from fixed bodies prove that any of their solid parts were employed in the composition of that air; as later discoveries have shown that air may be absorbed from the external atmosphere, and fixed in a great number of solid substances. His assertion concerning water deserves much consideration, and the experiment is well worth repeating; but it does not appear that he, or any other person, ought to have relied upon the experiment which was intended to prove this transmutation. The fact was this. Having designed to try the possibility of reducing water to earth by repeated distillations, he distilled an ounce of water three times over himself, and found a small quantity of earth always remaining. He then gave it to another, who distilled it 197 times. The amount of earth from the whole distillations was six drams, or $\frac{1}{8}$ths of the quantity of water employed; and this earth was fixed, white, and insoluble in water.— Here it is evident, that great suspicions must lie against the fidelity of the unknown operator, who no doubt would be wearied out with such a number of distillations. The affair might appear trivial to him; and as he would perhaps know to which side Mr Boyle's opinion inclined, he might favour it, by mixing some white earth with the water. Had the experiment been tried by Mr Boyle's own hand, his known character would have put the matter beyond a doubt.

The decomposition of water, however, in another way, by the combination of one part of it with the phlogistic, and another with the earthy part of a metal, is now well ascertained, and the experiments which led to the discovery are treated of under the articles Aerology and Water.

85 Existence of elements disputed.

Even the existence of earth as an element appears as dubious as that of the others; for it is certain that there is no species of earth whatever, from which we can produce two dissimilar bodies, by adding their other component parts.—Thus, the earth of alum has all the characters of *simplicity* which we can desire in any terrestrial substance. It is white, insipid, inodorous, and perfectly fixed in the fire; nevertheless, it seems to be only an element of that particular body called *alum*; for though alum is composed of a pure earth and vitriolic acid joined together, and Epsom salt and selenite are both composed of a pure earth combined with the same acid; yet by adding oil of vitriol to the earth of alum, in any possible way, we shall never be able to form either Epsom salt or selenite. In like manner, though all the imperfect metals are composed of inflammable matter joined with an earthy basis; yet by adding to earth of alum any proportion we please of inflammable matter, we shall never produce a metal; and what is still more mortifying, we can never make the earthy basis of one metallic substance produce any other metal than that which it originally composed.

86 Elements necessarily invisible.

A little consideration upon the subject of elements will convince us, not only that no such bodies have ever yet been discovered, but that they never will; and for this plain reason, that they must be in their own nature invisible.—The component parts of any substance may with propriety enough be called the elements of that substance, as long as we propose carrying the decomposition no farther; but these elements have not the least property resembling any substance which they compose. Thus, it is found that the compound salt called *sal ammoniac*, is formed by the union of an acid and an alkali: we may therefore properly enough call these two the elements of sal ammoniac; but, taken separately, they have not the least resemblance to the compound, which is formed out of them. Both the acid and alkali are by themselves so volatile as to be capable of dissipation into an invisible vapour by the heat of one's hand; whereas, when joined together, they are so fixed as almost to endure a red heat without going off. If, again, we were to seek for the elements of the acid and alkali, we must not expect to find them have any properties resembling either an acid or an alkali, but others quite different. Any common element of all bodies must therefore be a substance which has no property similar to any other in the whole system of nature, and consequently must be imperceptible.

87 Supposition of a fifth element, phlogiston.

To the above-mentioned four elements, viz. fire, air, earth, and water, a kind of *fifth* element has generally been added, but not usually distinguished by that name, though it has apparently an equal, if not a greater, right to the title of an *element* than any of the others. This substance is called the *phlogiston*, or inflammable principle; on which the ignition of all bodies depends. The existence of this element was first asserted by Stahl, and from him the opinion has been derived to other chemists; but of late a new doctrine was broached by M. Lavoisier, who denies the existence of phlogiston altogether. Though none of these substances therefore are properly the objects of chemistry, yet as they have so much ingrossed the attention of modern chemists, we shall here give an account of the most remarkable theories that have appeared concerning them.

Of the Elements of Fire.

Sect. I. *Of the Element of Fire.*

88 Two general theories of heat.

The opinions concerning the element of fire may be divided into two general classes; the one considering it as an effect, the other as a cause. The former is maintained by Lord Bacon, Mr Boyle, and Sir Isaac Newton; whose respectable names for a long time gave such a sanction to this theory, that it was generally looked upon as an established truth. Some learned men, however, among whom was the great Dr Boerhaave, always dissented, and insisted that fire was a fluid universally diffused, and equally present in the frozen regions of Nova Zembla as in a glass-house furnace, only that in the latter its motion made it conspicuous; and by setting it in motion in the coldest parts of the world, its previous existence there would be equally demonstrable as in the furnace above-mentioned.

89 Lord Bacon's definition of heat.

Lord Bacon defines heat, which he uses as a synonymous term with fire, to be an expansive undulatory motion in the particles of a body, whereby they tend with some rapidity towards the circumference, and also a little upwards. Hence, if in any natural body you can excite a motion whereby it shall expand or dilate itself, and can repress and direct this motion upon itself in such a manner that the motion shall not proceed uniformly, but obtain in some parts and be checked in others, you will generate heat or fire.

90 Mr Boyle's opinion.

The same opinion is supported by Mr Boyle in the following manner: "The production of heat discovers nothing, either in the agent or patient, but motion, and its natural effects. When a smith briskly hammers a small piece of iron, the metal thereby becomes exceedingly hot; yet there is nothing to make it so, except the motion of the hammer impressing a vehement and variously determined agitation on the small parts of the iron; which, being a cold body before, grows hot by that superinduced motion of its small parts: first, in a more loose acceptation of the word, with regard to some other bodies, in comparison of which it was cold before; then sensibly hot, because the motion in the parts of the iron is greater than that in the parts of our fingers; at the same time that the hammer and anvil, by which the percussion is communicated, may, on account of their magnitude, remain cold. It is not necessary, therefore, that a body should itself be hot in order to communicate heat to another."

91 Sentiments of Sir Isaac Newton.

The arguments made use of by Sir Isaac Newton are not intended positively to establish any kind of theory relating to fire, but are to be found in a conjecture, published at the end of his Treatise on Optics, concerning the nature of the sun and stars. "Large bodies (he observes) preserve their heat the longest, their parts heating one another; and why may not great, dense, and fixed bodies, when heated beyond a certain degree, emit light so copiously, as, by the emission and reaction of it, and the reflections and refractions within the pores, to grow continually hotter, till they arrive at such a period of heat as is that of the sun? Their

parts

Of the Element of Fire.

parts may be further preserved from flying away, not only by their fixity, but by the vast weight and density of the atmosphere incumbent on them, strongly compressing them, and condensing the vapours exhaled from them. Thus we see, that warm water, in an exhausted receiver, shall boil as vehemently as the hottest water exposed to the air; the weight of the incumbent atmosphere in this latter case keeping down the vapours, and hindering the ebullition till it has received its utmost degree of heat. Thus also a mixture of tin and lead, put on a red hot iron *in vacuo*, emits a fume and flame; but the same mixture in the open air, by reason of the incumbent atmosphere, does not emit the least sensible flame." In consequence of these experiments, Sir Isaac conjectures, that there is no essential distinction betwixt fire and gross bodies; but that they may be converted into one another. "Fire (he says) is a body heated so hot as to emit light copiously; for what (says he) is a red hot iron but fire?"

32 Fire now generally allowed to be an element *per se*.

The hypotheses of these great men produced long and violent disputes, which were never decisively settled: The discoveries in electricity, however, furnished such additional strength to the followers of Dr Boerhaave, that fire is now believed to be an element and fluid distinct from all others, by at least as many as espouse the contrary system; but the question is not decided, Whether the fire itself is to be considered as the agent? or, Whether its action is to be derived from the principles of attraction and repulsion, the natural agents supposed to influence other material substances?

33 Two other theories instituted.

This has produced two other systems of a kind of mixed nature, in which heat or fire is considered as a substance distinct from all others, but which acts in other bodies according to its *quantity*. These systems have been promulgated by Dr Black of Edinburgh and Dr Irvine of Glasgow.

34 In what they differ from the former.

They differ from the opinions of Mr Boyle, Lord Bacon, and Sir Isaac Newton, in supposing heat to be a fluid distinct from all other material substances; and they also differ from the hypothesis of Dr Boerhaave, Lemery, and others, in supposing different terrestrial substances to be hot according to the *quantity* of fluid contained, and not according to the force with which it moves in them.

35 General account of Dr Black's and Dr Irvine's theory.

Dr Black is of opinion that *heat*, which he seems to make synonymous with fire, exists in two different states; in one of which it affects our senses and the thermometer, in the other it does not. The former therefore he calls *sensible* heat, the latter *latent* heat. On these principles he gives the only satisfactory explanation of the phenomena of evaporation and fluidity that has yet appeared, as shall afterwards be more fully explained. At present we shall only observe, that, according to the theory of Dr Black, heat or fire itself seems to be the agent; but, according to that of Dr Irvine, as far as we can gather it from the treatises of Dr Crawford and others, the principles of attraction and repulsion are the agents by which heat, as well as other bodies, is influenced. Thus, on the principles of Dr Black, we say, that water is converted into vapour by a quantity of heat entering into it in a *latent* state, and thereby rendering it specifically lighter than the atmosphere: according to the principles of Dr Irvine, we say, that water is converted into vapour by having its capacity for attracting heat from the atmosphere increased. So that, according to the former, the absorption of heat is the *cause*; according to the latter, the *effect*, of its conversion into vapour.

36 Dr Irvine's theory explained by Dr Crawford.

Dr Crawford, in his Treatise on Heat, published in 1788, informs us, that *heat*, in the philosophical sense of the word, has been used to express what is frequently called the *element of fire*, in the abstract, without regard to the peculiar effects which it may produce in relation to other bodies.

37 Absolute heat defined.

This, with Dr Irvine, he calls *absolute* heat; and the external cause, as having a relation to the effects it produces, he calls *relative* heat. "From this view of the matter (says he), it appears, that *absolute heat* expresses, in the abstract, that *power* or *element* which, when it is present to a *certain* degree, excites in all animals the sensation of heat;

38 Relative heat.

and *relative* heat expresses the same power, considered as having a relation to the effects by which it is known and measured.

39 How divided.

"The effects by which heat is known and measured are three; and therefore relative heat may admit of three subdivisions. 1. This principle is known by the peculiar sensations which it excites in animals. Considered as exciting those sensations, it is called *sensible* heat. 2. It is known by the effect which it produces upon an instrument that has been employed to measure it, termed a *thermometer*. This is called the *temperature of heat in bodies*. 3. It has been found by experiment, that in bodies of different kinds the quantities of absolute heat may be unequal, though the temperatures and weights be the same. When the principle of heat is considered relatively to the whole quantity of it contained in bodies of different kinds, but which have

40 Comparative heat defined.

equal weights and temperatures, I shall term it *comparative heat*. If, for example, the temperatures and weights being the same, the whole quantity of heat in water be four times as great as that of antimony, the comparative heats of these substances are said to be as four to one."

41 Experiments by which Dr Black was led to the discovery of latent heat.

In order to have a proper conception of what is meant by a difference in absolute heat, when the temperatures are the same, it will be necessary to relate some experiments, by which Dr Black was first led to the discovery of latent heat. He observes, that when two equal masses of the same matter, heated to different degrees, are mixed together, the heat of the mixture ought to be an arithmetical mean betwixt the two extremes. This, however, only takes place on mixing hot and cold water together; but if instead of cold water we take ice, the case is remarkably different.

42 A quantity of heat lost in the melting of ice.

Here the temperature of the mixture is much below the arithmetical mean, and a quantity of heat is apparently lost. Now we know that the temperature of ice newly frozen is generally 32 degrees of Fahrenheit; supposing therefore the temperature of the water which dissolves it to be 120°, the arithmetical mean is 71; but if the mixture indicates a temperature only of 60°, then we must suppose that the ice contained 11° of heat less than was indicated by the thermometer; and consequently, that water at 32° contains 11° more of absolute heat than ice at 32°.

43 Great quantity of heat produced by the condensation of vapour.

The same thing is made still more evident from the condensation of vapour. The fluid of water is not capable of sustaining a great degree of heat; and 212° of Fahrenheit is the utmost it can be made to bear, without an extraordinary degree of pressure, as in Papin's pin's digester, or the admixture of saline substances: the temperature of the steam emitted by it therefore never can exceed 212°, except in the cases just mentioned; and it is often capable of bearing a great degree of cold without being condensed. When the condensation takes place at last, however, a very considerable degree of heat is always produced; and Dr Black has shown, that, in the condensation of steam by the refrigeratory of a common still, as much heat is communicated to the water in the refrigeratory as would be sufficient to make the water which comes over as hot as red hot-iron, were it all to exist in a sensible state.

44 Dr Black's method of calculating it.

His method of making the calculation is very easy. For, supposing the refrigeratory to contain 100 pounds of water, and that one pound has been distilled; if the water in the refrigeratory has received 10 degrees of heat, we know that the distilled pound has parted with 1000. If in passing through the worm of the refrigeratory, it has been reduced to the temperature of 50° of Fahrenheit, having been at 212° when it entered it, then it has lost only 162° of sensible heat; all the rest communicated to the water of the refrigeratory amounting to more than 800°, having been contained in a latent state, and such as could not then affect the thermometer.

45 Mr Watt's experiment on the distillation of water in vacuo.

This experiment was tried by Mr Watt in a manner still more striking, by a distillation of water *in vacuo*. Thus the steam, freed from the pressure of the atmosphere, could not conceive such a degree of sensible heat as in the common method of distilling. It came over therefore with a very gentle warmth, scarce more than what the hand could bear; nevertheless it had absorbed as much heat as though the distillation had been performed in the common way; for the refrigeratory had 1000 degrees of heat communicated to it.

46 Difference of absolute heat in different fluids.

The difference of absolute heat is likewise perceptible betwixt any two bodies of different density, water and mercury for instance; and in comparing these, it will always be found that the thinnest fluids contain the greatest quantity of absolute heat; as water more than mercury, spirit of wine more than water, ether more than spirit of wine, and air more than any of them.

47 Thinnest fluids contain the greatest quantity of heat.

Dr Black having brought equal bulks of mercury and water, the former to a temperature of 50 degrees higher than the latter, found that, on mixture, there was a gain of only 20 degrees above the original; but on reversing the experiment, and heating the water 50 degrees above the mercury, there was a gain of 30 degrees on the whole.

48 Great difference betwixt the calculations of Drs Cleghorn and Crawford.

"Hence (says Dr Cleghorn in his thesis *de Igne*) it appears, that the quantity of heat in water is to that in mercury, when both are of equal temperatures, as 3 to 2." Dr Crawford, however, tells us, that "the same quantity of heat which raises a pound of water one degree, will raise a pound of mercury 28 degrees; whence it follows, that the comparative heat of water is to that of mercury as 28 to 1; and consequently, the alterations which are produced in the temperatures of bodies by given quantities of absolute heat, may properly be applied as a measure of their comparative heats; the alterations of temperature and the comparative heats being reciprocally proportional to one another.

49 Crawford's account of sensible heat.

"Sensible heat (continues Dr Crawford) depends partly on the state of the temperature, and partly on that of the organs of feeling; and therefore if a variation be produced in the latter, the sensible heat will be different, though the temperature continue the same. Thus water at the temperature of 62° of Fahrenheit appears cold to a warm hand immersed in it; but on the contrary, that fluid will appear warm if a hand be applied to it which has a lower degree of heat than 62°. For this reason, the thermometer is a much more accurate measure of heat than the senses of animals. As long, however, as the organs remain unchanged, the sensible heat is in proportion to the temperature; and therefore those terms have generally been considered as synonymous.

50 Dr Reid's observation concerning temperatures.

On this subject Dr Reid observes, that until the ratio between one temperature and another be ascertained by experiment and induction, we ought to consider temperature as a measure which admits of degrees, but not of ratios; and consequently ought not to conclude, that the temperature of one body is double or triple to that of another, unless the ratio of different temperatures were determined. Nor ought we to use the expressions of a *double* or *triple* temperature, these being expressions which convey no distinct meaning until the ratio of different temperatures be determined."

51 Difference betwixt the calculations of Drs Crawford and Black.

In making experiments on the comparative quantities of heat in different bodies, our author chooses rather to use equal *weights* than equal *bulks* of the substances to be compared. Thus he found the comparative heat of water to be to that of mercury as 28 to 1 by weight, and 2 to 1 by bulk; which differs very considerably from the conclusion of Dr Black, who makes it only as 3 to 2, as has been already mentioned.

52 Capacities for containing heat explained.

From the differences observed in the quantities of absolute heat contained in different bodies, our author concluded, that "there must be certain essential differences in the nature of bodies; in consequence of which, *some* have the power of collecting and retaining that element in greater quantity than *others*." These different powers he calls the *capacities* for containing heat. Thus, if we find by experiment that a pound of water contains four times as much absolute heat as diaphoretic antimony, when at the same temperature, the capacity of water for containing heat is said to be to that of antimony as 4 to 1.

53 How the capacity, temperature, and absolute heat, are to be distinguished.

"The temperature, the capacity for containing heat, and the absolute heat contained, may be distinguished from each other in the following manner:

"The capacity for containing heat, and the absolute heat contained, are distinguished as a force distinct from the subject upon which it operates. When we speak of the capacity, we mean a power inherent in the heated body; when we speak of the absolute heat, we mean an unknown principle which is retained in the body by the operation of this power; and when we speak of the temperature, we consider the unknown principle as producing certain effects upon the thermometer.

"The capacity for containing heat may continue unchanged, while the absolute heat is varied without end. If a pound of ice, for example, be supposed to retain its solid form, the quantity of its absolute heat will be altered by every increase or diminution of its sensible heat: but as long as its form continues the same, its capacity for receiving heat is not affected by

an

an alteration of temperature, and would remain unchanged though the body were wholly deprived of its heat."

54 Crawford's opinion concerning heat in the abstract.

In the course of his work, Dr Crawford observes, that "he has not entered into the inquiry which has been so much agitated among the English, the French, and the German philosophers, Whether heat be a *substance* or a *quality*? In some places indeed he has used expressions which seem to favour the former opinion; but his sole motive for adopting these was, because the language seemed to be more simple and natural, and more consonant to the facts which had been established by experiment. At the same time, he is persuaded that it would be a very difficult matter to reconcile many of the phenomena with the supposition that heat is a *quality*. It is not easy to conceive, upon this hypothesis, how heat can be absorbed in the processes of fusion, evaporation, combustion; how the quantity of heat in the air can be diminished, and that in the blood increased, by respiration, though no sensible heat or cold be produced.

"Whereas, if we adopt the opinion that heat is a distinct substance, or an element *sui generis*, the phenomena will be found to admit of a simple and obvious interpretation.

55 Fire contained in bodies partly by its attraction to them, and partly the pressure of the external fluid.

"Fire will be considered as a principle; which is distributed in various proportions throughout the different kingdoms of nature. The mode of its union with bodies will resemble that particular species of union, wherein the elements are combined by the joint forces of pressure and attraction. Of this kind is the combination of fixed air and water; for fixed air is retained in water partly by its attraction for that fluid, and partly by the pressure of the external air; and if either of these forces be diminished, a portion of the fixed air escapes. In like manner, it may be conceived that elementary fire is retained in bodies, partly by its attraction to these bodies, and partly by the action of the surrounding heat; and in that case a portion of it will be disengaged, either by diminishing the attractive force, or by lessening the temperature of the circumambient medium. If, however, fire be a substance which is subject to the laws of attraction, the mode of its union with bodies seems to be different from that which takes place in chemical combination: for, in chemical combination, the elements acquire new properties, and either wholly or in part lose those by which they were formerly characterised. But we have no sufficient evidence for believing that fire, in consequence of its union with bodies, does, in any instance, lose its distinguishing properties."

56 Dr Berkenhout's opinion concerning the nature of heat.

Dr Berkenhout, in his First Lines of the Theory and Practice of Philosophical Chemistry, informs us, that "heat, or the *matter of heat*, is by Scheele and Bergman substituted for fire, which they believe to be the action of heat when increased to a certain degree. The first of these celebrated chemists believed this *matter of heat* to be a compound of phlogiston and pure air. He was certainly mistaken. It seems more philosophical to consider heat as an *effect*, of which fire is the sole cause.

57 His division of fire into fixed and volatile.

"Heat I consider not as a distinct substance, but as an effect of fire, fixed or volatile; in both which states fire seems to exist in all bodies, solid and fluid. Fixed fire I believe to be a constituent part of all bodies, and their specific heat to depend on the quantity of fixed fire in each. This fixed, this latent fire, cannot be separated from the other constituent parts of bodies but by their decomposition: it then becomes volatile and incorrcible. If this hypothesis be true, fire exists, in all natural bodies that contain phlogiston, in three different states: 1. In that volatile state in which it perpetually fluctuates between one body and another. 2. Combined with an acid, probably in the form of fixed inflammable air or phlogiston. 3. Uncombined and fixed, as a constituent principle, determining the specific heat of bodies.

58 Pure or volatile fire defined.

"Pure (or volatile) fire is distinguished by the following properties. 1. It is essentially fluid, invisible, and without weight. 2. It is the immediate cause of all fluidity. 3. It penetrates and pervades all bodies on the surface of the earth, and as far beneath the surface as hath hitherto been explored. Water hath never been found in a congealed state in the deepest mines. 4. It has a constant tendency to diffuse itself equally through all bodies, howsoever different in point of density. A marble slab, a plate of iron, a decanter of water, and a lady's muff, at the same distance from the fire, and other external circumstances, being equal, possess an equal degree of heat, which is precisely that of the atmosphere in which they stand. 5. It is perpetually in motion from one body to another, and from different parts of the same body, because external circumstances are continually varying. 6. In fluctuating from one body to another, it produces a constant vibration of their constituent parts; for all bodies expand and contract in proportion to the quantity of fire they contain. 7. Accumulated beyond a certain quantity, it effects the dissolution of bodies, by forcing their constituent parts beyond the sphere of mutual attraction, called the *attraction of cohesion*, which is the cause of solidity. Hence the sovereign agency of fire in chemical operations."

59 Dr Crawford's definition of fire.

Dr Crawford, besides the opinions already quoted, tells us, that fire, in the vulgar acceptation of the word, expresses a certain degree of heat accompanied with light; and is particularly applied to that heat and light which are produced by the inflammation of combustible bodies. But as heat, when accumulated in a sufficient quantity, is constantly accompanied with light; or, in other words, as fire is always produced by the increase of heat, philosophers have generally considered these phenomena as proceeding from the same cause: and have therefore used the word *fire* to express that unknown principle, which, when it is present to a certain degree, excites the sensation of heat alone; but, when accumulated to a greater degree, renders itself obvious both to the sight and touch, or produces heat accompanied with light. In this sense, the element of fire signifies the same thing with *absolute heat*.

Having premised these general definitions and remarks, he gives the properties of heat in the following words:

60 Heat has a tendency to diffuse itself equally over bodies.

"I. Heat has a constant tendency to diffuse itself over all bodies till they are brought to the same temperature. Thus it is found by the thermometer, that if two bodies of different temperatures are mixed together, or placed contiguous, the heat passes from the one to the other till their temperatures become equal; and

and that all inanimate bodies, when heated and placed in a cold medium, continually lose heat, till in process of time they are brought to the state of the surrounding medium.

"From this property of heat it follows, that the various classes of bodies throughout the earth, if they were not acted upon by external causes, would at length arrive at a common temperature when the heat would become quiescent; in like manner as the waters of the ocean, if not prevented by the winds and by the attractions of the sun and moon, would come to an equilibrium, and would remain in a state of rest. But as causes continually occur in nature to disturb the balance of heat as well as that of the waters of the ocean, those elements are kept in a constant fluctuation.

61 It is contained in considerable quantity in all bodies.

"II. Heat is contained in considerable quantities in all bodies when at the common temperature of the atmosphere.

62 Great degree of cold at Glasgow.

"From the interesting experiments which were made on cold by Mr Wilson, we learn, that at Glasgow, in the winter of the year 1780, the thermometer on the surface of snow sunk 25 degrees below the beginning of Fahrenheit's scale.

63 In Siberia, and at Hudson's bay.

"We are told by Dr Pallas, that in the deserts of Siberia, during a very intense frost, the mercury was found congealed in thermometers exposed to the atmosphere, and a quantity of that fluid in an open bowl placed in a similar situation, at the same time became solid. The decisive experiments of Mr Hutchins at Hudson's Bay prove, that the freezing point of mercury is very nearly 40° below the zero (or 0°) of Fahrenheit. From which it follows, that at the time of Dr Pallas's observation, the atmosphere in Siberia must have been cooled to minus 40. By a paper lately transmitted to the Royal Society we are informed, that the spirit-of-wine thermometer in the open air at Hudson Bay fell to — 42 in the winter of 1785; and from the same communication we learn, that by a mixture of snow and vitriolic acid, the heat was so much diminished, that the spirit of wine sunk to — 80, which is 112 below the freezing point of water.

64 Quantity of heat limited in all bodies.

"Hence it is manifest, that heat is contained in considerable quantities in all bodies when at the common temperature of the atmosphere. It is plain, however, that the quantity inherent in each individual body is limited. This, I think, must be admitted, whatever be the hypothesis which we adopt concerning the nature of heat; whether we conceive it to be a force or power belonging to bodies, or an elementary principle contained in them. For those who consider heat as an element, will not suppose that an unlimited quantity of it can be contained in a finite body; and if heat be considered as a force or power, the supposition that finite bodies are actuated by forces or powers which are infinite is equally inadmissible.

65 Bodies universally expanded by heat.

"To place this in another light, we know that bodies are universally expanded by heat, excepting in a very few instances, which do not afford a just objection to the general fact; because, in those instances, by the action of heat a fluid is extricated that previously separated the particles from each other. Since, therefore, heat is found to expand bodies in the temperatures which fall within the reach of our observation, we may conclude that the same thing takes place in all temperatures."

Our author, by a set of very accurate and laborious experiments, determines that the expansions in mercury and some other fluid, are proportionable to the quantities of heat applied; "from which (says he) it is manifest, that the quantities of heat in bodies are limited, because an infinite heat would produce an infinite expansion.

66 Expansion of mercury, &c. proportionable to the degrees of heat.

"It is manifest, that the number of degrees of sensible heat, as measured by the thermometer, and estimated from the beginning of the scale, must be the same in all bodies which have a common temperature; for by the first general fact it is proved, that heat has a constant tendency to diffuse itself uniformly over bodies till their temperatures become equal. From which it may be inferred, that if a quantity of heat were added to bodies absolutely cold, the same uniform diffusion would take place; and that if a thermometer, altogether deprived of its heat, were applied to such bodies, it would be equally expanded by them, the whole of the sensible heat which they had acquired being indicated by that expansion.

67 Homogeneous bodies of the same temperature, contain quantities of heat proportionable to those of their matter.

"III. If the parts of the same homogeneous substance have a common temperature, the quantity of absolute heat will be proportional to the bulk or quantity of matter. Thus the quantity of absolute heat in two pounds of water is double that which is contained in one pound when at the same temperature.

"IV. The dilatations and contractions of the fluid in the mercurial thermometer are nearly proportional to the quantities of absolute heat which are communicated to the same homogeneous bodies, or separated from them, so long as they retain the same form. Thus the quantity of heat required to raise a body four degrees in temperature by the mercurial thermometer, is nearly double that which is required to raise it two degrees, four times that required to raise it one degree, and so in proportion."

Thus we find, that Dr Black, Dr Irvine, Dr Crawford, and Dr Berkenhout, agree in speaking of fire or heat as a fluid substance distinct from all other bodies.

68 Mr Kirwan's opinion concerning fire.

Mr Kirwan, in his Treatise of Phlogiston, agrees in the same opinion. "Some (says he) have thought, that I should have included the matter of heat, or elementary fire, in the definition of inflammable air; but as fire is contained in all corporeal substances, to mention it is perfectly needless, except where bodies differ from each other in the quantity of it they contain."

69 Mr Cavendish's opinion that it is not a distinct substance.

On the other hand, Mr Cavendish, Phil. Transf. lxxiv. p. 141. tells us, that "he thinks it more likely that there is no such thing as elementary heat:" but, as he gives no reason for this opinion, it seems probable that the greater part of philosophers either positively believe that heat is an elementary fluid distinct from all others, or find themselves obliged to adopt a language which necessarily implies it.

70 Difficulty in defining the phrase quantity of heat.

The only difficulty which now remains therefore is, to affix a proper idea to the phrase *quantity of heat*, which we find universally made use of, without any thing to determine our opinions concerning it.

71 This phrase cannot be used in the common acceptation of the word with regard to fire.

That we cannot speak of a *quantity* of fire or heat in the same sense as we speak of a quantity of water or any other fluid is evident, because we can take away the quantity of water which any substance contains, but cannot do so with heat. Nay, in many cases we are sure, that a substance very cold to the touch does

Of the Element of Fire.

yet contain a very considerable quantity of heat. The vapour of water, for instance, may be made much colder than the usual temperature of the atmosphere without being condensed, when at the same time we are certain that it contains a great quantity of heat; and the same may be said of water, which, in the act of freezing, throws out a great quantity of heat without becoming colder; and in the act of melting absorbs as much without becoming warmer. It is not therefore by the mere presence or absence of this fluid that we can determine the real quantity of this fluid; nor does it appear that the word *quantity* can be at all accurately applied to the element itself, because we have no method of measuring it.

72 Dr Cleghorn's opinion.

Dr Cleghorn, in his inaugural dissertation *De Igne*, throws some light on this subject, by observing, that "the thermometer shows only the quantity of heat *going out* of a body, not that which is really contained in it:" and he also insists, that "we can neither assent to the opinion of Dr Boerhaave, who supposed that heat was distributed among bodies in proportion to their bulks; nor to the hypothesis of others, who imagined that they were heated in proportion to their densities." But in what proportion, then, are they heated; or how are we to measure the *quantity* which they really contain, seeing the thermometer informs us only of what they part with?

73 The latent heat of bodies cannot be considered.

As this point is by no means ascertained, we cannot form a direct idea concerning the absolute quantity of heat contained in any body; and therefore when we speak of quantities of this fluid, we must in fact, if we mean any thing, think of the sensible quantity flowing out of them; and though we should suppose the whole of this sensible heat to be removed, it would still be impossible for us to know how much remained in a latent state, and could not be dissipated. This difficulty will still appear the greater, if with Dr Cleghorn and others we suppose the fluid of heat to be subject to the laws of attraction and repulsion.

74 Dr Cleghorn's hypothesis concerning fire.

This gentleman supposes, that the particles of heat (like the particles of electric fluid according to the Franklinian hypothesis) are repulsive of one another, but attracted by all other substances. "If any body (says he), heated beyond the common temperature of the air, is exposed to it, the heat flows out from it into the atmosphere, and diffuses itself equally all around till the air becomes of the same temperature with itself. The same happens to bodies suspended *in vacuo*. Hence it is justly concluded, that there exists between the particles of heat a repulsive power, by which they mutually recede from each other. Notwithstanding this repulsive power, however, the quantities of heat contained in different substances, even of the same temperature, are found to be altogether different; and from Dr Black's experiments it now appears, that the quantity of heat is scarce ever the same in any two different bodies; and hence we may conclude, that terrestrial bodies have a power of attracting heat, and that this power is different in different substances.—From these principles it evidently follows, that heat is distributed among bodies directly in proportion to their attracting powers, and inversely according to the repulsive power between the particles of heat themselves.

75 Equilibrium of heat defined.

Such is the distribution of heat among bodies in the neighbourhood of each other, and which is called the *equilibrium of heat*, because the thermometer shows no difference of temperature among them. For seeing the heat is distributed according to the attracting power of each, the thermometer having also a proper attraction of its own, can show no difference in the attracting power of each; for which reason all bodies in the neighbourhood of each other are soon reduced to the same temperature."

76 The quantity of heat cannot be determined by this hypothesis.

If we assent to Dr Cleghorn's hypothesis, the quantity of heat contained in any substance depends, in the first place, on the attracting power of that substance, which is altogether unknown; and, in the second place, on the repulsive powers of the particles of heat themselves, which are equally unknown. To determine the *quantity*, therefore, must be impossible. Neither will the mixture of two different fluids, as in Dr Black's experiments, assist us in the least; for though water, heated more than mercury, communicates a greater heat to that fluid than the latter does to water; this only shows that water more readily parts with some part of the heat it contains than mercury does, but has not the least tendency to discover the quantity contained in either.

77 Dr Crawford's method of determining the proportional quantities of heat.

Dr Crawford, as we have already seen, calls the *degree*, or, if we may vary the phrase, the *quantity of power or element (fluid*, if we may substitute a synonymous word) existing or present in any body, its *absolute heat*; and lays down a rule for determining the proportional quantities of heat in different bodies. "It will appear (says he) from the experiments afterwards recited, that if a pound of water and a pound of diaphoretic antimony have a common temperature, the quantity of absolute heat contained in the former is nearly four times that contained in the latter." —The manner in which he illustrates this is as follows.

"If four pounds of diaphoretic antimony at 20 be mixed with one pound of ice at 32, the temperature will be nearly 26: the ice will be cooled six degrees, and the antimony heated six. If we reverse the experiment, the effect will be the same. That is, if we take six degrees of heat from four pounds of antimony, and add it to a pound of ice, the latter will be heated six degrees. The same quantity of heat, therefore, which raises a pound of ice six degrees, will raise four pounds of antimony six degrees.

"If this experiment be made at different temperatures, we shall have a similar result. If, for example, the antimony at 15, or at any given degree below the freezing point, be mixed with the ice at 32, the heat of the mixture will be the arithmetical mean between that of the warmer and colder substance. And since the capacities of bodies are permanent as long as they retain the same form, we infer, that the result would be the same if the antimony were deprived of all its heat, and were mixed with the ice at 32. But it is evident, that in this case the ice would communicate to the antimony the half of its absolute heat. For if 200 below frost be conceived to be the point of total privation, the antimony will be wholly deprived of its heat when cooled to 200 degrees below 32, and the heat contained in the ice when at 32 will be 200 degrees. If we now suppose them to be mixed together, the temperature of the mixture will be half the excess of the hotter above the colder, or the ice will

be

Of the Element of Fire.

be cooled 100 degrees and the antimony heated 100. The one half of the heat, therefore, which was contained in the ice previous to the mixture will be communicated to the antimony; from which it is manifest, that after the mixture the ice and antimony must contain equal quantities of absolute heat.

"To place this in another light, it has been proved, that the same quantity of heat which raises a pound of ice six degrees will raise four pounds of antimony six degrees. And as the capacities of bodies, while they retain the same form, are not altered by a change of temperature; it follows, that the same quantity of heat which raises the ice 100 degrees, or any given number of degrees, will raise the antimony an equal number of degrees.

"A pound of ice, therefore, and four pounds of antimony, when at the same temperature, contain equal quantities of absolute heat. But it appears from the third general fact (n° 67.), that four pounds of antimony contain four times as much absolute heat as one pound of antimony; and hence the quantity of absolute heat in a pound of ice is to that in a pound of antimony as four to one."

78 His method insufficient.

From this quotation it is evident, that, notwithstanding all the distinctions which Dr Crawford has laid down betwixt absolute heat and temperature, it is only the *quantity* of the latter that can be measured; and all that we can say concerning the matter is, that when certain bodies are mixed together, some of them part with a greater quantity of heat than others; but how much they contain must remain for ever unknown, unless we can fall on some method of measuring the quantity of heat as we do that of any other fluid.

79 Nicholson's account of the theories of heat.

Mr Nicolson, who has collected the principal opinions on the subject of heat, seems undetermined whether to believe the doctrine of Boyle or of Boerhaave on the subject. "There are two opinions (says he) concerning heat. According to one opinion, heat consists in a vibratory motion of the parts of bodies among each other, whose greater or less intensity occasions the increase or diminution of temperature. According to the other opinion, heat is a subtile fluid that easily pervades the pores of all bodies, causing them to expand by means of its elasticity or otherwise. Each of these opinions is attended with its peculiar difficulties. The phenomena of heat may be accounted for by either of them, provided certain suppositions be allowed to each respectively; but the want of proof of the truth of such suppositions renders it very difficult, if not impossible, to decide as yet whether heat consists merely in motion or in some peculiar matter. The word *quantity*, applied to heat, will therefore denote either motion or matter, according to the opinion made use of, and may be used indefinitely without determining which.

80 Advantages of the doctrine that heat is caused by vibration.

"The chief advantage which the opinion that heat is caused by mere vibration possesses, is its great simplicity. It is highly probable, that all heated bodies have an intestine motion, or vibration of their parts; and it is certain that percussion, friction, and other methods of agitating the minute parts of bodies, will likewise increase their temperature. Why, then, it is demanded, should we multiply causes, by supposing the existence of an unknown fluid, when the mere vibration of parts which is known to obtain may be applied to explain the phenomena?"

81 Answer to Mr Nicholson's argument.

To this the reply is obvious, that the vibration of parts is an *effect*; for matter will not begin to move of itself: and if it is an effect, we must suppose a cause for it; which, though we should not call it a fluid, would be equally unknown and inexplicable with that whose existence is asserted by those who maintain that fire is a fluid *per se*. Dr Cleghorn, however, in the dissertation already quoted, asserts, that "heat is occasioned by a certain fluid, and not by motion alone, as some eminent writers have imagined; because, 1. Those who have adopted the hypothesis of motion could never even prove the existence of that motion for which they contended; and though it should be granted, the phenomena could not be explained by it. 2. If heat depended on motion, it would instantaneously pass through an elastic body; but we see that heat passes through bodies slowly like a fluid. 3. If heat depended on vibration, it ought to be communicated from a given vibration in proportion to the quantity of matter; which is found not to hold true in fact. On the other hand, there are numberless arguments in favour of the opinion that heat proceeds from elementary fire. 1. Mr Locke hath observed, that when we perceive a number of qualities always existing together, we may gather from thence that there really is some substance which produces these qualities. 2 The hypothesis of elementary fire is simple and agreeable to the phenomena. 3. From some experiments made by Sir Isaac Newton, it appears, that bodies acquire heat and cold *in vacuo*, until they become of the same temperature with the atmosphere; so that heat exists in the absence of all other matter, and is therefore a substance by itself."

82 Dr Cleghorn's proof that heat is occasioned by a fluid.

83 Difficulties concerning the nature and properties of fire.

But though these and other arguments seem clearly to establish the point that fire or heat is a distinct fluid, we are still involved in very great difficulties concerning its nature and properties. If it be supposed a fluid, it is impossible to assign any limits to its extent; and we must of necessity likewise suppose that it pervades the whole creation, and consequently constitutes an absolute plenum, contrary to a fundamental principle of the received system of natural philosophy. But if this is the case, it is vain to talk of its being absorbed, accumulated, collected, or attracted by different bodies, since it is already present in all points of space; and we can conceive of terrestrial bodies no otherwise than as sponges thrown into the ocean, each of which will be as full of fluid as it can hold. The different capacities will then be similar to the differences between bits of wood, sponge, porous stones, &c. for containing water; all of which depend entirely on the structure of the bodies themselves, and which, unless we could separate the water by pressure, or by evaporation, would be for ever unknown. Supposing it were impossible to collect this water in the manner we speak of, we could only judge of the quantity they contained by the degree to which they swelled by being immersed in it. It is easy to see, however, that such a method of judging would be very inadequate to the purpose, as substances might contain internal cavities or pores in which water could lodge without augmenting the external bulk. This would suggest another method of judging of the quantity, namely, the specific gravity;

Elements of Fire.

vity; and we might reasonably suppose, that substances of the greatest specific gravity would contain the smallest quantity of water, though still we could by no means determine what quantity they did contain, unless we could lay hold of the element itself.

This seems to be very much the case with elementary fire, if we suppose it to be a fluid *per se*. We judge of its presence by the degree of expansion which one heated body communicates to another; but this is only similar to the calculation of the quantity of moisture a sponge or any other body contains, by what is communicated to wood when it comes into contact with it; which never could be supposed to carry the least pretensions to accuracy, though we should ascertain it with all imaginable exactness. It is likewise probable that the most dense bodies contain the smallest quantity of fire, as they generally communicate less when heated to an equal temperature than those which are more rare, though we are far from having any perfect knowledge in this respect.

84 Difficulty arising from the supposition that heat diffuses itself equally.

But the greatest difficulty of all will be, on the supposition that heat is a fluid, and an omnipresent one (which it must be, or there would be some places where bodies could not be heated), to answer the question, Why are not all bodies of an equal temperature, excepting only the differences arising from their specific densities, which render some capable of containing a greater quantity than others? — The difficulty will not be lessened, though the omnipresence of the fluid should be given up, if we suppose, as is generally done, that heat has a tendency to diffuse itself equably every way. If it has this tendency, what hinders it from doing so? Why doth not the heat from the burning regions of the torrid zone diffuse itself equally all over the globe, and reduce the earth to one common temperature? This indeed might require time; but the experience of all ages has shown that there is not the least advance towards an equality of temperature. The middle regions of the earth continue as hot, and the polar ones as cold, as we have any reason to believe they were at the creation of the world, or as we have any reason to believe they will be while the world remains. This indeed is one of the many instances of the impropriety of establishing general laws from the trifling experiments we are capable of making, and which hold good only on the narrow scales on which we can make them, but are utterly insufficient to solve the phenomena of the great system of nature, and which can be solved only by observing other phenomena of the same system undisturbed by any manœuvres of our own.

85 Another from the seeming disappearance of the heat.

Again, supposing the objection already made could be got over, and satisfactory reasons should be given why an equilibrium of temperature in the earth and its atmosphere should never be obtained, it will by no means be easy to tell what becomes of the heat which is communicated to the earth at certain times of the year.

86 Dr Crawford's solution.

This difficulty, or something similar, Dr Crawford seems to have had in view when treating of the effects of the evolution and absorption of heat. Thus, says he, "the Deity has guarded against sudden vicissitudes of heat and cold upon the surface of the earth.

"For if heat were not evolved by the process of congelation, all the waters which were exposed to the influence of the external air, when its temperature was reduced below 32°, would speedily become solid; and, at the moment of congelation, the progress of cooling would be as rapid as it was before the air had arrived at its freezing point.

"This is manifest from what was formerly observed respecting the congelation of different fluids. It was shown, that if the velocities of the separation of heat were equal, the times of the congelation would be in proportion to the quantities of heat which the fluids gave off from an internal source in the freezing process. Whence it follows, that if no heat were evolved, the congelation would be instantaneous.

"In the present state of things, as soon as the atmosphere is cooled below 32°, the waters begin to freeze, and at the same time to evolve heat; in consequence of which, whatever may be the degree of cold in the external air, the freezing mass remains at 32°, until the whole is congealed; and as the quantity of heat extricated in the freezing of water is considerable, the progress of congelation in large masses is very slow. — That the absorption and extrication of heat in the melting and freezing of bodies has a tendency to retard the progress of these processes, is remarked by Mr Wilkie in his Essay on Latent Heat. — The same doctrine is likewise taught by Dr Black in his lectures.

87 Severity of the cold in the northern regions mitigated by the production of ice.

"In the northern and southern regions, therefore, upon the approach of winter, a quantity of elementary fire is extricated from the waters, proportional to the degree of cold that prevails in the atmosphere. Thus the severity of the frost is mitigated, and its progress is retarded; and it would seem that, during this retardation of the cooling process, the various tribes of animals and vegetables which inhabit the circumpolar regions gradually acquire power of resisting its influence.

88 Inundations prevented by the slowness with which congealed water melts.

"On the contrary, if, in the melting of ice, a quantity of heat were not absorbed, and rendered insensible, that substance, when it was exposed to a medium warmer than 32°, would speedily become fluid, and the process of heating would be as rapid as if no alteration in its form had taken place. If things were thus constituted, the vast masses of ice and snow which are collected in the frigid zones would, upon the approach of summer, suddenly dissolve, and great inundations would annually overflow the regions near to the poles.

"But by the operation of the law of the absorption of heat when the ice and snow upon the return of spring have arrived at 32°, they begin to melt, and at the same time to imbibe heat; during this process, a large quantity of elementary fire becomes insensible; in consequence of which the earth is slowly heated, and those gradual changes are produced which are essential to the preservation of the animal and vegetable kingdoms.

89 Equal distribution of heat promoted by its absorption and evolution.

"We may remark, in the last place, that this law not only resists sudden changes of temperature, but that it likewise contributes to a more equal distribution of the principle of heat throughout the various parts of the earth, in different seasons and climates. Thus the diurnal heats are moderated by the evaporation of the waters on the earth's surface, a portion of the fire derived from the sun being absorbed and extinguished by the vapours at the moment of their ascent. On the approach of night the vapours are again condensed, and falling in the form of dew, communicate

Element of Fire.

to the air and to the earth the fire which they had imbibed during the day.

"It was before shown, that, in the regions near to the poles, when the vernal and summer heats prevail, provision is made for tempering the severity of the winter cold, a quantity of elementary fire, upon the dissolution of the ice and snow, being absorbed by the waters, and deposited, as it were, in a great magazine for the purpose of mitigating the intensity of the cold when the frost returns.

90 Heat of the torrid zone thus mitigated.

"From the experiments of Hales, Halley, and Watson, it appears, that vast quantities of water are continually converted into vapours by the action of the solar rays upon the portion of the earth's surface which is exposed to the light; and by the celebrated discovery of Dr Black, it is proved, that, in the process of evaporation, much elementary fire is absorbed. It is manifest, that this cause will have a powerful influence in mitigating the intensity of the heat in the torrid zone, and in promoting a more equal diffusion of it through the earth. For a considerable portion of the heat, which is excited by the action of the solar rays upon the earth's surface within the tropics, is absorbed by the aqueous vapours, which being collected in the form of clouds, are spread like a canopy over the horizon, to defend the subjacent regions from the direct rays of the sun. A great quantity of elementary fire is thus rendered insensible in the torrid zone, and is carried by the dispersion of the vapours to the north and to the south, where it is gradually communicated to the earth when the vapours are condensed."

91 This solution totally insufficient to remove the difficulty.

That all this takes place, as the Doctor has advanced, cannot be denied; but, by allowing it, the difficulty is not removed in the smallest degree, as will appear from a due consideration of the phenomena which he himself has mentioned.—He owns that the sun communicates fire to the earth: the question is, What becomes of it, seeing the emission is continual? In summer, the air, the earth, and the water, are heated to a certain degree. On the sun's declining southward, the air first loses its heat. Whither does it go? It does not ascend into the higher regions of the atmosphere, for these are constantly found colder than the parts below. It does not descend to the earth and water; for these give out the quantity they had absorbed, as Dr Crawford observes. Neither does it go laterally to the southern regions; for they are constantly very hot, and ought to impart their heat to those farther north, instead of receiving any from them. How comes it then, that the atmosphere seems perpetually to receive heat without ever being satiated? or if the heat cannot be found going off either upwards, downwards, or sideways, how are we to account for its disappearance?

92 Heat most probably the action of an omnipresent fluid.

This question seems to be altogether unanswerable on the supposition that heat is occasioned by the mere presence of a fluid; but if we suppose it to be only a particular mode of action of an omnipresent fluid, the whole difficulty vanishes at once. On this supposition indeed the question will naturally arise, Whence does this motion proceed, or by what is its action in general determined? Dr Berkenhout, in enumerating the properties of matter, exempts fire from two of those usually ascribed to other material substances, viz. gravitation and the vis inertiae. "According to the philosophers (says he), matter cannot move without being either impelled or attracted. I doubt much whether this be true of fire, and whether, when uncombined, motion be not one of its essential properties.—Gravitation seems also to be no property of fire, which moves with equal facility in all directions, and may be accumulated in hard bodies to any degree without increasing their weight. Fire, being the cause of volatility, seems rather to be in constant counteraction to gravity."

93 Fire seems destitute of gravity and vis inertiae [illegible].

But however essential we may suppose the motion of fire to be to it, there cannot be any self-existent mobility in its parts, otherwise it would soon be diffused equally throughout the universe, and the temperature of the whole reduced to an equilibrium. According to the present constitution of nature, we see that the distribution of heat is principally owing to the sun; and what we call its *quantity*, depends on the position of the sun with regard to terrestrial objects and the length of time they are exposed to his rays. Heat is not produced while the rays have a direct passage; and therefore fluids through which they pass easily, as air, are not heated by the rays of the sun. But when the rays are impeded in their course, and reflected in considerable quantity, a degree of heat takes place, which is always greater or less in proportion to the intensity of the rays.—In the reflecting substance, the heat will be comparatively greater in proportion to the quantity of rays which are absorbed or stopped in their course by it; but in any substance interposed betwixt the sun and the reflecting body, the heat is proportionable to the quantity of rays reflected.—Now it is plain, that when the particles of light fall upon any opaque substance, and enter its pores, which by their extreme subtilty they are well calculated to do, they must make an attempt to pass directly through it in their natural course; but as this cannot be done, they will push laterally, and in all directions, in consequence of being perpetually urged by the impulse of the light coming from the sun: and thus an action will be propagated in all directions as radii from a centre towards a circumference, which when it takes place in that subtile fluid always produces what we call *heat*.

In contemplating the system of nature, we perceive 94
three kinds of fluids of extreme subtilty, and very much resembling one another, viz. fire, light, and electricity. That it should be agreeable to vulgar conceptions to suppose these all to be ultimately the same, is not surprising; and on examining the evidence of their identity, it will certainly be found exceedingly strong. They all agree in the property of exciting the sensation of heat in certain circumstances, and in not doing so in others. Fire, we know, in the common acceptation of the word, always does so; but when it assumes the latent and invisible state, as in the formation of vapour, it lays aside this seemingly essential property, and the vapour is cold to the touch.—Light, when collected into a focus by a burning-glass, i. e. when its rays converge towards a centre, and diverge or attempt to diverge from one, produces heat also: and so does the electric fluid; for it has been found that the aura converging from a very large conductor to the point of a needle, is capable of setting on fire a small cartridge of gunpowder, or a quantity of tinder, surrounding it *. There seems also to be a connection betwixt fire

Fire [illegible]

Proofs of [illegible]

* See Dr [illegible]

Element of Fire.

fire and electricity in another way; for in proportion as heat is diminished, or the bodies are cooled, electricity succeeds in its place. Thus all electric bodies by heat
97 *Connection between fire or heat and electricity.*
become conductors of electricity, and cannot be excited or made to show any signs of containing that fluid; but as soon as the heat is removed, their electric property returns. Water is naturally a conducting substance: by being frozen its conducting power is lessened, which shows an approach to electricity; and, by being cooled down to 20° below 0 of Fahrenheit, the ice actually becomes electric, and will emit sparks by friction like glass*. The atmosphere is a natural electric; but by a certain degree of heat it loses this property, and becomes a conductor; nor is there any doubt that its electric properties are increased in pro-
98 *Excessive electricity of the polar regions in winter.*
portion to the degree of cold imparted to it. In the winter time, therefore, we must consider the frozen surface of the earth, the water, and the atmosphere of the polar regions, as forming one electrical machine of enormous magnitude; for the natural cold of these countries is often sufficient to cool the water to more than 20° below 0, and consequently to render it an electric. That this is really the case, appears from the excessively bright aurora borealis and other electric appearances, far exceeding any thing observed in this country. In the summer time, however, no such appearances are to be seen, nor any thing remarkable except
99 *Heat in summer becomes electric fluid in winter.*
an excessive heat from the long continuance of the sun above the horizon. This quantity of heat then being succeeded by a proportionable quantity of electricity in winter, it is impossible to avoid concluding that the heat in summer becomes electric fluid in winter, which, going off through the celestial expanse, returns again to the grand source of light and heat from which it originally came; thus making room for the succeeding quantities which are to enliven the earth during the following summer.

* See Electricity.

100 *Why thunder and lightning take place in summer and not in winter.*

Thus the disappearance of heat in winter, and of electricity in summer, in these countries, will be very naturally and easily accounted for. It is true, that the phenomena of thunder and lightning show the existence of this fluid in vast quantities during the summer season: but these phenomena are only partial, and though formidable to us, are trifling in comparison with the vast quantities of electric matter discharged by the continual flashing of the aurora borealis, not to mention the fire balls and meteors called *falling stars*, which are very often to be seen in the northern countries. In the summer-time, the air which is an electric, heated by the rays of the sun, is excited or made to part with the fluid to the vapours contained in it: and it is the unequal or opposite electricity of the clouds to one another, or to the earth, which produces the lightning. But in winter, when the air, earth, and vapours, all become electric, they cannot discharge sparks from one to another as before; but the whole, as one connected and vast electrified apparatus, discharges the matter almost in a continued stream for many months.

101 *Heat, light, cold, and electricity, the effects of one universal fluid.*

From a consideration of these and other phenomena of nature, as well as of the best experiments which have hitherto been made, we must consider fire in the abstract as an omnipresent fluid, of such subtilty as to pervade all terrestrial substances. When by any means it is made to diverge every way as from a centre, there it operates as heat; expands, rarefies, or burns, according to the intensity of its action. Proceeding in straight
Nature of Heat
and parallel lines, or such as diverge but little, it acts as light, and shows none of that power discoverable in the former case, though this is easily discoverable by making it converge into a focus. In a quiescent state, or where the motion is but little, it presses on the surfaces of bodies, contracts and diminishes them every way in bulk, forces out the expanding fluid within their pores, and then acts as cold. In this case also, being obliged to sustain the vehement action of that part of the fluid which is in motion, it flies with violence to every place where the pressure is lessened, and produces all the phenomena of Electricity.

§ 1. *Of the Nature of Heat.*

102 *Particular solution of the phenomena of heat.*

The manner in which the phenomena of heat may be solved and its nature, understood, will appear from the following propositions.

1. It is in all cases observed, that when light proceeds in considerable quantity from a point, diverging as the radii of a circle from its centre, there a considerable degree of heat is found to exist, if an opaque body, having no great reflective power, is brought near that point.

2. This action of the light, therefore, may be accounted the ultimate cause of heat, without having recourse to any farther suppositions; because nothing else besides this action is evident to our senses.

3. If the point from which the rays are emitted is placed in a transparent medium, such as air or water, that medium, without the presence of an opaque body, will not be heated.

4. Another cause of heat, therefore, is the resistance of the parts of that body on which the light falls, to the action mentioned in Prop. 1. Where this resistance is weak, as in the cases just mentioned, the heat is either nothing, or very little.

5. If a body capable of reflecting light very copiously is brought near the lucid point, it will not be heated *.

* See the article Burning-Glass.

6. A penetration of the light, therefore, into the substance of the body, and likewise a considerable degree of resistance on the part of that body to the action of the light, are the requisites to produce heat.

7. Those bodies ought to conceive the greatest degrees of heat into whose substance the light can best penetrate, *i. e.* which have the least reflective power, and which most strongly resist its action; which is evidently the case with black and solid substances.

8. By heat all bodies are expanded in their dimensions every way, and that in proportion to their bulk and the quantity of heat communicated to them.

9. This expansion takes place not only by an addition of *sensible* heat, but likewise of that which is *latent*. Of this last we have a remarkable instance in the case of snow mixed with spirit of nitre. The spirit of nitre contains a certain quantity of latent heat, which cannot be separated from it without effecting a change on the spirit itself; so that, if deprived of this heat, it would no longer be spirit of nitre.—Besides this, it contains a quantity of sensible heat, of a great part of which it may be deprived, and yet retain its characteristic properties as nitrous acid. When it is poured upon snow, the latter is immediately melted by the action of the latent heat in the acid. The snow cannot

Nature of Heat.

be melted or converted into water, without imbibing a quantity of latent heat, which it receives immediately from the acid which melts it. But the acid cannot part with the heat without decomposition; to prevent which, its sensible heat occupies the place of that which has entered the snow and liquefied it. The mixture then becomes exceedingly cold, and the heat forces into it from all the bodies in the neighbourhood; so that, by the time it has recovered that quantity of sensible heat which was lost, or arrived at the temperature of the atmosphere around it, it will contain a considerably larger quantity of heat than it originally did, and is therefore observed to be expanded in bulk. Another instance of this expansive power of latent heat is in the case of steam, which always occupies a much larger space than the substance from which it was produced; and this whether its temperature is greater or less than the surrounding atmosphere.

10. The difference between latent and sensible heat, then, as far as we can conceive, is, that the expansive power of the former is directed only against the particles of which the body is composed; but that of the latter is directed also against other bodies. Neither doth there seem to be any difference at all between them farther than in quantity. If water, for instance, hath but a small quantity of heat, its parts are brought near each other, it contracts in bulk, and feels cold. Still, however, some part of the heat is detained among the aqueous particles, which prevents the fluid from congealing into a solid mass. But, by a continuation of the contracting power of the cold, the particles of water are at last brought so near each other that the internal or *latent* heat is forced out: By this discharge a quantity of air is also produced, the water is congealed, and the ice occupies a greater space than the water did; but then it is full of air-bubbles, which are evidently the cause of its expansion. The heat then becomes *sensible*, or, as it were, lies on the outside of the matter; and consequently is easily dissipated into the air, or communicated to other bodies. Another way in which the latent heat may be extricated is by a constant addition of sensible heat. In this case the body is first raised into vapour, which for some time carries off the redundant quantity of heat. But as the quantity of this heat is continually increased, the texture of the vapour itself is at last totally destroyed. It becomes too much expanded to contain the heat, which is therefore violently thrown out on all sides into the atmosphere, and the body is said to burn, or be on fire. See Combustion, Flame, and Ignition.

11. Hence it follows, that those bodies which have the least share of latent heat, appear to have the greatest quantity of sensible heat; but this is only in appearance, for the great quantity they seem to contain is owing really to their inability to contain it. Thus, if we can suppose a substance capable of transmitting heat through it as fast as it received it; if such a substance was set over a fire, it would be as hot as the fire itself, and yet the moment it was taken off, it would be perfectly cool, on account of its incapacity to detain the heat among the particles of which it was composed.

12. The heat, therefore, in all bodies consists in a certain violent action of the elementary fire within them tending from a centre to a circumference, and thus making an effort to separate the particles of the body from each other, and thereby to change its form or mode of existence. When this change is effected, bodies are said to be dissipated in vapour, calcined, vitrified, or burnt, according to their different natures.

13. Inflammable bodies are such as are easily raised in vapour; that is, the fire easily penetrates their parts, and combines with them in such quantity, that, becoming exceedingly light, they are carried up by the atmosphere. Every succeeding addition of heat to the body increases also the quantity of latent heat in the vapour, till at last, being unable to resist its action, the heat breaks out all at once, the vapour is converted into flame, and is totally decomposed. See the article Flame, and Prop. 10.

14. Uninflammable bodies are those which have their parts more firmly connected, or otherwise disposed in such a manner, that the particles of heat cannot easily combine with them or raise them into vapour.

15. *Heat* therefore being only a certain mode of the action of elementary fire, it follows, that the capacity of a body for containing it, is only a certain constitution of the body itself, or a disposition of its parts, which can allow the elementary fire contained in it to exert its expansive power upon them without being dissipated on other bodies. Those substances which allow the expansive power of the fire to operate on their own particles are said to contain a great deal of heat; but those which throw it away from themselves upon other bodies, though they feel very hot, yet philosophically speaking they contain very little heat.

16. What is called the *quantity* of heat contained in any substance, if we would speak with the strictest propriety, is only the apparent force of its action, either upon the parts of the body itself, or upon other bodies in its neighbourhood. The expansive force of the elementary fire contained in any body upon the parts of that body, is the *quantity of latent heat* contained in it; and the expansive force of the fire exerted upon other bodies which touch or come near it, is the *quantity of sensible heat* it contains.

17. If what we call *heat* consists only in a certain action of that fluid called *elementary fire*, namely, its expansion, or acting from a centre to a circumference, it follows, that if the same fluid act in a manner directly opposite to the former, or press upon the particles of a body as from a circumference to a centre, it will then produce effects directly opposite to those of heat, i. e. it will then be absolute *cold*, and produce all the effects already attributed to Cold. See that article.

18. If heat and cold then are only two different modifications of the same fluid, it follows, that if a hot body and a cold one are suddenly brought near each other, the heat of the one ought to drive before it a part of the cold contained in the other, *i. e.* the two portions of elementary fire acting in two opposite ways, ought in some measure to operate upon one another as any two different bodies would when driven against each other. When a hot and a cold body therefore are brought near each other, that part of the cold body farthest from the hot one ought to become colder than before, and that part of the hot body farthest from the cold one ought to become hotter than before.

19.

General Effects of Heat.

19. For the same reason, the greatest degree of cold in any body ought to be no obstacle, or at least very little, to its conceiving heat, when put in a proper situation. Cold air, cold fuel, &c. ought to become as intensely heated, and nearly as soon, as that which is hotter.

The two last propositions are of great importance. When the first of them is thoroughly established, it will confirm beyond a doubt, that cold is a *positive*, as well as heat; and that each of them has a separate and distinct power, of which the action of its antagonist is the only proper limit; *i. e.* that heat can only limit the power of cold, and *vice versa*. A strong confirmation of this proposition is the experiment related by M. Geoffroy; an account of which is given under the article Cold. Another, but not so well authenticated, is related under the article Congelation. —De Luc's observation also, mentioned by Dr Cleghorn, affords a pretty strong proof of it; for if the lower parts of the atmosphere are cooled by the passage of the sun's rays at some distance above, and it hath been already shown that they do not *attract* the heat from the lower parts, it follows, that they must *expel* part of the cold from the upper regions.—The other proposition, when fully established, will prove, that heat and cold are really convertible into one another; which indeed seems not improbable, as we see that fires will burn with the greatest fierceness during the time of intense frosts, when the coldest air is admitted to them; and even in those dismal regions of Siberia, when the intense cold of the atmosphere is sufficient to congeal quicksilver, it cannot be doubted that fires will burn as well as in this country; which could not happen if heat was a fluid *per se*, and capable of being carried off, or absolutely diminished in quantity, either in any part of the atmosphere itself, or in such terrestial bodies as are used for fuel.

§ 2. *Of the general Effects of Heat.*

Having said thus much concerning the nature of heat in general, we come now to a particular explanation of its several effects, which indeed constitute the whole of the active part of chemistry.—These are,

I. *Expansion*, or increase of bulk in every direction. This is a necessary consequence of the endeavour which the fluid makes to escape in all directions, when made to converge into a focus. The degree of expansion is unequal in different bodies, but in the same body is always proportionable to the degree of heat applied.

103 Instruments for measuring the expansion of bodies.

There are two different instruments in use for ascertaining the degrees of expansion; and as we have already shown, that the degree of heat can only be known by the expansion, these effects of heat upon the instrument are usually taken for the degrees of heat themselves. These instruments are called the Thermometer and Pyrometer. The former is composed of a glass tube, with a globe or rather oval tube at one end, and exactly closed at the other; it is most usually filled with mercury or spirit of wine; but mercury is generally preferred on account of its expansions being more equable than those of any other fluid. It has the disadvantage, however, of being subject to congelation; which is not the case with spirit of wine, when very highly rectified. Spirit-of-wine thermometers, therefore, ought not to be entirely disused, but seem rather a necessary part of the chemical apparatus, as well as those made with mercury.

104 Wedgewood's improvement of the thermometer.

As no thermometer made with any fluid can measure either the degrees of heat above the point at which it boils, or the degrees of cold below which it congeals, instruments have been contrived by which the expansion of solid bodies, though much less than what is occasioned by an equal degree of heat in a fluid, may become visible. These were usually called *Pyrometers*; but Mr Wedgewood has lately contrived a method of connecting the two together, in which the highest degree of heat, exceeding even that of a glass-house furnace, may be measured as accurately as the more moderate degrees by the common mercurial thermometer. See Thermometer.

105 Instances of bodies expanding by cold.

Expansion in some cases does not appear to be the effect of heat, of which we have two remarkable instances, viz. of iron, which always expands in cooling after it has been melted; and of water, which expands with prodigious force in the act of freezing. The power with which iron expands in the act of passing from a fluid to a solid state, has never been measured, nor indeed does it seem easy to do so; but that of freezing water has been accurately computed.

106 Prodigious force exerted by water in freezing.

This was done by the Florentine Academicians, who having filled an hollow brass ball of an inch diameter with water, exposed it to a mixture of snow and salt, in order to congeal the water, and try whether its force was sufficient to burst the ball or not. The ball, being made very strong, resisted the expanding force of the water twice, even though a considerable part of its thickness had been pared off when it was perceived too strong at first. At the third time it burst; and by a calculation founded on the thickness of the globe and the tenacity of the metal, it was found that the expansive power of a spherule of water only one inch in diameter, was sufficient to overcome a resistance of more than 27,000 pounds, or 13 tons and an half.

107 Used as an argument for the existence of cold as a positive substance.

A power of expansion so prodigious, little less than double that of the most powerful steam-engines, and exerted in so small a body, seemingly by the force of cold, was thought to be a very powerful argument in favour of those who suppose cold to be a positive substance as well as heat; and indeed contributed not a little to embarrass the opposite party.

108 Explained by Dr Black's discovery of latent heat.

Dr Black's discovery of latent heat, however, has now afforded a very easy and natural explication of this phenomenon. He has shown, that, in the act of congelation, water is not cooled more than it was before, but rather grows warmer: that as much heat is discharged, and passes from a latent to a sensible state, as, had it been applied to water in its fluid state, would have heated it to 135°.

109 The expansion produced by the extrication of air-bubbles.

In this process the expansion is occasioned by a great number of minute bubbles suddenly produced. These were formerly supposed to be formed of *cold* in the abstract; and to be so subtile, that, insinuating themselves into the substance of the fluid, they augmented its bulk, at the same time that, by impeding the motion of its particles upon each other, they changed it from a fluid to a solid. Dr Black, however, has demonstrated, that these are only air extricated during the congelation; and to the extrication of this air he very justly attributes the prodigious expansive force exerted by freezing water. The

General Effects of Heat.

only question, therefore, which now remains is, By what means this air comes to be extricated, and to take up more room than it naturally does in the fluid? To this we can scarce give any other answer, than that part of the heat which is discharged from the freezing water combines with the air in its unelastic state, and, by restoring its elasticity, gives it that extraordinary force, as we see also in the case of air suddenly extricated in the explosion of gunpowder. Thus expansion, even in the case of freezing, is properly an effect of heat; and must therefore be considered as a phenomenon uniformly and certainly attending the action of heat, and in all cases to be ascribed to it.

110 This air extricated by part of the heat contained in the water.

111 Capacity of a body for containing heat, the same with the action of heat upon that body.

The only way in which the element or fluid of fire can be supposed to act, and the way in which we can have a rational idea of its being able to produce both heat and cold according to the diversity of its action, has been already explained so fully, that it is needless at present to enter into any further discussion of the subject. It will easily appear, that the *capacity* for containing heat is nothing different from the action of heat upon that body in expanding, and at last altering its form in such a manner, as either to be able to insinuate itself among the particles in much greater quantity than before, still retaining its internal action, though the external one becomes imperceptible; or scattering them in such a manner, that it breaks forth in great quantity in its peculiar appearances of fire and light; in the former case producing vapour or smoke, and in the latter flame, as shall afterwards be more fully explained. It must likewise appear, that to determine the quantity of heat in any body is altogether impossible; and with regard to the lowest degree of heat, or a total expulsion of that fluid, so far from being able to determine what it is, the probability must be, that nature does not admit of any such thing; for if heat consists in the expansive action of a certain fluid, and cold in its opposite or contractile action, there is very little reason to suppose that the constitution of nature will allow any one of these actions entirely to cease, as it does not appear by what means it could again be renewed. Cold, as we have already seen, always tends to produce electricity; and the connection betwixt that and fire is so strong, that we cannot suppose the former to be carried to any great extreme without producing the latter. Whatever we may therefore suppose concerning the capacities of different bodies for containing heat, or concerning the point of total privation of heat, must be altogether void of foundation. A rule, however, has been given by Mr Kirwan for finding the point of total privation, which, together with its demonstration, we shall subjoin; and as it is necessary for the better understanding of this, to call to remembrance what has been said concerning the difference between the temperatures and specific heats of bodies, we shall insert an epitome of the doctrine from Mr Nicholson.

112 Impossibility of determining the quantity of heat any body contains.

113 Mr Nicholson's account of the capacities of bodies for containing heat, &c.

"If two equal bodies of different kinds and temperatures be brought into contact, the common temperature will seldom, if ever, be the mean betwixt the two original temperatures; that is to say, the surplus of heat in the hotter body will be unequally divided between them, and the proportions of this surplus retained by each body will express their respective dispositions, affinities, or capacities for heat.—If, therefore, a given substance, as for example fluid water, be taken as the standard of comparison, and its capacity for heat be called one, or unity, the respective capacities of other bodies may be determined by experiment, and expressed in numbers in the same manner as specific gravities usually are. And because it is established as well from reason as experiment, that the same capacity for heat obtains in all temperatures of a given body, so long as its state of solidity, fluidity, or vapour is not changed, it will follow, that the whole quantities of heat in equal bodies of a given temperature will be as those capacities. And as the respective quantities of matter, in bodies of equal volume, give the proportions of their specific gravities, so the respective quantities of heat in bodies of equal weight and temperature give the proportions of their specific heats.

"A greater capacity for heat, or greater specific heat, in a given body, answers the same purpose with respect to temperature as an increase of the mass; or the quantity of heat required to be added or subducted, in order to bring a body to a given temperature, will be as its capacity or specific heat.

"The capacities not only differ in various bodies, but also in the same body, according as it is either in a solid, fluid, or vaporous state. All the experiments hitherto made conspire to show, that the capacity, and consequently the specific heat, is greatest in the vaporous, less in the fluid, and least in the solid state.

"The quantity of heat that constitutes the difference between the several states, may be found in degrees of the thermometer. Thus, if equal quantities of water at 162° and ice at 32° of temperature be mixed, the ice melts, and the common temperature becomes 32°; or otherwise, if equal quantities of frozen and fluid water, both at 32°, be placed in a like situation to acquire heat from a fire, the water will become heated to 162°, while the ice melts without acquiring any increase of temperature. In either case the ice acquires 130° of heat, which produces no other effect than rendering it fluid. Fluid water, therefore, contains not only as much more heat than ice, as is indicated by the thermometer, but also 130°, that is in some manner or other employed in giving it fluidity. And as fluid water cannot become ice without parting with 130° of heat besides what it had above 32 in its temperature; so also steam cannot become condensed into water without imparting much more heat to the matters it is cooled by, than water at the same temperature would have done.

"The heat employed in maintaining the fluid or vaporous form of a body, has been called latent heat, because it does not affect the thermometer.

114 Mr Kirwan's theorem for finding the point of total privation of heat.

"From the consideration of the specific heats of the same body in the two states of fluidity and solidity, and the difference between those specific heats, is deduced a method of finding the number of degrees which denote the temperature of any body immediately after congelation, reckoned from the natural zero, or absolute privation of heat. The rule is; multiply the degrees of heat required to reduce any solid to a fluid state, by the number expressing the specific heat of the fluid: divide this product by the difference between the numbers expressing the specific heat of the body in each state; the quotient will be the number

General Effects of Heat.

of degrees of temperature, reckoned from an absolute privation of heat.

"This theorem is Mr Kirwan's, and may be proved thus. Let s represent the required temperature of the body just congealed, l = the number of degrees that express the heat required to reduce it to fluidity, n = the specific heat of the solid, and m = the specific heat of the fluid. Then $s+l : s :: m : n$. Whence

$$s = \frac{ln}{m-n} = \text{the temperature from the natural zero}$$

in thermometrical degrees of the fluid. But because the actual fall of the thermometer is to be produced by cooling the solid, must pay attention to its capacity. The quantity of heat required to produce a given change of temperature in a body is as its capacity; and consequently the changes of temperature, when the quantity of heat is given, will be inversely as the capacities: therefore, $n : m :: \frac{ln}{m-n} : \frac{ln}{m-n} = s$. which is the rule above mentioned.

"If the data l, m, and n, be accurately obtained by experiment, in any one instance, and the difference between the zero of Fahrenheit's scale and the natural zero be thence found in degrees of that scale, this difference will serve to reduce all temperatures to the numeration which commences at the natural o. So that s being known in all cases, if any two of the quantities l, m, or n, be given in any body, the other may be likewise had. For $l = \frac{sm-sn}{n}$; and $m = \frac{sn}{s-l}$; and $n = \frac{sm-ln}{s}$.

"To give an example of this curious rule, let it be required to determine how many degrees of refrigeration would absolutely deprive ice of all its heat? The degrees of heat necessary to melt ice are 130; and the specific heats of ice and water are as 9 to 10. The number 130 multiplied by 10, produces 1300, and divided by the difference between 9 and 10 quotes 1300: therefore if ice were cooled 1300 degrees below 32°, or to −1268 of Fahrenheit's scale, it would retain no more heat."

II. *Fluidity* is another effect of heat, and is capable of taking place in all bodies hitherto known, when the fire is carried to a certain pitch. Theories have been invented, by which fluidity was ascribed to the smoothness and round figure of the particles whereof bodies were composed, and solidity to an angular or irregular figure. It has also been ascribed to a stronger degree of attraction between the parts of solids

115 Fluidity to be ascribed to the absorption of heat.

than of fluids. Dr Black, however, has shown, that in the case of melting ice, we are certainly to ascribe the acquired fluidity of the water to the absorption of heat. This was determined by a decisive experiment, in which he exposed a Florence-flask full of water to the atmosphere in a warm room, when he found that the heat in the air evidently left it, to flow into the ice in the bottle, and reduced it to fluidity. The air thus deprived of its heat, he felt sensibly descending like a cold blast from the bottle, and continuing to do so as long as any of the ice remained unthawed; yet after it was all melted, the temperature of the fluid was no more than 32°. Different degrees of heat are requisite for converting different solids into fluids, for which see the *Table of Degrees of* HEAT.

General Effects of Heat.

This theory receives an additional confirmation from the quantity of heat which is always known to be produced by the conversion of a fluid into a solid. And that this is really the case appears, 1. From what happens in

116 Sensible heat produced by the conversion of a fluid into a solid.

the congelation of water, it appears that ice is formed very slowly, and with several circumstances which support the theory.—Thus, if we expose equal quantities of water to the air, which is perhaps 10 below frost, and add to one of these a small quantity of salt or spirit of wine, and observe the cooling of each, we shall find them both grow gradually colder, until they arrive at the temperature of frost; after which the water containing the salt will continue to grow colder, until it has arrived at the temperature of the air, at the same time that only a small quantity of the other water is converted into ice. Yet were the common opinion just, it ought all to have been congealed by this time; instead of which, it is scarce grown a degree colder during the whole time. Its remaining at the same temperature for so long time, shows that it has been communicating heat to the atmosphere; for it is impossible that any body can remain in contact with another that is colder, without communicating heat to it. Whence then comes this heat? There must be some source adding to the sensible heat of the water, so as to keep up its temperature to the freezing point: and this source of heat must be very considerable; for it will continue to act for a very long time before the water is changed into ice; during all which time, even to the last drop, the water is not a degree colder than 32° of Fahrenheit's thermometer. This, therefore, is the *latent heat* of the water, which had formerly entered into it during its transition from ice to a fluid state.

117 Argument in support of the theory from water remaining fluid tho' cooled below 32°.

A still stronger argument is derived from the following experiment; which evinces that the fluidity of water really depends upon its latent heat, and that the sensible heat is only a mean or condition to its containing the latent heat. This experiment consists in exposing water contained in a covered beer-glass to the air of a cold frosty night; and when the atmosphere is at the temperature of perhaps 10° or 12 below frost, the water will acquire that temperature without freezing: so that the fluidity of the water does not altogether depend on the quantity of sensible heat contained in it. The congelation, however, may be brought on by touching it with a bit of ice, with the extremity of a wire, by a shock upon the board, or otherwise disturbing it; and we then find the temperature suddenly raised up to 32°. This shows plainly, that the water has a disposition to retain the quantity of latent heat, upon which its fluidity must immediately and necessarily depend; and it retains it with a certain degree of force, so as to keep the water fluid in a temperature below that in which it usually parts with the latent heat and congeals. By disturbing it, however, we instantly bring on the congelation, which cannot take place without an extrication of the latent heat; which then, being changed into the ordinary or moveable heat, raises the thermometer as usual. The quantity of heat discharged from the first small portion of ice formed in the water is sufficient to prevent any more latent heat from separating, and consequently from any more ice being produced till more of the sensible heat is abstracted.

This doctrine extends not only to such bodies as are actually converted from a solid to a fluid, but from

General Effects of Heat.

a fluid to a solid state, but to such as are in a kind of middle state betwixt solidity and fluidity; for every degree of softness depends on a certain degree of heat contained in the body. Thus, for instance, melted wax, allowed to cool slowly, soon becomes opaque and consistent; but it must be colder still before it attains its utmost degree of hardness. There is therefore a certain degree of heat below which every body is solid, and above which every one is fluid; the former being called the *congealing*, and the latter the *melting*, point of bodies.

118 How the cause of the softness of bodies approaching to fluidity.

119 Absorption of heat the universal cause of fluidity.

By making experiments upon different substances, the Doctor was convinced that latent heat is the universal cause of fluidity; and the doctrine holds good in all the experiments that have hitherto been made upon spermaceti, bees-wax, and some of the metals. If they are melted, allowed to cool slowly, and a thermometer be immersed into them, we find, that as long as they continue fluid, their sensible heat diminishes very fast; but as soon as they begin to grow solid, the sensible heat continues greater than that of the air to which they are exposed; and during all this time it is communicating heat to the air, without having its sensible heat diminished; for the latent heat within the fluid gradually receives a sensible form, and keeps up the temperature, proving a source of sensible heat, which is communicated to the neighbouring bodies as well as the surrounding air. The softness and ductility of bodies depend on this also.

120 Vapour formed by the absorption of latent heat.

III. *Evaporation.* A third effect of the action of heat is that of converting bodies into vapour, by which they are rendered specifically lighter than the surrounding atmosphere, and enabled to rise in it. To account for this, many theories have been invented; but that of Dr Black, who accounts for it, as well as fluidity from the absorption of latent heat, is now universally received. The circumstances by which he proves and illustrates his doctrine are the following:

1. When we attend to the phenomena of boiling water, in a tea kettle for instance, it may, when first put upon the fire, be about the temperature of 48° or 50°. In a quarter of an hour it will become heated to 212°. It then begins to boil, and has gained 162° of vapour in that time. Now, if the conversion of it into vapour depended on the quantity of sensible heat introduced, we may ask how long it will be necessary to raise it all in vapour? Surely another quarter of an hour should be sufficient; but this is far from being the case. Dr Black made some experiments upon this subject in conjunction with another gentleman. Having the opportunity of what is called a kitchen-table or a thick plate of cast iron, one end of which was made sensibly red-hot, they set upon this some iron vessels with circular flat bottoms, of about four inches diameter, and which contained a quantity of water. The temperature of the water was noted, as also when it began to boil; and when the whole of it was boiled away, it was found, that when set on the table its temperature had been 54°; in four minutes it began to boil, and in that space of time received 158° degrees of heat. Had the evaporation, therefore, depended merely on the quantity of sensible heat introduced, it ought to have been dissipated entirely in a single minute more. It was, however, 18 minutes in dissipating; and therefore had received 807 degrees of heat before it was all evaporated. All this time, therefore, while the water continued to boil, it was receiving a great quantity of heat, which must have been flowing equally fast out of it; for the vessel was no hotter, and the iron plate continued equally hot, the whole time. The vessels were of different shapes, some of them cylindrical, some conical, others widening upwards; one of the designs of the experiment being to show how far the evaporation was retarded by the particular form of the vessels. By suspending a thermometer in the mouth of one of the evaporating vessels, the heat of the steam was found to be exactly 212°; so that as the great quantity of heat absorbed was found neither to have remained in the water, nor to have been carried away by the steam in a sensible manner, we have nothing left to suppose, but that it flew off as one of the component parts of the steam in a latent state.

121 Experiments by Dr Black on the conversion of water into vapour.

2. In an experiment to show the fixedness of the boiling point of water, Dr Black inclosed some of that fluid in a strong vial having a thermometer in it, and stopped close with a cork. By the application of heat he hoped now to be able to raise the thermometer some degrees above the boiling point, which would be the natural consequence of the confinement of the steam. When this was done, he pulled out the cork, and supposed that the water would now all fly out in vapour; but in this he was totally disappointed; a sudden and very tumultuous boiling ensued, which threw out some of the water; but though some quantity of steam likewise issued, the quantity of water was not considerably diminished. The vial had been heated to 20° above the boiling point, but almost instantly cooled down to 212°, when the cork was taken out.

3. Mr Watt, in making some experiments on the force of steam, had occasion to use Papin's digester, with a pipe proceeding from its side; the orifice of which was shut with a valve pressed down by one end of a lever. Thus he heated steam to 400° of Fahrenheit; after which, having suddenly struck off the lever, a quantity of steam flew out with considerable noise, and with such violence as to make an impression on the ceiling of the room; but this noise gradually diminished, and after ten minutes ceased entirely; and upon opening the machine, he found the greatest part of the water still remaining.

122 Boiling point of water in vacuo determined by Mr Boyle.

4. The change of sensible into latent heat in the formation of vapour, appears still more evident in the boiling of water *in vacuo*. Mr Boyle took a quantity of water which had been previously boiled to purge it of its air, and put it whilst hot under the receiver of an air-pump. In consequence of this it began again to boil, and continued boiling till it was only lukewarm, and it soon arrived at this temperature; so that in this case also the heat had disappeared during the conversion of the fluid into vapour. Others have repeated the experiment, as Boerhaave, Muschenbroeck; and Robinson, who lectures on chemistry in Glasgow, says that the heat diminishes very fast till it comes to 90° or 95°, which seems to be the boiling point of water *in vacuo*. As a considerable part of the heat thus disappears, and is to be discovered neither in the water nor in the vapour, we must conclude that it enters the latter as part of its composition.

123 And by Mr Robison of Glasgow.

5. Thus also we may understand some curious experiments made by Dr Cullen upon ether and other vo-

latile

General Effects of Heat.

latile fluids. He employed some persons to make experiments upon the cold produced by evaporation; and willing to repeat them himself *in vacuo*, he put some of the most volatile liquors under the receiver of an air-pump. One of these was ether. It was contained in a glass, in which there was also placed some water. When the air was extracted, the ether began to boil, and to be converted into vapour, till it became so very cold that it froze the water contained in the vessel, though the temperature of the room was about 50°. Here therefore there was a quantity of heat which disappeared all of a sudden; which it is plain could not be owing to its having any communication with that of the atmosphere or other cold bodies, as they could not render it colder than they were themselves. Ether therefore is to be considered as a fluid so volatile, that were it not for the pressure of the atmosphere it would be perpetually in the state of vapour.

124 Dr Cullen's experiment on cold produced by evaporation.

125 Heat expelled in great quantity by the condensation of vapour.

6. That this heat which enters into the vapour is not destroyed, but remains in a latent state, is easily proved; for we find that a great quantity of heat is expelled from vapour when it is condensed again to form the body it composed originally. This is easily ascertained by observing the quantity of heat communicated to the water in the *refrigeratory* of a still by any given quantity of liquid which comes over. Thus, if the refrigeratory contain 100 pounds of water, and the distillation be continued till only one pound has come over, supposing the water in the refrigeratory to have received 8° of heat; it is plain, that if the whole of the quantity thus received could be thrown into one pound of water, the latter would be heated to 800°; which is sufficient to make an equal space of iron red-hot. But that this quantity of heat is received by the water in the refrigeratory has appeared from several experiments, which show that water, by being converted into vapour, absorbs between 800° and 900° of heat.

126 Mr Watt's experiments on the evaporation of fluids *in vacuo*.

On this principle we may explain some curious experiments made by Mr Watt with regard to the evaporation of fluids *in vacuo*. That gentleman had formed a design of converting water into steam with less expence of fuel, which he imagined might be done by removing the pressure of the air from the water, which he thought would thus require a much smaller quantity of fuel to convert it into vapour. Dr Black, however, perceiving that only the small quantity of sensible heat the steam possessed could thus be carried off, informed him beforehand that his project would not be found attended with the advantages he imagined. The experiment, however, was made in the following manner: A still was procured of tinned iron, the body of which resembled that of a retort, with a vessel serving as a condenser; the whole apparatus being close, excepting a little hole in the extremity of the condensing vessel. He first exhausted this vessel of air by holding the condenser over the retort, in which some boiling water was contained, until it was entirely converted into steam. He then suddenly stopped the little hole, and removed the vessels from the fire; when, after they were cooled, there was a pretty perfect vacuum formed by the condensation of the steam. The retort was then put on the fire, and turned so that the pipe and condensing vessel should hang downward; and plunging them into cold water, heat was applied to the still till the water boiled, as could be known by the noise. It was kept boiling, till a quantity of steam was pushed over and condensed with a very gentle heat, the still feeling little warmer than his hand. After a certain quantity had been distilled, the apparatus was removed, and he had noted the heat of the water in the refrigeratory; but though the steam all along came over with so gentle a heat, he found the quantity communicated to the water in the refrigeratory to be surprisingly great, not less than 1000°; so that it would have been more than sufficient to heat the quantity of liquor which came over red-hot.

127 Ignition a [illegible] and steady effect of heat.

IV. *Ignition*, or the causing bodies to shine or emit light in the dark. This may be considered as a species of inflammation, and shall therefore be explained under that head: here we shall only observe, that ignition is a more steady and constant effect of heat than either the production of fluidity or vapour; and appears not only to be the same degree with regard to any particular body, but the same with regard to all kinds of matter. Dr Martin imagines, that a red hot piece of iron is hotter than a red hot piece of stone; but if you put into a crucible an hundred different kinds of matter, as metals, glass, &c. that are capable of bearing a red heat, they will all begin to appear luminous about the same time, and their brightness will increase equally as their heat increases. But it is difficult to know at what point this begins, as we have no way of ascertaining the beginning or lowest degree of ignition but by the effect it produces on our sight, and we cannot be sure that we perceive the lowest degree of light; for we know that other animals see objects with such light as appears perfect darkness to us. Sir Isaac Newton's method of determining this has been already mentioned.

128 All ignited bodies equally hot.

129 Metals may become vastly hotter after they are brought to fusion.

Dr Boerhaave entertained a notion, that some metals, after being once brought into a state of fusion, could be made no hotter; and proposes the possibility of this as a question, "Whether the heat of metals can be increased after they are melted?" There is not, however, the least doubt but that their heat may be vastly increased after they are melted; and we know certainly that such as are of easy fusion may be heated to a vastly greater degree after being melted; and why may not those requiring stronger heats be the same? We are sure that this is the case with silver, which, after being melted, may be brought to such a heat as to become too dazzling for the eye to bear it. If Boerhaave's opinion were just, it would be impossible to cast any metal into moulds, because it must lose a little heat in being removed from the fire and in entering the mould; nor would they receive a proper impression if they did not contain a greater quantity of heat than was necessary for their fusion.

130 Ignition an universal effect of fire.

131 Water may be made sufficiently hot to melt lead.

Ignition appears to be universal; and all bodies capable of supporting it without being converted into an elastic vapour that cannot be confined, are affected the same way. Water, which in its ordinary state seems very little capable of enduring this heat, may be confined in strong vessels so as to become capable of melting lead, which is more than half way betwixt a red heat and that of boiling water. Experiments with the eolipile show also that it can be made red-hot; for when the steam passes through burning fuel, it can-

General Effects of Heat.

not miss of being made red-hot. Dr Black has also frequently seen the vapour of water heated by throwing it into the ash-pit of a furnace, so as to produce a very large and transparent flame in rising up through the vent. There is reason therefore to conclude, that ignition is one of the more general effects of heat, only that some bodies are incapable of it until they be reduced to a state of vapour.

132 Difference between ignition and inflammation.

V. The last of the effects of heat here to be taken notice of is *inflammation*. It differs from ignition in this, that the bodies subject to the latter gradually grow cooler as soon as they are taken out of the fire, without undergoing any considerable change; while those subject to inflammation become continually hotter and hotter, communicating a vast quantity of heat to others, and undergoing a kind of decomposition themselves, insomuch, that by this means they have been thought to be reduced to their constituent principles or elements.

133 Inflammation decomposes but does not destroy bodies.

Some substances indeed seem to be an exception to this, as in the open air they burn totally away, without leaving any residuum or producing any soot. These are spirit of wine, sulphur, and especially inflammable air; which last, by a proper mixture with dephlogisticated air, may be so totally consumed, that scarce a fiftieth part of the two will remain. On a careful examination of these substances, however, we find that there is by no means a total consumption, or indeed, properly speaking, any consumption at all, at least if we measure the quantity of matter by the weight of the substance employed.

134 Spirit of wine yields a great quantity of water by being burned.

Thus, if we are at pains to collect the vapour of burning spirit of wine, we will find, that an aqueous dew is collected, which sometimes equals the spirit of wine itself in weight. With regard to sulphur, the case is still more evident; for the vapour of this, when collected, not only equals but greatly exceeds the weight of the sulphur employed; and on burning dephlogisticated and inflammable air together, as much water is found to be produced as nearly equals the weight of both airs.

135 Water produced by the deflagration of dephlogisticated and inflammable air.

In like manner, when we collect the ashes, water, soot, and oil, procured by burning any of the common inflammable substances, we will find, that they in general exceed the weight of the matter employed. The great waste of bodies by fire, therefore, is owing to the dissipation of the volatile principles they contain, which are carried off and rendered invisible by being mixed with the atmosphere.

136 Of the existence of phlogiston.

The process of inflammation has long been explained from the presence of a substance called *Phlogiston* in those bodies which are subject to it, and which is supposed to be the same in all bodies belonging to this class; the differences between them arising from the principles with which it is combined.

137 Denied by M. Lavoisier.

This doctrine, which was first introduced by Stahl, has given occasion to such various and discordant theories, that the existence of phlogiston has been lately denied altogether by M. Lavoisier, who brought in a new method of solving the phenomena of fire, heat, and ignition, without any assistance from this principle.

138 Arguments against it drawn from the increased weight of metals by calcination.

The foundation of M. Lavoisier's doctrine is the increase of weight in metals by calcination. This increase he finds to be precisely, or very nearly so, proportionable to the decrease of weight in the air in which they are calcined. His theory, therefore, is, that in the act of calcination, the pure part of the air, which he calls the *acidifying* or *oxygenous* principle, unites with the metal, and converts it into a calx.

139 His theory of inflammation.

In like manner, in substances truly inflammable, the heat and flame are supposed to proceed from the union of the pure air, or the oxygenous principle, with the substance, and converting it into those principles which are found to remain after inflammation. Thus the increased weight of the substance is easily accounted for; while the inflammation, in his opinion, is nothing more than a combination of the inflammable body itself with pure air, which has an attraction for it; and in confirmation of this it is urged, that when combustion is performed in empyreal or dephlogisticated air, the whole of the latter is absorbed; but in common atmospherical air only one fourth, being the quantity of pure air contained in it.

140 Arguments for the non-existence of phlogiston, from the reduction of the calces of perfect metals without addition.

Other arguments in favour of this opinion are, that the calces of the perfect metals may be reduced without addition by the mere emission of the oxygenous principle, (dephlogisticated air); by an union with which they assume the form of a calx. Thus he evades a very strong argument used by the opposite party; who adduced, as a proof of the existence of phlogiston, the use of charcoal in the reduction of metals to their proper form.

141 Dispute between Lavoisier and Priestley.

A dispute indeed took place betwixt M. Lavoisier and Dr Priestley concerning the reduction of the whole of a mercurial calx formed by an union with the nitrous acid without addition; the Doctor maintaining, that the whole could not be reduced by mere heat, but that a very perceptible quantity was always lost; but on a thorough examination of the subject, the truth seemed rather to lie on M. Lavoisier's side. See Aerology.

142 Dr Lubbock's theory.

Another theory, somewhat similar to that of Lavoisier's, has been published by Dr Lubbock, in an Inaugural Dissertation in 1784. In this he supposes two kinds of matter to exist in the universe; one he calls the *principium proprium*, the other the *principium sorbile*; and it is this latter, which, according to our author, is the principle of mutability, or which, by being united in various proportions with the other, forms bodies of all the different kinds we see in nature. It is this principle, therefore, which he supposes to be absorbed in the calcination of metals, and not empyreal air, as M. Lavoisier supposes; and he contends, that this same principle extends throughout the whole system of nature, even to the utmost celestial bounds.

143 Disputes concerning phlogiston now entirely decided.

It would exceed the limits of this treatise to give an account of the various theories which have been invented, and the arguments used for and against them; nor indeed is there any occasion for doing so, as late experiments have reduced the dispute into a much narrower compass than before, and furnished the most decisive arguments in favour of the existence of phlogiston.

144 Objections against the existence of phlogiston from its invisibility and supposed want of gravity.

The greatest objection to the belief of this principle was, that it could neither be seen nor felt by our senses directly, nor discover itself indirectly by the weight it communicated to the bodies with which it was united; on the contrary, the latter always became lighter in proportion to the quantity they contained; so that it was imagined, instead of being possessed of any specific gravity of its own, to be a principle of positive levity, such as that of heat or light may be reasonably supposed. This objection, however, is now entirely removed; and phlogiston in the abstract is

fixed

General Effects of Heat.

found to be no subtile principle capable of eluding our researches, but one very common, and easily met with, being no other than common charcoal. In the last edition of this work, under the article PHLOGISTON,

145 Common charcoal and phlogiston the same.

it was shown, that inflammable air, deprived of its elasticity, and combined with metallic substances, is really their phlogiston; and that in the inflammable bodies commonly used, what we call their phlogiston, is really their oil; and that which exists in charcoal, and cannot be driven off by distillation, is part of the empyreumatic or burnt oil of the subject which adheres so obstinately. A similar doctrine soon after appeared in the Philosophical Transactions for 1782, and the identity of phlogiston and inflammable air was clearly proved by Mr Kirwan.

146 Decisive proofs of the identity given by Dr Priestley.

Still, however, it was insisted by the French philosophers and others, that no *facts* had been adduced against M. Lavoisier, nor any decisive proofs appeared of the existence of phlogiston as a substance *per se*. Facts of this kind, however, have now been discovered by Dr Priestley, and are related under the articles AEROLOGY, CHARCOAL, PHLOGISTON, &c. It is sufficient at present to mention, that he

147 Spirit of wine and metals convertible into charcoal.

has been able to convert the purest spirit of wine, and one of the hardest metals, viz. copper, as well as several others, into a substance entirely resembling charcoal; that by means of the heat of a burning glass in vacuo, he has dissipated this metallic charcoal, as well as the common kind, *entirely* into inflam-

148 Charcoal entirely dissipated by heat into inflammable air.

mable air, with the assistance only of a little water, which seems necessary to make it assume the aerial form, and perhaps is the true solvent of it; and by a combination with the element of heat, with the aid of the charcoal, is enabled to resist condensation in the common way[*]. This inflammable air, when absorbed by metallic calces, again reduces them to their metallic

* See *Elastic Vapour.*

149 Metallic calces reduced by inflammable air.

form: so that here is one fact by which the phlogiston not only appears to our senses, but we are able to ascertain its quantity with the utmost precision. Nor can it here be any objection, that the reduced metal is lighter than the calx; for this only proves that the metallic earth, while a calx, is united to a heavy ingre-

150 Why metals are lighter in their metallic than in their calcined state.

dient (the basis of dephlogisticated air), and in the latter to a light one, viz. charcoal, the basis of inflammable air.

Another case in which the existence of phlogiston is made equally evident to our senses, and where no such objection can occur, is related under the article

151 Dephlogisticated air converted into aerial acid by charcoal.

AEROLOGY, n° 112. It is there shown, that "by the loss of one grain of charcoal of copper (formed by the union of spirit of wine with the metal), and which like common charcoal was consumed without having any residuum, he reduced four ounce-measures of dephlogisticated air till only one-ninth remained unabsorbed by water; and, again, with the loss of one grain and a half of charcoal, six and an half measures of dephlogisticated air were reduced till five and an half measures were pure fixed air."—Here, then, is an absolute and undeniable evidence, that fixed air is composed of dephlogisticated air, and charcoal or phlogiston, and elementary fire. There were no other ingredients present, and the charcoal must either have been annihilated or disposed of in the manner just mentioned; but the superior weight of the fixed air evidently shows that some ingredient had been added to the dephlogisticated air; and which increase was more than we can suppose to arise from the condensation of the dephlogisticated air during the operation, for this sometimes amounted to no more than one-thirtieth part.

152 Objections drawn from the total combustion of dephlogisticated air in some cases.

The strongest objection which can be made against the doctrine of phlogiston may be drawn from the total consumption of pure air in certain cases of combustion, for instance, in that of phosphorus, inflammable air, and iron. It must be observed, however, that in no case whatever is the air totally consumed; and in that of inflammable air water is produced by the union of the basis of the latter, that is charcoal, with the basis of dephlogisticated air, the oxygenous principle of M. Lavoisier, and which appears to be one of the component parts of WATER. In the case of phosphorus, the latter is converted into an acid; and in all probability a quantity of water is also pro-

153 Little phlogiston expelled from iron by being burnt in dephlogisticated air.

duced, by which part of it is converted into crystalline flowers. The case of the iron, therefore, alone remains to be considered. Dr Priestley's experiments on this subject are related at length under the article AEROLOGY, n° 67 *et seq.* In them the iron burnt briskly in dephlogisticated air, which, according to the common theory, should have indicated the expulsion of a great quantity of phlogiston; yet the whole residuum, of which the fixed air, produced by the supposed union of the phlogiston or principle of inflammability, was only a part, scarce amounted sometimes to one-fourteenth of the air originally employed.

154 The objection invalidated.

This argument, however, instead of contradicting the existence of phlogiston, only shows, that in some cases the dissipation of a very small quantity of phlogiston is necessary to inflammation; or that the aerial principle may combine with the iron in its metallic state. In this case only a very little quantity of

155 Iron is not reduced to a calx by burning in dephlogisticated air.

the phlogiston of the iron was dissipated; for it was not reduced to a calx, but to that kind of scoriae which flies off in scales by beating the metal when red-hot with an hammer. A decisive proof of this was had by uniting iron thus combined with the basis of dephlogisticated air with inflammable air.

156 Water produced in the reduction of it by inflammable air.

By this the metal was indeed reduced to perfect iron again; but water was produced at the same time from the union of the basis of the two airs, that of the inflammable air being capable of furnishing a superfluous quantity, which united with the other into the form of a fluid.

157 Heat produced in the combustion of inflammable bodies coming from the air.

The existence of phlogiston being thus proved, and its nature ascertained, we may now proceed to determine the question, Whether the great quantity of heat produced by the combustion of inflammable bodies proceeds from the bodies themselves, or from the air which must be admitted to them in order to make them burn? That the heat in this case proceeds from the atmosphere is evident; because in all cases of combustion there is a certain diminution undoubtedly takes place by means of the conversion of the dephlogisticated part of the atmosphere into fixed air. It is proved, under the article *Elastic Vapours*, that elementary fire is the universal cause of elasticity in fluids. By uniting a certain quantity of it with any substance, the latter at length assumes an aerial or vaporous form; and it is this vapour alone which is inflammable[*]. Different vapours no doubt contain different quantities of these ingredients; but in all cases the basis of the dephlogisticated part of the atmosphere must

* See the article *Flame.*

General Effects of Heat.

must unite with the phlogiston of the inflammable body, or with something else, so that a decomposition may ensue; and it is this decomposition which produces the heat and light; for then the fire contained in the atmosphere having no longer any thing to absorb it, must appear in its proper form. But in those cases where there is a great quantity of phlogiston, and consequently much fixed air produced, the latter absorbs so much heat in a latent state, that the quantity communicated to surrounding bodies must be greatly diminished; and if by an excess of this ingredient, not only fixed air, but the phlogisticated kind and gross smoke be also produced, this diminishes the heat still farther by the great absorption, and will even destroy it altogether. The remedy for this is either to diminish the quantity of phlogiston, or to augment the quantity of air; which, by furnishing a greater quantity of dephlogisticated basis, affords an opportunity for the evolution of a greater quantity of heat. On the other hand, when the quantity of air is too great, the phlogistic matter cannot combine with the basis of the pure air in sufficient quantity to effect a decomposition; and therefore the heat is absorbed in a latent state, and the fire goes out.

158 Too much phlogiston prevents the heat from rising.

159 Too great a quantity of air has the same effect.

From this theory, which is further illustrated under the articles Fire, Flame, Heat, Phlogiston, &c. we may not only have a rational idea of the manner in which inflammation is generally accomplished, but see why a fire may be put out both by too great a quantity of fuel, and by too great a quantity of air. We may also see why the solar beams and electric fluid, which contain no phlogistic matter, excite a much more powerful heat than any we can raise in our hottest furnaces. The difference between ignition and inflammation will now likewise appear; such bodies as are capable only of ignition containing little or no phlogiston, but inflammable bodies a great deal.

160 Why the solar heat and that of electricity are so intense.

The following table shows the most remarkable degrees of heat from the congelation of mercury to that of Mr Wedgewood's hottest furnace.

161 Table of the various degrees of heat.

Mercury freezes at	40
Weak spirit of wine	32
Brandy at	10
Cold produced by snow and salt mixed	0
Strong wine freezes at	20
Vinegar freezes at	27
Water freezes at	32
Temperature of spring and autumn	50
Ordinary summer weather	65
Sultry heat	75
Heat of human blood	97 to 100
Feverish heat	108
Bees wax melts	142
Serum coagulates	156
Spirit of wine boils	174
Water boils	212
Tin melts	408
Bismuth melts	460
Oil of vitriol boils	550
Oil of turpentine boils	561
Lead melts	585
Quicksilver and linseed-oil boil	600
Iron begins to shine in the dark	635
Iron shines briskly in the dark	750
Iron shines in the twilight	884
Iron red-hot from a common fire	1050
Red heat fully visible in day light according to Mr Wedgewood	1077
Heat by which his enamel colours are burnt on	1857
Brass melts	3807
Swedish copper melts	4587
Fine silver melts	4717
Fine gold melts	5237
Least welding heat of iron	12777
Greatest ditto	13427
Greatest heat of a common smith's forge	17327
Cast iron melts	17977
Greatest heat of Wedgewood's small air-furnace	21877
Extremity of the scale of his thermometer	32277

Elective Attraction.

Sect. II. *Of the Doctrine of Elective attraction, and of the different Objects of Chemistry.*

Before we proceed to give a general theory of the changes which happen upon the mixtures of different bodies together, or exposing them singly to heat, we must observe, that all depend on certain qualities in bodies, by which some of them are apt to join together, and to remain united while they have an opportunity. The cause of these qualities is totally unknown; and therefore philosophers, after the example of Sir Isaac Newton, have expressed the apparent effects of this unknown cause by the word *attraction*. From them the word has been adopted by the chemists, and is now generally used in speaking of the phenomena which are observed in the mixture of different substances; but to distinguish it from other kinds, it is usually called *Elective*.

162 Chemical attraction.

This attraction is not equally strong between all substances; in consequence of which, if any body is compounded of two others, and another is presented to it which has a greater attraction for one of the component parts than they have for one another, the substance will be *decompounded*. A new compound is then formed by the union of that third substance with one of the component parts or *elements* (if we please to call them so) of the first. If the attraction between the body superadded and either of the component parts of the other is not so strong as that between themselves, no decomposition will ensue; or if the third substance is attracted by both the others, a new composition will take place by the union of all the three.

The objects of chemistry, as we have already observed, are so various, that an enumeration of them all is impossible. To ease the mind, therefore, when speaking of them, and render more useful any thing that is said or wrote on chemistry, it is necessary to divide them into different classes, comprehending in each class those bodies which have the greatest resemblance to one another, and to which one common rule applies pretty generally.—The division formerly used, was that of vegetables, animals, and minerals; but this has been thought improper, as there are many substances in each of those kingdoms which differ very widely from one another, and which are by no means subject to the same laws. The most approved method,

163 Objects of chemistry how classed.

thod, at present, of arranging the objects of chemistry, is into salts, earths, metals, inflammable substances, waters, animal and vegetable substances.

SECT III. *Salts.*

164 Salts. SALTS are either *fusible*, that is, capable of abiding the fire, and melting in a strong heat, without being dissipated; or *volatile*, that is, being dispersed in vapour with a small heat. Their other properties are, that they are soluble in water; not inflammable, unless by certain additions; and give a sensation of taste when applied to the tongue.

The most general characteristic of salts is, that they are all soluble in water, though some of them with much more difficulty than others. Most of them have likewise the property of forming themselves, in certain circumstances, into solid transparent masses of regular figures, different according to the different salt made use of, and which are termed *crystals* of that salt. In this state they always contain a quantity of water; and therefore the utmost degree of purity in which a salt can be procured, is when it has been well crystallized, and the crystals are freed of their superfluous moisture by a gentle heat. They generally appear then in the form of a white powder.

165 Phenomena attending their solution. In the solution of salts in water, the first thing observable is, that the water parts with the air contained in it; which immediately rises to the top in the form of bubbles. This, however, is most remarkable when the salt is in the dry form we have just now mentioned, because there is always a quantity of air entangled among the interstices of the powder, which rises along with the rest; and this discharge of air is sometimes so great, as to be mistaken for an effervescence. From this, however, it is essentially different. See EFFERVESCENCE.

Another thing observable in the solution of salts is, that a considerable change happens in the temperature of the water in which they are dissolved; the mixture becoming either a good deal warmer or colder than either the salt or the water were before. In general, however, there is an increase of cold, and scarce any salt produces heat, except when it has been made very dry, and deprived of that moisture which it naturally requires; and thus the heating of salts by being mixed with water may be explained on the same principle with the heat produced by quicklime. See QUICKLIME.

After salt has been dissolved in a certain quantity by water, no more of that salt will be taken up unless the water is heated; and as long as the heat continues to increase, the salt will be dissolved. When the water boils, at which time it has attained its greatest heat, and will take up no more salt, it is then said to be *saturated* with that salt. This, however, does not prevent it from taking up a certain quantity of another salt, and after that perhaps of a third, or fourth, without letting go any of the first which it had dissolved. How far this property of water extends, has not yet been ascertained by experiments.

To the above rule there is only one exception known as yet; namely, common sea-salt: for water dissolves it in the very same quantity when cold as when boiling hot. It has been said by some, that all deliquescent salts, or those which grow moist on being exposed to the air, had the same property: but this is found to be a mistake.

This property of solubility, which all the salts possess in common, renders them easily miscible together; and the property by which most of them shoot into crystals, renders those easily separable again which have no particular attraction for one another. This is likewise rendered still more easy by their requiring different proportions of water, and different degrees of heat, to suspend them; for by this they crystallize at different times, and we have not the trouble of picking the crystals of one out among those of the other. 166 Mixture and separation of salts.

The manner in which the solution of salts in water is effected, is equally unaccountable with most of the other operations of nature. Sir Isaac Newton supposed that the particles of water got between those of the salt, and arranged them all at an equal distance from one another; and from this he also accounts for the regular figures they assume on passing into a crystalline form; because, having been once arranged in an orderly manner, they could not come together in disorder, unless something was to disturb the water in which they were suspended; and if any such disturbance is given, we find the crystals are by no means so regular as otherwise they would have proved. Others have thought that these figures depend on a certain *polarity* in the very small particles into which the salt is resolved when in a state of solution. These things, however, are merely conjectural; neither is it a matter of any consequence to a chemist whether they are right or wrong. 167 Hypotheses concerning the solution of salts.

Though solution is that operation which salts undergo the most easily, and which should seem to affect them the least of any, a repetition of it proves wonderfully very injurious to them, especially if it is followed by quick evaporation; and the salt, instead of being crystallised, is dried with a pretty strong heat. Newman relates, that a pound of sea-salt was reduced, by 13 solutions and exsiccations, to half an ounce; and even that was mostly earth. Where solution is required, therefore, it ought always to be done in close vessels, in which also the subsequent evaporation should be performed, (see EVAPORATION); and in all cases where crystallization is practicable, it ought to be preferred to violent exsiccation. 168 Salts destructible by repeated solutions.

The two great divisions of salts are into acids and alkalies. The former of these are known by their peculiar taste, which is called *acid* or *sour*. They are not found in a solid form; neither are any of them, except the acids of vitriol, of tartar, of phosphorus, and of borax, capable of being reduced to solidity. The others, when highly concentrated, that is, brought to the utmost degree of strength of which they are capable, always become an invisible vapour, permanently elastic, until it comes in contact with water, or some other substance with which they are capable of uniting. For such acids the name of *salts* seems less proper, as we can scarcely say that a vapour, which is already much more fluid than water, can be *dissolved* in that element. 169 Acids.

The acids are divided into the mineral, the vegetable, and the animal; expressing their different origin, or where they are most commonly to be found. The mineral acids are commonly reckoned three; the

vi-

Salts

vitriolic, the nitrous, and the marine. To this the acid of borax ought to be added; but its weakness makes it much less taken notice of as an acid than the others. A Swedish chemist, however, Mr Scheele, hath lately added several others, which are afterwards taken notice of.

The vegetable kingdom affords only two distinct species of acids, at least without the assistance of some chemical operation. The one appears fluid, and when concentrated to the utmost degree becomes an invisible vapour. This is produced from fermented liquors, under the name of *vinegar*. An acid similar to this, and which is thought not to be essentially different from it, is extracted from most vegetables by distillation with a strong fire. The other is likewise a consequence of fermentation; and crusts on the bottom and sides of casks in which wine is put to depurate itself. In its crude state it is called *tartar*; and when afterwards purified, is called the *cream*, or crystals, of tartar. As for the various acids produced in the different chemical processes to be afterwards related, we forbear to mention them at present, it being justly suspected that some of them are artificial.

The animal acids, which have hitherto been discovered, are only two; the acid of ants, and that of urine, which is also the acid of phosphorus. The first of these is volatile; and consequently must be supposed a vapour when in its strongest state: the other is exceedingly fixed; and will rather melt into glass than rise in vapours. Besides these, it is said an acid is contained in blood, in wasps, bees, &c.; but no experiments have as yet been made on these to determine this matter with any degree of precision.

170 Alkalies.

The alkalies are of two kinds; fixed and volatile. The fixed kind are subdivided into two; the vegetable, and mineral or fossil alkali. The vegetable is so called, because it is procured from the ashes of burnt vegetables; the fossile, because it is found native in some places of the earth, and is the basis of sea-salt, which in some places is dug out of mines in vast quantity. They are called *fixed*, because they endure a very intense degree of heat without being dissipated in vapour, so as even to form a part of the composition of glass. The volatile alkali is generally obtained by distillation from animal substances. In its pure state this alkali is perfectly invisible; but affects the sense of smelling to such a degree, as not to be approached with safety.

171 Different action of alkalies and acids.

The acids and alkalies are generally thought to be entirely opposite in their natures to one another. Some, however, imagine them to be extremely similar, and to be as it were parts of one substance violently taken from each other. Certain it is, that when separated, they appear as opposite to one another as heat and cold. Their opposite action indeed very much resembles that of heat and cold, even when applied to the tongue; for the alkali has a hot, bitter, burning taste, while the acid, if not considerably concentrated, always gives a sensation of coldness. In their action too upon animal substances, the alkali dissolves, and reduces the part to a mucilage; while the acid, if not very much concentrated, tends to preserve it uncorrupted.

172 Neutral salts.

If an alkaline salt, and moderately strong acid in a liquid state, be mixed together, they will immediately unite; and, provided the alkali has not been deprived of its fixed air, their union will be attended with a very considerable effervescence; (see AEROLOGY.) If the alkali has been deprived of air, no effervescence will ensue, but they will quietly mix together; but if a due proportion of each has been added, the liquor will neither have the properties of an acid nor an alkali, but will be what is called *neutral*. The bringing the liquor into this state, is called *saturating* the acid or alkali, or combining them to the point of saturation.

If the liquor after such a saturation be gently evaporated, a saline mass will be left, which is neither an acid nor an alkali, but a new compound formed by the union of the two, and which is called a *perfect neutral salt*. The epithet *perfect* is given it, to make a distinction between the salts formed by the union of an acid and an alkali, and those formed by the union of acids with earthy or metallic substances; for these will likewise unite with acids, and some of the compounds will crystallize into regular figures; but, because of their weaker union with these substances, the salts resulting from combinations of this kind are called *imperfect*.

173 Vegetable colours changed by acids and alkalies.

All acids, the volatile sulphureous one excepted, change the blue infusions of vegetables, such as violets, to a red; and alkalies, as well as some of the imperfect neutrals, change them to green. This is the nicest test of an acid or alkali abounding in any substance, and seems the most proper method of determining whether a solution intended to be neutral really is so or not.

174 Difference in the degree of attraction between acids and alkalies.

Though between every acid and alkali there is a very strong attraction, yet this is far from being the same in all; neither is it the same between the same acid and alkali in different circumstances of the acid. When the acids are in a liquid state, and as free as possible of inflammable matter, between which and the nitrous and vitriolic acids there is a very strong attraction, the vitriolic will expel any of the rest from an alkaline basis, and take its place. Thus, if you combine the acid of sea-salt, or marine acid, to the point of saturation, with the fossil alkali, a neutral salt will be formed, which has every property of common salt: but, if you pour on a certain proportion of the vitriolic acid, the acid of sea-salt will immediately be expelled; and the liquor, upon being evaporated, will contain not the neutral salt formed by an union of the marine acid with the alkali, but another consisting of the vitriolic acid joined with that alkali, and which has quite different properties from the former.

When the acids and alkalies are applied to one another in a liquid state, the vitriolic acid always shows itself to be the most powerful; but when applied in a solid form, and urged with a violent heat, the case is very much altered. Thus, the acid of borax, commonly called *sal sedativus*, is so weak as to be disengaged from its basis by every acid applied in a liquid form, that of tartar alone excepted; but if even the vitriolic acid combined with an alkali be mixed with this weak acid, then exsiccated, and at last urged with a vehement fire, the vitriolic acid will be disengaged from its basis, and rise in vapours, leaving the weaker acid in possession of the alkali. The same thing happens on adding the phosphorine or urinous acid,

Salts. acid, or the acid of arsenic, &c. to combinations of the vitriolic or other acids with alkaline salts.—When the acids are in a liquid state, therefore the most powerful is the vitriolic; next the nitrous; then the marine; then vinegar; acid of ants; and lastly the sal sedativus and tartar, which seem to be nearly equal in this respect.—If they are applied in a solid form, the most powerful are the sal sedativus and phosphoric acid; then the vitriolic, nitrous, marine, and vegetable acids.

When they are reduced to vapour, the case is exceedingly different; for then the marine acid appears to be the most powerful, and the vitriolic the least so of any. It is impossible, however, to preserve the vitriolic acid in the form of vapour, without combining it with a certain quantity of inflammable matter, which must necessarily destroy its strength. Dr Priestley found, that the marine acid, when reduced to vapour, was capable of disuniting the nitrous acid from a fixed alkali.

Though the vitriolic acid sometimes assumes a solid form, it is by no means easy to reduce it to this state by mere concentration, without the assistance of nitrous acid. Baldasari, however, pretends that he discovered, in the neighbourhood of a volcano, a pure and icy oil of vitriol, from which nothing could be precipitated by alkaline salts; though there is certainly very great reason to doubt the accuracy of this observation. Of late the nitrous acid has also been found capable of assuming a solid form. This was first observed by M. Bernhard in distilling a very large quantity of the acid. At that time he perceived a white salt adhering to the inside of the receiver, which on examination proved to be the acid of nitre in a concrete form; being extremely corrosive, emitting red vapours copiously on being exposed to the air, and at length totally evaporating in it. Its specific gravity, however, was far inferior to that of the glacial oil of vitriol.

175 Acids unite with phlogiston. The acids have the property of uniting themselves to many other substances besides fixed alkalies, and forming neutral compounds with them. Of these the chief is the principle of inflammability or phlogiston. In the vitriolic, nitrous, and phosphoric acids, the attraction for this principle is very strong; so great, that the two former will even leave a fixed alkali to unite with it. In the marine acid it is less perceptible; in the liquid vegetable or animal acid still less; and in the acid of tartar, and sal sedativus, not at all.

176 With metals and earths. Besides this, all acids will dissolve metallic and earthy substances; with these, however, they do not in general unite so firmly with alkaline salts; nor do they unite so strongly with metals as with earths.

177 Elective attractions. In general, therefore, we may expect, that after having dissolved a metal in any acid whatever, if we add an earthy substance to that solution, the acid will quit the metal, which it had before dissolved, to unite with the earth. In this case the solution will not be clear as before, but will remain muddy, and a quantity of powder will fall to the bottom. This powder is the metalline substance itself, but deprived of one of its component parts; and in this case it is said to *precipitate* in the form of a *calx*.

If to this new solution of the earthy substance in an acid liquor, a volatile alkaline salt, not deprived of its fixed air, is added, the acid will quit the earth, and unite with the alkaline salt. The earth thus disengaged will again *precipitate*, and lie at the bottom in fine powder, while the volatile alkali and acid remain combined together, and the liquor again becomes clear.

The attraction between volatile alkalies and acids is considerably less than between fixed alkalies and the same acids. If, therefore, a fixed alkali be now added to the liquor, the volatile alkali will be separated, and the acid will unite with the fixed alkali. The volatile alkali indeed, being perfectly soluble in water, cannot precipitate, but will discover its separation by the pungent smell of the mixture; and upon evaporating the liquor, the volatile alkali will be dissipated, and a saline mass, consisting of the acid and fixed alkali, will remain.

178 Detonation of nitre. Lastly, If the acid employed was the nitrous, which has a strong attraction for the principle of inflammability, if the saline mass be mixed with a proper quantity of inflammable matter, and exposed to a strong heat, the acid will leave the alkali with vast rapidity, combine with the inflammable matter, and be destroyed in flame in a moment, leaving the alkali quite pure.

179 Exceptions to the above rules. Though the above-mentioned effects generally happen, yet we are not to expect that they will invariably prove the same whatever acid is made use of; or even that they will be the same in all possible variety of circumstances in which the same acid can be used.—The acid of tartar is one exception, where the general rule is in a manner reversed; for this acid will quit a fixed alkali for an earth, especially if calcined, and even for iron. If lead, mercury, or silver, are dissolved in the nitrous acid, and a small quantity of the marine acid is added, it will separate the stronger nitrous acid, and fall to the bottom with the metals in form of a white powder.—The vitriolic acid, by itself, has a greater attraction for earthy substances than for metals; and greater still for fixed alkaline salts than for either of these: but if quicksilver is dissolved in the nitrous acid, and this solution is poured into a combination of vitriolic acid with fixed alkali, the vitriolic acid will quit the alkali to unite with the quicksilver. Yet quicksilver by itself cannot easily be united with this acid. The reason of all these anomalies, however, is fully explained in the following section.

§ 1. *Of the Operations of Solution and Precipitation.*

The chemical solution of solid bodies in acid or other menstrua, is a phenomenon which, though our familiarity with it has now taken off our surprise, must undoubtedly have occasioned the greatest admiration and astonishment in those who first observed it. It would far exceed the limits of this treatise to speak particularly of all the various circumstances attending the solution of different substances in every possible menstruum. The following are the most remarkable, collected from Mr Bergman's Dissertation on Metallic Precipitates.

180 Phenomena attending the solution of a metal. 1. On putting a small piece of metal into any acid, it is dissolved sometimes with violence, sometimes gently, according to the nature of the menstruum and of the metal to be dissolved.

2. The nitrous acid is the most powerful in its ac-

Solution and Precipitation.

tive upon metallic substances, when unassisted by heat. So great indeed is the violence with which this acid sometimes acts, that the metal, instead of being dissolved, separates instantaneously from it in the form of a calx or powder scarce soluble in any menstruum, at the same time that the heat, effervescence, and noxious vapours issuing from the mixture, render it absolutely necessary to moderate the action of the menstruum, either by dilution or cold, or both. In other cases, however, as when put to gold or platina, the nitrous acid has no effect until it be united with the marine, when the mixture acts upon those metals, which neither of the acids singly would touch.

181 Nitrous acid the most violent in its operation.

182 Vitriolic acid acts more weakly.

3. The action of the vitriolic acid, though in the highest degree of concentration, is more weak. It does not readily attack silver or mercury unless assisted by a boiling heat, nor will even that be sufficient to make it act upon gold or platina.

183 Marine acid generally more weak than either, except when dephlogisticated.

4. The action of marine acid, unless on some particular substances, is still more weak; but when dephlogisticated, or deprived of part of the phlogiston essential to its constitution as an acid, it acts much more powerfully, and dissolves all the metals completely.

184 The rest of the acids much weaker still.

5. The other acids, as those of fluor, borax, with such as are obtained from the animal and vegetable kingdoms, are much inferior in their powers as solvents, unless in very few instances.

185 Different degrees of solubility in metals.

6. Metals vary very much in their degrees of solubility; some yielding to almost every menstruum, and others, as has been already observed, being scarce acted upon by the most powerful.

186 Solution of some metals promoted by abstracting a certain proportion of phlogiston.

6. Zinc and iron are of the former kind, and gold and silver of the latter, eluding the marine; and gold, unless in one particular case, viz. when assisted by heat in a close vessel, the action of the nitrous acid also. These metals, however, which in their perfect state resist the action of the most powerful menstrua, may be dissolved much more readily when deprived of a certain quantity of their inflammable principle. But though the separation of this principle in some degree renders metals more soluble, the abstraction of too much of it, particularly in the case of iron and tin, renders these metals almost entirely insoluble. Manganese is the most remarkable instance of this power of the phlogistic principle, in depriving metals of their solubility by its absence, or restoring it to them by its presence; for this substance, when reduced to blackness, cannot be dissolved by any acid without the addition of some inflammable matter; but when by the addition of phlogiston it has become white, may be dissolved in any acid.

187 But totally prevented by taking away too much; exemplified in manganese.

188 Solution of metals attended with an effervescence.

7. The dissolution of metals by acids, even to their very last particle, is attended by a visible effervescence; this is more perceptible according to the quickness of the solution; but more obscure, and scarcely to be seen at all, when the solution proceeds slowly.

189 Various kinds of elastic fluids extricated.

8. The elastic fluids extricated by these solutions are various, according to the nature of the acid and of the metal employed. With the nitrous, the fluid produced is commonly that called *nitrous air*; with vitriolic and marine acids the produce is sometimes inflammable air, sometimes otherwise, according to the nature of the metal acted upon.

9. Heat in a greater or smaller degree is always produced during the dissolution of metals; and the degree of it is in proportion to the quantity of the matter and the quickness of the solution; and hence, in small quantities of metal, and where the solution proceeds very slowly, the temperature of the mass is scarcely altered.

190 Heat produced during the dissolution of metals.

191 Little air can be obtained from metals when calcined.

10. The calces of metals either yield no air at all, or only the aerial acid, unless when urged by a violent heat almost to ignition; when, by means of vitriolic or nitrous acid, they yield a quantity of pure air, after other elastic fluids, such as vitriolic, nitrous, or phlogisticated air. None of the dephlogisticated air is usually produced by the marine acid in conjunction with metallic calces.

192 Various colours of metallic calces.

11. The solutions of some metals are coloured, others are not. The colour of the former is only that which is proper to the calx, but rendered more vivid by the moisture. Thus solutions of gold and platina are yellow; those of copper, blue or green; solutions of nickel of a bright green; but those of cobalt are red, although the calx is black. We may observe that even this red colour may be heightened to blackness. Iron moderately calcined is green; but this rarely continues upon further dephlogistication. The white calces of silver, lead, tin, bismuth, arsenic, antimony, and manganese, are dissolved without colour; but solutions of lead, tin, and antimony, are somewhat yellow, unless sufficiently diluted. Mercury, however, forms a singular exception to this rule; for the orange-coloured calx of this metal forms a colourless solution. The metals yielding coloured solutions are gold, platina, copper, iron, tin, nickel, and cobalt; the rest, if properly depurated, give no tinge. A solution of silver is sometimes of a blue or green colour at first, although there be no copper present; the vitriolic acid becomes blue with copper; the nitrous may be made either blue or green at pleasure; the marine varies according to the quantity of water with which it is diluted. Manganese, when too much dephlogisticated, renders both the vitriolic and marine acids purple.

193 Bergman's account of the cause of chemical solution.

With regard to the cause of chemical solutions, our author observes, that though attraction must be looked upon as the fundamental cause, yet we may also lay it down as a maxim, that no metal can be taken up by an acid, and at the same time preserve the whole quantity of phlogiston which was necessary to it in its metallic state. A certain proportion of the principle of inflammability therefore may be considered as an obstacle which must be removed before a solution can take place. Thus, of all the acids, the nitrous attracts phlogiston the most powerfully, and separates it even from the vitriolic. A proof of this may be had by boiling sulphur slowly in concentrated nitrous acid. At length all its phlogiston may be separated, and the vitriolic acid will remain, deprived of its principle of inflammability. The extraordinary solvent powers of this acid, therefore, is conformed to the peculiarity of its nature in this respect. For this menstruum dissolves metals fit for solution with the greatest ease, most commonly without any assistance from external heat; which in some instances would be hurtful, by separating too much of phlogiston, as appears in the case of iron, tin, and antimony; all of which may be so far dephlogisticated by the nitrous acid, as to be rendered extremely difficult of solution: for this reason it is very often necessary, as has already been observed, to temper the activity

194 Solution impeded by too great a quantity of phlogiston.

195 Sulphur dephlogisticated by nitrous acid.

196 Calces of some metals prepared by nitrous acid almost insoluble afterwards.

www.ingramcontent.com/pod-product-compliance
Lightning Source LLC
Chambersburg PA
CBHW022145300426
44115CB00006B/359

* 9 7 8 3 7 4 1 1 6 8 1 0 9 *